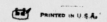

MAYA HIEROGLYPHIC WRITING

[This volume is No. 56 in the Civilization of the American Indian Series, published continuously since 1932 by the University of Oklahoma Press on the aboriginal cultures of North, South, and Central America.]

FRONTISPIECE—THE JOURNEY OF TIME

Adaptation from full-figure glyphs forming Initial Series of Copan D to represent arrival at the *Inb*, "the resting place," of the deified numbers bearing the periods as loads, at the completion of the tun. At the same moment the night sun, as ninth lord of the night, rises from the ground to start his nocturnal journey. The IS is 9.15.5.0.0 10 Ahau 8 Ch'en. See figure 60. Specially drawn for this publication by Jean Charlot.

MAYA HIEROGLYPHIC WRITING

An Introduction

J. Eric S. Thompson

UNIVERSITY OF OKLAHOMA PRESS : NORMAN

Books by J. ERIC S. THOMPSON

Maya Archaeologist (Norman, 1963)
A Catalog of Maya Hieroglyphs (Norman, 1962)
Maya Hierogylphic Writing (Norman, 1960)
Thomas Gage's Travels in the New World (ed.) (Norman, 1958)
The Rise and Fall of Maya Civilization (Norman, 1954)
Excavations at San José, British Honduras (Washington, 1939)
Mexico before Cortez (New York, 1933)
Archaeological Investigations in the Southern Cayo District,
    British Honduras (Chicago, 1931)
Ethnology of the Mayas of Southern and Central British Honduras
    (Chicago, 1930)

New edition copyright 1960 by the University of Oklahoma Press,
Publishing Division of the University, reproduced from the
first edition published by the Carnegie Institution of Washington in 1950.
Manufactured in the United States of America.
First printing, January, 1960; second printing, March, 1962;
third printing, August, 1966.

Preface to the Second Edition

THE NINE YEARS passed since this book was first published have witnessed a growing interest in the study of Maya hieroglyphic writing and some significant advances which are outlined below. Were I writing this book anew, I would omit some ideas advanced in 1950 and expand others and advance interpretations which had no place in the 1950 edition, but the process used in publishing the present edition makes such textual alterations impossible.

New hieroglyphic texts, the nourishment of our research, have been found at various sites. The splendid program of excavation at Palenque carried forward by the Mexican Instituto Nacional de Antropología e Historia, under the leadership of Alberto Ruz, has uncovered several important and excellently preserved texts. The University of Pennsylvania's program at Tikal has recovered others, and those are particularly welcome because good texts from that region are not numerous as a result of the severe weathering of the poor limestone of the northern Petén, of which most monuments are composed. During the 1959 field season, Edwin Shook, field director, discovered the earliest known Maya monument. This carries the Initial Series 8.12.14.8.15, almost surely a date nearly contemporaneous with that of the monument's erection, and twenty-eight years earlier than any previous text. Other inscriptions have been found at Tortuguero, Tabasco; Caracol, British Honduras; Dzibilchaltun, Yucatán; Kuna, Chiapas; and Kaminaljuyú, Guatemala, as well as at other sites of lesser importance.

Gunter Zimmermann (1956) has carried to a successful conclusion the immense task of cataloguing all the glyphs in the three surviving Maya codices. He uses a new and highly efficient system of numbering main signs and affixes which makes identification simple. This much-needed work is far superior to the earlier one by W. Gates, *An Outline Dictionary of Maya Glyphs.*

T. S. Barthel (1952, 1953, 1954, 1955, and 1955a) has contributed very valuable papers on the decipherment of glyphs in the Dresden codex and at Chichén Itzá. In his 1954 paper he successfully demonstrated that the affix I had labeled *te* (2) (pp. 282–85) represented the sound *al*. This well illustrates the difficulties of translation and so I will outline the problem. I had seriously considered this value *al* for the affix, but I finally rejected it because it appears apparently as a numerical classifier on Stela 19 be-

neath head numerals, but *al* is not a numerical classifier in Yucatec or, so far as is known, in other lowland languages. My fault was that I had not looked with sufficient care; I had not noted that this affix is attached only to heads representing numbers ten to nineteen inclusive, all of which are composed by incorporating the features of the death god. By seeing the affix, not as a numerical classifier but as having a connection with the death god, objections to the *al* interpretation immediately disappear. Unfortunately, Barthel has for the present abandoned his promising work on Maya hieroglyphs, but only temporarily, one hopes.

Heinrich Berlin (1959) has opened up a new front by his acute discernment in isolating what, to avoid being too specific, he terms "emblems." He has noted that each principal Maya city has one particular glyph which appears over and over again in its texts, but rarely or ever appears elsewhere (cf. p. 58). Nevertheless, the affixes of these local "emblem" glyphs are often the same everywhere, and it is only the main sign which is variable. Berlin suggests that these glyphs may have served as signs of local rulers, groups, or political entities.

A somewhat similar break-through has been achieved by Tatiana Proskouriakoff (1959, 1959a) in identifying patterns of dates with their associated glyphs with the subject matter of stelae, particularly at Piedras Negras. As I write, the first of Miss Proskouriakoff's papers has just been read and the second is still unfinished. As her ideas and interpretations are still fluid and tentative, and conclusions may be modified before they appear in print, I shall only say that the implications of her work are of the greatest importance. It may well be that they will lead me to revise my views on the impersonality of the texts on Maya monuments (pp. 64–65).

Linton Satterthwaite (1951) has discovered a pattern of recording katun-endings by carving the top of an altar with a giant glyph of the particular day Ahau on which the current katun ended. This forges one more link between archaeological practice of the Classic Period and the later pattern transmitted to us by colonial writers. Satterthwaite (1951a) continues his investigations of Maya lunar groupings. Andrews (1951) has brought together all records on monuments of the Maya lunar series.

The most widely publicized event in Maya glyphic decipherment is the claim of the Russian, Y. V. Knorozov, to have solved the problem by what he terms a Marxist-Leninist approach, but this does not differ greatly from the interpretation used by Whorf (pp. 311–13). Like Whorf, he has great confidence in the Landa alphabet, and he credits the Maya with a sort of cross between an alphabetic and a syllabic writing, a glyphic element representing the consonant or the consonant and vowel with which its sound value opens. There is not space here to deal justly with his ideas, and the reader is referred to his writings. Both Barthel (1958) and I (Thompson, 1953, 1959) have expressed complete skepticism concerning his claims. Barthel has pointed out that a high proportion of Knorozov's readings have been made by others, but of those which originate with Knorozov he finds only one which is worth consideration as possibly correct. A point of some importance, I feel, is that with a phonetic system, as in breaking a code, the rate of decipherment accelerates with each newly established reading. It it now eight years since it was announced that, after nearly a century of abortive bourgeois effort, the problem had been solved by Knorozov. Yet the first flow of alleged decipherments has not swollen to a river, as it should with the successful solving of a phonetic system; it has fallen to a trickle. Knorozov has deserted his Maya studies to become the first man to solve the enigma of the Easter Island writing, according to announcements from Moscow.

Much of my time over the past nine years has been given to the preparation of a catalogue of all non-calendrical glyphs, a task not yet finished. One paper (Thompson, 1958) discusses divinatory almanacs for diseases in the Maya codices and glyphs for disease in general and individual diseases; and the article, in which I expressed my skepticism of Knorozov's achievements, also contains a discussion of the nature of glyphic writing in Middle America and its development.

An indirect contribution of great value to glyphic work is the study by Ralph Roys (1954) of katun prophecies in the books of Chilam Balam.

The new Carbon-14 method of dating has produced a series of readings, some of which support the 12.9.0.0.0 correlation, others the 11.16.0.0.0 (p. 303–10). The technique is still undergoing refinement, and the newer gas process (CO_2) is proving more reliable. Single readings must be accepted with great reserve. The discovery of a 260-day almanac surviving among the Mixe of Oaxaca which is synchronous with Maya almanacs surviving in the Guatemalan highlands reinforces the argument against a pre-Columbian break in the Maya calendar (p. 310).

I deeply appreciate the uncommercial emprise of the University of Oklahoma Press and its director in publishing this new edition of a singularly long book on a very specialized subject. Likewise, it is a pleasure to acknowledge the gracious co-operation of Carnegie Institution of Washington in this emprise.

J. Eric S. Thompson

Harvard, Ashdon,
Saffron Walden, England
July, 1959

REFERENCES

Andrews, E. W.
1951 The Maya supplementary series. *Proc. 29th Int. Cong. Amer., New York, 1949*, 1: 123–41. Chicago.

Barthel, T. S.
1952 Der Morgensternkult in den Darstellungen der Dresdener Mayahandschrift. *Ethnos*, 17: 73–112. Stockholm.
1953 Region des Regengottes. Zur Deutung der unteren Teile der Seiten 65–69 in der Dresdener Mayahandschrift. *Ethnos*, 18: 86–105. Stockholm.
1954 Maya epigraph; some remarks on the affix 'al.' *Proc. 30th Int. Cong. Amer., Cambridge, 1952*, pp. 45–49. London.
1955 Maya-Palaeographik: die Hieroglyphe Strafe. *Ethnos*, 20: 146–51. Stockholm.
1955a Versuch über die Inschriften von Chichen Itza viejo. *Baessler Archiv*, n.s., 3: 5–33. Berlin.
1958 Die gegenwärtige Situation in der Erforschung der Mayaschrift. *Proc. 32 Int. Cong. Amer., Copenhagen, 1956*, pp. 476–84. Copenhagen.

Berlin, H.
1958 El glifo "emblema" en las inscripciones mayas. *Jour. Soc. des Amer. de Paris*, 47: 111–19. Paris.

Knorozov, Y. V.
1952 Drevnyaya Pis'menost' Tsentralnoy Ameriki [The ancient script of Central America]. *Sovietskaya Etnografiya 1952*, no. 3, pp. 100–18. Moscow.
1953 La antigua escritura de los pueblos de la América Central. *Boletin de Información de la Embajada de la U.R.S.S.* Año 10, no. 20. Mexico.
1955 La escritura de los antiguos mayas (ensayo de descifrado). In Russian and Spanish. *Institut Etnografi Akademii Nauk*. Moscow.
1958 The problem of the study of the Maya hieroglyphic writing. *Amer. Antiq.*, 23: 284–91. Salt Lake City.
1958a New data on the Maya written language. *Proc. 32nd Int. Cong. Amer., Copenhagen, 1956*, pp.

467–75. Copenhagen.

PROSKOURIAKOFF, T.

1959   A pattern of dates and monuments at Piedras Negras. *Ms.*

1959a   Implications of the Piedras Negras pattern of dates for glyph decipherment. *Ms.*

ROYS, R. L.

1954   The Maya katun prophecies of the books of Chilam Balam, Series ·1. *Carnegie Inst. Wash.* Pub. 606, Contrib. 57. Washington.

SATTERTHWAITE, L. S.

1951   Reconnaissance in British Honduras. *Univ. Mus. Bull,* vol. 16, no. 1, pp. 21–37. Philadelphia.

1951a   Moon ages of the Maya inscriptions; the problem of their seven-day range of deviation from calculated mean ages. *Proc. 29th Int. Cong. Amer.,*

New York, 1949, 1: 142–54. Chicago.

THOMPSON, J. E. S.

1953   Review of Y. V. Knorozov—The ancient writing of the peoples of Central America. *Yan,* no. 2, pp. 174–78. Mexico.

1958   Symbols, glyphs and divinatory almanacs for diseases in the Maya Dresden and Madrid codices. *Amer. Antiq.,* 23: 297–308. Salt Lake City.

1959   Systems of hieroglyphic writing in Middle America and methods of deciphering them. *Amer. Antiq.,* 24: 349–64. Salt Lake City.

ZIMMERMANN, G.

1956   Die Hieroglyphen der Maya-Handschriften. *Universität Hamburg, Abhandlungen aus dem Gebeit der Auslandkunde,* vol. 62. Hamburg.

Preface

THE PREFACES of many archaeological publications might be likened to Poets' Corner, for they hold many tributes in a small space, the unimportant jostling the important. There is, however, one salient difference: the tributes, for the most part in that horrendous grave-yard style of the late eighteenth and early nineteenth centuries, which crowd Poets' Corner could not be read by those to whom they were addressed; in prefaces the tributes are to the quick.

In this volume I have set forth in the section "Search and Research" my indebtedness to my fellow students of the Maya glyphs and related subjects, both the quick and the dead. However, I take this opportunity to mention in the time-honored place my lively gratitude to a group of students of ethnology, a field more closely related to that of the hieroglyphic writing than many realize. Robert Redfield, Sol Tax, Antonio Goubaud, and Mr. and Mrs. Wilbur Aulie have treated my requests for much and varied information with great forbearance, have answered with all the detail at their command, and made special investigations at my behest. I have acknowledged in the text my great obligations to Ralph L. Roys, but his help has been so unfailing that I would mention it also in this foreword. Dr. A. V. Kidder, Chairman of the Division of Historical Research, has made many helpful suggestions, and more than once has coaxed me off a dangerous limb. From his initiation of staff meetings to discuss general strategy and specific problems I, together with every participant, have derived great benefit. One could hardly ask more than a free hand to follow one's own investigations when that is coupled with the advantages and profitable obligations of teamwork.

The drawings of hieroglyphs, totaling nearly two thousand, form a most important part of this volume, and I would pause to express my heartfelt thanks to the artists responsible for them. Figures 2–10, the first five rows of figure 11, figures 16–19, 22–27, 30–34, 37, and 40 were drawn by Mrs. Huberta Robison, of Salt Lake City. Figures 1, 41–45, and the greater parts of figures 12–15, 20, and 21 are the work of Mrs. Eugene C. Worman, Jr. Miss Kisa Noguchi drew figures 36 and 46, the intricate full-figure glyphs of figures 28 and 29, and the last three rows of figure 11, as well as sundry final corrections of detail on other pages. To Miss Tatiana Proskouriakoff is due the credit for the glyphs of figure 35, and to Mr. Jean

Charlot, my room-mate at Chichen Itza for several months in 1926, I am indebted for the charming way in which he has interpreted for me the Maya concept of the journey of time. Mrs. Katherine B. Lang made some of the drawings of figures 12–15, 20, and 21. Miss Avis Tullock made the drawing for Table 6 and added glyphs to figure 46 and to sundry other figures.

All drawings were compared by me with photographs before inking, and so at my door must be laid any blame for errors. For a few glyphs, not more than half a dozen, good photographs were not available, and in such cases it was necessary to depend on drawings, principally those of Morley. As far as possible the best-preserved examples of each variant of a glyph were chosen. Eroded details are restored where there can be no serious doubt about them; broken lines are used or details are omitted where there is uncertainty. Omission of details tends to give a false impression but can hardly be avoided. As an example of omission I might cite the Moan bird. As used as a month sign or a personification of the tun sign, this seems to have as one of its characteristics crosshatched spots or little circles on the temple or projecting from the forehead. These probably indicate the tufted ears of the owl. However, such small details are easily lost through erosion, and in those cases in which there is no longer a hint of their former existence, they are omitted (e.g. fig. 18,35,39).

The series of glyphs of days, months, and periods (figs. 6–11, 16–19, 26, 27) as well as those of personified numbers (figs. 24, 25) are arranged in chronological order to illustrate variations in delineation with the passing of time. I have tried to make these complementary to the Bowditch (1910) series, but some duplication was unavoidable.

I would, also, express my deep gratitude to Mr. Giles G. Healey for his kindness in making a number of special photographs for this volume. Those friendly offices were not without pains to himself, for on one photographic mission in my behalf to Yaxchilan he was unjustly cast into ignominious prison by a grafting official. Stripes there were none, and his incarceration by the Sovereign State of Tabasco was of short duration, but it is not pleasant to suffer such indignity in the course of giving disinterested aid to another.

A number of contractions are employed, principally in the captions of the illustrations. These are:

Aguas Cal.	Aguas Calientes	Nar.	Naranjo
Alt	Altar	96 Gl.	Tablet of 96
Alt. de Sac.	Altar de Sacrifi-		Glyphs
	cios	Olvidado	El Templo
Balak.	Balakbal		Olvidado
Bl	Glyph block	Oxkin.	Oxkintok
Bonam.	Bonampak	Pal.	Palenque
Calak.	Calakmul	Palmar	El Palmar
Chichen	Chichen Itza	Pan	Panel
Chinik.	Chinikiha	PE	Period ending
Chinkul.	Chinkultic	P.N.	Piedras Negras
Cop.	Copan	P. Uinik	Poco Uinik
CR	Calendar Round	Pusil.	Pusilha
Cross	Tablet of Cross	Quir.	Quirigua
Fol. Cross	Tablet of Foli-	Seib.	Seibal
	ated Cross	S. Rita	Santa Rita
Gl	Glyph	Str	Structure
Hatz. Ceel	Hatzcap Ceel	Sun	Tablet of Sun
HS	Hieroglyphic	T	Temple
	stairway	Tab.	Tablet
Inscr.	Tablet of In-	Thr	Throne
	scriptions	Tik.	Tikal
IS	Initial Series	Ton.	Tonina
L	Lintel	Uax.	Uaxactun
LC	Long Count	u.h.	upper half
l.h.	lower half	Xcal.	Xcalumkin
Mor.	Morales	Yax.	Yaxchilan
MSS	Miscellaneous		
	sculptured stone		

In addition, the full titles of the books of Chilam Balam are contracted from "Book of Chilam Balam of Chumayel" etc. to "Chumayel," "Tizimin," "Mani," "Kaua," "Ixil," "Nah," and "Tekax." Similarly, the word "Codex" is dropped before Dresden, Madrid, Paris, and Mexican codices.

From the epigraphic viewpoint, it is not usually of much consequence whether a given monument is a stela or an altar, but it is necessary that there should be no confusion in abbreviations. Accordingly, the designation of the type of monument is not given in sites such as Copan, where all the monuments, whether stelae or altars, are numbered or lettered in a single sequence; such monuments are here called Cop. B, Cop. 7, Cop. S etc. instead of Stela B, Stela 7, Altar S etc. In sites such as Piedras Negras, where the stelae, altars, lintels, and thrones have different series of numbers or letters, stelae are numbered without designation of their nature, whereas other monuments have the number or letter preceded by the contraction used for the monument in question. Thus, P.N. 3 refers to Stela 3 at that site; P.N. L 3 indicates Lintel 3 at Piedras Negras; P.N. Alt 3 similarly indicates Altar 3 of that city. There is a slight irregularity at Quirigua. No designation of type of monument is given except in the cases of the altars of Zoomorphs O and P, which are referred to as Quir. Alt O and Quir. Alt P; the designations Quir. O and Quir. P are given to the two zoomorphs originally so lettered. The same system applies to the few altars, such as those of Stela 5, attached to stelae at Copan.

Standard nomenclature for monuments is followed with the exception of those at Chichen Itza, to which I have

assigned numbers with the purpose of avoiding the present clumsy system. These are:

Temple of the Initial Series
  1. Lintel
Temple of the Four Lintels
  2. North facade lintel, left doorway
  3. North facade lintel, right doorway
  4. West facade lintel
  5. West lintel of inner room
Temple of the Three Lintels
  6. North facade, left lintel
  7. North facade, middle lintel
  8. North facade, right lintel
Temple of the One Lintel
  9. Temple of the one lintel
House of Hieroglyphic Door Jambs
  10. East and west jambs of doorway in north side of enclosure
The Monjas
  11. Lintel, doorway east facade
  12. Lintel, doorway on left (east) north facade
  13. Lintel, doorway second from left, north facade
  14. Lintel, doorway middle, north facade
  15. Lintel, fourth doorway from left, north facade
  16. Lintel, doorway on right, north facade
  17. Lintel, doorway west facade
  18. Lintel, doorway east facade, East Annex
Akabtzib
  19. Lintel, inner doorway south end
Casa Colorada
  20. Band of glyphs outer chamber, under spring of arch
Caracol
  21. Stela
  22. Altar of same
  23. Hieroglyphic frieze
  24. Middle element of fillets, mask panels
  25. Stone head
La Iglesia
  26. Band of glyphs in stucco under spring of arch
Water Trough
  27. Lintel from water trough in hacienda
High Priest's Grave
  28. East face of southeast column
  29. Re-used blocks
  30. Stones at four exterior corners of sanctuary
Temple of the Wall Panels
  31. Re-used lintel in serpent-tail
Miscellaneous
  32. Round roughly spherical altar, several hundred meters west of south end of west wall of large Ball Court
  33. Painted capstone. Temple of the Owl
  34. Painted capstone. Tomb in terrace east of main corral of hacienda.

In citations of figures italicized numbers refer to positions on the plate, e.g. fig. 13,*6* is number 6 of figure 13; semicolons separate citations of different figures. References to sections of pages of the codices conform to standard practice in lettering the horizontal compartments of pages a,b,c, and, in some cases, d.

A number of current names for glyphic elements, such as "serpent segment," "bone affix," and "down-balls," largely coined by Beyer, are used, but their employment does not imply acceptance of the identifications; it is for simplicity of designation.

As there is a full table of contents and a summary at the end of nearly every chapter, I have not deemed it necessary to give at the start of each chapter an outline of the subjects covered. The index incorporates the illustrative material, and should be used to supplement references in the text to drawings of glyphs and affixes. To avoid unnecessary expense, sources of drawings are not given; with few exceptions they are in books listed in the bibliography, and are familiar to students.

A word should be said about the presence of a quotation at the head of each chapter, a fine custom cold-shouldered, alas, by our age. These serve to accent the theme which runs through the book, although often hidden by detailed discussion, to wit, the essentially poetical, even mystical, concept which underlies the individual glyphs and is discernible in the complete texts. They are also, so to speak, illuminated letters offering their tribute, chapter by chapter, to a glory which has now departed.

In this introductory volume I have essayed interpretations of glyphs, some of which may not hold water. These more dubious cases are included as examples of the new techniques in decipherment which are employed, for a primary objective of this study is to suggest new methods of tackling an old problem. Hence, I would pray readers to be guided in their judgment of my effort by two lines written of another book nearly four centuries ago:

> Be to its virtues very kind
> And to its faults a little blind.

Contents

CONTENTS

CONTENTS

Illustrations

(*at end of text*)

Tables

All excellence has a right to be recorded.

—Samuel Johnson, in *Memoirs of David Garrick Esq.*

I

Introduction

Together let us beat this ample field,
Try what the open, what the covert yield;
The latent tracts, the giddy heights, explore
Of all who blindly creep, or sightless soar;
Eye nature's walks, shoot folly as it flies,
And catch the manners living as they rise.
—ALEXANDER POPE, *An Essay on Man*

PURPOSE OF THIS STUDY

MAYA ARCHAEOLOGY is more than a dry catalogue of pots and pans, of studies of potters' methods and flint-knackers' strokes; it is more than a framework of history painfully erected from the timber of ceramic evolution; it is much more than a bare structure of material culture, for it has the animate beauty which the bricks and mortar of bygone ways of thought give it. In the New World only Maya culture extends to us the privilege of sharing its thoughts and its struggles, its triumphs and its failures, for in the glyphs the dead past has left a chart to guide the living present along the corridors of time to the treasures of its inspiration. That chart has permitted first one student and then another to take a few steps forward, but the half of it is yet ill-understood. The riches to which it leads may never be truly ours, for the accidents of centuries and differing mentality may prove a gulf too wide to bridge, denying us a true comprehension of the causes that channeled Maya thought into that strange, poetic absorption in the passage of time.

In this age when superlatives are used with a freedom that has made them all but meaningless, the commonplace or mediocre seldom lacks the label of remarkable. Yet the achievements of the Maya can be described only in words of grandeur, and no one who has studied Maya concepts of time can do aught but stand humbly in the presence of their records.

Down the centuries dominies have striven with scant success to deck the dull primers of Latin and Greek with a modicum of the beauty to which they are the key. It would be arrogance to think that where they have so often failed I could succeed, for the drudgery of Maya arithmetic, as of Latin paradigms, is the path to knowledge. Yet understanding is the overture to beauty, and if some student, advancing step by step to a comprehension of that symphony of time which is the Maya calendar, is inspired with a growing wonder at its magnificence and poetry, I shall not have written in vain.

The rhythm of time enchanted the Maya; the never-ending flow of days from the eternity of the future into the eternity of the past filled them with wonder. Like a miser counting his hoard, the Maya priest summed the days that had gone and the days that were to come, stacking them in piles, juggling combinations to learn when the re-entering cycles of time would again pass abreast the turnstiles of the present.

There is a quiet nobility in this concept of time's orderly flow which had a compelling appeal to the Maya, whose life was guided by a desire for moderation and consistency in all things. Yet there was a strange mysticism, too, in the striving of the priest-astronomers to bring into harmonious patterns the circling planets, the changing seasons, the shifting sun, and the errant moon. Not only the planets, but the very days were divine, for the Maya held, and in some parts still hold, the days to be living gods. They bow down to them and worship them; they order their lives by their appearance. Truly it might have been written also of the Maya priests, "In the handy-work of their craft is their prayer." It is because that attitude so clearly pervades the hieroglyphic texts, that I have scant patience with those whose sole objective is to assault the mysteries of that orchestrated symphony with slide rules, charts, and adding machines. Had those iconoclasts never heard of the Maya calendar they would have been equally content modernizing Hamlet or planning hydroelectric dams on the River Arno.

Scanning the centuries, our eyes rest on epochs, in which one group or another has produced individuals who, by their paintings or their poetry, their architecture or their prose, their music or their saintliness, have given the world spiritual comfort. Yet beauty, whether it be in the arts or in the lives of individuals or of communities, is all too rare.

In Maya civilization, culminating and finding its expression in the hieroglyphic writing, we have one such summit, perhaps not comparable to such towering ranges as Athens of the sixth and fifth centuries before Christ, Italy of the renaissance, or England of the fifteenth and sixteenth centuries, yet no mean peak. We can scale it

1

only with effort; we must first wander long in the foot-hills of glyphic decipherment, garnering beauty as we go. That is a pleasant and not unprofitable task, for Maya hieroglyphic writing embodies the religious concepts of its users, and in it is embedded a mythology of surpassing richness. In many, perhaps most, of the glyphs are to be found references to beliefs concerning the important gods, their activities, their powers, their kindlinesses, and their ill humors. These sagas are the expression of the Maya soul. Wherefore, in seeking decipherments we must rove in those green pastures of poetry, which we prosaically call mythology. In this study that poetical setting must always be in our thoughts, even when we are deep in minutiae as dreary as the dullest passage in Wordsworth, but for me it has not been easy to keep that beauty ever to the fore since argument and beauty are poor bed-fellows. The quotation at the head of each section is my apology for not having succeeded better in the body of the chapter. Each is a signpost to the reader, whose way I have not clearly marked.

It is not unbridled enthusiasm which bids me describe the Maya calendar, too, as poetry. It is that, indeed, and of a form not unduly remote from that of the Hebrews, which, as preserved in the King James version of the Bible, has molded the culture of our race for three centuries. There are close parallels in Maya transcriptions of the colonial period, and, I am convinced, in the hiero-glyphic texts themselves to the verses of the Psalms, and the poetry of Job. Those magnificent verses, which were sung antiphonally in the Gothic churches of England, studded with the effigies of recumbent knights of another faith, or recited in the spired and wooden churches of Puritan New England, rising with the leaven of Wren's inspiration, have much in common with Maya poetry. It is a subject to which I shall return, for on it depends the whole concept of the Maya calendar.

At first thought, the flow of time may seem hardly the material from which a national poetry could be fashioned, but a little reflection will show that it has all the needed qualities. Time past has the sadness of irrevocability, as Omar Khayyam, through the pen of Fitzgerald, reminds us in moving lines; time to come has the grandeur of the approaching dawn. Man can hardly fail to be moved in spirit as he gazes into the ever-receding past, or ponders the immeasurable future. He faces eternity which-ever way he turns. Appreciation of this concept is the key to Maya thought, I truly believe.

In the beautifully carved blocks of Maya glyphic writing are embodied the accumulated knowledge of the centuries, the Maya ways of thought, and perchance the answers to other problems. Perhaps a full understanding of this glyphic literature may reveal the workings of that strange mentality which led the Maya to chart the heav-ens, yet fail to grasp the principle of the wheel; to visualize eternity, as no other primitive people has ever done, yet ignore the short step from corbeled to true arch; to excel in the impractical, yet fail in the practical.

The study of the highest achievements of Maya cul-ture has as its goal not merely the enrichment of the store of factual knowledge, although there should be no limits to the acquisition of beauty and knowledge, be they in nature, art, or way of life. There is a more distant end: the intellectual and spiritual progress of the Maya, as the most mature expression of New World civilization, is prime material for a comparative study of the growth of culture and for speeding the quest for those elusive laws of human conduct.

The civilizations of the Old World formed a loose unit of culture, the members of which benefited from the ad-vances and discoveries of one another. A comparison of one civilization with another in the Old World will, therefore, not yield reliable criteria for the formulation of any laws that may govern human progress. For evidence of independent growth it is necessary to turn to the New World, where pre-Columbian civilizations developed without marked stimulation from the Old.

Naturally, the greater the progress, the greater the field for comparative study. One cannot weigh potsherds and flint points against the full range of Athenian civiliza-tion. One must seek the most advanced culture of the New World for that purpose. Maya temples and Maya sculpture can be compared with the products of Phidias or Praxiteles, but that is not the whole story. Only a com-plete elucidation of Maya hieroglyphic texts and early colonial transcriptions will reveal the breadth of Maya life. The intellectual progress, the poetry, the philosophy of life, and, indeed, the whole spiritual achievement of the Maya are contained therein, and these alone are worthy of comparison with the products of the minds of Pythagoras and Plato, Pindar and Aristotle.

To chart the diverging and converging paths that lead independently to the cultural peaks must be the final aim of students of history. That is a task far in the future, for in his most optimistic moment every student of the pres-ent generation must in truth echo the words of A. E. Housman:

> I see the country far away
> Where I shall never stand;
> The heart goes where no footstep may
> Into the promised land.

For the present, the nearer objective must engage us. Understanding and patience to continue the study of Maya hieroglyphic writing will be richly rewarded. In the jargon of journalists, archaeologists wrest secrets from the past; I feel rather that our studies win us the privilege of sharing them with the past. In the drudgery of addition and substraction, let us ever bear in mind the poetry of time. The road to that sublime concept of the expanding universe was thickly strewn with rocks of the most arid mathematics; in comparison Maya calculations are but grit.

In the next few pages I have attempted to sketch a geographical and cultural setting for the Maya hieroglyphic writing. Within such a short space it is impossible to give more than the barest summary. Unfortunately, the presentation must be somewhat of a cut-and-dried nature, which largely ignores alternative reconstructions and blurs the transitions from certainty to reasonable conjecture. Its purpose is solely to provide nonspecialists in Maya archaeology with a cultural background for the study of the hieroglyphic writing, for it is to be hoped that this subject will engage increasingly the attention of specialists in the fields of primitive astronomy and the development of writing.

GEOGRAPHY AND ENVIRONMENT

At the time of the Spanish conquest the Maya area covered all Guatemala except parts of the low coastal strip on the Pacific, sections of western El Salvador, the western fringe of Honduras, the whole of British Honduras, and, in Mexico, the entire states of Yucatan and Campeche, the Territory of Quintana Roo, the state of Tabasco except for a small area in the west, and the eastern half of the state of Chiapas. The area forms a rough quadrilateral with a north-south axis of nearly 900 km. The east-west extension is rather less than 550 km. toward the bottom of the rectangle; about 400 km. at the top of the Yucatan Peninsula. The whole area falls within the tropics, the southern boundary being about latitude 14° 20′ (fig. 1).

Like the early Victorian novel, the government of the United States, or, for those who like an old favorite, Gaul, the Maya area is divided into three parts. The southernmost, comprising the Guatemalan highlands and adjacent parts of El Salvador, is highly mountainous. Peaks, many of volcanic origin, tower to great heights. Towns nestle in mountain-girt valleys or sprawl on plateaus. Plants and animals of temperate climates flourish in this region, which only geographical co-ordinates place within the tropics. The temperature is never excessively hot nor unduly cold. A rainy season extends from May to October, nearly 30 cm. of rain usually falling in the peak month of June, but during the dry season there is often a distinct lack of water. The soil, largely of volcanic origin, is fertile.

The highlands had other advantages in addition to good soil and good climate. Stone of volcanic origin formed a handy supply of building material, and from it excellent metates (rubbing stones on which maize was ground) were fashioned. Deposits of obsidian furnished the raw material for sharp knives and spearpoints, and volcanic tuff was a first-rate temper for potters. Iron pyrites served the highlanders for mirrors, and specular hematite was the basis of a much-used red paint. In later times gold was probably washed from streams and copper perhaps mined. All these products were exported to less favorable parts.

The commodity which contributed most to the wealth of the highland Maya was the very highly prized tail feathers of the quetzal, for this bird inhabits only restricted regions of considerable elevation. The feathers were traded far and wide. It is not improbable that jade, also highly esteemed in ancient Central America, was obtained from stream-beds, and perhaps even mined in the highland regions, although no deposits have yet been located. A jade boulder weighing some 200 pounds in a cache at Kaminaljuyu, near Guatemala City, is the largest known piece. It has the marks of stream-rolling. The highland area had every advantage in climate, fertility of soil, variety of flora and fauna, mineral wealth, and strategic position. Nevertheless, although Maya culture here was advanced in a material sense and in political organization, yet in aesthetic development, notably in architecture and sculpture, it lagged far behind the other two areas.

The Central Area, the second main territorial division, is that in which Maya culture reached its greatest height, and in this region hieroglyphic texts are most frequent. It is, for the most part, a low-lying limestone country, 30–180 m. above sea level, intersected by rivers and dotted with lakes and small ponds, although many of these are now swamps because of silting. However, much of the southern part is higher where it bounds the highland area. The large city of Copan in the southeast, for instance, has an elevation of some 600 m., and in the southwest, which is the central part of Chiapas, elevations of over 1500 m. occur. There are also smaller Maya sites at altitudes of around 600 m. in the Maya Mountains of British Honduras, but by and large the region is lowland and in marked contrast to the Guatemalan highlands. Although the southern boundary of the Central Area is pretty clearly defined, it is hard to draw a northern line since the Central Area merges imperceptibly with the Northern Area, geographically and culturally. The northern limits of the Central Area are drawn to include the region in which the Initial Series system of dating was used but where there is no evidence at present of an intensive occupation in later times.

Annual rainfall in the Central Area is very high. In the north it is 1.50–2 m.; in parts of the southern lowlands it averages as high as 2.5–3.1 m. There is a dry season from January to the end of May, but during the rest of the year rainfall is heavy except for a letup some years in September and October or in December. The country is densely covered with mixed tropical rain forest, up to 50 m. high, in which are many varieties of palms, mahogany, cedar, sapodilla (or zapote, from which chewing gum is bled), breadnut (not to be confused with breadfruit), occasional rubber trees and vanilla vines, and incredible quantities of aerial plants and lianas. It is not a friendly country, particularly to those with any tendency to claustrophobia. The fauna is tropical: jaguars, tapirs, deer, peccary, agouti, monkeys of the spider and howler varieties, turkeys, macaws, parrots, boa constrictors, small crocodiles, and, along the coast, alligators abound.

The great core of this region, embracing the Peten district and adjacent parts of British Honduras and Mexico, is now largely uninhabited. Groups of chewing-gum gatherers spend several months in the heart of the forest during the rainy season when the zapote sap flows, but their primitive camps are not permanent, and until a year or two ago one could travel north from Flores, the tiny capital of the Department of Peten, for a distance of about 250 km. through the heart of ancient Maya country without striking a single village. The lack of population at the present time is largely due to the prevalence of malaria and hookworm—both almost certainly introduced from the Old World since the Spanish conquest—lack of roads and resources, and difficulty in controling the forest.

The numerous Maya ruins in this area are buried beneath the thick forest, and our knowledge of them is largely due to their chance discovery by natives cruising for zapote stands to bleed. Consequently these sites came to be known only long after the more accessible cities of Yucatan and of the southern edge of the Central Area had been visited by early travelers.

The more mountainous country to the southwest forms a subarea transitional to the Guatemalan highlands. Parts of it are covered with pine and savanna. Geographically, it is closer to the highlands, but for cultural and linguistic reasons it is best grouped with the Central Area. Unlike the Peten, it has a considerable Indian and mestizo (mixed Indian-Spanish) population.

The central core of the Peten is singularly deficient in natural resources, and the soil is scant except in the valleys. The ubiquitous limestone supplies first-rate stone for building and for sculpture, owing to its softness when first exposed, and it also contains deposits of flint, a good

substitute for the absent and more useful obsidian of the highlands. Minerals and metals are notably rare. The area is off the most important commercial routes of ancient Middle America, but it did produce in some quantity the highly valued cacao (chocolate) bean which served as currency throughout Central America and southern Mexico, and no doubt it exported to the highlands other tropical products such as macaw, trogon, and toucan feathers, jaguar pelts, cotton goods, logwood dye, vanilla, chile, copal incense, and rubber.

The Northern Area, the third division, comprises Yucatan and most of Campeche and Quintana Roo. As one travels northward from the Central Area the climate becomes drier until at the extreme northern tip the annual rainfall averages a scant 45 cm., about one-sixth of that registered for parts of the Southern Area. This, however, is rather exceptional, the rainfall over much of the region averaging 90–125 cm. annually. This greater aridity is reflected in the vegetation which becomes more scrublike as one goes northward. Much of the land is covered with thorny bushes, little resembling the lush rain forest of the Central Area, and many parts of Campeche are covered with savanna. Jaguars are found in Yucatan, but monkeys, tapirs, and macaws are unknown or extremely rare.

The limestone which covers the whole land is much more porous than that of the Central Area, and lets the rain seep through to an underground drainage system, with the result that surface rivers are nonexistent, and lakes occur only along certain fault lines. Much of the land would be quite waterless were it not that in places the surface crust of limestone has caved in, giving access to deposits of water beneath. These natural wells, known as *cenotes,* a corruption of the Maya word *tz'onot,* together with some artificial wells and catch pools, were, and still are, the sole sources of water throughout Yucatan. Yet the country had and now has a considerable population.

The Northern Area is extremely poor in natural resources. Limestone is everywhere, and flint beds are reported, but I suspect that the fine dark flint, used for the choicest work, is not local. Some products of the Central Area, such as rubber, vanilla, and cacao, do not do well in this more arid region. The last was grown to a certain extent in dry cenotes, but not in sufficient quantities to take care of the needs of the region. Cotton, however, grew well, and was widely exported in the form of woven and decorated mantles. There was also an active trade in salt in early colonial times and perhaps before the Spanish conquest. Yucatan is of prime importance because from there we have the fullest information on how Maya culture functioned at the time of the arrival of the Spaniards.

OUTLINE OF MAYA CIVILIZATION AND HISTORY

ORIGINS OF MAYA PEOPLE

Of the origins of the Maya nothing is known. It may be assumed that the ancestors of the Maya reached America from the Old World via the Bering Strait, as supposedly did those of all other American Indians. Physical anthropologists now incline to the view that the round-headed Indians of the New World are the descendants of a strain that was one of the latest to reach America. Since the Maya are one of the most round-headed people in the world, this would tend to place the arrival of their ancestors in this hemisphere at a fairly recent date.

It is uncertain exactly how much culture was brought to the New World from Asia. Until a few years ago it was generally believed that extremely few cultural elements were thus introduced from the Old World, but there is now a tendency to credit more cultural traits of the American Indian to importation by later arrivals from northeastern Asia. Be that as it may, there can be little doubt that the component elements of Maya culture are overwhelmingly of American origin.

It can be supposed that in the millennium prior to the birth of Christ the various peoples of Mesoamerica (roughly definable as the area of high culture between a line drawn slightly north of Mexico City and another crossing Central America through Honduras) shared a fundamentally uniform culture. General similarities in techniques, economy, social organization, and patterns of religious observances presumably were much more striking than local variations found in pottery or in the skill with which stone implements were chipped. Agriculture (principally maize, beans, squash, and perhaps sweet manioc) was without much doubt shared at an early date by the Maya and their neighbors; monochrome pottery of the Formative Period, pleasing in form and burnished slip, reveals in the variety of its temper a lengthy pedigree. There were many seedlings in the cold frame of Middle American culture, and on the Maya plant, indistinguishable from all others, the first pair of leaves can have given no indication of the profuse and rare bloom which the summer of New World civilization would later bring forth.

The Maya area at that time may have been somewhat larger than it was in the sixteenth century, for the Maya-speaking Huaxtec, who now live in northern Veracruz, detached from the main body of the Maya, may then have occupied parts of southern Veracruz or western Tabasco adjacent to the Maya area.

HISTORY

In *The Everlasting Mercy* John Masefield puts into the mouth of the parson some lines which well summarize the slow growth of culture.

> The social states of human kinds
> Are made by multitudes of minds,
> And after multitudes of years
> A little human growth appears.

and

> States are not made, nor patched; they grow,
> Grow slow through centuries of pain
> And grow correctly in the main.

Maya history divides rather conveniently into four great periods: The Formative, The Initial Series, the Mexican, and the Mexican Absorption.

The Formative Period or Middle Culture Horizon. During the second half of the millennium before the birth of Christ the Maya began to develop in the lowlands the distinctive traits which characterize their culture. The intricate Maya calendar, which bursts upon us full grown, like Pallas Athena springing from Zeus' head, can hardly have evolved in a few years. It seems to have the marks of slow growth. The evolution of medicine men into a caste of priests, capable of guiding or forcing the people to such stupendous feats of construction to the glory of their gods, must have been a matter not of years but of generations.

Differentiation was taking place in those elements which were to develop into what I have termed the hierarchic cult, but in the material culture of everyday life a general uniformity appears to have continued. There are no Maya hieroglyphic texts attributable to the Formative Period, although it is to be supposed that certain of the simpler elements of the calendar, such as the 260-day almanac and, possibly, the 365-day year, were shared by the Maya, Zapotec, Olmec, and other peoples of the region. By the close of the period hieroglyphic writing had made enough growth to permit of the development of different glyphic writings for the main centers of culture. The end of this period is marked by the earliest known Maya carving dated in terms of the Maya calendar. This corresponds to A.D. 320 in the Goodman-Martinez-Thompson correlation, followed in this publication. This first Initial Series, together with the appearance of corbeled vaulting and polychrome pottery, marks the change from the Formative Period to the fully developed Maya culture of the Initial Series Period.

The Initial Series or Classical Period. This, the second

stage of Maya history, takes its name from the use of the Initial Series method of dating (p. 154), which was current throughout its length. It spans the six centuries (A.D. 320–909) during which the lowland Maya were erecting stelae with Initial Series inscriptions or related forms of dating. The earliest inscription now known, which is coeval with its carving, is the Leiden plaque, which carries the date 8.14.3.1.12   1 Eb 0 Yaxkin (A.D. 320); the latest is 10.4.0.0.0 12 Ahau 3 Uo (A.D. 909), incised on a jade bead from Tzibanche, Quintana Roo, and probably recorded on the Caracol at Chichen Itza and on the Monjas at Uxmal, both in Yucatan. The Initial Series Period is the classical age of Maya history, to which belong the great architectural developments of the Central Area and the pre-Mexican buildings of the Northern Area and which is marked by the peaks in sculpture and ceramics. To it belong all the great "cities" of the Central Area. It was the period during which the hierarchic cult was at its highest. Interchange of ideas and products, the absence of fortifications, and the tremendous surge of building activity presuppose a period of relative peace. The hierarchic culture is composed of sundry traits, all of which conform to a rather uniform standard. The most important are: hieroglyphic writing; advanced arithmetic and astronomy; calendarial calculations of a nature more complex than those connected with the 260-day almanac; stone architecture, embodying the erection of temples and "palaces," the building of pyramids, and the use of the corbeled vault; typical Maya art, especially in sculpture; and the development of a series of deities not directly of the soil or the elements. To these undoubtedly should be added a theocratic government or one that was deeply influenced by the priesthood, although there is no direct evidence for such an organization.

These elements are in contrast to the traits composing the lay culture. The latter consists of the sum of such activities as agriculture, hunting, pottery making, weaving, and other home industries, together with a social and family organization of a simple form (in the primitive sense, but probably complex as among many less advanced peoples), and a simple religion, built around the personification of the powers of nature, which was served by a nonprofessional priesthood.

The hierarchic culture overspread divergent local cultures, and produced a false appearance of unity, just as Islam, with its Arabic script, mosque architecture, and art style evolved from the prohibition against representing the human figure, gives a superficial uniformity to the various cultures which have embraced its tenets. The various elements of the Maya hierarchic culture did not spread uniformly, with the result that one Maya city may have erected buildings with corbeled vaulting but set up no stelae, and vice versa. However, from the viewpoint of our study, the important fact is that the stela cult never penetrated to the Maya of the Guatemalan highlands.

Certain influences from central Mexico made themselves felt during the Initial Series Period. They are discernible in representation of the Mexican rain god Tlaloc on sundry Maya stelae (some of relatively early date) and are more manifest in certain ceramic forms which appear in the earlier of the two main horizons into which the Initial Series Period is divided. A Maya baroque, brighthued as autumn leaves, appears toward the close. As the period drew to its end, the leaves began to fall.

In all Maya cities there was a collapse of the stela cult and of intensive building activities at or shortly before the close of the Initial Series Period. At one time it was thought that the whole Central Area was then abandoned, but it now appears more probable that the people continued to occupy the region, although the great cities or ceremonial centers, to use a more fitting term, were deserted. In fact, many, perhaps most, great religious centers throughout the Maya area, both in the Guatemalan highlands and in the Northern Area, were deserted at about that time. It is not impossible that this was owing to the overthrow of the hierarchic government. Perhaps this was the work of the common people in revolt against the oppressive demands on their time in the name of a religion which meant little to them; perhaps it was the result of pressure from non-Maya groups, for the tenth century seems to have been a period of unrest and tribal movement in Mexico.

Following the close of the Initial Series Period there is an interlude of about 80 years. During this transitional phase, or at the close of the Initial Series Period, metal first makes it appearance in the Maya area. The exact date of its arrival probably varied from city to city, those nearest the great gold-working regions to the east (Panama and Costa Rica) apparently receiving trade pieces first; but the intensive excavation of Uaxactun, which erected its last stela at 10.3.0.0.0 (A.D. 889), failed to produce a trace of metal.

The Mexican Period. About 10.8.0.0.0 (A.D. 987), according to Maya chronicles of the colonial period, the Itza, a group from the region of Tabasco who may have been Chontal Maya or even Mexicans, conquered and settled several of the large cities of Yucatan. Their culture was profoundly affected by influences from central Mexico, particularly from Tula. During their domination of Chichen Itza, the great religious center of Yucatan, they introduced many Mexican elements and religious concepts, notably new ideas in architecture, the cult of

Quetzalcoatl the feathered-serpent god, and a militaristic organization, the fighting orders of Jaguars and Eagles. There is some evidence of a shift at this time or somewhat later to fortified sites; the adoption of Mexican terms for sundry elements of warfare serves to substantiate this change to a warlike society. Native sources record that at that time several city states in alliance dominated Yucatan.

At or about the same time very similar influences from Tula were modifying Maya culture in the Southern Area. Accordingly, this part of Maya history is known as the Mexican Period. It terminates at 10.19.0.0.0 (A.D. 1204) when, again according to the same sources, the Itza at Chichen Itza were overthrown.

The Mexican Period witnessed a profound change from the apparent theocracy of the Initial Series Period to the aggressive militarism of the new rulers. The old religion in its simple lay-culture form continued to be the prime factor in the lives of the common people, but among the new rulers the new religion, evolved from an uncohesive amalgamation of elements of the old Maya theocratic cult and of Mexican rituals and beliefs, lost ground to political and militaristic institutions. Warfare, once a means to an end—that of obtaining victims for sacrifice to the gods—became more important than the end. The culture changed from one of moderation in all things to one in which excess was the standard; an essentially extrovert pattern replaced one which was, I believe, profoundly introvert. The Mexican Period was to its predecessor as the pretentious formalism of Pope is to the simplicity of the Elizabethan poets.

Few traces of the Mexican Period have been found in the Central Area, which at that time was in cultural eclipse. No hieroglyphic stone monuments are assignable to this horizon, although a few non-Maya glyphs were carved on walls of buildings in the style of the Mexican Period at Chichen Itza; the stela cult had fallen into complete desuetude, but it is probable that two of the three known Maya hieroglyphic codices date from this time.

The Period of Mexican Absorption. This final division of Maya history lasted from 10.19.0.0.0 to 11.16.0.0.0 (A.D. 1204–1539), when it was terminated by the Spanish conquest. During its span Mexican influences gradually became attenuated in both the Northern and Southern Areas. Maya attitudes reasserted themselves, Mexican concepts and deities were discarded or nationalized, and the ruling families became Maya in speech and outlook. By the time of the Spanish conquest there remained little Mexican save a claim by all ruling families to descent from chiefs of Mexican Tula, a dying cult of Quetzalcoatl, and some architectural features.

At the start of the period there was strong centralized government. The Cocom family dominated Yucatan with their seat at the fortified city of Mayapan; in the south at approximately the same time the Quiche Maya, from their fortified capital, ruled the neighboring tribes. Yet there was a very marked retrogression in the arts and in architecture. Taking into consideration also the total lack of hieroglyphic inscriptions and the limited subjects covered in the one codex attributable to this horizon, one can not hesitate to class this as a decadent period.

Mayapan was overthrown about 60 years before the Spanish conquest, and the Northern Area dissolved into many petty chiefdoms, constantly at war with one another. In the Southern Area Quiche rule was also replaced by a process of Balkanization. Of the history of the Central Area during this period we know little, but at the time of the Spanish conquest it, too, was divided into small chiefdoms which fought among themselves. It was the Maya Götterdämmerung.

The parallel developments in the various parts of the Maya area may some day supply material for the students of cultural evolution.

Political and Social Organization During the Initial Series Period

There is no direct information on how the Maya were organized during the Initial Series Period in the Central and Northern areas, but the tremendous amount of religious building, the wholesale manner in which religious structures were altered and enlarged, the effort which went into the erection of dated monuments, the overwhelming dominance of religion in all works of art, the lack of reference to lay activities, and the evidence for a pacific culture all point to theocracy or a government over which the priests had complete control. War was not unknown, but probably was waged primarily to obtain sacrificial victims.

Lack of fortifications, evidence for the rapid spread of new discoveries in the intellectual field, the essential uniformity of the elements of the hierarchic culture from one end of the lowlands to the other, apparent scenes of conferences on astronomy by delegate priests from various groups, and much trading in commodities suggest a general unity. Perhaps one would not be far in error in postulating a loose federation of states each ruled by a small group of sacerdotal aristocrats. Perhaps the Jesuit organization of the Guarani in seventeenth-century Paraguay supplies the closest parallel.

During the Initial Series Period the whole Central Area and the greater part of the Northern Area were dotted with the great religious centers usually termed cities. However, it is virtually certain that these were not cities in our sense of the word, but rather ceremonial centers to which the people repaired for religious exercises and such lay activities as markets and courts of justice. The buildings are little suited to permanent habitation and in fact show no evidence of prolonged occupation. It is, however, probable that priests and novices took up residence in the temples and "palaces" for the long periods of fasting which preceded important ceremonies. Such temporary residence would account for the rather slight traces of occupation sometimes visible in Maya buildings. The general population undoubtedly lived in small scattered groups in the surrounding country. They must have been forced to work for long periods on the erection of the innumerable courts, platforms, pyramids, and temples of their sacred cities.

INDUSTRIES

Maya civilization was based primarily on maize, but many other plants were cultivated. The importance of maize and the deep religious feeling of the Maya toward it are alike illustrated by the fact that in many parts the Maya do not refer to maize directly by its name but in a reverent manner address it as "Your Grace." Land was held by the community and allotted to the heads of families for as long as they were able to work it. Perhaps over 90 per cent of the Maya were farmers, for many of those that had other occupations also cultivated their lands. We can presume that only the small ruling class and a restricted group, comprising such trades as masons and merchants, did not farm.

Not a few masons must have been permanently employed in construction of the religious centers, for the amounts of mortar alone that were used were enormous. Presumably the rank and file were made to work so many days a year hauling supplies and doing unskilled work on the buildings. The Maya had no domesticated animals, except dogs and fowl, and therefore no beasts of burden; they never learned to apply the principle of the wheel (except, perhaps, to use on toys, such as were constructed in Veracruz); and, to make life still more onerous, they had no tools except those of stone to clear the forest from their lands (copper axes appeared only shortly before the Spanish conquest, and even then were not too common).

SCULPTURE

Maya sculpture is one of the great glories of pre-Columbian America, but the newcomer to this field may at first have difficulty in appreciating it because its conventions are very different from those of western art. The primary interests of the artist lay in exactly reproducing the attributes of each god and in conforming to the traditional style of presentation. The necessity of introducing so much symbolism led to over-elaboration of certain aspects and to consequent distortion of proportions and failure to allow the design to stand forth by leaving the background plain. Thus, in many sculptures the head, with its elaborate headdress, may occupy over a third of the total height of the portrait because these were the vehicles principally employed to convey full information on the deity portrayed. At first this disproportion strikes our western eyes as uncouth, and seems to indicate lack of aesthetic development, but as one grows accustomed to Maya conventions, one takes them as much for granted as the lack of western conventions in oriental art, or many of the standards of our own art.

That tradition dictated the somewhat awkward positions of gods or their impersonators is demonstrated by the fact that subsidiary figures are quite frequently delineated with much greater skill, and with a vitality lacking in the static postures of the principal personages. In such details, the artist, unstifled by religious convention, showed his real worth. A true appreciation of the great heights to which Maya sculpture rose can be attained only through the study of such minor details.

The problem of perspective was sometimes tackled in a pleasing way by combining high with low relief, so that the principal figure in high relief stands against a background of low relief or even incised work. Size of figure was used not to convey perspective but to designate the relative importance of the participants in a scene. Thus captives and attendants are usually shown as about one quarter the size of the principal figure. On occasion, deities, other than the one occupying the central position, are on a small scale because their rôles were subsidiary to that of the principal god.

The employment of blocks of glyphs to counter disharmonic groupings, the treatment of feathers, particularly in the way the long sweeps were broken by carving one or two feathers with a forward swirl, as though ruffled by a breeze, the not infrequent use of a diagonal and secondary axis, and the way in which a three-dimensional effect was achieved in low-relief sculpture by allowing details of the design to overflow the frame, are a few among the many ways in which Maya sculpture attains true greatness.

Maya sculptural portraiture is distinctly static. It conveys a message of calm self-assurance and obviously reflects the temperament of a group that had chosen a philosophy of life in which moderation and dignity were dominant.

In contrast to sculptural portraiture, Maya murals of the Classical Period have remarkable animation. The artist, unshackled by the conventions of the stela cult, reveals his mastery of problems of grouping and of techniques, such as foreshortening. All stiffness disappears; the figures are quickened; the chatter and movement of real life are reproduced with amazing charm and vivacity. The same is true, although to a lesser degree, of portraiture on polychrome pottery. Even when tackling that refactory substance, jade, the artist reveals great powers of composition.

ARCHITECTURE

The large ceremonial centers or cities of the Maya were sometimes of considerable size. Tikal, the largest, occupies an area about 1150 m. long by 750 m. wide. A ceremonial center consists of many courts flanked by platforms and pyramids in astonishing numbers. On the platforms often stood large buildings of many rooms, to which the convenient but slipshod term "palace" is applied; the pyramids were usually crowned with small temples containing only one or two or three rooms. From the doorways of the highest of these one now looks across the tops of the trees growing in the courts beneath, the range of green hues not unlike the contrasting shades in shoal water, with perhaps the white walls of one or two temples rising like coral islands above the sea of foliage. In ancient times one would have had an uninterrupted view across the city with its clusters of smaller pyramids topped by temples, its multichambered buildings facing courts at different levels, and its endless surfaces of cream-white stucco relieved only by shadow and an occasional building finished in red.

There is a bewildering amount of local variation in minor details which serves to counteract the lack of deviation in major aspects from the pattern tradition had imposed on the builders. Tikal, in its crowded buildings and soaring pyramids, and even in its sculptural art, has the restless quality of a Tschaikowsky symphony, whereas at Palenque the rhythm of architecture and art beats more peacefully. The restful lines of its bas-reliefs in stone and stucco, and the less pretentious elegance of its smaller and fewer buildings, with their traceried roof-crests, are indicative of a greater cultural self-assurance. They are best translated in terms of an eighteenth-century minuet.

In the great court and in various smaller courts stood the stelae, like sentinels, before the approaches to platforms and pyramids. One can visualize the priest-astronomer, anxious to check his theories on the length of the solar year or the lunar month, threading his way from stela to stela to see what calculations his predecessors recorded in the then dim past, or one can conjure up the acrid, sooty smoke of copal incense which rose on special occasions from braziers placed before each stela. Just as one now forces one's way through the tangled vegetation that crowds the courts and surges up mound and across terrace, so, in ancient times, a late arrival at some ceremony must have shouldered his way through the congregation, which, packed in the court, intently witnessed some ceremony held on the platform top of a pyramid before the temple door. I once espied a troop of monkeys sporting in the ceremonial court of Tikal, converting it into a New World court of Jamshyd.

The Maya employed the corbeled vault familiar to students of Old World archaeology, the stone courses of the vault overlapping each other like inverted staircases, until the two sides were sufficiently close to be bridged by a line of capstones. Because Maya architects usually adhered to this type of vaulting, rooms were narrow, never exceeding about 4 m. in width. To balance each half of the vault thick walls were necessary, and as the overlap of each course was small, vaults were high. The Maya, accordingly, carried the façade up to or somewhat above the level of the roof, and thereby produced a large area which could be, and often was, used as a field for decoration.

Some buildings had flat roofs of stone and mortar laid on beams, others were of perishable materials, and still others had walls of stone and roofs of thatch.

As already noted, there is no evidence that Maya cities of the Initial Series Period were fortified in any way. Small mounds on the outskirts of the ceremonial centers supported huts which were probably the dwelling places of the priests and other members of the ruling class; the huts of the rank and file were probably scattered through the surrounding country. They, too, were of perishable materials.

A perusal of Miss Proskouriakoff's album of architectural renderings will bring to life the Maya cities to a degree which no description can hope to rival.

RELIGION

A review of Maya religion within the compass that can be allotted to it in this introduction can hardly claim to satisfy the general reader; it certainly fails to pleasure the writer. It is, in truth, regrettable that there exists no comprehensive publication on the subject because the religious concepts of the Maya are extremely complex, and that complexity throws light on their history and on their mental and spiritual outlook. Moreover, the matter is of outstanding importance to this study owing to the close relationship between Maya hieroglyphic writing and religion, for there is no doubt that many of the forms and perhaps the names of hieroglyphs have religious connotations. A knowledge of Maya theology and myth is essential to the student of Maya epigraphy.

Information on the subject preserved by Spanish writers of the sixteenth and seventeenth centuries is scant; it must be supplemented by data gathered from modern ethnological sources and from the related fields of Mexican religion. The religious concepts of the Maya and of the peoples of central and southeastern Mexico were fundamentally the same at the time of Spanish conquest, but we have no good means of knowing how much foreign intrusions during the Mexican Period altered those of the Maya, or what effects the still earlier Mexican influences of the first half of the Initial Series Period had on them. In the brief outline given below certainty and theoretical reconstruction are cheek by jowl, for space does not permit distinguishing them.

Cosmology. The Maya appear to have believed that the sky was divided into 13 compartments, in each of which certain gods resided. These may have been arranged as 13 horizontal layers or as six steps ascending on the east to the seventh and then six more descending on the west, so that compartments 1 and 13, 2 and 12, etc. were on the same level. In the latter case there were 13 heavens but seven layers. The sky was sustained by four gods, the Bacabs, who were placed one at each side of the world. An association of supreme importance in Maya religion is that of colors with directions. Red is the color of the east, white of the north, black of the west, and yellow of·the south; there may have been a fifth color, green, for the center. Almost every element in Maya religion and not a few parts of the Maya calendar are connected with one world direction and its corresponding color. Thus the red Bacab stood at the east, the white Bacab at the north, the black Bacab at the west, and the yellow Bacab at the south.

At each of the four sides of the world (or perhaps at each side of one of the heavens) stood a sacred ceiba (the wild cotton tree), known as the Imix ceiba, and these, too, were associated with the world colors. They appear to have been the trees of abundance, from which food for mankind first came; their counterparts in Aztec mythology helped to sustain the heavens. There is a group of 13 gods which appear to symbolize the sky and daylight; they fought with the group of nine gods who represent the underworld and night.

Of the Maya's ideas on the form of the earth we know little. The Aztec thought the crust of the earth was the top of a huge saurian monster, a kind of crocodile, which was the object of a certain cult. It is probable that the Maya had a similar belief, but it is not impossible that at the same time they considered the world to consist of seven compartments, perhaps stepped as four layers.

There seems no reason to doubt that the Maya, like the Aztec, believed that there were nine underworlds, one below the other or again stepped with the fifth the bottom-most. At any rate, the nine lords of the nights, who have an evil aspect, are as prominent in the Maya calendar as in the Aztec. In Aztec belief these ruled the nine underworlds; Mictlantecutli, one of the nine lords and chief god of the underworld, and his wife ruled the fifth. The numbers 13, 9, 7, and 4 have great ritualistic and divinatory importance in both Maya and Aztec cultures.

The Aztec believed the world had been created five times and had been destroyed four times, the present age being the fifth. Each age had been brought to a violent end, the agents being respectively ferocious jaguars, a hurricane, volcanic eruptions, and a flood. The traditions that have survived among the Maya on the number of creations and destructions of the world are somewhat at variance. That we are now in the fourth age is the view expressed in two sources. Nevertheless, it is probable that Maya belief was in agreement with the Aztec in assigning the number 5 to the present age.

Mexican sources allot varying lengths to these ages. The total as given in the Historia de Colhuacan y de Mexico is 2028 years; that of Codex Vaticanus A is 18,028 years. There seems little doubt that each age was believed to have been a multiple of 52 years (after which the cycle of year names starts to repeat), to which in some cases were added a few years to mark the interregna. There is no information on the periods the Maya assigned to their past ages. The theoretical start of the Maya calendar was over 5,000,000 years in the past according to Long (1919). As will be demonstrated (App. IV), there are good grounds for believing that the Maya reckoned backwards not five, but hundreds of millions of years, and one can, perhaps, assume that the Maya grasped the concept of a calendar, and therefore a world, without beginning. This idea would have existed alongside a belief in various creations and destructions of the world.

General Characteristics of Maya Deities. Most Maya gods were in groups of four, each associated with a world direction and world color, but at the same time, as in the Christian doctrine of the Trinity, the four were regarded as one. Thus there were four Chacs (rain gods) but at the same time one could speak of the four as a single personality. In this, as in very many respects, Maya and Mexican concepts and even deities are remarkably alike.

Gods could have both good and bad aspects. The Chacs sent the rain, but they also sent hail and long periods of damp which produced rust on the ears of corn. The Chac might therefore be shown as a beneficial deity or as a death-dealing power. In the latter case he could be presented with a skull replacing his head, and with other insignia of death. Gods could change their localities and resultant associations. The sun god was, naturally, a sky god, but at sunset he passed to the underworld to become one of the lords of nights, and emerged at dawn with the insignia of death. To depict him during his journey through the underworld it was necessary to add attributes, such as those of the jaguar or black, the color of the underworld, or maize foliage, which also connoted the surface of the world and the underworld. In a similar manner celestial dragons could become terrestrial monsters. These varying aspects of deities make the elucidation of Maya religion more difficult. Many, perhaps we can say most, Maya gods blend the features of animals or plants with a human aspect. The Maya may have made their gods in their own mental image, but hardly in their physical image.

Sky Gods. Of the sky gods perhaps most important from the epigraphical viewpoint were the sun and moon (figs. 14,*18,23,24;* 15,*15,16*). Around them was built a veritable cycle of legends. Sun and moon, prior to their translation to the skies, were the first inhabitants of the world. Sun is patron of music and poetry and was a famed hunter; moon was the goddess of weaving and of childbirth. Sun and moon were the first to cohabit, but moon, who was unfaithful to her husband, earned an unenviable reputation for looseness, and her name became synonymous with sexual license. As the flowers of the *plumeria* tree (frangipani) were the symbol of sexual intercourse, they came to be associated with both sun and moon. The monkey had the same symbolic qualities. We find both these traditions reflected in the hieroglyphic writing. From parallel beliefs in central Mexico we can add to the functions of the moon that of being goddess of maize and of the earth and probably all its crops. Sun and moon were finally translated to the sky. Moon's light is less bright than that of sun because one of her eyes was pulled out by sun. A widespread belief, still prevalent in Middle America, but clearly not shared by the Maya priest-astronomers, is that eclipses are due to fights between sun and moon. In Yucatec the sun is *Kin,* and in most Maya languages or dialects the word is similar or a slight variant thereof. The moon is *U* or *Uh* in Yucatec and other lowland dialects; *Po* or *Ikh* in several highland languages or dialects. Honorific titles such as "lord" and "lady," "our father" and "our mother," or "our grandfather" and "our grandmother" were bestowed on sun and moon almost throughout the Maya area.

Itzamna was perhaps the most important deity in the Maya pantheon. Again there were actually four Itzamnas, one assigned to each world direction and color. There can be little doubt that the Itzamnas are the four celestial monsters (often represented as two-headed alligators or lizards; sometimes shown as serpents with one or two heads) which are so prevalent in Maya art of all periods. To evidence on this point gathered some years ago (Thompson, 1939, pp. 152–62) may be added the important facts that *itzam* is translated in the Vienna dictionary as "lizard" and Izamal is said to have meant the place of the lizard. Anthropomorphic forms of Itzamna existed. Among the Chorti Maya of the eastern fringes of the Central Area sky monsters, known as Chicchan, are thought to be half human, half snake, and they are associated with world directions and colors. There are also terrestrial manifestations of the Chicchan. These celestial monsters are deities of the rain and, by extension, of the crops and food.

Other dwellers in the skies were the deities who were the planets and the Chacs. Of the former the Venus god was of supreme importance in the Maya hieroglyphic records; the Chacs, like the Itzamnas, are rain gods, and have ophidian attributes. It is possible that they merely represent a different manifestation of the Itzamnas, but it is, perhaps, a shade more probable that they are elements of the simpler and older religion which survived particularly among the peasants in rivalry with the more occult deities, such as the Itzamnas, favored by the hierarchy.

Kukulcan, as Quetzalcoatl was called in Yucatan, appears to have been but a flash in the Maya pan. Of supreme importance in the art of the Mexican Period, he appears to have been regarded as alien by the great body of the Maya. His ephemeral character is well illustrated by the fact that his name is quite unknown among the present-day Maya, although the Chacs and other gods of the soil are still worshipped. His portraits are very rare or unknown in the codices and during the Initial Series Period.

Earth Gods. Of the gods of the soil those who have charge of the crops are most important. A deity of vegetation in general and of maize in particular, a youthful personage who incorporates features of the young corn, is frequently represented in Maya art (fig. 13,*1,2*). His head is used as a symbol for the number 8 (fig. 24,*42–49*). In the more rugged parts of the Maya area gods of the soil are associated with prominent mountains, springs, the confluences of rivers, and other outstanding manifestations of nature. There is a little evidence suggesting that there may have been a group of seven deities associated with the surface of the earth, just as there were 13 sky gods and nine gods of the underworld.

It is almost certain that the Maya, like the Mexicans, believed that the world rested on the back of a huge alligator or crocodile, which, in turn, floated in a vast pond. I am inclined to think that there may have been four of these terrestrial monsters, each assigned to a world direction and each with its distinguishing features (fig. 12,*1–4*), although at the present time there is some doubt as to whether the sundry attributes of these saurian monsters are interchangeable or whether they serve to distinguish the various reptiles from one another.

The jaguar god, corresponding to the Mexican Tepeyollotl, god of the interior of the earth, is an important Maya deity of the surface of the earth or its interior, for the two regions overlap (fig. 12,*12–15*). Of importance, too, is the old god, the Mam, who carries the symbol of the year, and generally has a conch shell on his back, and is believed to cause earthquakes when he moves in his residence beneath the earth (fig. 21,*1–7*). The earth deities share a number of attributes, of which the water lily, shells, and other aquatic symbols, the Imix sign, and attributes of death are the most prominent.

Gods of the Underworld. The Aztec believed that there were three abodes of the dead. Warriors who had died in battle or on the sacrificial stone and women who had succumbed in childbirth went to a celestial paradise. The former escorted the sun from the eastern horizon to the zenith; the latter from the zenith to the western horizon. Persons who had died of sundry diseases, such as dropsy and epilepsy, and those who were drowned or had been struck by lightning (the axes hurled by the rain gods) went to Tlalocan, the home of the Mexican rain gods, called Tlalocs. This was a paradise in which all edible plants grew in great profusion, and, according to one source, formed the lowest celestial compartment. The third abode of the dead was Mictlan, apparently the lowest compartment of the underworld, whither departed those who had not qualified for either of the other two lands of the dead. The god and goddess of death ruled this realm.

How closely these concepts were paralleled in Maya belief is not certain. There is no evidence for a celestial abode for warriors, which may have been an outgrowth of Mexican warrior cults, but there was definitely a Maya equivalent of Tlalocan, and, at least in later times, an underground abode of the dead, ruled perhaps by Kisin, whose name implies the stench of the charnel house, and who is probably the death god so frequently represented in Maya codices (fig. 13,*11,19*).

In the pantheons of the peoples of Mexico and of the Maya there was a group of nine deities, called in Yucatec Bolon-ti-Ku, "nine gods," who were the lords of nights, and gods of the underworld. They ruled in succession over the nights in contrast to the 13 sky gods who apparently ruled the days in sequence. The glyphs of the Maya nine lords of nights and underworlds are known (fig. 34), but not all of them can be identified, although the first of the

series, the night sun or the sun god in Hades, is easily recognized.

Deification of Periods of Time and Numbers. The 20 days, which formed the Maya "week," were regarded as gods, and were the recipients of prayers. The days were in a way embodiments of gods, such as the sun and moon, the maize deity, the death god, and the jaguar god, which were drawn from their various categories to be reassembled in this series. The numbers which accompany the days were also gods and perhaps correspond to the 13 sky gods, although they are also in the same sequence as 13 of the day gods. The fact that in this series of 13 occur gods of the underworld or the surface of the earth does not seriously militate against their identification as the original 13 gods of the heavens, for Maya deities pass elusively from one region to the other. Similarly, all periods of time appear to have been regarded as gods, and Maya divinities form and reform in bewildering aggroupments, thereby supplying the priest-astrologer with means to hedge on his prophecies but sorely perplexing the modern student.

Sundry Gods. In addition to the deities assigned to sky, earth, and underworld, there were various gods not so easily placed, albeit temporarily, in those categories. At the time of the conquest, the Maya had various gods who were the patrons of trades, such as the patron deities of merchants, beekeepers, and tattooers. It is not improbable that several of these were merely manifestations of specialized aspects of gods, whose main functions were of a more general nature. Various deified heroes reported for sixteenth-century Yucatan probably reflect Mexican influences, but deities of animal origin, such as the dog and the Moan bird, surely were worshipped during the Initial Series Period, as was the god of the flint or obsidian blade. On the other hand, we have no information on a Maya god of fire, although among the Mexicans that deity was of considerable importance. The Maya recognized a supreme being, the creator god, but, like the Mexicans, appear to have accorded him little worship, presumably because he was regarded as remote from human affairs.

Several of the Maya gods have various names reflecting their functions and their calendar days; their glyphs will be discussed as occasion arises.

I believe the outstanding characteristics of Maya religion to be: (1) Reptilian origin of deities of the rain and of the earth; features of snakes and crocodiles, merged and fantastically elaborated, alone or blended with human characteristics, distinguish those gods. Deities with purely human form are not common in Maya art. (2) Quadruplicity of various gods together with association with world directions and colors, yet a mystic merging of the four in one, a process somewhat comparable to the Christian mystery of the Trinity. (3) Duality of aspect, for deities could be both benevolent and malevolent, and in some cases, seemingly, could change sex. This duality also extends to age, for in the case of several deities, functions are shared between a youthful and an aged god. Malevolence is expressed in art by the addition of insignia of death. (4) Indiscriminate marshaling of gods in large categories so that a god might belong to two diametrically opposed bodies, becoming, for instance, a member of a sky group as well as of an underworld group. (5) Great importance of the groups of gods connected with time periods. (6) Inconsistencies and duplication of functions arising from the imposition of concepts originating among the hierarchy on the simpler structure of gods of nature worshipped by the early Maya.

Sacrifices. In Maya eyes the gods were not benevolent dispensers of indiscriminate charity; they did not grant favors but traded them for offerings of incense, food, and blood. It is a rather pleasant concept, revealing somewhat of a desire on the part of the Maya not to be over-beholden to anyone and disclosing also an absence of abasement.

Human sacrifice almost certainly was practiced by the Maya in all periods of their history, but never on a scale approximating that reached by the Aztec. At one time it was thought that mactation was introduced during the Mexican Period, but evidence has now been uncovered which shows that the rite was observed during the Initial Series Period. Devotees customarily drew blood from various parts of their bodies to offer to the gods. The drawing of blood from the tongue and the offering of the sacrifice to a snake god are depicted on lintels from Yaxchilan. Sundry animals, such as dogs, deer, and turkeys, and large quantities of foodstuffs, particularly those made of maize, were also offered to the gods. Pictographic glyphs representing these offerings are prominent in Dresden. Copal and rubber were burned in sacrifice; the smoke represented the rain-filled clouds, an example of sympathetic magic. Jades, most cherished possession of the Maya, were also offered.

Character and Mental Outlook of the Maya

Some years ago Dr. Morris Steggerda persuaded a small group of American ethnologists, archaeologists, and missionaries who had been in rather close contact with Yucatec Maya to rate them on certain psychological traits. The majority opinion was: The average Yucatec Maya is socially inclined and likes to work in groups. He has strong family ties but shows little outward affection. He is not quarrelsome. Though good-natured and sympathetic toward those in distress, he is fond of practical jokes. He is a keen observer and has a very good memory. He is fairly intelligent, but not particularly inventive or imaginative or inclined to wander. He is very fatalistic and superstitious, and not particularly afraid of death. His sexual life is not over-emphasized, but he has a strong tendency to alcoholism. He is thrifty and unusually honest and exceptionally clean in his person. His wife is a neat housekeeper. Individuals vary in their desire to excel, in their religious enthusiasm, and in their attitude toward change. Murderers and beggars are exceptional in a Maya community.

My own answers agreed fairly closely with those of the majority replying to the questionnaire except that my observation in remote Maya villages of British Honduras leads me to believe that as individuals and groups the Maya like to move from one place to another. I would also list corporal modesty as a very marked trait, and give them a high rating for industry. I have noticed that a Maya, unless strongly influenced by Spanish contacts, is little inclined to sing and is even less given to whistling a tune. I would deem the Maya deeply religious, and would say that in his dealings he is formal. I have noticed in trials for small offenses that the presiding judge (the "mayor" of the village) seeks a verdict that will satisfy both parties rather than a strict application of the law. He will discuss the decision with each side, put himself in turn in the position of plaintiff and defendant, try to see both points of view, sympathize with both sides, and coax them to a reconciliation. I think this attitude epitomizes the Maya attitude of "live and let live."

On the whole this description applies pretty well to all Maya groups of the present time, although in some regions the Maya are not so clean and pacific as in Yucatan. It probably would have fitted the mass of Maya in pre-Spanish days except in two regards: intelligence and artistic attainments. The Maya of today is fairly intelligent but not exceptionally so, and he shows little artistic inclination at the present time except in such minor arts as the brocading of textiles and the shaping of pottery. This retrogression is largely attributable to the submergence of the ruling class in colonial times, although there were clear signs of a decline in the centuries immediately prior to the Spanish conquest.

The Maya outlook on life has a direct bearing on the content of the hieroglyphic texts and therefore merits a brief review. It is a subject which, despite its obvious importance, has never been discussed in any book dealing with the Maya.

The Maya philosophy is best summarized in the motto "Nothing in excess" which was inscribed over the temple of Delphi. Harmonious living, moderation, and a full comprehension of that spirit of toleration for the foibles of one's neighbors contained in the expression "live and let live" characterize Maya civilization. The development of a somewhat similar philosophy has been generally considered one of the greatest achievements of Athenian civilization, and rightly has been put before material progress.

The various books of Chilam Balam (p. 34) which have survived reveal unconsciously that the preceding paragraph correctly summarizes the Maya philosophy of life. This is particularly apparent in the descriptions of the two occasions when the Maya felt the impact of alien ideas and ways of living: first when they were conquered by the militaristically minded Mexicans, second when the imposition of Spanish rule required tremendous mental and physical adjustments. Both conquests were accompanied by great bloodshed and cruelty, but it is highly significant that it was the disappearance of harmonious living, not the temporary slaughter and cruelty, which impressed itself on the Maya mentality. This is reflected in the following passage in the Chilam Balam of Chumayel (Roys, 1933) contrasting life before and after the Itza conquest:

In due measure did they recite the good prayers; in due measure they sought the lucky days, until they saw the good stars enter into their reign. Then they kept watch while the reign of the good stars began. Then everything was good. Then they adhered to the dictates of their reason; in the holy faith their lives were passed. There was then no sickness. . . . At that time the course of humanity was orderly. The foreigners [the Itza] made it otherwise when they arrived here. They brought shameful things when they came. They lost their innocence in carnal sin; they lost their innocence in the carnal sin of Nacxit Xuchit, in the carnal sin of his companions. . . . This was the cause of our sickness also. There were no more lucky days for us; we had no sound judgment. At the end of our loss of vision and of our shame everything shall be revealed. There was no great teacher, no great speaker, no supreme priest when the change of rulers occurred at their arrival. Lewd were the priests. . . .

The mention of carnal sin and lewdness refers to certain erotic practices introduced by the Itza, which were not at all in accordance with the Maya concept of purificatory rites before interceding with the gods. The Maya clearly attributed the subsequent outbreaks of sickness and general disaster to these erotic practices. In another passage referring to the immodesty of the Itza we read:

They twist their necks, they twist their mouths, they wink the eye, they slaver at the mouth, at men, women, chiefs, justices, presiding officers . . . everybody, both great and small. There is no great teaching. Heaven and earth are truly lost to them; they have lost all shame. . . . Understanding is lost; wisdom is lost. . . . Dissolute is the speech, dissolute the face of the rogue to the rulers, to the head chiefs.

Of the change resulting from the Spanish conquest the Maya scribe writes:

Before the coming of the mighty men and Spaniards there was no robbery by violence, there was no greed and striking down one's fellow man in his blood, at the cost of the poor man, at the expense of the food of each and everyone. [And elsewhere:] It was the beginning of tribute, the beginning of church dues, the beginning of strife with purse snatching, the beginning of strife with guns, the beginning of strife by trampling of people, the beginning of robbery with violence, the beginning of debts enforced by false testimony, the beginning of individual strife, a beginning of vexation. . . .

There had been tribute before the Spanish came, but it had not been onerous; and doubtlessly violence was not entirely unknown, but what an indictment of our civilization! All through these quotations and similar passages the Maya spirit of moderation is revealed. Wisdom, restraint, orderliness, honesty, respect for one's fellow men, reasonableness and nonresort to violence are the elements stressed. The flouting of them by the new rulers is deplored. These writings are not nostalgic recollections of an idealized past. The same attitude is revealed in the customary prayers of hunters, wherein it is promised that only what is needed will be killed. The Maya believes that it is wrong to slaughter wild life indiscriminately, and that he must show consideration for the animals themselves, and for others who also depend on hunting to augment their food supplies. The desire to see both points of view survives in the simple judicial proceedings to which I have referred.

There are historical instances of this Maya spirit of toleration. After the overthrow of Mayapan, the Mexican mercenaries were not massacred or even expelled from the country, despite the fact that they had been instrumental in keeping a tyranny in existence. Instead, they were given territory in which to settle.

Early in the seventeenth century two friars visited the still independent Itza of Tayasal. On being taken on a tour of the city, one of them on a sudden impulse smashed the chief idol in its temple, and, with his face alight with fanatical joy, exhorted the enraged Itza to become Christians. After resting in the guest house, the friars visited the chief ruler and told him what they had done. He, of course, already knew of the incident but showed no outward sign of anger, and in the subsequent conversation did not once refer to the matter. Far from suffering the death which in Maya eyes they must have merited for this sacrilege, the two friars were permitted to continue their stay on the island and to say their daily masses in public. The only outward manifestations of anger were a refusal to supply the friars with men to accompany them when they finally departed and a shower of stones and some jeering as they set out. How many other peoples would have displayed equal moderation?

The art of the Initial Series Period reflects cultural tranquility as clearly as the restless art of the Mexican Period mirrors the turbulent, extrovert influences of that epoch; but it is the superb compromise which the Maya made between their own religion and Christianity, amalgamating elements of both in a harmonious and living whole, which most clearly illustrates this philosophy of life. A people that could adjust itself and its culture so well, and eschew excess so uncompromisingly, had achieved an intellectual advance which we may well envy.

Bearing of Maya Mentality on Glyphic Writing

The mental characteristics of the Maya have, I think, affected their glyphic writing and its subject matter to a considerable degree. So far as the glyphs themselves are concerned, the marked artistic sensibilities of the Maya must be partly responsible for the extreme diversity permissible in their delineation, although without the Maya concept of the personification of glyphs, this variation would have been less extreme. In theory, every glyph could seemingly have at least two distinct outlines: a symbolic (or normal) form and a head (or personified) form. In addition, there were many elements which could be substituted for one another, and many of these must have had their origins in the poetical and artistic concepts which enriched the figurative speech and, in turn, expanded the range of glyphs.

In the content of the glyphic texts Maya mentality and character are more evident. Without infinite patience, the methodical recording of all pertinent data, and a willingness to correct previous errors, progress in astronomy would have been scant, and the bulk of the material on the stelae would never have been recorded. The motto *per ardua ad astra* would have served Maya astronomers as well as modern aviators. I am persuaded that inscriptions were longest around 9.13.0.0.0 (A.D. 692) because the Maya scientists were then deep in argument on two problems: the length of the solar year and how best to record lunar data. A century later, after these matters had been solved to the satisfaction of the priest-astronomers, the inscriptions on stelae were much abbreviated.

The poetical endowment of the Maya also, I believe, affected the form of the inscriptions, and glyphs were added, like enough, not in a spirit of witless tautology, but because they corresponded to the antiphonal character of the spoken word (p. 62).

One wonders, too, whether the not infrequent mistakes in texts may not in some cases reflect Maya mentality. Some errors may have arisen from hasty transference

to stone of the drawings on the work sheets of the priest-astronomer in charge, or, if the glyphs were outlined in charcoal on the smooth stone, smudging of the design might have caused mistakes, such as the carving of a crescent instead of a dot or the omission of a numerical bar; but some errors, such as the carving of a wrong glyph, can not be blamed on the sculptor. Naranjo 18 has the Initial Series introductory glyph corresponding to Yax, whereas it should be Zac; Pusilha H has Glyph G9 instead of G1. These mistakes are so obvious that a tyro could hardly have made them. Did they result from plain carelessness in calculation or is there some other reason for them? The erection of a stela must have been an event of great importance, and it seems incredible that no one proofread the inscription before it was carved. Perhaps, therefore, G. B. Gordon was on the right track many years ago, when he suggested that the Maya may have deliberately made mistakes, holding the oriental view that no human undertaking should be perfect, as perfection belonged to the gods. This theory, if acceptable, gives a fresh insight into Maya mentality.

Finally, because of the deprecatory attitude toward individual assertiveness which characterizes Maya culture, glyphic inscriptions on the monuments, unlike those of almost every other civilization in the history of mankind, almost certainly do not record the deeds of individuals; instead, they are utterly impersonal records of calendarial and astronomical data and of religious matters.

Language

At the present time there are 15 Maya languages or major dialects spoken or recently extinct, and several of these are further divided into minor dialects, so that altogether there are about 23 Maya languages or dialects; it is impossible to be more definite because some have not yet been well studied, and many of them hardly differ sufficiently from one another to deserve separate ranking (fig. 1). The Maya stock may be compared to the Romance group of languages: some Maya languages are closer than Spanish is to Portuguese, others stand in approximately the same relation as French to Italian. Quite possibly we should speak of only two Maya languages, a highland and a lowland, and classify the rest as dialects.

Authorities on linguistics are noncommittal as to what wider affiliations Maya may have. There is a tendency to consider that it may be related to the Mixe-Zoque-Huave group of languages spoken in central Chiapas and southern Veracruz, just west of the Maya area. Should that be so, it is possible that Maya fits into a yet larger category. This embraces the Aztec group of languages and some spoken in the western United States and northern Mexico, such as Shoshonean, Piman. Kiowan, Tanoan. Others of

California and Oregon belong to the same group. However, one would have to go back very far to reach their mutually ancestral tongue.

The various Maya languages and dialects fall readily into two groups, highland and lowland. In the Northern Area only Yucatec (often called Maya) is spoken; in the north of the Central Area Yucatec is also dominant. Southeast of this is Mopan, and across the base of the Central Area are spread from west to east Chontal, Chol, and Chorti. In the transitional area in the southwest (eastern Chiapas) are found Tzeltal, Tzotzil, Chaneabal, and Chuh, the last extending into the Guatemalan highlands. Except for Chuh all are quite closely related, and as one travels southwestward there appears to be a slow and uniform transition from Yucatec to Tzotzil. Mopan differs little from Yucatec. Chontal, Chol, and Chorti are all very close to one another, and nearer to Mopan than to Yucatec. Tzeltal and Tzotzil form another fairly closely related group. Halpern (1942) thinks the Chiapan languages diverged from the Maya stock at an early date, but there are grounds for questioning this (p. 283).

Thus for the Northern and Central Areas this gradual transition in language is strong evidence that no large movements of peoples have taken place in recent centuries, and that therefore Maya classical art and architecture and the considerable achievements in astronomy and arithmetic must be credited to lowland Maya groups.

Jacalteca, the first highland language in the geographical sense, is closest to Chuh, the last of the languages of this transitional area, and is in turn closely related to its southern neighbor, Motozintlec. All three have been classified by some authorities as lowland, by others as highland. The same dependence of language change on distance is true of the highland languages. The late Dr. Manuel J. Andrade, the foremost authority on Maya languages, has remarked that in the central highlands the transition from one language or dialect to another is so gradual that it is impossible to say where Quiche stops and Cakchiquel or Tzutuhil starts. As he put it, one would have to make the language map in blending pastel colors, not harsh reds and greens and yellows. The Indians themselves do not visualize definite boundaries. This correlation of distance and change applies also to the other highland tongues—Kekchi, Pokoman, and Pokomchi, and Ixil and Mam—a good indication that the same static conditions have persisted for many centuries. This does not imply that no changes have taken place. There is evidence that the Quiche expanded at the cost of their Zutuhil neighbors, and the Kekchi have absorbed Chol areas, but these were minor matters.

Entirely cut off from the Maya area is Huaxtec, a Maya language spoken by the Indians around Tampico, Veracruz, and contiguous territories in San Luis Potosi and Tamaulipas. It is now fairly definite that Huaxtec is closer to the lowland group of languages than these are to the highland group. This is a matter of considerable historical importance, since it means that the Huaxtec were separated from the lowland Maya after they had diverged from the highland group, and linguistic evidence suggests that this may not have taken place much over a couple of thousand years ago.

All these languages and dialects, listed at such dreary length, are still spoken by large numbers of Indians, and in the remoter villages the number of Maya who speak Spanish is often very small, particularly in the case of women, who have fewer contacts beyond their village or with the local schools. Yucatec is so virile that many whites in Yucatan are bilingual, and not a few mestizos speak no Spanish.

The inventors of the Maya hieroglyphs almost surely spoke a lowland language, because Maya hieroglyphic texts occur only in the area covered by peoples of the lowland group, and because the hieroglyphic writing presumably developed after the lowland and highland groups began to diverge.

I am convinced that the inventors of the hieroglyphic writing spoke a language which was very close to modern Yucatec and to Chol-Chorti-Mopan. Unless there have been unsuspected shifts in population, a view which is contradicted by the gradual transitions from one contiguous group to another, the glyphs probably originated among the ancestors of the people who spoke Yucatec, Chol, or Chorti at the time of the Spanish conquest. To judge by the dated monuments, Maya hieroglyphic writing spread later to the territories in which Tzeltal, Tzotzil, and Chaneabal now live, and never reached the highland peoples. In fact, the Cakchiquel used the 400-day year until after the Spanish conquest. This is complete proof of the inability of the Maya long count to spread across the highlands. Two or three thousand years ago the differences between the various lowland dialects were presumably even less than they are today.

Accordingly I believe that we shall not err greatly in supposing that the language of the glyphs would have been understandable by present-day Yucatec or Chol. Phonetic elements in the glyphic script, particularly examples of rebus writing, suggest that the inventors of the glyphic writing spoke a language closest to sixteenth-century Yucatec (p. 285).

There is a great deal on Yucatec in the form of vocabularies, grammars, and religious manuals, but available material on Chol and Chorti is scant. Chorti is merely a dialect of Chol, chiefly differentiated by the substitution of *r* for the *l* of Chol. Unfortunately, Chol word lists, published or photostated, are in no way commensurate with the historical importance of the language. There exist only the short vocabularies of Moran, Fernandez and Fernandez, and Starr, and the longer one compiled by Becerra. Western (or Palencano) Chol is somewhat different from eastern (or Manche) Chol, which is quite close to Yucatec. A vocabulary of western Chol has been compiled by Mr. and Mrs. Wilbur Aulie, and it is to be hoped that this will be published.

There is a fair amount of material on Tzeltal and Tzotzil but less on Chaneabal. This can be used in comparative work. For example the occurrence of a word in the same or slightly changed form in both Yucatec and Tzotzil is evidence that it is an old lowland root. There are certain phonetic changes. For example the *ch* (as in *chai*, "fish") of many words in Tzeltal, Tzotzil, Chol, and Chaneabal is the equivalent of hard *c* in Yucatec *(cai,* "fish"), and the *t* (as in *te,* "wood") of the same dialects is often the equivalent of *ch* in Yucatec *(che,* "wood").

Perhaps it would be well to warn the reader at this point that I am not a trained linguist.

The highland languages and dialects can also be used for comparative purposes. If, for example, a word runs through several highland languages or dialects but is not found in dictionaries of the lowland group, there is a reasonable expectation either that chance has decreed the absence of the word from available lowland dictionaries or that the word has become extinct in Yucatec (the dialect with the largest vocabularies available) but survives although unrecorded in the incomplete dictionaries of other lowland tongues. An example of this is supplied by the Kekchi word *hix* which means "jaguar." The Yucatec day name Ix or Hix is the equivalent of the Aztec Ocelotl, "jaguar," and the glyph clearly shows the markings of the jaguar, yet *hix* or *ix* does not connote jaguars in any lowland tongue so far as is known. In Kekchi alone the connection remains. Perhaps *hix* was a ceremonial name for the jaguar which has disappeared elsewhere. Whatever the explanation may be, we are fully justified in going to the highland group of languages for such interpretations when the lowland group fails us. Outstanding vocabularies are listed under the respective lowland language or dialect in the bibliography.

Language will play an ever-growing part in the decipherment of the Maya hieroglyphs, and the day may not be far distant when texts will have first to be rendered in Maya to conserve their full richness. A start in that direction will be made in this publication.

Physical Appearance

The Maya are fairly homogeneous in their physical appearance despite the language differences. Generally speaking, the Maya is stocky with strong muscular development in his legs. He is broad-faced and has prominent cheekbones. The features are soft, and one can describe both sexes as handsome. The Yucatec are among the most broad-headed of the world, for the average cephalic index for males is 85, with isolated cases reaching 93. Among the Tzotzil and Tzeltal there seems to be a strain which has produced a group with narrow heads. Other Maya groups are very definitely in the brachycephalic column. Maya of pure blood have straight (sometimes slightly wavy) black hair and dark brown eyes, but the eyelids often show a rather pronounced Mongolian fold, which makes the eyes appear almond-shaped. Many Maya have a fleshy, hooked, or rather aquiline nose, and somewhat drooping lower lip. These are features which combined with the deformed forehead to produce the type of classical beauty found everywhere in the art of the Central Area during the Initial Series Period.

Estimates of Population

The descendants of the Maya still exist in large numbers in many parts of the area they formerly ruled, but in some areas they have been absorbed culturally and, to a certain extent, physically into the mestizo population. Sapper estimated in 1904 that there was then a Maya-speaking population of approximately 1,250,000, three-fifths of whom belonged to the highland linguistic group.

Estimates on the preconquest population vary from the one of 1,250,000 by Kroeber (1934) to that of over 13,000,000 for the Peninsula of Yucatan alone by Morley. Taking as a basis the tribute list of 1549 for Yucatan and Campeche and Sapper's figures for the present population, and allowing for areas now depopulated or occupied by mestizos, I reach a figure of about 3,000,000 for the Maya population at A.D. 800. Estimates that the Central Area toward the close of the Initial Series Period was one of the most densely peopled in the world, and that its population may have surpassed the 50,000,000 mark are surely fantastic.

SOURCES OF HIEROGLYPHIC TEXTS

Stelae

The great bulk of Maya hieroglyphic texts occurs on stelae and altars, as adjuncts to buildings, or in hieroglyphic codices.

The stelae and altars vary considerably in material. Throughout the greater part of the Peten and Yucatan they were made of limestone, which differs greatly in quality from one region to another. For example, the limestone used for stelae in several sites of northern British Honduras, northern Peten, and southern Quintana Roo is so poor that I have made perceptible scratches on the under side of a fallen stela with my thumbnail, and have been unable to scrub surfaces with a hard-bristled brush without seriously injuring the carving. Consequently, very few hieroglyphic texts have survived in that region; at the most, there remain vague outlines of glyphs which can be identified only because of their positions in a text. However, at some sites, notably Lubaantun in southern British Honduras, a fine crystalline limestone of marblelike consistency was used. The stone in many Peten sites ranges in quality between these two extremes. Naturally, when a stela has fallen, the design on the under side is likely to be better preserved than that on the sides still exposed to the weather.

The best-preserved inscriptions come from the southern part of the Maya lowlands. At Palenque and at some sites of the Usumacinta Valley dolomite was used for the carving of some hieroglyphic inscriptions, and this is superior to most limestones. At Quirigua the stelae and altars are cut from sandstone which has withstood the ravages of time remarkably well; at Copan, on the extreme eastern fringe of the Maya area, a beautiful greenish trachyte was employed for buildings, stelae, and altars. This has proved the most enduring of all materials. Unfortunately, time and climate have destroyed or rendered illegible a high proportion of glyphic texts, but we can take some consolation in the thought that, generally speaking, the most interesting inscriptions occur at cities which had the most enduring stone. The texts of the northern part of the Central Area are the poorest preserved, but, by and large, they are short and in subject matter of meager interest; the inscriptions of the belt covering the Usumacinta basin and extending eastward to Copan are in fairly good shape, are longer, and in their content demonstrate greater scholarship.

Stelae are usually about 3–3.50 m. high, about 1 m. wide, and about 30 cm. thick; the height includes an undecorated butt, set in the ground, which may be as much as 75 cm. long. There is, however, considerable variation in the size of stelae. At Quirigua, in the Motagua Valley, some tall graceful shafts were erected, the tallest of which, Stela E, has a height of 10.50 m. (including a butt 2.50 m. long) and a width of 1.50 m. The weight of this stela has been estimated at 65 tons. On the other hand, stelae may be less than 3 m. high.

Stelae at Quirigua throw some light on the method of quarrying the stone. Quarry stumps remaining on one narrow side of the butts of both Stelae A and E indicate that the profile of the shaft was outlined in the ledge of rock by a ditch which was cut to a depth slightly greater than the desired width. The mass was then undermined from back and front and cut through at intervals until the shaft stood detached except for slender stumps left in the process of undercutting. With levers those stumps could be snapped and the shaft moved for trimming, transportation, and carving.

The wheel was unknown in Middle America except as a relatively late development in Mexico, where its use appears to have been confined to toys (small pottery animals have been found with four wheels). It is therefore probable that stelae were hauled to the points of erection with the aid of rollers. Peter Martyr has an account of transportation in ancient Mexico which is doubtlessly applicable also to the Maya area:

They have also certain hearbes, with the which, in steed of broome, and hempe, they make ropes, cordes and cables: and boaring a hole in one of the edges of the beame, they fasten the rope, then sette their slaves unto it, like yoakes of oxen, and lastly in steede of wheels, putting round blocks under the lumber, whether it be to be drawn steepe up, or directly downe the hill, the matter is performed by the neckes of the slaves, the Carpenters onely directing the carriage. After the same manner also, they get all kind of matter fitte for building, and other things apt for the use of manne.

There is evidence that some, but not all, decorative elements for buildings were carved at or near the quarries, feathered serpents and parts of decorated friezes having been found in open country; the stones composing the panels of Copan Temple 11 clearly were carved before assembly (fig. 54,4, Gl B1, B5, C3). If stelae were carved at the quarry, great care would have been necessary to avoid damage in transit. Moreover, the shaft would presumably have to be upended to facilitate carving on all four sides, particularly when the design was carried round to another face. For those two reasons it was probably advantageous to erect the stela in its final position before starting to carve it, despite a possible hardening of the limestone which the delay might entail. Strömsvik (1941, p. 92) has discussed the methods by which the Maya probably raised stelae into position. He deems it most likely that a temporary ramp or incline of earth was built, up which the stela would have been pulled on skids until its butt could be tipped into a prepared socket. Alternatively he suggests prying up one end with levers and blocking under until leverage could be had for a final pull with ropes. The ropes might have passed over a stout A-frame. Possibly both methods were employed: the first for the huge shafts at Quirigua, the second for the stelae of more normal size.

Usually the butt of a stela was placed in a hole dug in the earth or through the artificial fill of a platform, and then wedged with rubble or dirt and stones. At Copan a number of stelae were erected over cruciform vaults, which frequently contained dedicatory caches. The butt of the stela was held in position by a close-fitting crib of long stone blocks. At Quirigua stelae were typically supported by large slabs, and held in position by rubble packed between the butt and the stone-lined walls of a pit especially prepared for it.

There is evidence that stelae were sometimes moved from their original positions and re-erected elsewhere. There is therefore some danger in dating buildings by the stelae with which they are associated, and similarly caution must be observed in associating cache material beneath stelae with the dates recorded thereon.

Stelae may be carved on one, two, three, or four sides or they may be plain. It has been supposed that plain stelae were covered with stucco, on which hieroglyphs were painted. Usually the front of a stela is carved with the figure of a deity or of a priest impersonating a deity. I believe, although proof escapes me, that the choice of subject for portrayal was directly governed by the dedicatory date of the monument. The designs are usually complex.

The principal figures on stelae are almost always presented full face with feet turned out so that they are almost in a straight line, heel to heel, or the head is in profile and the body full face, or the whole figure may be in profile. The stiffness of these awkward postures must not be considered a symptom of immaturity. There is little reason to doubt that they were demanded by tradition, and probably represent a rigid adherence to a style evolved at a time when Maya sculptors had not yet mastered the art of foreshortening. This is not surprising, for religious art throughout the ages has tended to adhere to the canons of past usage. Foreshortening can often be detected in the portraits of captives or minor figures, or in the complex vignettes which served as full-figure glyphs. Tremendous vivacity is to be seen in little figures of gods who clamber around lianalike motifs, or peer like startled fawns from behind a cornstalk. Sometimes a scene was enclosed within a frame, but more often the border was omitted or reduced to a very low and hardly noticeable line.

Maya sculptors seldom failed to achieve good balance in their compositions. Sometimes the symmetry was a little too patent, as in the tablets at Palenque, where a central motif is flanked by individuals of almost equal size, and they, in turn, by columns of glyphs of the same length and breadth. Generally, however, the columns of glyphs are used to counter disharmonic groupings. Where a smaller figure faced a larger one, a mass of glyph blocks above the former restores the balance. Too obvious balance is often avoided by subsidiary glyphs in the diagonally opposed corner. In fact, many sculptures have

a subsidiary quality of diagonalism which results from the two-headed dragon element, usually called the ceremonial bar, which many personages carry at a cant across their breasts. These introduce a secondary axis: the headdress with its sweeping feathers and massed masks at the top right corner and a kneeling captive in the bottom left corner countering it.

Because religious considerations dictated a narrow field within which to work, Maya sculptural portraiture of Late Classical times, which is that we have been discussing, is distinctly static. Yet, as we have seen, subsidiary figures were often vibrant with life. The maize god, in particular, was treated with gay abandon, for he was loved and regarded almost as a comrade by the Maya. This combination of static portraiture of the main figure and vivacious treatment of subsidiary figures reminds one of mediaeval Christian art. Reposeful statues of saints dominate, but in odd nooks and corners or on the under sides of choir stalls are carefree little scenes which reveal how alive that sculpture, too, could be when freed of ecclesiastical formality.

This restrained portraiture of the Initial Series Period contrasts strongly with the restless art of the Mexican Period, as exemplified by Itza sculptures at Chichen Itza. Never-ending lines of warriors, as awkwardly grouped as figures on an old-style fashion plate, face in toward an altar or sun disk. There is an incredible stiffness in their poses, and a depressing monotony in their dress and weapons. Since this was primarily a secular art, these defective qualities can not be attributed to the restraining influences of religious conservatism.

Maya sculpture was not, like mediaeval Christian art, a form of pictorial education for the masses. It was executed for the edification of the gods and a small sacerdotal group, the members of which were thoroughly acquainted with all the intricacies of its symbolism. Also, the confused polytheism of the Maya, in which gods blended into one another and overlapped in their functions, naturally required a more complicated representation than would be necessary in the art of a monotheistic culture.

Frequently small areas not utilized in the presentation of the main personage or for details subsidiary to his portraiture were filled with short panels of glyphs. This was invariably the case when only the front of the stela was carved. Generally, however, the bulk of the hieroglyphic text is presented on the sides and sometimes on the back of the stela. The back, nevertheless, is more often plain or devoted to the portrait of some other divine personage. Very rarely figures are found on the sides. All four sides of a very few stelae are carved with glyphs, but there is no known case of a stela with figures in relief but lacking glyphs. From this it may, I think, be inferred that the primary purpose of these stelae was to record hieroglyphic texts.

Sylvanus G. Morley evolved an elaborate system for classifying the stelae in 10 groups according to whether the various surfaces of the stelae are plain or carved with glyphs or personages. Although such a system has some value, the group to which a stela belongs must have been largely a matter of how many subjects were to be discussed in the hieroglyphic texts, just as the length of a letter depends on how much the writer wishes to say. At one period lively discussions concerning lunar and solar computations were going on between the various cities, and calculations far into the past were recorded as evidence for the varying viewpoints. Finally, these matters were settled, and as a consequence, I believe, inscriptions became much shorter. Thus, an increase in the space devoted to hieroglyphs is indicative that the text dates from 9.12.0.0.0 to 9.17.0.0.0 in the Maya calendar, and even that applies only to cities which were intellectual leaders. Other cities, having no controversial views to air, recorded only abbreviated inscriptions.

On those stelae carved on three or more sides, the hieroglyph inscription usually starts on the (observer's) left side, and then passes to the back or to the right side, but at Copan it commences on the back. The final date is not infrequently given or repeated on the front of the stela. There is no fixed rule in this matter.

Stelae were usually erected in the courts of Maya cities, at the foot of some pyramid or mound so that their fronts faced toward the center of the court. Sometimes they were placed on the terraces or on the summit of a pyramid, or they could be set in the stairway of a structure. Quite commonly several stelae stand in a row before a single building. An example of this method is to be found at Piedras Negras where no less than eight stelae were in line before Structure J-4, six or seven of these occupying a single low platform. Indeed, low platforms were frequently built to carry one or more stelae. Sometimes stelae were housed in small shrines, which may be vaulted with corbeled arching, and very occasionally they were placed in temple rooms.

Some stelae still retain traces of stucco in sheltered nooks of their surface, and sometimes traces of paint (red of more than one tone commonest; also green, and light and dark blue). The reprehensible Maya custom of painting the lily has, however, been beneficial to epigraphists; the stucco, which is often of considerable hardness, has done much to save the texts from weathering.

Frequently fragments of incense burners are found in the ground immediately in front of stelae, indicating that they were the object of a cult. Present-day Maya of Yucatan and Quintana Roo still burn copal and candles before certain stelae of Coba which are regarded as guardians of the forest. A. M. Tozzer (1907, p. 82) reports finding five incense burners in a line before a stela at Tzendales. They were of the type ordinarily made by the present-day Lacandon. At the ruins of Benque Viejo in western British Honduras an altar with a small cross on it has been erected on top of a fallen stela, and passing Indians place flowers or stones on it, and say an Ave Maria or Pater Noster.

Among the Maya of eastern Yucatan and Quintana Roo special stones, either stelae or rocks of odd shapes, are known as *tzimin tun,* a term which originally meant "stone tapir," but which now signifies "stone horse," or can be translated "stone ridge" or "stone trestle." These are believed to be alive. By day they are motionless; at night they wander around. They will protect one's milpa (cornfield), aid one while hunting, and keep one in health, if placated with offerings of food, copal, or candles; but they will punish with sickness anyone who fails to make them offerings. It is believed that they can be brought to life by a *h-men* (priest-sorcerer). The ritual, which consists of sprinkling the stone with water and offering it copal, posol (maize gruel), and tortillas (maize cakes), is preceded by a nine-day vigil.

These simple rituals are presumably the last surviving elements of a stela cult, for we know that the image of each katun (period of 20 approximate years), which must have been very closely associated with the stelae, was worshipped during its "reign."

ALTARS AND ZOOMORPHS

Altar is a convenient term under which are grouped many Maya monuments which cannot be called stelae because of their shapes. They comprise two main categories: squat rectangular blocks and drum-shaped stones. The former usually rest directly on the floor of a court; the latter sometimes stand on three oblong supports also of stone. They vary considerably in size. Altar T, Copan, one of the largest, is 70 cm. high, 1.80 m. wide, and 1.30 m. thick. Altar 1, Piedras Negras, which is drum-shaped, has a diameter of 2.16 m. and is supported by three feet of solid stone, each 1.39 m. high.

Many of these altars are placed before stelae; others are in no way associated with stelae or even with structures, but stand entirely by themselves. Those that are carved frequently carry glyphs on their sides or perimeters, and sometimes on their tops; they may be all glyphic or may be carved with designs but no glyphs. The supports also may be inscribed with hieroglyphic texts. Altars have been designated by separate numbers or letters or have been referred to by the stela in front of which they stand (e.g. Altar of Stela 1, Copan). The system followed in this publication is explained in the preface.

The unmelodious term "zoomorph" has been applied to certain large sculptured boulders at Quirigua which are indistinguishable, except for size, from the more elaborate altars. In recent years other sculptures which are in the same category, have been discovered in front of two of these zoomorphs, and they have been called respectively "Altar of Zoomorph O" and "Altar of Zoomorph P." Naturally such nomenclature makes no pretense to being functional. Zoomorph P, at Quirigua, in the intricacy of its carving and in its massive presentation (girth 10 m., height 2.20 m., estimated weight approximately 20 tons) is an amazing testimonial to Maya sculpture. The late W. H. Holmes, former director of the National Art Gallery, presently Collection of Fine Arts, considered it the finest example of ancient American sculpture extant. The subject, a favorite one in Maya art, is a two-headed celestial dragon. The hieroglyphic text is grouped around the two heads in a felicitous blending with the intricacies of the monstrous deity.

There is no definite evidence that altars ever functioned as such. Possibly those that are directly associated with stelae served as tables for sacrifices of various kinds. Occasionally (e.g. at Piedras Negras and Calakmul) outcroppings of rock in or near ceremonial centers were carved.

TEXTS IN BUILDINGS

Lintels. In most Maya cities the lintels of doorways were of wood, but along the Usumacinta Valley, particularly at Yaxchilan, and at Chichen Itza (during the Initial Series Period) and at a few other scattered sites, notably Xcalumkin and other Puuc cities, they were often hewn from a single stone. Many of those of stone are carved with hieroglyphic texts and representations of deities or ceremonies performed in their honor.

Usually the under side and the front of the lintel are carved, and if there are several doorways thus treated, the inscription is continued from one lintel to another. Stone lintels are usually about 2 m. wide, 85 cm. deep, and 30 cm. thick, the width includes plain borders at each end which rest on the jambs, and, naturally, are hidden from view. The length of the sculptural panel is usually around 1.25 m. The design on many lintels can be viewed by looking upward as one enters the doorway, but in other cases the design or hieroglyphic text follows the long axis of the lintel.

Presumably, many wooden lintels were once sculptured, but none with hieroglyphic texts has escaped the ravages of time, except a handful at the large site of Tikal. The material in some cases is sapodilla wood (*Achras zapota* L.), the tree which yields chewing gum.

There are grounds for believing that nearly all the stone "lintels" from Piedras Negras were actually wall tablets. As they are so well known under their classification as lintels, much confusion would arise if they were renamed now.

Jambs. Hieroglyphic texts in stone on the jambs of doorways are rare. They are confined to Copan, and parts of Yucatan and adjacent Campeche.

Columns. A few stone columns, round and square, which supported lintels or roof beams, carry hieroglyphic texts. They are rare and confined to a few sites in Yucatan and adjacent Campeche.

Wall Panels or Tablets. These were usually set in the rear walls of temples. All that have survived are of stone. Most famous are those of the Temples of the Cross, the Foliated Cross, the Sun, and the Inscriptions at Palenque. The last of these consists of three panels. Two are set in the back wall of the outer room; the third is in the back wall of the rear room, the sanctuary. The three together have a total of 620 glyph blocks, the longest inscriptions still intact in the Maya area. As already noted, some texts labeled as lintels, are almost certainly panels. A variant form of panel, a long narrow text on a vertical band which starts close to the capstone of a building and continues to near floor level is found at the Campeche site of Xcalumkin.

Another form of panel sometimes decorates the surfaces of short walls on each side of a doorway. In most cases the hieroglyphic texts are subsidiary to the portraits of deities or their impersonators, but at Copan the panels are purely textual.

Moldings. In the Red House, Chichen Itza, a stone molding with a line of glyphs in low relief runs the length of the rear wall of the front room at the level of the vault spring. At Xcocha a similar band apparently ran around the whole room, and was carried around three sides of the capitals of the columns in the doorways. Temple 26, Copan, once was decorated in a similar manner with full-figure glyphs. At Halal a painted band of glyphs extends on either side of a carved glyphic lintel, along the inner wall of a room, as though forming a single text.

Thrones. This term has been applied to some immovable tables of solid masonry or of stone partially supported by stone legs. These are rectangular, and set against the rear wall of a building, sometimes occupying a specially designed alcove. There is evidence that on occasions a throne served as a sort of dais, on which an important personage sat while others stood or sat in front. The sides, the screen at the back, and the supports may carry hieroglyphic texts, which may be carved or incised (Piedras Negras) or worked in stucco (San Jose).

Ceilings. The only example I know of hieroglyphic texts on ceilings occurs at Tzibanche, in southeastern Quintana Roo. There it seems to have been customary to lay flooring across the vault a few feet below the level of the capstones so as to form a small attic running the length of the room. In profile the vault and ceiling·take the form of an A with blunted apex. These floors are of wood and in one case the under side, which forms the ceiling of the room, was carved with hieroglyphs.

Capstones. A few stucco-covered capstones were painted with designs, which include short hieroglyphic texts. The known examples are confined to Uxmal, Chichen Itza, Xkichmook, and Dzibilnocac. At Kiuic there is a carved capstone with glyphs.

Murals. Hieroglyphic texts painted on the stuccoed walls of rooms, alone or accompanying religious scenes, are scarce. The most important are the sequence of 72 day signs on a wall of Structure B-XIII at Uaxactun, certain texts from the palace at Palenque, and various lots of glyphs, including an Initial Series (hereinafter contracted to IS; p. 154), on the magnificent murals recently found at Bonampak. Vertical or L-shaped panels of two or three glyphs placed near individuals are common on the Bonampak and Uaxactun murals, and should some day prove a fruitful field for investigation.

Naturally, inscriptions which were inside buildings have been less exposed to weathering, and therefore supply prime study material.

Texts Connected with the Exteriors of Buildings

Hieroglyphic Stairways. Flights of stone steps, one or all of which are inscribed with hieroglyphs, are fairly common. As a rule, only the riser is carved, but both treads and risers of the hieroglyphic stairway at Palenque carry glyphs. The most magnificent hieroglyphic stairway is that of Structure 26, Copan. It has been estimated that this originally·consisted of 62 steps, each 8 m. wide. At intervals were seated five heroic figures of gods or priests, as though guarding the ascent to the temple which once crowned the summit. Unfortunately the stairway is partially destroyed, much of it having slid down to the base of the mound, with the result that only two sections, comprising approximately one-half of the text, are still intact. Most of the remainder of the inscription has been recovered, but the stones are hopelessly jumbled; the inscription originally consisted of about 1000 glyph blocks.

Sills and Single Steps. Each of the three doorways of Structure 44, Yaxchilan, has a carved sill, and a second carved step giving access to it. The surfaces are decorated with hieroglyphic texts and personages in low relief.

Some of the riser faces of these stones are also carved. The text of the so-called Reviewing Stand at Copan falls in this category.

Retaining Walls. Rarely, short hieroglyphic texts are carved on the stone retaining walls of the platforms of structures. The best known examples are at the Palace, Palenque.

Façade Decoration. Glyphic texts on façades are rare. The outstanding examples are the hieroglyphic molding of Structure 1, Quirigua, and that of the south building, Xcalumkin, and the various elements from the exterior of the Caracol, Chichen Itza. There is some doubt as to how these last were arranged except that they were inscribed on the bodies of two-headed snakes. The fronts of piers between the exterior doorways of Palenque buildings were generally ornamented with representations of personages and hieroglyphic texts in stucco.

Occasional short texts are scattered in odd places. At Labna a few glyphs are incised on the long snout of the mask of a celestial monster, and the medial molding of one structure at Palenque has glyphs cut in the under surface of the lower element. The exterior walls of a small temple at Santa Rita, British Honduras, were largely covered with murals. Figures of gods, probably the patrons of a succession of approximate years (tuns), predominate, but a few hieroglyphs also occur.

Texts Connected with Ball Courts

The Maya, like several other peoples of Mesoamerica, erected courts for the playing of a certain game which involved the use of a large solid rubber ball. The rules forbade propelling the ball with hands or feet, and shots were usually taken on the upper thigh immediately below the hip. The game had a strongly ritualistic connotation and occupied an important place in Maya culture. The court consists of a playing alley which varies considerably in size but in most instances is about 17–22 m. long and 3.5–6.5 m. wide. On the long axis the sides of the playing alley are bounded by solid masonry masses with low faces toward the alley. Typically, the upper surface of each masonry mass slopes upward and outward for a distance of about 4 m. and then becomes vertical, or more sharply sloped, to form the faces of a flat-topped section, on which a temple is often situated. Transverse playing areas may exist at each end of the playing alley, converting the ground plan into two T's placed base to base. Sometimes a stone ring projects from the center of the vertical face of each flanking mass. The main scoring point in the game, at least in the form of the game played in the sixteenth century, was achieved when the ball was driven through the ring.

Hieroglyphic texts may occur in various parts of the

ball court. Frequently stone markers are set in the floor of the playing alley along its long axis, with their surfaces flush with the floor. There are usually three, set at equidistant intervals, and round, with diameter about 65 cm., or sometimes rectangular. The surfaces of these markers may carry hieroglyphic texts or may be carved to represent players in the game with or without the addition of hieroglyphs. Alley markers with hieroglyphs have been reported from Yaxchilan, Copan, Chinkultic, Cancuen, Laguna Perdida, Lubaantun, and Hatzcab Ceel. In the last case the inscription is worn nearly smooth, presumably by Maya feet.

Panels are sometimes set in the surfaces of the sides flanking the playing alley. These panels may be rectangular or circular or long vertical bands. Rectangular panels with figures and glyphs have been encountered on the slopes of ball courts at Coba and Tonina; circular panels with glyphs occur at Yaxchilan; and long bands with glyphs are reported from ball courts at Copan and Piedras Negras.

Short hieroglyphic inscriptions cover both faces of each ring of the ball court at Uxmal.

Hieroglyphic Codices

Form and Material. Only three Maya hieroglyphic codices have survived; many were destroyed by order of the church because they were considered, quite rightly, to be an integral part of the old Maya paganism. Some were probably destroyed by the Maya themselves because their existence endangered the souls of their owners if these were Christians; their bodies, if at heart they remained heathens. Others must have fallen victims to neglect and to the ravages of time. From sixteenth-century Spanish writers we learn that sometimes codices were buried with Maya priests. This information has been confirmed by the discovery of heaps of thin flakes of lime with painting on them in tombs at Uaxactun and San Agustin Acasaguastlan. These surely represent the sizing of pages after the vegetal backings had disintegrated. A tomb at Nebaj yielded a codex in a slightly better stage of preservation.

Spanish (and hispanicized Maya) writers state that the subjects noted in their codices were: historical records, lives of outstanding people, prophecies, information on the planets, songs in meter, ceremonies, the order of sacrifices to their gods, and their calendars. We can be reasonably sure that, like the peoples of central Mexico, the Maya had also hieroglyphic documents covering distribution and ownership of land, tribute lists, dynasties, and mythology.

The contents of the three surviving Maya codices deal with the passage of time, rituals and perhaps prophecies

for sequences of katuns and tuns, arrangements of the 260-day sacred almanac for the purposes of divination with special sections dealing with particular professions, tables covering the movements of the planet Venus, eclipses, and perhaps for correcting the vague year to solar time, various "multiplication" tables, pictures of certain ceremonies, and numerous vignettes representing the deities and rituals connected with all these activities (figs. 61-64). Short glyphic passages give the luck of the day, the pictures illustrating and supplementing the texts.

No historical records have survived so far as is known, although it is possible that historical and prophetic data are concealed in the unelucidated texts of Paris. Moreover, certain passages in books written since the Spanish conquest in European script but employing the Maya language give the appearance of deriving from hieroglyphic predecessors.

Maya books consist of a single sheet of paper, of varying length (the longest, that of Madrid, is approximately 6.70 m.) and height between 29.5 and 22.5 cm. The long sheet of paper was folded like a screen to produce pages 8.5-13 cm. wide. The pages were made of a paper, really a refined bark-cloth, made by soaking and then pounding the inner bark of certain trees until a thin sheet was obtained. The tree generally used was a wild fig (*Ficus*). The tree, the paper, and the books were called *amatl* (hispanicized form *amate*) in ancient Mexico. Some Spanish colonial writers apply the variants *analte* or *analteh, anares,* or *amales* to the books or the glyphs of the Maya. It is probable that all are corruptions of *amatl* or its hispanicized form, *amate.* The Yucatec word for a book or paper is *huun,* and to read, *xochun,* literally "to count a book."

The sheets of paper were covered with a fine lime sizing which formed a smooth white surface on which the glyphs and pictures were painted on both sides of the sheet. Texts run from left to right the whole width of the obverse, and then from left to right on the reverse side. The pagination is a modern addition for convenience of reference. Each fold of the obverse is numbered consecutively from left to right, and those of the reverse continue the sequence from right to left. Thus a codex of 10 leaves (folds) would have page 20 as the verso of page 1. The covers of Maya codices have not survived, but among the few Mexican codices of pre-Columbian date is one with covers of wood with jade inlay.

Codex Dresden. This, the finest of the Maya codices in draughtmanship and the most interesting in content, takes its name from the city of Dresden, for it was and presumably still is in the former Royal Library of Saxony but suffered some damage from water in World War II. Nothing is known of its history prior to its purchase in

1739 from an unknown vendor in Vienna by the director of the Dresden library, but its appearance in Vienna suggests that it may have been sent to the Emperor Charles V.

It is 3.5 m. long and 8.5 cm. high, and is folded into 39 leaves, of which all except four are painted on both sides. Like other codices both Maya and Mexican, it consists of various sections—chapters we might almost call them —which deal with different subjects. There are, however, usually no lines or other obvious indications of a change of subject, such as the start of a new divinatory almanac, when that occurs in the middle of a page; many pages, on the other hand, are divided into two, three and, in one case, four horizontal sections which are independent or semi-independent of one another. For example, the eclipse table starts in the upper half of page 53 and passes across the tops of pages 54–57, as far as the middle of page 58, where a vertical line divides the page in half, indicating a change of subject. At that point the table passes to the lower half of page 51 and then continues across the lower halves of pages 52–57 to terminate on page 58 immediately below the conclusion of the upper half of the table.

The contents of the codex, so far as is known, are as follows:

p. 1: Badly damaged.

pp. 2–23: Divinatory almanacs in all sections except for a scene of human sacrifice on p. 3. Pp. 16–23 presumably devoted to affairs of women, since a goddess, probably the moon goddess, patroness of childbirth, weaving, etc., dominates the scene (figs. 62,5,6; 63).

p. 24: Multiplication table for synodical revolutions of Venus together with adjustments. Glyphs of various deities connected with the revolution of the planet.

pp. 25–28: Pictorial representations with explanatory texts of ceremonies leading up to new-year celebrations (fig. 64,1).

pp. 29–45: Divinatory almanacs, interrupted only by multiples of 91 and 364, occupying top sections of pp. 31, 32 and 45, and IS probably associated therewith on top section of p. 31 (fig. 46,10). Sacrificial scene at top of p. 34, 260-day almanac and lords of night in a combined cycle occupy the lower parts of pp. 30–33. IS and multiples of 78 are on middle of pp. 43, 44 (figs. 61,1–4; 62,1–4; 64,2–4).

pp. 46–50: Tables of movements of planet Venus.

pp. 51–58 (left): Eclipse tables.

pp. 58 (right)–59: Multiples of 78 and 780 days. By some these are thought to be tables for calculating the synodical revolutions of Mars; more probably, they are divinatory almanacs with accompanying tables. IS lead to them.

p. 60: Pictures and glyphs of unknown meaning, but reference to Katun 11 Ahau. Last page of obverse.

pp. 61–62 (left): Long distance numbers reckoned from far in the past set in folds of serpents.

pp. 62 (right)–64: Multiples of 91 and 364 days up to 145,600 days and IS leading thereto.

pp. 65–69 (left): Subdivisions of the periods of 91 days in the preceding section, each into 13 unequal parts. Almost surely prognostications of the weather, and its effects on the crops.

pp. 69 (right)–70 (left): Long distance numbers, reckoned from far in the past, set in the folds of a serpent, and accompanying IS. These preface the following pages.

pp. 70 (right)–73 (left): Multiples of 65 and 1820 days and of 54 and 702 days. The tables are carried to 109,200 days in the first table, and probably to 168,480 days in the second table. Periods of rain, cloudy weather, and drought; and their effects on the crops (fig. 46,1–9).

p. 74: Scene showing water descending from celestial monster, the god Itzamna. Probably representing the destruction of the world by flood.

It should be noted that the pagination is irregular. Ernst Förstemann, the great commentator and interpreter of Dresden, at first thought he was dealing with two separate codices. Accordingly he numbered the first part pages 1–24 obverse and 25–45 reverse (the four blank pages were left unnumbered). The second section carried the pagination 46–60 on the obverse; 61–74 on the reverse. The order should be 1–24, 46–60, 61–74, 25–45. Förstemann's arbitrary arrangement, based on very weak evidence, divided the Venus chapter in two, for pages 46–50 belong with page 24, which they follow in the original. Raynaud (1893) rectified the arrangement, but Förstemann's pagination is retained to avoid confusion.

The portraits of deities and the glyphs are delineated with extreme neatness. Presumably a thin brush was employed. Many of the pages are merely in red and black, but in some sections details or backgrounds are in bluish green, light and dark yellow, brown, or red.

The codex is without much doubt a copy, or rather a new edition, of an earlier and now lost original, for certain tables are included which were out of date when the present copy was made, but additions bring them up to date. Certain Mexican influences are discernible. To cite a particular example, the Mexican blindfold god Ixquemilli is portrayed, whereas this deity is nowhere represented in Maya art of the Initial Series Period. Furthermore, a few of the pottery vessels depicted in the codex appear to be of forms typical of the Mexican Period in Yucatan, which at Chichen Itza started about A.D. 1000 or very shortly prior thereto.

The latest date in the codex written in the notation generally used for transcribing Maya dates is 10.17.13.12.12. This corresponds to A.D. 1178 in the correlation followed in this publication. The starting and ending dates of the eclipse tables are apparently 10.12.16.14.8 and 10.14.10.0.8, respectively A.D. 1083 and A.D. 1116. Probably, therefore, we are not far in error in dating Dresden as twelfth century. To guess as to the area in which the codex was composed would be hazardous; as it does not conform to Yucatecan methods of writing, it almost certainly did not originate in that area.

Dates in the Long Count (Chapter 6) consist of various (usually five) units of time in the vigesimal system arranged in descending order; in transcriptions these are given in arabic numbers separated by periods. The transcription 10.17.13.12.12 corresponds to 10 baktuns (units of 400 tuns), 17 katuns (units of 20 tuns), 13 tuns (approximate years of 360 days), 12 uinals (periods of 20 days), and 12 kins (days). These total 4353 approximate years and 252 days, and the reckoning is made from the usual point of departure for the Maya calendar, corresponding in function to the A. U. C. of ancient Rome.

Codex Paris. This codex is commonly known as Codex Perez or Codex Peresianus, but as certain manuscripts dealing with the Maya calendar are also known as the Codex Perez (they were collected and annotated by the Maya scholar Juan Pio Perez), it seems best to follow the lead of W. E. Gates in calling this hieroglyphic manuscript after the city in which it now lies. It was found by Leon de Rosny in 1859 in a basket amid a mass of old papers, deep in dust, which lay forgotten in a chimney corner of the National Library in Paris. It was wrapped in a piece of paper which bore the name Perez, in a writing claimed to be of the seventeenth century, and from this circumstance derives the name by which the codex is generally known.

The codex in its present state is approximately 1.45 m. long and 22 cm. high and is folded into 11 leaves, all with writing on both sides. One may assume that this is merely a fragment of the original codex. Actually there is internal evidence that at least two pages are missing at the end or perhaps one at the start and one at the end, as W. E. Gates (1910) supposed.

The obverse is a record of 11 successive ends of katuns (20 approximate years, 7200 days), one to each page, such as were used in Yucatan at the time of the Spanish conquest (and almost certainly for several centuries before) as a framework for recording historical events and prophecies, and for noting the deities that ruled over each katun and, probably, the ceremonies appropriate thereto.

Since these katuns were arranged in sequences of 13, after which the series started to repeat itself, it is clear that two pages are lacking to complete the series. These probably followed the present sequence to make the important Katun 4 Ahau the last of the series; Gates thought that the series could best be completed by adding a page at each end, and so he numbered the obverse pages 2–12, and the reverse 15–25, leaving the numbers 1, 13, 14, and 26 for the missing pages. A pagination of 1–11 for the obverse and 16–26 for the reverse, with 12–15 for the two lost leaves at the end, would be better, but such a

change at this date would merely add to the confusion. Accordingly, I shall adhere to the Gates pagination, which is well established in the literature of the subject.

The center of each page is occupied by figures which undoubtedly depict the deities ruling over the katun recorded on that page. Each picture is framed with a fairly lengthy hieroglyphic text. Little progress has been made in elucidating their content, but it is a fair assumption that ritual, prophecies, and perhaps historical events are discussed. The upper third of each page lists two or perhaps three days Ahau spaced to show that the whole formed sequences of tuns.

The reverse of the codex is in poor condition. Remains of some divinatory almanacs, new-year ceremonies (pp. 19, 20), what is probably a kind of Maya zodiac with divisions of the 364-day year associated with it (pp. 23, 24), and miscellaneous scenes can be recognized. The material on pages 12 and 25 is almost completely obliterated.

Deities and glyphs are painted with care, but the general standard is somewhat lower than that of Dresden. Colors are brown, black, red, pink, blue, and bluish green. There are several intermediate tones.

There is little stylistic evidence to date the codex. The glyphs show a certain intermingling of styles, as in Dresden. I think that, as in the case of Dresden, this may be due to the fact that the present codex was copied from an earlier one painted during the Initial Series Period, and that the scribe sometimes copied glyphs in their original forms and sometimes changed them to conform with the style then current. Paris can hardly be earlier than Dresden, and is probably of slightly later date.

Writing in Spanish, apparently a commentary, is visible on several pages, but cannot be read.

Codex Madrid. This codex, also called Codex Tro-Cortes, is in Madrid. It became divided, and the two parts fell into separate hands. The first part, the Tro manuscript, was brought to the attention of the scientific world by the famous Americanist the Abbé Brasseur de Bourbourg, who, during the course of a visit to Madrid in 1866, found it in the possession of Juan de Tro y Ortolano, professor of palaeography. By one of those twists of fate which readers enjoy in histories but deprecate in works of fiction, the owner of the fragment was himself a descendant of Hernando Cortes. There is no information as to how long Sr. de Tro y Ortolano, or perhaps his family, had been in possession of these pages, but it is not improbable that the professor acquired them as a result of his researches in palaeography.

The second part, discovered in Spain in 1875, was bought by the Spanish government and named Codex Cortes. It was soon recognized by Leon de Rosny as forming with the Tro part a single codex, which is now known as Tro-Cortes or as Codex Madrid.

The codex is approximately 6.55 m. long by 22.6 cm. high and is folded into 56 leaves, painted on both sides. The pagination starts at the left of the obverse of the Cortes (pp. 1–21) and then continues with the obverse of the Tro (pp. 22–56); the codex is then reversed, the pages of the Cortes part following those of the Tro.

The codex contains no astronomy, no multiplication tables, no prophecies, and no reckoning in the "long count." It appears to have served purely as a book of divination. Divinatory almanacs cover many subjects including hunting, beekeeping, weaving, rain-making, sowing, and crops. One must assume that all these almanacs had as their purpose the enumeration of days propitious for each activity. As in the other two codices, there are pages devoted to the ceremonies which ended the old year and began the new. These, too, were of a divinatory nature.

Much attention is paid to world directions and world colors, the various glyphs for which appear with monotonous regularity. An almost complete 260-day period crosses the centers of pages 13–18, arranged in four horizontal lines, each of 52 sequent days. Apparently the scribe miscalculated the length of this table, and did not have room to complete it, as the addition of the 13 missing columns would have required another page. The right half of the last page (18) was left incomplete, and the scribe arranged the day signs on the left half of that page so that there were only five vertical columns. Consequently, after coming to the end of one horizontal line, one could pass to the left of the horizontal line immediately below on page 18 and count off 13 days in the usual left-to-right and top-to-bottom sequence, and then pass to the start of the next horizontal line on page 13. It was an ingenious solution of the problem raised by a misjudgment of space available. A 260-day cycle with fuller commentary occurs on pages 65–73b.

The delineation of the codex is hasty, and is far inferior to that of the other two codices. Gods are portrayed in a grotesque and crude manner, and little attention is paid to shaping the glyphs; lines are too heavy and spacing is often irregular. Colors include reddish brown, light brown, light blue, dark blue (very rare), and black.

On stylistic grounds (glyph styles and portraits of gods) the codex can be dated as quite late, perhaps as late as the middle of the fifteenth century. The pottery vessels depicted on several pages appear to be of late types. Among these should particularly be noted storage jars on tripod supports. Absence of real learning, as exemplified by the astronomical sections of Dresden and the katun pages of Paris, may be accidental, but it is suggestive of a period of cultural decline when the primary interests of the priesthood had sunk to mechanical divination. Such a period of decline marks the close of Maya history, the Period of Mexican Absorption, immediately prior to the Spanish conquest.

The treatment of the deities finds its closest parallel in frescoes from late temples at Tulum, on the east coast of Quintana Roo. This serves to confirm the lateness of the codex, and at the same time to suggest a provenience. This would not necessarily be the east coast of Quintana Roo, since the art and architecture of that region clearly reflect influences from northwestern Yucatan. It is not impossible that the codex was obtained at Tayasal by one of the participants in the overthrow of that last Maya stronghold in 1697, for the people or, at least, the rulers of Tayasal had migrated thither from Yucatan during the Period of Mexican Absorption.

Reproductions of Codices. There have been many editions of these three codices during the past century; the best facsimile reproductions are listed in the bibliography. All are very rare, and in default of them, the reader is advised to use the accessible edition published by Villacorta and Villacorta (1930). The various editions published by Gates should be avoided because of the casting of the glyphs in type, a treatment which greatly reduces their value for students. Gates also restores glyphs, usually without any indication of the fact. The Kingsborough version of Dresden has some value for checking damaged glyphs, because it was copied half a century before the first Förstemann edition.

OTHER SOURCES OF GLYPHIC MATERIAL

Short hieroglyphic texts were also incised on jade, hard stones, bone, and shell; embossed on metal; and painted, carved, or molded on pottery.

Jade and Hard Stone. The most famous jade from an epigraphic viewpoint is the Leiden plaque, which records the earliest Maya IS which was current time when the glyphs were incised. This is 8.14.3.1.12 1 Eb o Yaxkin (A.D. 320). Actually this plaque was found in apparent association with copper bells which were not manufactured in Mesoamerica until five or six centuries later. However, because of the style of the glyphs, there can be no question of the antiquity of the date (Morley and Morley, 1938).

The Tuxtla statuette, a large figure of jade found at San Andres Tuxtla, Veracruz, was at one time thought to bear the earliest inscribed date in the Maya calendar (Holmes, 1907), but more complete information on Middle American cultures now makes it virtually certain that this piece is of Olmec (La Venta) workmanship, and it has also been suggested that the calendarial system employed may not be that of the Maya (Thompson, 1941a).

Several jade pieces, both pectorals and beads, carry short inscriptions of calendarial import. In two cases the cities where the glyphs were incised can be traced from the inscriptions they carry, for two of the jades recovered from the Sacred Cenote at Chichen Itza repeat or refer to dates which were of great importance at Piedras Negras and Palenque. Other pieces, both jewels and celts, of jade, diorite, and other hard stones carry glyphs, but their meanings are unknown. In a few cases the glyphs are apparently Olmec, although the pieces were found in the Maya area. Rarely, glyphs were incised on obsidian.

Bone and Shell. Texts incised on bone and shell ornaments are short and for the most part undecipherable. One on a peccary skull, found at Copan, is of importance because of the early style of the glyphs.

Metal. The only objects of metal with glyphs are some disks dredged from the Sacred Cenote at Chichen Itza.

Painted Pottery. Hieroglyphs painted on pottery vessels appear to have been largely decorative. On a few vessels from the Alta Verapaz, Guatemala, short sequences of day signs, without coefficients, are painted (fig. *6,12,28,62,63,* etc.), but these can bear no relation to the deities depicted, and appear to have functioned as ornamental divisions between scenes. A few vessels carried Calendar Round (hereinafter contracted to CR) dates but as some of these contain obvious errors (e.g. Imix followed by 13 Zip), one may presume that their function is purely decorative.

Senseless mistakes of a rather singular nature occur in the only IS so far found on a vessel, the famous IS vase at Uaxactun. There is internal evidence that the artist who painted the details was ignorant of hieroglyphic writing. The blunders must have worried the priest who owned this vase and, indeed, may not have ceased to do so after his death, for the vase was buried with him, and its "soul" accompanied him to the next world. Many vessels carry repetitions of the same glyph, and in these cases obviously the glyphs had only a decorative function. In the Uloa Valley and southward to El Salvador these decorative glyphs degenerate into semigeometric patterns hardly recognizable as glyphs.

A few vases from the Alta Verapaz have short vertical or L-shaped glyphic panels which do not add to the composition and give the appearance of being explanatory. They resemble those found on murals. In the study of these lies the best hope of progress in the field of ceramic texts. A cylindrical tripod vase from Uaxactun with fresco decoration is in the same category, although of earlier date, and there are scattered examples from elsewhere.

Carved and Molded Pottery. Generally speaking, glyphs carved and molded are more conventionalized and tend more to the purely decorative than those that are painted. A short text incised on a vessel from Uaxactun has been used for helping to date pottery sequences, but the sign identified as Ahau is, as a matter of fact, an entirely different but well-known glyph. The reading must be rejected.

Two or three small figurines from Lubaantun, British Honduras, are molded to represent stelae with hieroglyphic texts. The glyphs are hard to make out, and doubtlessly are not supposed to convey any meaning.

AREA AND EPOCHS OF HIEROGLYPHIC WRITING

The area in which Maya hieroglyphic writing was employed does not correspond to that of Maya speech in the sixteenth century, for we have no evidence that hieroglyphs used in the Guatemalan highlands were Maya, and the stela cult never penetrated to that area. Furthermore, the Cakchiquel reckoned their years in the Long Count (hereinafter contracted to LC) by periods of 400 days, not the 360-day tuns of the hieroglyphic texts. We have no information on the LC practices of other highland peoples, but because of their close cultural ties with the Cakchiquel, it is probable that the Quiche and Zutuhil had the same 400-day count. There is actually some evidence suggesting that some of the ruling families of the Guatemalan highlands used Mexican hieroglyphs.

The evidence of rebus writing and the forms of the head variants for the numbers 11 and 12 (p. 51) tend to confirm the supposition that Maya hieroglyphic writing originated in the lowlands.

The area of Maya hieroglyphic writing corresponds pretty closely with that occupied by Maya of the lowland group of languages and dialects. In defining the area of hieroglyphic writing the distribution of polychrome vases or jewelry with glyphs is not considered, for in both cases trade might, and in fact did, carry pieces far afield, and in the case of polychrome pottery the use of conventionalized glyphs as a decorative design (as in the Uloa–western El Salvador region) is hardly evidence on which alone to postulate a knowledge of Maya hieroglyphic writing in the area.

The various sites in which hieroglyphic inscriptions have been found are superimposed on a linguistic map in figure 1. It should be remembered that the linguistic boundaries are based on colonial and modern data.

The Zapotec, Olmec, and perhaps other peoples of Middle America used hieroglyphs at an early date, but their writings never passed the rudimentary stage, and little progress has been made in their decipherment. The general homogeneity of day names and, perhaps, certain glyphs in those areas points to a single center of origin, but present evidence does not suggest which, if any, of these three peoples invented glyphs. As Zapotec and La Venta (Olmec) influences on Maya writing were probably very slight once the formative stage had passed, I shall not discuss their glyphs. Readers are referred to Caso (1928, 1947) for Zapotec writing; to Holmes (1907), Stirling (1940, 1945), and Thompson (1941a) for Olmec writing.

Maya hieroglyphic inscriptions on stone, with a few dubious exceptions, are confined to the Initial Series, or Classical, Period, and no text inscribed on stone can be surely assigned to the Mexican Period, although there are a few non-Maya glyphs in buildings of that period at Chichen Itza. It is evident that the stela cult ceased at the close of the Initial Series Period, perhaps because of foreign influences or a revolt against the hierarchy. There are, however, mural texts which date from the Mexican Period or Period of Mexican Absorption, and to those epochs must be assigned the three surviving codices, as well as a scattering of glyphs on copper disks.

SEARCH AND RESEARCH

Maya hieroglyphic writing was first brought to the attention of the modern world by Abbé Brasseur de Bourbourg, the French antiquary and historian, whose enthusiastic delving into the past of Middle America uncovered a great mass of material and saved many manuscripts from the dangers of ignorant neglect. It is a sad commentary on our supposed progress that more manuscript treatises on every aspect of Indian life were destroyed through negligence, bigotry, and ignorance during the second half of the nineteenth century than were lost during the three preceding centuries. The abbé had the good fortune to be in Chiapas at the time the convents were suppressed in Mexico, and was thus able to save many manuscripts from destruction. His interest in the Maya was aroused by his contact with the Quiche when he served as priest of the Quiche town of Rabinal. Above all things we are indebted to the abbé for bringing to light and publishing the copy, or rather abstract, of Bishop Diego de Landa's *Historia de las cosas de Yucatan.*

This book, by the third bishop of Yucatan, was written somewhere about 1566. It gives a history of Yucatan from native informants, an account of the Spanish conquest, a good deal of straight Maya ethnography, and a rather full description of the Maya calendar together with some of the ceremonies connected therewith. The description was illustrated with drawings of the glyphs for the days and the 20-day months. There was also a "key" to the hieroglyphic writing which was to prove a source of much contention. When efforts to decipher the Maya codices with its aid were fruitless it was declared a Spanish fabrication; it was probably neither a key nor a hoax. Landa appears to have asked the Maya glyphs for the letters of the Spanish alphabet, and the informant drew a glyphic element resembling the sound. Thus, when Landa said *b* (pronounced bay in Spanish) the informant drew a foot, the symbol for travel because the Maya word *be* (pronounced bay) means road, journey, etc. I have found the Landa alphabet of some assistance.

Landa's description of the calendar and his illustrations of day and month signs supplied a firm foundation on which to reconstruct Maya hieroglyphic writing; it is as close to a Rosetta Stone as we are ever likely to get.

Brasseur de Bourbourg (he discarded his title with the fall of Napoleon III) published Landa's book, omitting, however, the final and least important part, in 1864, the year following its rediscovery. He had immediately recognized as Maya the Dresden and Paris codices on the strength of the identity of glyphs they contained with those illustrated by Landa, and he had realized that the inscriptions at Palenque and Copan belonged to the same class.

Dresden had already been published in Lord Kingsborough's monumental work *Antiquities of Mexico,* and the inscriptions of Palenque and Copan were known through the descriptions or drawings of Del Rio, Dupaix, Castañeda, Stephens, and Catherwood. A photographic reproduction of Paris appeared in the same year as Landa's *Relación.* Probably the enthusiastic support of the abbé hastened its publication. Two years later Brasseur de Bourbourg collaborated with Count Waldeck in a work on Palenque which reproduced in 40 lithographed plates many of the drawings made by Waldeck during the three years he spent at Palenque. It is interesting to note that despite his long residence in the tropics, the count lived to the age of 109.

In that same year of 1866, or very shortly after, the indefatigable Brasseur de Bourbourg had discovered the Tro part of Madrid; this he published with a lengthy introduction and a Yucatec grammar and vocabulary in 1869–70. The introduction has little value because the abbé followed that will-o'-the-wisp, the Landa alphabet, and failed disastrously in the attempt to decipher the glyphs. He did, however, recognize the day signs.

Some idea of the stupendous activity of this French priest can be gained by noting that between 1857 and 1859 he published his *Histoire des nations civilisées du Mexique et de l'Amerique centrale;* he translated the Popol Vuh and published it in 1861, and in the same year he produced a charming travel book *Voyage sur l'isthme de Tehuantepec*. In 1862 he followed this with a grammar and vocabulary of Quiche. Landa appeared in 1864; the Palenque report and studies of the ruins of Merida, Izamal, and Mayapan in 1866. In 1868 his *Quatre lettres sur le Mexique* were printed; during the next two years he was engaged in his studies of the Tro part of Madrid and in travel in Central America, and in 1871 his *Bibliothèque Mexico-Guatémalienne* saw the light.

Various smaller studies and articles appeared during this fruitful decade despite the fact that he also gave courses on New World archaeology at the Sorbonne. Before residing in Guatemala (1855–57) the abbé had written extensively on the history of the Roman Catholic Church in Canada. His acquisitions of many manuscripts, including the indispensable Motul dictionary of Yucatec, the Rodaz material on Tzotzil, and the Aguilar dictionary of Tzeltal, rescued so many priceless works from destruction that we are forever indebted to the learned antiquary.

It is well to cite the record of this remarkable man, for with the recent progress in Maya archaeology the great contributions of the pioneers in the field are easily forgotten.

An earlier student in the field, but one whose work could not be fully utilized until after the publication of Landa, was the Yucatecan Juan Pio Perez, one-time *Jefe Politico* of Peto in Yucatan. Pio Perez did very valuable service in preserving, copying, and collating the various books of Chilam Balam and land titles in Maya, and in copying Yucatec-Spanish dictionaries. His published works start with *Cronología antigua de Yucatan* which he presented to J. L. Stephens in 1842, and which the latter published as an appendix to his *Incidents of Travel in Yucatan*. A much fuller version was published in 1846 in the *Registro Yucateco* and was also printed by Brasseur de Bourbourg in his edition of Landa. The Pio Perez dictionary of Yucatec-Spanish is largely derived from the older San Francisco and Ticul dictionaries and Beltran's *arte*, but contained many additions by Pio Perez. It was completed after Pio Perez's death (1859) by Dr. Berendt, and published in 1866–77.

The manuscript compilation by Pio Perez of material in the Maya language is of great importance; it is known as the Codex Perez, and among its contents are lengthy abstracts from the Book of Chilam Balam of Mani, the original of which is lost. Tozzer (1921) lists the contents; Barrera Vasquez (1939) gives a more detailed description. A full summary is given by Roys (1949a), and a translation by Ermilo Solis Alcala is in press.

Brasseur de Bourbourg had failed in his attempts to interpret the Tro fragment with the Landa key, but he had recognized the day signs and the kin signs and had learned the meaning of the bars and dots. Leon de Rosny (1876) identified at least one month sign and correctly deciphered the world direction glyphs; A. Pousse (1884) found how the red and black numbers in the codices were used, and the glyph for twenty; Cyrus Thomas (1882) identified the ceremonies for the departure of the old year and the start of the new in the Tro fragment, and wrote extensively on the subject of Maya numeration (1901) and the calendar (1901 and 1904) without, however, making any fundamental contribution to the subject.

It was in 1880 that the most important figure in Maya hieroglyphic research entered the field: Ernst Förstemann, head librarian of the Royal Public Library at Dresden. In that year he published a reproduction of Dresden (a somewhat inaccurate edition had been published by Lord Kingsborough nearly 50 years before).

Dr. Förstemann was 58 years old when he took up his Maya studies; six years later the first results of his investigations were published, and thereafter scarcely a year passed without a significant contribution from his pen. Even in 1906, the year of his death, at 84, two papers of his appeared, following the publication of no less than five during 1905. The whole framework of the Maya calendar was elucidated by him. At first his studies were largely confined to Dresden, but subsequently he extended his interest to the other codices and to the stelae.

In papers published in 1880, 1886, and 1887 Förstemann identified the month signs in Dresden, recognized that the shell and moon symbols had the respective values of 0 and 20, and demonstrated the abbreviated system of the almanac of 260 days. In addition, he showed that the Maya employed a vigesimal system (except for the uinals), and used this to the sixth degree (the pictun of 2,880,000 days) by means of superposition. He also recognized and deciphered the complex Venus tables, and seems to have grasped the lunar significance of the eclipse tables in Dresden. He had also worked out the numerous "multiplication" tables.

In 1887 he was able to announce that the Maya LC was reckoned from the base 4 Ahau 8 Cumku, and he was able to give the correct explanation of the ring numbers. In 1891 he identified the glyphs for the uinal, tun, and katun in Dresden. To these he added in 1893 the definite recognition of the lunar series in that codex. In the following year he identified the baktun glyph on the monuments (it does not occur in Dresden) and the hand and normal symbols for zero used with period glyphs on the monuments. Actually he calls them symbols for 20, but he recognized their functional value. As a result of these identifications he was able to decipher the head variants of kin, uinal, tun, katun, and baktun used on the monuments. In that same paper, written in 1894, he read correctly the IS on seven monuments at Copan.

In 14 years this brilliant man had wrested the secret of the Maya calendar from codex and stela; he stands shoulders above any other student of Maya hieroglyphs. Furthermore, one must bear in mind that these studies had to be pursued in the time he could spare from his duties as chief librarian of the Royal Library at Dresden. The title of Privy Councillor bestowed on him was a just recognition of his remarkable achievements. In the remaining 12 years of his life Förstemann added much to our knowledge of the glyphs. For example, he was probably the first to recognize distance numbers on the monuments, for in his study on the Temple of the Cross (1897) he uses them as though they were no novelty to him. However, Goodman's work, which also includes distance numbers, was published as early as February of the same year. In a discussion of Piedras Negras 3, published in 1902, Förstemann recognized the lunar character of the lunar or supplementary series, and came near a solution, but was misled by giving the lunar glyph a value of 28 instead of 20, thereby reaching a value of 37 instead of 29 for Glyph A of that series. A dozen years later, Förstemann's discovery overlooked, the lunar character of this series was hailed as a new and great discovery.

J. Thompson Goodman's important work *The archaic Maya inscriptions* appeared in February 1897, as an appendix to Maudslay's great work, the archaeological part of *Biologia Centrali-americana.* As Goodman made no acknowledgments in his text to the work of any other student of the glyphs, it is difficult to know what he thought were his own discoveries, and what he assumed his readers would know were those of others. It has often been claimed that Goodman produced his results quite unaware of Förstemann's and others' work, and it has been suggested that the credit for the various decipherments should be divided between them, to Förstemann being attributed those in Dresden, to Goodman those on the stelae.

I find some details in Goodman's study which convince me that Goodman had knowledge of Förstemann's discoveries. Strong evidence is to be found in a casual reference by Goodman to the lunar tables in Dresden. Had he discovered these himself he would hardly have been content with a passing remark, for that was an achievement of very considerable importance. I can only conclude that Goodman had read Förstemann's paper of 1893 in which the interpretation was set forth. Förstemann called the 20-day period the Chuen, because of the resemblance of its glyph to that day sign; Goodman, who relied largely on the writings of Landa where that period is clearly named uinal, also calls the 20-day period the Chuen. Förstemann thought the zero or completion symbol attached to period glyphs on the monuments should be read as 20; Goodman also renders it as 20, although it is more logical to translate it as zero. It would be strange had both these students hit upon this same rather artificial rendering independently.

Irrefutable evidence, however, that Goodman had read Förstemann comes from his own pen. In discussing the chronological calendar, Goodman writes, "It has been known that the Mayas reckoned time by ahaus (i.e. tuns), katuns, cycles (i.e. baktuns), and great cycles (i.e. pictuns)." That information is in none of the early sources, but was brought to light only through the studies of Förstemann. Furthermore, Brinton (1895) gives many details of Förstemann's researches, including the reading of IS, and such matters as the glyphs for the katun and tun, in his *Primer of Maya hieroglyphics,* which surely must have come into Goodman's hands.

In view of the above facts, it is amazing to find in Goodman's work such statements as: "I had discovered the secret of the ahau and katun count," "I determined the character of the chuen and great cycle periods. . . . I ascertained the first cycle was composed of twenty katuns. . . . I finally deduced a chronological calendar . . . and, by reversing the process, succeeded in reconstructing the outline of the entire Archaic chronological scheme. I expect my calendar to be challenged," and, of the results of other students of the glyphs, "A deal of learned and pompous kowtowing to each other, but not a single substantial gain toward bottoming the inscriptions." Every one of these discoveries had been made previously by Förstemann, who, of course, had for his own use tables like Goodman's "archaic chronological calendar," for without such tables or their equivalent in some other form, he could not have checked his reckonings from 4 Ahau 8 Cumku. One wonders what Maudslay, whose modesty was his outstanding characteristic, felt about such vaingloryying.

Withal, Goodman has to his credit the identification of the head variants 0–19 (except 2, 7, 11), a discovery of prime importance. This Förstemann himself had just failed to make when he successfully read the IS of Copan I (for the coefficient of Ahau on that stela is the head variant for 5). Goodman also recognized the half-period glyph (the misnamed lahuntun sign) and the 5-tun glyph (the so-called hotun glyph). His very full tables of Maya dates have been of great aid to scholars, and are still in constant use. Some of his ideas on numerical values have been rejected by subsequent students, but I myself am often amazed at how many correct leads he gave us. Except on the subject of numbers Goodman displayed sound judgment, and *The archaic Maya inscriptions* remains a reference book of the highest importance.

In 1905 Goodman published a short paper in the *American Anthropologist* in which he advocated a correlation of the Maya and European calendars which involved the addition of 584,283 to a Maya date to reach the equivalent Julian day. For over 20 years his ideas on the subject were rejected by other workers in the field, but in 1926 the Yucatecan scholar Juan Martinez Hernandez reaffirmed the correlation, producing new evidence from the times of the conquest. This synchronization is now known as the Goodman-Martinez correlation. In 1927 I applied the tests of the lunar data and the Venus calendar to the various correlations, and offered an amended version of the Goodman correlation, using an addition of 584,285 to the Maya day to reach the Julian day. This correlation bears the name Goodman-Thompson, and has received rather wide acceptance. I have now amended this to the equation 584,283 (App. II).

Goodman's renown does not rest only on his achievements in the field of Maya hieroglyphs. As owner and editor of "The Territorial Enterprise" of Virginia, Nevada, he gave Mark Twain his start as a journalist; the two were lifelong friends. Subsequently Goodman founded "The San Franciscan," a literary publication of some importance.

Goodman's studies and, indeed, those of all his contemporaries would have been impossible had it not been for the great contribution of Maudslay. Alfred Percival Maudslay, after some years in the British colonial service, visited Guatemala in 1881 with the primary purpose of passing the winter in a warm climate. Visits to the nearby ruins of Copan and Quirigua interested him so greatly in the Maya that he returned the following year with more suitable equipment for recording the inscriptions. Altogether Maudslay made seven expeditions to Central America, spending considerable periods at the ruins of Copan, Quirigua, Palenque, Yaxchilan, Tikal, and Chichen Itza. The results, in the form of casts, magnificent photographs of the ruins and particularly of the hieroglyphic texts, maps and plans, and the extremely good drawings of the glyphs, made by Miss Annie Hunter under Maudslay's supervision, were published between 1889 and 1902. They formed four volumes of plates and one of text and included Goodman's study on the inscriptions as an appendix. They set a new standard of accuracy, and are a fitting monument to the tireless enthusiasm which enabled this pioneer to overcome the obstacles with which those remote and fever-ridden jungles strove to daunt him.

Maudslay's work was acclaimed by all those interested in the subject. With characteristic generosity he placed his results at the disposal of the leading scholars in the field, content to have provided them with the material for their studies in usable form. Goodman pays a well-merited tribute to the value of Maudslay's work which every student of Maya hieroglyphs will echo.

No prophet is without honor save in his own country. Maudslay's magnificent collection of casts was ignominiously consigned to the basement of the South Kensington Museum. It was not until 1923 that they were removed from obscurity and placed, together with some original sculptures, in the Maudslay room of the British Museum. In 1925 Cambridge University tardily recognized her son by conferring on him an honorary degree. I count it among my privileges to have been present at that ceremony. The words John Drinkwater wrote of another Cotswold man—"a life complete is a great nobility"—well encompass the achievements of this lovable scholar and gentleman.

Other figures were crowding the stage of Maya research in the last two decades of the nineteenth century. Their contributions were of great importance, but Maya hieroglyphs were but one of the many subjects that engaged their attention. The great Eduard Seler, Nestor of Middle American studies, turned from his primary interest in the field of Mexican religion and codices to put his shoulder to the wheel. In addition to his studies on the inscriptions of Copan and Quirigua and his commentaries on the codices, he wrote extensively on the ruins of Palenque, Chichen Itza, Uxmal, and the Chenes country. Perhaps his greatest single contribution was his demonstration of the essential unity of the advanced cultures of Middle America.

The early explorer Waldeck had been a soldier of Napoleon in Egypt, and perhaps had stood in the shadow of the pyramids to hear Bonaparte's historic address to his troops; Daniel Garrison Brinton was a surgeon of the Union at the battle of Gettysburg, and may have heard Lincoln's still more memorable speech on that battlefield. In the years following the Civil War Brinton devoted such time as he could spare from his medical duties to the study of linguistics and ethnology, particularly those of the Maya field. His translations of the chronological passages in the various books of Chilam Balam (1882) and his researches into the Maya calendar (1893, 1895) and Maya mythology (1881) are of particular importance to the student of the hieroglyphs.

Count Hyacinthe Charency was another scholar primarily interested in the linguistic field. Among his publications are two Tzotzil-Spanish vocabularies and the names of the Tzotzil months, the latter from a Spanish manuscript. He made special studies of Maya terms for numbers and the cardinal points.

The turn of the century saw a notable recruit to the study of Maya hieroglyphs, Charles Pickering Bowditch, also a veteran of the Civil War. He contributed generously to the various expeditions of the Peabody Museum, Harvard University, to the Maya area, and by his own example and tireless efforts persuaded others to support this work. He was largely instrumental in creating the magnificent library for Maya research at the same museum, donating most generously from his own pocket for rare items and paying the cost of large numbers of photographic copies of inaccessible works. As an adjunct to this work, he supervised the translation into English of the leading papers on Middle America written by Förstemann, Seler, and other German scholars. In his book *The numeration, calendar systems and astronomical knowledge of the Mayas* he set forth in a concise manner the progress to date in that field, subjecting the take-it-or-leave-it statements of Goodman to arithmetical tests, and proving or discarding them one by one. In various short papers he offered many new readings of inscriptions at Yaxchilan and Piedras Negras and drew together many of the loose ends left by previous workers in the field.

Teobert Maler, born in Bonn in 1842 but subsequently naturalized as an Austrian, came to Mexico in the train of that most pathetic figure in Mexican history, the Emperor Maximilian. Subsequently, he explored many Maya sites for Peabody Museum, Harvard University, as well as a considerable number in Yucatan and Campeche without outside backing. He had had some training as an architect and engineer, to which he brought a determination and patience to overcome difficulties, many, alas, of his own making. He was a first-rate photographer and paid special attention to making as complete a record as possible of the texts and sculptures he found; his photographs of Tizimin are of great value, for subsequently the manuscript deteriorated. His excellently illustrated reports supplement Maudslay's work.

Students of Maya linguistics and hieroglyphs owe a deep debt to William E. Gates for his unflagging zeal in gathering or photographing every available manuscript or rare book on Maya linguistics in particular and Middle American culture in general. Gates' death in 1940, at the age of 76, left unfinished the tremendous task he had set himself of collating the vocabularies and grammars of all the Maya languages. His principal publications in the hieroglyphic field were a study of Codex Paris (1910) and his dictionary of Maya hieroglyphs (1931), but many other papers from his pen, particularly in the short-lived *Maya Society Quarterly*, are of very considerable importance to that discipline. Gates was a descendant of General Horatio Gates who took a prominent part in the French and Indian wars and later in the Revolutionary War.

Early in 1907 Morley, then a young student at Harvard, stepped ashore in Yucatan on his first visit to the Maya area. Until his death, in 1948, there passed only one year which did not find him in Central America. Of this first journey Morley says, "My great-aunt Virginia offered me a trip anywhere in the world I might choose. When I said Yucatan, she replied 'And where, pray, is Yucatan?' She was horrified no end at my choice when she found out where it was."

Sylvanus Griswold Morley in the past four decades visited almost every known site in the Maya field in his unfaltering quest for hieroglyphic texts. A man of indifferent physique, he endured the discomforts and the monotony of travel at the slow pace of a mule train for months at a time in his search for new sites and new stelae. His first long trip through the forests of the Peten was made in 1914. This, with characteristic enthusiasm, he financed with the proceeds of a bequest of a thousand dollars from a relative, although that sum would have measurably relieved the strain on his personal finances. It was his persuasive advocacy that induced Carnegie Institution of Washington to enter the Maya field. Morley's faculty, almost uncanny at times, for wresting dates and distance numbers from crumbling stelae enabled him to produce a huge number of decipherments. These have been presented in his two monumental works, *The inscriptions at Copan* and *The inscriptions of Peten*. The later earned for him the Loubat Prize and the Guatemalan Order of the Quetzal. With the amassing of so much raw material, Morley had little time for the decipherment of glyphs of unknown meaning. However, he proved the identifications of the so-called hotun and lahuntun glyphs first made by Goodman, and, with the aid of R. K. Morley and Professor Robert W. Willson, established the general lunar significance of the supplementary series. He was the first to solve the meaning of the end of a tun glyph.

Morley's unshakable enthusiasm has been an inspiration to me since my first meeting with him on the trail from the hacienda of Chichen Itza to "old Chichen" on a January afternoon in 1926 and his unfailing friendship I have ever cherished. His death in 1948 was a grievous blow to Maya research.

Herbert Joseph Spinden entered the Maya field at approximately the same time as did Morley. His greatest contribution has been in the field of art (1913). In 1909 Morley had proposed a correlation of the Maya and European calendars which placed the Katun 13 Ahau of the Spanish conquest in the LC position 12.9.0.0.0 13 Ahau 8 Kankin. Ten years later Spinden announced a day-for-day correlation of the calendars which equated 12.9.0.0.0. 13 Ahau 8 Kankin with April 22, 1536 (Gregorian) and called for an addition of 489384 to a Maya date to reach its Julian day equivalent. Spinden's writings on Maya hieroglyphs (1924, 1928, 1930) have been entirely confined to the advocacy of that correlation. At one time the Spinden correlation had a large following, but in recent years opinion has turned against it. Nevertheless, the cogency with which he has advocated his ideas has enormously stimulated interest in the glyphs. His outstanding successes in many branches of Maya study place him in the very forefront of Middle American research.

Richard C. E. Long, an Irish solicitor who had for many years studied ethnology, interested himself in Maya hieroglyphs toward the close of the second decade of this century. In the numerous short papers he has written there are many important discoveries, notably arithmetical proof for the identification of the pictun glyph, data on the "burner" period, identification of the haab as a period of 360 days, the elucidation of dates in the *Annals of the Cakchiquels,* and the identification of the frescoes at Santa Rita as a count of tuns. Through many years of his friendship I have derived much pleasurable benefit. As I write, Maya calendar names subtly changed by his soft brogue echo in my ears.

John Edgar Teeple, a chemical engineer of outstanding merit, took up the subject of Maya hieroglyphs to while away time on the long train journeys his professional work entailed. In articles published in the *American Anthropologist* from 1925 to 1928 he proved that Glyphs D and E of the lunar (or supplementary) series recorded the age of the moon, and Glyph C of the same series indicated the number of the moon in a group of six with which Glyphs D and E were to be associated. He also showed that a uniform system of moon numbering spread to all Maya centers, and that this eventually gave way to something else. He also solved the problem of the various entries in the Venus tables in Dresden, showing that the different sets of dates represented corrections to bring the calculations into agreement with actual revolutions of the planet.

In 1930 his brilliant study *Maya astronomy* was published by Carnegie Institution. This was in part an expansion of ideas he had previously published, but it gave to the public for the first time his determinant theory, the elucidation of a system by which the Maya kept track of the difference between solar time and their vague year of 365 days. I had the pleasure of hearing this revolutionary idea from Teeple's own lips at a lunch in New York in the summer of 1929. Death cut short the career of this brilliant and productive student early in 1931 when he was just getting into his stride.

Hermann Beyer began his long series of publications on Mexican archaeology as early as 1908, but it was not until 1921 that he published anything on Maya hier-

oglyphs, and not until 1926 that he began to devote the greater part of his attention to the subject. During the next 15 years he wrote on a great number of topics connected with the study. Beyer's greatest contribution to the field was, undoubtedly, *Studies on the inscriptions of Chichen Itza,* not because of the actual result (conclusions were insignificant and his chronological scheme was quite unacceptable) but because of his approach. The glyphs were systematically classified, variants in affixes noted, and clauses isolated with a methodical thoroughness thitherto unknown in the Maya field. The same systematic classification characterized all his numerous studies on Maya glyphs. Of his discoveries the most important are: the function of the variable element in the IS introductory glyph (1931), Glyph G8 (1936d), the use of the moon sign in distance numbers in the inscriptions (1938a), and rules for affixes and infixes (1934). An unbending opponent in the field of archaeology, Beyer had a kindness of heart and a queer pawky humor, more Scottish than German, which endeared him to his colleagues. Apart from the direct results of his studies, he has an outstanding monument in his great pupil, Alfonso Caso. Beyer was the plodder, but folklore tells us and Beyer's work confirms it, that the tortoise may get first to the tape. Beyer died in 1942, leaving much manuscript material, which, one fervently hopes will eventually be published. In this book I have made much use of the Beyer approach.

Four astronomers of distinction in their own field have studied Maya inscriptions from the astronomical point of view, and have added their important contributions to the subject, although not directly contributing to the decipherments. They are Robert W. Willson, Hans Ludendorff, Arnost Dittrich, and Maud W. Makemson. Their publications are listed in the bibliography. The high hopes entertained for decisive results from a strictly astronomical approach have not been fulfilled. I think that is because the Maya priests did not use astronomy as an exact science. Instead, they fashioned it to their mystical and poetical approach. Associations of celestial phenomena with lucky or unlucky days, or connections deep in mythology were, I am sure, of more importance than an exact record of when they occurred. Since these are the methods of the astrologer rather than of the astronomer, the precise technique of the latter is often of little value in augmenting knowledge of the meaning of the inscriptions. Among the astronomers who have taken up this study only Mrs. Makemson has realized this fundamental difference in approach.

Interest in Maya epigraphy in Mexico has not been great. With so many ancient cultures in the center of Mexico to be investigated, it is not surprising that the

Maya area, remote from Mexico City, has received little attention. However, the Mexican archaeologist Enrique Juan Palacios, whose primary interests lie in Veracruz, has made important contributions, of which the most outstanding are the identification of the head form for the number two, and various discoveries in Chiapas and Campeche. Another Mexican who has made valuable researches in Maya epigraphy is the journalist Cesar Lizardi Ramos. A star on the horizon is Raul Pavon Abreu, now director of the museum at Campeche. Heinrich Berlin is a notable student of the Mexican school which stems from Palacios.

Attention should also be called to the writings of E. Wyllys Andrews, Samuel K. Lothrop, Thomas A. Joyce, Lawrence Roys, and Linton Satterthwaite on the inscriptions, and of Oliver La Farge, Robert Burkitt, Sol Tax, Antonio Goubaud, and J. Steward Lincoln on modern survivals of the Maya calendar.

Indirect contributions of outstanding importance to the study of Maya hieroglyphic writing have been made by Ralph L. Roys through his published translations of Chilam Balam of Chumayel (1933), the titles of Ebtun (1939), the prophecies for the Maya tuns (1949), and his many unpublished translations. Roys combines a wide knowledge of the Yucatec language with a deep understanding of Maya culture. My personal debt to him is great, for he has vouchsafed me of the full stores of his wisdom and advice on a hundred occasions, invariably answering my queries with a conscientious thoroughness rarely found in this age. Most vivid of my impressions of Roys harks back to an evening on the deck of *The Ulua,* when we settled, to our fleeting satisfaction, the problems of the Maya, as the sun's afterglow suffused with soft violet the tree-clad hills of Tela. To him I could repeat the lines from *Henry IV:* "My voice shall sound as you do prompt my ear, and I will stoop and humble my intents to your well-practised wise directions."

The translations from the various books of Chilam Balam by the Yucatecan scholars Juan Martinez Hernandez, Alfredo Barrera Vasquez, and Ermilo Solis Alcala and his son are also of prime importance. Until all this source material is accessible in translations, hieroglyphic research must suffer.

Outstanding figures in Maya research, such as A. V. Kidder, A. M. Tozzer, and G. C. Vaillant, are omitted from this brief survey because their work bears only indirectly on glyphic problems, although of enormous importance in the reconstruction of Maya civilization. Were they and their many colleagues in the fields of dirt archaeology, architecture, and ethnology to be included, this section would have to be expanded to a considerable extent.

BOOKS OF CHILAM BALAM

The books of Chilam Balam are manuscripts written in Yucatec with European characters; their compilers were Maya of the colonial period interested in preserving a knowledge of the old culture. The books take their name from a Maya called Chilam Balam who reputedly prophesied the coming of the white man; with that is coupled the name of the town in which each was preserved. The most important contain chronicles of native history set in the frame of the Maya calendar; fragments of historical narrative; prophecies for years and for katuns (of 20 approximate years), in which are embodied much history, mythology, and ritual; almanacs of lucky and unlucky days (App. I); medical lore, European and Maya; and astrology, mainly European. Roys (1933, 1946) details their contents.

Some of the material, particularly in the prophecies for years and katuns, may well have been transcribed from glyphic sources comparable to the pages of Paris giving the katun round and to the pages of year prophecies in all three codices. Indeed, we have the statement of one transcriber of a framework of Maya dates (Chronicle of Oxkutzcab, p. 66) that he compiled it from a glyphic source. Many of the expressions and set phrases are paralleled in glyphs or pictures (p. 270) in the codices, but it is highly probable that the glyphic and pictorial frame was strengthened with material culled from ancient chants and traditions. When the surviving editions were written, much of the old lore had been lost, and there is considerable garbling of rituals and phrases. The historical frameworks were probably made in colonial times by drawing historical material from the prophecies, but often events seem to have been assigned to wrong rounds of the katun count (p. 181). Moreover, these eighteenth-century antiquaries deliberately tampered with their sources, inventing a 24-year katun and then rewriting dates to fit the new scheme. Withal, the ritual and wording of the prophecies are rich veins of glyphic ore.

The most important books are those of Chumayel, Tizimin, and Mani. The last, incorporated in Codex Perez, closely parallels Tizimin, but the text is somewhat corrupt. Kaua also contains katun prophecies. Principal translations are by Martinez Hernandez (1927), Roys (1922, 1933, 1949), Barrera Vasquez (1943, 1949), Solis Alcala (1949), and Gates (1931a).

APPROACH USED IN THIS STUDY

In this volume I have tackled the problem of decipherment in what I deem to be a new way, although one which has in it elements which have been tried before. It is my conviction that we shall interpret the glyphs only by relying heavily on the beliefs, the religious symbolism, the mythology, and, to a lesser extent, the everyday activities of the Maya, because such concepts surely are imbedded in the structure of each glyph, but at the same time we must follow Beyer's lead in paying careful attention to affixes and infixes, particularly with regard to their assignment to groupings of synonyms and near synonyms.

The same glyphic elements, such as yax and water signs (pp. 274–79), appear over and over again in different combinations. Sometimes these signs are not readily recognizable, as they may appear in a horizontal position in one glyph, in a vertical position in another, as happens, for instance, with the jade symbol (cf. figs. 8,4–7; 17,14–22; 43,30,31). It is essential, therefore, to learn to recognize such elements, and then to seek to identify their meanings by turning to the mythology of the Maya and their neighbors. If a dog glyph appears sometimes in a context which suggests fire, but at other times in one indicative of death and the underworld, we must pore over the vast body of Maya and Mexican religion to seek a link connecting these different concepts. Sometimes, as in the case of the dog, it is apparent; at other times direct evidence is not forthcoming. There may be a hint of what the context of the glyph leads us to surmise, or we may not be able to recover the connection.

Argument must be from the known to the unknown, and for that reason many pages are given to elucidating the meanings of the day names and glyphs and other signs, the names and functions of which are known. I believe I have had some success in that task; of those who are not convinced by my views I would fain echo, although, I trust, with less complacency, that passage in *Sense and sensibility,* in which the pompous Mr. Dashwood remarks, "Well may you wonder, Marianne, at the obstinacy which could resist such arguments as these."

From the study of the known glyphs a fair vocabulary, or, rather, list of ideographs and symbolic concepts, can be garnered, and this can be tested on glyphs of unknown meaning. The study of the affixes will yield some idea of the structure of the glyphic writing, and a due appreciation of the poetical inspirations of Maya thought and writings (for mythology is poetry) will teach us that a Maya, when dealing with sacred matters, never calls a spade a spade.

I am not unmindful of the pitfalls in the path of one who would stray in the tangled woods of Maya mythology. There is too much danger of finding what one seeks, for many opposed ideas exist in the religious concepts of the peoples of Middle America, and one is free to pick and choose. To take an extreme instance, I have built a structure, the walls of which are assumptions with a light bonding of fact, to explain the religious significance of the day Cib (pp. 84–86). Is this a well-reasoned reconstruction of the Maya ideas behind that day, or have I built on sand? I take confidence from the realization of how the same religious ideas pervade the Maya area in particular and Middle America in general. Agricultural prayers practically throughout the Maya area are cast in the same mold. Snakes are not really a great danger to milperos, yet a petition for protection from the bites of snakes occurs in these prayers almost throughout the region; elements of the creation legend are equally widespread, as, for instance, the story of the origin of monkeys, which is repeated in substantially the same form from the Maya Dan to the Maya Beersheba. Similarly, the Tlalocs of Mexico, the mountain gods of Guatemala, and the Chacs of Yucatan merge their identities, and the same story of the discovery of maize by ants is spread from central Mexico across Guatemala to British Honduras. The extension is not only geographical; it is temporal. The incident of a captive deceiving his enemy by substituting a firefly for the glow of his cigar occurs in the preconquest traditions of the Popol Vuh, and reappears in a twentieth-century story of the imprisonment of our Lord before the Crucifixion. Such continuity in time and space encourages me to feel that although there may be some misses in identification, there are plenty of hits.

The excursions into mythology are time-consuming, but it is meet and right to make them; they represent the unromantic staff work which must be done before the attack can be launched. They take up much space, and it is only as the book draws to a close that we can take the offensive into new territory. In truth, this new approach to the glyphic problem holds great promise; it has enabled me to grasp, at least to my own gratification, the general purport of the glyphic texts in Dresden. Old friends argued over in discussing day glyphs and names are later ready to help interpret the unknown, and the identification of synonymous affixes in glyphs of ascertained meaning greatens the possibility of deciphering glyphs of unknown significance. Those are the two principal methods which will be used in subsequent chapters.

2

Principles of Maya Glyphic Writing

And in the handywork of their craft is their prayer.
—*Ecclesiasticus*, ch. 38

A SMALL PRIMER, entitled *French without tears,* enjoyed a large circulation in Victorian and Edwardian days. It was the precursor of a whole series of books, even systems of education, based on the optimistic assumption that any one can master a subject quickly and without effort by ignoring or hastily covering its more tedious and toilsome sections. In contrast, between the appearance of the present editions of Codices Dresden and Madrid, Geoffrey Chaucer had written: "Ther nys no werkman, whatsoevere he be, That may bothe werke wel and hastily," and assuredly Chaucer has the best of the argument. A hasty review of the fundamentals of Maya hieroglyphic composition is a poor foundation for research in that subject; there can be no *Maya glyphs without tears,* or, at least, without a smothered yawn of tedium.

Surprisingly, no one has hitherto attempted to elucidate or even to list such rules of that peculiar form of writing as may exist. Naturally, with the greater part of the glyphs still undeciphered, a definitive study of the subject can not be made, but progress is hindered by the lack of any attempt to formulate such rules as can be accepted tentatively or affirmed with certainty. Hence the greater part of this chapter is a primer of Maya hieroglyphic writing, a hornbook one day to be replaced by the ample treatise of some grammarian. Its contents must be mastered by him who would essay glyphic decipherment. Withal, the subject is not without interest because of the effect of Maya temperament on the glyphic writing. The Maya had orderly minds, as their calendar, their philosophy, and the symmetrical groupings of their gods make clear; they were also poets and artists. Theoretically, rules closely prescribed the pattern of writing; in practice considerable deviation was conceded to the artistic and poetical temperament.

Hieroglyphic texts on the monuments consist of a number of blocks of varying size but usually rectangular with slightly rounded corners. The glyph blocks may be of the same height and width, or they may be wider than they are high, or, in rare cases, higher than they are wide; approximately equal height and width is the commonest practice. A height and width of about 15 cm. is average, but there is a wide range in dimension, de-

pending on the space available and the length of the text.

A text may have the glyph blocks arranged in one or more areas or masses. Where the whole surface is devoted to a hieroglyphic text there is usually only a single glyph-block area (fig. 51,2); where the glyph blocks occupy spaces not utilized by sculptured figures of gods or priests, they may occur in several masses.

Within a glyph-block area all glyph blocks are usually of the same size except that the one at the head of the inscription may occupy the space of two or four glyph blocks if it holds the IS introductory glyph (fig. 53,*1–3*); other glyph blocks in an area may be divided into two, three, or four sub-blocks (figs. 47,*2;* 54,*1;* 57,*1*), for the size of a glyph block bears no relation to the importance of the glyph or glyphs it contains. The subdivision, if it occurs, is in the lower part of an inscription and is purely a question of squeezing in more text without undue disturbance of the symmetry of the pattern (fig. 47,*3*). This is confirmed by the fact that the IS introductory glyph is not of outstanding importance as regards content, merely as regards position. The treatment is comparable to that of initials in an illuminated manuscript.

In those texts arranged in more than one glyph-block area, the glyph blocks within each area are of the same size, but the set size for the glyph block may vary from one mass to another. Again this is not a question of import but of space and balance. For ready reference vertical columns are lettered A, B, C, D, etc. from left to right, and the glyph blocks within a vertical column are numbered consecutively from top to bottom. Thus C4 would be the fourth glyph block down in the third vertical column. In the case of a quartered glyph block the two left quarters are distinguished by the addition of *a*, u.h. and *a*, l.h. (u.h. and l.h. standing for upper half and lower half respectively); the two right quarters similarly are designated by the addition of *b*, u.h. and *b*, l.h. Thus D5a, l.h. is the lower left quarter of the fifth glyph block in the fourth vertical column from the left.

Morley has introduced the system of continuing the lettering of the vertical columns in sequence through various lintels of a single building. Thus at Yaxchilan Structure 10 contains Lintels 29, 30, and 31. There are four vertical columns of glyph blocks on Lintel 29, lettered A–D. The left-hand column of Lintel 30 accordingly is given the letter E, and since there are also four columns in that lintel, the first column in Lintel 31 carries the letter I. The same sequence of lettering is used for the various sides of an inscription. The system has the drawback that later investigations have in more than one case shown that the order in which the sides are read is different to that originally supposed, thereby throwing the latter sequence into confusion. That, however, is a fairly unimportant detail. Morley's system is followed in this book.

With extremely few exceptions an inscription starts at the top left corner and passes to the glyph block in the adjacent column (B1); next to the second glyph block in the first column (A2), and then to that in the adjacent column (B2). The text continues in pairs of glyph blocks A3, B3, A4, B4 etc. until the bottom of the second column is reached. The reader then passes to the top of the third and fourth columns C1, D1, and from the bottom of those to the next pair. Generally the columns reach an even number. If there is an extra column, the glyph blocks it contains are read from top to bottom after the last pair of columns is finished. In short texts of three columns this system may be used (fig. 59,2–5), or the sequence may be across each line in turn from left to right (fig. 48). Single horizontal lines of glyphs are deciphered left to right. These rules have exceptions (e.g. a longer column at the left read by itself), but the context will usually resolve the point.

The quarters of a glyph block are generally read in the order *a*, u.h.; *b*, u.h.; *a*, l.h.; *b*, l.h. before passing to the next glyph block. Where a glyph block is halved the left half precedes the right half. Sometimes a single glyph may occupy the left half of a glyph block, whereas two glyphs one above the other occupy the right half.

In the codices the same general rules for reading apply, although, if, as is probable, multiplication tables are to be read in ascending order, the sequence on certain pages runs from right to left starting at the bottom right corner.

A glyph block or its half or quarter division may contain one or two glyphs, arranged so that the edge of one impinges on the edge of the second. I believe, although with our present knowledge of Maya writing the belief can not be substantiated, that this welding together of glyphs was practiced only when both formed part of the same clause.

GLYPH FORMATION

INFIXES

A glyph may consist of a single element, a main element to which have been added various infixes or affixes. An infix is a detail added to the interior of a glyphic element; an affix is attached to its outer edge. Few glyphs lack affixes, and probably features in nearly every main element would qualify as infixes did we but know more of the history of the development of Maya writing. At the present stage of glyph decipherment it is best to treat as infixes only those details known to have been added to the main element of a glyph to change its meaning. For example, the carving inside the dot of the Imix glyph of a small face like that of Ahau changes the meaning of the glyph (fig. 2,*1,2*) and the addition of a small crosshatched area, the symbol for black, to the cauac element indicates that the month Ch'en is meant (fig. 2,*5*). Both of these additions are therefore infixes. The number of infixes as defined above is not great, although there is little doubt that they will become more numerous as decipherment progresses. It will probably prove impossible to draw the line between fused glyphs (p. 41) and infixes, for many of the latter are probably the ultimate step in glyph mergence. There are also cases where a prefix is merged with the main element, thereby becoming an infix from the technical point of view. Examples of this process are found in representations of the month signs Uo and Zip (figs. 2,*7; 16,13*). Affixes, too, can have infixes added. Technically the head variants of numerical coefficients can be considered to be prefixes. The heads for the numbers 14–19 are formed by adding the diagnostic character of the head for 10, a jawbone, to the head of the second digit. The jawbone of 10 as an infix of the head for 4 converts the latter to the head for 14. It is, therefore, a prefix with an infix.

AFFIXES

Certain elements may be added to the main element, to the left (prefix), above (superfix), to the right (postfix), or below (suffix). In the vast majority of cases an affix can be moved from the left to above the main element or vice versa without altering the meaning of the whole one iota. For example, the superfixes of certain months are sometimes moved to the left for purposes of symmetry without in any way affecting the meaning. Cases of such transpositions occur in the glyphs of the months Uo, Zip, Zec, Yaxkin, Ch'en, Yax, Zac, and Ceh (fig. 2,*4,6*). Contrarily the forward element of the posterior date indicator is usually placed to the left of the main element, but sometimes it occurs above (fig. 2,*8,9*), or it may appear as in infix (fig. 2,*10*).

Correspondingly, the affixes to the right and below are generally interchangeable without effect on the meaning of the symbol (figs. 11,*1–8; 33,15–20*). The postfix of the posterior date indicator is usually below the main element but it can occur to the right without altering the meaning (fig. 2,*43–45*).

I think we can assume that prefix and superfix positions and postfix and suffix positions were always interchangeable and could shift in the same way. We can also assume that tradition alone led to the employment of only one position in those cases where an affix does not occur in both the positions open to it. For example, there is no known case of the affix of the katun glyph being placed to the left of the main (tun) element, but presumably the Maya priest would not have hesitated to put it there had consideration of space made it advisable. On the other hand, tradition dictated that the affix which served as a count indicator, a component element of a distance number, should be placed beneath the glyph (fig. 2,*13*), yet on Lintel 30 Yaxchilan it appears to the right of the katun sign. There the glyph block is somewhat elongated, and the use of both superfix and suffix would have produced a distorted glyph. Consequently the artist disregarding tradition moved the element from below to the right of the main sign (fig. 2,*14*). In this publication the terms *prefix* and *postfix* will be used in the more comprehensive sense: the former indicating that the affix stands above or to the left of the main element; the latter that it is below or to the right of the main element. The terms *superfix* and *suffix* will be used only when it is desired to record the actual positions of the affixes.

The same side of an affix, as Beyer (1934, 1934a) has pointed out in his admirable discussion of the subject, generally touches the main element whatever the position it occupies. Usually it merely pivots around the main element as the Plough swings around the north star. This is not a hard and fast rule, for certain affixes used above or below the main element may point either way. One example of this is the *"ti"* element of the anterior and posterior indicators, which may have the "flame" element pointing to left or right (fig. 2,*8–12*). Another exception to the practice is supplied by the *te* (1) classificatory element. This, as a prefix, may occur to the left or above the main element. When placed to the left the circle may be at top or bottom and the curve against the main element; when placed above, the circle may be to left or right, and the curve against the main element or away from it (fig. 2,*15–22*). Perhaps such latitude was permitted only with affixes which were not likely to be misinterpreted.

A few affixes usually retain the same axis whether above or below, to right or to left of the main element. The most common example of this is the inverted Ahau, which almost always keeps its inverted position. This is almost certainly because the Ahau sign developed a new meaning when inverted (fig. 2,*24–27*). Were the rule of always attaching the same side of the affix to the main

element here followed, this particular affix would lose its characteristic, the inverted position, when used as a suffix, and could be confused with other symbols.

It is clear, then, that rules for attaching affixes were not rigid, but were modified as circumstances demanded.

INTERCHANGEABILITY OF AFFIXES AND MAIN ELEMENTS

Affixes and main elements do not form two separate groups, rigidly restricted as to function, for affixes could be used as main elements, and many main elements were also used as affixes. Figure 2,*29* shows a main element with the "comb" variant of the count sign as postfix to right and an inverted Ahau postfix below; in figure 2,*30* the main element has become a prefix, the "comb" variant of the count sign has been replaced by the personified or head variant of the same symbol which serves as the main element. The same inverted Ahau postfix is still below, but now attached to the new main element. The positions of these glyphs in almost identical clauses make it virtually certain that the essential meaning they convey is the same, although there may be small grammatical variations involved in the change, just as we convey the same information by saying either "that book is mine" or "that book belongs to me."

Similarly, in glyphs for the month Mac the "count" element may be the "comb" symbol used as a postfix (fig. 18,*1,2,10–13*), or it may be the corresponding head form (the head of the *xoc* fish, highly conventionalized) used as the main element (fig. 18,*3–6,14,15*). Another example is supplied by the month sign Zec. The normal form of this glyph consists of a geometrical main element with a "comb" prefix (fig. 16,*45–49,51*), but in one case the comb is replaced by its corresponding head variant, the *xoc* fish, recognizable by the upsweeping barbels in front of the forehead, and the "chuen" symbol, which is normally the main element, becomes an infix (fig. 16,*50*).

Another case of an affix becoming a main element is supplied by Glyph F of the lunar series. This sign usually has a postfix which I have termed *te* (2) (fig. 34,*58–62,64–66*), but occasionally the corresponding head form, which is almost certainly that of the maize god (p. 283), replaces it, becoming the main element, and the knot, which is normally the main element, becomes a prefix (fig. 34,*21,63,68*). The same happens when the *"ti"* postfix is replaced by its personified form, a vulture head, in rare examples of the anterior date indicator (cf. fig. 2,*43–45,* with fig. 4,*29,30*).

The rule seems to be that when the head or personified form of an affix, replaces the geometric or symbolic form, the affix becomes the main element. There are, however, exceptions to this rule, for where the *xoc* head replaces the comb as a prefix (fig. 5,*26,42*), and where the death head is substituted for the "death eyes" as a prefix (fig. 32,27) these head forms remain prefixes. This is probably because they do not normally form part of the glyph but are attached to modify its meaning. In one case the prefix becomes a separate glyph on changing from its symbolic, or normal, form to its personified form (fig. 33,26).

Theoretically any affix could become a main element, but in practice many do not, or a more elaborate variant is used, as in the case just cited. It is also impossible to draw a hard and fast rule as to whether a certain combination is a single main element with an affix or two main elements joined together. One can be reasonably sure that the Maya themselves did not always make such a distinction, but were guided primarily by questions of spacing and appearance.

Were the text long for the area to be occupied, the glyphs were compressed and affixes used; were there plenty of space the reverse could happen. At Chichen, particularly, affixes are frequently detached, and stand alone in separate glyph blocks or are attached to an adjacent glyph. In fact, Maya glyphic writing has a flexible quality, and could be easily expanded or compressed without loss in the essential meaning. Figure 35,16 shows a text of nine glyphs from the hieroglyphic stairway at Copan. Four glyphs could be eliminated, and one prefix added to produce a shorter version which would convey all the information now embodied in the text, although, as we shall see, melodic qualities might be lost by abbreviations.

Transference of Affixes to Adjacent Glyphs

There is evidence that some affixes could be shifted to an adjacent glyph without substantially altering the meaning of the passage. In the divinatory almanacs of Dresden the same glyph or pair of glyphs frequently occurs with each division of the almanac. In the divinatory almanac on pages 13b–14b the same pair of glyphs opens the text in each division, but in the last three sections the postfix of the second glyph is transferred to the first glyph, and one of the prefixes of the first glyph disappears, but a postfix of the same meaning as that prefix (p. 40) is attached, in its place, to the second glyph (fig. 2,58–61). That is to say, this is a change roughly the equivalent of that of *ab,cd* to *bd,ca'* (*a'* denoting that it is a synonym for *a*). This mutation is surely about the same as changing an expression such as "he gave him hearty thanks" to "he heartily thanked him." I make no doubt that the flexibility of such affixes corresponds to the flexibility of spoken Maya. Naturally, affixes such as those possessed by most month signs could not be transferred to another glyph, because they qualified the elements to which they

were attached, and served to identify the glyph. At Chichen the *tu* prefix is sometimes attached to the previous glyph as a postfix, but the sequence, of course, is unchanged (fig. 39,3–6). This shift is comparable to wrong punctuation. Similarly, the tail of the kin is incorrectly attached to the adjacent sky sign in figure 3,14.

Interchangeability of Prefixes and Postfixes

Generally speaking, an affix attached to a given element always occupies either the prefixal or postfixal position, and in the case of most glyphs of known meaning the positions either could not be, or in practice never were, interchanged, but there are cases in which an affix may appear in either position with the same main element, or may be used as prefix to one main element, but as postfix to another. Unfortunately, it is not yet known what effect a shift from one position to the other had on the meaning of the whole glyph. This is, naturally, a matter of very great consequence in the interpretation of the glyphic writing.

There is, however, one clear instance of a change in position of the affix having no affect on the meaning of the whole glyph: all examples of the month sign Zec in the inscriptions have the "comb" element as a prefix, but in all examples of Zec in Dresden the "comb" element is a postfix (fig. 16,45–52). Another possible example of this shift in position producing no change in meaning may be supplied by the hand glyph with infixes (fig. 42,58–61). This sign, followed by a sun glyph with dotted outline, occurs in the three divisions of the divinatory almanac of Dresden 12c and in the two divisions of the almanac on Dresden 15c (figs. 62,5; 63,1). In the divisions of Dresden 12c its only affix is the "ak" postfix (fig. 42,59), but on page 15c it appears in the first compartment with "ak" postfix to right and "down-balls" postfix below, whereas in the second compartment it has a saw-bracket prefix to left and the "down-balls" element now a prefix above (fig. 42,61). The same main element is found also on Dresden 2d, but there it has the *u* bracket to left and the "down-balls" as postfix. In all six cases this is the initial or action glyph of its compartment, and it is, therefore, highly probable that the shift of the "down-balls" element from prefix to postfix makes no important alteration in the meaning of the whole element, but is probably a result of the addition of other affixes.

A very common glyph at the end of texts is composed of two Imix signs, the second of which has the comb prefix (figs. 5,15; 40,13,15), but in one text this prefix becomes a postfix without seemingly any change in general meaning (fig. 40,14). Conspicuous among the glyphs which accompany the 260-day almanac occupying Madrid 65–72 is the tun sign with a variable coefficient and usually with the *il* postfix and a second affix, apparently a numerical classifier, perhaps *piz* or *p'el* (p. 197). In 10 cases this latter is a postfix; four times it is absent; thrice (including one haab substitution) it is a prefix (fig. 12,23,24). Here again the transposition from postfix to prefix clearly does not affect the meaning. The clenched hand and crossed-bands glyph at Chichen Itza (Beyer, 1937, figs. 450–56) supplies another instance of transposition of postfix to prefix (cf. fig. 51,4, Gl C1,C2). The conclusion is inescapable that under certain circumstances prefixes and postfixes could be interchanged without major modification in meaning.

In the case of one of the tun signs with the Madrid almanac just discussed, the numerical classifying affix is missing, but appears as prefix of the next glyph, the cross-bands sign. As nowhere else does that common sign have this affix, it is extremely likely that it really belongs with the tun sign, and, accordingly, supplies another instance of an affix transferred to an adjacent glyph.

SUBSTITUTION OF PREFIX FOR POSTFIX OF SAME VALUE

Most IS at Quirigua are followed by a distinctive glyph with a crosshatched area and usually with a lunar postfix, but in two cases the lunar postfix is absent, and is replaced by the *u* bracket prefix (fig. 11,37–41). This is a situation rather similar to that of the interchange of affixes on Dresden 13b and 14b, where the *u* bracket prefix replaces the lunar postfix, but with a shift from the second to the first glyph of the clause (p. 39; fig. 61,5,6). In these Quirigua texts the lunar glyph is probably used rebus fashion to indicate the possessive *u* (p. 47), and Landa informs us that the bracket prefix corresponds to the sound *u*. The two affixes therefore have the same sonal value, and we can be reasonably sure that both stand for the possessive *u*.

Tradition or need for clarity has resulted in certain affixes, among which is the *u* bracket, nearly always occupying a prefixal position, whereas others, including this lunar sign, are generally found as postfixes. If, then, this prefix and this postfix have precisely the same meaning, it follows that the order of reading does not necessarily correspond to the order in which the parts of a glyph are carved or written. This case, therefore, presents evidence that in translating glyphs into spoken Maya, the word corresponding to a postfix may come before the main element, and, reciprocally, a prefix may follow the main element in the spoken word. This confirms the evidence of transfer of the affixes of Zec and Imix, to which attention has already been called. There are other glyphs which can take either the *u* bracket prefix or the lunar postfix, but, unfortunately, they are of unknown meaning.

CHARACTERISTICS OF AFFIXES

There is fairly good evidence that affixes could be suppressed, when the meaning of the main element was not clouded by their suppression; the postfix of the month signs Uo and Zip (fig. 16,13,14,16,17,26,28–31) was often suppressed, presumably because the meaning of the glyph was perfectly clear without it. In Madrid 43b and 43c are two divinatory almanacs, the first divided into eight compartments, the second, into seven, with the result that the glyphs are crowded. The same glyph (Gates' Glyph 141) appears in all 15 compartments, but only the first and last compartments of each almanac show this glyph with the *u* prefix attached. These examples without prefix are the only known cases of this main element standing alone, and, accordingly, I think it very probable that the affixes were suppressed because of crowding. Affixes could be fused with one another, as noted in the discussion of that subject. They could also be duplicated without affecting the meaning, as pointed out under the heading "Duplication of Details."

In brief, the following characteristics of affixes should be remembered: They can become infixes and they can change places with the main element of the glyph. Like main elements, they can be personified as head forms, and they can be duplicated without change of meaning. They can, in some cases, be suppressed, and they can be fused with one another, and they can have their own infixes. Under certain conditions an affix can be transferred to an adjacent glyph in a clause without serious modification of meaning, and, also, under certain conditions a postfix can become a prefix without altering the meaning of the whole glyph, although there is, as yet, no evidence that such interchanges never affected the meaning of the whole passage.

The meanings of most affixes are still unknown; those which have been identified, definitely or tentatively, include adjectives (color symbols), numerical classifiers (*te*), prepositions (*ti, tu,* and signs for backwards and forwards), relationship terms (*u, il*), attributive elements which confirm the identity of the main element ("*ak*," "*te*," and the "death eye" prefix), elements which indicate a restricted usage of the main element (postfixes of time periods to indicate that period glyphs record a distance number or mark the lapse of time, the "Ben-Ich" prefix with katun signs and Ahau), and nouns directly joined to the word corresponding to the glyph to which they are affixed (hand, count, and demise prefixes). Affixes may be found in more than one category; for instance, the symbol for black may be used as an adjective or, as a symbol of the underworld, it may denote a connection with that region, as in the glyph of the night sun. A main element may be an adjective, and the affix, the noun it qualifies, if the emphasis is on the adjective. The glyphs for the world directional trees supply examples of this (p. 56). Finally, it should be observed that there are groups of synonymous or nearly synonymous affixes, the members of which were under certain conditions interchangeable.

Affixes, then, are of tremendous importance, and I heartily disagree with the view that some of them are meaningless, and were merely added for decorative reasons. Attributive affixes and affixes indicating a specialized use of the main element could be, and not infrequently were, suppressed because they were not essential, but served to permit more speedy identification of the function of the whole glyph; affixes in other categories were, for the most part, essential and could not be suppressed. If the main elements can be regarded as the skeleton of Maya glyphic writing, the affixes and infixes are the flesh, without which the dead bones can not take life. In subsequent chapters much will be said concerning them, but I fully apprehend that these are but quick forays against a subject of outstanding importance. Until most of the affixes can be deciphered, the purport of Maya texts will not be within our ken.

Compound Glyphs

In some glyphs there is more than one main element: the symbolic form of the baktun glyph has the main element doubled, and usually a postfix is added (fig. 26,*15–23*); the sunrise glyph has three main elements (fig. 2,*32*). Glyphs of this nature may be termed compound glyphs. A compound glyph may also have affixes (fig. 2,*33*), and it may be expanded into two or more glyph blocks, as occurs once with the drought glyph (p. 271; fig. 46,*6*).

Overlapping Glyphs

Frequently two glyphs are joined together so that one slightly overlaps the other, leading to the suppression of some of the details of the latter as though they were hidden from view (fig. 40,*13,44,52*). In such cases it is the glyph on the right or below (rarely above) which is given in full, hiding details of the glyph to the left or above. It does not necessarily follow that glyphs which are paired in this way are intimately related to one another, although that is often the case.

Fusion of Glyphic Elements

Sometimes glyphs are fused together. This process not infrequently happens in the case of Glyphs G and F of the lunar series. Glyph G can stand by itself, but Glyph F apparently was never used without Glyph G. In a number of cases the essential variable element of Glyph G was placed in the center of Glyph F (fig. 2,*35–37*). As already noted, this is a transition to the use of an infix. Examples of the symbol which Beyer has termed the o-tun glyph (although I am inclined to translate it as the seating of the haab; p. 119) carries the process a step farther. The fusion is complete so that a new glyph emerges, the tun sign with a special infix (fig. 19,*37–39*). The first glyph of the clause used in discussing the 819-day cycle supplies an interesting case of fusing two elements, the second of which might be treated either as a postfix or a separate element subsequently fused or infixed (fig. 2, *38,39*). Morley (1945) cites examples of the fusing of Glyphs C and A of the lunar series. The general custom of fusing the two glyphs which together denote the half-period is another example of this practice (fig. 32,*46–53*) but sometimes the second glyph becomes a postfix of the first illustrating the fluidity of the rules of Maya glyphic writing (fig. 32,*50*).

Affixes, too, could be fused when questions of space or aesthetic treatment were involved. The month Kayab normally has two postfixes, which are usually placed to the right and below the main element, or both may be suffixes, placed one below the other. Occasionally the two are arranged alongside one another as suffixes. There was little room for such an arrangement, and consequently the two postfixes were sometimes merged, an unessential element being omitted from one of them (fig. 2,*40–42*). There is also an example from Copan of the two postfixes of the anterior date indicator being fused (fig. 2, *43–45*), and the postfixes of Glyph D of the lunar series are sometimes fused (fig. 37,*7*).

Duplication of Details

Beyer has shown that the duplication of details does not alter the meaning of a glyph, and produces and illustrates a number of cases to prove his point. He shows that the doubling of an affix was merely a matter of appearance and of space. Where a single affix might appear distorted in the space assigned it, the artist doubled or tripled it. Presumably tradition dictated what elements might be duplicated.

Examples of duplication of affixes without alteration of meaning are to be seen in representations of the months Zec and Mac (figs. 16,*49,51*; 18,*1,2,11,12*), and in the inverted Ahau element of that variant of the kin sign (fig. 2,*24,27*). An example of Yax at Chichen Itza supplies another good case of duplication of the main element without change in meaning (fig. 17,*44*). The duplication of the cauac element to form the baktun sign is discussed on page 147. It may be noted that the element can be tripled without, apparently, affecting the meaning.

Naturally, if an element which is usually single can be doubled, an element which is usually in duplicate can also appear only once. The prefix of the katun sign usually consists of a cauac element flanked by two small combs, thereby producing a good balance. However, sometimes when the katun sign overlaps another glyph or for some reason space is limited, the left comb was omitted (fig. 2,*46*). Similarly one of the "legs" in the superfix of a glyph common at Quirigua could be suppressed (fig. 2,*47–49*).

SIZE OF ELEMENTS

The size of one of the elements composing a glyph bears no relation to its importance, just as the size of the glyph block similarly fails to reflect the significance of its content. Again artistic considerations were paramount. Generally speaking, affixes are smaller than the main element, but they may be larger. A good example of this is supplied by the Yax sign on the Caracol at Chichen Itza just cited. The prefix becomes the largest element, although normally it is about half the size of the latter, and the main element is doubled (fig. 17,*44*). Were there not other forms known, we would consider the yax prefix to be the main sign, and the doubled cauac to be postfixes. Variation in size and duplication are well illustrated by the compound variant of the kin (fig. 31,*12–20*).

The four months signs, Ch'en, Yax, Zac and Ceh, are distinguishable only by their prefixes, and their names partially correspond to their prefixes. Were the value of the meaning of an element to guide its size, these four prefixes should be larger than the main element which they share. The fact that normally that is not the case confirms the conclusion that size and import are not related. Moreover, in the numerous texts which have the date which they commemorate recorded as a period-ending (hereinafter contracted to PE) date at or near the close of the inscription, the glyphs which carry that information are in no way differentiated by size, spacing, or arrangement from their neighbors.

ELIMINATION OF DETAILS

Most Maya glyphs could be elaborate or simple, the complexity of the design depending on the date when the glyph was carved (the early inscriptions are the most elaborate), the space available, the skill of the artist, the standard of glyph writing in each city, and the rarity of the glyph. Because many a glyph contains certain details which are not essential to its meaning or its identification, there was usually opportunity to simplify by eliminating the unessential, a process comparable to the kind of writing evolved for sending telegrams.

Morley (1915, p. 23) has illustrated the range of elimi-

nation in Glyph B of the lunar series, an excellent example of the process. The series can be amplified.

The glyph generally consists of four elements: (1) the head of a rodent; (2) an oval element, identified by Beyer as a conventionalized bone; (3) one of three prefixes: the possessive *u* bracket (fig. 2,*51*), the head of the *xoc* fish with the meaning of "count," (fig. 2,*55*), or the death eyes and hair, with the meaning of "expiration" (fig. 5,*33*); and (4) a doubled "sky" element which forms an elbow, the two arms flanking the top and right edge of the rodent's head (fig. 2,*50*).

This glyph could undergo the following changes without any loss of essential meaning: the oval element could lose its independence, and become an infix of the rodent's head (fig. 2,*51*); the head of God C could replace the rodent and oval, although that is very rare (fig. 2,*52*); the symbolic form of the "count" prefix could be used in place of the *xoc* head (figs. 2,*53; 5,31*), or it could replace the rodent and oval (fig. 2,*56*); the symbolic form of the rodent's head could be used (fig. 2,*55*); problems of space or symmetry could cause the elimination of either arm of the sky elbow (fig. 2,*53–54*); or the prefix could be entirely eliminated. Finally, it should be noted that the entire glyph could be dropped from its position in the lunar series without any essential loss of meaning to the whole clause.

The sky glyph, which forms the elbow, is a very common sign, the St. Andrew's cross being one of several infixes it can take (figs. 2,*57; 31,52–72*). It is a frequent element in the sunrise compound, where it occupies a space across the right top corner of the glyph, roughly corresponding to the elbow shape it assumes with Glyph B (fig. 31,*41–51*).

Another example of elimination of detail is supplied by the cauac element in the katun sign (fig. 26,*24–32*). The glyph was such a common and distinctive one that there was no danger of its being confused with any other if a detail was dropped from the cauac part of the prefix, consequently the "bunch of grapes" element was often omitted, or the side infixes could be left out. Such omissions could be compared to contractions, such as "Mr." or "Inc." in our writing.

ADDITION OF DETAILS

For reasons of balance or at the whim of the sculptor certain details could be added to most glyphs. The numerical classifier *te* was unessential; it was never used with day signs because it was not so used in speech, but was sometimes employed with month signs and period glyphs, corresponding to its oral use in Yucatec (*tu hunte Pop,* "on first of Pop"). Since only about 5 per cent of the month signs and an even smaller percentage of period glyphs have the *te* prefix, it is clear that it was not essential. The reasons for adding it must have been aesthetic; that is to say, to avoid distortion of the glyph (fig. 2,*15–23*).

Similarly, there are a few cases where both the tripedestal and distance number postfixes occur with a period glyph (fig. 3,*1*). Normally, the second replaced the first when a distance number was recorded (fig. 2,*34*).

Examples of elimination or elaboration of detail are particularly evident in head variants. The presence of the normal kin element as an infix plus position in the clause were sufficient to identify the head variant of the kin sign, yet other details were often added which were not essential for the identification (fig. 27,*53–66*). Again, the long-nosed snake, one of the head variants of the tun sign, is unmistakable when it occurs in an IS or in a distance number. Nevertheless, the normal tun element is almost always present as a headdress, a quite unnecessary elaboration (figs. 27,*28,30–33,35; 28,16,17; 30,6*). The occasional presence of the katun prefix with head variants of the katun is another instance.

The sporadic use of only half the normal Venus symbol to represent the day Lamat is an example of simplification (fig. 7,*57*); extreme conventionalization of the Ahau face, in which the features are reduced to three circles representing the eyes and mouth is another (fig. 11,*13*). Generally speaking, elimination of unnecessary detail is commoner in the codices than in the carved texts. This, of course, is to be expected in view of the great rapidity with which glyphs could be reproduced on paper.

PREFATORY GLYPHS

There are some cases in which a separate glyph qualifies the glyph it precedes. The term "prefatory" will be applied to glyphs of that type. Sometimes the prefatory glyph can be substituted for a prefix. The commonest prefatory glyph is the completion sign which has as its main element an outstretched or partially outstretched hand. Sometimes the hand alone or with only the tassel as an addition serves as a prefix; sometimes it stands alone with its own affixes (fig. 33,*25,26*). The hand in that position has the meaning of completion and is followed by the glyph of the period which is completed. Few glyphs now fall in this category but, with greater knowledge, more should be classified as such. The prefatory glyph and that which it qualifies really form a short clause, but a prefatory glyph is differentiated by the fact that it can be replaced by an affix.

CLAUSES

The word clause is used to denote a combination of glyphs which is repeated elsewhere in the same or some

other text, and which appears to represent a single sentence. A clause need not always consist of the same number of glyphs or be in precisely the same order. There should, however, be certain obvious repetitions of glyphs in a clause. Naturally, the IS, distance numbers, and lunar series are clauses, but scattered through the text there are many more combinations which are clearly clauses, although often their meanings are still unknown.

As early as 1897 Goodman isolated clauses of unknown meaning; Beyer, in his studies of the inscriptions of Chichen Itza, identified a considerable number of what he called glyph pairs and glyph series. These are also clauses.

An example of a clause on the stelae of the Central Area is supplied by the six glyphs which discuss the 819-day cycle. The first and last are the same in four cases, and the intervening glyphs show certain relationships between the various texts (fig. 35,*1–5*). Examples of another clause which is of the expandable type occur on two stelae at Naranjo. There are usually four glyphs in the same order, but the first in the series may be dropped, and extraneous ones may be added (fig. 3,*3–9*). This sentence of unknown meaning appears four times on Stela 24, Naranjo, and four times on Stela 29 at the same site.

World-direction signs form a two-glyph clause, in which the first glyph (that of the world direction) is variable but the second remains the same. The first sign theoretically could be of four, or perhaps five, forms corresponding to the four world directions and perhaps to the center. Among surviving texts all directions are reasonably sure. The second glyph has two main elements, the cauac and muluc signs. The "down-balls" prefix of Mac stretches above both (fig. 4,*1–4*). A clause of six or seven glyphs occurs at Palenque (fig. 3,*10–12*), and one with coefficients appears at three cities (fig. 3,*13–15*). A long clause may contain one or more subordinate clauses. Glyphs G and F form one within the lunar series, which is a long sentence dealing with nocturnal matters.

Possibly the overlapping of glyphs within a clause is indicative of subclauses. Glyph B of the lunar series is sometimes omitted, but it is never present if Glyph X is absent. However, on Quirigua B Glyph B (reproduced as a full-figure variant) carries Glyph X on its shoulder, just as day signs and their coefficients are similarly linked together when produced as full-figure variants (fig. 29, *14*). It is a good assumption, although nothing more, that Glyphs X and B form a subclause within the lunar series and should be read together.

Needless to say, the various glyphs which compose a clause often stand alone or they can reappear in other sentences. Cities appear to have shown a certain independence in the development of clauses, for a number occur only at a single ceremonial center. A clause, which usually contains the "Ben-Ich" katun, is common at Yaxchilan, but does not seem to have been used elsewhere. Its composition varies greatly (figs. 46,*10–16;* 49,*1* Gl G1–G2; *2* Gl G1–H1; 50,*2* Gl C7–C8; 51,*2* Gl B3–B4; 56,*4* Gl G2–G3, *6* Gl Q3–R4). Clauses are of great importance to the epigrapher because they supply examples of synonyms and near synonyms.

Because of fusion a clause may at times consist of only one glyph: the world-direction sentence normally comprises two glyphs, one of which is a compound, but there is at least one case of the two being fused to form a one-glyph clause (fig. 41,*22*). The fusion of Glyphs G and F of the lunar series supplies several examples of a sub-clause reduced to one glyph.

Sequence of Glyphs

Generally speaking, sequences of glyphs conform to established patterns, particularly when matters of the calendar or arithmetic were under discussion, but certain variations in the order were permitted, and these probably reflect the flexibility of the spoken word. For example, at Yaxchilan the sign of the "Ben-Ich" katun is sometimes combined with a lunar glyph which has certain established affixes, but the moon sign may either precede or follow the "Ben-Ich" katun (fig. 33,*36–38*). The same is true of the pictun glyph and "one moon" on the Tablet of the Inscriptions, Palenque (fig. 3,*10–12*). In the illustrations the pictun glyph comes first, but elsewhere in the text the order is reversed. A reversal of the order of glyphs in clauses also occurs at Chichen Itza (Beyer, 1937, figs. 101, 102). There is even a case, on Copan 16, of the day sign following the month sign, and occasionally distance numbers are arranged in descending order instead of the usual ascending order (p. 158). This occasional variation in the order of reading applies also to some compound glyphs. For example, in the "count of the year" compound, either the haab or the count element may come first (figs. 4,*1–4;* 41,*6,8,20,22*).

Glyph Variants: Symbolic and Personified Forms

A peculiar quality of Maya hieroglyphic writing is the very extensive use of variant forms of the same glyph or of quite different forms to express the same idea. Of those glyphs that have been identified there are very few which have not at least two shapes. These are a symbolic or geometric form and a human form, and they are usually known respectively as the normal form and head variant, but the first term is not very felicitous since it carries the implication that the symbolic is the regular and most common shape, whereas in many cases the personified

form is far commoner. For example, the so-called normal form of the baktun glyph is somewhat rare, the head variant being far more frequent. The latter is true of certain days signs, as, for example, the glyphs for the days Chicchan and Cimi (fig. 7,*1–34*).

In some cases, as, for instance, with the tun sign (figs. 26,*33–40;* 27,*28–39*) the head variants (for there is more than one) are totally distinct from the symbolic form; in other cases (fig. 5,*14,24,44*) the personified variant is formed by converting the outline of the symbolic form into a profile head, or infixing the symbolic form in a head (fig. 30,*52–54*). The "normal" form may consist of some symbol which is in some way connected with the head variant or is one of the attributes of the deity involved. For example, the symbolic form of Cimi is the percentage sign (fig. 7,*26,29,31*), one of the attributes of death; but Cimi means death, and the head variant is a skull (fig. 7,*18–25*). Similarly the personified form of Lamat is the head of the god of the planet Venus, who is often shown with the Venus symbol in his headdress or on his cheek; the geometric form of Lamat is that sign in its single or double form (fig. 7,*51–68*).

Sometimes there is no obvious connection between the head and geometric forms, but we can be reasonably sure that a relationship would be apparent had we a greater knowledge of Maya mythology and symbolism. The symbolic form of the count element is identical with the day sign Muluc (fig. 30,*37–40,42–44*); the personified form is the highly conventionalized head of a mythological fish (fig. 30,*41,45–47*). The connection would not be apparent were it not known that Muluc corresponds to the Aztec day Atl, "water," and the symbol itself probably represents a jade bead. In the ritualistic speech of the Aztec, jade is used as a honorific term for water. With these various connections known, it is obvious that the two forms of the "count" glyph are linked, the connection between fish and water being very obvious.

In a few cases (e.g. the main element of the IS introductory glyph) no head variant has yet been found; in others the head variant is very rare. I know certainly of only two head variants of the distance number introductory glyph. The symbolic form of this has as its main element what looks like an unfinished swastika; in the personified variant that element is replaced by a youthful head with what seems to be the swastika on his temple (fig. 30,*9–16*), but there are a few examples of possible head variants of this glyph at Palenque (fig. 30,*17–19*).

In the case of a few affixes there are also head forms which replace symbolic affixes. The comb form of the "count" affix can be replaced by the head of the mythological *xoc* fish. The comb affix may be the conventionalized dorsal fin of a fish, although it is also possible that it is the stylized picture of the flower of a water lily (fig. 5,*29–31;* p. 72). The head of the Chicchan god, god of number nine (fig. 24,*50–55*), is the personification of the yax affix and of the synonymous kan cross (figs. 3,7, penultimate glyph; 31,*49–51*).

Another prefix partly interchangeable with the count prefix has the meaning of "expiration of," "demise of," and hence "end," and takes the form of a small skull (fig. 5,*22,36,43*). The symbolic form corresponding to this has two circles with an intervening element. Each circle usually has a small circular or oval infix attached to its left edge, the interior of which is frequently crosshatched (fig. 5,*21,27,33,45,52*). This decorated circle is one of the attributes of the death god, who frequently has this identical circle immediately before his forehead (fig. 24,*56–62*); several may be set in his hair or in his headdress or attached to the edge of his ruff, or one may be at the end of the rod of each earplug. They may even be painted on the mantle, or attached to the ankles (fig. 13,*11,19*). Schellhas (1904, p. 11) identifies them as rattles or bells; Beyer (1937, p. 151) as death eyes. For our purpose the identification is not important. However, it is worth noting that representations of the death god in central Mexico often have rather similar circles set in their hair; these have been recognized as symbols of darkness, the eyes of night, that is, the stars. The death god lived in the underworld, the land of darkness, therefore this was a natural attribute, and one can be reasonably sure Beyer is correct. Note how, for lack of space, the death eye may be placed below the affix (fig. 5,*22*).

It is clear that the attribute of the deity serves as the symbolic form of this prefix; the skull of the deity as the head form. The skull may also stand alone as a prefatory glyph (fig. 5,*26*). The lines between the two eyes may well represent the hair of the death god as Beyer has suggested. Doubtlessly, a greater knowledge of Maya mythology and symbolism would reveal connections between many symbolic forms and their equivalent head forms.

FULL-FIGURE FORMS

In a few texts complete bodies are attached to the head variants of a number of glyphs. The full-figure glyphs are largely confined to the elements which form the IS, although the complete texts of Quirigua B and Copan D are of this type. Full-figure variants are extremely useful in identifying the animals or beings which the head forms represent. For example, the various full-figure representations of frogs as uinal signs make the identification of the corresponding heads certain (figs. 28; 29; 60).

Full-figure glyphs are among the finest examples of Maya carving extant. The artists, unrestricted by the rigid traditions which prescribed certain styles of presentation for religious art, were able to show their mastery of the technique of foreshortening. The static poses of the gods and their impersonators, which Maya religious portraiture demanded, yield to the utmost vivacity in treatment. These full-figure variants appear "a sort of bustle or hubbub in stone," as G. K. Chesterton says of mediaeval carving in *Tremendous Trifles,* but they are merely elaborations of the regular signs.

GLYPH SUBSTITUTION

In many cases one glyph may be substituted for another in a clause or one affix may replace another with the same glyph. Substitution of one element for another may or may not change the meaning of the whole. Naturally there is no way of telling in the cases of glyphs of unknown meaning whether substitution involves change in meaning. Even in the cases of glyphs of known meaning, further research has shown that changes in affixes vary the meaning of the whole. For example, it is now known that a number of the 26 affixes that Beyer (1937, pp. 150–58) groups together as ending signs mean something quite different. Every case of substitution must be examined on its own merits, and a decision as to whether a change of meaning is involved can be reached only after all examples of the use of the element in question have been tested. For example, the tun and katun signs can take three different postfixes. The tripedestal type appears to be purely ornamental (fig. 26,*25,26,28,40*). The type formed by two crescents flanking two or three circlets (and variations thereof) occurs only in distance numbers, and clearly serves to express the fact that a distance number is to be counted forwards or backwards (fig. 26,*27, 30,36–38*). The third type, the so-called bundle postfix, is used only to record that the accompanying date is a definite distance of so many tuns or katuns from some other CR date (hereafter called an anniversary count) but is not used to record distances counted from the conventional starting point of Maya chronology (fig. 33,*21–23*).

In order to preserve the full savor of Maya hieroglyphic writing, it is essential that our translations render, as far as is possible, those minor glyphic variations, which, in turn, surely reflect alternative phrases in the spoken word. Were a translator or paraphraser to encounter such expressions as "the day is ended," "the day draws to its close," "the day is no more," "the light has waned," "darkness has fallen," "night is here," and were he to render them uniformly as "at the end of the day," he would convey the general sense, but his work would show an impoverishment not in the original. In the case of the decipherment of Maya texts such treatment in the past has obscured many clues to the translation of glyphs of unknown **meaning.**

The various affixes and prefatory glyphs found with PE supply a case in point. There are five main signs: the hand, the bracket, the fish head, the comb, and the eye of death. All five have been given indiscriminately the meaning of "end of," although only the first and last carry, and indirectly at that, the meaning of "ending." The fish head and comb correspond to the word *xoc,* "count" or "sum"; the bracket, which is listed in Landa's alphabet with the value *u* is the possessive "of" but also converts cardinals to ordinals; the death eye and its sundry variant forms is without much doubt the symbol for *hitz',* "death throes of," "demise of," and, by extension, "end of"; the hand symbol can be accepted with some assurance as the equivalent of *tz'oc,* "end of" or "completion of." Sometimes the hand appears as a prefatory glyph, and one of the affixes, usually the bracket, is attached to the period glyph. The whole then reads "completion of *n*th katun" (fig. 32,*8*). Thus by careful attention to variations we can enrich the translation, and pave the way for fresh decipherments; to translate all such expressions as "end of *n* katuns" is a sorry performance.

Convergence in Glyph Delineation

Elaboration of glyphs and the latitude allowed the sculptors occasionally cause some confusion, producing fortuitous resemblances between two distinct glyphs. There are cases where only the context serves to differentiate between the day signs Ben and Kan (figs. 6,*53–58;* 9,*3–12*). In the case of some head forms there is also a certain difficulty in distinguishing between different glyphic elements. Weathering, of course, is a much more serious cause of misidentification, but that can hardly be blamed on the Maya.

MAYA GRAPHOLOGY

Landa's Alphabet

For three-quarters of a century scholars have discussed whether Maya hieroglyphs represent a true writing or an embryo writing, and have argued as to whether the glyphs are ideographic or phonetic or are based on the ebus system or are a combination of all. The discovery of Landa's supposed alphabet raised high hopes of a rapid decipherment of the glyphic texts, but those hopes were soon dashed to the ground. All attempts to apply Landa's alphabet met with failure and the alphabet was pronounced a fraud.

There seems little doubt, as Valentini surmised (1880), that Landa pronounced the letters of the alphabet to an educated Maya, and the latter drew a glyphic element which resembled the sound. Not all the symbols are clear, but there is little doubt that that was how the famous alphabet was composed. There is also no doubt at all that Landa was wrong in trying to extract a Maya alphabet from his informant. Maya symbols appear usually to have represented words, occasionally perhaps syllables of compounded words, but never, so far as is known, letters of the alphabet. Elements in the Landa list identifiable with varying degrees of probability are: a, *ac* (turtle); b, *be* (road); c, *Zec* (month sign); e, *elel* (burn, cf. fig. 43, *53–55*); h, *ach'* (apply pressure when tying something); ca, *cai* (fish; p. 146); k, *kab* (hand, deed, cf. fig. 42,*58–61*); p, *pek* (dog); pp, Xipe (a Mexican god); cu, element in *cuch,* "burden," glyph (cf. fig. 43,*37,49,61*); ti, *ti,* locative preposition used as an affix; u, *u,* affix meaning "of"; u, *u* (moon), conventionalized lock of hair, the main attribute of the moon goddess.

I myself have found the Landa alphabet of some value and confidently expect that it will be of aid in deciphering other elements, although in a manner very different from that which Landa supposed.

Rebus Writing

The use of homophones (words with similar sounds but different meanings) seems to have been fairly general among the Maya. It also appears in Aztec writing, although, as Long (1935, pp. 25–26) has shown, it is far more prevalent in postconquest glyphic writing than in that of the pre-Columbian period. It survives among us as a children's pastime. For example, pictures of an eye, a tin can, waves, an ant, and a rose are decipherable as "I can see Aunt Rose."

The Maya language with its wealth of monosyllabic words and verbal roots was particularly well supplied with homophones. A few examples of rebus writing among the Maya will be given.

The word *xoc* or *xooc* in Yucatec is the name for a mythological fish. The word *xoc* also means a count, or the root of the verb to count. The head of a fish is the main element of a glyph which can only mean "count forward to" or "count back to" or something very similar, the direction varying with changes in affixes (figs. 2,*43–45;* 30,*45–47*). The evidence is too lengthy to be presented here, but there is little reason to doubt that *xoc* fish stands for *xoc* count (Thompson, 1944).

The general lowland Maya word for the moon is *u* perhaps *uh* in some dialects). *U* also is used before consonants as the possessive of the third person in Yucatec, eastern Chol, Tzeltal, and probably other dialects (*u col Juan,* "Juan's milpa," literally "his milpa Juan"). In Maya texts the moon sign usually refers to the moon itself, and in combination with numbers can give the age of the moon (figs. 36; 37). In one form it can also have the meaning of 20, and with numbers affixed can serve as a short distance number (fig. 4,*16–18*). Occasionally, however, a moon sign appears with a hand before a period glyph (figs. 4,*15*; 32,*2–5,7,11*). There is no doubt that the hand is a symbol for completion, the whole signifying the completion of so many katuns or tuns; the moon sign, as here used, can not possibly have a lunar connotation, but must be read as a rebus for the possessive *u*. This may be used here to convert the following number from a cardinal to an ordinal, "the completion of the *n*th katun," or it may correspond to the possessive, "their completion, *n* katuns." In neither case would the moon sign have a lunar significance. There are other cases in which the moon glyph is used as the possessive (p. 40; figs. 2,*59*; 11,*37–41*).

The glyph for Bolon-Yocte (p. 56) presumably supplies another instance of rebus writing. The name probably means "Nine Strides," but *oc*, "stride," is represented by the head of the dog used for the day Oc (fig. 12,*1–3*).

The symbolic form of the tun is among the commonest glyphs of known meaning. As used in IS, distance numbers, and PE, it always represents the period of 360 days, called in Yucatec tun. Occasionally, this sign becomes a prefatory glyph or a prefix attached to a month sign (fig. 19,*21–26*). Elsewhere I have shown (Thompson, 1935, pp. 101–03) that when thus used, this tun affix (sometimes with the addition of its own affix) must mean completion of the month in question. I am indebted to Ralph L. Roys for suggesting to me the reason for this use: the word *tun* means in Yucatec not only "stone" (jade) and the 360-day period, but also carries the connotation of finality. Thus we find in the Motul dictionary "*tun: postpuesta a la primera diccion, ya ó finalmente. Cimen tun, muerto ya, zame hoppoc in xachetic, ca tun chictahi ten, rato ha que començé á buscarlo y finalmente lo hallé.*" The San Francisco dictionary gives "*Finalmente. tz'ocebali tun, tu tz'oc tun.*" The Vienna dictionary has "*Ya no mas, u lahi tun, u nak, u xuli tun.*"

Mr. Roys, on supplying the above citations, comments, "Its most frequent meaning in my texts seems to be 'then, after that.' It can mean 'finally,' as per the dictionaries; often it seems to me to emphasize and put the seal on an immediately preceding word which has already expressed the idea of completion or something done. This, of course, is merely my personal view. Certainly *tz'oc tun* is a familiar term to me, but the most frequent expression is *ca tun* or *caa tun.*"

The tun sign used as a prefix with a month sign can be substituted for the so-called zero sign with the following month. The combination tun Yaxkin has the same apparent meaning as o Mol. Therefore it must mean Yaxkin ended, which is the same as Mol not yet started. The interpretation made independently of the glyph

agrees with one of the meanings of the affix. *Tun*, "360-day year," is, therefore, used in the sense of "end," another example of rebus writing.

The use of the frog or toad as a symbol for 20 is probably another case of homophonic substitution. In a number of Maya dialects, highland and lowland, the generic name for the frog or toad is *po*. In Yucatec a special variety of frog (*Rhynophrynis dorsalis*) is called *uo* and this same word denotes frog in Chaneabal. Yet there is a variety of toad called *ampo* in Yucatec, listed in the Vienna dictionary as Mr. Roys informs me. There seems little doubt that both *po* and *uo* are onomatopoeic words corresponding to the croaking noise emitted.

In Kekchi, Pokomchi, and Pokoman, Maya dialects of the Guatemalan highlands but occupying an area bordering on the lowlands, the moon goddess, who is also the goddess of weaving, is called Po. In Pokoman the month also bears the name *po*, and it is probable that this word was originally applied to the 20-day period known in Yucatec as the uinal. Mr. Aulie informs me that the Palencano-Chol word for full moon is *pomol*. The Yucatec name for the wife of the sun, who was also the goddess of weaving, was Ix Azal-Uoh, according to Lopez de Cogolludo. However, as the sun's wife was considered to be the moon in most parts of the Maya area, we can be reasonably certain that Ix Azal-Uoh was the moon. Thus we have *po*, "frog," and *po*, "moon" in one area (but except for the Palencano term for full moon, not that in which the glyphs presumably originated); *uo* and *po*, "frog," *po*, "toad," *uoh*, last name of a goddess who was almost certainly the moon in Yucatan. The word *po* seems to be connected with weaving. *Pot*, "huipil," in Chol, Kekchi, and Pokomchi; *poh*, "to sew something," and *potal*, "something connected with the huipil or dress of the natives," are Pokomchi words.

The Maya moon goddess, like other Middle American deities, seems to have had three names, an honorific title, a functional title, and a real name. Honorific titles are "The Lady" or "Our Mother" (Chaneabal, *hanantic ixau*, "our mother, the lady"; Chorti, *ca tu*, "our mother," a term used also to denote queen; Jacalteca and Mam, *xau*, "the lady"; Chuh, *ix cu chich*, "our lady [grand?] mother"; San Miguel Acatan, "our mother"; Lacandon *na*, "mother," and *ekna*, "star mother" (?); and Pokomchi, *atit*, "old lady").

Functional titles are less common. Po, as already noted, appears to refer to the moon as the lady who introduced weaving. Ix Azal-Uoh may also be a functional title. In the Ritual of the Bacabs Ixchel, who is almost certainly the moon goddess, is addressed as the virgin of the jade needle and reference is also made to her 13 balls of dyed thread. The real name for the moon appears to be U or

Uh. The highland name *ik* may be honorific since *ixik* means in Yucatec a woman of rank and in western Chol and Chontal a woman. *Ix* is the feminine prefix.

With three names available, one might become common in one dialect; another in some other dialect. Thus in present-day Yucatec the real name, *u,* remains. The functional title may have been Ix Azal-Uoh, as given by Lopez de Cogolludo, but the honorific title had disappeared. Another of her names, Ixchel, which perhaps means the stretched-out woman, may refer to an incident in the moon's life on earth. On the other hand, in Kekchi territory the functional title came into general use and appears to have supplanted the honorific title and real name. In Pokomchi both the functional and the honorific title were used in counting time, for we find both *hinah po* and *hinah r atit* given as the equivalents of one month; in Palencano *uh* is the usual name for the moon, but *po* appears to survive in the term *pomol,* "full moon."

Thus the absence of a title such as Po or Uo from the vocabularies of lowland Maya dialects is not a serious argument. These vocabularies were largely collected by Roman Catholic missionaries who were constantly on the watch for signs of heathenism. The less the informant said about titles of important deities, the better for everyone save his auditor.

In the hieroglyphic texts 20 days can be expressed by a moon glyph (p. 167; fig. 4,*16–18*), the head of a frog or toad (figs. 27,*40–52;* 29,*1–4*), or a geometric sign. In the lunar series the moon glyph can be replaced by an up-ended head which without much doubt also represents a toad or frog (fig. 37,*11,36*). The employment of the moon sign to represent 20 days is of very ancient usage since it thus appears in a distance number on the very early Balakbal 5. The Yucatec species *ampo* also suggests a connection between frog or toad and moon. The name would be translatable as "spider toad," but the moon goddess is also connected with the spider (Thompson, 1939, pp. 147–49). In short, moon sign and frog are interchangeable in the glyphic texts presumably because their names were once phonemes in the lowlands, as they still are in the northern highlands. Thus *po,* "frog" or "toad," is a rebus for *po,* "moon."

Other examples of rebus writing will be discussed in following chapters. There are excellent grounds for affirming that the Maya made much use of this kind of writing.

PICTORIAL GLYPHS

In the codices there are a considerable number of pictographic glyphs, for when we find glyphs shaped as fish or haunches of animals above scenes which show offerings of fish or deer haunches we can hardly err in classifying these glyphs as pictographic (fig. 5,*54–56,58–60*).

A fairly common glyph shows the symbols for earth and sky arranged so that their contiguous edges touch at the right edge of the glyph, but diverge from one another to the left, forming an angular opening like the open jaws of a crocodile. In this wedge is set the sun glyph (fig. 31,*41–51*). This compound glyph has been variously interpreted as observation of sun at the horizon, daybreak, sun in the day sky, and sunset (p. 168). A Yucatec word for daybreak is *hatzcab.* The Chol equivalent is given in the Moran vocabulary as *pazcab,* "de mañana," but again the Moran vocabulary often fails to distinguish between *z* and *tz* (there is an occasional shift from *p* to *h*). The Yucatec word *hatz* means "to divide"; *cab* means "earth." There can be little doubt that in the Maya mind sunrise marked the cleaving of the earth, perhaps the division into sky and earth. The hieroglyph under discussion represents this action; the sun is in the cleft betwixt sky and earth.

A number of glyphs may be pictographic, although there is a possibility that they may eventually prove to be examples of rebus writing. The Yucatec name for the fourth month is Zotz', and the corresponding glyph is the head of the leaf-nosed vampire bat, called *zotz'* in Yucatec and in most lowland dialects (fig. 16,*35–44*). This month may have been called the month of bats, or it may have had a name with some quite different meaning, but resembling the word *zotz'.* For instance, *zutzil* is given as the equivalent of winter in Moran's vocabulary of eastern Chol. Should that have been the meaning of the month, the bat head would be in rebus writing.

Pop, the name of the first month, means "mat" in Yucatec and in most lowland Maya dialects, and the glyph shows as its main element plaited rushes (fig. 16, *1–9*). It thereby qualifies as a pictographic symbol, but there is also an ideographic element, since "mat" is a symbol of authority or overlordship in Maya because the chiefs sat on special mats or mat-covered cushions (corresponding to the West African use of the sunshade as a symbol of authority). Indeed, the word means chief in Pokomchi. Thus the first month of the series might well be named Pop because of the idea of elevated rank contained therein.

IDEOGRAPHIC GLYPHS AND GESTURE SIGNS

Some Maya glyphs can clearly be classed as ideographic. The hieroglyph for west is the back of a partly opened hand over the sun symbol. The hand in that position symbolizes completion or perhaps ending. "End of sun" is an ideographic sign for west. The Yucatec expression for west is *chikin,* and sunset is *ocol kin,* "the entering of the sun." West in Manche Chol is given in the Moran manuscript as *u yochib cin* (should be *ḳin*), "the entrance of the sun." Thus the glyph does not correspond to the spoken word but expresses a parallel idea.

The winged cauac glyph (figs. 5,*40–46*; 32,*24–31,35–45*) is used in the inscriptions to denote the passage of a certain number of tuns, but never in IS and never in combination with uinals and kins. It is probably the hieroglyph of the word *haab* or *hab,* which is used in a somewhat similar manner in the books of Chilam Balam. The cauac symbol which forms the main element of this glyph represents water, and is almost certainly a section of the body of one of the celestial dragons which send the rain; the tail part is one of the distinguishing marks of the sun glyph. Thus the glyph appears to symbolize rain and sun, that is to say the rainy and dry seasons, in other words the year.

The western and eastern Chol, the Chontal, the Kekchi, and the Pokomchi also call the year *hab;* the Tzotzil, Tzeltal, Chaneabal, and Jacalteca use the word *habil.* Tzotzil also uses *abil;* the Ixil word is *yab.* The general word for water or rain throughout the Maya group of languages is *ha* (rarely *a*). *Hab* means rain in Kekchi and shower in Cakchiquel, and the same word is given as water in Pokomchi. It is therefore probable that the word for year carries the idea of rain and the rainy season, just as the glyph does.

The glyph in its more usual form, as already noted, seems to combine symbols for the rainy and dry seasons, but the addition of the latter appears to be an afterthought, perhaps for the purpose of avoiding confusion with other glyphs. The evidence for this assertion lies in the existence of another cauac glyph without the wing (but with a prefix), which also means year (fig. 33,*27–32*).

Glyphs for the tun (year of 360 days) supply interesting examples of ideographic writing. The commonest head form for the tun is the profile of the Moan bird (fig. 27,*29,34,36–39*). These creatures, the Yucatecan screech owl or horned owl, were believed to be set in the sky above the celestial dragons, and to participate with the latter in the task of sending rain to earth. In fact, the Yucatec word *moan* means shower. As the year carried the idea of rain or rainy season, it was perfectly logical to use the head of the Moan bird to represent it (p. 145). Another head form of the tun is that of a snake, which, because of its association with water, carries the same connotation (figs. 27,*28,30–33,35;* 28,*12,16,17*).

The symbolic form of the tun sign is also in part ideographic. One of its elements is the sign for jade. Jade was "the precious thing," and among the Mexicans,

and doubtlessly, too, among the Maya, a ritualistic name for rain or water because rain was so essential for the crops. Thus the use of this jade symbol in the tun sign once more demonstrates the association of the year with the rainy season. In full confirmation of this identification, it may be remarked that *tun* means jade (p. 144).

The jade symbol, as a sign for rain, "the precious thing," is also used to form the day sign Muluc, which corresponds to the Aztec day Atl, "water." Again, the day Muluc has as its guardian the *xoc* fish. This *xoc* fish, as already noted, is used as a rebus for *xoc,* "to count." The symbolic form corresponding to it is again the jade sign because water and the *xoc* fish were already closely connected through their identification with the day Muluc, and perhaps because the *xoc* deity also sent water to mankind. With growing knowledge as our guide, we shall tread such trails with surer foot.

Religious symbolism is the basis of many ideographic glyphs. For example, shells, particularly the conch and other univalves, symbolize the earth, the underworld, and the realm of the dead situated therein. Shells added as a prefix to the glyph of the sun convert that deity to his nocturnal form, as lord of the night, because during the night the sun was believed to travel through the underworld from west to east to reach again his point of rising in the east. Similarly, a conventionalized univalve shell, inverted and flanked with additional elements (fig. 41,*28,31,34,36*), is the glyph for south on the monuments (but not in the codices), because that direction is under the guardianship of the death god, the lord of the underworld. Again, the glyph for day commonly used in lunar calculations and in distance numbers is a conventionalized shell because the count appears to have been by nights or sunrises (fig. 31,*1–9;* p. 174).

The glyph for Caban, "earth," is the glyph of the moon goddess, with a lock of hair as its most prominent feature (fig. 10,*1–15*), because in Maya (and also Mexican) mythology the moon goddess was also an earth goddess (fig. 14,*18,23,24*). Many other examples of ideographic glyphs will be noted in succeeding chapters, and I feel that were our knowledge of Maya mythology more extensive, a great number of other ideographic glyphs based on legendary incidents or associations would be identifiable.

Some elements may have either a direct or an ideographic meaning, depending on their use. Thus, the symbol for black may represent black as opposed to some color, or it may be found on glyphs connected with denizens of the underworld, not to denote that they are black, but to show that they are connected with the world of darkness. Similarly, vegetation may represent actual growth or it may be a symbol of the earth and the underworld. As the latter it sometimes replaces the shells as a prefix to the glyph of the sun god to indicate that it is the night sun, the lord of the night, who is under discussion. As the former, it may, for example, be shown emerging from the kan glyph, the symbol of ripe maize and of maize seed. Likewise, the jade symbol may denote the actual jade in addition to its secondary meaning of rain, and its tertiary meaning of year. Thus, a straightforward division of glyphs into ideographic and pictorial is not possible.

There are a few signs which derive from gestures. The back of the outspread hand in a horizontal position or at an angle of 45 degrees signifies completion. A thumb or single finger stands for one. Possibly the open hand pointing downwards signifies completed, a past participle form. I suspect, but cannot prove, that the hand in a vertical position has a different meaning. It occurs in this position with Manik, which so far as is known has no connection with completion. The hand is also the main element of various glyphs of the action group (p. 265), which may derive from gestures.

PLACE NAMES AND PERSONAL NAMES

No glyphs representing the names of persons (other than gods) and places have been identified. That glyphs of personal names existed is shown by a statement by Oviedo y Valdes (1851–55, 3:246), which has been cited by Genet (1934b, p. 41) to the effect that beehives were identified by the marks of the individuals who owned them. This can hardly mean other than the glyphs of the owners' names. There is inconclusive evidence that persons of importance had their name glyphs tattooed or painted on their arms or hands. Landa (Tozzer ed., p. 40) states that Ah Kin Chel "wrote on the fleshy part of his left arm certain letters which were of great importance and such as to be respected." Similarly in Chumayel we read of a certain Uooh-puc, "There was a glyph written on the palm of his hand. Then a glyph was written below his throat, was also written on the sole of his foot and written within the ball of the thumb." Here attention is probably drawn to the glyphs because the man's name contained the word for glyph (*uooh*). On the Bonampak murals one warrior has glyphs painted on his arm; another has them on his thigh.

One of the very few place names concerning which there is any glyphic information is Campeche, called in Maya Campech. The author of the relacion de Chunchuchu y Taby (Relaciones de Yucatan, 11:146) writes that Campeche is the name of an idol which had on its head as insigne a curled-up snake with a tick on its head. This precisely corresponds to the name, for *can* is

snake and *pech* is tick (*n* not infrequently becomes *m* before a labial). It is possible, but not probable, that the god was an anthropomorphized blending of a snake and a tick, although such a deity would hardly reflect much dignity. It is therefore likely that *campech*, "snake tick," is a rebus glyph worn in the headdress of the god and later adopted as the glyph of the town.

It is possible that titles of rank, individual names, and names of groups, perhaps even of totemic clans, eventually will be recognized. They may occur in the short panels of glyphs accompanying figures on murals and polychrome pottery or the minor glyphs, often incised, on some stelae and lintels, notably at Piedras Negras.

The glyphs for various gods found in the codices will be discussed in the following chapers. Several of the better-known deities have two glyphs, one a pictorial representation, the other a symbolic form, perhaps corresponding to a ritualistic name or an attribute. Thus the symbolic form of the glyph of God B has as an infix part of a hand, reminding one of the title of Kabul, "he of the working hand," applied to Itzmna and perhaps other deities.

SENTENCES

In deciding what is a sentence, one must remember that the distinction between noun and verb is vague in many of the Maya stems, many verbs are really nouns used with the possessive pronoun as subject (Tozzer, 1921, p. 9). Gender is absent except for particles attached to some nouns. In the opinion of Ralph L. Roys, tense is of much less importance to the Maya than to us. This blending of verb and noun may well be reflected in the hieroglyphic writing. The posterior date indicator is associated with distance numbers. The prefix is the adverb forward; the main element expresses the idea of count; the postfix is the preposition *ti,* "to, at or from" (fig. 30,42–47). The whole, therefore, reads "count forward to" and shows the direction in which the distance number is to be reckoned. The elimination of the prefix and the addition of a second postfix changes the meaning to "count backward to" or something very similar (fig. 30,37–41). The central element pretty clearly corresponds to the word *xoc* which can be a noun, or the root of a verb derived therefrom. We can not say which it is, and I do not suppose that the Maya would have attempted to do so. On the other hand, I doubt that the Maya could or did add other affixes to take care of pronouns or to express tenses. In other words, they could give a number of tuns, uinals, and kins, followed by the glyph meaning "count forward to," but I suspect that they had not evolved elements to record "you counted forward to," or "we shall count forward to," although, having a glyph for the pronoun of the third person, they could have written "his count forward to."

The interchangeability under certain circumstances of the positions of affixes shows, I think, that the arrangement of glyphs and the elements which compose them does not always correspond to the order of the spoken word. There are two identified (and other suspected) affixes representing the possessive pronoun *u*. One of these, the bracket, is nearly always a prefix; the other, the lunar glyph, is usually a postfix. However, in spoken Yucatec the possessive pronoun *u* precedes the object possessed, and the possessor comes last, e.g. *u pek uinic,* literally "his dog man" (the man's dog). When therefore, as in the case of the shift of prefixes on Dresden 13b–14b (p. 40), we find that the *u* prefix, probably used as a nominal pronoun with a verbal stem, is moved in the last three clauses of the almanac to the second glyph, and changed from the prefixal bracket form to the postfixal lunar form, we can feel reasonably sure that in the second case the sequence does not correspond to that of the spoken word. Similarly, the attributive *il* in the speech of Yucatan is always a suffix, whereas in glyphic writing it can be either a prefix or a postfix (p. 285).

The short clauses on the monuments which record the world direction to which the haab (year of 360 days) belonged, usually consists of two glyphs. The first records the point of the compass; the second is a compound comprising the cauac (haab) glyph, the "down-balls" prefix of unknown meaning, and the symbolic form of the count glyph (fig. 41,5–8,19,20,28,29). The whole clearly means "the east (or north, west, or south) the count of the year," and corresponds to *u xocol haab ti lakin,* "the count of the year to the east," as given in Mani. However, in the texts, the order of the haab and xoc glyphs can be reversed, so one can perhaps conclude that the order of the glyphs is not supposed to correspond without deviation to the spoken sentence, but that all the essential parts are given so that the reader could arrange them and supplement them with speech particles (e.g. the possessive *u* in this clause) not represented in the text, to correspond to the spoken word, whether the reader was a Yucatec, Chol, Tzeltal, or Chontal priest.

MAYA COUNTING

All Maya dialects and languages made use of a vigesimal system for general purposes of counting. Twenty units of the first order made one of the second order. Twenty units of the second order made one of the third order, and so on.

There is no specific name for the first order, for the Maya use a large number of numerical classifiers to indicate the nature of the object that is being counted just as we speak of three head of cattle, two lengths of cloth, etc. The numerical classifier is a suffix attached to the numeral. Tozzer (1921, p. 290) lists some 80 examples in Yucatec, and other Maya languages and dialects are equally rich in these suffixes. These numerical classifiers are reduced to a very few in the second order and disappear with the third order.

The general unity in Maya numeration is illustrated in Table 1. The representation of Maya dialects or languages could be increased, but without revealing any different arrangements or tendencies. I have taken the liberty of standardizing the spelling in some cases and of not giving every unimportant variant.

It is noteworthy that the names for numbers 1–10 are approximately the same in all languages, but that the numbers 11 and 12 are distinctive names in the lowlands, whereas in highland languages and dialects they are formed by combining the words for 10 and 1 and 10 and 2 respectively. Exceptions in the lowland groups to this system are in eastern and southern Yucatan and some western Chol vocabularies. Starr (1902) and Tozzer (1921) report that the words for 11 and 12 in the Valladolid and Tekax regions of Yucatan are *hunlahum* or *unlahun* and *calahun* respectively, that is to say they follow the highland style of combining the two digits. The same is true of western Chol (Palencano) vocabularies collected by Stoll (1938) and Marcos Becerra (1935), but not of vocabularies from the same group made by de la Fuente Albores (1789, reproduced by Fernandez and Fernandez, 1892), by Sapper (1897), and by Starr (1902). As Huaxtec conforms to the highland system in that respect, it is not improbable that the lowland groups (including the Maya peoples of Chiapas) coined these separate terms for 11 and 12 after they had separated from the Huaxtec and from the highland groups. That the personified glyphs for those numbers do not combine with that for 10 (p. 135) is evidence that the glyphs are of lowland origin.

All Maya languages, so far as is known, parallel English in compounding the two orders to form the numbers 13–19, inclusive. All Maya languages start the second order with 20. In Yucatec, Chol, Chuh, and Jacalteca the word for 20 is *hun kal,* "one score," but several dialects, both highland and lowland, call 20 *hun uinic* or such variations of it as *hun uinac,* literally "one man." Nevertheless, in some highland languages where *kal* does not occur with 20 it reappears as *ox kal,* "60" (Mam, Ixil, Aguacatec, Quiche, Uspantec, Kekchi, Pokomchi, and Cakchiquel), and again, in most cases as *ho kal* or *o kal,* "100." At first thought *kal* and *uinic* (together with the rarer *mai, tab,* and *tom*) would appear to be no more than different numerical classifiers. Nevertheless, the

TABLE 1—NUMBERS IN VARIOUS MAYA LANGUAGES

	Yucatec (Beltran, Kaua)	Chol (Moran; Sapper, 1897; Becerra, 1935; Aulie)	Tzeltal (V. Pineda, 1888; Sapper, 1897; Blom and La Farge, 1926-27)	Tzotzil (Rodaz, 1688; Seler, 1901)	Chaneabal (Berendt, 1870; Seler, 1901; Stoll, 1884)	Kekchi (Thomas, 1901; Burkitt, 1902; Wirsing, 1930)	Pokomchi (San Cristobal Cahcoh Vocabulary; Thomas, 1901)	Quiche (Stoll, 1938; Sapper, 1891; Thomas, 1901)	Mam (Stoll, 1938; Thomas, 1901)
1	hun	hun	hun	hun	hun	hun	henah, hun	hun	hun
2	ca	cha	che(eb)	chi(m)	cha	ca	ci, ca	ci	ca
3	ox	ux	ox	ox	ox	ox	ux, ix, ox	vuox	ox
4	can	chuum, chan	chan	chan	chan	ca, cah	cih	cah	ciah
5	ho	hoo, o, oo	hoo	ho	ho	o, ho	ho	ho	ho
6	uac	uöc	uac	uac	uac	uac	uac	uac	uac
7	uuc	huc	uuc, huc	huc	huc	uuc	uuc	uuc	uc
8	uaxac	uaxöc	uaxac	uaxac	uaxac	uacxac, uahxac	uaxac	uaxac	uacxac, uahxac
9	bolon	bolon	balun	balun	balun	bel(eb), belo	beleh	beleh	belehuh, belhuh
10	lahun	luhum	lahun	lahun	lahun	lah(eb)	lah	lahun	lahuh
11	buluc	buhluch, hun e luhum	buluch, muluch	buluch, baluch	buluch, bulu, huluch	hun lahu	hun lah	hu lahuh	hum lahuh
12	lahca	lahchöm, cha e luhun	lahche, laschai	lahcha	lahcha, lahchan	cab lahu	cab lah	cab lahuh	cab lahuh
13	ox lahun	ux e luhum	ox lahun, ux lahun	ox lahun	ox lahun	ox lahu	ox lah	ox lahuh	ox lahuh
14	can lahun	chum e luhun	chan lahun	chan lahun	chan lahun	ca lahu	cah lah	cab lahuh	ciah lahuh
15	hol hun	ho lum	ho lahun	ho lahun	ho lahun	vuo lahu, ho lahu	ho llahuh	o lahuh	ho lahu, oo lahuh
20	hun kal	hun kal	tab, tap	hun uinic, tom, tob	hun tab, hun tahb	hu mai, hun mai	hun inac, hu uinac	hu vinac	huing, vuincim
30	lahu ca kal	luhun cha kal	lahunes-cha uinic	lahun-cha uinic	lahunez-cha uinic	lah x-ca kal	lah(eb) ni-ca vuinac	hu vinac-lahuh	vuinac lahuh
40	ca kal	cha kal	cha uinic	cha uinic	cha uinic	ca kal	ca vuinac	cavinac	cauinac
60	ox kal	ux kal	ox uinic	ox uinic	ox uinic	ox kal	ox kal	ox kal	ox kal
80	can kal	chun kal	chan uinic	chan uinic	chan uinic	caa kal	ca vuinac	hu much	hum mucx, hu much
100	ho kal	ho kal, o kal	hol uinic, hoo uinic	ho uinic	ho uinic	ho kal	ho kal	o kal	o kal, ho kal
200	lahun kal	luhun kal	lahun uinic	laghun uinic	lah uinic	lah kal, ho tuc, hun lah	ho tuc	o tuc	o chuc
400	hun bak	hun bakh, hun bak	bak	bok, hbok	hun xan	hun okob, ca(ib) lah	hun icom	o much	o mucx, o much
800	ca bak	cha bahk	cha bak	cha bok	cha xan	ca(ib) okob	ca icom	ca go, ca ko	lahuh much
8000	hun pic	hun pik, hun kal ti bak	pic, tabuc bak	hpic, pic	hun hiquipil	hun chin, hun mai	hun chui okob	hu chuvy	......
160,000	hun calab	......	bak baketic	......	......	hun calab	un cilab	......	......

regularity of the use of *kal* compounded with *ox* and *ho* or *o* to represent 60 and 100 suggests something more than chance. I can offer no explanation.

Typical of Maya speech is that numbers beyond two-score are counted as so many on the next score. Fifty for example is called "ten on (or to, or lacking to) three-score"; 41 is "one on (or to, or lacking to) threescore." Similarly two and a half is called "half on (or to, or lacking to) three." We shall find this system reflected in the use in hieroglyphic texts of the glyph for a half period, which is not infrequently followed by the next highest number (p. 192).

There are traces in several highland languages or dialects of a count by 40's and 80's. Thus in Quiche, Cakchiquel, Pokomchi, Kekchi and Mam 200 is called *ho* (or *o*) *tuc* or *chuc*, i.e. five *tuc*. Brasseur de Bourbourg (1862) says that *tuc* appears to signify a certain herb, and has also the meaning of 40; Beltran (1859) notes that *tuc* has in Yucatec the meaning of "to count heaps" or "to count by heaps"; the Motul dictionary has for *tuc*, "heap of small things brought together such as salt, earth, stones, fire-wood, etc." The author of the Pokomchi dictionary of Cahcoh (pp. 443*v*, 490*v*) notes that this term for 40 is used only for counting cacao, wild cacao (*pataxtle*), chile, and ears of corn, but with the number five prefixed (i.e. as 200) "*este se dice ad omnia generaliter.*"

For 80 we find in Quiche, Cakchiquel and Mam *humuch, humuch,* and *hum mucx* or *humuch* (one *much*) and for 400 in the same three languages *o much, o much,* and *o mucx* (five *much*); the Motul dictionary defines *much'* as "in composition many together" and "pile of grains and small things. *Hun much' ixim.*" The last means one pile of maize.

There is no way of judging whether the Yucatec used *tuc* and *much'* in a vague way or defined them as heaps of 40 and 80 small objects. The word *tuc* occurs once in connection with a time count in Chumayel, for in a rather obscure passage with reference to a Katun 3 Ahau there appears the expression *oxtuc ti hab,* "three heaps of years." However, there is no way of telling whether this means three years, three heaps of years, or 120 (3×40) years. At any rate this counting by 40's and 80's undoubtedly was much more highly evolved in the highlands, and may have been a local development which never reached the lowlands.

The third order (400) is called *bak* or *bök* (the western lowland shift from *a* to a sound between *o* and *u*) in all recorded examples from lowland languages except Chaneabal, which unaccountably has *xan*. One can, therefore, be fairly certain that *bak* was the word in use in the place and at the time Maya hieroglyphic writing was produced. Kekchi and Pokomchi have respectively *okob* or *ocob* and *icom;* the Quiche word is *go,* not reported as 400, for that is given as 5 *much,* but appearing as *ca go,* "800," *oxo go,* "1200."

For the fourth order (8000) we have *pic* in Yucatec and Tzotzil: *pic* or *tabuc bak* (20 *bak*) for Tzeltal; and *chui* in various highland languages. The Chaneabal *hiquipil* is a direct borrowing from Nahuatl.

The fifth order (160,000) is termed *calab* in Yucatec and Kekchi; *cilab* in Pokomchi, and *bak baketic* (400 *bak*) in Tzeltal. It is interesting to note that the first syllables of *calab* and *cilab* mean "two" in the respective languages in which the words occur. This, however, may well be coincidence, since the number two could scarcely be involved. The Cahcoh vocabulary also gives *ca quilab* as 320,000.

Vicente Pineda (1888, pp. 155–72) gives the terms *tab sbak baketic, mam, mechum,* and *muculmam* for the Tzeltal equivalents of 3,200,000, 64,000,000, 25,600,000,000, and 10,240,000,000,000.

Yet another unit, 200, occurs in Kekchi according to the Wirsing dictionary, where the words *hun lah, caib lah, oxib lah, cahib lah, hoob lah,* and *laheb lah* are listed for 200, 400, 600, 800, 1000, and 2000 respectively, but

there are alternatives for expressing these numbers. The number 200, for instance, can be translated as *laheb kaal* (10 *kaal*), *ho* or *hoob tuc* (5 *tuc*), or *hun lah* (1 *lah*). Similarly for 400 one can say *laheb tuc* (10 *tuc*), *caib lah* (2 *lah*) or *hun ocob* (1 *ocob*). The term *lah,* as used for 200 and its multiples, presumably is a contraction of *laheb kaal* (tenscore). Again, the possibility must be borne in mind that these terms *tuc, much,* and *lah* were originally restricted to the count of certain articles, but have attained a wider use owing to the breakdown of the old systems of counting. It is worth noting that all three are multiples of 20, and therefore were probably developed within the framework of the vigesimal system.

This brief summary of names for higher numbers in several Maya languages and dialects suggests that counting in scores of millions may not have been restricted to the sacerdotal class, but may have been employed also in commercial transactions, perhaps in reckonings of cacao beans. That, in turn, implies the use of standard measures of weight or volume, with a sack or load of given weight or content representing a higher unit in the arithmetical count. One is amazed at the mastery over tremendous numbers implied in the various terms for higher units which have survived. Surely no other people on a comparable level of material culture have had such a concept of vast numbers, and a vocabulary of terms for handling them.

It has been suggested that as *lah* means completion and *hun* one, *lahun,* the word for 10 in most Maya languages and dialects means one completed. From this it has been deduced that the Maya system once had a decimal basis. It has further been suggested that the one completed refers to the 10 fingers. The proponents of this theory fail to note that if *lahun* means one completed, the word for 12, *lahca,* must similarly mean two completed. If 10 marks one completion, 12 can scarcely be two completions. Furthermore, one completion would normally be written *hun lah* not *lah hun.*

It would appear more likely that *lahun* means not one completion, but a completion plus one, and *lahca* a completion plus two. As a rule added digits are prefixed in Maya (e.g. *ox lahun,* "three and ten"), but in Huaxtec we find the reverse (e.g. *lahu ox*), suggesting that in the developmental stages of the language the added digit could equally well appear as a suffix.

On the above assumption the first completion is not 10, but nine; the second is not (twice) six, but 10. Nine is a number of the greatest ritualistic importance in Maya. There are nine lords of the underworld, and almost certainly nine underworlds. Nine is commonly used in magic and medicine as a lucky number, and caches frequently contain nine offerings. Various Maya deities have the number nine in their names: Bolon-Mayel, Bolon-Tz'acab, Bolon-Hacmatz, Ah Bolon-Yocte, Ah Bolon-Caan-Chaac, Bolon-Hobon, and Cit-Bolon-Tun in Yucatan; and Bolomac among the eastern Chol. The deified days 9 Imix and 9 Kana are regarded as tribal ancestors by the Jacalteca, and the day 9 Toh was an important god of the Cakchiquel. Among the Ixil one picks a day with a coefficient of 9 or 13 to send one's nagual into another person. Also in the interrogation of the chiefs in Chumayel the novice replies to the question as to when he prays: "On the ninth day and on the thirteenth day: it is to Bolon-ti-Ku [nine lords of the underworld] and Oxlahun-ti-Citbil [thirteen sky gods] that I count my beads."

Redfield and Villa note that *bolon* also has the meaning of uncontaminated, something which is apart or with which man has not been in contact. *Bolon* also implies, I think, the idea of the superlative. For example, *pixan* means lucky, fortunate or happy; *ah bolon pixan* is a man who is lucky or fortunate. *Hobon* combined with the words *puczikal* or *ol* ("heart," "soul") means clever, wise or inventive; *ah bolon hobon* is one who knows many trades and one who is very clever in one trade; *ah bolon makap*, "great hunter." *Tz'acab* means lineage, but *Bolon-Tz'acab*, the name of an important god, is translated in the Motul dictionary as a thing without end.

The use of the lucky nine in inscriptions is well illustrated by the IS of Altar 1, Uxul, which reads 9.9.9.9.18 9 Etz'nab 16 Zac. I feel that this date must have been chosen because of its lucky or divinatory aspect.

I think, therefore, that it is not impossible there was once a count of nine, and 10 was one over the completion of that count. Later, 10 may have become important as a count of fingers, and 12 was then called one completion (of the finger count) and two. Twenty was one man presumably because fingers and toes reach 20. After all, languages grow in a somewhat illogical manner; they are not composed in any ordered arrangement. In English we have traces of counting by 7's, 10's, 12's, and 60's, and historical evidence of importations of these sundry conflicting systems. There is no reason to believe that Maya counting was an orderly and autochthonous growth. Reckoning by 9's, 10's, 13's, and 20's may have arisen among a number of neighboring groups and as a result of mutual influences a tally by 10's replaced one by 9's, and at the same time or later a count by 20's may have come into vogue. The decimal system seems to have been transitory in all Maya languages and dialects and there are no traces of a decimal count in the hieroglyphic texts. Huaxtec, it is true, enumerates 100's by the decimal system, but as lower numbers are counted in the vigesimal system, and the term for 100 means five 20's, we can be

reasonably certain that the old vigesimal system has been modified in the higher, and therefore less frequently used, numbers as a result of European contacts.

I see no evidence that the Maya count ever had a quinary basis; there is no linguistic evidence for a system of that type. In the hieroglyphic texts there is much emphasis on the 5-tun and 5-katun intervals, but I am convinced that this emphasis is because these are quarter periods, and are stressed just as the 15-minute interval is of importance in our own civilization merely because it is a quarter of an hour. There is no emphasis on the 5th, 10th, and 15th uinal because these are not quarters of a tun. Had the number five had importance in its own right as a unit in a quinary system, one would presumably find the 5, 10, and 15 uinals stressed.

The hieroglyphic texts reveal evidence of counts by 7's, 9's, 13's, and 20's, but all, save the last, appear to have a ritualistic origin. There are also special glyphs used when recording five or seven days, and a corresponding linguistic term in many Maya languages or dialects. It is not improbable that this term refers to the interval between markets (p. 170; fig. 31,33–36).

NUMERICAL CLASSIFIERS

The books of Chilam Balam supply many examples of the uses of numerical classifiers in time counts, illustrating entries in various dictionaries and grammars. It must be remembered, however, that these were for the most part written or copied in late colonial times when the old usages were losing their value. Below are listed the principal numerical classifiers.

Te. The Motul dictionary says this was used for counts of years, days of the months, leagues, cacao, calabashes, and eggs. Examples show that when used with *tu* (contraction of *ti u*) the number changes from an ordinal to a cardinal. Examples in the various books of Chilam Balam and the Chronicle of Oxkutzcab: *oxlahunte ti katuns,* "13 katuns [they reigned]"; *oxlahunte katun u cuch,* "13 katuns was the burden," but *oxlahunte katun catac uacppel haabi,* "13 katuns and six years [it took to build the mounds]"; *buluc Hix tu hunte Pop,* "11 Ix on first of Pop"; *tu bulucte xul,* "on eleventh of Xul"; *uucte hab kintunyabil,* "seven years of drought"; *tu holhunte (tun),* "in the fifteenth [tun]."

Piz. The Motul dictionary says of *piz,* "count for days and years and reales." It also has the meaning of ordinary, common, simple, without malice. It is used with katuns, tuns, haabs, and European months. Examples are: *cankal haab catac lahunpiz haab,* "fourscore years and ten years"; *lahunpiz katun,* "in katun 10 [was established]"; *tu uucpiz tun uaxac Ahau u katunil,* "in the seventh tun [or tun 7?] of Katun 8 Ahau"; *bulucpiz Junio,* "eleventh of June." The substitution of *tu* for *ti* probably converts *piz* into an ordinal.

Ppel is a general classifier for numbers. The Motul dictionary says "general count for everything there is" and also gives the meaning "only," "not more than." Perhaps it corresponds to our "no more no less." It is used with the kin, tun, haab, katun, and Spanish time periods: *hun ppel katun,* "one katun"; *uacppel hab u binel,* "six haab shall pass until"; *uucppel kin ichil hunppel semana,* "seven days in one week." It is very likely that the use of *ppel* with periods of time arose in colonial times, and is part of the general decay in the use of numerical classifiers which has continued to this day.

Tz'it. The Motul dictionary lists this as used for counting candles, thin rods, or spindles, and cotton or silk threaded on a needle. To this list the Pio Perez adds, "particle for counting long things such as candles, sticks, sections of cane, ears of young corn, etc., and also persons." Beltran (1859) adds to the list mamey apples, bananas, and alligator pears, although the mamey apple and alligator pears hardly qualify as long. The books of Chilam Balam use the particle occasionally with katun and tun: *u bolontz'it katun,* "the ninth katun [of the count]"; *huntz'it tunil,* "in the first tun." I have the impression that *tz'it* may be used as a numerical classifier only when reference is made to the position of a katun, tun, or other period within the round of 13, that is to say in the rotation of Katun 11 Ahau, 9 Ahau, 7 Ahau, etc., or the equivalent rotation of the tuns. On page 17 of Chumayel there occurs the phrase *huntz'it katun yanobi,* which Roys (1933, p. 81) translates, "They were there one katun." The incident refers to the Spanish occupation of Campeche which started in 1531 (the text has 1513). Twenty tuns counted from 1531 would fall largely in Katun 11 Ahau, which, if the suggested explanation is correct, would be the *huntz'it katun* of the new round of the katuns which started in 1539.

On page 13 of Tizimin is the expression *tu tz'oc katunob u uutz' huntz'it katun* which is translated as "at the completion of the katuns, the fold of one katun." The whole passage ostensibly treats of a Katun 5 Ahau, but there is fair evidence that the seventeenth-century scribe transferred a prophecy from a Katun 11 Ahau to a Katun 5 Ahau. Katun 11 Ahau would be the first of the cycle of 13 katuns. The passage may, therefore, well mean "from the completion of the katuns, the fold of the first katun [of the new series]."

In the katun prophecies *tz'it* is used with the number giving the position in the sequence of 13, thereby greatening the possibility that the suggested interpretation of *tz'it* may be correct.

Tic. The Motul dictionary defines *tic* as something which is untied, such as bundle or a load. It occurs in the story of the birth of maize in Chumayel: *ix huntic, catic, oxhuntic,* which Roys (1933, p. 108) translates "the first, the second, the thirteenth unfolding." Later in the text we are told that the only son of God, God the Father, and Expleo-u-caan were born in the *huntic, catic, oxtic* katuns. This might mean the first, second, and third katuns, but it is also possible that it refers to three different creations of the world, since there appears to be a reference to the final creation at the bottom of the same page. This affix, therefore, in all probability has a purely mystical sense, and can be ignored so far as the calendar is concerned.

Tuc. This occurs once in Chumayel. It may mean 40. *Oxtuc ti hab* would then be "120 haab" (p. 53).

From the above it would appear that *te* and *piz* were more or less interchangeable as numerical classifiers with the counts. When *tu (ti u)* precedes them they are, it would seem, converted into ordinals. This interchangeability may, however, be due to decline in the strict use of numerical classifiers in colonial times. A copyist may sometimes have retained the original classifier and at other times may have changed it to conform with the usage then current. In pre-Spanish times there may well have been a definite distinction. *Tz'it* may refer to the position within a re-entering cycle, and would be used as an ordinal. The use of *p'el* with dates may, one suspects, be a colonial innovation. *Tic* and *tuc* probably have a significance not at present apparent. Finally mention should be made of *tzuc* which appears to indicate a fraction. In the Chronicle of Chicxulub (1882, p. 216) there occurs the expression *u hotzuc ca culhi ah buluc Ahau lai katun.* This has been translated as "the fifth division of Katun 11 Ahau had been placed." It has, furthermore, been assumed that the said division is a tun. This last, however, is open to question, although probably correct.

The affix *il,* sometimes attached to the coefficients of day names, is the possessive or rather the relationship termination, showing that the word to which it is attached belongs to or is related to the word that follows. That is to say, it affirms the close connection between the coefficient and the day name. The glyphic affix corresponding to *il* has now been identified with considerable certainty (p. 285).

Numerical classifiers have not hitherto been recognized in the glyphic texts. Nevertheless, it is reasonably certain that the sign which Beyer calls "greenstone disk and teeth element" is a classificatory affix with the meaning of *te.* I designate it *te* (1) since there are two other elements, termed *te* (2) and *te* (3), apparently with the same phonic value. *Te* (1) occurs not infrequently in the inscriptions with period glyphs and with month signs, but never with day signs. Thereby, it conforms to the use of *te* in the books of Chilam Balam. Its position is almost invariably between coefficient and glyph (fig. 2,*15–23*). It is found with 9 baktuns (Copan 6, 19; Tila B); with 2 tuns (Copan T 11); with 1 tun (Yaxchilan 11; fig. 56,*6*); with 8 uinals (Copan Z); with 4 uinals (Xcalumkin IS); with 3 uinals (Copan HS, Date 1); with month signs (Copan 1, 7, C, G, J, M, N [pedestal], HS, Dates 21, 34; Yaxchilan 11, 19, L 3, Str 44; Quirigua G, P; Palenque Olvidado; Calakmul 9; Yula 1; Halakal 1; Naranjo 10; and La Amelia HS). I make no doubt there are other examples. There seems to be no rule governing the presence or absence of this element; it may have been inserted to obviate possible distortion of the glyph when a low coefficient would have left a somewhat elongated space for the glyph, for it usually appears with bar and dot coefficients of 5 or less. However, there are rare cases in which it accompanies 8 and 13. It does not occur with period glyphs or month signs in the Dresden, where space was always at a premium, but *te* (3) is present once in Madrid (66a) with 13 tuns.

Te (1) appears five times in the codices as a postfix to the head form of Oc, and in each case there is a coefficient of 9 (fig. 12,*16,17*). I think we can safely read this glyph as that of a rather obscure deity, Bolon-Yocte, whose name may mean "9 strides," the *y* before *oc* probably being the possessive. Bolon-Yocte is mentioned in Chumayel, Perez, and Kaua as patron of Katun 11 Ahau and in connection with the second year of the Tizimin prophecies. On Dresden 60 his glyph appears in a short text dealing with a Katun 11 Ahau (the affixes of 11 Ahau indicate a katun count; p. 200) confirming the identification of the glyph. However, his glyph is also recognizable on Paris 7 and 8, which treat of Katuns 5 Ahau and 3 Ahau. This does not weaken the identification, for the patrons of the katuns in Paris are not in agreement with our information from Yucatec sources. There is a variant form of this glyph on Madrid 70b.

The fact that *te* (1) is placed not between numeral and glyph, but as postfix to the Oc head is interesting, because the order thereby agrees with that of the syllables of the god's name, 9, Oc, *te;* as a numerical classifier with periods and months, its position between numeral and sign similarly reflects the spoken word, 3, *te,* Pop. Its presence with period glyphs and month signs taken in conjunction with its absence from day signs is strong evidence that we are dealing with a numerical classifier; its uses in other contexts strengthen the case for identifying it as a symbol for *te.*

Te (1), like the other *te* affixes, occurs with glyphs which do not have a numerical coefficient. This is understandable, for *te* is a word with sundry meanings (p. 283),

and the affix is often used in an attributive sense to indicate a connection with vegetation. Indeed, the sign appears to have developed from the vegetal motif which forms the headdress of God E, god of vegetation in general and of maize in particular.

Among other things *te* signifies tree, and the affix *te* (1) is used in that sense. On Dresden 30c–31c (fig. 62,*1,2*) are pictures of God B seated on a tree, and the corresponding text in each compartment contains the glyphs of God B and of one of the four world directions. Accordingly, we can feel confident that the section deals with God B and the trees set up at the four sides of the world, to which were assigned the colors red, white, black, and yellow. The glyphs for these in that order precede the corresponding world directions in each of the four compartments, and postfixed to those for red, black, and yellow is the *te* (1) affix. These combinations must read "red tree," "black tree," and "at· [*ti* prefix] the yellow tree." The passages fully confirm the identification of the *te* (1) affix. The white affix is joined to the tun sign which replaces *te* (1). The heart of the habin tree is called *tun cuy,* "stonelike hardening," presumably because of the hardness of the wood of that tree. *Zac tun* could mean "substitute for stone" or "not quite the same as stone," both of which would be applicable to a very hard wood (cf. *quiebra hacha,* "axe breaker," a name for *Krugiodendron ferreum*). The element containing three dots placed between red and *te* (1) may be the sign for *le,* "leaf" (note its use on Madrid 42c with snaring [*le*] of animals. *Te* (1) is also affixed to the yax element (Dresden 67b; Paris 16b, 18a; Madrid 95d) to form a glyph which, I think, we are justified in reading as that of the *yaxche,* the ceiba tree (with *te* (2), fig. 62,*4*).

These glyphs make it clear that *te* (1) was used not only as a numerical classifier and as the termination *te* in Bolon-Yocte, but also for *te,* "tree."

A second and very common affix, which for other reasons (p. 282) appears also to have the value *te,* can be used, as well, as a postfix of numerical coefficients (figs. 24,*62;* 25,*20,36*). On Copan 19 it is postfixed to all the numerical heads of the IS except that of the baktun, which has instead the regular *te* (1) postfix. The reason for this unusual display of postfixes is that the numerical heads occupy separate glyphs blocks on this monument. On two or three other Copan stelae, where this same situation obtains, postfixes do not occur, but enlarged earplugs fill the spaces. The fact that these two postfixes are reciprocals on Copan 19 and with *yaxche* strengthens the case for identifying the second form as also a *te* symbol. This element I call *te* (2). There is a third affix, *te* (3), seemingly with the same value (p. 283).

Another affix occurs with the tun and haab glyphs

when used as declarants of anniversaries, but never when they are used in IS or PE. This may correspond to either *piz* or *p'el*, both numerical classifiers used with years (pp. 54–55).

An element which resembles, but is not identical with, this last is found with month signs and the winged cauac in Yucatecan texts, but it stands outside the coefficient, sometimes even being placed beneath the previous glyph. Because of that placement and because the *te* affix may also be present, we can feel reasonably sure that we are not dealing with a numerical classifier. It appears to correspond to the Yucatec *tu*, a contraction of *ti* and *u*, which commonly precedes the number of the month or the year in the books of Chilam Balam. The *u* converts the number from a cardinal to an ordinal; *ti* is the locative (figs. 38; 39; p. 163).

GLYPH STYLES

There are certain variations in glyph presentation which represent differences in material, space, and time.

Glyphs painted in the codices are much more cursively treated than those carved in stone. The variations are not entirely due to the lateness of the codices, because they also exist, although to a lesser degree, on murals and pottery vessels of the Initial Series Period. They are to be expected because glyphs could be painted with rapidity; they could be carved only with painstaking slowness. The ranges of difference can be seen in the series of day signs and month glyphs (figs. 6–11; 16–19), and in individual glyphs, as, for instance, the glyph for south (fig. 41,23–31,34,36).

There is little variation in glyphic styles between one city and another of the Central Area during most of the Initial Series Period, but well-preserved texts from the early stages of that period are not sufficiently numerous to indicate whether the same uniformity holds good for the first two centuries of the inscriptions.

Hieroglyphic texts from Chichen Itza and northwest Yucatan are somewhat different from those of the Central Area. As this was a peripheral region during the Initial Series Period, the local style never conformed entirely to that of the area to the south. There are traces of archaism which appear to have survived there long after their disappearance in the south (Thompson, 1937, pp. 191–92). The "centipede" affix of day signs and the occasional absence of a true cartouche from day signs are examples (figs. 38,5,6; 39,4,5).

Late inscriptions at Sacchana, Chiapas, are of a style not found elsewhere, but it is possible that those deviations from standard practice are due to the lateness of the dates, and do not have a geographical explanation (Seler, 1901, figs. 5,6; this work, fig. 27,14,39,52,65).

Some sites in Campeche, notably Xcalumkin, have a local style of writing which is quite marked (fig. 53,3). The style is dissimilar to that of Chichen Itza, although in both regions the same peculiar method of recording dates existed.

Despite these differences there is a marked homogeneity in glyphic delineation throughout the Maya area, and a Maya priest from Copan would have had no difficulty in reading contemporaneous inscriptions at Piedras Negras or Palenque, at Macanxoc or Naranjo. He would have had a little trouble at Xcalumkin or Chichen Itza, but more because of the content of the texts than because of stylistic differences.

Temporal variations are fairly evident. In some texts from the early part of Baktun 9 (ca. A.D. 500) there are certain features which later disappear. The most characteristic of these are complex elaboration of detail of glyphs, decoration in some detail of numerical dots, rarity of filler crescents on each side of numerical dots, a certain irregularity in the outline of glyphs, the centipede infix or prefix of day signs (fig. 47,4), the use of a monkey face in full view for the day Ahau (fig. 10,50,51; Morley's notched day sign), the circular outline of the right infix of the cauac glyph (fig. 26,15,17), a peculiar headdress (fig. 27,31,32,42), and a tendency to shallow relief. With two or more of these stylistic features present, Maya texts can be dated as early with as much certainty as the writings of Oscar Wilde can be placed by style and content in the Yellow Book period.

Yet earlier texts, from Baktun 8, display a number of these early features, but the carving is more crude, and lacks the complexity of the sequent style (figs. 10,48; 26,24,33,41,49). The outline of the glyphs is even more irregular and relief tends to be quite shallow (fig. 7,37). In the earliest known text, that of the Leiden plaque, some of the period glyphs lack their identifying characteristics (fig. 27,3,15).

By the close of the first half of Baktun 9 (A.D. 633) the classical style is well established. This endured for approximately two centuries, but toward the close of Baktun 9 and in the first katuns of Baktun 10 changes appear. Glyphs are carved with less care. For example, in the interiors of the tun and katun signs straight horizontal lines replace the more elegant design of the previous period (fig. 26,31,39). The numerical filler may take the form of a St. Andrew's cross instead of the more usual crescent, and the same element appears between the double "eye" of death as a prefix (fig. 5,27). The "grape" infix of the cauac glyphs becomes angular (fig. 17,61); hands lose their beauty and become pudgy (fig. 32,22).

Beyer (1932, 1937) has discussed the stylistic sequence of glyphs at some length, but in my opinion all his classification of the glyphs at Chichen Itza is incorrect, for I believe the various texts to which he assigns a span of over 500 years actually were carved within a very few decades of one another, and that the stylistic differences result from a mingling of styles in a period of uncertainty and do not correspond to great differences in time (p. 197). A similar mingling of styles is to be seen on the pages of Dresden. Glyphs of types which Beyer on stylistic grounds would separate by hundreds of years occur almost cheek by jowl in that codex.

The lunar series supplies a good example of the addition of new glyphs as needed. In inscriptions of Baktun 8, Glyphs X, B, and A are absent, but Glyphs X and A appear at the start of Baktun 9; the first occurrence of Glyph B is not until 9.8.15.0.0 (Piedras Negras 25).

REGIONAL GLYPHS

Certain glyphs are common at one site or in one region but unknown elsewhere. These are clearly local developments which for some reason were not widely accepted.

At Palenque a small prefix in the form of a snake or an eel is sometimes placed over day signs to indicate that that is the starting point of a count forward (figs. 4,*24,25; 30,48–51*); the glyph really serves as a short substitute for the anterior date indicator. The element occurs with that meaning nine times at Palenque; never, so far as is known, at any other site except once at Xcalumkin (fig. 4,*26*). Beyer (1943a) has called attention to the composite glyph which he names "ending day," but which actually must have a meaning such as "forward to sunrise" (or sunset?; p. 166). This occurs 19 times at Piedras Negras and once at the nearby site of El Cayo, but nowhere else in the Maya area, although the elements composing the glyph are frequent in other combinations or alone. On some inscriptions at Copan the IS introductory glyph is not followed by an IS. This practice is not observed elsewhere.

A peculiar composite glyph consists of a sky sign below a small cauac flanked by flippers or legs and with the addition of a double flame element which, being a prefix, may be to the left or above (fig. 2,*47–49*). This glyph is quite common in certain clauses at Quirigua but is unknown elsewhere.

Quirigua also has a peculiar head form of the winged cauac with a very beaked nose and larger square eye of a type not reported from other sites. Together with the corresponding symbolic form it is used as a substitute for the more general "end count of tun" glyphs (fig. 4,*27*). At Palenque, but not elsewhere, the Moan bird can replace this glyph (fig. 4,*28*).

The substitution of the eagle or a vulture for the *ti* or torch element in anterior date indicators occurs only at Quirigua and Copan (fig. 4,*29,30*). The reason for this substitution is that the *ti* element is the characteristic frontal ornament of the vulture.

In Yucatan and Campeche alone is the kin sign placed immediately after the day sign (fig. 4,*31–35*). This corresponds to a Yucatecan method of writing dates, as, for instance, *ti hoo ahau tu ḳin*, "on 5 Ahau on its day," on page 2 of Tizimin. Also, in Yucatan and Campeche alone are month signs supplied with a prefix which almost certainly means *tu* as in expressions such as *tu hunte Pop*, "on first of Pop" (figs. 38; 39).

Examples of these local glyphs are very numerous. There are also small local variations in the delineation of common glyphs, particularly noticeable in the case of Ahau, with its regional and temporal variations. The Ahau sign with death-eyes prefix and bundle postfix is very frequent at Yaxchilan, but unknown or rare at other sites.

Many clauses, also, are local. One expandable clause is of common occurrence at Yaxchilan, but unknown elsewhere (fig. 46,*10–16*), and the same is true of a clause which appears several times at Naranjo (fig. 3,*3–9*).

REGIONAL METHODS OF FIXING DATES

In Yucatan a special system of recording dates was employed. The CR date is followed by a winged cauac glyph with its coefficient and a day Ahau also with coefficient, and almost invariably with the "Ben-Ich" prefix and the "ak" postfix. There is good evidence that this arrangement means that the given date fell in the declared tun of a katun ending on the day Ahau recorded (pp. 197–99). Even though the interpretation may be challenged, the local character of the arrangement is beyond doubt.

In the Jatate drainage of Chiapas there appears to be special emphasis on a system of counting not from the last date recorded, as is the general Maya practice, but directly from the IS (p. 158). At Palenque there is a system of reckoning from suppressed dates which is still not entirely understood. However, certain glyphs appear to indicate whether the count is to the "seating" of a tun or to a date which does not mark the end of a tun (p. 120).

Beyer's glyph for 0 tuns, which I read as "the seating of the tun" (p. 119), appears to be confined to Palenque, and to Chinikiha, which lies a short distance to the east; it has not been reported from elsewhere, and presumably was a local development. The special postfix to indicate an anniversary is also a localism, being confined to the Usumacinta Valley (p. 195; fig. 4,*13,14*).

Perhaps with more thorough investigation, other regional variations in methods of date recordings will be discovered.

THE BURDEN OF TIME

Time has been the subject of many similes in the history of man. In our own civilization the most familiar symbol is that of aged Father Time with his scythe. He reminds us of the brevity of our span of life but fails to convey the idea of the eternity of time. A far better picture is that of the poet which compares time to an ever-flowing stream, but the concept is narrowed to the experience of the individual when Isaac Watts conceives of this stream as bearing its sons away. These and other similes reflect the attitude toward time in our own culture; time is regarded not as an abstract, but rather as to its effect on us as individuals. It is as though we were surprised and a trifle offended that we, the self-styled lords of creation, should have to bow to the passing years.

The Maya concept of time was something which in its broad outlines is not unfamiliar to us, but which in its philosophical aspect reflects a very different mentality. The Maya conceived of the divisions of time as burdens which were carried through all eternity by relays of bearers. During the Initial Series Period these bearers were the numbers by which the different periods were distinguished; each number carried the period with which he was associated over his allotted course. This imagery differs strikingly from any picture of time our civilization has produced, for time was not portrayed as the journey of one bearer and his load, but of many bearers, each with his own division of time on his back.

The concept is well illustrated in the full-figure glyphs, particularly those of Copan D. The date of that monument is 9.15.5.0.0 10 Ahau 8 Ch'en, an important subdivision of Maya time (fig. 60). The numbers are the bearers; the periods, the burdens. The glyphs depict the moment when the period comes to an end, symbolized by the arrival of the procession at the *lub*. That Yucatec term customarily signified the place where porters set down their burdens, and also the distance between one resting place and another. The word undoubtedly is a noun formed from the root *lub* with the meaning of falling (*lubul*, "to fall"; *lubzah*, "to upset something," literally, cause to fall). The Motul dictionary gives *lubay* as "the great resting places, or the destination at the end of a journey." In Kekchi, according to the Wirsing dictionary, *lub* means "weary," "tired."

The glyphs of the IS of this Copan stela depict the weary bearers starting their rest. For the gods of the numbers 9 and 15 this is a momentary respite; for the others it is the end of the journey. The 9 and 15 must carry their burdens more stages on the journey, for the current baktun and katun have still considerable distances to travel before the *lubay* is reached. The god of number

5 will be immediately replaced by the god of number 6 as bearer of the tun; the deity of number 1 will assume the loads of the uinal and kin now fallen from the backs of the impersonators of the god who personifies completion. A charming picture of these bearers and their loads in a living group, from the pen of the famed artist, Jean Charlot, forms the frontispiece to this volume.

In the hieroglyphic pictures the resting gods hold the periods or support them in their laps. The god of number 9, the bearer of the baktun, still has his load on his back, held there by the tumpline (the *mecapal*) which passes across his forehead. His hand is raised as though to slip off the load; the pad between tumpline and forehead is clearly delineated. Beside the god of number 10, with his arm linked in the cartouche of Ahau, is the lord of the night who is clearly in the act of rising from the ground; the tumpline and the load (Glyph F) it supports are in position. With his left hand the nocturnal god eases the weight on the tumpline; with his right hand on the ground he steadies himself as he starts to rise. Furthermore, the artist has subtly conveyed in the strain reflected in the god's features the physical effort of rising from the ground with his heavy load. It is the typical attitude of an Indian carrier as he resumes his journey, which anyone familiar with present-day Maya of the highlands of Guatemala must have seen a score of times.

The lord of the night takes up his burden as the day comes to rest. The combination pictures feelingly the never-ceasing journey of time. True, there was not in the Maya concept of time a measurable period of repose with the burdens fallen to the ground, for it was a relay race; as soon as one bearer set down his burden, his successor hoisted it on his back, but the glyphs had to conform to the general presentation of the IS. It is the very moment that the period ends and there was, accordingly, no need to show the new bearers waiting to assume their loads. Such an enlargement of the picture would not have been in conformity with use and wont so far as the IS was concerned, and would have caused an undesirable confusion in the hieroglyphic text.

Other inscriptions also show the dropping of the burdens. On Copan D' what is apparently the month coefficient bears the month by means of a tumpline, still in position across his forehead; on Quirigua B and D most of the period glyphs rest on the legs of the gods that represent the numbers. The latter for the most part are seated or reclining in positions suggestive of exhaustion after their journey (figs. 28; 29). On the other hand, the god of the night has his burden on his back, although he does not appear to be rising from the ground. The picture of the completed moons portrays the goddess of number 1 with the moon held with both her hands on her left shoulder. Glyph B of the lunar series carries Glyph X of the same series on his back, the tumpline being very clear (fig. *29,14*). This last picture is of importance since it clearly shows that Glyph B should be read with Glyph X, not with Glyph A, as has been rather widely supposed. The artist who carved the full-figure glyphs of Quirigua D depicts the bearers in attitudes of exhaustion on completing the stages of their journey.

This interpretation of the Maya concept of time does not rest only on a diagnosis of the attitudes of these full-figure glyphs, for there are many passages in the books of Chilam Balam which reveal the same pattern of thought.

In the Chronicle of Mani the phrase *lai año cu ximbal,* followed by a note on some historical event, occurs eight times. Brinton (1882, p. 104) translates this "as this year was passing"; Martinez Hernandez (1927) as *"en el transcurso de este año."* *Ximbal,* however, means "to walk, to journey," and the whole clearly expresses the concept of the year traveling. Elsewhere the phrase recurs with the Maya *haab* or *hab* substituted for *año,* for in the eight passages where *año* is employed the associated events fall after the Spanish conquest, and the European year is given.

In the series of year prophecies at the start of Tizimin, which appear also in Mani (which supplies two words lacking in Tizimin), we read *"lai u lukul u cuch . . . hoote u cuch ca ti luki ti yahaulil."* This Roys translates: "This is the removal of his burden . . . five is his burden, and then he departs from his reign." The reference is to a Katun 5 Ahau. Again, on page 9 of the same manuscript occurs the phrase *"u kax cuch katun ti ho ahau katun u lubul uale tu hunte uil katun,"* translated by Roys as "the binding of the burden [of] the katun in Katun 5 Ahau. It would fall in the first katun." On page 10 of the same manuscript we read: *"ti ah oxil kan tu hunte pop u kax cuch katun,"* "On Lord 3 Kan on 1st of Pop the binding of the burden [of] the katun." On page 11 of Tizimin there occurs the expression *"tu kin u kaxal u cuch ah ho ahau,"* "On the day of the binding of the burden of Lord 5 Ahau." Furthermore, in connection with the end of the katun we are told in Roys' words: "He [Katun 5 Ahau] gives up his mat, his throne. There comes another cup, another mat, another throne, another reign. The burden of Lord 5 Ahau falls (*u lubul u cuch ah ho ahau*)." Again we find in this same passage *tu tz'oc u cuch katun,* "at the completion of the burden of the katun," and in Chumayel *u cuch u ximbal katun,* "the burden of the journey of the katun."

Again, in Tizimin, page 10, we find *"u ximbalte kin, u ximbalte akab,"* "the march of the day, the march of the night," and in Chumayel, page 90, in connection with the prophecy for the evils of Katun 7 Ahau, *"ti u hoppol u tzintzin loc katun,"* "the katun begins to limp."

In the account of the Manche Chol calendar in the manuscript by Tovilla, recently brought to light by Scholes, it is stated that, "According to what [the Indians] say, [these four first days] are those which take the road and bear the load of the month (*cargan el mes*), changing in turn." It is, therefore, clear that this concept of the periods of time traveling with their loads was not confined to Yucatan at the time of the conquest. The "first four days" are, of course, the year bearers. Indeed, the expression year bearer is a direct translation of the Yucatecan compound *cuch haab,* and similar expressions occur in other Maya languages and dialects, notably Jacalteca and Chuh (La Farge and Byers, 1931, p. 180).

In a passage of Chumayel (p. 45) there is a sentence which Roys translates as: "Then the charge of the katun was sought; nine was its charge when it descended from heaven. Kan was the day when his burden was bound to him." Actually, the mention of nine has nothing to do with the coefficient of the day Ahau in this particular case, for the katun ended on 11 Ahau. The reference is probably to the association of nine with the katun because Ah Bolon-Tz'acab was regent, his name meaning "Lord Nine Generations." Here *cuch* might rather have the meaning of misfortune, for, by extension, *cuch* can mean the burden of office and the burden of life's misfortunes, for holding office was a burden. The same meaning can be attached to the katun's burden.

The above quotations are somewhat contradictory. The first implies that the coefficient was the burden, as Roys has pointed out; the others suggest that both the day and his coefficient were the bearers. It is tolerably certain that the day and his coefficient were the bearers of the katun in Yucatan, at least in the sixteenth century, but in the somewhat different system of the Initial Series Period the number of the katun was the bearer. These distinctions appear to reflect somewhat different usages, for in Yucatan the custom of numbering katuns in sequence according to the position of each within the baktun seems to have been on the verge of extinction, having given place to the numeration of katuns by the day on which each ended. It is, therefore, not illogical that in the south, during the Initial Series Period, the bearer should have been the number of the period; in Yucatan, at the time of the Spanish conquest, the day name and number on which the katun ended.

Possibly there was a shift, spatial or temporal, or the old idea may have persisted in Yucatan until the Spanish conquest, but its details were reversed by the eighteenth-century chroniclers who may have misunderstood the concept. More probably, we are insisting on too sharp a definition of what was really a flight from realism, for the outlines of such poetic imagery• are by their very nature blurred.

That the Maya were not too precise in defining this concept is perhaps indicated by the full figure kin of Yaxchilan L 48, which holds the head for six in his outstretched hand and supports the head for 10 on his feet (fig. 47,2). This, taken in conjunction with the reversed treatment at Quirigua and Copan might indicate that the Maya of the Initial Series Period had not made up their minds as to which was the bearer and which the borne. Nevertheless, the conclusion is not beyond criticism, for the numbers on this Yaxchilan lintel are represented as heads, not as full figures, and a head could scarcely carry a full figure. Yet there was nothing in Maya artistic canons to prevent the artist from depicting the kin as a head and the number 16 as a full-figure glyph, had the burden concept been sufficiently defined as to demand that arrangement.

That, however, is a minor detail not seriously affecting the Maya imagery of time on its journey.

In the katun prophecies given in the various books of Chilam Balam the names of towns are generally accompanied by the designation of the katun and the words *u hetz' katun*. For example on page 97 of Chumayel there is the sentence: *"Lahun Ahau katun. Chable u hetz' katun."* This has generally been rendered as "Katun 10 Ahau, the katun is established at Chable." In the Perez dictionary *hetz'* is translated as *"apoyar, sellar, asentar con firmeza, elegir lugar, fundar, establecer usos,"* and the intransitive *hetz'el* is given the meanings *asentarse, apoyarse con firmeza algo que pesa, establecerse, fundarse, cimentarse."* It is just possible that *hetz'* refers not to the act of setting up a stela (for none appear to have been erected at so late a date, Landa notwithstanding), but to the symbolic adjustment of the burden of the katun to the bearer's back. It is possible that important towns took turns in celebrating the advent of a new katun by religious pageantry, and in such celebrations impersonators of the time periods may have performed the ceremonies involved in the transference of burdens from the backs of one set of divine bearers to those of the new group of carriers.

Another method of expressing this association may involve the word *ch'a*. For example, in Chumayel, page 80, we read: *"Lahca Ahau te ch'abi Otzmal u tunile."* This has been customarily rendered as "12 Ahau, the stone was taken at Otzmal." The Motul dictionary translates *ch'a* as *"tomar, llevar, traer"*; the Perez dictionary gives *tomar, apropriarse.* It has been widely assumed that the word refers to the act of setting up a stela, although movement is definitely implied in the Motul dictionary.

It is possible, therefore, that the sentence means "12 Ahau, his stone was carried at Otzmal," supposing that the day 12 Ahau was regarded as starting from Otzmal on his burdened pilgrimage of 20 tuns, or, perhaps, the sentence implies that the pageant which acted this poetic fantasy was held at Otzmal. The suggested interpretations of *hetz'* and *ch'a* may not hold water, for *ch'abi* could also come from *ch'ab,* "create something from nothing, which power belongs to God," although this is not a very probable derivation. In any case, the evidence for the general concept of the burdens of time being borne by relays of divine carriers is beyond dispute.

It has been necessary to interlard this poetical imagery with dull discussions of Maya etymology. It is as though one discussed the geology of Mount Helicon in an introduction to a brief essay on Clio. Nonetheless, deviations along arid paths are necessary in assessing such an unknown quantity as the mental outlook of the Maya. We are, accordingly, fortunate in having the aid of Jean Charlot in bringing to life this vivid concept. He has captured its qualities of mysticism and striking beauty in the frontispiece of this volume.

MAYA POETRY

In many hieroglyphic texts there are glyphs which, so far as the general meaning is concerned, are redundant. In some texts these glyphs are inserted; in others they are omitted; and I had thought that their presence was evidence of an inherent love of tautology (Thompson, 1932b, p. 386; 1944, p. 14). There are also some grounds for believing that unnecessary glyphs were sometimes introduced to fill a space so that an important glyph might occupy a prominent position. Now, however, I am convinced that these extra glyphs were interpolated to improve the cadence of a passage.

In the introductory paragraph of this book I have referred lightly to Maya poetry, comparing it to the poetry of the Psalms and other parts of the Old Testament. Both have an antiphonal arrangement in which the second line of a verse answers or repeats a variant from the first. In addition, Maya poetry plays on the sounds of words, bringing together words which have approximately the same sound. Compare:

"The sea is his, and he made it; and his hands prepared the dry land."—*Psalms,* 95:5.

"Surely against me is he turned: he turneth his hand against me all the day."—*Lamentations,* 3:3.

"They shall roar together like lions: they shall yell as lions' whelps."—*Jeremiah,* 51:38.

"Katun 11 Ahau is set upon the mat; is set upon the throne, When their ruler is set up: Yaxal Chac its face to their ruler.

The fan of heaven shall descend; the wreath of heaven, the bouquet of heaven, shall descend.

The drum of the Lord 11 Ahau shall resound: his rattle shall resound,

When knives of flint are set in his mantle.

On that day there shall be the green turkey: on that day there shall be Zulim Chan: on that day there shall be Chakanputun.

They shall find their harvest among the trees: they shall find their harvest among the rocks, those who have lost their harvest in the katun of Lord 11 Ahau."—*Chumayel*, p. 13 (Roys translation with slight emendations).

"Accept in person my offering of meat.

I have given you, my father, the offering of meat, the heated sacrifice, for many days, for many years:

Ground meat, fine ground maize, cooked meat, ground meat, fine ground maize.

This will be the offering of meat, this will be the offering of meat for many days, for many years, for many days to come, for many years to come."—*Lacandon prayer* (Tozzer, 1907, Chant 36).

"They moved among the four lights: among the four layers of the stars.

The world was not lighted. There was no day: there was no night, there was no moon.

Then they perceived that the [first] dawn was coming: Then dawn came.

Until [during] the dawn thirteen eight thousand *tz'ac* to seven was the count of the [first] dawn. Then the world was theirs."—*Chumayel*, p. 44 (Roys translation with slight emendations).

There is a fine cadence in the original Maya, as for example some of the lines in the first quotation:

"Buluc Ahau katun
Cumaan ti pop: cumaan ti tz'am
Ti ualaac yahaulili: Yaxal Chac u uich ti yahaulili.
Emom caanil ual: emom caanil tz'ulub, caanil utz'ub
Pecnom u pax: Pecnom u zoot Ah Buluc Ahau,
Ti yokte tok yubte.
Tu kin yan yax cutz: tu kin yan Zulim Chan, tu kin yan
Chakanputun
Uiilnom che: uiilnom tunich, ah zatal uiil ichil
Ah buluc Ahau katun"

Single sentences often possess a vibrating melody, as for example:

"Ca tz'oci u lohol balcah: ca tz'oci u caput cuxtal" (Chumayel, p. 42).
"Ca yalah u chich; ca yalah u tz'e naa,
"Ca yalah u mim; ca yalah u muu" (Chumayel, p. 60).
"Yan xin mac xin ahan, uale" (Chumayel, p. 59).

Tizimin presents many similar passages. For example on page 6:

"Yalab u t'an yetel u caan" and
"Hol can be, hol can lub," and, as a variation
"U tz'oc tzotz, u tz'oc sitz'il

Note the rhythm of the lines, the free use of iambs, and the antiphonal character of every line. This is blank verse of high quality. The same poetry is in the Lacandon prayer and in other prayers from Yucatan and British Honduras, but Maya poetry has little imagery. It depends for its effect on simplicity of language and cadence.

The playing on the sounds of words is well illustrated by the following passages:

"U uacunic u luch: yetz'cunic u pop" (Tizimin, p. 6).
"Bal bin c'alab ca bin c'ilab uinic ti be?" (Chumayel, p. 60).
"Ba la hex u kabatahob ca patlahobe" (Chumayel, p. 58).
"Hex u zilic u pice: u tz'ilic u pach" (Chumayel, p. 40).
"U chun tz'alpach p'ax; u chun pakpach p'ax" (Chumayel, p. 14).

This, however, is a quite minor and infrequent feature of Maya poetry.

With such a melodious cadence in the Maya of the books of Chilam Balam and in that of modern prayers, it is logical to expect a similar setting for the hieroglyphic texts, and, accordingly, we may believe that the redundant glyphs were inserted to better the flowing harmony.

In many cases a katun completion not only chronicles the number of katuns elapsed, but notes, furthermore, that the date is also the completion of the tun count. Since a katun consists of 20 tuns, obviously a date ending a katun must also end a tun. It is as though we wrote "December 31, 1900, end of nineteen centuries, end of a year."

On Tikal 16 the first five glyph blocks (fig. 4,36) record: "6 Ahau 13 Muan, completion of the count of 14 katuns, the completion of the tun." There is a certain reverberant measure in the English translation, which echoes the majesty of the glyphs. In Yucatec the text may have run: *Uacil Ahau tu oxlahunte Muan, tz'ococ u xocol canlahunte katunob, u tz'ocol haab.* This, too, is not lacking in antiphonal melody.

Seven glyph blocks of Palenque Inscriptions Tablet (east) read: "Completion of a haab, 1 Ahau 8 Kayab, the seating of the tun, tenth katun, expiration of a half baktun" (fig. 4,37). The Yucatec equivalent may have been: *u tz'ococ haab, Hunil Ahau tu uaxacte Kayab, u cutal tun, u lahunte katunob, u hitz' xel baktun.* Here three glyphs would have conveyed all the information: "1 Ahau 8 Kayab, tenth katun."

Similarly the secondary series was often expanded to a length unnecessary for clarity, but perhaps contributing to euphony. The IS itself could in many cases have been replaced by the much shorter PE without raising any doubt as to the date recorded. That its numerous glyphs were patiently carved is, I think, good evidence that the Maya strove for a euphonious grandeur in their texts. The passage of time had for them a mystical beauty which called for beauty in recording it.

I often wish that I could summon some Maya priests from the shades to listen to the grandeur of our music. Their hearts would be uplifted by it. In the third movement of Beethoven's Fifth Symphony, to cite a single instance, they would hardly fail to recognize their own antiphonal poetry transmuted into melody beyond their mortal ken. A Maya, were he of the majestic period of the stelae or of the sixteenth-century eclipse, could have repeated with sincerity the words of Elihu, "For the ear trieth words, as the mouth tasteth meat." My belief is strong that the glyphic texts are words tried by the ear, and deemed worthy of perpetuity graven in stone.

SUBJECT MATTER OF HIEROGLYPHIC TEXTS

The subjects covered in Maya writings depend on the media in which they are contained. The inscribed monuments carry texts dealing with one group of subjects; the codices, for the most part, record information on different matters. Single sheets, none of which has survived, were probably used for recording data in yet other categories. For that reason it is advisable to discuss separately the two main groups, texts inscribed on monuments of the Initial Series Period, and writings on paper.

Inscribed Texts

In this book the words *inscribed* and *inscriptions* apply only to texts which were carved in low relief or incised in stone and wood, and serve to differentiate them from texts written in the codices.

With very rare exceptions the inscriptions deal with the passage of time, with particular reference to the end of the period which was approaching when each inscription was carved. As we have seen, the unending journey of time was of transcendental importance to the Maya; it was the main theme of their philosophy of life, but, because of its effect on human life, it was much more than the focal point of a cult of mysticism. The powers wielded by the succeeding rulers of the divisions of time affected life to its very roots: the ruler of one day was a beneficent deity who brought happiness and prosperity with him; the lord of another day was a malevolent power, whose passage was fraught with misery and evil.

The same subjection of man to the caprice of each god extended to that of each god of a year and each god of a katun. Years which were the burdens of Kan and Muluc (i.e. began with those days, and were under their influence) were favorable; those borne by Ix and Cauac were calamitous. A few katuns were ruled by benign day gods; one or two were affected by influences which were neither good nor bad; most were under the sway of malign powers. Naturally, the longer the period, the more important were its aspects.

Few prophets are over-positive in forecasting the future or in charting the path of divine action for many years to come; they generally provide some loophole of escape, some way of substituting gray for uncompromising black and white. From Landa's account of the ceremonies held in Yucatan for the incoming years we learn that the gods who bore the burdens of the years could be influenced for the better by appropriate ceremonies; it was possible to ease the woes of Ix and apply balm to the ills of Cauac. Maya philosophy was not a simple form of predestination, for many indirect influences allowed man some latitude. Evils could be ameliorated by some forms of propitiation, and doubtlessly the fate of each katun could also be bettered by appropriate action.

In the sixteenth century Maya culture was both mature and decadent. Formulae had been established for achieving certain results: so many offerings of food, so many grains of copal incense, would produce the desired result. In the earlier and more vigorous period of the inscriptions the priest-astronomers, I believe, dedicated much of their effort to an investigation of the complex influences that decided the aspect of the katun. Were it merely a question of the temperament of the ruling god, the problem would have been relatively simple, but it is a fair assumption that other factors, the positions of sun and moon and the wanderings of the planets, influenced the periods. Some of these may have been known; others were unknown equations. The investigation of these problems, I think, occupied the priest-astronomers, and the computations involved presumably form the subject matter of most inscriptions.

As an illustration, let us assume that we are Maya priests living at 9.15.10.0.0 (A.D. 741). In another ten tuns Katun 13 Ahau (9.17.0.0.0 13 Ahau 18 Cumku) will enter. It is necessary to prepare our calculations for the new katun. The god 13 Ahau is somewhat ill-disposed toward man. Are there factors which might alleviate the expected evils, or, alas, augment them? Calculations show that the day on which the katun will end will also be the occasion of a solar eclipse, but we do not know whether that eclipse will be visible or not. Our only recourse is to turn to our records to see whether a visible eclipse has ever occurred before, on a day 13 Ahau.

When the katun ends Venus will be at, or very close to, superior conjunction, and therefore invisible. The sun will rise on that day (13 Ahau 18 Cumku) at a point 20 risings north of the winter solstice, but so far as the true solar year is concerned, the situation is very different. Our most modern calculations show that at that date the sun will be 940 days behind our calendar, a loss accumulated by our failure to use leap days in the 3960 tuns that have elapsed since the last creation of the world at

13.0.0.0.0 4 Ahau 8 Cumku. Subtracting two years (730 days) from the sun's lag, we have a correction of 210 days to apply. Therefore, in weighing the various aspects of the katun ending, we must take into account that the day in the year of the last creation on which the sun was 20 risings north of the winter solstice was 8 Mol (210 days before 18 Cumku), and, contrariwise, the sun will now rise on 3 Zac at the same point at which it rose on 18 Cumku at 13.0.0.0.0 (3 Zac is 210 days after 18 Cumku).

These various possibilities give us material with which to gauge the factors which will have a bearing on the aspect of the coming katun. If we can find dates in the past which unite celestial and divine influences comparable to those which will occur at the end of the coming katun, and note what were their fortunes, we shall have data to check the effects of the various influences for good and evil which will shape the destiny of Katun 13 Ahau.

Such motives, I would hazard, governed the Maya priests. I further believe that the calculations they made to find precedents for the various combinations which would influence the end of a katun occupy the bulk of the inscriptions. That is to say they were using astronomy to develop laws of astrology, and combining the results with what they knew of the direct influences of the days themselves. It was a scientific approach, but the original premises were false. The CR dates in the inscriptions (p. 123) are, I think, for the most part those which reproduced conditions duplicating or related to those expected to obtain at the end of the katun. All the data which would throw light on the problem were examined, and the most pertinent incorporated in the texts.

I do not believe that historical events are recorded on the monuments. The almost complete absence of dates, other than period endings, common to two cities (there are only three such dates known) is, I believe, due to the almost limitless choice of dates in gathering information on the katun endings. A priest in one city, gauging the aspects of a katun ending, might put more emphasis on lunar influences, and be governed accordingly in his choice of dates; priests in other cities may have regarded solar influences as paramount, and chosen dates with that in mind. In that matter, too, there was room for divergences, for calculations as to the amount the Maya year was ahead of solar time varied from city to city. Furthermore, the correction might be applied in various ways, and at any time during the journey of the katun. Thus, in solar corrections alone there were perhaps a hundred dates which might have been used in connection with every katun ending. The choice would have been more restricted had there been complete agreement as to the aspects of every day, but that, in all probability, was one of the variables, as it certainly is among the present-day Maya. There must have been rather general agreement that such and such a day was lucky, and such and such a number lucky or unlucky, but the appraisal of the combination of the two may have varied from city to city, and perhaps from one individual to another within a city. Such divergences of opinion, although they may not have been great, would have affected the choice of pertinent dates.

A few texts deal with new formulae for reckoning the length of a lunation and for grouping moons, but I feel rather certain that celestial phenomena, such as eclipses, heliacal risings of Venus, sun at zenith, or equinoxes, were not recorded unless thay had some bearing on the end of the current period (p. 217).

A number of the undeciphered glyphs record doubtlessly the names of gods whose influences affected the calculations, and probably the ceremonies and offerings necessary to ameliorate those influences. Many glyphs, I think, will be found to correspond to set phrases, paralleling those in the katun prophecies of the books of Chilam Balam. Others, I believe, will prove alternative forms or variants reflecting choice of expression in the spoken word, just as we can choose among such words as "count," "reckon," "sum," and "calculate." I do not, therefore, look to the emergence of much directly factual material in the untranslated portions of the texts.

I have stressed what I believe to be the impersonal nature of the stelae records. It might be objected that some lintels and stelae may portray scenes of conquest and glorify the individual. For instance, Piedras Negras 12 carries a design representing a richly attired individual on the top of what is probably a small structure or conceivably a throne; two attendants and nine captives are grouped on the steps below. This has been identified as the commemoration of a conquest, but can we be sure that it is not a scene preceding some important ceremony, in which the captives are to play their dire parts as sacrificial victims? The number of the captives leads to the suspicion that they are being groomed to impersonate the nine lords of the underworld, and the fact that each one has been delineated with such care points to a rôle greater than that of the conquered in a triumphal procession. The attitude of the main personage is not that of an arrogant conqueror, but of a person intent on the scene being enacted beneath him.

One captive alone is regally dressed. Is it not as logical to suppose that he has been attired in the costume he is to wear in the ceremony (cf. the attirement scene on the Bonampak murals) as to assume that he is a captive of rank who has not been deprived of his jewelry. Soldiers the world over are much alike, and it is not, therefore, rash to argue that had he been a captive thus attired in battle, his beautiful necklace, earplugs, and headdress would have been stripped from him long before he got to his captors' base camp. On this thesis the other victims are waiting to be attired for their tragic rôles in the ceremony. There are, I submit, as good grounds for identifying this scene as ceremonial as for regarding it as one of conquest.

Again, Piedras Negras L 2 shows a richly clad individual behind whom stands an official, and before whom kneel six persons, also sumptuously dressed. All eight carry spears. This scene, too, has been identified as a representation of an historical event, but Morley (1937–38, 3:96–98) makes out a good case for the scene's having an astronomical connotation. He also shows that the somewhat similar scene on Piedras Negras L 4 may treat of astronomical or calendarial matters. It is, perhaps, not beside the point to note that two of these monuments, and perhaps the third, were dedicated to commemorate periods ending on the highly important 4 Ahau. As I have remarked, I am inclined to think that the choice of deity or subject to be sculptured on a monument was governed by the dates recorded. This is not the place to enter into a lengthy discussion of the matter, but as good a case may be made for such scenes' being ritualistic as for their being historical. It is noteworthy that there are no scenes of actual battle, such as one finds in the Mexican Period of Chichen Itza; it is the aftermath of battle with its ritualistic connotations which is presented.

WRITTEN CODICES

The subject matter of the three surviving codices has already been discussed (pp. 23–26). Madrid is a book of divination, crowded with information which would aid a priest in choosing days suitable for the sundry activities of everyday life; it is essentially the book of a priest catering to the requirements of the rank and file. Dresden is a mixture of simple divination and a compilation of astronomical data, doubtlessly used in the more important branches of that work—for matters of church and state— in contrast to the simple almanacs for everyday life. Paris appears to deal with the divinatory aspects of katuns and tuns, with the new-year ceremonies, and to a limited extent with manipulations of the 260-day almanac.

Codices recording history are said to have existed, but none has survived, unless there is some historical matter in those pages of Paris dealing with the sequences of tuns and katuns. The missing codices, one would expect, would have followed the general pattern of the historical codices of central Mexico, either of the type of Codex Nuttall or of the type of Codex Xolotl or the Codex of 1576. Much historical matter was, of course, the warp into which the prophecies were woven, and such books of prophecy undoubtedly existed in addition to the purely divinatory sections of Dresden.

Roys writes me that he seriously doubts that chronicles in the Mexican or European sense of the word existed in pre-Spanish Yucatan. He calls attention to the remarks of Fuensalida and Avendaño to the effect that at Tayasal prophecies and histories were the same thing, and that knowledge came from their Yucatecan experiences. He also notes the lack of postconquest chronicles in sixteenth-century Yucatan (the only exception being the short Xiu Chronicle, the historical elements of which are perhaps the result of European influence) in contrast to the comparative frequency of chronicles in Mexico and probably in the highlands of Guatemala. This comment refers, of course, to records other than those incorporated in the prophecies.

We can be reasonably sure that such matters as land maps and titles, and genealogical records were also written on paper, perhaps single large sheets rather than books, but none of these has survived. Probably a good deal of the information in these last categories, as well as that in the historical outlines and prophecies, was presented as pictures supplemented with glyphs or, perhaps, as in the divinatory almanacs, as glyphs supplemented with pictures. An attempt to decipher in broad outlines the general tenor of the divinatory almanacs in Dresden will be found in Chapters 11 and 12.

With the conclusion of this brief review of the general principles of Maya glyphic writing, let us pass to the details of the complex Maya calendar.

3

The Cycle of 260 Days

What hath this day deserved? What hath it done,
That it in golden letters should be set
Among the high tides in the calendar?
—SHAKESPEARE, *King John*

THROUGHOUT HISTORY man has ascribed favorable or malevolent powers to certain days. At different times and in varying places, the supposed influences of days have played a not inconsiderable part in the functioning of cultures. Nowhere did those influences attain the importance with which they were invested by the peoples of Middle America. There the life of the community and the acts of the individual were rigidly adjusted to the succession of days with their varying aspects. Each day belonged to a god who took a lively interest in his duties; happy and sorrowful days succeeded each other. The day ended; the officer of the day was relieved. The one next in charge might be of a very different nature to his outgoing comrade; the mood changed as abruptly as in a Tschaikowsky symphony.

The 20 days of the Maya calendar followed one another in unbroken succession, each bringing its charge of weal or woe. The dread jaguar god of the underworld was in command one day. As his powers were malign, the life of the community was partially paralyzed for the day and night he ruled; no important activity save hunting was undertaken. That alone would be a profitable occupation, because the wild animals were in the care of the jaguar god. Children born on that day were doomed to an existence of misery and misfortune. The following day was that of the maize god. Everything changed. As the youthful god of vegetation was kindly and well disposed toward man, one could face the day with a good heart, certain of the benevolence of that friendly god. Every prospect pleased: crops sown on that day would be bountiful; children born then would be rich; they would excel in crafts and wisdom. Two days later, the god of death ruled, and evil cloaked the land; misfortunes multiplied, vexations were rife. It was a day that would have tested Job; it did not try the patience of a Maya. He took it with good grace or resignation because the source of the misfortune was known and was inevitable; his cultural heritage had taught him that it is senseless to kick against the pricks when the god who administers them is firmly in the saddle.

Life passed in this pattern of sunshine and shade was not monotonous. It is not improbable that this strange semblance of predestination molded the Maya character, or was itself a manifestation of that character which was imbued with the insignificance of man's part in the universe. Other peoples of Middle America lived their lives under similar arrangements of shifting influences. Yet the system appears to have been less onerous among the Aztec, for example, because their days had ceased to be gods. Gods still influenced their lives, but their powers were less direct; they ruled the days which influenced life. Among the Maya the days themselves were very gods.

The most important element of the Maya calendar was the sequence of the 20 days with their attached numbers. The series of 20 names of days and the numbers 1 to 13 ran concurrently, repeating themselves in immutable sequence through all eternity.

The combination of number and day was a unit, and the one part was as meaningless without the other as a telephone number is without the name of the exchange. The Maya said "today is 13 Ahau"; they did not say "today is Ahau" or "the day 13." This very close relationship between the name and number of a day is illustrated in the Yucatecan language. For example the day 3 Imix is often written not *ox Imix*, which would mean 3 Imix, but *oxil Imix,* the termination *il* denoting a relationship with the word that follows, that is to say, "Three related to or belonging to Imix."

Although the Maya would not say "today is Ahau," they would pay attention to the fact that Ahau rules on that day, but he shared the rule with the attached number, and the luck of the day was a combination of the influences of the name and the attached number, that of the name outweighing that of the number, to judge by present-day practice in the Guatemalan highlands. Lincoln (1942, p. 106) reports that among the Ixil tallies of names and numbers are kept by separate priests who specialize in their respective counts. This statement, if correct, surely can mean no more than that the tally of the days was thus farmed out as a precaution against error, for as augural values for the numbers no longer survive among the Ixil, a priest in charge of numbers would have as his only specialized knowledge the ability to count from 1 to 13! Lincoln's account of the calendar nowhere bears out this idea of division, and there is no confirmatory information from students of any other group which retains the day count. All informants, however, agree in the greater importance of the name. This fact presumably accounts for day numbers having been lost among the Mam of Santiago Chimaltenango, although the day names survive (Wagley, 1941, p. 17). The same is true of the very late compilations of Nah and Tekax.

Since 13 and 20 have no common factor, it is obvious that the same combination of name and number will not recur until 260 days have elapsed. At each repetition of any name the attached number will be seven greater provided the sum is not in excess of 13; if the sum is greater than 13, that number has to be subtracted from it. The first day of the cycle was 1 Imix; accordingly, 20 days later Imix will repeat, but this time with the number 8 attached. At its next appearance the attached number will be 2 (8 + 7 = 15; 15 − 13 = 2), so that the sequence of numbers attached to a given day name will run 1, 8, 2, 9, 3, 10, 4, 11, 5, 12, 6, 13, 7.

Below is given a short section (65 days, the first quarter of the cycle) to illustrate the system. It will be noted how after 20 days the same Imix and the rest of the names repeat themselves, but the cycle of numbers has already completed one turn, and progressed seven spaces through the next turn. Now the number attached to Imix is 8, as explained above.

frame has a support consisting of three elements, although in a number of the earlier inscriptions this was dispensed with. A few glyphs which are not day signs appear at first glance to be within cartouches, but a closer examination will show that the frame is open at one point or another (e.g. the uinal frame open at the bottom).

There are very rare exceptions to this rule. Day signs on some of the very earliest inscriptions lack a fully developed cartouche (figs. 9,52; 10,48), and one or two at Chichen Itza, where there are distinct signs of archaisms in late inscriptions, also are without frames (figs. 7,44; 11,2,8).

In a number of early inscriptions, and some late ones at Chichen Itza, a peculiar element sometimes projects from the top of the cartouche or is placed above it (figs. 38,5,6; 42,2,4). Morley (1920, p. 69) has shown that this is a very early feature which soon disappears in the Central Area. Its survival at Chichen Itza is another example of the persistence of an archaism in that peripheral region. Except for this rare element, day signs never have affixes other than added elements such as the ti and "Ben-Ich" signs which modify the meaning (pp. 163, 202). Both personifications (head variants) and symbolic (geometric) variants of most day signs are known. In some cases (e.g. Imix, Ik, Kan) symbolic variants are much more numerous than head variants; in other cases (e.g. Chicchan, Cimi) the reverse is the case. There seems no reason to doubt that there existed both head and symbolic variants of all day signs, and, for that matter, probably of all glyphs, although in the

TABLE 2—SECTION OF 260-DAY CYCLE
(Read down left column and continue vertically with next to right)

1 Imix	1 Ix	1 Manik	1 Ahau	1 Ben
2 Ik	2 Men	2 Lamat	2 Imix	2 Ix
3 Akbal	3 Cib	3 Muluc	3 Ik	3 Men
4 Kan	4 Caban	4 Oc	4 Akbal	4 Cib
5 Chicchan	5 Etz'nab	5 Chuen	5 Kan	5 Caban
6 Cimi	6 Cauac	6 Eb	6 Chicchan	6 Etz'nab
7 Manik	7 Ahau	7 Ben	7 Cimi	7 Cauac
8 Lamat	8 Imix	8 Ix	8 Manik	8 Ahau
9 Muluc	9 Ik	9 Men	9 Lamat	9 Imix
10 Oc	10 Akbal	10 Cib	10 Muluc	10 Ik
11 Chuen	11 Kan	11 Caban	11 Oc	11 Akbal
12 Eb	12 Chicchan	12 Etz'nab	12 Chuen	12 Kan
13 Ben	13 Cimi	13 Cauac	13 Eb	13 Chicchan

The last (260th) day of the cycle is 13 Ahau, after which the whole almanac starts to repeat with 1 Imix.

GLYPHS FOR DAYS

In the texts of the Initial Series Period day signs are differentiated from most other glyphs by being enclosed in a frame or cartouche (figs. 6–11). Often this

case of some glyphs, both variants have not survived or have not as yet been recognized.

It is not necessary to describe the glyphs at this point. They will be discussed in reviewing the evidence as to the meanings of the day names. It should be noted that for the most part they bear little resemblance to their equivalents in the Aztec texts, although in some cases

TABLE 3—DAY NAMES IN VARIOUS MAYA LANGUAGES

Yucatec	Tzeltal or Tzotzil[4]	Chuh S. Mateo[10]	Jacalteca[24]	Ixil[30]	Quiche (1722)[35]	Quiche (Goubaud)[36]	Pokomchi[46]
Imix	Imox[5]	Imox	Imox[25]	Imux[31]	Imox	Imox	Mox
Ik	Ikh	Ic[11]	Ikh[26]	Ikh	Ikh	ikh	Ik
Akbal	Uotan	Woton[12]	Watan	Akbal	Akhbal	Akhabal[37]	Acabal[47]
Kan	Khanan	Cana[13]	Cana	Katch	Kat	Kat	Kat
Chicchan	Abakh	Abak	Abac[27]	Can	Can	Can	Can
Cimi	Tox[6]	Tox	Tox	Camel	Ceme	Came[38]	Cime[48]
Manik	Moxic	Ceh[14]	Che	Tche	Ceh	Cieh[39]	Kih[49]
Lamat	Lambat	Lambat	Khanil	Kanil	Khanil	Khanil[40]	Kanil
Muluc	Mulu[7]	Mulu[15]	Mulu	Tcho	Toh	Toh	Toh
Oc	Elab	Elab[16]	Elac	Tchii	Tzih	Tz'i[41]	Tzi
Chuen	Batz	Bats[17]	Batz	Batz	Batz	Batz[42]	Batz[50]
Eb	Euob	Ehub[18]	Euup	E	Ee	Eeh	Ih[51]
Ben[1]	Been	Been[19]	Ah	Ah	Ah	Ah	Ah
Ix[2]	Hix	Iix[20]	Hix[28]	Ihx	Iix	Ix[43]	Ix
Men	Tzikin[8]	Tzikin[21]	Tzicin	Tzicin	Tzicin	Tzicin	Tzicin
Cib	Chabin	Chabin	Chabin[29]	Ahmac[32]	Ahmac	Ahmac	Ahmac[52]
Caban	Chic[9]	Kixcab[22]	Noh	Noh	Noh	Noh	Noh
Etz'nab[3]	Chinax	Chinax	Chinax	Tihax[33]	Tihax	Tihax	Tihax[53]
Cauac	Cahokh	Chavuc[23]	Cak	Cauoc	Caoc	Cauac[44]	Cahuc[54]
Ahau	Aghual	Ahau	Ahau	Hunahpu[34]	Hunahpu	Hunahpu[45]	Ahpu[55]

[1]Also written Been.

[2]Hix or Hiix also used, and probably more correct, but Ix retained because of its long-established usage.

[3]Landa, who paid little attention to Maya spelling, has Eznab; Books of Chilam Balam generally use Etz'nab.

[4]This is the list given by Nuñez de la Vega (1702, p. 10) without any information as to provenance other than Chiapas. Presumably it is Tzeltal, but might be Tzotzil.

[5]The text has Imos in one place; Mox in another.

[6]Vicente Pineda (1888, p. 132) has Tog. He states that he corrects some of the sounds as he thought necessary, apparently to make them agree with Tzeltal words.

[7]Molo given as alternative. The Spaniards generally hesitated between o and u in translating a certain native sound.

[8]Vicente Pineda (1888) has Tzigquin.

[9]Vicente Pineda (1888) has Chigc.

[10]Termer (1930, pp. 385–86) gives four lists of Chuh names: that of San Mateo Ixtatan, here listed, a second from the same village collected by Gustav Kanter (here called Kanter I), one from Santa Eulalia, and another from El Quetzal. La Farge and Byers (1931, p. 224) reproduce the Kanter list in an improved form (here called Kanter II), apparently made to conform with the second list, and on p. 176 another list, presumably that of the Santa Eulalia Chuh who had migrated to Zapotal, Chiapas. Since the preparation of the above table La Farge (1947, p. 164) has published a list of day names from Santa Eulalia. This lies between the San Mateo and Jacaltenango lists, having features of both.

[11]Ikh in El Quetzal, Kanter II, and Zapotal lists; Ek in the Santa Eulalia list.

[12]Watan in El Quetzal, Zapotal, and Kanter II lists.

[13]Khana in Zapotal and Kanter II lists.

[14]Cheh in El Quetzal, Kanter I and II, Santa Eulalia, and El Quetzal lists; Che in Zapotal list.

[15]Molu in Santa Eulalia list.

[16]Elap in Zapotal and Kanter II lists.

[17]Variant forms Baatz, Batz, and Baats.

[18]Eu in Santa Eulalia list; Ihob in El Quetzal list; Ayu in Kanter I; Aiyup in Kanter II and Zapotal lists.

[19]Ben in Santa Eulalia list.

[20]Ix in all other lists.

[21]Tsicin in Kanter II and Zapotal lists.

[22]Kaah in El Quetzal list; Cuxkhap in Kanter II and Zapotal lists.

[23]Cak in Santa Eulalia list; Kahk in El Quetzal list; Chauoc in Kanter II and Zapotal lists.

[24]La Farge and Byers, 1931, pp. 167–68. Burkitt (1930–31) gives the day names of Saloma, supposedly Jacalteca-speaking. These vary a little from the La Farge and Byers list. Iac, Cheh, Elap, and Yup replace Ikh, Che, Elac, and Euup, but, more

important, Saloma follows Chuh in using Lambat, Ben, and Kixcap, although it agrees with Jacalteca and Santa Eulalia in the employment of Cak. Thus, it is very similar to the Chuh of Santa Eulalia, as is to be expected from its geographical position.

[25]Or Imux.

[26]Or Ik.

[27]Or Aba or Abax, or Apac.

[28]Or Ix.

[29]Or Chapin.

[30]Lincoln, 1942, pp. 107–09. Burkitt (1930–31) also gives some Ixil day names.

[31]Or Ikabal.

[32]Burkitt gives Aama for Nebaj.

[33]Or Kiuitz.

[34]Or Kitix. Burkitt gives Pu for Chajul.

[35]Quiche calendar, 1722. Ximenez, 1929–31, bk. 1, ch. 36, differs in giving Balam in place of Iix, and Hunhapu which is probably a copyist error for Hunahpu. He has Camey as in modern Quiche. The Ximenez list is a few years earlier than the calendar of 1722. Cakchiquel day names, as given in the Annals of the Cakchiquels (Brinton, 1885), agree well with the list of 1722, but have the variants of Khanel, Tzi, and Ey. The day Ix does not appear in the list.

[36]Goubaud, 1935. Other lists from Momostenango are published in Burkitt (1930–31) and Lothrop (1930). Except for minor variations in spelling the Burkitt names are the same as those given by Goubaud, except that he gives the last day as Ahpu. Lothrop's list is also in agreement when the unusual German spelling is discounted. Another Quiche list is published by Sapper, 1925. This agrees with the others except as noted. Yet another list of Quiche days was written by Hernandez Spina (Bunting, 1932) in 1854. This is from the town of Santa Catalina Ixtlauacan, 15 km. south of Totonicapan. This, too, conforms to the pattern save that Bacbal resembles the Tzutuhil form rather than the Quiche Akhbal. Quiche day names from Santa Maria Chiquimula are published by Lincoln (1942, p. 107). These differ from the Goubaud list only in orthography and in having Camel and Cauoc for Came and Cauac.

Tzutuhil day names have been collected at San Pedro Laguna by Rosales, and a transcription was sent me by Tax. They do not differ markedly from Goubaud's Quiche list. Differences are noted in footnotes.

[37]Santa Catalina has Bacbal; the Tzutuhil name is P'akhp'al.

[38]The Tzutuhil day is C-he'mel; Santa Maria gives Camel.

[39]C-heh in Tzutuhil; Cikh in Sapper.

[40]Kha'nel in Tzutuhil.

[41]Tis in Sapper. A misprint?

(e.g. Cimi and the head variant of Imix) both subject and general treatment are the same. The resemblance to Zapotec glyphs is also very scant. Perhaps future discoveries will bring to light the 20 day glyphs of the La Venta culture, and they might well prove closer to the Maya signs.

DAY NAMES

The names given above are those which were in use in Yucatan at the time of the Spanish conquest. These are the terms which are invariably used in all discussions of the Maya calendar because they were the first Maya names of days brought to the attention of the modern world, first by Pio Perez (1843) and later by Brasseur de Bourbourg, in his edition of Landa's *Relación de las cosas de Yucatan.* I retain Etz'nab, rather than Landa's Eznab, because it is so used in the books of Chilam Balam.

Lists of day names for various groups are given in Table 3. In Spanish versions I have converted *j* to *h,* and *qu* before *e* or *i* to *c* or *k,* and *gh* to *kh.* The various transcribers of the day names have had difficulty in distinguishing between *k* simple, aspirated, or with glottal stop. The Ixil list I have altered to conform to what appear to have been the current pronunciations, for, as I remarked in the introduction to the paper in which the list was published, the author had not evolved a clear-cut system of transcription when death left his material unfinished. The Pokomchi list of Narciso also fails to differentiate between *k* simple, glottalized, and aspirated. I have tried to make these sounds conform to those of neighboring peoples so far as the glottal stop is concerned, but have not added aspirates. This is somewhat a case of the blind leading the blind since I myself have no linguistic training and a poor ear for sound.

In addition to those listed and the Cakchiquel and

Tzutuhil series referred to in the footnotes, the 20 day names are still current among two other branches of the highland Maya according to Burkitt (1930–31), who gives variant forms of sundry day names as used by the Mam and the Aguacatec, noting, however, that in all essentials these lists do not differ from those of other towns. He records Imix as the form of Imix current among the Mam, and gives Akbal as the Aguatec form of the third day. Wagley (1941, p. 17.) gives the year bearers at the Mam village of Santiago Chimaltenango as Ik, Cheh, Ek, Noh, and also notes the days Imix and Kan.

MEANINGS OF DAY NAMES

In the lengthy and, I fear, involved discussion of the 20 days, I shall try to uncover the identity of each one, or rather of the god which each glyph represents and which its corresponding names once recalled, for we seek not animals or natural objects but divine beings. The days are alive; they are personified powers, to whom the Maya address their devotions, and their influences pervade every activity and every walk of life; they are, in truth, very gods. I believe, not without evidence, that this was not a gradual process of deification, but that the days were always held to be divine because from the very beginning each day was named after the god who ruled it; days did not represent the abstract ideas of darkness, death, and storm, but gods who were closely connected therewith or had dominion over them.

The concepts behind each day may be found by reviewing its sundry names in the various languages, particularly in Aztec, by studying its auguries, as preserved in the books of Chilam Balam and among the present-day Maya of the Guatemalan highlands, and by examining its glyphic representations.

As previous students have done, we shall make the assumption, for which there is ample support, that Maya and Mexican glyphs have the same ancestors, and that, therefore, a Maya day is probably related in meaning to the Aztec day in the corresponding position in the series. This assumption will not always hold good, for evolution and mutations in the course of a score of centuries have affected glyphs in both almanacs, but in most cases it can be demonstrated that the same idea underlies the day in both series. The Maya days are entities in an esoteric count, veiled in symbolism and mythological anecdote; the Aztec days are prosaic and largely secularized, in keeping with the Aztec tendency to call a spade a spade. Maya day glyphs are often so conventionalized that the object they represent can not be identified, and a goodly proportion of their names are meaningless, for they have been corrupted or are now obsolete; Aztec glyphs are straightforward pic-

---

[42]P'atz' in Tzutuhil.

[43]Itz in Sapper; Balam in Ximenez.

[44]Ca'uok in Tzutuhil. Sapper gives Canyoc, perhaps a *u* in original manuscript misread as *n.* Santa Maria has Cauoc.

[45]Ahpup' in Tzutuhil; Burkitt has Ahpu.

[46]Santa Cruz Verapaz (Goubaud, Rosales, and Tax, 1947, pp. 149, 151). The Narciso list from San Cristobal (Gates, 1932a) has variations from this noted below.

[47]Narciso gives Nakaual, and the second Santa Cruz list has Abalh.

[48]Narciso gives Cemeh.

[49]Second Santa Cruz list gives Ceh; Narciso has Cieh.

[50]Narciso writes Uatz.

[51]Narciso gives Eh.

[52]First Santa Cruz list is written Hamac.

[53]This day name is omitted in the second Santa Cruz list. In place of it appears Cauom, to which the meaning "hard" is assigned.

[54]Narciso has Cohoc; the second Santa Cruz list has Kohok.

[55]Narciso writes this Ahpuhm; the second Santa Cruz list gives Ahpuh.

tures of such things as eagle, dog, lizard, skull, and reed, and the names correspond to the pictures—plain Jane and no nonsense. Naturally, this complete lack of subtlety in the Aztec list is of considerable help in identifying the more recondite Maya glyphs and names.

The names of the Maya days, as recorded from the sixteenth century to the present, vary from group to group, and, as just noted, they do not always lend themselves to straightforward translation. Some names are unfathomable; others have meanings which are not related to the glyphs, as, for example the day name Eb, which in Yucatec signifies stairway, although there is no allusion to this in the glyph. A possible explanation of this partial lack of correspondence might lie in borrowing of names from some non-Maya language, such as Zoque, for foreign and, in time, uncomprehended words would more readily be corrupted. It has been rather widely assumed that the cycles of 260 days was a Maya invention, and that may well be the case, but no good evidence for the assumption has ever been produced. Nevertheless, I do not deem it likely that many Maya day names are derived from foreign words; rather I should expect them to have originated from esoteric and mythological sources. In time, the meanings of some of these would be lost and garbling would result. Thus, we find Lambat used by one group, Lamat by another, Muluc in Yucatan, Mulu in the northwestern corner of Guatemala. It is a fair guess that the latter of each pair is a corruption of the former, which in turn may have changed from the archaic form of the name, and there is evidence that the process of adulterating the names still continues. La Farge and Byers (1931, pp. 163, 167) cite four variants of one day at Jacaltenango alone—Aba, Abac, Apac, and Abax—while the Chuh and Chiapas equivalents are Abak and Abakh. There can be little doubt that all six sounds derive from a single original, the process being accelerated by the loss of the original meaning (probably that of some mythological serpent).

In discussing the auguries of the days, I shall not list every one lest this chapter become a volume; I shall note only those that fit the general picture. Readers who do not approve of this subjective approach can work the slag heaps for ore I may have discarded. Such a treatment is, I think, necessary because most of the old associations have been lost, and fortuitous sonic resemblances apparently have given rise to auguries of recent invention. Such spurious accretions must be ignored. For example, the forms of the eighth day, Khanil and Kanil, current in the Guatemalan highlands probably derive from a word resembling kanal, "star" or "planet," which survives in Tzotzil as *canal* (*ḳanal?*). However, the present names of this day resemble local terms for ripe maize, and the

auguries are now based on that resemblance, although there is no reason to believe that the day originally had anything to do with maize. It is somewhat as though we had forgotten the origin of our name of March and, supposing that it was connected with marching, came to believe it was a month favorable for outings or was the month of marching ants.

In discussing names and auguries of the days I shall cite the sources for each group only once, since references to all days are within a page or two of one another. For instance, all material on the Ixil calendar will be found at the place, or within two or three pages of it, in Lincoln's paper first cited.

The personifed glyphs are surely conventionalized portraits of the gods who ruled the days they represent; the symbolic forms supposedly picture some attribute of the god in question. Thus the glyph of the day Manik, which is a hand, presumably does not carry any direct connotation of grasping or taking or passing, but must be regarded as a once recognizable attribute of the god who ruled that day. With our deficient knowledge of the esoteric features and the symbolic values of Maya religion, we are handicapped in recognizing some of those associations; the reduction of such symbols to a few lines, forming unidentifiable designs, greatens our task.

Many writers have tried their hands at interpreting the day names, although, in most cases, with indifferent success; far and away the best discussions are by Seler (1902–23, 1:449–503) and Barrera Vasquez (1943). The latter author, in assembling and translating the various passages in the books of Chilam Balam that deal with the influences and divinatory aspects of the days, has made available a mass of vital information. The best and far the fullest of these passages is the first list in the Kaua manuscript which gives, in some detail, the aspects of the day names and the animals or deities accompanying them. The identities of the animals or beings associated with the days are powerful aids in tracing origins of day names; they give new leads and confirm past surmises.

Let us, then, follow the tracks of the marching days, scanning their footprints and other clues to their identities, and endeavoring not to stray on false trails, or be deflected where signs of passage are but faint.

Imix, Imox, Imux, Mox (fig. 6,*1–17*). It is quite clear that this day symbolizes the earth and, by extension, abundance. The Ixil attach the meanings of world or earth to it (Lincoln, 1942, p. 109); at Santa Eulalia, in Chaneabal territory, Imux is the holy earth (La Farge, 1947, p. 172); the Jacalteca connect Imox with weaving (La Farge and Byers, 1931, p. 165), but weaving is the special function of the moon and earth goddess (p. 83). For the Mam of Santiago Chimaltenango this is a day most favorable for maize (Wagley, 1941, p. 34), and the same is true of Yucatan, for the Kaua I list gives maize dough, *"iximil uah,"* as its symbol (Barrera Vasquez, 1943, p. 15). Schultze Jena (1946, p. 34) remarks that the Quiche of Chichicastenango connect Imox with *Mo'x,* a name for the earth god, although he believes that this association has arisen as a result of a fortuitous resemblance between the two names. In view of the Ixil and Santa Eulalia ideas, I feel that Schultze Jena must be mistaken, and that this is not a case of sonic convergence but, rather, that the two terms have a single origin, and that Imox, or some term close to it, was the old name of the earth god, surviving only in Quiche as Mo'x. In fact, one of the forms given for this day by Nuñez de la Vega is Mox, and that is the way this name appears in all Pokomchi lists.

Cipactli, the equivalent day of the Mexican plateau, also symbolizes the earth, for Cipactli is the earth crocodile, whose gnarled and spiny back forms the crust of the earth. Cipactli seems to mean "spiny creature," and the term *cipaque* yet survives in parts of Mexico to denote the crocodile or perhaps the alligator. In Mexican codices the day glyph is usually represented as the head of a crocodile with upper jaw, eye, and snout, the lower jaw being omitted; sometimes the whole body, replete with spines, is shown (Beyer, 1921b). The Zapotec name for this day also signifies crocodile (Seler, 1904, p. 38). According to Mexican belief this great crocodile, whose back was the earth, floated in a great pond. There is evidence in Maya art that the same concept obtained among the Maya.

Nuñez de la Vega (1702, p. 9) remarks that in Chiapas the worship of the day Imox "alludes to the ceiba, which is a tree which they have in all their town-plazas, in view of the town hall. Below them they elect their alcaldes, and they cense them with braziers. They hold it for very certain with regard to the roots of that ceiba that it was through them their lineage came." This last sentence must surely mean that the ancestors of the group (Tzeltal or Tzotzil) emerged from mother earth through the roots of the ceiba.

At first thought, this connection with the ceiba would appear to be in conflict with the association with the earth, and the maize it produces. Actually, the two concepts are allied because of the part played by the ceiba in Maya religion, for the ceiba was a symbol both of abundance and of mother earth.

In Yucatan there exists a belief that a giant ceiba tree, growing in the exact center of the earth, rears its branches through the successive heavens or layers of heaven to the highest. The spirits of the dead ascend by it to that highest heaven (Tozzer, 1907, p. 154). The Lacandon believe that the sun enters the underworld each evening by climbing down the trunks of trees and through the roots (Soustelle, 1936, p. 188). The trees are not identified but, in view of the above quotations, presumably they are ceibas, called in Yucatec *yaxche,* "first tree" or "green tree" (*Ceiba pentandra* (L.) Gaertn.).

Landa states that one of the abodes of the dead was a land of milk and honey, where there was no lack of delectable food, and where the souls of the dead rested in the shade of a giant *yaxche.* This description puts one in mind of Xochitlan, "the land of flowers," one of the abodes of the Aztec dead, situated in the skies, yet the construction of Landa's next sentence suggests that this Maya paradise was not in the sky, but on or under the earth, for, after describing it, he turns to Metnal, the Maya underworld, and says that it is "lower than the former." In Chumayel (p. 44) there is mention of the *yaxcheel cab,* "the first tree of the world," which was rooted fast, and Roys (1933, p. 102) notes that the Itza of Tayasal believed that the *yaxcheel cab* was the first tree of the world, from which the first man of the world ate. This, in turn, reminds one of a legend of the Mopan Maya that after the creation man first obtained all the produce of cultivated plants by cutting down a mamey tree (Thompson, 1930, p. 135). Probably my informant, through ignorance, had substituted mamey for *yaxche.* In the account of the creation in Chumayel (p. 1) four trees, each with its appropriate directional color (red, white, black, and yellow), are set at the four sides of the world, and the context indicates that with them were placed the produce of the land, such as maize and beans. These trees are called *Imix yaxche.* It is also worth noting that in the Yucatec village of Chan Kom little girls are warned not to play with the fruits of the *yaxche* or *ch'oy* trees, as such action will cause their breasts to grow too large (Redfield and Villa, 1934, p. 207). This superstition would seem to be referable to the qualities of abundance possessed by the *yaxche,* rather than to the category of sympathetic magic, in which like produces like, for the fruit of the ceiba is not mammiform. It should also be realized that throughout the Maya area the ceiba is a holy tree.

From the above quotations we learn that the *yaxche* is the tree of abundance; that it was set up at the time of the creation, in the center of the earth or (and?) at the four sides, providing the first man with food; that it serves as a path from one celestial or terrestrial layer to another; and that it is prominent in the land of abundance, beneath the earth, where the dead repose. It is clear that such concepts are in no wise alien to those of the earth, the earth monster, and abundance of maize with which Imix is allied in the rituals of other Maya groups; the concepts do not conflict, they supplement one another.

The Imix glyph is used in a noncalendarial sense in many passages in the codices and on the monuments (fig. 40). It is frequently compounded with a Kan symbol, and this dual glyph is frequently associated with offerings of food (fig. 43,46–48). Gates (1931, p. 19) notes that there are nearly 200 examples of the Kan-Imix compound in the codices, and suggests that it signifies food and drink. Kan certainly represents the ripe maize (p. 75), but, by extension, it covers food in general (cf. uah, "bread," used also to signify food and abundance, and our own "Give us this day our daily bread"), but I think that the discussion has shown that Imix symbolizes abundance, and the compound accordingly signifies abundance of maize or food in general, and is probably the glyphic form of the augury for Imix as given in Kaua I.

The symbolic form is usually favored in representations of the Imix glyph, but there is one personified form of the day sign at Piedras Negras (fig. 6,8), and another on Tzendales 1, although only a drawing of this exists. There are, too, several personified Imix glyphs used in a noncalendarial sense (fig. 40,1–4). All show the head of a saurian or ophidian monster with a long pendulous nose and usually without a lower jaw, or with a jawbone replacing the lower jaw, and with the Imix glyph or the flattened u (p. 278) as his headdress, from which vegetation usually sprouts (fig. 12,1,2,4). This deity is an actor with a large part on the stage of Maya art. Commonly water lily plants or maize vegetation emerge from his head (fig. 12,1,4,8; Tablets of Cross and Foliated Cross, Palenque, and Maudslay, 1889–1902, IV, pl. 93). His body occasionally carries celestial symbols, but that is not a serious objection to recognizing him as an aquatic god of the surface of the earth because denizens of the underworld passed to and from the sky, and were as at home in one place as the other (p. 13). Imix glyphs are associated with the two subsidiary monsters of the Tablet of the Foliated Cross, Palenque. In one case Imix is set in an eye of the monster; in the other case on the shell from which what may be the long-nosed god emerges with the maize plant growing from his hand (fig. 21,8). The shell itself is a symbol of the interior of the earth, and is worn by many deities, Aztec and Maya, connected with the earth and its interior (p. 133). This same deity sometimes has the number 7, also a symbol of the earth (p. 278; fig. 12,2), before his face.

The jawbone and other symbols of death which this earth monster usually displays denote his connection with the interior of the earth, the abode of the god of death; the vegetation, particularly maize plants and lilies (they are edible), which sprout from his body, bear witness to the fact that he forms the surface of the earth, and is the symbol of abundance, and that he floats in a great pond, for in the Peninsula of Yucatan small lakes and backwaters are often covered with a mantle of lily pads, liberally sprinkled with white flowers. Crocodiles love such patches of water where the stream flows sluggishly or there is no current at all. I myself have journeyed through mile after mile of the upper reaches of the New River in British Honduras, where the river broadens into long wide lagoons, and there is only a narrow channel free of water lilies, along which the dugouts of the Maya glide and the launch of the Belize Estate and Produce Company chugs its noisy way. It is truly a moving sight to see the water lily pads swaying gently in one's wake.

This Imix monster, therefore, is the earth dragon, the exact counterpart of Cipactli, even, at times, to the absence of a lower jaw. He symbolizes the earth and the abundance it brings forth.

Presumably because the great earth crocodile floats in a vast pond beneath its coverlet of water lilies, that plant became a common attribute of the earth crocodile in particular, and of all terrestrial and subterrestrial gods in general. Water lilies are attached to the paws of the great crocodile which sprawls across Altar T, Copan (Maudslay, 1889–1902, I, pl. 95); water lilies grow from the head of this saurian monster (fig. 12,4,8; Spinden, 1913, fig. 79; Yde, 1938, fig. 24; Maudslay, 1889–1902, IV, pl. 93), or are attached to the jaguar, another denizen of the interior of the earth (fig. 12,12,14,15: Spinden, 1913, figs. 101, 185). On the Madrid slab (Lothrop, 1929, pl. 1a) the personage is seated on the head of the Imix monster, with the Imix glyph set in his headdress, and holds in his hand the flower and leaf of a water lily. Furthermore, water lilies may be set as pendants in the earplugs of deities, such as the god of death, who are connected with the surface or interior of the earth, or are attached to the body of a terrestrial serpent (fig. 28,15).

In view of this intimate connection of the Imix monster with the water lily, we can be reasonably certain that the symbolic form of the Imix glyph (fig. 6,1–7,9–17), with its large circle surrounded by smaller dots, and with slightly curving lines at the bottom, represents the water lily. As can be seen by comparison with the drawing (fig. 12,4), the glyph is a perfect reproduction of the somewhat stylized flower of the water lily which emerges from the head of the earth monster of House D of the Palace, Palenque. Other illustrations of water lilies, often with fish nibbling at them, are shown on the same figure. The flower of the water lily presumably was chosen as the symbolic form of Imix, partly to avoid confusion with other reptilian monsters, but, perhaps also because, owing to its food value for man, fish, and bird, it signified abundance, and at the same time kept before everyone's eyes the aquatic nature of the earth monster.

I know of only one reference to the water lily (*naab*) in Maya mythology. In the account of the creation in Tizimin, page 21, there is a passage tentatively translated by Roys and myself as "Then sprouted the red deep calyx, the white deep calyx, the black deep calyx, and the yellow deep calyx, the water lily face upward, the water lily that sways [on the surface of the water], the budding water lily."

On the recently discovered murals at Bonampak, Chiapas, several impersonators of gods of the earth, including the old god, the Mam, with the tun sign under his arm instead of on his head, and the crocodile monster, are assembled for a dance. Everyone of them is lavishly decorated with water lilies, naturalistically represented as handsome white blossoms. *Naab* is also the palm of the hand, and it is possible the lily got its name from the resemblance of a lily pad to the palm of the hand.

Imix, therefore, was the earth monster, the crocodile, whose back formed the surface of the earth; the water lily was probably his symbolic form; abundance was his aspect, and the earth his domain. It is surely not chance that the first day of the series belongs to the provident, bountiful earth, object of the deep love of all Maya, be they of the mountains or the plains, the uplands or the forest.

Ik, Ikh (fig. 6,*18–34*). Almost all sources agree that the name of this day means wind. It directly corresponds to the Aztec Eecatl, who was the wind god. The T-shaped sign, which is the only element in the glyph, is also prominent in the name glyph of Schellhas' God B (fig. 12,*11*). The gods of this group, however, are not primarily wind gods but deities of rain, perhaps the Itzamnas, the celestial dragons who sent the rain, but more probably the Chacs, closely allied gods of rain, thunder, and lightning.

Gates has pointed out that this glyph must be considered to be not a personal name but an appellative because it is sometimes used with other gods and sometimes occurs where God B is not pictured. Ik and the equivalent Ikh of the highlands mean not only wind but breath and by extension life itself. The name glyph then might have a meaning, such as "giver of life," which would be applied also to other gods.

The Ik sign itself appears to have the meaning of life. For instance on Madrid 28, which deals with the germination and growth of the maize crop, the young maize god is pictured several times. Twice he carries the kan (seed corn) sign, thrice the Ik sign. The latter must refer to germination or to the life-giving powers of the food in his care. The lower halves of Madrid 97 and 98 are occupied

by two divinatory almanacs of 260 days. The eight gods associated with the various subdivisions are for the most part the maize god and God B. Each one holds in his hand an Ik sign from which a plant, probably of maize, is growing (fig. 12,*9*). Here again, the Ik must carry the idea of germination, of coming to life. Maize plants growing from an Ik sign also appear on stelae (fig. 12,*10*).

In the Kaua divinatory list the winds are associated with Ik, and the tree connected with the day is the frangipani (the plumeria). The plumeria symbolizes fruitfulness, and is also found as the augural of Imix, but that day, as we have just seen, has the secondary value of abundance and fertility.

The day sign Ik, therefore, represents Schellhas' God B, god of rain in particular, and of life, germination, and fruitfulness in general because these are dependent on rain. Whether God B was also a god of wind is uncertain. The rains are so closely connected with the winds that it is possible that the latter, too, were once under the dominion of the God B, although in the belief of the present-day Maya of Yucatan the wind gods are separate and rather unimportant.

Akbal, Akabal, Uotan, Watan (fig. 6,*35–50*). The Ixil and Quiche associated this day with night. Akbal is given in western Chol as the word for night, its equivalents in Chaneabal, Tzeltal, Jacalteca, and Yocotan are *acual, akahbal, a'balil* and *akhup;* in Yucatec and eastern Chol it is *akab.* The equivalent Zapotec day means night; the Aztec, house. In view of these close resemblances and of Quiche and Ixil associations, there can be no doubt that these names mean night or darkness. The first Kaua list of auguries for the days gives Yalam as the animal of the day. *Yalam* means the young of animals in general, and a small deer in particular. In view of the relationships which will be brought out, the meaning of young animals in general fits quite well, although it is possible that *balam* (jaguar) has been miscopied.

Uotan or Watan, which replaces Akbal in the Chuh, Jacalteca, Santa Eulalia, and supposedly Tzeltal lists, is said by Nuñez de la Vega to have been the tribal ancestor who divided the land among the people. He put tapirs (mantles? *dantas* misreading of *mantas?*) and a great treasure of hieroglyphic material and jades in a dark house which he formed by blowing. This house was identified with a cave near Huehuetan, on the Pacific coast of Chiapas. Uotan was much venerated and in some provinces was considered to be the heart of the people (or towns). He was the lord of the hollow wooden drum, the *teponaztle* or *tunkul.*

Brinton (1882b, p. 217) and Seler (1902–23, 1:458) both consider that Uotan means the heart, just as a deity in the Popol Vul is called "The heart of heaven." Seler

(1904–09, p. 235), furthermore, considers that he is the Maya equivalent of the Mexican god Tepeyollotl, the eighth of the nine lords of the nights, and the god of the day Calli. There seems no reason to doubt this identification.

Tepeyollotl, according to commentators of Codex Telleriano-Remensis, was the echo, and the lord of animals; his name means "heart of the mountain." In the various codices he is invariably depicted in association with a temple, which in one case has its façade shaped as the open jaws of the earth monster. He usually has features which suggest the jaguar, and his ornament is the conch shell; in some cases he is merged with Tezcatlipoca. Seler considers him to be a god of caves and of the interior of the earth who was regarded as a jaguar. He is probably a manifestation of Tecciztecatl, the earth god. The conch shell (p. 133) confirms his terrestrial origin, apparent in his name; the association with the echo suggests a connection with Uotan who was god of the wooden drum, the *teponaztle,* for deep rhythm emerging from its cavity carried for leagues. Furthermore, both gods were associated with the third of the sequence of 20 days. Night and blackness have a natural affinity with the interior of the earth.

The present-day Kekchi Maya believe in a number of earth deities, the Tzultacah (Mountain-Valley) who inhabit the interior of the earth, frequenting deep caves, and who are often worshipped in caves. When they stir they cause earthquakes. They are lords of the animals, like Tepeyollotl, and the sounds of the thunder echoing in the hills are their voices talking among themselves (Sapper, 1897, p. 272; Burkitt, 1918, p. 285). They have an association with the tapir, according to verbal information of Wirsing.

La Farge and Byers (1931, p. 222) record a Chuh prayer, addressed to "my father Day-Night . . . under the hills, under the woods, under the cliffs, under the lakes," again associating night and darkness with the interior of the earth. The Lacandon have a belief that the god of the underworld, Cisin, has a number of jaguars under his control, and eventually they will end the world by eating the sun (Cline, 1944). That the jaguar symbolized night and the underworld for the Maya is, I think, obvious from the fact that the burden of the lord of the night in the full-figure glyphs of Copan D (fig. 60) is a roll of jaguar skin. The burden of the lord of the night is, of course, the night itself, since it was during the hours of darkness that he ruled. This roll of jaguar skin is Glyph F (p. 212).

Thus in Mexico the lord of the third day was an anthropomorphized jaguar with attributes of the earth and a connection with the earth deity. His name meant "the heart of the mountain," and the echo was associated with him, presumably because echoes generally are produced where cliffs and caves abound. He was lord of animals. The jaguar symbolized for the Mexicans both night and the earth (Beyer, 1921a, p. 43).

The third day in the Maya series is the day of darkness or night. In Chiapas and adjacent areas this is the day of Uotan, "the heart of the people," lord of the drum (with consequential connection with the echo?), who was the owner of a treasure stored in a dark house, identified with a cave. A Chuh prayer is addressed to a deity Day-Night who lives under the ground. Uotan had tapirs to guard his treasure; the Kekchi earth gods, who live under the earth and whose speech is the echoing thunder, have an unspecified association with tapirs and are the lords of the wild animals. The day Akbal is related with young animals. These tenuous connections, taken together, establish beyond much doubt a relationship between Uotan and the earth gods of the Kekchi and Chuh. On the other hand, the jaguars are closely connected with the earth in Lacandon tradition and in Maya art, for the jaguar god is often adorned with water lilies, a symbol of the earth. Furthermore, as we have noted, the jaguar's skin represents the night on Copan D.

There can be little doubt that the two groups of concepts are identical, and that the Maya god of the third day was the jaguar god of the dark interior of the earth. I think that *yalam,* given in the Kaua list as the augury of this day, may be a faulty transcription of *balam* (jaguar), although, as the gods of the earth are also guardians of the animals (Thompson, 1930, pp. 58, 142), *yalam* would also fit.

The Akbal glyph consists of looped lines around hooks above an undulating line formed of three connected curves. The upper part of the glyph is a fairly common Maya infix with animal glyphs. It is to be seen at the tops of heads representing the months Xul and Zotz' in Dresden (fig. 16,42–44,62,63) and with various representations of animals, usually dogs (fig. 42,76), on the monuments. As the head of the centipede, it is a prefix to the moon glyph when used as part of the name of God D, and on two occasions forms the headdress of deities connected with death. Zotz', the leaf-nosed bat, is a deity of the underworld, and the dog, because of its duty of conducting the dead to their last resting place in the nether regions, has a similar association. The moon also is a deity of the earth. It is, therefore, possible that this symbol represents the interior of the earth. It is noteworthy that the jaguar glyph sometimes has a shield with the Akbal glyph (fig. 46,10,12,16).

The undulating line has been explained by Beyer (1928a) as a section of the conventionalized body of a snake, the looped lines representing the vertical scales. He considers this to be the feathered serpent, to which he attributes a nocturnal symbolism. It would seem better to regard this sign rather as a conventionalization of the ventral scales of the earth monster. Both elements, then, would represent the interior of the earth, for as the back of the terrestrial crocodile is the surface of the earth, so the under side of that monster must correspond to the interior of the earth, but the identification is highly speculative.

Kan, Cana, Kat (fig. 6,51–68). The first list of the Kaua augury supplies the key to this day, for with the second repetition of Kan is the sentence *u yumil ixim,* "the lord of the maize grain." *Kan* in Yucatec means cord and any netted cord and also yellow and, by extension, ripe. The word signifies ripe also in Kekchi (Wirsing), and the same meaning is given to *Kanaan* in Manche Chol; *kun* is yellow and *kunix* ripe in Palencano, which frequently substitutes *u* for *a*. There can be no question that the Kan sign represents grains of maize since young maize plants are frequently depicted in the codices issuing from a Kan sign, and not infrequently a young maize plant, growing from a Kan sign, forms the headdress of the maize god and other deities (figs. 13,1; 20,14; 63,3). As noted (p. 48), Kan signs frequently appear in the codices with offerings of food, and the word seems to have the extended meaning of food in general, corresponding in that respect to the English "our daily bread."

There is also a Yucatec word *kanan,* "a thing which is precious and highly esteemed," which might also supply a connection with maize, since that was the most precious possession of the Maya. Indeed it is called *"gracia"* by the present-day Maya of Yucatan, and "holy maize" by some highland Maya groups (La Farge, 1947, p. 77; Stadelman, 1940, p. 123).

The equivalent of Kan on the Mexican plateau was Cuetzpalin, "lizard," a symbol of abundance, but at Meztitlan, on the border of the Huaxtec country, the day was Xilotl, "the green ear of corn." There is not the slightest doubt, therefore, that Kan is the ripe grains of maize, symbol of the young maize god.

The symbolic form of the Kan glyph is a geometric design, too conventionalized to be any longer recognizable. The only personifications of the day sign are the poorly executed example on the Uaxactun mural (fig. 6,52), and one at Chinikiha (fig. 49,4, last glyph). The latter is rather weathered, but may have been the youthful maize god. There is also a personified form of the zero-Kan compound (Copan B, A8), which shows a youthful personage who might well be the maize god (fig. 11,51).

Chicchan, Abac, Can (fig. 7,1–17). Chicchan is the Chorti name for an important group of ophidian deities,

who may take the form of giant snakes or of half-human, half-feathered serpents. There are four principal Chicchans who live in the sky at the four points of the compass. They send the rains, and thunder is the noise of one Chicchan shouting to another. There are also Chicchans living on earth, either within the mountains or in lakes and streams (Wisdom, 1940, pp. 392–97). *Chan* is the Chorti name for snake and corresponds to the Yucatec and Quiche *can*. The Ixil and the Quiche (Schultze Jena, 1946, p. 35) also give the meaning of snake to the corresponding day in their calendars; Coatl, the Mexican equivalent, also means snake, but the Zapotecan name for this day has a most tenuous connection with the serpent.

Seler has pointed out that the crosshatched infix, the main element of the Chicchan glyph in the codices, undoubtedly represents the markings of the snake. This same element is also the characteristic attribute of the Chicchan god, Schellhas' God H (fig. 13,17,18). The head form on the monuments might be that of some fantastic snake (fig. 7,1–3,5,6,8); the symbolic variant has two diagonal marks, which are the usual element of the yax affix, but that affix, in turn, is a distinguishing attribute of the Chicchan god, and the god of number 9, who is the same personage (figs. 13,17,18; 24,50–52,54; 25,32,34,35,46) and also is a mark found on snakes and water (figs. 13,15; 44,3,5,7). In fact, the head of God 9, the Chicchan god, can serve as the personified form of this yax prefix (pp. 45, 278). Truly, the Chicchan, the snake god of number 9, and the yax affix are closely related—partly synonymous and partly interchangeable elements.

The fifth day, therefore, without question is the day of the snake deities who send the rains.

Cimi, Tox, Came, Camel (fig. 7,18–34). Almost all sources are in agreement in connecting this day with death. The Yucatec name is beyond question from the same root as *cimil,* "to die," "death." Furthermore the augural animal of this day is the *cui* owl, which in Maya belief was a portent of death. According to the Popol Vuh, the lords of Xibalba, which is the underworld, were 1 Came and 7 Came, and this day name has the same root as the Quiche word for death. The Quiche still recognize its connection with death, for if the divination for a sick person falls on the day Came, the person will die (Schultze Jena, 1946, p. 35). Ximenez gives the meaning "Lord of hell" for this day, and the Mexican equivalent is Miquiztli, "death." Tox, the name for this day in Tzeltal, Jacalteca, and at Santa Eulalia, appears to be a name for the lord of the underworld, the god of death, for Nuñez de la Vega writes that 13 Tox was a demon with horns like those of a ram. Ram's horns are not aboriginal, and it is therefore probable that Tox acquired them as a result of European ideas concerning the devil, for the natives had been subject to a century and a half of Christianity prior to the publication of the bishop's writings. As horns would be added only to a god of the underworld, we can be reasonably certain that 13 Tox, like 1 Came and 7 Came, was a god of the underworld, that is to say a death god, and that Tox also was a day of death.

The day glyph bears out this aspect, for the personified form is the skull of the death god; the symbolic form is the peculiar percentage sign, an attribute of the death gods (figs. *7,18–34; 13,11,14,19*), but, strangely, the day is considered lucky in one respect or another by the Quiche, the Ixil, and the people of Santa Eulalia.

The name and picture of the sixth day unquestionably refer to the death god.

Manik, Moxic, Che, Ceh, Cieh (fig. *7,35–50*). This is one of the most puzzling of all days. The Mexican equivalent is Mazatl, "deer," and the highland Ceh and Cieh have the same meaning, but that might be a late borrowing from Mexican intruders. The names Manik and Moxic appear to have no connection with deer; neither does the glyph, which is a hand, shown sideways with thumb and one finger touching or extended with back to the observer.

As in the cases of several of the day signs already examined the design has been shown to reproduce a characteristic attribute of the deity to whom the day was dedicated, it is virtually certain that the hand is the symbol of the god of the seventh day. Because of the association with deer in the names for this day current in the Mexican and Guatemalan highlands, one would expect this day to be that of the guardian of the deer or of animals in general. This conclusion is strengthened by the fact that the augury for this day among the Jacalteca is abundance of animals.

The hand is the characteristic of the head of the number 2 (fig. *24,8–11*), a personage who appears to be the same as God Q (p. 131), but God Q (fig. *15,1–3*) is almost certainly a deity of sacrifice, not a god connected with deer or with hunting. The hand is also associated with Itzamna, and, on the jaw of a deity, is the symbol for completion; in the same position it is also the identification mark of the head for the baktun (400-tun) glyph. None of these suggests any connection with deer.

In Yucatan the chief god of hunting in general and of deer in particular is Zip or Ek Zip, "the black Zip," as he is addressed in hunting prayers by the Yucatec of Chan Kom (Redfield and Villa, 1934, pp. 350–51). He is the guardian of the deer; in the Guatemalan highlands deer, and game in general, are under the protection of the gods of the mountains, that is, the earth gods.

Mixcoatl, the god of the chase on the Mexican plateau, is invariably depicted wearing black paint on his face, and we are informed that in a ceremony of the Quiche of Mazatenango, in which a live deer in a cage received offerings, the participants had their faces covered with soot (Vasquez, 1937–44, bk. 3, ch. 19). There seems, therefore, to be a fairly widespread connection between gods of the deer (and hunting in general) and black features.

In Madrid a black deity with many of the features of God B is represented 12 times (fig. *13,20–23*). On three occasions he wears the head of a deer above his own; on one page his hand supports a snare in which a deer is caught; in three of the pictures he is in the act of hurling a spear; in another he has an axe in one hand, a brand in the other. Obviously he bears a close relationship to God M, since his eye is the name glyph of God M, and he has the peculiar drooping lip of God M. Furthermore, their costumes are often the same.

God M has been identified as Ek-Chuah, the black god of cacao and, by extension, of merchants, because of the fact that cacao beans were the most widespread form of currency. God M engages in sundry activities, but I think the identification with Ek-Chuah was made because 40 years ago no other black god had been reported. The tumpline almost invariably on his head and the pack or net bag which he sometimes carries have been cited in support of this identification, but these attributes might equally well be those of a hunter. In fact the netted game bag which he carries is one of the identifying attributes of Mixcoatl. Furthermore, on Dresden 13c an antler rises from his head. God M is also depicted on two or three occasions drilling with fire-sticks, and in that connection it is worth recalling that Mixcoatl was credited with the introduction of the fire-drill. There seems, therefore, little doubt that God M is primarily a god of hunting.

Not infrequently both God M and the other black god wear scorpion tails (fig. *13,23*). The scorpion, also, is closely connected with hunting deer, for on Madrid 44 and 48, part of the section on trapping deer and other animals, huge scorpions rope deer (fig. *13,24*). In two of the pictures the rope is held by a human hand at the point of the scorpion's tail; in the third picture the rope is grasped by a black claw. On Madrid 39 two deer are pictured one above the other. The upper deer has a scorpion tail ending in a hand. This hand holds the hilt of a dagger which is plunged into the body of the lower deer.

At the top of each of the four pages of Dresden depicting the ceremonies which close the old year and start the new there is an individual who has the head of some animal, a human body, and a long curly tail. In his right hand he carries a staff which terminates in a human hand. The staff itself has a series of ovals set along its length. These ovals are similar to those used to form the scorpion's tail.

Seler (1902–23, 4:509) identifies the head with that of the opossum, and the naturalistic representation of the tail appears to confirm this. In the accounts of the festivals for the new year there is nothing concerning opossums. However, if the hand is the symbol of the scorpion, it is worth noting that on the Mexican plateau the scorpion was a sign of penance and in particular symbolized blood-letting. The five nameless days, with which these new-year ceremonies commence, were an occasion for fasting and confession. However, the hand also symbolizes the flint blade, which one would expect to see here, for the hand is an attribute of the god of sacrifice and of the knife with which it was performed (p. 131).

The Yucatec word for scorpion is *zinaan*, which could be a participle of *zin*, "to get ready a lasso or bow." This may explain why the scorpion catches the deer in the noose of a rope, and gives a reason for the connection between the scorpion and the gods of hunting. In the Tzeltal, Tzotzil, and Chaneabal languages scorpion is called *tzec*, a word which in Yucatec means punishment or penance. This would indicate that the association the Mexicans recognized between scorpion and penance was also prevalent in the Maya area.

The Manik glyph in that case would be the hand with which the scorpion's tail sometimes terminates. The word *Manik* has no recognizable meaning, and the same is true of *Moxic*. However, the Pio Perez dictionary gives *moch'*, the back of the hand, fingers, or the foot of a bird. This is probably a coincidence since *ch'* is not the Yucatec equivalent of *x* in any Maya language or dialect.

The animals associated with Manik in the first Kaua list are Ah Xop and Ah Yaxum. No such animal as the *Xop* is known. Barrera Vasquez suggests a derivation from *Oop* or *Xoop* given in the Pio Perez dictionary as a species of parrot, but such a derivation implies the addition of both the masculine (*ah*) and the feminine (*x*) prefixes, an arrangement which I believe never occurs. In Yucatec the masculine or the feminine prefix may be added to the name, but not both at the same time. The name is given by Pacheco Cruz as *ix oop*, "macaw."

It seems possible that the word is a corruption of *ah xob*, "the whistler," for Roys informs me that quite occasionally a final *b* in Yucatec becomes *p*. *Xob* is to whistle by putting a finger in one's mouth, and is also the call of the turkey to its young. In the hunting prayer given by Redfield and Villa (1934, p. 351) there is a request that the black Zip, the deer god, may be silenced.

In a footnote the authors explain that the Zip warns the deer of the approach of hunters by whistling through closed hands, and that this whistling is called *xob. Ah xob*, "the whistler," would then be a name for the deer god.

The second animal of Manik is the Ah Yaxum, which Roys has shown to be in all probability the quetzal. The associated tree is the cacao, which raises the possibility that the black god of hunting and the black god of cacao may have been related.

The evidence, such as it is, points to Manik as the day of a god of hunting, whose symbol was the scorpion. This was shown by a hand because the scorpion's tail is thus terminated in Maya art. However, the god of Manik is really the God of number 11, an earth god (p. 88), but the earth gods were gods of hunting and had the deer in their charge (p. 135).

Lamat, Lambat, Kanil, Khanil (fig. 7,*51–68*). The glyph for Lamat is the sign for the planet Venus. In head variants the Venus monster or, perhaps more correctly, the celestial dragon with Venus symbols on his body is clearly recognizable. The equivalent day on the Mexican plateau is Tochtli, "rabbit."

The highland forms Kanil and Khanil are perhaps corruptions of K'anal, the name for star in Tzotzil, Chaneabal, and Chuh. The Tzotzil-Spanish dictionary (Charency, 1885) has *Mucta canal, "lucero." Mucta* appears to mean great, "the large star."

The first Kaua list, as translated by Barrera Vasquez, gives as the augury: "Drunkard, deformed dog is his prognostic. The head of a jaguar; the rear of a dog. A meddler, a prattler, dishonest in his speech, an experimenter in mutual hatred, a sower of discord. Great." This category of unpleasant characteristics fits the description of Lahun-Chan, "10 Sky," the principal god of the planet Venus (fig. 14,*1,2,4*) who, according to Chumayel, walked abroad like one drunk, and who was ribald and insolent in his speech. He had the head of a jaguar and the body of a dog. There is excellent evidence that he is the same as 1 Ahau, and was so called because on that day the Venus cycle always ended. The whole matter is discussed in full in the review of the planet (p. 218).

The day names Lamat and Lambat have no obvious connection with Venus. Tochtli, "rabbit," is a symbol of drunkenness on the Mexican plateau, thereby supplying a tenuous connection with the Maya conception of Venus as a drunkard. Here, again, the Aztec have lost the religious significance of the day.

Lamat, then, is the day of the Venus god.

Muluc, Mulu, Toh, Tcho (fig. 8,*1–16*). The Mexican equivalent of this day is Atl, "water." In a recent paper (Thompson, 1944) I was able to prove that the personified form of the Muluc glyph, when used as the central element of the directional glyph, was the head of a fish. Further evidence made it virtually certain that this fish was the *xoc,* a large mythical fish identified with both the shark and the whale. At that time I had not read Barrera Vasquez' translations of the day auguries, and was not aware that the first list of Kaua gives Ah Xoc and the jaguar as the animals of this day. This, of course, is overwhelming evidence for the correctness of the identification.

The symbolic forms of the day sign have been identified by Beyer (1926) as the signs for jade. Beyer's case is a strong one, and there seems no reason to doubt its validity. As he notes, jade was the symbol for water; jade-water was a ritualistic name for rain on the Mexican plateau, and the goddess of water in that same area was "she with the jade skirt." It is interesting to note that the jade sign also forms part of the glyph of the month Mol. The connection between jade and water also holds good for the Maya area, for jade disks decorate water in some Maya pictures (fig. 14,3,5). Barrera Vasquez connects Muluc with the Tzeltal root *mul,* "sink beneath the water." Most authorities, however, would derive the word from the root *mul,* "to collect, pile up, congregate." The suggestion that this refers to water or clouds collecting is somewhat forced, yet an inverted pyramid of circles is one of the two elements that compose the cauac glyph, and that without the slightest doubt is the symbol for rain. There is also a Quiche word *mulul* with the meaning of pottery jug, which reminds one of the jugs in which the rain gods stored water.

Toh appears to be connected with water. Seler (1902–23, 1:473) notes that Brasseur de Bourbourg gives the translation "shower"; *Tohoh* is thunder or the roaring of a river, and Tohil or Tohohil was the Quiche god of thunder. Ximenez says the day signifies a shower. It may be no more than a coincidence that *ton,* which is the Yucatec equivalent of *toh* (for Quiche final aspirate shifts to *n* in Yucatec and other lowland languages) is very close to *tun,* the Yucatec word for jade.

Be that as it may, there is every evidence that the day was under the mythical *xoc* fish, and water was its sign. The symbol for jade was used to represent water. In central Mexico, at least, water was given the ritualistic title of jade because of its precious nature and because of its green and blue color, and the connection holds good for the Maya area since jade symbols are sometimes set on pictures of water in the Maya codices.

Oc, Tzi, Elab, Elac, Chi (fig. 8,*17–34*). The tenth day has the meaning of dog (*tzi*) in several highland lists, and the glyph itself is the head of an animal which may well be that of a dog; the equivalent day on the Mexican plateau is Itzcuintli, "dog." Strangely, the words for dog in Yucatec (*pek, ah bil, tzul, bincol*) are quite different from the usual word *tz'i* or *chi* which is found in all other Maya languages and dialects except Huastec, Chontal, and Chicomucelteca. Even Manche Chol, which is so close to Yucatec, uses *tz'i,* but Becerra (1937), who does not distinguish between *c* and *k,* gives *ok* as Palencano for dog.

We have no information concerning a canine deity among the Maya, but in central Mexico the god Xolotl had the form of a dog (fig. 14,7). Xolotl is closely connected with the underworld, for according to the Mexican story of the creation he descended thither to obtain from Mictlantecutli, lord of the abode of the dead, the bone from which the human race was made (another version attributes this journey to his twin brother Quetzalcoatl). He also became the sun.

In Mexican belief the dog, sacrificed at the death of his master, conducted the deceased to Mictlan, the land of the dead. He was of particular aid in assisting his master to cross a wide stretch of water which barred his path. The same belief existed among the Maya, for the Lacandon place at each corner of a grave small dogs made of palm leaves, and these are thought to accompany the soul to its final resting place (Tozzer, 1907, p. 47), and remains of dogs were found in several tombs at Kaminaljuyu (Kidder, Jennings, Shook, 1946, p. 155). More direct evidence for this belief is supplied by the Tzeltal of Tenejapa who say that one should treat dogs well because they lead the souls of the dead to the underworld (Barbachano, 1946, p. 124), and by the people of Chenalho who believe dogs help their masters to cross the river of the land of the dead (C. Guiteras Holmes, 1946, p. 306).

Xolotl's connection with the underworld is further emphasized by symbols of death with which he is sometimes decked. As lord of the week 1 Cozcaquauhtli, he is shown in Bourbon with a knife in his mouth, a symbol of death, and he has black wavy hair which appears to be similar to that worn by the gods of death. The famed jade figure of Stuttgart portrays him with a skull and with his ribs showing (fig. 14,7).

The glyph for the dog in the Maya codices is a symbol which has been generally accepted as representing the animal's ribs, combined with a death sign (fig. 14,*10*). Occasionally, pictures of dogs show the ribs (fig. 14,*8*); more frequently the symbol of darkness is set above the eye (fig. 42,*74,76*). This, as noted (p. 74), probably indicates a connection with the underworld.

Seler regards Xolotl as the canine god who conducts the sun each evening to the underworld. There is strong support for this idea in the fact that Xolotl shares with Tlalchitonatiuh the patronage of the week 1 Cozcaquauhtli in Bourbon and Telleriano-Remensis and in the Aubin Tonalamatl; Tlalchitonatiuh is the dawn manifestation of the sun (Thompson, 1943b). It is natural that the evening manifestation of the sun should share this day. Further confirmation of this hypothesis is supplied by the Stuttgart jade. This skeletal form of Xolotl bears on its back a large sun disk, clearly symbolic of Xolotl's guidance of the sun to the underworld.

In Maya inscriptions the head of what is probably a dog, usually decorated with a pair of crossed bones, is sometimes used as a kin (day) sign in the secondary series and in the lunar series, and there is evidence for identifying this variant of the kin sign as the night sun. The crossed bones, of course, refer to the dog's connection with the underworld. The substitution of this glyph for the more usual sun glyph, particularly in its use in the lunar series, is very strong evidence for a Maya association of the dog with the sun at night when it descended to the underworld to emerge next sunrise in the east.

The dog is often depicted in the Maya codices carrying a torch, perhaps a reference to the Maya tradition that the dog brought fire to mankind (Thompson, 1930, p. 151) and the head of a dog is sometimes part of the compound glyph which represents the fire-drill (figs. 42, 76; 43,55). On the Mexican plateau, also, the dog symbolized fire (Sahagun, 1938, bk. 4, ch. 25).

Attention should also be called to the close relationship between Xolotl and Nanauatzin, the syphilitic god. The one can be substituted for the other in the series of days and weeks, and the two are confused in mythology. Indeed, there seems little reason to doubt that Nanauatzin is merely a variant of Xolotl. One of the characteristics of the dog in Mexican art is that his ears are eaten away or blood (pus as well?) pours from them. The dog is often portrayed in Maya art with ragged ears (fig. 14,9) and I think this must have reference to the syphilitic character of the god. Xolotl is usually portrayed with the same sore ears, and in Fejervary-Mayer an ear with a jagged edge generally replaces the complete head of the dog as the glyph for the day Itzcuintli (fig. 14,15a). The ear similarly replaces the complete head of the dog in the symbolic form of the glyph for Oc in the Maya codices (fig. 8,28–33). A constant feature is the presence at the base of the ear of two black spots. Is it fanciful to suppose that these symbolize syphilitic sores?

In the Kaua list and the auguries for the Quiche reported by Schultze Jena adultery is among the aspects of the day. The nature of the dog presumably gave rise to this association. The Quiche believe that persons born on this day will be habitual fornicators; La Farge (1947, p. 174) reports that "on 5 Elab our cross told him [the informant] that we had dirty thoughts."

Xolotl is really the hairless dog called *xol* in Aztec. In this connection it is worth remarking that the word for dog in the aberrant Maya language of Chicomucelo is *sul*, and *xul* is the Kekchi term for animal in general. There is a possibility of a single origin for this word, because the Aztec sound was between Spanish *u* and *o*, and is sometimes transcribed as *u*, sometimes as *o*.

The first augural list of the Kaua manuscript associates Oc with "the adorned one," *Ah zuli*, which Barrera Vasquez translates as he who lives a life of entertainment, a parrot, adulterer, one without judgment or discretion, without understanding. Can it be a corruption of *tzul*, given in the San Francisco dictionary for domestic dog?

There are two other expressions *Ah ocencab* and *Ah oczahya*. Barrera Vasquez translates the first as pining or languishing. *Oc* is the root of the word *ocol*, "to enter," and is applied to sunset, for *ocol kin* is sunset; *em* is the root of the verb *emel*, "to descend," and *emel cab* is "the sun falls, late afternoon." It seems, therefore, that *Ah ocencab* is "he who descends, and enters the earth," which is precisely the rôle of the dog.

Ah oczah ya means "He who causes to enter pain or sores." Barrera Vasquez translates this as trouble-maker, but it might well refer to the syphilitic aspect of the canine god. The sores are not metaphorical, but physical, the syphilitic sores the god sends. Elab, the Chiapan and Chuh name for this day, may refer to the dog's rôle of bringer of fire to mankind. *El* is the stem of a group of Yucatec words connected with burning (*elel*, "burn," *elzah*, "to set fire to," *elnac*, "something which is burning") and *ab* is the instrumental termination. A hasty check does not reveal this root with the same meaning in dictionaries of other Maya languages, but there seems no valid reason to assume that it is not widespread.

Oc may well be connected with the root of *ocol*, "to enter." Since this is used to describe sunset, when the sun entered the earth, a connection exists with the dog of the underworld who was closely connected with the sun during its nocturnal passage through the nether regions. The survival of *oc* or *ok* as a name for the dog in Palencano Chol is significant, checking with *tzi* of the highlands.

The tenth day, therefore, was under the patronage of the Maya equivalent of Xolotl. The name of this canine deity is unknown, but he appears to have led the sun across the underworld each night from west to east. In some way he actually represented the sun since his apparent glyph is used sometimes in Maya texts to show counts of days which had some special connection with the night (e.g. to count the age of the moon).

On the Mexican plateau Xolotl merges with the god of syphilis, and the bleeding sore ears of Xolotl and of glyphs of the day Itzcuintli are prominently displayed; in the

Maya codices, as in the Mexican Fejervary-Mayer, the ear alone usually replaces the whole head of the dog. Certain markings on these ears may represent syphilitic sores.

The three principal names for this day, Tzi, Oc, and Elab, may therefore recall respectively, dog in general, the dog as conductor to the underworld and Xolotl, his personification, and the dog as the bringer of fire to mankind; the glyph may allude in its infix, to the underworld, and in its mutilated ears to the syphilitic character of Xolotl.

Chuen, Batz (fig. 8,35–50). The eleventh day in the sequence represents the monkey god. In the Popol Vuh, 1 Chouen and 1 Batz are personages named after the day on which they were born. They were rivals of their half-brothers, the hero-gods, Hunahpu and Xbalanque. Indeed, 1 Chouen and 1 Batz were skilled in all the arts. They were great singers and orators, sculptors in high and low relief, writers of hieroglyphs, and in all respects extremely wise; they passed their time in praying and singing. Because of jealousies between the two pairs of brothers, Hunahpu and Xbalanque decided to get rid of their elder brothers. They persuaded them to climb a tree to fetch some birds, and then changed them into monkeys.

Batz' is the generic name in Maya for the howling monkey; *chuen*, which is surely the same as Chouen, has in Yucatec the meaning of craftsman, for the Motul dictionary gives *ah chuen*, "artificer, craftsman of some art." Combined with the words *kak* (fire), *kat* and *luum* (terra cotta and earth), and *mazcab* (iron), it means respectively metal-smith, potter, and iron-smith.

This relationship of 1 Chouen and 1 Batz with the arts and crafts is reflected in the auguries for the day Chuen in the first list of days in the Kaua manuscript. As translated by Barrera Vasquez, this section reads: "Carpenter, weaver, is its augury. Masters of all arts. Very rich all their lives. All the things they may do are very good. Judicious as well."

In the Quiche list of Schultze Jena this is a good day for prayers to do with furnishings of the house. This rather suggests an association with craftsmanship. The Chichicastenago informant of Tax (1947, p. 486) says the day is good for learning, which is definitely in accord with the significance of Chouen.

Among the Aztec the equivalent day was Ozomatli, which also means monkey. The same association with the crafts holds, for Sahagun (bk. 4, ch. 22) writes: "They say that boys born on this day would be of good disposition, happy and friendly to all. They would be singers or dancers or painters or they would learn some good craft because they had been born in that sign."

In the scant information on Maya religion that has come down to us there is no mention of a monkey god or of a god that was patron of the arts. The head of a monkey sometimes replaces that of the sun god as the kin sign (figs. 27,53,64; 29,10), indicating a connection between the two. There is good but indirect evidence that the Maya regarded the sun as a patron of singing and music (Thompson, 1939, pp. 140–41); among the Chorti the sun is also a god of knowledge and power, and patron of medicine men (Wisdom, 1940, p. 399). In central Mexico, too, the sun was the inventor and patron of music. The replacement of the sun god by the head of a monkey might therefore be due to an overlapping of functions.

Schellhas' God C (fig. 14,12), whose head is the main element of the glyph for the north, usually has the mouth of a monkey, although not when he is god of the north in Dresden, and it has been suggested that the Maya may have regarded the constellation of the Great Bear as a monkey. Be that as it may, there is what at first sight seems to be evidence for attributing a planetary or stellar rôle to God C, because his glyph occurs on three occasions on planetary bands (fig. 14,13), yet all three of these are in a special context, for they serve to divide the pictures corresponding to the ceremonies saying farewell to the old year and welcoming the new.

Another connection between the monkey and celestial phenomena is supplied by a version of the story in which the youth climbing a tree is changed into a monkey. According to this the monkey, brother of the sun, is converted into one of the planets (Thompson, 1930, p. 138).

Nevertheless, I think that Gates (1931, p. 106) is correct in seeing in the head of God C, as used as a separate glyph, an honorific title which might be applied to almost all the gods. Gates suggests some interpretation such as "Lord." In view of the associations of the monkey, it is perhaps more likely that the title should be interpreted as *Ah Men*, "the wise one" or "the one who accomplishes much," which is listed as one of the aspects of the day Chuen, or as Ah Chuen, "the craftsman."

The symbolic form of the glyph itself is too stylized to yield any meaning. Except for the infix at the top it is rather similar to the darkness element in the Akbal sign. This resemblance, however, may well be fortuitous. The two personified day glyphs probably represent monkeys (fig. 8,37,42).

The day Chuen, then, was the day of the god of arts and crafts who was regarded as having the form of a monkey or standing in some close relationship to the monkey.

Eb, E, Euob (fig. 8,51–68). The twelfth day of the Maya list corresponds to the Aztec Malinalli, which is given the meaning of grass, but which in some of the codices originating in southern Mexico is a jawbone without any vegetation or with vegetation no more emphasized than the jawbone. In the Aztec codices the jawbone is usually replaced by a complete skull. A third feature of many representations of this day sign is the presence of an eye, often on the end of a longish kind of tenon which rises from the jawbone.

Peñafiel (1885, p. 135) says Malinalli is a grass known as "grass of the charcoal burners" because it is used for making their sacks and tumplines, and adds that it is hard, rough and fibrous. The sister of Huitzilopochtli was known as Malinalxoch, "Malinalli flower," although she was more generally called Coyolxauhqui.

On the Maya inscriptions Eb is depicted as a human head with prominent jawbone and with elements of the cauac sign inserted around the temple. In the earliest examples of this glyph the jawbone appears instead of the complete head; in the codices the jawbone is less evident, but the cauac element is more emphasized.

In the Maya glyphs the combination is rain (cauac element) and death or the underworld (jawbone); in the Mexican equivalents, grass and death. One recollects, too, that the cauac symbol also represents the haab, the tun, and that in central Mexico grass similarly stood for the year.

Rain combined with death calls to mind the Mexican tradition that the Tlalocs, who sent rain to mankind, stored it in various receptacles. One of these receptacles contained bad rain which caused mildew and cobwebs. Naturally, such rains, or rather drizzles and mists, were regarded as evil and destructive; because of them crops would fail. It would be logical to show the rain god responsible for such calamities with symbols of death.

Borgia 28 shows the five principal Tlalocs of the four world directions and the center. The Tlaloc of the west and Acatl years, who is garbed in black, pours down water sprinkled with flint knives; below, these flint knives pierce the growing corn, tearing gaps in the cobs. This scene must surely represent the harmful mists which cause smut in the corn.

In the Motul dictionary we find *akab yeeb*, "*niebla oscura*." This could mean dark mildew, smut, or dark mist, or fog, *akab* signifying dark or night. Pacheco Cruz gives *eb* as mist; the Pio Perez dictionary has *yebha*, "drizzle" (*ha* is "water"); the San Francisco dictionary lists *yeeb* for dew. The Moran vocabulary terms *yeeb* "mist," and Mr. Aulie informs me that *ye'ep* is Palencano for the same. For Tzotzil the Charency dictionary lists *eboc*, "soot from the fire." Mildew in Central America usually takes the form of a growth of black powder, like soot, to which it would be logical to apply the term for soot.

As we have noted, the Eb glyph combines the symbols for death and water, which would be a perfect way of writing noxious moisture, whether mist or dew. Moreover the Eb sign is set in the water which falls from the jar of the aged goddess in the scene on the last page of Dresden (fig. 14,*14*), and since this scene represents the destruction of the world by a deluge, the Eb sign is very appropriate. Although I think that the case is a strong one, Roys is less convinced. He writes: "I have always hesitated to associate *yeeb* with Eb, but you may well be right."

Nevertheless, I think, that the Yucatec name for this day does correspond to the glyph, and Malinalli, the Mexican equivalent day, appears to express a similar idea (vegetation ruined). E, the Quiche name, means tooth. I suppose the name has been corrupted.

The aspect of this day in Yucatan is entirely favorable. The translation given by Barrera Vasquez reads: "The tz'iu [identified by Roys as the red-eyed cowbird] of the hills is its augury. Rich, the richness is that of the community. Good rich man. His belongings are those of the community. Generous. Good man. Not parsimonious. Very good as well." Among the Quiche, according to Schultze Jena, this is a good day for prayers for prosperity and for good advice concerning misfortunes. It is strange to find such favorable aspects from a day that has such ominous associations. There are two explanations for this paradox: the original meaning of Eb may have been entirely lost when these auguries were transcribed, or some factor counterbalancing the evil effect exists, although not known to us.

On the other hand, in two of the Chuh lists reproduced by Termer the day is classified as unlucky; Malinalli, the Aztec equivalent, was also calamitous, for things would start well but would end in disaster. Sahagun (1938, bk. 4, ch. 15) writes: "They said that this sign was unlucky and to be feared like a wild beast. Those who were born under it had bad fortune. They were prosperous for some time but then all of a sudden they fell from their prosperity. Many children were born to them, but suddenly all would die one after the other. Greater was the anguish and sorrow that the death of their children caused them than was the pleasure of having had them."

Here death and calamity follow prosperity. It suggests a parallel with the rain clouds that seem to bring the rain needed for good harvests, but instead produce the mildew that destroys the young crops.

Eb, then, is the day of the malignant rain deity who sends the mists, dew, and damp weather that produces mildew in the crops.

Ben, Been, Ah (fig. 9,*1–17*). The thirteenth day in the Maya list corresponds to Acatl, "reed," of the Mexican plateau. Ah, the name used in the highlands of Guatemala, appears to stand for the green corn, and also reed or cane; both meanings are given for that day by the Quiche, with an apparent preference for reed or cane. According to Ximenez, the day represents young maize which has not ripened, and cane. The word *caña* has the general meaning of cane or reed but specifically it is sugar cane. That would, of course, be a colonial mutation since sugar cane was unknown in pre-Columbian America; the resemblance of the sugar cane to a maize plant is quite striking. An extension of meaning, staff, is supplied by Lothrop. Cane is also the significance given for the day among the Ixil; in Jacaltenango the day is assigned the meaning of reed, but it is a day favorable for prayers for the cornfields; at Santa Eulalia it is a day for maize; the Quiche regard it as very favorable for children.

According to the Kaua list the Yucatec Ben was under Ah Kauil. Roys has produced evidence that *kauil* is a word connected with the crops. It is a title borne by Itzamna. Nuñez de la Vega says that Been was a person who left his name inscribed on the upright stone which is situated in the town of Comitan.

The word Ben or Been does not appear to have any connection with plant life or a deity thereof. It is a somewhat sterile root in Yucatec, supplying only a series of words connected with the idea of going or departing.

A personification of the day sign Ben on Piedras Negras L 3 shows a young head with oval eye and the IL on the cheek, but with a rather prominent and somewhat Roman nose (fig. 9,9). There is a small circle on the forehead with a curved line through it, such as occurs in the kan sign. This type of circle is often set in the heads of deities of the soil connected with vegetation. It is very prominent on the forehead of the fantastic deity who forms the stalk of the maize plant which is the "tree" on the Tablet of the Foliated Cross, Palenque, and is generally to be discerned on the forehead of the manikin god with maize leaves growing from it.

Accordingly, it is probable that Ben represents the growing maize plant, whereas kan is the grain of ripe maize and the seed. The fact that this day is favorable for children among the Ixil and the Quiche may well be an extension of the concept of growth to the human race.

Ix, Hix, Balam (fig. 9,*18–34*). The fourteenth day in the Maya list corresponds to Ocelotl, "jaguar," of the Mexican plateau. The word *hix* appears to have been a Maya name for that animal, but it has survived only in Kekchi. The Quiche name Balam, given by Ximenez, means jaguar in almost all Maya languages and dialects including Quiche. According to Schultze Jena, Ix is a designation for the earth god, but we have already seen that the jaguar is associated with the underworld in Maya and Mexican thought. The Ixil connect the day

with the mountains and with animals. Both mountains and game are generally placed in the domain of gods of the underworld, and a similar association of animals with the jaguar god exists for Akbal (p. 73). Schultze Jena, in discussing Ix as a sacred name for the world divinity, adds that prayers are said on that day to the mountain gods who represent that deity, and that it is a propitious day to pray for rain, for maize of good quality, and for the general well-being of a person.

The first Kaua list, as translated by Barrera Vasquez, reads: "The fierce jaguar. Bloody his mouth; bloody his claws. A slayer as well. Devourer of flesh. Killer of men." The Mani list also gives this day as pertaining to the fierce jaguar with its bloody mouth and claws.

The glyph itself is quite stylized. Seler (1902–23, 1:487) sees in it the hairy ear and spots of the jaguar. There can, I think, be little doubt that the circles represent the spots on the jaguar's skin, and, in view of the close resemblance of the Maya glyph to the obvious ear of a jaguar used in Fejervary-Mayer to represent the equivalent day Ocelotl (fig. 14,*15*), Seler is almost certainly correct in his identification. There is, in any case, overwhelming evidence that this day represents the jaguar god.

Men, Tzikin, Tzicin (fig. 9,*35–49*). The fifteenth day of the Maya list corresponds to Quauhtli, "eagle," of the Mexican plateau, and the Zapotec Naa, "mother." The name current in Chiapas and throughout the Guatemalan highlands means bird, but the Yucatec *men* has no connection with bird or eagle. Instead, it is the root of the verb "to do" or "to make"; *Ah men* is the name current in present-day Yucatan for the prayer-makers or curers.

In central Mexico the eagle was a symbol of the sun and, more particularly, of the priests who officiated at human sacrifices in honor of the sun or as the functionary who carried the sacrificial heart or blood to the sun. Over and over again in Mexican art the eagle is represented as carrying the heart of the victim to the sun. The heart of the sacrificial victim was called "the prickly pear fruit of the sun"; the basin in which the blood of the victim was collected bore the name *quauhxicalli*, "gourd of the eagle."

The orders of warriors whose task it was to keep the sun fed with the hearts of victims were known as jaguars and eagles. Finally "Ascending eagle" and "Falling eagle" were names for the sun. Thus in Mexican belief the eagle was a name for the sun itself, and also symbolized the priest, and in some way functioned as an intermediary between man and that divinity.

In the minds of the Maya the eagle or the king vulture also symbolized the sun, for the head of one of these two birds is sometimes used to represent the day Ahau (fig.

11,8,30–32). Nevertheless, the Maya glyph for Men does not bear any marked resemblance either to an eagle or to the sun. We must follow some other clue.

The glyph for Men in the codices is a head with a prominent line of dots running back from the eye, and a mouth which is bereft of teeth save for one, sometimes two, large molars. These, however, are precisely the features usually found in the glyph which represents 20 in the codices (fig. 25,60). This in turn is a moon symbol (p. 139). Thus, we can assume that Men represents an aged deity of the moon. Maya dualism in religion is a complex affair. Deities may be dual-sexed or may be in pairs: they may be both benevolent and malign; they may be denizens of the sky yet have terrestrial or subterrestrial connections. This dualism appears to extend also to age. There is evidence for the existence of both a youthful and an aged sun god, and Seler many years ago assumed the existence of a youthful and an aged moon goddess with, I think, complete justification. This dualism in all its aspects is also a feature of the religion of the Mexican plateau.

From the appearance of the glyph the head seems to be that of the old goddess of the moon. It remains to show a connection with the eagle.

The young moon goddess in Middle America is also the mother goddess and patroness of medicine, weaving, sexual license, the soil, and the crops, and she was the first woman in the world (Thompson, 1939). The aged moon goddess presumably had parallel powers. Among the goddesses of the Mexican plateau was Ciuacoatl, also known as Tona, "our mother," Ilamatecutli, "the old princess," Quilaztli, and Cozcamiauh, "jewel ear of corn." She was an earth goddess and agricultural deity, as the song in her honor makes abundantly clear (Seler, 1902–23, 2:1048–58). The commentator of Vatican A mistakenly calls her Mixcoatl, but states that she was the inventress of weaving and embroidery, a fact amply confirmed by the weaver's sword she carries in her hand. It was said that she was the first woman in the world and the mother of the human race. She had the custom of walking among the people, and then disappearing; she would leave a cradle behind on those occasions, and when the people looked inside, they found it contained a stone knife. Her headdress, too, was decked with stone knives. She was also a goddess of war and of death, but these probably represent extensions of her functions at a late date. I think she may well be a manifestation of Toci.

Seler (1902–23, 2:1000) considers Ilamatecutli to be the old moon goddess, an identification which I believe to be correct. She is not directly connected with the moon, but exercises most of the functions of lunar deities. Throughout Middle America moon goddesses are asso-

ciated with the earth and the maize crop, and are patronesses of weaving and childbirth; they are regarded as mothers of the gods or of the human race, and are generally given a licentious character.

Ilamatecutli-Ciuacoatl is a goddess of the earth and of the maize and a patroness of weaving; she has an association with childbirth because of the cradle she carried, and because she was the goddess of twins. She was called "our mother," and a licentious character is indirectly ascribed to her, for she was believed to appear in human form and lure away young men, whom she subsequently slew. The flints in her headdress and the flint in the cradle she carried suggest a lunar connection since in Mexican codices a flint knife is frequently set in the moon sign.

The goddess was closely connected with the eagle, for she wore a headdress set with eagle feathers and carried a shield conspicuously decked with the same feathers (fig. 14,17), and her special day was 13 Quauhtli (13 Eagle). In the song of Ciuacoatl she is called "the eagle," "the eagle woman," and her throne is said to have been of eagle feathers. Accordingly, in central Mexico, the eagle is the symbol of the old moon goddess. The Zapotec name "mother" agrees with this, because in Middle America "our mother" is a usual term for the moon.

In the Maya area the fifteenth day is represented by a picture of the aged moon goddess; in central Mexico, the equivalent day is not a picture of the aged goddess, but of the eagle which is her symbol.

An aged goddess is depicted frequently in the Maya codices (Schellhas' Goddess O and the aged representation of Goddess I). She frequently wears a snake on her head, and that would suggest a name corresponding to Ciuacoatl, "Snake woman"; sometimes her hair is arranged in two diverging cones, a characteristic, too, of Ciuacoatl. This aged goddess is also pictured in several vignettes in Madrid as engaged in weaving. In the large design on Madrid 75 and 76, which shows the divisions of the universe and their guardians, this old goddess shares the center with God D. Both have the symbol of life, the Ik sign, before them. One can scarcely fail to see in this aged goddess, the deity Ixchebelyax, inventress of weaving, or Ixchel.

The glyph of this aged goddess takes four forms: (1) the head of an aged person of indeterminable sex with a red prefix (fig. 14,16c) or the head of an aged woman, characterized by the Caban curl, with the same prefix and a knotted postfix (fig. 41,41), (2) Men or its variant (Gates' Glyph 25) with the knotted prefix and the head of the aged goddess to the left (fig. 14,16d), (3) the same Men sign or variant with the same knotted prefix, but with the red prefix replacing the head of the senile goddess (fig. 14,*16a*), (4) the knotted sign converted from a prefix to a main sign and with the sign for red as its prefix (fig. 14,*16b*). As the goddess is frequently painted red, the color prefix surely refers to that distinctive feature. The Men element can well be translated "the craftswoman"; the knotted element, I would suggest, refers to weaving. Attached to the Men glyph or Men variant, it appears above two scenes of weaving on Madrid 102d, once with the head of the aged goddess prefixed (fig. 14,*16d*), above a picture of her weaving, and once with the glyph of the death god prefixed, above a picture in which that god is weaving.

Barrera Vasquez gives the combined prognostications for this day as "The happy and cheerful (?) one is its augury. Masters of all the arts. Very good. (Children born under this sign) soon talk. Very holy their words." The last sentence, however, might equally well refer to the patroness of the day: "Very quick her words, very holy her words." Through an oversight there is omitted from this summary the expressions *ah sacal* and *ah men sacal* which occur in three of the four lists. *Ah zacal* is defined in the Motul dictionary as "woman who weaves," and *ah men sacal* would mean expert woman weaver or craftswoman in weaving. There is, therefore, direct mention of this aged goddess of the moon and of weaving, with whom we have identified the day, or of the group which would be under her special protection.

Ah men sacal is evidently identifiable in the glyphs of this aged goddess. The four forms of the glyph would mean "the red goddess" (no. 1), "aged lady *ah men zacal*" (no. 2), "red *ah men zacal*" (no. 3), "the red weaver" (no. 4).

I make no doubt in view of these various lines of evidence that Men was the day of the aged patroness of weaving, the aged moon goddess, who was the Maya equivalent of Mexican Ilamatecutli-Ciuacoatl, the "eagle woman" who gave her name to the Aztec day and who was patroness of weaving.

It is difficult to say why Tz'ikin should have become current as the name for this day in Chiapas and the Guatemalan highlands. The resemblance to the word for bird may be fortuitous, and some deeper meaning, now lost, may be concealed in the name. Alternatively, bird may refer to the eagle, although the Maya are as a rule specific when it comes to naming members of the animal kingdom.

Cib, Chabin, Ah Mac, Ah Mak (fig. 9,*50–68*). The sixteenth day in the Maya list corresponds to Cozcaquauhtli, "king vulture," of the Mexican highlands, but in the list given by Serna the picture is that of a metate, and Temetlatl is given as an alternative name for the day. Moreover, Caso (1946) notes that the equivalent

day in the Matlatzinca list means "day" or "sun," and in the Meztitlan list "day of god." The Kaua list connects the day with deer, and places it under the patronage of Ah Zip, the deer god; at Santa Eulalia the day is very bad, and one informant said that a child born on that day must die. The name among the Chuh signifies spider monkey.

Cib means wax; Ah Mac is said to signify sinner; Chabin survives in Hun Chabin, "1 Cib," the name of a pyramid on the outskirts of Comitan in Chiapas. This suggests that the Chaneabal name for this day was also Chabin. As the *ch* of Maya languages of Chiapas often corresponds to Yucatec *c*, the Yucatec equivalent would be *cabin*. *Cab* means bee, honey, beehive, a thick liquid, and also the earth. The first meanings suggest a connection with the Yucatec *cib*. Schultze Jena, in discussing the Quiche Ahmac, gives the usual derivation of sinner, but adds that "it would seem that the real meaning of this word is associated with an insect, which the Indians call *ahmak* [*ahmac*]. This agrees with the fact that on this day the Indians make offerings to the souls of their ancestors, and beg of them to visit their homes on a day Ahmak. The Indian visualizes the souls of the ancestors in the form of this insect which is smaller than a fly." Tax (1947, p. 486) reports that at Chichicastenango the day is that of ancestral spirits. Adding yet more to the obscurity, the head variant of the day Cib on Yaxchilan L 48 is the jaguar god of the number 7.

Notwithstanding this confusion, there are certain threads connecting some of these diverse elements. One group of bee gods of Yucatan bears the name Balam-Cab. The balam are a group of guardian deities not now associated with the jaguar, but the word *balam* does, in fact, mean jaguar. It would, therefore, be perfectly licit for a Maya to depict the god of the bees with the features of the jaguar, either as an example of rebus writing or because the Balam-Cab were once regarded as having the bodies of jaguars.

A strip across the centers of Madrid 103–106 is divided into 13 pictures of insects receiving offerings of food. Each scene is accompanied by three day signs, Cib, Caban, and Etz'nab, with sequent coefficients. The series starts with 7 Cib, 8 Caban, 9 Etz'nab, and then an addition of 17 carries to the next picture with its accompanying glyphs, 1 Cib, 2 Caban, 3 Etz'nab, and so on, until the 260 days are completed at the thirteenth picture. It can be assumed that the first day of the series, Cib, is closely connected with the insect depicted, and which most authorities identify as the bee, but which Seler (1902–23, 4:733–40) thinks is the Maya equivalent of the Tzitzimime, gods and the souls of the dead warriors and of women who have died in childbirth. Actually, the two concepts can be reconciled, but only after the presentation of a mélange of facts and assumptions.

The symbolic variant of Cib is almost surely a section of a univalve shell, for the outline, save that it is upsidedown, is practically the same as that of the shell variant of the kin (fig. 31,*1–9*), and is almost the same and in the same position as the form of the glyph for the south, which in turn is associated with the dead (fig. 41,*28,30,31,34,36*). The conch shell is a symbol of the underworld and darkness (p. 133), although it has another association which we shall discuss shortly. The personified form of Cib has, as we have seen, features of the jaguar god, a deity of the underworld and of darkness.

The Aztec equivalent day is Cozcaquauhtli, "the king vulture," and the regent is Itzpapalotl, "the obsidian butterfly," who is one of the Tzitzimime, and who is provided with claws, which are sometimes like those of a jaguar. Thus we have possible associations with both the Tzitzimime and jaguars in Maya and Mexican ideas centering around this day.

In Mexican belief the Tzitzimime were certain stellar deities who had at one time been posted at the four corners of the earth, and supported with upraised arms the heavens. They were believed to fall head first to earth at certain times, notably during the darkness of eclipses, and in the course of these descents to eat men and women. They were monstrous beings who took the form of insects (Thompson, 1934, pp. 228–32), and they were also called Tzontemoc, in allusion to their habit of descending head first. On Magliabecchi 76 a Tzitzimitl (singular of Tzitzimime) is depicted as a skeleton with claws for hands and feet, and decked with such symbols of death as hands, hearts, and sacrificial banners.

With the concept of the Tzitzimime was confused that of the rôle of the souls of warriors who had died in battle and women who had died in childbirth. The author of the *Historia de los mexicanos por sus pinturas* says that Cicimime was a name for the Tezaucigua, "the fleshless women," in the second layer of heaven, who would descend to earth at the end of the world and eat all men. This is certainly a reference to the Ciuateteo, the women who had died in childbirth and who were believed to descend to earth every 52 days, to harm mankind. At those times they afflicted people, particularly children, with sundry diseases, and mothers kept their children indoors. They were propitiated with offerings, particularly of corncakes in the shape of butterflies (the Obsidian Butterfly was one of their number). Dead warriors, in the guise of hummingbirds and white butterflies, also descended to earth on certain occasions, but, at the same time, they were likewise regarded as stars (Seler, 1902–23, 3:298–304).

The Maya also had gods set at the four sides of the earth to uphold the heavens. They were the Bacabs, and to them were assigned the four directional colors: red, white, black, and yellow. They were patrons of beekeeping, according to Landa, and in the story of the creation, as given in Chumayel, wild bees were at the four sides of the earth, to each group of which a directional color was also allotted. The Bacabs are well represented in Maya art of the Mexican Period, each in the same posture, with uplifted arms, and each wearing a conch shell, or a shell probably the *planorbis,* or a turtle shell, or a spider's web (Thompson, 1934, p. 235), all of which are features identified with Mexican Tzitzimime. In addition, some of the Bacabs even appear to have wings or body markings like those of the bee, and nearly all have a special loincloth with a crisscross design which suggests the markings on the wings of bees.

Perhaps connected with this concept is the Quiche belief (Tax, 1947, p. 465) that bees had once been people. They decided when the flood came to go underground in boxes to save themselves. God did not approve of that, and converted them into bees. It is related of the Bacabs that they escaped when the world was destroyed by flood. The significance of this relationship is enhanced by the fact that flood myths are not overly important among the Maya.

We have no direct information that the Bacabs were regarded as stellar deities, but such was probably the case in view of their insignia and of the close parallels with Mexican sky bearers. On the other hand, the Maya definitely associate the dead with stars and with insects. Tax informs me that the souls of the dead are related to insects in the beliefs of the people of Panajachel, and that "there is a clear notion that when a person dies he becomes a star. The better the person, the bigger the star. There is also a notion that when a baby is born, it is one of the stars in the sky come back to earth as the soul of a person." He also cites field notes by Rosales on the Tzutuhil of San Pedro Laguna, of which the following is a translation:

They believe that in September of every year God gives license to the spirits of the dead to come to visit this world. They stay until about twenty days after All Saints' Day. In September certain large green flies begin to come out. These the natives call *ci uech' camina'k* (eyes of the dead), and they are most abundant in October. They enter and leave the houses, and frequent all the street corners, but they do not molest anyone, and for that the people of San Pedro say that they are the spirits of the dead members of their families. For that reason they do not harm them or chase them away.

At Chan Kom, Redfield tells me, the souls of the dead are believed to return to earth in the form of insects on All

Souls' Day. The idea that the dead return to earth in the form of small insects, such as flies, is found in distant Nayarit (Toscano, 1947, p. 55); it must have been widespread.

If we now assemble these tesserae, a design, albeit incomplete, appears. The Bacabs who support the heavens are patrons of beekeepers, and, to judge by their insignia and their similarities with Mexican sky bearers, they are the equivalents of the Tzitzimime, stars that change into insects, turtles, and molluscs, to fall headlong to earth on certain occasions. With these Mexican concepts are fused ideas relating to the souls of dead warriors and the souls of women who died in childbirth. These also descend to earth in the guise of insects, birds, and monstrous forms. The males are also stars; the women are much feared because in their descents they afflict mankind, and particularly children, with sickness.

For the Guatemalan highlands we have the beliefs that the souls of the dead becomes stars and also that at a certain time they return to earth as insects. Tying these sundry concepts to the day under discussion is the Quiche belief recorded by Schultze Jena that the souls of the dead return on this very day in the form of an insect, and that Ahmac, the Quiche name for the day, means "flying insect," according to an aged informant. The evil character of the day, and the belief in Santa Eulalia that a child born on this day will die remind us of the Mexican belief that the descent of the Ciuateteo to earth was fraught with peril for all mankind, but particularly for children. Finally, we have the Yucatecan association of the souls of the dead with unspecified insects.

As we have seen, the symbolic form of Cib on the monuments in all probability represents a shell, and that calls to mind the shell insigne worn by some of the Bacabs; the personified glyph has features of the jaguar, a symbol of darkness, and it was under screen of darkness that the Tzitzimime descended. The belief that Cib is connected with the Maya equivalents of the Tzitzimime is greatened when we note that the corresponding Mexican day, Cozcaquauhtli, was under the rule of Itzpapalotl, "the obsidian butterfly," who is stated to have been one of the Tzitzimime. Cozcaquauhtli, the king vulture, was a symbol of death, of eating of entrails, an idea not too remote from the concept of the Ciuateteo with their emblems of death.

The case is not proved, but it is a fair assumption that Cib was the day of the Bacabs, patrons of beekeeping, who, converted into diverse creatures, merge with the earth-bound souls of the dead in insect form.

Caban, Kixcab, Noh, Chic (fig. 10,*1–15*). The seventeenth day corresponds to the Aztec Ollin, "movement" and "earthquake." Caban and Kixcab contain the root *cab,* "earth." *Kixcab* means "earthquake" in Chuh, and "valley" or "plain" in Pokomchi, according to Stoll; the same word appears to connote earthquake also in Santa Eulalia, La Farge notes. The Jacalteca cognate Noh is associated with the earth, and Seler states that among the Quiche *noh* means "strong," "powerful," and "earthquake," although none of those derivations is given in more recent works on the Quiche. There is fair unanimity in associating the day with the earth or with earthquake.

The symbolic form of the glyph has as its main feature a design resembling a query mark. As first pointed out by Seler (1902–23, 1:548), and as subsequently agreed by most specialists in the field, this represents the lock of hair worn by the Goddess I in the Maya codices (fig. 14,*23,24*). This identification was effectually confirmed by the decipherment of the full-figure representation of Caban on Stela D, Quirigua. This glyph shows the head of the youthful goddess with the corkscrew lock on the side of her face (p. 131; fig. 10,*7*). Absolute proof that this is the symbol of the moon goddess is in Landa's so-called alphabet, where it is given the phonetic value of the letter *u,* which is the Yucatecan name for the moon. It is the same profile which serves as the head variant for the number one and as that of the deity of the month Kayab. The head is that of the young moon goddess who is at the same time goddess of the earth and of the crops. The glyph appears in various contexts. Sometimes the meaning is uncertain; in others it clearly refers to the earth, as when plants grow from it or gods are seated on it (fig. 14,*19,20*). In view of the moon's connection with marriage, it is not surprising to find that among the Quiche this is regarded as a day suitable for asking the consent of a girl's parents to her marriage.

The Kaua and Mani lists give the position of augury to the woodpecker. The reason for this is probably to be found in a tradition of how the woodpecker helped to obtain maize for man by pecking the rock under which it was hidden to find the weakest point. This incident is preserved in legend and in Chumayel (p. 111), save that in the latter case the bird is the macaw. It is, therefore, not inappropriate that the day of the goddess of the earth, maize, and moon should be associated with the bird who aided in bringing maize to mankind. The day is also associated with medicine and successful commerce, the first of which was very definitely under the patronage of the moon goddess.

Caban, then, is the day of the young goddess of the earth, the moon, and the maize.

Etz'nab, Tihax, Chinax (fig. 10,*16–30*). The nineteenth day in the Maya list corresponds to the day Tecpatl, "flint knife," of central Mexico. The auguries in the

Kaua list are in complete agreement with this. As translated by Barrera Vasquez these read: "The bleeder for fevers. The sharpened flint. The mot-mot bird is its augury. In good health. Medical bleeder, medical healer also. Valiant also." It is the custom among the present-day Maya to bleed for fevers by opening a small vein in the temple with a chip of flint or glass. The term here used is *Ah tok chacuil*, which actually means "the user of flint for fevers."

The names Tihax and Chinax contain the words *ti* and *chi*, which mean mouth in almost all Maya languages and dialects (*ti* in the Chiapas group; *chi* in the others). Representations of flint or obsidian blades in Mexican codices are quite generally supplied with a mouth and a formidable set of teeth. The knife clearly was regarded as something that bit into the flesh, and this is the idea apparently behind the word in the highlands of Guatemala, for Schultze Jena connects it with the Quiche root *ti*, which carries the idea of biting. It is just possible that the endings *nax* and *hax* convey the idea of downward motion.

Ximinez says Tihax means "death cutting asunder" and that it signifies obsidian knife. The Jacalteca associate the day with the earth; in Chiapas, according to Nuñez de la Vega, Chinax was a great warrior who was always pictured with a banner in his hand. He was slain and cremated. Barrera Vasquez has shown that Etz'nab is a sharpened implement, and the words he cites from the Motul dictionary give the impression that the action carries the idea of pressure-flaking, which, of course, was used in preparing the finest blades of flint and obsidian.

The standard glyph of Etz'nab has been identified as a picture of a pressure-flaked blade, and it has been noted that the same design is frequently depicted on the stone or obsidian heads of spears. In the early representations of Etz'nab (fig. 10,*16–19*) the resemblance is much more apparent.

In central Mexico there was a deified form of the obsidian knife, the god Itztli, who was one of the nine lords of the underworld and of the nights, but of whom little else is known. To judge by the pictures in various codices, he is sometimes merely a manifestation of Tezcatlipoca. Xipe, the god of flaying, was also an obsidian god, but apparently of the rare red obsidian or of the white flint.

Chai Abah, a block of obsidian, was supposed to have been one of the principal deities of the Quiche, but our knowledge concerning this deity is very unsatisfactory, for it is largely derived from the *Recordación Florida* of Fuentes y Guzman, a work in which, unfortunately, the *florida* (flowery) presentation is usually more important than the accuracy of the *recordación* (remembrance).

A deity Hunpictoc, "8000 flints," is said to have been worshipped at Izamal in Yucatan, but nothing further is known concerning him. So far as I am aware, no representations of anthropomorphized blades of flint or obsidian exist in the art of the Initial Series Period.

The sacrificial knife was known in Yucatan as *u kab ku*, "the hand of the god" (Scholes and Adams, 1938, 1:142). This may well be the reason why hands are substituted for blades at the ends of the staff carried by the animal impersonators in the new-year ceremonies pictured in Dresden.

Etz'nab accordingly is the day of some god connected with the flint or obsidian knife, perhaps an anthropomorphized blade, but more probably a deity that presided over human sacrifice, not improbably God Q (p. 131). The only known head variant of Etz'nab presumably represents this deity.

Cauac, Caoc, Chavuc, Cak (fig. 10,*31–45*). The nineteenth day corresponds to Quiauitl, "rain," of the Mexican plateau. The sundry names for this day in the Maya lists are clearly related, and signify "storm," "thunder," "rain." A few of these words are: *chauc*, "thunder," "thunderbolt" in Tzotzil; "lightning" in Chaneabal; "storm, thunder, thunderbolt, shower" in Tzeltal. *Cahok* is "lightning" in Pokoman and *kakh* is the Kekchi word for storm, and somewhat similar forms occur in other highland languages (cf. Gates, 1931b).

Ximenez assigns the meaning "rain" to the Quiche day. The elements of the day sign frequently appear on the bodies of celestial dragons, which represent the Itzamnas, gods of rain (fig. 15,*11–13*). They also form the haab, "year," glyph. Sometimes, particularly at Quirigua (fig. 32,*31*), this haab glyph is the head of a deity with reptilian features and the cauac symbols.

Cauac, then, is the day of the celestial dragons which send the rain and the storms.

Ahau, Hunahpu, Ahpu, Ahpum, Pu, Kitix (figs. 10,*46–68*; 11,*1–36*). The last day corresponds to the Mexican Xochitl, "flower." Ahau means chief or lord in a number of Maya languages or dialects, notably Tzotzil, Chaneabal, Chol, Chontal, and Yucatec. With the female prefix *ix* substituted for the masculine *ah*, it is the name for the moon in Chaneabal, Mam, Aguacatec, and Jacalteca. Since the sun was the husband of the moon, it is logical to assume that the title Ahau, "lord," was given him, since moon was called Ixau, "lady." Kitix, the alternative name for this day among the Ixil, means sun.

Ahpu is "he of the blowgun." In the Kekchi and Mopan myth of the sun and moon, the blowgun is the weapon of the young sun god. The Zutuhil day name P'up' must surely mean blowgun.

The glyphs of Ahau may take the form of a conventionalized face or, in the personified forms, they may represent a handsome young man in profile, who is almost certainly the young sun god. Sometimes the head of an eagle or a vulture replaces this youthful face, recalling the fact that in central Mexico eagle was a name for the sun. That this same concept existed among the Maya is proved not only by the substitution of the eagle head for the usual Ahau head, but by the scene of human sacrifice on Dresden 3, which shows the eagle consuming the blood of the sacrificial victim. Moreover, the Kaua list gives rapacious eagle as the animal of the day Ahau.

There is a close connection between the sun and flower. Both the sun and moon are associated with the frangipani, symbol of sex, because they were the first couple to cohabit. The normal form of the kin sign is a four-petaled flower. In a version of the sun's courtship of the moon in Chumayel (p. 105) we read "Four-fold was the plate of the flower, and Ah Kin Xocbiltun [a name for the sun god] was set in the middle." In central Mexico Xochipilli, "Flower prince," was the young sun god, and his day was Xochitl. It is, accordingly, clear that the Mexicans called the sun god's day Xochitl, "flower," because that was a symbol of the sun.

Ahau, then, was the day of the sun god.

In Table 4 the day signs are listed, together with their symbols and the gods they appear to represent. The last column requires an explanation. The numbers 1–13 are usually written by means of bars and dots. Sometimes heads, each with its characteristic attribute or distinguishing mark, replace the bars and dots (figs. 24; 25). The characteristics and meanings of these heads are discussed elsewhere (pp. 131–36). Suffice it to say that starting with the head for one, there is a remarkable correspondence between the gods of the days, beginning with Caban, and the gods of the numbers 1–13.

1. Head of the young goddess of the moon, earth and maize. Caban.
2. God with hand over his head. The connection between hand and stone knife has been noted. Etz'nab.
3. The youthful head of the number 3 is not that of the celestial dragon, but it carries the Ik sign on the cheek, and that is the symbol of life, which has a natural association with Itzamna, who sends the life-giving rains. Cauac.
4. Head of aged sun god. Ahau.
5. Head of aged god, Schellhas' God N. Perhaps Mam, the earth god. He often wears a shell on his back, denoting his connection with the earth (p. 133). Imix.
6. God with axe in his eye. God B is usually shown carrying an axe. Ik.
7. The jaguar god with the cruller ornament on the bridge of his nose, god of the underworld and darkness. Akbal.
8. The maize god. Kan.
9. The god with spots or hair on his chin, the Chicchan god. Chicchan.
10. The death god. Cimi.
11. The god has the Caban sign, indicating that he is a god of the earth. Earth deities were also gods of hunting and protected deer and other wild animals. Manik.
12. The head on two occasions wears the sky sign as a headdress. This element enters into the glyph and name of Lahun-Chan, the Venus god. Lamat.
13. A god with reptilian features, in all probability an earth monster. On two occasions at Palenque his headdress is decorated with what is probably a water-lily flower. Muluc.

The deities of the days Oc to Cib do not seem to correspond with any numerical sequence. Why the series should start with Caban is not clear. There is not complete agreement between the deities of the days Caban to Muluc and the heads for the numbers 1–13, but the correspondence in most cases is too striking to be fortuitous. The subject is discussed in more detail on pages 131–36. Goodman (1897, pp. 53–63) also believed that the day signs, starting with Caban, represented numbers or, rather, could be used as numbers, but many of his deductions were so fantastic that his theory was discredited. He also assigned numerical values to the month signs, and scores of other glyphs.

INFLUENCES OF DAY NAMES

There is a striking disagreement as to the values of the days in terms of benevolence and malevolence. In fact this variation is carried so far that there are cases in which a day is lucky in one Quiche town and unlucky in another town of the same speech.

It is difficult to account for such opposing concepts unless one assumes that there has been a serious deterioration in the art of divination since the Spanish conquest. One must suppose that when the calendar was functioning undisturbedly there was a fairly wide agreement as to which days were lucky and which were unlucky, but at the present time so many of the old concepts have been lost that there has been room for new ideas to develop independently.

It is virtually certain, for example, that at the present time no diviner in the highlands of Guatemala is aware that Lamat was the planet Venus. With the loss of that association, a new influence had to be sought. The highland name for this day, Kanil or Khanil, probably came from the Chiapan word for star. With that origin no longer remembered, the diviners noted a resemblance to an old word for ripeness and ripe corn, and proceeded to regard the day as lucky for the maize crop. A comparable change in meaning has taken place among the Quiche with regard to Ah Mac. It formerly meant the souls of the dead; now, sinners.

TABLE 4—MEANINGS, AUGURIES, AND GODS OF THE DAYS

YUCATEC NAMES	INTERPRETATIONS OF GLYPHS	MEANINGS OF YUCATEC NAMES	ASSOCIATIONS AND AUGURIES	AZTEC NAMES	PRESIDING GODS	ASSOCIATED NUMBERS
Imix..........	Flower of water lily	Earth monster	Earth (H) Maize and fruitfulness (Y)	Earth monster	Earth crocodile	5
Ik............	Life, breath	Life, breath	Breath, wind	Wind	God B	6
Akbal.........	Interior of earth	Darkness	Darkness Jaguar ? (Y)	House	Jaguar	7
Kan..........	Maize	Ripe maize	Ripe (H) Maize (Y)	Lizard	Maize	8
Chicchan.......	Celestial snake	Celestial snake	Snake	Snake	Celestial snake	9
Cimi..........	Death god	Death	Death god (H) Owl (Y)	Death	Death	10
Manik........	Hand, sting of scorpions?	Uncertain	Whistler ? (Y) Deer (H)	Deer	Earth	11
Lamat........	Venus symbol	Uncertain	Lahun-Chan (Y)	Rabbit	Lahun-Chan (Venus)	12
Muluc........	Jade or water	Collected?	Xoc fish (Y)	Water	Ah Xoc	13
Oc............	Dog	Enter (the underworld)	Adulterer (Y) Dog, adulterer (H)	Dog	Dog of underworld	..
Chuen........	Uncertain	Craftsman	Craftsman (Y) Howling monkey (H)	Monkey	Ah Chuen	..
Eb...........	Destructive Water	Mist, drizzle, rust on plants	..	Twisted grass	Destructive rain god	..
Ben..........	Uncertain	Uncertain	Food (Y) Green maize (H)	Reed	Maize	..
Ix............	Jaguar skin or ear	Jaguar	Jaguar	Jaguar	Jaguar	..
Men..........	Old moon goddess of weaving	Wise one	Weaver Wise one (Y) Bird (H)	Eagle	Old moon goddess	..
Cib...........	Section of shell?	Wax	Deer god (Y) Souls as insects (H)	King vulture	Bacab-Tzitzimime?	..
Caban........	Lock of earth goddess' hair	Earth	Woodpecker (Y) Earth (H)	Movement	Youthful earth and moon goddess	1
Etz'nab.......	Knife blade?	Sharpened instrument?	Bleeder (Y) Tear flesh (H)	Flint	God of sacrifices	2
Cauac.........	Rain	Storm	Quetzal (Y) Storm (H)	Rain	Celestial dragon; Itzamna	3
Ahau.........	Sun god	Lord	Eagle (Y) He of the blowgun (H)	Flower	Sun	4

H stands for highlands of Guatemala; Y, for Yucatan.

The same process took place in Yucatan as is shown by page 61 of Chumayel, on which the 20 days are associated with the creation of the world. In that account 2 Eb is the day on which God made the first stairway, and on 6 Cib the first candle was made. *Eb* means stairway and *cib* means candle, but it is abundantly clear that these were not the original meanings of the days. In fact candles were a post-Columbian introduction. Yet some of the old associations remain, for Muluc is the day of the flood, and Imix, that on which rocks and trees were created.

adversity, are marble constant. The miracle is that any part of the calendar has survived four centuries of European domination; one could hardly expect that the delicate arrangement of checks and balances stemming from the characters of a forgotten mythology would remain. The spiritual contexts of the days have been lost; ignorance has produced haphazard substitutes.

The chaotic conditions which this decay has produced are manifest in Table 5, which lists the auguries for the days according to various sources. The column of good and bad days of Tizimin is an averaging of the auguries

TABLE 5—GOOD AND BAD DAYS

Day	Yucatec (Kaua)	Yucatec (Tizimin)	Quiche (Sapper)	Quiche (Schultze Jena)	Chuh (Ixtatan 1)	Chuh (Ixtatan 2)	Chuh (El Quetzal)	Santa Eulalia	Jacalteca	Ixil	Average	Aztec (Sahagun)	Maya Inscriptions
Imix	B	B	B	B	G	B	G	G	G	G	I	G	G
Ik	B	B	G	B	B	B	B	B	G	G	B	B	I
Akbal	B	B	B	BG	G	G	G	G	G	B	I	B	B
Kan	G	B	B	B	G	B	B	I	B	B	B	G	G
Chicchan	B	G	B	B	B	G	B	G	—	GS	B	G	B
Cimi	B	G	B	G	G	G	BG	G	BGS	G	G	I	I
Manik	B	I	G	G	B	G	B	B	B	G	B	G	G
Lamat	B	B	G	GS	G	G	G	G	I	G	G	G	I
Muluc	G	B	B	GS	G	G	B	B	B	B	B	G	I
Oc	B	G	B	B	B	B	B	B	B	B	I	G	B
Chuen	G	B	B	GS	B	B	G	G	B	G	I	G	B
Eb	G	B	G	GS	G	B	B	B	GS	G	I	B	G
Ben	I	B	G	GS	G	B	G	G	GS	G	G	B	I
Ix	B	B	G	G	B	B	B	B	G	G	I	B	I
Men	G	I	G	GS	B	G	G	G	B	G	G	B	B
Cib	B	I	B	G	B	B	B	B	B	G	B	G	I
Caban	G	I	B	BG	B	B	G	B	G	GS	I	I	G
Etz'nab	G	G	B	B	G	G	G	G	G	G	G	G	B
Cauac	I	I	I	GS	G	G	G	G	G	G	G	B	B
Ahau	G	I	I	I	G	G	G	G	G	G	G	I	I

G, good; B, bad; I, indifferent; GS, day favorable for prayers for some special matter, usually of secondary nature; BG, one town or good informant regards the day in question as bad whereas another of same speech considers it lucky.

The Maya calendar of today is a pitiful survival. It is not unlike those many ecclesiastical buildings of colonial Middle America which have fallen into such disrepair that now all that stands is some corner, used as a jail or as quarters for a detail of soldiers. A section of ornate balustrade, the stump of a wide-flung arch, or the mildewed stucco of some ornamental frame are clues to a glory that has departed. The structure of the Maya calendar remains, but the embellishments are no more. The nobility of the Maya concept of eternal time has gone, the gods are largely forgotten, and the pomp and much of the meaning of the count are lost, but the 260 days, the rock which has withstood the buffetings of

for the 13 repetitions of each day (to form the complete cycle of 260 days). Where over seven of the 13 occurrences of a day are listed as good or bad the day is entered accordingly in the table. Where the lucky and unlucky days are divided seven and six the day is entered as indifferent. This series of auguries may, however, have shifted from one set of days to another, as is noted in App. I. The Aztec material is derived from Sahagun's list of "weeks." It is the one list which is truly aboriginal. The final column is based on the occurrences of all day signs on the monuments in order of frequency: the seven days most commonly recorded on the monuments are listed as good, the next six as indifferent, and the last

TABLE 6
DISTRIBUTION OF DAYS OTHER THAN PERIOD ENDINGS ON THE MONUMENTS

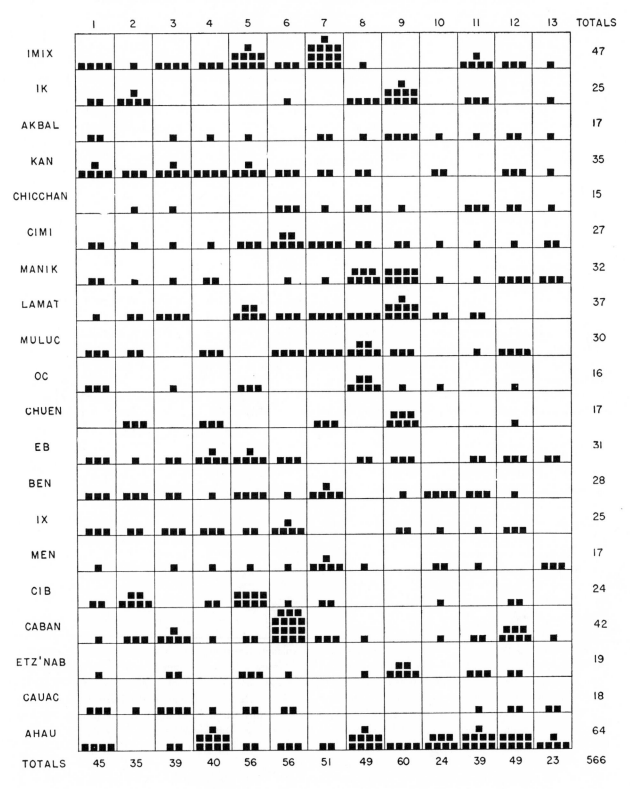

	1	2	3	4	5	6	7	8	9	10	11	12	13	TOTALS
IMIX														47
IK														25
AKBAL														17
KAN														35
CHICCHAN														15
CIMI														27
MANIK														32
LAMAT														37
MULUC														30
OC														16
CHUEN														17
EB														31
BEN														28
IX														25
MEN														17
CIB														24
CABAN														42
ETZ'NAB														19
CAUAC														18
AHAU														64
TOTALS	45	35	39	40	56	56	51	49	60	24	39	49	23	566

seven as bad. It should be noted, however, that a point is given for each repetition of a date, such as 6 Caban 10 Mol of Copan. This is done because repetition shows a date was important, and one may suppose that important dates were also lucky ones. The data from the monuments may present a distorted picture because conditions were probably such that the priest had a choice of several days in picking determinants. He might have a choice between, say, 8 Ahau 13 Mol and 9 Chicchan 13 Mol, a year later. He probably chose the Ahau date because Ahau, the day of the sun, was very favorable for such calculations.

The distribution is very interesting. Ahau leads the field with 64 occurrences, followed by Imix (47), Caban (42), Lamat (37), Kan (35), and Manik (32). It will be noted that each of the first five day-signs belongs to a different group if the 20 days are divided in five groups at four-day intervals. As will appear later, a division of this nature in fact existed, for, owing to the construction of the calendar, only those days which are five places apart in the series can fall on the same month position. For example, only Akbal, Lamat, Ben, and Etz'nab fall on first of Pop, and only Kan, Muluc, Ix,

TABLE 7—FREQUENCIES OF DAYS WITHIN GROUPS

GROUP 1		GROUP 2		GROUP 3		GROUP 4		GROUP 5	
Imix (2)	47	Ik (11)	25	Akbal (16)	17	Kan (5)	35	Chicchan (20)	15
Cimi (10)	27	Manik (6)	32	Lamat (4)	37	Muluc (8)	30	Oc (19)	16
Chuen (16)	17	Eb (7)	31	Ben (9)	28	Ix (11)	25	Men (16)	17
Cib (13)	24	Caban (3)	42	Etz'nab (14)	19	Cauac (15)	18	Ahau (1)	64
Totals	115		130		101		108		112

Therefore, the rare occurrences of Chicchan on the monuments may not indicate that that was an unfavorable day, but merely that Ahau was luckier for such purposes.

This table has the disadvantage that it does not take into account the influences of numbers on days, but in the whole range of the almanac these tend to cancel out.

The closest correspondence is between Tizimin and the Aztec series if one treats the various highland lists as a single unit. The material from the monuments of the Initial Series Period does not agree well with any other list, but there is a logical explanation for this. Most Maya dates, other than period endings, are of an astronomical or astrological nature. A day which is rated as favorable in the other lists because it is auspicious for farming or hunting, may be unfavorable for recording solar or lunar phenomena. The present-day lists of the Guatemalan highlands and the somewhat earlier list of Tizimin have as their function the rating of days as they affect the daily activities of the Maya peasant; the choice of days on the monuments was governed by problems of solar, lunar, and planetary calculations.

Table 6 lists all decipherable days on the inscriptions of the Initial Series Period other than those which marked the ends of baktuns, katuns, and 5, 10, 13, and 15 tuns arranged to show the frequency of each of the 20 days in combination with the numbers 1–13. In the preparation of this list I have retained only those day signs which have been deciphered with reasonable accuracy. The propensity to repeat certain dates, such as Copan's 6 Caban 10 Mol and Palenque's 5 Lamat 1 Mol, causes some over-weighting. Yet the repetition of these days on various monuments presumably reflects their importance.

and Cauac can fall on second of Pop, and only those of the Ahau group on third of Pop.

The 20 days are thus grouped in Table 7 above; the position of each in the frequency listing is noted in parentheses, together with the number of times it occurs. It is abundantly clear that Ahau is so popular in its group that it occurs more frequently than the other signs combined. Accordingly, we can be sure that if a solar correction reached third of Pop, the priest-astronomers would try to arrange for a year in which Ahau coincided with that month position.

The luck of the various days in the groups is shown below, the days within each group being arranged in descending order of benevolence:

Group 1   Imix (G), Cimi (I), Cib (I), Chuen (B)
Group 2   Caban (G), Manik (G), Eb (G), Ik (I)
Group 3   Lamat (G), Ben (I), Akbal (B), Etz'nab (B)
Group 4   Kan (G), Ix (I), Muluc (I), Cauac (B)
Group 5   Ahau (G), Men (B), Oc (B), Chicchan (B)

Good (G) represents the top seven in the listing; indifferent (I), the next six; bad (B), the last seven. An explanation for the poor showing of all days except Ahau in Group 5 has been offered.

Landa associates only one celebration with the 260-day almanac, although several of the feasts he attributes to the months are probably almanac celebrations. He states that a very great festival lasting three days was held in connection with the day 7 Ahau, and that it was preceded by a period of fasting. It will be noted, however, that 7 Ahau was not a popular day in the inscriptions of the Initial Series Period. Among the Aztec the equivalent day, 7 Xochitl, was the occasion of a festival in honor of the goddess Xochiquetzal and of the god called 7 Xochitl (probably the calendar name of a deity). Prayers of hunters reproduced by Alarcon show that 7 Xochitl was a ritualistic name for the deer or their patron. In this connection it is worth noting that Landa describes a festival of hunters immediately before noting the festival on 7 Ahau. There is a bare possibility that the two paragraphs belong together, and that 7 Ahau was a hunting festival among the Maya.

The divinatory aspects of the various almanacs of the books of Chilam Balam are discussed in App. I (p. 297).

INFLUENCES OF DAY NUMBERS

The frequencies of the numbers attached to the days in texts of the Initial Series Period are of considerable importance. In descending order (with occurrences in parentheses), they are: 9 (60), 5 and 6 (56), 7 (51), 8 and 12 (49), 1 (45), 4 (40), 3 and 11 (39), 2 (35), 10 (24), and 13 (23).

It is surprising to find 13 at the bottom of the list, as one would have expected that number to have been regarded as favorable because it represents the number of heavens and of the chief celestial gods. The lucky character of 9 has already received comment (p. 54); one would expect it to head the list. Ten, associated with the death god, is naturally near the bottom of the list.

Closer scrutiny of Table 6 brings some surprises. Although 9 is the most popular number, it does not appear in combination with Imix, Kan, or Caban, all of which are favorite days, and is not common with Ahau. The combination 2 Ahau is absent, but Ahau is quite often preceded by the unfortunate 10. One cannot entirely rule out the possibility of chance, but it would appear that in these combinations, we see the results of the laws of divination.

There is strong evidence (p. 131) that the gods who ruled over the numbers 1–13 also were the deities of the day names Caban to Muluc. Accordingly the combinations 1 Caban, 2 Etz'nab, 3 Cauac, 4 Ahau, 5 Imix to 13 Muluc must have represented the overwhelming influence of a single deity, whereas other combinations would involve influences of two deities (e.g. 4 Caban would be affected by the god of number 4, the sun, and the deity of Caban, the moon). Of the 13 days which have the same deity for day and name, only 4 Ahau (sun god) and 5 Imix (earth deity) rank high in the list. Since 9 is so fortunate, one would expect 9 Chicchan to be most favorable, yet there is only one example. 7 Imix, combining jaguar god (number) and earth god (name) is very popular but its reciprocal 5 Akbal (earth god number, jaguar god name) has a low rating. 6 Caban (rain-and-storm god number, moon-earth goddess name) is a favorite, but its reciprocal, 1 Ik (moon-earth goddess name, rain-and-storm god number) is poorly represented.

The scheme of lucky and unlucky days is far from simple, and its solution probably depends on factors concealed in an elaborate mythology now largely lost.

There is a certain conformity within each group with regard to lucky and unlucky days, although this may be chance. Thus 9 (together with 10, 11, and 13) is not favored in Group 4, and there is only one coefficient of 2 in Group 5; Group 1 does not favor 8, 10, or 13, and Group 2 appears to avoid 10 and 7.

The desire to reach a lucky day probably was an important factor in the choice of dates for solar and other corrections. Copan's famous base for a solar correction was 9.16.12.5.17 6 Caban 10 Mol. This was probably chosen in preference to 9.16.13.6.2 7 Ik 10 Mol, because 7 Ik appears to have been an unlucky day. Sundry factors probably influenced the calculations, but, other things being equal, the Maya would almost certainly have chosen a date falling on 6 Caban rather than on 7 Ik.

The choice of dates was sometimes influenced by a desire to get a series of days with the same coefficients. Thus Lintels 27, 58, and 28 at Yaxchilan carry a single text, the dates of which fall on the following days: 6 Chicchan, 6 Ix, 3 Ix, 10 Akbal, 6 Caban. Obviously it was not chance that three of the five days have coefficients of 6, and a fourth repeats one of those three day names. Other inscriptions show a similar repetition of the same day number or the same day name.

An interesting example of this desire to reach a lucky number is supplied by the first IS of Altar 2, Uxul. This reads 9.9.9.9.18 9 Etz'nab 16 Zac. The prominence of the number 9 (and in one case a multiple of it) can not have been fortuitous. At Coba there appears to be a variation of this reading on Stela 4 of the suburb at Macanxoc. This date is 4 Ahau 18 Yax with the position 9.9.9.9.0 in the LC; one 9 was sacrificed, but the lucky day 4 Ahau was reached. There is a little doubt, however, as to the correctness of this decipherment. The Jacalteca regard 8 as the most fortunate number and 1, 4, and 13 are important. When these numbers coincide with Ahau the prayer-makers place candles before the church. The day 8 Ahau is particularly important; outstandingly good days are 8 Ben, 8 Ik, 8 Cauac, 8 Ahau, 8 Akbal, and 8 Manik; in addition, 8 Cimi and 8 Lamat are good. The ancestors of the Jacalteca are 9 Kan and 9 Imix, yet Kan is a bad day, and one should not pray to it (La Farge and Byers, 1931, p. 157). At Santa Eulalia 13 is very good; 9 very bad, with 4, 8, and 12 good, and 3, 5, and 11 bad in certain combinations (La Farge, 1947, pp. 172–76). Here the even numbers seem to be good; the odd ones, except for 13, bad, suggesting that the influences of the old gods of the numbers have little value. The present arrangement may derive from customs of divination, for even numbers usually mean "yes" and odd numbers indicate a negative response.

Tax (1947, p. 486) lists a number of the most lucky and unlucky combinations at the Quiche town of Chichicastenango. The best are 5 Imix, 8 Imix, 13 Imix, 9 Ik, 13 Eb, 13 Ben, 13 Ix, 9 Caban, 13 Caban, 10 Etz'nab, and 11 Cauac. The worst days are 8 Cimi, 13 Cib, and 9 Ahau. Of these only 5 Imix and 9 Ik appear to have the same significance on the monuments, where they are both very popular numbers.

The luck of the day may have influenced the erection of stelae to mark period endings. The peaks of stelae erection are 9.15.0.0.0 and 9.18.0.0.0 with 9.19.0.0.0 close behind. The days on which these periods end are 4 Ahau, 11 Ahau, and 9 Ahau. The first is the repetition of the formal start of the Maya calendar; the second is the day on which the katun of the creation ended, according to Chumayel; the third falls on the lucky day 9 Ahau. There is a rather marked drop at 9.16.0.0.0, although this was at a time when the custom of erecting stelae was at its peak. That katun ended on 2 Ahau, which has been listed as unlucky in the list of Ahaus that do not end periods. Another plunge occurs at 10.0.0.0.0. This ends on 7 Ahau, also an unpopular day in the earlier list. The peak of half-katun recordings is at 9.17.10.0.0, which ends on 12 Ahau, a popular day in the earlier list.

These figures for katun and half-katun endings can not, however, be given too much weight since they were undoubtedly influenced by the prosperity of the cities during the last quarter of Baktun 10. The half-katun 9.18.10.0.0 is the second highest peak in that series. That ended on 10 Ahau. The number 10 was generally unlucky, but 10 Ahau has a rather high place in the list of Ahaus that do not end periods. The point about which one cannot be sure is how many stelae would have carried this date had it ended on an unlucky day, for example 2 Ahau.

From what has been said above I think that the desire to avoid unlucky days, the state of prosperity of the Maya people, and the influence of the priesthood all contributed to the decision as to whether a new monument should be erected.

RITUALISM OF DAYS

This statistical analysis of the days and their number is irksome and, in a sense, outrageous: it is as though one were to discuss the glowing colors of the mediaeval glass of Chartres in terms of Ridgway's color chart or to record Gregorian chants in decibels. Unfortunately, it is the only way in which we can get information on the incidence of good fortune in the Maya count of 1200 years ago.

To give an idea of the importance the calendar still retains in the life of Maya communities in the highlands of Guatemala, and to counteract the metallic taste of numbers in the mouths of my readers, I quote at length from Antonio Goubaud's description of the ceremonies at Momostenango on the occasion of the celebration of the feast of 8 Batz (8 Chuen), the most important day in that Quiche town (1937, pp. 20–27).

All the natives of the village of Momostenango feel bound to observe this day, and for this purpose all those who happen to be away return to their place of birth. They firmly believe that breaking this rule causes illness or even death.

In spite of the fact that 8 Batz is a general ceremony for all, it is in itself individual for each person, so that, although large groups come together to celebrate it, there is no established routine for its observance, such as happens, for instance, for the dramatic dances. . . .

The celebration of this feast begins in the evening of the previous day, and in the afternoon the Indians begin to arrive at the church of Momostenango. By eight in the evening of that day the church is completely full of Indians, kneeling in parallel rows, face to face, and filling the whole width of the church. They light candles which they place on the floor, and, burning native incense in clay censers, they pray aloud with deep faith. The murmur of the fervent prayers, the thin light of the candles in the cloud of pale gray smoke of the aromatic incense, give the entire scene an atmosphere of intense spiritual emotion. . . .

On the day 8 Monkey [8 Batz] (which in this case happened to be the 24th of August), at dawn, the Indians go to a place called Chuti-mesabal, "little broom," which is about half a mile west of Momostenango, where the pagan altars . . . are found. These altars are mounds, three to ten feet high, the tops of which are covered with potsherds. . . .

By nine in the morning a multitude had already gathered there. It is estimated that from fifteen to twenty thousand Indians congregate at Momostenango for this ceremony. In front of each altar were the *chuch-ḳahau* [shamans who are those best acquainted with the calendar]. Men officiated at some of them; at others, women, for the profession of shaman is not restricted to men. . . .

Around the *chuch-ḳahau* gathered the Indians for whom they were praying. One person or a group—a family for example—arrive at one of the altars and deposit at one side of it pieces of broken pottery which they bring as an offering to the divinity. . . .

One person, or at most two, go to the *chuch-ḳahau* at one time, that he might make his prayers for them. The shaman asks them their names, and the object for which he must pray, which is: the expiation for sins committed, for physical, moral, spiritual and economic well being as well as to express gratitude to the divinity for gifts received. Upon payment of a tiny sum of money, usually a penny, the *chuch-ḳahau* begins the rite. He takes a package of native incense [of the most sacred kind] . . . [and offers it] to the divinity, burning it in the niche which is built in each altar for that purpose. These niches are of semi-circular shape, about twenty inches wide by fifteen inches deep, formed by potsherds that on this occasion are decorated with pine boughs.

Located at one side of the incense which the *chuch-kahau* burns, a little bag of cotton . . . may be seen, which is the visible sign that he who officiates at the altar is an authorized intermediary between man and the divinity. This bag contains the objects used by the *chuch-kahau*. . . .

The ceremony for each person is very long, because the shaman prays interminably, mentioning to the deity all kinds of the most intimate details of the life of the suppliant. Sometimes the shaman offers a little liquor, *aguardiente,* to the divinity, and afterwards takes the offering himself. . . . When the shaman is slightly intoxicated, he believes himself closest to the supreme deities. . .

Near the big altars, on secondary altars, pray the recently initiated shamans, who are not so sought after as the older ones to celebrate the ceremony. For the families of the shamans there are exclusive altars at another place. . . .

The rites last at Chuti-mesabal until twilight. At dusk the ceremony moves to the brow of a hill called Nim-mesabal, "big broom." . . . There, during the whole night, the shamans pray before other altars similar to those below at Chuti-mesabal, and burn incense continually. So great is the gathering of people at this place that for these days they put up rows of booths where all kinds of edibles, drinks, candles and incense are sold.

The two days following 8 Monkey are also dedicated to the world divinity, and almost all the Indians remain in Momostenango praying during those days.

Lincoln (1942, p. 213) describes more briefly the celebration of 5 Noh (5 Caban in Yucatan) by the Ixil on its return 260 days after it had occurred as New Year's day.

This shrine [of Huyl], two hours' ride from Chajul, is built on an archaeological site on the mountain of the same name, and is the most sacred spot of the whole Ixil people. "Angel Huyl is what holds the world together" they say. The building itself outwardly resembles any Ixil house with tiled roof and veranda. Inside are six large crosses on a raised stone altar, and three average-sized ones wrapped in leaves and palm fronds and draped with *alamek (cola de leon),* the sacred plant. Below at the back were six crosses, only about four inches high. In front of the crosses were many large stones from a pre-Columbian structure, and great heaps of copal ash. In addition, there was a long wooden bench in front of the shrine.

About a quarter of a mile up the mountain are the ruins of a pre-Columbian ceremonial center. . . . Actually the whole mountain is regarded as a deity, and long before reaching the shrine one removes one's hat, and approaches with great reverence.

Before sunset Indians . . . began to arrive. They lit candles and copal, and prayed before the crosses. All were professional calendar priests, most of them accompanied by their families. Women and children moved in, lit fires, and cooked while the calendar priests recited their long prayers. The calendar priest, who accompanied us, offered our candles and copal, prayed for us by name, and let off four rockets, one for each Dominical day [days on which new year can fall, among the Ixil the equivalents of Ik, Manik, Eb, and Caban]. . . . Later more and more Indians arrived. . . . Praying, drinking, and music went on all night in the hut, attended by possibly 300 Indians. By morning the night crowd had thinned out, but all during the day (November 26—6 Noh) calendar priests kept coming up from Chajul and other towns.

La Farge and Byers (1931, pp. 173–75) give an outline of the ceremonial year at Jacaltenango from March 15, 1927. A section of this is given below in abbreviated form since it well summarizes the rhythm of ritual. The Jacalteca day names have been converted to their Yucatecan equivalents.

6 Eb (March 15). Preparations completed for the new-year ceremony. Prayer-makers and laymen prayed in front of the church and the crosses all day.

7 Ben (March 16). New year entered with 7 Ben as year bearer. The whole village prayed at the church between dusk and midnight. At midnight the *cahampal* rite, which involves the sacrifice of a turkey or fowl, was performed by prayer-makers and private families. Prayer-makers began a "follow-up" prayer lasting 20 days.

8 Ahau (April 12). Very auspicious. Prayer-makers held *cahampal* for the animals of the village. Deer dance began in neighboring village as the start of the festival of St. Mark, 13 days later.

8 Ben (April 25). Feast of St. Mark. Prayer-makers begin 20 days of prayer preceding rain ceremony.

2 Ben (May 15). Climax of prayer for rain. Followed by another 20 days of prayer. Fourth recurrence of day (but not number) of year bearer.

4 Ahau (July 30). A very good day. *Cahampal* in celebration of first green corn was probably held on this day.

4 Ben (August 3). Start of 13 days of prayers against locusts.

11 Ben (August 23). Start of 30 days of prayer preceding the *cahampal* of the boundaries.

12 Ahau (September 19). Feast of the new beans or "flute tamales" was probably on this day. Bean tamales made by all. A clay flute was played while the beans were cooking. Afterwards it was broken into the pot.

2 Akbal (September 22). *Cahampal* of the boundaries in which a bull is sacrificed.

4 Kan (November 2). Sixty days before civil new year's day. Election of ceremonial officers for following year.

7 Ben (November 30). Recurrence of year bearer. Prayer-makers held a *cahampal.*

4 Akbal (December 11). New and retiring prayer-makers start 20 days of prayer preceding the installation on civil new year's day.

1 Etz'nab (February 24). Start of 20 days of prayer prior to new year bearer.

3 Ben (March 10). Last day of year. Souls of little children visit this world. Five nameless days (p. 117) intervene.

8 Etz'nab (March 15). Entry of the year bearer of the new year.

It will be noted how the ceremonies tend to follow the day Ben, which is that of the year bearer. In the following year there would have been a similar concentration on the day Etz'nab. Such an arrangement is, of course, perfectly logical. Ben was the year bearer, he was in charge of the year; it is natural that ceremonies should be held when his interest was, so to speak, doubled, through a combination of his influence as regent of the year in general and of that day in particular.

Such, then, is the important rôle the cycle of 260 days plays on the modern stage, for the actor is seldom off the boards, and even from the wings his influence is felt. How much richer must have been this part in the pageantry of Maya life before Columbus sailed westward. Today Orson Welles, not David Garrick, is in the green room.

DIVINITY OF THE DAYS

In discussing the meanings of the day names evidence has been produced to show that the days were originally gods, and it has been suggested that they were always regarded as such. This idea is well exemplified by the attitude of the present-day Maya of the highlands of Guatemala toward the days.

The divinity of the days is strongly emphasized by La Farge (La Farge and Byers, 1931, pp. 172–73). He writes:

When speaking of these day-names I have called them "he" instead of "it," and referred to them as being "in charge" of a day, or in the case of the year bearer, "coming into office." This is in strict accordance with local usage, and also is done to emphasize the fact that strictly speaking these names are not the names of days, but of "men" who control days. . . . These twenty men have charge of their respective days, the informants spoke of "his day". . . . The soothsayers stated definitely that "these men" granted the prayers, and would say of a given day-god "he does so-and-so."

La Farge also notes that the year bearers are sometimes given the highly honorific *komam*.

Lincoln (1942, pp. 112, 123) relates that in Ixil prayers "the 20 sacred day-lords of the calendar with their respective 13 numbers are invoked," and in one prayer gives the sentences "At this time, it is the day 1 Kan [1 Chicchan], it is the day 2 Kamel [2 Cimi]. To you two Day-Lords I come to offer gifts" and "At this time, too, to you, our fathers, Day-Lords, 13 I'x, 1 Tzikin, 2 Amak, 3 Noj, 4 Tijax, 5 Kauok, 6 Hunahpu, 7 Imux, 8 I'q, 9 Akbal, 10 Katch, 11 Kan, 12 Kamel, 13 Tche. O Thirteen kings who are seeking their substance and food."

The days which can serve as year bearers in the Ixil calendar are, like those of the Jacalteca, given a special title of respect which also emphasizes the concept that they are living beings, for they are called "our father," or "our father king" (*cubal rey*), or by the Spanish word, now completely indianized, *alcalde*. This literally means "mayor" but in function corresponds to our word "chieftain." The current year bearer is the *"alcalde mayor"* roughly translatable as "principal chieftain."

Evidence that the Maya of Yucatan regarded the days as alive, and presumably also as gods, is to be found in the prefixing of the masculine gender *ah* to the day 5 Ahau, as the name of a katun in an archaic passage in Tizimin. He is called *ah ho Ahau*, literally "he, 5 Ahau," for *ah* denotes the masculine gender for both gods and men. In this same text the year bearer is called *ah oxil Kan*, "he, 3 Kan." The masculine gender is also prefixed to day names in Chumayel and Kaua, although the custom was by no means general. Similarly we find in the chronicle of Mani *ah oxlahun Ahau*, "he, 13 Ahau." This refers to a katun.

In the passage in Chumayel describing the birth or creation of the 20 days, we read: "Then they [the days] went to consider and spoke as follows. . . . Then the reason was sought by the first ruling day why the meaning of the word to them was not repeated so that they could declare themselves. Then they went to the center of heaven and joined hands." One could hardly ask for a clearer proof that the Maya regarded the days as animate and sentient beings.

The living nature of the days is to be seen also in Nuñez de la Vega's description of the Chiapan calendar, for he speaks of them as heathens or gentiles, and says of 13 Tox that he is the devil. Furthermore, Roys calls my attention to the faces which precede day names in the first part of Ixil.

In the discussion of the series of days it has been made abundantly clear that the day names derive from gods. There does not seem the slightest reason to doubt that each day name referred to the god who was in charge during its course; days did not represent abstract ideas, such as darkness, storm, or death, but the gods who had dominion over them.

NAMES OF THE 260-DAY CYCLE AND OF ITS DIVISIONS

The Maya name for the 260-day period is not surely known. For many years the Mexican word *tonalamatl* was used by archaeologists as a name for this period in the belief that that was the true Aztec term. Recently, however, Caso (1937, pp. 131–33) has shown that tonalamatl means not the period of 260 days, but the book in which the 260 days with their divinatory material were painted (*amatl* is the name of trees of the genus *Ficus* from which paper was made, hence the derived meaning of paper and book). The name for the period itself, Caso points out, was tonalpohualli.

Gates (verbally about 1921, subsequently in print) suggested that the Maya name for the cycle of 260 days was *tzolkin,* which means literally the counting in order of the days. This word has come into rather general use in recent years despite the fact that Long (1934) has demonstrated that *tzol* is a general word that can be used for any sort of count of days, weeks, or nights and serves both for a reckoning of 365 days and for a count of 260 days. Indeed, Wisdom tells me, the Chorti use *tzohrkin* (shift to Chorti *r*) for the European calendar! The word should be dropped, for an erroneous term masquerading as the true one is worse than none at all.

Friar Francisco Vasquez (1937–44, bk. 1, ch. 15), speaking of the efforts of one friar to eradicate superstitions and traces of idolatry among the Cakchiquel of Comalapa, says "he drew them away from many bad and superstitious customs of their heathenism, especially a count of days which they called *utzilahquih,* full of errors and computations of judiciary astrology." The mention of astrology and superstition makes it virtually certain that Friar Vasquez was speaking of the count of 260 days. *Utzilahquih* perhaps means "the completion of the days," but more probably is "the good luck of the days" (*utz,* "good," "lucky"; *quih,* "day," "sun").

So far as I am aware, no equivalent name in a lowland language and dialect has been noted. In the absence of any Maya word other than the Cakchiquel *utzilahquih,* it seems best to use an English term. I shall refer to this count as "the 260-day cycle" or "the divinatory almanac" or "the sacred almanac." The period of 20 days (from Imix to Ahau), 13 of which formed the sacred almanac, appears to have been called *uinal.*

In Chumayel (pp. 60–63) there is a passage recounting the birth of the uinal. The uinal there listed started with the day 13 Oc and runs to 6 Muluc; a second one runs from 8 Muluc to 1 Lamat. This suggests that any sequence of 20 days was a uinal. *Uinal* is also used in the same source (p. 23) as a name for the months. These, too, are of 20 days, but start with Akbal, Lamat, Ben, or Etz'nab (Ik, Manik, Eb, and Caban if the month is regarded as commencing with 0). Landa states that the months of 20 days were called *uinal hun ekeh;* the San Francisco dictionary gives *"can uinal, ochenta dias,"* and *hun uinkehe* and *ho uinkehe* for 20 and 100 days ago. One suspects that Landa's *hun ekeh* may be a corruption of a word incorporating the past time *he* (more correctly *he'*) suffix. Uinal is used by epigraphers for any period of 20 days, but principally for the span of 20 days,

running from Imix to Ahau, which forms part of the IS. Here it is a true division of the 260-day cycle.

The Maya were extremely precise in their calendarial nomenclature. It does not therefore seem probable that they would use a single term for any period of 20 days, but rather would have one name for the divisions of the sacred almanac, running from Imix to Ahau, and another for the "months."

The word *uinal* appears to be connected with *uinic,* "man," a root used in most Maya dialects for 20. Among the Jacalteca the word *xahau,* "moon," is used for the period of 20 days from the year bearer to the return of the same day name, which is roughly the equivalent of the month; we are not informed whether the same term is used for the 20 days from Imix to Ahau. The use of the moon's name for a period of 20 days is in agreement with hieroglyphic material of the Initial Series Period, for the moon glyph frequently represents 20 days (p. 167). The Pokoman dictionary of Friar Moran lists *hun uinak* as 20 days. In this case *uinak* definitely has the original meaning of man.

RANGE OF 260-DAY CYCLE

Beyond the Maya area the use of the 260-day almanac extended at least as far north as Hidalgo. The twenty day names are reported for the Aztec and neighboring peoples in and around the Valley of Mexico, the Matlatzinca, the Zapotec, the Otomi, and a people of Meztitlan. There is an incomplete list from the Mixtec, and from the proveniences of codices it is known that the almanac was current among the Tlapanec and the Cuicatec. Mention of day names in historical codices adds the Toltec and various peoples in the region of Puebla to the list. Calendarial names of gods and places allow such people as the Totonac and Mazatec to be ranked as users of the almanac. As the Middle American year of 18 months and five extra days is based on a round of 20 days, we can be fairly certain that users of that type of calendar also had the 260-day calendar. Groups reported as using this calendar include the Chiapanec, the Chinantec, and the Tarascan. Taking into account the distribution of monuments carved with day signs, it becomes virtually certain that the almanac was in use in all Mexico south of latitude 21°. It has not been reported from the Huaxtec or Zoque, but one can feel sure that it was used by those peoples. The evidence of stelae assures us that it was an important feature of La Venta culture.

East and south of the Maya area the almanac was used by the Pipil and Mexican-speaking Nicarao, but it was probably brought to those regions at a relatively late period from Mexico. An unnamed group in Honduras used the 18-month pattern.

I know of no evidence as to where in this large area the almanac originated, save that some of the fauna which give their names to days in some of the almanacs are inhabitants of the *tierra caliente,* as noted by Hans Gadow. My guess would be that the first development took place somewhere in an area extending from slightly west of the Isthmus of Tehuantepec to the Golfo Dulce, a region which would include the Maya, the Zapotec, and the builders of La Venta culture. It would also seem probable that the almanac was in use before the Maya fully developed those characteristics which differentiate their culture from those of their neighbors.

ORIGIN OF 260-DAY CYCLE

The choice of the number 260 has given rise to much speculation. It has been suggested that the number was chosen because it approximates the period of human pregnancy, but that is not a very happy explanation because there is no logical reason why the period of pregnancy should be considered in establishing a divinatory almanac. Moreover, it is probable that the 260-day almanac evolved before the exact length of gestation was known, for one must be able to count days before such a reckoning can be made. Furthermore, once the biological facts of pregnancy were known, it should have been simple to get a closer estimate of its duration than 260 days. It has also been suggested that the period derives from nine lunar months each of 29 days, although why the Maya should have regarded the lunar month as of 29 days is not clear, and even at that one has to reckon one lunation as of 28 days.

A better explanation is that offered by Mrs. Nuttall (1928), and recently supported by Merrill (1945). According to this thesis the 260 days represent the interval each year between the passages of the sun across the zenith. In the approximate latitude of 14° 30′, which passes a little south of Copan through Amatitlan to Retalhuleu, the sun crosses the zenith on April 30, and is north of it at midday until August 13, when it is again at the zenith on its passage southward. The period that the sun is north of the zenith at midday is 105 days; it is south of it for 260 days.

There are serious drawbacks to this thesis. Were the interval from sun overhead to sun overhead 260 days in much of the area in which the sacred almanac was in use, the explanation would be very logical, but the interval varies from about 260 to about 311 days in that area. One must assume then that the cycle of 260 days originated on the periphery of the area in which it was current, and that, spreading northward and westward, it was eagerly adopted by peoples for whom it had no solar significance. For example, the cycle was appropriated by the inhabitants of the Valley of Mexico, although there the interval it was supposed to commemorate was about 291 days. In Meztitlan (approximate latitude 21°), the most northern outpost from which the 260-day almanac is reported, the interval was about 311 days, and it could not have been much less for the Otomi, also users of the almanac.

Furthermore, had the 260-day period a zenith-to-zenith significance, surely there would have been a complementary period of 105 days to maintain a correspondence with the solar phenomena. Repetition without that intervening period immediately breaks all contact with the zenith-to-zenith period.

There is, moreover, absolutely no evidence that the 260-day cycle originated in the vicinity of Copan or anywhere along latitude 14° 30′, which is on the periphery of the area it covered. It might equally well, so far as our present knowledge goes, have been a Zapotec, Mixtec, or La Venta invention, or even have been developed by the Mazatec or Totonac. If we assume that it was a Maya invention, there is no evidence, apart from the zenith-to-zenith interval in that area, that the calendar originated at Copan. The earliest known date at Copan is about 100 years later than Stela 9, Uaxactun, and later still than the Leiden plaque, which certainly was not carved at Copan.

At first sight the coincidence between the length of the zenith-to-zenith interval and the 260 days of the sacred almanac appears very striking, but one must remember that the same explanation would cover many periods of varying length. There are approximately 70 intervals from zenith to zenith of less than a year, in the area in which the sacred almanac was used (70–105, 260–95 days). Accordingly the fact that one of these 70 coincides with the length of the sacred almanac is not so very remarkable.

Merrill carries the argument a step farther, suggesting that the start of the Maya year was made to coincide with sun at the zenith on August 14. In the amended Goodman-Thompson correlation (App. VI) the formal base of the LC, the date 13.0.0.0.0 4 Ahau 8 Cumku actually falls on August 10, but that presumably is coincidence. When the LC was invented, it is very doubtful that the Maya could have calculated backwards some 3000 years with an error of only four days. Furthermore, the logical thing in that case would have been to reach a day 13 Ahau (the end of the 260-day cycle) as the end of the 13 cycles which preceded the present era. Then the present era would, like the 260-day cycle, have started with 1 Imix.

The same argument holds good if, as Merrill supposes, the 260-day interval started with the first day of Pop. That was the day 9 Etz'nab, not 1 Imix. As a matter of fact, there is some evidence that the Maya regarded that part of the year lying between 1 Pop and the last day of Mac as forming a sort of compartment of 260 days at the start of the year (p. 113), but there is also some evidence that there may have been a balancing compartment of 260 days at the end of the year, stretching from the end of Zec to the end of Cumku.

Whatever may be the explanation of the origin of this cycle of 260 days, I think it is very unlikely that it arose from the fact that the interval from sun overhead to sun overhead happens to be 260 days at about latitude 14° 30'. That is not to say that the Maya did not pay attention to that solar phenomenon.

A number of years ago I suggested that the cycle of 260 days perhaps had developed in a rather haphazard way from two counts, one of 20, the other of 13 (Thompson, 1931, pp. 349–53). The Maya used a vigesimal system, and it was therefore natural for days to be grouped in 20's. The vigesimal system was also used by nearly all the other peoples of Middle America, and we have seen that there is ample evidence that the 20 days are really 20 gods, each one of whom ruled over his day.

There was a general belief in Middle America in the existence of 13 heavens (arranged one above the other or in a stepped pattern of seven layers with two compartments on six levels and a single compartment at the top) and in 13 gods of the heavens. The Maya account of the creation in Chumayel speaks of the struggle of the 13 gods against the 9 gods, and although the fact is not actually stated, there can be little doubt that this represented a fight between the 13 celestial deities and the 9 gods of the underworld. In the same passage there is mention of the thirteenth heaven or celestial layer.

The nine gods of the underworld ruled the nights; the 13 sky gods presumably ruled the days. An arrangement of this nature existed in central Mexico, for a series of 13 gods of the days, which forms a re-entering cycle, accompanies the day signs in Bourbon and in the Tonalamatl of the Aubin collection. The nine lords of the underworld similarly accompany the days.

This series of 13 gods of the days appears to have been of great antiquity, for if, as is almost certainly the case, the days from Caban to Muluc represent the gods whose heads stand for the numbers 1 to 13, it would seem that the concept of the 13 gods was older than the 20 day signs. In that case there was originally a cycle of 13 days each ruled by its own god. Then the 13 days were increased to 20 to conform to the vigesimal system, by the addition of seven more gods. Yet the old series of 13 was not dropped, but continued to function at the same time as the new series.

From there it would not have been a great step to re-place the gods of the original cycle of 13 with the numerical positions they held in the sequence. The old gods were not forgotten, as the head variants of the numbers show, nor were the associations of the gods lost. Ten, for instance, continued to be unlucky because it corresponded to the death god. In fact, the association of the 13 numbers with gods still survives, for Lincoln writes that among the Ixil, "The 13 numbers and the 20 day names are both regarded as sacred beings or deities who are worshipped and petitioned in prayer. The 13 numbers with their days are referred to as the thirteen kings."

Perhaps a memory of this expansion of the series of 13 days to 20 is contained in a sentence in Chumayel describing the birth of the period of 20 days—*Oxlahun tuc, uuc tuc, hun.* This Roys (1933, p. 118) translates as "Thirteen entities, seven entities, one." *Tuc* means something piled up; Roys, in a footnote, expresses his opinion that this refers to the fact that the 20-day period comprises a series of 13 days and a remainder of seven.

The main objection to this explanation of the origin of the sacred almanac is the absence of complete proof that the 13 celestial gods gave rise to the days, and not vice versa. If one could be certain that the days from Caban to Muluc were the same as the heads for the numbers 1 to 13, one could be reasonably certain that the concept of 13 gods was earlier than the 13 gods of the days. I myself regard the evidence in favor of the identity of the gods of the numbers with the gods of that sequence of days as overwhelming.

RITUALISTIC AND DIVINATORY DIVISIONS OF THE SACRED ALMANAC

The Maya, like the other peoples of Middle America, associated periods of time with the world directions. There were subdivisions of the period of 260 days with ritualistic connotations, and of these the most important were the year bearers and burner periods, each of which involved quartering that cycle. The manner in which the year bearers functioned is described in Chapter 4.

The details of the burner period are somewhat obscure, but of its importance in Maya ritual there can be no doubt. It is mentioned in Chumayel, Tizimin, Kaua, and Mani, and Landa describes one of the ceremonies although he was unaware of its context in the cycle of 260 days. The burner ceremony was first made known through the Pio Perez (1843) paraphrase of a Maya year 1 Kan. This calendar contains information on good and bad days, and days suitable for various activities.

Opposite the days 3 Chicchan, 3 Oc, 3 Men, and 3 Ahau are the words *"u ch'a kak ahtoc,"* translated as "the burner takes the fire" or "the burner handles the fire."

Following 10 Chicchan, 10 Oc, 10 Men, and 10 Ahau is

the sentence *"u hoppol u ƙak ahtoc,"* "the fire of the burner begins." Elsewhere *hopol* replaces *hoppol*. Roys, who remarks that either word fits the context, translates this as "the fire of the burner flares up."

With the days 4 Chicchan, 4 Oc, 4 Men, and 4 Ahau is the statement *"yalcab u ƙak ahtoc"* which J. L. Stephens translates from the Spanish of Pio Perez as "the burner gives the fire scope." Long (1923), who has made an invaluable study of the burner period, proposes the translation "the fire of the burner runs." Roys points out that the more reliable Tizimin gives *yal ƙaba,* and that version would mean "the declared name of the burner."

Opposite the days 11 Chicchan, 11 Oc, 11 Men, and 11 Ahau is written *"u tup ƙak ahtoc,"* which is translated as "the burner extinguishes the fire." Similar entries occur in the Maya year which starts on page 41 of Tizimin.

On page 38 of Tizimin is a passage which reads:

The record of the burners which are in the uinal. There are only four of them. There is 4 Chicchan: 10 Chicchan takes the fire; 11 Chicchan puts out the fire. The bearer of the uinal to the east. There is 4 Oc: 10 Oc takes the fire; 11 Oc puts out his fire. The bearer of the uinal to the north. There is 4 Men: 10 Men takes the fire; 11 Men puts out the fire. The bearer of the uinal to the west. There is 4 Ahau: 10 Ahau takes the fire; 11 Ahau puts out the fire. The bearer of the uinal to the south.

This is an unpublished translation by Roys incorporating minor amendments suggested by me. The omission of the days with coefficients of three is clearly due to carelessness. The intervals from 3 Chicchan to 10 Chicchan, to 4 Chicchan, to 11 Chicchan, to 3 Oc are 20, 20, 20, and 5 days. Thus this burner period divides the sacred almanac into four quarters, each of 65's, and each associated with a world direction. The four burners, 4 Chicchan, 4 Oc, 4 Men, and 4 Ahau, are called the four Ahaus, that is to say, the four chiefs or four rulers. In each quarter the burner takes the fire, begins the fire, lets it run (or names it), and extinguishes it.

The four burners are represented on Dresden 42–45 (fig. 61,*1–4*). Each of the four divisions of the sacred almanac is accorded a picture, and beneath the initial days of each division are the corresponding directions. The sequence is: 4 Ahau, south; 4 Chicchan, east; 4 Oc, north; 4 Men, west. There is, therefore, complete agreement with Tizimin in the assignment of directions to burners. Each period of 65 days is again divided, but not in conformity with the subdivisions of each burner period. The pictures show God B. With 4 Ahau he is opposite the seated god of maize; with 4 Chicchan he paddles a

canoe; with 4 Oc he is opposite an unidentified god, and there is a stylized fish between them; with 4 Men he is seated astride a dog (?) and holds in each hand an object generally identified as a flaming torch. Only the last suggests any connection with the act of letting the fire run. However, in view of the statement by Landa that the burner ceremony, as described by him, was held to assure rainfall, it may be significant that God B, who is a rain deity, appears in every picture. A specialized Oc sign above a bundle and with what may be a fire prefix appears with each picture. It may be the burner glyph, particularly since the dog, whose glyph is Oc, is closely associated with fire (p. 79). This is one of the few almanacs in Dresden divided into sections of 65 days, a second being on page 29. The day glyphs in the latter almanac are badly damaged, although their coefficients are clearly 11. Förstemann reads the day signs as Lamat, Ben, Etz'nab, and Akbal, but details cannot be made out in the edition of 1880. The possibility that they are the burner group 11 Ahau, 11 Chicchan, 11 Oc, and 11 Men is worth bearing in mind.

Landa describes a ceremony which he calls *tuppƙak,* and which, as Long points out, must be the same as the *u tup ƙak ah toc.* A large fire was lit, and into that were cast the hearts of sacrificed animals, or, if those were not available, copal formed in their shapes. When the hearts were burned the assistant priests, called Chacs, extinguished the fire by pouring water from their jugs. Landa says the ceremony took place in Mac, and was to insure copious rains, and that it was also held in Pax.

Long has shown that in Landa's typical year, which began with 12 Kan, the burner would extinguish his fire on 11 Oc 7 Mac and 11 Men 12 Pax, so that there is agreement in name and dates of the ceremony. Landa does not mention the other three occasions on which the ceremony would fall during the year, but Long has several plausible explanations for that omission. One is that Landa's description of the ceremonies is very brief and surely incomplete; the other, that the burner period indicated days on which the ceremonies might be held, not days on which it must be held.

Actually, the two occurrences mentioned by Landa fell in the dry season, one late in March, the other on June 2. The first was at the height of the dry season, the other just at the time when the rains were expected; whereas the remaining four occurrences fell in the rainy season. One would hardly expect the Maya to indulge in sympathetic magic imitating the fall of rain, when day after day water was cascading earthward.

The author of the *Relación de Valladolid* describes a fire-walking ceremony, in which a pile of wood, more than 25 feet long, as much wide, and taller than a man,

was prepared. This was set alight with appropriate ceremonies, and when the whole was turned to hot embers
it was smoothed out. The chief priest sprinkled balche
wine on the embers by means of a hyssop, made of the
tails of rattlers and other poisonous snakes. All four sides

each subdivision are indicated by black numbers to represent the number of days to be counted forward and red
numbers to declare the coefficient of the day reached.
Thus a typical almanac (Dresden 6 and 7) appears as
follows:

TWO LINES OF GLYPHS ACROSS TOP. TOTAL 16,
MAKING FOUR GLYPHS FOR EACH HORIZONTAL DIVISION.

1 Chuen	17	5	19	11	6	4	10	1
	(black)	(red)	(black)	(red)	(black)	(red)	(black)	(red)
Akbal								
Men								
Manik								
Cauac								

WRITTEN IN FULL THIS WOULD HAVE BEEN AS FOLLOWS:

1 Chuen	+ 17 =	5 Lamat	+ 19 =	11 Manik	+ 6 =	4 Ben	+ 10 =
1 Akbal	17	5 Ahau	19	11 Cauac	6	4 Chicchan	10
1 Men	17	5 Eb	19	11 Chuen	6	4 Caban	10
1 Manik	17	5 Kan	19	11 Akbal	6	4 Muluc	10
1 Cauac	17	5 Cib	19	11 Men	6	4 Imix	10

of the fire having been sprinkled in this way, the high
priest removed his sandals, and walked across the embers
unharmed, followed by the rest of the procession. The
ceremony is said to have been held at various times of
the year. Fire walking, as a purificatory rite, is still
practiced by the Tzotzil.

Landa also mentions this fire-walking ceremony, but
says that it was held during years which had Cauac as
the year bearer. Here, I think, the Valladolid *relación* is
more reliable, for it appears not unlikely that this is the
chief ceremony of the burners, on 4 Ahau, 4 Chicchan, 4
Oc, and 4 Men, when the fire of the burner spreads.

There may even be an explanation why Landa associates the ceremony with a Cauac year. Actually, the
ceremonies he describes are for a year commencing with
2 Cauac, in which the following day, 3 Ahau, would
start the 65-day period of the 4 Ahau burner, the most
important of all. His informant may well have told him
that on the day after the 2 Cauac new year, the ceremonies leading to the fire-walking climax began.

No special glyphs for the burner days have as yet been
recognized, with the possible exception of the Oc glyph
with special affixes, which occurs in Dresden, but the ceremony was obviously of considerable importance, perhaps the greatest connected with the 260-day almanac.

Various divisions of the sacred almanac occupy many
pages of Dresden and Madrid; most commonly the 260
days are divided into five sections of 52 days each. These
are in many, probably in all, cases the tools of divination,
recording days favorable and unfavorable for various
activities, but the exact manner in which these divinatory
almanacs functioned is not known. The subdivisions of
52 (rarely of 65) days are in turn partitioned into irregular intervals. Usually, the glyphs of only the initial
date of each subdivision are drawn. The dates within

The days of the subdivisional compartments presumably
were suppressed in order to save space, since the priest
making the divination could calculate them without much
trouble.

Thus, reading downwards, one gets the five subdivisions, each of 52 days; reading horizontally one reaches
the irregularly spaced intervals within each subdivision.
Below each interval there is usually the picture of a god,
presumably the deity who ruled those dates, and above
the numbers are the explanatory glyphs, usually four. In
the almanac under discussion the days 5 Lamat, 5 Ahau,
5 Eb, 5 Kan, and 5 Cib are ruled by the death god. The
next division 11 Manik, 11 Cauac, etc. was under God
D. The third was ruled by the Moan god. The last deity
who held sway on the days which form the last column,
but which are painted at the start of the almanac, is probably Schellhas' God H. Several almanacs are illustrated
(figs. 61–64) and briefly described in the captions.

Rules, if such exist, which govern the choice of the
various deities pictured, have not been discovered. The
kind of divination for which an almanac was devised is
fairly obvious in some cases, such as in those almanacs
which deal with apiary, but in this particular almanac no
clue as to its purpose has been found.

These divinatory almanacs, which clearly played an
extremely important part in Maya culture, will be discussed in more detail in a subsequent chapter.

STARTING POINT OF 260-DAY CYCLE

Landa states that the 260-day cycle commenced with
1 Imix. There are no grounds for doubting that the cycle
started with the day Imix, and small reason for not supposing that the accompanying number was one. The
Mexican almanac began with 1 Cipactli, as the "weeks"
given by all early authorities commence with that day.

The incomplete cycle of 260 days which stretches across Madrid 13–18 starts with the day Imix, but no numbers are given; Nuñez de la Vega says that Imox was the head of the count, and Ximenez opens his 20 days with Imox, and compares it to New Year's day; La Farge (1947, p. 179) notes that at Santa Eulalia he received a very strong impression that Imox led the list.

Full confirmation for Landa's statement, however, is to be found on Madrid 75 and 76, where the scheme of the calendar is laid out as the symbol for completion, together with world directions and their presiding deities. The day 1 Imix stands at the start of the count to the east, which is the direction with which Maya counting normally commenced. The fact that 13 Ahau, the day preceding 1 Imix, was regarded as the last day of the count of katuns is further evidence that the almanac started with 1 Imix, for if the round of katuns ended with 13 Ahau, the first day of the new round would be 1 Imix, the opening day of Katun 11 Ahau. According to Chumayel the (last?) creation occurred in a Katun 11 Ahau. The world may, therefore, have been regarded as having been inaugurated on 1 Imix, the first day of that katun.

On Madrid 65–73 the whole 260 days, complete with their coefficients, are again given. Here also the count leads off with 1 Imix, on page 65a, and terminates with 13 Ahau on page 73b. The evidence is overwhelming that the 260-day cycle started with 1 Imix.

The moment when each day of the sacred almanac started is a matter not easily settled. Among the present-day Maya of Jacaltenango the day commences at sunset. The same is true of the Ixil days, according to Lincoln. Goubaud, in his account of the ceremony held at Momostenango, at 8 Batz (p. 94), describes the ceremonies as having started at sunset of August 23, 1930, and continuing all through the day and night of August 24. The ceremonies accordingly lasted 36 hours.

A peculiar custom existed in Yucatan at the time of the Spanish conquest, whereby each katun was "the guest" of the preceding katun for the second half of the latter's reign, sharing its power. A katun, accordingly, had power for 30 tuns. For the first 10, it shared power with the preceding katun, then for the next 10, which formed the first half of its true length, it ruled alone. For the last 10 it shared its power with the next katun in the sequence (p. 204).

It has seemed to me not improbable that a similar arrangement may have existed for all periods of time, including the day. The great importance which the Maya give to the eve of Christian festivals might be a survival of this practice, but the idea also is European, and so this custom may not indicate Maya influence. Tax informs

me that he feels fairly sure that there is no idea that the day starts in the afternoon or evening of the previous day among the Maya groups of the midwest highlands which he has studied. These, however, have lost the old Maya calendar in its entirety.

The Aztec day, apparently, ran from midnight to midnight; for Yucatan there is no information. Had the Yucatecan day started at sunset, it is strange that Landa fails to mention the fact, seeing that he obviously had a first-rate informant on the calendar, probably Gaspar Antonio Chi, and although he did not comprehend every detail of his information, such a straightforward fact as that the day started at sunset could hardly have led to confusion. The evidence is negative, but the failure of Landa or any other writer on Yucatan to mention a matter which to them would have seemed very peculiar, viz. that the day commenced at nightfall, tends to support the view that the Yucatecan day started at sunrise, although it might have been the "guest" of the preceding day during the night. On the other hand, Redfield reports that in the Yucatec village of Chan Kom the appropriate name for a child born after noon is that of the saint of the following day. If this has a bearing on the subject, it would indicate that the Yucatec day ran from noon to noon.

There is some glyphic evidence that during the Initial Series Period the day ran from sunrise to sunrise (p. 174), and while this is not conclusive, it is sufficient to cause one to hesitate before assuming that the day's span was unquestionably from sunset to sunset. I regard the question as unsettled, and have a slight preference for the view that during the Initial Series Period the rising of the sun heralded the new day (see also p. 177).

The days on which the years started had great influence on the years which they initiated. Because of the construction of the calendar only four of the 20 day names could fall on the first day of the year. They were known as the year bearers, and they are discussed in Chapter 4.

Every endeavor was made by the Maya to adjust all their time periods, such as the synodical revolutions of the planets and lunar cycles, to the 260-day cycle so that they could establish equations, e.g. 65 synodical revolutions of Venus uncorrected equaled 146 cycles of 260 days; 405 lunations equaled 46 cycles of 260 days. This subject will be discussed in later chapters.

So far as is known, the individual cycles of 260 days were not numbered or arranged in larger groupings, such as in 20's, 400's, and 8000's.

SUMMARY

The cycle of 260 days is the core of the Maya calendar. It is a divinatory and sacred almanac which bears no known relation to any celestial phenomenon. It consists of 20 day names combined with the numbers 1–13. Not until the 260 combinations of names and numbers have been completed does the cycle start again. It repeats through all eternity regardless of the positions of sun, moon, and stars.

The 20 days were—and still are—regarded as gods, and the accompanying numbers hold similar rank. The glyphs for these day names appear to be stylized portraits of those gods or highly conventionalized pictures of attributes or insignia of those deities. The numbers 1–13 are sometimes personalized as the heads of the gods which they represent. It is almost certain that a sequence of 13 of the day names running from Caban to Muluc represent in the same order the identical series of gods ruling the numbers 1–13.

The individual combinations of day names and numbers wielded enormous influence over the daily life of the Maya from prince of the church to humble peasant. The luck of each day name and number decided when crops should be planted, when wars should be started, whether individuals would be suitably mated, and when the marriage should take place, and, indeed, the aspects of the days dominated practically every activity, whether of the group or of the individual. A rigid system of predestination encompassed the individual because the influences of the day of his birth molded his entire life; there is even some evidence that these same controls swayed the course of history.

The cycle of 260 days was not used by itself in the counting of time, and, so far as is known, these cycles were not grouped in large units, such as by 20's, 400's, and 8000's. On the other hand, all other Maya cycles, whether of vague years (365 days), approximate years (tuns), synodical revolutions of the planets, or lunations, were coordinated with the sacred almanac by utilizing the lowest common multiples of the 260-day period and the astronomical cycle.

In the Maya fane this cycle was the sanctuary, to the glory of which the subordinate transepts of solar and lunar counts, the nave of the tun reckoning, and the crypt of the lords of the nights were integrated in one grand fabric. From its 20 choirstalls, with their changing occupants, radiated the essence of Maya life through the temple, and, beyond its doors, to every corner of Maya land.

4

The Year of 365 Days

Thou crownest the year with thy goodness.
—Psalm 65

For ritualistic and divinatory purposes the Maya had their sacred almanac, the cycle of 260 days, but for agriculture and for the yearly round of mundane activities this did not suffice; a calendar approximating the annual travels of the sun was necessary. To fill this need the Maya had a year of 365 days, and, although they were were well aware that this period fell short of the true length of the year, they did not intercalate days to make it conform to the solar year of 365.2422 days. However, careful calculations of the accumulated error were made, and the results set down as separate entries in the hieroglyphic texts, whereby the priests could easily calculate how much their year had gained on the true year in the 4000 years elapsed since the official point of departure of their calendar (App. V).

The intercalation of leap days would have wrecked the whole Maya scheme of utilizing the points at which the initial dates of the various cycles of time coincided. For instance, the interval of 37,960 days was of prime importance to the Maya because it was the lowest common multiple of 365, 260, and 584. Only after that number of days would the vague year, the sacred almanac, and the synodical revolution of Venus again coincide. The Maya paid a great deal of attention to such intervals, and many of their computations deal with the problem of obtaining numbers divisible by a maximum number of their cycles; the main purpose of seeking such periods was to relate all cycles to the sacred almanac so that it would be known after what interval celestial phenomena, such as heliacal risings, would repeat on the same day of the sacred almanac. The day 1 Ahau was particularly important in the Venus calendar. It was therefore necessary to know when a heliacal rising of Venus would again coincide with 1 Ahau: the answer was, after 146×260 days. Positions in the sacred almanac and the tun (approximate year of 360 days) would be the same after 18×260 days, but any intercalations of days to adjust the vague year of 365 days or the tun to the solar year would have upset all such schemes. The year of 365 days accordingly gained nearly one day in four years over the solar year, and no direct correction offset this.

NAMES OF THE MONTHS

The year was divided into 18 "months" of 20 days each, and there was a final period of five days, which was regarded as very unfortunate. "Month" is an incorrect term but will be retained because of its convenience and because it is well established in the literature.

As in the case of the day names, the month names employed by modern investigators of the Maya calendar are those which were in use in Yucatan at the time of the Spanish conquest. These differed radically from those in use in other parts of the Maya area. Information on month names for the whole Maya area is less satisfactory than for the day names; in some cases series are incomplete, and in others the sequence of the months is uncertain.

These sundry lists are given in Table 8. It will be noted that the position of the five unlucky days varies considerably. The least reliable set of months is that of the Ixil. Lincoln (1942) published six lists of Ixil months, but his informants were in complete disagreement as to the order, and, in one case, the same informant gave two different sequences. Clearly the whole arrangement is in the last stages of decadence; the combined series contain more than 19 names. I have arranged the names to make the few obvious correspondences (e.g. Yaxki, Molche, Chentemac, etc.), and filled in the rest more or less haphazardly.

I have started the Tzeltal and Tzotzil lists with Huc Uincil and Nichilkin, respectively, so as to correlate Yaxkin and Mac with their Yucatecan namesakes. We have no information as to when the sequences began.

La Farge's sundry informants on the Kanhobal months varied considerably in their lists, and in the number of months they could name; they were in fairly good accord for the sequence starting with Oneu and ending with Bak, but for the rest of the series I have depended on one informant. The order of two or three months is open to doubt, but I have confidence in the general reliability of this important list.

The Pokomchi list dates from the last period of regression, and one can be reasonably sure that there are errors in the arrangement. To check with lowland calendars Kazeu, Mox kih, Olh, and the sequences Yax and Zac and Chentemac to Muuan should be moved one or two places.

That changes in the succession do take place when the calendar ceases to function is demonstrated by innovations in the sequences of the Tzeltal and Tzotzil months for which some informants are responsible. Thus Barbachano's Tzeltal informant at Tenejapa placed Yaxkin before Pom, and Vicente Pineda does the same thing; Pineda also has Olalti Tzun and Chaikin misplaced; Becerra, in one list, gives Chaikin after Tzun. With disintegration months are misplaced or forgotten.

We can, therefore, assume that the same sort of errors have crept into the Pokomchi, Kanhobal, and Ixil lists. This is a different situation from that which obtains so far as the 260-day cycle is concerned. In that case we are dealing with a highly ritualistic count divorced from seasonal influences, and with an immutable sequence, any tampering with which would send all divinations awry. Moreover, the almanac has for its maintenance a body of priests or shamans. Consequently, wherever the 260-day almanac still is used there is no confusion in the order of the days.

From the reports of ethnologists one gets the impression that among the Tzeltal and Tzotzil, who alone have lost the day series but retained the month names, there is no organized body of priest-shamans, such as keeps the tally of the days in the Guatemalan highlands. The greater impact of Christianity on these peoples is probably the cause of the absence of that group. Instead, the count of the months appears to be in the hands of the laity, who use it as an agricultural almanac. Mistakes in the sequence might occur more readily with no authoritative guardians of the count. The fates of the two systems reflect, I think, their degrees of sacredness.

PATRONS OF THE MONTHS

In texts of the Classical Period which give IS, the first glyph is the IS introductory glyph, the central element of which is a variable. Beyer (1931) has proved what Bowditch (1910) suspected, namely, that the variable element changes according to the month of the IS, and that there are 18 forms (several with variants) corresponding to the 18 months. A nineteenth form pertaining to Uayeb has not been identified because no IS falling in the five unlucky days has yet been found. There can be no doubt that these variable elements symbolize the patron deities of the months, and correspond in function somewhat loosely to the day gods. There was an analogous patronage of the months in the Valley of Mexico, for among the Aztec an important feast was held each month to at least one deity, and attributes of those deities became the symbols of the months, although a picture of the patron god more usually indicates the period of 20 days.

It will be necessary to identify briefly the patrons of the Maya months before the meanings of the names of the months can be discussed. In many cases the heads are readily recognized (figs. 22; 23).

Pop. The jaguar, usually depicted in a naturalistic manner.

Uo. The jaguar god of the underworld, whose head serves also as the head variant of the number 7. Note jaguar ear and loop under eye and over bridge of nose.

Zip. The head of a monster, whose snout turns upward and backward to form a fret design. The lower jaw is generally, but not always, suppressed. An animal with this same unusual head appears several times in Dresden (pp. 43–45, 68) in the act of plunging downward from the sky, represented by bands of planetary symbols. Similar animals, but with human heads and legs, are depicted on Madrid 2 in the act of falling earthward. They carry axes in their hands and have a background of falling water (as does the animal on Dresden 68). Tozzer and Allen (1910, p. 352) identify this creature as a peccary; Seler (1902–23, 4: 551) regards it as a mythical monster, the lightning beast, which cannot for that reason be classified zoologically. A variant form from Piedras Negras 36 gives a clue to the identification of this creature, since it is the same as a conventionalized head frequently seen in planetary bands (fig. 22,*11*). As is well established, planetary symbols not infrequently hang from planetary bands, but there is no reason to suppose that symbols or personifications of clouds, thunder, or lightning might not also figure in these bands or be pendent therefrom.

The fact that this head is prominent on pages dealing with the 780-day period led Willson (1924, p. 33) to identify it as that of the god of Mars, but there is considerable doubt that these pages really refer to that planet. Makemson believes that they may deal with Jupiter, although probably referring also to Mars; Spinden believes they are tables for Saturn; I myself am confident they are for prognosticating rain (p. 258).

The identification with the peccary made by Tozzer and Allen is a possibility that cannot be overlooked, but mythological animals elude rigid classification. The animal is not unlike a deer (the brocket), a determination not without elements in its favor, for deer are sometimes shown in Mexican art falling from the sky, and, as we shall see, this month bears the name of a deer god.

Zotz'. The patron is the mythical *Xoc* fish, which is also the god of the day Muluc. The fins behind the nose and around the corner of the mouth are unmistakable (Thompson, 1944, p. 3).

Zec. The symbol for this month is usually one of two glyphs: the first is the sign commonly accepted as the sky symbol (p. 172); the second is the Caban sign, which represents the earth. On Morales 2 these are replaced by the head of a youthful deity, perhaps the god of number 11.

Xul. The patron of the month is not surely identified. The best-preserved head is that of a youthful deity with a line curving from his eye.

Yaxkin. The old sun god is the patron. His head or his glyph, the kin sign, is the variable element. (See also fig. 23,*33,38*.)

Mol. The head of an aged god, perhaps Schellhas' God D; the symbolic form is well established, but can not be identified.

Ch'en. This month belongs to the moon. The moon glyph or the moon goddess emerging from the moon sign constitutes the variable element.

Yax. Venus is the patron, and is represented by the Venus symbol or the head of the Venus monster.

Zac. The head corresponding to this month is probably that of the frog deity.

Ceh. The variable element is the upper part of the sky symbol

TABLE 8—NAMES OF MONTHS IN VARIOUS MAYA LANGUAGES

YUCATEC[1]	CHOL(?)[7]	TZELTAL[8]	TZOTZIL[18]	KANHOBAL[26]	IXIL[32]	POKOMCHI[33]	CAKCHIQUEL[40]
Pop	......	Huc Uincil[9]	Nichilkin[19]	Nabich	Metchki	Kanhalam	Likinka
Uo	Icat	Uac Uincil	Hum Uincil[20]	Moo	Mu	Makux	Nabei Tokik
Zip	Chaccat	Ho Uincil	Xchibal Uinicil[21]	Bak[27]	Zilki	Kazeu	Rucac Tokik
Zotz'[2]	......	Chan Uincil	Yoxchibal Uinicil	Canal[28]	Tchotzcho	Kanazi	Nabei Pach
Zec[3]	Cazeu	Ox Uincil	Xchanibal Uinicil	Cuhem	Xetki	Kanahal	Rucam Pach
Xul	Chichin	Pom[10]	Pom	Huachsicin	Tzicinki	Tzikin Kih	Tzikin Kih
Yaxkin[4]	Ianguca	Yaxkin[11]	Yaxkin	Yaxacil	Yaxki	Mox kih	Cakam
Mol	Mol	Mux[10]	Mux[23]	Mol	Mol	Tih txehk[34]	Ibotan
......	......	......	......	......	......	KAXI K LAHKIH	
Ch'en[2]	Zihora	Tzun[12]	Tzun[24]	Khek Sihom	Petzetzki	Yax	Katic
......	......	......	......	......	......	......	......
Yax	Yax	Batzul	Batzul	Yax Sihom[29]	Avaxki	Zac	Izcal
Zac	Zac	Zacilab[13]	Zizac	Sah Sihom	Huiki	Tzi	Pariche
			CHAIKIN				TZAPIKIH
Ceh	Chac	Ahelchac[14]	Muctazac	Khak Sihom	Kohki	Txip[35]	Tacaxepual
Mac	Chantemat	Mac	Moc	Mac	Chentemac	Chantemac[36]	Nabe Tumuzuz
Kankin	Uniu	Olalti	Olalti	Oneu	Ochki	Uniu	Rucab Tumuzuz
Muan	Muhan	Hulol[15]	Ulol[25]	Sivil	Muen	Muuan	Cibixik
......	......	CHAIKIN[11]	......	......	......	......	......
Pax	Ahkiku	Hoken Ahau[16]	Okin Ahual	Tap[30] OYEBKU[31]	Pactzi	Tam[37]	Uchum
Kayab	Kanazi	Alauch[17]	Uch	Uex	Talcho	Sackohk[38]	Nabei Mam
Cumku[5]	Olh	Mucuch	Elech	Sakmai	Nimcho	Ohl[39]	Rucab Mam
UAYEB[6]	MAHI IKABA	......	......	......	OKI	......	......

[1]Various books of Chilam Balam. Sometimes vowels are doubled as in Uoo, Mool, Ch'een, Yaax, and Paax. This doubling appears to have no significance.

[2]Landa gives Zotz and Chen which has been generally accepted by modern epigraphers; Zotz' and Ch'en are almost certainly the old forms. Landa paid little attention to glottal stops.

[3]Landa gives Tzec, but the books of Chilam Balam and Sanchez de Aguilar use Zeec or Zec.

[4]Tz'eyaxkin is an alternative form.

[5]Landa has Cumhu which has been accepted by most present-day students. Nevertheless, the books of Chilam Balam and Sanchez de Aguilar give Cumku. Probably the bowdlerizer of Landa's manuscript read a k as an h. Cunku is another spelling.

[6]Sanchez de Aguilar (1892, p. 95), who wrote in 1613, gives as alternative names for these five days *Uayeab, u tuzkin,* "the falseness or dissimulation of the days," *u lobol kin,* "the evil of the days"; Pio Perez (1864, p. 384) gives the names *Uayeb haab* and its contraction *Uayab,* which he translates "the bed or compartment of the year." He also lists *u yail haab* or *u yail kin,* "the misfortune of the year or of the day." The days were also called *Xma kaba kin,* "nameless days"; the Motul dictionary gives *u hitz' haab,* "last day of the year." *Hitz'* means "end or death."

[7]Based on Gates (1931c, pp. 30–32) and Thompson (1932). In that paper I give evidence suggesting that this is a Chol, not a Kekchi year, principally because of the use of *y* in *Yax;* in Kekchi one would expect *Rax;* Gates regards the month names as Kekchi. The accompanying text is Kekchi.

[8]Based on Redfield and Villa (1939) and Schulz (1942). Earlier lists are published by Vicente Pineda (1888, pp. 130, 31) and others are given by Marcos Becerra (1933), Villa (1945), and Barbachano (1946).

[9]Most sources give Huc Binkil, etc. There is no doubt that *binkil* or *uincil* is the word for twenty, and the first five months record 140, 120, 100, 80, and 60 days. Perhaps this refers to a feast held in Mux.

[10]V. Pineda has Pom and Mux interchanged; Barbachano reverses Yaxkin and Pom.

[11]V. Pineda has Chaikin immediately after Pom which would be Mux in the present calendar.

[12]V. Pineda has Tzun after Olalti; Becerra has Chaikin after Tzun.

[13]Schulz, Becerra, and V. Pineda have Sacilha; Villa has Zacilab.

[14]Schulz has Ahilchac, as does Villa.

[15]V. Pineda has Hulhol.

[16]V. Pineda has Hoken Hahab; Schulz Hokin Ahau.

[17]V. Pineda has Yaluch; Becerra gives Yalahuch, Yahuch, Alaluch, Alahuch, and Bikituch for various towns; Villa and Barbachano have Chinuch.

[18]Based on Rodaz (1688) and Schulz (1942). Emeterio Pineda (1845), Starr (1902, p. 72), Becerra (1933), Barbachano (1946a), and Guiteras (1946) also give lists of Tzotzil months.

[19]Modern authors have Nichikin.

[20]Modern authors have Sba Bincil or Sba uincil.

[21]Schulz has Xibal Bincil.

[22]Schulz has Xanibal Uincil; Starr, Chanim Uincil.

[23]Rodaz has Muy.

[24]Starr has Tzim.

[25]Rodaz gives Ulol or Hoyoh.

[26]Kanhobal is the name used by La Farge for a linguistic group comprising two main languages, Kanhobal and Chuh, with Jacalteca as a major dialect of the former. In the lists of day names those of the Jacalteca and of the Chuh village of San Mateo Ixtatan are separated because of significant differences. The following list of months is based on Antonio Juarez list in La Farge, 1947, p. 168. See also Termer (1930, p. 391). I assume that Antonio Juarez was mistaken in saying that the sihom was a period of 80 days; I think that he should have said that the four sihoms total 80 days. They conform to the four Cauac months with their colors. I have made two transpositions in his sequence, and suppressed Bactan which no other informant lists. For variations in spelling see Table 2 in La Farge, 1947.

[27]Two of La Farge's informants place Cuhem here.

[28]Juarez has Yaxacil here. I have transposed it with Canal, and suppressed Bactan.

[29]Juarez places Sah Sihom here. I have transposed it with Yax Sihom to retain the color sequence of the glyphs: black, green, white, red.

[30]Termer has a month Tam, which corresponds to the Pokomchi.

[31]Termer gives Oyebin, with which all La Farge's informants disagree. Oyebku means "five days."

[32]Lincoln (1942). As already noted, there is complete confusion as to the order of the months, and the present arrangement makes no pretense to being correct.

[33]Termer (1930, pp. 394–95) and Gates (1932a). Both derive from a list made in 1906 by a certain Sr. Vicente or

with St. Andrew's cross infix. Sometimes this is worn as the head-dress of the earth monster.

Mac. The head of a deity with a peculiar cap represents this month. He is probably the god of the number 3. The symbolic variant is the Ik sign which is an insigne of the god of number 3. It has been shown that this deity is connected with the rains.

Kankin. The symbolic form of the element is a doubled arch of unknown meaning; the head variant is that of a fantastic monster with a row of prominent fangs which curve backward.

Muan. A head which appears to vary from youth to old age, and is supplied with a prefix. Conceivably the Moan bird.

Pax. The personified form may be that of the night sun, since the features are those of the sun god, but without a lower jaw, the lack of which indicates a connection with the underworld and death. Before the face there is generally an affix which forms part of Glyph G7 (fig. *34,32,35*) and of a form of Glyph X (fig. 37, *9,34,38,55,60,69*). The symbolic form (fig. *23,36*) has this same element before what is seemingly a jade symbol. (See also fig. *23,34.*) Conceivably a puma god (p. 116).

Kayab. The young moon, earth and maize deity, patroness of Caban and the number 1, and goddess of childbirth. (See also fig. *23,37,39,40.*)

Cumku. The head of a monster is the variable of this month, no symbolic form being yet reported. There is considerable variation in the details. Beyer considers that the identifiable element may be the ornament at the back of the head. The monster is most probably the Imix crocodile.

MEANINGS OF NAMES OR GLYPHS OF MONTHS

In discussing the meanings of the various names given to the months by the Maya, those which come from the Pokomchi, Chuh, and Ixil will receive less attention than those of the Yucatec and Chol lists, chiefly because their order is uncertain, but also because there is doubt as to how carefully they have been recorded. The Quiche and Cakchiquel month lists will be largely ignored because of the Mexican influences they show, and because there is no information even as to what the names are supposed to mean.

Pop, Huc uincil, Nabich, Nichilkin (fig. 16,*1–9*). The glyph for this month is a plaited pattern with the kan cross, a water symbol, as an infix. Pop means straw mat in almost all Maya languages and dialects, and therefore is in agreement with the sign, for the plaited symbol suggests

the mat pattern. The kan cross probably reinforces the idea that the mat was of reed. Pop, however, has a secondary meaning of chief in some Maya languages or dialects because the mat was the symbol of authority, and this mat of authority is sometimes called the jaguar mat (Roys, 1933, pp. 66, 74); it was probably a mat only in name, being in actual practice a throne with a jaguar skin over it or a seat carved as a jaguar, of which there are many representations in Maya art. The term corresponds to the Mexican *icpalli*.

The extension of Pop to mean chief is natural. In the Pokomchi dictionary of Cahcoh occur *Ah Pop,* "chief," and *Im pop im camha,* "I am chief." The jaguar, too, was a symbol of authority. Thus "jaguar mat" is a reinforced term for authority. Accordingly the first 20-day period of the Maya year was the symbol of chieftainship as shown by the glyph itself and by its Yucatecan name. Its patron was the jaguar god, the jaguar, too, connoting authority.

In the Tzeltal calendar the name Huc uincil means seven periods of 20 days, and presumably refers to a feast to be held seven months later. This system of numbering months in descending order may well represent a rather late innovation. Nichilkin means in Tzotzil "festival of the flowers." Schulz (1942, p. 13) makes the very interesting suggestion that this may correspond to the Aztec month Tlaxochimaco with the meaning "flowers are given." Evidence that Schulz's identification may well be correct is to be found in the fact that at the time of the Spanish conquest the first month of the Maya year and Tlaxochimaco were concurrent, both starting late in July. We might also deduce from this evidence that the Tzotzil and Yucatec years started at the same time, or within a few days of one another, but Nichilkin now starts on July 22, and there is some evidence that leap days are not intercalated; in that case it could not have fallen in July at the time of the Spanish conquest.

Uo, Mo, Icat, Uac uincil, Hum uincil (fig. 16,*10–22*). The glyph for the second month consists of celestial crossed bands, such as occur in planetary bands, with the symbol for black as a prefix or infix. The jaguar god of the underworld, who is the night sun and whose head is the symbol for the number 7, is the patron. We have already seen that this god is also the deity of Akbal, "night, darkness, and the interior of the earth." There is therefore a direct connection between this glyph with its black symbol and the patron deity.

Icat, or Ikcat as it should be, in the Chol list from the Alta Verapaz carries the idea of darkness. The months Uo and Zip are similar except that the former has the color symbol for black as a prefix or infix; the latter has the symbol for red as its prefix. The names in the Chol

---

Victor A. Narciso. The dictionary of Cahcoh gives Petcat and Canazi, corresponding to the 2nd and 17th. months. See Thompson (1932).

[34] Gates has Tik-cheik.

[35] Gates has Kchip.

[36] Termer has Txantemac.

[37] Gates has Cham.

[38] Termer has Sacgohk.

[39] Termer has Oh.

[40] Calendario Cakchiquel (1685). Quiche lists are omitted for lack of space. The best are the Ahilabal Kih (c.1722), which is reproduced in La Farge (1934), and the Hernandez Spina (1854) list from Ixtlauacan. Quiche months do not differ radically from those of the Cakchiquel. Both diverge greatly from other Maya lists, and show fairly marked influences from Mexico.

list for these two months are respectively Icat and Chaccat. *Kat* or *cat* (both forms are given) must correspond to the crossed bands since *chac* is the word for red in most lowland dialects, and *ek* or *ihk* means black in the same lowland group. These names, too, are evidence that this calendar is not Kekchi, since the Kekchi names for red and black are *cak* and *kehk*, respectively, whereas the Chol names are *chacchac* and *ik, ikh,* or *ek.* The meaning of *cat* in Chol is unknown, apart from jar or vase. However, there is a Yucatec root *kaat* which means something transverse or oblique, and is used for such actions as placing a beam transversely, and crossing from one side to another. One derivative, *kat cunah* for example, means to place one thing transversely across another. Such meanings correspond rather closely to the crossed bands of the glyph, but the correspondence may be fortuitous. The Chol name for the month therefore means the black *kat.*

Uo is the Yucatecan name for a variety of small frogs which are almost black in color but with a yellow line down the spine. They are usually found in the ground (p. 144). According to Maya legend they are the musicians of the Chacs, the rain gods, probably because the croaking of frogs announces rain. Nevertheless, I do not believe that the name of this month can have any connection with these small frogs, unless it be that because of their burrowing habits they were regarded as symbols of the interior of the earth. It is not improbable that the name Uo refers to some ceremony held during this month.

In the Tzeltal calendar the corresponding month is Uac uincil, "six periods of 20 days," but in the Tzotzil calendar of Rodaz this is Hum uincil, "one period of 20 days." This is the first of a series of numbered uinals in ascending order in contrast to the descending order of the Tzeltal. The only logical explanation is that the start of this month once fell 20 days after the start of the year. In the modern Tzotzil calendar this sequence is disrupted.

Zip, Chackat, Ho uincil, Xchibal uincil, Bak (fig. 16, 23–34). As already noted, the glyph for the third month is formed of the crossed bands with the symbol for red as the prefix, and the Chol name for it is red *kat* or *cat* (crossed bands?). The Yucatec name Zip is almost surely due to the fact that an important festival in honor of the gods of hunting was held in this month (on the seventh day, Landa tells us). One of the chief gods of hunting was Zip or Ek Zip, "Black Zip" (p. 76). The Yucatec, therefore, appear to have named this month after that god, but this was probably a later innovation since a reference to the color red in all probability once was featured in the month's name, as in the Chol list.

The identity of the patron of the month, an animal with hoofs and an upper jaw which terminates in a fret, has been discussed. It seems possible that these beasts represent an early Maya form of Mixcoatl, the Mexican god of hunting who has features of the deer. His name, which translates "cloud serpent," suggests that he was once a bringer of rain, but that idea, if it did once exist, had disappeared before the sixteenth century. Such an identification would account for the ophidian character of the beast's snout, and the crosshatched spots, like those on snakes, on the bodies of those depicted in Madrid, and also for the axes (insigne of the rain gods) carried by the beasts, and the glyphic texts which appear to deal with rain (p. 258). At the same time the connection with hunting would remain. The fact that Mixcoatl, as one of the Tzitzimime, fell head first to earth, whereas this beast is depicted in the same attitude in the codices, perhaps adds some force to this speculation, on which, however, I do not insist. Even though the identification with Mixcoatl may not stand, the fact that the patron deity has an animal form, whether deer, peccary or something else, might be the reason why the hunters held their chief festival in this month. The Tzeltal month is Ho uincil, "five periods of 20 days"; the Tzotzil is Xchibal uincil, "two periods of 20 days." The former a step in a descending order; the latter in an ascending series.

Zotz', Chan uincil, Yoxchibal uincil (fig. 16,35–44). The glyph for the third month is the head of the leaf-nosed bat; the word *zotz'* has that same meaning. The equivalent month is missing from the Chol list. The patron deity is the *xoc* monster, a mythical fish (p. 108). It is very strange that one animal should form the glyph and another, totally unrelated to it, should be the patron of the month. So far as I know, there is no season of the year when bats are abundant, and no reason in nature why a month should bear the name of the leaf-nosed bat, and it is, therefore, not improbable that we have in the name of this month an example of rebus writing, and that the head of the leaf-nosed bat was chosen as the glyph of this month because its name resembled that of some activity which took place during this month. The Moran dictionary of Manche Chol, which completely fails to recognize glottal stops, lists *zutz,* "bat," *zutzil,* "winter," and *zutzil quiui,* "annatto of Christmas," presumably a variety ripening at that season. The first word is clearly the same as Yucatec *zotz',* and appears also in Palencano and Chontal as *zutz',* "bat."

The month Zotz' could not have fallen near Christmas during the colonial period. There is therefore the possibility (and it is no more) that *zotz'* had the meaning of winter, or rather the period when the days were shortest. There is also a Yucatec root *zutz'* which carries the idea of laying down or stretching out long objects.

Here, however, the connection with winter is not apparent. Pio Perez also gives *zuutz'*, "bitter," "vinegar." In Ixil *zutz'* is cloud.

The Tzeltal and Tzotzil lists continue their numbered months.

Zec, Cazeu (or *Kazeu*), *Oxuincil, Xchanibal uincil* (fig. 16,45–53). This is a geometric design resembling the uinal with the comb (count) prefix, which in personified forms becomes the headdress of a grotesque being. Once the count prefix is personified, becoming the main element with the uinal symbol infixed (fig. 16,50). The uinal-like sign is too conventionalized to give any clue as to its meaning. The patron of the month is a youthful deity, perhaps the god of 11. However, this head is extremely rare, and is in nearly every case replaced by the signs caban, "earth," or caan, "sky."

As noted, Landa writes this month as Tzec, and in that way the month has been spelled by modern writers. Nevertheless, the spelling Zec or Zeec of the books of Chilam Balam is supported by Sanchez de Aguilar, and Pio Perez also uses Zeec or Zec. I know of no satisfactory translations of Zec or of Cazeu or Kazeu, the corresponding month in the Chol and Pokomchi calendars, although displaced in the latter list. The Tzeltal and Tzotzil equivalents are units in the series numbered, respectively, three and four periods of 20 days.

The presence of the count prefix in the glyph for Zec may be significant. It occurs also with Mac, the glyph for which, to anticipate, probably indicates the count of the 260-day period, for the end of Mac actually is 260 days from the start of the year. If one counts from the end of Zec to the end of the year the distance is also 260 days. In other words there may be in the glyphs for these two months recognition of compartments of 260 days set within the year (exclusive of the five unlucky days). The evidence so far as Mac is concerned is fairly strong; in the case of Zec it is much weaker.

Bishop Landa states that the beekeepers held a festival in honor of the gods of the bees, especially the god Hobnil in the month Zec, but as Hobnil was the Bacab who ruled the Kan years, and as Bishop Landa's typical year had the year bearer 12 Kan, it is not improbable that this was a festival of the 260-day cycle. In effect the day 1 Kan chanced to fall in the month Zec of Landa's typical year. Accordingly it is probable that this festival had nothing to do with that month, but was a commemoration of 1 Kan.

Xul, Chichin, Pom, Tzikin kih, Huachsicin (fig. 16,54–64). The sixth month has as its glyph the head of an animal, generally recognized as that of a dog, to which is attached the "sun tail" such as is found with the kin sign (fig. 26,51–57). Only one glyph of the

patron deity is sufficiently well preserved to yield information. Morley draws this as a human head with an irregular line which is placed vertically on the face, passing through the eye. There is a prefix before the face, the *il* relationship element (p. 285). There is also a large circle at the back of the cheek which may represent an earplug. In view of the apparent canine associations, discussed below, it is worth remarking that Xolotl, the Mexican canine god, is sometimes shown with a line through his eye, and the Maya canine god is usually depicted in Dresden with a curved line on his face. This starts from the eye, and may represent a change of color of the hair.

Xul means "end" in Yucatec, but I think it probable that this month name was not used in that sense. In Kekchi *xul* is a general name for animal. In central Mexico Xolotl, or Xulotl, as the name is often transcribed, was the canine god who descended to the underworld, and who may well have been the deity who led the sun each evening into the underworld, and in time came to be associated with the sun immediately after setting. Among the Nahua-speaking people of Nicaragua the name for dog was *xulo*. This suggests a derivation from the Mexican *xolot(l)*, and implies that that word is an ancient term for dog, although the usual word at the time of the conquest was *itzcuintli*.

The Zapotec name for the native hairless dog is *peco xolo*, but the word *xolo* also enters into the composition of the term for the tapir *peche xolo*. The Lenca name for dog is given in one vocabulary as *xuxu*, which suggests a connection. Elsewhere it is recorded as *xui* or *xuiy*, *xu* being given as the first letters (syllable?) of the names for coyote, rat, squirrel, and the mapache. Jicaque names for dog include *shio, soyo, choyo*, and *tzoo*. The Sumo word for dog is given as *sul* or *suul* or *sulu*.

In the various Maya languages and dialects the generic names for dog are *ch'i* (or *tz'i*) and *pek*, but Chicomucelteca which differs from most Maya tongues and seems to have affinities with Huaxtec, uses the word *sul*, and *xolo* is the generic name for swine, domestic and wild.

Lehmann (1920) appears to regard some of the above terms as derived from Xolotl, the implication being that they were carried to Central America in Mexican penetration of relatively late date. I would be inclined to consider the distribution too widespread to be explained in that way unless we are to assume that the word was widely adopted to describe some new species of dog. Furthermore, the word appears to have become extinct in the Valley of Mexico, at least, by the early part of the sixteenth century, surviving only as the name of the canine god, Xolotl. I am inclined to believe that the term *xul* or a word with that root was used by the Maya of the Initial Series Period for a dog, although it may have been a ritualistic word used only to describe the dog which led the sun to the underworld.

It is barely possible that Chichin, the Chol month, may convey the idea of the dog since *chichi* is a nickname for the dog in many parts of Central America and Mexico, and the picture of a dog represents the sound chichi in Codex Mendoza.

Tzikin kih is usually rendered as feast of the birds, but it is perhaps worth noting that the first syllable means dog.

The Chiapan name, Pom, signifies copal incense in most Maya languages. There is, nevertheless, another meaning, that of pus, perhaps because of a resemblance of pus to the yellowish white gum. Thus we find in Yucatec *pomactel*, "a fresh sore with pus," and *pomkak*, "smallpox," although *kak* by itself is the more usual word for smallpox. One is reminded of the sore ears exuding pus and the syphilitic character of Xolotl. It is therefore possible that this Chiapan name for the month refers to that feature of the canine god (cf. p. 79).

The evidence is far from satisfactory, but I am inclined to consider that this month was under the patronage of the canine god who appears to have conducted the sun to the underworld. That might account for the presence of the sun tail. With greater hesitation I would assume that *xul* was the liturgical name or the root of the name of that deity.

Yaxkin, Ianguca, Yaxacil (fig. 17,1–13). There is better agreement here than in any of the months so far discussed. Yaxkin appears in Yucatec, Tzeltal, and Tzotzil, and there is an Ixil month Yaxki, which has the same meaning; the Chuh name Yaxacil may belong here. Yaxkin means "new sun" or "green sun" or "first sun" or "dry season." The glyph itself is in complete agreement with this name, for it is the kin sign with the yax element as prefix. Furthermore, the patron of the month is the sun god, for his head or his glyph is the variable element in the IS introductory glyph corresponding to this month.

New sun or first sun is in accord with the suggested interpretation of the preceding month, for if the sun was believed to have been in the underworld during the previous month, a new sun would logically appear in this month. However, the name more probably refers to the morning sun who, refreshed by the sacrifices offered him, sheds the symbols acquired during his nightly journey through the underworld to appear in all his vigor.

In the various books of Chilam Balam this month usually carries the prefix *tz'e,* which means "small," but is also prefixed to certain terms of kinship as though to carry the idea of "not quite," or "nearly," e.g. *yum*, "father"; *tz'eyum,* "father's brother"; *na*, "mother";

tz'ena, "mother's sister." In that case *tz'eyaxkin* might mean "little first sun," or "not quite new sun." I can offer no interpretation of the Chol name Ianguca.

Mol, Mux, and probably *Molche* and *Moxkih* (fig. 17,14–22). The eighth month in the Maya year has as its glyph the symbol for jade or water (p. 78) surrounded by small circles. The patron deity is not well identified. The best example, preserved on Piedras Negras 10, resembles the aged sun god, who is patron of the month Yaxkin, but there appears to be a curving line behind the corner of the mouth; two other portraits of the patron of this month are badly weathered. There are several examples of the symbolic variant of this element; they appear to represent the gaping mouth of some monster with what looks like a large tooth in the upper jaw, but none of the surviving examples is sufficiently distinct to make this identification certain.

Landa describes a ceremony held in Mol in which utensils were painted with the sacred blue, and the children were given nine light blows on the backs of their hands so that they would become skillful in their trades. The girls were brought there by an old woman, called Ix Mol, and she administered the raps to the girls. Landa translates Ix Mol as *la allegadera,* "the collector"; the Motul dictionary applies the term to the woman who supervised others engaged in spinning and weaving, and collected from each cacao to supply refreshment for all. The word presumably derives from the collecting duties of this position since *mol* means to collect. The Moran dictionary of Manche Chol lists *molo* with the meaning of "to congregate," and *moloc* is given as "collect" in Wirsing's Kekchi dictionary, the *oc* being a verbal termination.

On the other hand Tzotzil dictionaries give *mool*, "old man," and *moltot,* "grandfather"; in Kekchi *mol* means "to bud."

As the central element of Mol corresponds to that of the day sign Muluc, and symbolizes water or jade, it seems highly probable that the name of the month refers to the gathering of rain, that is to say, the gathering of clouds, an interpretation first proposed, I believe, by Spinden (1924, p. 128). The fact that the central element, representing water, is surrounded by a ring of circles, which are almost surely simplified symbols for water, tends to confirm the identification.

Ch'en, Tzun, Zihora, Khek Sihom (fig. 17,23–33). The ninth month in the Maya year is the first of four consecutive months which vary only in their prefixes, the main part in all four cases being the cauac element.

The cauac symbol is a section of the body of a celestial dragon, a rain-giving monster of Maya mythology; the name is that of the nineteenth day which is formed from this element. Since *cauac* and its cognates mean storm, there can be little doubt that the cauac sign means rain storms when used as a day glyph (p. 87), but it might refer to the celestial dragon when it forms part of these month signs.

The four prefixes are, in their order, those of black, green, white, and red. A knotted element sometimes appears as a secondary prefix with all four months. It clearly belongs with the cauac element, and it is particularly prominent with Ch'en merely because the individual prefix of that month is often changed to an infix, leaving a space, which the knotted prefix is expanded to occupy.

As the names for the sequent months are Yax (green), Zac (white), and Chac (red), one would expect the ninth month to bear the name Ek or Ik or Kek (black), but such is not the case in the Chol list, which preserves old color terms for Uo, Zip, and Ceh, but gives for the ninth month the name Zihora, which sounds Spanish and is certainly not Chol. Nevertheless, the Kanhobal name Khek Sihom does mean black Sihom.

Ch'en, the Yucatec name, signifies in nearly all Maya languages a hole in the ground, such as a cave or well, or a large rock or crag. Actually, the two meanings are connected, for a crag is a wedge of earth thrust into the air, whereas a cave or a well can be regarded as a wedge of air thrust into the earth. Other Maya words, for example, Peten, "land surrounded by water" or "water surrounded by land" or "one kind of vegetation surrounded by another," are further examples of a single term for things which at first glance appear to be diametrically opposite, but which in fact have much in common. *Ch'en* is also a Yucatec root meaning "to cease," "to finish," "to be silent" (cease making a noise?), "to become quiet." *Tzun* has in Tzeltal the meaning of sowing. Neither of these names seems to yield any clue as to why the month was thus termed, but the connection may lie in the fact that at conjunction the moon was believed to retire to a well (p. 238), and the patroness of the month is the moon goddess, for the symbol of the moon or the figure of the goddess emerging from the moon is the variable element in the IS introductory glyph which heads IS falling in the month Ch'en.

Yax, Batzul, Yax Sihom (fig. 17,34–47). The tenth month, the second of the series of four cauac months, has as its glyph the symbol for yax as a prefix to the cauac element. This same symbol is the prefix of the month Yaxkin. *Yax* means new, strong, blue and green in Yucatec, and has the meaning of blue or green in practically every Maya language or dialect (in various highland dialects the word is *rax* or *chax*). The significance of the element in this case will be considered in the gen-

eral discussions of the four cauac months. *Batzul*, occording to Vicente Pineda, means first amaranth, but this interpretation is somewhat dubious.

The patron of the month is the Venus monster, his head or the Venus symbol forming the variable element in the IS introductory glyph corresponding to this month.

Zac, Zizac, Zacilha or Zacilab, Sah Sihom (fig. 17,48–55). The eleventh month, the third of the series of four cauac months, has the prefix for white with the cauac element. The word *zac* means white in almost all Maya languages and dialects; *Sah* of Sah Sihom is Kanhobal for white. The patron of the month appears in only one text with full clarity of detail; it is the head of some reptile with a full complement of sharply serrated teeth. Beyer (1931) thinks that it is probably the head of the toad, which serves as the head variant of the uinal, an identification which must be accepted.

The patrons of the two cauac months already discussed are celestial bodies—the moon and the planet Venus. It is logical, therefore, to suppose that the patron of Zac should be a denizen of the sky. In effect, there is evidence that the frog respresented a constellation or planet. Across the center of Madrid 13–18 there stretches a celestial band on which is inscribed an incomplete cycle of the 260 days. Above and below this are planetary symbols, and around it are twined celestial snakes. On the right of page 17 there hangs head-down from the band a turtle, and beside him an unmistakable frog also head-down. The turtle reappears in the same position in other groups of constellations and is the name among the present-day Yucatec of the square of Orion. It is, therefore, fairly evident that the frog must represent another constellation or some planet.

Ceh, Chac, Ahelchac, Muctazac, Khak Sihom (fig. 17,56–65). The twelfth month, the last of the group of four cauac months, has the prefix for red with the cauac element. Chac, the name for this month in the Chol list, actually means red, as does Khak in the Kanhobal list, bringing this month into agreement with Yax and Zac, which are also named for the colors they represent.

The Tzotzil name, Muctazac, appears to signify "great Zac," and presumably contrasts with Zizac, "little (?) Zac," the preceding month. Similar pairings of months occur in the Quiche, Cakchiquel, and Aztec lists.

Ceh, the Yucatec name for the twelfth month, means deer. Presumably Ceh represents a more recent name for this month, which, perhaps arose from some hunting ceremony held in this period, although none is reported for this month in the scant ceremonies which have been preserved. On the other hand, it may be significant that the two months, Zip and Ceh, which share the color red in their glyphs and in their names in the Chol list should both be connected with deer. A hunting festival in honor of various gods including Ah Zip, god of the deer, was held in Zip, and Ceh, as noted, means hart. Furthermore, there is a god of the deer called Ah Ceh.

Be that as it may, the original association of this month appears to have been something quite different. The variable element of the IS introductory glyph corresponding to Ceh is a sky symbol with a superfix which consists of two or three circles of dots with a hook in the center. Spinden (1924, fig. 56) identifies the main element as a bundle of sticks and considers that it represents the sacred fire which "was kindled after the ends of important time periods." Beyer (1931) also accepts this identification.

Nevertheless, it is unnecessary to see fire in the pictures or to assume that new fires were kindled after (at?) the ends of periods, although such ceremonies in all probability did take place. The sign in question is merely the celestial symbol, so frequent in Maya texts. Arranged as an elbow, it surrounds Glyph B of the lunar series (fig. 5,28–33); with one of the two flanking elements placed beneath the cross, it is one of the three signs that compose the glyph representing sunrise or the sun at the horizon (fig. 31,41–51). In this same composite form the glyph appears in planetary bands (fig. 20,15) and, with a coefficient of 10, is almost surely the glyph of Lahun-Chan, "10 Sky," a deity who is a manifestation of Venus (fig. 14,2,4). The central element may be two vertical bars with a St. Andrew's cross between them, or the space between the bars may be left a blank. The cross might represent an infix, but its presence or absence appears not to affect the meaning.

The symbol, as already noted, is one of the elements that appear in planetary bands, and almost certainly has the meaning of sky. Since it appears in the glyph representing what is in all probability sunrise, it may have in addition the more specialized sense of eastern sky. Some confirmation for this supposition is to be found in the fact that red, the associated color, is that of the east.

The four cauac months, therefore, have the following associations:

> Ch'en—black (west)—moon goddess
> Yax—green (south?)—Venus monster
> Zac—white (north)—frog constellation (?)
> Ceh—red (east)—god of the (eastern) sky (?)

In all four cases the patron would appear to be a celestial being; the colors suggest associations with world directions. West in the Mexican cosmology is the region of goddesses and women who, by succumbing in childbirth, had qualified for divine rank. The west, therefore, is the natural home of the moon goddess both because

she was a woman, and because she was the patroness of childbirth. In view of the very close connections between Maya and Mexican mythology, the same assignment of the moon to the west presumably was made by the Maya.

Yax, as noted, means green, but that color is not associated with the world directions unless there was a fifth (center) direction assigned to that color. On the other hand, the central element of the glyph for south, as drawn in the codices (fig. 41,23–27), is the same as the codical form of the yax prefix, although the identity does not hold good for the corresponding glyphs on stelae of the Initial Series Period. The color assigned to the south in sixteenth-century Yucatan was yellow.

Nevertheless, it is not improbable that the yax prefix represented the south. One would expect Venus to be placed in the west or the east, but in Dresden all four directions are assigned the planet. South is the direction of death and calamity, commodities which that planet freely distributed (p. 217). It is not impossible that there has been a change in world directional colors, that at the time the glyphs were invented green was the color of the south, but later yellow replaced it; but the yax element in the codical form of south preserves this ancient form.

As the presumed constellation of the frog has not been identified, it is impossible to seek any connection with the north.

Chac and Khek Sihom, the Chol and Kanhobal equivalents of Ceh, have already been explained as signifying red, the color of the superfix. Red is the color of the east, so if the symbol of the patron deity represents not only the sky in general but by extension the eastern sky, the association would be complete.

The Cauac glyph, as previously noted, is a symbol for storm and rain. Nevertheless, this is a derived meaning. The cauac sign is composed of symbols which appear on the bodies of celestial dragons, the Itzamnas (fig.15,11–13). They are the beings who send the rain, and it is entirely appropriate that their markings should form the glyph of the day of rain and storms. On the other hand, in the cases under discussion the associations are primarily celestial. The celestial dragons usually carry planetary symbols, such as the signs for Venus, the moon, the sun, and the sky, on their bodies. Accordingly, there is reason to believe that when used as the main element of each of these four months, the cauac sign betokens not its secondary meaning of rain and storm, but its primary meaning, the celestial dragon. In that case, these four months were dedicated to, and named for, the four celestial dragons: the black dragon of the west associated with the moon; the green (?) dragon of the south (?) associated with Venus; the white dragon of the north associated with the frog constellation; the red dragon of the east associated with the god of the (eastern?) sky.

Mac, Moc, Chantemat, Chantemac, Chentemac (fig. 18,*1–20*). The thirteenth month has retained the same name or a variant form in most Maya languages, for Mac appears by itself or in a compound in seven different calendars.

The glyph itself shows considerable variability. In the personified forms the main element is the head of the *xoc* fish, with the meaning of "count"; in the symbolic form the main element is either a sign resembling Imix or the so-called snake markings, which forms the lower part of the glyph Akbal and a variant of the kin sign (fig. 31,*12–15*). In the latter case there are crosshatched (black) infixes. In the symbolic form the xoc element takes the form of the comb affix, often doubled, for the comb has the same value of "count" as the *xoc* fish (Thompson, 1944, pp. 5–10).

On the monuments the personified Mac usually has a well-known prefix, which is Landa's glyph for *ma,* and which Beyer has named the two balls of down. The symbolic Mac lacks this prefix but appears to incorporate one-half of it, although changed from the horizontal to the vertical position, as an infix of the main element, which has features of the Imix sign. The same process has probably taken place in the two examples on the monuments which lack this prefix. A very slight change in Morley's drawing of the Mac on Aguas Calientes 1, which I have followed (fig. 18,*13*), would convert this into the required infix corresponding to the codical form. Unfortunately, no photograph is available to check this point. Likewise, the Ahau-like infix of Yaxha 13 (fig. 18,*16*) may be the same element, for details of the photograph are not too sharp. What may be the same sign appears as an affix with certain examples of Glyph D of the lunar series (figs. 36,*25,39;* 37,*48,59,67*), and with other glyphs.

The word *mac* means "to enclose" or "to cover" in a number of Maya languages and dialects. I have suggested elsewhere that both the glyph and the name of this month may refer to the fact that with the end of Mac 260 days of the year have been counted, and that this period, equivalent to the length of the sacred almanac, was regarded as a sort of compartment within the year. The Imix and comb variant would then signify "the count of Imix" or perhaps "Imix counted," Imix referring to the 260-day cycle. Mac would then mean that the period was enclosed, forming a sort of compartment within the year. Nevertheless, I hesitate to reaffirm that explanation, for it now seems more probable that the main part is not Imix, but one of the "down-balls" of the prefix set upright and converted into a main element.

The patron of the month is a deity, identified by Beyer as the youthful head for the number 3. His distinguishing marks are a close-fitting cap and the Ik symbol on the side of the cheek or worn as an ornament. The symbolic form of this head is the Ik sign, clearly displayed in the introductory glyph of the IS of the Tablet of the Foliated Cross, Palenque. There is no obvious connection between this god and the glyph or names of the thirteenth month.

Kankin, Olalti, Uniu, Oneu (fig. 18,*21–30*). The fourteenth month is endowed with a plethora of names; the glyph itself presents some difficulties. The symbolic form on the monuments consists of an object resembling a leafless tree with a circular infix on the left, the interior of which is sometimes filled with crosshatching to indicate black. In the drawing of Kankin on the Tablet of the Inscriptions, Palenque, which Maudslay published, this infix is shown as a kin sign, but as in the photograph the interior of the infix is blurred, one hesitates to accept this kin infix since it does not seem to occur with other examples of Kankin.

The head variant of Kankin, which is somewhat rare, represents the head of an animal. The canine teeth are prominent, and so are the rather oddly shaped ears. There are quite a number of lines on the face, particularly behind the corner of the mouth, and the snout is large and slightly upturned. There appears to be an orbital plate, but that feature is not very clear.

The symbolic form of Kankin appears in the codices in combination with an apparent death sign as the glyph of the dog (fig. 14,*10*). As such it was recognized by Schellhas as long ago as 1897, and this identification is accepted by Förstemann, Seler, Beyer, and others, and tentatively by Tozzer and Allen. Most of these writers see in the symbolic form of Kankin the ribs of the dog (note prominence of ribs on dogs, fig. 14,*7,8*). The codical form certainly bears a resemblance to ribs, but the earlier forms of the monuments of the Initial Series Period are much more cursive, and twist and curve in a way that invalidates the identification. Whatever the symbolic form of Kankin may be intended to depict, there can, I think, be no doubt that it represents the dog. It is also worthy of note that dogs are almost always depicted in Maya codices with black markings, particularly around the eye (fig. 14,*8,9*). The circular infix with crosshatching (a well known symbol for black) in the symbolic form of Kankin presumably refers to the black spots on the dog.

In view of the probable identification of the symbolic form of Kankin as a canine sign, there can be little doubt that the animal of the head variant is a dog. In fact, these heads accord fairly well with representations of dogs in Maya and Mexican codices, particularly in such details as the ears and the snout. Possibly the orbital plate, which can be recognized in the best-preserved examples, represents the black markings around the eye.

The Yucatec name does not refer to the dog, for Kankin means "yellow sun." Likewise, whatever meanings Olalti and Uniu may have had, they do not contain Maya names for the dog. On the other hand, there is a Pokomchi month, Tzi, which signifies dog, but it probably does not correspond to this position. A number of the Pokomchi months clearly have been displaced, and the calendar was obviously in the last stages of decay when recorded by Sr. Narciso. There is, therefore, a bare possibility that Tzi and Uniu were alternative names for the same month. There is also an Ixil month called Tzihep. The order of the Ixil months is completely chaotic. The symbolic form of the variable element in the IS introductory glyph for the month Kankin takes the form of an arch above another, or of one arch above a double arch. The meaning of the design is not apparent. The two personified forms recorded (Pusilha P, Quirigua Alt O) are heads of a fantastic monster with prominent canines and fangs, but without a lower jaw. One would like to identify it as the head of the canine deity, since that god is sometimes depicted with prominent fangs in addition to canines (Dresden 36a, 39a) but the long arched snout hardly suggests the nose of a dog. There seems little doubt that this is an earth monster, similar to, but perhaps not identical with, the Imix monster. Thereby the association of the dog with the underworld is retained.

Muan, Muhan, Muen, Muenchin, Ulol, Hulol, Sivil (fig. 18,*31–45*). The Yucatecan name of the fifteenth month appears also, with minor variations, in the Chol, Pokomchi, and Ixil lists; Chiapas uses Ulol and Hulol, and Chuh has Sivil. No symbolic form of the glyph is known on the monuments; the head form is that of a bird with a prominent beaked nose. On the monuments of the Initial Series Period a tail, of the kind found with the kin sign, Xul, Yaxkin, and the winged cauac, is usually attached as a postfix, but this element is absent from the personified representations of Muan in Dresden.

One symbolic variant of the glyph occurs in Dresden (fig. 20,*18*). This consists of a spiral enclosed in a ring with two postfixes, one above the other. The lower is the tail, to which reference has just been made, and is the only example of this postfix with Muan in the codices; the upper is a common affix, which I identify as indicating a connection with vegetation, new growth, and rain, and to which I tentatively attach the meaning *ak* (p. 282). This sign, but with a different postfix, is one of the two glyphs of the Moan bird (fig. 20,*19,20*). In Middle America the spiral is a symbol of water. It is often set in representations of water in Mexican codices (fig. 20,*31–34*),

and is placed in the eyes of God B and other Maya deities, including the Moan bird, connected with water and vegetation (fig. 20,*13,14,16,21,35*). It is also an element of the codical form of cauac (fig. 20,*29*), the aquatic value of which is beyond dispute, and appears as a water symbol above pictures of water in Dresden (fig. 20,*30*). It is held by gods in divinatory almanacs (fig. 20,*21,22*) and appears in hands or in other combinations in texts of the Initial Series Period (fig. 20,*25–28*), although it should be pointed out that in those cases there is no direct evidence connecting the sign with water. This symbolic form of the glyph, therefore, indicates that the month is connected with water. As we shall see, there is ample evidence for this.

In Yucatec *moan* means cloudy and drizzle. Pio Perez lists in his dictionary *moankin,* "a cloudy and drizzling day," but *moan* is also the Yucatec name for the screech owl, and since *u* and *o* are not uncommonly interchangeable in Spanish transcriptions of Maya and Mexican words, it is very probable that the glyph and the Yucatec name refer to the screech owl, although so far as the pictures are concerned, it is perhaps being too precise to indicate the actual species. The Chol vocabulary of Friar Moran gives sparrow hawk or kite as the translation of Muhan.

The rôle of the Moan bird in Maya mythology has led to much confusion. The deified bird appears on three occasions in Dresden with a maize plant as headdress (fig. 20,*14*). Its glyph is the head of the bird itself with a coefficient of 13 or the sky sign also with a coefficient of 13 (fig. 20,*19,20,23,24*). Seler (1902–23, 4:615) has suggested that the Moan represents the 13 layers of clouds which are said to compose the sky. He based this conclusion on two lines of evidence: firstly, that one of the glyphs for the bird is the sky symbol with a coefficient of 13; secondly, that *moan* means in Yucatec cloudy and rainy. To these one might add that the vegetal aspect of the Moan bird, as emphasized in the headdress of maize leaves, accords well with a deity of clouds and rain.

Tozzer and Allen (1910, p. 336) take Stempell to task for confusing the Yucatan horned owl with the Yucatan screech owl. Since pictures of the first are distinguished by those writers through the "horns" or tufts of hair on the sides of the head, and the second is admitted to have similar horns, one can only conclude that the distinctions are of more importance to the zoologist than they were to the Maya artist.

I see no reason for not accepting the owl carved on the wooden lintel of Tikal, above the celestial serpent (fig. 20,*10*), as the same bird as that shown in the codices. In fact, there are several cases where an owl is placed on or immediately above celestial dragons (fig. 20,*11,15*).

Assuming that this is the screech owl, these designs can be brought into relation with the supposed associations of the screech owl. If the Moan god represents the 13 layers of clouds or the 13 skies, it would be perfectly natural to place him on or above the celestial dragons who send the rain.

Finally, attention might be called to the almanac which runs across the bottom of Dresden 33–39. The subject is rain, and God B occupies each of the 20 divisions. With the days 1 Chicchan, 1 Oc, and 1 Men he stands in the rain. On the days 13 Oc, 13 Men, 13 Ahau, and 1 Ahau he stands on a receptacle full of water; on 13 Chicchan he stands in the rain. On 9 Muluc, 9 Ix, 9 Cauac, and 9 Kan he is in his house, which in two cases has the celestial crossband on it, and in one case stands on a cauac glyph.

In the four pictures which accompany the days 7 Ahau, 7 Chicchan, 7 Oc, and 7 Men God B is seated. On 7 Ahau and 7 Chicchan his seat is the sky symbol with crossed bands, to which is attached a poorly defined prefix; on 7 Oc his seat is a planetary band, that is to say, a segment of the body of a celestial dragon; on 7 Men he is seated on the head of the Moan bird.

In view of the certainty that the subject of this divinatory almanac is rain, and in consideration of the similarity of the pictures with the subdivisions of each group, the close relation of the Moan bird to the sky symbol and to the celestial dragons is beyond dispute.

An interesting confirmation of the above thesis comes from Mexican sources. On the Mexican plateau one of the names for the celestial abode of the gods, the land of flowers and abundance, was Tamoanchan. In the hymn to Xochiquetzal we read, "From the land of the rain and the mist, from Tamoanchan I, Xochiquetzal, come." This name is pure Maya of the Chiapan group. *Ta* is the locative "at," "in," or "from" in Tzeltal, Palencano Chol, and other languages of the Chiapan group, and corresponds to the Yucatec *ti; moan* is the Moan bird; *chan* is snake in nearly all the Maya languages of the Chiapan group, and also means sky in several of them, corresponding to the Yucatec *can* and *caan*. The Yucatec equivalent would be *Timoancan*. Tamoanchan, as the celestial land of rain and mist, the land of abundance, corresponds to the Maya representations of the celestial serpent surmounted by the Moan bird (fig. 20,*10,11,15,17*). The celestial snake surmounted by the Moan bird can be regarded either as a literal representation of a mythological concept of the heavens or as a form of rebus writing for rainy, misty sky, since Moan and snake (*can*) have those alternative meanings.

The idea of deriving Tamoanchan from Moan was first proposed by Seler (1902–23, 2:1034), but was not carried to its logical conclusion because Seler failed to identify the celestial snake surmounted by the Moan bird and, therefore, did not recognize the Maya origin of the syllable *chan*.

This digression has been necessary because of the general belief that the Moan bird is a symbol of death. This theory originated with Schellhas, who mistakenly identified a certain glyph with the Moan bird (Beyer, 1929). It has been repeated by a number of writers on Maya mythology. Actually, there is an owl of ill omen, but it is the *cui,* a different species.

Muan, accordingly, is the month of the Moan bird, a deity who lived in the sky, was intimately associated with the celestial dragons, and symbolized the cloud-filled heavens. Perhaps the Moan bird appears because this was originally a month of rains and clouds.

The variable element in the IS introductory glyph corresponding to Muan is not clear. Only head variants are known, and these, unfortunately, are not well preserved. That on Quirigua G appears to be a youthful head; that on Piedras Negras 3 seems to be aged and provided with a hooked nose. It might even be the Moan bird. In all known cases the head has a prefix.

Pax, Okinahual, Hokenahau, Tap, Tam (fig. 18,*46–52*). The symbolic form for the sixteenth month is the tun sign with a pair of stalklike objects which start from the center and curve outward immediately above the main element. The whole resembles a somewhat cursive Υ, and suggests a vegetal origin.

The tun sign (p. 144) is derived from the symbol for jade and, by extension, water. The picture might conceivably represent vegetation nourished by the precious water. The one personified form of Pax is the head of a frog with the same projecting stalks above its head.

Brinton has suggested that Okinahual, the Tzeltal name for this month, might be derived from *kin,* "time, day or season," and *aual,* "to sow," and the whole would mean "planting time." This would agree with the possible significance of the glyph, but both the translation and the interpretation of the glyph rest on shaky ground.

The patron of the month is an anthropomorphized feline, whose features recall those of the jaguar but are also reminiscent of those of the sun god (fig. 23,*18–20,34*). In the full-figure representation the god, like the jaguar, is decked with a water lily, which seems to emerge from his mouth, and he lacks a lower jaw. On his temple is the claw of some animal, and it is not improbable that this is a reference to *chac mol,* "giant paw," a name for the jaguar. On the three heads the lower jaw is vestigial or absent, and the mouth contains a variable element, in one case a St. Andrew's cross. In all three cases there is before the face a symbol, to which I shall refer as the three-circles-and-bundle variant. The early example on

Yaxchilan L 48 has a paw above the earplug; in another head a sign resembling the symbol for white replaces the earplug. The full figure has an ornament with a St. Andrew's cross, reminding one of the same sign in the mouth of one of the heads. This device seems rather closely connected with the jaguar god of 7, for it is prominent on the full-figure representation of number 7 on Quirigua D, and is worn as a pectoral by the jaguar gods on Quirigua A and C and on Piedras Negras MSS 19 (fig. 12,*15*). The sandals of the jaguar gods of Quirigua A and C are adorned with heads (but not of jaguars), each of which has a St. Andrew's cross in the mouth, and the same design is on one of the heads at the side of the chest of the jaguar god of Quirigua C. Moreover, the jaguar god of Stela C has this St. Andrew's cross in his mouth. Unfortunately, this creature has his feline character less emphasized, but that he is a jaguar god can, I think, be accepted without much question.

The patron of the month Pax, then, has features reminiscent of those of the jaguar, but the two are not identical, for the addition of various attributive affixes—the circles-and-bundle variant, the pseudo-white symbol, and the feline claw or paw—indicates that we are dealing with a variant of the normal jaguar god. Landa states that in the month Pax warriors held their ceremonies in the temple of Cit-Chac-Coh, "father red [or great] puma." This may have been a ritual brought to Yucatan by the Mexicans, but it is also possible that the patron of the month was from the earliest times Cit-Chac-Coh, and that he is the god under discussion. The jaguar also symbolized war in sixteenth-century Yucatan, but, again, this may be a concept of Toltec derivation, connected with the orders of Jaguars and Eagles. All that we can say for the moment is that the patron of Pax was a feline, possibly the puma but more probably a jaguar, and perhaps a representation of the night sun. We shall meet this unsatisfactory deity again as the seventh lord of the nights (p. 209) and as Glyph XI of the lunar series. No connection with the glyph of the month Pax is apparent.

Kayab, Kanazi, Alauch or *Yaluch, Uch, Uex* (fig. 18,*53–64*). The glyph of the seventeenth month is the head of a creature which has been identified both as that of a parrot and of that of a turtle. This confusion was a source of innocent merriment to G. Elliot Smith, as he gaily swam his elephants across the Pacific to the shores of Central America (Smith, 1924, pp. 14–18).

Förstermann, Seler, Gordon, and Tozzer and Allen recognize the Kayab glyph as the head of a turtle; Spinden sees in this hieroglyph the head of the blue macaw. It must be admitted that both parties can cite much evidence in their favor. I think the decision should go to Seler because of a feature which has hitherto been disregarded. That is the prominent kan cross in the creature's eye. The kan cross has two values: it is a symbol of water (p. 275) and also the sign for yellow. Whichever value it has in this case, it agrees better with the identification as the turtle, for that is an aquatic animal and has a brilliantly yellow under side. The blue macaw, on the other hand, has nothing to do with water, and has little yellow plumage.

In Maya legend the tortoise or turtle is connected with the sun because when he fled with the moon, he escaped destruction by donning the shell of a turtle (the moon sought safety in the carapace of an armadillo, a crab, or a turtle). This, however, is a slight connection. In codices from southern Mexico the sun is depicted on sundry occasions wearing the shell of a turtle. The turtle shell is also the insigne of one of the four Bacabs set at the cardinal points to sustain the heavens, although there is no information on which point of the compass was assigned to the Bacab who wears that costume.

There is also a Maya constellation called *ac,* "the turtle," which, according to an informant, is the square of Orion, although the Motul dictionary has: "*ac ek* 'the stars which are in the sign of Gemini, which with others form the outline of a turtle.'"

Finally, one of the Aztec hymns given by Sahagun is dedicated to Ayopechtli or Ayopechcatl. This name means without much doubt "the one on the tortoise seat." The content of the hymn makes it abundantly clear that the auditor is a goddess of childbirth. Sahagun's picture of the goddess and description of her attire reveal that she shares many features with Mayauel and with Teteo-Inan Toci.

After her name Sahagun adds the information "in the house of Tezcacoac [mirror-serpent]." On Magliabecchi 75 there is pictured a goddess who has as her glyph a rattlesnake above a mirror. She is identified as Atlacoaya, and the information is added that at her festival people were sacrificed to the 400 Tochtli gods. These are the gods of pulque; Mayauel is the goddess of pulque. In the pictures on Magliabecchi 58 Mayauel and Atlacoaya are rather similarly garbed. As a final link in the chain Mayauel is depicted on Laud 9 seated on the back of a turtle.

The turtle, therefore, was associated in Mexican thought with a goddess who was close to Mayauel yet shared features with Toci and Xochiquetzal and, like them, was a patroness of childbirth.

In Maya religion no goddess equivalent to Mayauel has yet been reported, but the moon goddess corresponds rather closely to Toci and Xochiquetzal who, without serious doubt, were the old and young moon goddesses of central Mexico.

The word *kayab* is not Yucatec, nor does the root *kai*, "to sing," produce any lead. As *ab* in an instrumental suffix, the whole could mean "with what one sings," but that is hardly a promising clue. *Kan*, the name for yellow, appears in *Kanazi*, the Chol name for this month, but the old Pokoman name was *Canazi*. Unless the initial letter is glottalized, the word yellow is not contained in this month name. *Uch*, the Tzotzil name of this month, means in the closely related Tzeltal the animal called *huiztlacualtzin* according to Vicente Pineda. Tlacuatzin is the Aztec name for the opossum. *Uch* presumably is the same as the Yucatec *och*, "opossum."

Disregarding the meaning of the month names, there seems to be a connection between the patroness and the glyph of Kayab. The patroness is the young moon goddess, patroness of medicine and childbirth, and a goddess of the soil and of maize. In Mexican mythology a goddess of childbirth is called "the one on the tortoise seat." The glyph for Kayab in all probability represents a tortoise.

Cumku, Olh, Ohl, Mucuch, Elech, Sakmai (fig. 19,*1–16*). The glyph for the eighteenth month is composed of the sign Kan, which represents the ripe maize, and an irregularly formed prefix. This prefix, as Beyer (1936d) has noted, is the main element of Glyph G8 in the series of lords of the nights (fig. 34,*39–45*), and it also occurs in a variant of Glyph X of the lunar series. Beyer considers that it represents the tail end of a serpent. I myself regard it as probably representing a section of a conch shell. The irregular outline, the three or more dots, sometimes joined with smaller dots, and the cleft at the base are all consonant with this interpretation (see fig. 21,*4–7*; Spinden, 1924, fig. 8,*a3–a5*). As the conch shell is a symbol of the earth and the underworld, its use as symbol for one of the nine lords of the underworld and of nights (p. 173) would be appropriate.

The patron deity of Cumku is a dragon, whose head is seen in the introductory glyphs corresponding to IS which terminate in Cumku. Usually he has a series of curved fangs set in his mouth, a projection before his forehead, and a somewhat unusual element at the back of the head.

The head at the top of the west side of Copan 3 is somewhat more anthropomorphized, but the element behind the head is the same as on portraits of this deity, supporting Beyer's belief that this feature served to distinguish the head from those of other snakes or dragons. In one case (fig. 23,*32*) the head shows barbels which would associate it with the *Xoc* monster; in another portrait (fig. 23,*30*) the quincunx sign is set in the headdress.

Cumku is listed in the Motul dictionary with the meaning of potters' oven; *cum* is used for oven and apparently for any large receptacle resembling an oven, for *cumche*, literally a wooden *cum*, is a maize granary. The Motul dictionary also lists *Cumhau*, "Lucifer, chief of the devils," which might be a contraction of Cum Ahau, "*Cum* lord," just as *Cumku* could mean "*Cum* god."

It is possible that the name means the god of the corn bin, who was associated with the garnered maize or the seed that was reserved for sowing. To judge by the portraits of the patron of the month, this deity would be a dragonlike monster. The glyph for the month—the apparent conch element, a symbol of the earth and its interior, over the sign for ripe maize or maize seed—appears to bear out this interpretation. The peculiar ornament at the rear of the head of the patron deity, with its three circles on what resembles a curling leaf, might well be a conventionalized maize plant.

In the earth crocodile we might have the origin of this presumed god of the stored corn. He often appears with maize leaves growing from his head, and he is a god of the soil. An objection to this interpretation is that earth monsters usually lack a lower jaw or have bared jawbones. In other respects they closely resemble the patron of Cumku. Since deities could don and doff the markings of death with facility, the objection is not fatal. It would, however, seem more probable that the head represents the sky monster, Itzamna, in view of the presence of a lower jaw. The Itzamnas sent the rain and thereby controlled the harvests. One of the names of these dragon monsters was Itzamna Kauil, the last word having as one of its meanings "food." Furthermore, sacrifices were made to the Itzamnas to petition good crops. The Itzamnas are usually depicted as saurian monsters but they were also represented as snakes. Usually they have a second head at the rear of the body.

The Tzeltal name, Mucuch, pairs with Alauch, just as Zizac and Muctazac do in the Tzotzil calendar. The prefix *muc* means "great" in Tzeltal, just as does *mucta* in Tzotzil. For Olh or Ohl I can suggest no plausible translation, although, just conceivably, it is connected with Olontic, the Tzotzil name for the underworld.

Uayeb or *Uayeab* or *Uayeb haab, u tuz kin, u lobol kin, u yail haab, u yail kin, xmakaba kin, u tich kin* (all Yucatan), *Mahi ikaba Chaikin, Oyebku, Oki, Kaxik lahkih* (fig. 19,*17–20*). The many names for the period of five days at the end of the year have four main meanings: the evil or deceptive or misfortunate days (*u lobol kin, u tuz kin, u yail kin, kaxik lahkih*); nameless days (*xmakaba kin, mahi ikaba*); five days (*oki, Oyebku*); the misfortune of the year (*u yail haab*); and the days left over (*u tich Kin*).

The Yucatec names uayeb, uayeab and uayeb haab have been translated as the bed (*uay*) of the year, but it is more probably that they derive from a homonymous root meaning poisoned, damaged, or infected, and therefore convey the same idea as the unlucky days.

Of the days of Uayeb Landa says that they were considered unlucky and bad. He lists a number of ceremonies for the entering year. These commenced in Uayeb and varied according to the year bearer. In another place he says that during these five days people did not wash

that reason nothing is known of the patron deity of the period save that Landa lists the names of deities connected with the five unlucky days.

Such information as can be garnered concerning the meanings and associations of the various months is given below in tabular form. Much chaff has produced a fistful of grain.

TABLE 9—THE MONTHS, THEIR PATRONS, AND THEIR POSSIBLE ASSOCIATIONS

NAME OF MONTH	PATRON	GLYPH	COMMENT
Pop..............	Jaguar	Mat, chief	Mat and jaguar symbols of chiefdom
Uo..............	Jaguar of underworld	Black sky symbol	Jaguar-night-blackness
Zip..............	Fret-nosed sky being. A deer?	Red sky symbol	Maya version of Mixcoatl?
Zotz'..............	*Xoc* fish	Bat (*zotz'*)	Rebus for winter?
Zec..............	Sky and earth	Count of uinals?	260-days to end of year?
Xul..............	Canine god??	Dog with sun tail	Dog who led sun to underworld?
Yaxkin..........	Sun god	Sun with yax prefix	New or strong sun
Mol..............	?	Water symbol	Clouds gather?
Ch'en...........	Moon	Black sky monster	Sky monster of west
Yax..............	Venus	Green sky monster	Sky monster of south?
Zac..............	Frog constellation	White sky monster	Sky monster of north
Ceh..............	Sky god	Red sky monster	Sky monster of east
Mac..............	God of number 3	Count set in order?	End of 260 days?
Kankin..........	Earth monster?	Dog	Both connected with underworld
Muan............	Moan bird	Moan bird	Deity of rain and clouds
Pax..............	Jaguar or puma	Water dispersing??	Rising sun disperses mist and dew?
Kayab...........	Moon goddess	Turtle	Turtle symbol of parturition?
Cumku..........	Crocodile?	Conch (?) over maize seed	Itzamnas, gods of rain and plants?
Uayeb...........	......	Tun with prefix	Deity perhaps Mam, the earth god

or comb their hair or rid themselves of fleas, and they did not undertake any arduous tasks for fear misfortune should overtake them. Instead, they kept to their houses as much as possible.

Lincoln reports that among the modern Ixil the five days, called Oki (*Okih?*), are regarded as dangerous and very unlucky. Everyone fasts, and nothing is eaten save a small piece of tortilla spread with chili sauce. Sins are confessed and certain ceremonies, involving offerings at the village crosses, are held or have fallen into desuetude only in recent years. It is believed that children born during these five days will be impotent, and boys will be effeminate.

The Jacalteca, who have lost all names for the months, still remember the five days at the end of the year. They call them *ho pix,* for which the translation "five women" has been suggested, but perhaps this is the numerical affix *bix* (p. 170). The Kekchi also have lost their months, but retain a memory of the five unlucky days. They have been transferred to Easter, and are called *rail cutan,* "grievous days" (Wirsing, 1930).

The Uayeb glyph is a tun sign with an indeterminate prefix. In view of what has been written above, the prefix might represent the idea of evil. There is no IS introductory glyph for Uayeb among surviving texts, and for

The evidence, although far from complete, suggests that the months were under the patronage of various deities, and that the glyphs of some of the months refer to those gods. The changing seasons may not have played any part in the formation of the glyphs or in the original names for the months. Thus, if this thesis is correct, one cannot attempt to arrange the months so that, for instance, Yaxkin falls in a hot dry spell and Muan at a time of cloudy or rainy weather. According to the interpretation here advanced, Yaxkin would mean "vigorous sun" because the morning sun, who is patron of the month, is vigorous as he renews his flesh after emerging from the underworld; Muan is so named because it was the month of the Moan bird, a deity of the sky connected with clouds and rain.

It is highly probable that in the various Maya languages there were often two or more names for a month. In some instances the old sacerdotal name was retained; in other cases a popular name became pre-eminent. Thus in Chol the old name for the twelfth month Chac, "red," was retained; in Yucatec Ceh, "deer," became the common designation for this month, perhaps because at that time special festivals in honor of the gods of venery may have been held. This duplication of names is illustrated in the Tzeltal and Tzotzil calendars, and in the many names for the five days that close the year. Similarly, there were alternative names for many of the Aztec months.

It will be noted that several of the gods, to whom the months were dedicated or, more probably, whom the months represented, are the same as those already noted in discussing the gods of the days and of the numbers 1–13.

The gods of the numbers 1–13 appear to have been associated with the following months:

1. Moon goddess. Ch'en (month 9).
1. Moon goddess. Kayab (month 17).
2. ?
3. God of storms. Mac (month 13).
4. Sun god. Yaxkin (month 7).
5. Old god of earth. Uayeb?
6. ?
7. Jaguar god of underworld. Pop (month 1).
7. Jaguar god of underworld. Uo (month 2).
8. ?
9. Chicchan god. Perhaps Mol (month 8).
10. ?
11. Hunting god. Perhaps Ceh (month 12).
12. Venus monster. Yax (month 10).
13. *Xoc* fish. Zotz' (month 4).

There is no clear parallel in the sequence.

NUMBERING DAYS OF MONTHS

Each of the 18 months consisted of 20 days. Numbers 1–19 inclusive are found with month signs.

These numbers are written in the various books of Chilam Balam with the month names as *tu hunte Pop,* "on first of Pop," *tu bulucte Zeec,* "on eleventh of Zec," etc. Such month positions are usually transcribed as 1 Pop, 11 Zec, but the Motul dictionary gives examples showing that when *tu* (contraction of *ti* and *u,* literally "on its") precedes the number with the numerical classifier *te,* the number should be translated as an ordinal. For simplicity I shall continue to write 3 Uo, 13 Xul, etc., although more correctly these should be written 3rd of Uo, 13th of Xul, etc. A prefix which almost certainly corresponds to *tu* has been discussed (p. 57; fig. 39,*1–8*).

SEATING OF MONTHS

A problem which has provoked much discussion in the past 40 years is how the day before, for example, 1 Pop (more correctly first of Pop) was designated. It can be easily proved by simple arithmetic that the sign commonly called the spectacle glyph is found with the Pop glyph under conditions which can only indicate that it represents the day before 1 Pop and, similarly, when attached to the sequent month glyphs, denotes the day before 1 Uo, 1 Zip, 1 Zotz', and all the other months.

It has been assumed that in designating the days of a month the Maya counted only elapsed time. Therefore, as the first day of Pop was not yet concluded, it could not be called 1 Pop. The deduction was made that the first day of the month was 0 Pop, and that the days of any month bore the designations 0–19, and that 0 Uo followed 19 Pop. This view has been widely accepted, but it is certainly fallacious. On the other hand, Seler (1902–23, 1:851–62) suggested for the spectacle glyph the interpretation "eve of" (*Vorabend*), but this meaning could hardly apply to its use with another glyph, now to be discussed.

The spectacle glyph occurs also in other combinations, of which the commonest is one in which it is attached to or merged with the winged-cauac glyph (fig. 19,*37–41*). The winged cauac is a variant form of the tun sign, never employed in IS but used to designate, customarily with the addition of prefixs for count or completion, an even tun from 13.0.0.0.0 4 Ahau 8 Cumku.

Beyer (1932a, pp. 105–13), who was the first to comment on the combination of spectacle glyph and winged cauac, interprets the sign as 0 tuns, having assumed that the spectacle glyph was correctly deciphered as zero. He cites a number of cases at Palenque where this combination occurs with the recording of the ends of katuns. There are, however, two very cogent reasons for rejecting his interpretation.

From all we know of the Maya philosophy of time and from all we can gather from the glyphs, the Maya were interested in recording the completion of time. Such and such a date marks the completion of a period, not its beginning. The date 8 Ahau 13 Ceh is the end of nine baktuns, not the beginning; 8 Ahau 8 Uo is the end of 13 katuns, not the beginning. In the books of Chilam Balam we read "the count of [Katun] 11 Ahau was not ended when . . . ," and "for six years the count of 11 Ahau will not be ended," and in the Chronicle of Chacxulubchen "in this year the katun ended." Instances of such references to the ends of time periods could be repeated; none refer to the beginning of a time period.

The spectacle glyph with a month sign, if it means zero, can only indicate the commencement of that month, not its end; if it is used with the winged-cauac sign to indicate that the tun was also that on which a katun ended, it can only mean completion. The ideas are diametrically opposite. Had the Maya failed to distinguish between a count not started and one completed—and the possibility is well nigh inconceivable—the spectacle glyph and the normal signs for completion (the hand with affixes, the shell, or the face with hand on cheek) should be interchangeable. They are kept rigidly apart.

The second objection to the Beyer interpretation is that his 0 tun glyph occurs with a date 9.8.13.0.0 5 Ahau

18 Zec, which is followed by the glyph for 13 tuns. A date can hardly be both 13 tuns and 0 tun. Beyer's explanation for this refutation of his thesis is not convincing.

There is probably a second case of the use of the spectacle-winged-cauac glyph with a date that is not a katun ending. The last two glyphs of the step leading to the inner chamber of Temple 22, Copan, are composed of the spectacle-winged-cauac glyph and a day sign, which is probably Ahau, with a coefficient of 5. No katun near the date of the erection of Temple 22 is completed on 5 Ahau, but 9.17.2.0.0 ends on 5 Ahau 8 Cumku. As this date occurs elsewhere at Copan, it is probably the one meant in this inscription, and in that case the supposed 0 tun glyph again occurs with a tun which is not 0. The Beyer interpretation of this glyph must be rejected.

The spectacle glyph also occurs in other combinations. Merged with the winged cauac and with an added postfix, it follows distance numbers which are counted forward or backward to reach the end of a katun or a tun that is not also a katun ending (fig. 19,42–44). In other forms the glyph follows distance numbers which lead to dates which are not even tun endings (fig. 19,46–51).

The problem is to seek an interpretation which will cover these different uses. In Tizimin (pp. 41–52) there is a combined Maya and Spanish almanac. Similar almanacs occur in most of the books of Chilam Balam except that of Chumayel, and all appear to derive from a single source since all begin with 10 Oc on January 1. At 20-day intervals the names of the months are given, starting with Pop on July 16 (as in Landa). Before each month name occur the words *u cutal*. With 10 names these words occur alone; in the remaining instances the word *licil*, "at that time," or *uai c*, "here," precedes the phrase. Similar phrases occur in Mani and Ixil.

U cutal means "the seating of." On July 16, then, Pop was seated. Twenty days later the seating of Uo took place, and so at 20-day intervals all 18 months were seated. The year is obviously based on the same one that was frozen into the European year, with the beginning of Pop falling on July 16 (O.S.). Thus it is virtually certain that the seating of each month took place at its start.

Actually the word *cutal* is a contraction of *cultal*, "the seating." The root of the verb to seat is *cul*. On page 76 of Chumayel we find *caanil Kan cumlahci Pop ti lakin*, "4 Kan, Pop was seated to the east"; on page 1 of Tizimin occur the words *ca bin culac hun Muluc*, "when 1 Muluc will be seated."

The expression is also used for the seating of the tun, for on page 7 of Tizimin is written *ti cutal ti tun*, "there the seating at the tun." It occurs also in the same book (p. 36) in connection with the katun: *Buluc Hix cu cutal*

oxlahun Ahau katun ti lah [ca] bil Cauac, "11 Ix, then the seating of katun 13 Ahau on 12 Cauac." The expression is similarly used for the night, for in the Motul dictionary we find *akab culen cul*, "entre dos luces," at nightfall. The seating, therefore, is when the period enters.

The problem then is whether the seating of the month took place on first of Pop, etc., or on the day previous, the so-called 0 Pop. The tun and katun obviously must have been seated at the time of the completion of the previous period. Katun 14 was, one can be reasonably certain, seated on the day 9.13.0.0.0 8 Ahau 8 Uo, not on 9.13.0.0.1, for it was immediately on the completion of one katun that the next one began. It is, therefore, logical to assume that the month was seated also at the moment it entered, and that would coincide with the exit of the old month.

It will be shown that for the spectacle glyph with one month can be substituted the glyph of the previous month with a tun sign as a prefix. The only deduction possible is that the day before the first of the month could also be regarded as the last day of the previous month.

If the spectacle glyph is translated as "the seating of," it agrees with the sundry occasions on which it is used. With month signs and with the winged cauac it would mean respectively "the seating of the month" and "the seating of the tun"; with the postfix and placed after a distance number, it would mean "[the distance number] leads to the seating of a tun." The last variant which lacks the wing (fig. 19,46–51) would mean "[the distance number] leads to the seating of a day," and the variant, in which the inverted Ahau is the main element, would have the same meaning as the last (p. 165).

THE LAST DAY OF THE MONTH

As noted above, there are cases where the spectacle glyph with a month sign is replaced by the tun sign used as a prefix or as a prefatory glyph of the previous month (fig. 19,21–27; Thompson, 1935, p. 101; 1943a). There are nine known occurrences of this substitution including two dubious examples (Table 10).

The IS values of only three are beyond question (1, 6, and 7). Calculations lead respectively to 13 Ik, Ch'en seated; 1 Caban, Mol seated; and 2 Eb, Pop seated. In nos. 1 and 6 the preceding month glyph is given without any question. In the case of no. 7 the bottom part of the glyph clearly shows the tun sign, the main element of Uayeb. The top part of the glyph is weathered, but I think I recognize on the left a hand; on the right, an indistinct element which might be the prefix of Uayeb. The hand, if it is present, would correspond to the tun sign, both conveying the idea of completion. It is just possible that the main element is the tun sign and is used

TABLE 10—DATES RECORDED AS TWENTIETH DAY OF MONTH

1. Palenque Cross, D9	13. 0. 1. 9. 2	13 Ik, Mol with tun prefix.
2. Palenque Palace, W. court	(9. 8.18. 3. 7)	13 Manik, Yaxkin with prefatory tun.
3. Yaxchilan 9, B1	? ? ? ? ?	11–13 day sign, Mac with tun prefix.
4. Yaxchilan L9, A2–A3	(9.11.11.16.12)	1 Eb, Yaxkin with prefatory tun.
5. Piedras Negras MSS 16, B1	(9.14.16. 1. 7)	8 Manik, Ceh with tun prefix.
6. Piedras Negras shell plaque	9.14.17.14.17	1 Caban, Yaxkin with tun prefix.
7. Naranjo HS, A1b	9.10. 3. 2.12	2 Eb, Uayeb completed?
8. Naranjo 19, C10–C11	(9.17. 5. 8.12)	9 Eb, Yaxkin with prefatory tun.
9. Quirigua G, U′2–V′2	9.17.14.13.17	13 Caban, Yax (?) with prefatory tun.

here with a hand to show that 2 Eb coincided with the end of the year (p. 122), but I do not consider this likely.

No. 9, at the close of the text on Quirigua G, follows three dates in this arrangement:

H′1–G′2	9.17.14.13. 0	9 Ahau 3 Yax
K′1–L′1	9.17.14.13. 2	11 Ik 5 Yax
U′1a	10	Add
U′1b–V′1a	9.17.14.13.12	8 Eb 15 Yax
U′2–V′2a	9.17.14.13.17	13 Caban tun glyph, Yax (?)

The day sign has a coefficient of 13, but is too weathered to show whether or not it represents Caban. The prefatory tun is very clear, but the subsequent glyph bears little resemblance to Yax in Miss Hunter's drawing. A good photograph is not available.

It is to be regretted that the position of several examples of the use of this tun glyph with month signs is not fixed in the LC. The fact that of the only three thus securely placed, two (nos. 1 and 6), which are perfectly clear, show the use of the glyph of the month prior to that normally to be expected, while the third (no. 7) almost certainly does the same, is full evidence for accepting the theory. One can not assume that mistakes have been made, when that involves classifying 100 per cent of the examples as errors.

There is linguistic confirmation for reading the tun sign in these cases as "end of" or "last of." Roys has called my attention to a very similar use of the word *tun* in Yucatec. The Motul dictionary lists among the many meanings of that word: *postpuesta á la primera dicción, ya, o finalmente.* The Vienna gives: *u lahi tun, u nak,* and *u xuli tun* as translations of *ya no mas.* In the San Francisco dictionary *finalmente* is translated as *tz'ocebali tun* and *tu tz'oc tun.* Roys, on supplying these quotations, adds that the most frequent meaning of tun in the texts seems to be "then, after that," but it can mean "finally."

The word seems to be used frequently with expressions of finality to give added emphasis.

As the prefix of the tun sign can be omitted (nos. 2 and 3), its meaning can not be of much importance. In the best preserved example (no. 8) it is identical with the prefix of Glyph F of the supplementary series, and other examples seem to confirm this identity.

We must conclude that the days of the months were numbered 1–19, and that the day between the nineteenth of one month and the first of the sequent month was usually called the seating of the new month, but sometimes was called the last of the old month. It is possible that "seating of" is not the correct translation, and that the glyph actually represents some other phrase, such as "entrance of." In any case we can be sure that the translation zero is incorrect.

HANDLING OF LEAP DAYS

The Maya made no attempt to intercalate days in the count of the years to bring the year of 365 days into conformity with the solar year. Such a correction would have played havoc with the whole orderly plan of the calendar and would have disorganized the elaborate system of lowest common multiples of different time cycles, which were of the highest importance for divinatory and ritualistic purposes.

Naturally, the Maya were well aware that their year and the solar year were at variance. They made excellent calculations as to the rate at which the error accumulated, but these were merely noted as corrections; they were not used to change the calendar (App. V).

NAMES OF THE YEAR AND ITS DIVISIONS

I think it is doubtful that the Maya had any distinct name for the year of 365 days, but instead they probably used the names for the year of 360 days loosely to refer also to the 365-day period, for actually, there was no year of 365 days, but one of 360 days, to the end of which were added the five nameless days.

Spanish writers and the Motul, as well as other dictionaries, give the meaning of year to the word *haab* or *hab.* This also occurs as *haab* or *hab* in western and eastern Chol, Chontal, and Pokomchi; as *habil* in Tzeltal and Tzotzil; as *habil* or *hail* in Chaneabal; as *ab* in Mam and Quiche; and as *yab* in Ixil. The word has been rather widely accepted by Maya epigraphers as meaning the year of 365 days. Long (1925), however, has shown clearly that as employed in the chronological passages of the books of Chilam Balam it refers to the year of 360 days, and that as used in the combination *cuch haab,* "year bearer," it also means the year of 360 days. He points out, furthermore, that in the hieroglyphic texts the year of 365 days does not have its own glyph, but that the period would be written as 1 tun and 5 kins.

Beyer (1936f), on the other hand, calls attention to passages on Copan U, in which two dates, 3 Caban, Pop seated, and 3 Eb, Pop seated, occur. Following the first date is a glyph "expiration of 13 tuns"; immediately before the second date are two glyphs. The first is that of 13 tuns with the postfix indicating that it is a distance number; the second is the anterior date indicator, which denotes that this number is to be counted back to reach the date which follows. Actually that is precisely the relationship between these two dates provided the tun is translated as a year of 365 days.

A1–B1	(9.18. 2. 5.17)	3 Caban, Pop seated
A2		Expiration of 13 tuns
O2–P2	13. [3. 5]	Count back
O3–P3	(9.17. 9. 2.12)	3 Eb, Pop seated

Perhaps the tun glyph is used in this passage because the count is made from the start (or end) of one haab to another, and the distance might be thought of as 13 haab because of the important positions the two dates hold. Also in this particular case there would be little danger of confusion between the tun alone and the tun plus the nameless days. Whatever may have been in the mind of the Maya priest, it is reasonably certain that in this unique arrangement the priest-astronomer twice used a tun glyph to indicate the year of 365 days. The lateness of the text may account for this aberrant treatment.

The rather pedantic differences the Maya established for the usage of the tun glyph and the cauac glyph, both of which stand for the period of 360 days, and for the words *tun* and *haab* are discussed on page 190. Suffice it to say that in the books of Chilam Balam only the word *haab* is used in describing the period of 18 months whereas *tun* is principally used to chronicle the passage of time in direct or indirect relationship to the LC. No word for the period of 365 days is surely known, although it is just possible that the term *buk* served that purpose.

The word *haab* appears in Mam with the meaning of rain, and as *hab* is translated in the Guzman dictionary of Cakchiquel as "shower," there seems little doubt that the word contains the root *ha,* "water." Perhaps the final letters *ab* represent the instrumental termination; that is to say, *haab* is that which causes water. The main part of the winged-cauac glyph is the section of the body of a celestial dragon, a creature which sent the rains. Similarly,

the main element in the tun sign of geometric form is the symbol for jade or water (p. 144). The word *tun* has a similar connotation since it means jade, the symbol for water. The head form of the tun may be that of the Moan bird, deity of the clouds, but that identification is open to question (p. 145).

The names for the divisions of 20 days which compose the 260-day cycle have been discussed (pp. 69–88). It was noted that there is some uncertainty as to whether those terms for 20 days refer to divisions of the divinatory almanac, which run from Imix to Ahau, or to the months which start with Akbal (or Ik, if the seating of the month is regarded as the first day). The difference may seem very small, but was almost certainly of sufficient importance to the Maya to require separate terms, just as slight variations in context led to the substitution of haab for tun.

Landa writes that the 18 months were called *uinal hunekeh.* It would appear that two names are here given: uinal and hun (one?) ekeh. The latter is probably the result of miscopying (p. 97).

Several words connected with moon are listed in various dictionaries with the meaning of month. It is not improbable that in some cases the word for the month of 20 days was transferred after the Spanish conquest to the Spanish months.

In Cakchiquel and Pokoman *uinak* was used for a count of 20 days, whereas the respective terms for month are *ikh* and *po,* both of which denote moon. In Yucatan, according to Landa, the 30-day month (more correctly, alternating months of 29 and 30 days) was called *u.* Expressions such as *canpel u,* "[the war lasted] four months," *oxte uu,* "three months," and *hun kalab ti u,* "one whole month," in the books of Chilam Balam, and the Motul dictionary confirm this usage. *U* is the Yucatec name for the moon. The Motul dictionary also lists *ho uen,* "a matter of five months." The Tzotzil word for month, *uh,* is close to Yucatec, and has the same meaning; the Chaneabal word is *ixauh,* which also denotes the moon. At Santa Eulalia *xahau* is the term used for the uinal, and also signifies moon. *Uinac* may have once described the 20-day period.

The reason for believing that some of these terms now used for the lunar or civil month may once have been used for the month of 20 days is that the moon glyph is used as a sign for 20 both in distance numbers (stelae and codices) and in the lunar series. Santa Eulalia use of *xahau* for both moon and uinal conforms to this supposition. I do not know the derivations of *toh amac* and *tachbal amac,* the Ixil terms for the uinal.

THE CYCLE OF FIFTY-TWO YEARS

The sacred almanac of 260 days and the year of 365 days were concurrent. Naturally at the end of the year of 365 days, one cycle of 260 days had been completed, and 105 days of the second cycle had elapsed. It is, therefore, clear that after one year of 365 days the day name had advanced five places, and the day number one place (105 ÷ 20, remainder 5; 105 ÷ 13, remainder 1). As the day name advanced five places each year, at the end of four years the same day name returned, but with a coefficient four points higher. It follows that only four day names could coincide with any one month position.

The originators or reformers of the calendar made Imix coincide with the fourth (or ninth or fourteenth) of each month, with the result that the day names which could accompany each month number were as follows:

Caban, Ik, Manik, Eb   on seating of month and 5th, 10th, and 15th days.
Etz'nab, Akbal, Lamat, Ben on 1st, 6th, 11th, and 16th of month.
Cauac, Kan, Muluc, Ix   on 2nd, 7th, 12th, and 17th of month.
Ahau, Chicchan, Oc, Men   on 3rd, 8th, 13th, and 18th of month.
Imix, Cimi, Chuen, Cib   on 4th, 9th, 14th, and 19th of month.

Thus there are only four day names which can occur with a given month position. If a date is deciphered as, for instance, 7 Ahau 14 Zip, there is an error in the decipherment or in the original text, or the standard system was not being used (p. 124), for the day Ahau could fall only on the third, eighth, thirteenth, and eighteenth of Zip. On the other hand, only the day names Imix, Cimi, Chuen, and Cib can coincide with fourteenth of Zip. This arrangement is often of great help in deciphering weathered or incomplete dates. For example, if the day sign is eroded, but the month sign is preserved, one knows from the latter's coefficient that the day sign must be one of the corresponding group of four. Thus if the month coefficient is 2, 7, 12, or 17 the day sign has to be Kan, Muluc, Ix, or Cauac. As these four signs are quite dissimilar, any small detail that has survived will usually lead to the identification of the glyph. In other cases the popularity of a day sign may be of assistance. If the month coefficient is 3, 8, 13, or 18, the day sign has to be Chicchan, Oc, Men, or Ahau, but as the last is more frequently represented than the other three together, one has a strong hint that the day is Ahau. Furthermore, as Ahau ends every period in the Maya count from the uinal to the great-great cycle, a month coefficient of 3, 8, 13, or 18 prompts one to be on the lookout for a tun ending.

Because of the surplus of 105 days of the year over the cycle of 260 days, Pop will be seated on 1 Ik one year,

on 2 Manik the next, on 3 Eb the third, on 4 Caban the fourth, on 5 Ik the fifth, on 6 Manik the sixth, etc. The thirteenth seating of Pop will be on 13 Ik, the fourteenth on 1 Manik, the twenty-seventh on 1 Eb, the fortieth on 1 Caban, the fifty-second on 13 Caban. After the fifty-second year the series starts again with 1 Ik. Naturally the same interval of 52 years of 365 days must pass before any combination of day and month sign can repeat. The reason for this can be shown in another way. The highest common factor of 260 and 365 is 5, therefore $260 \times 365 \div 5 = 52 \times 365$.

This interval of 52 vague years is called the Calendar Round, and any specific date, such as 13 Ahau 18 Cumku or 5 Muluc 17 Ceh, is a CR date. The Maya name for this period is unknown. It may have been an expression which included the word *uazaklom,* since that term is used to describe the cycle of katuns; the Motul dictionary lists *uaçaklom, cosa que es de buelta o que se vuelve.*

There are altogether 18,980 (52 × 365) CR dates, but the same day name and month will recur after 1460 days (four vague years) although the day number will be four units higher. For example, 13 Ahau 18 Cumku falls on 9.17.0.0.0. Four vague years later the date will be 9.17.4.1.0 4 Ahau 18 Cumku. This is so because the interval of 4 tuns, 1 uinal, and 0 days is 1460 days. This is four years of 365 days, and therefore the month position is unchanged. Dividing 1460 by 13 leaves a remainder of 4, the coefficient of the day sign therefore increases by that amount. As 1460 is divisible by 20, the day remains Ahau (p. 67).

POSITION OF MONTH GLYPH

The full CR date is almost always given in texts on the monuments of the Initial Series Period. Sometimes, however, particularly in the repetition of a PE date, the month position is dropped, but the month position never occurs without the day. The normal position of the month glyph is immediately after the day sign in the case of CR dates, but rather rarely they are separated by one or more glyphs, notably Glyphs G and F (p. 208), the first of which gives the name or emblem of the lord of the night. In the case of IS the day and month glyphs are usually separated by Glyphs G and F and the lunar series, the month sign following Glyph A of the lunar series (fig. 50,*1,2*); in about 15 per cent of the IS the two are together, and precede Glyphs G and F and the lunar series (fig. 53,*1*) or, more rarely, both follow Glyph A of the lunar series (Copan 10, 13). Quite rarely the month sign lies between Glyphs G and F and the lunar series, the day sign preceding Glyphs G and F. Glyphs connected with the cycle of 819 days form a sort of parenthetical clause, with its own day and month glyphs, between the day and month signs of the IS, so that, disregarding other glyphs, the order is: 1, day sign of IS; 2, day sign of cycle of 819 days; 3, month sign of cycle of 819 days; 4, month sign of IS.

THE YEAR BEARERS

The days which fell on first of Pop were of great importance at the time of the Spanish conquest. In the standard system first of Pop coincided with the days Akbal, Lamat, Ben, and Etz'nab, but in parts of Campeche and Yucatan a shift took place, starting as early as 9.12.0.0.0 (Proskouriakoff and Thompson, 1947; fig. 35,*8–15*) and was apparently accepted generally in Yucatan in the sixteenth century. The months were displaced one position so that 1 Pop was made to coincide with Kan, Muluc, Ix, or Cauac. Naturally this shift applied to all the days, so that, for example, Ahau fell only on the second, seventh, twelfth, or seventeenth days of a month (fig. 35,*9–11,15*) instead of the third, eighth, thirteenth, and eighteenth days, as was the practice during the Initial Series Period.

These days falling on first of Pop were called in Yucatan *ah cuch haab,* "bearer of the year." Among the present-day Jacalteca the year bearers are called *ikum habil* which means precisely "bearer ·of the year." The Chuh name is *cuchlum haabil,* which has the same meaning, and is very close to Yucatec, for the terminations *lum* and *um* denote the agent. Presumably, the Ixil term *ih yab* has the same meaning, for yab signifies year.

The codical form of the glyph for the burden of the year, now identified (p. 267; fig. 43,*37,49,61*), occurs several times, as would be expected, on the pages dealing with the new years and their prophecies. What is probably a postconquest variant appears in Mani (fig. 46,*32*).

FUNCTIONS OF YEAR BEARERS

The year bearers served two main purposes: they influenced the luck of the years and they served as a ready designation of the current year.

Landa gives a rather full description of the ceremonies, which commenced in Uayeb, for the installation of the new year bearer. The year bearers were associated with world directions and colors: Kan was placed to the east and its color, accordingly, was red; Muluc was set at the north, and its color was white; Ix ruled in the west and was associated with black; to Cauac fell the

south and yellow. Naturally, after four years the cycle started again with the association Kan-east-red. In addition, each year, through its association with a world direction, was under the patronage of important deities who ruled over that quarter. These included the four Bacabs who were stationed at the four points of the compass, and were known as the red Bacab, the white Bacab, etc., although they also possessed individual names. Other important deities connected with the years were: Bolon-Tz'acab, who held sway during the Kan years; Kinich-Ahau, the sun god, who ruled the Muluc years; Itzamna, the celestial dragon, patron of the Ix years; and Uacmitun-Ahau, a god of death, whose dire reign influenced the Cauac years.

Kan years were lucky and generally free of calamities, because, Landa informs us, the ruling Bacab, Hobnil, had never sinned, as his brother had done. Muluc was also an auspicious year bearer because the ruling Bacab was the greatest of the four. The fortunes of Ix years were calamitous. They were favorable for the cotton crop, but the maize harvest would be very meagre because of drought and hot spells; famine would follow, and this would lead to theft. Thieves would be sold into slavery, and that, in turn, would cause discords, wars, and revolutions. Locusts would plague the land, towns would be depopulated, and chiefs might die. Cauac years were also unfortunate, as one would expect since they were under the baneful god of death. Many persons would die; hot spells of weather, and plagues of birds and ants would destroy the crops in many parts. Some of these auguries are given in glyphs in Dresden (pp. 268–73).

Propitiatory ceremonies might alleviate distress, and these took place, according to Landa. Nevertheless one suspects, although there is no direct evidence to support the suspicion, that the coefficient of the year bearer affected the auguries. A lucky number probably offset the evils inherent in Ix and Cauac; an unlucky number presumably modified the good cheer of Kan and Muluc years. That would be normal procedure for the Maya, and would present those opportunities for hedging, so needful for all who essay to chart the future. The importance of the year bearer in the ceremonial round of the year is well illustrated in accounts of the practices of present-day Maya in the Guatemalan highlands, notably the Jacalteca and Ixil (p. 95).

Besides shaping the fortunes of the years, the year bearers served as names for the years, and thereby afforded a rapid and simple method for identifying any year within a CR. Assuming that the first of the 52 year bearers was 1 Kan, it is a very easy matter to find the position of any given year bearer in the sequence. One merely finds by subtraction the preceding year bearer with coefficient of 1, and notes the division it heads (Table 11, p. 127). Thus, to find the position of a year 10 Cauac, one subtracts nine years to reach 1 Ix, and notes that this heads the third division, and therefore is the twenty-seventh year. Adding 9 and 27 gives the answer that 10 Cauac is the thirty-sixth year bearer.

CONCEPT OF BURDEN

The term year bearer appears to have arisen because the Maya conceived of the year bearer carrying the year as a load on his back. The same concept was applied to other periods as well. Thus we find in Tizimin (pp. 2, 9, 10, 12, 13) statements such as *tu kin u ch'a cuch*, "at the time he takes the burden," apparently referring to the year bearer 3 Cauac; and *u kax cuch katun* which probably means "the binding of the burden of the katun"; and again in *tu kin u kaxal u cuch ah ho Ahau*, "on the day [or at the time] of the binding of the burden of Lord 5 Ahau," 5 Ahau being the day which gave its name to the current katun. Other references to the burden have been discussed at some length (pp. 59–61).

Each year has his burden with which he traverses his course to pass it at journey's end to his successor. It is a poetical imagery, not devoid of beauty, and in keeping with the Maya concept of time.

LOCATION OF YEAR BEARERS

Alfonso Caso (1939) has advanced evidence that among the Aztec the year bearer was the last (360th) day of the year; but Maya sources, such as the various books of Chilam Balam, are unanimous in placing the year bearers on first of Pop. The question arises as to the reliability of these colonial sources. It is known that late in the eighteenth century an attempt was made to reform the Maya calendar by making the length of the katuns 24 years instead of 20 tuns (p. 34). Could there have been in the seventeenth century a similar but more successful attempt to shift the year bearers from the end of the year to first of Pop?

Evidence in favor of first of Pop is as follows:

1. Page 66 of the Chronicle of Oxkutzcab lists the dates on which a succession of 13 tuns, running from 1532 to 1544, ended. There are also listed the year bearer as 13 Kan on first of Pop, etc. Despite certain inaccuracies in transcription this document bears every evidence of being the purest writing on Maya chronology which has survived. At the end Juan Xiu signs the entry, dates it May 29, 1685, and states that he copied it "from an ancient book, namely in characters as they are called, *Anares*" (p. 23). Entries on some events were probably added in script to a chronological frame in glyphs, but it is the latter which interests us for the moment.

2. A series of year bearers occurs on pages 1–13 of Tizimin in connection with prophecies for years or tuns for a Katun 5 Ahau (Roys, 1949). The sequence runs from 13 Kan to 8 Muluc, and in most cases the year bearer is stated to fall on first of Pop. The first in the series, 13 Kan, is said to have occurred in 1593. Under 13 Kan there is a reference to the Katun 5 Ahau declaring its name on 15 Zec. If by this is meant the CR date 5 Ahau 17 Zec, this actually fell in a year in which 13 Kan was on first of Pop. The sequence is in agreement with page 66 of the Chronicle of Oxkutzcab. In fact the authors probably drew from a single source. These prophecies in Tizimin are written in an archaic manner and are full of a ritualism which was certainly lost within a century after the Spanish conquest (Roys, 1949). This early material, provided it has not been tampered with by colonial transcribers, supplies very strong evidence for the year bearers having coincided with first of Pop.

3. Bishop Landa, after noting that Kan, Muluc, Ix, and Cauac were employed as Europeans use dominical letters, says that they begin the first days of the months of twenty days, and "the letter which is the dominical letter always comes out on the first day of their year. . . . the first of their month Pop" (Tozzer edition of Landa, pp. 135, 149–50).

4. Entries stating that the year bearers coincided with first of Pop are frequent in the books of Chilam Balam. For instance, Perez 130–31 lists year bearers for 1752 to 1796, and in every case 1 Pop follows the name of the year bearer. Similarly, year bearers are connected with 1 Pop on page 99 of Ixil (Berendt copy, p. 77). In Chumayel references to year bearers are very infrequent, and in no case is the position in the year stated. Of course, that information was not really required; every Maya must have known when the year bearers fell.

5. Tovilla, in his brief account of the calendar of the Manche Chol, does not specifically state that the year bearers fell on the first day of the year, but he does say that the month bearers fell on the first day of each uinal. There are traces in the sundry Chilam Balam that the year-bearer name had a secondary function as bearer of the month. Thus, we can indirectly infer from Tovilla's description that the year bearer coincided with the first day of the year.

6. In the calendars used by the present-day Ixil and Jacalteca, the year bearers fall on the day after the close of the five unlucky days. These five unlucky days do not occur in the same position as in the Yucatan calendar, but structurally the arrangement is the same, in that the year bearers are at the beginning of the year following the five unlucky days.

These six lines of evidence make a very strong case for the first of the month following the five nameless days as the position of the year bearer. During the Initial Series Period and in Yucatan in the middle of the sixteenth century that was Pop. Whether year bearers fell on the first of the month or on the seating of the month will be discussed below.

There are certain arguments which slightly favor the position of 1 Uayeb for the year bearers in sixteenth-century Yucatan:

1. The Maya named baktuns, katuns, and tuns by the days on which those periods were completed; it would be logical to apply the same system to the year. However, in this case, the presumed month position would not be the last day of the year, but the first day of the nameless days, 1 Uayeb, for Kan, etc., could not fall on the last day of Cumku.

2. There is a good case (Caso, 1939) for the thesis that Tititl was the last month of the Aztec year, and that the year bearer fell on the last day of that month. However, Weitzel (1948) has produced astronomical evidence against this thesis.

3. The series of prophecies in Tizimin for the years or tuns of a Katun 5 Ahau starts with the year bearer 13 Kan, which is dated 1593 (Roys, 1949). The katun therefore started in 1593 and ended in 1613, but the evidence is strongly against a katun having ended in that year; according to the 11.16.0.0.0 correlation a Katun 5 Ahau, which was also a baktun completion, ended in September 1618, and that was 12.0.0.0.0 5 Ahau 13 Zotz'. The year bearer for the end of the katun is given as 7 Kan or 8 Muluc, but 5 Ahau 12 Zotz' (as it would be in the Campeche-Yucatan system used in the books of Chilam Balam) could not fall in a year of which the first day was either 7 Kan 1 Pop or 8 Muluc 1 Pop. On the other hand, 8 Muluc 1 Uayeb does occur in the same year as 5 Ahau 12 Zotz', and the sequence of 20 year bearers from 1 Muluc to 8 Muluc would correspond to the katun which ended on 5 Ahau 12 Zotz'. In order to accept this arrangement of year bearers on 1 Uayeb one must assume that the statements as to the year bearers falling on first of Pop and the reference to 1593 are interpolations. In view of the innovations made by colonial scribes this assumption is not out of order. However, it is much more probable that the compiler of this text had access to the series of year bearers used by the compiler of page 66 of the Oxkutzcab chronicle, and added a CR, thereby getting the year bearers correct, but throwing a wrench into the katun chronology. The material can be used in favor of the 1 Uayeb hypothesis, but the argument is weak.

Against these arguments must be set the very much stronger case for the year bearers on first of Pop. I was attracted by the Caso thesis, and tried to apply it to Yucatan, but the arguments against it are too overwhelming.

CORRELATION OF YEAR BEARERS WITH EUROPEAN YEARS

The year bearers fell on the first of the first month after the five nameless days, but the position of the last varied, as can be seen in Table 8 (p. 106). The Yucatec system, however, agrees with that of the Initial Series Period in that Pop follows the nameless days, and the same is true of the Chol system, although in the Chol list the equivalent of Pop is missing.

Because the Yucatec year started in the middle of the Christian year, one cannot correlate the former with a single European year, but one must say that it corresponds, for example, to 1517–18, or that it started in 1517, or that it ended in 1518. Of these three methods, the last two appear to have been used in colonial Yucatan.

On page 66 of the Chronicle of Oxkutzcab a sequence of 12 year bearers is assigned to the years 1534–45, and in this sequence the year bearer for 1542 is given as 13 Kan. The *Crónica de Yaxkukul* states that the Spaniards settled permanently at Merida in 1542, and the year bearer was 13 Kan. The formal foundation of Merida was in January 1542, so we can deduce that the year bearer covered the period middle of 1541 to middle of 1542. The Tizimin prophecies (Roys, 1949) give 1593 as the equivalent of 13 Kan, and deducting a CR, one gets 1541 as the year when 13 Kan had previously been the bearer. We thus have statements that 1541 corresponded to 13 Kan, that January 1542 fell in a year 13 Kan, and that 1542 was the year 13 Kan.

From these statements it seems safe to assume that the Maya correlated the Maya year either with the European year in which the year bearer began his course, or with that in which he finished it. There is, however, a fragmentary entry in Perez 184, which equates an incomplete date in Zip with August 1537, and the year bearer (subsequently designated as such) was 8 Cauac. According to the system just discussed, 8 Cauac would have been the bearer of a year running from July 1536 to July 1537. The scribe, of course, was reckoning back, for we can be sure that in 1537 the year bearers had not been correlated with the European year. Did he associate 8 Cauac with 1537, and therefore add that information arbitrarily, or did 8 Cauac correspond to 1537–38, and 13 Kan, likewise to 1542–43?

Long has shown that Landa's typical year with year bearer 12 Kan can not be placed by the European dominical letters, as Spinden had supposed, but there is indirect evidence that his year must be that of 1553–54. Reckoning back from one of the calendars of the present-day Indians of the Guatemalan highlands, one finds that 12 Kan fell on July 15, 1553, whereas Landa places 12 Kan first of Pop on July 16. The nearest other occurrences of 12 Kan near July 16 in the middle of the sixteenth century can be reckoned by the same method to have been July 21, 1548, and July 9, 1558, neither of which agrees so closely with Landa's statements. Moreover, 12 Kan will not fall anywhere near July in 1554. We must, therefore, conclude that Landa's equation was 12 Kan first of Pop equals July 16, 1553. In that case the year 8 Cauac ran 1536–37, and the statement in Perez 184 is technically incorrect.

The round of year bearers from 1529–30 to 1580–81 is given in Table 11, together with source materials. Note that those cases, such as the Chronicle of Oxkutzcab, which give the year in which the bearer ended his course are included.

and Cauac. Is there any reasonable explanation of this lack of conformity?

On the assumption that the Akbal set was used by most cities of the southern area, the Yucatec system can be explained satisfactorily. It is now known that the Maya of Campeche, at least as early as 9.12.0.0.0 (p. 304) changed the month positions on which the day Ahau fell, so that under the new arrangement the end of Katun 12 was not 10 Ahau 8 Yaxkin, but 10 Ahau 7 Yaxkin. The days remained unchanged; the month positions advanced one place. Similarly, Kan, Muluc, Ix, and Cauac had perforce to fall on first of Pop in place of Akbal, Lamat, Ben, and Etz'nab. Why this shift took place we do not know, but that it did take place without loss of a day is now established. This explains the shift to the Kan set of year bearers, and also locates the original home of Codex Madrid.

If the month were seated on 0 Pop, to use the old

TABLE 11—YUCATEC YEAR BEARERS

1 Kan	1529–30	1 Muluc	1542–43[4]	1 Ix	1555–56	1 Cauac	1568–69[7]
2 Muluc	1530–31	2 Ix	1543–44	2 Cauac	1556–57	2 Kan	1569–70
3 Ix	1531–32	3 Cauac	1544–45[5]	3 Kan	1557–58	3 Muluc	1570–71
4 Cauac	1532–33	4 Kan	1545–46	4 Muluc	1558–59	4 Ix	1571–72
5 Kan	1533–34[1]	5 Muluc	1546–47	5 Ix	1559–60	5 Cauac	1572–73
6 Muluc	1534–35	6 Ix	1547–48	6 Cauac	1560–61	6 Kan	1573–74
7 Ix	1535–36[2]	7 Cauac	1548–49	7 Kan	1561–62	7 Muluc	1574–75
8 Cauac	1536–37	8 Kan	1549–50	8 Muluc	1562–63	8 Ix	1575–76
9 Kan	1537–38	9 Muluc	1550–51[6]	9 Ix	1563–64	9 Cauac	1576–77
10 Muluc	1538–39	10 Ix	1551–52	10 Cauac	1564–65	10 Kan	1577–78
11 Ix	1539–40	11 Cauac	1552–53	11 Kan	1565–66	11 Muluc	1578–79
12 Cauac	1540–41	12 Kan	1553–54	12 Muluc	1566–67	12 Ix	1579–80
13 Kan	1541–42[3]	13 Muluc	1554–55	13 Ix	1567–68	13 Cauac	1580–81[8]

[1]Given on p. 66 of Chronicle of Oxkutzcab. The first of a series of twelve year bearers covering the years 1533–34 to 1544–45, all of which are correct save the last, which gives 13 Cauac instead of 3 Cauac.

[2]Given in Ixil as the year bearer of 1743 (4 × 52 years later), but on this same page the wrong years are given for year bearers.

[3]Given in the Cronica de Yaxkukul (p. 18) and the parallel Cronica de Chicxulub as the year 1542, that in which Merida was founded in January 1542. This is correct. Given 52 years later in Tizimin (pp. 1–13) as the first of a series of 21 year bearers.

[4]Given in Mani (Perez 124) as the year bearer of 1750 (4 × 52 years later).

[5]Starts series of year bearers in Tizimin (p. 35) and Mani (Perez 130) with 1752 (4 × 52 years later).

[6]At the head of a sequence of 17 year bearers in Mani

(Perez 124–25). The series starts with 1758 (4 × 52 years later).

[7]The first of a series of 24 year bearers on page 36 of Tizimin correlated with 1776–99 (4 × 52 years later). However, on the next page all 52 year bearers are given in a table which starts with 1 Kan as the year bearer for 1758. This is incorrect, throwing the whole series awry. It should be 9 Muluc, as correctly given in Mani (see note 6 above).

[8]At the head of a sequence of 53 year bearers in Mani (Perez 122) starting with 1736 (3 × 52 years later). The references to year bearers could be expanded considerably by citing their occurrences in connection with the reformed katuns of 24 years. In one place (Perez 165) year bearers are given up to the year A.D. 2003, but the coefficients are uniformly one digit under the correct numbers. Corrections are made in the margin.

SHIFTS IN YEAR BEARERS

The Quiche, the Ixil, the Tlapanec of Guerrero, and the Zapotec and Cuicatec of Oaxaca used their equivalents of Ik, Manik, Eb, and Caban as year bearers; the Tzeltal, the Chuh, the Jacalteca, the Aztec, the Mixtec, and the compilers of the Dresden and Paris codices had Akbal, Lamat, Ben, and Etzn'ab as theirs; Codex Madrid and sixteenth-century Yucatan used Kan, Muluc, Ix,

designation, and the year bearer fell on the following day, that is first of Pop, it would not be difficult for the two events to be confused or merged by a people not overly strict on the preservation of old ways. The Quiche and Ixil, with no stela cult and, apparently, no LC, might have had little interest in keeping those two ceremonies apart; and in time the days on which the years were seated might have acquired more importance, and finally replaced the next group of days as bearers of the years.

One suspects that the two functions were confused by the colonial scribes of the books of Chilam Balam. The situation then might have developed thus:

	Chiapas, etc.	Yucatan and Campeche	Quiche, Ixil
Seating of year	1 Ik 0 Pop	2 Akbal 0 Pop	1 Ik 0 Pop for both events
Year bearer	2 Akbal 1 Pop	3 Kan 1 Pop	

One must suppose that in the Central Area during the Initial Series Period the year bearers were Akbal, Lamat, Ben, and Etz'nab, and that the month and the year were seated on the previous day. So far as the texts on the monuments are concerned, there is no direct evidence that the year-bearer cult existed; but I make no doubt that it did function, but probably in ways that did not call for its recording on stelae. No glyph for the year bearer has been isolated on the monuments, and the number of dates falling on seating of Pop or first of Pop is no larger than would result from chance. This is hardly strange, for with the elaborate IS system, a notation of the year bearer would have been superfluous. Such a system was convenient in Yucatan prior to the conquest when the IS method of dating had fallen into desuetude, for a combination of year bearer and katun ending would fix a year in a cycle of 260 tuns.

The identification of clauses which give the world direction glyph followed by a glyph which records the count of the year makes it highly probable that year bearers were in use in the Initial Series Period, for this information is closely related to the year-bearer system in sixteenth-century Yucatan.

Grouping of Year Bearers

It will be noticed that the table is readily divisible into four parts of 13 year bearers apiece. Each part starts with the coefficient 1 attached to a year bearer in its correct sequence. This naturally follows because the thirteenth year bearer has the same name as the first, and, consequently, the fourteenth (also twenty-seventh, and fortieth) is the next year bearer in sequence and has a coefficient of 1.

One would expect the Maya to have given some attention to such an arrangement since it conformed to the kind of division they sought in that the whole formed a re-entering cycle (of 52 years of 365 days). The divisions were four in number and therefore could be assigned to the four world directions and colors, and the day at the start of each division had a coefficient of 1.

In Tizimin (p. 37) the 52 year bearers are thus arranged in four columns, headed respectively by 1 Kan, 1 Muluc, 1 Ix, and 1 Cauac. Beside each of these four year bearers at the head of each division is written its

world direction, "to the east," "to the north," "to the west," and "to the south" respectively. Possibly the year bearers were arranged hieroglyphically in four quarters of a wheel (p. 247). There is some evidence that a wheel-like presentation of this kind was called *cuceb* from the root *cuc*, "to roll or turn like a wheel." This term heads the sequence of year bearers on Tizimin 1–13.

It is only in the last few years that such a system has been reported in use among a Maya group. Lincoln notes that these four divisions of the round of year bearers is of some importance among the present-day Ixil. The year bearer with coefficient of 1 at the start of each division of 13 years is known as *ih lenal ki* or *el presidente*. It dominates the whole period of 13 years in which it is in power, its influence combining with that of the year bearer of the current year to affect the fates. I do not know the meaning of the phrase, although *ki* or *kih* is "day" or "sun," and *ih* may be connected with the Jacalteca root *ik*, "bear a burden."

SUMMARY

The bulk of this chapter has been devoted to a somewhat tedious inquiry into the meanings and religious affiliations of the months. The results have been summarized in Table 9 (p. 118), and it is not necessary to repeat that information here. This was followed by a discussion of the meaning of the element which indicates the so-called zero position of each month, and evidence has been produced to show that that glyphic element probably had the meaning "the seating of." It has been demonstrated that the seating of a month coincided with the last day of the previous month; the Maya artist could carve "last of month *n*" or "seating of month *n* + 1."

Attention has been called to the Maya system of reckonings on the side to take care of the error accumulated by a calendar which did not intercalate leap days. It has been demonstrated that the various names for the year and tun, as well as for the sundry glyphs which correspond to them, without exception refer to water, and that the idea presumably derives from a count by rainy seasons. This was followed by a discussion of the structure of the CR.

Much space was devoted to the year bearers, particularly as to whether the generally accepted ideas on their placement on first of Pop and on their correlation with the European years were correct. It was shown that the evidence in favor of those ideas was overwhelming. An entirely new light on Maya mentality is shed by a reconstruction of their concept of time as a burden borne by relays of travelers marching without respite through all eternity. An explanation for the shifts in year bearers is offered, and the grouping of year bearers is discussed.

5
Methods of Recording Numbers

Dust-footed Time will never tell its hour,
—John Masefield, *Lollingdon Downs*

Numbers loom large in Maya hieroglyphic writing; there are few texts that entirely lack them. This is not strange in view of the Maya preoccupation with time and its multitudinous divisions, and in consideration of the part numbers played in divination. Not only were all periods of time accompanied by numbers, but numbers had to be combined with names to designate the days. Furthermore, numerals were incorporated in the names of many gods, and there is no reason to doubt that many of these were expressed hieroglyphically.

Among gods and goddesses with names of this description may be mentioned: Hun-Batz (One Monkey). Ox-Multun-Tzekil (Three Heaps of Skulls), Uac-Lom-Cham (Uac-Lot-Chaam, Six Molars), Ah Uuc-Cheknal (He Who Fertilizes the Maize Seven Times), Uucub-Cakix (Seven Macaw), Bolon-Tz'acab (Nine Generations; Bolon can also mean uncontaminated [Redfield and Villa, 1934, p. 356] or can be used as an intensive), Lahun-Chan (Ten Sky), Buluc-Ch'abtan (Eleven Penances?), Oxlahun-ti-Ku (Thirteen Gods), Hun-Pic-Tok (Eight Thousand Flints), and Hun-Pic-Tz'iu (Eight Thousand Cowbirds).

Some names of gods incorporating numbers are clearly of calendarial origin. These include Hun-Ahau (1 Ahau), Hun-Came (1 Cimi), Hun-Tihax (1 Etz'nab), Bolon-Imux (9 Imix), and Beleje-Toh (9 Muluc). In a number of cases the name glyphs of gods depicted in the codices are supplied with coefficients. Among these are God Q, whose hieroglyph is a picture of his head with the number 10 placed before it (p. 131; fig. 15,6,7). God Q is a god of death probably by sacrifice, and it is, therefore, fitting that the number 10 should form part of his name, since 10 symbolizes death and is the sign of the death god. The glyph of God R, whose head rather resembles that of the maize god and who is a benevolent deity, has a coefficient of 11 (fig. 15,9,10).

A glyph, like the Chicchan sign, but with a coefficient of 1, appears a number of times in the codices (fig. 42,19) as the name glyph of an unidentified god. The glyph for Lahun-Chan exactly depicts his name (p. 218). There is a hieroglyph of a god with coefficient of 6 attached to a Yax sign with "Ben-Ich" superfix; several others, notably the long-nosed gods with coefficients of 7 and 9, include numbers.

The name glyph of the Moan bird incorporates the number 13. This may be prefixed to the head of the bird itself or to the symbol for the sky. In the first case the meaning is "thirteen layers of clouds"; in the second, "thirteen skies [or layers of sky]" (figs. 20,19,20,23,24; 42,12,21).

Some hieroglyphs with numbers probably correspond to ritualistic terms. Gates (1931, p. 58) has suggested that the Oc glyph with a special suffix and a coefficient of 3 may correspond to the Maya salutation *oxtezcun*. This term, which Villa (1945, p. 159) gives as *oxtez*, is used in prayers and means "thrice greeted." It is highly honorific. There is, however, reason to believe that this glyph has the meaning of good tidings, and is used in passages indicating the good or bad luck of the day. In any case, *ox* surely does not have any directly numerical connotation, but rather has an intensificatory value, the term being attached to various words to add emphasis, more or less as in our own expressions "a thousand thanks," "a thousand times no," or "ten times better." Glyphs of the ritualistic offering of 9 tortillas to the bee god are on Madrid 103b, 106b.

In the books of Chilam Balam numbers are constantly used in passages describing the ritual of the current katun. For example, Chumayel (p. 89) says of Katun 9 Ahau: "Nine was its cup; nine was its plate," the number of the cup and the plate being in such cases, as Roys has pointed out, the coefficient of the day Ahau on which the katun ends. Something of that sort is probably expressed on Copan B, where three glyphs in succession have coefficients of 4. The inscription commemorates a katun (9.15.0.0.0) which ended on 4 Ahau. Likewise, numbers, principally 6, which accompany a succession of 10 glyphs on Quirigua P, probably have a ritualistic value.

Of the nine glyphs which represent the gods of the nights, three (1st, 4th, and 5th) have coefficients. These numbers—9, 7, and 5—almost certainly were incorporated in the names of those nocturnal powers (fig. 34; p. 209). Moreover, not a few animals, birds, and insects have numbers incorporated in their names (Roys, 1949). No wonder, then, that with such a constant use of numbers, Maya hieroglyphic texts are so freely larded with numerical expressions.

BARS AND DOTS

The most frequent method of expressing numbers under 20 is by means of bars and dots. Each bar represents five; each dot, one. Thus, to express the number 13, the Maya wrote two bars and three dots; 16 was transcribed as three bars and one dot; four as four dots. Numbers could be written horizontally or vertically. If the bars were placed horizontally, the dots were above them; if the bars were in the vertical position, the dots were to their left (figs. 30–35).

The clue to this system of numeration was in books of Chilam Balam, where examples were found of days, the coefficients of which were written both in Spanish script and by means of bars and dots. An explanation in Maya of the system, with drawings of bars and dots in the margin, occurs in Mani, and is dated 1793 (Perez 92). The text with a translation is given by Brinton (1882, pp. 47–48) without naming the source. The sequence of the coefficients with the series of 260 days on Madrid 65–73 supplies full confirmation.

In the sculptured texts there is often considerable ornamentation. The numerical bars may have decorative lines added, with the unfortunate result that sometimes it is difficult to tell whether a somewhat eroded coefficient is one quite thick bar with interior ornamentation or two rather thin bars (figs. 47,4; 48,2). Ornamentation of the interiors of both bars and dots is particularly frequent in texts dating from the first half of Baktun 9.

Rather than leave a dot (more correctly speaking, a circle) with large blank spaces to each side of it, the Maya sculptors frequently added decorative details, which generally took the form of small crescentic ornaments. Their presence or absence in no way affects the number. Thus the number 6 would frequently be carved as one circle flanked by crescents and a bar, 17 would be sculptured as two circles with an ornamental crescent between, and three bars (figs. 3,1; 4,12).

Usually crescents were added if there were only one or two circles to bring the sum of circles and ornaments to three. Quite rarely, two crescents are added to two circles, producing a less elegant and somewhat confusing coefficient (fig. 2,13,14). Early texts usually lack ornamental crescents, but after 9.10.0.0.0 they had become quite common, although some cities, notably Palenque, showed a preference for unembellished coefficients. In late times variations on the crescent became quite common. Of these the St. Andrew's cross was the most popular, appearing in many inscriptions carved between 9.17.10.0.0 and 10.3.0.0.0 (figs. 2,22; 4,34).

The use of crescents, too, is a snare and a delusion to the epigrapher, for when severe weathering has taken place, it is often difficult to distinguish between a numerical circle and an ornamental crescent. A coefficient which was written as 11 seems to be a damaged 13, or erosion converts circles into crescents so that a damaged 13 appears to be 11 or 12. In some cases the sculptors appear to have used circles which look remarkably like crescents, and crescents hardly distinguishable from circles; in other cases ovals or circles slightly larger or smaller than the numerical circles are used as decorative elements (fig. 35,16). These, too, are hard to distinguish from the numerical circles if any weathering has occurred. Nevertheless, one should not complain of such little difficulties; overcoming them brings an increment of zest to the epigrapher. No such troubles confront the student of the three codices, for that type of decoration is absent from the hieroglyphic books, although crosses were occasionally used.

In Dresden and Madrid color distinguishes the main uses of numerals. Coefficients of day signs are red; distance numbers and coefficients of month signs are black. This may have been an ancient custom since on the Uaxactun fresco the coefficients of the days are red, and on the Santa Rita frescoes numbers with day sign are red or yellow, whereas a coefficient with a glyph which is certainly not a day sign is gray. On the other hand, the coefficient of the day sign on the IS vase from Uaxactun is a yellowish cream outlined in black, but all other coefficients are similarly painted. Also all glyphs and coefficients of the text in House E, Palenque, are painted black.

In Dresden two IS sometimes occupy the same space, the coefficients of one being placed in the spaces between the coefficients of the other. In such cases the numbers of one IS are painted red; of the other, black. Symbols for zero or completion are invariably painted red.

Bars and dots may stand alone (p. 139), but more usually they serve as prefixes to glyphs. Like all prefixes, so far as is known, they could be placed to the left of the glyph they qualify or above it. In the earliest texts they usually stand above the glyph; in later texts they are more often to its left, but frequently are above it. For the sake of symmetry all coefficients in a passage usually occupy the same position with respect to the glyphs they modify.

In the case of Glyph A of the lunar series the coefficient is a postfix, and stands below or to the right of it (figs. 36; 37), and very rarely, other glyphs have numerical postfixes (fig. 3,3–9). The belief has been expressed that coefficients used as prefixes are to be read as multipliers; when used as postfixes they are to be taken as additions. This theory was formulated soon after the meaning of Glyph A of the lunar series was discovered. However, subsequent investigations have disproved it, for coefficients of the moon glyph as used as a distance number in the codices and in the inscriptions are added despite the fact that they usually occur as prefixes, and the same is true of Glyph E of the lunar series. It seems probable, therefore, that the coefficient of Glyph A of the lunar series appears as a postfix in order to distinguish that glyph from Glyph E (they are really identical, save that Glyph E sometimes has the distance number postfix). Actually, there is one case of the coefficient of Glyph A being a prefix (Quirigua K), the exception which proves the rule.

The addition of the *u* bracket converts cardinals to ordinals (p. 188); other affixes represent numerical classifiers (pp. 54–57).

HEAD VARIANTS: ONE TO NINETEEN

The Maya with their mystical attitude toward numbers were not satisfied to use only bars and dots to depict them. In many texts, although rarely in Dresden and never in the other codices, numbers are expressed by portraits of deities, whose features or attributes are the key to the number thus portrayed (figs. 24; 25).

It cannot be proved that every numerical profile is that of a god, but nearly all can be identified as such, and it is therefore safe to assume that all have a similar derivation. An explanation has been given for this association of numbers with gods (p. 99). The identification of these heads is largely due to the investigations of J. T. Goodman.

One (fig. 24,*1–7*). The head for 1 is that of a youthful deity with classical profile embracing almond-shaped eye, deformed head, prominent, straight nose, the edge of which continues upward in a straight line to form the forehead, open mouth, drooping lower lip, and receding chin. The distinguishing marks are a lock of hair which passes in front of the ear, and curves forward along the base of the jaw, and a long rod inserted in the earplug. There is usually a small ornament on the forehead, formed of one, two, or three circular elements. An IL sign frequently appears on the cheek as though to represent tattoo or paint marks.

The deity who rules during the month Kayab is the same individual (p. 117; fig. 23,*21–27*) and there is very little doubt that the head variant of the day Caban on Quirigua D (fig. 10,7) is again the same deity. In fact, the main element of Caban is in all probability the lock of hair. A lock of hair is the distinguishing mark of the goddess whom Schellhas (1904) designates with the letter I, and who, I have shown, is the moon goddess (Thompson, 1939). She is also a goddess of the earth

(*cab* means earth) and of the maize. Furthermore, this curl appears in Landa's alphabet to represent the letter *u,* but that is precisely the Yucatec name for the moon. Thus the identification of the head form of one with the moon goddess can be accepted as fully proved.

Two (fig. 24,*8–11*). The identification of the head which represents the number 2 is due to the acumen of Enrique Juan Palacios (1935), who deciphered several examples on the Tablet of the 96 Glyphs at Palenque. The distinguishing characteristic is a hand which surmounts the head; the features are those of a youthful individual. There is a double curve on his cheek, and the IL mark may be present.

In discussing the day Etz'nab it was noted that it was not improbable that God F was connected with the sacrificial knife. Before investigating this matter further, it should be pointed out that Schellhas (1904) confuses two distinct gods and classifies them together under the letter F. One god is distinguished by a curving line which starts on his forehead, passes through his eye or immediately behind it, and terminates below the ear (fig. 15,*1–3,6,7*); the other god has a sharper curve which faces in the opposite direction, and is placed behind the eye (fig. 15,*4,5,9,10*). The latter I call God R; to the former I assign the letter Q, thereby avoiding any confusion by discarding the letter F. God Q is closely associated with death both in his ornaments and attributes and in many of the scenes in which he appears; he shares with the death god rulership of the north in the diagram of world direction on Madrid 76; God R is benevolent, and his associations are with the maize god. The curving line on his face resembling the Caban sign perhaps is indicative of his connection with the soil. The respective glyphs of these two gods are distinguished by faithful delineation of these facial markings. Furthermore, God Q has a numerical coefficient of 10 before his name glyph; God R has the number 11. Part of Schellhas' confusion of these two gods undoubtedly arose from the fact that God Q has in front of his face, as one of his attributes, the eye of death. In the reproductions of the codices this often resembles a numerical dot, and as a consequence, Schellhas and others after him (e.g. Gates, 1931, p. 117) have supposed that this should be added to the two numerical bars beneath to yield a coefficient of 11. It has, however, no numerical value; it merely identifies the wearer as a god closely connected with death (fig. 15,6). Lastly, God Q usually has a long strip of material, perhaps bark cloth, pendent from his earplug; God R has a short rod. In the illustrations of his paper Schellhas shows a picture of God R to typify his merged God F, but in the text the description of the god applies rather to God Q. This same illustration is similarly labeled by subsequent writers including, I regret to say, myself. Thus are errors perpetuated, gathering authority with each fresh appearance.

The resemblance of God Q to the Mexican god Xipe was first noted by Schellhas, for both gods are distinguished by the line curving through the eye or immediately behind it. In the case of Xipe it is known that these lines appear on both sides of the face and represent the seams of the mask of human skin usually worn by that bloody god. Moreover, it is not unreasonable to suppose that the lines of dots on God Q's body correspond to the crescentic markings on Xipe, which, in turn, represent the human skin he wore. As evidence that God Q, like Xipe, was a deity of human sacrifice, it should be noted that he, in the company of the god of death, presides over a scene of human sacrifice, in the diagram on Madrid 76. On Madrid 84–86 he appears three times, on each occasion with a knife in one hand, a torch in the other. On another occasion he is thrusting a stone-pointed lance in the mouth of God M.

In Mexican art the hand is a symbol of death. The figure identified as Tzitimitl on Magliabecchi 76 has a headdress of hearts and hands surmounted by paper banners, all three being well-recognized symbols of human sacrifice and death; hearts and hands alternate on the collar of the same fearful being. Noguera (1927) reports the occurrence of human hands in a combination with hearts and skulls, on one of the two sacrificial altars of Tizatlan, Tlaxcala, and presents a brilliant discussion of their distribution in art and their undoubted use as symbols of mortality. He cites examples of the hand associated (1) with skull, a bleeding foot, and what was probably the glyph for jade (precious substance, a symbol for blood); (2) with skull and an unidentified symbol; (3) with flint knives; (4) with scorpions, sacrificial bone needles, blood, human hearts and hands. All of these elements represent sacrifice or death. It might also be noted that the Aztec god of death not infrequently wears human hands pendent from his ears.

I think the reason for associating human hands with sacrifice is not too recondite. The Mexican god of human sacrifice was Xipe, who was the god peculiarly associated with the gruesome custom of donning the flayed skin of the sacrificial victim. It must have been difficult to step into the skin of the victim; it was practically impossible to insert one's fingers in the human gloves. Accordingly the human skin was cut at the wrists, so that the wearer's hands were not encased. The skin of the victim's hands hung from the wearer's wrists. These dangling hands form a prominent characteristic of Xipe and his impersonators. In that way the hand may have become a symbol of death and sacrifice through its conspicuousness

in the Xipe costume. Xipe, as noted (p. 87), was also the god of the sacrificial knife, and, because war was waged for sacrificial victims, he further served as a god of battle.

God Q has the same facial markings as Xipe and, too, seems to have been connected with human sacrifice. He carries stone knives or points on a number of occasions. This may show his connection with those implements, since stone knives are not over-common in the codices, but the fact that he holds them may have no significance, and the human hand is nowhere associated with God Q. Maya art was less preoccupied with death than were the various schools of art in central Mexico. Skulls and crossbones, bleeding hearts, and other symbols of the morbid imagination of their northern neighbors are rare in the healthier religious art of the Maya of the Initial Series Period (they appear in battle scenes, understandably, on the Bonampak murals). Nevertheless, there is one clear example of the association of human hands and death in Maya religious art. The head form which represents completion or zero has as its identifying characteristic a hand across the lower jaw (fig. 25,37–45). The head itself frequently displays death symbols such as the percentage sign, the death eye, on the forehead or on the collar, and the three dots placed horizontally on the forehead. Thus the association of hand with death holds also for the Maya area.

Another association which brings together death or sacrifice, stone knife, and hand is to be found in the Yucatec name for the sacrificial knife *u ḳab cu* (*ḳu*), "the hand of god" (Scholes and Adams, 1938, 1:142).

The head for number 2, as carved on the Tablet of 96 Glyphs at Palenque, has a curved line on his face, like that of God Q, but well behind the eye instead of passing through it. Each has a hand on his head suggestive of death and sacrifice. Furthermore, we have seen that there is evidence indicating that the days Caban to Oc are connected with the numbers 1 to 13. To Etz'nab, accordingly, corresponds the number 2, but that is the day "knife," more particularly "sacrificial knife."

The garment of near-certainty to cast around the shoulders of our surmise has been woven from these various threads of evidence. It may be taken as practically proved that the head variant for the number 2 is that of a god of sacrifice and of the sacrificial knife. He corresponds closely to Xipe, and may well be the same as God Q of the codices.

Three (fig. 24,12–17). The head for 3 is also that of a youthful god with classical profile, and often with the IL design on his cheek. His distinguishing characteristics are the Ik symbol, a disk edged with circlets which is set on the forehead, and a banded headdress.

The Ik sign may be engraved on an oval shield which covers the ear or it may be set farther forward; the headdress can be better studied in the illustrations than described. The banding and the circular area at the top seem to be characteristic.

The Ik symbol is the principal element of the day Ik, which signifies wind and breath. It replaces the eye in the hieroglyph of God B (fig. 12,11), and, as that god is a deity of the rain and the storm, it is clear that the Ik sign symbolizes rain and wind. The disk edged with circlets is also a rain symbol (p. 277), and, clinching the argument, the god of number 3 is associated with the day Cauac in the proposed scheme (p. 87). The glyph for cauac is the symbol for rain, and the word itself means storm. Furthermore, a cursive form of Ik is frequently one of the component elements of the cauac sign (fig. 26,10,11). Accordingly, there is no doubt whatever that the god of the number 3 is a deity of wind and rain.

Four (fig. 24,18–25). The head of the aged sun god represents the number 4. He has a large, almost square eye with the pupil set in the top inner corner, so that he squints. In fact Akanchob, whose name means "he with the squint who cried aloud," is the Lacandon name for a deity who is the husband of the moon, and as we know from many sources that the sun is the husband of the moon (Tozzer, 1907, p. 95; Thompson, 1939, p. 133), there can be little doubt that this was a nickname for the sun. The god of number 4 sometimes wears the kin (sun) glyph on the side of his face, and often has the upper incisors filed to a T-shape, as was the custom of the sun god. Final proof, were that needed, that the god of number 4 is the sun is to be found in the use of the symbolic form of the kin (sun, day) sign on one occasion as the symbol for 4 (fig. 25,52; p. 137). Ahau, the day with which the number 4 is associated in the day sequence, is the day of the sun god (p. 87). There is, accordingly, irrefutable evidence that the sun is the god of number 4.

Five (fig. 24,26–31). The personification of 5 is an aged god, as indicated by the single tooth in his jaw, who wears the tun sign as his headdress. This ancient deity is recognizable in the Dresden and Paris codices, since there, too, he is depicted sometimes wearing the tun headdress (fig. 21,1–3). His glyph is the cauac sign with a coefficient of 5 and a looped prefix. Schellhas, who assigns him the letter N, accepts him as the god who ruled the days of Uayeb, an identification first made by Förstemann (1901a, pp. 189–92). This old god, known as Mam, "maternal grandfather," was worshipped during the five nameless days, and at the end of that period was undressed and discarded in an irreverent manner (Lopez de Cogolludo, 1867–68, bk. 4, ch. 8). It should be noted, however, that

in the codices this god is not directly associated with the Uayeb days. Mam is also the name of the aged earth god of the Kekchi and Pokomchi, with whom important mountains are associated, and whose home is beneath the earth, where he lies bound. He is generally regarded as an evil god in the Alta Verapaz, although in southern British Honduras, where he is merged with the mountain-valley gods, his aspect is benignant. That this Mam is the same as the Mam that ruled the days of Uayeb in Yucatan is apparent from a Kekchi survival of an old tradition. As already noted, the Kekchi no longer retain their old native calendar, but the five unlucky days have survived in a curious form, for they have been transferred to Easter. According to a letter to Mrs. McDougall from Mr. Helmrich, who has lived many years in the Alta Verapaz, the Kekchi have the custom of burying a Mam during these five unlucky days, clearly a fusion with Christian practices. He states that the Mam holds power only during those five days.

That the old god of number 5 is also an earth god is evident from the vegetation which usually decorates his tun headdress. An excellent example of this is supplied by the murals of Bonampak. Among the impersonators of gods of the underworld assembled for the dance, all bedecked with water lilies, is this aged god of number 5. He carries the tun sign under his arm instead of on his head, but from the presence of the water lilies and from the nature of his companions, it is clear that he is a god of the earth. The water lily, as we have seen (p. 72), is the most important symbol of gods of the underworld.

Not infrequently God N carries a large conch shell on his back or is depicted emerging from it (fig. 21,3–7); a variant of his name glyph consists of a conch shell with the same prefix as in his usual glyph.

The conch shell has two symbolic associations. By a natural process it represents water, and as the earth was believed to be on the back of a crocodile who floated on the surface of a cosmic sea, the conch shell became a symbol of the subterrestrial region and its divine inhabitants. As such it was also the symbol of the great mother, the moon goddess, who was also a deity of procreation, of the earth, and of water. From this, combined with a certain physical resemblance, developed the association of the conch shell with birth. In the words of the interpreter of Vatican A, "They placed on its [the moon's] head a marine shell to denote that just as the [shell] fish issues from the shell, so emerges man from the womb of his mother." This employment of the conch shell as a symbol of birth was certainly an extension of the earlier association with the earth.

The conch shell is the constant symbol of Tepeyollotl, the Mexican god of the interior of the earth with jaguar features (fig. 21,9,13; p. 74), and in the Bourbon and the Aubin Tonalamatl it appears, usually in conjunction with the night eye (also a symbol of death and the underworld), with certain deities, notably Itztlacoliuhqui with death symbols, the jaguar night-sun, Tecciztecatl, Xiuhtecutli, and Chantico, all of whom are connected with the interior of the earth (fig. 21,10–12). It should be mentioned in passing that one of the names of Xiuhtecutli was "the navel of the earth," and that Chantico, another fire deity, presumably has a similar association. I very much doubt that Tecciztecatl was actually a moon god, as is generally believed. He does not have lunar attributes, and in Middle America the deity of the moon is generally feminine. Because Tecciztecatl became the moon in the legend of the conversion of Nanahuatzin into the sun, it does not follow that he should be regarded as the moon god, any more than Nanahuatzin and the sundry other gods who served as the sun in the various creations should be viewed as sun gods. Tecciztecatl's white loincloth, the death eyes which are so prominent in his pictures, and his mergence with Tezcatlipoca indicate that he is probably an earth god. If that identification is accepted, he becomes a twin of the Maya god of number 5, who is aged and has as his symbol the conch.

The conch, as a pectoral, is worn by Quetzalcoatl and Xolotl. The former, I believe, is primarily the deity of fresh vegetation, of growth when the rains come, as is brought out in the hymn to Xipe; the latter is the god who leads the sun to the underworld. Both deities, therefore, are connected with the earth: in one case with its surface, in the other case with its interior. There is, accordingly, reasonably full evidence for recognizing the conch as a symbol of the earth, particularly its interior.

The god of number 5, therefore, is the aged god of the interior of the earth, the Mam, whose symbol is a conch shell. He is also the god of the day Imix, the day of the earth crocodile which symbolizes the earth.

Six (fig. 24,32–37). The god of number 6 is distinguished by a hafted axe set in his eye, which is squarish with a loop passing below it. The nose is Roman, and the central incisors of the upper jaw, which appear to be filed, are often somewhat prominent. A deity with an axe in his eye does not appear in the Maya codices, and is extremely rare in the sculptural art of the Initial Series Period. However, on Madrid 66 a deity, whose eye is covered by crossed bands in an oval, emerges from the jaws of a snake. The crossed bands may be a badly drawn axe.

The axe is the symbol of Schellhas' God B, a deity of the rains and storms. Over and over again he is depicted with an axe in one hand. The axe is similarly one of the

insignia of the Tlalocs, the Mexican gods of rain, who correspond closely to the Maya God B. God B is very intimately connected with serpents, a reason for supposing that the head on Madrid 66 is meant to represent the god of number 6. The close association of the god of number 6 with water and vegetation is confirmed by one of the very rare representations of this deity outside epigraphy. His head rises from the flower of a water lily on Pier F, House D, the Palace, Palenque (fig. 12,4). As noted, the water lily is a symbol of water and, by extension, of the primeval water and the alligator monster who rested in it. Indeed, the water lily plant in this design grows from the head of the alligator monster. For these reasons there is little cause to doubt that the god of number 6 is intimately associated with God B, and may in fact be a prototype of that deity, his most characteristic insigne being transferred to the eye because the numerical glyph shows only the head. The god, therefore, is a deity of rains and storms.

Seven (fig. 24,38–41). Heads of the god of number 7 are somewhat rare, but the distinguishing marks are easily recognizable. Of these the most important is a loop which passes under the eyes, and is loosely tied like a cruller, to use Spinden's expressive description, over the bridge of the nose. Characteristic, too, is the earplug which is oval and has a flamelike pendant with one tongue longer than the other. The eyes are square; the nose is Roman. The central incisors of the upper jaw are filed T-shape. There are two or three little circles below the loop under the eye.

The deity represented is the jaguar god as recognized first by Seler. This is shown by the jaguar paws of the only full-figure representation of the god of number 7, and by numerous representations of the god in sculpture and ceramics, which show the details noted above in combination with the peculiar ear of the jaguar, or the beard or spotted skin of that animal (fig. 12,14,15). Sometimes an impersonator wears the twisted loop of the jaguar god combined with the paws or beard of the jaguar; on one occasion the impersonator of the god has the number 7 on his cheek (fig. 12,13), and that number may appear on jaguar heads (fig. 52,2–E5).

As already pointed out, the jaguar is the god of the underworld, and appears to be merged with the night sun. As a god of the earth he carries the symbols of his origin, for frequently he wears the lily or shells, and not infrequently he has the symbol for night as an ornament of his ear or before his face (fig. 46,10–12,16). He is the Maya equivalent of Tepeyollotl.

Eight (fig. 24,42–49). The head of the god of number 8 has long been recognized as that of the maize god. Not infrequently he is depicted with a maize plant growing out of his head; more often this vegetation is replaced by a spiral on the forehead. There are grounds for thinking that this spiral is the symbol for the maize plant. The god usually has a string of maize grains on the side of his face, falling around or immediately before the ear, and reaching to the chin. The face is youthful and conforms to the classical style of Maya beauty; the IL mark on the cheek is sometimes present. The earplug has a short projecting element, perhaps of bark cloth.

Nine (figs. 24,50–55; 28,1–5). The god whose head serves as the number 9 is easily identified by the markings on his chin, for the area below the line of the lower lip is covered with dots, and the face is often bearded. The features are youthful, and conform to the classical type of Maya beauty. Sometimes the yax sign appears as an ornament on the forehead and the hair may be long. There seems to be no standard form of earplug, but a jaguar claw may be on the temple. The spots probably represent jaguar markings (cf. jaguar features of Tlaloc).

To Hermann Beyer (1933, p. 678) is due the credit for first identifying the god of the number 9 as the Chicchan god (Schellhas' God H). He points out that the heads for 9 and 19 frequently have the yax element on the forehead, a feature also found with the glyph of God H. Similarly the glyph of the Chicchan god has spots around the chin, the distinguishing attribute of the god of number 9. The head for 9, as carved during the Initial Series Period, never has the Chicchan circle on his temple, but in cases of full-figure numerals there is a pendent element which emerges behind the ear and extends some distance below the chin. This is almost certainly the lower jaw of a serpent. Beyer has also identified a head with Chicchan spots as the number 9 in Dresden, where it serves as the coefficient of the baktun glyph (fig. 25,46). In support of Beyer's argument, it should be noted that the symbolic form of the day Chicchan is composed of two parallel strokes set diagonally within the frame, but that is precisely the main feature of the yax element worn by the god of number 9. This same head for 9 can replace the yax prefix in certain glyphs (figs. 3,7; 31,51). There can be little doubt, therefore, that the head for the number 9 is the serpent deity, the Chicchan, as worshipped yet by the Chorti (Wisdom, 1940, pp. 392–97).

Ten (fig. 24,56–62). The head of the god of number 10 was recognized by Goodman as that of the death god 50 years ago, and has been accepted as such by all workers in the field. The principal characteristics are the bared jawbone, the fleshless nose, the percentage signs on the cheek, the "eye" on the forehead, and the three dots on the upper part of the head. Of these characteristics only the bared jawbone is constant, but one or more of the remainder is usually present.

Eleven (fig. 25,1,2). Heads of this god are rare. The distinguishing feature is the caban, "earth," sign, the crosshatched circle and curl, indicating that the god is of the soil or a lunar deity. I think we can eliminate the latter possibility; the individual is clearly masculine. The caban curl, but without the crosshatched circle, is the identifying feature of God R (p. 131), and occasionally appears on the glyph of the maize god in Madrid (pp. 60b, 65a, 97b). That is understandable in view of that god's intimate connection with the earth. With rare exceptions, the glyph of God R has a coefficient of 11. This could indicate either that he is the god of that number (cf. occasional appearance of 7 on face of jaguar god and of 5 with the glyph of the old earth god, Mam) or that number 11 is part of his name. Names of gods incorporating that number are rare; the most prominent is Buluc-Ch'abtan, perhaps connected with *ch'ab*, "to create." However, Mesoamerican creator gods are usually celestial. Alternatively, the name means "11 Penances," reminding one that Zip, name of the Yucatecan deer god, means sin. This tenuous connection is probably fortuitous. God R is not associated with deer in the codices, but he sometimes plays parts in keeping with an earth god.

The god of number 11 rules Manik, clearly the day of deer and of hunting. One of the prognostics for Manik in Kaua is *ah uitz*, literally "he of the hills," but the earth gods are generally mountain gods and have the deer and other wild animals in their keeping. Hunters petition them for success (Thompson, 1930). Moreover, for the Quiche, Manik is a good day for prayer to the mountain god, "who is in intimate relation with the concept or idea of the deer" (Schultze Jena, 1946, p. 35). We conclude that the god of 11 was an earth and mountain deity, patron of deer and other animals, perhaps God R, and conceivably identifiable as Buluc-Ch'abtan. See page 296.

Twelve (fig. 25,3–7). The god of number 12 is a somewhat youthful deity who is rarely represented in the texts. An example from the Temple of the Cross, Palenque, supplies the clue to the god's identification through the unusual headdress which he wears, for this is the sky sign. Evidence has been presented (p. 88) for identifying him with Lahun-Chan, a variant of the god of the planet Venus, whose glyph contains the sky sign as its main element (fig. 14,2,4).

Thirteen (fig. 25,8–14). The portrait which denotes the number 13 takes two forms. It may be the profile of 3 with the bared jawbone and other insignia of the death god, deity of the number 10 (fig. 25,8,11–13), or it may be a fantastic head with a long pendulous nose (fig. 25, 9,10,14). The former is commoner than the latter. The first form, which is a blending of the features of the heads for 3 and 10, is in agreement with the method of combining the insignia of the gods of the two digits, as seen in the heads for 14–19 inclusive. This arrangement appears to be a translation into glyphs of the spoken word, for in all Maya languages and dialects the numbers 13–20 inclusive have the second digit attached to the word for 10 (e.g. in Yucatec *uaxaclahun* [*uaxac,* "eight"; *lahun,* "ten"]). In the case of the heads for 13 the translation of the spoken word would seem to have conflicted with the old sequence of the 13 gods, with the result that 13 came to be carved either as the head of the thirteenth god in the series or as the combined features of the gods of 3 and 10. As a matter of fact, this did not involve a serious clash of rival claims to suzerainty of the number 13. The god of number 3, as we have seen (p. 132), was a deity of storms and rain; the individual god of number 13 without much doubt is a deity of water.

This deity of 13, as already noted, has a long pendulous nose. The eye is squarish with a loop beneath it, and sometimes there is set in it a hook, which rises from the lower edge. A fang emerges from the corner of the mouth. Details of the lower jaw are too worn in surviving examples to indicate whether it was characterized by the bared jawbone. I rather think not, although the jaw is somewhat angular. The headdress is variable; in two examples from Palenque it is composed of some material held in position by a knotted sash and surmounted by what is clearly a vegetal motif and which perhaps may be further classified as the water lily. The head closely resembles that of the Imix monster, save that the latter usually carries death symbols. It appears to be the same as a variant of the tun sign, in which a grotesque head is surmounted by the tun sign. The tun itself symbolizes water, and the Imix monster also has an aquatic significance, additional to his primary function as an earth deity. In the full-figure representation of the god of number 13 on Quirigua D (fig. 28,*15*), the head lacks a lower jaw. It is attached to the body of a snake decorated with a large water lily. This last item strengthens the identification of the vegetal motif on other heads as a water lily. The ophidian body confirms the identity of the god of number 13 with the tun variant noted above.

It is difficult to distinguish betwixt terrestrial and celestial snakes and dragons, and I suspect that the Maya themselves were uncertain as to where to draw the line. One of the chief characteristics of Central American mythology, and one which is exceedingly disconcerting to students, is the nomadic tendencies of the divine race. Deities passed from the upper to the nether regions at will, refusing to remain in neat categories of terrestrial and celestial beings. Furthermore, their shapes are not constant, for the dragons may be crocodiles, snakes, or fishlike beings, or a mingling of those creatures.

Whether the dragon of 13 is a celestial or terrestrial monster it would be hard to say. The evidence of the association of the god of 13 with Muluc and its patron the *xoc* monster rather suggests that the god of 13 is the *xoc.* Yet *xoc* is a mythical fish, whereas the head for 13 is that of a snake or, perhaps, a dragon. In that connection it is worth remembering that the Cipactli monster was at times regarded as a kind of fish, and the day Imox in the Quiche calendar, according to Ximenez, meant swordfish, whereas in Maya art the Imix monster is a draconian crocodile.

Because snakes were so closely linked in Maya thought with water, and because this same head could serve as a variant of the tun, which, too, was very intimately associated with water, I think there can be no serious reason to doubt that the head of number 13 is that of a serpent, perhaps capable of transmuting itself into a dragon, which represented water. The number 13 and Muluc are, accordingly, united by their aquatic values.

Fourteen to Nineteen (fig. 25,*15–36*). As noted, the heads for these numbers result from a merging of the two digits composing each number. In three texts the heads corresponding to both digits are given, the one above or beside the other. Thus in an early inscription (Yaxchilan L 48) the coefficient of the kin, which is 16, is shown by means of the head for 6 above that for 10. The former is held in the paws of the monkey which in this inscription represents the kin; the latter is immediately below the monkey's paws (fig. 29,*10*). The other examples of this practice are on Tila B (fig. 25,*12*), and at Xcalumkin (fig. 53,*3*).

A somewhat similar practice, but combining bars and dots with the head for 10, is shown on the east jamb of the south door of Temple 11, Copan. There the coefficient of Ceh is expressed by means of a bar and four dots at the side of the head variant for 10, the whole denoting 19. In this case the bar and dots are to the right of the head, which also faces to the right. This unusual arrangement is due to the fact that the whole inscription is reversed so that the glyph, being on the right jamb of the entrance, faces one on entering the temple. In the illustration (fig. 25,*36*) it has been reversed.

On the early Tikal 6, what is almost surely 18 Yax is shown as the death head of 10 with a bar and three dots prefixed; the Yax is a head variant with yax prefix to left (fig. 5,*53*). A third example, noted by Morley (1920, p. 166), is on the east altar of Copan 5, and serves as the coefficient of the tun sign. It is composed of a numerical bar before the death head of 10, the whole reading "15 tuns." The other cases cited by Morley are not acceptable, for in one text the IS reading is incorrect, and in the remainder the glyph given the value of 10 is a variant of the kin sign. However, there are two other examples of this practice. On Yaxchilan L 47 the co-efficient of Pax is expressed as a bar and four dots before the head for 10, making a reading of 19; on Chichen 16 the coefficient of Uo is written as a bar above the head for 10 (fig. 39,6). In all these cases the order of the digits corresponds to the spoken word, e.g. 9 and 10 (never 10 and 9) paralleling *bolonlahun*.

SYMBOLIC VARIANTS: ONE TO NINETEEN

In addition to bars and dots and head variants to represent the numbers 1–19, there are a few examples of symbolic variants for the numbers 1, 3, 4, and 8. There may be others not yet recognized.

One. This is a finger, recalling and partly confirming the belief that the commonest term for 20 in the Maya languages and dialects is the word for man, because 20 is the sum of a man's fingers and toes. The jade circle, generally shown at the wrist, is usually added to the finger (figs. 25,50; 33,18; 47,6; 48,2).

Three. On Dresden 9b the number 3 is represented as a cursive Ahau surrounded with crescents and with a prefix which may be a water symbol (fig. 25,51). Three is an aquatic god, and one would expect water symbols, particularly the T element.

Four. On an inscription at Copan the kin (sun) sign is used to express the number 4. The explanation of this usage is simple: the patron of number 4 is Kinich Ahau, the sun god, and his symbol replaces his face (fig. 25,52).

Eight. On both Copan I and its altar the number 8 is expressed by means of a bar and three dots inside an oval which is surmounted by maize foliage. This, again, is in accordance with the head variant of this number, for that is the head of God E, the maize god (fig. 25,53). A similar glyph occurs in Dresden, where it is almost surely a symbol for maize (p. 272; fig. 25,54).

COMPLETION (OR ZERO??)

For a number of years, around the turn of the century, the controversy 20 versus 0 raged. There was "great argument about it and about," with a final verdict in favor of zero. The matter boiled down to this: when, for example, the Maya wrote an IS which we would translate as 9.15.0.0.0 4 Ahau 13 Yax, did the symbols which we translate as zero mean 20 or zero? The argument was really triangular, for there was a suggestion that the symbols in question actually meant completion.

As in most, perhaps all, Maya glyphs, there is a head variant in addition to the symbolic form (fig. 25,37–45). The most characteristic feature of the former is the presence of a hand across the lower jaw. This is frequently combined with characteristics of the death god, such as

the percentage sign (Quirigua B), the death eye before the forehead (Copan 1 and 6), and the three dots across the top of the head (Quirigua J). In several cases there is a bifurcated ornament attached to the earplug, a spiral on one side, a long tapering element on the other (fig. 29,1,5,7). This element occurs rather frequently but by no means invariably in the aural ornaments of gods of the underworld (e.g. on the earth monsters beneath the crosses of the Tablets of the Cross and Foliated Cross, Palenque), on the earth monster, a true alligator, on Copan T; on the rear head of the double-headed snake, Tikal T 4 and L 3; on the main personage, Copan H; and on representations of the jaguar god, Quirigua A, and the jaguar god of number 7. It would appear, therefore, to symbolize death when used on the heads under discussion, for the underworld is the realm of the death god.

The principal meaning (there are others) of the hand is that of completion. In that sense it is used with period endings, preceding the required number of baktuns or katuns. Without much doubt its significance here is that of completion of so many baktuns or katuns. Even were the meaning not precisely that of completion, the sign cannot possibly have the meaning of zero as used in this sense. The hand is also placed below the winged cauac glyph, and the whole sign is formed usually with the addition of a "count" or a *u* prefix (figs. 5,40–46; 32,24–29). The whole surely means (count of) the approximate year completed; it cannot possibly refer to zero tuns since the glyph often occurs with the dates which are not katun endings. It is extremely unlikely that hand would signify completion in one place, zero in another. Furthermore, death symbols with the meaning of expiration (p. 189) are used as a prefix in phrases which carry the connotation of completion, and can substitute for the regular count bracket and replace the hand. Counting and expiration were the equivalent of completion in Maya thought; they are clearly the opposite of zero in the sense of the count not having yet begun.

Thus the evidence strongly indicates that the head and symbolic forms under consideration denote not zero but completion, and that a date which we read as 9.15.0.0.0 means that 9 baktuns and 15 katuns have ended, and that the count of the tuns, uinals, and kins has been completed. It is convenient to write this as 9.15.0.0.0, but with the understanding that 0 is here to be understood as it is in 10, 20, 30, etc.; that is to say, the first unit in our decimal system stands at nothing because the total has reached a multiple of the second unit. On the other hand, I am sure, although there is no evidence pro or con, that the Maya would not have used this sign in the sense of nil had they, for example, been required to report on the production of some crop that had been a total failure, or had they wished to write the zero day (if one existed) in their calendar.

Fulton (1947, 1948) has discussed at length the concept of zero. Although in agreement with many of the ideas he expresses, I am not sure that the cyclical arrangement can be applied to the LC in view of the Maya picture of time as relays of bearers marching ever forward from one *lub* to another (see also p. 59).

There is yet another symbol which is used interchangeably with the head variant and the hand with attached elements. This is the left or top half (depending on whether it is to the left or above the period) of a sign resembling somewhat a Maltese cross with the addition of loops or diagonal lines between the arms of the cross (figs. 25,55,56; 30,1,2). The complete design is not uncommon in Maya art. In Madrid and in Fejervary-Mayer, which is from southern Mexico, the 260-day cycle is arranged in a pattern which exactly conforms to this design, the days following the sides of each arm of the cross and each loop. The whole in each case is divided into four parts of 65 days apiece. The Maya divisions are marked by the glyphs of the four world directions; the Mexican, by world directional trees and birds. Both show, in addition, a pair of gods associated with each direction and a pair (only one in Fejervary-Mayer) in the center. It cannot be chance that the same design is used in both codices in view of the considerable distances and cultural differences which separate the two areas from which they emanate. One must conclude that the design has a special association with the sacred almanac in particular or time cycles in general.

As used with time periods (kin, uinal, tun, etc.) only half to three-quarters of the glyph is shown, but that is pretty obviously because of lack of space. It is either a prefix attached to the period glyph or it may be a separate element overlapped by the sign to its right. In one example of this overlapping style (Ixkun 2, B4) it is possible that a small piece of the right arm of the cross is visible behind the open mouth of the frog head of the uinal, although the available photograph is not sufficiently clear to permit of a positive identification. Lack of space allowed Maya sculptors to cut a glyph in half (e.g. the moon sign of Glyph A of the lunar series is cut in half and attached to Glyph B on Coba 20). It would therefore appear practically certain that the symbol under discussion represents the whole Maltese cross, and lacks an arm only or an arm and parts of two others merely because of lack of space.

This same element, with a special infix, a prefix, and with lines across the top, forms the half period (the so-called lahuntun) glyph (fig. 32,46–55). The form of this glyph is discussed elsewhere (p. 192). Suffice it to say at this point that the meaning of the whole corresponds in general to some such phrase as "half the completed period," or "half lacking to the complete period."

As will be noted shortly, the moon sign is sometimes used in distance numbers with the value of 20, the attached coefficient being added to that number. Thus, the moon sign with two bars and a dot attached has the value 31.

In one text (Palenque Cross, B13) a distance number of 20 days is expressed by means of a moon sign with this symbol resembling the Maltese cross attached (fig. 4, 17). To judge by the analogous cases the whole would mean 20 plus 0 or 20 only. This interpretation rather favors the proponents of the thesis that the symbols under discussion mean zero. On the other hand, it does not seem special pleading to offer the translation "completion of one lunar period of 20 days," although it must be admitted that zero fits this particular case rather better.

My purpose in discussing these slight variations in meaning, for they do not affect the general sense, is to show that some signs to which have been assigned the value of zero may actually correspond to verbal expressions.

The matter is discussed at some length by Spinden (1924, pp. 18–22) who appears to have been the first student of the subject to accept these signs as having the primary meaning of completion. The evidence is not entirely satisfactory, but so far as it goes, it rather suggests that this sign, like the hand and the head with hand across lower jaw, signifies completion, or perhaps it might have the slightly variant meaning of setting in order. Either interpretation would harmonize with the use of the sign as a frame for the cycle of 260 days. Translation of the sign as zero would be contrary to its use in the half-period glyph and as a frame for the cycle of 260 days.

In Dresden the above symbols are replaced by stylized drawings which have been generally accepted as representing shells. Förstemann (1886, pp. 4–5) identifies many of these as *Oliva*, a view upheld by Tozzer and Allen (1910, p. 297); many others appear to be bivalves, and one or two resemble conchs (fig. 25,59). In this connection it will be recalled that a shell is frequently combined with a hand in the symbolic variant already discussed.

If these representations of shells are examples of rebus writing, a Maya homonym, if such exists, must be sought among generalized words for shell. In this connection Roys points out that *xixim* is a general term for shell in Yucatec, and that might come from *xim* (duplication of syllable) or, more likely, from *xix*. *Xix* has a number of meanings, none of which would apply here, but Roys notes that in composition the term seems to signify "completely," e.g. *xix ich tah te,* "to look at someone fixedly from head to foot," *xix uouol oc,* "perfectly round, spherical." He suggests with some hesitation that this might account for the use of a shell to signify completion.

GLYPH FOR TWENTY

The moon sign is used constantly in Dresden and Madrid to represent the number 20 (figs. 25,*60; 63,1–4*). The coefficient attached to it does not, however, serve as a multiplier, as do the coefficients of the usual period glyphs, but it is added. Thus a moon sign with a coefficient of 8 (bar and three dots) represents 28, not 160. The use of the moon sign as 20 is restricted to distance numbers. It serves with its coefficient to express intervals between dates in the various divinatory almanacs provided those distances are not less than 20 and not more than 39 days. The system presumably could not be used above 39 days. It is a shorthand system of writing, a reckoning in days alone rather than in uinals and days, just as we might say either 18 days or two weeks and four days. Examples of this usage on the monuments will be found on page 167.

Gates (1931, pp. 89–90) expresses the belief that there is no evidence that the sign used for 20 in the codices is the moon glyph, although all other investigators accept it as such without hesitation. Proof that it does represent the moon is to be found in the fact that the inscriptional type of this sign, which it resembles in appearance and duplicates in function, also serves as the symbolic variant of the head of the moon goddess in IS introductory glyphs corresponding to Ch'en (fig. 22,*44–49*). Furthermore, this sign occurs in planetary bands, and can be substituted for the sun glyph in the darkness glyph (fig. 43, *51,52*). Moreover, it is paired with sun disks above planetary bands on several stelae at Yaxchilan. Finally, it appears in the lunar series to express the age of the moon: in two glyphs (E and A) to record a moon age of 20 days, and sometimes as Glyph D, but with a different infix, to record moon ages of less than 20 days (figs. 36; 37).

GLYPH FOR HALF

The Maltese cross with a line or lines cutting off the top and with an infix, a prefix, and occasionally a postfix was employed to record the completion of half a period (fig. 32,*46–55*). This glyph is mentioned above; it is discussed at greater length on page 192. It would seem that the lines across the top indicate that the whole element is cut in half. To the best of our knowledge, the Maya made no use of fractions except for a very limited use of the simplest fractions with denominator of 1, such

as in this case. Naturally, when the Maya divided their cycle of 260 days into four or five parts, each part was a fourth or fifth of the whole, but, so far as is known, there exist no glyphs to indicate that a division was a quarter or a fifth of the whole, and no evidence that the Maya regarded these parts as we do fractions. The fact that the Maya expressed the length of the moon either as 29 days or as 30 days, alternating these two numbers with necessary irregularities is good evidence that they did not employ fractions. The use of fractions is against the whole Maya philosophy of numbers based on the lowest common multiple of two or more periods. In its simplest form the relationship of the moon is to the day, not to the half-day.

SUPPRESSION OF NUMBERS

Occasionally in distance numbers a period was suppressed if its coefficient was zero (I shall continue to use the term zero in translating the signs which, I believe, represent completion). Examples of this practice are discussed on page 159 (fig. 30,*3,4*). There is possibly a unique example (Chinkultic 8) of the suppression in an IS of the baktun and its coefficient. The whole seems to read: A1-B2, IS introductory glyph; C1, 18 katuns; C2, 0? tuns; D1a, 0? uinals; D1b, 0 kins; D2, 11 Ahau. The suppression of the 9 baktuns may have been an error, or it may have been deliberate since there could have been no doubt of the correct number. The second IS of Lacanha 7 reads 9.6.(0).11.0 8 Ahau 18 Zac, the 0 tuns being omitted.

POSITIONAL NOTATION

In Dresden and certainly on one stela (Pestac 1; Blom, 1935) the Maya suppressed the period glyphs of IS, and used a purely positional system of numeration. The bar and dot coefficients of the five periods from baktun to kin were arranged in a vertical column, spaces between serving to eliminate the danger of confusion (figs. 46,*17; 64,2*). In a few cases six positions, including the pictun, are written in this system. Smaller numbers of two or more periods are also used. These numbers must first be read upwards, for it is necessary to start with the bottom number (the kin coefficient) in order to find out what period corresponds to the top number, because, naturally, with each additional coefficient, the period at the top is one higher. Such a preliminary reading was probably automatic, just as our eyes, in seeing the number 195238, register that there are six digits, and our brain automatically tells us that the first of these corresponds to the hundred thousands.

With this system of positional notation period glyphs were not essential; most probably they were retained because they enhanced the dignity of the text and exalted the grandeur of time. Presumably, they were generally suppressed in Dresden to save space in a book which was primarily a work of reference, but they occur in a few passages where their presence was required because of the elimination of zero coefficients of intermediate periods. For example, on Dresden 69 we find a distance number of one pictun, three uinals, one kin. All three glyphs are present. The baktun, katun, and tun are missing, and their suppression indicates that they are to be regarded as completed, that is, with coefficients of zero. Written with bars and dots without period glyphs, this statement would have required six spaces; with period glyphs it could be written in three.

In IS the periods are arranged in descending order from the highest, usually the baktun, to the lowest, the kin (figs. 47; 48,*1*), but in distance numbers the order is ascending, the coefficient of the kin being placed at the start of the series (fig. 49,*1,2*). There are two or three exceptions to this rule, in which the periods of a distance number are to be read in descending order.

SUMMARY

Numbers have a very important part in Maya hieroglyphic writing, not only because of the very many dates and the intervals between them recorded in the texts, but also because they are components of the names of a number of deities. Lunar calculations and perhaps ritualistic phrases involving numbers still further increase the total. There are three ways of writing the numbers 1–19. Most common is the employment of bars and dots, each bar representing five; each dot, one. Symbolic variants occur, but they are rare. In many texts numbers are expressed by head variants. The heads for the numbers 1–13 are those of the 13 gods associated with each of those numbers. The sequence is the same as for the deities which without much doubt were the days Caban to Muluc. The heads for the numbers 14–19 combine the features of the head for first digit with the bared jawbone, characteristic of the head for 10. The head for 13 is, more often than not, formed in the same way. This method appears to correspond to a linguistic construction, for the Maya terms for 13–19, like our English terms, combine the words for the two digits. With the head variants should be included the full-figure variants, which are merely head variants with the addition of the bodies pertaining thereto.

There were special signs for 20, and symbols which are usually translated as zero but which probably had a meaning akin to completion. Certain affixes convert cardinals to ordinals or represent numerical classifiers.

The Maya did not use true fractions, but they employed a special glyph to express the completion of half a period, provided that period was a multiple in the vigesimal system of their lowest unit of time, the tun.

In the codices and, very rarely, in inscriptions on stone, period glyphs are eliminated and numerals are arranged in vertical columns, a true case of positional notation. Aesthetic considerations and a desire to magnify the grandeur of time probably account for the scant use of positional notation save in the codices. Period glyphs were known to the users of Dresden, for they appear in a few passages where their presence is essential for clarity because of the suppression of zero coefficients of intermediate time periods.

6

The Long Count

. . . and the days of eternity, who shall number? The height of the heaven, and the breadth of the earth, and the deep, and wisdom, who shall search them out?

—ECCLESIASTICUS, 1:2–3

IN THE MAYA SCHEME the road over which time had marched stretched into a past so distant that the mind of man cannot comprehend its remoteness. Yet the Maya undauntedly retrod that road, seeking its starting point. A fresh view, leading farther backward, unfolded at the end of each stage; the mellowed centuries blended into millennia, and they into tens of thousands of years as those tireless inquirers pushed deeper and still deeper into the eternity of the past. For them time receded in endless vistas of hundreds of thousands of years; the resting places, those annual stages of the bearers of time, mounted to millions and even scores of millions. Theirs was an appraisal of the ages which would have been utterly inconceivable to us, had not our minds been gradually conditioned to that vastness by the writings of astronomers and geologists during the past century.

Time, in the Maya concept, leads into the future, too, with the endlessness of the straight roads of France. When Alfred sat in exile by the rude hearth of tradition, Maya astronomers at Palenque were recording calculations which sweep more than 1,250,000 years into the past, and then forward to dates over four millennia in the future. At about the same time, in another Maya city, there was recorded a computation which in all probability spans over 400,000,000 years. The brain reels at such astronomical figures, yet these calculations were of sufficient frequency and importance to require special glyphs for their transcription, and they were made some 10 centuries before Archbishop Ussher had placed the creation of the world at 4004 B.C.

THE TUN AS BASIS OF MAYA CALCULATIONS

For the manipulation of these calculations into past and future the Maya used the tun (approximate year of 360 days) and its multiples in the vigesimal system, just as we use the year and its multiples in the decimal system. Fractions of a tun were expressed in terms of uinals (20-day periods) and kins (single days).

Students of Maya epigraphy have been divided on the question of what is the Maya chronological unit. Some writers (e.g. Spinden, 1924, pp. 8–9; Morley, 1915, p. 37, and 1937–38, 5:274) consider that the unit of Maya time

was the day; others (Goodman, Gates, Teeple, and Thompson) have expressed the view that the unit was the tun, and that the uinals and kins are merely fractions of the lowest unit, just as our periods are reckoned in multiples of years with the months and days as fractions thereof.

Evidence in support of the second view is, I think, overwhelming:

1. In the various books of Chilam Balam the lapse of time is invariably expressed in tuns or haabs (another name for the period of 360 days used under certain conditions) and is never expressed in days unless the interval is less than a tun in length. Thus we find constantly statements such as: "during threescore and fifteen katuns (they [the mounds] were constructed)," *oxkal katun . . . catac holhunpiz katun* (Chumayel, p. 15); "eighty-one *haab* had passed since their departure," *cankal haab catac hun[p]pel haab* (Mani Chronicle); "six hundred and seventy-five *haab* after Chichen Itza was depopulated," *lahu ca bak haab catac holhu cankal haab* (Chumayel, p. 85).

2. The symbolic forms of the glyphs for all periods above the tun have as their principal element or elements one of the two main signs for the 360-day period, either the tun sign or the cauac symbol; the kin (day) glyph is a component of none of them.

3. The main element of the IS introductory glyph is the tun sign, a pair of duplicate affixes being symbols for counting. Thus these two elements mean a count of the tuns, with no suggestion of a count of days.

4. The sentences which precede the chronological tables in various books of Chilam Balam are: *u tzolan katun,* "the order of the katuns," or *u kahlay u xocan katunob,* "the record of the count of the katuns," or *u kahlay katunob,* "the record of the katuns." These sentences appear to correspond in part to the IS introductory glyph. There is no mention of a reckoning by days.

5. The only name of a period higher than the tun which is beyond question is that of the katun. This is probably an elided form of *kaltun* (20 tuns), and makes no reference to the kin.

6. Were the Maya count to have been based on the single day, it would be logical to expect a straightforward

vigesimal system with a year of 400 days, such as was used by the Cakchiquel.

GLYPHS AND NAMES OF PERIODS

KIN

This word means day or sun, and also time in a general sense, e.g. *u kin oczah,* "sowing time." The symbolic form of its glyph is the main element of the glyph of the sun god (fig. 26,49–57). It also appears frequently as an identifying attribute on the forehead, the earplug, or the headdress of that deity, and it is also the principal element of the month sign Yaxkin (fig. 17,1–13).

The glyph resembles, and in all probability represents, a four-petaled flower. It seems very probable that this is a conventionalized picture of some species of plumeria. The plumeria is a symbol of procreation (Roys, 1933, pp. 104, 121; Thompson, 1939, pp. 138–40), and there are some grounds for believing that it may have been a name for the sun. At any rate the sun and moon are closely connected with the plumeria, presumably because they were the first people to cohabit. The five petals of the plumeria were probably reduced to four because four is the number over which the sun god rules. In Chumayel there is an account of the wooing of the moon by the sun couched in esoteric language. The moon is described as the five-petaled flower; the sun is said to have been set in the center of a flower—"Four-fold [or four-branched] was the plate of the flower, and Ah Kin Xocbiltun [i.e. the sun god] was set in the center." In support of this identification, it should be noted that the Mexican equivalent of Ahau, the day of the sun god, is Xochitl, which both means and represents "flower." Furthermore, in the list of interpretations of Quiche day names recorded by Ximenez, the Quiche equivalent of Ahau is given the meaning of "flower." The value of this as independent evidence, however, is reduced by the strong possibility that such an identification may have resulted from Mexican influences in late times, perhaps even at the start of the colonial period.

This kin element has a postfix a streamerlike arrangement, which it has been suggested is the beard of the sun god and which is sometimes called the tail. The Motul dictionary gives two expressions for the sun's ray: *mex kin,* "the sun's beard," and *u tab kin,* "the cords of the sun." In Chol we find *u halal cin (kin),* "the arrow-shafts of the sun." Since these streamers do not usually issue from the god's chin, it would seem more probable that they represent the sun's cords. The word *kin* with mutations (e.g. highland *kih*) means sun in most Maya languages and dialects save Tzeltal, Tzotzil, and Chico-muceltec, where the word *kakal* (fiery?) replaces it, and

kin is used as the equivalent of festival. *Hun kak* (one fire) is a Lacandon name for the sun, although kin is in common use.

In the IS there are no less than three head forms for the kin, and there are others (pp. 167–75) which are used only in distance numbers and which will not be discussed here.

The most easily recognized and perhaps the commonest variant of the head form is that of the sun god himself (figs. 27,58–63,65,66; 29,5,7,9). The characteristic features of the sun god are: a squarish eye with squarish pupil in the top inner corner and with a loop, often with two or three circlets attached, which encloses the eye on the sides and bottom; a prominent Roman nose; the central incisors of the upper jaw filed to the shape of a squat tau; often a fang projecting from the corner of the mouth; and a hollow on the top of the head. In the glyphs the kin tail is usually present beside or below the head.

The second variant of the head is that of an animal (figs. 27,55–57; 29,6). The nose becomes a snout, often with a small scroll on it. The eye is still squarish, but the pupil moves to the center of the eye and becomes a short crescent, the ends of which are sometimes joined across the top by a straight line. A shell pendant hangs from the earplug, and on the cheek there is frequently an irregular crescent, the horns of which point toward the ears (Bowditch, 1910, pl. 14,9,10,21,22). A banded headdress is often shown. On the temple or the side of the face there are visible on most well-preserved examples two circles within an oval, although for lack of space they are frequently reduced to semicircles.

The presence of these two circlets within an oval is of prime importance, since there can be little doubt that they are the symbol for black. In the codices the symbol for black is distinguished from that for white usually by a black circular edging around the two (or more) circlets which constitute the main element of the sign (fig. 20, 1–5). However, in the sculptured texts (and occasionally in the codices; fig. 20,6,7) the black is omitted. In sculpture black is generally shown by hachuring (fig. 20,8,9). When the area involved is quite small and the text no longer retains its full clarity of detail, the crosshatched lines may no longer be visible. This weathering doubtlessly accounts for the absence of the symbol for black in some cases, but in others it is quite plain that the symbol never was present. Beyer (1925 and 1929) has discussed this matter at length and concludes that the surrounding black paint or hachure was often omitted when there was no doubt as to the meaning of the glyph.

The symbol for black is used in two ways: to denote that color, if one may so term it, and to represent the night, the interior of the earth, and death. Thus we find the symbol for black attached to a glyph of a skull, perhaps that of Multun-Tzek, presumably because the skull has a natural association with the dark underworld (fig. 20,*4–6*).

I hesitate in making a definite identification of this animal with the black infix which serves as a kin sign. It is most probably either a dog or a jaguar. Note the resemblances on the one hand to heads for Oc and Xul, which are definitely pictures of dogs; on the other hand, to the head in the introductory glyph of Copan P, which is that of the jaguar god (fig. 22,*2,3*). Both animals may wear the symbol of black, and both animals can wear it because they have much black in their natural coloring (dogs in the Maya codices are almost always painted black and white) and because both are connected with the underworld. Furthermore, both animals are intimately associated with the sun, particularly in connection with his nocturnal journey to the underworld and his passage through its shadowed recesses (pp. 78, 114). I slightly favor the identification of this creature as a dog since we shall later encounter yet another variant which is probably a jaguar (p. 173).

Sometimes a monkey serves as the symbol of the sun (fig. 27,*53*); a particularly fine example is to be seen in the full-figure variant on Yaxchilan L 48 (fig. 29,*10*). For a connection between monkey and sun we must turn to Mexico. In Mexico the sun god as patron of the arts of singing, music, and entertainment was Xochipilli ("Flower Prince"), and one of his guises was that of the monkey. Furthermore, the day Ozomatli, "Monkey," is under his rule. In the Maya area the sun god was also patron of poetry and music, and was likewise connected with flowers (the plumeria, symbol of procreation). The monkey also symbolized the arts and crafts as well as licentiousness and the act of procreation, but the sun god was the first person to cohabit. With these various threads forming a definite warp and woof, it is entirely appropriate that the monkey should substitute for the more usual representations of the sun.

Thus kin might be represented by the flower symbol, by the portrait of the sun god himself, by the monkey, or by another animal, probably the dog or the jaguar. These variant forms well illustrate how deeply the hieroglyphs are rooted in mythology.

UINAL

The derivation of the Yucatec name for the period of 20 days is uncertain. As already noted (p. 51) a fairly general term for 20 in many Maya languages and dialects is man (*uinic* and *uinac* respectively in lowland and highland stocks), the assumption being that this derives from the count of fingers and toes. Yucatec and Chol,

however, usually employ the word *ƙal* for 20 and its multiples, whereas Jacalteca, Chuh, Pokomchi, Uspanteca, Quiche, etc. use both terms, one for 20, the other for some multiple thereof. *Uinic,* the Yucatec word for man, in some cases can have the meaning of 20 in that language, for it is the term used for 20 *ƙaan* (a cord-length used in measuring milpas), but it should be noted that because of confusion in the various dictionaries, it is uncertain whether *uinic* and *uinac* were used for counts of days or for listing such items as bales of cotton or pods of cacao, or for both categories. We do know, at least, that uinac meant 20 days in Cakchiquel and Pokoman. The problem is to decide whether uinal derives from *uinic,* "man."

We shall see (p. 167) that a period of 20 days was often expressed by means of the moon glyph. In that connection it may be significant that the Motul dictionary lists the word *uen* with the meaning of a matter of a month or months, with examples given as *hun uen ual,* "my [her] child is one month old," *ho uen in paalil,* "my child is five months old." The word *uen* appears to be connected with the moon, for *uen uinic* is an albino, and albinos are associated with eclipses. Nonetheless, as Gates has pointed out, it is impossible to derive *uinal* directly from *u,* moon. Gates (1931, p. 90) seems to suggest that uinal is a contraction of *uinicil* or *uinical,* "manhood," but the trouble there is that *uinal* is a Yucatec word, whereas *uinical* is highland. Futhermore, as we have seen, *uinic* survives in Yucatec for a count of 20 cords. That being the case, it is most improbable that it would be changed to *uinal* to denote 20 days. It seems much more probable, therefore, that uinal is the Yucatec word for month (of 20 days?) with the termination *al,* which functions very vaguely to show an association, in many cases not apparent (e.g. *eb* and *ebal,* both meaning staircase; *cayom* and *ah cayomal,* both meaning fisherman but perhaps the former, a casual fisher, the latter a professional).

There is evidence that in some parts of the Maya area the 20-day period is named for the moon, for among the Jacalteca it is called *xahau,* "Lady," that is to say, the moon, but that term is applied by the uninitiated to the month of 30 days (La Farge and Byers, 1931, p. 157).

Finally, to terminate this tiresome subject, the fact that man is in no way connected with the glyphs for 20 days, whereas the moon glyph has that function, is fair evidence for accepting a derivation of uinal from *uen,* "month," and assuming that the word formerly referred to the period of 20 days, not to the month of 29 or 30 days.

The symbolic form of the uinal is too simple to give any good clue as to what it represents (fig. 26,*41–48*). The resemblance to the day sign Chuen has been remarked, but this may be fortuitous. The uinal sign not infrequently takes the bundle postfix, like the months Uo and Zip, and the glyphs of certain deities. The meaning of this postfix is uncertain (figs. 26,47,48; 27,46).

The personified form of the uinal is that of a frog, very clearly represented in several full-figure glyphs (figs. 27, 40–52; 29,1–4). There seems little reason to doubt that this is the *uo,* a small black frog with a yellow stripe down its back, which has burrowing habits. The *uo* is the musician of the Chacs, the gods of rain, in Maya legend and folklore (Thompson, 1941, p. 104). The reason why the picture of the *uo* may have been used to designate the period of 20 days has already been set forth (p. 47). The evidence is not beyond question but does suggest an example of rebus writing. The scroll emerging from the corner of the mouth, the serrated teeth, the peculiar form of the snout, the forehead ornament with its circle of beads, the eyelid covering half the eye, and finally the shield with its three circles, are characteristics which together clearly differentiate this head from those of other period glyphs. None is essential, but most are usually present. The three circles on the shield (Maudslay's drawing of the uinal head with four circles, on Copan B, appears to be incorrect) might conceivably represent warts, or might possibly be the symbol for fire, the three hearthstones (Thompson, 1930, pp. 93, 111), although a connection between the *uc* frog and fire is not apparent. However, in all probability these three dots refer to the god of number 3, who is a rain deity (pp. 132, 277), for the frog is closely associated with the rains and their patrons.

TUN

The name for the approximate year of 360 days means in Yucatec "precious stone." It is almost certain that the word was primarily used for jades and various green stones. According to the Relación of Campocolche and Chochola, the Maya made offerings in time of hunger of "green stones which they call *tun.*" The Yucatec word for stone in general is *tunich,* which becomes *tun* in compounds. In the Manche Chol dictionary of Moran *tun* is given as stone and *yax tun* as blue beads, although *yax* means both green and blue. Precious stone is listed as *sitzil ton* and *ghayalton* in the large Tzotzil dictionary. The first term suggests a meaning of cold stone, one of the properties of jade being its coldness to the touch. *Ton, tun,* and *tuun* have the general meaning of stone in Tzeltal, Yocotan, and western Chol respectively. It is therefore apparent that tun meant stone in general and precious stone in particular, although in Yucatec it had lost its general meaning except in compounds.

The symbolic form of the tun as used in IS almost surely contains the sign for jade, which, as already noted, is either a circle set on a larger disk or the same with the addition of two beads on the perimeter. As such it is the main element of the glyphs for Muluc and Mol (figs. 8, 1–16; 17,14–22), where it signifies not jade as such, but water, the ritualistic name for which was "precious stone, jade." It will be noted that the lower part of the tun sign contains the circle set on a larger disk. The upper part of the glyph is rounded, as in the extension of the jade sign, but differs from the latter in the presence of two vertical bars which are usually filled with crosshatching in the sculptured examples (to represent black) and with black paint in the codices (fig. 26,33–40). Beyer (1927) considers the two bars to represent the number 10 and to be a symbol of fire, but I do not regard his arguments as acceptable, since several of the examples he cites are late forms from the codices. These are clearly simplified versions of more complex originals, which have become pairs of straight lines because they could be painted that way with greater rapidity. Furthermore, the number 10 is associated with death, not with fire.

It seems possible that the two vertical bars might represent the element yax. In the forms of Yax and Yaxkin in the codices the principal feature of the prefix comprises two vertical bars painted black (fig. 17,11,12,45,46). In the corresponding elements in representations of Yax and Yaxkin in sculpture the two bars are usually set diagonally in the center of the prefix but two vertical bars or pairs of vertical lines often appear in its upper part (fig. 17,2–4,6,9,38,40). Yax signifies green or blue, and also is associated with the Chicchan deities, the celestial snakes who guard the rain (p. 135). If this identification is correct—and it must be admitted that a plausible case could be made for a quite different interpretation—the whole glyph would read "green precious stone," or "precious water of the celestial Chicchans."

The reasons for believing that this identification is correct are that the cauac glyph, which under certain conditions replaces the regular tun glyphs, undoubtedly means rainstorm (p. 87); and the word *haab,* which also signifies a period of 360 days, is almost certainly connected with *ha,* "water." Thus if our identification is correct, both the two glyph forms and the two names signify rain.

The original of the commonest personified form of the tun glyph will not be found in any picture book of Central American fauna, but is the product of a vivid imagination. Its most outstanding feature, and the one by which it can be most surely identified, is the bared jawbone which replaces the lower jaw (fig. 27,34,36–39). The beak is generally rather sharp. In nearly all cases there is a projection in front of the forehead, and a corresponding area at the back of the head. These are usually represented as partly black by the addition of areas of crosshatching; the absence of hachure is probably due to weathering. I think that these two projections can be identified with some assurance as the tufted horns of the Yucatecan screech owl. These tufts are always prominently displayed in representations of owls in the codices, and always have black markings (fig. 20,*13,14,19,20,23*).

We have already seen that there are excellent reasons for identifying the Yucatecan screech owl with the Moan bird (p. 114). The Moan bird, when it serves as the glyph of the month Muan and when it appears in sculpture, lacks a lower jaw. The absence of the lower jaw and its replacement by the bared jawbone have apparently the same symbolic value. Accordingly, the fact that the tun bird has a bared jawbone, whereas the Moan bird has no lower jaw at all in its glyphic form, is not an argument against the identification of both birds as screech owls.

It has been pointed out that the Moan bird is connected with rain, and that the word *muan* itself means shower. The identification of this head form of the tun glyph as the rain bird brings the head variant, too, into agreement with the other variants and the names of the period, all of which, as we have seen, have a pluvial connotation.

There is another personified form of the tun, the head of a long-nosed being, of either ophidian or saurian origin, which lacks a lower jaw, indicating a connection with the earth. Often this creature wears the tun headdress, although in early texts the headdress is of the voluted form much favored in the first half of Cycle 9 (fig. 27, *28,30–33,35*). In two full-figure representations of the tun this head, with tun headdress, is attached to the body of a snake (fig. 28,*16,17*), and the same is true of the example on the Leiden plaque (fig. 27,*28*). This snake is also the deity of number 13, god of the day Muluc, "water," and as such is intimately associated with water (p. 135; fig. 28,*15*). The absence of the lower jaw and the presence of the tun headdress, which is often decked with vegetation, also worn by the Mam, god of the interior of the earth (p. 133) greaten the possibility that this is the snake or crocodile monster which supports the earth. In any case, as god of the number 13, this creature represents rain, and so once again the tun is portrayed by the glyph of a being connected with rain.

In three full-figure representations of the tun at Quirigua a creature which one can tentatively identify as a crab is substituted for the Moan bird or the snake (fig. 28,*12,13,15*). The identification of this as a crustacean rests on the portrayal, on the murals of Bonampak, of an impersonator of a crab god, who is a member of the group of impersonators of terrestrial gods, including the Mam, all of whom are decked with water lilies to emphasize their connection with the earth. At El Baul there was a strong cult of the crab god, from whose body vegetation grows (Thompson, 1948, p. 20). The crab god, therefore, is a god of the earth and of fertility; his aquatic environment is obvious. Here, too, is another aquatic personification of the tun.

The glyphs for the 360-day year therefore stand, respectively, for jade, that is to say, precious water; rainstorm (cauac variant); the Moan bird (rains and showers); god of number 13 and the day Muluc; a serpent god of water; and, probably, the crab god, a deity with vegetal and aquatic associations. All have pluvial or aquatic associations, as do haab and tun, the names for the period. It is interesting to note that *xiuitl,* the Mexican name for the year, also meant turquoise and, by extension, rain, both because of its color, which is that of the Tlalocs, and because both turquoise and rain were precious things. Furthermore, the trapezoidal ornament usually worn by the Tlalocs is the sign for year in Mexican texts, and there are good reasons for identifying the head of Cocijo, the Zapotec rain god, as the year symbol in the glyphic writings of that people (Caso, 1928, pp. 45–64). The symbolic form is the kan cross which was an aquatic symbol for both the Maya and the Mexicans (p. 275). Thus the same association of the year with water, "the precious substance," holds good for Maya, Zapotec, and Mexicans.

KATUN (20 TUNS)

It has been rather generally supposed that *katun* is a contraction of *kal,* "twenty," and *tun.* The name is found constantly in the various books of Chilam Balam; an entry in the San Francisco dictionary reads: "It is said that the Indians counted their years in pairs, and when one reached twenty years, there they said *hun p'el katun* [one katun]."

In discussing the possibility that katun is derived from *kaltun* (20 tuns), Roys writes:

A good, but not incontrovertible, case can be made out for the contraction. The principal argument is the weakness of the *l* in Yucatec. Sometimes this is lost at the end of a syllable. An example of this is the numerical classifier *p'el,* which has become *p'e,* e.g. *hunp'el, cap'el* or *hunp'e, cap'e.* A village elder at Yaxuna chid me for speaking of Cetelac instead of Ceteac. The first is the Chumayel form; the second the present-day pronunciation, and presumably the spelling, for my brother Lawrence had Cetelac typed in a list of sites, and his spelling was pronounced wrong by his informants at Yaxuna, only 2 km. from the site. Thus it is apparently not a case of an *l* which is so lightly pronounced that we do not recognize it, but it has actually been lost in modern times. The only case I recall in which the Motul dictionary implies that an *l* has been lost, occurs with *bal, balx,* and *bax,* which are assigned the same meaning. However, those early lexicographers always had in mind the derivations of words, and I suspect they may have sometimes inserted an unpronounced *l* when they believed that it belonged there. An example of a contraction of *lt* to *t* is supplied by *beeltah,* as written in the Motul and San Francisco dictionaries, and *betah,* which we find in the Ticul dictionary. Another example is *ciioltzil,* listed in the Motul dictionary with the meaning of a happy or delectable thing; on Chumayel, p. 103, it is twice given as *ciotzil,* and I have seen that same contraction elsewhere. Similarly, the Motul dictionary gives *talzah,* whereas Pio Perez lists that word both as *talzah* and as *tazah;* the latter is the way it is pronounced at the present time.

Another example of the disappearance of *l* before *t* is supplied by *cutal* as in *u cutal Pop,* "the seating of Pop," which derives from the stem *cul* as in the verb *cultah,* "to be seated." All things considered, it is probable that katun is a contraction of *kaltun.*

Terms employed for the period of 20 years have not been preserved in most Maya languages and dialects. According to Friar Pedro Moran, that period was called *may* in Pokoman. *Mai* means tobacco or powdered tobacco, among other things, in some Maya languages. It has the meaning of 20 also in Kekchi, because, it is said, tobacco leaves are tied in bundles of 20.

The symbolic variant of the katun sign consists of the tun sign with a small cauac glyph, flanked by combs, as a prefix. The cauac sign has the same value as the tun glyph; the flanking combs usually denote "count." It has been suggested that the cauac here is to be taken as an example of rebus writing, *ca,* the first syllable representing the *ka* of katun, but Long (1935, p. 27) has called attention to the fact that *c* and *k* are two entirely different sounds in Maya, and it is therefore extremely improbable that the Maya would use a *ca* element to represent the glottalized *ka.* Apart from that, it seems unlikely that the Maya would take one syllable of a word in that way were it not the root of the word. Actually there appears to be no such root. That interpretation must, therefore, be discarded. Similarly, the comb element, to which Landa assigns the sound *ca,* presumably because that is the first syllable of *cai,* "fish," cannot stand for *ka.*

It will be noticed that all symbolic glyphs for multiples of the tun sign are composed of two glyphs for the 360-day period plus additional affixes. In the case of the katun sign the cauac glyph is combined with the tun sign; in all others the cauac glyph is doubled. In a rare variant of the baktun sign two cauacs appear above a tun sign (fig. 26,*19,22*). There is also a glyph, which may have the value of baktun, composed of three cauac signs arranged

as a pyramid (fig. 33,*57–60*). It is tempting to assign the added meaning of 20 to the cauac sign; attached to the katun sign it would mean 20 tuns, doubled it would signify 400 tuns, one baktun. The hand, as we shall see, also stands for the baktun (400 tuns) and the hand over the doubled cauac represents the calabtun (400 × 400 tuns), and, with another affix, the kinchiltun (400 × 8000 tuns). It must be admitted, however, that no evidence in support of this possibility has been uncovered in other passages.

The head variant for the katun is a birdlike creature (fig. 27,*15–27*). In most cases it resembles rather closely the head form for the tun save that the lower jaw does not show the bone; there is, in addition, a hollow area in the top of the head, such as occurs in the heads of several deities, and is most familiar to us in representations of the long-nosed god of the sculptured monuments.

In the full-figure text of Copan D and Quirigua Alt O the creature has a head which with its rapacious jaws suggests a bird of prey, perhaps a hawk, an eagle, or a vulture. Black markings on the wings rule out parrots and macaws (fig. 28,*8,10*). Sometimes the fore and aft ornaments of the tun sign which seem to represent the horns of the screech owl are present. In other texts there is on the top of the head a peculiar ornament, which looks like a tight-fitting cap, but also resembles closely the Imix sign (cf. fig. 55,*1,* Gl B2). Identification of this design, either as an attempt to show some feature of the bird's head or as a glyphic element with symbolic value, would doubtlessly solve the identity of this bird.

In a few cases the prefix of the symbolic form of the katun appears over a head which in most cases seems to be the usual katun head, but in one text (Copan 1) it is definitely the tun head with bared jawbone. This last is what one would expect, for if the prefix raises the value of the tun 20 times, one would suppose that the head beneath would correspond to the tun, not to the katun.

In view of the impossibility of identifying the katun bird, any attempt to find the meaning of the glyph is futile. It may be worth noting, however, that the Moan is not the only bird associated with celestial bands and, what is perhaps more probable, that there were four Moan birds, one for each world direction. On the front of Naranjo 32 a personage, now almost entirely obliterated, appears (seated?) above a mass composed of three, perhaps four, planetary bands. One must assume that the scene represents some deity in his celestial abode. The ends of each of three planetary bands in the lower parts terminate in heads which are clearly those of birds with prominent beaks (fig. 20,*15*). On the top of each head is the same element, vaguely resembling Imix, to which attention has already been directed. There can be little doubt, I think, that these heads represent the same bird as does the head variant of the katun.

It is well known that birds were associated with world directions. Although these fowl of the air are individually named in Chumayel, it is possible that they were known collectively as the Moan birds, although each had its characteristics. Hence, one type may have been used to illustrate the tun, another the katun, and a third the baktun. Naturally, since they were mythical creatures, primarily birds but with a dash of alligator and a strain of snake in their ancestry, their characteristics were no more constant than were those of the celestial dragons or the terrestrial alligator. They had this in common, however: all were associated with the celestial dragons, the rain-sending Itzamnas, and therefore could symbolize the haab or tun, "the rain," with complete propriety.

BAKTUN (400 TUNS)

The Maya terms for this and all higher periods are not surely known. They have been formed by modern investigators by prefixing the Yucatec terms for 400, 8000, 160,000, and 3,200,000 to the tun, on the logical assumption that katun is a contraction of kaltun and that its multiples are formed in the same manner. There is some support for the term baktun since the expression *bakhaab*, "400 haab," occurs in Chumayel. Haab and tun are synonymous, although their use depends on the texts. Previously, the terms cycle, great cycle, and great-great cycle were employed. Pseudo-Maya terms are to be eschewed, but in these cases I have retained them because cycle is an overworked word.

The symbolic variant of the baktun consists of two cauac signs to which is often added, as a postfix, a knotted piece of textile or similar material. A rare and apparently late variant has the double cauac over the normal tun sign. Should the cauac element have the value of 20, as is possible although hardly probable (p. 146), the one would multiply the other to produce the required 400. Against this should be set the established fact that the doubling of an affix makes no difference as to the meaning (p. 41; fig. 26,15–23).

The head variant is again a bird (figs. 27,3–14; 28,1–5). Tozzer and Allen (1910, p. 334) tentatively accept the full-figure variant of this on Copan D as the zopilote, the black vulture. The heads do not differ greatly from those of the katun, except for a hand covering the lower jaw, as in the head for completion (or zero?). I think there is in this symbol, and in the repetition of the main element of the baktun in higher periods, a little evidence that the Maya considered the baktun somewhat in the light of a basic unit, and that the pictun (8000 tuns) was

also regarded as 20 baktuns. This would roughly parallel our own custom of saying either one thousand nine hundred or nineteen hundred. The Maya did the same thing, for in Chumayel occurs the expression 8000 katuns, whereas one might have expected this number to have been expressed as one calabtun, or, perhaps, 400 baktuns.

PICTUN (8000 TUNS)

The symbolic variant of this sign is the baktun element, the doubled cauac, rarely with the postfix (fig. 3,*12*), but with an essential prefix, which consists of an oval outlined with dots and containing a double flare (fig. 26, *8–14*). This double-flare element is a matter of some confusion, since it closely resembles the conventionalized symbol for maize as worn by a number of terrestrial deities. The maize symbol is usually distinguished by the addition of circles (grains of maize?), but these are not infrequently omitted. In the codices, however, these two designs are more clearly distinguished. A cauac sign with the *te* (1) affix and with the flare (definitely not the maize element) as prefix occurs 13 times in the codices. Twice it appears with the dog who carries flaming torches and who has been generally accepted as a symbol of lightning; twice with God B, on one occasion when he carries a lighted torch, on the other when he lacks the torch. On six occasions the glyph follows that of the sun god, and in three of these the pair stands above the picture of the sun god. Once it is above the goddess who is probably the moon and who has the fire symbol on the load on her back. Once it is associated with the so-called Mars beast. The thirteenth appearance of this glyph is on a page in which picture and context are obliterated (fig. 43,*65–67*).

The cauac symbol is without doubt the sign for rain and storm. When, therefore, we find it with the flare prefix above a god of the rain and storms who carries a lighted torch, we can feel fairly certain that the picture represents a lightning storm. The dog was recognized many years ago by Seler as the lightning beast, and Gates (1931b, p. 33) has pointed out that there is linguistic evidence in Pokomchi for associating the dog with lightning or thunderbolts. The reason for linking this cauac glyph with its flame prefix to the sun god is not clear unless one turns to the language. The name for the rain god of the modern Maya who causes the lightning is Ah Lelem-Caan-Chaac, "the Chac who makes brilliant the sky" (Redfield and Villa, 1934, p. 115). *Lelem* means not only lightning but also brilliant light; *lelem caanil* denotes thunderhead, the storms of much cloud but little rain, and the term is used, as well, to describe the brilliant light of the sun, as *lelemac kin,* "the brilliant sun." The cauac sign, as already noted, is derived from a section of the body of one of the celestial dragons which form one of the layers of the sky and send the rains to earth. The glyph, therefore, has the general meaning of rain, but it could presumably be used to indicate the layer of heaven. The combination of this glyph and that of the sun god must mean "Kinich Ahau [the sun god] who fills the heavens with his brilliance" or words to that effect. In that sense it is also applicable to the moon goddess. In the section of the so-called Mars beast of Dresden (fig. 64,2–4), glyphs of light and darkness, of darkened skies, and of drought are prominent, and therefore the cauac with flames symbolizing an electric storm is not out of place. Indeed, this almanac probably indicates days when rain, drought, and storms might be expected (p. 258).

As used in the pictun glyph, the flames are enclosed in an oval of small circles or dots, similar to that which surrounds the glyph for Mol. The latter, it has been shown (p. 110), symbolizes the rain clouds, and the circles or dots probably represent raindrops. The prefix of the pictun, therefore, in all probability is yet another symbol for storm—the lightning flash and rain.

The head variant is the bird with hand across lower jaw which is the sign for the baktun. Above this stands the same prefix as found with the symbolic form of this glyph (fig. 27,1,2).

Calabtun (160,000 Tuns)

The term *calab* with the meaning of 160,000 appears in the Yucatec list of Beltran and also in Kaua (Berendt edition, p. 79). As *calab,* it is given by Burkitt (1902) as the Kekchi term for the same number.

The symbolic variant of the glyph has again as its main element the doubled cauac (fig. 26,1–3). The prefix is an outstretched hand, which often holds a rod or has some other minor embellishment. It will be recalled that the head variant of the baktun of 400 tuns has as its main characteristic a hand; now we find the hand with this period, which is 400 baktuns.

The head variant is some indeterminate species of bird with the same hand superfix, but in the best-preserved examples (Copan C) the hand is visible on the lower jaw converting the head into that of the baktun (fig. 26,4–6).

Kinchiltun (3,200,000 Tuns)

Only three examples of this period glyph occur in IS or distance numbers, where its numerical value can be demonstrated by its position in the sequence. Two are symbolic variants (Tikal 10, Coba 1); the other is a personified form, on the stone of Chiapa. In all three cases the main element is either the symbolic or personified

form found in the baktun, pictun, and calabtun. Clearly, then, the kinchiltun is differentiated from the other higher period glyphs by its affixes, which, unfortunately, are not well preserved in any of these three cases. Luckily, there are two examples, at Quirigua, in near mint condition, of what calculations show to have been the symbolic form of the kinchiltun (App. IV; figs. 26,7; 33,48,49). In each case the glyph is similar to the calabtun except for the addition of a prefix, which resembles somewhat the number 8, but with the greater part of each *o* filled with a crosshatched circle. The left edge of the prefix of the Tikal example of the kinchiltun is broken, but one can see a circle, and, on the right edge of that, an interior circle with crosshatching is plainly visible in the photograph (Maler, 1911, pl. 21), although only one *o* of the 8, together with a looping element, is present. The hand affix is placed above the glyph. So far as one can make out, this same 8-shaped prefix is attached to the kinchiltun glyphs on Coba 1 and on the Chiapa stone, but it is highly doubtful that the hand prefix is also present. We can, therefore, make the tentative deduction that the essential determinant of this glyph is this 8-shaped affix, and that the hand may, perhaps, be omitted. To the best of my knowledge, no one has previously attempted to distinguish this glyph from those of the other high periods.

Alautun (64,000,000 Tuns) and Higher Periods

Only one example of the alautun and yet higher periods may exist. On Coba 1 there are a number of glyphs preceding the record of 13 kinchiltuns, and each of these has a coefficient of 13. It is possible that one or more of these represents higher periods in the vigesimal system. The glyph preceding 13 kinchiltuns appears to have the tun sign as its main element, and this is surmounted by an effaced prefix. It may well represent 13 alautuns. In passages dealing with reckonings of millions of years into the past at Quirigua there are a couple of glyphs which have the tun as their main element, and which may represent the alautun or even higher periods, but their identification must remain unsolved for the present.

These, then, are the periods of Maya time: the tun (1 unit of 360 days), the katun (20 tuns), the baktun (400 tuns), the pictun (8000 tuns), the calabtun (160,000 tuns), the kinchiltun (3,200,000 tuns), and the alautun (64,000,000 tuns). Perhaps even higher multiples existed. The manipulation of these highest periods is discussed in Appendix IV. This was the count of the tuns, as the IS introductory glyph records; the uinals, 18 of which made a tun, and the kins, 20 of which made a uinal, were fractions of the tun. The system is a strictly vigesimal count of tuns.

STARTING POINTS OF THE LONG COUNT

The reckoning of the tuns and the multiples of the tun in the vigesimal system was usually made from a date which was nearly 4000 years in the past at the height of the Initial Series Period. Almost all IS contemporaneous with the monuments on which they are carved fall in Baktun 9, although a few of the earliest belong to the last third of Baktun 8, and the group of latest IS fall in the first three katuns of Baktun 10. It should be remembered that when we speak of a date, such as 9.15.10.0.0, belonging to, or falling in, Baktun 9, we are, almost without doubt, committing an error, for Baktun 9 had been completed over 300 years before that date, and the count was already more than three-quarters of the way through Baktun 10. However, as the Maya did not record a baktun or any other period before it was completed, it has become customary among specialists on the Maya to speak of a date belonging to the baktun which had expired. It is as though one referred to 1920, 1948, and 1965 as dates in the nineteenth century. Nevertheless, the custom of referring to such dates as 9.15.10.0.0 as falling in Baktun 9 is so firmly established, not only among epigraphers, but among students of all branches of Maya archaeology, that to start speaking of such dates as falling in Baktun 10 would cause inextricable confusion; the correction of the error would cause more harm than its perpetuation.

The base from which 9.15.10.0.0 and almost all other Maya dates are reckoned is 13.0.0.0.0 4 Ahau 8 Cumku. This was not the true starting point of the calendar, since 13 baktuns had already elapsed, for this position of 4 Ahau 8 Cumku is written as the completion of 13 baktuns (fig. 32,1). Moreover, some calculations deal with dates before 13.0.0.0.0 4 Ahau 8 Cumku. For example, the Tablet of the Cross, Palenque, has an IS 12.19.13.4.0 8 Ahau 18 Zec, which precedes 13.0.0.0.0 4 Ahau 8 Cumku and is linked with it (fig. 53,1). This is reckoned from a base 13 baktuns before 13.0.0.0.0 4 Ahau 8 Cumku, but there is no valid reason for supposing that this, either, was the true starting point of the Maya calendar. In fact, I feel confident that there was no such thing as an initial point of departure for the Maya calendar, but, rather, time was conceived of as without beginning or end, and therefore one could project one's calculations farther and farther into the past without ever reaching a starting point. Apart from that concept, it is to be doubted that zero as nothing could be expressed in glyphs.

For the sake of convenience, the Maya chose the point 4 Ahau 8 Cumku, completion of 13 baktuns, from which ordinarily to reckon the LC. Our typical date, 9.15.10.0.0, therefore was 9 baktuns, 15 katuns, and 10 tuns after this point of departure for the reckoning. It is not improbable, although the matter is not susceptible of proof, that 13.0.0.0.0 4 Ahau 8 Cumku was regarded as the date on which the world was recreated, perhaps for the fifth and last time. The LC was presumably invented in Baktun 7 or 8 of the current count, and an interval of that number of baktuns, and perhaps some katuns as well, was set aside to mark the time which was imagined to have elapsed since an event, which, if my supposition is correct, was regarded as the last creation of the world. Groups of 13 baktuns preceding that base would, perhaps, have been allowed for the earlier "suns" (p. 10).

When the LC was born, the highest period seems to have been the baktun. Baktuns were grouped in re-entering cycles of 13, after which a baktun would end with the same day Ahau; these cycles probably had no starting point, a Baktun 1 following a Baktun 13 in endless succession. Later, with progress in astronomy and growing skill in computation, the Maya priests burst the bounds of the baktun, and roamed farther into the past: they probed with their calculations outermost time, as modern astronomers with giant telescopes penetrate to the recesses of the universe. The re-entering cycles of 13 baktuns were unsuitable for such calculations, for they could be distinguished from one another only by a cumbersome system of nomenclature. The remedy was simple: baktuns were grouped in 20's to form a higher unit in the vigesimal count, the pictun; and the Baktun 13 of 4 Ahau 8 Cumku became Baktun 0 for purposes of calculation, although the old designation of Baktun 13 was retained for everyday usage.

Perhaps at the same time, perhaps later, periods higher than the pictun were invented, and the calabtun, kinchiltun, and alautun came into existence, each with its distinguishing glyphs. The date when the count was extended backward is not known; the earliest record of it is on Tikal 10, erected some time before 9.10.0.0.0. Around 9.13.0.0.0 the Maya priests were much interested in the backward projection of time, and not a few calculations millions of years into the past were made. These are discussed at length in Appendix IV. Suffice it here to say that there are good grounds for believing that in the extended LC our typical date, 9.15.10.0.0, held the position 1.13.0.9.15.10.0.0 3 Ahau 3 Mol. That is to say, there had elapsed 1 kinchiltun, 13 calabtuns, 0 pictuns, 9 baktuns, 15 katuns, 10 tuns, and no extra uinals or kins from the extended point of reckoning. This, however, was not the true zero date, for calculations at Quirigua carry the count very much farther into the past, and, to reiterate, there almost certainly was no such thing as a zero date.

Such calculations were, so to speak, for the senior

wranglers among the Maya priest-astronomers; for all practical purposes they can be ignored, and we can concentrate on the regular LC reckoned from the base 13.0.0.0.0 4 Ahau 8 Cumku. There is, of course, complete arithmetical evidence that all run-of-the-mill IS are computed from that base, and there are many ways of proving the sum. The most obvious, but not the quickest, method is to reduce all the orders of an IS to days and divide the total by 260 and 365, respectively, to obtain the number of days and position in the year of 365 days to be added to 4 Ahau 8 Cumku. Thus Piedras Negras 3 has the IS 9.12.2.0.16 5 Cib 14 Yaxkin (fig. 50,*1*). In terms of days the interval which has elapsed is:

9 ×	144000	1296000	(baktuns)
12 ×	7200	86400	(katuns)
2 ×	360	720	(tuns)
0 ×	20	0	(uinals)
16 ×	1	16	(kins)
	Total of days	1383136	

1383136 ÷ 260, remainder 196; 4 Ahau + 196 = 5 Cib.
1383136 ÷ 365, remainder 151; 8 Cumku + 151 = 14 Yaxkin.

Various methods for calculating Maya dates have been evolved by modern students, but as there is little evidence that any of them was used by the Maya priests, I shall not discuss them here; we are interested in Maya ingenuity, not that of the modern student. One may presume that the Maya priest-astronomer knew by heart the dates on which the various katuns and half-katuns of Baktun 9 ended, and merely checked his calculations from those points. Thus in the case of the date just discussed, the Maya priest must have known that 9.12.0.0.0 ended on 10 Ahau 8 Yaxkin. He could calculate in his head that 9.12.2.0.0. fell on 2 Ahau 18 Xul (p. 247) and an addition of 16 days would lead to 5 Cib 14 Yaxkin.

All sculptured IS were carved between the second half of Baktun 8 and the first quarter of Baktun 10 (the extremes contemporaneous with the carvings on which they occur are: 8.14.3.1.12 1 Eb 0 Yaxkin [Leiden plaque] and 10.3.0.0.0 1 Ahau 3 Yaxkin [Xultun 10 and La Muñeca 1]), and every legible IS on the monuments which carries a baktun coefficient of 8, 9, or 10 is calculated from 13.0.0.0.0 4 Ahau 8 Cumku. All the IS in Dresden which do not involve orders higher than the baktun are calculated from 4 Ahau 8 Cumku or bases very close thereto, and all record dates in Baktuns 8, 9, and 10. Altogether some 445 IS have been reported from the Maya area, all of which, with the exceptions noted above, have 4 Ahau 8 Cumku as their point of departure. The various dates and distance numbers which extend into pictuns and higher orders are discussed in Appendix IV.

THE INAUGURATION OF THE LONG COUNT

The date of the inauguration of the LC, and the reasons which led to the choice of the starting point have given rise to much speculation. In the absence of any authentic facts on that distant matter, one must regard the subject as ideal for the exercise of that joyous pastime, the building of theoretical castles on sand.

Conjectures as to the length of time necessary for the construction of the calendar vary from the adult life of one man (Spinden, 1924, pp. 157–58) to a span of 500 years for gathering only the data which enabled the length of the year to be calculated as approximately 365 days (Morley, 1937–38, 4: 271). I cannot believe that the whole Maya calendar was the work of one man, or that about half a millennium of research was necessary to fix the year as 365 days. Observation extending over many years surely would not have been necessary for a people as intelligent as the members of the Maya hierarchy. Merrill (1945), who made a series of experiments, reports that the length of the solar year to the nearest day is easily determined at the equinoxes and at the passage of the sun across the zenith. Once the idea of a line of sight is developed or it is decided to mark the shadows cast through the year by an upright pole, the approximate length of the year will soon be established. Merrill notes that observations at sunset are better than those at sunrise, and the equinoxes more sharply defined than the solstices.

I should regard the cycle of 260 days as being of considerably greater age than the completed calendar. It is very widely distributed in Central America, and in most areas it has more mythological and ritualistic association than the year of 365 days. Extent of diffusion and aggregation of mythological and ritualistic associations are not by themselves certain indications of antiquity, but taken together they tend to substantiate it. The year of 365 days also would seem to be of very considerable age. I should suppose that those two elements of the calendar functioned side by side for a long time before the evolution of the LC, and probably for some time before the CR came into existence.

There is no direct evidence for this last supposition, but this is one line of reasoning which leads to it: it would have been natural to make the vague year of 365 days start with Imix, so that every fourth vague year would be an Imix year (as 365 divided by 20 has a remainder of 5, the first days of the vague years would be Imix, Cimi, Chuen, Cib, Imix, etc.). Inasmuch as Imix is the starting point of the 20-day period, it would be logical, and in keeping with their constant desire to bring into harmony the various cycles of time, for the Maya to have arranged the contact in such a way that Imix fell on the first day of the vague year; it is reasonable to assume that they once did that. If, however, the relationship was at the beginning somewhat indefinite, it could well be that the starting point of the vague year was shifted by the intercalation of days to keep associations with stations of the solar year. Had such intercalation taken place at a time when the CR date was not firmly fixed, Imix would have lost its contact with the start of the year. Intercalation of days was absolutely against the Maya philosophy of time because the addition of leap days would have thrown the whole delicate system of the calendar awry, but shifts could easily have occurred before the CR system was firmly established without interfering with the mechanism of the calendar because that mechanism had not then been evolved. From this very indirect evidence of the noncoincidence of Imix with the start of the year I think one may tentatively assume that after the invention of the 260-day cycle and the recognition of the vague year of 365 days there was an interval of some duration before the two were engaged to form the CR.

The construction of the LC would appear to be a still later stage in the building of the complex calendar. Much speculation has centered on the reason for the choice of an approximate year of 360 days: it has been suggested that the round of 360 days represents an early attempt to guess the length of the solar year, but from what has been said above, I consider that extremely unlikely. Observation of only two succeeding spring or fall equinoxes or of northward or southward passages of the sun across the zenith would show the Maya that the year was of longer duration than 360 days.

I am inclined to think that the period of 360 days was chosen because the Maya desired a formal year which would invariably start with Imix and end with Ahau. To fulfill that condition, 360 days was the logical choice, for 380 days (it had to be a number divisible by 20) are nearly 15 days beyond the true length of the year. Furthermore, with an approximate year of 360 days the same lord of the night always governs the same nights in each tun. Moreover, at the moment the sum of tuns reaches the sacred figure of 13, 18 (twice the important number 9) sacred almanacs are completed, 4680 being the lowest common multiple of 360 and 260 (13 × 360 or 18 × 260 = 4680).

The only good alternative to a year of 360 days is one of 400, such as was used by the Cakchiquel and possibly, too, by the people of La Venta (Thompson, 1941a, pp. 15–16; 1943, pp. 108–09). Such an arrangement has the advantage of conforming to the vigesimal count, and making the 400-day and 260-day cycles coincide after 13 "years" of 400 days, but with that system each "year" does not start with the same lord of the night, nor is there a reasonably close relationship with the true year.

In seeking the date when the LC was inaugurated one must assume that the choice of the starting point was governed by ritualistic or astronomical considerations, or perhaps a combination of both. From what we know of the Maya we can, perhaps, suppose that the start of the year of 365 days would have coincided with some significant point in the tropical year, but I doubt that that was the case at the time the LC was inaugurated, for even should the assumption be correct that the length of the vague year was corrected with occasional additions of days while it was still unrelated to any other count, intercalation would hardly have been permissible once the CR came into being. Intercalation would have upset the relationship between the two counts or broken the unending succession of the days and their bearers. Thus, if the further assumption that there was an interval of some duration between the development of the CR and the inauguration of the LC be justified—and I feel strongly that it is—then there would be no grounds for supposing that the start of the year was at some significant point when the LC came into being. It would have slipped, the gap depending on the length of the period between the invention of the CR and the inception of the LC.

Accordingly, it is logical to suppose that in the choice of a starting point for the LC the placement of first of Pop at some significant point in the solar year was not a factor. That matter would have been beyond control, since, on the assumption made above, the vague year was already in being and could not be changed. Had first of Pop coincided with, for example, the autumnal equinox at the time the year of 365 days was launched, it might have fallen in mid-June by the time the IS was devised, the distance from the autumnal equinox depending, of course, on the number of years that elapsed between the inception of the CR and the birth of the LC. Only if one assumes with Spinden that the whole Maya calendar emerged fully developed from the womb of time can one expect first of Pop then to have coincided with a significant station in the tropical year.

On the other hand, the start of the count of the tuns might have been arranged in such a way that the first day of the tun fell on that same point of the tropical year, although by then the position in the Maya vague year might have been 18 Uo or 13 Zec or somewhere else, depending on the interval that had elapsed between the inception of the CR and the inauguration of the LC. It would also be natural to assume that the first day of the LC would fall on 1 Imix. In seeking the starting point of the LC, therefore, one would expect to find 13 Ahau coinciding with an important point in the tropical year.

More complications ensue. Can one be certain that the correlation of the Maya and European calendars used in this book is correct? What point in the tropical year would have had most significance for the Maya? There are sundry possibilities: vernal and autumnal equinoxes, the winter solstice, the northward and southward passages of the sun across the zenith, the start or end of the rainy season, and the start of the agricultural year. This last in turn could be reckoned as either when clearance of the land starts or when the seed is sown, and the dates for those two activities vary from one part of the Maya area to another. There are too many possibilities.

The earliest object with a contemporaneous date yet found in the Maya area is the Leiden plaque which has the IS 8.14.3.1.12 1 Eb 0 Yaxkin. By that time the IS was fully developed; the inscription gives the name of the current lord of the night, and may have a rudimentary record of the lunar count (Nottebohm, 1944). It is possible that there has survived a calculation of still earlier date, for it is highly probable that most of the IS in Dresden are records of actual observations of celestial phenomena, the earlier ones having been copied from previous editions of Dresden. Seven of these IS fall in Cycle 8, occupying positions slightly later than the IS of the Leiden plaque; two of them are earlier. These last record respectively the dates 8.6.16.7.14 9 Ix 7 Mac and 8.11.7.13.5 3 Chicchan 8 Kankin. It is, I think, a fair assumption that these dates represent ancient records handed down from the times when they were current observations. In that case the LC was established before 8.6.16.7.14.

At one time and another 7.1.13.15.12 8 Eb 0 Pop (Spinden, 1924, pp. 152–55), 7.6.0.0.0. (Teeple quoted in Thompson, 1932, p. 370), and 7.13.0.0.0 (Thompson, 1927, p. 12) have been advanced as dates for the inauguration of the LC. I now think that the reasoning which led to these several choices is in each case defective.

On the assumption that the Maya, between the inception of the CR system and that of the LC, kept a record of the number of CR's and odd years that had passed, it is logical to suppose that they would fix the date of the inception of the CR as the end of a baktun or of a katun, and from that point allow so many baktuns or katuns for the period prior to the inception of the CR and add to that the number of years that had elapsed since that event (bringing the figure perhaps to an even katun) so as to obtain a LC position in the following way:

A	13.0.0.0.0	Base. Last creation of world?
B	7.0.0.0.0	Theoretical passage of time.
C	7.0.0.0.0	Inauguration of CR.
D	5.0.0.0	Time elapsed between inauguraton of CR and IS.
E	7.5.0.0.0	Inauguration of LC.

Since there is no evidence at present for the lengths of B and D, it is impossible to make a fair guess as to the true position in the LC of C and E. The date given above is, I think, the very earliest at which the LC could have been inaugurated; 8.5.0.0.0 is probably about the latest. I would rather expect the figure to be closer to the latter position than to the former. In the hieroglyphic texts as now deciphered there is no definite evidence that the Maya paid attention to the date when the LC was inaugurated. There are a handful of references to dates in Baktun 7 and the first half of Baktun 8, but not one is repeated elsewhere. According to the various assumptions already set forth, Date E should fall on 13 Ahau but would no longer have any significance in the solar year. Theoretically at Date C the start of the vague year should occupy a position of significance in the solar year, but if Interval D is a poor approximation to that which actually elapsed between the inauguration of the CR and the birth of the IS, the relationship of first of Pop with the solar year would be in error according to how far Date E, the reconstructed date, is distant from the actual date of the inauguration of the CR. At Date C minus an unknown quantity 1 Imix probably fell on first of Pop.

Whether 13.0.0.0.0 4 Ahau 8 Cumku has any solar associations depends on the accuracy of the Maya calculations as to the length of the solar year at the time of the inauguration of the LC; I doubt that they were then capable of estimating it much better than as 365.25 days. According to the correlation followed in this book, 13.0.0.0.0 4 Ahau 8 Cumku fell on August 10, on which date the sun crosses the zenith somewhat north of Quirigua and Copan. This, however, I believe is merely coincidence because of the probable inaccuracy of Maya computations at the time the LC was launched, and because there is no valid reason for assuming that any part of the calendar originated in that latitude.

According to the Spinden correlation of Maya and Christian dates, a lunar eclipse occurred on 13.0.0.0.0 4 Ahau 8 Cumku, and, moreover, several planetary events of note took place on and around that date. This has been cited as evidence for the correctness of the correlation in question. However, when Maya astronomy was at its peak of perfection, the priests were unable to calculate lunations over thousands of years without an error of several days, and so it is certain that at the time of the inauguration of the calendar they could not have correctly deduced a lunar eclipse some 3000 years in the past. Indeed, according to their best lunar calculations, the moon age at 13.0.0.0.0 4 Ahau 8 Cumku was 22–24 days, not a full moon. Such evidence merely serves as a warning that the path to the secrets of Maya astronomy is liberally sown with pitfalls of coincidence.

After much argument we go out by that same door through which we entered, still empty-handed but with the satisfaction of knowing that some possible solutions have been eliminated, and some conditions which the true solution must meet have been outlined.

The LC presumably came into being to meet two needs: with the general development of the concept of the eternity of time which was to become the supreme mystery of Maya religion, some greater and handier unit than the CR was a necessity; with an awakening interest in astronomy and a desire, withal, to reduce all time counts to cycles in harmonious relationship with one another, a count by CR alone did not suffice. For example, it is possible that the relationship between the CR and the synodical revolutions of Venus had been solved at a somewhat early date (65×584, 104×365, 146×260). The Maya priest may have desired to bring the moon into harmony with the other factors. Multiples of CR's would have been necessary, but there was no way of distinguishing one CR from another. All started and ended with the same day and month positions. A LC was practically essential for computations of that nature.

INITIAL SERIES INTRODUCTORY GLYPH

An integral part of the IS on the monuments is the IS introductory glyph which stands at the head of the inscription. The variable element in the center of the prefix is the glyph of the deity who rules or is closely associated with the month in which the IS falls (p. 105; figs. 22; 23). One of the IS on Coba 1 lacks this introductory glyph, and the glyph very rarely (Copan 4) stands above a distance number. In a few texts at Copan, notably those of Stelae P and 7, the IS introductory glyph which is above the IS on one side of the monument, is repeated on other sides, although the glyphs which it heads do not comprise an IS. Here the repetitions probably respond to aesthetic considerations.

Copan C has an IS introductory glyph on each face, but these are not followed by IS. Instead there are in each case declarations of 11, 12, or 13 calabtuns followed by dates but without any record of the intervening periods (p. 315). Similarly Copan F has an IS introductory glyph followed by a declaration of "5 Ahau 3 Mac, half period," without the requisite IS, 9.14.10.0.0. The inscription on the lower step of Mound 2, Copan, also has an IS introductory glyph but lacks an IS. Such presentation is highly irregular. For long it has been believed on stylistic grounds that Stelae F, C, and 4, which do not carry IS but have IS introductory glyphs, form with Stela H a group of monuments erected at almost the same time (circa 9.15.0.0.0?).

The constant elements of the IS introductory glyph are the tun sign, the upper prefix, and the pair of lateral elements of the lower prefix. These last are formed of the so-called comb symbol, which in a few inscriptions is replaced by pairs of fishes (fig. 23,37,39). It has been suggested (Thompson, 1944) that since the fish and comb signs represent the word "count," the whole glyph, less the variable element and the first prefix, has the meaning of "the count of the tuns" (u xocan [or xocol] tunob), and is comparable to the words "the record of the count of the katuns" (u kahlay u xocan katunob) which stand at the head of the first chronicle of Chumayel. In Tizimin and Mani the equivalent expression is u tzolan katun, "the arrangement in order of the katuns." Allowing for the fact that in the hieroglyphic texts the count is of tuns, whereas in the books of Chilam Balam it is of katuns, the correspondence is close. In the various chronicles there is no mention of the deity of the month, but that is natural since there follows a sequence of katuns, not a specific date.

An IS which we write 9.15.0.0.0 4 Ahau 13 Yax actually reads, so far as we can now tell: "The count of the tuns. The planet Venus [is the patron]. Nine baktuns, fifteen katuns, the tuns complete, the uinals complete, the kins complete [since 13.0.0.0.0 4 Ahau 8 Cumku]. 4 Ahau [the day on] 13th of Yax." Matter in brackets is understood.

A full-figure IS which we would write 9.15.5.0.0 10 Ahau 8 Ch'en, the Maya would interpret with the aid of the pictorial grouping of the signs somewhat as follows: "The count of the tuns. The moon goddess [is the patroness]. The Chicchan god bears the burden of the baktun. The earth god of the realm of the dead bears the katun. The earth god carries the weight of the tun. The deity who symbolizes completion doffs the burden of the uinal, and has run his course with the kin. The god of the dead rests from carrying the day Ahau, and our divine youth of the maize likewise has reached the end of his stage with Ch'en upon his back" (fig. 60 and frontispiece).

INITIAL SERIES OF CODEX DRESDEN

The IS of Dresden (figs. 46,17; 64,2) differ in three respects from the kind usually inscribed on the stone monuments. (1) They lack period glyphs, being formed of bars and dots arranged in vertical columns, true positional notation. (2) They lack IS introductory glyphs. Morley (1937–38, 4:315) claims that five have this glyph, but it is the common "Men variant" with an unusual prefix. (3) A number of them depart from bases shortly anterior to 13.0.0.0.0 4 Ahau 8 Cumku. In such cases the interval between the bases and 4 Ahau 8 Cumku is expressed by means of a distance number the kin coefficient of which is enclosed within a ring. Thus on page 70 of the codex there are no less than six IS. The first two read 9.13.12.10.0   9 Ix and 9.19.11.13.0   9 Ix. Under them are the numbers 1.12.6 and 4.10.6, the six kins in both cases being enclosed within a ring which has a knot at the top. Beneath each ringed number is the date 4 Ahau 8 Cumku. If these two IS are counted from 4 Ahau 8 Cumku they will not reach 9 Ix. That is obvious because the coefficient of the kin in each case is 0, and 0 kins added to Ahau reaches Ahau. If the ringed numbers are first subtracted from 4 Ahau 8 Cumku and the IS then added, the required day position is reached:

(13. 0. 0. 0. 0)	4 Ahau 8 Cumku
1.12. 6	*subtract*
(12.19.18. 5.14)	9 Ix 7 Xul)
9.13.12.10. 0	*add*
(9.13.10.15.14)	9 Ix (12 Muan)
13. 0. 0. 0. 0	4 Ahau 8 Cumku
4.10. 6	*subtract*
(12.19.15. 7.14)	9 Ix 2 Ch'en)
9.19.11.13. 0	*add*
(9.19. 7. 2.14)	9 Ix (17 Ch'en)

It is clear that in these two examples, bases before 4 Ahau 8 Cumku were chosen so that the IS might be multiples of 260 days. Matter in parentheses does not appear in Dresden. Other IS with ring numbers are shown in figure 46,*17* and translated in the caption.

It is often difficult when treating of Dresden to draw the line between IS and distance numbers, since both are arranged in descending order and both lack IS introductory glyphs. Period glyphs, however, do occur in Dresden (p. 140; figs. 26,*13,14,32,40,48,57;* 42,*43–53*).

IS without period glyphs are not confined to Dresden, for one IS of this type is sculptured in stone (Pestac 1) and records the date 9.11.12.9.0   1 Ahau 8 Cumku. Why this single example of an IS without period glyphs should have been sculptured it is difficult to say. Pestac is an outlying part of the important site of Tonina, the other surviving IS of which are of normal type. Unfortunately a number of the IS at Tonina have been destroyed, for they were on the backs of the heads of statues since decapitated. Their former existence is assured by the pattern of glyphs which remain. Tonina is not far from the western boundary of the Maya area, and it is possible that foreign contacts may have led to this unusual presentation, so far as stone sculpture is concerned. On the other hand it is probable that the original from which Dresden derives also employed positional notation for the presentation of IS, and therefore the idea was not unknown to the Maya of that earlier period.

IS or inscriptions resembling IS, also without period glyphs, are found in sites of La Venta culture, generally attributed to the Olmec, and also occur on the Pacific slope of the Guatemalan highlands. To the culture of La Venta can certainly be attributed the famous Tuxtla statuette, for many years regarded as bearing the earliest known Maya inscription. A discussion of La Venta hieroglyphs and the calendar of that people is outside the scope of this book. Suffice it to say that there is no conclusive evidence that these bar-and-dot inscriptions served as IS, and still less grounds for assuming that they should be reckoned from 4 Ahau 8 Cumku (Thompson, 1941a).

POSITION AND FUNCTION OF THE INITIAL SERIES

The Initial Series was thus named by Maudslay because it stands, with very rare exceptions, at the start of a text (i.e. the top left corner). Usually there is only one IS on each monument, but in some cases there are two. There are two monuments with three IS (Uxul Alt 2, Lacanha 7) and one with four (Coba 1). Commonly, the second IS, if present, occurs on a different face of the monument. An IS is a LC plus required CR date.

The IS usually serves one of two purposes: it may declare the date which the monument was erected to commemorate, usually either the end of a katun, the completion of a half-katun, or the end of one quarter (5 tuns) or three quarters (15 tuns) of a katun (figs. 47,*3;* 48,*1;* 53,*2*); alternatively it records a date not ending on a tun, which, almost without exception, is prior to the dedicatory date (figs. 50,*1,2;* 53,*1,3*). There are good grounds for believing that an IS which does not fall at the close of a period was in almost all cases chosen because the date it carries was connected with the dedicatory date of the monument or the end of the current katun, usually declaring the correct position in the solar year of the date in question or recording a position of lunar importance. The latter may or may not be directly related to the dedicatory date. There is not at present evidence that all IS which do not declare the end of a period fall into this category, but I believe that future research will reveal a relationship of some kind between nearly all IS and the dedicatory date of the monument or the katun current at the time of its erection.

On the other hand, there are a few IS (e.g. Quirigua F, Copan T 11) which repeat dates recorded on earlier monuments, or give their anniversaries in the LC, as in the case of Piedras Negras L 3 (fig. 57,*1*). Such dates, being of outstanding importance for sundry reasons, were repeated on more than one occasion. Somewhat rarely a date was recorded as an IS apparently because of its ritualistic importance. Thus, we find some emphasis placed on the date 9.4.0.0.0 13 Ahau 18 Yax as a starting point for calculations in the past, presumably because 13 Ahau ends the round of 13 katuns, as noted above; the IS 9.9.9.9.18 9 Etz'nab 16 Zac (Uxul Alt 2) was probably chosen because of the profusion of "lucky" nines.

When the IS is not the dedicatory date of the monument, one or more distance numbers carry the reckoning forward to the PE which the monument commemorates. There are some texts, however, notably at Yaxchilan, which, so far as they can be deciphered, do not record a PE, but I am not sure that these are exceptions to the rule, for the information may be given in a way we do not understand (the "Ben-Ich" katuns?), or the count may have been carried forward to altars or lintels no longer existing.

It has been held by some that Maya dates recorded on stelae may refer to historical events or even recount the deeds of individuals; to me such a possibility is well-nigh inconceivable. The dates on stelae surely narrate the stages of the journey of time with a reverence befitting such a solemn theme. I conceive the endless progress of time as the supreme mystery of Maya religion, a subject which pervaded Maya thought to an extent without parallel in the history of mankind. In such a setting there was no place for personal records, for, in relation to the vastness of time, man and his doings shrink to insignificance. To add details of war or peace, of marriage or giving in marriage, to the solemn roll call of the periods of time is as though a tourist were to carve his initials on Donatello's David. Stelae and other monuments chimed the passing hours; they were dedicated to mark the passage of time, that is to say, its arrival at the major *lub* of the katun, or those wayside halts which are the half- and quarter-katuns. Cities which had a highly developed stela cult erected a monument every quarter-katun; those less religiously inclined or less wealthy consecrated a monument every katun.

Some writers have compared the IS to a counting machine of boundless accuracy. Tosh! Accuracy does not enter when it is a question of counting years and days one by one: the IS was a sublime poetic concept; to regard it as a machine is on a par with discussing fan vaulting only as a problem in engineering.

Of the sculptured legible IS, approximating 340, some 230 record the ends of baktuns, katuns, half-katuns, or quarter-katuns. None of the IS of Dresden fall into this category.

DEDICATORY DATES OF MONUMENTS

There are no foolproof rules for determining the commemorative date of a monument, but one is fairly safe in assuming that the latest period ending recorded is that of the monument's dedication, particularly if that is given at the close of the text, although there are exceptions. For instance, Copan S has an IS 9.15.0.0.0, which is followed by a period ending 10.0.0.0.0, but there is good evidence that the latter was not the dedicatory date of the altar but was probably inserted because 9.15.0.0.0 marked the completion of three-quarters of Baktun 9 (more correctly 10). The glyphs lack late features (the tun with horizontal lines, and the St. Andrew's cross as a numerical filler are absent; the Ahau with its crescentic eyes is a type in use around 9.16.0.0.0, but not two katuns later). Furthermore, Copan had abandoned the use of IS by 9.18.0.0.0, and without much doubt had ceased to erect hieroglyphic monuments before 10.0.0.0.0.

Style of the glyphs, detailed treatment of elements of costume and attributes of personages (Proskouriakoff, MS.), location of the monument (not infrequently monuments which follow in a sequence of erection are grouped in a single court), methods of recording lunar data, and length of text and its subject matter (late monuments tend to have abbreviated texts which ignore problems to the fore in earlier times) are all helpful in deciding on the dedicatory date of a monument, if that is in doubt.

Generally speaking, the dedicatory date of a monument is posterior to any non-tun ending date recorded in the text, but, here again, there are exceptions which prove the rule: Los Higos 1 has an IS 9.17.10.7.0 9 Ahau 3 Zec, but a distance number of 7 uinals followed by the anterior date indicator leads back to 9.17.10.0.0 12 Ahau 8 Pax. This is probably the dedicatory date, although on the opposite side there is what may be the start of a distance number (0 kins, 0 uinals), which might have been 10.0.0, and, therefore, carried the count forward to 9.18.0.0.0.

THE GRANDEUR OF THE INITIAL SERIES

As will be set forth in Chapter 7, dates were recorded by other methods which to all intents and purposes are just as good as the IS. For example, a statement "1 Ahau 8 Kayab, end of a katun" fixes the position of a date in a period of 949 katuns. Only after that interval of over 18,000 years will 1 Ahau 8 Kayab again mark the end of a katun, and it will be 18,980 katuns, over a third of a million years, before 1 Ahau 8 Kayab can once more be the closing day of a Katun 10. Such accuracy should have satisfied the Maya. That statement requires three glyphs; the IS, eight.

There is little doubt in my mind that the IS was carved because its majesty and rhythm did justice to the honor in which time was held. The roll call of the periods has a grand cadence when spoken, and is a panorama of harmonious glyphs when written; an IS is in itself a prayer and a noble offering to the divine powers. Because it embodied a living creed and a philosophy which was the core of Maya character, it was carved with the same faith, humility, and loving patience as guided the hands that embroidered the magnificent vestments of mediaeval Christendom; the bewildering intricacies of the full-figure IS, veritable pageants in stone, have a deep religious emotionalism comparable to that which inspired the best carving in Gothic—not only of reredos but also of hidden misericord.

Dull pages of dull discussion about the identity of this god or of that, or why jade is an element in one glyph, or why the Moan bird is the form of another, have led us into the swamps of minutiae. If we lift our eyes thence to the heights we may perceive dimly the sublime poetry of time into which the tools of the graver and the legends and myths of the storyteller have transmuted its periods. It is not given to us to see it in the whole clarity of its beauty nor fully to share the exhilaration of its poetry, for differences in mentality and in outlook on life, as well as unperfected knowledge, are veils before our eyes. Yet what we can perceive fills us with reverent wonder at this sublime achievement of the Maya. In truth, the Initial Series, that opening movement of the symphony of time, is a shining nobility, a treasure in history's store of beauty.

7
Distance Numbers

Each night since first the world was made hath had
A sequent day to laugh it down the skies.
—JAMES THOMSON, *Why Are Your Songs All Wild?*

FUNCTION OF DISTANCE NUMBERS

VERY MANY hieroglyphic texts of the Initial Series Period carry several dates. The distances between these are expressed in terms of kins, uinals, tuns, katuns, etc., so that by the addition of these to the adjacent date or subtraction therefrom the positions in the LC of dates which do not end periods are established. Thereby the necessity of repeating the IS for every date is avoided; space is saved and the IS is not cheapened by frequent repetition. Usually these figures, which are known as distance numbers or secondary series, lie between the dates they connect, although there are exceptions to that procedure. Generally, then, a distance number follows the IS and leads to the next date. Another distance number carries the reckoning forward or backward to the next date, and so on to the end of the inscription. With the position of one date in the LC fixed by means of an IS or by a PE (p. 181), the positions of all other dates are established by the distance numbers. The functions of dates thus connected are discussed elsewhere (pp. 64, 259).

The inscription on the back of Piedras Negras 3 presents a clear example of the use of distance numbers (fig. 50,*1*). The text, so far as dates are concerned, reads as follows:

A	A1–A4,B7	9.12. 2. 0.16	5 Cib 14 Yaxkin (IS)
B	C1–C2a	12.10. 0	count forward to
C	C2b–D2a	(9.12.14.10.16)	1 Cib 14 Kankin
D	D4a–C5	1. 1.11.10	count forward to
E	D5–C6	(9.13.16. 4. 6)	4 Cimi 14 Uo
F	E1–F1	3. 8.15	count forward to
G	E2–F2	(9.13.19.13. 1)	11 Imix 14 Yax
H	F6–E7	4.19	count forward to
I	F7–F10	(9.14. 0. 0. 0)	6 Ahau 13 Muan, completion of 14th katun

The inscription starts with an IS and ends with a PE, for 6 Ahau 13 Muan is stated to be the completion of the 14th katun. The four distance numbers lead to three intermediate CR dates and thence to the PE. All are quite straightforward and, as can be seen, together they bridge the distance from the IS to the last date recorded on the back of the monument. That fact alone is proof that the various additions are correctly stated, but as a further check, let us reduce the various distance numbers to days, and find the remainders by dividing by 260 and 365 and then add as per tables. This is the same process as was followed in checking the IS (calculations given overleaf).

Thus this modern method of proving the four distance numbers, which certainly is not that used by the Maya, reveals the Maya calculations to be entirely without fault.

. A preliminary check on any addition is to note the kin coefficient, which should indicate the right day sign. For example, the kin coefficient of Distance Number H is 19, and 19 added to Imix reaches Ahau. Should the day of Date I be Ik one would know that the distance number should be subtracted since Imix minus 19 is Ik. As a matter of fact most distance numbers are followed by a glyph which indicates whether the count is backward or forward. In the example cited all four distance numbers are followed by this glyph indicating a forward count (fig. 50,*1*, glyphs at C2a, C5b, F1, and E7). This glyph and the form with variant affixes which declares that a count is to be made to an earlier date are discussed below (p. 162).

There is no limit to the number of periods which may occur in a distance number. The longest so far reported occurs on the stone of Chiapa and reads 13.13.13.1.1.0.11.14. The text opens with 14 kins and 11 uinals and closes with 13 kinchiltuns. The tun glyph is omitted, but in such cases the omitted period is understood to have had a coefficient of o (p. 159). The shortest distance number is one day, recorded twice at Tikal.

Occasionally either the starting point or the terminal date of a distance number is suppressed. Although there is not at present complete substantiation, yet I am inclined to believe that Maya literary canons required that the terminal date be expressed. As we shall see (p. 164), there were special glyphs to indicate what kind of day the terminal point recorded.

In some texts, notably those from central and eastern Chiapas, distance numbers sometimes link a date not to that last given, but to the IS (Thompson, 1944c). That is to say, the distance numbers are not cumulative. An

Distance Number B	*Distance Number D*	*Distance Number F*	*Distance Number H*
	$1 \times 7200 = 7200$		
$12 \times 360 = 4320$	$1 \times 360 = 360$	$3 \times 360 = 1080$	
$10 \times 20 = 200$	$11 \times 20 = 220$	$8 \times 20 = 160$	$4 \times 20 = 80$
$0 \times 1 = 0$	$10 \times 1 = 10$	$15 \times 1 = 15$	$19 \times 1 = 19$
Total days 4520	7790	1255	99

$4520 \div 260$, remainder 100	5 Cib + 100	= 1 Cib
$4520 \div 365$, remainder 140	14 Yaxkin + 140	= 14 Kankin
$7790 \div 260$, remainder 250	1 Cib + 250 (or −10)	= 4 Cimi
$7790 \div 365$, remainder 125	14 Kankin + 125	= 14 Uo
$1255 \div 260$, remainder 215	4 Cimi + 215	= 11 Imix
$1255 \div 365$, remainder 160	14 Uo + 160	= 14 Yax
	11 Imix + 99	= 6 Ahau
	14 Yax + 99	= 13 Muan

example of this is supplied by Poco Uinik 3, the text of which reads:

A1–A8	9.18. 0. 0. 0	11 Ahau 18 Mac (IS)
A10–A11	1. 4. 7. 4	*subtract*
B11–B12	9.16.15.10.16	2 Cib 14 Ceh
C12–A13	8. 7. 2	*subtract from IS*
C15–B16	9.17.11.10.18	5 Etz'nab 16 Mol?
C16–B17	8. 3. 4	*subtract from IS*
C17–B18	9.17.11.14.16	5 Cib 14 Ceh
C20–B21	7.17. 0	*add to preceding date*
C21–A22	9.17.19.13.16	5 Cib 14 Ch'en
C22	4. 4	*Distance to IS*

One distance number is added to the preceding date; the rest are subtracted from the IS. This method is known elsewhere, but its prominence in the Jatate drainage represents a regional variation.

ARRANGEMENT OF PERIODS IN DISTANCE NUMBERS

Whereas the periods of an IS are arranged in descending order so that one reads in the order baktuns, katuns, tuns, uinals, kins, the periods of a distance number are in reverse order so that one reads first the kins and uinals and then the tuns, katuns, and baktuns if they are present. This arrangement is not followed in Dresden where, because of the general absence of period glyphs, its adoption would have caused much confusion. The three or four distance numbers in that codex which do have period glyphs retain the arrangement of the periods in descending order. There are a very few cases in the inscriptions of the Initial Series Period where the periods of the distance number are in descending order. Thus at P7–P8, west panel of Inscriptions, Palenque, a distance number 9.7.11.3.0 is written in that way, the 9 baktuns being at the start, the uinals and kins at the end. In this case the distance number is subtracted from the first of the two dates between which it lies:

O7	9.12. 3.6.6	7 Cimi 19 Ceh
P7–P8	9. 7.11.3.0	*subtract*
O10–P10	13. 4.12.3.6	1 Cimi 19 Pax

Apart from any other consideration, a count that is reckoned backward could under no circumstance be regarded as a somewhat unusual IS.

Another example of a reversed distance number occurs on the Foliated Cross, Palenque, at C3–D4. There the distance number is 1.14.14.0, 1 katun coming first, 0 kins last. This connects 1 Ahau 13 Mac with the end of 2 baktuns:

A1–A9	1.18. 5. 4.0	1 Ahau 13 Mac (IS)
C3–D4	1.14.14.0	
C7–D7		Forward to completion of 2 baktuns
C8–D8	2. 0. 0. 0.0	2 Ahau 3 Uayeb

There is a second reversed distance number in this same text at D15–D17, although there appears to be an error in the computation. Ixlu 2 also carries a distance number in reverse. This is somewhat damaged, and Morley (1937–38, 3:442) has reconstructed the dates in a manner which is not entirely satisfactory, but of the reversed position of the distance number there can be no doubt. Another reversed distance number occurs on Copan 4 (p. 178); Berlin (1945) calls attention to two more on the platform of the Temple of the Cross, Palenque.

The existence of these rare distance numbers arranged in descending order is of some importance, not as exceptions to a rule but for their linguistic evidence. Distance numbers in the books of Chilam Balam are written in descending order (e.g. *hunkal haab catac canlahun pizi,* "a score of years with fourteen"); I know of none written in ascending order. Therefore, it would seem probable that the ascending order of the distance number does not correspond to a linguistic arrangement, as Whorf (1935, p. 372) maintained, but was primarily a device to differentiate the two kinds of counts, as Long (1935, p. 28) thought. It is very possible that in Maya speech one could reverse the periods, saying "so many kins, so many uinals, so many tuns," etc., but the fact that for reasons of clarity (because of general absence of period glyphs) distance numbers are in descending order in Dresden, whereas they are normally arranged in ascending order in the inscriptions, clearly indicates that they do not reflect a rigid speech pattern.

SUPPRESSION OF KIN GLYPH

In the majority of distance numbers the kin glyph is suppressed, and its coefficient is attached to the uinal glyph. With few exceptions the kin coefficient is to the left of the uinal sign; that of the uinal itself is placed above that glyph (fig. 30,*1,2*). The few cases in which these positions are reversed, the uinal coefficient being to the left and the kin coefficient above, may be permissible departures from normal procedure, the larger perhaps placed above to save space where the glyph is squeezed into a half-block (fig. 50,*1*, Gl D4a, E1), but I am not at all sure that they should not be regarded as errors. The Maya took considerable pains to write with clarity and to conform to established rules, and for that reason it is hard to believe that they would countenance such sloppiness. It is as though one could express the difference between $50.75 and $20.50 either as $30.25 or as $25.30. License to reverse the coefficients introduces an element of ambiguity which is more than annoying to the modern epigrapher, and must have been equally detestable to the Maya reader of a thousand years ago.

In those cases in which the kin sign is not suppressed, special glyphs were used, and still other forms were utilized to express distance numbers of less than 20 days. These variant forms are discussed on pages 167-75.

SUPPRESSION OF OTHER PERIOD GLYPHS

In a few distance numbers a period glyph other than the kin is suppressed, together with its coefficient, if the coefficient is 0. Thus on Yaxchilan 12 there is a distance number of 10 tuns 0 uinals 6 kins which connects the CR dates 6 Ix 12 Yaxkin and 11 Ahau 8 Zec (fig. 30,*3*).

A1–B1	(9.15.10.17.14)	6 Ix 12 Yaxkin
A6	10. 0. 6	
C1–D1	9.16. 1. 0. 0	11 Ahau 8 Zec

The distance number is presented as a tun sign with a coefficient of 10 above and 6 to the left; the uinal sign and its coefficient of 0 have been omitted, and the kin coefficient has been attached to the left of the tun sign. This distance passage is irregular in another respect: the distance number introductory glyph (p. 160) has a lunar sign attached to it as a postfix, an arrangement,

which, so far as I am aware, occurs in no other text. Since the moon glyph under certain circumstances has the same value as the uinal sign, it is possible that its presence here in some way not at present obvious declares that the uinal glyph with its coefficient of 0 is suppressed or, what is more probable, serves as a substitute for it (fig. 51, *2*, Gl B5).

On Copan J there is a distance number of 13.10.0.0. The 13 katuns occupy a separate glyph block, but the preceding glyph block is shared by 0 kins and 10 tuns, the uinal sign and its coefficient of zero being suppressed (fig. 30, *4*).

So far as I am aware only in these two distance numbers and that of the stone of Chiapa (p. 315) are an intermediate period and its coefficient of 0 eliminated. In all other cases of suppression of periods and their zero coefficients, those thus treated are the lowest units in the series. Thus, on Copan U, there is a distance number of 1.10.0.0 which connects the dates 3 Caban 0 Pop and 6 Caban 10 Mol (Thompson, 1935a). This consists of a katun glyph with an eroded coefficient above, which for reasons of space cannot be greater than 5, and a clear coefficient of 10 to the left. Beneath the katun sign is the postfix indicative of a distance number, and the following glyph is the anterior date indicator which announces that the distance number is to be subtracted to reach the following date (fig. 30,*5*). The whole therefore reads:

A1–A2	9.18. 2. 5.17	3 Caban, Pop seated. Expiration of 13 tuns
I1–J1	1.10. (0. 0)	Subtract
K1–L1	9.16.12. 5.17	6 Caban 10 Mol

The record of 0 uinals and 0 kins is completely suppressed. Morley (1937-38, 2:266) has called attention to a similar case on Seibal 7, where the distance number, too, is 1.10.0.0, and the uinal and kin signs are omitted together with their zero coefficients. The posterior date indicator is given. Another instance which Morley cites, that of a supposed distance number of 13.2.0 at A2 on Copan U, cannot be accepted, for the supposed coefficient of 2 is in fact the prefix "expiration," as noted in the transcription just made. Yet another example of a distance number, this time with tuns, uinals, and kins suppressed, occurs on Palenque, Tablet of 96 Glyphs. This consists merely of a katun sign with a coefficient of 1 (fig. 55,*1*, Gl H6). The presence of the distance number postfix, the distance number introductory glyph, and the posterior date indicator confirm that this is a distance number—vanguard and rear guard with a corporal's file in the middle!

Tila B supplies an example of baktuns, complete with distance number postfix, being employed as a distance number. The remaining periods are suppressed. The whole reads:

A1–B5	10. 0.0.0.0	7 Ahau 18 Zip
A6–B6	10.(0.0.0.0)	Anterior date indicator
A7–B8	13. 0.0.0.0	4 Ahau 8 Cumku, 13 baktuns

Nonetheless, in most distance numbers all period glyphs with coefficients of 0, save that of the kin, are carved. The custom of omitting them was never general, and does not appear to have been in good taste at the height of the Initial Series Period; it is more frequent after 9.17.0.0.0, although Copan J was erected at 9.13.10.0.0. There are rare cases of omission of periods from IS (p. 179).

DISTANCE NUMBER POSTFIX

A good example of how one can overlook the obvious is supplied by the specialized postfix which usually occurs with the period glyphs of distance numbers. For some 50 years the period glyphs and their different uses in IS and distance numbers have been known, yet it has until now not been noted that the period glyph takes a special postfix (almost always beneath, but rarely to the right). This postfix usually consists of a pair of abbreviated scrolls or roughly U-shaped elements which flank one, two, or three dots usually arranged in a vertical or slightly diagonal line. There is considerable variation, however, in the arrangement of the design (fig. 30,*1–5,7,8*), and sometimes, particularly at Palenque, there are three or four circles or U-shaped elements (it is sometimes difficult to distinguish between an abbreviated scroll and a circle). In nearly all cases this distance number postfix replaces the normal pedestal support of some of the period glyphs, such as is found under the symbolic variants of the tun and katun (fig. *26,25,26,34,40*), but in some examples both postfixes are present, the distance number postfix being placed below the normal support. It is accordingly probable that the examples which show several circles or abbreviated scrolls merely represent merging of elements, a matter already discussed (p. 41). That is to say, the two postfixes merge to form one. Examples of the postfix being to the right to avoid this are sometimes seen (fig. 55,*1*, Gl E1, F7, F8; see also fig. *26,27,42*).

The distance number postfix is not always present in distance numbers and it may be omitted from one or more period glyphs of a distance number but be attached to the remaining glyphs of the series (fig. 53,*1*, E5–F6). As an aid in translating texts this postfix has scant value, but there are a few cases in which its presence throws a little light on style, and is of aid in deciding whether a passage should be read as an IS or as a distance number.

This same postfix is the distinguishing characteristic of the anterior date indicator (p. 162), its presence as a postfix with the count glyph immediately following a distance number denoting that the distance number should be counted backward to reach the date which follows; placed with a CR date which precedes a distance number, the glyph indicates that it is the earlier of the two dates to be connected by the distance number, and its significance in such cases is that of anterior in time or a backward count. Such a meaning will hardly apply when it is attached to the periods of a distance number, since it is used with dates counted both forward and backward. It does, however, appear possible that it might have originated in a desire to show that the order of the periods of a distance number is to be read backward, starting with the lowest rather than the highest. The presence of this postfix in those irregular distance numbers which are arranged in descending order would appear to negate this surmise. Yet the fact that this postfix came to be almost an integral part of a distance number may have led to its inclusion, almost automatically, in those occasional distance numbers in descending order, although its significance of backward cannot have been lost because of its use in other glyphs.

DISTANCE NUMBER INTRODUCTORY GLYPH

Many, but by no means all, distance numbers are preceded by a glyph which to us has the function of announcing that a distance number is to follow, although there can be little doubt that to the Maya reader it corresponded to a definite expression or sentence. As is the case in so many, perhaps all, Maya glyphs there are both a symbolic form and a head outline; the former is much the commoner.

The symbolic form of this glyph consists of a central element, which vaguely resembles a simple swastika, with prefix and postfix attached (fig. 30,*9–14*). The prefix may be any one of the half-dozen or so which form the "count" group (p. 187); the postfix, another of the group, is always the same one—the eyes and hair of the death god or of the underworld. This rather resembles the number 7, but the hairs arranged as short lines between the two circles (the eyes) serve to differentiate it from the numerical coefficient except in the most weathered examples, and even then the context usually shows which glyph it should be.

The main element, the swastika sign, but with different prefixes and postfixes or lacking one or both of them, occurs with considerable frequency in various compounds: in a number of passages it has a numerical coefficient (highest known is 16), and in almost all cases the "Ben-Ich" prefix (fig. 30,*20,21,24–28*). It is one of the combination in the 9-16-9 group of glyphs, where the sequence runs 9 sky sign, 16 kins (?), 9 swastika, a puzzling formula, the meaning of which is unknown (fig. 30, 22,23).

The glyph, almost always with the "Ben-Ich" prefix, occurs over 80 times in the codices, particularly in Paris and Madrid (fig. 30,29–35). It is found, among other places, on the pages of Dresden and Madrid which record the ceremonies at the change of the year. That led Gates (1931, p. 151) to hazard the suggestion that the glyph might represent the year of 365 days, an opinion in which few would concur.

The main design, the kind of swastika, is rather like the Aztec glyph Ilhuitl, "day" or "festival," which occurs rather infrequently in the Mexican codices (fig. 30,36). It appears four times on Mendoza 19, where, as Long (1942) has shown, it indicates the four days (on which monthly festivals fell) of the year on which tribute was due. Long demonstrates that the interpreter's translation of these signs as 80 days is not strictly correct, since the glyphs do not imply four consecutive monthly festivals, but rather four quarterly festivals. This same glyph again appears four times on Mendoza 57. Here it represents four consecutive days, not four festivals. A parallel use of a single word (kin) to describe both day and festival is found in some Maya languages and dialects.

If the Maya glyph has the same value as the Aztec, it would mean, in conjunction with its prefix and postfix, something like "the count of days expired," but there are other possibilities. This swastika-like element suggests circular motion. There is a Maya expression bukxoc which is translated in the Motul dictionary as contar generalmente o sumar la cuenta; the latter definition certainly would appear to cover distance numbers, since they are addition (or subtraction). Under buk the Motul dictionary says "count to count years: hun buk, ca buk: one year, two years, etc." This specialized meaning would agree with the use of the glyph in the pages covering the new-year ceremonies in Dresden and Paris. The expression bukxoc occurs in various passages in the books of Chilam Balam. In Ixil there is a wheel showing the year bearers running anticlockwise from 1 Kan to 12 Cauac (Bowditch, 1910, fig. 62). The number 13 is written under 1 Kan, so that by allowing for the shift in numbers one can reckon the position of any year bearer in the round of 52 with comparative ease. The words "bux xoc" are in large letters beneath the wheel. Perez (1864, p. 394), who may have had this wheel before him when he wrote (1842), says that the wheel of the year bearers was called bukxoc. In Ixil there is a table giving the coefficient of the opening day of each uinal of a year, the numbers rising by 7, since 20 minus 13 equals 7. The heading above this table is u bukxoc nohxibcabob uchi

hunp'el haab, "the reckoning of the ancients formerly for one year."

The word buk seems to convey the idea of turning over. As a verb it means to whip wax until it becomes spongy; buklah luum is to spade land for planting; bukul is to interweave or insert. The action of turning over does not seem at first sight to have much connection with adding because we count by summing vertical columns of figures. The Maya, on the other hand, appear to have done much of their summing of periods of time by counting around wheels or four-sided figures.

Nevertheless, I do not believe that this swastika element corresponds to bukxoc. I have summarized the case as an example of how easily one can sometimes find support for an idea in pairing words with glyphs. I think it is much more probable that the swastika sign corresponds to the word hel, "change, successor."

The Motul and Perez dictionaries give for this word, as a substantive, the meanings successor in office, replacement for something or somebody lacking or worn out, or quit, exchange, return payment; as a verb they list to move, to exchange, to put one in place of another, change one's clothes; as a past participle (helan) they give the extended meaning of different, as a thing different from what it used to be or different from another thing. Helep is to change in custom or nature, and, by extension, new year when the incoming officers take over their duties from those retiring; helep akab is past midnight; helehel is at times, and there are numerous other compounds.

In Chumayel there is mention of canhel or cangel, a word which Beltran translates as dragon. Ralph L. Roys (1933, pp. 67, 110) discusses at some length the canhel, which he concludes is a wind god or rather that there were four of them, and that the word could well be translated the four changing ones. He also notes that as the canhel was held in the hand by God, the word was presumably applied to the manikin scepter or something of that nature. The passage in question, as translated by Roys, reads: "Here was the first heaven where God the Father was set up, grasping in his hand his stone, grasping his cangel, grasping his wheel on which are hung the four angels of the winds." The angels of the winds are identified in the preceding paragraph as the red, white, black, and yellow Pauahtun, who are closely related to, if not identical with the Bacabs set at the four sides of the world to sustain the heavens. I would suppose that the cangel (i.e. canhel) was the wheel on which the four angels (canhel) hung. "The changing ones" is a reasonable interpretation since the one succeeded the other (hel can mean successor) in counterclockwise rotation as rulers of the years. Thus, there does seem to be a definite association between *hel* and the rotating movement involved in this succession of deities with their changing world directions and numbers. The swastika sign could, accordingly, have the meaning of *hel*. As a distance number involves a rotation of rulers and perhaps was counted in a rotary manner, the use of the *hel* concept would not be out of place.

Hel or *helep* appears several times in the prophecies for the divisions of Katun 5 Ahau in Tizimin (Roys, 1949). The terms occur in contexts dealing with the end of one katun and the entry of its successor, and are linked to such paraphernalia of the changing katuns as the mat, the throne, the cup, the bowl, the rule, and the law: on page 10 we find the expression "when the katuns change with one another."

Because of the prominence of the swastika glyph (but with the "Ben-Ich" prefix) on the pages in the codices which deal with the new years and the accompanying change over from one set of rulers to another (p. 124) and its even greater prominence on the pages of Paris which record the sequence of the 13 katuns with their rulers, I feel fairly confident that the swastika element means *hel,* and that such a meaning would fit a count of days as well as the "successor" aspect of the new years and the new katuns. The symbol might also represent the four world directions and their rulers because of the rotary arrangement of the calendar and because of the apparent use of the word *canhel* for the four wind deities. Nevertheless, I do not think that this identification can be accepted as entirely proved (see also p. 202).

The head form of the distance number introductory glyph is not always identifiable save through its position at the start of a distance number, and because it retains the prefix and postfix of the symbolic form. However, on Copan T 11, there occurs a head form with the swastika-like symbol on the side of the head (fig. 30,*16*), and there are other possible examples which may indicate the subject matter of the date reached (fig. 30,*17–19*).

ANTERIOR AND POSTERIOR DATE INDICATORS

These glyphs indicate by means of their affixes whether the date with which they are associated is the earlier or later of the two dates connected by a distance number. They correspond roughly to our plus and minus signs.

The posterior date indicator consists of a main element, a prefix, and a postfix (fig. 30,*42–47*). The symbolic form of the main element is the jade symbol, which is used for the more usual variant of the day sign Muluc (fig. 8,*4–7,10,11*) and has the meaning of water. The head form, which is nearly as common as the symbolic form, is that of a strange creature I have shown to be without question a fish (Thompson, 1944). The animal

associated with the day Muluc is the *xoc* (p. 78), according to the Vienna dictionary a species of shark. The Perez dictionary lists *hkan xoc* as a species of shark, and this Gaumer (1917, pp. 32, 35) identifies as "pilot or caaing whale" and as "short-finned blackfish." Roys, who supplied these references, also points out that there is mention on page 2 and *passim* of Tizimin, part of section of prophecies for the tuns of a katun, of Chac uayab xooc, "the great or red demon shark or whale." For the year 1 Ix there is a passage which he translates: "Chac uayab xoc. At that time the fire was set; it clings to the tail of the shark. When it is set, it clings to the sky, to the clouds; at that time it is beheld everywhere." He notes that this being seems to be connected with the Yucatec god of fishermen, said by Landa to be Ah Kaknexoi, but which he had previously reconstructed as Ah Kaknexoc, "fire-tailed shark or whale" (Roys, 1949). He concludes that *xoc* or *xooc* refers to an ill-defined group of large fish or whales. In the Pokomchi dictionary of Cahcoh shark is one of the meanings given for the word *xoc*. I have been unable to trace the word in other lowland tongues, but, as I have pointed out, the compilers of such dictionaries, being with few exceptions men of God, would hardly worry about obtaining the native equivalents of such denizens of the deep as whales, sharks, and mythical fish unless they contemplated a sermon on Jonah. Moreover, only a small part of the Maya lived near the coast or went down to the sea in ships.

In view of the association of the *xoc* with the day Muluc, I think there can be little reason to doubt that the fish here used as a head form is the *xoc,* and that the *xoc* was a mythological monster connected with water (p. 44). There is considerable variation in portraits of this *xoc* monster, as is the case with all creatures of imaginative zoology. The characteristic feature is supplied by what appears to be barbels which sweep upward before the forehead and curve down behind the mouth to form a sloping S-like design, but equally prominent is the finlike prolongation at the back of the top of the head, which probably represents the start of the dorsal fin. The gill opening is sometimes marked but generally blends with the barbels; serrated teeth are usually displayed. These features would militate against the identification of the creature as a whale were it not that mythology and zoology have but a nodding acquaintance.

The head of this fish is also that of the patron of the month Zotz' (fig. 22,*17–22*); in an abbreviated form it is used as the head form of the count prefix (fig. 5,*24,34, 41,49,50*), its corresponding symbolic form being the "comb," a conventionalized picture of the dorsal fin (fig. 5,*14*). A series of illustrations of fish are shown in figure 5,*1–7;* the replacement of the "comb" element by pictorial representations of fish is well illustrated by the IS introductory glyph (fig. 23,*34–40*).

Xoc is also the Yucatec word commonly used for counting. I have not encountered the word in other languages save Kekchi. In that language there is a verb *xococ,* "to collect, to bring together" (Wirsing, 1930), which is very probably the same. The final *oc* is a verbal termination. There seems not the slightest doubt that the picture of the *xoc's* head is used here to represent the noun and verb *xoc,* "count" or "to count," a perfect example of rebus writing. The symbolic form (fig. 30,*37–40,42–44*), on the other hand, is ideographic, the symbol for water or rain representing the creature which inhabits water and in all probability gave rain to the earth. The meaning of count fits the use of this glyph perfectly.

The prefix of the posterior date indicator, which resembles Landa's glyph for the letter *i,* occurs in several combinations, where its meaning must correspond to "leading to," "forward to," "falling on," "ending," the interpretation Beyer (1937, p. 154) favored, or something very similar. It occurs most frequently in combinations which lie between distance numbers and period endings (figs. 31,*45–48;* 32,*11*), but in all cases these distance numbers lead forward, not backward, to the dates in question. There are, therefore, really good grounds for attaching to this prefix the meaning of "forward." I have no suggestion to offer as to the actual Maya word or words it represents. Nonetheless, terminations were attached to numbers in some, and perhaps all, Maya languages and dialects to differentiate a time count into the future or into the past. Thus we find *er* added to numbers in Kekchi and Pokomchi to denote a count into the future; *eh* to indicate a count into the past in the same languages. The termination *eh* appears to be used for a lapse of time in which time relationship to the present is not indicated, but with the addition of the number one, e.g. *hun cabeh,* "a period of two days"; *hun oxeh,* "a period of three days."

The prefix usually stands to the left of the main element, but quite frequently it is above it. Occasionally it becomes an infix of the main element, when that is the head form, serving as the headdress of the head in question, for the Maya saw nothing incongruous in supplying with headgear a somewhat anthropomorphized fish.

The postfix of the posterior date indicator is also a postfix of the anterior date indicator. It is the so-called torch or vulture symbol, which seems to be the same as Landa's glyph for the sound *ti. Ti,* however, is the Maya locative, which in practice corresponds not only to "at" and "in" but also to "with," "to," and "from." As we have already established the meaning of "count forward" for the main glyph and its prefix, the locative value

of *ti* fits extremely well, and the whole then reads "count forward to," the only doubtful part being the exact meaning of the prefix, but that at least must be something very similar to "forward."

The anterior date indicator has the same main element, the *xoc* monster or the precious water as the symbolic form. There is no prefix, but two postfixes. These may be placed one above the other, or merged in one line, below the main element; or one may be below, the other to the right (fig. 30,*37–41*). One of the two postfixes is the locative sign *ti,* which appears in the posterior date indicator; the other is the same as the postfix of periods of distance numbers, already discussed. As this glyph is used to denote that the CR date to which it is adjacent is the earlier of two dates joined by a distance number, and as it differs from the posterior date indicator only in the substitution of this postfix for the prefix of the latter, it stands to reason that this reversal in the direction of counting must be expressed by that substitution. The second postfix, therefore, indicates anteriority in time, and the whole glyph means "count backward to" or "count from the earlier date to," indicating the point of departure.

A short passage comprising Dates 22 and 23 of the Hieroglyphic Stairway, Copan (fig. 35,*16*), illustrates the usage of the various elements which compose a distance number. Translated as pure arithmetic, it would be transcribed

$$\begin{array}{ll} (9.14.15.\ 0.0) & 11\ \text{Ahau}\ (18\ \text{Zac}) \\ 11.14.6 & \\ \hline (9.15.\ 6.14.6) & 6\ \text{Cimi}\ 4\ \text{Zec} \end{array}$$

Translated as the Maya wrote it, it would run something like this: "A change of time by addition [*hel?*], 6 kins, 14 uinals, 11 tuns in reverse order [? the postfixes]. The count is from the earlier date 11 Ahau [18 Zac], the count forward to 6 Cimi 4 Zec."

The presence or absence of the anterior and posterior date indicators appears to have depended on the decision of the priest-astronomer who prepared the drawings for the texts, and he was probably guided in his choice largely by problems of space. No doubt, too, individual taste played a part in the decision, for among the Maya priesthood, as among modern writers, there were probably devotees both of a polished style and of telegraphic journalese. Two citations are given below to texts in which these glyphs are particularly prominent.

The Tablet of the 96 Glyphs, Palenque (fig. 55,*1*), supplies five examples of posterior date indicators of the head form, at A6, C4, E2, G1, and G7. There are four examples of this glyph on the back of Piedras Negras 3: head forms at C2a and E7, symbolic forms at C5b and F1 (fig. 50,*1*).

At Palenque, but nowhere else save perhaps at Xcalumkin, an entirely different form of the anterior date indicator is used. This is a wriggly creature, perhaps a snake or an eel or even a tadpole, which is attached to the day sign from which the distance number is counted forward, or which is reached by subtracting the distance number from the other date. The best preserved and delineated example is on the Tablet of the 96 Glyphs, Palenque (fig. 30,48–51). The creature is to the left of the day 13 Ahau. The passage runs

H7–I1	(9.17.13.0.7)	7 Manik 0 Pax, Completion of
		first katun
L1	7	(*subtract*)
K2–K3	9.17.13.0.0	13 Ahau 13 Muan, 13 tuns

The nine examples of this sign so far discovered are listed elsewhere (Thompson, 1944, p. 21). In one case the prefix is attached to the tun sign, not the day sign, to which the distance number leads back (Inscriptions, west panel, H8). A tenth example may occur at Xcalumkin (fig. 4,26). See Addendum, page 296.

The presence of these directional indicators reflects the spoken word, but they are also of some value to the modern epigrapher in reconstructing damaged or defective texts, since they inform us which of two dates is the earlier. Thus, with a complete distance number, an anterior or posterior date indicator, and only one of the two CR dates, one can restore the missing or suppressed date with complete assurance. The front of Yaxchilan 25 opens with a distance number of 2.2.7.0, posterior date indicator, 3 Imix 14 Ch'en (fig. 49,1). Luckily, the under

With the posterior date indicator present, only the first reconstruction is permissible.

INDICATORS OF TUN AND OTHER DATES

In some cases distance numbers are followed, not by an anterior or posterior date indicator, but by other glyphs, the meanings of some of which are known.

Two of these glyphs, which are commonest at Palenque, have as one of their main elements the sign for which the meaning *cutal*, "the seating of," has been suggested. The postfixes attached to this main element differentiate this glyph (fig. 19,42–44,47–51) from the merged form, identified tentatively as the symbol for the seating of the tun (fig. 19,37–41).

In the first glyph the wing is attached as a postfix, as in the case of the merged form of the supposed glyph of the seating of the tun, but there is a second postfix. This generally consists of a decorated crescent, the horns of which touch the edge of the main element, and the affix tentatively named *ak* (p. 282). This postfix and the wing postfix can change positions. If the wing is to the right of the main element, the tripartite postfix is below; if the wing is below, the tripartite element is to the right (fig. 19,42–44). The identity of this glyph with the merged form of the supposed glyph of the seating of the tun, save for the addition of a postfix, suggests a very similar meaning. The glyph, however, is not directly associated with a CR date but immediately follows a distance number. It would appear that its meaning is something along the lines of "leading to the seating of a tun." I find the following examples:

Text	Site	Inscription	Initial Point	Distance Number	Terminal Point
A	Palenque	Inscr. (E.), A11	Suppressed	12.10. 3?	9. 5. 0.0.0 11 Ahau 18 Zec
B	Palenque	Inscr. (E.), G6	Missing or suppressed	1.12?	9. 6.13.0.0 9 Ahau 18 Muan
C	Palenque	Inscr. (E.), L3	Suppressed	9.14.12	9. 8. 0.0.0 5 Ahau 3 Ch'en
D	Palenque	Inscr. (E.), L10	Suppressed	1. 8.10	9. 8.13.0.0 5 Ahau 18 Zec
E	Palenque	Inscr. (E.), M12	Suppressed	10. 2	9. 9. 0.0.0 3 Ahau 3 Zotz'
F	Palenque	Inscr. (E.), R10	Suppressed	17.13.12	9.10. 0.0.0 1 Ahau 8 Kayab
G	Chinikiha	Throne, A2	Suppressed or missing	8. 7. 8	Suppressed or missing
H	Chinikiha	Throne, G1	9.9.2.8.4 3 Kan 17 Zac	3. 2. 9.16	Missing
I	Tortugero	1, A4, u.h.	1 Men 8 Cumku?	12. 5	9.11. 0.0.0 12 Ahau 8 Ceh

side of this lintel is excellently preserved, and shows clearly the date 5 Imix 4 Mac, but were it to have been completely destroyed, one could still restore this date, for the presence of the posterior date indicator at N1 shows that 2.2.7.0 has to be added to the first CR date to reach 3 Imix 14 Ch'en. Were this glyph lacking, and the under side of the lintel destroyed, one would be faced with two possibilities:

5 Imix 4 Mac + 2.2.7.0 = 3 Imix 14 Ch'en
1 Imix 4 Xul − 2.2.7.0 = 3 Imix 14 Ch'en

It will be noted that in all the examples for Palenque the starting point of the count is either missing or omitted, but in every case the ending point is the seating of a tun. In the case of F the starting point is 9.9.2.4.8 5 Lamat 1 Mol, a date prominent at Palenque. The glyph in this example is not correctly drawn in Maudslay, for there it is shown with another element replacing the wing or tail, whereas this latter is discernible in the photograph. In the case of Date H there is doubt as to the accuracy of the reading. Here the glyph follows the

CR date which appears to be 3 or 1 Kan 16–18 Zac. The reconstruction would be:

D2–F1 3.2.9.16
E2–F2 (9. 9.2.8. 4) 3 Kan 17 Zac
_____
       (9.12.5.0. 0 3 Ahau 3 Xul)

Because of a break in the text, it is impossible to verify this reading.

Date I differs from the reading given by Morley and Blom (Blom and La Farge, 1926–27, p. 151). Unfortunately we must depend on an extremely poor drawing. The last four glyphs appear to record 12 Ahau 8 Ceh, 11 katuns completed, the last glyph probably being the hand which is scattering drops of water. The prefix of the month sign in B3b, l.h, appears to be that of Cumku since the nick in the lower part is very clear in the

distance numbers to indicate intervals of less than 20 days. The inverted Ahau over the regular kin sign is the symbol for east, sunrise. Ahau is the day of the sun, and the glyph is a picture, naturalistic or conventionalized, of the sun god. It is therefore fairly certain that the inverted Ahau has the meaning of sun, or perhaps sunrise. Possibly it was inverted to avoid any danger of confusion with the many glyphs of which the Ahau sign is a component. With its prefix of the "seating element," it would appear to have the meaning of *u cutal kin,* "the seating of the day," and, in that case, it should refer only to CR dates which do not mark the ends of tuns, thereby differentiating such dates from those which call for the use of the glyphs of "seating of the tun," or of "leading to the seating of the tun." I find the following examples:

Text	Site	Inscription	Initial Point		Distance Number	Terminal Point	
A	Palenque	Fol. Cross, N7	9.12.11.12.10	8 Oc 3 Kayab	6.11. 6	Suppressed	
B	Palenque	Inscr. (W), R8	9. 9.13. 0.17	7 Caban 15 Pop	2. 7. 6. 1	9.12. 0. 6.18	5 Etz'nab 6 Kankin
C	Palenque	Inscr. (W), T7	9.12.11. 5.18	6 Etz'nab 11 Yax	4. 1.10.18	Suppressed	
D	Tikal	Temple 4, L2	9.15.16. 4.18	12 Etz'nab 11 Zac	13.10. 2	9.15. 2.12.16	5 Cib 14 Zotz'
E	Copan	HS, E, Ra	9. 7. 5. 0. 8	8 Lamat 6 Mac?	2. 9.16.17?	9. 9.14.17. 5	6 Chicchan 18 Kayab?

drawing. That would eliminate Yax, as preferred by Blom. The suggested reconstruction would be:

A1–A2 9.10.13. 0. 0 1 Ahau 3 Kankin tun 13,
                       Count of tuns completed

B3a, u.h.   12. 5
B3b   (9.10.19. 5.15) 1 Men 8 Cumku
_____
A4a, u.h.   To the seating of the tun
B4   9.11. 0. 0. 0 12 Ahau 8 Ceh, 11 katuns completed

It will be noted from the components of Glyph Block B4 that the glyphs within the glyph block are to be read in the sequence a, u.h.; a, l.h.; b, u.h.; b, l.h.

These examples from Chinikiha and Tortuguero are too defective to be used as evidence either for or against the suggested interpretation, but they are of interest in showing that the glyph in question is not confined to Palenque.

In the second form of the glyph the tail or wing is replaced by an entirely different element, and for the crescents and scroll postfix is substituted one composed of a small oval or pointed object flanked by scrolls. The main element is the same (fig. 19,47–51).

A glyph on Palenque, Foliated Cross, N7, seemingly represents the unmerged form of this glyph and, if that is so, supplies the clue as to its meaning (fig. 19,46). The main element is an inverted Ahau with a double postfix which is essentially the same as that just discussed. The inverted Ahau is an element which enters in a glyph which, together with its coefficient, is used in certain

The suppressed terminal point of A is 9.12.18.5.16 2 Cib 14 Mol, prominent at Palenque; that of C is 9.8.9.13.0 8 Ahau 13 Pop, which occurs elsewhere in this inscription and also on the hieroglyphic stairway at this same site. What may be a variant of this sign occurs at Palenque Sun, A14. The postfixes are those of the glyph under discussion; the central element may be a head variant. Text D has inverted Ahaus as one postfix, and the little head in the center can not now be seen. Nevertheless, I think the glyph may be accepted as "the seating of the day." The Copan example is somewhat damaged, but there appears never to have been a wing, and therefore the glyph is classifiable as of the second category. On Copan J there is another example, but this lacks both the wing and the element which replaces it in examples of "the seating of the day."

These few swallows hardly assure us that we may bask in the summer of certainty, but so far as they go, they confirm the suggested decipherments. It might be argued that such glyphs, if rightly deciphered, would be entirely redundant. Such a view would be fallacious, for the glyphs reflect the spoken word. Frequently in the books of Chilam Balam one finds expressions such as *hun Imix u kin,* "1 Imix, the day." Similarly in the texts of Yucatan the kin glyph usually follows the day sign, and precedes the month sign: "9 Lamat, the day, on 11th of Yax" (fig. 38,1–3). The statement that 9 Lamat is a day is quite unnecessary by modern standards of journalese English, but neither Shakespeare nor the Maya poets shaped their styles to reduce the charges of cable and telegraph companies. Fine concepts deserved fine words. Sentences reduced to the bare words necessary to convey their ideas may have their place in modern life, but they are seldom great literature. Time was the great mystery of Maya philosophy; resounding sentences were its due.

"FORWARD TO SUNRISE" GLYPH

There are quite a number of glyphs which lie between distance numbers and terminal dates. I would not venture to hazard interpretations of many of them at this moment but there is one which should be discussed because of the light it may throw on other problems.

The glyph in question is a compound, to which is attached the "forward" prefix we have already encountered in the posterior date indicator (fig. 31,*45–48*). The compound without the forward affix means day in general, and quite probably sunrise, or perhaps dawn, in particular (fig. 31,*41–44*). Its derivation and implications are explored on page 168. Beyer (1943a), who has discussed the glyph, believes that it means "ending day," because he gave that interpretation to the prefix, which we have found has a meaning analogous to "forward." He notes that the glyph with this prefix is confined to Piedras Negras, with one fairly certain example at nearby El Cayo, and lists 21 occurrences, of which 19 follow distance numbers which are counted forward. On Stela 22 and Lintel 4 the distance numbers are illegible; on Throne 1 the distance number was probably on a missing fragment, some glyphs intervening between it and the "forward to sunrise" glyph. The glyph on Stela 36 lacks the forward prefix. This text is rather irregular so far as Piedras Negras is concerned, for the distance number precedes the starting point, and that is not connected by a distance number with the preceding date. As the astronomers of Piedras Negras usually took care to connect all their dates with distance numbers, this variation may in some way, not now apparent, account for the absence of the forward prefix. On Altar 2 (twice) and perhaps on Lintel 3 *ti* is prefixed to the day sign of the terminal date. This locative prefix must here signify "on" or "at," the whole reading in the second case on Altar 2 "1 katun forward to sunrise on 2 Ahau 13 Zec." On Altar 1, Lintel 3, and the shell plaque the posterior date indicator precedes the glyph under discussion, introducing a repetitive statement which probably corresponds to a speech variation (see p. 296).

On Stela 37 the "forward to sunrise" glyph is not directly preceded by a distance number, although the count is forward. The text reads:

A1–D1	9.12. 0. 0. 0	10 Ahau 8 Yaxkin
C2–C3		Haab completed. Completion 12th katun
D4–D5	3. 6.14	Anterior date indicator?
C6–D6	9.11.16.11. 6	5 Cimi 9 Pop
D10		Forward to sunrise
C11–D11	9.12. 0. 0. 0	10 Ahau 8 Yaxkin
C12–D12		Haab completed, 2 "Ben-Ich" katuns

Thus the reckoning is forward, but a second distance number, which would have been precisely the same as the first, was supplied mentally; the glyphs in D9–C10 may convey that information. Similarly, on Piedras Negras Thr 1 the distance number is suppressed, but from analogous cases it would seem that the presence of the glyph "count of 15 katuns" at M1 indicates a count forward through that PE.

It is possible, of course, that this "forward to sunrise" glyph could be substituted for the posterior date indicator, which it closely parallels in function, only on certain occasions, but if there exists any such regulation, I have failed to find it. The glyph occurs with some period endings, not with others; with some determinants and anniversaries, not with others. I believe its use depended on the caprice of the priest-astronomer who prepared the blueprints of the inscription. One could say "count forward to *n* day, *n* month," or "forward to sunrise [or day] of *n* day, *n* month." Such flexibility surely reflects the pattern of the language.

There appear to be a number of somewhat similar signs, notably that which Spinden (1924, p. 202) has called the sacred fire glyph. It would seem that this is probably the sky symbol, not that for fire. It is essentially the sky symbol set horizontally and doubled. A series of glyphs of which this sign is an element is shown in figure 31,*52–72*. It will be seen that all are basically the same except for a variable infix, and that in several cases (fig. 31,*60,61*) the identification of this symbol as that of sacred fire will not fit the context, whereas the text is not violated if the element is translated as sky (perhaps eastern sky). One cannot identify an element as "sky" in one glyph (Spinden's "Observation of the sun at the horizon") and as "fire" in another (his "new fire" or "sacred fire" glyph) unless one can show a reason for the transmutation.

In some Maya languages the term for light, brightness, and day is the same. Obviously, by brightness and light is to be understood not the direct rays of the sun, but the diffused light of day, since the term is not confined to days on which the sun is visible. Thus, I think it is fairly clear that light and brightness refer to the sky. Accordingly, this glyph which Spinden translates as new fire in all likelihood means "light or bright sky," that is to say, "day," probably sunrise, but perhaps dawn with its fiery light. If that assumption is granted, the glyphic interchangeability of "bright sky" and "day" corresponds to their synonymous use in the spoken language. I further assume that the curls surrounded by dots represent fiery light, an identification already made in connection with the discussion of the pictun glyph (p. 147), for the Maya use a single word (in Yucatec and Kekchi *lem*) to describe the brightness of the lightning flash, of the full moon, and of the sun. The whole glyph would therefore correspond in a general way to the "count forward to" or "forward to sunrise" glyphs. It reflects a slight variation in the spoken word. Nevertheless, this as well as other interpretations offered in this section, must be treated as tentative; the last word on them has not been said.

USE OF LUNAR GLYPH IN DISTANCE NUMBERS

Mention has been made more than once of the use of the moon glyph with circular eye, Glyph E of the lunar series, to represent the number 20. In the lunar series Glyph E has the value of 20 days or nights; its coefficient is added to it to give the age of the moon. Thus 7E indicates a moon age of 27 days or nights. The glyph in question is used in contexts other than that of the lunar series with the value of 20.

In the divinatory almanacs of Dresden distance numbers between 20 and 39 days inclusive are expressed by the moon glyph to represent the number 20 and an attached coefficient of bars and dots to cover the balance. The coefficient may be in line with, but detached from, the moon glyph; in other cases it is above it, as with Glyph E of the lunar series, or to the right of it, as a postfix, in precisely the same way as the coefficient is usually attached to Glyph A of the lunar series (figs. 63,*4;* 64,*4*).

There are five known cases in the inscriptions of distance numbers of over 19 but under 40 days which are expressed by a lunar glyph with a value of 20, and a coefficient to represent the balance (fig. 4,*16–18*).

On Palenque Cross and Yaxchilan L 10, moon signs with coefficients of 0 and 4 respectively serve as distance numbers of 20 and 24 days (Beyer, 1938a). On Balakbal 5 the same sign with a coefficient of 11 is used to record a distance number of 31 days (Thompson, 1940b). Another example occurs on Piedras Negras L 3, where a distance number of 23 days is expressed by means of a moon glyph with a coefficient of 3; on Quirigua Alt O a distance number of 22 days is similarly expressed by a moon sign with coefficient of 2 (Thompson, 1945b).

Presumably the Maya would never have written a distance number of, for example, 385 days as 1 tun, moon sign with coefficient of 5, for this use of the moon sign appears to have been confined to distance numbers between 20 and 39 days inclusive. The associations of 20 with the moon signs have already been discussed.

FORMS FOR KIN USED IN DISTANCE NUMBERS

In the investigation of the period glyphs of the IS it was noted that there are at least five forms of the kin: the head of the old sun god, the head of a monkey, a beaked head which may represent the eagle, the head of a youthful person, perhaps the young sun god, and the four-petaled symbolic form. None of these is normally used in distance numbers.

The only two examples which I know of the use of IS types of kin glyphs are to be found in the two distance numbers of the Foliated Cross, Palenque. These are atypical, as already noted (p. 158), because the period glyphs are arranged in descending, not ascending, order. In one case the symbolic variant of the kin is employed; in the other, the head of the sun god. The arrangement of these two distance numbers as though they were IS may have led to the carving of kin forms of regular IS types. In a third distance number in reversed order (Palenque Inscriptions (W), P7–P8) the kin glyph is suppressed, and its coefficient of 0 is attached to the uinal glyph. Another possible exception to the rule of not employing normal kin glyphs in distance numbers can be discarded. In a drawing of the glyphs on the right side of Altar de Sacrificios 9, Morley (1937–38, 2:324) shows the kin of a distance number with the cartouche outline and tail of the normal four-petaled kin, although the center is left blank. This, however, is not a correct drawing, for the photograph from which it was made shows quite clearly the upper part of the shell variant of the kin.

There are five different glyphs which replace the IS forms of kin in distance numbers.

Shell Variant

The form of the kin most generally used in distance numbers is an irregular design which has been identified by Beyer (1936a) and seemingly by Spinden (1924, fig. 8*d*) as a conventionalized shell (fig. 31,*1–9*). This form is the same as that of the so-called Glyph Z of the lunar series except that the latter is provided with legs (fig. 31,*10,11*), the attachment of which gives the whole glyph a certain resemblance to a turtle, but the central part does not resemble the design or the outline of the carapace of a turtle. Instead, it is very similar to Maya carvings of univalve shells of the conch type. Accordingly

Beyer's identification is more acceptable, although it is hard to explain the legs attached to Glyph Z unless one makes the somewhat farfetched supposition that they are the humanized legs of a hermit crab. In reversed position and with various affixes attached, this shell sign is the glyph for south on the monuments (fig. 41,*28,30,31,34,36*), and almost surely has the same origin as Cib.

A fairly careful but not exhaustive examination of Maya inscriptions reveals some 45 examples of this glyph in distance numbers: it appears in descending order of numerical occurrence at Copan, Naranjo, Piedras Negras, Palenque, Pusilha, Yaxchilan, Seibal, Uxul, Tonina, Uaxactun, Altar de Sacrificios, and Quirigua. Frequency of examples with coefficients 0–19 are in ascending order: 6,1,1,1?,1,1,2,3,2,1,1,3,4,1,0,2,1,10 (including two probables), 0,4. The large number of examples with coefficients of 17 is noteworthy; the six examples with zero are somewhat high, but may reflect only the predominance of distance numbers in which the kin coefficient is 0. The first glyph of the sculptured panel on the west of the doorway to the sanctuary of the Temple of the Cross, Palenque, with coefficient of 10, might appear at first glance to be an example of this glyph. But there are a number of reasons for not accepting this as a kin glyph: It does not connect a pair of dates, for it stands at the head of a short inscription completely devoid of day signs; it has a "count" bracket to the left, and a suffix different from that found with any certain example of this glyph; the vertical lines joining the base of the loop to the base of the central element are missing, and there is an unusual circle in the bottom right corner. Finally, it should be noted that were this a distance number of 10 days, it would be the only known example of the use of this variant to record an interval of less than 20 days. As will appear later, the Maya usually employed special glyph forms for distance numbers of less than 20 days.

Long-Snouted-Animal Variant

The head form of the kin most generally used in distance numbers is that of some animal with a long snout (fig. 31,*22–29*). In several cases the eye is replaced by a pair of crossed bones. The head, except for the crossed bones, seems to be the same as that which forms the main element of Glyph B of the lunar series, and rather closely resembles the head form of the day Oc. It lacks the infix on the cheek and usually does not have the pointed ear, the characteristics of the month Xul. There has been considerable divergence in guesses as to the identity of this creature, for the head has been variously recognized as that of a dog, a jaguar, an agouti, and a squirrel.

A search reveals twelve examples of this variant of the kin, all occurring in distance numbers:

1. Copan J (W) (Maudslay's Glyph 17). Coefficient 0.
2. Copan J (E) (Maudslay's Glyph 33). Coefficient 12.
3. Copan J (N) (Maudslay's Glyph 41). Coefficient 0.
4. Pestac 1, C6. Coefficient 15.
5. Palenque Sun, C14. Coefficient 16.
6. Palenque Inscriptions (E), G5. Coefficient 12.
7. Palenque Inscriptions (E), M6. Coefficient 14.
8. Palenque Inscriptions (W), G8. Coefficient 8.
9. Naranjo 32, X5. Coefficient 0.
10. Tikal 19, B19. Coefficient 19.
11. Copan HS, Step S11. Coefficient 0. This does not closely resemble the long-nosed animal, but has crosshatched spots which suggest the jaguar. However, as the related animal heads of Glyph B of the lunar series at Copan diverge considerably from the normal, I feel that this head probably belongs with the group of kin variants.
12. Quirigua H, S2. Coefficient damaged. Perhaps 0; might be 14.

Crossed bones replace the eye in Examples 1, 4, 5, 7, 9, and 12. In Examples 3, 6, and 10 the glyphs are too weathered to indicate whether that detail is present. In Example 8 the treelike central element of Kankin appears as an infix on the cheek. In this connection it is worth recalling that the head form for Kankin is that of some animal, conceivably a dog although the long thin snout is absent.

This kin variant takes one of two postfixes, the same pair as occur with the shell variant of the kin previously discussed. One is the "*ak*" affix; the other, *te* (2), is closely related (p. 284). See Addendum, page 296.

Skull-with-Quincunx Variant

A second head form is exceptionally rare, there being but one known example of its use in a distance number (fig. 31,*33*). This occurs on the Tablet of the 96 Glyphs, Palenque, with a coefficient of 7, and comprises the whole distance number, for there are no uinals or tuns. The head has death symbols and the quincunx sign as a headdress. This variant is discussed in detail on page 170.

Sun-at-Horizon Variant

The glyph which has been called sun at the horizon (fig. 31,*41–43*) is used solely when the distance number is of only one day. Two examples occur at Tikal; a third on Naranjo 32. Morley (1937–38, pl. 16) illustrates in a drawing of the inscription on Ixkun 2 another example of this variant with a coefficient of 1, but the calculations do not indicate any addition or subtraction of one day. The photograph appears to show the supposed dot and upper crescent merging into a single element. It is accordingly doubtful that this glyph is a true parallel to the two examples from Tikal and the one from Naranjo.

A kin glyph with a coefficient of 1 is also found on Naranjo 35 at B11a. There is no doubt that this is a distance number of one day because of the dates it connects, but the glyph itself is weathered beyond identification.

Seler (1902–23, 1:731) first proposed the reading of "daybreak" for this glyph, because he considered that the kin element issues from between a cleavage of the sky and earth symbols. Spinden (1924, pp. 147–48) suggests the decipherment "observation of the sun at sunset," similarly recognizing the sky and earth elements; Beyer (1943a, p. 346) interprets the glyph as representing the sun in the day sky. He believes that it means merely day, considering that the Caban element represents not earth, but, like the upper element, sky.

INVERTED-AHAU-OVER-SERPENT-SEGMENT VARIANT

In several cases a distance number of less than 20 days is expressed by a coefficient attached to an inverted Ahau above what has been called the serpent-segment glyph. This serpent-segment element may be replaced by the bundle sign without affecting the meaning, or the inverted Ahau may be duplicated (fig. 31,*12–20*). The Ahau element is inverted when used as an affix, and it has been shown that duplication of an affix does not alter the meaning (Beyer, 1934a, p. 101). One form of the glyph, that with a single inverted Ahau of considerable size, was identified first by Bowditch (1901d, p. 6). Many years later, Beyer (1935b, 1936i) identified two examples with the inverted Ahau duplicated and one with a single Ahau inverted over the "bundle" sign, and Morley (1937–38, 3: 223) adds two with a single Ahau to the list. The remaining identifications are mine (mainly in Thompson, 1944b). Inverted Ahau is a poor name for this variant, because sometimes the inverted Ahau is not the main element, but a prefix. This variant of the kin occurs in the following texts:

1. Quirigua C, I1, with coefficient of 8 (Morley, 1915, p. 72).
2. Piedras Negras 1, F3, with coefficient of 5 and *u* bracket prefix to left (Bowditch, 1901d, p. 6).
3,4. Piedras Negras L 3, L1 and U4, with coefficients of 2 and 3 respectively, but in the latter case, and probably the former, too, the serpent segment is replaced by a diamond-bundle element (Morley, 1937–38, 3:223).
5. Piedras Negras, Altar Support, B4a, with coefficient of 6. Element beneath is diamond bundle. The glyph is somewhat worn, leading Morley to suggest that it may be a winged kin, but the wing is clearly the diamond-bundle element, and the large circle of the mouth of the inverted Ahau is plainly visible.
6. Calakmul 89, D1, with coefficient of 2 and *u* bracket prefix above. Element beneath not identifiable (Morley, 1937–38, 3:223).
7. Yaxchilan L 10, E5a, u.h., with coefficient of 4 and *u* bracket

prefix above. Element beneath is diamond bundle (Beyer, 1935b).
8. Quirigua G, U'1a, with coefficient of 10. Element beneath is diamond bundle. The glyph is worn but there is a circle at the top of the large element which probably represents the mouth of the inverted Ahau. Above is what is almost certainly the *u* bracket. Since this occurs also in Examples 2, 6, and 7, the identification of the whole glyph may be accepted without much hesitation.
9. Naranjo 28, G8, with coefficient of 12 and what may be *u* bracket above. The element beneath appears to be the diamond bundle. The weathered central element might pass as the shell variant of the kin sign, but that variant never has a superfix nor are there any certain instances of its occurrence in distance numbers of less than 20 days.
10. Piedras Negras, Shell Plaque 1, H1, with a coefficient of 6. The Ahau element is duplicated (Beyer, 1936i).
11. Naranjo 29, F18, with coefficient of 3. Two partially defaced circles, forming a superfix, may be duplicated Ahau glyphs in inverted positions. There is a flame prefix to the left (Beyer, 1936i).
12. Naranjo 12, C8b, with coefficient of 4. The serpent segment is fairly clear, and above it are two small circles, presumably inverted Ahau signs.
13. Piedras Negras 8, B24, with coefficient of 3. The serpent segment is fairly clear, and above it are two inverted Ahau signs.
14. Piedras Negras 8, C1, with coefficient of 3. There are two circles above, and these presumably are inverted Ahau signs. To the left of the coefficient is an element which looks like a bar, but must surely be the *u* bracket in view of its presence with Examples 2, 6, 7, and probably 8.
15. Piedras Negras 8, L3. In poor condition. Coefficient may be 3, certainly not over 10. Two circles over main element presumably inverted Ahau faces.
16. Quirigua Alt O, U1a, with coefficient of 8 and *u* bracket above. Morley reads this as "end of Katun 6," but his drawing shows the lower part to resemble the "serpent segment" rather than the tun sign. In the photograph one can, I think, make out the mouth circle of the inverted Ahau. More important, however, is the following glyph which is surely the posterior date indicator. This makes it virtually certain that the glyph under discussion represents a distance number (Thompson, 1945b).

The calculations in connection with all these short distance numbers are straightforward, and can be found in Morley (1937–38) with the exception of no. 6 (Ruppert and Denison, 1943), no. 7 (Beyer, 1935b), nos. 13, 14, and 15 (Thompson, 1944), and no. 16 (Thompson, 1945b).

In nos. 1–9 the inverted Ahau is the largest sign; in nos. 10–14 the single inverted Ahau is replaced by two small elements which in the two cases where details are clear are seen to be pairs of inverted Ahau signs. Beyer (1934a) illustrates examples in which the inverted Ahau, when used as affix, may be carved as a single large sign or as a pair of small signs. One must conclude, therefore, that in all these examples the Ahau is an affix despite the fact that it is frequently larger than the main sign.

Madrid 66b has an inverted Ahau over a postfix lacking detail, and with a coefficient of 3 to the left. This pretty clearly denotes three days, but is not a distance number. Other compartments of this almanac have records of tuns, uinals, and, perhaps, days.

What is probably another example of this glyph occurs on Piedras Negras 9, D7. The glyph is somewhat weathered, but one can distinguish a *u* bracket to the left and a coefficient of 5 above a large glyph with suffix. No cartouche is visible, but there is a circle at the top such as normally marks the mouth of the inverted Ahau; and two smaller circles, which would be the eyes, are perhaps distinguishable below. However, it is possible that this is the shell variant of the kin sign, although nowhere else does that form occur with a *u* bracket. Morley (1937–38, 3:195) reads this as "end of a hotun," connecting it with the date immediately above, and assuming that the distance number of five days is suppressed. However, it is clear that the central element cannot be the cauac sign since it lacks the unmistakable three-quarter cartouche of that element.

There are a few damaged glyphs which form distance numbers of less than 20 days. These occur with coefficient of 1 on Seibal 11 and with coefficients of 2 on Naranjo 12 and Piedras Negras 35. The example from Seibal has a bundle beneath, but of the main element little is clear. The glyph on Balakbal 5 is complex; it certainly is none of the normal forms of the kin. The examples on Piedras Negras 35 and Naranjo 12 have high superfixes and might therefore be the form with inverted Ahau, but they are too weathered to make this identification more than a guess.

Thus we have the following kin variants occurring with distance numbers: shell, long-snouted animal, skull with quincunx, sun at horizon, inverted Ahau and serpent. It is to be understood that these designations are merely handy terms, and do not necessarily imply acceptance of the identifications involved therein.

OCCURRENCES OF KIN VARIANTS IN LUNAR SERIES

Every one of these variants of the kin or some of their component elements occur also in the lunar series. The shell variant with arms and legs attached becomes the so-called Glyph Z of the lunar series (fig. 31,*35,37*). There are four occurrences of the long-snouted animal in lunar series. Together with its coefficient of 15, it is attached to Glyph D of the lunar series of Yaxchilan L 29 (fig. 31,*30*), the combination indicating a moon age of 15 days. A second example of this coalescence, but with a coefficient of 7, on Quirigua E (fig. 31,*31*) declares a moon age of seven days. On Quirigua B this head, with a coefficient of 7 expressed as a full figure, is combined with Glyph E to record a moon age of 27 days (fig. 29,*12*).

On Quirigua Alt O a not very distinct head which is probably the same as that under discussion has a coefficient of 5 and precedes Glyph D of the lunar series. There is no doubt the whole indicates a moon age of five days.

The skull-and-quincunx headdress with a coefficient of 7 is attached to Glyph D of the lunar series of Yaxchilan L 21, the combination declaring a moon age of seven days (fig. 31,*36*). It should be noted that Glyph D is the variant with slit eye, not the form with circular infix which converts the whole to Glyph E. Another example of the skull-with-quincunx headdress attached to Glyph D of the lunar series, but this time with coefficient of 5, is to be seen on the Tablet of the Cross, Palenque, the combination indicating a moon age of five days (fig. 36,*19*).

The skull with quincunx also forms the so-called Glyph Y of the lunar series (fig. 31,*37*), or the skull may be suppressed, the quincunx alone replacing it (fig. 31,*38*). In either case the designation "Glyph Y" should be dropped, since the glyph is not an integral part of the lunar date. As Glyph Y, the quincunx glyph has a coefficient of 5 on Lintels 21, 29, 56, Yaxchilan; it may occur with a coefficient of 7 as Glyph Y on the upper step of the middle doorway, Yaxchilan Str 44, but neither the glyph nor the coefficient is certain. A very clear example, with coefficient of 5, is on a fragment of Yaxchilan 4; as it is apparently followed by a date indicator and a CR, it probably represents a distance number. As already noted, on the Tablet of 96 Glyphs, Palenque, the quincunx skull with coefficient of 7 records a distance number of seven days. With a coefficient of 5 it appears on the murals of Room 1, Bonampak, but not in a calendarial passage.

There are, therefore, six certain occurrences of this glyph with coefficients of 5, two certain and one possible occurrence with coefficients of 7, and no occurrence with any other coefficient on monuments of the Initial Series Period. However, once in Madrid (p. 52) the quincunx is inserted between the numeral 10 and the head of God Q. Nevertheless, there can be little doubt that in this case the coefficient is used primarily in an appellative sense, the number 10 forming part of the name of God Q.

In view of the use of this glyph only with coefficients of 5 and 7, it should be noted that there is a numerical classifier *bix* or *uix* which is used only with the numbers 5 and 7. This occurs with one or both of these numbers in Yucatec, Pokoman, Kekchi, Quiche, and Cakchiquel (Noyes, 1935). Where only one of the two (days 5 and 7) are given, information is lacking on the other number. The Motul dictionary lists *u bix* as an interval of seven days, a week, but it seems probable that after the Spanish conquest only *uuc bix* (seven days) was retained, *ho bix* (five days) falling into desuetude, like other Maya time periods, because it did not correspond to any European time period. With the disappearance of *ho bix, bix* would refer only to the seven-day week and it would be unnecessary to retain the numeral. The Motul dictionary also gives *uucbix,* "a week hence," *uucbixhi* or *uucbixi,* "a week ago," but *u bix pascua,* "the eighth [seventh in our system] day from Easter." The use of this term *bix* for intervals of five and seven days suggests two new time periods. The first perhaps corresponded to the intervals between markets, the fourth part of a uinal (just as the quarters of the katun and of the 260-day cycle were of importance); the second perhaps also denotes a market interval, but it might represent a cycle of the seven days under the rulership of seven lords of the soil. Elsewhere I have discussed the possibility of such a period (Thompson, 1943d). *Bix,* then, would appear to have had some such connotation as cycle of days, the attached number indicating whether it was composed of five or seven days. I do not think that *uuc bix* can be a colonial innovation produced to supply a Maya equivalent to the Spanish week. Had such a term been coined, it is quite probable that it would have been *uaxac bix,* corresponding to the Spanish ocho dias (eight days—one week). Maya, like English but unlike Spanish, does not count both the starting and ending days of a period, but with the breakdown of the old system in the sixteenth century, a Maya term coined as the equivalent of the Spanish week might well have had the number 8 as one of its component elements. Furthermore, it would seem unlikely that the same term would be coined by Yucatec, Pokoman, Kekchi, and Cakchiquel in colonial times when the cultural ties binding the various parts of the Maya area had become very weak; the wide distribution of the expression 5 and 7 Bix is strong evidence for pre-Spanish usage. The same word probably appears in the Jacalteca name for the five days at the end of the year, ho pix (p. 118).

The words *bix* or *uix* supply no likely leads of a phonetic nature. The quincunx, however, was the badge of Venus as morning star (Tlauizcalpantecutli). In the pages of Borgia and Bologna dealing with Venus, this deity has a skull, whereas in Vatican B he has a normal head with the quincunx painted on it. I shall recur to this matter later (p. 172).

The sun-at-horizon combination does not occur in the lunar series, but the *caan,* "sky," element with an unknown element to its left and no coefficient substitutes for Glyph D of the lunar series on Quirigua E to record a moon age of no days (perhaps conjunction). It is possible, although far from certain, that there is a four-petaled kin sign in the center of this element to the left (fig. 36,29).

The inverted-Ahau-over-serpent-segment variant is probably recorded in the lunar series of Copan 9 (fig. 31,21). The main element is the head of God C with a coefficient of 5 above, and an Ahau face set on its side as a prefix to the left. The whole substitutes for the regular form of Glyph D of the lunar series and indicates a moon age of five days. By the rules of Maya affixes, a prefix may be placed above or to the left of the main element without altering the meaning in the slightest way, and the same edge of a prefix usually adjoins the main element whether the prefix be placed to the left or above it. Thus if the Ahau is inverted above the main element, its corresponding position to the left is on its side with top of glyph (the eyes) touching the main element. This is precisely the arrangement in this lunar text.

God C is perhaps the most elusive deity in the Maya pantheon. With the *u*-bracket prefix he is god of the north, but with color prefixes he is associated with all four world directions; with a coefficient of 9 and held in the hand, he functions as the first of the nine lords of the nights. Most significantly, the shell variant of the kin with legs, and also with a coefficient of 9, replaces him as lord of the night on Yaxchilan 6. Therefore God C equates with the shell variant of kin. God C can also substitute for the long-snouted animal of Glyph B of the lunar series (Copan P, 3, and 19, and perhaps Pusilha H) and, inserted in the jaws of a celestial dragon or serpent, he is an important element of one of the forms of Glyph X of the lunar series. In a somewhat similar manner his head sometimes serves as the headdress of the long-nosed skull which is inserted in, or by itself forms, the rear head of the double-headed celestial monster. More usually, however, the headdress of this long-nosed monster with bared lower jaw consists of the four-petaled kin sign surmounted by a triple ornament (see Seler, 1915, figs. 101–16). In one case the *caan,* "sky," sign replaces the four-petaled kin. Thus again God C equates with a kin sign, this time the four-petaled variant. (See p. 296.)

We conclude, therefore, that as God C can replace both the shell and the four-petaled variants of the kin sign, he also can function as a kin sign. This conclusion is reinforced by noting that he can substitute for the animal head of Glyph B of the lunar series, which, in turn, seems to be closely allied to the animal-headed variant of kin.

An examination of the so-called serpent-segment element makes it abundantly clear that the circle at the left with its curving line is an exact reproduction of the peculiar mouth of God C. This identification does not necessarily conflict with that of serpent segment, for the serpent segment may well represent the body of the serpent dragon from which God C emerges.

The head of God C without an inverted Ahau attached may also replace Glyph D of the lunar series. An example of this may be seen on Copan N, where God C has a coefficient of 1, indicating a moon age of one day (fig. 36,1). Here again, therefore, God C equates with kin.

SYMBOLISM OF KIN VARIANTS USED IN DISTANCE NUMBERS

As yet a common symbolism or meaning to link these various forms of kin is lacking. Such must be sought in order to give a coherent interpretation of these sundry signs used in distance numbers.

Of the five variants, the so-called caan-kin-caban or sun-at-horizon glyph appears the most promising from an ideographic point of view. Seler and Spinden independently concluded that the glyph represented the sun at the horizon because the sun is squeezed between two symbols which for many years have been accepted as representing sky and earth respectively. Beyer (1943a) appears to be the only writer who has challenged this interpretation; he considered that both symbols represent day sky, and therefore the whole means sun in day sky, that is, merely day. However, the evidence is strongly against such an interpretation.

Seler and Spinden differ, however, in one respect. Seler writes: "The sun disk issues from a cleavage between the hieroglyphs sky and Caban, an easily comprehensible picture of daybreak"; Spinden considers the glyph to represent sunset. Actually we have no information as to the starting point of the Maya day (24-hour period) during the Initial Series Period or, in fact, until modern times. Among the modern Jacalteca and Ixil it starts at sunset.

Ralph L. Roys, in a correspondence with me on the linguistic side of this problem, points out that the sky-sun-earth glyph seems to correspond very nicely to a Yucatec term for morn, *hatzcab,* which appears to be compounded of *hatz,* "divide or part," and *cab,* "earth." There is no linguistic evidence, however, for the use of the numeral one with this term, but this lack of numerical corroboration is purely negative, and there is similarly no evidence for the use of the number one with any Maya word for sunset. Yet it is not without importance that Seler should have recognized this form as depicting dawn by a cleavage of sky and earth by the sun, although apparently unaware of the fact that this action closely parallels one of the Maya terms for morning.

An examination of the inverted-Ahau-over-serpent-segment reveals its similarity to the symbol for east in the Maya codices, which is an inverted Ahau over (sometimes to the side of) the four-petaled kin sign (fig. 41,1–4). We have already noted that serpent segment probably

equates with God C, and that that in turn can serve as a substitute for the four-petaled kin under certain circumstances. It is, accordingly, a fair assumption that inverted-Ahau-over-serpent-segment and inverted-Ahau-over-four-petaled-kin may have the same symbolic value. Inverted-Ahau-over-four-petaled-kin is the glyph for east, but in Yucatec *likin,* "east," means literally sunrise. Similarly the words for east in Tzeltal and Cakchiquel mean sunrise, whilst the eastern Chol term appears to mean "where the sun grows strong." There is therefore good, but not unchallengeable, evidence that the glyph inverted-Ahau-over-serpent-segment means sunrise, and therefore agrees with the best interpretation of the caan-kin-caban glyph.

The long-snouted and quincunx variants have in common a rather marked tendency to display symbols of death, although these are not always present. The quincunx, as already noted, is a symbol of the Mexican deity Tlauizcalpantecutli, the god of Venus as morning star. The complete Maya glyph for the planet Venus resembles a quincunx, consisting of four circles, one at each corner of the glyph, and a central element which is usually a sort of diamond with incurving sides (figs. 7,52–56; 42, 31). The quincunx is frequently set on the regular four-petaled kin glyph, apparently without altering its value in any way (fig. 26,51).

In Mexican and Maya belief the sun, after setting, traveled during the night through the underworld, land of the dead, so as to emerge next morning once more in the east (Cline, 1944). The Mexican manifestation of the sun at the eastern horizon, Tlalchitonatiuh (literally "sun on the ground"), appears in Bourbon as a mummy; on Borgia 18 a deity who is apparently the sun god, for he has a sun disk on his back, is depicted as aged and with a bared jawbone, and as the scene is the underworld, one may assume that the jawbone indicates his nocturnal transit through the realm of death. According to tradition, Quetzalcoatl appeared as morning star after being dead for eight days, the period between disappearance of Venus as evening star and the planet's reappearance as morning star. As Venus as morning star is frequently depicted with death symbols, one may assume that he obtained these in his journey through the underworld during the eight days between his disappearance in the west as evening star and reappearance as morning star in the east.

There is therefore evidence that both the sun and Venus were believed to take on characteristics of death during the passage through the underworld, and to retain these at the moment of rising. Parenthetically one might remark that the purpose of human sacrifice to the sun (and perhaps to Venus, too) may not actually have been to nourish an already plump solar deity, but more specifically to clothe the skeleton of the sun with flesh in replacement of what he had lost in his nocturnal journey through the underworld. This act of donning a carnal garment may be reflected in the Manche Chol term for the east, *tzatzibcin* (*tzatzibkin*), which seems to mean strengthening of the sun (*tzatz,* "strength"; *kin,* "sun").

Provided the above assumption is valid, the deity with skeletal features and the four-petaled kin on his forehead, who frequently forms the rear head of the celestial dragon or emerges from it, is some manifestation of the sun at the moment of rising. The presence of the long ophidian or draconian snout makes it doubtful that these heads directly represent the sun, but there can be no doubt that they have an intimate association with the solar deity.

These various incursions into the realms of Mexican and Maya mythology supply cogent reasons for accepting the quincunx and death symbols as indicative of dawn or sunrise.

The identification of the long-snouted head is not easy. Because of the shape of the nose and the general resemblance to heads of Oc and Xul, I am inclined to recognize it as a dog. On the other hand, Tozzer and Allen (1910, pl. 35, nos. 6, 9) class as jaguars heads which closely resemble those under discussion. Both the dog and the jaguar are intimately associated with the underworld, the former because he led the sun and the dead to the underworld; the latter because the jaguar god is a denizen of the underworld (p. 74). The crossbones which are frequently set over the eye confirm the association with the underworld.

This head, therefore, whether it be that of a dog or of a jaguar, clearly refers to the sun in the underworld or at the moment of its emergence therefrom at sunrise.

In Maya symbolism the shell represents the earth, the underworld, and death. The association perhaps arose from the water in which the earth crocodile floats, just as the water lily symbolizes both water and earth because of its intimate association with the earth crocodile. Alternatively, the conch or similarly shaped shells were the symbols of parturition, an idea prevalent in central Mexico, and since birth and the surface or interior of the earth were intimately associated in Mexican and Maya thought, the univalve shell came to have the more general meaning of earth.

The earth god, the Mam, is frequently depicted wearing a shell on his back or emerging from a shell (fig. 21,3–7). The glyph of the sun god (G9) as lord of the night consists of the head of the sun god or the four-petaled kin sign surmounted by three shells (or death eyes) or by a vegetal motif, also a symbol of the earth (fig. 34,46–57). Often, too, part of the four-petaled kin

sign, whether standing alone or worn as the headdress of the sun god, has part of its area crosshatched, the symbol for black, to denote either the interior of the earth or darkness.

The glyph for south on the monuments is an inverted shell with certain affixes (fig. 41,28,30,34,36), but south is the land of the death god, the realm of the dead, the underworld. A design of great frequency in the art of the Initial Series Period, as noted above, is a representation of the long-nosed dragon god without a lower jaw or with a skeletal jawbone, but wearing the four-petaled kin sign on his forehead. The head is usually surmounted by three elements, a central leaf-shaped ornament which is flanked on one side by crossed strips of such frequent occurrence in planetary bands; on the other side, by what has been generally recognized as a conventionalized shell. Sometimes the design appears as the rear head of the dragon, and it forms a glyph (fig. 21,14–18).

In Mexican art the conch is the symbol of Tepeyollotl, the jaguar god of the interior of the earth, and is frequently placed beside the "night eye," the symbol of darkness (fig. 21,9–13). It is also a symbol of birth, a function of which the moon goddess was the patroness, but the moon goddess among the Mexicans, as among the Maya, was also a deity of the earth. Xolotl, the canine god who led the way to the underworld, wears the conch ornament and so does Quetzalcoatl, who after residing eight days in the underworld, emerges as Venus the morning star, and as such was known as Tlauizcalpantecutli, "Lord of the dawn."

Tecciztecatl, "he of the conch shell," is a somewhat elusive deity. He is the god of the week 7 Miquiztli on Bourbon 6, where he is opposite Tezcatlipoca, and has the conch shell and night eye in close proximity. Since the day Miquiztli (the sixth week and the sixth day are both Miquiztli) is the sign death, we cannot fail to see in this deity a god of the interior of the earth, a Mexican equivalent of the Maya conch man, the Mam. Itztlacoliuhqui, as lord of the twelfth week, also has the conch as his symbol, and the night sky is in the picture. His name means "god of frost," and he appears to be merely a variant form of Tlauizcalpantecutli, god of the morning star, who was also Cetl, god of cold. Since the dawn hour is the coldest of the day, it is not unnatural that the god of the morning star should also be a god of frost and cold. Furthermore, Itztlacoliuhqui is one of the manifestations of Venus as morning star in Dresden (p. 50).

As lord of the twentieth week, 7 Tochtli, Xiuhtecutli has the conch and night eye near his person in Bourbon and in the Aubin Tonalamatl; as I have shown (p. 134), he was believed to dwell in the interior of the earth.

It is thus apparent that both in Maya and Mexican

symbolism the univalve shell betokens the earth, the underworld, and darkness. Used in distance numbers as a substitute for the normal kin signs, it would appear to have the meaning of night, or, since it is associated closely with the morning star, it may stand for dawn or sunrise.

It is not immediately apparent why these variants should occur in distance numbers but not in IS, or why the sun-at-horizon glyph should be used only in recording intervals of one day. Similarly, no explanation is forthcoming as to why the inverted Ahau variant should be used only to record intervals of eight days and less (there are, however, two or three possible examples of this variant with coefficients above 8 but below 20). It is probable that these variations correspond to linguistic differences.

If the use of the skull-with-quincunx variant only with the numbers 5 and 7 really corresponds to a linguistic arrangement, as is strongly suggested by the use of *bix* with those two numbers, it is probable that the sun-at-horizon and inverted-Ahau-over-serpent-segment forms have similar linguistic correspondences. Yet, as already noted, there is no known case of the use of a number with *hatzcab,* the assumed translation of the sun-at-horizon variant.

In connection with the possibility that the inverted Ahau variant might correspond to some specific term or numerical classifier, Ralph L. Roys calls my attention to the use in Yucatec of *pach,* a numerical classifier given in the Motul dictionary. This is used for enumerating birds and certain animals, but only in counts of 9–19 inclusive. Since there is this numerical classifier for numbers 9–19, there should be another attached to the numbers 2 (or 1) to 8. *Pach,* so far as we know, was not used as a numerical classifier in reckoning days, but as there was a special classifier used in counting birds from 9 to 19, and presumably another term for counts of less than nine birds, there may well have been a similar arrangement in telling days, in which some term with the meaning of sunrise was employed for intervals of two to eight days. In that case this would correspond to the glyph of the inverted-Ahau-over-serpent-segment (provided, of course, that that glyph can not be used with coefficients of more than 8).

In English we can speak of an interval of less than a month as so many mornings later—"He left, but returned three mornings later"—but we can hardly say, for example, "two years, a month, and three mornings later." To express intervals composed of months and days, or years, months, and days we would use only the word "day" to denote the lowest unit; the glyphic material suggests a similar arrangement may have existed among the Maya.

The suggested interpretations of these variant forms for kin are summarized below.

COUNT BY SUNRISES, NIGHTS, OR SUNSETS

GLYPHIC EVIDENCE

We have seen that in distance numbers kin is expressed by:

1. A glyph which appears to represent parting of the earth, and which probably corresponds to the Yucatec term *hatzcab.* This word has precisely that meaning, and is used to denote daybreak, although the Motul dictionary says the term applies to the whole morning.

2. A glyph (inverted-Ahau-over-serpent-segment) which corresponds indirectly to that used by the Maya for the east, called in Yucatec *likin,* "sunrise."

3. Two glyphs (the animal head and the *"bix"* glyph) which customarily display prominent emblems of death. It has been shown that in Mexican and Maya mythology the sun was believed to pass through the underworld, the land of the dead. Representations in Mexican codices of the sun and Venus at the moment of rising not infrequently carry symbols of death, as though to imply that at the moment of rising the elements of death acquired in the journey through the underworld had not yet been shed. A combination of death symbols with insignia of the sun on the rear heads of sky monsters probably carries the same connotations.

4. A glyph which is almost certainly a conventionalized picture of a conch or some other species of univalve. Such shells in Maya and Mexican symbolism represent the earth and its interior, the underworld and death, the last because the abode of the dead was in the interior of the earth. By the addition of what may be death eyes or shells the sun god becomes, as lord of the night, the night sun; the deities who are connected with the interior of the earth or who have sojourned there wear conch shells or ornaments made from them. The shell glyph, therefore, would indicate a count by nights, or perhaps by dawns, or sunrise if the symbols of the underworld were still undoffed at sunrise.

All these variants, therefore, have associations with the night or with dawn or sunrise. This conclusion is reinforced by finding these same variants, with the exception of the *hatzcab* glyph combined with glyphs of the lunar series. The lunar series presumably was a count by nights. On the whole, I think it is most probable that together the glyphs in question point to a count by sunrises, for whereas two of the glyphs appear to have the restricted meanings of dawn and sunrise, the other three stand for night in a general sense but probably have, in addition, the specific meaning of dawn or sunrise. One is therefore led to the conclusion that during the Initial Series Period distance numbers were reckoned by dawns or sunrises, or even perhaps by nights. If distance numbers were counted in that way, IS dates must surely have been reckoned in a similar manner; otherwise terrible confusion would have arisen.

PRESENT-DAY USAGE

The present-day Jacalteca (La Farge and Byers, 1931) and the present-day Ixil (Lincoln, 1942) count their days from sunset to sunset, but it is far from certain that a sunset-to-sunset count was widespread in the Guatemalan highlands. Goubaud (1937) in describing the 8 Batz ceremony at Momostenango (p. 94) rather gives the impression that the day begins at sunrise, although he describes ceremonies which start the previous evening and continue through the second night. In answer to a letter from me he writes (April 1945) that he has no additional information on the 8 Batz ceremony to clarify this matter, but he supplies some very interesting information on practices elsewhere in the Guatemalan highlands:

As regards religious ceremonies, it may be well to distinguish between those of a decidedly preconquest character, and those of Catholic origin. For the first Rosales has given me a very good case which would show that the day in the ceremonial calendar of 260 days begins immediately after midnight. He consulted a shaman for a propitious day in which to do a certain task. The shaman recommended the day Kan to do the ceremony in the hills. They went to the place on the night previous to the day Kan, about eleven o'clock at night, when the shaman performed certain rites. But he did not start his rites to Kan until past midnight. The previous rites may have been to Akbal, Rosales could not tell me. This happened in San Pedro la Laguna.

In San Pedro la Laguna the staffs of office for the town official are changed at midnight of the 31st December, as at Chichicastenango. The holy day Todos Santos begins at midnight too. Indians believe that at midnight the souls of the ancestors come out of the graves. The officials of the religious brotherhoods (*cofradías* [sodalities]) receive their offices from former officials at 4 P.M. of the previous day to the day in which the change of office actually should take place. The saint is taken to the church at 12 noon of the following day, when formal exchange of office takes place. But the receiving brotherhood has a marimba playing in the church past midnight of the day when formal exchange of office takes place. Visiting of altars in the hills (*en el monte*) takes place at midnight.

Lastly, and general for all municipio cultures that I know of for Guatemala, the Indians have a system of ceremonies whereby they celebrate a Catholic religious day during two days, i.e. on the day preceding the actual day in the Catholic calendar, and the actual saint's day. This previous day is called *visperas* by the Indians in the central part of Guatemala.

As against the day beginning past midnight, I have information from San Juan Sacatepequez, for religious ceremonies in which the day begins at daybreak. Candles are placed in the church early in the morning of a holy day. But my informant was not conversant with shaman practices in the hills, so we cannot say that for the 260-day calendar they do not place them at midnight in the hill altars.

I am a little more conversant with the Kekchí of Chamelco. There, the 260-day calendar is not in use. Old shamans to whom I spoke did not know of it. The sacred days are called by the Spanish names of *Martes, Jueves,* etc. Although a shaman woman performed health rites for me in Chamelco, I am unable to say (from my field notes) the precise hour at which this woman went to light candles at various places of the village for my health. I only know that she told me that she would place some candles at night in the *hermitas,* or wayside shrines, and other candles during the day, in the church.

The Kekchí, as you know, have the Tzultaká as their main deity. Since they do not use the tzolkin, they do not seem to have geared their religious ceremonies to specially significant days, as far as I know. The Chamelco Kekchí have a special ceremony against the wind which blows down their corn fields in September. The ceremony is held about the middle of September in the various caves in the vicinity of Chamelco. Groups of men and women, elders of the community, hold a prayer meeting in a house, at night, about 9 P.M. of the day previous to which they go to the caves. They go to the caves before the day breaks.

Furthermore, the pattern of the dual day is seen among the Kekchí of Chamelco in the Catholic rituals connected with the *cofradías.* The outgoing cofradía takes the saint to the church, from the cofradía house, on the day previous to the change of office. At 5 P.M. they go to the church to take it back to the cofradía, where the incoming cofradía awaits them. Ceremonies and a ritual meal are held that evening, and all during the night there is ceremonial drinking at the cofradía house. On the following day, the saint is taken to the church where the Catholic priest does the formal exchanging of cofradía *varas* [wands of office], by handing them to the new *cofrades.* The saint stays in church all day, until 5 P.M. when it is taken back to the new cofradía house. Both cofradía groups (outgoing and incoming) spend the night in ceremonial eating and drinking.

The custom of the *visperas* probably has a European origin so far as church festivals are concerned, or it may be a blending of Maya and European concepts. There is, however, a possible explanation of the 24-hour day starting at sunset among the Ixil and Jacalteca. In Yucatan, as we shall see (p. 204), there existed a peculiar arrangement by which katuns began to hold power 10 tuns before they officially entered. The incoming katun was the "guest" of the old katun and shared power with him. Thus Katun 13 Ahau officially ran from 1519 to 1539. In 1509 he began to share power as the guest of the preceding katun; from 1519 to 1529 he held sway alone; from 1529 to 1539 he was host to his successor. Unless this arrangement was a regional development, one would expect tuns, months, and days to share their powers in a similar way throughout the Maya area.

If a day started to hold power at sunset, 12 hours before

his real entry, that would supply an exact parallel to the katun practice of Yucatan, for 10 tuns are half the span of a katun just as one night is half the length of the kin. Alternatively, if the day officially began his reign at midnight, he may have held power also for the first half of the night. This arrangement, too, would be a parallel to the katun as guest, although the parallel would not be quite so close as in the other case. In time such a practice, assuming that it existed, might have given rise to the habit of attaching the name of the day, not to his true reign, but to the interval during which he held power. Alternatively, the all-night vigil, which seemingly originated in a desire to insure group continence (Thompson, 1930, p. 44) may have produced the shift for the start of the day to the preceding evening.

Evidence in Literary Sources

For Yucatan there is, so far as I am aware, no direct evidence as to when the day started. Had it been at sunset one would have expected some mention of that fact by Bishop Landa, for such an arrangement could not have failed to arouse the curiosity of that first student of Maya culture. Moreover, Landa had the benefit of well-educated informants, two of whom clearly had an intimate knowledge of the calendar. Had they been accustomed to a sunset-to-sunset count, the midnight-to-midnight reckoning of the Spaniards would have seemed equally strange to them and should have elicited comment on the difference. There is one piece of evidence that favors a count by sunrise: according to the Relación de Valladolid, at new year all arose to await the rising of the sun. In early colonial times sacrifices took place at night, but according to a Maya chief the reason for that was the danger of being caught by the Spaniards (Scholes and Adams, 1938, 1:108). At the present time the Yucatec Maya consider that the day runs from midnight to midnight, but that may be a result of European influence.

Evidence for a count by dawns or midnights is scant in the books of Chilam Balam. In the story of the birth of the uinal in Chumayel (p. 60) we read that the uinal was created in the east. "This was the count after it had been placed in order by 13 Oc, after his feet were joined evenly, after they had departed there in the east." And later: "The uinal was born, the dawn was created. . . . the setting in order of the sequence of the days according to the count, beginning in the east, as it is arranged." From these passages one can infer that the count of the first day started in the east, and therefore in all probability this took place at dawn or sunrise. On page 96 of the same book occurs the sentence, "This was when it dawned on our account"; on page 87 in connection with the prophecy for Katun 11 Ahau, "You shall see its dawn."

It seems to me that the idea of a count from sunset is contrary to the whole philosophy of the Maya. The real start of time, as opposed to the theoretical extension of time far into the past, was the creation of the sun, presumably the last sun. The sun could hardly have been created at the moment of sunset. Such an arrangement, involving the disappearance of the new glory almost as soon as it had manifested itself, would have lacked all dignity. Indeed, the accounts of the creation of the sun, both Mexican and Maya, indicate that the orb first appeared in the east.

In the story of the creation as given by Sahagun (1938, bk. 7, ch. 2) the sun appears in the east; in the Codex Chimalpopoca we are not told directly where the sun first appeared, but, after being stationary some time, he crossed the sky, so one can infer that he rose in the east. According to Popol Vuh (8th tradition), the people awaited the first sunrise. The morning star rose, and then the sun. At the time of its appearance the sun had little strength, presumably because it had just emerged from the land of death (p. 172). The world as it is today therefore began at sunrise both in Mexican and Maya tradition.

Most students are of the opinion that the Aztec day ran from midnight to midnight. The great ceremony of the kindling of the new fire at the end of every 52 years took place at midnight (Sahagun, 1938, bk. 7, ch. 11), and that would suggest a count from that moment. In fact elsewhere Sahagun (1938, bk. 4, appendix, final section) says that as soon as the constellation of the Pleiades had passed the zenith the people were assured that the world would not end but would endure another 52 years. On the other hand, we are informed that the great fear was that the sun would not rise. That rather suggests that the new cycle may have started at sunrise, and that new fire was kindled at midnight so that it could be distributed to the surrounding towns before sunrise.

Another possible line of evidence in favor of a count by sunrises is to be found in the remark which, according to Sahagun (1938, bk. 7, ch. 1), the Mexicans made at sunrise: "Now the sun begins his task. What will it be? What will happen on this day?" Had the day commenced at midnight, the latter part of this remark should have been made then. Furthermore, a count from midnight to midnight would have raised complications with regard to the rule of the lords of the nights. Each ruler of a night would have held sway over parts of two days.

Thus there would appear to be evidence favoring a count among the Mexicans from midnight to midnight and also from sunrise to sunrise; among the Maya, from sunrise to sunrise or sunset to sunset or perhaps midnight to midnight.

BALANCING OF EVIDENCE

The evidence of the kin variants used in distance numbers strongly supports a count by dawns, sunrises, or nights; literary testimony, particularly that connected with the creation of the world, favors a count by sunrises. I know of no evidence suggesting that the Aztec may have counted from sunset to sunset. Instead, the contestants are midnight and sunrise, with arguments in favor of both. Despite the importance of midnight in the new-fire ceremony, I think it unlikely that such an artificial point of departure was employed, and I would imagine that emphasis on midnight among the present-day Maya of the highlands of Guatemala is due to European contacts.

The Maya custom of counting in elapsed time might be thought to favor a reckoning by sunsets, yet sunset was not journey's end for the sun, for he spent the night traveling across the underworld. As it was at sunrise that the sun renewed his strength, once more clothing his skeleton in flesh, that would appear to be the moment when one sun ended and another began. The use of the word *kin,* "sun," to describe the whole period of 24 hours negatives the possibility that the Maya, like many primitive peoples (Nilsson, 1920) counted preferably by nights. That attention was paid to a count by nights is shown by the importance attached to the lords of the nights (pp. 208–12). Furthermore, on page 21 of Chumayel, which contains notes on both the European and Maya calendars, occurs this entry: "the count of days in one year, 365; the count of nights in one year, 365." Roys calls attention to the significance of this reference to a count by nights in a document of such late date.

The evidence is far from conclusive but, so far as it goes, rather favors a count from sunrise to sunrise during the Initial Series Period. The Jacalteca and Ixil reckoning from sunset to sunset may have arisen from the "guest" concept or from the custom of all-night vigil.

DIVISIONS OF THE DAY

The discussion of the point from which days were reckoned brings us to the question of divisions within the day. No glyph for a period of less than a day has yet been identified, and it is clear that "hours" did not enter into the LC or distance numbers recorded in the inscriptions and in the codices. Nevertheless, it is more than probable that the day and night were divided into parts. In truth, some such division would have been almost indispensable for astronomical computations.

The Motul dictionary gives *lat'ab kin* as meaning hour, and lists *"hun lat'ab kin, ca lat'ab kin, una, dos horas."* *Hech* is another numerical classifier which, according to Beltran and the Motul dictionary, was used in counting hours and pages of a book. The existence of these terms is fair evidence that the Maya had regular divisions of the day, for usually the Spanish word for an entirely new concept was borrowed by the Maya, as, for example, the term *semana,* "week"; and as the Spanish term *hora,* "hour," was also adopted by the Maya, one can assume with a fair degree of certainty that *lat'ab kin* was a term for divisions of the day in use prior to the Spanish conquest.

That the Maya were interested in divisions of the day and night is perhaps to be seen in a notation in Perez, page 93, of the numbers of hours of day and night throughout the year. The Spanish months are listed with their lengths in days, the length of the moon (alternating 30 and 29 days), the hours of day, and the hours of night:

January, 31 days; moon, 30 days [written *horas* here; *dias* correctly for other months]; the day, 8 hours; the night, 14 hours (*sic*).
February, 28 days; moon, 29 days; the day, 10 hours; the night, 14 hours.
March, 31 days; moon, 30 days; the day, 12 hours; the night, 12 hours.
April, 30 days; moon, 29 days; the day, 16 hours; the night, 8 hours, etc.

The alternating moons of 30 and 29 days are a pre-Columbian survival; the peculiar divisions of the hours must result from some blending of ancient Maya practice and Spanish custom. It certainly does not reflect actuality, for the length of the day varies little throughout the year in the latitude of Yucatan, and a variation from eight hours of daylight to 16 is far from nature's division. Can these figures have been copied from an almanac printed for use in Flanders? Even then the transcription shows an interest in divisions of the day.

Seler has suggested that the Mexicans divided the day into 13 hours, and the night into nine, the compartments corresponding to the 13 day lords and the nine night lords. There is no confirmatory evidence of this suggestion, but it is what one might expect. The Aztec priesthood appear to have divided day and night into nine ritualistic periods, for they made offerings at fixed intervals, four times during the day and five times during the night. These divisions, of course, may have had nothing to do with standard parts of the day, but may reflect only a ceremonial rhythm.

So far as is known, the Maya had no way of measuring with accuracy the length of their divisions of the day and night; according to Rodaz (1688), the Tzotzil did not distinguish hours but used the term *oc* for a short indeterminate time. Pantaleon Guzman gives Cakchiquel terms for divisions of the day. The English equivalents of some of these are: now the sun has jumped up, now the sun is out, now the sun is high, midday, afternoon, after eating, sun falling, night entering, first cockcrow, second cockcrow, midnight, third cockcrow, very early in the morning, before dawn, and becoming light. There is some confusion and obvious repetition. Altogether 28 terms are listed. Thus for the period before sunrise we find seven terms, the Spanish equivalents of which are given as *al amanecer, cuando ya para amanecer se va obscuriendo, la obscuridad para amanecer, antes de amanecer, ya está claro, por la mañanita, por la mañana, ya amanece*. Obviously all or most of these must be alternative ways of expressing the same period.

Antonio Goubaud sends me a list of 19 divisions of the day and night collected by Juan Rosales at the Cakchiquel town of Panajachel. The same divisions, he informs me, hold good also for Solola and San Pedro de la Laguna. They are: coming out of the sun, sun already up, sun already far away, a little to midday, noon, past midday, falling sun, a little for the fall of the sun, sun has fallen, night has entered, night already up, a little to midnight, night already far away, midnight, first rooster, second rooster, third rooster, fourth rooster, and becoming light.

The occurrence in both lists of various cockcrows must indicate European influence, but in neither list is there a division into 24 hours. The Rosales list gives nine divisions of the day and 10 of the night. The fifth division in the one group corresponds to midday; to midnight, in the other. If the last cockcrow is regarded as the same as "becoming light," we would get nine hours of day and nine hours of night symmetrically arranged with four hours on each side of midday and midnight. Such an arrangement is, of course, purely conjectural. I would have expected to find 13 day hours and nine night hours to bring the count into relation with the 13 gods of the upper world and the days and with the nine gods of the underworld and the nights. The trouble with such an arrangement is that the night hours would then be longer than the hours of daylight. It is perhaps worth noting that the 18 hours, as amended, are just twice the number of ritualistic periods at which the Aztec made offerings (p. 177). Moreover, the Zapotec divided our 24-hour day into 18 parts, apparently nine for the night and nine for the day. As listed in Cordova's *Arte* the terms correspond approximately to those of the Cakchiquel. It is therefore quite possible, although far from certain, that among the Maya day and night each may have had nine divisions,

and in that case the Maya hour may have been of approximately 80 minutes duration. Elsewhere (Thompson, 1935, pp. 90, 91) I have cited some very dubious evidence for a division of the night into hours of 80 minutes.

LITERARY CURIOSITIES

There were definite canons of literary style, to which Maya writers were expected to conform. In the main they so did, but there are a few examples of glyphic presentation which are definitely in bad style. For the most part these date from the last katuns of the Initial Series Period, an age in which art styles, also, show some evidence of failure to maintain orthodox standards. Two or three examples of this decadence will be reviewed.

The text of Quirigua C opens on the east side with the IS 13.0.0.0.0 4 Ahau 8 Cumku, presented in perfectly regular manner save that the lunar series is defective. At the top of the west side there is an IS introductory glyph followed by what at first sight appears to be an IS recording the date 9.1.0.0.0 6 Ahau 13 Yaxkin. There are, however, three features which are irregular: (1) There is no lunar series. (2) The posterior date indicator, which has the special function of indicating that a distance number is to be counted forward to the date which it precedes, is present between the 0 kins and 6 Ahau. (3) The distance number postfix is attached to the tun sign. These irregularities are such that one can only conclude that the priest who prepared the drawings for this text was no respecter of literary style, a kind of forerunner of Gertrude Stein. He, too, lived in an age when literary standards were debased. The paragraph is neither an IS nor a distance number. It is a literary curiosity.

The opening glyphs on the back on Copan 4 have been read as the IS 9.8.15.0.0 10 Ahau 8 Zec by Morley (1920, pp. 356–57). To reach that reading it was necessary to suppose that Glyph Block B2, then missing, carried 15 tuns, 0 uinals, 0 kins. The compression of three periods of an IS into one glyph block would be without precedent. Recently, Glyph Block B2, which had flaked off, was found by Gustav Strömsvik and cemented in its original position. It does not show tuns, uinals and kins, but instead the anterior date indicator, which follows distance numbers, and indicates that the CR date to which it is juxtaposed, in this case 10 Ahau, is the earlier of the pair united by a distance number.

Most irregularly the inscription opens with the head variant of the distance number introductory glyph, and this is followed by the IS introductory glyph, the central variable of which is somewhat weathered, but as drawn in Maudslay is clearly the moon element, indicative of the month Ch'en. The distance number postfix shows with perfect clarity beneath the baktun and katun signs.

The month sign is gone, but presumably it was in the right half of A3, alongside the day Ahau. The baktun coefficient lies between 6 and 10; the katun coefficient is clearly 8.

The presence of the distance number introductory glyph, the prominence of the distance number postfixes, and the addition of the anterior date indicator show that this is a distance number; the IS introductory glyph alone supports the idea that an IS is given. However, attention has already been called to several examples at Copan of IS introductory glyphs not followed by IS.

At A5b there is another distance number introductory glyph, but this is not followed by a distance number. In A6–A7 there is recorded the date 11 Ahau 18 Zac which is declared to fall on the fifteenth tun: the LC position of this date is 9.14.15.0.0.

If the baktun coefficient is restored as 9, the text can, perhaps, be reconstructed as follows:

A3	(13. 6.15.0.0)	10 Ahau (18 Uo)
A2	9. 8. (0.0.0)	Add
A6	9.14.15.0.0	11 Ahau 18 Zac

Such an arrangement disagrees with the IS introductory glyph which appears to demand the month Ch'en. Alternatively, one can regard 10 Ahau as an error for 5 Ahau, and reconstruct the text as:

A2	9.8. (0.0.0)	Add (to 4 Ahau 8 Cumku)
A3	9.8. 0.0.0	5 Ahau (3 Ch'en)

Whether this reconstruction is correct or not, there is no doubt of the irregularity of the presentation, for the passage breaks all the canons of Maya literature; it is unforgivable.

An even more irregular presentation is that of Chinkultic 7 (Blom and La Farge, 1926–27, p. 432). There are only five glyphs on this monument, and these record an irregular IS 9.17.10.0.0, but the IS introductory glyph and the terminal date, 12 Ahau 8 Pax, are missing. The suppression of the CR date represents a most extraordinary failure to supply what in Maya eyes was the essential part of the text. Furthermore, the baktun glyph consists of only one cauac element, instead of the normal two, and the tun part of the katun glyph is in two parts, the lower half forming what one would regard as a postfix did one not know better. The tun sign has an irregular postfix. These strange aberrations may be due to the location of Chinkultic, almost the ultima Thule of the Maya area, on the border of the Guatemalan highlands.

Two stelae from Santa Rosa Xtampak, Campeche, which is also a peripheral site, have IS which appear to lack terminal dates. although because of weathering this is not absolutely certain. One has an IS 9.15.19.0.0; the other, what appears to be 9.15.19.17.13, although the katun coefficient is open to question. One wonders whether in these three cases the missing terminal dates may not have been recorded on altars which have not been recovered; as the inscriptions stand, they are highly irregular. The second IS of Lacanha 7, 9.6.0.11.0 8 Ahau 18 Zac, lacks the tun sign and coefficient, presumably because the latter is 0, or could this have been an error of omission on the part of the sculptor?

SUMMARY

Distance numbers, also called secondary series, bridge the interval from one Maya date to another by addition or subtraction. As the LC position of at least one date in a text is usually given by means of an IS or a PE, distance numbers serve to place CR dates also in the LC by linking them by addition or subtraction to dates, the positions of which in the LC are given directly or by calculation.

Distance numbers may be as little as a single day or they may span millennia. The periods of which they are composed are customarily arranged in ascending order, in contrast to the descending order of the IS.

Period glyphs used in distance numbers are the same as those used in IS, with the exception of the kin glyph. A special postfix indicative of a distance number is usually attached to one or more of the period glyphs, and thus serves to differentiate the periods of a distance number from those of an IS. It probably reflects a linguistic usage.

The kin glyph is often suppressed, and its coefficient attached to the uinal glyph. If the kin sign is present, it may take one of five different forms, none of which ever occurs with an IS, but three of which are of frequent occurrence in the lunar series. Elements of the remaining two also appear in the lunar series.

In all five variants there are indications of a reckoning by sunrises, dawns, or nights. A review of material on the subject in the literature suggests rather strongly that the Maya counted by sunrises, not by sunsets as appears to be the custom among the present-day Jacalteca and Ixil. The start of the day at sunset may have arisen in a development similar to that of the guest katun, in which a katun began to have power 10 tuns before its official beginning, or it may have evolved from the vigil of continence before a ceremony.

One kin variant, with a quincunx design, appears only with coefficients of 5 and 7. It may well correspond to the numerical classifier *bix*, which is used only to record five days and seven days, and which may indicate the intervals between markets. Another variant, used only to express an interval of one day, appears to be a picture of sunrise or dawn, and probably corresponds to the Yucatec word *hatzcab.*

Distance numbers of 20–39 days inclusive are expressed in the divinatory almanacs of the codices by means of a moon glyph, with a value of 20, and a coefficient which is added to the 20. Thus 31 would be represented as a moon glyph with a coefficient of 11. This method was also employed in inscriptions of the Initial Series Period to denote distance numbers within the same limits. The practice must be of considerable antiquity since it is found on Balakbal 5, a Baktun 8 inscription.

Periods with coefficients of 0 could be suppressed. Thus 1.10.0.0 is given as a distance number on Copan U as a katun glyph with one dot above and two bars to the left. At Yaxchilan, 10.0.6 is written as a tun sign with two bars above, a bar and dot to the left. Distance numbers are often preceded by an introductory glyph, the central element of which vaguely resembles a swastika. It is possible that the whole glyph corresponds to the Yucatec *hel,* "change." There is a head variant of this introductory glyph.

Frequently there stands between the distance number and the terminal date one of two glyphs, which indicates whether the distance number is to be counted forward or backward to reach the terminal date. The main element of the glyph is the same in both cases, consisting of the head of the *xoc* monster or, in the symbolic form, the sign for jade (water). In the case of a count forward (posterior date indicator) the forward glyph is used as a prefix; the locative *ti,* "at" or "to" or "from," as a post-fix. In the case of a count backward (anterior date indicator) there is no prefix, but two postfixes, one of which is the locative *ti;* the other, a sign indistinguishable from the distance number postfix. These glyphs may also be attached to the starting date of a distance number to indicate whether the count is backward to or forward from that point. At Palenque there is a special variant, a squiggly eel or snake, which replaces the anterior date indicator in some texts.

There are other glyphs which lie between distance numbers and terminal dates, and reveal the nature of the count. One form probably indicates that the distance number leads to the seating of a tun; another may warn that the terminal date is not a tun ending. At Piedras Negras and El Cayo there is a combination which means "forward to daybreak" or "forward to sunrise," and there are yet other glyphs with such general meanings, the use of which surely corresponds to variations in the spoken sentence.

The discussion of the point from which days were counted leads to the question of a possible division of the day into hours. The evidence is far from complete but, such as it is, rather suggests nine "hours" of daylight and nine "hours" of night. The Maya "hour" in that case would equal 80 of our minutes, although it is to be doubted that the Maya accurately measured the subdivisions of the day.

The chapter is concluded with some examples of degeneration in Maya literary style.

8
Period Endings, Anniversaries, and Katun Counts

Mellow'd by the stealing hours of time.
—SHAKESPEARE, *Richard III*, Act 3, Scene 7

PERIOD ENDINGS

THE RESTING PLACES, the *lub*, of the eternal march of time were of transcendent consequence to the Maya. Each birthday of creation was celebrated, were it the end of a tun, a katun, or a baktun, the importance of the event naturally depending on the length of the period which was concluded. The end of the tun was of such frequent occurrence that it received little or no attention in the inscriptions, although if a date chosen for some other reason happened to coincide with the end of a tun, a note was made of that fact. Likewise, the priest-astronomers tried to manipulate their calculations so that they could reach the end of a tun. Let us suppose that the priest-astronomer found that the date 9.12.6.13.16 was the solar anniversary of some date he wished to note. I think we are safe in assuming that, unless there was some special reason for that choice, he would shift the calculation forward 16 solar years, and make it fall on 9.13.3.0.0, a tun ending.

The ends of katuns were of supreme importance to the Maya and around them revolved many, probably most, of the calculations contained in the inscriptions of the Initial Series Period. The end of a baktun was naturally of even greater importance, but this was such a rare event that a dozen generations of priest-astronomers made their contributions to science and passed to the bosom of Abraham without the privilege of witnessing such an outstanding event. Baktun 9 ended before the stela cult was well developed; Baktun 10 completed its journey in a period of decadence. Here I am speaking of baktuns in the Maya sense; in the incorrect modern usage these would be called Baktuns 8 and 9.

As presumably the Maya were then, as now, short-lived, the average priest-astronomer witnessed two or, at the most, three katun endings in his lifetime, and one of these would have fallen before his graduation in sacerdotal lore. Considerable attention was paid to the half-katuns, and the quarter-katuns, too, received their meed of honor.

Morley has shown how the largest cities strove to erect a monument to commemorate every quarter-katun. There is an almost complete sequence of texts marking the quarter-katuns (the so-called hotuns) at Piedras Negras and Quirigua; other cities set up stelae and altars to honor the katuns and half-katuns, whereas still others frequently solemnized the quarter-katuns in stone but did not habitually do so. In some cases more than one stela was erected in connection with the end of a katun: Calakmul, where 103 stelae have been discovered, on various occasions erected several stelae in homage to the same katun, and even dedicated three or four at each of several half-katuns, but carved very few at quarter-katun intervals. A few monuments were dedicated at the ends of 13 tuns, and there are a handful of inscriptions which have as their latest date the end of an odd tun, but no regular PE. Naranjo 29, with the date 9.14.3.0.0 7 Ahau 18 Kankin, is a case in point. This date apparently was chosen because it is the katun anniversary of 9.13.3.0.0 9 Ahau 13 Pop, also given in this text, which presumably had for the Maya some astronomical significance not now apparent.

INFLUENCE OF THE KATUNS ON DAILY LIFE

From the abundant material on the subject, it is manifest that the divinity of each katun exercised full power during his reign over mankind, although that may not have coincided with the duration of the katun because of the guest concept (p. 204). As in the case of the gods of the days, some katun rulers were benign; others, malevolent. It must be confessed that the Maya, who were hardly given to facile optimism, expected a harsh rule more frequently than benevolence. The influences of 13 lords of the katuns (i.e. the days on which each katun ended) are set forth in the various prophecies for the katuns contained in the books of Chilam Balam. The tidings of the katuns according to Chumayel (pp. 87–100) are as follows:

11 Ahau "Niggard is the katun; scanty are its rains . . . misery."
9 Ahau No definite information, but Tizimin has: "Bread is mourned, then water is mourned . . . excessive adultery."
7 Ahau Carnal sin, roguish rulers.
5 Ahau "Harsh his face; harsh his tidings."
3 Ahau Rains of little profit, locusts, fighting.
1 Ahau "The evil katun."
12 Ahau "The katun is good."
10 Ahau "Drought is the charge of the katun."

181

8 Ahau "There is an end of greed; there is an end to causing vexation . . . much fighting."

6 Ahau "Shameless is his speech."

4 Ahau "The quetzal shall come . . . Kukulcan shall come."

2 Ahau "For half the katun there will be bread; for half the katun there will be water."

13 Ahau "There is no lucky day for us."

Thus, only the reigns of Katuns 4 Ahau, 8 Ahau, and 12 Ahau were beneficent; Katun 2 Ahau was halfway lucky; the portents for the other nine were direful in the extreme. The luck of the katuns in Tizimin and Mani is not precisely the same as in Chumayel. Mani assigns to Katun 4 Ahau drought, poor crops, and epidemics. Nevertheless, I think the expected return of Kukulcan in Katun 4 Ahau places it in the lucky class. The association of the Itza with Katun 4 Ahau would have caused that katun to have been lucky for them, but the unpopularity of the Itza due to their arrogant and sinful behavior, perhaps at first not evident, may have caused their special katun to become baleful for other groups in Yucatan. Accepting 4 Ahau as beneficent, we note that the favorable rulers have coefficients which are 4 and its multiples, 8 and 12. These, presumably, were well inclined toward man because four is the lucky number of the sun and the milpa. It is interesting to note that in the frequency of day signs (p. 91) 4 Ahau, 8 Ahau, and 11 Ahau tie for first place; 12 Ahau follows immediately behind, and at Santa Eulalia (p. 93) 4, 8, and 12 are good and 13 is very good. The multiples of 4, accordingly, may represent an ancient and widespread grouping for good luck, and from this one can perhaps infer that the aspects of the katuns had been generally established far in the past. Nevertheless, if we are correct in supposing that the aspect of 4 Ahau was affected by its association with the Itza, it follows that the pattern of the luck of the katuns was not inviolate. That is quite understandable. The Maya were both intelligent and conservative: they started with the premise that a katun brocaded the same design each time the stuff of history was in its hands, but their experience showed them that that was not always the case, for an evil design might be produced by a katun listed as favorable. Their reasoning would impel them to revise the aspect of that katun; their conservative instincts would warn them not to make innovations in an ancient and sacred formula. Probably, as seems to be the case with Katun 4 Ahau, one group would revise the aspect of the katun; another, more conservative, would retain the old pattern. Withal, the important point is that the aspect of the katun was predicted, and that form of predestination profoundly affected Maya life, both corporate and individual.

The fortunes of the katuns not only influenced the everyday life of the community, they also affected history, noted by Roys (1933, p. 184) and elaborated by Morley (1938, pp. 558–62). Roys says: "A katun of the same name recurred after approximately 256 years, consequently, at the end of that time history was expected to repeat itself. The events recounted in the Maya chronicles . . . offer excellent grounds for believing that this belief was so strong at times as to actually influence the course of history. A surprising proportion of the important upheavals in Maya history appear to have occurred in some katun named either 4 Ahau or 8 Ahau."

In Yucatec the fortune of the katun was generally called *u uich,* "his face," or *u kuch,* "his burden" (p. 202).

Changes, conquests, and migrations seem to have been the burden of Katun 8 Ahau, although it is not improbable that one of the events, which is referred to separate recurrences of Katun 8 Ahau, may in fact have been assigned two different positions 13 katuns apart by the compilers of the chronicles, although in reality it happened but once. Furthermore, coincidences invariably receive more attention than they warrant. Apparently great changes were expected in any Katun 8 Ahau; when they occurred they were given prominence, but one suspects that lots of important events in other katuns were less well remembered because they did not happen to conform to the expected patterns. Those who plotted to overthrow the Cocoms of Mayapan were probably fortified in their hopes of success by the fact that a Katun 8 Ahau was then running its course, but under the circumstances the revolt would probably have taken place whatever the katun, save that waverers would have shown more inclination to join the revolt in a Katun 8 Ahau because they would have taken into consideration its bellicose aspect. Although, therefore, the destinies of the katuns certainly affected the pattern of Maya history, and imposed on the individual a marked fatalism, yet the results of such influences can be exaggerated. At least, it can be said of Hunac Ceel, the one live actor on the stage of Maya history, that he shaped his own destiny. Many accept predestination in theory but disregard it in practice.

The sundry matters probably involved in assaying the fortune of the katun have been briefly sketched. They are not directly pertinent to the present discussion of methods of recording the ends of katuns, and will be dealt with as occasion arises in other chapters.

COUNT BY ENDING OR BEGINNING DAYS

It is now taken for granted that Maya periods, be they tun, katun, or baktun, are not counted until they are completed, and that they are named for the day on which they end. Goodman held the opposite view, namely that the katun was named for its beginning day. Even Morley (1910) was of the same opinion as late as 1910, but subsequently accepted the contrary view. Since the above was written Fulton (1947, 1948) has challenged our complacent acceptance of these ideas. Withal, the evidence for a reckoning by the ending day is very strong, for throughout the books of Chilam Balam the completion of the katun receives constant attention.

Roys has called my attention to a passage in Tizimin (p. 13), which gives the prophecy for the last tun of Katun 5 Ahau. One sentence reads: "13 Oc would be the day when the katun is measured by paces, and 4 Cauac would be the turn of the fold of the katun, the time when he gives up his mat, his throne. There comes another mat, another throne, another reign. The burden of 5 Ahau falls. He looks back, when he took what was granted to him. Gone is his cup, gone is his mat, gone is the bearer of his command."

As 4 Cauac is the day before 5 Ahau and is placed in the last tun of the katun, there is good evidence in this passage that Katun 5 Ahau ended on the day 5 Ahau.

If the proposed method of reading Maya dates in the Yucatec system is correct—and I feel reasonably certain that it is—then the katun must be named for its closing day, otherwise the system will not work (p. 196). A date, such as the IS of Xcalumkin which reads 9.15.12.6.9 7 Muluc 1 Kankin in Tun 13 in Katun 2 Ahau, will be incorrect if the katun was named for its opening day. Katun 9.16.0.0.0 opens on 4 Ahau (or 5 Imix) and ends on 2 Ahau. This system, therefore, provided it is correct, is strong evidence for the naming of katuns by their ending days.

Apart from any other considerations, the opening day of a katun was almost certainly Imix, not Ahau. Thus, had katuns taken their names from their opening days, in all probability they would not have been called 11 Ahau, 9 Ahau, etc., but 1 Imix, 12 Imix, 10 Imix, etc. That the opening day of a katun was Imix, not Ahau, rests on two lines of reasoning: the katun of the creation according to Chumayel was Katun 11 Ahau (Tizimin and Mani start the story in Katun 13 Ahau), but if 11 Ahau is assumed to be the last day of the katun, 1 Imix was the opening day; we know from various sources that 1 Imix was the starting point of the cycle of 260 days, and one can assume that it was similarly the start of other counts. Likewise, the books of Chilam Balam state that 11 Ahau was the first katun of the count, and it is so marked in at least one katun wheel. The information is added that 11 Ahau became the first katun because the Spaniards conquered Yucatan in Katun 11 Ahau, a statement which is surely incorrect, for the whole mechanics of the Maya calendar would have been disrupted had the

starting point of the katun round been shifted. Furthermore, had the katuns been counted by their starting days, the elaborate system of matching the various cycles by finding their lowest common multiples would have gone awry, for it would have been contrary to the fundamentals of the Maya calendar to try to harmonize the sacred almanac of 260 days, running from 1 Imix to 13 Ahau, with a long count which ran from 11 Ahau to 8 Cauac.

In the Chronicle of Chicxulub, paragraph 33 (Brinton, 1882, pp. 210, 236), it is stated that Ah Naum Pech told the people that on 1 Imix the bearded ones would come with the sign of Hunabku (the one God), and that the people must go to receive them. This reference to the coming of the Spaniards and Christianity is a condensation of the prophecy for Katun 11 Ahau which speaks of the sign of Hunabku and of the reception of the bearded men (Chumayel, pp. 87, 88). Ah Naum Pech gives the gist of the prophecy but does not name the katun by its day 11 Ahau, on which it would end; instead he refers the event to the day on which the katun begins. A second version of this prophecy in Chumayel (pp. 105–06) immediately follows a statement that the katun will expire (*u hitz'i uil katune*) on 13 Ahau, but the Tizimin and Mani versions change that to the establishment of the katun (*u hetz'i uil katun*) on 13 Ahau, thereby shifting the prophecy from Katun 11 Ahau to Katun 13 Ahau. This is clearly an error due to careless copying.

If Katun 11 Ahau began on the day 11 Ahau, the reference to 1 Imix has little meaning, but if the katun is completed on 11 Ahau, as seems almost certain, then the choice of 1 Imix, its opening day, as that on which action was to be taken on the prophecy is very much to the point. This statement from the Chronicle of Chicxulub is, accordingly, good evidence for the thesis that a katun was named for the day on which it was completed.

The Annals of the Cakchiquels (Brinton, 1885) throw some light on this subject. The Cakchiquel reckoned by years of 400 days, 20 of which formed a cycle called *may*, comparable to the katun although of 8000, not 7200, days. The zero point of the count was a day 11 Ah, which marked a revolt. The day 3 Ah is marked as the completion of one *may* from that date, and, indeed, it is precisely 8000 days from 11 Ah. I do not know whether Brinton is correct in his use of the word "completion" in this and similar passages, but if 11 Ah is the start of the first year of a *may*, then 3 Ah is not the completion of the twentieth year, but the start of the twenty-first, yet the passage indicates that the twenty-first year coincided with 13 Ah. There are numerous other statements noting the conclusion of sundry years and *mays* after 11 Ah, all of which fall into the pattern.

Direct evidence from Maya sources and the indirect evidence of all we know of the mechanics of the Maya calendar and of the Maya philosophy of harmonizing concurrent cycles of time support the view that the katun was named for its ending day.

RECORDS OF BAKTUN AND KATUN ENDINGS

The ends of baktuns and katuns are expressed by means of the respective glyphs with the required coefficients and one or more of a number of prefixes or prefatory glyphs or both, which express such ideas as "completion of" or "count of." These statements, the precise meanings of which are discussed on page 187, almost invariably follow immediately a record of the date in question, so that the whole reads, for example, "6 Ahau, 13 Muan, completion of count of 14 katuns, haab completed" (fig. 4; 36). That is to say, 14 katuns have elapsed since the completion of the last baktun, in this case Baktun 9 in Maya thought. The endings of baktuns are similarly recorded. The first three glyphs on the front of Uaxactun 13 read: "7 Ahau 18 Zip, tenth baktun" (Morley, 1937–38, vol. 5, pl. 6, *a*). Rather rarely, the order may be reversed. Palenque, Foliated Cross, C7–D8, reads: "Forward to the completion of the second baktun, 2 Ahau 3 Uayeb" (fig. 32,*11*).

A statement, such as 6 Ahau 13 Muan, completion of count of 14 katuns, fixes the position of a date without equivocation, for such a date can not repeat for 949 baktuns, approximately 375,000 years. Even a simpler statement, in which the katun number is unspecified, places a date in the LC with sufficient precision for most purposes, for 6 Ahau 13 Muan will not again end a katun for 949 katuns, which is slightly less than 19,000 years. This is so because there are 73 month positions on which a katun can end and 13 possible coefficients of Ahau. Even the statement "count of tun completed" at tached to a date is sufficient for most purposes, for any given tun ending can not recur until the lapse of 949 tuns (the same combination of 73 month positions and 13 coefficients of Ahau).

Naturally, such a system of recording was to all intents and purposes as accurate as the IS. That the Maya generally used IS to record PE dates at the start of an inscription merely demonstrates that they were not interested in efficiency, but sought to honor time with the grandiloquence of the IS.

Because in sixteenth-century Yucatan katuns were not numbered according to their positions within the current baktun, but were identified by the day on which each ended and sometimes by its position in the round of

13 katuns, there exists no close parallel between glyphic texts such as "6 Ahau 13 Muan, count of 14 katuns" and references to katun endings in the books of Chilam Balam.

HAND SYMBOLS FOR COMPLETION

The most ornate, but not the commonest, ending sign is a prefatory glyph which consists of a hand with fingers pointing to the right and generally upward. This is usually combined with either a moon sign or a conventionalized element which has been identified as a shell (Spinden, 1924, fig. 8). Sometimes both are present (fig. 32,*1–11*).

The position of the hand appears to have been important both in Maya art and in hieroglyphic writing. In sculpture and in paintings on pottery the hand is often shown in the same position, as though gestures were as significant as in Buddhist and Brahmanic art. The hand which serves as the glyph for Manik is the right, and is almost invariably shown with tips of forefinger and thumb touching or nearly meeting. Position varies from the vertical to near horizontal, and the back of the hand is exposed to view. Examples on the early Uaxactun murals are the only exceptions (fig. 7,*35–50*). In contrast, when used as an ending sign the right hand is usually outstretched with thumb parallel to the fingers and, as noted, in a horizontal or slightly diagonal position, palm inwards. Sometimes the fingers, other than the index, are slightly flexed at the first joint; usually the index finger points to a small bonelike tassel (fig. 32,*1–11*). Less commonly, the left hand serves as a completion sign. It is upright with palm outward, and fingers other than index slightly flexed sometimes grasping lightly some bent object which might be a wand or even a snake. When the hand is used in an IS with period glyphs to express zero or completion, it occupies the same position as with a PE (fig. 25,*57,58*).

With Glyph C of the lunar series the right hand is generally used in a horizontal position, pointing to right, with the dorsal part to front and without noticeable flexing of the fingers. In Glyph D the hand is in a more diagonal position, and may be the right hand, with back to the observer, or the left hand, with palm to the front. In either case the index finger is in a pointing position, the other fingers somewhat flexed, although there are a few exceptions in which the index finger does not point. The problem is to determine whether these are badly carved or whether the pointing forefinger is an unimportant element in this presentation of the hand (figs. 36; 37).

In a number of glyphs of unknown meaning the hand is placed horizontally with fingers pointing to left, but thumb vertical. The variable element—kin, head of God C, inverted Ahau, uinal, etc.—rests on the side of the hand in the angle formed by the horizontal line of the fingers and the vertical line of the thumb (fig. 46,18–23). To the best of my knowledge, the position of the hand is invariable in this group of compound glyphs and it is, I think, always the left hand. Again in the glyph of the hand holding a fish the hand is always the left, and is always shown palm to front with the fingers and thumb flexed to grasp the fish (fig. 30,60–63). The hand glyph, identified on rather weak evidence as the sign for grasping, is common in Dresden (fig. 42,62–64). So far as the hand itself is concerned, it is always placed in the same gesture as Manik, and is always the right hand. In the codices the hand in the sign for west is like that of Manik, but in the inscriptions it takes another form (fig. 41, 14–19).

Other examples of the use of the hand in glyphs could be cited, but enough has been written to show that the position of the hand does vary to a certain extent according to the glyph in which it occurs. Nevertheless, the divisions are not clear cut; the glyphs showing horizontal position with fingers slightly flexed blend with those which favor the diagonal position with pointing index, and in those, in turn, occur examples which approach the Manik form. In the case of Glyph G1 of the lunar series the normal form of the hand with fingers pointing to the left and thumb upright is in one text replaced by a grasping hand in the same position as in the glyph of the hand holding the fish (fig. 34,1–7). From the above we are led to conclude that whereas certain positions were favored for certain glyphs, there was a good deal of overlapping. This was probably artistic license permitted only in the case of well-known glyphs, easily recognizable by their positions in the text. In the case of lesser known glyphs, such as hand grasping fish, and inverted Ahau, kin, God C, etc., enclosed in the right angle between thumb and fingers, no such deviations appear to have been tolerated.

There is inconclusive ethnological evidence that the position in which the hand is held affects the meaning. Wirsing, in some fragmentary ethnological notes on the Kekchi, shows a drawing of the left hand held in an almost vertical position, with fingers tightly flexed and thumb resting on top of the index finger. He notes that the hand is held in that position to indicate height or growth of children, animals, and crops, adding, "the other sign is not allowed. It stops growth." Unfortunately the other sign is not described or drawn. I had assumed that this implied that some other position of the hand indicates stoppage of growth, that is to say, completion. However, I have since been informed by Mr. Joe Cason,

who has made ethnological investigations in the Guatemalan highlands, that in some areas use of a hand gesture which refers to the height of an inanimate object will endanger an animate object if employed to indicate its height. This, of course, does not eliminate the possibility that a hand gesture may indicate completion of growth, but it does emphasize that categories of gestures are as distinctive as those of numerical classifiers.

Antonio Goubaud has most kindly taken the trouble to gather information for me from various ethnologists in the highlands of Guatemala on the use of the hand to express size or growth. Although these do not bear directly on the subject, they are listed below as examples of the Maya preciseness in detail and of the importance they attach to variations in gestures:

1. Hand vertical with fingers and thumb close together to indicate height of a person. Distance is from ground on which one stands to the hand of the speaker (San Pedro de la Laguna); same but with fingers cupped to show height of person (Nahuala).
2. Hand vertical with fingers together but thumb slanting out to indicate size of a vessel or gourd (San Pedro de la Laguna). Same position with back of hand toward questioner to show size of person or child (San Bernardino Suchitepequez).
3. Hand horizontal with palm toward questioner to indicate height of quadrupeds, such as horses and cattle (San Pedro de la Laguna); same but with thumb upright used for quadrupeds (San Bernardino Suchitepequez).
4. Hand horizontal with palm down to show size of birds (San Pedro de la Laguna).
5. Hand horizontal with palm up to indicate growth or height of plants and depth of rivers or lakes (San Pedro de la Laguna). The same position is used at San Bernardino Suchitepequez to indicate size of young plants of maize, cotton, rice and yucca.
6. Hand horizontal with fingers closed to indicate height or size of a bundle or bag of maize, beans, etc., or of a bottle of rum or beer (San Pedro de la Laguna).

Early writers on the Maya describe two signs with the hands: the right hand on the left shoulder was a sign of submission (Villagutierre Soto-Mayor, 1933, bk. 2, ch. 2); raising the hands together was a sign of peace (Lopez de Cogolludo, 1867–68, bk. 3, ch. 6).

That the hand, as used with counts of katuns, must mean end, or completion, or something very similar rests on four arguments:

1. Evidence already given that katuns (and therefore their multiples or divisions) were counted by their ending days.
2. Deduction that the hand sign as used in IS must signify completion or zero (p. 137), but the zero concept is eliminated by Argument 1.
3. A word meaning end or completion is constantly used

in connection with the ends of katuns in the various books of Chilam Balam.

4. Whereas it might be argued that the hand sign with, for example, 15 katuns might mean "start of Katun 15," the use of the hand with katun anniversaries proves that it cannot have the meaning of start. The date 9.14.13.4.17 12 Caban 5 Kayab is very prominent at Quirigua. Quirigua D has as one of its two IS the second katun anniversary of that date, to wit 9.16.13.4.17 8 Caban 5 Yaxkin. This date is followed by a hand sign, the head of the *xoc* fish, signifying count, and then the katun sign with a coefficient of 2 (fig. 33,*26*). This must mean "end of the count of two katuns." It cannot mean "start of the count" because in that case the coefficient of the katun would have to be 3, for the date would be the start of the third katun after 12 Caban 5 Kayab. The hand must indicate the completion or end of two katuns. There are other examples of the use of the hand with one-katun anniversaries (fig. 33,*25*).

The Maya words used for end or completion of a katun derive from the root *tz'oc*, which as a noun means "end, finish, conclusion." It occurs in verbal forms, as *tz'ocol*, "finish or conclude something," and the participle *tz'ocaan*, "just finished or completed." In Mani we find: *ma tz'ococ u xocol oxlahun Ahau*, "Will not be ended the count of [katun] 13 Ahau." In Chumayel occur passages such as *He ix bin tz'ocbal nicte katun lae*, "This shall be the end of the katun of the plumeria" (p. 96); *Ya ix bin tz'ocebal nicte katun*, "In sorrow shall end the katun of the plumeria" (p. 65); *Tz'oc ix u kuchul tu kinil u tz'ocol yahaulil yetel u tepal halibe*, "The time has come for the end of his [Katun 3 Ahau] rule and reign. It is finished" (p. 28); *Tz'oci lay lae*, "Then he [Katun 11 Ahau] ended" (p. 21); *tu kin u tz'oc katun*, "at the time of the ending of the katun" (p. 12); *U tz'oc katun talzabi Ix Tziu nene*, "at the end of the katun when *Ix Tziu nene* was brought." The term *tz'oc* is similarly used in Tizimin: *tu tz'oc u cuch katun*, "at the end of the burden of the katun" (p. 13) and again on the same page *tu kin u tz'oc katunob*, "at the time of conclusion of the katuns."

There is another term for end or, more precisely, expiration, used in these pages of Tizimin, namely, *hitz'*. This is discussed on page 189. As we shall see, there is probably a distinctive prefatory glyph and a distinctive affix which correspond to this linguistic expression.

The root *tz'oc* does not appear to have any connection with the hand, but that is understandable, for the hand sign is without much doubt derived from gesture language. I think, then, that we can be positive that the hand sign in these contexts means "end" or "completion," and fairly certain that it corresponds to the word *tz'oc*.

Although the use of the hand to express completion is probably a case of gesture language, it might be an ex-

ample of rebus writing: *lah* is a root meaning "to complete," "to end," but it also signifies "to slap with the open hand."

In some cases the hand sign is combined with a lunar glyph to form a prefatory glyph. In that compound the moon sign appears to be an example of rebus writing, for *u* not only signifies moon but is also the term for the possessive. Thus the combination could correspond to *u tz'oc* or *u tz'ococ* as given in the books of Chilam Balam.

This was the interpretation I suggested a few years ago (Thompson, 1944, p. 19), but I am now less certain that it is correct, although I believe that the lunar sign is still to be read rebus fashion. Among other uses of *u* is that of converting a cardinal number into an ordinal. As we shall see under the next heading, the bracket element also stands for the sound *u*, and the lunar postfix and the bracket prefix are interchangeable under certain conditions. However, the *u* bracket occurs with numbered katuns and other period glyphs which lack a prefatory glyph, and it can hardly represent the possessive *u* in such cases. A good example of this practice is supplied by the so-called hotun glyph (fig. 32,*36–40*), which never has a prefatory glyph. Moreover, when the *u* bracket follows the hand glyph, the lunar glyph does not appear with the latter, indicating that they have the same meaning in these clauses as in others, and the appearance of both would be pure redundancy. Accordingly, I feel confident that hand, moon, 15 katun, for example (fig. 32,*4*), should be read "completion of the fifteenth katun." This question of the conversion of cardinal numbers into ordinals is discussed below at greater length.

To return to the hand as a prefatory glyph, there is commonly below the outstretched hand an element which has been rather generally identified as a shell. Shell also has the meaning of completion, for it is used as such (the so-called zero sign) in the IS and distance numbers of Dresden (fig. 25,*59*). Why this meaning should have arisen is not now apparent, although it may have developed from the use of a shell to mark the completion of each unit in a primitive count (cf. Spinden, 1924, p. 158). As thus used it does not appear to have any connection with the shell as a symbol of the underworld, unless conceivably it represents the idea of death as the finish. It appears also with the hand symbols for completion used with period glyphs in IS. Perhaps its purpose is to indicate that the hand is to be read in such cases as completion. (See also p. 138.)

"COUNT" GROUP OF PREFIXES

There are four distinct prefixes and two or three variants of these which are used with tun, katun, and baktun glyphs with coefficients to mark the ends of periods. They are:

The *u* bracket (figs. 32, *12,13;* 33,*21,23,25,27,30*).
The flattened fish head (fig. 32,*14,34*).
The bracket with line of dots (figs. 4,*36;* 5,*48;* 32,*15*).
The death eye (figs. 32,*17–19;* 33,*22,24*).

All four have generally been translated as "end of," but it is extremely probable that only the last actually has that meaning.

The fish head, as already pointed out (p. 162), is a rebus for the word *xoc*, "count," which is used in connection with periods in the various books of Chilam Balam. For example, the first chronicle of Chumayel starts with the words *u kahlay u xocan katunob*, "the record of the count of the katuns." In Mani we find *tz'ococ u xocol oxlahun ahau*, "ended the count of [Katun] 13 Ahau," and in Tizimin, *uacp'el hab u binel ca tz'ococ u xoc oxlahun ahau*, "six years to go to the end of the count of [Katun] 13 Ahau." The Motul dictionary lists *u xocan haab, u xocan kin*, "all the years or each year, all the days or each day." The actual meaning must be "the count of the years, the count of the days." The Chronicle of Chicxulub gives *lai cu xocol yabil*, "here the count of the years." There is, therefore, ample evidence that the root *xoc* was used for counting periods and for recording their ends.

In spite of this, the glyph of the *xoc* fish occurs only rarely with a PE date; instead, we find the flattened head of a fish to which reference has already been made above. Moreover, the comb affix, the symbolic variant of the *xoc* fish (p. 162), does not appear with PE; instead, we find the bracket with line of dots. Similarly, the flattened fish head never replaces the comb affix in a number of combinations, notably the glyphs of the months Mac and Zec and the double Imix glyph (fig. 5,*14,15*).

As affixes have from their very nature to be narrow, one would normally expect a fish head flattened to the breadth of an affix to correspond in meaning and function to the regular *xoc* head used as a main element, but the issue is clouded by the confinement of each form to separate categories. Fortunately, there are enough exceptions to this rule of mutual exclusion to justify the extension of the meaning of *xoc*, "count," to the flattened fish head:

1. In the only case of which I know where the fish is used as a prefatory glyph to a PE, this takes the form of the *xoc* fish (fig. 5,*50*). This indicates that when the flattened head prefix is converted to a main element it assumes the regular *xoc* form.

2. Very rarely the anterior date indicator (p. 163) has the *ti* part as its main element (personified as the head of a vulture with the *ti* on its forehead). In one such case the *xoc* head, displaced from its position as the main ele-

ment, becomes a prefix and takes the form of a flattened fish head (fig. 4,*29*). Therefore when the *xoc* main element is changed to a prefix it can be carved as the flattened fish head.

3. The flattened fish head is a common prefix of the distance number introductory glyph, Glyph B, completion of the haab glyph, and the caban glyph, but in all four glyphs there are rare cases of the *xoc* head being substituted for the flattened form (fig. 5,*20,31,42*, perhaps *26;* Copan I, D2a). These four cases, accordingly, supply full confirmatory evidence that the *xoc* head and the flattened fish head are interchangeable, the latter being a prefixal form, the shape of which was imposed by spatial considerations.

The comb, as noted, does not appear with PE or with a number of other glyphs with which the flattened fish head is used. In its place we find the bracket with line of dots, usually three or four in number, but this appears to derive from the same original as does the comb, for comb and dots are combined in the lateral appendages of the IS introductory glyph (fig. 5,*8*). Yet we again have the situation of one affix occurring with some glyphs; the other with a different set. The question again arises whether we are dealing with two distinct signs, and once more the answer must be in the negative, for there are rare cases of one being substituted for the other:

1. The double Imix glyph, often the final glyph in a text, almost invariably has the comb affix, but according to Miss Breton's drawings (the photographs are not sufficiently distinct to supply confirmation) it is replaced by the bracket with line of dots on Yaxchilan L 13 and L 56. Once the bracket with line of dots replaces the comb as the postfix of the glyph with crosshatched center (Palenque Inscriptions, east, S12). These three cases show that comb and bracket with line of dots have the same value. In both cases the head of the *xoc* fish or a full-length fish (figs. 5,*16;* 11,*60*) can replace the comb, assuring the *xoc* identification.

2. Once the bracket and line of dots as a prefix replaces the *xoc* head as main element of the anterior date indicator (Pusilha D, C10). In this case two things (bracket with line of dots and comb) being equal to a third (the *xoc* head) must be equal to one another.

3. In one postfix of the glyph with crosshatched center (Copan Q, west side) dots and comb appear together, blended into a single element.

Although there is good evidence for giving the same value to comb and bracket with line of dots, the situation is somewhat fogged by the substitution in Madrid of what appears to be the comb element for the *u* bracket. Withal, this is probably a case of fortuitous convergence, for in all likelihood this Madrid affix is a simplification of the bracket with sawtooth (fig. 61,*5*, Glyphs C1,E1) which in Dresden has the same value as the *u* bracket. At Quirigua and Copan the *v* of the *u* bracket is occasionally shown as a circle (fig. 11,*40*). Such examples closely resemble the bracket with line of dots, but in the latter glyph the circlets are always small, often more than three in number, and often enclosed by a line connecting the two horns of the bracket.

With our present knowledge it is difficult to surmise why certain glyphic forms, such as those just discussed, should be confined to one group of compounds, whereas others, with precisely the same meaning, should be used exclusively with another set. Probably it is a matter of traditional usage, but I have wondered if grammatical construction may not enter: a substantive might call for one form; a verb, with the same root, for another.

Having established that the flattened fish head and bracket with line of dots have the value of *xoc,* "count," let us return to the discussion of this group of prefixes. The *u* bracket prefix casually resembles the Venus half-glyph, but this resemblance, as well as that to the decorative design often seen on the pottery vessels in the codices, is surely fortuitous. It is difficult, almost impossible, to hazard an acceptable guess as to its derivation because of the extreme conventionalization which has apparently taken place, and because of its lack of any outstanding resemblance to anything in nature.

The *u* bracket is one of the commonest elements in Maya glyphic writing, and it occurs with many glyphs, particularly in Dresden, which clearly have nothing to do with ending, the meaning commonly assigned it. For example, it is prefixed to the burden glyph on the pages of Dresden devoted to the ceremonies for the new year. This burden glyph on all four pages accompanies glyphs giving the luck of the coming year. On Dresden 26 it follows the glyph for drought, and the two glyphs together clearly read "drought is its burden" or, more probably, "drought is the burden of the year." In Maya the former would be *kintunyabil u cuch* (fig. 43,60,61). The *u* bracket here clearly corresponds to the use of *u* in the spoken word; it can not signify ending, since this is a prophecy for the incoming year. This element also appears with verbal glyphs of action (fig. 42,63,67) where it probably corresponds to *u* as used as a nominal third person pronoun. It also appears as a prefix in the name glyphs of gods (figs. 41,10–13; 42,1), where a meaning such as "ending" is hardly to be expected.

The *u* bracket figures in Landa's alphabet where it is assigned the sound *u.* Landa's drawing lacks the two circlets, but that is not a serious objection to its identification, because these circlets are usually omitted in examples of this prefix at Chichen Itza (they are absent from nearly 75 per cent of the examples of this prefix which appear in the drawings by Beyer [1937]). At Xcalumkin, too, the circlets are usually suppressed, whereas at Sayil they may be present or absent; scattered records from

other sites in Campeche show the circlets. It is clear, then, that the absence of the circlets is a regional variation which was in force in the area in which Landa obtained his so-called alphabet.

There is, moreover, evidence that the *u* bracket prefix can be substituted for the lunar postfix without apparent change of meaning. A good example of this is supplied by a glyph with a crosshatched area which at Quirigua normally follows immediately after the IS if that is a PE (fig. 11,37–41). In most cases this glyph has a lunar postfix, but the *u* bracket, as a prefix, occasionally replaces it (fig. 11,40,41). Although the exact meaning of this glyph is not known, we are justified from its constant position at the close of the IS in assuming that the substitution of one affix for another makes no change in the meaning, and that both have the value of *u,* probably used as a possessive. In a pair of glyphs which repeats through all the divisions of a divinatory almanac the same shift takes place (fig. 2,58–61). This text is discussed on page 39, where it is concluded that the substitution occasions no alteration in meaning. In many glyphs of uncertain interpretation the same interchangeability rules, probably without affecting the meaning.

I see no reason not to accept the identification of this bracket as a sign for *u,* as Landa indicates, especially as *u* is one of the commonest words in Yucatec and this bracket is one of the commonest glyphic elements. Certainly, the meaning of "ending" generally attributed to the *u* bracket has little to recommend it, for it will not fit interpretations of many of the glyphs to which it is attached.

As has been noted, the prefixing of *u* to a number in Yucatec converts it from a cardinal to an ordinal, and this is surely the sense in which the *u* bracket is to be used when it is attached to period glyphs with coefficients. Thus we have records such as tenth katun, fifteenth katun, and tenth baktun (fig. 32,12,13,16), and completion of the fourteenth katun (fig. 32,8) following the CR dates which coincide with the ends of those periods. The same interpretation, of course, would apply to records of anniversaries which use this prefix (fig. 33,21,23,25, 27,28,30). Generally the *u* bracket attached to the katun sign and the lunar glyph postfixed to the hand used as a prefatory glyph surely function in the same way, but there are very rare examples where both the lunar sign and *u* bracket are present (fig. 33,23 and Yaxchilan 3). In such cases I assume that the lunar postfix must be read as a possessive *u;* the bracket prefix, as converting cardinal to ordinal.

The *u* bracket, therefore, has the value *u,* and, as used with time periods with coefficients, it converts the coefficient into an ordinal.

Another prefix in this group is the death eye which

takes a number of forms. The commonest is shaped as a bar with a design on its outer side which usually consists of two circles with inset details, and which are separated by a number of short parallel lines (fig. 5,*19–22,27,33, 45,51,52*), more rarely, by a St. Andrew's cross. This last variant appears only in late inscriptions, and so far as I know, is not found in carved texts prior to 9.17.0.0.0. Sometimes, the circles have been mistaken for numerical dots (Morley, 1920, p. 301; 1937–38, 3:443). Beyer (1937) was the first to identify the elements that compose this sign. The circles with their inset details are the eyes of darkness or the eyes of death which are commonly set before the foreheads of pictures of deities connected with death. These eyes of death commonly adorn the dress and accoutrements of God A, the death god (fig. 13,*11,19*), and God Q, the god of human sacrifice (p. 131; fig. 15,2). They are also associated with gods of the underworld in Mexican art (fig. 21,*10–12*). Usually one of these eyes is set before the forehead in glyphs of Gods A and Q (figs. 13,*14*; 15,6). In the latter case the eye has sometimes been mistaken for a numerical dot, and added to the coefficient of 10 which forms part of that god's name glyph (p. 131), but the diagnostic circle inset at the edge (the pupil?) is clear in most cases.

A peculiar arrangement of the hair or a wig is characteristic of Mictlantecutli, the Mexican god of death. This is frequently set with the eyes of darkness or the eyes of death (e.g. Fejervary-Mayer 32, 37). We can, therefore, accept without hesitation Beyer's identification of the short parallel lines in this affix as the peculiar hair or wig of the death god. The whole prefix, then, is a symbol of death. As a skull is sometimes used as an ending sign in cases where one would expect to find the eye-and-hair prefix or one of the count prefixes, we can be certain that the death-eye prefix is the symbolic variant pairing with the skull, its equivalent head variant (fig. 5,*22,36,43*).

In the books of Chilam Balam *hitz'* is sometimes used where one would expect to find *tz'oc* or *xoc* or *tzol*. For instance, in the discussion in Tizimin of the end of Katun 5 Ahau we find: *u ch'a be katun . . . tu hitz' katun,* "the katun takes his departure . . . at the demise [death throes] of the katun" (p. 12), and *u hitz'il katun uale tu kin u kaxal u cuch ah ho ahau,* "at the expiration of the katun it would be at the time of the binding [falling?] of the burden of [Katun] 5 Ahau." In Chumayel (p. 104) we find *cu hitz'ibte katune,* "at the end of the katun." As used in Perez 156 its sense is even more explicit: *u hitz'il cabil ahau katun lae ca culac oxlahun ahau katun,* "the expiration of Katun 2 Ahau, there is then the seating of Katun 13 Ahau." The old katun passes; the new one is seated in its place.

The Motul dictionary gives for *hitz'* the translation "death throes," and notes that it is applied to the end or last day of the year or month or week, *u hitz' haab,* "the last day of the year." The expression clearly implies the concept of the death of the period, and corresponds to our expression "the dying year" or to our extension of the words expire and expiration to periods of time.

Hitz' is not confined to Yucatec; in the Manche Chol vocabulary of Friar Moran is listed *hitzhitz,* "pains," "to palpitate." The Chol word has a milder connotation than the death throes of its Yucatec equivalent. It is accordingly perfectly logical to accept the death-eye prefix and its variants as signs for the word *hitz',* "death throes," "expirations," and, by extension, "end."

The Maya priest, therefore, had a choice of words derived from the roots *tz'oc, xoc,* and *hitz'* to denote the end of a katun, and he had one or more glyphs or prefixes to express each of them.

One or two other terms occur frequently in the books of Chilam Balam in connection with the counting of time, and particularly with reference to PE. The commonest of these is *tzol,* "to set in order." For instance, the chronicle in Mani is headed *lai u tzolan katun,* "here the setting in order of the katuns." I have not found a glyphic element to correspond to this expression. Another term used in the various books of Chilam Balam, which appears to be roughly comparable to *tzol, tz'oc* and *hitz',* is *uutz'.* The Motul dictionary assigns to this root the meanings "crumple, fold, turn over, double." The word appears in the various chronicles in connection with Katun 8 Ahau. The starting point of the chronicles, in which the expression occurs, was either 8 Ahau or 6 Ahau. Each repetition of 8 Ahau, therefore, marked the completion of one round of 13 katuns. Several of these repetitions carry the words *Oxlahun uutz' katun,* "thirteen foldings of the katun," indicating the completion of the round of 13 katuns. Similarly, in connection with the prophecy for the last tun of the 20 of a Katun 5 Ahau given in Tizimin, we read *u uutz' hun tz'it katun,* "the folding of one katun" and *canil cauac uil u ualak u uutz' katun,* "4 Cauac would be the turning over (or the return) of the fold of the katun" (Roys, 1949). The day 4 Cauac is the eve of 5 Ahau, on which the katun ended. Thus it is perfectly clear that *uutz'* in some way symbolized the completion or at least the passage of time. So far as I know, it is used only with katuns. I have not noted any glyph or affix which would appear to correspond to it. The word *xul,* "end," is also used occasionally with time periods, but again I have not succeeded in identifying a corresponding affix or prefatory glyph.

Two other matters should be mentioned before we leave

the discussion of the hand as a prefatory glyph. Morley (1937–38) draws several of these prefatory glyphs as ending hands over shells and with *u* bracket prefixes. In no case is the original sufficiently well preserved to be sure of the details, and in one or two instances I believe the main element is not a hand, but the prefatory glyph with curving medial line discussed below. The *u* bracket prefix could be used with this prefatory glyph (Tikal 3), but the combination is rare. So far as I know the *u* bracket and moon sign do not appear together in this prefatory glyph. Secondly, the death-eye prefix appears never to be attached to the period glyph and its coefficient when the prefatory hand glyph is used. The fish prefix is extremely rare in such clauses. The noting of such small details may appear hairsplitting, but they must be considered in assigning different meanings to the elements which compose these glyphs.

There is another prefatory glyph which takes a prefix of the *u* bracket–fish-head group, but in no case are the details sufficiently clear to permit of a definite identification. The main element has a curving line which rises vertically from the base. There seem to be circlets attached to this line, and there appears to be a second line paralleling it (fig. 32,20,21,23); the element is slightly reminiscent of the "swastika" sign (fig. 30,9–15,20–35). In that connection it will be remembered that the translation *hel*, "successor," "change," has been offered for this glyph, and it has been noted that *hel* is used in passages which deal with the change of rule when a new katun takes over from an old one. This prefatory glyph, with the fish-head prefix, might mean "change of the count," a reasonable interpretation for a glyph with katun endings.

Sometimes, the period glyph stands alone without any prefatory glyph or symbol. This is particularly true of Tun 13, but katun endings and tun endings sometimes lack those additions (fig. 32,35).

There is yet one more prefix which must have a general meaning equivalent to "count" or "set in order," but which does not occur with period glyphs other than the tun when the CR position is stated. This is a double link, which we shall encounter in reviewing the variant forms of the count of the tuns. It is used with higher period glyphs at Palenque, notably with the baktun and pictun glyph, but never when these are in association with CR dates (fig. 5,46). From its use as a substitute prefix in the glyph for the count of the tuns concluded, it is clear that its meaning must be closely akin to that of count or expiration or set in order.

COMPLETION OF HAAB

Very frequently a glyph, which must mean "count of haab completed," "completion or expiration of the haab,"

or something very similar, accompanies or replaces the regular PE glyphs. This consists of the winged cauac sign above a hand placed horizontally with fingers almost always to right. A prefix of the *u* bracket–fish-head group may or may not be present (figs. 5,40–46; 32,24–29). This glyph was first identified as a tun-ending sign by Morley (1920, p. 153) and has been discussed at length by Beyer (1932a). When it accompanies a regular PE glyph, it is redundant so far as fixing a date in the LC is concerned, but surely reflects a ceremonial phrase. It is the second half of an antiphonal chant: "Completion of the fourteenth katun; the end of the count of a haab" has a fine literary swing. Sometimes, particularly at the close of the Initial Series Period, the actual lapse of katuns was not noted, and only this glyph identifies the date as a PE. Prefixes used with the glyph are the *u* bracket, fish head, death eye, skull, dots, and links. In one or two cases a yax prefix appears over the winged cauac. The significance of this is not obvious, but I am inclined to think it is an additional symbol of rain, since the yax sign is intimately associated with the Chicchan snakes (p. 135). The cauac sign, it will be remembered, is a sign of rain and storm.

Not infrequently the tun sign and the cauac sign stand alone without hand or prefix, but have the same function of denoting the end of a tun, just as a katun sign with coefficient, but without prefatory glyph or affixes is sometimes used as a PE. In such cases the winged cauac is most commonly used, sometimes converted into a head (fig. 32,30,31) or, rather rarely the head form, the Moan bird, of the regular tun sign may be used (fig. 32,32,33). Almost invariably the winged cauac sign is used, the substitution for it of the regular tun sign, either the symbolic form or the head form, being quite rare. In those few cases where a half-period glyph is followed by a statement that 10 tuns have been counted or completed, or have expired, the normal form of the tun sign is used or occasionally the winged cauac.

TUN OR HAAB

In assigning the word *tun* to the glyphs shown in figure 26,33–40, and *haab* to the sundry glyphs representing the period of 360 days which incorporate the cauac element (fig. 32,24–31,35–45), I run the risk of making a false identification. This risk, I feel, is small, and is outweighed by the confusion which would arise were one to use a single term for both glyphs; to avoid the issue by referring to those periods as years of 360 days would add clumsiness to a subject which does not easily lend itself to clear exposition.

Haab, it was once thought, referred only to the year of 365 days, but Long (1925) showed conclusively that it is employed in the books of Chilam Balam in the sense of a year of 360 days. He notes the distinction that the Maya make in the use of tun and haab in the chronicles. The word tun is employed for tun endings, e.g. *tu lahun tun uaxac ahau,* "at the tenth tun of 8 Ahau," and in all cases these are tuns in the LC. That is to say, they are counted from the start of a katun. *Haab,* on the other hand, when it has a number attached to it, "is used as a mere counter to give the distance between points of time which need not be either katun-endings or tun-endings." Haab was also used as a term for the year of 365 days in colonial times, e.g. *u tzol kin ichil hunppel haab,* 365, "the setting in order of the days in one haab, 365." This secondary usage may have been a colonial innovation, but I incline to the belief that both uses were correct in pre-Columbian times.

The various uses of the tun glyph and the winged cauac do not agree with these linguistic differences. The tun sign is used both in the LC and as a distance number, whereas the first would require the word *tun,* the second the word *haab,* to conform to the style of the books of Chilam Balam. The tun sign is used to denote the end of 10 tuns, the half-katun; the winged cauac, to mark the end of the fifth and thirteenth tun, but there are exceptions: on Palenque Sun a half-katun is recorded as 10 winged haab, and on Yaxchilan L 2 the tun glyph with a coefficient of 5 and a prefix of the death eyes marks the end of 5 tuns (fig. 33,22). In the books of Chilàm Balam this usage would be covered by the word *haab.* With other anniversaries, however, a form of the cauac glyph is used (fig. 33,27-31). A clear case of failure to conform to colonial practice is supplied by the employment of the winged cauac to mark both the fifth tun and five tuns lacking to the end of the katun. The books of Chilam Balam use *tun* to express the first; *haab* to signify the second (fig. 32,36-45).

One must conclude, I think, that the use of these two words in colonial Yucatan differed widely from their use during the Initial Series Period. The meanings of words change in all languages, and so it is not strange that a difference should have arisen in the millennium which separated the Initial Series Period from eighteenth-century Yucatan.

The tun sign, because it contains the symbol for tun, "jade," must, I think, be correctly translated. Similarly the winged cauac glyph, with its prominent symbols of rain, must surely correspond to haab, which means rain in several Maya languages and dialects.

GLYPHS FOR FIFTH HAAB AND FIVE HAAB LACKING

Special glyphs exist for recording the fifth and fifteenth haab. The glyphs were first interpreted by Goodman

(1897), and first proved by Morley (1917a). It was not until 1934 that it was shown that these were really two different signs with slight changes in affixes to differentiate that used with the fifth tun from that used with the fifteenth tun (Thompson, 1934a). These variations supply a good example of the importance of studying the humblest affix.

The fifth haab glyph consists of the winged cauac glyph with a coefficient of 5 and the *u* bracket as a prefix above or to the left. In most examples the *u* bracket lacks the two circlets, and the central element sometimes develops into a sort of flare. These abnormalities might lead one to suspect that in the cities of the Central Area the absence of the circlets might affect the meaning of this prefix. This suspicion is allayed, however, by one certain and two possible examples of the bracket complete with circlets attached to this glyph (Copan J and Alt of I; Piedras Negras 9). Moreover, there are cases where the *u* bracket without these circlets is prefixed to other period glyphs (Palenque Inscr. (E), D6; Tikal 3, B8), and, as we have noted, that variation is extremely common at Chichen Itza. Here, as with other period glyphs, the *u* bracket presumably functions to convert the attached number from a cardinal to an ordinal. The prefix is arranged so that the coefficient is included within the span of its points. The whole reads "fifth haab" or "fifth tun" (fig. 32,36-40).

The glyph used with dates which fall at the end of a fifteenth tun likewise has the winged cauac as its main element, and a coefficient of 5. The affix, however, is not the bracket, but takes one of two forms: it may be an oval containing a crosshatched area on which impinges a smaller circle, or it may be a flaring flamelike element (fig. 32,41-45).

The Maya were accustomed to count toward a number not yet reached. For example, 63 would be called "three to the fourth score"; 97, "seventeen to the fifth score." Similarly, half was reckoned toward the next number. The Motul dictionary gives *tancoch tu yoxppel lub,* "half lacking to three leagues," i.e. two and a half leagues. In Tizimin (p. 35) we read of a certain event: *uacppel hab u binel ca tz'ococ u xoc oxlahun ahau,* "six haab to go until the completion of the count of Katun 13 Ahau." This is not quite the same as the method of counting, but corresponds precisely to the use of the winged cauac with a coefficient of 5 to represent not the fifth, but the fifteenth tun. It is clear, therefore, that this glyph corresponds to the expression "5 haab [or tuns] lacking to the end of the period," or, more correctly, as the Maya pictured time as traveling toward its destination, "5 haab to go to the end of the period." In fact, the word *binel* means "to go" and by extension is used for lacking and to express the future. Presumably the oval with crosshatched area expresses the idea of "lacking" or "to go."

GLYPH FOR HALF-PERIOD

Period endings which coincide with the end of 10 tuns or the end of 10 katuns are usually accompanied by a glyph which denotes that half the next highest period (usually the katun, very rarely the baktun) is completed. This glyph was also first identified by Goodman (1897, p. 99), but his interpretation was not accepted by his colleagues until its correctness was proved by Morley (1917a). Morley, however, failed to recognize the true elements of the glyph, and, in addition, caused some confusion by baptizing it lahuntun (10 tuns) glyph, although, as we shall see, the glyph denotes not 10 tuns but the half-period.

The most usual form of the glyph consists of the completion (or zero) sign cut across the top with one or more horizontal lines, and with a peculiar infix, which shows a "mouth" and three circles placed irregularly around it, set in its center. There is usually a suffix and the "down-balls" prefix found with Mac and other glyphs (fig. 32, 46–55). Actually, this is not a single glyph, but a fused glyph, as can be seen by examining those examples which consist of two separate glyphs (fig. 32,47,49,51,54) or a single glyph with the completion sign as a postfix (fig. 32,50).

The first glyph consists of the "mouth" with three circles, to which the te (2) affix is postfixed. A ti, "at," "to," "from," prefix may be present. The central element with its "mouth" and three circlets is a shell, as can be seen by comparing it with representations of shells in sculptural art. The shell which is attached to the kin sign on the rear head of the double-headed monster from which water flows (Rands, 1946) generally has those three circlets similarly arranged. Maudslay (1889–1902, vol. 4, pls. 92, 93) has brought together a number of examples, and where the three circlets are not visible, one can probably assume that they have been obliterated by weathering. There can be little doubt, I think, that these designs represent cross sections of conch shells, and that the mouth is the orifice, and the three circles are knobs on the shell (fig. 21,4–7,14–19). Seler (1915, p. 93) says of this design: "In some instances it looks like the cross-section of a large marine univalve. The little circles in the wide portion, or the globular pendants filled with small circles lead me to assume that this design was a shell ring, comparable to the *oyoualli* of the Mexicans also cut from a univalve." Spinden (1913, p. 53), too, identifies the decorative element as a shell. The shell, as we have seen, is a symbol for a completed period.

The second glyph is again a symbol for completion, being the so-called zero sign which is used with period glyphs in IS, but which, I have argued, must mean completion (p. 137). One or more bars across the top cut it in half or, more strictly, cut off about one-third. There can be little doubt, I think, that this implies that completion is cut in half, and that the whole therefore means half-completion. This is approximately the interpretation Morley (1917) gives to the glyph, although, influenced by the belief that the four-petaled glyph means zero, he argues that the Maya regarded 10 as half of zero.

I cannot hazard a guess as to the linguistic value of the "down-balls" prefix; the meaning of the postfix is discussed on pages 282–85. Neither affix can be of vital importance, since both can be omitted. The prefix is rarely absent; the postfix frequently. When the two glyphs are fused, the St. Andrew's cross in the center formed by the diagonal loops is omitted to make room for the shell element.

Finally, it should be noted that the two glyphs can be fused to form an affix. In two cases at Tikal the fused glyphs are affixed to a katun sign (fig. 32,53). The matter is a little confused by the fact that the katun signs, both head variants, have a hand on the lower jaw. This is, strictly speaking, a symbol of the baktun head, but there are a few cases where it appears on katun heads, notably on the Leiden plaque, and Oxkintok L 1. Apparently, there was some doubt in early times as to which period should be denoted by a hand.

Sometimes the day on which the current katun ends is given in the adjacent glyph block. I presume this is to indicate the complete period to which this glyph denoting half to completion of the period refers. This surmise is strengthened by the fact that in such cases the half-period seems to be the date which the monument was erected to commemorate. Examples of this practice are to be seen on Tulum 1 (9.6.10.0.0, half-period, 7 Ahau), Copan 6 (9.12.10.0.0, half-period, 8 Ahau), Calakmul 9 (9.11.10.0.0, half-period, same repeated as distance number, 10 Ahau 8 Yaxkin), Quirigua F (9.16.10.0.0, half-period, 13 Ahau), and Copan F (9.14.10.0.0, half-period, obliterated [ti 4 Ahau], demise of 15 katuns). I am inclined to think Uaxactun 22 belongs in this series, for I believe the IS is 9.2.10.0.0. This is followed by half-period, 2 Ahau, completion of Katun 3.

In the case of Quirigua F the half-period glyph impinges on 13 Ahau (fig. 32,55). Such impingement, I believe, is evidence of direct relationship between the two glyphs involved.

A close parallel to sixteenth-century usage is supplied by Naranjo 25, where a three and half katun anniversary is followed by the half-period glyph and 4 katuns. Half lacking to four katuns is precisely how this would be said in Yucatec—*xel u can ḵatun* or *tancoch tu can ḵatun.*

A somewhat different arrangement obtains at Piedras Negras, for on Stelae 4 and 7 of that city distance numbers of 10 tuns lead forward to the end of the current katun. In each of these two cases there are good reasons for believing that the dedicatory date is the half-katun. The second half-period glyph on Calakmul 9 probably serves as a distance number.

Of the use of the half-period glyph with the PE 10 katuns I know of only one example, that on the Tablet of the Inscriptions, Palenque, but that particular PE is rare in Maya inscriptions. Nevertheless, the evidence is conclusive that this glyph expresses the idea that half the period is lacking to its completion. To continue to refer to the sign as the lahuntun glyph is inaccurate, and fails to reflect the pattern of Maya thought and linguistic usage.

As noted above, the Maya of Yucatan generally expressed half by placing it before the next highest number. Two and a half leagues was *tancoch tu yoxp'el lub,* "at the half span lacking to the third league." The addition of the days of the current katun, therefore, corresponds closely to this linguistic arrangement. Thus, the text on Tulum 1 would mean half-period lacking to completion of Katun 7 Ahau. The Motul dictionary also lists the word *xel* as meaning half, but notes it is used only with numbers less than 20—*xel u ca cuch,* "a load and a half." *Xel* means "piece," and is also used as half on the next number. The San Francisco gives *xel u ca ḵatun,* "30 years," more correctly a katun and a half, or literally half on the second katun.

VARIOUS ENDING GLYPHS

There are two or three glyphs which almost certainly are signs used to denote the ends of periods, and several others which I feel reasonably sure have the same function, but which I shall not discuss at this time.

About 9.17.0.0.0 Copan tired of recording the ends of katuns, half-katuns, and quarter-katuns with the usual glyphs such as "count of *n* katuns," "half-period lacking" etc. In a few cases (e.g. G³ and I″) merely the CR date was inscribed, and supposedly, it was assumed that the reader knew that the date marked the end of a period. Such brevity is surely a mark of decadence. However, Copan partly atoned for this lapse by employing two rare glyphs.

The first consists of a stylized shell with a water symbol as prefix (fig. 32,*56–60*). The prefix I identify as a water symbol on the strength of the circle of dots, like those of Mol, which is its most distinctive feature. In some cases the circle is reduced to a semicircle. There

may be other prefixes, namely "the forward" element or the "down-balls" superfix.

This glyph occurs in the following texts at Copan:

Monument	Glyph	Associated Date
Z	B3	9.17.0.0.0 13 Ahau 18 Cumku
T 21a	Pb?	" " "
Review Stand	Q7b	" " "
11	B1	9.17.5.0.0 6 Ahau 13 Kayab?
Q	F1	" " "
G²	B2	9.18.5.0.0 4 Ahau 13 Ceh
F′	A3b	Date uncertain

In the last case the glyph follows a record of 1 katun 4 tuns (p. 197), although there is no information on the PE date. It may be an anniversary (p. 196). This sign also occurs with the PE 9.10.10.0.0 at Palenque (Sun, P16 and I1) and a somewhat similar glyph is associated with 9.17.0.0.0 on Quirigua E. What appears to be the chac prefix is present in some cases, perhaps with the value "great." See Addendum, p. 296.

The shell, as we have seen, has the meaning of period completed; water is the symbolic equivalent of the *xoc* fish which means "to count." It is accordingly logical to translate the whole glyph as "count of completed period" or words to that effect. Alternatively, water stands for haab, "rainy season."

A second glyph to denote a PE appears in the last years of Copan's devotion to the hieroglyphic cult. Examples are to be seen on U, N5 (with 9.18.5.0.0), G¹, A2 (9.18.10.0.0), and S, 9b (10.0.0.0.0). The tail of the winged cauac is attached to an element with lines of dots and a peculiar prefix (fig. 33,*1–3*). At one end of this prefix is a ring of little circles suggesting jade or water. The rest of the prefix might pass as a distorted hand. In that case the ring of circles would represent the jade ornament commonly worn on the wrist. However, I am inclined to doubt the identification of the hand (cf. fig. 37, 55,60,69). Be that as it may, I think the glyph may be tentatively accepted as a PE sign.

A glyph which most probably connotes completion is the hand scattering water (fig. 33,*4–8*). At one time I had thought that the circles falling from the hand represented grains of maize, as in the scene on Piedras Negras 40, but the many cases in which, as Rands (1946) has shown, streams fall from the hand held fingers down, have convinced me that the glyph in question represents the sprinkling of water. Furthermore, in some cases the circles falling from the hand are enclosed within lines, indicating more clearly a liquid stream (fig. 44). One of the names given the Chacs, the rain gods of Yucatan, is *Ah hoyaob,* "the sprinklers," because they are supposed to sprinkle water on the earth from their stores; this is apparently the action shown in the glyph. A connection between the root *hoya* and the completion of a period is not obvious. Conceivably, the glyph symbolizes the rainy season and, by extension, the whole year, just as haab has the primary meaning of rainy season but stands for the whole year by the *pars pro toto* principle. The arrival of the Chacs, the sprinklers, still marks the start of the rainy season (Redfield and Villa, 1934, p. 116).

The glyph is common, and is associated with PE dates with a few exceptions. One exception occurs on Naranjo 23, following the date 9.13.18.9.15 1 Men 13 Yaxkin. There are several *u* brackets with glyphs of unknown meaning, and then the hand sprinkling water, but without a prefix of the count group, attached to a glyph resembling Muluc. Clearly on 1 Men 13 Yaxkin several unknown matters were set in order, and those events may have accounted for the presence of the water-sprinkling symbol. A second exception is on Tonina 7 where the glyph precedes (9.14.17.9.0) 1 Ahau (3 Uo).

That the sign is not a prefatory glyph is established by the fact that not infrequently it directly precedes the PE date; that it does not modify the glyph it follows is shown by its occasional presence immediately after a PE.

Normally there is a prefix, either the *u* bracket, fish head, comb, or death eye. On Copan J (W) the prefix is a symbol, such as occurs with frequency at Quirigua (fig. 33,8–14).

Attention was called to the presence of a shell as one of the two glyphs which, separated or merged, indicate together the half-period. This shell, with its peculiar mouth and three little circles, reappears as a distinct glyph, either without a coefficient or with a coefficient of 1. The little circles are in line or in an arc around the mouth, there is a *te* (2) postfix, as with the glyph for half-period, and commonly a prefix of the bracket group (fig. 33,15–20). I find the following occurrences with coefficient of one:

Palenque Inscr. (M), F7	9.11. 0. 0. 0	12 Ahau 8 Ceh
Palenque Inscr. (W), S11	9.12.11.12.10	8 Oc 3 Kayab
Palenque Fol. Cross, N17	9.12.18. 5.16	2 Cib 14 Mol
Naranjo 24, D8	9.13. 7. 3. 8	9 Lamat 1 Zotz'
Piedras Negras 3, C7b(?)	9.13.16. 4. 6	4 Cimi 14 Uo
Morales 2, B11	9.13.19. 8. 1	2 Imix 14 Zec
Pusilha M, C7	9.14. 0. 0. 0	6 Ahau 13 Muan
Pusilha E, C4	9.15. 0. 0. 0	4 Ahau 13 Yax
Tikal T 4, L 3, H5	9.15.15. 2. 3	13 Akbal 1 Ch'en
Tikal T 4, L 2, K1	9.15.16. 4.18	12 Etz'nab 11 Zac
Yaxchilan 10, H1	9.16.15. 0. 0	7 Ahau 18 Pop(?)
Palenque 96 Glyphs, I8	9.17.13. 0. 7	7 Manik, Pax seated

Palenque Cross, doorway   No associated date

As to the exact usage of this glyph I would not hazard a guess, but the sign must mean something like "period completed" in view of its employment in other texts, but its use clearly is not restricted to the time periods of the LC. Note how on Copan A this glyph, but with "down-

balls" postfix, precedes fifteenth katun (fig. 32,*10*), and replaces the more conventionalized shell postfix.

The pursuit of all glyphs derived from a shell would take us too far afield, but before leaving the subject I desire to call attention to one other glyph. This is a right hand held vertically with back to observer, and only the thumb shown. It has as an infix the "mouth" and three circlets of the shell, the latter arranged as a triangle. There is a prefix and sometimes, in addition, four dots which may or may not have a numerical value. The derivation of the merged glyph is obvious (fig. 33,*9–13*). Sometimes the katun prefix is present (fig. 33,*12,13*). The glyph probably means the completion of a period.

It may seem strange that the meaning "completion of a period" should be assigned to so many diverse glyphs. Yet, such variation merely reflects the paramount importance of such events in the Maya concept of time. The orderly completion of each stage of time's march through eternity was a matter of prime concern to the Maya priest; it is a subject treated at considerable length in the measured phrases of the books of Chilam Balam. If, as I first assumed and, I trust, have now furnished evidence, the set phrases of the books of Chilam Balam reflect the patterns of speech incorporated in the glyphic texts of the Initial Series Period, then one would expect various glyphs to express those phrases. Some we have identified; others are still dubious.

Moreover, it must be remembered that the surviving writings on the ends of periods are without any doubt but a fraction of the ritual on the subject which existed in the sixteenth century, and that in turn was but a bedraggled survival from the great cantatas of time which the Maya priests of 1200 years ago composed, recited, sang, and wrote. Those infinite variations on the theme which the different glyphs denote are its magnificence. Much of that beauty is now lost because our present knowledge does not permit us to identify and translate those antiphonal changes, or to reproduce the meter.

KATUN AND TUN ANNIVERSARIES

The term anniversary is here used to designate CR dates other than baktun and katun endings, and the ends of fifth, tenth, thirteenth, and fifteenth tuns, which by declaration or by implication are an exact number of tuns or katuns later than a date already recorded in the same or some other text in the same city. Thus 9.18.2.5.17 3 Caban, seating of Pop, is the one and one-half katun anniversary of 9.16.12.5.17 6 Caban 10 Mol. Both dates with the required distance number are declared on Copan U. The anniversaries observed are generally those with a span of one katun, but 1½, 2, 3, and 5 katun anniversaries are recorded, as well as 5, 7, 10, and 13 tuns. The dates thus commemorated are for the most part those which had particular importance in solar and other astronomical calculations; most of them appear to be solar determinants.

The glyphs used to denote these anniversaries are the usual PE signs, together with their prefatory glyphs and affixes, with two exceptions. The first of these is the occasional presence of a "bundle" suffix with the katun or tun sign (fig. 33,*21–23*). This postfix appears with period glyphs only when they are anniversaries. The other is a peculiar cauac glyph which lacks the wing postfix but has a peculiar prefix (fig. 33,*27–32*).

As anniversaries have received little comment, it seems advisable to list all known examples in the order of their appearance within each site, together with the dates they commemorate.

TABLE 12—LIST OF DATES WITH THEIR ANNIVERSARIES

Letter	Monument	Date		Associated Glyphs
		PIEDRAS NEGRAS		
A	L 4	9.10. 6. 2. 1	5 Imix 19 Kayab	
B	L 2	9.11. 6. 2. 1	3 Imix 19 Ceh	
C	3, 7, 8	9.11.12. 7. 2	2 Ik 10 Pax	
D	7	9.14. 9. 7. 2	8 Ik 5 Uo	Hand bracket, 17 haab,[1] 2 katuns?
E	8	9.14.12. 7. 2	9 Ik 10 Pop	Hand, moon, bracket, 3 katuns[2]
F	33, 36, 38, etc.	9.10. 6. 5. 9	8 Muluc 2 Zip	
G	34	9.10.19. 5. 9	8 Muluc 2 Cumku	13 haab, completion of haab
H	38	9.12. 6. 5. 9	4 Muluc 7 Zac	Hand? 2 katuns?
I	7, 8	9.12.14.11. 1	6 Imix 19 Kankin	
J	1	9.13.14.11. 1	4 Imix 19 Ch'en	Bracket 1 katun?
K	3, 7, 8	9.12.14.13. 1	7 Imix 19 Pax	
L	Jade	9.13. 7.13. 1	7 Imix 14 Mac	Hand 13 tuns
M	1	9.13.14.13. 1	5 Imix 19 Zac	
N	Jade	9.13.14.13. 1	5 Imix 19 Zac	Hand 1 katun
O	8	9.13.14.13. 1	5 Imix 19 Zac	Hand, moon (?), bracket, 1 katun
P	3	9.13.19.13. 1	11 Imix 14 Yax	Hand, bracket, 5 haab,[1] 1 katun
Q	11, Alt·2	9.14.18. 3.13	7 Ben 16 Kankin	
R	9	9.15. 5. 3.13	5 Ben 1 Mac	Hand, bracket, 7 tuns
S	L 3	9.15.18. 3.13	5 Ben 16 Ch'en	Bracket 1 katun[2]
T	Not found	(9.14.18.16. 7	1 Manik 5 Ch'en)	
U	Alt Sup.	9.15. 5.16. 7	12 Manik 10 Yaxkin	Bracket-tun (?) hand
V	Thr 1	9.15.18.16. 7	12 Manik 5 Zotz'	
W	12	9.18. 4.16. 7	10 Manik 0 Zac	Bracket 6 haab,[1] bracket 3 katuns
X	Thr 1	9.17.10. 6. 1	3 Imix 4 Zotz'	
Y	L 3	9.17.11. 6. 1	12 Imix 19 Zip	
		COPAN		
Z	5, W. alt	9. 7.19.17.11	9 Chuen 14 Mol	
A'	1, altar	9.12.19.17.11	12 Chuen 19 Pop	Hand (5) katuns?
B'	3	9.10.19. 5. 0	12 Ahau 13 Kayab	
C'	A	9.14.19. 5. 0	4 Ahau 18 Muan	
D'	1	9.11.15.14. 0	11 Ahau 8 Zotz'	
E'	I	9.12. 3.14. 0	5 Ahau 8 Uo	
F'	Q, R, U, T, 8 etc.	9.16.12. 5.17	6 Caban 10 Mol	
G'	T	9.17.12. 5.17	4 Caban 10 Zip	*u* bracket katun
H'	U	9.18. 2. 5.17	3 Caban Pop seated	
		NARANJO		
I'	25	9. 5.12. 0. 4	6 Kan 2 Zip	
J'	25	9. 6.12. 0. 4	4 Kan 7 Pax	1 katun, completion of haab
K'	25	9. 7.12. 0. 4	2 Kan 7 Zac	2nd katun, completion of haab
L'	25	9. 8.12. 0. 4	13 Kan 7 Xul	3 katuns
M'	25	9. 9. 2. 0. 4	12 Kan 17 Zip	1/2 period lacking to 4th katun
N'	29	9.13. 3. 0. 0	9 Ahau 13 Pop	
O'	29, 30	9.14. 3. 0. 0	7 Ahau 18 Kankin	

TABLE 12—*Continued*

LETTER	MONUMENT	DATE	ASSOCIATED GLYPHS
		QUIRIGUA	
P'	E, F, etc.	9.14.13. 4.17 12 Caban 5 Kayab	Hand, fish, 2 katuns
Q'	D	9.16.13. 4.17 8 Caban 5 Yaxkin	
		YAXCHILAN	
R'	Str. 44	9.11.18.15. 1 7 Imix 14 Zotz'	
S'	L 25	9.14.11.15. 1 3 Imix 14 Ch'en	
T'	L 27	9.13.13.12. 5 6 Chicchan 8 Zac	
U'	L 26	9.14. 8.12. 5 11 Chicchan 13 Yaxkin	
V'	11	9.15.19. 1. 1 1 Imix 19 Xul	
W'	L 8, L 41	9.16. 4. 1. 1 7 Imix 14 Zec	
X'	L 1	9.16. 1. 0. 0 11 Ahau 8 Zec	Death eye 5 tuns[2]
Y'	L 2	9.16. 6. 0. 0 4 Ahau 3 Zotz'	
Z'	L 26	9.14.12. 6.12 12 Eb 0 Pop	
A''	L 9	9.16.17. 6.12 1 Eb, End of Yaxkin	
		PALENQUE	
B''	96 Glyphs	9.16.13. 0. 7 9 Manik 15 Uo	Hand, *u* bracket, 1 katun
C''	96 Glyphs	9.17.13. 0. 7 7 Manik Pax Seated	
		BISHOP JADE	
D''		9.10.10. 6.14 4 Ix 7 Zip	Hand, bracket with dots, katun
E''		9.11.10. 6.14 2 Ix 12 Pax	

[1]Cauac with unusual prefix.
[2]Bundle suffix.

Probably a more careful scrutiny of texts would reveal other anniversary dates. In one or two cases, notably on Yaxchilan 3, much of the inscription is obliterated, but two glyphs record "completion of first katun," and it is probable that the missing date which these two glyphs explain was an anniversary. Similarly, the date 9.10.4.16.2   8 Ik 5 Kankin on Naranjo HS is declared to mark the completion of one katun, but a date one katun earlier has not survived. The date on Copan I perhaps is not an intentional anniversary, for it is eight tuns after the original date, but the eighth tun had, so far as we know, no significance for the Maya. The date on Copan A also may not be meant as an anniversary of that on Stela 3, for the distance of 19.5.0 which each records in excess of the katun ending is of lunar significance, since the interval is 6940 days, the Metonic cycle, as first pointed out by Spinden (1924, p. 175). This is one katun less one 260-day cycle and equals 19 tropical years or 235 lunations. In both these texts there is a winged-cauac glyph, but I am not certain that these refer to the anniversaries.

The various anniversaries at Yaxchilan, with the exception of the pair X' and Y', are somewhat open to doubt because of the nonplacement of several of the CR dates in the LC. The incised text on the Bishop jade (D'' and E'') is certainly a katun anniversary, but the LC positions of the dates are not given: the assigned position is

probably correct, since it proves to be an excellent determinant of 9.11.0.0.0   12 Ahau 8 Ceh (p. 205). Another possible anniversary may be given on Quirigua Alt O, where there appears to be a record of 9.16.6.14.6   4 Cimi 9 Cumku, which is the katun anniversary of 9.15.6.14.6   6 Cimi 4 Zec, a date very prominent at Quirigua.

THE HAAB VARIANT

As already noted, a special glyph for the 360-day period is used with several of these anniversaries. This consists of the cauac sign without the wing, but with the addition of a prefix with a crosshatched oval (fig. 33,27–32). This haab variant never stands alone, but is always followed by the katun sign (once by another tun sign), and is apparently used only with anniversary dates, that is to say to mark a count forward from some determined position which is not chosen because it is a PE in the round of tuns or katuns. What is probably the same element occurs frequently with the tun sign and once with the haab glyph without wing in the 260-day almanac on Madrid 65–72 (fig. 12,23,24). In every case the tun and haab signs have coefficients; the affix may be a prefix or postfix, lying between the coefficient and main element in the former case. Here, also, it is clear that no PE in the LC are involved. On the other hand this affix almost surely is not the same sign as that used with month glyphs and sometimes with the winged cauac at Chichen

Itza and other sites in the Northern Area (figs. 38; 39), tentatively identified as the *tu* element. The *tu* element has an infix with three circlets which is lacking in this affix, and it stands outside the coefficient, whereas this affix lies between coefficient and main element or may even be postfixed to the main element.

The situation is somewhat unsatisfactory, but perhaps we shall not be much amiss if we assume that this affix is a numerical classifier, possibly *piz* or *p'el*, both of which may be used with the word haab, corresponding to a specialized use of haab in the recording of anniversaries, but not in marking regular PE. The presence of this affix (once) with the half-period glyph when that is used as a distance number leading to the end of the current katun (fig. 32,*48*) and its attachment to glyphs without coefficient do not militate against its identification as a numerical classifier, for both *piz* and *p'el* have other uses: both words can also mean "only," and *piz* has the additional significance of "simple," "ordinary," and *p'el* in the compounds *p'el hun* and *p'elech* denotes "exactly." This affix should be distinguished from another which terminates in a ring of circlets (fig. 33,*8–14*), and which probably has a different meaning.

In the list of anniversaries given above, this haab variant occurs with Dates D, P, and W. It also appears at Copan on Temple 11 and Stela 8. On Temple 11 (west panel of north doorway) there is a damaged IS, which Morley has read as 9.14.15.0.0　11 Ahau 18 Zac, a decipherment which can hardly be challenged. Immediately after 18 Zac follow two glyphs, which, like all on this panel, are reversed. The first is a katun glyph with a coefficient of 3; the second is this haab variant with a coefficient of 5 (fig. 33,*29*). Unfortunately, the following glyphs are not recognizable (they are probably on an adjacent panel.) If this is to be regarded as an anniversary, the date commemorated is 9.11.10.0.0　11 Ahau 8 Ch'en. On the east panel of the south doorway there is a date 11 Ahau 8 Ch'en or 8 Uo. In view of what has been said about anniversaries, it is highly probable that these fragments of the texts should be reconstructed as follows:

(9.11.10.0.0)　11 Ahau 18 Ch'en
9.14.15.0.0　11 Ahau 18 Zac
3 katuns 5 *haab*

I suspect, but have no proof, that the next occurrence of 11 Ahau at the end of a katun—9.18.0.0.0　11 Ahau 18 Mac—was also inserted in this inscription.

The second occurrence of this combination of 3 katuns 5 haab variant is on Copan 8, and precedes the date 10.0.0.0.0　7 Ahau 18 Zip. One would expect to find the date 9.16.15.0.0　7 Ahau 18 Pop in this text, but it is not present on what remained of the inscription when it was photographed. Several glyphs are entirely gone, and

there is therefore a possibility that originally the date occurred on this monument (fig. 33,*30*).

This particular form of the cauac glyph occurs rather rarely in other texts. For example, it appears with a coefficient of 2 on Copan U in an obscure passage immediately before a record count of 4 tuns, 9.18.5.0.0　4 Ahau 13 Ceh. It follows a date 9.18.1.13.2　9 Ik 10 Mol, which actually falls in a second tun, and if four completed tuns are counted from that point the date 9.18.5.0.0. will be reached. The passage would then read "(9.18.1.13.2)　9 Ik 10 Mol in the second haab. Fourth tun (from 9 Ik 10 Mol) to (9.18.5.0.0) 4 Ahau 8 Ceh." Such methods of recording dates are not in conformity with practice in the Central Area during the Initial Series Period, but old usage was breaking down at 9.18.5.0.0, and the suggested interpretation may be correct (fig. 33,*32*).

This same cauac glyph appears also on Altar F' with a coefficient of 4. It is followed by 1 katun, and what is apparently a PE glyph. This is probably an anniversary, but the associated date is not recoverable to give a definite answer.

A YUCATECAN METHOD OF RECORDING DATES

The hieroglyphic texts of Chichen Itza and some other cities of Yucatan and Campeche are set apart from those of the cities of the south by the rarity of IS and by the complete absence of PE. In none of the 20-odd inscriptions recovered so far at Chichen Itza is a statement such as "13 Ahau 18 Cumku, completion of [or count of] 17 katuns." Such PE, as we have seen, abound in the texts of the Central Area, and in their abundance and ease of general decipherment perhaps delude epigraphers, leading them to regard their task as less onerous. They are absent from the texts of Yucatan; they do not appear in the pages of the books of Chilam Balam.

In the books of Chilam Balam, events are referred to katuns identified not by the numerical positions of those katuns within a baktun, but by the day on which each closes. An event, in their narrative, took place in a katun ending on the day *n* Ahau, or in tun *n* of a katun ending on *n* Ahau. For instance on page 80 of Chumayel are the statements: *Tu hunpiz tun Buluc Ahau, laix u katunil*, "In the first tun of 1 Ahau, that of the katun"; *tu hunpiz tun ichil hun Ahau u katunile*, "in the first tun in the katun of 1 Ahau." In Mani we read: *tu lahun tun uaxac Ahau*, "in the tenth tun, 8 Ahau."

Similarly, each sentence of the various chronicles commences with the day Ahau of the katun: *Uaxac Ahau paxci u Chich'een Itza*, "8 Ahau, the abandonment of Chichen Itza." That the katuns were named for the day Ahau on which each ended is further seen in statements such as: *Can Ahau u kaba katun emciob,* "4 Ahau was the name of the katun when they descended."

Nowhere is an event said to have taken place in Katun 7, 2, or 3, etc., except in one passage in Tizimin which appears to state that the Katun 8 Ahau of the Hunac Ceel incident was the seventeenth (Roys, 1922, p. 46), and that is almost surely incorrect, perhaps a reference to the tun number. Nowhere is a CR date declared to be a PE.

In the Central Area there is no exact parallel to the Yucatecan custom of omitting the word katun, and giving merely the day on which it ended, with the clear understanding that so and so happening on *n* Ahau does not mean on that day but on the katun that ended on that day. There are indications, however, of an approach to that system. The somewhat rare practice of following the half-period glyph with a notation of the day on which the current katun will end (p. 192) is analogous, for the whole clearly means something like "half-period lacking to the completion of *n* Ahau," the katun glyph being omitted. Another parallel, although somewhat weaker, is to be found on the Tablet of the Inscriptions at Palenque. The katun endings, 9.9.0.0.0 3 Ahau 3 Zotz', 9.10.0.0.0 1 Ahau 8 Kayab, and 9.11.0.0.0 12 Ahau 8 Ceh, are followed after a lapse of several glyphs by the day Ahau on which each ends, namely 3 Ahau, 1 Ahau, and 12 Ahau. I think there can be little doubt that these repetitions are references to the katun endings, for in each case Ahau is followed by a tun glyph. In each case Ahau is supplied with an unusual postfix, which perhaps serves to indicate that the day Ahau represents an abbreviated reference to the katun ending. In this connection attention should be called to the *ak* postfix with 8 Ahau, which appears on Copan 6 as an abbreviated reference to the katun ending 9.13.0.0.0 (fig. 11,59).

This system of naming a katun by the day on which it ended was not confined to Yucatan and to the few uncertain examples of the Initial Series Period of the Central Area just discussed; it was clearly favored by the users of Paris, for that codex contains a series of pages giving the round of the katuns, each apparently with its prophecy, and each katun is designated by the day Ahau on which it ends. There is also on these pages a sequence of tuns similarly labeled. Moreover, a clouded passage in Ordoñez y Aguiar (1907, note 57, par. 119) suggests that the author may have had a confused knowledge of this practice among the Tzeltal. A jade from Ocosingo has a 4 Ahau (note typical forehead ornament) with the katun prefix and the *ak* postfix (fig. 11,58), and this must surely indicate a Katun 4 Ahau.

The murals at Santa Rita, British Honduras, name a sequence of tuns by the day on which each is completed,

and it is a fair assumption that the people of that part of Chetumal did the same for the katuns. The Itza of Tayasal, of course, used the same system, but presumably they brought it with them from Yucatan. I think that had the Maya inscribed full prophetic material for the katuns on their monuments, we would have encountered complete evidence for the existence of this system of nomenclature throughout the Maya area in the Initial Series Period.

The calendarial inscriptions at Chichen Itza largely fall into a single pattern of which those of Chichen 2–5 (Four-Lintels) is typical. Ignoring for the moment certain affixes, we read them as: 9 Lamat the day, on the 11th of Yax, haab 13, 1 Ahau (fig. 38,*1–3*).

Morley (1918) at first tried to reach a decipherment which would make the CR date fall in a Tun 13 ending on the day 1 Ahau, but as that was not possible within historical limits, he (1925) abandoned the idea, and treated the two parts of the text as separate items: a CR date 9 Lamat 11 Yax, and a reference to a Tun 13 which fell on 1 Ahau, viz:

$$(11.8.19.5.8)\quad 9\ Lamat\ 11\ Yax$$
$$(11.9.13.0.0)\quad 1\ Ahau\ (13\ Pop)$$

Beyer (1937) accepted these readings, although by the time he wrote, enough architectural evidence had been accumulated to brand as preposterous such late datings.

In that year I suggested an entirely new interpretation of this and similar dates at Chichen Itza, proposing that the whole should be read as: 9 Lamat 11 Yax falling in a Tun 13 of a katun that ended on 1 Ahau (Thompson, 1937). The decipherment offered was: 10.2.12.1.8 9 Lamat 11 Yax which fulfills the required conditions in that it falls in a Tun 13 of a katun (10.3.0.0.0 1 Ahau 3 Yaxkin) which ended on the day 1 Ahau.

The one surviving IS at Chichen Itza is 10.2.9.1.9 9 Muluc 7th of Zac. Later in this text occur the glyphs 10 Winged Cauac and 1 Ahau (fig. 39,2). Beyer reads this last as (10.9.10.0.0) 1 Ahau (3 Zac), thereby placing the second date some 140 years after the first. Morley misread the "Ben-Ich" prefix of Ahau as a coefficient of 2, and thereby obtained a reading 10.2.9.1.9 tun ending on 2 Ahau (10.2.10.0.0). By the system I proposed, the reading would be 10.2.9.1.9 9 Muluc 7th of Zac in Haab 10 in [Katun] 1 Ahau, which is in agreement with the thesis since 10.2.9.1.9 is in the tenth haab or tun of a katun (10.3.0.0.0 1 Ahau 3 Yaxkin) which ends on 1 Ahau.

In this last case, if one does not accept the suggested association between the CR date and the latter half of the chronological statement, one must suppose that the tun-and-Ahau combination agrees with the thesis merely by chance. As there are 260 tun-and-Ahau combinations

(Tuns 1–20; 1–13 Ahau), the chances of a coincidental agreement are 1 in 260. In the case of the 9 Lamat 11 Yax text the chances of coincidence are somewhat less, since 9 Lamat 11 Yax theoretically might occupy two or three places in the LC, thereby reducing the odds to a mere 80 or 100 to 1.

It has been objected that there is no mention of katun

bad weathering, the proposed reading requires one to assume that the 1 haab and the month sign have been transposed. Such transpositions are contrary to all Maya practice, and so, in view of the bad condition of the glyphs, one is very hesitant to accept the Beyer reconstruction involving such drastic irregularity in the arrangement.

TABLE 13—RECORDS OF DATES BY YUCATECAN METHOD

INSCRIPTION	CALENDAR ROUND		HAAB	KATUN	
Chichen 27	10. 1.17. 5.13	11 Ben 11 Cumku?	18	(10. 2.0.0.0)	3 Ahau
Chichen 27	10. 1.18. 6. 5	6 Chicchan 18 Cumku??	19	(10. 2.0.0.0)	3 Ahau
Chichen 20	10. 2. 0.11. 3	5 Akbal 1 Zec??	1	(10. 3.0.0.0)	1 Ahau
Chichen 20	10. 2. 0.15. 3	7 Akbal 1 Ch'en	1	(10. 3.0.0.0)	1 Ahau
Yula 1	10. 2. 4. 8. 4	8 Kan 2 Pop?	5	(10. 3.0.0.0)	1 Ahau
Yula 2	10. 2. 4. 8.12	3 Eb 10 Pop	5	(10. 3.0.0.0)	1 Ahau
Chichen 1	10. 2. 9. 1. 9	9 Muluc 2 Zac	10	(10. 3.0.0.0)	1 Ahau
Chichen 12, 15, 16	10. 2.10.11. 7	8 Manik 15 Uo	11	(10. 3.0.0.0)	1 Ahau
Chichen 2–5	10. 2.12. 1. 8	9 Lamat 11 Yax	13	(10. 3.0.0.0)	1 Ahau
Chichen 2	10. 2.12. 2. 4	12 Kan 7 Zac?	13	(10. 3.0.0.0)	1 Ahau
Chichen 23	10. 3. 0. 2. 1	3 Imix 4 Ch'en??	1	(10. 4.0.0.0)	12 Ahau (written 14 Yax)
Chichen 28	10. 8.10.11. 0	2 Ahau 18 Mol?	11	(10. 9.0.0.0)	2 Ahau
Xcalumkin IS	9.15.12. 6. 9	7 Muluc 1 Kankin	13	(9.16.0.0.0)	2 Ahau
Uxmal, Monjas	10. 3.17.12. 1	5 Imix 18 Kankin	18	(10. 4.0.0.0)	12 Ahau?

in these texts, but such an objection is easily surmounted; frequently, the word katun is omitted in the books of Chilam Balam, and an event is said to have occurred in *n* Ahau with the understanding that *n* Ahau refers to the katun ending on that day (p. 197). Thus carved glyph and written word once more agree.

As a number of other readings conform to the thesis, I think one can not hesitate to accept the suggested interpretation in view of the impossibility of explaining a succession of agreements as coincidences when the chances against each coincidence vary from about 80 to 1 to 260 to 1. Furthermore, the suggested method of reading very closely parallels that used in the books of Chilam Balam.

The list of dates of this type so far deciphered is given in Table 13. The reading of the date of Chichen 23 is quite doubtful. The text is irregular, for certain affixes, to be discussed shortly, are wanting. The head coefficient of the day Ahau is best as 12 (Beyer's reading). Furthermore, a position in a Katun 12 Ahau (10.4.0.0.0) is in closer agreement with other dates associated with the Caracol. I assume that the month was written 14 Yax instead of 4 Ch'en. Naturally, this can not serve as support for the proposed method of reading, but errors do occur. The form of Yax is most irregular, and were it not for the prefix would be quite unrecognizable.

It is not proposed to discuss these readings one by one. They have been threshed out by Beyer (1937), Thompson (1937, 1941), and Satterthwaite (1944). I have not included the date on Halakal Lintel 1 because on top of

These texts introduce affixes attached to the haab and Ahau glyphs not previously encountered. In most cases the prefix or prefatory glyph of the haab is a sign with four or five dots arranged in a vertical line; often the topmost is considerably larger than the rest and is a regular circle. A *ti* element is present as a prefix to the prefatory glyph (suppressed when the glyph is a prefix) and one or two inverted Ahaus serve as a postfix (fig. 38,*1–7*). I know of no similar glyph in the inscriptions of the Initial Series Period, but the vertical arrangement of dots is a not uncommon motif on late pottery of that period (R. E. Smith, 1936, pls. 13*b*, 14*a*), and it is of fairly frequent occurrence in the codical forms of the day sign Caban, although not in the inscriptional forms. However, its use with the codical forms of Caban is of little assistance to us, since it is an element secondary in importance to the lock of hair. Beyer (1937) designates it an ending sign ("end of") without adducing any evidence in support of that identification. However, as Beyer translated a formidable number of prefixes as "end of" on the flimsiest of evidence, there is no reason for assuming that in this case he was right.

In view of what has been written above, it seems more probable that the affix or prefatory glyph has some such meaning as "in the course of" (cf. *cu ximbal,* "when [the year] was marching," in Mani) or, conceivably "forward to."

In a few cases other prefixes replace the one just discussed. On Monjas L 4 (fig. 39,*4*) the prefix consists of the forward element, Landa's *i,* above a hand, held in the

Manik position. Since the hand is in that position, we have at present no evidence for interpreting it as a sign for completion, but perhaps as a sign for grasping (p. 267), and conceivably corresponding to the expression *te ch'abi Otzmal u tunile,* "there it was taken at Otzmal, its tun." This, however, is not probable since *ch'a* carries the implication of movement, and the sense is that of taking away, not of seizing *per se.*

Be that as it may, the presence of the forward element appears to confirm the assumed association of the CR date with the haab. In this particular text a number of glyphs intervene between the date 8 Manik 15 Uo and "forward,—, 11 haab."

In the Casa Colorada text (no. 20) the haab sign appears six times, on each occasion with the *tu* prefix. In two places the glyph forms part of a full date, declaring the CR date to lie in the first haab in (Katun) 1 Ahau; in the other examples the haab does not directly determine the position of a CR date. In all six texts there is a conglomeration of small elements between the coefficient and the haab (fig. 39,7,8). The 13 haab of Xcalumkin similarly has a *tu* prefix. This use of the *tu* prefix gives a clue to the use of the haab glyph, since, together with the haab and its number, it means "in, at, on, or from the *n*th haab." The *ti* prefixed to the element with dots in a vertical line is the same locative, but does not call for the use of ordinal numbers unless the sign with dots in a vertical line has the value *u*. A translation "in the *n*th haab" would, of course, be in agreement with the proposed decipherment of these texts.

The two dates of the ball-court rings of Uxmal also show the *ti* element as part of the prefatory glyphs before the haab signs. These last are rather weathered; they may represent the element with dots in a vertical line.

On Stone 18 of the Caracol there is a clear 3 Imix 9 (or 14) Yax, 1 haab, 12 (or 4?) "Ben-Ich" Ahau, but there is no prefix attached to the 1 haab (fig. 38,8). A prefix is similarly absent from the 10 haab of the Initial Series Lintel, and probably from the 11 haab of Chichen 28 (the High Priest's Grave), although it is possible that the badly weathered glyph which precedes 11 haab is a prefatory glyph.

The day Ahau also has unusual affixes. In almost all cases (exceptions: Chichen 1, 8, 28, and Yula 1, 2) Ahau is surmounted by the "Ben-Ich" prefix. Nowhere in the texts of the Central Area is this prefix attached to a day sign. In the codices Ahau appears hundreds of times, but on only three occasions does it have this prefix: twice (Dresden 60, Paris 4) it has a coefficient of 11; in its third appearance it lacks a coefficient (Madrid 34). No other day sign ever has this prefix either in the inscrip-

tions or in the codices, although it is one of the commonest of affixes.

It has been pointed out by Gates (1931, p. 39) that the Ik part of Ben Ik, here called "Ben-Ich," is not an Ik at all. This element has also been identified as Lamat because of its resemblance to the center of that glyph (Teeple, 1930, p. 71; Beyer, 1937, p. 161). I accept this identification because of the resemblances of early forms of this superfix to Lamat (fig. 33,47).

Of its three occurrences with Ahau in the codices, it is fairly certain that it refers to a Katun 11 Ahau in Paris, and there is a strong probability that it is similarly used in Dresden. In the first case it occurs on Paris 4, but that is precisely the page which deals with Katun 11 Ahau in the sequence of katuns on pages 2–11, and is immediately below what is probably a haab glyph with a coefficient of 15, suggesting the possibility that the two together indicate a Tun 15 in Katun 11 Ahau. In the second case it is associated with a page (60) of Dresden which is not connected with any divinatory almanac and apparently not with any astronomical tables, but which conceivably relates the struggles of the gods of the underworld with those of the heavens at the creation. This occurred in Katun 11 Ahau according to Chumayel. Be that as it may, with 11 Ahau in the same box of six glyphs is a katun glyph without a coefficient, the only katun without an attached number in the codical writings. That makes the identification of this unattached 11 Ahau as a katun ending more probable.

The third occurrence of "Ben-Ich" Ahau, but this time without a coefficient, is in Madrid 34. Ahau has a comb postfix below, and probably a second postfix to the right—a unique combination.

As we shall see, the "Ben-Ich" prefix is commonly used with a count of katuns, with coefficients from 1 to 5 (possibly 6) frequently encountered in the inscriptions of the Central Area. This numbering of katuns may refer to an enumeration in some way linked to the cycle of 13 katuns (p. 203). Should that be the case, it would tend to strengthen the surmise that the "Ben-Ich" prefix indicates the specialized use of Ahau as a station in the round of the katuns.

The "Ben-Ich" superfix, with the addition of a common postfix, converts the symbolic glyph for kin into the name glyph of the sun god. In sixteenth-century Yucatan the commonest name for the sun god was Kinich Ahau, "Lord sun face" (figs. 33,44; 42,3).

This "Ich" element decorates the earplug of a head glyph on a recently discovered stone at Palenque. The portrait is that of a deity with the features of God D, the Roman-nosed god, with the barbels of the *xoc* monster.

It also is a glyph in its own right enclosed within a solid or broken line (Gates' Glyph 341). It may take affixes and a numerical coefficient. In Madrid it once appears with a coefficient, which is 8; its four appearances with coefficients in Dresden are on the four pages dealing with the new-year ceremonies. It is followed in each case by a moon glyph with a coefficient, the arrangement being:

Eb-Ben (p. 25)	9 "Ich"	7 moon glyph
Caban-Etz'nab (p. 26)	7 "Ich"	16 moon glyph
Ik-Akbal (p. 27)	11 "Ich"	5 moon glyph
Manik-Lamat (p. 28)	6 "Ich"	6 moon glyph

I have no idea what these glyphs and numbers signify save that I think they should be read together, and that the moon glyph may have the value of 20.

The examples of "Ben-Ich" on Yaxchilan L 35, 37, and 49 are both early and detailed. What is without much doubt a "Ben-Ich" prefix over B1 of L 35 shows the "Ich" as a straightforward Lamat sign, and in other examples on these lintels the element is a small cross, such as frequently occupies the center of the Lamat sign in place of the rhomboid as seen in some Lamat signs and the usual "Ben-Ich" (fig. 33,*46,47*). It is highly probable, therefore, that the prefix was originally Lamat-Ben, but that to save space in the crowded area of the prefix the four little circles were eventually dropped.

Lamat, as we have seen, is the day of the planet Venus. One of the names for Venus is *Noh Ich* or *Nohoch Ich*, "big eye" or "big face." The stars in Mexican art are commonly represented as eyes from which rays of light radiate, so it is probable that *ich*, in addition to meaning eye or face, was a general term for stars; Venus was merely the big star or the big eye. It is, therefore, not improbable that the Lamat sign stands for *ich* when used in the "Ben-Ich" prefix. This would satisfactorily account for its employment with the kin sign to convert that to the symbol for Kinich Ahau, the sun god.

It will be remembered that one of the ways of stating *n* tun in (Katun) *n* Ahau in the books of Chilam Balam was, for example, *hunpiz tun ichil hun Ahau u katunile*, "in the first tun in the katun of 1 Ahau." The word *ichil* means "in" or "within." The preposition is *ich;* the addition of *il* denotes relationship with the adjacent word, converting it into a relative noun. The Motul dictionary says that *ichil* replaced *ich* when a possessive is used, e.g. *bini ich col*, "he went to the milpa," but *bini ichil u col*, "he went to his milpa." In the passage quoted there is of course a possessive—the katun of 1 Ahau. However, in the books of Chilam Balam the form *ichil* is retained even when the words *u katunile* are suppressed.

In view of the possibility that the Lamat of the "Ben-Ich" has the value *ich* it is interesting to note that the

translation of the prefix as *ich* or *ichil* would be in agreement with the phrase of the books of Chilam Balam. The occasional absence of the prefix would agree with linguistic usage, for *ichil* is sometimes suppressed in sentences, and one finds *tu lahun tun uaxac Ahau*, "in the tenth tun of 8 Ahau." The weakness of this translation is that it leaves the Ben element unexplained. I am far from convinced of the correctness of this interpretation but offer it as a possibility.

Another possibility, and one which I prefer, is that the "Ben-Ich" prefix corresponds to the use in the books of Chilam Balam of the word *ich* to indicate the aspect of the katun or its associated god, for *ich* means both eye and face. As examples of this usage may be cited: *Ek cocohmut u uich ti yahaulil*, "Black Cocahmut his [Katun 3 Ahau] aspect (face) in his rule" (Chumayel, p. 92); *Yaxal chuen u uich Buleu caan chac u uich ti yahaulil*, "Yaxal-Chuen his [Katun 12 Ahau] aspect (face), Buleu-Caan-Chac his aspect (face) in his rule" (Chumayel, p. 96); *chich u uich*, "harsh his [Katun 5 Ahau] face" (Chumayel, p. 91); *och u uich ti yahaulil*, "the opossum is his [Katun 1 Ahau] face in his rule" (Chumayel, p. 93, inserted). In the prophecies of the years of a katun in Tizimin we find *te u uich ti caan ti yahaulil*, "there is his [the new occupant of the throne, the new katun] face in the sky in his rule," and, again, "the day shall march before his face." One gets the distinct impression that *ich* has in these contexts the meaning of countenance and, by association, patronage, almost augury.

There seems to be a lot of symbolism connected with this idea of the countenance of the katun, for passages in the prophecies for the years in Tizimin suggest that at the beginning of the katun his eyes were unbound when he arrived (*choch ich*); *kaxan u uich ti ualac yahaulil*, "his eyes were bound in the time of (or during) his reign" seems to refer to the departure of the katun (Tizimin, p. 10). The same expression, *kaxan u uich*, "blindfold his face," on page 12 of the same manuscript certainly refers to the departure of the old katun, although there is no indication whether he was blindfold when he departed or had been so for some time.

There is also an indication that a more drastic treatment might be in store for the departing katun, for in another passage, in which the katun is depicted as loath to give up his rule, we read: *u kin pacat col ich ah tzai kanche*, "the time of viewing the tearing out of the eye of him who clings to the chair [i.e. the departing katun]." Again: *ti ho muluc u kin u ch'aic u bel tu kin u hoch' ich*, "On 5 Muluc the time he takes the road, on that day (at that time) his eye is pierced" (Tizimin, p. 3). However, Mani, in the parallel passage, has not *hoch' ich*, but *choch ich,* "unbound his eyes," and as the context suggests the beginning of the katun, when the katun takes its road (that is, begins his journey), I would think that the Mani version was the correct one, but Roys tells me that the Tizimin paragraphing would permit the piercing of the eye to refer to 4 Kan, who had run his course.

In connection with the piercing of the eye, it should be noted that the eye of Kinchil Coba, lord of Katun 13 Ahau, the last in the katun cycle, is pierced with an arrow in the series of katun prophecies in Mani (Perez 85); the same is true of the regent of Katun 13 Ahau in the Kaua series, and of the ruler of that katun in the Europeanized katun wheel of Lopez de Cogolludo (Morley, 1920, fig. 73) although the numerical coefficients are absent from that picture. It can hardly be coincidence that the eye of the ruler of the last katun in the series is the only one pierced, for, as pointed out previously (p. 183), Katun 11 Ahau which starts on the day 1 Imix is the first of the series, and Katun 13 Ahau the last. Piercing of the eye might therefore be a ritualistic expression for the end of a period; among the Aztec it symbolized penance.

In the Lopez de Cogolludo picture all heads of katun rulers have their eyes closed, and most of them have a tear or a drop of blood on the cheek (the pierced head has several tears or drops of blood on the cheeks). The faces of the 13 rulers of the katuns in Chumayel, page 84, are blackened and almost obliterated, that of 13 Ahau being the worst besmudged of all. Roys has suggested that this blackening may represent the blindfolding of the gods. Roys has also called my attention to the fact that the patrons of the first eight katuns .of the series on pages 87–100 of the same manuscript lack eyes, although their brows are prominent (the head of Katun 3 Ahau is perhaps an exception), whereas the last five patrons, starting with 8 Ahau, have eyes. He suggests the possibility that the original manuscript, from which Hoil made the present copy, may have been composed during Katun 8 Ahau; should that be the case, the preceding katuns may have been represented as sightless because they had passed at the time the volume was written (late seventeenth century ?).

In any case, one gets the impression from this material that at the beginning of the katun the eyes of the katun are unbound, and at its end the eye of the departing katun is pierced or he is blindfolded. This rather suggests the concept of the uncovering of the face at the start of the period; the covering of it or the extinction of its power of seeing at the close. Whether that is so or not, the primary concept of the countenance of the katun is well established.

Benel ich, which, with the addition of the attributive *el,* would correspond to our "Ben-Ich" prefix, means to lose one's sight. *Benel* signifies to depart or absent oneself, and the whole would therefore mean literally that the sight had gone. Can the "Ben-Ich" prefix have that meaning? I doubt it. As used in the Yucatecan system of writing dates with Ahau, this prefix should indicate that the katun (*n* Ahau) to which it is attached is running its course, not that it is ended. Moreover, a meaning of sight gone would not fit the name glyph of Kinich Ahau, the sun god, unless this can be construed as the name glyph of the elusive Colop-u-Uich-Kin (sun with plucked-out eye).

Ignoring the Ben part of the prefix and applying to the *ich* part the meaning of countenance or patronage, we see that it would fit well the Yucatec system of dating: 9 Lamat 11 Yax in Haab 13; the ich (countenance or patron) is that of (Katun) 1 Ahau.

As prefixed to the swastika glyph, tentatively assigned the value *hel,* "change," or "succession in office," the meaning of countenance or patron would fit very nicely the use of that glyph on the pages in Dresden and Madrid dealing with the entry of the new year. There it normally precedes the glyph of the god of what I have taken to be the expiring year (that of the entering year would serve as well), and the whole would mean "the change of the patron (or countenance), God so-and-so" (figs. 30,29–35; 64,1). In the last illustration, that of Dresden 27, the glyph may be seen in the center of the page, followed by that of God D and the *ahaulil* glyph, the whole perhaps translatable as *u hel ich—Itzamna—yahaulil,* "the change of the patron (of the year), Itzamna, his rule." Below, Itzamna (or God D should that identification not be acceptable) is seated in the temple.

This interpretation of the glyph would similarly fit its appearance, repeated three or four times, on the left of each of the pages (2–12) of Paris which deals with the sequence of katuns. In each case our swastika glyph with "Ben-Ich" prefix is followed by the glyph of a god, but owing to the poor condition of these pages, one cannot be certain of the identities of the patrons of the various katuns. The suggested interpretation would also appear to fit, so far as we can tell, the use of "Ben-Ich" katuns on the monuments (fig. 33,33,35–40).

Later research may well prove the proposed meaning of the "Ben-Ich" prefix to be incorrect; provisionally it will serve, although the failure to bring the Ben element into the interpretation speaks against the translation.

Sometimes the Ahau has a different prefix, to wit, the so-called centipede glyph. This may occur as the only prefix or may share the honors with the "Ben-Ich." This "centipede" element not infrequently accompanies day signs in texts which date from the early stages of the Initial Series Period (fig. 47,2,4). Its importance can not be very great because it does not always occur in the early texts, and entirely disappears as a prefix of day signs in texts of the Central Area inscribed from 9.5.0.0.0 onward. Its appearance in these Chichen Itza texts of considerably later date probably reflects the conservatism of a peripheral center. There are other examples of archaism in the inscriptions of Chichen Itza.

There is another and far commoner prefix or prefatory glyph with these Ahau signs. This consists of crossed bands above what is probably Beyer's serpent segment (fig. 39,*1,3,6,7*). The precise interpretation of this prefix must remain undetermined for the present.

There are a number of records of *n* haab *n* Ahau which stand alone, and do not determine the LC positions of CR dates. These, one must suppose, are to be read in the same way because of the presence of the "Ben-Ich" prefix in most cases, and are to be regarded as PE. Examples include 10 haab, crossed bands 1 Ahau (Text 8). This presumably represents 10.2.10.0.0 2 Ahau 13 Ch'en which falls in a katun (10.3.0.0.0) 1 Ahau. On Chichen 19 we find 1 haab, centipede 1 "Ben-Ich" Ahau, presumably 10.2.1.0.0. On the Akab Tzib lintel (Text 19) there is also a record of 11 haab, crossed bands 1 (?) "Ben-Ich" Ahau. The haab prefix may be the death eye, and the whole would then read "Expiration of haab 11, ——, in 1 Ahau," that is, 10.2.11.0.0. On Yula 2 there may be a record of thirteenth haab, 1 "Ben-Ich" Ahau. However, it is far from certain that the haab prefix is the *u* bracket.

Attention should be called to the postfix almost invariably attached to Ahau in these katun references. No other day sign has this suffix. The only occasion in texts of the Central Area in which a postfix, other than the tripedestal support of the cartouche, is used are precisely those in which the day Ahau definitely or probably represents a katun ending (p. 198). In fact in one case (Copan 6) the postfix of Ahau has the same form, except for the addition of a crosshatched spot, as do those of the katun Ahaus of Chichen Itza. This postfix very frequently accompanies the "Ben-Ich" prefix with other glyphs. It is discussed at greater length on page 281; Beyer calls it the owl-plume suffix; I tentatively name it the *ak* affix.

In favor of the suggested interpretation of these CR dates, haab, and Ahau combinations the following points may be cited:

1. It is in close agreement with the method used in the books of Chilam Balam for fixing dates.
2. In most cases the method works, whereas the chances of accidental agreement are exceedingly slim.
3. The suppression of the katun glyph with the Ahau sign corresponds to the frequent suppression of the word

katun with the day Ahau in the books of Chilam Balam.
4. The interpretation securely places all the associated CR dates in the LC. If it is not accepted, there is no known way of telling what positions these dates should occupy in the LC. Yet preciseness of dating was of supreme importance to the Maya.
5. The two occasions where the method involves IS dates supply striking evidence for the correctness of the method. In each case only one out of 260 combinations of Ahau and tun can be correct, and in both cases that precise combination is given.
6. There is slight evidence that something approximating this method of recording dates made its appearance on a late text at Copan (U, p. 197), and the practice of adding the terminal day of the current katun after the glyph of the half-period is perhaps an earlier stage in this system.

"BEN-ICH" KATUN

In a considerable number of texts of the Central Area there are isolated katun glyphs with coefficients of 2–5. There is one case (Yaxchilan L 27) of a coefficient of 6, and two or three head coefficients which might represent the number 1, but which I am more inclined to read as 3. Frequently, but by no means always, the "Ben-Ich" prefix is present (fig. 33,*33–43*). We have seen in the case of the Chichen Itza texts that the "Ben-Ich" prefix could be suppressed almost certainly without affecting the meaning. The same is without doubt true of these katun records. The date 9.16.1.0.0 11 Ahau 8 Zec on Yaxchilan L 31 is accompanied by 3 "Ben-Ich" katuns; on Yaxchilan L 1 the same date is followed by 3 katuns (the head coefficient has the Ik sign on the cheek assuring its identification). This seems to confirm that in these scattered references to numbered katuns, the general meaning is not affected by the presence or absence of the "Ben-Ich" prefix. There are some grounds for believing that different katun coefficients can occur with the same date: on Yaxchilan 12, 5 "Ben-Ich" katuns may follow a reference to 9.16.1.0.0 11 Ahau 8 Zec, although on Lintels 1 and 31 this date is followed by 3 katuns. There is every reason to suppose that the coefficient of the "Ben-Ich" katun is not affected directly by the CR date, but by the accompanying glyphs. In fact, the "Ben-Ich" katun at Yaxchilan is one of a group of about five glyphs which shows variation in its composition (fig. 46,*10–16*), but repeats the same combinations in many texts. Lunar glyphs are prominent. I suspect that these glyphs serve to determine the LC position of the CR dates with which they are associated, but the problem is too complex to offer a ready solution.

The numbering of the katuns in the katun prophecies of Chumayel (pp. 87–100) may hold a clue to these numbered "Ben-Ich" katuns. There the series of 13 katuns are numbered 1, 2, 3, 4, 5, 1, 2, 3, 4, 5, 1, 2, 3, starting with Katun 11 Ahau as the first. The numbers are given in Spanish, *primero, segundo,* etc., but there is no reason for supposing that this grouping of the katuns by fives indicates Spanish influence.

The solution of the problem of the "Ben-Ich" katun must await correct placement of the associated dates at Yaxchilan. For the moment it is worth bearing in mind the suggested meaning of "countenance" proposed above for the "Ben-Ich" prefix.

THE GUEST KATUN

Bishop Landa, discussing the strange arrangement of the guest katun, writes:

They had in the temple two idols dedicated to two of these characters [days Ahau on which the katuns ended]. They worshipped and offered homage and sacrifices to the first according to the count from the cross on the circle shown above [the katun wheel with cross above 11 Ahau] as a remedy for the calamities of his twenty years. But for the 10 years lacking [to the completion] of the 20 of the first, they did no more for him than burn incense to him and reverence him. When the 20 years of the first had been completed, they began to be guided by the destinies of the second and to make sacrifices to him, and, that first idol having been removed, they set up another to venerate it another 10 years.

For example, the Indians say that the Spaniards had just arrived at the city of Merida in the year of our Lord 1541 which was precisely the first year of the era of Buluc Ahau [11 Ahau], which is that which is in the "house" where the cross is. . . . If there had been no Spaniards, they would have adored the idol of Buluc Ahau until the year of '51, that is to say 10 years. The tenth year they would have set up another idol, to Bolon Ahau [9 Ahau], guiding themselves by the prognostications of Buluc Ahau until the year '61. Then they would have removed it from the temple, and [in '71] they would have set up the idol of Uuc Ahau [7 Ahau], and they would have been guided by the prognostications of Bolon Ahau another 10 years. Thus they gave to each its turn, so that they worshipped these katuns 20 years, and [for] 10 [years] they were ruled by their superstitions and deceits, which were so numerous, and sufficed so well to trick the simple people that it astonishes one [Englished in part by me].

From the above account, it is reasonably clear that a katun became the guest of the ruling katun halfway through the latter's rule, it then held power alone for the first 10 years of its own reign, but during the last 10 years it received as its guest the incoming katun. I have followed Roys' suggestion, given in a footnote by Tozzer, that words such as "in 10 years" were omitted, perhaps by the copyist, from the sentence discussing Katun 7 Ahau. Landa tends to contradict himself as to whether the ruling katun or the guest katun influences life during the last ten years of the former's reign, but he appears to favor the belief that the power of the katun coincides with its actual reign, and such a view is in agreement with data in the books of Chilam Balam.

In the tun prophecies which occupy pages 1–13 of Tizimin there may be allusions to the installation of the guest katun in the tenth tun, but somewhat similar statements occur with other tuns.

PATRONS OF KATUNS

Although the day of the katun was a god and the ruler of the katun, other deities were associated with the katuns. In the various katun prophecies each katun usually has assigned to it a deity who is called the countenance (*u uich*) of the katun. There are gaps in the sequence probably due to faulty copying. The three best lists are given in Table 14.

Concerning most of the deities listed as patrons of the katuns little or nothing is known. The two or three who are known do not fit any recognizable pattern of the katuns, based either on their sequence or on the co-efficients of Ahau. Thus, one would expect Kinich Kakmo, as a manifestation of the sun god, to be associated either with the fourth katun in the sequence or with a katun ending on 4 Ahau. Such is not the case. Perhaps the deities are associated with the world directions to which the katuns are assigned, but not enough is known about the subject to make an examination profitable.

I would expect the personages depicted on stelae to conform to a pattern of katun rules, but if such a system does in fact exist, its elucidation still escapes me.

DETERMINANTS

A word should be said at this point about determinants because of their close connection with the ends of katuns; a fuller discussion of the subject will be found in Appendix V. The term "determinant" was coined by Teeple (1930) to designate those Maya dates which, as he first demonstrated, give the correction which should be applied to convert dates in the Maya year of 365 days to their positions in the solar year, the reckoning being made from 13.0.0.0.0 4 Ahau 8 Cumku. One of the most noteworthy of these corrections is the date 9.16.12.5.17 6 Caban 10 Mol. The current katun was 9.17.0.0.0 13 Ahau 18 Cumku. Since 4 Ahau 8 Cumku, 3876 years have passed. For that interval, according to the Gregorian system of intercalating 97 leap days every 400 years, there is required a correction of 940 days, that is to say, 210 days after removing the two complete years. The problem the Maya wished to solve was to find the solar position in the year of 4 Ahau 8 Cumku which corresponded to

18 Cumku, the day on which the current katun would end. Using the Gregorian system, we would note that the Maya calendar had gained 210 days in that interval of 3876 years, therefore by subtracting 210 days from 18 Cumku, we would get the day in the year of 4 Ahau 8 Cumku on which the sun rose or set at the same points on the horizon. Subtracting 210 days from 18 Cumku, we would reach 8 Mol as the answer. The Maya calculations tended to run a couple of days under the Gregorian; their equation was 208 days, which, subtracted from 18 Cumku, gives 10 Mol as its equivalent at 4 Ahau 8 Cumku.

It was mentioned on page 196 that 9.10.10.6.14   4 Ix 7 Zip was a preferable position for the earlier date on the Bishop jade because, by design or accident, it is an excellent determinant of 9.11.0.0.0   12 Ahau 8 Ceh, for 7 Zip at 13.0.0.0.0   4 Ahau 8 Cumku occupies the same position in that year as 8 Ceh in the year then current. The distance from 4 Ahau 8 Cumku is 3755 years, requiring a correction of 181 days by Gregorian. The Maya equation would have been 7 Zip+181 days=8 Ceh. Piedras Negras, on 36, 38, and L 2, made the same calculation in reverse order four years earlier, using the date 9.10.6.5.9   8 Muluc 2 Zip. Here 2 Zip is the present

TABLE 14—COUNTENANCES OF THE KATUNS

Katun	Kaua	Tizimin	Chumayel
	(pp. 167–71)	(pp. 23–28)	(pp. 13, 72, 73, 87–100)
11 Ahau	Yaxhal Chac	Yaxal Chac	{Yaxxaal Chac (p. 13) {Yaxhaal [Chac] (p. 73)
9 Ahau	Sac Uacnal	Sac Uacnal	
7 Ahau	Ek Chuuah	Ek Chuuah	Yaxal Chac
5 Ahau	P'es sahom Kauahom	Pus hom[1]	{Puzkohom (p. 72) {Kauil (p. 91)
3 Ahau	Yax Cocaymut	Yax Cocaimut[2]	{Ek Cocahmut (p. 92) {Yax Cocaymut (p. 72)
1 Ahau	Amayte Ku	Amaite Kauil	
12 Ahau	Yaxhol Chuen	Yaxal Chuen	{Yaxal Chuen (p. 96) {Yaxaal Chuen (p. 72)
10 Ahau	Lahun Channal	[La]hun Chaan[3]	
8 Ahau	Amayte Kauil	{Amaite Kauil {Cit Bolon Ua	Kinich Kakmo (p. 98)
6 Ahau	Kinich Kakmo	Kinich Kakmo	
4 Ahau	Ah Bacocob[4]	Ah Bal Cab	Ah Bacocol (p. 73)
2 Ahau	Buluc Ch'abtan?[5]	Buluc Ch'abtan?	Buluc Ch'aabtan? (p. 73)
13 Ahau	Ytzamna Ytzam Tzab[6]	Itzamna Chac Sabin	Ytzamna Ytzam Tzab (p. 73)

[1]Perez 160 has *piz kouhom uil*. Kaua also has *uil*, but in both cases there is little reason to doubt that *u uich* has been wrongly copied. Mani (Perez 77) has P'uzhan.

[2]Perez 161 has yax cocat mut, but on page 78 ya cocah mut.

[3]Perez 164 has lahun ch'an, which is certainly wrong, and, on page 81, hun chaan and citbolon ua.

[4]Kaua has *Ah-bacocob macan u uich, cimen u uich*. Gates translates this "Ah Bacocob. Covered its [his] face, dead its [its] face." Mani (p. 83) has ahba cocol. Ah Bac alone, would be "the bone one." Perez 154 has Uac chu ahua.

[5]Buluc Ch'abtan is not given as the countenance of the katun but as the bearer of the burden. Mani (Perez 84) has buluc chaab tan.

[6]Mani (Perez 85) has ytzamna: zab, and on Perez 156 itzamna followed by an illegible word, perhaps cabib.

Thus the numerous representations of the date 6 Caban 0 Mol indicate that the astronomers of Copan had decided that on 10 Mol at 13.0.8.10.7   10 Manik 10 Mol the sun rose and set at the same position as at 9.17.0.0.0   13 Ahau 18 Cumku. The equation might be reversed, and the present-day solar equivalent of 18 Cumku at 13.0.0.0.0   4 Ahau 8 Cumku might be sought. On Copan Z occurs the date 9.17.0.0.0   13 Ahau 18 Cumku, and a distance number leads to a suppressed 9.16.18.9.19   12 Cauac 2 Zac. The date is six years later than the 6 Caban 10 Mol, and the correction therefore is one or two days greater; 18 Cumku plus 209 days is 2 Zac. Then 13.0.0.0.10   1 Oc 18 Cumku occupied the same position in that year as did 9.16.18.9.19   12 Cauac 2 Zac at the time the monument was erected.

position of 8 Ceh at 13.0.0.0.0   4 Ahau 8 Cumku. The interval is 3751 years, calling for a correction of 180 days by Gregorian, but the Maya correction, as in the case of Copan, runs a day or so less than Gregorian, viz. 8 Ceh+179=2 Zip. At 9.11.0.0.0 the LC dates were just half a year ahead of solar positions, hence the interest in solar corrections at that time.

The Maya also applied corrections to reach the solar positions in current time of 8 Cumku at 13.0.0.0.0   4 Ahau 8 Cumku, or the reverse (solar equivalent at 13.0.0.0.0 of 8 Cumku in current time). Copan I carries the date 9.10.19.15.0   4 Ahau 8 Ch'en which is a determinant of 8 Cumku. Gregorian calls for a correction of 183 days; the Maya calculation is 8 Ch'en+180=8 Cumku.

At Palenque the date 9.12.18.5.16   2 Cib 14 Mol, together with its sequent day, 9.12.18.5.17 3 Caban 15 Mol, occurs several times, and on more than one occasion is linked to 13.0.0.0.0 4 Ahau 8 Cumku. The interval is 3802 years, calling for a correction of 191½ days. In Palenque calculations of that time 14 Mol at 13.0.0.0.0 occupied the same position as 8 Cumku in the year then current. The calculation is: 14 Mol+194=8 Cumku, with 15 Mol+193=8 Cumku given as an alternative. These last are not so close to the mark as the determinants already cited. The subject is discussed in greater detail and illustrated with a table of determinants in Appendix V. At one time I accepted Teeple's suggestion that 7.6.0.0.0 was used in addition to 13.0.0.0.0 as a base for calculating determinants (Thompson, 1932b). Subsequently, I expressed skepticism as to the Maya use of that second base (Thompson, 1936), a view I continue to hold. Of the correctness of the determinant theory, as first outlined by Teeple, I have no doubts, although I would hesitate long before accepting Teeple's views as to the corrections having been calculated with the aid of lunar-solar equations.

These calculations concerning positions in the solar year were of great value to the Maya in determining the auguries of each katun (p. 64). Another kind of count, the 819-day cycle (p. 212), relates positions, both solar and lunar, with the close of the current katun.

SUMMARY

The ends of periods, particularly the ends of katuns, were of great importance to the Maya, not only because each marked the completion of one more stage in the endless journey of time, but also because with the end of each period a new set of gods, wielding new powers, took command. The luck of the katun changed, thereby affecting the whole community.

In the books of Chilam Balam are found many terms and set phrases to describe the ends of periods; in the hieroglyphic texts there are arrangements of hieroglyphs to mark those endings. There is fairly strong evidence for the identification of some prefixes and prefatory glyphs used in these groupings with the terms *xoc*, "count," *tz'oc*, "completion," and *hitz'*, "expiration," which occur in chronological passages of the books of Chilam Balam. Special glyphs were employed to mark the end of the tun as well, and also to indicate completion of five tuns from the end of the preceding katun, and five tuns lacking to the end of the current katun. A special affix served to convert cardinal numbers to ordinals.

The glyph for completion of half a period, misnamed the lahuntun glyph, is used to mark the half-katuns and half-baktuns. It illustrates in an interesting manner the use of the shell symbol for completion, and, as well, the

Maya practice of fusing glyphs so that the main element of one becomes an infix of the other.

There are several other glyphs which appear to be associated with period endings.

The Maya frequently recorded in the inscriptions anniversaries of important dates which did not end a period. Most commonly the first katun anniversary was thus signalized, but 5-tun, 13-tun, 1¼-katun, 1½-katun and 2-katun anniversaries were also noted. All known cases of such anniversaries are listed. A special postfix, the bundle, was sometimes employed with the katun or tun signs to mark such anniversaries, and in such dates a variant of the haab glyph could be substituted for the usual tun sign or the winged cauac.

A method of recording dates, which was almost certainly used in parts of Yucatan, involves a record of the tun in which the given CR falls, together with the day Ahau on which the current katun ends, e.g. (10.2.12.1.8) 9 Lamat 11 Yax falling in Tun 13 of (Katun) 1 Ahau. The interpretation corresponds closely to the method of writing dates, even to the omission of the word katun, followed in the books of Chilam Balam. The various texts supply some interesting prefixes and prefatory signs, and hint that the so-called "Ben-Ich" prefix may mean "countenance."

The appearance of katun glyphs, often with this same "Ben-Ich" prefix, and with coefficients running from 2 to 6 but most generally 3, 4, and 5, presents a difficult problem. Solution is hindered by the fact that the best series of occurrences of this glyph is at Yaxchilan, where the correct positions of most of the CR dates are uncertain.

The strange custom of the "guest" katun is outlined, and the patron gods of the katuns, as given in various passages of the books of Chilam Balam, are listed. The chapter concludes with a brief outline of the determinant theory.

Most unfortunately, we who style ourselves Maya epigraphers tend to regard the ends of katuns primarily as units in a mathematical system, and transcribe them as a jumble of digits, periods, and strange-sounding words. We forget that ringing sentence of Elihu: "for the ear trieth words, as the mouth tasteth meat." Despite the danger of being repetitious I feel the need to emphasize once again the very different position the ends of katuns held in Maya eyes. They were the climaxes of the great mysteries, every whit as sacred as were those of Eleusis to the early Greeks. Each marked the end of a major stage in that great imaginative concept of the Maya, the majestic journey of time through eternity. Each was celebrated in the antiphonal chants of the Maya. Each was honored by the painstaking hewing and arduous transportation and erection of great shafts of stone. Glyphs, laboriously carved, told in measured lines of the greatness of the event. The grand cadences of the Initial Series sang its glory and the concluding hieroglyphs echoed its praise; towering pyramids rose to exalt it and stone lintels intoned its majesty. Captives lost their lives in sacrifice to it; priests shed their own blood in its honor. The whole pomp and wealth of each community was directed to its greater glory in a degree not seen by western eyes since the passing of mediaevalism.

9

Ritualistic and Astronomical Cycles

My planets, these live embers of my passion,
These children of my hurricanes of flame,
Flung thro' the night, for midnight to refashion,
Praise, and forget, the splendour whence they came.
—ALFRED NOYES, *Watchers of the Sky*

THE DAYS and the months, the tuns and the katuns, did not march alone through eternity: others marched with them. Gods succeeded one another as rulers of the hours of darkness; the planets and that other wanderer of the sky, the moon, traveled the bourneless road. The Maya sought agreement between these stages of varying length, so that they would know when all the voyagers rested together at the *lub*. In the case of ritualistic groupings, such as that of the lords of the nights, the task was easy; when the unequal revolutions of planets were involved, and when fractions of days frustrated agreement, the task was difficult.

LORDS OF THE NIGHTS

IDENTIFICATION OF THE SERIES

The existence among the Aztec of a group of nine gods who ruled over the nights in sequence has been known for a long time. They are named by Serna (1892, p. 345), who wrote in 1656, and discussed by Boturini (1746, p. 57) and Leon y Gama (1792). The corresponding glyphs were identified at the close of the last century by del Paso y Troncoso in Codex Bourbon and by Seler in other Mexican codices. Slightly more than 30 years later I showed that Glyph G of the lunar series really consisted of nine different glyphs (only eight of them were identified), and that these repeated in sequence and clearly corresponded in function to the nine lords of the nights of central Mexico (Thompson, 1929). It was demonstrated that "in order came the grand Infernal peers." For instance, the commonest of the nine glyphs, the night sun, was found only with days that ended tuns or were removed therefrom by multiples of nine days. Subsequently, Beyer (1936d) identified the eighth form, and in other papers (Thompson, 1935, pp. 84–85; 1940b; 1942; 1944c; and Beyer, 1935b; 1935d) it was established that Glyphs G and F of the lunar series were not truly a part of that series at all because both, or Glyph G alone, could accompany any CR dates, whereas the regular glyphs of the lunar series are found only with IS. Nevertheless, in view of the established custom of speaking of Glyph G of the lunar series, the term will be retained, just as the manifestly incorrect terms Chacmool and Baktun 9 when we mean Baktun 10 have been retained in the literature for convenience.

The employment of Glyph G is of considerable antiquity, for G5 accompanies the IS of the Leiden plaque, and is also found with a CR date on the very early Balakbal 5 (fig. 34,25,26). As is the case with most hieroglyphs, there are personified forms and symbolic variants, although all of these have not been identified. Glyphs G1, G4, and G5 have coefficients, the numbers 9, 7, and 5, respectively. I see no reason for doubting that these numbers form parts of the name glyphs of the gods in question.

IDENTIFICATION OF THE GODS

The names of the nine lords of the nights of the Aztec have been preserved for us by Serna. With necessary and perfectly justifiable corrections in orthography, these are:

Xiuhtecutli	God of fire, year or grass	Bad
Itztli	God of flint	Bad
Piltzintecutli	Lord of the youths or youthful lord	Very good
Centeotl	God of maize, ears of corn, and bread	Very good
Mictlantecutli	God of infernal regions	Good
Chalchihuitlicue	Lady with skirt of jade	Good
Tlazolteotl	Goddess of love	Bad
Tepeyollotl	Heart of the mountains	Good
Quiauitecutli	Lady [Lord] of the rain	Good

The identifications of the deities and the fortune of each night are as given by Serna. The former are quite correct save that Quiauitecutli should be the lord of the rain. Serna notes that *yohua*, "night," was added to the name of each deity when he or she functioned as a lord of the night.

The glyphs of the nine lords as given in the various codices agree with Serna's list, although there are minor variations. Tlaloc, god of rain, is the ninth lord corresponding to Quiauitecutli, which is a designation rather than a proper name.

The glyphs of the Maya lords of the nights do not correspond closely to the Mexican gods. The series presumably starts with G1, which is used with the first day of a tun, and therefore corresponded to 1 Imix, when that day opened Katun 11 Ahau, the first katun of the round of 13, the katun of the creation.

G1. This glyph invariably has a coefficient of 9. Generally the main element consists of a hand with fingers horizontal and thumb vertical. In the angle between the forefinger and the thumb there is a head (fig. 34,*1–7*). This is generally the head of God C, his features blending with those of a monkey. A circle of dots, partly hidden by his profile, is generally in front of his face, precisely as in Glyph X of the lunar series (fig. 36). In one text (fig. 34,*2*) the head of God C within the angle of the hand is replaced by what is almost certainly a fish grasped by a hand (cf. fig. 30,*60–63*). The connection here probably lies in the fact that God C has a water symbol (circlets, kan cross) before his face, and fish is a symbol for water. This is just one more complication with regard to this very perplexing god.

G2. A few symbolic variants and one head variant of this glyph exist (fig. 34,*8–13*). The most detailed and best preserved example is on the ball-court marker at Chinkultic, with the early IS 9.7.17.12.14 11 Ix 7 Zotz'. Above the main element, a kind of cross between the lower part of the tun sign and the upper part of Imix, there is a double scroll, perhaps a vegetal motif. To the left there is a second prefix, in the form of an arc outlined with small circles, and with more circles within the points of the arc. It has already been noted that outlining with small circles symbolizes water. Mol is an example of this. The head variant is that of a youthful deity without any distinguishing characteristics. On the rather weathered IS lintel of Chichen Itza there is a poor example of Glyph G2 with three circles as a prefix in place of the double scroll. These may be numerical dots, in which case Glyph G2 is associated with the number 3. Thus we have for the identification of this deity: a resemblance to the jade part of the tun sign, scrolls possibly a vegetal motif, a second prefix which probably symbolizes water, and a possible association with the number 3. Three, however, is associated with rain and storms (p. 133), so there is a fair probability that the second lord of the night was a rain deity.

G3. One head variant and several symbolic variants of this form exist (fig. 34,*14–21*). The head is that of a bird which on the strength of its beaked nose and projecting ears can be identified probably as the Moan bird, the bird of the rain clouds. The symbolic variant consists of two ovals with simple designs on the interior, one of which is the propeller sign (cf. fig. 30,*52–54*). These ovals are enclosed on two or three sides with lines of little circles, which, as already noted, usually represent rain. It is therefore fairly evident that Glyph G3 represents some pluvial deity.

G4. Both head variants and symbolic variants of this glyph have been recovered, and to both forms a numerical coefficient of 7 is attached as a prefix. The head is that of a Roman-nosed deity with a prominent oval on the crown of the head (fig. 34,*22–24*). The personified forms are clearly the symbolic elements given head form. The design is rather close to that of the Kan glyph, but none is sufficiently well preserved to make this identification certain. In central Mexico, at least, the number 7 is closely connected with deities of maize (Chicomecoatl, Chicomollotzin, and Chicomexochitl).

G5. Only symbolic forms of this glyph exist. The main element has no outstanding characteristics, and in the most ornate example, Yaxchilan L 48, the interior can be compared only to the last period of Picasso (fig. 34,*25–30*). Characteristic are an oval infix with curved interior lines, and an affix which has a bent line of dots. A numerical coefficient of 5 is always present. The number 5 is associated with the earth monster and with the Mam, the god of the interior of the earth, the conch man (p. 133). Whether Glyph G5 corresponds to him is another matter; on present evidence it can be regarded as no more than a possibility.

G6. Only one moderately well preserved example of Glyph G6 has survived. It is the head of a youngish deity with a bracket in front of his face. There are no outstanding characteristics (fig. 34,*31*).

G7. Both head variants and symbolic variants of this glyph are recorded (fig. 34,*32–38*). One of the heads is surmounted by a hand, although a hand is not visible in the other. The symbolic variant may take one of two forms: it may be a sign closely resembling that for white (cf. fig. 34,*33* and probably *37* with fig. 17,*48–54*), or it may consist of the elements seen in figure 34,*32*, which for clarity I tentatively call the three-circles-and-bundle variant. The pseudo-white symbol and the circles-and-bundle variant may be fused (fig. 34,*35*). In discussing the head which serves as the variable element of the IS introductory glyph corresponding to Pax (p. 116), it was noted that to it were attached various symbols, but those are the same as the elements which appear in Glyph G7, namely, the circles-and-bundle variant which is before the face (fig. 23,*18,19,34*), the pseudo-white symbol, worn as an earplug (fig. 23,*34*), and what is surely the paw of some large animal, probably that of a jaguar, corresponding to the hand of Glyph G7, and worn on the temple of two of the patrons of Pax (fig. 23,*18,20*). We shall find these elements recurring in various combinations to form Glyph X1. It is also noteworthy that the original of the Glyph G7 shown in figure 34,*36* has a distinctly feline appearance, and has a treatment of the area where the lower jaw should be which is reminiscent of that of the Pax regents. Unfortunately, this glyph is rather weathered, and one can not be certain of details.

Accordingly, it is reasonably certain that the seventh lord of the night is the same deity as the one who presides over the month Pax, and who appears to be a variant of the jaguar god of number 7, or perhaps a puma. The likelihood of this identification's being correct is greatened by the fact that one example of G7 has a coefficient of 7 (fig. 34,*35*), and another example may have the same numerical coefficient, although this might well be a non-numerical prefix (fig. 34,*33*). Seven is the number of the jaguar god, who being a deity of the interior of the earth is eminently suited to be a lord of the night, as was his Aztec counterpart, Tepeyollotl.

G8. Beyer, who first identified Glyph G8, believed that the queer-shaped element was a conventionalized snake (fig. 34,*39–45*); I am of the opinion that it is a section of conch shell (pp. 117, 278). The conch, as a symbol for water in general, came to stand in particular for that primeval body of water in which floated the saurian monster whose back was the earth. By extension, the conch became a symbol of the surface and the interior of the earth (p. 133), and for that reason it is an attribute of several deities who inhabit the interior of the earth, notably the god Mam, lord of the number 5, and Tepeyollotl, the Aztec jaguar god who inhabits the interior of the earth. The conch shell, therefore, as the symbol of one of the lords of the underworld, would be highly appropriate.

G9. The last of the lords of the nights is by far the commonest in the inscriptions because he ruled over the nights of tun endings. Accordingly, he is represented on almost every IS with lunar series commemorating a katun, half-katun, or quarter-katun, and, in addition, by the law of averages occurs on a number of dates that do not end periods. It was the observation of the fact that this deity occurred only on PE and on days removed therefrom by multiples of nine days, that led to the discovery of the lords of the nights. The ninth god is the night sun. Head and symbolic forms are represented in about equal numbers. The main element in the first case is the head of the aged sun god; in the second case it is the kin glyph (fig. 34,*46–57*). Not infrequently half the kin sign, whether the main element of the symbolic form or the headdress of the head form, is crosshatched to indicate blackness. There is also a prefix which usually takes the form of three death eyes or perhaps shells in a row, but sometimes is a vegetal motif.

Black, death eyes, shells, and vegetation are all symbols of the earth or its interior (pp. 189, 280). The presence of one or more of these symbols, therefore, converts the sun god into the night sun, the manifestation of the sun on his nocturnal journey from west to east through the underworld. They correspond to the addition of *yohua,* "night," to the Aztec lords of the nights, as reported by Serna.

Nowhere in the books of Chilam Balam or in any other writings have the names of the lords of the nights been discovered, although there is a bare possibility that they may yet be found in the Ritual of the Bacabs. There are, however, fairly obvious references to the group as a whole. Collectively, they seem to have been known as the Bolon-ti-Ku, "the nine gods," in contrast to the Oxlahun-ti-Ku, "the thirteen gods," who are almost certainly the 13 gods of the days and of the 13 heavens. The struggles between the two groups are recounted briefly in Chumayel (pp. 42, 43), as well as in Tizimin and Mani. This event took place in the interval between the creation of the world and its destruction by flood. The details are not clear, but the nine gods appear to have fought and defeated the 13 gods, and despoiled them of their insignia, a kind of forerunner of the famous plot of Anatole France.

We have no information, such as Serna gives for Mexico, on the influences for good or evil of the Maya lords of the nights.

Correspondence with Mexican Series

There is a certain, but far from satisfactory, correspondence between the Maya and Mexican lords of the nights. In several cases the same deity occurs in both lists, but the sequence is not the same, and, in view of the uncertain identifications of the gods in the Maya series, there is little profit in comparing the two groups at the present time.

Relationship with Other Counts

A fundamental Maya practice was to bring the various cycles of time into relation with one another, so as to know after what interval the starting points of each would again coincide. The outstanding example of this is the CR which harmonizes the 260 days of the sacred almanac with the 365 days of the vague year.

The Maya were also interested in relating the cycle of the nine lords of the nights with other cycles. So far as the relationship with the LC is concerned the matter was extremely simple, for 360 is divisible by 9, and therefore the starting points of both counts will coincide every tun.

The cycle of 260 days and the nine lords of the nights have no common factor. Accordingly, the starting points of the two series will not coincide until after the lapse of 2340 days (9×260), which is 6.9.0 in Maya numeration. This round of the two counts was of interest to the Maya, and is recorded on Dresden 30c–33c (fig. 62,*1–4*). That section consists of nine sacred almanacs with 20 major sections, each of 117 days. These in turn are divided into nine subdivisions, of 13 days apiece. The series starts with 11 Ben, passes to 11 Oc, then to 11 Manik and so in order until each day has appeared in the sequence. In that way every day with a coefficient of 11 appears nine times, each time with a different lord of the night. The table closes with God G9 ruling the day 11 Ahau, on the assumption that the series opens with God G1 as ruler. The arrangement is shown in part in Table 15. The accompanying pictures, however, are not vignettes of the nine lords of the nights, but all portray God B. The first four

position of the deity associated with any date will advance one place at each repetition of a CR. Therefore, a CR date if it is accompanied by the corresponding Glyph G is firmly placed in a cycle of nine CR. That is to say, an interval of 1.3.14.9.0 must elapse before the same combination of CR and Glyph G can occur. This fact is of considerable help in restoring damaged IS when Glyph G is legible, and also for placing a CR date in the LC, when Glyph G is present.

The earliest application of this method was to a date on Copan I (Thompson, 1935, pp. 84–85). In that text a position 10 Lamat is linked by a distance number of 10.8

TABLE 15—RELATIONSHIP OF LORDS OF NIGHTS WITH THE 260-DAY CYCLE (DRESDEN 30c–33c)

G1	G2	G3	G4	G5	G6	G7	G8	G9
(east, red)	(north, white)	(west, black)	(south, yellow)					
11 Ben	11 Cimi	11 Cauac	11 Eb	11 Chicchan	11 Etz'nab	11 Chuen	11 Kan	11 Caban
11 Oc	11 Akbal	11 Cib	11 Muluc	11 Ik	11 Men	11 Lamat	11 Imix	11 Ix
11 Manik	11 Ahau	11 Ben	11 Cimi	11 Cauac	11 Eb	11 Chicchan	11 Etz'nab	11 Chuen
11 Kan	11 Caban	11 Oc	11 Akbal	11 Cib	11 Muluc	11 Ik	11 Men	11 Lamat
11 Imix	11 Ix	11 Manik	11 Ahau	11 Ben	11 Cimi	11 Cauac	11 Eb	11 Chicchan, etc.

compartments carry glyphs of the world directions and world colors. These last are combined with the *te* (1) affix, and refer to the world-direction trees (p. 56). Each compartment has the usual four glyphs, the first of which is in each case a highly conventionalized hand in an inverted position (Gates' Glyph 141; p. 266). This glyph, however, appears in several other divinatory almanacs, and therefore can not refer to the lords of the nights. Nevertheless, I think that this arrangement of nine sacred almanacs almost certainly was set down because it harmonized the 260-day sacred almanac with the round of the lords of the nights. Since the above was written Satterthwaite (1947, pp. 24–27) has made the same identification.

Of attempts to relate the lords of the nights with the year of 365 days no record has survived. Again, there is no common factor shared by 365 and 9. Accordingly 3285 days—9.2.5 in Maya notation—would have to elapse before the same lord of the night would again rule over the night of any given month position. Whether the lords of the nights also ruled in sequence over the hours of the night, as Seler thought, is still uncertain. It seems to me that there is a fair possibility that some such system obtained with the god who was ruler of the whole night also reigning (p. 177).

As 9 and 18,980 (the number of days in a CR) have no common factor, a different lord of the night will rule over each repetition of a CR date, and since 18,980 has a remainder of 8 when divided by 9, it is clear that the

to a damaged PE which was almost certainly the end of a Katun 6, 7, or 8. The Lamat date is accompanied by Glyphs G1 and F; the PE, by Glyphs G9 and F. Morley had suggested the reading 9.11.19.15.8 10 Lamat 16 Zotz', but this had to be rejected because it requires Glyph G2. The right solution was 8.6.0.10.8 10 Lamat 16 Pop. The sum of the uinals and kins is 208, and that divided by 9 leaves a remainder of 1, that is to say Glyph G1; the PE was 8.6.0.0.0 10 Ahau 13 Ch'en, which, of course, demands Glyph G9.

A better example is supplied by the elucidation of a date on Tonina 7 (Thompson, 1942). A CR date 11 Manik 15 Mac is accompanied by Glyph G2. The problem is to find its position in the LC. Clearly the inscription fell in Baktun 9. The CR in question occurs in the following positions in that baktun:

```
9. 1.13. 9.7  (G7)
9. 4. 6. 4.7  (G6)
9. 6.18.17.7  (G5)
9. 9.11.12.7  (G4)
9.12. 4. 7.7  (G3)
9.14.17. 2.7  (G2)
9.17. 9.15.7  (G1)
```

The corresponding forms of Glyph G, obtained by taking the remainder after dividing the uinals and kins by 9, are given in parentheses. Clearly the only position in Baktun 9 corresponding to 11 Manik 15 Mac with the required form of Glyph G is 9.14.17.2.7. The sum of uinals and kins is 47, which, divided by 9, leaves a remainder of 2, calling for Glyph G2 as required. Other examples of the use of Glyph G to place dates in the LC are given in Thompson (1940b, 1942, 1944c) and Beyer (1935b, 1935d, the former published in 1936).

A possible harmonizing of the lords of the nights with the four divisions of the 364-day count is discussed below in reviewing the functions of the 819-day cycle.

GLYPH F

Glyph F of the lunar series is very closely associated with Glyph G. When it is complete in itself it follows Glyph G, but not infrequently the two glyphs are fused. Glyph F consists of a central element, of which both head and symbol forms exist, to which are attached a prefix and a postfix (fig. 34,*58–62,64,67*). The symbolic form is a tied or knotted cord; the head form varies considerably. In many cases it is a grotesque head with a beaked nose of unusual prominence, but in a number of texts at Yaxchilan a peculiar element, consisting of a grotesque head set on its side, replaces this head.

The prefix, always above the main element, consists of two or three dots in a diagonal line, which are flanked to left by a leaflike element, to right by an inverted crescent. This prefix, with slight variations, is seldom omitted. The postfix, a bracket with a couple of nicks on the base and two or three circlets near the top is tentatively labeled the *te* (2) affix (p. 282). It is sometimes omitted from the fused G and F glyphs, more rarely from the symbolic variants.

There is a personified form of this postfix in the shape of a youthful head, apparently that of the maize god (p. 283; fig. 34,*21,63,68*). When the postfix is thus personified it becomes the main element, and the knot becomes a prefix.

On Copan D the full-figure glyph of G9 is rising from the ground. He carries on his back, as his burden, a roll of jaguar skin, indicated by the crosshatched spots and the triangular arrangements of dots as in Ix, the day of the jaguar (fig. 60, Gl B4). I think there can be no doubt that this jaguar bundle represents Glyph F, for it is not part of Glyph G9, and it is in the correct position between Glyph G and the month sign to be Glyph F. Beneath the roll of jaguar skin is a small element which looks rather like the knot, but which, on the evidence of other glyphs, must be something else.

On the mural of House E, Palenque, Glyph F consists of this jaguar bundle as the main element, together with the usual prefix of Glyph F and an obliterated postfix (fig. 34,*58*). A jaguar skin spread on a throne which is part of the design incised on a shell from Jaina has this same pinked border. The jaguar bundle also occurs as the main element of Glyph F on Tila B. The *te* (2) postfix is present, but most unusually the flattened fish head serves as prefix, if one accepts Beyer's drawing. The Palenque and Tila specimens indicate that the jaguar skin corresponds to the knotted element. What the connection may be between these two signs is not apparent. The jaguar bundle is rare, but its wide distribution indicates that it is not a local caprice.

The main element of Glyph F, then, may be a knot, a jaguar skin, a head with a large hooked nose, or the head, in a vertical position, of what appears to be a frog. The jaguar, as we have seen (p. 74), symbolizes darkness and the interior of the earth, and I should not be surprised to learn that the jaguar skin represented the starry sky of night. The up-ended head of the frog may also have a nocturnal connection because of its use in the lunar series. Glyph F, because it never appears without Glyph G and is often fused with it (fig. 34,*14–17,29,39, 40,42,49* etc.), should explain or amplify the function of Glyph G. The pair should translate "God G*n* is the lord of the night," or that he is power, or that he rules the darkness, or words to that effect. The jaguar skin, as a symbol of darkness and the interior of the earth, or, conceivably, the night sky, would fit such an interpretation, but it is not now apparent how the knotted element or the face with the hooked nose could have that meaning. At present, no translation for them can be offered.

THE 819-DAY CYCLE

In five Maya texts the month position is separated from the rest of the IS by the insertion of a parenthetical clause. In four texts and almost certainly in the case of the fifth, which is damaged, a distance number of less than two tuns is subtracted from the IS to reach a day with a coefficient of 1. There are six explanatory glyphs in four of these inserted clauses (only four glyphs survive in one damaged text). Four of these glyphs are the same in the four undamaged texts; two are variables (fig. 35,*1–5*). In announcing these unusual constructions, I demonstrated that the dates of the parenthetical clauses occurred at intervals of 819 days (Thompson, 1943d).

These IS with their associated dates are:

Palenque 1

A	A1–B5	9.12. 6. 5. 8	3 Lamat	(IS)
	A9–B9	1.10. 1		(subtract)
A'	A10	9.12. 4.13. 7	1 Manik 10 Pop	
	A11–B11		Explanatory glyphs	
	B12		Missing. Probably 6 Zac, month of IS	

Yaxchilan L 29 and L 30

B	A1–A4	9.13.17.12.10	8 Oc	(IS)
	E1–F1	1. 1.17		(subtract)
B′	E2–F2	9.13.16.10.13	1 Ben 1 Ch'en	
	E3–F5		Explanatory glyphs	
	G1		13 Yax	(month of IS)

Yaxchilan 11 (right and left sides)

C	B′1–B′7	9.16. 1. 0. 0	11 Ahau	(IS)
	C′2–C′3	1. 3. 6		(subtract)
C′	C′4–C′5	9.15.19.14.14	1 Ix 7 Uo	
	C′6–C′9		Explanatory glyphs	
	C′10		8 Zec	(month of IS)

Yaxchilan 1

D	A1–D3	9.16.10. 0. 0	1 Ahau	(IS)
		(1. 1.10)	Presumably on eroded section	(subtract)
D	E2	(9.16. 8.16.10	1 Oc) 18 Pop	(day sign obliterated)
	E3–F6		Explanatory glyphs	
	E7		3 Zip	(month of IS)

Quirigua K

E	A1–A5a	9.18.15. 0. 0	3 Ahau	(IS)
	A6	10.10		(subtract)
E′	B6b–A7a	9.18.14. 7.10	1 Oc 18 Kayab	
	A7b–C2a		Explanatory glyphs	
	C4		3 Ahau 3 Yax	(day and month of IS)
	D4		Further explanatory glyphs	

Another example may perhaps be added. This differs from the rest in that it does not interrupt the IS but immediately follows the lunar series thereof (fig. 53,*1*):

Palenque Cross

F	A1–A9	12.19.13.4.0	8 Ahau 18 Zec (IS)	
	B13	1.0	(subtract, lunar variant for 20)	
F′	A16–B16	12.19.13.3.0	1 Ahau 18 Zotz'	
	A14–B15		Explanatory glyphs	

There is probably yet another example. This is to be seen on the south panel of the east doorway of Copan T 11. The accompanying date is not preserved, but may have been 9.17.2.10.4 1 Kan 7 Yax. The text is too uncertain to use (fig. 54,*4*). See Addendum, page 296.

In the case of the other texts only that of D′ is clouded because of weathering. However, the month position 18 Pop is perfectly clear, and in view of the parallel cases, the restoration suggested is almost certainly correct. For reasons of brevity it will be assumed that this reading is not open to question.

The explanatory glyphs obviously treat of the same subject, although there are certain differences, owing possibly to the use of variable forms of the same glyph or substitution of another glyph with the same meaning (fig. 35,*1–5*). All five texts include a glyph with a coefficient of 1, which, except in Text A′, occupies the last place, immediately preceding the detached month sign of the IS. This is the head of a rodent with the so-called bone glyph as affix, which forms one of the elements of Glyph B of the lunar series.

The principal features of the various glyphs, numbered in the sequence in which they occur, are as follows:

1. Obviously the same glyph in all cases. In all texts except A′ it, like the month sign Pax, has at the top an opening through which in three cases pass two diverging curls. There is an infix resembling the Chuen sign, and in three cases a lunar infix or postfix. This is Gates' Glyph 92, which occurs very frequently in the codices.

2. In Text B′ this is a kin sign with a half-kin as superfix. In Texts C′ and D′ this is replaced by the head of a god with a Roman nose and with a sign in front. In view of the kin sign in Text B′ these may be portraits of the sun god but they may represent Glyph G6. In Text E′ the second glyph is a cauac sign but the partly obliterated third glyph appears to be the same face with a Roman nose.

3. In Texts C′ and D′ the central element consists of crossed bands. There is a "flame" affix and, in the case of Text C′, what may be a coefficient of 9, but the details are hard to make out, and it is possible that this element is not numerical. One is reminded of the crossed bands in planetary bands. In Text B′ a grotesque head with affix replaces this sign. In Text E′ this glyph appears to be suppressed.

4. In Texts B′–D′ this is the "shell" glyph with arms and legs added, the so-called Glyph Y, which occurs in some lunar series, particularly at Yaxchilan, and which must mean dawn or night (p. 174). The corresponding glyph in Text E′ is largely obliterated.

5. In Texts B′, C′, and E′ this is a grotesque head with a branching flamelike element emerging from the forehead. In Text A′ this same head occurs but not in the correct sequence. In Text D′ a grotesque head can be made out, but it is not possible to say whether the flamelike element is present.

6. This is the "rodent" glyph to which attention has already been called.

In F' the explanatory glyphs differ from those already discussed. The first is the glyph with Pax and Chuen elements but without a lunar postfix. The second glyph has the branching "flame" element emerging from a glyph which from other examples can be shown to represent the top of the head of the god who normally has this element. The other two glyphs do not figure in the texts already reviewed.

In several of the texts there are supplementary glyphs before or after the parenthetical clauses, to which they appear to be related (fig. 35,6,7). Also, on Quirigua K the Pax-Chuen glyph is repeated, complete with lunar postfix, after the detached conclusion of IS and lunar series.

As in all six texts the day sign coefficient reached by subtraction is 1, the intervals between these positions must be multiples of 13. In days these intervals are 11,466, 15,561, 3,276, 16,380, and 1,433,250, but the highest common factor of these is not 13 but 819. Such a high common factor could hardly be the result of chance; the odds are over a thousand to one against it. This number is composed of 91 × 9, or 117 × 7, or 273 × 3, or 9 × 7 × 13.

The numbers 9, 7, and 13 are of great ritualistic importance. Nine represents the nine underworlds and the nine lords of the nights, seven probably the seven layers of the earth, and thirteen the thirteen heavens. The number 91 is ritualistically and arithmetically important, but its multipliers are four, five, and twenty in Dresden, not nine.

Since 819 is divisible by nine, the same form of Glyph G of the lunar series, G6, is required by all the parenthetical clauses. In this connection it is interesting to note that Texts B, C, and D, all of which are from Yaxchilan, are followed by a glyph with a coefficient of 6. The glyph itself is a simplified face above what is probably a lunar affix. In one case half the face is covered with crosshatching, a symbol for black and presumably, by extension, darkness. (Cf. crosshatching of kin sign when employed as lord of the night, p. 210.) One wonders whether this face with coefficient of 6 can refer to the fact that the sixth lord of the night and underworld rules over the parenthetical dates. It is also worth noting that it was this same sixth lord of the night and underworld who ruled over the opening night of the 13-day week in which 13.0.0.0.0   4 Ahau 8 Cumku fell. His reign started at 12.19.19.17.17   1 Caban 5 Cumku, three days before 4 Ahau 8 Cumku. In fact this 1 Caban 5 Cumku is the starting point of the 819-day cycle.

As only once in every 63 times will a day with a co-efficient of 1 also mark the start of the 819-day cycle, the fact that this first day with a coefficient of 1 before 4 Ahau 8 Cumku is a base in the 819-day cycle argues strongly for that count's being primarily ritualistic.

The fact that the base of the 819-day cycle falls three days before 4 Ahau 8 Cumku implies that the gods who were in power at the start of the period continued to exercise certain influence throughout its span, thereby giving further scope to the balancing of good and bad influences inherent in the calendarial divination of the Maya. Such a concept certainly existed. On the Mexican tableland the god of the 13-day "week" shared power with the patron of each day until a fresh god of the "week" entered into power with the return of a day with a coefficient of 1. Similarly among the Ixil Maya the year-bearer deity who rules over a year bearer with a co-efficient of 1, continues to influence human affairs until, 13 years later, another year bearer with coefficient of 1 enters (Lincoln, 1942, p. 115).

It is obvious that this cycle of 819 days must involve more than a grouping of lords of the skies and underworlds. The number is too high, for after 117 days the cycle would have been completed, each lord of the night would have ruled over a 13-day period. However, only after 819 days would sequences of nine lords of the underworlds, 13 lords of the heavens, and the presumed seven lords of the earth once more coincide. There is no strong evidence for the existence of a group of seven terrestrial deities, but in the account of the creation in Chumayel there is mention of a certain Ah Uuc-Cheknal, "he who fertilizes the maize seven times," who came from the seventh stratum of the earth (or the seven strata of the earth). Since both the group of 13 gods and the group of nine gods bear collective names used in the singular, it is not impossible that Ah Uuc-Cheknal is really the name of a group of seven gods who are associated with the seven layers of the earth. Ralph L. Roys informs me that he sees no valid reason why the Maya text should not be taken to refer to seven deities and seven strata, not necessarily to a single deity from the seventh stratum.

It is possible, therefore, that the 819-day cycle developed from a desire to mark the coincidence of the starting points of these three series of deities. It is also possible, however, that 819 days represent the interval which must elapse before the cycle of nine lords of the nights and that of the 91-day period will again coincide. As we shall see (Chapter 11), the period of 364 days and its four quarters, each of 91 days, were of considerable importance to the Maya, both for calculations and as a handy quartering of the year to indicate approximately equinoxes and solstices. There is some evidence that the 819-day cycle was related in some cases to divisions of the year, so it is probable that the 91-day interval is one of its components to which the Maya attached importance. The possibility that the 819-day cycle had an astrological or astronomical meaning cannot be overlooked. The cycle is 117 × 7. In 117 the Maya had a good approximation to the synodical revolution of Mercury (115.877 days). Such an approximation would have suited them admirably because it complied with one of their most important desiderata, in that it constituted a re-entering cycle in terms of the 260-day almanac. At the end of 117 days the day coefficient would be the same. However, in order to achieve a return to the same coefficient and day, the 117-day cycle would have as its next highest order 117 × 20; in this case the multiplier of 117 is 7. Therefore, it is clear that any connection with Mercury would be a secondary, not a primary, purpose of this 819-day cycle. Moreover, it is very doubtful that the Maya paid attention to the synodical revolution of Mercury, which is short and difficult to observe accurately.

The position of the parenthetical clauses immediately after or, in one case, in the middle of, the lunar series, and the lunar elements which enter in them suggested the possibility that a lunar meaning might also be involved in this count.

Faced by these astronomical problems, I turned to Dr. Maud W. Makemson, Director of Vassar Observatory, and to Dr. Alexander Pogo, both of whom most kindly undertook the many laborious calculations needed to determine the positions of Mercury and the moon on the various dates in question. Because both specialists possess that rare combination, a mastery of both practical and Maya astronomy, their many suggestions were most useful.

An examination of the positions of Mercury on the 10 dates in question, using the Ahau equation 584,285, produced no pattern. Periodicity would, of course, be absent whatever correlation was used. It was clear that the 819-day cycle did not primarily involve Mercury (Thompson, 1943d, p. 144).

In connection with the possibility that a lunar significance might be attached to this cycle, Dr. Pogo pointed out that 819 days are within a day of 30 sidereal months and at the same time they approximate 27¾ synodical months. After 819 days, therefore, the moon would be in about the same position in relation to the stars but its age would have decreased by one phase. However, Dr. Pogo notes that as 30 sidereal revolutions of the moon are actually 819.65 days and 28 synodical revolutions are 826.86 days, an error will rapidly accumulate. Thus the 819-day cycle could not have been used without correction to calculate the actual positions of the moon against her stellar background, except for relatively short periods.

Again Drs. Makemson and Pogo kindly volunteered

to calculate the positions of the moon on Dates A–E and A′–E′ in view of the possibility that the IS in question might record observed positions of the moon with regard to the stars, whereas the parenthetical clauses might record calculated positions in an uncorrected cycle, or, alternatively, the parenthetical clauses might record occasions when the moon was in conjunction with certain important stars, both by observation and according to the uncorrected cyclic reckoning. Again no pattern emerged.

Dr. Makemson has suggested other ways in which the 819-day cycle might have been used. A discussion of these would take us too far afield and, in any case, would come best from her pen.

There remains another line of approach, that of linking the endings of the 819-day periods to the katuns current when the monuments in question were dedicated.

The dedicatory date of the lintels with which Date B′ is associated is 9.17.0.0.0. The distance from Date B′ to 9.17.0.0.0 is 22,827 days. This is within a day of 197 revolutions of Mercury (22,827.8 days). It is also 773 moons (22,827.15 days), and exactly 62½ solar years. Also 1 Ch'en is a determinant of 18 Cumku: 1 Ch'en + 197 = 18 Cumku (Gregorian correction is 197½ days). The Maya priest may have reasoned more or less as follows:

The 819-day cycle ended 377 days (just one synodical revolution of Saturn) before the IS. As a rule we do not record these cycle endings, but in this case it can be brought into an interesting relation to the dedicatory date, 9.17.0.0.0 13 Ahau 18 Cumku. On both dates there was a new moon, and on both dates Mercury was at the same point in the heavens (maximum eastern elongation). Moreover the sun is just half a revolution away at 1 Ben 1 Ch'en (Date B′) from where it will be at 9.17.0.0.0 13 Ahau 18 Cumku. In the first case it is 31 days after the summer solstice; in the second, 31 days after the winter solstice. Finally, 1 Ch'en occupied at Cycle 13 the same position in the solar year that 18 Cumku occupied in the year then current.

The lower part of Palenque 1, on which Date A′ is recorded, is missing, but it is probable that the dedicatory date was 9.12.10.0.0 or 9.13.0.0.0. If the latter, a reason for giving the end of the 819-day cycle exists in the fact that 9.13.0.0.0, Date A, and Date A′ all have the same moon age, which according to the lunar series was 19 days. Also the moon number of both 9.13.0.0.0 and Date A′ would be 5 according to the uniform lunar system, since the interval between them (186 moons) is divisible by 6. The lunar series is not in the uniform system, but records the moon number as 5. It is an interesting possibility, although nothing more, that when Stela 1 was erected Palenque had adopted the uniform system, but gave the moon age of the IS by the old system, thereby reaching the same moon number and moon age for all three dates. Lastly, 9.13.0.0.0 and the IS (not in this case the parenthetical date) are separated by 13½ solar years (the remainder is 183.8 days), the two dates lying about eight days before the vernal and autumnal equinoxes. The IS is also, as Teeple pointed out, a determinant of 9.13.0.0.0, for by Maya reckoning the sun on 6 Zac at Cycle 13 was in the same position as at 8 Uo in current time. 6 Zac + 187 = 8 Uo (Gregorian calls for a correction of 189 days).

Date C' was a new moon according to Maya calculation. Date C is recorded on this monument as 5 moons 12 days in the uniform system. The distance number of 1.3.6 equals 14 moons and 12 days, thereby indicating a moon age for Date C' of three moons no days. The dedicatory date of this monument is uncertain. The IS falls in Katun 9.17.0.0.0 13 Ahau 18 Cumku, which, as we have already seen, was also the date of a new moon,

rection calls for 209 days). Also 16 Ch'en is the same moon age as 18 Pop, since 207 days is within a third of a day of seven moons (206.7 days). In other words 16 Ch'en is half a year away from 18 Cumku, and 18 Pop is the anniversary of 16 Ch'en placed at Cycle 13, and the two linked dates of 18 Pop and 16 Ch'en have the same moon age. Also God G6 ruled on both dates.

Quirigua K, which carries Date E', has the dedicatory date 9.18.15.0.0. (Date E) as the IS, and the current katun was therefore 9.19.0.0.0 9 Ahau 18 Mol. The interval between Date E' and Katun 19 is 2010 days, which is one day more than five and a half solar years (2008.8 days). The katun ended, according to the correlation here followed, on June 26; Date E' fell on December 24, both dates being a few days after the solstices.

As Date E gives the moon age as 18 days, the moon must have been thought to have been full (15 days old) at Date E'. The moon at 9.19.0.0.0 would have been 17 days old by calculation from either of those points.

TABLE 16—THE 819-DAY CYCLE AND ITS ASSOCIATIONS

Text	Parenthetical Dates	Katun Ending	Interval in Days	Lunar Associations	Solar Associations
A'	9.12. 4.13. 7	9.13.0.0.0	5,493	Same moon age	Half-year advance over IS[1]
B'	9.13.16.10.13	9.17.0.0.0	22,827	Same moon age (new moon)	Half-year advance.[2]
C'	9.15.19.14.14	9.17.0.0.0	7,266	Same moon age (new moon)	None.[3]
D'	9.16. 8.16.10	9.17.0.0.0 } 9.16.8.6.3 }	207	Same moon age	Half-year advance.[4]
E'	9.18.14. 7.10	9.19.0.0.0	2,010	Two days difference in moon age.	Half-year and one day advance.[5]

[1]Date A also same moon age. Solar positions close to equinoxes.

[2]Mercury at same position on both dates. Same god in series of seven.

[3]Same god in series of seven ruled on both dates.

[4]Association is with 9.16.8.6.3 2 Akbal 16 Ch'en, the current determinant of 9.17.0.0.0, but this is not actually given in the text. Same lord of night (G6) ruled both dates. 16 Ch'en + 182 = 18 Cumku.

[5]Solar positions close to solstices. Moon at E' was full.

and furthermore was the third moon. Date C also occurs on Lintels 29 and 30, the dedicatory date of which was certainly 9.17.0.0.0. Accordingly, it is quite probable that 9.17.0.0.0 is the dedicatory date of Stela 11 as well or, failing that, marked the end of the current katun. There is no solar association linking these two dates, but it may be significant that on both dates the first god of the series of seven (terrestrial?) deities was in power.

Yaxchilan 1, which carries Date D', was erected at 9.16.10.0.0 (Date D). The current katun was, therefore, again 9.17.0.0.0 13 Ahau 18 Cumku. There is no direct relation between Date D' (1 Oc 18 Pop) and the katun ending, yet we have seen that solar half-years and the same moon age seem to be the matters which interested the Maya in these particular texts. Half a year back from the current 18 Cumku is 9.16.8.6.3 2 Akbal 16 Ch'en. However, 16 Ch'en is itself the determinant of 18 Pop at that date: 16 Ch'en + 207 = 18 Pop (Gregorian cor-

The precise secondary meaning of the early date (Date F') on the Temple of the Cross inscription is not clear. It is of interest to note that, as pointed out by Teeple several years ago, the IS is a determinant of 9.10.10.0.0 13 Ahau 18 Kankin. This last date, however, can not be connected with Date F', but the correction according to the Gregorian calendar would be 182 days. The Maya reckoned this as 180 days. Furthermore, as Bowditch pointed out many years ago, the early date 1.18.5.3.2 9 Ik 15 Ceh falls at a time when a correction of half a solar year was required. It is, accordingly, possible that this date, indirectly grouped with the series already discussed, is, in some way at present not clear, associated with solar time.

The various associations just discussed are presented in Table 16.

If the above interpretations are correct, the Maya did not bother to record every starting point of the 819-day cycle but only those on which there were lunar or solar relationships, or both, with the current katun ending, presumably links with the series of nine and 13 gods. As already noted, lunar elements occur in all the parenthetical clauses except Text A'. Text B' has a kin glyph surmounted by a second kin glyph cut in half, conceivably to indicate a solar half-year. The corresponding glyph in the remaining complete texts is the head of a deity, possibly the head of the sun god, although the usual attributes are lacking. Alternatively this head might represent God G6, who reigned over the first night of the 819-day cycle.

The ritualistic cycle of 819 days, therefore, was probably recorded only when its importance was enhanced by associations of an astronomical or calendarial nature with the end of the current katun, possibly only when the sun or moon or both were involved in the computations. The accompanying glyphs tend to bear out this thesis, since both solar and lunar glyphs are recognizable. The period of 819 days not only marked the return to the same starting point of the series of thirteen, nine, and seven deities, probably corresponding to the celestial, infernal, and terrestrial deities, but also embraced the two re-entering cycles, of nine and 91 days. The nine-day cycle, we know, was a nocturnal count. In addition, there is some evidence that this computing year of 364 days, together with its four divisions of 91 days apiece, was connected with the positions of the sun, as Dr. Makemson (1943, p. 217) has pointed out. She also notes that two IS connected with the computing year, namely 8.17.11.1.10 13 Oc 3 Mol and 10.1.1.1.5 13 Chicchan 3 Cumku, reach the autumnal equinox and the winter solstice respectively in the Goodman-Thompson correlation.

THE PLANET VENUS

Maya and Mexican Beliefs Concerning the Planet

Man has ever cherished the beauty of the planet Venus, wondered at its brilliance, and been astonied at its swift wayfaring. Poems, myths, and folk-tales bear witness to the high place that most moving of the stars of dawn and that most splendent lamp of the evening sky holds in our affections.

The Maya, with their deep appreciation of beauty, cannot have failed to see the splendor of the great planet, but their discrimination was warped by the baleful influences which surrounded the person of the stellar god. Our knowledge of the Maya attitude toward Venus is not so full as we would wish, but the pictorial scenes which accompany the Venus tables in Dresden are so similar to those in Mexican codices (Vatican B, Borgia, and Bologna) that we can be certain that the same concepts concerning the god existed in both areas, as first pointed out by Seler (1904a). Sundry details of the deities in the Dresden table show Mexican influence, but the general concept is Maya.

In Mexican belief Venus was particularly malignant at the moment of heliacal rising. Sahagun (1938, bk. 7, ch. 3) states that the Mexicans shut the doors and windows so that the light of the newly risen planet should not enter the houses, for it was unlucky and was believed to bring sickness. However, on some occasions which depended on the time (the day?) on which Venus appeared, heliacal risings of the planet were of good augury.

In a passage in the Anales de Cuauhtitlan (Codex Chimalpopoca, 1945, par. 51) the various influences are listed:

They (the old men) knew when he [Quetzalcoatl as Venus] appears, on what number and what particular signs he shines. He casts his rays at them, and shows his displeasure with them. If it [the sign which coincides with heliacal rising] falls on 1 Cipactli, he spears the old, men and women equally. If on 1 Ocelotl, if on 1 Mazatl, if on 1 Xochitl he spears the children. If on 1 Acatl he spears the great lords, just the same as on 1 Miquiztli. If on 1 Quiauitl, he spears the rain, and it will not rain. If on 1 Ollin, he spears the youths and maidens; if on 1 Atl, everything dries up. For that the old men and the old women venerated each of these signs.

Seler (1904a, pp. 384–87), in a fine exhibition of scholarship, compared this passage with the pictorial representations of the revolutions of Venus in the Mexican codices. The five days on which the planet consecutively rose in the cyclic Venus calendar are Cipactli, Acatl, Coatl, Ollin, and Atl. Below are listed the targets of Venus' spear in the pictures which accompany these signs.

Sign	Codex Victim	Anales de Cuauhtitlan
1. Cipactli	Water goddess	Venus spears aged
2. Acatl	Jaguar throne	Venus spears lords
3. Coatl	Various deities	...
4. Ollin	Warriors of jaguar order	Venus spears young
5. Atl	Maize deity with symbols of drought	Drought

The jaguar throne symbolizes chieftainship; the jaguar itself, with the sign Ollin, doubtlessly represents the military order of Jaguars, the young warriors. Indeed, in Borgia the jaguar is replaced with a shield and spears, the symbols of war. In such highly militaristic and masculine cultures as those of central Mexico, it is logical to personify youth as a warrior. A serious discrepancy occurs in the case of 1 Cipactli: according to the Anales de Cuauhtitlan, Venus spears the aged on that day; the codices show him spearing the water goddess, that is to say, drought was to be expected.

In Dresden 46–50 the five sets of pictures accompanying the Venus tables similarly portray the spearing of victims. These are respectively, an aged deity, a jaguar, the maize god, a frog deity, and a youthful personage, perhaps God R. There can, therefore, be not the slightest doubt that Venus at heliacal rising was regarded by the Maya also as dangerous to sundry categories of humanity and to those forces of nature on which he was most dependent.

In the cycle of myths concerning the life of sun and moon on earth, the Venus god is the older brother of the sun (Thompson, 1930, pp. 119–40). He is described as rather stupid, and very ugly with a heavy beard. He is the patron of the animals of the forest, from which his Kekchi name Xulab (*xul*, animal) derives. Hunters must keep vigil the night before hunting, and offer copal and prayers to him before he rises high above the horizon. In connection with his ill repute in the books of Chilam Balam, it is noteworthy that in this cycle of myths he commits adultery with his sister-in-law, the moon.

The sun and his brother play an important rôle in the Popol Vuh of the Quiche, but according to the extant version the brother becomes the moon. I deem it most probable that this identification with the moon is due to degeneration in the period of Spanish influence which preceded the reduction of the legends of the Popol Vuh to writing. The brother could hardly have been the moon because the Maya almost everywhere regarded and still regard the moon as a woman, the wife of the sun. On the other hand, the cycle of stories clearly belongs with those in which the sun and Venus are brothers, and the moon is the wife of the former. Accordingly, we can be reasonably sure that the brothers of the Popol Vuh legend were in the pre-Spanish version the sun and Venus. Hunahpu was the name of the brother we assume to have become the planet Venus but Hunahpu is the Quiche equivalent of the day 1 Ahau, which is precisely the day sacred to Venus, and, as we shall see, a name for the Venus god in Yucatan.

Names for the Planet Venus

There are various names in Yucatec for Venus. These include *Nohoch ich,* "great eye," *Chac ek,* "red star," or "giant star," and *Xux ek,* "wasp star." They are listed in the Motul dictionary as morning star, but we are doubtlessly justified in using the more specific rendering of Venus as morning star. The affix for red is almost invariably prefixed to the glyphs for Venus in Dresden. The use of this affix perhaps derives from the fact that red is the color of the east, but more probably it is a rebus for *chac,* "giant," which agrees with the other names. *Nohec* (Manche Chol), *ah no ic* (Yocotan), *mucta canal* (Tzotzil), *niuan canal* (Chuh and Chaneabal), *nim cheuh* (Mam of Tectitan), *nim ch'umil* (Ixil), and *nima*

ch'emil (Quiche of Rabinal) appear to mean "great star," showing how widespread that designation is. Indeed, among the Aztec the name for the planet was *Uei citlalin,* "great star." The Kekchi *cac chaim* probably means "red star," corresponding to the Yucatec *chac ek.* Other names for the morning star, but which might have been applied to whatever planet occupied that position, are the Yucatec *ah zahcab,* roughly corresponding to our "herald of the dawn," and *ah p'iz akab,* "measurer of the night." The latter occurs also in Manche Chol.

None of the early writers gives any direct information on the Venus gods, but it is possible to piece together a number of veiled references in the books of Chilam Balam.

Let us first recall the augury in the first Kaua list of the day Lamat, for that was the day of Venus. It reads: "Drunkard, deformed dog is his prognostic. The head of a jaguar; the rear of a dog. A meddler, a prattler, dishonest in his speech, an experimenter in mutual hatred, a sower of discord." That description exactly fits Lahun-Chan. Roys (1933, p. 101) notes that this name would mean "10 Sky" in Tzeltal, Chontal, and those other languages which often substitute *ch* for the Yucatec *c* (*caan* is "sky" in Yucatec). He points out that the glyph "10 Sky" accompanies the picture of a deity, previously identified by Seler as the Venus god, on Dresden 47, one of the pages dealing with the Venus cycle (fig. 14,*1,2*).

Lahun-Chan has a part in the story of the creation, as narrated in Chumayel (p. 46). We are told that he was envious, ribald, and insolent in his speech, and that sin was in his face and talk. He was forgetful of his father and mother; he walked abroad like one drunk, one without understanding, and there was no virtue in him. Mighty were his teeth (alternative translation, "Great is his madness"); his hands were claws (Roys, 1933, p. 105). Lopez de Cogolludo writes that he had ugly teeth (the spelling Lakunchan in the second and third editions is a misprint). The allusions to his mighty teeth and his claws suggest the jaguar, since the large canine is one of the identifying attributes of the jaguar in Maya art; the other details conform to the prognostication for the day Lamat. Let us see whether we can find any further reference to this unpleasant god.

The katun of the creation in which Lahun-Chan makes his disagreeable appearance is Katun 11 Ahau. Since deities recur at each return of the same katun, one would expect to encounter Lahun-Chan in other references to a Katun 11 Ahau. In a prophecy, which according to Chumayel (p. 64) is for the tenth katun but which Tizimin and Mani assign to the first katun, that is Katun 11 Ahau, there is indirect mention of this god. His head is said to be that of a jaguar, his body that of a dog; his tooth is long, his body is withered (like that of a rabbit in the Mani version). He is called Ah Chich, "the forceful one," in Mani; "9 Mountains" and Yuma-Une-Tziuit in Chumayel. Roys, who sees references to Quetzalcoatl in this passage from Chumayel, has interesting footnotes to his translation.

In Chumayel, page 87, there is another prophecy for Katun 11 Ahau. This has generally been taken as alluding to the second coming of Quetzalcoatl, but two mentions of a white (or artificial) circle in the sky suggests a reference to Quetzalcoatl as the Venus god. In one case the word for circle is replaced by a large O. The two conflicting sets of ideas can be reconciled: Lahun-Chan, if my thesis is correct, was the original Maya god of Venus; Quetzalcoatl, a later importation perhaps grudgingly accepted by the Maya, was also a deity of that planet. In time, we may suppose, the two were partly fused with resulting allusions to both in the prophecies for Katun 11 Ahau. References were made to Quetzalcoatl in the prophecies because those were partly directed to the new ruling caste with its Mexican affiliations; in Dresden, which was a new edition of a pre-Mexican book, Lahun-Chan seemingly is pictured, and so, too, is Quetzalcoatl.

There is still further proof that this jaguar-faced god, Lahun-Chan, is the Venus god. In almanacs in the books of Chilam Balam the prognostic for 8 Lamat is "jaguar-faced 1 Ahau with the protruding teeth" (p. 299). As Lamat is the day of Venus and as 1 Ahau is the base, the *lubay,* of the Venus cycle, we can rest assured that "jaguar-faced" 1 Ahau is another name for the Venus god, that is to say Lahun-Chan. Furthermore, as we have seen, Hunahpu, "1 Ahau," of the Popol Vuh was in all likelihood the Venus god. Other reasons for associating 1 Ahau with Venus as morning star are noted on page 224.

The picture of Lahun-Chan in the Venus tables (fig. 14,*1*) does not show the features of a jaguar, but his ribs are prominently displayed, reminding one that that is the most salient feature of the glyph of the dog (fig. 14,*10*), whose body he has.

The Venus god as patron of the month Yax is represented either by the Venus symbol or by the head of a dragon which may carry the Venus symbol (fig. 22, *50–59*). Celestial dragons frequently have Venus glyphs on their heads, but as they form the canopy of heaven, it is not unnatural that their function should be emphasized by setting on their bodies the star of dawn and dusk.

It would seem that the Mexicans associated various gods with each of the five appearances of Venus as morning star in the eight-year division, and it is not impossible that the same idea obtained among the Maya. At least, it is clear that the five deities shown in the middle pictures of the Venus table of Dresden 46–50 represent five distinct manifestations of the god in the act of hurling the shafts of affliction at mankind and his world, but it is possible that five-fold representation is a borrowing from Mexico.

The deity on page 46 has a partially blackened face, but the area around the mouth is white. His features are not unlike those of God D, but I deem the resemblance fortuitous, for the glyph of the god has an Imix sign as prefix, a feature never found with the glyphs of God D (fig. 42,*24*). In fact, Schellhas (1904, p. 34) segregates the examples of this god, to which he assigns the letter L. He is a rare body, appearing only four times in Dresden and not at all in the other codices. Once (p. 14b) he lacks the black coloring, and twice he wears a fish in his headdress. The fish and the Imix prefix to his glyph are probably the clues to his identification, for we have seen (p. 72) that both are primarily symbols of the earth crocodile, and secondary attributes of all deities of the soil and the underworld. The Venus god in some Mexican codices carries death symbols, and Lahun-Chan on page 47 of the Venus tables in Dresden is similarly decked; those I have explained as indicative of his residence in the underworld prior to heliacal rising as morning star. It is, therefore, highly probable that the Imix prefix and the fish similarly record that Venus as morning star has just emerged from the underworld. God L, therefore, can be provisionally identified as one of the manifestations of Venus as lord of the dawn.

The god on page 47 has been identified as Lahun-Chan (fig. 14,*1,2,4*).

The deity on page 48 is clearly an animal. He wears the Mexican *oyoualli* ornament on his breast and in his headdress. This pectoral is carried by certain Mexican gods with animal characteristics, particularly those connected with amusement (the pisote, monkey, etc.), and by the gods of sport, dancing, and amusement, the Macuil gods. His face is black save for a yellow area around his mouth, and a small green oval around his eye; his body is set with circles containing three dots, similar to those usually carried by the frog when it serves as the head form of the uinal. What is probably the same deity is depicted on page 37a of this codex, and this picture has been identified by Seler (1902–23, 4:701) as that of a frog. If this is, indeed, a frog god, I am unable to offer any suggestion for connecting him with Venus. I would be inclined rather to regard the portrait as that of Xolotl, the canine god, and twin brother of Quetzalcoatl.

The god on page 49 is distinguished by a broad black band edged with white, which crosses his face horizontally at the level of the eyes, and a second, narrower one which passes across the upper lip. Horizontal bands on the face are typical of Mexican rather than Maya gods. One can, accordingly, surmise that it is a deity of Mexican origin. In the lobe of one ear there is a bird and, on the other side of the face at the same level, is a snake, which from its position appears to have emerged from the lobe of the other ear, hidden from sight. The god wears a circular pectoral with a design of linked crescents; his loincloth is of jaguar skin. His foot is painted white. A conch shell may be set in his headdress. This deity, I think, can be identified with some assurance as Quetzalcoatl-Kukulcan. The principal objection to the identification is that Quetzalcoatl is usually provided with vertical, not horizontal, face markings. On the other hand, the bird and snake suggest very strongly Quetzalcoatl's rebus. Furthermore, Sahagun lists among the attributes of Quetzalcoatl the loincloth of jaguar skin and the white sandal. The pectoral is of Mexican design, and something very similar is frequently worn by Quetzalcoatl and one or two other gods; the conch ornament is one of his attributes. Lastly, we know that Quetzalcoatl was the god of the morning star in Mexico, and in view of the very close similarities in the legends and beliefs concerning Venus in both areas, one might well expect to find Quetzalcoatl-Kukulcan in an edition of a Maya codex which is subsequent to the start of the Mexican period. The facial painting may have derived from some local variation of the god in southern Veracruz or Tabasco.

The deity on page 50 is blindfold. This is not a Maya divinity but Ixquimilli, the blindfold god of the Mexicans. Ixquimilli is a shadowy deity, who partakes of the attributes of both Tezcatlipoca and Itztlacoliuhqui. He is the god of the day Atl, and as such he wears the smoking mirror of Tezcatlipoca. As lord of the twelfth week, 1 Cuetzpalin, in Borgia, Bourbon, and Telleriano-Remensis, as well as in the Tonalamatl of Aubin, Ixquimilli wears the hood of Itztlacoliuhqui which curves backward; only in Vatican B, where Ixquimilli is shown as a mummy bundle, is the curved hood missing. On Bologna, page 12, occurs a deity with the curved hood of Itztlacoliuhqui, the bandaged eyes of Ixquimilli, and the facial bands of Tezcatlipoca. Sahagun (1938, bk. 2, ch. 30) says that this hood was called Itztlacoliuhqui, "which means god of frost." One commentator of Telleriano-Remensis remarks that Itztlacoliuhqui is "a star which they say goes backward [a reference to the retrograde motion of a planet?]." Another commentator says he was lord of the frost. In that connection it is important to note that according to the Codex Chimalpopoca (1945, p. 122) Tlauizcalpantecutli, the morning star, lord of the dawn, shot an arrow at the sun to make him move but missed his mark. Thereupon the sun shot at and hit Tlauizcalpantecutli with his spears with red feathering, and immediately "covered his face with the nine skies together, for Tlauizcalpante-

cutli is the god of frost." Lehmann (1906, par. 45) translates this sentence "he threw him face down, on the ground, to the river of the underworld [Chiconauhapan, 'nine rivers'], so Tlauizcalpantecutli is the god of cold." Both translations come from different versions. One has "nine skies," the other "nine rivers," which Sahagun gives as the name of the river of the underworld. The latter seems more reasonable, for the underworld was the place of cold, and Venus spends time there before his emergence as morning star. In view of what has been set forth above, I deem it virtually certain that Itztlacoliuhqui is merely a variant form of Tlauizcalpantecutli, the god of Venus as morning star, and that the concept of lord of frost derives from a natural association of the morning star with the coldness of dawn. I feel, too, that there can be little doubt that the blindfolding is merely an attribute generally added to representations of Itztlacoliuhqui.

Of the five Venus gods pictured in the Venus tables, Lahun-Chan and God L are Maya; the remaining three are almost certainly Mexican. One is probably Quetzalcoatl, another almost surely Itztlacoliuhqui blindfold, and the third, although unidentified, can be attributed to the Mexican pantheon because of the *oyoualli* ornament he wears. We can therefore be reasonably sure that this idea of having five manifestations of the Venus god, one corresponding to each of the five Venus years in a group, derives from Mexico.

GLYPHS FOR VENUS

The hieroglyphs for the planet have been identified with very little doubt, since they occur in profusion on every page of the Venus tables of Dresden. The first form is clearly that of the day sign Lamat without its cartouche (fig. 42,31). The design consists of a small rhomboid in the center, and four small circles set in the corners of the glyph. The Venus glyph is differentiated from the Lamat signs by the addition of a squat cross, in the angles of which the circles are set. Yet this is not a fundamental difference, since even in the Lamat glyphs the points of the rhomboid (the "Ich" of the "Ben-Ich" sign) are prolonged so as to produce a cross. The second form of the Venus glyph consists of an inverted *w* with a circle set in each loop (fig. 42,33). This form, too, occurs as the day sign Lamat (fig. 7,57,61). It has been suggested that it is merely the first variant cut in half. This is plausible, but it should be noted that the end lines of the inverted *w* do not occur in the first variant.

The Venus glyph in the Dresden tables with two exceptions has the prefix for great or red (*chac*) attached to it. This prefix is very seldom found with Venus signs in the inscriptions; an example on Copan T 11 is a rare exception (fig. 54,5). In this connection, it is interesting to recall that the Motul dictionary lists *chac ek,* which could mean "red star" or "giant star," as one of the names for the morning star. The Venus glyph appears twice in the eclipse tables, both times without the red. The total number of Venus glyphs without prefix or with the *chac* prefix in the codices is 50. There are also half a dozen occurrences of Venus glyphs with quite different affixes, notably the seated man placed upside down (twice in the eclipse tables, once on Paris 4; fig. 42,32), a death symbol (Madrid 59c), and with a suffix (Paris 23 and perhaps 5). Once (Dresden 71a) the Venus sign is affixed to a glyph no longer legible.

The Synodical Revolution of Venus

The synodical revolution of Venus averages 583.92 days. It may be as little as 581 or as much as 587 days. The interval of 584 days therefore was a very good approximation to the mean. This number was of prime importance to the Maya because of the facility with which it could be related to the year of 365 days, and to the sacred almanac of 260 days. The common factor of 584 (8×73) and 365 (5×73) is 73. Therefore in 2920 days (5×584 or 8×365) exactly five synodical revolutions of Venus and eight years of 365 days will have completed themselves, and the two periods once again share the same *lub.* A longer period, but an extremely convenient one, is necessary to harmonize the synodical revolution of Venus with the sacred almanac, for the highest common factor is 4. A total of 37,960 days will pass before the two cycles will end on the same day. That number, however, is two CR (5.5.8.0), at which time the vague year of 365 days also ends on the same day. In other words after two CR there will have elapsed 65 synodical revolutions of Venus, 104 years of 365 days and 146 rounds of the sacred almanac. All three periods will reach the *lubay,* "the great resting place," together.

There is no reliable evidence that the Maya were acquainted with the sidereal revolution of Venus or of any other planet.

Venus Tables in Codex Dresden

The tables of Venus in Dresden, identified as such by Förstemann many years ago, apportion the synodical revolution in four uneven divisions of 236, 90, 250, and 8 days. From Mexican sources we know that the period of invisibility at inferior conjunction was reckoned as eight days. It is therefore obvious that the cycle was counted from heliacal rising, four days after inferior conjunction, when the planet is first visible as morning star. To the period of visibility as morning star were assigned 236 days, at the end of which Venus was lost to view in the solar light. In 90 days Venus, continuing its unseen

course, passed through superior conjunction to its second heliacal rising, as evening star. After 250 days as evening star it was once more lost in the sun's rays to pass four days later through inferior conjunction and then, at the end of eight days, to reappear as morning star, thereby completing the revolution of 584 days.

As 584 divided by 20 has a remainder of 4, it is clear that heliacal risings of Venus as morning star can occur only on days at intervals of four days in the official revolution of the planet, but observed risings could occur on any day because actual revolutions of Venus vary in length from 581 to about 587 days. These official days of heliacal rising were. Ahau, Kan, Lamat, Eb, and Cib. As 584 divided by 13 has a remainder of 12, it follows that the coefficient of the day increases by 12 (or decreases by 1) at each new heliacal rising. Heliacal risings, therefore, follow in the sequence 1 Ahau, 13 Kan, 12 Lamat, 11 Eb, 10 Cib, 9 Ahau, 8 Kan, etc., an arrangement which greatly simplified calculations.

In the table of Venus which occupies Dresden 46–50 the days on which the revolutions end, and the intervening days of disappearance before superior conjunction, reappearance, and second disappearance occupy the upper compartment of the left half of each page. The material is transcribed in Table 17. The starting point is the end of the table, the day 1 Ahau. The number 236 in line 26 is counted from 1 Ahau to reach 3 Cib, at the left of line 1. This is the day of disappearance. The addition of 90 days (line 26) leads to reappearance as evening star at 2 Cimi (line 1), and 250 additional days carry the count to second disappearance at 5 Cib. Inferior conjunction, four days later, is not noted. Instead, the tally advances eight days (line 26) to a new heliacal rising at 13 Kan (line 1).

The process repeats: Venus passes through the three stages to a third heliacal rising at 12 Lamat (line 1, last column of p. 47), to a fourth at 11 Eb (line 1, last column of p. 48), to a fifth at 10 Cib (line 1, last column of p. 49), and to a sixth at 9 Ahau (line 1, last column of table). Thence the sequence is across the second line, passing through the intermediate points to heliacal risings at 8 Kan, 7 Lamat, 6 Eb, 5 Cib, and 4 Ahau. The series succeeds line by line until the table is completed when the day 1 Ahau is again reached as the date of a heliacal rising (line 13 extreme right), the total of 65 revolutions of the planets having been counted. The series then repeats in the same sequence.

Line 19 gives the totals of days elapsed in the course of the five revolutions comprised in a horizontal line. Line 15, omitted from the table, repeats the same glyph, a hand under shell with lunar postfix (fig. 42,55), 19 times. In the last appearance of the glyph the lunar postfix is

TABLE 17—SCHEME OF THE VENUS CYCLE ON DRESDEN 46-50

Line	Cib	Cimi	Cib	Kan	Ahau	Oc	Ahau	Lamat	Kan	Ix	Kan	Eb	Lamat	Etz'nab	Lamat	Cib	Eb	Ik	Eb	Ahau
1	3	2	5	13	2	1	4	12	1	13	3	11	13	12	2	10	12	11	1	9
2	11	10	13	8	10	9	12	7	9	8	11	6	8	7	10	5	7	6	9	4
3	6	5	8	3	5	4	7	2	4	3	6	1	3	2	5	13	2	1	4	12
4	1	13	3	11	13	12	2	10	12	11	1	9	11	10	13	8	10	9	12	7
5	9	8	11	6	8	7	10	5	7	6	9	4	6	5	8	3	5	4	7	2
6	4	3	6	1	3	2	5	13	2	1	4	12	1	13	3	11	13	12	2	10
7	12	11	1	9	11	10	13	8	10	9	12	7	9	8	11	6	8	7	10	5
8	7	6	9	4	6	5	8	3	5	4	7	2	4	3	6	1	3	2	5	13
9	2	1	4	12	1	13	3	11	13	12	2	10	12	11	1	9	11	10	13	8
10	10	9	12	7	9	8	11	6	8	7	10	5	7	6	9	4	6	5	8	3
11	5	4	7	2	4	3	6	1	3	2	5	13	2	1	4	12	1	13	3	11
12	13	12	2	10	12	11	1	9	11	10	13	8	10	9	12	7	9	8	11	6
13	8	7	10	5	7	6	9	4	6	5	8	3	5	4	7	2	4	3	6	1
14	4 Yaxkin	14 Zac	19 Zec	7 Xul	3 Cumku	8 Zotz'	18 Pax	6 Kayab	17 Yax	7 Muan	12 Ch'en	0 Yax	11 Zip	1 Mol	6 Uo	14 Uo	10 Kankin	0 Uayeb	5 Mac	13 Mac
16	N.	W.	S.	E.	N.	W.	S.	E.	N.	W.	S.	E.	N.	W.	S.	E.	N.	W.	S.	E.
17	A	B	C	D	E	F	G	H	I	J	K	L	M	N	O	P	Q	R	S	T
18	Red ½ Venus	Red ½ Venus	Red ½ Venus	Red ½ Venus	Red Venus	Red Venus	Red Venus	Red Venus	Red Venus	Red Venus	Red Venus	Red Venus	Red Venus	Red Venus	Red Venus	Red Venus	Red Venus	Red Venus	Red Venus	Red Venus
19	236	326	576	584	820	910	1160	1168	1404	1494	1744	1752	1988	2078	2328	2336	2572	2662	2912	2920
20	8 Zac	18 Muan	4 Yax	12 Yax	3 Zotz'	13 Mol	18 Uo	6 Zip	2 Muan	7 Pop	17 Mac	5 Kankin	16 Yaxkin	6 Ceh	11 Xul	19 Xul	15 Cumku	0 Zec	10 Kayab	18 Kayab
21	T	A	B	C	D	E	F	G	H	I	J	K	L	M	N	O	P	Q	R	S
22	Winged Chuen	Winged Chuen	Winged Chuen	Winged Chuen					Winged Chuen	Winged Chuen	Winged Chuen	Winged Chuen	Winged Chuen	Winged Chuen	Winged Chuen	Winged Chuen	Chuen	Winged Chuen	Winged Chuen	Winged Chuen
23	Red Venus	Red Venus	Red Venus	Red Venus	Red Venus	Red Venus	Red Venus	Red Venus					Red Venus	Red Venus	Red Venus	Red Venus	Red Venus	Red Venus	Red Venus	Red Venus
24	E.	N.	W.	S.	E.	N.	W.	S.	E.	N.	W.	S.	E.	N.	W.	S.	E.	N.	W.	S.
25	19	4	14	2	13	3	8	16	7	17	2	10	6	16	1	9	0	10	15	3
26	Kayab 236	Zotz' 90	Pax 250	Kayab 8	Yax 236	Muan 90	Ch'en 250	Ch'en 8	Zip 236	Yaxkin 90	Uo 250	Uo 8	Kankin 236	Cumku 90	Mac 250	Mac 8	Yaxkin 236	Zac 90	Zec 250	Xul 8

Page 46 (columns Cib, Cimi, Cib, Kan) — Page 47 (Ahau, Oc, Ahau, Lamat) — Page 48 (Kan, Ix, Kan, Eb) — Page 49 (Lamat, Etz'nab, Lamat, Cib, Eb) — Page 50 (Ik, Eb, Ahau) omitted (fig. 42,*56*). I think there can be little doubt that this is merely a completion sign, the lunar postfix being the rebus for the possessive *u* (p. 188).

Lines 18 and 23 are monotonously filled with Venus glyphs which, with one exception, have a red prefix. The single omission probably has no significance. On page 48, line 23 is omitted, presumably because of lack of space. A glyph resembling the Chuen sign but with various post-fixes is repeated across the lower half of each page, except page 47, where its omission is presumably due to lack of space. It appears in lines 21 or 22 (fig. 42,*70,71*).

Line 14 gives the month positions corresponding to the 65 days recorded at the top. As the table extends horizontally for five Venus revolutions, which equal eight years of 365 days, the month positions follow in sequence, and each is used with all the 13 day signs above it. The table starts with 13 Mac, passes to 4 Yaxkin 236 days later, next to 14 Zac 90 days later, then to 19 Zec 250 days later, and reaches heliacal rising at 7 Xul. Passing through the various stages, heliacal risings are attained at 6 Kayab, 0 Yax, 14 Uo, and finally, once more, at 13 Mac. Thus, if 1 Ahau 13 Mac marks a heliacal rising, 9 Ahau 13 Mac will again be a heliacal rising, five revolutions later, to be followed after the same interval by 4 Ahau 13 Mac.

Lines 20 and 25 set forth two other sets of month positions, arranged in precisely the same way, but counted respectively from (1 Ahau) 18 Kayab and (1 Ahau) 3 Xul. The manner in which these two series may have been used will be reviewed later. The only major error in the table is 0 Xul instead of 0 Yaxkin (p. 50).

Line 16 gives the glyphs for the four world directions in the sequence east, north, west, south, with east corresponding to heliacal rising, so that page 46 starts with north assigned to the disappearance of Venus before superior conjunction, west appropriately to its reappearance as evening star, south to the day of its disappearance in the sun's rays four days before inferior conjunction, and east to its reappearance as morning star. The sequence then repeats on the following pages.

Line 24 repeats the world directions but in the sequence south, east, north, west, with south beneath the dates of heliacal risings after inferior conjunction. It will be recollected that whereas line 19 gives the accumulation of days, line 26 gives the intervals between the points in the synodical revolution. It is therefore probable that the first set of world directions refers to the actual dates of the synodical revolution of the planet; the second set gives the world directions of the intervals between those points. That is to say, heliacal rising after inferior conjunction is assigned to the east, and so, too, are the 236 days during which Venus is a morning star. The day of disappearance before superior conjunction is assigned to the

north, and so are the 90 days of invisibility which follow. Heliacal rising after superior conjunction, when Venus becomes the evening star, is allotted to the west, as are the following 250 days during which the planet is visible in the west. Disappearance and the period of invisibility around inferior conjunction fall to the north.

DIRECTIONAL GODS IN VENUS TABLES

Line 17 is occupied by the glyphs of 20 deities, some of whom are recognizable (fig. 42,*1–20*). These are lettered from A to T. The same series of glyphs, with immaterial variations, is repeated in lines 21 and 22 (the drop to line 22 on pp. 48–50 is due to the winged Chuen glyph being inserted above). However, the twentieth god of line 17 becomes the first god of lines 21 and 22, and the whole series is thereby moved forward a space. This displacement corresponds to the shift in the world-direction glyphs. God A is in the top line associated with the north and disappearance of Venus before superior conjunction; in the lower line he is assigned again to the north, but the association is, I hazard, with the 90 days of invisibility around superior conjunction.

Grouped by directions, these gods are:

East:

D. Almost certainly God A, god of death (fig. 42,*16*).

H. The tun sign in one line; the Cauac element in the other. The two glyphs are more or less synonymous. In both cases there is a coefficient of 4 and the same prefix. The latter glyph, but with a coefficient of 5, is that of God N, the old god. However, on Dresden 4a this same glyph with coefficient of 4 appears above a portrait of an aged god indistinguishable from God N. All in all, it is not unlikely that both glyphs represent God N, or a deity very closely connected with him (fig. 42,*17,22*).

L. The moon goddess, identifiable by the lunar postfix. Save for the two appearances in this table and a third appearance on page 24, which belongs to the ephemeris of Venus, this glyph occurs in only one other place in the codices. That is above one of the pictures in the eclipse tables of Dresden (fig. 42,*18*).

P. The Chicchan god with a coefficient of 1. The Chicchan, it will be recalled, is a celestial serpent (fig. 42,*19*).

T. A long-snouted monster with crossbands in the eye, and a death eye above the root of the snout. The crossbands are absent from the representation on page 24, and not recognizable on the glyph at the start of page 46 (fig. 42,*20*). With crossbands in the eye the glyph appears also in the eclipse tables (p. 56a). Its only other occurrence is on Madrid 71b, where, in a decidedly more conventionalized form, it accompanies one of the compartments of the sacred almanac, that starting with the day 3 Muluc.

These five glyphs follow one another in descending order in column B of Dresden 24a. That page, as already noted, is really a part of the Venus tables, and in the original pagination (p. 24) immediately preceded page 46. The glyphs, as arranged on page 24, take the order: H, L, P, T, D. That is the same as noted above save that D comes at the end of the series, not at the start.

North:

A. A geometric element above a bundle and with a *u* bracket as prefix. The central element has a death eye at top right, and in the center a motif which is similar to the closed eye with eyelashes of the death god (fig. 42,*1*). It is Gates' Glyph 344 and, as he has shown, is of frequent occurrence with varying affixes. Without the bundle it appears on all the Venus pages in apposition to other name glyphs of gods. Sometimes an object which looks like a rope crosses the glyph diagonally. It cannot be assigned to any known deity, although it would appear to represent some god of the underworld.

E. The head of a bird (?) with Etz'nab infix (fig. 42,*2,23*).

I. The glyph of the sun god; God G (fig. 42,*3*).

M. The head variant of the glyph of God B (fig. 42,*4*).

Q. The head of the maize god, God E. On page 24 the head of the maize god, but with a different prefix, appears in Column C (fig. 42,*5,28*).

West:

B. A glyph with a *te* (2) postfix and a prefix which is like that of white save for the addition of two antennae (fig. 42,*6*).

F. A deity with prominent lips and what is probably a death eye on his forehead. He wears a headdress which resembles the "Akbal" sign (fig. 42,*7*). Presumably a god of the underworld. This deity does not appear elsewhere in Dresden, but occurs a few times in Madrid with different affixes, and once with a coefficient of 9.

J. A symbolic glyph with a coefficient of 6. The glyph consists of a yax sign over a hand, like that of Manik (fig. 42,*8*). In the second example a "Ben-Ich" superfix is present. This glyph, in all cases with a coefficient of 6, occurs on Dresden 34c and on Paris 4, 9, and 10 in connection with the Katun regents. On the Santa Rita murals, again with coefficient of 6 and "Ben-Ich" prefix, it is attached to a deity resembling God D who is the regent of Tun 11 Ahau.

N. The head of the god of death with the *il* prefix and eye with loop in it (fig. 42,*9*).

R. The black-headed variant of God D. The black is surely added because the god here rules in the west, with which black is associated (fig. 42,*10*).

South:

C. A head with the red prefix, an oval of dots around the mouth, peculiar curls at the corner of the eye and the Etz'nab sign on the side of the cheek (fig. 42,*11*). One would be inclined to identify this as the head of a deity of sacrifice. Xipe, it will be recalled, is the red god, the god of sacrifice. The head is not uncommon, with varying affixes, in Paris.

G. A composite glyph with a coefficient of 13. The top part of the first glyph is the sign for misfortune; the lower half the sky sign. There is a *te* (3) prefix (p. 285). The second glyph is precisely the same, save that the sky sign is above the misfortune element. The glyph vaguely suggests a deity of the 13 skies or the thirteenth layer of heaven (fig. 42,*12,21*).

K. The glyph is the "Akbal" over serpent scales with "Ben-Ich" prefix above, and another prefix to left (fig. 42,*13*). Could this mean something like night countenance (p. 201)?

O. A well-known head with two volutes emerging from an oval inserted in the forehead. It is the glyph of God K (fig. 42,*14*).

S. A symbolic glyph with a coefficient of 7. The main element resembles Mol, and there is a prefix like that of the month sign Cumku (fig. 42,*15*).

Although many of the deities to which these glyphs pertain cannot at present be identified, the listing of the glyphs by the directions with which they are associated may prove beneficial for later studies. I do not think they are directly associated with the planet Venus. The directional gods are in poor agreement with those given in Landa and on Dresden 25–28. God K is associated with the south on the Venus pages; with the east in the other two sources. The death god is associated with east and west on the Venus pages; with the south in the other two sources. The sun god and God D are associated with north and west, respectively, in all three sources (Thompson, 1934, p. 226).

Long Count Positions of Venus Tables

There are, as we have seen, three sets of month positions running through the Venus revolutions and clearly to be associated with the days given above.

These three sets of month positions end on 1 Ahau 18 Kayab, 1 Ahau 3 Xul, and 1 Ahau 13 Mac; what is undoubtedly the base for a fourth set, the date 1 Ahau 18 Uo, is given on page 24. It is pretty clear that they represent corrections to keep the Venus revolutions in step with the year of 365 days. After the table has been used once, that is to say after 65 synodical revolutions of Venus, the average appearance of the planet at heliacal rising will have dropped back slightly over five days ($65 \times 583.92 = 37954.8$; $104 \times 365 = 37,960$). Thus if heliacal rising fell on 1 Ahau 18 Kayab at the start of the table, it would be expected to fall on 9 Men 13 Kayab at the end, but because there is considerable variation in the length of a synodical revolution of Venus, one cannot say definitely that it would fall on that particular day. It is obvious that the table would accumulate a huge error if one waited until the sixty-fifth revolution fell on 1 Ahau 13 Mac, and a still greater error over thousands of years if one waited until it fell on 3 Xul. Teeple (1926) was the first to tackle this problem. He showed that if the Maya subtracted four days at the end of the sixty-first revolution of Venus, they would again reach 1 Ahau, but with a different month position. Similarly, as a correction of eight days occasionally had to be made, because the error was slightly over five days, not four, the subtraction of eight days at the end of the fifty-seventh revolution of the planet would also lead to 1 Ahau. These four bases would then be connected as follows:

```
1 Ahau 18 Kayab
    add 4.12. 8.0   57 revolutions of Venus less 8 days
1 Ahau 18 Uo
    add 4.18.17.0   61 revolutions of Venus less 4 days
1 Ahau 13 Mac
    add 4.18.17.0   61 revolutions of Venus less 4 days
1 Ahau 3 Xul
    add 4.18.17.0   61 revolutions of Venus less 4 days
(1 Ahau 8 Ch'en    not recorded)
```

The table can, of course, be extended indefinitely, with three corrections of four days at the end of 61 revolutions and one correction of eight days at the end of 57 revolutions. This correction of 20 days for 240 revolutions of the planet is remarkably accurate. The true correction should be 19.2 days, an error of less than a day in nearly 384 years.

This reconstruction was a brilliant piece of work on Teeple's part. It is moreover supported by the numbers on Dresden 24, which, as already noted, comes immediately before page 46, the break in the pagination being due to the incorrect arrangement made by Förstemann, and retained ever since.

The table on the right side of the page starts at the bottom right corner, and proceeds to the left and upwards, precisely the reverse of the way we write. Rearranged, with minor restorations and one change (260 days added to 9100), the material is presented in Table 18.

be a correction of about 25 days. If, however, the amended figure of 9360 days is subtracted from 185,120, the result (175,760 days) equals 301 revolutions of 584 days less 24 days, that is to say, four groups of 61 revolutions and one group of 57 revolutions. That is precisely how the correction should be made to achieve the greatest accuracy.

The figure 9360 is my own amendment, for the number is actually written as 9100 (1.5.5.0). However, there are good grounds for supposing that this is incorrect, for every other number of this table is either an exact multiple of 584, or a multiple of 584 with a small correction which is a multiple of 4, made in such a way that the total is a multiple of 260. The figure 9100 is $15 \times 584 + 340$, and, therefore, is far removed from any multiple of 584. In two or three cases in the tables of Dresden there are apparent mistakes which can best be corrected by the addition or subtraction of 260 days. If 260 is subtracted from 9100, the remainder still fails to approximate

TABLE 18—MULTIPLES OF VENUS REVOLUTIONS ON DRESDEN 24

Maya	Day	Days	Revolutions of Venus	
8 . 2.0	9 Ahau	2920	5	
16 . 4.0	4 Ahau	5840	10	
1 . 4 . 6.0	12 Ahau	8760	15	
1 . 12 . 8.0	7 Ahau	11680	20	(3 dots restored in uinal coefficient)
2 . 0 .10.0	2 Ahau	14600	25	
2 . 8 .12.0	10 Ahau	17520	30	
2 . 16 .14.0	5 Ahau	20440	35	
3 . 4 .16.0	13 Ahau	23360	40	
3 . 13 . 0.0	8 Ahau	26280	45	
4 . 1 . 2.0	3 Ahau	29200	50	
4 . 9 . 4.0	11 Ahau	32120	55	
4 . 17 . 6.0	6 Ahau	35040	60	
1 . 6 . 0.0	1 Ahau	9360	16	plus 16 days (260 days added)
4 . 12 . 8.0	1 Ahau	33280	57	minus 8 days
9 . 11 . 7.0	1 Ahau	68900	118	minus 12 days
1 . 5 . 14 . 4.0	1 Ahau	185120	317	minus 8 days
(5).(5). 8.0	1 Ahau	37960	65	
(10).(10).16.0	1 Ahau	75920	130	
(15).(16). 6.0	1 Ahau	113880	195	
(1).(1). 1 .14.0	1 Ahau	151840	260	

The figures in the table are regular multiples of the group of five revolutions of Venus ($2920 = 8 \times 365$) with the exception of those in the fourth row. These embody the corrections employed. The 57 revolutions minus 8 days lead from 1 Ahau 18 Kayab to the base 1 Ahau 18 Uo, given at the bottom of this page; the 118 revolutions minus 12 days carry the reckoning from 1 Ahau 18 Kayab to 1 Ahau 13 Mac (57 revolutions with a correction of 8 days plus 61 revolutions with a correction of 4 days).

The figure of 185,120 represents 317 (260 + 57) revolutions less 8 days, but after 317 revolutions there should

a multiple of 584, but if 260 is added, the new figure of 9360 is $16 \times 584 + 16$, the remainder being, as required, a multiple of 4. I shall revert to the discussion of this number.

The question next arises as to what positions in the LC were occupied by these bases. On the left of page 24 there are two IS with the distance number that separates them, expressed as a ring number, that is to say, part of it is encircled.

9.9.16. 0.0	4 Ahau 8 Cumku
6. 2.0	
9.9. 9.16.0	1 Ahau 18 Kayab

This means that to a base 6.2.0. before 13.0.0.0.0 4 Ahau 8 Cumku the number 9.9.16.0.0 is added to reach 9.9.9.16.0 1 Ahau 18 Kayab.

The first number is 72 CR, which are equal to 2340 uncorrected synodical revolutions of the planet. During that interval Venus would have moved forward until heliacal risings would be 184 days earlier in the year (24 days correction for 301 Venus revolutions). The accumulated error of 184 days is very close to half a year, but that may be coincidence.

In no correlation so far suggested which is not derived solely from astronomical data does 9.9.9.16.0 coincide with a heliacal rising of Venus after inferior conjunction. In the Goodman-Thompson correlation heliacal rising occurs at about 9.9.9.16.16, that is to say about 16 days later. This error of some 16 days immediately reminds one of the corrected number 9360 days in the table, which equals 16 Venus revolutions and 16 days. If that is added to 9.9.9.16.0 1 Ahau 18 Kayab, one gets a new and correct base for the table, to which groupings of 57 and 61 Venus revolutions can be added as shown below:

A	9. 9. 9.16.0	1 Ahau	18 Kayab
A'	1. 6. 0.0	16 V. R.	+ 16 days
B	9.10.15.16.0	1 Ahau	8 Zac.
B'	4.18.17.0	61 V. R.	− 4 days
C	9.15.14.15.0	1 Ahau	18 Zip
C'	4.18.17.0	61 V. R.	− 4 days
D	10. 0.13.14.0	1 Ahau	13 Kankin
D'	4.18.17.0	61 V. R.	− 4 days
E	10. 5.12.13.0	1 Ahau	3 Yaxkin
E'	4.18.17.0	61 V. R.	− 4 days
F	10.10.11.12.0	1 Ahau	18 Kayab
F'	4.12. 8.0	57 V. R.	− 8 days
G	10.15. 4. 2.0	1 Ahau	18 Uo
G'	4.18.17.0	61 V. R.	− 4 days
H	11. 0. 3. 1.0	1 Ahau	13 Mac
H'	4.18.17.0	61 V. R.	− 4 days
I	11. 5. 2. 0.0.	1 Ahau	3 Xul

It will be seen that this table embodies all four of the corrections given in the third row of page 24:

9360 (as amended)	is 16 × 584 − 16	= A'
33280	is 57 × 584 − 8	= F'
68900	is 118 × 584 − 12	= F to H or E to G
185120	is 317 × 584 − 8	= A to G

One may also note, although it may be pure coincidence, that the highest figure in the table clearly restorable as 1.1.1.14.0 (151,840) is the distance between the two positions of 1 Ahau 18 Kayab (A and F).

The positions which end the tables in the codex are 1 Ahau 18 Kayab (A and F), 1 Ahau 13 Mac (H), and 1 Ahau 3 Xul (I), while 1 Ahau 18 Uo (G) is given on page 24.

This, of course, is not the only reconstruction that can be made, but it fits the 11.16.0.0.0 correlation, and it satisfactorily explains the large correction of 317 Venus years minus eight days. One would normally expect 301 Venus years minus 24 days. The drawback to the solution offered is that the bases 1 Ahau 8 Zac, 1 Ahau 18 Zip, 1 Ahau 13 Kankin, and 1 Ahau 3 Yaxkin, are nowhere written. The explanation of this probably lies in the fact that those bases were far in the past when the present edition of Dresden was written. Probably the 1 Ahau 18 Uo base was current when the present edition was produced. The Maya astronomer, accordingly, gave the old base, and with the correction of 185,120 days reached the base then current, and added those which would follow, 1 Ahau 13 Mac and 1 Ahau 3 Xul.

There remains unexplained the reason why a base 9.9.9.16.0 1 Ahau 18 Kayab, with a positive error of some 16 days, was chosen. There are several factors which may have led to its choice. Mrs. Makemson (1943, p. 214) has pointed out that the planet Mars is probably involved. She has shown that the Mars revolution of 780 days is a factor, and also that 9.9.9.16.0 1 Ahau 18 Kayab was just three days before conjunction of Mars with the sun. The synodical revolution of Mars is 779.936 days. The number 780 was therefore a very close approximation, and had the tremendous advantage in Maya eyes that it was a multiple of 260. Thereby the uncorrected Mars cycle would always fall on the same day. A point perhaps of some importance is that with the return of 1 Ahau at the end of each group of 65 uncorrected revolutions of Venus, the lord of the night will be different; only after the 65-year cycle has repeated nine times will the same lord of the night return to power. That is to say, only at the end of 585 uncorrected Venus years will the theoretical date of heliacal rising both fall on 1 Ahau and have the same lord of the night regnant. The interval 9.9.16.0.0, equivalent of 2340 uncorrected Venus years, being four times the lowest common factor, reproduces this condition.

The interval 9.9.16.0.0, accordingly, has a number of properties which gave it importance in Maya eyes. It is the equivalent of:

2340	uncorrected revolutions of Venus (584 days)
3744	uncorrected years of 365 days
5256	cycles of 260 days
1752	uncorrected revolutions of Mars (780 days)
3796	tuns (360 days)
4	Venus great cycles with same lord of night (341,640 days)

Perhaps the corrections applied to the Venus calendar prior to 9.10.0.0.0 were too great, with the result that the calendar showed a heliacal rising of Venus at 9.9.9.16.0, whereas it actually took place 16–18 days later. Accordingly the uncorrected date for Venus was first given, and then this was corrected by the addition of 16 Venus revolutions and 16 days. This number of Venus revolutions was chosen because it was the only one which with the addition of 16 days once more brought heliacal rising back to the desired base of 1 Ahau. It also had the property of being equal to 12 synodical revolutions of Mars. The Maya could therefore say: "Mars was in conjunction with the sun at 9.9.9.16.0, when Venus should have been at heliacal rising after inferior conjunction. However, our calculations have been in error. The new base is 9.10.15.16.0 1 Ahau 8 Zac. On that date Mars will again be very near conjunction with the sun, and on the same day there will be a heliacal rising of Venus."

Because of variation in the length of the synodical revolutions of Venus, it would be difficult at first to approximate the true correction. Assume, for instance, that the Maya correction was originally made by dropping 12 days at the end of every 118 Venus revolutions, as given in the list of corrections on page 24. This would have been too much by 2.56 days, and the positive error of some 16 days would have accumulated in about three baktuns. On the other hand, it is possible that there was a shift from heliacal setting to heliacal rising at 9.9.9.16.0. The total error in that case would be only some eight days, and would have accumulated with the same overcorrection in about 30 katuns.

The possibility that the Venus cycle was once counted not from heliacal rising, but from heliacal setting eight days before should not be disregarded. The arrangement of the tables in the present edition of Dresden makes it abundantly clear that the reckoning was then from heliacal rising after inferior conjunction, but it does not necessarily follow that that arrangement had always been in force. The position 1 Ahau and the day Lamat are closely associated with the planet. If heliacal setting was on a day Ahau, heliacal rising would occur eight days later on Lamat. Furthermore, disappearance of the planet seems a trifle more logical as the point to complete the revolution than does the day of reappearance.

These tables demonstrate how accurately the Maya reckoned the synodical revolutions of Venus. With the correction of four days at the end of 61 revolutions repeated four times, and then a correction of eight days at the end of the 57 revolutions they attained a rare precision. For this is a correction of 24 days in 301 revolutions (approximately 480 years), whereas the accumulated error would in reality have been 24.08 days. The tables also demonstrate how important it was to the Maya to associate their various cycles with the sacred almanac so as to find when together they would reach the same *lub*.

In the case of the uncorrected revolution of Venus that was a relatively simple matter, for 65 revolutions of Venus equaled 146 cycles of 260 days, but the corrections had to be made so as to retain that association. This could be achieved only by corrections of four days and its multiples. It was for that reason that a correction of four days was made at the end of 61 revolutions, although a reduction of five days was called for; with an adjustment of five days it would have been impossible to retain 1 Ahau as the base, but that was essential.

The elucidation of the Venus tables illustrates well how one student after the other has taken up the torch of research. Förstemann, Seler, Willson, Teeple, Makemson, Long and I have contributed in varying degree to our present appreciation of this beautiful and subtle product of Maya mentality. Satterthwaite (1947) has shown how the Venus tables are very handy for calculation.

VENUS GLYPHS IN THE INSCRIPTIONS

There are few, if any, references to observed positions of Venus in the hieroglyphic texts of the stelae. If one takes all the Venus glyphs in the inscriptions and computes the positions of the planet, no pattern will emerge whatever correlation is used. Some of those entries, therefore, must be of a ritualistic nature. As I have pointed out, there is no reason to believe that celestial phenomena, save data on the moon, were generally noted in the inscriptions. However, if the current katun was, for example, associated in some way with the planet Venus, then one might reasonably expect to find references to that planet on the monuments dedicated to that katun. The day 1 Ahau, as we have seen, was the day of Venus, it would be natural therefore to make a passing reference to Venus on those katuns that ended on 1 Ahau, particularly if Venus was prominent at the date in question. Two katuns during the Initial Series Period ended on 1 Ahau. These were 9.10.0.0.0 and 10.3.0.0.0.

Three texts commemorate 9.10.0.0.0 1 Ahau 8 Kayab, but two of these are badly eroded. The only one in good condition is the so-called lintel re-used in the hieroglyphic stairway of Naranjo. This carries the following arrangement of dates:

$$9.\ 7.14.10.\ 8 \quad 3 \text{ Lamat } 16 \text{ Uo}$$
$$2.\ 5.\ 7.12$$
$$\overline{9.10.\ 0.\ 0.\ 0 \quad 1 \text{ Ahau} \quad 8 \text{ Kayab}}$$

The distance number reduces to 16,352 which is equal to 28 synodical revolutions of Venus. Furthermore, 41 synodical revolutions of Jupiter reach 16,353.5 days. Therefore, on the two dates both Venus and Jupiter would have been in the same positions in the sky. The presence of a Venus glyph and the fact that a day Lamat and the day 1 Ahau are involved in the calculation make it fairly certain that the astronomical values of the distance number are not fortuitous.

At both dates, according to the Goodman-Thompson correlation, Venus and Jupiter were morning stars. The former was approximately 40 degrees above the horizon at sunrise; the latter approximately 20 degrees. There was nothing outstanding about the planets on those dates, although sun, Jupiter, and Venus, evenly spaced in the dawn sky, are ever a sight to rejoice one's heart. I think, therefore, the Maya recorded this appearance of the two planets because their thoughts were turned to Venus by the fact that the katun they were commemorating ended on 1 Ahau. Furthermore only after 28 revolutions of Venus and 41 of Jupiter will the cycles of the two planets come within a day or two of coincidence.

Another calculation involving 1 Ahau 8 Kayab occurs in the hieroglyphic stairway, and again a Venus glyph is found with the secondary date:

$$9.\ 9.18.16.\ 3\quad 7\ Akbal\quad 16\ Muan$$
$$\underline{1.\ 1.17}$$
$$9.10.\ 0.\ 0.\ 0\quad 1\ Ahau\quad 8\ Kayab$$

Jupiter, too, appears to be involved, since the interval of 1.1.17 reduces to 397 days, which is slightly less than two days short of a synodical revolution of that planet. Jupiter, therefore, was in approximately the same position at both dates, that is to say, a morning star about 20 degrees above the horizon at sunrise. Venus on the first date was invisible, having passed through superior conjunction about 11 days earlier.

On the Tablet of the Inscriptions at Palenque the date 9.9.2.4.8   5 Lamat 1 Mol is linked with 9.10.0.0.0   1 Ahau 8 Kayab. The interval is 6392 days, which equals 16 revolutions of Jupiter (399.5 days) and 10 revolutions of Venus plus 552 days. Thus Jupiter was in the same position as on the dates discussed. Venus was about 148 days past heliacal rising, just about halfway between heliacal rising and superior conjunction. It is not likely that this interval was chosen because of Venus; there is no Venus glyph in the text, and the period is not an integral number of synodical revolutions of the planet. The second katun to end on 1 Ahau was 10.3.0.0.0   1 Ahau 3 Yaxkin. At 10.3.0.0.0 Venus was within a day or so of superior conjunction in the Goodman-Thompson correlation. According to the reconstructed calendar, this was exactly one CR before 10.5.12.13.0   1 Ahau 3 Yaxkin, the next base for the Venus cycle. As two CR equal 65 Venus revolutions, one CR equals 32½ revolutions. Venus, therefore, at 10.3.0.0.0   1 Ahau 3 Yaxkin was not at heliacal rising, but half a revolution away, that is to say, three or four

days past superior conjunction, at the opposite extreme of the Venus revolution.

The date 10.3.0.0.0 is commemorated by Uaxactun 12. There is at least one Venus glyph in the text, but there is no other date recorded. The same date appears as an IS on Xultun 10. On the front of this monument there is a distance number, and a CR date. The whole is read by Morley as follows:

$$10.1.13.\ 7.17\quad 6\ Caban\quad 10\ Zip$$
$$\underline{1.\ 6.10.\ 3\quad \textit{Add}}$$
$$10.3.\ 0.\ 0.\ 0\quad 1\ Ahau\quad 3\ Yaxkin$$

The interval reduces to 9563 days, which equal 16 synodical revolutions of Venus plus 219 days and 24 synodical revolutions of Jupiter (398.5 days) less 1 day. Here again, therefore, we find an apparent connection with Jupiter. Venus was very close to greatest elongation, rising about three hours before dawn; Jupiter on the other hand was setting at about 1 A.M. No Venus glyph is recognizable, and it is doubtful that the text treats of that planet.

I think the reason for bringing Jupiter into the discussion lies in the fact that the heliacal rising of Venus prior to 10.3.0.0.0 fell on 10.2.19.3.12 according to the set pattern of the cycle beginning with 10.0.13.14.0 1 Ahau 13 Kankin, and the conjunction of Jupiter with the sun took place around 10.2.19.3.17, some five days later. The close proximity of the conjunction of those two planets with the sun must have interested the Maya in view of the fact that the katun was associated with Venus because it ended on 1 Ahau. This exhausts the recordings of katuns ending on 1 Ahau and their associated dates so far as the Central Area is concerned. There are other examples at Chichen Itza but as the readings are not as yet generally accepted, I do not deem it advisable to prolong this discussion by including them.

I do not propose to discuss at this time all dates with Venus glyphs; in any case that is a problem for an astronomer. As I have already noted, they cannot fall into any regular pattern of heliacal risings or oppositions or points of greatest elongation whatever correlation is used. Furthermore, I feel confident that the Maya did not record such events as eclipses, heliacal risings of planets, equinoxes, or solstices unless there was some special association, actual or ritualistic, to warrant a reference. Even in the cases of katuns ending on 1 Ahau the evidence that any attention was paid to Venus is unsatisfactory. Instead, Jupiter seems to have engaged the attention of the Maya priests. There are a number of cases in which Venus glyphs are combined with other elements, both known and unknown. It is a fair assumption that such glyphs refer to conjunctions of Venus with other planets or important constellations. A good example is supplied by the Tablet of the 96 Glyphs at Palenque (fig. 55,*1*). Glyph Block E7 shows a Venus glyph and moon glyph with certain affixes. The associated date is 9.16.13.0.7 9 Manik 15 Uo. At that time the moon was about 25 days old; Venus was an evening star, approximately 123 days past heliacal rising in the Goodman-Thompson correlation.

It is suggested elsewhere (p. 233) that the Venus glyph, with a human figure head down as affix, might represent the tzitzimime, demons which were believed by the Mexicans to fall to earth during eclipses.

SUPPOSED CYCLES OF OTHER PLANETS

Tables in Dresden which may refer to other planets are reviewed in Chapter 11. Suffice it at this point to note that there is wide divergence of opinion as to which tables refer to the various planets. I myself do not believe that they are in any way connected with revolutions of planets, but, instead are multiples to be used in connection with the divinatory almanacs which follow them.

SUMMARY

In this chapter are discussed two ritualistic cycles, and one astronomical, that of the planet Venus. The ritualistic cycles are that of the nine lords of the nights, and the 819-day count.

The nine lords of the nights ruled in the same endlessly repeating sequence as many nights. The glyph of the lord of the night usually follows the day sign, and immediately precedes Glyph F. It is known as Glyph G of the lunar series, although it is now realized that it has no direct connection with that series. There are nine glyphs, with both head forms and symbolic forms, each representing a god in the sequence. The Maya lords of the nights correspond loosely with the equivalent group in central Mexico, but the two series are not identical and the gods do not occur in the same order in the two series. The cycle of nine nights is brought into harmony with the sacred almanac of 260 days in Dresden.

As the lengths of the CR and the cycle of the lords of the nights have no common factor, any given CR date will repeat with a different lord of the night until the series is completed, a fact of considerable value in establishing the LC position of such CR dates as are accompanied by Glyph G. Likewise the presence of Glyph G is often a great help in the elucidation of damaged IS.

The Maya had a cycle of 819 days, which appears to have been used to relate the 13 lords of the days, the nine lords of the nights, and, perhaps, the seven lords of the earth to the solar year and to the moon. The ending point of this cycle always fell on a day with a co-

efficient of 1. Apparently those ending points of the 819-day cycle which had a solar or lunar relationship to the end of the katun in which the monument was erected were noted; others were ignored. For instance, the ending date of an 819-day cycle which had the same moon age as the end of the current katun or occupied the same position in the solar year, or was distant half a solar year from it might be recorded. Ending dates of the 819-day cycle are accompanied by about five explanatory glyphs which are approximately the same in all examples. The ending dates with their accompanying glyphs are inserted as parenthetical clauses between the day and month signs of the IS.

The planet Venus was of great importance to the Maya as an object both of worship and of astronomical exercises. Among the peoples of southern and central Mexico heliacal rising of the planet after inferior conjunction was regarded as fateful in the extreme: according to the day on which the planet rose, different categories of humanity and nature suffered affliction. It is certain that similar ideas existed among the Maya at the time the present edition of Dresden was written. There can be little doubt that the concepts of Venus, as recorded in Dresden, show profound influences from Mexico. Of the five manifestations of the planetary god, three are almost certainly Mexican; only two are Maya. The 20 directional gods who accompany the Venus tables are discussed.

The synodical revolutions of Venus (approximately 584 days) were related to the 260-day cycle and the year of 365 days in a very simple manner by equating 65 Venus years with 104 years of 365 days (146×260). In that way 1 Ahau, the sacred day of Venus, was retained as the closing day of the cycle. A brilliant system of correcting the small error which accumulated in these tables in such a way as always to retain 1 Ahau as the closing day of the cycle was developed by the Maya and first recognized by Teeple. In the discussion of this method of corrections certain emendations are suggested whereby all the correctional totals in Dresden are utilized, and the corrected bases brought into agreement with the Goodman-Thompson correlation. The principal factor which is new is the utilization of the number 9360 (amended from 9100), which equals 16 revolutions of Venus plus 16 days.

Venus glyphs in the inscriptions are not reviewed in detail because there is full evidence that no pattern of significance will emerge whatever correlation is used. The possibility that attention was paid to Venus on monuments erected to commemorate katuns ending on 1 Ahau is explored. The results are inconclusive. There is a suggestion that several of the associated dates refer primarily to Jupiter.

IO

The Moon

Night seems endless and the day
In fear or shyness stays away.
—J. H. B. Peel, *Mere England*

THE MOON GODDESS IN MYTH AND LEGEND

THE MAYA MOON, who treads her constant path across her stellar fields, yet shows her fickle nature in every human deed, is a moving figure of pathos, whose waywardness should be presented in a bitter setting comparable to that of Rachmaninoff's second concerto. Instead, the atmosphere, surcharged with arithmetical computations, is more reminiscent of Shostakovich or even of five-finger exercises. The Maya story of the moon goddess is "an empty tale, of idleness and pain, of two that loved—or did not love—and one whose perplexed heart did evil, foolishly, a long while since, and by some other sea." It is a moving tragedy, the only one that has survived in Maya folklore. Perforce, it must be compressed and bowdlerized in the worst tradition of the monthly digests to make room for the too arid discussion of the intellectual patterns to which the Maya scientists sought to reduce her erratic ways. We can only glance at that unhappy goddess who still holds the affections and receives the prayers of countless living Maya, before turning our full gaze upon the tailor's dummy on whom the Maya astronomers draped their involved calculations. For the argent moon, which in the skies of Central America seems so much closer and so much more effulgent than in these northern climes, failed not to arouse the curiosity of the Maya astronomer and to stir the imagination of those of humbler rank.

The Maya, like many peoples of the Old World, regarded the moon as the goddess of love, but they endowed her with a harshness of character which sharply differentiated her from Aphrodite and Venus. According to Maya legend (Thompson, 1930, pp. 119–40), the moon goddess is called Xt'actani. At the time the story opens, in the period before the creation of the sun, she lives with her grandfather and spends much of her time weaving.

The young man, who later becomes the sun, decides to woo her. He poses as a great hunter and wins her admiration. Later he borrows the skin of the hummingbird, and in that guise flies to the hut where moon lives. While sipping the honey from tobacco flowers he is hit by a clay pellet from the blowgun of the girl's grandfather. She picks up the unconscious bird and takes it to her room, where it recovers. During the night Sun resumes his human shape, and persuades Xt'actani to elope with him. This they do. The girl's grandfather, seeking to recover her, enlists the aid of one of the Chacs, who hurls a thunderbolt at the pair fleeing in a canoe. Sun turns himself into a turtle, Moon into a crab (alternative versions convert her into an armadillo or another turtle). Sun escapes injury, but Moon is killed. Dragonflies collect her flesh and blood in 13 hollow logs (perhaps those used as beehives). After 13 days Sun uncovers the logs. Twelve contain various noxious insects and snakes, which, escaping, spread all over the world; the thirteenth holds Moon restored to life.

Moon has no vagina, but with the aid of the deer this defect is remedied. Thereupon Sun and Moon have intercourse, the first persons ever to do so. The future god of the planet Venus, Sun's elder brother, comes to live with them. Later, Sun suspects that Moon is having relations with Venus (a Kekchi version has Cloud as the suspected adulterer). In revenge, he plays a trick on them. Moon is very upset. As she is crying on the riverbank a vulture persuades her to go with him to the house of the king vulture (a devil with four horns in another version). This she does, becoming the wife of the king vulture. Sun, seeking his errant wife, borrows the skin of the small deer and hides under it. When the vultures come to eat the carcass of the supposedly dead deer, Sun puts out a hand, and seizes one of them. He rides on its back to the vicinity of the home of the king vulture. Eventually he recovers Moon, who is somewhat reluctant to return with him.

Sun and Moon then ascend to heaven to take up their celestial duties. Moon is so bright that the people on earth complain that they cannot sleep as it is always day. To dim her brightness Sun plucks out one of her eyes.

The myth from which the above incidents are extracted is current among the Kekchi, and is also found in its entirety among the Mopan Maya of southern British Honduras. Various incidents in the narrative occur in myths and stories almost throughout the Maya area, and even among the Zapotec and other non-Maya peoples of southern Mexico. The popularity, the length, and the strong qualities of survival of this story attest to its importance and to the esteem in which its principal characters were held by the Maya. The antiquity of the myth is demonstrated by the painting of the incident of the deer guise on a vase of the Initial Series Period (Thompson, 1939, p. 151).

Other Maya groups say that Sun and Moon are always quarreling, and that eclipses are due to fights between them. The Tzutuhil Maya, living in the vicinity of Lake Atitlan, relate that the fights arise because Moon tells Sun lies about the conduct of the people on earth; the Quiche say that Moon is erratic, difficult to understand, a deceiver. These concepts also occur among people of Nahuatl and Nahuat speech. Although, so far as I know, cause and effect are no longer related by the modern Maya, one can assume that the quarrels and actual blows between Sun and Moon are renewals of the old grievance of Sun against Moon because of her promiscuity.

FUNCTIONS OF THE MOON GODDESS

Among most Maya groups the moon is recognized as the wife of the sun, and is usually given the title of "Our Mother," "Our Grandmother," "The Lady." She is the patroness of weaving, of medicine, of procreation, pregnancy, and birth. In central Mexico her counterpart is also a deity of the earth and of the crops. There is no direct evidence for the moon's being a goddess of the earth among the Maya, but the indirect evidence is very strong. The glyph of a goddess whom I identified many years ago as the moon goddess has as its principal characteristic a sign like a query mark, which actually appears to represent a lock of her hair. This same symbol is the principal element of the day sign Caban, "earth," which was under the patronage of the moon goddess, the deity of number 1. At the time I made that identification I had not realized that the Maya informant had given Bishop Landa for the sound u a drawing of this conventionalized lock of hair. The reason for his choice was that u means moon in Yucatec. This evidence is complete confirmation of the correctness of the identification of this glyph as that of the moon goddess (fig. 14,23,24). It is therefore virtually certain that the moon goddess was also a goddess of the earth and, by extension, of the crops it yields.

As the first person to weave, the moon goddess was patroness of the art of weaving, and was the object of reverence of all engaged in that craft. There is some evidence that a spider and its web symbolized that aspect of her functions.

Because of her adulterous conduct, the moon goddess symbolized promiscuity, and because she and Sun were the first to cohabit, both of them were regarded as closely associated with the sexual act. Furthermore, the moon, as the first woman, was the mother or grandmother of mankind. Yet, the attitude of the Maya to the moon goddess is not one of filial affection. It would be difficult to maintain such an attitude toward a mother who was manifestly a wanton. The moon goddess, rather, is regarded as capricious, quarrelsome, and a prevaricator.

The Mexicans, whose ideas concerning the moon were very close to those of the Maya, believed that the moon goddess lived in the layer of the heavens which was the abode of the Tlalocs, the gods of rain, and that this was the land of rain and mist. Indeed, the moon crescent is frequently filled with water in Mexican codices. There is some evidence, both in folklore and in the glyphs themselves, that a somewhat similar idea existed among the Maya (p. 238).

There is a possibility that the Maya personified the moon not as one woman, but as two, a young goddess and an old goddess, the former perhaps representing the waxing, the latter the waning, moon. There is a great deal of material on the subject of the moon goddess which I have discussed elsewhere (Thompson, 1939). It should be noted that evidence forthcoming since that study was written has considerably strengthened the thesis (Wisdom, 1940; Siegel, 1941; Amram, 1942; Cline, 1944).

Although the Maya, particularly those from the lowlands, generally regard the moon as the consort of the sun, among the Tzeltal and Tzotzil of Chiapas she is thought to be the mother of the sun (Barbachano, 1946, p. 122; Guiteras, 1946, p. 97) and also the spouse of the lord of the realm of the dead, which is called Olontic. The sun goes thither each night to visit his father and the newly deceased (Pozas Arciniega, 1947, p. 452). This belief reaffirms the connection of the moon with the earth and its interior. The confusion between the spouse and the mother of the sun may be reflected in the two forms of the moon, the youthful goddess and the aged woman, just as there are some reasons for believing that the Maya worshipped both a youthful and an aged sun god. This dual concept probably accounts for the obscurity in the relationship between the Yucatecan goddesses Ixchebelyax and Ix Azal-Uoh.

In representations of the moon in Mexican codices a rabbit or a stone knife may be set in the crescent of the moon (really a recurved u apparently made of a section of shell or bone). Mythology accounts for the presence of the rabbit, which also serves to connect the moon with the earth, for 1 Tochtli (1 Rabbit) is a name for the earth, and the rabbit is sometimes depicted emerging from the jaws of the Quetzal snake, which symbolizes the surface of the earth covered with vegetation. The connection between the flint blade and the moon is not apparent, but flint knives are sometimes set in the night sky.

So far as is known, neither the rabbit nor the flint knife is connected with the moon in the sculptural or graphic arts of the Maya.

GLYPHS OF THE MOON GODDESS

The various names and titles bestowed on the moon goddess have already been discussed (pp. 47-48, 87). Several glyphs can be identified as belonging to the moon goddess. These include glyphs corresponding both to functions and to titles. A functional glyph of the moon goddess has been noted in the series of directional gods listed with the Venus tables (p. 223; fig. 42,*18*). This same glyph, it will be recalled, appears also in the eclipse tables of Dresden. A similar glyph, combining the features of the youthful goddess with the symbol of the moon, appears with some frequency in the lunar series of the inscriptions, particularly in the full-figure glyphs (fig. 29, *12,17*).

A glyph which clearly corresponds to an honorific is that which embodies the curl of hair (fig. 14,*23,24*). This pretty certainly means something like "the woman," for the moon was "the woman" to the Maya. (She had something in common with Irene Adler of "A Scandal in Bohemia.")

There are certain variations in prefixes which probably refer to descriptive titles. Thus the prefix for white is often attached to her glyph, and "the white lady" is a natural title to bestow on the moon. Moreover, this emblem for white is sometimes set in her hair (fig. 14,*18*).

So far as the hieroglyphic texts are concerned, the observed or predicted movements of the moon are of greater consequence than the mythological aspects of the goddess, and we shall now turn to that interesting but vexatious problem.

A great deal of ink has flowed in discussing Maya methods for recording the age of the moon on a given date, for grouping moons, and for establishing tables of dates on which eclipses might fall. Other matters which have engaged the attention of students include Maya ideas as to the length of the lunation as revealed by their computations over nearly 4000 years to learn the age of the moon at dates in the neighborhood of 13.0.0.0.0 4 Ahau 8 Cumku.

Brilliant studies by scholars, particularly Meinshausen, Willson, Guthe, Teeple, Pogo, Makemson, Beyer, and Satterthwaite, have revealed much concerning the achievements of the Maya in that field. As an illustration of how each student has builded on the foundations of his predecessors, I purpose on another page to give a brief

outline of the history of the elucidation of the eclipse tables of Dresden.

Such studies are, of course, more than a tribute to modern scholarship; they reveal the wondrous achievements of the Maya scholar, and replace many tesserae in the mosaic of the Maya intellect. He who would display the peaks of Maya achievement for the general reader, yet would not neglect to chart for the specialist the confusion of foothills with which they are girt, faces a problem in the presentation of data which is not easily solved. A literature of frightening proportions on the subject has already appeared, and there is little that I can add either to a discussion of the arithmetical and astronomical angle or to the dissection of the explanatory texts. I shall accordingly confine myself largely to a résumé of the subject.

THE ECLIPSE AND LUNAR TABLE OF CODEX DRESDEN

Pages 51-58 of Dresden have for long excited the curiosity of students and aroused the interest of astronomers. They follow the Venus table already discussed, and conform to the same general pattern in so far as a lower row of numbers gives the interval between the accompanying date and the previous one; an upper row of numbers gives the accumulated totals (reproductions of the table are given in Guthe, 1921, and Willson, 1924). The lower numbers are for the most part intervals of 177 days or, occasionally, of 178 days, but before each of the nine "pictures," which interrupt the tables at somewhat irregular spacing, the interval is 148 days. There is a tenth picture at the end of the table, which is not preceded by an interval of 148 days and which in fact has an entirely different function, for it appears to have served primarily to mark the conclusion of the cycle.

The total number of days recorded is 11,958 by the upper row of additions; 11,959 by the intervals. Actually, there can be no reasonable doubt that the table is meant to record a re-entering cycle of 11,960 days (1.13.4.0). Month signs are omitted, but with each column are given three sequent day signs. The first entry (p. 53a, left) records an addition of 177 days leading to 6 Kan, 7 Chicchan, 8 Cimi. By subtracting 177 days, the bases of the table are easily obtained. They are 11 Manik, 12 Lamat, and 13 Muluc.

THE PICTURES

Eight of the pictures which follow intervals of 148 days hang from stylized planetary bands representing the heavens; in the ninth picture this celestial band is missing, presumably because the picture is that of the death god, a deity of the underworld. Pictures 4, 5, 7, 8, and 9 represent the kin, "sun," glyph against a background part black, part white. No. 2 shows the head of the aged sun god in a black frame with a white design overlaying a part of it. The head of Picture 3 is that of God D. It is within a cartouche, half black and half white, and a kin glyph immediately above indicates that the solar aspect of God D is intended. Picture 1 is the death god; Picture 6 a dead woman with a black spot on her cheek. A rope, joined to the celestial band, passes loosely around her neck. Emblems of death and darkness or the underworld, such as crossed bones or death eyes, accompany Pictures 2, 5, 7, and 8.

The kin glyph or head of the sun god against a background of black and white can be reasonably interpreted as pictures of darkness (p. 272), the black areas presumably indicating the obscurity associated with eclipses. The deities of death and the mortuary symbols logically express the same idea, for at a solar eclipse the sun may have been thought to depart to the underworld, his abode during the hours of darkness.

The tenth picture, which ends the table, is that of a monster who plunges head first from a celestial band, to which are attached two pairs of black and white ovals, one of which has a kin sign in the center, the other a lunar glyph. The head of the monster is hidden by a large glyph of the planet Venus. One is instantly reminded of the Aztec belief that during eclipses the monsters called Tzitzimime or Tzontemoc (head down) plunged earthwards from the sky. These monsters include Tlauizcalpantecutli, the god of Venus as morning star (Thompson, 1934, pp. 228–30). It is therefore highly probable that this picture represents a Tzitzimitl plunging head down toward earth during the darkness of an eclipse. A glyph immediately above the picture appears to confirm this identification, for it shows the glyph of Venus with a prefix which is a picture of a person placed upside down (fig. 42,32). It has been supposed that the presence of the Venus monster in this picture indicates some relationship with the revolution of that planet. It is very much more probable, however, that the Venus monster is depicted merely because Venus is the most conspicuous or most easily recognizable of the Tzitzimime and that, in consequence, the synodical period of Venus in no way enters into the calculations.

HISTORICAL OUTLINE OF INVESTIGATIONS ON THE LUNAR TABLE

As early as 1901 Förstemann (1906, pp. 200–15) deduced that the table had to do with the moon, surmising that the intervals of 177 days represented groups of six lunations, thus arranged to conform as far as possible to the solar half-year. A dozen years later, a young German student, Martin Meinshausen (1913), established that the tables dealt with eclipses, for, by comparing the intervals in the lunar table of Dresden with tables of observed solar and lunar eclipses of the eighteenth and nineteenth centuries, he was able to demonstrate that the intervals in Dresden were such as normally occur between observed or predicted eclipses. Meinshausen also suggested that pictures came after the intervals of 148 days because when a solar eclipse followed another at an interval of 148 days, a lunar eclipse would occur 15 days later. Unfortunately, the career of this young student, which had opened with such brilliance, was cut short by his death on the Russian front in the early days of World War I.

Professor Robert W. Willson started his studies of Dresden 51–58 in 1910, and continued them at intervals until his death in 1923. His findings appeared in 1924. Willson recognized that the table dealt with eclipses some time before the publication of Meinshausen's conclusions, for he says of Bowditch's transcription of the Dresden tables:

At the first glance [I] saw the number 6585.32, conspicuously displayed. . . . The idea was at once suggested that the table had to do with the Saros, or, at any rate, with a series of eclipses. . . . The codex showed . . . a series of dates on which eclipses may possibly occur, when the sun happens to be near the node of the moon's orbit on the day of new moon. For proof of this compare the upper numbers from the Dresden Codex . . . with those in column 1 of Table 11 of Schram's "Table of the Phases of the Moon," and it will be found that the numbers are identical. . . . If there is a central eclipse on a given date, there will be a central eclipse somewhere on the earth after 1033, 1211, 1388, and 1565 days, and there may be a central eclipse after 1742 days. The intervals of the pictures in the codex are 1742, 1033, 1211 thrice repeated, making three periods of 3986 days each.

With a most ingenious construction Willson (1924, pp. 13–14) compared the intervals between eclipses visible in the Maya area from 31 B.C. to A.D. 1508 with those between the nine pictures in Dresden, with the primary object of discovering whether the pictures corresponded to observed eclipses, and the secondary object of solving the correlation question. This secondary aim, naturally, could only be realized in the event that the primary object was attained. The results were disappointing: no group of nine eclipses at the requisite intervals were visible in any one part of the Maya area, and there was no series in which visible eclipses corresponded to eight of the nine pictures. Willson felt that a solution along those lines would not be found. He concluded that the purpose of the table was that of listing positions in the Maya calendar on which solar eclipses could occur.

Carl Guthe (1921) devoted considerable time to the

study of Dresden 51–58, acknowledging the great help he received from Willson. Guthe's report is largely devoted to a discussion of the pattern of the eclipse table. He brought out the manner in which the table consists of three equal parts, each with 23 unequal subdivisions. He believed that the table served both for predicting eclipses and for lunar reckonings.

In 1930 John E. Teeple, who had already solved the problem of the lunar series on the monuments of the Initial Series Period by his elucidation of Glyphs C, D, and E of that series, published his great work *Maya Astronomy*. Starting where the others had left off, he was able to make two important contributions to the subject. First, he showed that if the days in the table are plotted on a wheel of 520 days, that is to say, two almanacs of 260 days apiece, the possible eclipse dates fall in three groups. That is so because an eclipse must occur within approximately 18 days of the node, and the moon's path and that of the sun cross every 173.31 days. Thrice 173.31 is less than a tenth of a day short of 520 days, the double almanac. Thus, in a wheel with 520 spokes, matching the number of days in a double almanac, there will be three main radii 173 days apart, corresponding to the node days. If the count starts with 12 Lamat (Day 168), that will be the first main radius. The second will be 173 days later at 3 Imix (Day 341); the third will correspond to a 7 Ix (Day 514). Another eclipse half-year will carry the count back to 12 Lamat. One would expect the possible eclipse dates to be clustered on both sides of these three points with a spread in each direction of about 18 days, and such is the case.

By comparing the various dates in the table, Teeple was able to establish that the three node days were 11 Manik (Day 167), 2 Ahau (Day 340), and 7 Ix (Day 514). It is a remarkable fact that three eclipse half-years correspond so closely to twice the length of the divinatory almanac, and there is no reason to doubt that the Maya priests took full advantage of the fact. The assumption has been made that the period of 260 days was chosen because twice its length was practically the equivalent of three ecliptic seasons, but that is surely another case of putting the horse before the cart, for the 260-day almanac must have been in being centuries before the Maya priests learned how to predict dates of possible eclipses. Furthermore, had an almanac been developed to conform to the eclipse half-years, why should the cycle have been 260 days rather than 520? Teeple was also the first to call attention to the importance of the recession of the node days in the double almanac. After the table has been used once, that is to say, after the lapse of approximately 33 years, the node days will have receded about 1.6 days, be-

cause 69 eclipse half-years are approximately that much less than 46 cycles of 260 days. After the table has been used a couple of times some possible eclipse dates falling 16–18 days after the nodal points will have lost their significance, for with the recession of the nodal points, the sun will be too far from the point of intersection with the moon's path on those days for an eclipse to occur. An extra group of five moons would in time have to be inserted in order to recover all possible eclipse dates.

An important contribution to the problem of the eclipse table was made by Alexander Pogo (1937), who returned to the theory, first advanced by Meinshausen, that the nine pictures in the Dresden table represent lunar eclipses following 15 days after the end of a group of five lunations. He concluded that an alert Maya astronomer could have constructed this table in Dresden from data obtained by observation of lunar eclipses over a third of a century, and by careful handling of the intervals between observed eclipses and combinations thereof.

Maud Makemson (1943) calls attention to the three IS at the start of the table, which throw light on the problem of node days. These are the dates 9.16.4.10.8 12 Lamat 1 Muan, 9.16.4.11.3 1 Akbal 16 Muan, and 9.16.4.11.18 3 Etz'nab 11 Pax. Obviously, she notes, they must represent two solar eclipses with a lunar eclipse between, or two lunar eclipses with solar eclipse in the middle. In either case 1 Akbal must have coincided with the node passage, or fallen not more than a couple of days from it. The IS date 9.16.4.10.8 12 Lamat 1 Muan was, therefore, 13–15 days before node passage, whereas Teeple had shown that the 12 Lamat of the table was at node passage or within a day thereof. It follows that when 1 Akbal coincided with the node passage, certain dates, such as 5 Imix which ends the sixth lunation group, 4 Ahau which ends the twenty-first lunation group, and 3 Cauac which ends the thirty-sixth lunation group, will be too far from node passage (22, 23, and 24 days) to coincide with solar eclipses. The table, now lost, which accompanied the IS 9.16.4.10.8 12 Lamat would have had a different arrangement of the 148-day groups, and a consequent shift of 29–30 days in many of the possible dates for eclipses. That indicated that the tables were constructed in their present form at a date sufficiently removed from the IS to account for a recession of the node passage of approximately 15 days, from 1 Akbal to 12 Lamat. As Teeple had shown that the node passage recedes at the rate of 1.61 days each time the table (1.13.4.0) is used, approximately 9 × 1.13.4.0 must have passed between the 12 Lamat of the IS (9.16.4.10.8) and the 12 Lamat of the table, and therefore the 12 Lamat of the table was within three or four katuns of 10.10.0.0.0:

9.16. 4.10.8 12 Lamat
14.19. 0.0   (9 × 1.13.4.0)
_____
10.11. 3.10.8 12 Lamat

This was an exceedingly important point, for it eliminated consideration of 9.16.4.10.8 as the base of the table, and enabled the date of the table to be fixed approximately in terms of the Maya calendar, and without reference to the conveniences of advocates of the several correlations.

The date Dr. Makemson favored for the start of the eclipse calendar was 10.12.16.14.8 12 Lamat 1 Ch'en, because in the 11.16.0.0.0 correlation this corresponded to Julian day 2,116,732. Dr. Makemson further demonstrated that with that base for the table, pairs of partial

Maya moons		*260-day cycles*	*Astronomical moons*	
5 × 405 moons	= 59800 d. =	5 × 46 × 260 :	5 × 405 moons =	59799.44 d.
361 moons − 1 d.	= 10660 d. =	41 × 260 :	361 moons =	10660.54 d.
2386 moons	= 70460 d. =	271 × 260 :	2386 moons =	70459.98 d.

eclipses of the sun, enclosing lunar eclipses, occurred at the same intervals as those that mark the positions of the nine pictures in Dresden.

Satterthwaite (1947) has made many experiments in grouping of moons, and has discussed how the Maya might have constructed the eclipse table.

That is the history in brief of progress in that one small field of Maya hieroglyphic research. It illustrates well how the torch has passed from one hand to another.

POSSIBLE METHOD OF CORRECTING THE LUNAR TABLE

One should not paint the lily nor lose sight of creation in a pollen count. The construction of the eclipse table was a magnificent feat; its reconstruction by scholars in the past half-century from defective source materials is also a resounding triumph. I do not wish to dim these achievements or to lose the reader in a fog of speculative reconstructions, and for those reasons I shall suppress some pages of discussion about groupings of moons which I had written, and deal with only one point.

It is very probable that the equation 405 moons = 46 × 260 (11,960 days) was used for lunar calculations before it was adapted by changes in its internal structure to the prediction of eclipses. Indeed, its use at Palenque before the initiation of the eclipse calendar, as demonstrated by Teeple, is strong evidence for this view. I am inclined to believe that corrections were made to this equation for reckoning lunations, but not for its use as a table of possible eclipse dates. It is reasonable to suppose that the Maya, had they realized that 11,960 was a trifle too long, would have applied corrections to it in approximately the same way as they corrected the Venus tables with the primary object of retaining the *lub* at 12 Lamat.

The Venus table, it will be remembered, was corrected by dropping four days at the sixty-first revolution or eight days at the fifty-seventh revolution so that with the correction the count could start again with 1 Ahau still as the *lub;* the lunar (but not the eclipse) count can be corrected by dropping one day at the three hundred and sixty-first lunation, and starting the count over again at 12 Lamat. The three hundred and sixty-first lunation ends on 13 Muluc, but the correction is greater than the error in the 11,960-day equation. The latter would have to be used five times before a sufficient error had been accumulated to be offset by the correction at the three hundred and sixty-first moon:

This correction is remarkably accurate, but we have no reason to believe that the Maya knew that the 405-moon table should be repeated five times before 44 moons and a day were dropped from the sixth round. Yet there is some evidence that this correction was applied, although not at a 1:5 ratio.

The red IS of page 52e reads 9.19.8.7.8 7 Lamat, but this is an impossible combination, for the date does not reach 7 Lamat nor does it reach the expected 12 Lamat. Previously, I had suggested to Mrs. Makemson that it should be corrected to 10.19.9.12.8 12 Lamat, so as to reach a date which was a multiple of 1.13.4.0 removed from 9.16.4.10.8, but that amendment calls for drastic changes. The scribes were careless, but three errors in five numbers is an unwontedly low level of accuracy. Furthermore, with three periods of an IS corrected, one can get almost any result one wants. With my thought centered on a multiple of 1.13.4.0, I ignored the much simpler correction which, I now believe, should have been made, namely, the change of the tun coefficient from 8 to 7. This correction was first proposed by Schulz (1940). The resulting position is distant one cycle of 405 moons plus 361 moons less a day from 9.16.4.10.8:

9.16. 4.10.8 12 Lamat
 1.13. 4.0   (405 moons : 46 × 260 d.)
_____
9.17.17.14.8 12 Lamat
 1. 9.11.0   (361 moons − 1 d. : 41 × 260 d.)
_____
9.19. 7. 7.8 12 Lamat

The date 9.19.7.7.8 cannot be a position in a table for eclipse predictions, for it is an odd number of 260-day cycles from the starting point of the eclipse table and, furthermore, does not occur as one of the endings of a lunation group, but it could have been used for reckonings in lunations.

There is some evidence that the Maya combined two groups of 405 moons to one 361-moon group, although the ratio is not constant. The distance 9.16.4.10.0 which leads from the 12 Lamat immediately after 4 Ahau 8 Cumku at Baktun 13 can be resolved into 70 × 1.13.4.0 and 54 × 1.9.11.0, which is a ratio of 1:1.3. The distance number of 2.10.16.3.0 on Copan I' has been long suspected to have lunar significance. It reduces to 19 × 1.13.4.0 and 13 × 1.9.11.0, a ratio of 1:1.46. If the count is then projected backward not to 13.0.0.0.0, as Teeple suggested, but to the nearest occurrence of 9 Ahau, just 60 days earlier, the interval of 7.1.14.0.0 equals 55 × 1.13.4.0 and 34 × 1.9.11.0, a ratio of 1:1.6. The ratio has to be kept nearly constant, in these cases at approximately 2:3, or one can make any recurrence of a day far in the past or future the same moon age as one's starting point. Actually, the two formulae used in a 2:3 ratio are less accurate than the 1.13.4.0 equation used by itself, but we have no reason to assume that the Maya were aware of that.

On present evidence one can not assert that the Maya used this 361-moon formula in combination with the 405-moon equation, but I think there are enough hints to justify us in watching for further indications of its existence.

THE MAYA AND THE ASTRONOMICAL NEW MOON

The point from which the moon age is counted is not surely known. The possibilities are disappearance of the old moon, conjunction, or appearance of the new moon. Teeple assumed that the age of the moon was reckoned from conjunction; Beyer (1937a) believed that the calculation was made from disappearance of the old moon. The latter method of counting is still current in some Tzeltal, Chol, and Tzotzil villages of Chiapas, for Schulz (1942) says: "the day in which the moon was last seen before sunrise is counted as the last day of the old moon. The following day is the first of the new moon, even though the moon be not yet visible."

According to Schulz, the villagers of the three linguistic groups cited say that when the old moon disappears "the moon has now died." The Aztec used a similar term for the disappearance of the old moon, saying "now the moon dies; now it sleeps a lot." At the time of conjunction they said "now the moon is dead." The Kekchi and Pokomchi, also, say of the waning crescent "the moon sleeps." In the Carcha district, according to Dieseldorff, the Kekchi say for new moon *x'cam li po,* "the moon is dead." Unfortunately, it is not clear whether Dieseldorff referred to the astronomical new moon, or

the moon when first observed. In view of the other evidence, the reference is more probably to conjunction.

The Kekchi say of the first phase of the moon "the moon is born." A similar concept appears to have existed among the Yucatec, for the Motul and San Francisco dictionaries give for new moon *pal u. Pal* means child.

The Motul dictionary also lists as a term for the waning moon when it is about to disappear *benel u tu ch'een,* the translation of which appears to be "the departure of the moon to its well." As noted on page 238, this appears to be an obscure reference to a supposed sojourn of the moon, during her period of disappearance, in the heaven of the rain gods, or possibly in a well sacred to the rain gods (cenotes assuredly were regarded as places for offerings to the rain gods).

In the Vienna dictionary the same expression is given for the moon when it is no longer visible, although only the first two letters of *luna* are now legible: *lu . . . no se ve, binaan u, binan u tu ch'en* (literally "the moon gone, the moon gone to her well").

Two distinct concepts or metaphors are contained in these sundry terms: after disappearance the moon is said to die and, at reappearance, to be reborn as a child, or to go at disappearance to the heaven of the rain gods, or to enter some body of water on or under the surface of the earth. Venus similarly was believed by the Mexicans to die at disappearance, and to come to life again at heliacal rising.

The linguistic evidence, I think, rather favors a count from disappearance or, perhaps, from conjunction. It is certainly not in conformity with Spinden's thesis that the Maya reckoned the moon age from full moon. That thesis was adopted by Spinden and by Ludendorff, his fidus Achates, because Maya dates which were declared to be new moons actually fell some 10 days after new moon in the Spinden correlation, published before Teeple had discovered the meanings of Glyphs C, D, and E of the lunar series. To reconcile his correlation to the new data, Spinden made two assumptions: one that the Maya reckoned lunations from full moon to full moon; the other that the Maya calculated the length of the moon slightly under its true length, and allowed that error to accumulate, with the result that Maya full moons are recorded four days before they actually occurred. Ludendorff offered a somewhat more complicated explanation. According to his theory, the Maya overcalculated the length of the lunation, and when the error had reached about three days, they applied a correction, but the correction was approximately twice as great as the accumulated error, and produced full moons four days before they actually occurred.

Nevertheless, so far as is known, no American Indian

group reckoned lunations from full moons. At one time the Haida were believed to have been an exception in that respect, but more careful observation of their customs revealed that they reckoned their months only from new moon to new moon (Murdock quoted in Thompson, 1932b, p. 412).

LUNAR SERIES ON THE MONUMENTS

Most IS on the monuments of the Initial Series Period are expanded to include a number of glyphs which record the age of the current moon, the position of that moon in a lunar half-year, and the number of days in the current moon or, perhaps, that immediately past. These glyphs, together with others, such as Glyphs G and F which actually do not belong with the group, are known as the lunar or supplementary series. The latter name, now somewhat obsolete, was applied to the group before its main function was known to indicate that the glyphs of which it is composed appeared to supplement the IS.

The lunar series sometimes follows the day and month glyphs of the IS, but more often it lies between them; occasionally it precedes both, intervening between the kin glyph and the day sign. In exceptional cases the sequence is: day sign, Glyphs G and F, month sign, remaining glyphs of the lunar series.

The number of glyphs in the lunar series varies. Generally there are eight, including, for convenience and because of their nocturnal associations, Glyphs G and F in the tally. The others are Glyphs E, D, C, X, B, and A. Occasionally two other signs, the so-called Glyphs Y and Z, are inserted between Glyphs F and E.

The desire to record with an IS data concerning the moon appears to have existed from the earliest times. There are hints of a lunar reckoning on the Leiden plaque (Nottebohm, 1944), and definite lunar series accompany some early IS, namely that of Uaxactun 18 (8.16.0.0.0) and Balakbal 5 (8.18.10.0.0), although these are of a somewhat abbreviated form, giving merely the moon age and the number of moons of the current group. Glyphs A, B, and X were later additions to the series, the first making its appearance at an early date, followed by Glyph X (present on Uaxactun 22, 9.3.10.0.0, and on Yaxchilan L 48, 9.4.11.8.16). The first appearance of Glyph B is seemingly on Piedras Negras 25, 9.8.15.0.0. At Copan it is first recorded on Stela 7, dedicated at 9.9.0.0.0, whereas at Pusilha it does not appear until 9.11.0.0.0 (Stela H).

The decipherment of Glyphs C, D, and E, which are the kernel of the group, was made by John E. Teeple (1925, 1925a, 1930). The discovery of their meaning had a significance far greater than the disclosures of their general import, for it not only supplied a new test which

correlations of the Christian and Maya calendars must pass, but also threw light on the intellectual processes and the spirit of scientific co-operation which animated the Maya astronomers. Correlations which failed to produce new moons close to the dates on which the lunar series indicated them had to be rejected. The rapid spread to important Maya centers of the uniform system of grouping moons in lunar half-years (p. 244) reflects a close co-operation in scientific advance and a marked absence of local jealousies and intellectual isolationism.

Glyphs D and E record the age of the current moon (figs. 36; 37). When the moon is less than 20 days old, Glyph D, with coefficient of 1–19 inclusive, alone is used; when the moon age is 20 days or over, Glyph E, which has the value of 20 days or nights, is included. Its coefficient does not exceed 9. To record a moon age of exactly 20 days, Glyph E appears without a coefficient. When Glyph E is necessary, Glyph D also appears, but without a coefficient. It is clear that Glyphs D and E function as a distance number, corresponding broadly to kins and uinals. In fact, they often have the distance-number postfix and Glyph E sometimes occurs in distance numbers which are in no way part of a lunar series (p. 167). Thus to express a moon age of 27 days, both Glyphs D and E would be used. Glyph D would lack a coefficient; Glyph E would have a coefficient of 7. On the other hand, a moon age of seven days would be expressed by the attachment of a bar and two dots to Glyph D. Glyph E would not be present.

GLYPH D

The most usual form of Glyph D is composed of three or four elements. On the left there is a hand (usually the right with back to the observer, but sometimes the left with palm visible) which is placed in a position usually about halfway between vertical and horizontal with wrist to left. The forefinger usually points diagonally to the right; the other fingers are usually bent. On the right there is half of the normal moon sign but with three dots, arranged diagonally, replacing the circle generally found in the interior of the moon sign. A postfix, the attributive *il* sign (p. 285), is beneath the hand or underlies both hand and half-moon sign. Sometimes, the distance-number postfix is added as a second postfix, or, more rarely, the two postfixes are merged. The coefficient is usually to the left; quite rarely, above. Most irregularly, Glyph D of Pusilha K is formed of what seems to be a complete moon sign above a hand placed horizontally with wrist to right (figs. 36,*11,15,35,39,44,57,61;* 37,*7, 11,27,36,41,46,53,58*).

I had formerly thought that the half-moon indicated the crescent of the waxing moon, but such an assumption is surely erroneous. The moon sign is halved to economize space, for in variants which lack the hand the full glyph is used, and in a few instances (e.g. Glyph A, Coba 20) moon signs, which are normally shown as full glyphs, are cut in half when combined with another glyph. The normal form of Glyph D is essentially the same as Glyph C, which is known to declare the number of complete moons. The different position of the hand in Glyph C is in all probability due to the need to place it in such a position that it would not obscure the variable element added to Glyph C, which is absent from Glyph D. It is, accordingly, probable that Glyph D represents a completed moon, to which the coefficient is added, rather than a lunar period of 24 hours which is multiplied by the coefficient. Apart from the testimony of the resemblance of the normal form of Glyph D to Glyph C, there are two other lines of evidence in favor of this interpretation. In a number of cases glyphs which stand for day (more probably a count by nights, p. 174) are inserted between the coefficient and Glyph D, but these would be redundant had Glyph D the meaning of a lunar period of 24 hours. The *il* postfix is usually present with Glyph D, as with Glyph C, and there seems little doubt that this should be read with the lunar element (*u*) to produce *uil*, a term used in reference to moons, the *il* being an attributive or relationship suffix. There is a third, but weaker, argument in favor of the thesis: did Glyph D refer to a single night, there would be no need to carve the glyph when Glyph E was also present. I think, therefore, that we have good reason to accept Glyph D as meaning completed moon, the coefficient, together with the distance-number postfix, indicating a distance number of *n* days (or nights or dawns) from the last completed moon.

This normal form of Glyph D can be modified in several ways, of which the most important involves the elimination of the hand, the conversion of the half-lunar element to a complete lunar disk, and, sometimes, the addition of a prefix (figs. 36,6,25,49; 37,23,67). Beyer (1941) has ably discussed at some length the various forms of Glyph D, and in particular the variant with full lunar disk. He notes that when this is employed as a symbol for 20, it has in its center a circle (figs. 4,16–18; 37,5,10, 25,31,40,46 etc.); when it serves as Glyph D the circle is replaced by an eye (figs. 36,6,25,49,54; 37,1,23) or two or three circlets (fig. 37,67). Beyer thinks the eye in moon means "shining moon," but it is much more probable that the eye represents the death eye, and the whole means death of the moon.

In a number of cases in which the hand is eliminated, a jade symbol, which we have previously encountered with the meaning of water, is prefixed (figs. 36,49; 37,23). Beyer (1941a, p. 65) also recognizes the affix as a jade

symbol, but attributes to it the meaning of shining, for he writes: "the polished (that is the shining) green stone. In this connection the symbol evidently is used to characterize the shining of the moon." With this interpretation I hardly agree. The primary symbolism of jade is that of water, and, so far as I know, the value of brilliance, as that of the argent moon, would not normally be expressed by the symbol of jade. Furthermore, Beyer accepts the meaning of moon completed ("end of moon" in his terminology) for the normal form of Glyph D, and, therefore, he should have sought a similar idea for this variant to express; "shining moon" is the exact antithesis.

According to Mexican belief the moon resided in Tlalocan, the abode of the rain gods; Vatican A speaks of one of the celestial layers as "the kingdom of the rain god and the moon," and the moon symbol in the Mexican codices usually contains water. Moreover, both Maya and Mexican goddesses of the moon are closely associated with water (Thompson, 1939, p. 143). The Cakchiquel of Panajachel, for instance, consider the moon goddess to be the "owner" of Lake Atitlan, and believe that she has a palace beneath its waters.

In Yucatan, as we have seen, one of the terms for the disappearing of the moon was *benel u tu ch'een*, "the departure of the moon to her well." This, I think, must mean that the Yucatec believed that when the waning moon disappeared, she went to the land of rain, the abode of the Chacs, the rain gods, or in line with the Cakchiquel association of the moon with a lake, she entered some lake or well or cenote, perhaps connected, in thought, with the primal waters in which the earth monster floats, or, in view of the association in Yucatan and among the Chorti (p. 75) of rain gods with wells and cenotes, a temporary abode of those deities. It will be remembered that the month Ch'en, "well," has the moon goddess as its patroness.

It is at least possible, if not highly probable, that this variant of Glyph D with the jade prefix expresses the idea of the moon disappearing, after it wanes, to the land of water. Thereby, this variant connotes the same general idea as is conveyed by the variant with outstretched hand, namely, a count from the completion of the moon. In one variant a hand indicates the completion of the moon; in the other, a jade symbol appears to represent the abode of the rain gods to which the moon goddess at her death may have been thought to retire for the period between disappearance and reappearance.

There is, however, a slight complication. A Yucatec word used for the setting of the moon, and also for the setting of the sun, is *t'ubul*, which means to sink or be submerged in water or some hollow or concave object. The root also appears in *t'ubtal* with the meaning of being submerged in water, but also used in the sense of being (deep) in a hammock or cradle. It does not necessarily follow, therefore, that the Maya thought of the moon and sun as sinking into water when they used this expression, and I know of no combination of kin and a jade symbol which could represent the setting sun. The expression was probably used in precisely the same way as we speak of the sinking sun or moon, without any image in our minds of sinking into water. Moreover, as we have seen, Glyph D almost surely refers to the completed moon, not to its daily setting.

In another variant of Glyph D the jade prefix is attached to an element resembling a little head on its side, and the distance-number postfix is below (fig. 37,48). This element sometimes occurs with head variants of the completion sign. Beyer (1941a, pp. 67–68) regards it as a death or an ending symbol, with which identification, so far as death is concerned, I am in agreement. The element with its jade prefix, accordingly, would seem to be translatable as "the dead one (the moon) in the land of the rain gods." The meaning therefore would be the same as that of the variant just discussed.

In two instances (Naranjo 13, Xcalumkin IS) the hand element of Glyph D is present, together with the normal suffix of that glyph, but the moon sign is suppressed. Presumably it was so obvious that the completion referred to the moon that the latter glyph could be omitted without any danger of ambiguity.

A head variant of Glyph D is common at Palenque but quite rare at other sites. This takes the form of a grotesque head, clearly that of an animal or a reptile, which is placed mouth upward (figs. 36,20; 37,36). Beyer regards this as identical with the frog head used as the personified form of the uinal glyph (fig. 27,40–52). The resemblance is certainly close, but this head variant of Glyph D invariably has an upturned snout, not a characteristic of the uinal head, although it occurs in a vestigial form in some examples of that glyph. Also, this Glyph D variant lacks the triangular arrangement of dots almost invariably found in the ear of the uinal head. These differences are sufficient to enable the two heads to be distinguished easily from one another, quite apart from differences in affixes and positions, but they are probably not sufficient to require us to seek outside the frog or toad groups for the prototype. As noted (p. 47) the generic name for frog or toad in many Maya languages and dialects of the highlands is *po,* a word which also is the name of the moon in Kekchi and Pokoman. Nevertheless, I would be inclined to regard this head as signifying in some way as yet not clear disappearance of the moon.

On Quirigua G there is an unusual variant of Glyph D, consisting of a hand, with distance-number prefix below, a skull or death head in a vertical position, and a vestigial moon sign (fig. 37,17). The whole must surely mean "completion of the death of the moon."

The variants of Glyph D with their probable meanings are accordingly:

1. Hand and moon sign. "Completion of the moon."
2. Hand. "Completion."
3. Moon with eye infix. "Death of moon?"
4. Moon with eye infix and jade. "Dead moon (?) in the heaven of the rain gods."
5. Little head on side and jade. "The dead one in the heaven of the rain gods."
6. Head of frog or toad in vertical position. Meaning uncertain.
7. Hand, skull, moon. "Completion of death of moon."

The evidence of the glyphs themselves seems to indicate that Glyphs D and E were not counted from observed new moon, but either from the disappearance of the old moon or from conjunction with the sun during the period of disappearance. Thus the glyphic evidence appears to substantiate deductions from the linguistic data.

These seven variants of the Glyph D provide a good example of how richness in glyphic combinations reflects the flavors of a wealth of metaphors and synonyms in the spoken language. The wide choice of glyphs emphasizes how numerous and how diverse may be glyphs with the same general meeting and function, but each with its individuality corresponding to the wide range of idiomatic expression. The Maya priest could pick the glyph he wanted as the author chooses the word that adds most flavor or beauty to a passage.

Glyph E

In contrast to Glyph D, Glyph E is confined to a single variant of the main element. That is the complete moon sign with a circle or dot in the center. This element may be personified (fig. 37,16). Generally the distance-number postfix is added, and rarely other affixes appear (figs. 36,25,34; 37,46,67), but sometimes there is no postfix (fig. 36,66). Glyph E has a value of 20; the coefficient, never greater than 9, has to be added to this. As already noted, Glyph D, without a coefficient, is usually present when Glyph E is recorded, but in a few texts Glyph D is omitted after Glyph E (Yaxchilan 6, Chichen Itza 1).

Glyphs for Day, Dawn, or Night

Beyer (1936a) has called attention to certain extraneous glyphs which sometimes intervene between Glyphs D or E and their coefficients. He identifies them as symbols for day, and supposes they were inserted at the whim of the sculptor or because of considerations of space. I have already discussed some of these variants, and concluded that they probably refer to a count by nights or dawns (p. 174). The variants encountered with Glyph D and, very rarely, with Glyph E are the *bix* glyph (fig. 31,*11,34,36–38*), the conch (fig. 31,*10,35,37*), and the head of an animal, either a jaguar or a dog (figs. 31,*30–32; 37,26*). Copan 9 has a most unusual sign with a coefficient of 5 (fig. 37,*32*). The moon age corresponding to the IS (9.6.10.0.0) is about 28 days. Teeple read the glyph in question as 5E, but I think it must be meant for 5D, although that involves a considerable error in the calculation. Nevertheless, no element which would seem to have the meaning of 20 is present. The glyph consists of the head of God C with a water symbol before his face and, to the left, an Ahau sign on its side as a prefix. There is a second prefix above the main element. As noted (p. 171), the glyph would appear to mean 5 dawns. Apparently Glyph D has been suppressed, and one must understand that the 5 dawns or, more probably, sunrises are reckoned from the completion of the previous moon.

Copan N has a somewhat similar sign. In that case the head of God C has a single prefix; water symbols, to the left of the head, flank a numerical dot (fig. 36,*1*). The whole would then mean "1 dawn," and, again, Glyph D, indicating the departure point of this count, has been suppressed. The lunar age corresponding to the IS (9.16.10.0.0) is, in effect, about one day.

GLYPHS FOR LAST DAY OF MOON

There are two or three unusual glyphs which seem to refer to disappearance of the moon or perhaps to conjunction. They replace the normal forms of Glyphs D and E. Unfortunately, the details in none are entirely clear. Texts which seem to refer to the completion of the moon accompany the following IS:

1.	Copan 1	9.12. 3.14. 0
2.	Quirigua E	9.17. 0. 0. 0 (fig. 36, *29–33*)
3.	Quirigua D	9.16.15. 0. 0
4.	Quirigua F	9.16.10. 0. 0 (fig. 37, *63–66*)
5.	Piedras Negras 13	9.17. 0. 0. 0
6.	Quirigua Alt O	9.17.14.16.18 (fig. 37, *26–31*)

In Text 1 Glyph D is present, but it is upside down, and has three little circles as an infix instead of the eye. There is a superfix, perhaps a jade symbol, flanked by little death heads of the type already discussed. To the left there is a queer combination. The main element appears to be a Cauac sign, above which is a knotted element and, above that, again, an element of unknown meaning, conceivably but not probably a stylized hand. The whole might indicate dead moon in the house of storms.

Quirigua D has a head in a vertical position surmounted by a second glyph, possibly, although not probably, a sign for darkness.

In the text of Quirigua E also there is a pair of glyphs. That on the right is a variant form of the normal sky sign; that on the left is somewhat eroded. Quirigua F is equally unsatisfactory. The right glyph is a frog head in a vertical position; the left glyph is hard to identify, although a Cauac infix is recognizable. Maudslay's drawing leaves much to be desired. Piedras Negras 13 is also defective. There is a complete moon sign to the right; probably two signs to the left, the topmost having a large crosshatched dot in the center. Quirigua Alt O is also a little dubious. There seems to be a manikin death sign before the first glyph. These signs which indicate a moon age of no days are too uncertain to be used in reaching any conclusions but I think the future will produce special glyphic arrangements to indicate the completion of the moon. See Addendum, page 296.

GLYPH C

Glyph C indicates the number of complete moons. It consists of a minimum of three elements, and a maximum of six including the coefficient (fig. 36,*2,7,12,16,21,26,*etc.). The essential elements are:

1. A hand in a horizontal or nearly horizontal position with fingers to right and back toward observer. This hand occupies the bottom part of the glyph, often extending the whole width of the sign.

2. A half-moon which occupies the right part of the glyph. It rests on the forefinger of the hand or is at the right of the hand.

3. A small head or other sign, a variable factor, which occupies the top left corner of the glyph.

The elements which may or may not be present are:

4. A coefficient between 2 and 6 inclusive.

5. A prefix which may be the flattened fish head ("count of"), the *u* bracket ("of" or converting number to an ordinal), or the skull or death eyes ("expiration of").

6. The *il* postfix, similar to that found with Glyph D but seldom used.

Teeple, who deciphered the meaning of Glyph C as a count of completed lunations, showed that Glyph C without a coefficient should be read as one month completed, for calculations during the period of uniformity (p. 244) prove that Glyph C without a coefficient falls one lunation after Glyph C with coefficient of six (written 6C) and one lunation before Glyph 2C. Glyph C without a coefficient usually has the *u* bracket or *xoc* prefix, the whole presumably declaring "count of completion of a moon" or merely "the completion of a moon." It is strange that the numerical coefficient should be omitted when one lunation is recorded, since that practice was not followed in recording other counts (but see "Ben-Ich" katuns). The omission probably corresponds to a linguistic variation.

Teeple thought that Glyph C recorded moons in the group already completed, and that a record of, say, 12D 4C meant that 12 days of the fifth moon had been counted. This is perhaps the more logical interpretation, but Glyph C may well refer to the current, not the last elapsed moon, as both I (Gann and Thompson, 1931, p. 218) and Satterthwaite (1947) have suggested.

Three texts which apparently record conjunction or disappearance or new moon, since no moon age is given, favor the interpretation of C as the current moon. These are on Quirigua F, D, and E and have 6C, C without coefficient, and 2C for the dates 9.16.10.0.0, 9.16.15.0.0, and 9.17.0.0.0. According to the uniform system and a reading of Glyph C as elapsed moons, these dates call respectively for C without coefficient, 2C, and 3C. That is to say, in each case one moon more than is recorded. Yet, other lunar series on Stelae D and E are in agreement with lunar groupings of the period of uniformity, and it is logical that all five texts should give the moon number in the uniform system. However, if Glyph C denotes the current moon, the coefficients of C are what one would reasonably expect in the uniform system, for, as the new moon has not yet started, the moon just ending is current, and it is logical so to record it. In the suggested arrangement of a count by current moon three consecutive days with that of Quirigua F in the middle would run: 6C 29DE (or 28DE if this were a 29-day moon), 6C no moon age, C without coefficient 1D. In this text Glyph A records a 30-day moon, but if the cyclic base has no number the coefficient of DE can not exceed 29. These three texts do not prove the contention, but they weigh the scales in its favor.

The function of the small head, occasionally replaced by a symbolic element, is not certain. In about half the legible texts the head is that of the death god or an aged being; in other cases it is that of a youthful personage. The head of the Chicchan god, the god of number 9, and that of the moon goddess herself, as deity of number 1, occasionally occur, as well as the jaguar god of number 7 and the head of number 6. Unfortunately, these heads are carved on such a small scale that they are veritable miniatures. A small amount of weathering suffices to obliterate characteristics with the result that in most texts an exact classification is not possible.

GLYPH X

This glyph, which follows Glyph C and is dependent on it, is thus named because of its great variability. Teeple (1931, pp. 61–62) demonstrated that the form of

Glyph X was governed by the coefficient of Glyph C; Lawrence Roys numbered the principal variants X1 to X6 inclusive. The form which consists of the head of God C (X2) in the jaws of a celestial monster, and with varying prefixes indicative of water is carved only when the coefficient of Glyph C is absent or is 2 (fig. 36,3,8,17,27,37). A form (X3) which has as its main element a horizontal band enclosing two or more vertical or up-curving lines, and usually a tassel-like prefix, and a postfix placed on its side and with lines cut in it, occurs only when the coefficient of C is 2 or 3 (fig. 36,22,31,41). A skull over crossed legs or crossed legs over a skull, or crossed legs over a kin sign or a complete moon sign (X4, fig. 36,46,51,56,69) may occur when the coefficient of C is 3 or 4, but is present once when the coefficient of C is 2 (Yaxchilan L 46). It has been supposed that it follows Glyph C5 on Yaxchilan L 29, and is thus given by Teeple (1931) and by Morley (1916 and 1937–38), but a photograph of the lintel shows that the coefficient of Glyph C is probably 3, and that this text may not, therefore, be an exception to the rule. Another form (X4a) has as its most distinctive feature a double fret, like an angular reversed S, which divides the glyph into two fields (fig. 36,59). This may occur when the coefficient of C is 3 or 4. A form (X5) which is commonly used when the coefficient of C is 4 or 5 consists of a face with a beaked nose and a hollow in the top of the head. This has a prefix, usually the completion sign (probably used here with the value of water), but often the cauac sign, also a symbol of water, which may be an infix of the head (figs. 36,63; 37,3,13,19,29). There is a symbolic variant which is a water sign, and appears to correspond to the beak-nosed combination.

There are various forms which occur when Glyph C has a coefficient of 6, but they do not at first glance conform to a single type. In two cases (X6) the sky sign is one of the elements; in another the kan cross with a "Ben-Ich" superfix forms Glyph X (fig. 37,47,50). The commonest form with C5 or C6 is X1, consisting of three or four elements, the most constant of which appears to be an elaboration of the bundle element used as an affix with some glyphs (figs. 16,13,14,16,17,28–31; 26,47,48). With this may be joined or fused an element which resembles, but probably is not, the symbol for white, or a small element containing three circles, like an inverted Ahau. A human fist and/or yet another element may be present (fig. 37,9,34,38,43,55,60,69). These seem very diverse elements, but the bundle variant, the pseudo-white symbol, the three circles, and the fist also appear together in various forms of Glyph G7, corresponding to the seventh lord of the night (fig. 34,32–35,37), and in the variable element of the IS introductory glyph assigned to

Pax (fig. 23,*18–20,34*). As they appear in three distinct glyphs we can be sure that they belong together.

When Glyph C has no coefficient (given the value C1), Glyph X, with one definite exception, is always X2, that is, the variant with the head of God C in the jaws of a monster. The clear exception, on Copan J, is an obvious example of X1 (fig. 36,*13*). Andrews (1934), who published Lawrence Roys' chart showing the correspondences between Glyphs C and X, put forward this one example as evidence that just as each of the other forms of Glyph X accompanies two consecutive coefficients of Glyph C, so this variant of Glyph X covered two sequent lunations, namely, C6 and C1, and that was evidence that the two cycles overlapped. Nevertheless, this theory will not hold water because this form is commonly found with C5 and C6. If it occurs also with C1, the whole pattern of each form of Glyph X following two sequent forms of Glyph C breaks down, for in that case it would be found with three sequent coefficients of C, to wit, C5, C6, and C1.

As every other Glyph C1, with the possible exception of the lunar series of Copan 7 where the combination C1 and X3 may be given, is accompanied by X2, I think either that the pattern of a form of Glyph X with two sequent coefficients of C is not a rigid one or that this appearance of X1 with C1 represents an error on the part of the Maya who prepared the blueprint of this text.

As this is only one of several disagreements with the Glyphs X and C cyclic pattern, I feel that we are not justified in labeling as Maya errors these exceptions to the rule which we ourselves have formulated. Rather, I would suppose that there is some factor, still unknown to us, which causes these divergences from the regular pattern. It is surely wrong to charge the Maya with errors until we are certain that the supposed mistakes are not the result of an incomplete knowledge of the subject on our part.

The solution of this problem is made more difficult by the presence of yet other forms of Glyph X, as, for instance, the kan cross with "Ben-Ich" prefix (fig. 37,*47,50*). This may be an independent form of Glyph X or it may be an unrecognized variant of X6. I am inclined to think it was an independent form, appearing only with C6.

The close connections between X2 and Glyph G1 and between X1 and Glyph G7 suggest that the lords of the nights, or some of them, may be involved; it is worth noting that one variant of X1 (fig. 37,*38*) has the distinguishing feature of Glyph G8 as one of its elements. The preponderance of symbols denoting water, death, and the underworld suggests that Glyph X is connected in some way with the aquatic abode of the moon goddess during conjunction.

There is inconclusive evidence that whereas the coefficient of Glyph C restricts the form of Glyph X to two choices (perhaps three in one group), the head accompanying Glyph C may determine which of those alternative forms is to be used.

The heads attached to Glyph C are perhaps assignable to two main groups: Group 1, comprising youthful heads; Group 2, heads representing death or old age, together with the symbolic variant, the "pack" or "eye" sign (fig. 36,*2,58*,etc.). The apparent relationship of Glyph X to the head and coefficient of Glyph C is shown in tabular form:

GLYPH C		GLYPH X	
Number	*Head Group*		*Form*
0	2	2	(God C in snake's jaws)
2	2	2	(God C in snake's jaws)
2	1	3	(tassel variant)
3	1	3	(tassel variant)
3	2 (usually death)	4	(crossed legs)
3	2 (aged and "pack")	4a	(fret)
4	2 (aged and "pack")	4a	(fret)
4	2 (usually death)	4	(crossed legs)
4	1	5	(beaked nose)
5	1	5	(beaked nose)
5	2	1	(hand-bundle-"white")
6	2	1	(hand-bundle-"white")
6	2 ("pack" only)	6a	(kan cross)
6	1	6	(sky combination)

Because of weathering and the smallness of the heads, one cannot say how strictly these categories were observed, and there appear to be cases which fail to conform to the apparent arrangement, just as there are exceptions to the apparent relationship between Glyph X and the coefficient of Glyph C. Nevertheless, the general pattern is too regular to be the result of chance.

GLYPH B

Glyph B comprises four elements (figs. 2,*50–56;* 5,*28–33*): (1) the sky sign shaped as an elbow, but sometimes reduced to one arm, (2) the head of an animal of uncertain species within the elbow, (3) an oval sign which may be a postfix or an infix usually replacing the animal's ear, and (4) a prefix of the "count" group, the *u* bracket, the fish head, or the death eye. The prefix is lacking in a few texts at Copan. There is a symbolic form of the animal head. This consists of two circles containing what appear to be drops of water or cursive Ik signs (fig. 2,*55*). Occasionally the head with its infix or postfix is replaced by the muluc (water or *xoc*) symbol, and in two texts the head of God C is the main element within the elbow (fig. 2,*52,56*).

Glyph B is lacking in a number of texts, particularly those of early date; it is never present when Glyph X is suppressed. Teeple and Lizardi Ramos (1941) have supposed that Glyph B is to be read in conjunction with Glyph A, but the text of Quirigua B suggests that Glyphs B and X be read together, for the animal of Glyph B carries Glyph X on his back (fig. 29,*14*). Moreover, B is never present when X is absent.

With regard to the identity of the animal, Lizardi Ramos (1941) has demonstrated that the two circles with drops of water or cursive Ik signs replace the head of this animal in other contexts. We can assume, therefore, that those circles are the glyph for the animal in question. They do not correspond to the name glyph of the species of dog found in Dresden, for that is the composite sign consisting of the rib sign and another symbol (fig. 14,*10*).

The oval suffix or infix has been identified by Beyer (1930, p. 14; 1937, p. 55) with some plausibility as a long bone. The combination of two circles with Ik centers over the supposed bone element is given three times in Dresden in this simple form: on page 57 it occurs in the group of glyphs above one of the pictures in the eclipse table; on page 46 it appears above the picture of the Venus god preparing destruction for dwellers on earth; on page 58 the glyph is in the introductory text to the IS which head the table of multiples of 78 and 780. To make the matter still more complex, the rare substitution of the muluc, "water," symbol for the head of this animal must be taken into account in interpreting the animal heads. Furthermore, in one case (fig. 2,*50*) there is a kan cross on the animal's cheek. This symbol has the values of both yellow and water; presumably it is to be interpreted as the latter in this case in view of the substitution of the water symbol for the head and "bone" elements.

The elbow element which stretches across the top and down the right side is clearly the sky sign distorted to occupy this space (fig. 2,*57*). It has been suggested that this is a symbol for house or temple. Be that so, or be it not, the important point is that the elbow is merely the usual sky symbol, bent to that shape. It is conceivable that in view of the aquatic associations already noted, the whole represents the celestial realm of the rain gods in which the moon, according to the cosmological ideas of the Mexicans, had her abode. As we have seen, there is some evidence that a similar concept was current among the Maya. That interpretation must be regarded as extremely tentative, for the link between the little animal with the "bone" affix or infix and water is tenuous. If the two circles which form the symbolic variant corresponding to the animal head do, indeed, have the meaning of water (jade), the case would be much stronger. Should some such meaning in reality correspond to Glyph B, the three glyphs C, X, and B would convey

some such idea as "completion of *n* moons, Glyph X*n* in power, in the celestial realm of the rains."

GLYPH A

It has long been known that Glyph A indicates whether the month be of 30 or 29 days. It consists of a moon glyph with a coefficient of 10 or 9 in the form of a postfix. At one time it was thought that the coefficient appeared as a postfix instead of as a prefix in order to indicate that the number was added to the number 20, for which the moon glyph stands, and did not serve as a multiplier. That idea, of course, no longer holds good, for it was subsequently learned that the coefficient of Glyph E also is added, but that is a prefix, not a postfix. Furthermore, there is one case in which the coefficient of A is a prefix (Quirigua I). Therefore, the postfixal position of the coefficient is not necessarily indicative of addition. In the absence of any better information, one may surmise that the coefficient was placed below or to the right of the moon glyph as a ready means of distinguishing Glyph A from Glyph E.

Teeple (1931, p. 63) writes: "There is a regularity about the 29 and 30 of Glyph A that makes one believe it is a predicted and not an observed figure. Whenever Glyph C has an odd coefficient, 1, 3, or 5, the chances are about three to one that Glyph A will show 30 days; whenever Glyph C has an even coefficient, 2, 4, or 6, the chances are about three to one for a 29-day Glyph A. This goes beyond the bounds of probability for observation, hence I regard Glyph A as a more or less arbitrary prediction of the length of the current moon."

This interpretation must be accepted except conceivably for the designation of Glyph A as a record of the current moon, for if Glyphs C, X, and B should refer to the lunation last completed, Glyph A might similarly deal with the last completed moon, indicating whether it was of 29 or 30 days. The minority of 29-day lunations with C1, C3, and C5 and the minority of 30-day lunations with C2, C4, and C6 presumably reflect the occasional conversion of a 29-day span to one of 30 days, and a consequent derangement of the sequence. As the lunar half-year is 177.18 days, a 29-day moon would have to be converted to one of 30 days every fifth or sixth lunar half-year.

GLYPHS Y AND Z

Except that both Glyph Y and Glyph Z appear to indicate dawn or night, and that Glyph Z is the same as that called the *bix* glyph, I have no idea as to how they function in those cases in which they are not to be read with Glyphs D and E, because they are inserted between those glyphs and their coefficients.

GROUPINGS OF MOONS

Teeple (1928 and 1931) in a brilliant analysis of the coefficients of Glyph C was able to establish three periods, which he named the periods of independence, uniformity, and revolt.

During the period of independence which lasted from the start of the lunar series to around 9.12.10.0.0, each city appears to have been attempting to coordinate its lunar calendar to the solar calendar by interpolations which varied from city to city. The second, which he named the period of uniformity, is marked by the standardization of the lunar groups into lunar half-years which were always of six months. This system spread rapidly and was soon adopted by most Maya cities, although it does not appear to have been accepted in outlying sites in Campeche, such as Calakmul. During this period one can predict what the coefficient of Glyph C will be for any date found on a monument erected during this period at any city that had adopted the system. This is simple, because as five tuns are just about one day less than 61 moons, one knows that as, for example, the standard system calls for 3C at 9.14.0.0.0, at 9.14.5.0.0 (61 moons later) the coefficient of C will be 4: 3C+1 (61÷6=1)= 4C, and five tuns later still it will be 5C. Therefore, to get the coefficient of Glyph C for any date in a city that was using the standard system, one has merely to take the interval from some recorded example in that system, convert the figure into lunations, divide the result by 6, and add the remainder to the base. As an example, we wish to check the moon age of Piedras Negras L 3, which carries the date 9.15.18.3.13 and for which the moon age is given as 9D 1C (fig. 57,1). Stela 10 at this site gives the moon age of 9.15.10.0.0 as 9D 3C (fig. 57,7) which is in agreement with the system of uniformity. The interval between the two dates is 8.3.13 which reduces to 2953 days; 100 moons are 2953.06 days. Therefore the interval is 100 moons without remainder. When these are divided by 6, the remainder is 4, which must be added to the moon age of 9.15.10.0.0: 3C 9D+4C=1 (7−6) C 9D. The lunar record of Lintel 3, therefore, is given in the uniform system, and the moon age of 9D is correct.

This is a very simple calculation. Let us try one that is somewhat more involved. At Piedras Negras the IS 9.12.2.0.16 appears on both Stela 1 and Stela 3. On the former the moon age is recorded as 3C 8D; on the latter it appears as 2C 7E (fig. 36,25–28). There is not only a difference in the coefficient of Glyph C, but a difference of 10 or 11 days or of 19 days in the age of the current moon (i.e. the interval from 7E to 8D or 8D to 7E). Stela 6 at Piedras Negras gives the moon age of 9.12.15.0.0 as 4C 5E, and is in agreement with the uni-

form system. The interval between the two dates is 12.17.4, which reduces to 4664 days. This is the equivalent of 157 moons and 27.7 days, which must be subtracted from the moon age of Stela 6 after casting out all multiples of six lunations:

Moon age Stela 6	4 C	25 D
Subtract interval	1 C	27.7
Calculated moon age of Stelae 1 and 3	2 C	26.8

The moon age of 9.12.2.0.16 is, accordingly, in the uniform system 2C 7E, and is correctly given as such on Stela 3. Stela 1 is not in agreement with the uniform system, and records a moon age of 8D, whereas it should be about 7E.

Teeple has supposed that these two texts at Piedras Negras record the change from the old system of the period of independence to that of the period of uniformity, and that one text gives the new method, the other the old. This seems logical, particularly in view of the two IS at Naranjo for the date 9.12.10.5.12, one of which gives the lunar count 1C 18D, the other 6C 19D, one month less one day earlier, the former being in the system of uniformity. However, if these two dates at Piedras Negras do treat of the inauguration of the uniform system, it is surprising that the Maya priest should have made an error in one of the three or four glyphs which are essential to the exposition of the problem, for the substitution of one glyph for another (D for E) can hardly be attributed to the sculptor.

At 9.16.5.0.0 Copan abandoned the uniform system of grouping lunations, and instituted a new system which, in Teeple's opinion, was probably of the type found in the eclipse tables of Dresden. That is to say, instead of a straightforward grouping of lunations in sixes, an occasional group of five lunations was inserted so as to make each group of lunations end on a date on which an eclipse might fall. As Teeple points out, there are insufficient lunar series for Copan after 9.16.5.0.0 to make the proof complete.

For other cities, except Quirigua, the number of lunar series after 9.17.0.0.0 is too small to indicate what system was used. All that can be said is that the uniform system was not followed. On late monuments at Quirigua there is an apparent tendency to keep the same moon age for two or three consecutive quarter-katun endings. Thus, for 9.16.10.0.0, 9.16.15.0.0, and 9.17.0.0.0 the moon age is nil; for 9.17.5.0.0, 26 days; for 9.17.10.0.0, 27 days; for 9.17.15.0.0, 9.18.0.0.0, and 9.18.5.0.0, 23 days; for 9.18.10.0.0 and 9.18.15.0.0, 18 days, but the former may read 16 days.

Normally the moon age at each succeeding quarter-katun should be reduced by one or two days, for 1800 days (five tuns) are 1.36 days less than 61 moons. Apparently the astronomers of Quirigua liked to equate five tuns with 61 moons, and at intervals reduce the moon age by three, four, or five days to offset the error which had accumulated or which would accumulate in the next two or three quarter-katuns.

THE INTRODUCTION OF THE UNIFORM SYSTEM

The period of uniformity at Copan first appears in the lunar series of Altar H'. The inscription on Altar H' is continued on Altar I', and there is not the slightest doubt that the two should be read together. Their dedicatory dates are either 9.12.10.0.0 9 Ahau 18 Zotz', which is declared on both monuments, or the current katun ending, 9.13.0.0.0 8 Ahau 8 Uo, which is recorded on Altar H'. Attention has already been called to the apparent use on these monuments of combinations of 405 and 361 moons in lunar calculations far into the past which lead from 9.12.10.0.0.

The IS is 9.12.8.3.9 8 Muluc 17 Mol which is recorded in the uniform system as 5C 22D. The distance to 9.13.0.0.0 is 4251 days, whereas 144 moons are 4252.4 days. Teeple believed that the people of Copan may have set the moon age of 9.13.0.0.0 as 22 days; 144 months are 12 lunar years. Thus, Copan inaugurated the uniform system with a date 12 lunar years before the current katun ended.

The uniform system is marked at Naranjo by Stela 24, which gives the date 9.12.10.5.12 4 Eb 10 Yax as 1C 18D. Stela 24 was dedicated at 9.13.10.0.0, which is the closing date of the text. The interval between these dates is 7088 days which is .66 days less than 240 moons. As 240 is divisible by 6, the lunar data for 9.13.0.0.0 at Naranjo would have been calculated in the uniform system as 1C 18D, or 1C 17D. The interval between the two dates is 20 lunar years.

As in both these texts the dates chosen to inaugurate the uniform system are within a day or so of an even number of lunar years from the dedicatory date of the monument, one would expect the same to happen at Piedras Negras. There the uniform system is inaugurated with the IS on Stela 3, which records 9.12.2.0.16 2 Cib 14 Yaxkin as 2C 27D. The dedicatory date of this stela is 9.14.0.0.0 6 Ahau 13 Muan, which occurs on the left side of this stela as an IS. The corresponding moon age, as first read by Morley, is 3C 17D. There is, therefore, no lunar relationship between the two dates. However, there is a relationship with the moon age of the current quarter-katun. On Stela 39 the moon age of 9.12.5.0.0 is given as 1C 27D in the system in use at Piedras Negras prior to the introduction of the uniform system. The interval between the two dates is 1064 days,

within a day of three lunar years (36 moons=1063.1 days).

No inauguration dates of the period of uniformity are known from other cities, for it is hardly reasonable to suppose that the double lunar recording of 9.16.1.0.0 on Yaxchilan 11 refers to the inauguration of the uniform system by that city, for at the date (9.17.0.0.0) on which that monument was probably erected, the uniform system had run its course and had already been replaced by another at Copan.

At Copan and Naranjo, therefore, dates to mark the inauguration of the uniform system were chosen apparently because they were calculated to be 12 and 20 lunar years, respectively, before the dates which the monuments commemorated; at Piedras Negras the inaugural date of the uniform system was three lunar years before the end of the quarter-katun, then running its course. The dedicatory date of the monument was considerably later:

Copan H'	9.12. 8. 3. 9	8 Muluc 17 Mol
	11.14.11	(4251 d.; 12 lunar years
	———————	= 4252.4 d.)
	9.13. 0. 0. 0	8 Ahau 8 Uo
Naranjo 24	9.12.10. 5.12	4 Eb 10 Yax
	19.12. 8	(7088 d.; 20 lunar years
	———————	= 7087.3 d.)
	9.13.10. 0. 0	7 Ahau 3 Cumku
Piedras Negras 3	9.12. 2. 0.16	2 Cib 14 Yaxkin
	2.17. 4	(1064 d.; 3 lunar years
	———————	= 1063.1 d.)
	9.12. 5. 0. 0	3 Ahau 3 Xul

SUMMARY

The moon goddess was the wife of the sun, and patroness of weaving, childbirth, women in general, the earth, and probably, too, the maize crop. Because of her promiscuity, she symbolized wantonness. Her very human nature is unfortunately lost beneath the furbelows of arithmetic and astronomy with which she is decked.

Dresden 51–58 comprise an arrangement of moons which produces the equation 405 moons=46×260=11,960 days, thereby constituting a re-entering cycle of the type beloved by the Maya which brings the period under discussion into relationship with the 260-day cycle by seeking the lowest number divisible by both. The *lub* of the series is the day 12 Lamat. The equation 405 moons=46×260=11,960 days was apparently used by the Maya for making calculations to obtain the age of the moon at dates far in the past.

The arrangement of the groups of moons within the table in Dresden is such that there is no doubt whatsoever that the cycle of 11,960 days had been divided in such a way as to give a series of days, at intervals of 177 (occasionally 178) and 148 days, on which eclipses might, but not necessarily would, occur. After each occurrence of a five-lunation group of 148 days there is a picture. Most of these carry symbols indicative of an eclipse or at least of conjunction (areas of black and white, solar and lunar glyphs together, the sun with symbols of death, etc.). It has been suggested that these pictures may indicate lunar eclipses between two partial eclipses of the sun one lunation apart.

Teeple showed that because three eclipse half-years (519.93 days) almost exactly equal a double 260-day cycle, possible eclipse dates of the table cluster around three points in a 520-day wheel, and from those clusters the nodal points may be deduced. The starting point of the table, 12 Lamat, was about one day from the node day. On the other hand, Mrs. Makemson proved that 12 Lamat of the IS 9.16.4.10.8   12 Lamat 1 Muan, fell 14 or 15 days before node day. Therefore, the date of the table in Dresden cannot have been 9.16.4.10.8, but 9 or 10 × 1.13.4.0 later (because the node day recedes approximately 1.6 days each time the table is used), that is to say, about 10.12.0.0.0. The actual date Mrs. Makemson favored was 10.12.16.14.8   12 Lamat 1 Ch'en.

I doubt that the Maya had any inkling of the passage of the nodes. If an addition of six lunations to a possible eclipse date carried to a position in the 520-day wheel beyond the segment of 36 consecutive days, the priest would have known that an interval of five lunations would be necessary, for thereby the next date of a possible eclipse would fall within the allowable spread of 36 days.

For calculating the age of the moon on any given date far in the past or far in the future, the Maya of Palenque, as Teeple has demonstrated, appear to have used the equation 1.13.4.0=405 moons. This, of course, is the same as the length of the eclipse cycle in Dresden. There is some evidence, here presented for the first time, that the Maya, perhaps realizing that 1.13.4.0 was a trifle more than 405 moons, may have tried to correct the equation by the addition of twice 1.9.11.0=361 moons to approximately thrice 1.13.4.0=405 moons. This formula may have been used at Copan, and there are some grounds for believing that it appears in Dresden, for one of the IS is probably 9.19.7.7.8, which is 1.13.4.0+1.9.11.0 from 9.16.4.10.8. It is a variant of that which Teeple attributed to Copan.

The various glyphs of the lunar series are reviewed with regard to their functions and probable meanings, and evidence is adduced that the Maya probably counted their moons from disappearance. A relationship between the head attached to Glyph C and the variant of Glyph X is noted. The three periods of lunar groupings, as demonstrated by Teeple, are briefly reviewed. Evidence is presented that the inaugural dates of the uniform system were chosen so as to be an exact number of lunar years before the dedicatory date of the monument in question or, in one case, of the current quarter-katun. A review of three lunar series at Quirigua suggests that, contrary to general belief, Glyph C may refer to the current, not the elapsed, moon.

It should be noted that in Chapter 9 and in this chapter the expression "new moon" does not refer to any definite astronomical point, such as new moon visibility, but is used to indicate the cyclic base—disappearance, conjunction, or reappearance—from which the Maya reckoned moon age. This is done because of the uncertainty as to what point was used as the cyclic base. Indeed, it may well be that that point shifted from time to time and from city to city, as Satterthwaite believes.

I I

Soulless Mechanisms and Magical Formulae

Amiddes
His Magick bookes and arts of sundry kindes,
He seekes out mighty charmes, to trouble sleepy mindes.
—EDMUND SPENSER, *Faerie Queene*

NOT A FEW PEOPLE are content to draw inspiration from the outward appearance of some work of beauty without overly concerning themselves with mechanical problems, such as stress in buildings or application of pigments in a painting. I must confess to being among that number. I consider the lily of the field, but pay scant attention to its stamens and pistil. Nonetheless, it is meet and very right that we inspect, albeit briefly, the structural elements in the Maya fabric of time, and tour the quarries and kilns whence come its stone and brick.

SHORT CUTS IN COMPUTATIONS

Computations in the Maya calendar are involved, and, unless short cuts are taken, they can be both long and tedious. Modern students of the subject have evolved various systems of shortening the labor of computation. Some are along lines that might have been followed by the Maya; others involve special charts or slide rules. It is not my intention to discuss these, for each student will choose the system which best agrees with his bent of mind.

Numerical sequences hold the key to the quickest ways of making calculations in the Maya calendar. For example, the coefficients of Ahau have different sequences according to the period of time in question. This, of course, is so because the number of days involved has a different remainder in each case when divided by 13. The uinal sequence rises by 7: 13, 7, 1, 8, 2, 9, etc. The tun sequence falls by 4: 13, 9, 5, 1, 10, 6, etc. The katun sequence falls by 2: 13, 11, 9, 7, 5, 3, etc. The baktun sequence falls by 1: 13, 12, 11, 10, 9, 8, etc. For ready reckoning it is extremely useful to remember these quick cuts, for with a few dates firmly fixed in one's mind, one can quickly calculate from them the coefficient of Ahau for any other date. Thus, if one knows that 9.15.0.0.0 fell on 4 Ahau 13 Yax, one can calculate immediately that katun 9.18.0.0.0, for example, has an Ahau coefficient 6 less, that is to say, 11 Ahau.

In Kaua (pp. 275–76) there are notations which give the correct sequence of Ahau coefficients for uinals, tuns, and katuns, although the tun series is labeled uinals.

Vinales 1, 8, 2, 9, 3, 10, 4, 11, 5, 12, 6, 13, 7.
Vinales (tuns) 13, 9, 5, 1, 10, 6, 2, 11, 7, 3, 12, 8, 4.
Katunes 13, 11, 9, 7, 5, 3, 1, 12, 10, 8, 6, 4, 2.

The accompanying explanation is given in bad Spanish and involves the year bearers for the last years of the eighteenth century. In Perez (pp. 100–01) the same arrangement is repeated, the second line representing the tuns, being wrongly labeled *Katunes*. The passage is copied from Mani.

A somewhat similar arrangement of the sequence of coefficients of the year bearer day for the uinals of a year, but written in Maya, occurs in Ixil (Perez, p. 174; probably p. 2 of original). The series runs 1, 8, 2, 9, 3, 10, 4, 11, etc., concluding with "10 to 4 Muluc on first of Pop." There is something wrong with the table, for no note is made of the five nameless days, which would lead not to 4 Muluc on first of Pop, but to 2 Muluc. Perhaps the copyist erred, writing *can* (4) instead of *ca* (2).

WHEELS

I think these sequences of coefficients must have been illustrated by wheels, of which a few colonial examples have survived, the best known of which are those in Chumayel and in Landa. Both wheels give the order of the katuns starting with 11 Ahau and proceeding clockwise 9 Ahau, 7 Ahau, 5 Ahau, etc. In Ixil (Perez, p. 172; probably p. 1 of original) is a wheel of year bearers, which, however, is to be read anticlockwise, starting with 1 Kan. I do not purpose to describe these wheels in detail, for the subject has been thoroughly discussed by Bowditch (1910, pp. 324–34). One might note, however, that it is probable that wheels giving the sequence of coefficients for tuns and uinals, and perhaps baktuns, once existed. There is a wheel of the days in the Quiche calendar of 1722. Similar wheels were also used in Mexico proper, and have been reproduced by Sahagun, Duran, and Veytia. It is possible that the circle was a development from an earlier design, an elaborated Maltese cross, representing the completion sign, such as forms the framework of the 260-day cycle which occupies Madrid 75 and 76 (Thompson in Caso, Stirling, et al., 1946). There

247

again the arrangement is anticlockwise. The count starts with 1 Imix, to the east, at the left upper edge of the bottom section. Twelve dots (erroneously written as 11) lead down to 13 Ben, next to which is 1 Ix. Twelve dots (erroneously written as 13) lead across the bottom of the page to 13 Cimi, next to which is 1 Manik.

Thereby the days continue the circuit, each of 20 lines that form the pattern of four petals and four loops being assigned to each 13-day "week" starting with 1 Imix 13 Ben, and ending with 1 Lamat 13 Ahau. Each petal has three lines; each loop has two. A petal and the contiguous leaf in the anticlockwise direction are assigned to a world direction, thereby dividing the cycle into four divisions, each of 65 days.

The center of the picture is surrounded by the 20 day signs, without coefficients, but there are almost certainly errors in this arrangement. It is probably meant to run sinistrally:

Right:	Kan	Lamat	Eb[1]	Cib[1]	Ahau[1]
Top:	Imix	Chicchan	Muluc	Ben	Caban[1]
Left:	Ik[2]	Cimi[2]	Oc	Ix	Etz'nab
Bottom:	Akbal	Manik	Chuen	Men	Cauac

[1]Transposed pairs.

[2]Partly obliterated, and perhaps transposed.

This elaborate design, accompanied as it is by portraits of gods associated with the world directions, must have been decorative rather than useful. As a ready reckoner, it can have functioned only to give the sequence of the "weeks" and their association with world directions. It closely resembles the design in Fejervary-Mayer.

THE FOOTSTEPS OF THE YEAR

La Farge and Byers (1931, p. 158) note that among the Jacalteca the only subdivision of the year which is recognized is that of 40 days (two uinals). The recurrence of the year bearer with a coefficient one higher is called "one foot of the year." This, of course, happens after 40 days because the sequence by uinals runs 13, 7, 1, 8, 2, etc. Forty days later is two feet of the year and so on until eight feet of the year is reached at the end of 16 uinals, where the count is terminated. The completion of the last couple of uinals is not regarded as adding another (ninth) foot to the year. Nevertheless, one may presume that there once was some term to denote that the footsteps of the year carried to the three hundred and sixtieth day, although that term may have made no reference to the feet. The foot of the year is termed *yoc habil*. The word *oc* in Yucatec means not only foot, but also footprint or track, and the same is possibly true of Jacalteca. Roys (1933, p. 116), in a somewhat parallel passage next to be considered, translates the word as both footprint and footstep.

This text, in Chumayel, recounts in recondite language the creation of the uinal before the sun first rose. It forms one of the mysteries of Maya religion:

These were their words as they marched along, when there was [as yet] no man. Then they arrived there in the east and began to speak, "who has passed here? Here are footprints. Measure it off with your foot." So spoke the mistress of the world. Then our Lord God the father measured his footstep. This was the reason of his ordaining the count of the whole world by footsteps on 12 Oc. This was the setting in order, after it had been given life by the action of 13 Oc, after his feet were joined evenly, after they had departed there in the East.

The above translation is based on that of Roys, but with certain amendments which have been approved by him. There follows a description of the birth of the uinal in the era before the first dawn, and then the 20 days which follow 13 Oc are listed in order with some detail of the creation assigned to each day. The fact that the interval from 12 Oc to 13 Oc is 40 days, taken in conjunction with the fact that *oc* means foot or footstep and the whole text is full of the word *oc*, is surely significant. One footstep or pacing off was taken before the uinal was created. The simile, of course, is in keeping with the Maya concept of time being carried on the backs of gods. Apparently the same imagery of measuring by paces was applied in some way to the katun. In the series of prophecies for the tuns of a Katun 5 Ahau in Tizimin (p. 13) there is a statement in the text dealing with the twentieth tun of the katun: "13 Oc would be the day when the katun is measured by paces" (*u chek oc katun*). This is 70 days before the end of the katun, and I see no way to reconcile this with a 40-day arrangement, which would lead to a day 5 Ahau, but it may not be coincidence that 13 Oc marks the termination of the measuring before the birth of the uinal.

Roys, who translates the above, calls my attention to a confused passage on Perez 151–52, where the colonial fallacy of a katun starting on the day after a Cauac year bearer is rehashed. The table which follows this indicates that the katun was paced off from the day Oc immediately preceding the day on which it begins (for these 24-year katuns are named for the days on which they start). I do not believe that either of these arrangements is correct, but they are evidence that in some way the katun was paced off, just as the years were divided into periods of 40 days. The present-day Maya of British Honduras use *oc* in the sense of "last chance"; *oc pak* is the last chance to sow before the rains. I do not know if there is any connection with the calendarial use of *oc*.

OTHER SHORT CUTS IN RECKONING

There must have been a number of other "rules" of the calendar, of which the Maya priest was cognizant; many of them would probably have been of more value to the priests of the Initial Series Period than to those of the period before the Spanish conquest. For example:

1. The coefficient of a half-katun is one less than the preceding katun, e.g. 9.15.0.0.0 4 Ahau, 9.15.10.0.0 3 Ahau.

2. The coefficient of a 5-tun date is seven less than that of the preceding katun, and that of a 15-tun date is eight less, e.g. 9.15.0.0.0 4 Ahau, 9.15.5.0.0 10 Ahau, 9.15.15.0.0 9 Ahau.

3. Any Ahau date repeats as the end of a 5-tun division after 3.5.0.0, e.g. 9.15.0.0.0 4 Ahau, 9.18.5.0.0 4 Ahau.

4. At the end of each tun the month position is five days less than at the preceding tun, e.g. 9.15.0.0.0 4 Ahau 13 Yax, 9.15.1.0.0 13 Ahau 8 Yax.

5. With the passage of a half-katun the month position drops 50 places, and at the end of a katun it has receded 100 places (five months less), e.g. 9.15.0.0.0 4 Ahau 13 Yax, 9.15.10.0.0 3 Ahau 3 Mol, 9.16.0.0.0 2 Ahau 13 Zec.

Formulae for reckoning the age of the moon and the position of the planet Venus over long periods have been indicated in the chapters dealing with those subjects. There is a good body of evidence that the Maya purposely recorded the glyph of the current lord of the night to denote the LC position of a CR date within the span of slightly over 23 katuns (p. 211).

WORLD DIRECTIONS AND COLORS

The great attention paid to the four quarters of the world, and the association with them of colors, is typical of all the high cultures of Mexico and Middle America, and not improbably represents a local development of Old World cosmology.

It is very definitely established that at the time of the Spanish conquest the associations in Yucatan of year bearers, colors, and world directions were as follows:

Year bearer	Direction	Color
Kan	East (*Likin*)	Red (*Chac*)
Muluc	North (*Xaman*)	White (*Zac*)
Ix	West (*Chikin*)	Black (*Ek*)
Cauac	South (*Nohol*)	Yellow (*Kan*)

The directional names in parentheses are those most commonly used in Yucatan. *Likin* means sunrise; *chikin* may perhaps be a contraction of *chinkin*, "lowering of the sun"; the derivation of *xaman* is unknown; that of *nohol* is almost as elusive. *Nohol* means the greater or greatest and is a superlative form derived from *noh*, "great." From what we know of Maya cosmology we can be rea-

sonably sure that the south was not the most important direction. However, *noh* also means the right hand or on the right hand, and in several languages the right hand is the "big" or important hand; the left, the less important (cf. Kekchi: *chi tze*, "left"; *chi nim*, "right"). I am inclined to think the south originally was called "on the right hand," and this it would be when one faces the east, which to the Maya is the most important direction. Indeed, east is at the top of the two native maps accompanying the land treaty of Mani (Roys, 1943, p. 184). I am aware that this interpretation is opposed to Seler's, based on the Palmo vocabulary of Nahuatl which assigns the left hand to the south, but I offer it as a matter worth investigating. Another possibility is offered by the Moran vocabulary of Chol. South is listed as *nool*, to which the meanings "very bad" and "headache" are also given. Father Moran frequently omits light aspirates (e.g., *no*, "great"), and it is accordingly evident that *nool* and *nohol* are the same words, and may indicate "very evil." As the south was ruled by the god of death and as Cauac years were calamitous, there was every reason for regarding the south as evil. I prefer the meaning of right for *nohol*, but that does not necessarily preclude the Manche Chol analogy.

Andrade (1946) gives the Lacandon term for south as *yaram k'in*, the Yucatec equivalent of which would be *yalam k'in*, "below the sun"; Blom and La Farge (1926–27, p. 477) list as a Tzeltal term for that direction *nitaa lan*, "here below." Wirsing (1930) gives the Kekchi for south as *sacque*, the name for the sun. Such descriptive terms presumably refer to where the sun is at midday except for the time when it is north of the zenith in midsummer.

In some Maya languages north also bears a descriptive name, such as "from here the water," in reference to the cold northers which make life so unpleasant in the winter, but in the Moran vocabulary of Manche Chol north is given as *no ec*, which is probably meant for *noh ek*, "great star," presumably a reference to the pole star or perhaps the great bear.

Maya names for east and west generally mean sunrise and sunset, but Moran gives the Manche Chol word for east as *tzatzibcin*, and that may indicate something like "where the sun gets strength," and perhaps refers to the clothing of the sun with flesh on its departure from the underworld (p. 173).

Charency (1899) has collected linguistic material on this subject, and a great deal more is available. Unfortunately, these linguistic terms are of little help in interpreting the directional glyphs. The associations of gods and year bearers with directions have been discussed by various writers, and as I have covered that ground at some length

(Thompson, 1934), I shall not enter into detail. There are, however, a number of points still unsettled, notably:

1. Seler and I have supposed that the directions north and south and their corresponding colors have been transposed on Dresden 26 and 28, corresponding to Caban-Etz'nab and Manik-Lamat. However, it is possible that the Dresden scheme is clockwise, and represents a regional variation from the counterclockwise arrangement recorded by Landa.

2. Is Kan always associated with the east, or only when it functions as a year bearer, or only when it is a year bearer in the years starting with 1 Kan?

3. In the round of 20 days, does the world direction change with each day, or only at each fifth day?

4. At the time Akbal was the year bearer, was it, as the first of the year bearers, associated with the east, or with the south, or did it rotate?

5. Madrid 75–76, as previously noted, assign the weekly divisions of the 260-day cycle to world directions. In the rectified arrangement of the center, Akbal is set to the east, together with days at intervals of four days therefrom. Can this double page have been copied without alteration from some other codex which conformed to the Akbal set of year bearers? Whether that be the case or not, the arrangement does suggest that to each sequent day was reserved a different world direction. On the other hand, in the late and degenerate Kaua, Kan to Lamat are set to the east, Muluc to Ben are to the north, and so with the other divisions of the 20 days. I believe this wheel, made toward the close of the eighteenth century, does not mirror true usage. Indeed, it assigns Katuns 2 Ahau, 13 Ahau, and 11 Ahau to the east, contradicting in that respect also the views of its elders and betters.

The year bearers on Paris 19–20 run Lamat, Ben, Etz'nab, Akbal. Although the glyphs of the first and third are now completely obliterated, there seems small reason to doubt that the series begins with 1 Lamat. There are no directional glyphs or colors, but the picture corresponding to Ben has the background blackened, which suggests assignment to the west.

6. It is possible that the directions of year bearers changed every 13 years. Thus when a year bearer entered with a coefficient of 1, he may have been set to the east. In that case, for 13 years Kan would be set to the east, then Muluc would enter as chief year bearer for 13 years, and would be moved to the east, Kan passing to the south. Thirteen years later, Ix would enter with 1 Ix, and would be set to the east, sending Muluc back to the south. The latter, in turn, would cause Kan to pass to the west. Finally, 1 Cauac would be supreme for 13 years in the east, thereby completing the cycle of 52 years.

Such an arrangement might account for the year bearers of Dresden starting with Ben; those of Paris with Lamat, and those of Madrid with Cauac. (But why 10 Cauac in the top line? Did the scribe start with 1 Cauac, and then, finding there was no room at the bottom of the page, add the last row of four year bearers at the top of the column on each page?) Each scribe would have started with the year bearer which had ushered in the 13-year period current when each codex was painted. That theory might also take care of the apparent mistakes in Dresden, for this could be the result of converting one sequence of year bearers to another when the new edition was prepared.

There is a passage in the account of the Ixil calendar which may supply a parallel. Lincoln (1942, p. 115) says that the Ixil recognize these four divisions of the round of 52 year bearers. The year bearer with coefficient of 1, which starts each period of 13 years, is known as *Presidente* or *Ij lenal'ḳi*, and "it dominates the whole period [of thirteen years] over and above the year bearer of the current year." In Yucatecan terms that would mean, for example, that in a year 11 Muluc the influence of 1 Cauac would still make itself felt, as the *"Presidente"* of the 13-year period then current. Perhaps such an arrangement accounts for the dextral circuit of the year bearers in the wheel of Ixil, for the year bearers would rotate clockwise if, at the start of each period of 13 years, the incoming year bearer replaced its predecessor at the east, for, of course, 1 Muluc as *"Presidente"* succeeds 1 Kan, which would move clockwise to the south, and is in turn replaced by 1 Ix which then would move down from north to east. Note that I am speaking of the wheel in rotation; if it is stationary, the eyes of the reader move sinistrally.

Landa's account of the year bearers is so confused that various interpretations are possible. I have given one explanation (Thompson, 1934) but the text can be read to make Muluc the year bearer to the east, which, of course, it would have been in 1553, if the suggested theory is correct, for 1 Muluc entered as *"Presidente"* in 1542. The statement in various books of Chilam Balam that the year bearer 4 Kan was set to the east in 1536 contradicts the above assumption, but that statement is itself at fault since 4 Kan was not the year bearer for that year. I am by no means convinced that there was a shift of year bearer in relation to world directions every 13 years, but I believe the possibility should be borne in mind.

I think that we can assume that during the Initial Series Period the year bearers were generally Akbal, Lamat, Ben, and Etz'nab, but that in the region (principally Campeche), where the shift of one place in month positions almost certainly took place as early as 9.12.0.0.0 (Proskouriakoff and Thompson, 1947), the Kan-Muluc-Ix-Cauac year bearers came into use at the time the shift was made. It is, accordingly, highly probable that the two sets of year bearers existed side by side for a very long period. By the time of the Spanish conquest, Yucatan had switched to the Kan set, but not improbably peoples living in much of the Central Area retained the Akbal set until the arrival of the white man. A weak explanation of why the Quiche and the Ixil may have come to use the equivalents of Ik, Manik, Eb, and Caban as their year bearers has been offered (p. 127).

I have discussed at some length (Thompson, 1934) other problems involved, and, with no better guidance than I had then, I do not now propose to venture further on those shifting sands.

The ceiba glyph and what I call the double-sky element once follow the world directions and trees (fig. 62,4); the latter may represent center above.

In the codices the sign for east consists of an inverted Ahau above a winged kin; the inscriptional form comprises a kin or a kin cut in half above a winged kin. Sometimes a yax, "new," prefix may be added and in such cases the kin may be infixed in the yax prefix (fig. 41,1–9,32). The inverted Ahau, either through carelessness or because the change did not affect the meaning, is sometimes right side up in Madrid, and it may be placed beneath the kin. It will be recalled that the inverted Ahau is one of the elements in a compound, perhaps with the meaning of sunrise, which can be substituted for the kin sign in distance numbers (p. 172). We shall probably not be far in error if we read these two forms as signifying "sun at sunrise" and "new sun," respectively. The locative ti, "to the east," etc., can be prefixed to all directional glyphs (fig. 41,2).

The glyph for west both on the monuments and in the codices is a hand over the winged kin, presumably to be read as "completion of sun or daylight" (fig. 41,14–22,33). One apparent glyph for west (fig. 41,22) seems to represent the sun with death markings, which would have a parallel meaning of end. The hand takes the form on the monuments of an upright clenched fist with kin infix, and this, when slightly eroded, is hardly distinguishable from the yax prefix of east.

The head of a god with u bracket before his face represents north in the codices (fig. 41,10–13). It is open to question whether this is really God C, as Schellhas (1904) supposed; more than one deity is probably present in the figures he grouped under the name of God C. If that is so, the god of the north may not be connected with the one with monkey features. To complicate matters further, this same head, without u bracket, can be assigned to all world directions and colors (fig. 41,40,49,58,67). In the inscriptions the glyph for north is not surely identifiable, although it would appear that a glyph on Copan A represents that direction because it follows those for east, west, and south (fig. 41,35). It consists of a yax prefixed to a crosshatched triangle, reminiscent of snake markings and definitely identifiable with an element sometimes occupying one of the segments of a celestial band or celestial serpent. The glyph may represent a snake, and perhaps be that of some constellation in the northern sky; our constellation Draco would qualify as such.

The glyph for south in the codices is the yax symbol with "down-balls" prefix and usually two or three little u's on each side; the inscriptional form has the same affixes, but the main element is a section of shell, and small inverted Ahaus may be postfixed (fig. 41,23–31,34,36). The shell is the same as that used as a kin variant except that it is inverted (fig. 31,1–8). South was anciently associated with the god of death by both the Maya and Mexicans (Thompson, 1934), although Wisdom (1940) reports that the present-day Chorti connect death with the west. The shell, as a symbol of the underworld, fits this assignment nicely. A possible connection between yax and south has been discussed (p. 112).

Glyphs for world directions are of considerable antiquity, for they appear to be inscribed on Piedras Negras L 12 (c. 9.4.0.0.0) and, perhaps, on Tikal 12 (c. 9.4.13.0.0).

Often world-direction signs are followed by a glyph which consists of the muluc and cauac elements conjoined and surmounted with the "down-balls" prefix, (fig. 41,6,8,20,22,29). The muluc element here must be read as xoc, "count"; the cauac element represents haab "year." Taken in conjunction with the world-direction glyph, it reads "To the east (north, west, or south) the count of the year," and corresponds to the expression "The count of the year to the east" (u xocol hab ti lakin), which occurs in Tizimin. I have been unable to discover what governs the appearance of these glyphs. It is possible that more than one sequence is involved.

On the murals at Santa Rita there is a sequence of tuns represented as gods roped together. Beside each god is the day Ahau on which each ends; the tun ending on 13 Ahau is accompanied by the glyph for west (Gann, 1900, pl. 29, no. 5). It may be significant that the personification of that tun wears a black mark, for black is associated with the west.

Glyphs which might represent the world colors, other than color elements affixed to main elements (fig. 41,42, 45,51,71,72,81,83–90), have not as yet been recognized on the monuments, although they are frequent in the codices (fig. 41,38,46,47,55,56,64,65,73,74). That the association of colors with directions as given on page 249 holds good also for the codices is beyond question, for colors and world directional glyphs are constantly linked (fig. 62, 1,2), but there is a possibility that yellow may have replaced green as the color for south, perhaps a regional shift or perhaps a general time change. The evidence for this is far from satisfactory, but it may be significant that the prefixes of the four months, Ch'en, Yax, Zac, and Ceh, which have the cauac sign as their main element, are those of the colors black, green, white, and red. Indeed, those color names survive in the names of the months in some languages (p. 111). Moreover, as we have just seen, yax (green) is one of the elements in the glyph for south. In the Popol Vuh (1927, pp. 219, 259) the four colors of Yucatan and the codices are given in one passage, but in another, green is substituted for yellow. In neither case are the associated directions given, but the fact that both passages treat of the four roads makes it evident that these sets of colors were assigned to world directions. It is possible that either green or yellow may have been once assigned to the center, a region almost ignored in Yucatecan sources of the sixteenth and later centuries.

Research subsequent to the writing of the above reveals that the kan cross, identified above as a symbol for both yellow and water, represents turquoise in the glyphic writing of Monte Alban, for it is prominent on the front of the *xiuhuitzolli* (the turquoise headband), which is the Zapotec symbol for the year. Moreover, an interpretation of turquoise would fit its constant use with representations of Tlaloc in the art of Teotihuacan. Turquoise was unknown or extremely rare in the region and period which witnessed the development of Maya glyphs, but I think one should give serious consideration to the possibility, suggested above, that the assignment of the south to yellow was a recent, and perhaps local, innovation. It is not impossible that when or where the surviving codices were compiled or copied, blue or green (one word covers both in Maya) was the color of the south. In that case the kan cross would represent blue or blue-green, and the symbol for yellow would be unidentified. Should that be so, the presence of the kan cross in sky bands, often beside the sign for darkness, presumably would indicate the blue sky of day; combined with the yax sign, it might indicate jade and turquoise (fig. 45,13,14). A symbol for blue or turquoise would naturally stand also for water.

Color names have secondary meanings in Yucatec, and probably other Maya languages, and such extended usages may be expected to occur in the glyphs. *Zac* signifies not only white, but also artificial or not what a thing seems; *zacmul* is an artificial mound, whereas *mul* may be either natural or man-made; *zacyuum* is stepfather, whereas *yuum* is father; *zacyaom* is applied to a woman who gives the appearance of being pregnant but is not so; *yaom hal* is pregnancy. There is a glyph for great fainting, *chac zac cimil* (fig. 41,54). Barrera Vasquez (1944) also points out that *zac* can mean pure, and is thus used in describing a sacrificial victim who had to be uncontaminated. Red and white are frequently paired in the Ritual of the Bacabs, and Roys is under the impression that the two are contrasted, red for strength and white for weakness. In a legend of the Guatemalan highlands (Redfield, 1946, p. 134) the red rain god pours from his large gourd heavy rains and storms, but the white god sprinkles from his small gourd only drizzling rain. The white prefix usually appears with the glyph of the young moon goddess (fig. 41,50), probably to indicate white goddess but perhaps with one of the secondary meanings of *zac,* although that of purity could scarcely be applied to that vivacious lady; red is usually prefixed to the glyph of the old clawed goddess, whom I take to be the aged moon goddess (p. 83).

The red prefix is usually found with the Venus glyph (fig. 42,31,33), but rarely on the monuments (fig. 54,5). One is reminded that one of the names for Venus was *chac ek,* "red star" or "giant star." *Yax,* in addition to meaning green or blue in nearly all Maya languages (shift to *rax* in the Guatemalan highlands), signifies new or strong, and these secondary meanings appear in the glyphs, as for instance in Yaxkin and *yaxil haab* (figs. 32,25; 43,62), and other glyphs (fig. 33,57–60). It is also the symbol of the Chicchan god of number 9, and the two are interchangeable (figs. 13,17,18; 24,50–52,54,55; 25, 32,34,35,46,49; 41,90). The glyph for yellow also serves as a symbol for water, probably because *kan* means both yellow and precious (p. 275). Much remains to be done in elucidating the uses of color affixes in the glyphic writing.

This elaborate structure of years, katuns, and probably other periods, as well as colors, associated in rotation with world directions is in keeping with Maya mentality, which forever sought an orderly arrangement of the spiritual and material world. The periods of time and the gods who rule them change positions in ordained succession and, completing their rounds, return to their original places like participants in a square dance or a set of lancers.

TABLES OF MULTIPLES OF THIRTEEN

In the second half of Dresden are given the 4, 5, 6, and 7 × 13 tables, and another table lists multiples of 54. The tables are constructed to reach 260 days or one of its multiples, and usually continue with multiples of that figure in the vigesimal system; the exception to this rule, multiples of 19 × 780, is perhaps due to an error in computation. At first glance the tables appear to have been constructed by simple addition, that is to say the scribe would have obtained, for example, 1.9.6. (546) as the total for 7 × 78 by adding 3.18 (78) to 1.5.8 (468), the total for 6 × 78 given in the adjacent column. That, however, cannot have been the case, for in that event errors, which are not unusual, would have been repeated through the higher entries in the table. Occasionally, a dot is dropped or added, and that might be due to the carelessness of the copyist who prepared the present edition of the codex, but the omission or addition of 260 days in one total is not repeated in higher multiples. The possibility that such additions or omissions were intentional must not be overlooked, but I think that if the explanation I shall offer for the use of these tables is correct, omissions or additions would throw everything out of gear.

Most of the tables are preceded by one or more IS, which are counted from bases short distances before 13.0.0.0 4 Ahau 8·Cumku. At the base or to the side of each IS is a short distance number, the kins (exceptionally the uinals too) of which are enclosed in a circle with a knot at the top, apparently to indicate subtraction. Robert Willson coined the term "ring number" to designate distance numbers of this type. For instance, there is a ring number on page 43b (fig. 64,2). The whole, with the IS, can be transcribed as follows:

13. 0. 0. 0. 0	4 Ahau (8 Cumku)
17.12	Ring number. *Subtract*
(12.19.19. 0. 8)	3 Lamat (1 Uayeb)
9.19. 8.15. 0	*Add*
(9.19. 7.15. 8)	3 Lamat (6 Zotz')

Data in parentheses do not appear in the codex. The dates reached by the IS are those which form the bases of the adjacent tables. Thus the table which follows the IS given above has 3 Lamat as its base. Month positions are not given in the tables, presumably because the latter could be used at different places in the LC and they are also generally absent in the IS.

Each table has its particular day or days for its *lub* just as we found that 1 Ahau was the *lub* of the Venus table. The tables with their days and the pages on which they occur are as follows:

4 × 13	13 Chicchan (?)	pp. 71a–73a
5 × 13	4 Eb	73b–70c
6 × 13	3 Lamat	44b–43b
6 × 13	13 Muluc	59
7 × 13	13 Akbal etc.	32a–31a
7 × 13	13 Oc	45a
7 × 13	13 Akbal, 3 Chicchan	64c–63a
6 × 9	9 Ix	71a–73a, 71b–70a

The 4 × 13 table is presented in a most unusual manner, for it is grafted on the first part of the 6 × 9 table. This was a fairly simple matter to arrange because 52 (4 × 13) is only two less than 54 (6 × 9). It was achieved by placing a ring number under each multiple of 54, each ring number being two greater than the preceding one. As, however, the basal date of the 54-day table was 9 Ix, and the desired basal date of the 4 × 13 table was 13 Chicchan, the ring number of the first entry is 11. The first five entries of the table are reached as follows:

9 Ix	+ 54 = 11 Lamat.	Subtract ring number 11 = 13 Caban
11 Lamat	+ 54 = 13 Ik.	Subtract ring number 13 = 13 Muluc
13 Ik	+ 54 = 2 Cib.	Subtract 13 + ring number 2 = 13 Imix
2 Cib	+ 54 = 4 Oc.	Subtract 13 + ring number 4 = 13 Ben
4 Oc	+ 54 = 6 Kan.	Subtract 13 + ring number 6 = 13 Chicchan

The entries continue thus until 12 × 52 is reached, at which point the 4 × 13 table ends. The entries can be transcribed as:

$$1 \times 52 = 52$$
$$2 \times 52 = 104$$
$$3 \times 52 = 156$$
$$4 \times 52 = 208$$
$$5 \times 52 = 260$$
$$6 \times 52 = 312$$
$$7 \times 52 = 364$$
$$8 \times 52 = 416$$
$$9 \times 52 = 468$$
$$10 \times 52 = 520 \ (2 \times 260)$$
$$11 \times 52 = 572$$
$$12 \times 52 = 624$$

The 5 × 13 table on pages 73b–70c is longer and more complicated. The multiples are in sequence as far as 28 × 65, which is the same as 7 × 260 or 5 × 364. Then follow 14 × 260 and 21 × 260. The next step, 28 × 260, which is the same as 20 × 364 (20 computing years, p. 256), is missing, but the following entries are all multiples of 1.0.4.0 (20 computing years). The entries are:

65 =	1 ×	65		
130 =	2 ×	65		
195 =	3 ×	65		
260 =	4 ×	65		
325 =	5 ×	65		
390 =	6 ×	65		
455 =	7 ×	65		
520 =	8 ×	65		
585 =	9 ×	65		
650 =	10 ×	65		
715 =	11 ×	65		
780 =	12 ×	65		
845 =	13 ×	65		
910 =	14 ×	65		
975 =	15 ×	65		
1040 =	16 ×	65		
1105 =	17 ×	65		
1170 =	18 ×	65		
1235 =	19 ×	65		
1300 =	20 ×	65		
1365 =	21 ×	65		
1430 =	22 ×	65		
1495 =	23 ×	65		
1560 =	24 ×	65		
1625 =	25 ×	65		
1690 =	26 ×	65		
1755 =	27 ×	65		
1820 =	28 ×	65;	7 × 260;	5 × 1.0.4
3640 =	56 ×	65;	14 × 260;	10 × 1.0.4
5460 =	84 ×	65;	21 × 260;	15 × 1.0.4
14560 =	224 ×	65;	56 × 260;	2 × 1.0.4.0
21840 =	336 ×	65;	84 × 260;	3 × 1.0.4.0
29120 =	448 ×	65;	112 × 260;	4 × 1.0.4.0
36400 =	560 ×	65;	140 × 260;	5 × 1.0.4.0
43680 =	672 ×	65;	168 × 260;	6 × 1.0.4.0
50960 =	784 ×	65;	196 × 260;	7 × 1.0.4.0

58240 =	896 ×	65; 224 × 260;	8 × 1.0.4.0 (uinals written 10)
65520 =	1008 ×	65; 252 × 260;	9 × 1.0.4.0
72800 =	1120 ×	65; 280 × 260;	10 × 1.0.4.0 (0 kins omitted)
87360 =	1344 ×	65; 336 × 260;	12 × 1.0.4.0 (added in red; 0 kins omitted)
94640 =	1456 ×	65; 364 × 260;	13 × 1.0.4.0
109200 =	1680 ×	65; 420 × 260;	15 × 1.0.4.0

There is a final entry, written 1.0.12.3.0 (?), which is obviously in error. It should perhaps be 1.0.4.8.0, which is 14,5600 (2240 × 65; 560 × 260; 20 × 7280).

The 6 × 13 table is given on pages 44b–43b of Dresden. It is connected with the IS and ring number transcribed above, with 9.19.7.15.8 3 Lamat 1 Zotz' as the base. The arrangement (fig. 64,2,3) is:

78 =	1 × 78	3 Cimi	
156 =	2 × 78	3 Kan	
234 =	3 × 78	3 Ik	
312 =	4 × 78	3 Ahau	
390 =	5 × 78	3 Etz'nab	
468 =	6 × 78	3 Cib	
546 =	7 × 78;	6 × 91	3 Ix
624 =	8 × 78	3 Eb	
702 =	9 × 78	3 Oc	
780 =	10 × 78;	3 × 260	3 Lamat
1560 =	20 × 78;	6 × 260	3 Lamat
2340 =	30 × 78;	9 × 260	3 Lamat
3120? =	40 × 78;	12 × 260 (written 9.7.0; 13 × 260)	3 Lamat
3900 =	50 × 78;	15 × 260	3 Lamat
7800? =	(100 × 78;	30 × 260)	3 Lamat
or			
13260? =	(170 × 78;	51 × 260)(written 1.16.2.0; 50 × 260)	3 Lamat
15600 =	200 × 78;	60 × 260	3 Lamat
31200? =	400 × 78;	120 × 260 (written 4.5.17.0; 119 × 260)	3 Lamat
62400? =	800 × 78;	240 × 260 (written 9.13.6.0 for 8.13.6.0)	3 Lamat
72800 =	.... ;	280 × 260; 200 × 364	3 Lamat
109200 =	1400 × 78;	420 × 260; 300 × 364	3 Lamat
131040 =	1680 × 78;	504 × 260; 360 × 364	3 Lamat
151320 =	1940 × 78;	582 × 260	3 Lamat

There are in the table two apparent errors which can be rectified by the addition or subtraction of 260 days. The last four numbers are seemingly attempts to relate the 780-day period to the computing year. If that assumption is correct, the last number probably needs the addition of 6 × 260 to reach the number 1.1.4.12.0 (152,880: 1960 × 78; 420 × 364), but so many alternative rectifications are possible that one can not feel sure that the correction is justified. Indeed, it is possible that no changes in this and the other tables are required, and that in the seeming errors lie the clues to the correct application of the tables.

A second table of multiples of 78 occupies page 59 of Dresden. The *lub* is 13 Muluc. The following multiples are given:

78 =	1 × 78
156 =	2 × 78
234 =	3 × 78
312 =	4 × 78

390 =	5 × 78	
468 =	6 × 78	
546 =	7 × 78	
624 =	8 × 78	
702 =	9 × 78	
780 =	10 × 78	
2340 =	30 × 78	
3120 =	40 × 78 (written 8.13.0 for 8.12.0)	
3900 =	50 × 78	
4680 =	60 × 78 (written 13.13.0 for 13.0.0)	
5460 =	70 × 78	
6240 =	80 × 78	
7020 =	90 × 78	
7800 =	100 × 78	
8580 =	110 × 78	
9360 =	120 × 78	
10140 =	130 × 78	
10920 =	140 × 78	
11700 =	150 × 78	
12480 =	160 × 78	
13260 =	170 × 78	
14040 =	180 × 78	
14820 =	190 × 78;	19 × 780
29640 =	380 × 78;	2 × 19 × 780
44460 =	570 × 78;	3 × 19 × 780
74100? =	950 × 78;	5 × 19 × 780
88920? =	1140 × 78;	6 × 19 × 780
103740 =	1330 × 78;	7 × 19 × 780
118560 =	1520 × 78;	8 × 19 × 780
133380 =	1710 × 78;	9 × 19 × 780
134160 =	1720 × 78	
138840 =	1780 × 78	
140400 =	1800 × 78	
144300? =	1850 × 78	

One wonders whether the compiler of this table intended to give the multiples of 19 × 780, for such an arrangement is quite different from that found in other multiplication tables. I would be inclined to suppose that when the number 19 × 780 (14,820) was reached, he thought he had reached 20 × 780 (15,600), and proceeded to multiply 14,820 by 2, 3, 5, 7, 8, and 9 under the mistaken impression that he was recording 20, 40, 60, 100, 140, 160, and 180 × 780. However, it must be borne in mind that other tables show no evidence of having been composed in that manner, for mistakes do not repeat, and one must not ignore the possibility that 14,820 is the key number, and a reasonable explanation for it may yield an entirely new interpretation of the table. The explanation, however, must be reasonable and not a forced interpretation offered only because it agrees with the correlation its author supports.

Tables of multiples of 91 and 364 days are given on Dresden 31a–32a, 45a, and 63–64. They are imperfect, owing both to wear and to mistakes by the Maya scribe, probably through hasty copying from an earlier edition of the codex. The computations are reproduced in figures, obliterated material being restored in dotted outline. The totals are added in Arabic figures. Readings and restorations do not differ materially from those made by other students. They are discussed in some detail, so that the reader may follow their arrangement, which is in general that observed by all the tables.

In the first case (fig. 46,*17*) the calculations, based on the day 13 Akbal, start at the bottom right corner of the right upper half of page 32a, and read as is the usual, but not the invariable, custom in these tables, right to left. After four places the table passes to the right of the upper horizontal row and, on reaching the left of that row, it continues leftward from the bottom right corner of the left half of the page as far as the right column of page 31a (four places). It then follows the second, third, and fourth horizontal rows in the same manner from right to left. Only the zero kins of the first two numbers of the fourth row remain. The series starts with 91 and its multiple up to 1001 (11 × 91). The fourth and eighth multiples (364 and 728) are omitted from this first part of the table, and placed instead at the start of the second half of the table, where, as units in the 364-day count, they more correctly belong. The calculations, restored, corrected, and rearranged to conform to our method of transcribing tables, are:

Days

91	= (	1 ×	91)
182	= (	2 ×	91)
273	= (	3 ×	91)
455	= (	5 ×	91)
546	= (	6 ×	91)
637	= (	7 ×	91)
819	= (	9 ×	91)
910	= (	10 ×	91)
1001	= (	11 ×	91)
364	= (	1 ×	364)
728	= (	2 ×	364)
1092	= (	3 ×	364)
1456	= (	4 ×	364)
1820	= (	5 ×	364; 7 × 260) (zero transposed)
3640	= (	10 ×	364)
5460	= (	15 ×	364)
7280	= (	20 ×	364) or 1 unit of second order
14560	= (	40 ×	364) or 2 units of second order
21840	= (	60 ×	364) or 3 units of second order
29120	= (	80 ×	364) or 4 units of second order
36400??	= (	100 ×	364) or 5 units of second order
72800??	= (	200 ×	364) or 10 units of second order
109200??	= (	300 ×	364) or 15 units of second order
145600??	= (	400 ×	364) or 1 unit of third order

Beneath the right of the table the 20 days are arranged to read from right to left and top to bottom in five horizontal rows of four glyphs each. The series starts with 13 Ix, which is 91 days after 13 Akbal (the *lub* of the series), and proceeds horizontally through 13 Chicchan, 13 Cib etc. (i.e. at intervals of 91 days). If the columns are read vertically, the intervals are 364 days (i.e. 104 days plus one round of the 260-day cycle). On reaching the end of a horizontal line, one passes to the right edge of the row below. Since the counts are re-entering, the last glyph of the table, that is the one in the bottom left corner, is 13 Akbal, the *lub,* from which a new count starts. In vertical reckoning one passes from bottom to top of each column.

As an example of how the table can be used, let us suppose that one wishes to count 819 days from 13 Akbal. The table shows this to be 9 × 91. To get the correct day sign, count forward nine places horizontally from the starting point (always one step horizontally for each 91 days; one step vertically for each 364 days). Nine places forward will carry to the first (right) glyph of the third column, the day 13 Ik. Accordingly, 13 Akbal + 819 = 13 Ik. Similarly, to reckon forward 11 × 364 + 2 × 91 from 13 Ahau count 11 spaces vertically from 13 Ahau to reach 13 Kan, and then two spaces horizontally: the answer is 13 Cimi. The numeral 13 can naturally be replaced by any other number in making the calculation. The same sum added to 4 Ahau will lead to 4 Cimi.

The table at the top of Dresden 45 handles only multiples of 364 days. The top line is almost entirely obliterated, but its restoration as given below conforms to the pattern of the table. The multiples are: 1, 2, 3, 4, 5, 10, 15, 20?, 40, 60, 80, 100?, 200?, 300?, and 400. On the left is an IS 8.17.11.3. (0) and a ring number of 1.10 which together lead to 13 Oc (3 Mol), indicating that that day is the base of the table. Beneath 2 × 364 stands 13 Etz'nab, which is 728 days from 13 Oc. Beneath 3 × 364, 4 × 364, and 5 × 364 stand respectively 13 Ik, 13 Cimi, and 13 Oc, which are those distances from the base. The last is a repetition of the *lub* of the table because 5 × 364 = 7 × 260. The day 13 Ix, reached by an addition of 364 days, is not found at the right of the row because for some reason 364 days is not in the bottom division of the table, but occurs on the right of the second division.

A multiplication table, formed in the same way by additions, occupies the whole of Dresden 64 and the right half of 63. It starts at the bottom of page 64, to be read from right to left, and then passes to the right edge of the second division of the table. The multiples are:

91	= (	1 ×	91)
182	= (	2 ×	91)
273	= (	3 ×	91)
364	= (	4 ×	91; 1 × 364)
455	= (	5 ×	91)
546	= (	6 ×	91)
637	= (	7 ×	91)
728	= (	8 ×	91; 2 × 364)
819	= (	9 ×	91)
910	= (	10 ×	91)
1001	= (	11 ×	91)
1092	= (	12 ×	91; 3 × 364)
1183	= (	13 ×	91)
1274	= (	14 ×	91)
1365	= (	15 ×	91)
1456	= (	16 ×	91; 4 × 364)
1547	= (	17 ×	91)
1638	= (	18 ×	91)
1729	= (	19 ×	91)
1820	= (	20 ×	91; 5 × 364)
3640?	= (	10 ×	364)
5460	= (	15 ×	364)
7280	= (	20 ×	364)
14560	= (	40 ×	364)
21840	= (	60 ×	364)
29120	= (	80 ×	364)

$$36400? = (100 \times 364)$$
$$72800? = (200 \times 364)$$
$$109200 = (300 \times 364)$$
$$145600 = (400 \times 364)$$

Beneath the calculations are five sets of glyphs, spaced (right to left) at intervals of 91 days, as far as the column giving 5×364. Beyond this the same date repeats, since 5×364 and its multiples are divisible by 260. The starting points of the calculations are 3 Chicchan, 3 Kan, 3 Ix, 3 Cimi, and 13 Akbal. These are precisely the days reached by the so-called serpent numbers, on pages 61 and 62, which precede this table.

THE COMPUTING YEAR

In a previous paper (Thompson, 1941c) I have discussed the possible use of multiples of 364 days for rapid computation of dates, and I have shown how with pebbles or something of that nature, perhaps even a mechanism approaching a simple abacus, it is easy to calculate positions in the Maya calendar with great rapidity. This is so because in all reckonings in 364 days and its multiples the day number remains unchanged. The addition of 364 days involves only two changes: moving four places in the list of day names and subtracting one day from the month position:

9.17.0.0.0	13 Ahau 18 Cumku
1.0.4	*Add*
9.17.1.0.4	13 Kan 17 Cumku
1.0.4	*Add*
9.17.2.0.8	13 Lamat 16 Cumku

Twenty of these years of 364 days, which I have called computing years, are handled with greater ease, for the addition of 20×364 involves no change in the day, and merely the subtraction of one month:

9.17.0.0.0	13 Ahau 18 Cumku
1.0.4.0	(20×364)
9.18.0.4.0	13 Ahau 18 Kayab

In subtraction one reverses the processes, adding the same amounts instead of subtracting them. For example, one wishes to find the CR date corresponding to 9.16.12.5.17 and one knows the date 9.10.10.0.0 13 Ahau 18 Kankin. Add six of the 20 computing years (subtracting six months), and then add one computing year (advancing the day sign four places, and subtracting the day from the month position):

9.10.10.0.0	13 Ahau 18 Kankin
6.1.6.0	$(6 \times 20 \times 364)$
9.16.11.6.0	13 Ahau 18 Mol
1.0.4	(364)
9.16.12.6.4	13 Kan 17 Mol

The calculation has overshot the mark by seven days. These can be readily subtracted in one's head, and the answer 6 Caban 10 Mol thereby obtained.

For a fuller examination of this method of computing the reader is referred to the paper already cited. Nevertheless, it appears probable that these tables of multiples of 91 and 364 days have some further use in addition to that of serving as ready reckoners. That other purposes are involved is, I think, indicated by three factors: the association with IS; the presence of various bases for counting, such as 13 Oc, 13 Akbal, 3 Chicchan; and the presence of three such tables in the codex where one would have sufficed had simple computations been the only factor involved.

There is another use for this table, although I would not regard it as of primary importance. The 5×13 table has all the simple multiples until it reaches 28×65, which is 1820. Thenceforward 1820 is the multiplicand. Similarly the 78 table on pages 44b–43b switches in its higher numbers to multiples of 364. Accordingly, tables of multiples of 364 could have served for calculating over long intervals positions in the 5×13 and 6×13 tables.

There may be a reference to the computing year on Tikal Alt 5, where the last date, 9.13.19.16.9 1 Muluc 2 Kankin, is exactly 20 computing years after the date 9.12.19.12.9 1 Muluc 2 Muan, which opens the inscription. The former is followed by a completion sign of the hand type, another hand, and a head.

SIX TIMES NINE MULTIPLICATION TABLE

This table starts on Dresden 71a and proceeds, unlike other tables, to the right, as far as page 73a, where 12×54 is reached. It then passes to page 71b and continues from left to right as far as page 70b, whence it passes to 71a, and ends at 70a. An odd high number ($20 \times 13 \times 54$), apparently omitted by mistake, is inserted on the right of page 73a. The arrangement is:

54 =	1×54
108 =	2×54
162 =	3×54
216 =	4×54
270 =	5×54
324 =	6×54
378 =	7×54
432 =	8×54
486 =	9×54
540 =	10×54
594 =	11×54
648 =	12×54
702 =	13×54
1404 =	$2 \times 13 \times 54$
2106 =	$3 \times 13 \times 54$
2808 =	$4 \times 13 \times 54$
3510 =	$5 \times 13 \times 54$
4212 =	$6 \times 13 \times 54$
4914 =	$7 \times 13 \times 54$
5616 =	$8 \times 13 \times 54$

```
 6318 =    9 × 13 × 54
 7020 =   10 × 13 × 54;  27 × 260;   1 × 7020
14040 =   20 × 13 × 54;  54 × 260;   2 × 7020
28080 =   40 × 13 × 54; 108 × 260;   4 × 7020
42120 =   60 × 13 × 54; 162 × 260;   6 × 7020
56160 =   80 × 13 × 54; 216 × 260;   8 × 7020
70200 =  100 × 13 × 54; 270 × 260;  10 × 7020
84240 =  120 × 13 × 54; 324 × 260;  12 × 7020
98280 =  140 × 13 × 54; 378 × 260;  14 × 7020
112320 = 160 × 13 × 54; 432 × 260;  16 × 7020
126360 = 180 × 13 × 54; 486 × 260;  18 × 7020
140400 = 200 × 13 × 54; 540 × 260;  20 × 7020
154440? = 220 × 13 × 54; 594 × 260;  22 × 7020
168480? = 240 × 13 × 54; 648 × 260;  24 × 7020
```

The basal date of the table is 9 Ix. It requires 7020 days to recover this *lub*.

INITIAL SERIES ASSOCIATED WITH THE TABLES

Initial Series, together with their ring numbers (p. 253), are associated with all the tables, except the short one of 4 × 13, which, as noted, was seemingly an afterthought. There are errors in several of the dates, and corrections can not be safely made because month positions are usually omitted.

In some cases the number to be added is a multiple of the basic number handled in the adjacent table, but I am far from sure that the numbers were deliberately chosen because they were multiples of the basic multiple; they may well possess those properties through coincidence. Thus one of the dates associated with the 780-day table (p. 43b) has already been transcribed (p. 253). The addition (1,435,980 days) is 1841 × 780 and 3945 × 364.

With the table of the 364-day computing year on pages 32a–31a there are three IS, two of which are multiples of 364 days:

```
13. 0. 0. 0. 0    4 Ahau 8 Cumku
          6. 1        Ring number. Subtract
─────────────────
12.19.19.11.19   (13 Cauac) 7 Ceh
 8.16.14.15. 4        Add
─────────────────
 8.16.14. 9. 3   13 Akbal (16 Pop)

13. 0. 0. 0. 0    4 Ahau 8 Cumku
             17       Ring number. Subtract
─────────────────
12.19.19.17. 3   (13 Akbal) 11 Kayab
 8.16. 3.13. 0        Add
─────────────────
 8.16. 3.12. 3   13 Akbal (11 Yaxkin)
```

The first addition (1,272,544 days) is 3496 × 364; the second (1,268,540 days) is 3485 × 364. The third IS contains mistakes, but can be restored because it is repeated on page 63. It has the largest ring number in the codex, 7.2.14.19 (51,419 days). It is not divisible by 364.

It is far from clear what objectives the Maya astronomer-priests had in picking the bases for these sundry tables. A ring number to reach the *lub* of the table immediately before 4 Ahau 8 Cumku is understandable,

but why should they have used a ring number of over 50,000 days? Presumably the date far in the past thus reached had certain ritualistic or astrological values, which it is our business to discover. It has been claimed that the additions represent multiples of planetary revolutions, but over such long distances one can reach agreement between the number and the revolution of a planet by juggling the figures below the decimal point of the mean synodical revolution of a planet. I myself do not believe that the tables have to do with the revolutions, synodical or sidereal, of planets.

One might suppose that these tables of 4, 5, 6, and 7, times 13 and of 6 times 9 were used only as ready reckoners. That is surely one of their purposes but, in all probability, not the only one, for in that case there would be no apparent need for the sundry IS which introduce them.

PLANETARY TABLES?

Several students of Maya astronomy have supposed that these tables are connected with the revolutions of the more conspicuous planets. Teeple, on the other hand, has expressed his doubts as to the validity of that assumption. Because of the very close approximation of the synodical revolution of Mars (779.936 days) to 780, Willson (1924) was convinced that the two tables of multiples of that number referred to that planet, and on that conviction he largely based his correlation. He took the date 9.19.7.15.8 3 Lamat 6 Zotz', and assumed that one of the subdivisions (19 + 19 + 19 + 21) in the divinatory almanac connected with the table gave an important position of Mars.

In the correlation, as he finally developed it from the Venus and eclipse tables with the supposed Mars table as a check, Mars was in conjunction with the sun 39 days after the date 3 Lamat 6 Zotz'; and, as this was within one day of one of the subdivisions of the table, Willson regarded it as of great significance. He seemingly did not realize that there are no less than 40 subdivisions of the 780-day period, and, except in the case of 3 Lamat, there is no reason to suppose that any one of them would be of outstanding significance in a Mars pattern. This was, indeed, strange reasoning. In the Venus table the important dates are 1 Ahau, the *lub,* and dates at intervals of 584 days therefrom. In this table 3 Lamat is the *lub,* and should by analogy coincide with the most important point in the revolution of Mars, if the table does in fact deal with that planet. Dates 19, 38, 57, 78, 97, . . . and 759 days later can hardly be more than of minor importance. The huge number of subdivisions of the period, patterned in regular intervals, must make one very suspicious of any planetary association.

Mrs. Makemson (1943, p. 243) shares Teeple's uncertainty as to the use to which the multiples of 780 are to be put. Spinden (1942, p. 43) believes that the 3 Lamat table refers to Jupiter. He points out that the IS 9.19.8.15.0 (1,435,980) represents 3600 synodical revolutions of Jupiter. The revolutions would average 398.883 days as against the true average of 398.867. One must beware, however, of the long arm of coincidence; division of large numbers by small numbers allows of much unconscious manipulation. Actually, 3600 average revolutions of Jupiter amount to 79 days less than the IS. Naturally, no one supposes that the Maya had measured Jupiter's synodical revolution so accurately that they were able to calculate its length to their equivalent of the third decimal point. On the other hand, one must use great care in assigning a table to a planet and one is not justified in doing so on the grounds that the IS is divisible by an approximation to the true length of a planet. A shift in the supposed Maya calculation of the length of the revolution by only one-tenth of a day would make a difference of 360 days in this calculation.

The second table, on page 59, of multiples of 78 and 780 has been interpreted by Willson as pertaining to Mars; Spinden assigns it to Saturn. In an unpublished manuscript of another student the case is presented for regarding this as a table to be used in connection with the revolutions of Jupiter, and the 780-day table on pages 44–43 with Mercury. It must be remembered that some of these are attempts to fit those tables into correlations regarded by their authors as proved.

It is almost inconceivable that there could be 40 points, such as conjunction, opposition, stationary points, and heliacal rising and setting, in the synodical revolution of Mars which could be reflected in the formalized pattern of subdivisions of the 780-day period. The possibility that any planet other than Mars could be associated with the table is even less, for one would have to seek some number that is a multiple of 78 or 780 and is also divisible by the average synodical revolution of the planet in question. It would then be necessary to account in terms of astronomy for the scores, perhaps hundreds, of subdivisions which would be produced by the intervals of 19, 19, 19, and 21 days, into which every 78 days is divided.

It would seem, then, highly improbable that the 780-day table refers to Mars, and even more improbable that it refers to any other planet. The same is even more certain so far as the other tables are concerned, for none has a basic number close to the synodical revolution of any planet. Furthermore, none of the glyphs found in the planetary bands is prominent in any of the multiplication tables, yet the introductory page to the Venus table displays massed Venus glyphs, and with the eclipse table prominence is given to solar and lunar glyphs.

FARMERS' ALMANACS?

If these tables do not concern planets, of what do they treat? The head of an animal with a prominent snout which is bent back accompanies 3 Lamat at the head of the 780-day table. The four pictures of the almanac on pages 44b–45b, which is clearly to be read with the table, show this animal hanging from planetary bands, and its glyph stands above each picture (fig. 64,3,4).

The animal has cloven hoofs, drawn with great clarity in all four pictures. Tozzer and Allen (1910, pp. 351–53) identify it as a peccary. Seler (1902–23, 4: 549–52), remarking that the pictures evade zoological determination, calls attention to the parallel passage on Madrid 2, where these same beasties are given human hands which hold axes and, in one case, what may be a torch. Glyphic elements in both texts include axes and reversed comb elements. Eight of the animals are distinguishable on page 2, and there may have been more on page 1. They form a divinatory almanac, the visible intervals of which are 19 and probably 21 days. There are good grounds for supposing that they are closely associated with rain, for alternate pictures are streaked with falling rain, and the adjacent texts—in fact, the whole of this section of Madrid—have a markedly pluvial character. In Madrid the bodies are covered with crosshatched patches, circular to oval in shape, which are the characteristic markings of snakes. Furthermore, the upturned snouts are usually diagnostic of snakes or crocodiles in Maya symbolism. Lastly, this same beast reappears on Dresden 68a in a section clearly dealing with rain. The skies, from which it is pendent, pour streams of rain on the seated maize god, who holds the Kan-Imix sign; the flanking pictures are also rain-swept. His glyph appears elsewhere only on Dresden 71a and 72a, and in both cases the compartment is filled with falling rain, and the axe is prefixed to the glyph. There are, accordingly, good grounds for believing that this beast is a symbol of rain or, conceivably, of some planet or constellation regarded as a sender of rain.

With each creature there are six glyphs which in a number of cases parallel those found with the 6 × 9 and 5 × 13 table and which, as we shall see (p. 260), probably treat of agricultural activities, particularly the planting and germination of the crops. They probably denote, too, days which are unfavorable for such activities.

It would seem, therefore, that the pendent beasts and the glyphs above them together indicate the weather and general agricultural prospects for the days associated with each of the four divisions they occupy. These, with their intervals of 19, 19, 19 and 21 days, have the following pattern when fully expanded:

9 Manik + 19	2 Cimi + 19	8 Chicchan + 21	3 Cimi + 19
9 Chicchan	2 Kan	8 Akbal	3 Kan
9 Akbal	2 Ik	8 Imix	3 Ik
9 Imix	2 Ahau	8 Cauac	3 Ahau
9 Cauac	2 Etz'nab	8 Caban	3 Etz'nab
9 Caban	2 Cib	8 Men	3 Cib
9 Men	2 Ix	8 Ben	3 Ix
9 Ben	2 Eb	8 Chuen	3 Eb
9 Chuen	2 Oc	8 Muluc	3 Oc
9 Muluc	2 Lamat	8 Manik	3 Lamat

The arrangement is not that of a simple divinatory almanac, but of a triple one. If rain, let us suppose, was to be expected on a certain 3 Lamat or on 9 Manik, 19 days later, the same expectations would not be in order for the following appearance of 3 Lamat or 9 Manik; three cycles of 260 days would have to pass before the same conditions would recur. To judge by page 2 of Madrid, rains should occur on days in the columns of 9 Manik and 8 Chicchan because those panels are filled with falling rain; thunderstorms, perhaps with little or no rain, might be expected on days in the columns of 2 Cimi and 3 Cimi because the symbols of thunder and lightning are present, but rain is not pictured.

One might ask what purposes the multiples of 780 days and the IS serve. Let us suppose that the Maya priests are engaged in collecting all data which will throw light on the luck of the coming Katun 2 Ahau, which has the LC position 10.9.0.0.0. The priests know that 2 Ahau is a day on which, let us assume, no rain may be expected because it is in the 2 Cimi column, but that is true only of every third appearance of 2 Ahau. If the 2 Ahau of 10.9.0.0.0 is one of those on which no rain is to be expected, it may, let us suppose, be indicative of a katun of scant rains. The Maya priest turns to his codex. He finds the IS 9.19.7.15.8 3 Lamat 6 Zotz' as a day on which the table ends (p. 253). By the addition of 272 (3 × 78 + 38) he arrives at the 2 Ahau of the table. He then adds multiples of 780 until he reaches or passes 10.9.0.0.0:

$$
\begin{array}{ll}
9.19.\ 7.15.\ 8 & 3\ \text{Lamat} \\
\hphantom{0.00.0}13.12 & (3 \times 78 + 38) \\
\hline
9.19.\ 8.11.\ 0 & 2\ \text{Ahau} \\
\hphantom{0}8.13.\ 6.\ 0 & (80 \times 780) \\
\hline
10.\ 8.\ 1.17.\ 0 & 2\ \text{Ahau} \\
\hphantom{0.0}19.\ 9.\ 0 & (9 \times 780) \\
\hline
10.\ 9.\ 1.\ 8.\ 0 & 2\ \text{Ahau}
\end{array}
$$

+ 19	9 *Etz'nab*	+ 59	3 *Caban*
+ 19	9 Ix	+ 59	3 Ben
+ 19	9 *Oc*	+ 59	3 Muluc
+ 19	9 *Cimi*	+ 59	3 Chicchan
+ 19	9 *Ik*	+ 59	3 *Imix*

His calculations show him that 10.9.0.0.0 ends on a 2 Ahau, to which the luck of the 780-day table does not apply. He can disregard that aspect of the day in preparing his Jeremiad for the current katun. The tables, of course, could be used for predictions of much less importance, such as those of days suitable or unsuitable for planting, burning milpa, or fishing.

There is some confirmation of the suggested interpretation of the 780-day table as a triple almanac for predicting storms in Kaua (Maler photos 72*v*) and Perez (93–94), where there are listed series of days, against each of which is written *u syan chac*, "the birth of Chac," or "the beginning of the storm." The Kaua entries run: 9 Etz'nab, 3 Caban, 9 Cib, 3 Oc, 9 Chuen, 3 Eb, 9 Cimi, 3 Manik, 9 Ahau, 9 Imix, 9 Ik. It will be noted that the coefficients of 9 and 3 are two of those found in the 780-day table, and these two numbers are closely associated with rain or water, for the god of 3 has the Ik sign on his cheek and is patron of the day Cauac, "rain storm," and the god of 9 is the Chicchan god, the celestial water snake. Presumably the last three days have errors in their coefficients as the pattern seemingly is 9-3-9-3-9-3. One must assume that the day Lamat was omitted. With these corrections it is possible to form a 260-day cycle divided into four parts of 65 days each, the first interval being the distance from the last entry, as in the re-entering almanacs of Dresden:

+ 46	3 *Ik*	+ 6	9 *Lamat*	+ 13	9 *Imix*
+ 46	3 *Manik*	+ 13	3 *Ahau*	+ 6	9 *Cimi*
+ 46	3 *Eb*	+ 6	9 *Etz'nab*	+ 13	9 *Chuen*
+ 46	3 *Caban*	+ 13	3 *Oc*	+ 6	9 *Cib*

Italics represent what is given in the Kaua list (the Perez has Cib for Cimi and Tz'ib for Cib). Forty-six is not a very promising number, although the four numbers add to 78. In an expanded form, and assuming that the *u syan chac* was in the last stages of decay when these entries were made, we could get:

+ 19	9 *Cib*	+ 59	3 Men
+ 19	9 *Eb*	+ 59	3 Chuen
+ 19	9 Lamat	+ 59	3 *Manik*
+ 19	9 Kan	+ 59	3 Akbal
+ 19	9 *Ahau*	+ 59	3 Cauac

This forms a triple almanac comprising 10 sections of 78 days apiece, each of which is subdivided into groups of 19 and 59 days. This is very similar to the Dresden arrangement of 10 sections of 78 days, each of which is subdivided into groups of 19, 19, 21 (=59), and 19 days. In Dresden the coefficients are reversed, running 3 Etz'nab, 9 Caban, 3 Cib, etc., since 3 Lamat, not 9 Lamat, is the *lub* of the table. The coefficients of the Kaua and Perez lists could be reversed to attain conformity with the Dresden table, although that would involve more corrections.

Of course, other reconstructions of this *u syan chac* material are possible, but I think the resemblances noted are of sufficient significance to lead us to believe that we are on the right track. It should be noted that in the Dresden table the accompanying glyphs indicate rainless storms for the column of days with coefficients of 3.

Dates given for the birth of the Chacs in the almanacs do not agree with this table, either because of mistakes in their compilation or because of the existence of more than one arrangement for predicting the birth of the Chacs. It is perfectly consonant with Maya practice for different patterns to exist, the choice being governed by the year bearer.

In both the 6 × 9 and the 5 × 13 tables certain compartments have backgrounds of falling rain, and it would, therefore, seem probable that those tables were constructed also for predicting rains, storms, and such matters. In the case of the 6 × 9 table (Dresden 71a–73a) alternate days with coefficients of 11, 8, 10, 1, and 7 occupy the rain-swept compartments, that is to say, 11 Lamat, 11 Oc, etc.; 8 Etz'nab, 8 Ahau, etc.; 10 Eb, 10 Ix, etc.; 1 Ahau, 1 Ik, etc.; 7 Ik, 7 Kan, etc. As the table in its fully expanded form gives 130 days each 54 days apart, no date will repeat for 7020 (130 × 54; 27 × 260) days. Therefore, to make prognostications one needs multiples of 7020 and one or more positions in the LC from which to make the reckoning. The higher multiples are, in fact, based on 7020.

In the 5 × 13 table (Dresden 73c–71c) compartments with rainy backgrounds are: 15 × 65, 4 Manik; 16 × 65, 4 Eb; 18 × 65, 4 Ik; 20 × 65, 4 Eb; and 28 × 65, 4 Eb. Are we to assume from these occurrences of rain that a rainy day can be expected to coincide with 4 Manik only at its fourth occurrence within the cycle of 1820 (28 × 65) days, and with 4 Eb only at its fourth, fifth, and seventh occurrences? That is, perhaps, the most logical assumption, firstly because it presents a pattern similar to those of the 78- and 54-day tables, and secondly because each multiple of 65 up to 28 × 65 is accompanied by three glyphs. Although certain glyphs tend to accompany certain days—for example, the kin or kin-darkness signs with 4 Manik—there is no absolute repetition of the explanatory glyphs. I think, therefore, we can assume that the same conditions were not expected to repeat at each

occurrence of the same day, but only at the indicated positions within the cycle of 1820 (28 × 65; 7 × 260; 5 × 364) days.

I feel reasonably sure that the sets of three glyphs are the equivalents of the entries in the farmers' almanacs in the books of Chilam Balam, and that they indicate what days were favorable for planting maize and other crops, and when drought might be expected. An Ik sign, of frequent occurrence, might well signify strong winds (fig. 46,1,9). A sky sign, on its side, with three rain drops before it appears several times—thrice above compartments filled with rain—and seems a natural sign for a rainy sky (fig. 46,1,9). A glyph, the main element of which consists of a small oval or circle with a vertical line joining it to the top and bottom of the border, is particularly frequent (fig. 43,38–43). In other texts this is often combined with the Caban, "earth," glyph. This is the glyph for seed, germination, and sowing (p. 271). Other glyphs in this and other tables include the Kan, "ripe maize," sign, the head of the maize god, the drought glyph, and the sign for misery and misfortune (fig. 20, 3,7). The sun-darkness glyph (fig. 43,50) which also occurs might well stand for the darkening of the sky before a storm. Should that be the case, divinatory passages probably occur also on the stelae, for this same glyph is of common occurrence on the monuments. These signs are also represented in the texts which accompany the so-called Mars beasts of the 780-day almanac of pages 44 and 45, although new elements are there combined with them (fig. 64,3,4).

On Paris 23–24 there is an incomplete cycle of 1820 days (65 × 28; 7 × 260; 5 × 364) which appears to have started with 10 Ahau. It advances from right to left at intervals of 28 days with five rows of 13 columns. The table is surmounted by a planetary crocodile. Beneath this various members of the animal kingdom, such as a tortoise, a scorpion, a rattlesnake, and birds, grasp in their mouths or beaks sun disks which dangle from the planetary band. Actually, there are only seven animals, but there are six, perhaps seven, more in the section below the table. Stansbury Hagar (1917) identified this table as a zodiac, and this identification later received support from Spinden (1916; 1924, p. 56). It is hard, however, to see how such a table could have been used in connection with the sidereal year, for it has a length of 1820 days, whereas five sidereal years are 1826.28 days. I would rather suppose that this again was a divinatory almanac of the expanded type, reaching, as in the case of the 5 × 13 table and the 7 × 13 table, 1820 (7 × 260) days. The glyph which I have suggested means seed is prominent in the text above the planetary crocodile. Perhaps the same general idea is behind the incomplete almanac of 260 days which stretches across Madrid 13–18, and, with its repetitive sections of rain and drizzle, is faintly evocative of an English (or New England) landscape in early spring.

Following the 7 × 13 table on Dresden 31a–32a, there is an arrangement of additions which carry the dates forward 208 days. Förstemann (1906, p. 138) supposes that this leads from a day with coefficient of 1, but there can be little doubt that the count is from a day with coefficient of 13, presumably 13 Akbal. The additions are: 11, 28, 13, 26, 12, 19, 5, 1, 20, 12, 6, 8, 5, 7, 11, 5, 8, and 11, a total of 208 days, from 13 Akbal to 13 Chuen, another of the five day signs in the 13 Akbal group on page 32a (fig. 46,17). Förstemann has supposed that the additions of 208 days represent an incomplete cycle of 260 days, but there is no need to make such an assumption, for additions of 208 days lead from 13 Akbal to 13 Chuen, to 13 Cauac, to 13 Manik, to 13 Men, and, at the end of 1040 days (5 × 208; 4 × 260) once more to 13 Akbal.

As in the case of the divisions which follow the 6 × 13 table, the series must repeat until the *lub* is once more reached. In this case it is reached after 4 × 260, in contrast to the 3 × 260 total of the 6 × 13 table. I take it that the days in the remaining three columns of page 32a, 13 Ix, 13 Chicchan, and 13 Cib, could also be bases.

The first five pictures associated with the divisions of the 4 × 260-day cycle are of unusual size, for they occupy the width of a half or a whole page instead of the customary third. This may have no significance, for the arrangement may have been imposed on the artist by spatial considerations. Of the 17 pictures or groups, four show water or falling rain, three represent deities with torches in their hands, apparently a symbol for thunder and lightning, one represents a sacrifice of a head decked as that of the maize god, and the remainder are nondescript, although several have secondary characteristics which suggest that rain and crops are the subjects under discussion. God B holds the earth symbol in one picture; a Kan (ripe maize) glyph in another; in a third God B with a Kan sign in his hand lies on the roof of a temple, inside which is seated God C also holding a Kan sign. This scene may correspond to that which Roys (1933, p. 182) cites from Tizimin: Chilam Balam lay prostrate in a trance while the god or spirit, perched on the ridgepole of the house, spoke to him. The trance aspect of the ceremony may well have been a later accretion. The primary date associated with this picture is 13 Imix.

The glyphs connected with the pictures are noncommittal, at least to us at the present state of our knowledge. The sun-darkness glyph for which the meaning of darkened day has been suggested (p. 272) occurs, as well as the glyph tentatively identified as storm with lightning

(p. 147), and the axe comb and *u* glyph, found also with the Mars beast (p. 258). The glyph which represents planting or seed, however, is absent. It is, all things considered, not improbable that these divisions were used for divinations in connection with agricultural activities. Nevertheless, it is difficult to relate the arrangement to the 364-day year, for not until the passage of 7280 days (1.0.4.0), that is 20 × 364 or 28 × 260, will the two series 364 and 208 reach again their common *lub*.

I think, therefore, that the main purpose of these tables was to supply ready reckoners to be used in conjunction with divinatory almanacs, not of the simple type of 260 days, but multiples thereof. As the divisions were arranged in such a way that, for example, the day 3 Lamat will not reappear until the 260-day almanac has repeated three times, it was necessary to list multiples of 780 so that the priest could quickly discover whether a particular 3 Lamat was that affected by the aspect of the day, or whether it was one of the other two which were passed over. This arrangement, of course, parallels that of advancing by multiples of two CR in order to recover correct days in the uncorrected Venus calendar.

There is, however, one line of evidence which appears to contradict the interpretation I have advanced. If, for example, the 9 × 6 times table supplies us with a series of days, starting with 9 Ix, for which certain prognostications were made, not at each occurrence of the day but only at every 27th occurrence, that is at intervals of 7020 days, then one would expect the final dates of the four IS which lead to 9 Ix to be separated by multiples of 7020 days. That, however, is not the case. Accordingly, if the IS were used, as I have suggested, as bases for calculating whether any given repetition of a day qualifies for the prognostications, a priest calculating from all four 9 Ix IS would get different results. This is an argument against my thesis, for which at present I can offer no convincing rebuttal, other than to note that we are very much in the dark as to how the mechanism of these divinatory almanacs was manipulated.

Despite this objection, I believe that these tables have nothing to do with the synodical revolutions of planets, but were used in connection with stations in almanacs expanded to some multiple of 260 days. These stations, I am strongly inclined to think, were primarily for agricultural divination, and marked days when rains or storms might be expected. Probably they record, also, days which were suitable for planting and perhaps for sacrificial ceremonies in connection therewith, for Maya thought is like a glade in a woodland, in which are two altars: one is dedicated to the earth; the other, to eternal time. No matter what path is followed, it will lead to one or other of the twain.

GENERAL OBSERVATIONS

It would be difficult to summarize adequately the diffuse and tedious contents of this cave of Adullam which I have labeled Chapter 11. The argument of its final pages prefaces much in Chapter 12.

The discussion of these various multiplication tables, the short cuts in computations, and the rotation of periods in relation to world directions and colors do not take us far along the path of decipherment, but they are of indirect aid because they give us an insight into the workings of the Maya mind. Moreover, the divinatory aspects of the tables present a purpose different to that which the manipulation of time served.

The IS, with its divisions, the coordination of the moon and Venus with the 260-day cycle, and the unintermitting engagement of the vague year with the tun stand forth as mighty monuments of the Maya concept of the inherent orderliness of time. The various divisions served also astrological ends, but the grandeur of the whole is breath-taking. In its contemplation, as in contemplation of the soaring tracery of Lierne vaulting, man is made to realize how transitory and trivial is his part in the pageant of eternity. That exalting nobility is not to be found in the divisions and manipulations of segments of the count of time for divinatory purposes, for in seeking their domination man would exalt himself, and would claim divine knowledge of the laws which govern the actions of the gods themselves. The mystery of eternity is dispelled; man deludes himself that he has learned how to control its goings out and comings in; the village *hmen* pries into the control of eternity for a few tamales, and tells man's birthright for a mess of potage.

Man has ever found it hard to divorce magic from religion and to acknowledge that there are no hocus-pocus formulae to control destiny. It is disappointing to find that the Maya were no better in that respect than others at a comparable level of civilization, although, one has the consolation of knowing that that aspect of the calendar was practiced, so to speak, in booths around the portals of the temple.

It might be argued that there is little difference between the priest-astronomer, with his astrological practices, and the village *hmen* who told the farmer on what days to burn his milpa or plant his crop. Actually there was a great gulf between them. The one probed the recesses of heaven and pried deep into the past to gain guidance in assessing the fortunes of the katun; he weighed the factors, and followed what were, to his way of thinking, scientific lines, making his deduction objectively. His premises were at fault, but that he did not know, and, in any case, the same charge can be made against not a few modern scientists who start with the premise that the stone of materialism will satisfy mankind, ignoring man's far greater need for the bread of spiritual life. On the other hand, the village *hmen* made no attempt at deduction; he relied entirely on magical formulae from a book, believing that rules had been mastered which permitted man to control his fate, provided rigid conformity to certain practices was enforced. The priest-astronomer would ascribe failure to foretell the future to incomplete data or a faulty interpretation of the data he possessed; the village *hmen* would lay the blame for his failure to some little irregularity which caused the magical formula to go awry.

It has been necessary to view this somewhat tawdry aspect of Maya culture in order to present a more complete picture of the whole, just as no study of Florence, which confined itself to the Giottos, Brunelleschis, and Donatellos, but ignored the more ignoble of the Medicis, would be a true portrait of that culture.

I am convinced that the almanacs placed after the multiplication tables are primarily for predicting weather and crops, but it does not necessarily follow that the use I suggest for the multiplication table is correct. The explanation is weak. I can only echo the words of Hilaire Belloc: "The student should be warned that they are theories, and theories only, that their whole point and value is that they are not susceptible to positive proof; that what makes them amusing and interesting is the certitude that one can go on having a good quarrel about them, and the inner faith that when one is tired of them one can drop them without regret. Older men know this, but young men often do not...."

12

Aids to Decipherment

Helpe then O holy virgin chiefe of nine,
Thy weaker novice to perform thy will.
Lay forth out of thine everlasting scryne
The antique rolles, which there lye hidden still.
—EDMUND SPENSER, *Prologue to Faerie Queene*

PATHS TO THE SCRYNE

THERE ARE FOUR PATHS which may profitably be trodden in search of that scryne wherein Clio, granting her dominion in the New World, hides the decipherment of Maya writing. Three, which hold most prospect of leading to success, are: an intensive study of the glyphs in the divinatory almanacs of the Dresden and Madrid codices; a careful search for interchangeable elements in glyphs so as to expand the groups which are synonymous or nearly synonymous; a listing of glyphs which have the same main element, but the meanings of which appear to change radically through variation in positions of the main sign (such as being inverted or placed on its side) or by the addition of sundry affixes, always bearing in mind that sometimes a radical change in meaning may be due to secondary use as a homonym. Lastly, the mathematical approach, which involves computing the distances between dates, with which a given glyph is associated, and seeking a common factor to account for those distances, has not yet come to a dead end, as the recent discovery of the 819-day cycle and the differentiation in the last few years between the glyphs for the fifth and fifteenth tun of a katun attest.

In this chapter I purpose to note progress in these various methods of solving our problems, and to sketch the ways in which these studies may be expanded. These blasts will not fell the walls of our Jericho, but they will, I trust, make some sizable breaches in it.

GLYPHS WHICH ACCOMPANY DIVINATORY ALMANACS

TYPES OF GLYPHS

A fundamental misconception has, I think, handicapped nearly all those who have endeavored to decipher the glyphs which are above the pictures in the divinatory almanacs of the codices. That misconception, I believe, arises from regarding the glyphs above each picture as serving to explain the pictures. Thus, for example, Whorf (1933) assumed that the glyph of a hand referred to the actions of the god depicted below it, and on that assumption based a large part of his argument; Gates (1931, pp. 136–39) similarly linked glyphs to pictures.

I myself prefer to suppose the opposite, namely, that the pictures are subordinate to the glyphs and supplement them. I believe that whereas one or more of the glyphs, particularly the name glyphs of gods, are illustrated in the pictures, the actions of the gods do not necessarily correspond to the texts. For example, a long divinatory almanac starts on Dresden 4a and continues to 10a. Although some of the glyphs are missing, there is no good reason to doubt that the same pair stands at the head of each of the 20 divisions into which the whole is partitioned. The first of these is an animal head with an Etz'nab infix, a lunar postfix, a peculiar curved line around the eye, and dots around the mouth (fig. 42,84). According to Tozzer and Allen (1910), pictures of various mammals, notably deer, dog, peccary, and jaguar, show this curved line through the eye. The Etz'nab infix suggests either a knife or sacrifice.

The second glyph of each pair consists of two hands, held in the positions used for the Manik sign in the codices, and placed one above the other. There is a prefix to the left (fig. 42,64). The third glyph in each group is that of a god, almost invariably the deity depicted in the picture below. It is very improbable that the double-hand glyph refers to anything which the god in the picture below is doing with his hands, for the deities in all the illustrations to this almanac are doing nothing in particular.

The sundry almanacs in the books of Chilam Balam (pp. 297–302) should be of some assistance in identifying the general characters of the messages, albeit the sorry versions that have reached us are of the eighteenth century, and have clearly lost much of their old paganism in two centuries of Christian dominance. As they now stand, they list the good and bad influences of the days, and contain entries against certain days regarding the prospects for hunting, sowing, rain, and drought. There are also a few notes, no longer fully understandable, on old pagan rites. We should therefore expect the glyphs in the divinatory almanacs to contain information of the same general nature, together with such items as the name of the god who is the author of the luck of the day and perhaps the appropriate ceremonies.

The glyphs of the gods have already been identified in most of these texts, and we can therefore be reasonably sure that their actions are under discussion. We can also be reasonably sure that one or more of the signs refers to the luck of the day. As we shall shortly note (p. 268), a glyph to which in all likelihood the general meaning of misery can be applied usually occurs in texts which also carry the glyph of the death god or stands above pictures of malevolent action; other glyphs appear to indicate favorable aspects. Such symbols usually conclude each text, and it is a fair assumption that they give the luck of the day.

The first two glyphs in each text are quite often repeated in all the compartments of the almanac in question. They may therefore indicate the general subject under discussion, or perhaps be of a still more general nature. I assume one is a verb or verbal noun; the other the object.

As an illustration, let us take the very simple almanac that runs across Dresden 13b–14b (fig. 61,5,6). In all six sections the first two glyphs are the same so far as their main elements are concerned, although there are changes in the affixes in the last three pairs of glyphs which may correspond to slight variations in the spoken word. The first glyph is a hand with the "comb" infix and the "down-balls" prefix; the second is the Kan with affixes (maize sign). The hand presumably represents the action and is perhaps verbal; the Kan (maize) glyph I take to be the object. The third glyph in each compartment is that of the god in question; the fourth is what I assume to be the resulting luck of the day. A tentative translation of the glyphs would be:

6 Ben. His influencing the maize, the death god. Heaped-up death (*multun tzek*).
2 Ik. His influencing the maize, the maize god. Change of aspect (?).
9 Muluc. His influencing the maize, God C. Very good tidings.
3 Cib. The black god influences his maize. Good crop (??).
10 Akbal. The god of number 10 influences his maize. Evil.
6 Eb. The rulership of God D influences his maize.

Here the construing of the hand glyph as "influence" is offered as a general term. The subject is discussed in greater detail on page 266. The translation for the glyphs denoting the luck of the day is no better than a guess in two of the texts; of the general correctness of the other three I am reasonably confident. Variation in the subject of the verb is to suggest the transposition of affixes (p. 39).

In the short almanac on Dresden 12b, there appear to be no verbal nouns but, instead, two glyphs denoting influences (fig. 62,6). The opening glyph is a Muluc sign with two postfixes, one of which is the moon sign, probably here used as the possessive. The second glyph is the name of the god; the third and fourth appear to record the resultant luck of the day:

1 Manik. The water of the death god. Death. Evil.
1 Ben. The water of the Chicchan god. Abundance of maize is his rule.
1 Cimi. The water of the death god. Death. Evil.

GLYPHS OF ACTION

A number of these glyphs which usually stand at the head of the text in each compartment of divinatory almanacs are shown in figure 42,58–87. Many of them possibly correspond to verbal nouns or verbs. They are for the most highly conventionalized signs which for that reason are hard to translate.

Flare-uinal-moon Glyph (fig. 61,3, Col. 1, Gl 2). The conventionalized head with the Chuen-uinal infix, flame at the top, and lunar postfix, usually occurs immediately after month signs or adjacent to world-direction glyphs. It is often followed by the head of a dog. Coming after the month sign, it might correspond to the use of the kin glyph after day signs in the inscriptions of Yucatan, and merely indicate that the preceding glyph records the month sign. The explanation, however, is probably not so simple, because in all such cases the associated dates are far in the past and represent points of departure for the count. There are also a few instances where this sign precedes glyphs that are symbols neither of the months nor of world direction. For example, it precedes the burden glyph with "thatch" prefix on Dresden 34a–35a, and occurs before an earth-seed symbol (milpa?) on 38b.

What is clearly the same sign occurs as the opening glyph in all known recordings of the 819-day cycle, although the second postfix is different (the lunar postfix becomes an infix in one example: fig. 35,1–5). In one text the glyph is followed by the symbol for east; in other texts the sequent glyph is a head or a cauac with a count prefix. The closing glyph of the clause is that of an animal, with coefficient of 1, reminding one of the dog glyph of the codices.

On pages 48c–50c of the Venus table in Dresden there is what is probably a variant form (fig. 42,71). This stands between the month sign and the name glyph of the god in each of the 12 divisions. It is omitted from page 47, and is shifted to below the gods on page 46, probably through carelessness. Is the absence of this glyph from section *b* of the table fortuitous, or is it due to the fact that the numbers in that section are cumulative, or that the month positions are not the earliest? The fact that the variant glyph in question is closest to the earliest set of month positions, that is to say the 1 Ahau 18 Kayab table, may be significant in view of the association of the regular form with the points of departure of a number of the IS on Dresden 61, 62, 63, and 70, probably on 45, and 58, and possibly on 51, and its appearance with records of the 819-day cycle, all of which involve a backward count in time. It would appear, therefore, that a translation must be sought which is applicable both to a point of departure in the past and to world direction. Such a word should also be related to the name Chuen, Zec, or uinal, or their equivalents in some other Maya language or dialect. With much hesitation I would suggest that the root *uin* may be involved. The Motul dictionary gives *uinan* as order or manner, *manaan u uinan u than . . . u beel*, "he has no order in his words nor in his works." The word *uinba*, "image, figure or portrait," and perhaps *uinal*, too, may derive from the same root. This root may have served to indicate both the setting in order or sequence of the world directions and the priority of one date or series of dates over another. This interpretation, however, must be regarded as no more than a hazard, for the possibilities are numerous, because three unrelated glyphic forms, each with variant names in different languages and dialects, are involved. However, we probably shall not err greatly in translating this glyph and the direction symbols as indicating together "it is set in the east" etc., or "it moves in order to the east" etc., or the subject may be the glyph of the god, "god *n* is set in the east" etc. That the meaning of the glyph is not fundamental is, I would suppose, indicated by its presence before the world directional sign in only one of the four divisions of the almanac which occupies Dresden 42c–45c (fig. 61,3). On the other hand, the dog glyph, which so frequently follows the glyph under discussion, is present in all four sections. The head with a uinal glyph infixed in the eye (Gates' Glyph 91) does not appear to be the head form corresponding to this glyph, for its associations in Dresden are entirely different.

Drilling Glyph (figs. 42,76; 43,53–55). The difficulties of interpreting glyphs with the aid of pictures is well illustrated by the so-called glyph of the fire drill. In two almanacs of Madrid 38, the fire drill glyph accompanies scenes of making fire with a drill. The main element prefixed to a dog head accompanies pictures showing the use of the fire drill on Dresden 5b–6b. On the other hand, the glyph, following the so-called burden glyph, occurs above pictures on Dresden 8b and 9b (figs. 42,77; 43,54), which show no evidence of fire-making. Twice the glyph accompanies pictures which illustrate spikelike implements being driven into heads of human forms.

These scenes have been identified as depicting the manufacture of idols.

However, if the postfixes are not neglected, a more logical classification can be made. The horseshoelike glyph is associated only with the dog head or the curving postfix with crosshatching when it occurs above pictures, showing the use of the fire drill. The dog is closely associated with fire, and, in view of the scenes depicted, we are probably not over-imaginative in seeing in the crosshatched extension, which emerges from the base of the main element, a pictorial representation of smoke. The main element, with a different postfix and with the three dots of its infix differently arranged, is above two figures showing the eye of a head being pierced. It is, again, perhaps not over-imaginative to suppose that the maker of idols is engaged in drilling the eyes. In Yucatec the word *hax* means to drill a hole, and to twist cord by rubbing between the palms of the hands; as a noun it signifies hole in general and holes made by wood lice and other insects, and twisted cord. *Hax kak* is to drill fire, and *haxab*, with the instrumental *ab*, is the drill. The same word occurs in Manche Chol, but only the meaning "to twist cord" is given in the Moran dictionary. Pio Perez lists also the verb *haxah* with the meaning "to twirl a drill between the palms of the hand, to twist cord in the same way, and to stir chocolate by twirling a swizzle stick between the palms of the hands." It is, then, highly probable that the main element of the glyph refers to the action of twirling with the hands, whereas the affixes indicate the particular use.

In the case of the fire drill, the infix of three dots arranged as a triangle may be significant, as this may represent the three stones of the hearth. The postfix, as noted, may be a stylized picture of smoke or, perhaps, fire. The replacement of this postfix by the head of a dog in Dresden is consonant with this interpretation, as the dog symbolizes fire. In the pictures which show the piercing or boring of the eye of the statue, the gods' hands are not indicated in the act of twirling, but neither, for that matter, are they correctly held for drilling fire. The postfix of the drill symbols on Dresden 8b and 9b is hard to explain. It resembles the symbol for jade. Could the whole glyph represent jade beads which have been drilled?

Clenched-hand Glyphs (fig. 42,58–61,65–68). The hand appears to serve in many instances as a glyph of action. Usually, unlike the outstretched positions indicative of completion (p. 184), the hand is clenched, and may be upright or upside down. There is also a group of glyphs in which the main element is a hand or two hands, one above the other, held in the position of Manik (fig. 42,62–64).

The clenched hand with Ik infix and vestigial mouth

and nose is the very common glyph for God B (fig. 42,57). In that case we are reminded that a hand was the symbol of Itzamna, and corresponded to his name *Kabul,* "the hand that works," according to Lizana, but Ah Kabul would be "he who works with his hands." The hand not infrequently appears in the headdress of figures on stelae, but in such cases it is usually outstretched in a vertical position.

The closed fist similar to that of the glyph of God B might therefore represent the act of doing something. In most lowland languages and dialects the word for hand is *kab,* but in Yucatec there is also a verb *kab,* "to do something with one's hands." To judge by the example in the Motul dictionary, which employs *kab* to indicate working in one's milpa, the word could be employed for any action which involved the hands, although their use was not necessarily stressed. The hand often appears above pictures which show a deity holding something. For example, in the almanac which runs across Dresden 15c each god holds the sign for the sun in his hand, and the texts for both divisions open with the same pair of glyphs (fig. 62,5). The first is a hand with a comb infix and Landa's *ma* symbol as an affix; the second is the sun glyph. In passing it is interesting to note that the *ma* sign is a postfix in the first compartment, a prefix in the second compartment. The same hand glyph, but followed by the Kan (ripe maize) sign, is at the head of the six compartments of the almanac on Dresden 13b–14b, already discussed (fig. 61,5,6), and in the pictures below gods hold the Kan sign in their hands. The act of holding ripe maize is understandable, but it is less likely that the glyphs tell us that the death god and God D hold the sun or day in their hands, unless we are to take the glyph as having a figurative meaning.

It is tempting to translate the glyph as *etma,* "to hold in one's hand," or as *machma,* which has the same meaning, thereby resting in part on Landa's translation of the affix as *ma.* The clause would then read: the action (the hand glyph) of the death god (Glyph 3) on the sun (Glyph 2). Evil (Glyph 4). A freer rendering of that would be: the death god is in power, and affects the sun, causing evil. Similarly, the other gods affect the ripe maize in the almanac previously discussed. Both *etma* and *machma* appear in ritualistic passages in Chumayel. Thus we find that Yaxal Chac, the patron of the katun, grasps the heavenly fan, the heavenly bouquet (*u machma canal ual canal utz'ub;* Perez, p. 75). There is a passage which Roys translates, "He set up the planets, Saturn, Jupiter, Mars, Venus, which he said were held in the grasp of the god (*u machma kui*) in heaven where he created them." Here, then, is a passage in which the god holds the planets in his hand, just as the picture depicts the gods holding the sun in their hands. The employment of this term permits us to give greater consideration to the possibility that this expression is a figurative one to denote that the god in control wields power over activities in heaven and on earth, be they planets or crops or rains.

The various books of Chilam Balam employ several forms derived from *et,* "to hold," in ritualistic passages where the influences of the gods are under discussion. Roys notes that the term is used in connection with the heavenly fan and bouquet to which reference has already been made: *Etbom ual, etbom, utz'ub,* "The fan shall be displayed, the bouquet shall be displayed" (Chumayel, p. 73), *yetbal canal ual* (Tizimin, p. 23), *Etlahom utz'ub* (Chumayel, p. 100), *minan yutz kinnob yetzahob toon,* "no lucky days were displayed to us" (Chumayel, p. 20).

Other possibilities are *men,* "to do something, preferably with one's hands," *ch'a,* "to take," *tz'a,* "to give," and *kamac,* "to receive," all of which involve the use of the hand. Perhaps the expression *minan yutz kinnob yetzahob toon,* "there were no lucky days displayed to us," is the key to this passage. The *z* added to the root *et* is causal. "The god holds out in display to mankind the day," may be a ritualistic phrase indicating that the god controls the luck of the day.

Unfortunately, there appear to be no texts in European writing which explicitly refer to the influences of the gods over the days, although there are a few terms which appear to designate the influence of a god over his katun. The word *ich,* "face" or "eye," is frequently used in connection with the name of a god associated with a katun, presumably to indicate that he is the regent (p. 204); *tepal,* a word of Nahua origin meaning rule, and *t'an,* "command," appear often in contexts which imply a similar concept. Among the Lacandon the word *can* occurs in chants in the sense of protection by the god of the individual (Tozzer, 1907, chants 14, 21). The form *canan* is used in a similar way in Yucatec (Brinton, 1882, p. 241). None of these, or, for that matter, words of less currency, convey the idea of the hand. The only expressions of that nature in the various books of Chilam Balam which conceivably refer to the influences of the gods are *machma* and *et.* I am far from certain that either corresponds to the glyph in question. However, my intent at present is to discuss the general meaning of the glyph rather than to pair it with any definite word. That general meaning is, I think, influence, sway, or control.

There are several other hand symbols which are probably glyphs of action. One common sign is an inverted hand which in Dresden with three exceptions is the first glyph of its compartment. This has a peculiar infix regarded by Beyer as a death eye, an identification which appears very dubious (fig. 42,65–68). In Dresden, with the exception of one example with entirely different affixes on page 46, this glyph appears only in almanacs which have to do with rain. Its distribution is:

29c–30c. First glyph in all four sections. All pictures are of God B. His glyph is the fourth. Second and third glyphs represent world direction and colors.

30c–33c. First glyph in all nine sections. All pictures are of God B. His glyph is the second in all sections. World-direction trees and colors are represented (fig. 62,1–4).

33c–39c. First glyph in all 20 sections. All pictures are of God B. His glyph is the second in 16 sections and third in two sections. Twice it is replaced by the head of a long-beaked bird with black markings, probably a king vulture, which is frequently shown in rainy settings (e.g. Dresden 38b), and appears to symbolize rain.

40c–41c. First glyph in all six sections. All pictures are of God B. His glyph is the third in all sections.

41b–43b. Probably first glyph Sections 2, 3, fourth glyph Section 1. Replaced by Cumku sign with lunar affixes Sections 4 and 5. Sections 1–4 show God B; Section 5 carries a portrait of the old red goddess pouring water from a jar. The glyph of God B is the second sign in all sections, including that in which the old goddess appears, but her glyph also is present there.

65b–69b. First glyph in all 13 sections. All pictures are of God B. His glyph is the third in all sections.

42a–44a. First glyph in four sections; opening glyph of other four sections obliterated, but presumably was this hand sign. God B is pictured in six sections; the old goddess and an unidentified deity occupy Sections 2 and 6, respectively. The glyph of God B appears in five sections. The glyphs in two sections are obliterated. In the section with the picture of the old goddess, Glyph B is omitted or obliterated, but the base of her glyph is recognizable.

Although this glyph does not appear in every almanac pertaining to rain, its close association with God B and his colleagues in divination for rain, and its absence from almanacs which deal with both rain and lightning storms suggest that when used with the given affixes, it conveys the idea of giving rain to mankind. The reversed position of the hand suggests the act of donation.

In Paris and Madrid the glyph occurs with different affixes; in the latter the main element is often doubled. It appears in almanacs of Madrid which closely parallel those cited in Dresden save that God C replaces God B. Compare, for instance, the almanacs on Madrid 10c–11c, and Dresden 33c–39c. Both have 13 Ahau as the point of departure, and several of the pictures in one almanac are repeated or closely paralleled in the other. However, in several places this glyph, but with other affixes, has no apparent connections with rain (e.g. Madrid 38a–39a).

Again, it would be premature to suggest a Maya equivalent for the glyph at this time, although the possibilities

of *tz'a,* "to give," and *matan,* "a gift" or "grace or mercy received" are worth bearing in mind.

Partly Open Hand (fig. 42,62–64). In a third use of the hand symbol apparently as a glyph of action, the position is that common to the day sign Manik. The main element in frequently duplicated. Where this sign is repeated through all sections of an almanac, it generally occupies the second place. Thus, it probably occupied the second position in all 20 sections of the almanac on Dresden 4a–10a, following the animal head with Etz'nab infix and lunar postfix (fig. 42,84). It follows a spiral glyph (water or fire?) on Dresden 4c–5c, or a queer element, conceivably a shellfish emerging from a bivalve, on Dresden 6b–7b.

Burden Glyph (fig. 43,37,61). This almost certainly corresponds to the word *cuch,* which is ritualistically applied to the luck of a period which shows deities carrying burdens. In such cases, I believe, the burdens symbolize the burden of good or bad luck of the period. The common form of affix with this glyph is the cauac element. It is tempting to read the whole as *cuch haab,* "the burden of the year." This would fit very well the appearance of the glyph on all four of the pages of Dresden (but not the equivalent pages of Madrid) devoted to the incoming year, where in three cases glyphs of good or bad augury (abundance of maize, evil, and drought) are juxtaposed (figs. 43,60,61; 64,1). In the fourth case the adjacent glyph is obliterated. The combinations would read:

p. 25. (Obliterated) the burden of the year.

p. 26. Drought the burden of the year. *Kintunyaabil u cuch haab.*

p. 27. Abundance the burden of the year. Kan-Imix (?), *u cuch haab.*

p. 28. Death the burden of the year, a year of evil. *Cimil u cuch haab, kaz tunil* (?)

Note the *u* prefix of the burden glyph, corresponding to the spoken word.

In the divinatory almanacs the burden cannot have been carried for a year, since the compartments refer to divisions of the 260-day cycle. Conceivably, the cauac element could refer to the year of 360 days in particular, but also time is general. Another possibility is that the burden glyph with cauac superfix represents the stem *cucuch.* The Motul dictionary lists *cucuchuc,* "things which go one above the other, like carrying them in a load one above the other." Landa, in his alphabet, gives to the cauac glyph the sound *cu.* This is not the primary sound corresponding to that sign, but it may be a secondary one. In that case it would agree well with this interpretation. A point which may be significant is that the "grape" element is always omitted from the cauac part of the cuch glyph, whereas it is seldom lacking from the day Cauac or from the cauac months in Dresden. However, the same occurs when the cauac element is an infix of the katun sign in the inscriptions, so perhaps the grapes may be omitted when there is little space. Despite these misgivings, I am strongly inclined to read the combination as *u cuch haab*, "the burden of the year."

Little success can be reported in positively identifying these and other glyphs of action, but the suggestion made here, I believe, for the first time that these glyphs describe the influences of the various gods on the affairs of earth and heaven provides a new approach to the solution of this oburate problem.

AUGURAL GLYPHS

The final glyphs in compartments of almanacs in the codices are, I feel reasonably sure, records of the luck of the day in question or the object which will benefit or suffer on the assigned day. A number of the glyphs, which I call augural, are illustrated (fig. 43,33–36,38–48,50–52, 56–70); below are brief discussions of some of them.

Evil Glyph (fig. 20,3,7). This glyph almost invariably occurs in sections in which God A (the death god) or his comrade in malignity, the God of number 10 (God Q) are represented either pictorially or glyphically, usually in both media. This association is so close that the sign has at times been confused with that of God A, but they are distinct. Gates (1931, p. 127) first identified it as "a determinative of the 'evil' force active," although he did not carry this identification a step forward, and recognize the evil force as the luck of the day. Beyer (1929) saw in the glyph the head of a dog; I (Thompson, 1939, p. 175) believed its prototype to be a monkey with death symbols. Whatever may be the position in the animal kingdom of this impish creature, there is no doubt concerning its connection with death, for it wears the collar with death eyes which is one of the most prominent and constant attributes of God A. In the glyph the black infix is prominent. Although this infix might refer to the color of the creature, as Beyer supposed, it can just as well symbolize the underworld, the land of death.

The monkey, for I think the simian features of this figure with its crest and 3-shaped design on the temple (Thompson, 1939, p. 145) are undeniable, symbolizes one aspect of evil, that of licentiousness. Furthermore, there are several words in Yucatec signifying rogue or ruffian into which the word *maax*, "spider monkey," enters. Whether the monkey could symbolize all forms of evil and misfortune is another matter.

The two Yucatec words which appear most likely to translate this glyph are *kaz* or *kazal* and *lob*. *Kaz* as an adjective means "bad," "perverse," "stupid," "useless," "roguish," and "mean, vile, or despicable." For *kazal*, the

noun derived therefrom, the same meanings apply. *Lob*, the adjective, and *lobil*, the substantive formed from it, have the same general range of meaning. *Lob* is used very extensively in the divinatory almanacs of the books of Chilam Balam to denote that a day was evil, in contrast to *utz*, "good." However, in Perez I, which is the least European of these almanacs (p. 297), the word *kaz* appears several times, usually in combination with *lob*, or as a negative: *utz, ma kazi*, "good, not evil." I rather favor *kaz* as the equivalent of this glyph, because it has a homonym which modifies the following term, and has a meaning equivalent to our "somewhat." This secondary usage is discussed below. The glyph can be rendered "misery."

Death Glyph (fig. 20,4–6). This glyph is easily recognizable as a symbol of death because of the closed eye, and the death-eye prefix (p. 189). Moreover, there is a symbolic form in which the percentage sign, a common attribute of the death god, replaces the skull. This has generally been regarded as a name glyph of the god of death, which in a sense it is, but the death god has his regular name glyph (figs. 13,14; 42,9,16), whereas the element under discussion frequently appears in augural passages from which the death god is absent, or it follows the glyph of the god of death. This would indicate that the sign must be a general sign for death rather than a specific designation of "hell's grim tyrant." A ritualistic expression for death in Yucatan is *multun tzek*, "heap of skulls," which is used to designate mass death as a result of plague or war or drought. One wonders whether this glyph could represent that term, for it is certainly used in passages where the glyph for drought also occurs (figs. 61,4), for the skull (*tzek*) is certainly present. Could the little pyramid of three dots in the postfix represent the heap, *multun*? Whether or not we are justified in accepting the definite tag *multun tzek* for this glyph, there can be no doubt that it represents widespread mortality.

The three dots in a triangle also occur as a postfix with the Imix, "abundance," glyph (fig. 46,2) for which a translation such as "heaped-up abundance" would not come amiss.

Good Glyph (figs. 43,33,34; 61,2,5). It is obvious that if we have correctly identified one glyph as a sign for evil, *kaz*, there should be a glyph denoting its opposite, good tidings. I think this is the dog-ear glyph, almost always with a coefficient of 3. The main element is the form for Oc used in the codices; the postfix is a sign which just possibly has the value *ak* (p. 282). The coefficient is probably not to be read as numerical, for *ox*, "three," has a secondary use, that of emphasizing or intensifying something, and is roughly equivalent to our use of "very." Thus *ox kanan* is something very necessary; *ox kaz ol* is a person who is vehemently lascivious; *ox numya* is miserable, presumably a more acute form of misery than is covered by *numya; ox tezcuntah,* "thrice hail," is a form of salutation. Other examples appear in the books of Chilam Balam. In English we have a similar use of thrice: "Happy, thrice happy are they, whom God hath doubled his spirit upon, and given a double soul unto to be poets" (Thomas Nashe, *The Unfortunate Traveller*). A monument in Salisbury Cathedral speaks of "that thrice worthie Lady Walsingham."

The dog-ear glyph occurs nearly a hundred times in the codices, almost invariably in favorable contexts, either with the glyph of gods who are generally well disposed toward man, such as Gods B, E, and K, or above their pictures. It is never found in association with a glyph or picture of the death god. Once, however, on Madrid 89d, it is juxtaposed to the glyph of God Q, but that sign occurs in this same position in six of the seven compartments of this almanac, and clearly has to do with the subject of the divination. The deity depicted in this compartment is the black god, God M, who is on the whole beneficent. In 19 texts the 3 Oc glyph is associated with the Kan-Imix compound (p. 271), and in a dozen others there are other associations with maize. The Ahaulil glyph (fig. 43,*36;* this page) is found with the 3 Oc glyph in 15 compartments, and if the identification I propose for the Ahaulil glyph, namely "rule," is correct, the combination of this glyph and the 3 Oc symbol probably signifies "His rule is very good, very favorable." Generally, the 3 Oc glyph appears in contexts which concern rain, crops, or agriculture, where *och,* "sustenance," would fit.

A few occurrences in texts apparently unconnected with food make an identification of the glyph as a sign of abundance less probable. It would appear, therefore, that we are dealing with a symbol of general good cheer. The corresponding word that first comes to mind is *utz,* "good," which is used throughout the divinatory almanacs of the books of Chilam Balam to designate lucky days. However, I must confess that I have not been able to recover any link connecting *utz* or any of its synonyms with dog. Furthermore, the expression *ox utz* is not apparently used.

There is one case where this glyph is combined with the sign for evil (fig. 43,*35*), and another in which the same combination occurs but with the *ox* element omitted. Both of these are in the almanac which stretches from Dresden 65a to 69a. The identification of the evil glyph as *kaz* has been suggested above, but in addition to its general meaning of evil, *kaz* can be used also as a modifier, corresponding roughly to our "rather" or "somewhat." The Motul dictionary cites as examples *kaz calan,*

"a little drunk," and *kaz takan,* "half roasted." Such a meaning would fit this use, indicating that the luck of the day was half-way good.

Ahaulil Glyph (fig. 43,*36*). This, perhaps, is not truly an augural glyph, but it occurs very frequently in connection with what I take to be auguries. It is discussed at this point because of the reference to it in a preceding paragraph. The glyph consists of the day sign Ahau with the so-called knife element as a prefix and suffix. It is a very common symbol, occurring over 100 times in the codices. It has been generally accepted as a second name glyph of God D (Schellhas, 1904, p. 22), but it appears in many contexts which have nothing to do with that god, and not infrequently it is the last glyph of a text, following those which I assume to be augural.

There is a term in Yucatec, *ahaulil,* which signifies "rule, reign," and is both a noun and a verb. This is clearly the word Ahau, "ruler," with the addition of *lil; il* is the termination often added to form abstract nouns. It is, of course, possible that the inventors of the glyph used a slightly different word (Manche Chol has *ahaoilia,* "pity," which is probably the same root), and on the strength of this one glyph we should not be fully justified in translating the affixes as *il.* There are, however, a number of cases where such an identification works well. For example, the glyph of the death god has this affix (fig. 42,*9,16*); *cimil* is "death" and Yum Cimil, "Lord of death," is a name of that god. The element also occurs in the glyph of the maize god, whose Yucatec name is not surely known, but may be Ah Uaxac-Yol-Kauil, "He-eight-heart-of-food" (Roys, 1949), perhaps named also Kauil. The identification of the affix as the sign for *il* is demonstrated by its use with the drought glyph (see below).

Naturally, the ahaulil glyph could be construed with the glyph of the supreme God D, or could be read with augural glyphs, as suggested above, "his rule is good."

Drought Glyphs (figs. 43,*57–60,63;* 64,*1*). The usual term in Yucatec for a year of drought is *kintunyaabil.* Glyphs for each of the first three syllables, *kin, tun, haab* (the *y* is a change to denote relationship) are known, and the affix for *il* has been tentatively identified. Since a combination of these four elements occurs in contexts where a reference to drought would not be out of place, we can be reasonably sure of the correctness of the identification.

There runs across Dresden 42c–45c (fig. 61,*1–4*) an almanac divided into four sections of 65 days apiece. Each section is referred to a world direction; God B is depicted in all four. There is a column of six explanatory glyphs with each section. The directional glyph and that of God

B appear near the head of each column; augural glyphs at the bottom. The arrangement is as follows:

Page	Picture	Direction	Augural Glyphs
42	God B attacks maize (hail?)	South	Maize god; drought glyph
43	God B in canoe	East	3 Oc; maize seed; Kan-Imix
44	God B and unidentified god	North	Maize god; partly obliterated, but surely Kan-Imix
45	God B above fallen deer	West	Maize god; drought glyph; death sign

It will be noted that the glyph for year of drought appears with the sections assigned to south and west, but these are precisely the directions connected with droughts, for Landa tells us that in Cauac and Ix years, which were associated with south and west respectively, droughts were expected. On the other hand, the glyphs associated with the east, a direction connected with favorable harvests, are favorable. The first is the 3 dog-ear symbol, identified above as the sign of good tidings; the next glyph is that of maize seed; and the last is apparently the Kan-Imix sign, a symbol of abundance. Unfortunately the augural glyph for the north (p. 44) is obliterated, but enough of the prefix remains to make it virtually certain that it is the Kan-Imix sign (cf. fig. 43,48). Abundance is to be expected from the north. The *kintunyaabil* glyph in both cases consists of a small kin over a small cauac sign, with a larger tun sign over the postfix tentatively identified as the sign for *il*.

One of the two pictures illustrating the times of drought shows God B, axe in hand, attacking the cowed maize god; the other shows the same god above a prostrate deer. The Yucatec word *baat* signifies both axe and hail, and stone axes of the old times are called by their finders, the present-day Maya, *baat chac,* "axes of Chac," and are believed to be thunderbolts which the Chacs hurl to earth during storms. The first picture can, accordingly, be read with some confidence as giving the cause of the drought, namely destruction of the maize crop by hail and storms.

The second illustration accompanying the time of drought depicts God B above a prostrate deer. One is instantly reminded of the Maya expression *cim-cehil,* "when the deer die," a set phrase to indicate drought (Roys, 1933, p. 122). I think it is reasonable to see in this illustration a portrayal of that term for drought. This, then, supplies a good instance of the illustration supplementing or paralleling the glyphs, not the glyphs explaining the picture. The glyphs inform us straightforwardly that there will be drought (*kintunyaabil*); the picture depicts *cim-cehil,* "death of deer," a metaphor for drought. Similarly, in the other section, the glyph announces drought; the picture tells us that it will be caused by hail and storm damage to the crops.

The same drought glyph, but without postfix, appears on Dresden 40b, above a picture of a macaw holding a flaming torch in each hand. According to Lizana, a macaw personified the sun at midday; a macaw with torches in both hands might, therefore, well symbolize burning drought. The same compound appears again on Dresden 72c, where it is the first of three glyphs. The second is the maize sign but without the usual affix, the third is the glyph for evil (fig. 46,5). Surely these three together read, "Lengthy drought. Evil for the maize, or the maize crop is bad." Another appearance is on Dresden 71b, where it is followed by the Kin-Akbal glyph and that of maize seed. The whole perhaps reads: "Lengthy drought. Time of darkness. Maize seed."

The glyph is present on three of the pages in Dresden dealing with the ceremonies at the change of years. On page 27c (Akbal years) it again appears with the affix in a text which includes the glyph for west and the death god, whose picture appears below (fig. 64,1). On page 26a (Etz'nab years) the postfix is lacking. The glyph is followed by the sign cuch haab, the whole reading "Lengthy drought is the burden of the year." On page 25c the glyph has a slightly different arrangement: the kin and cauac signs are above the tun sign, and the postfix is absent. The glyph is in the same line as the sign for east. The ceremonies are connected with the entry of Ben years.

There are certain difficulties in the assignment of these pages and directions. Seler and I have both suggested that certain glyphs have been transposed. I have previously (Thompson, 1937, pp. 213–26) assigned the Etz'nab years to the west, the Ben years to the north, and the Akbal years to the south, but no longer feel so certain that the years are correctly allotted. On the assumption that these identifications are justified, the drought years are correctly assigned to west and south. This leaves unexplained the glyph of the year of drought assigned to the Ben years or, more probably, the Uayeb ceremonies of the preceding years. Is it possible that the glyphs state that unless such and such a ritual is carried out there will be drought?

The glyph also appears on Dresden 37a, above a picture of God B, who is merely striding along. As this almanac deals with thunder and lightning, a prophecy of drought is not out of place. On Paris 11, middle right, there is a partly obliterated glyph consisting of a kin and obliterated element above a cauac sign with *il* postfix. Perhaps we are justified in restoring the missing element as the tun sign. This page corresponds to a Katun 10 Ahau of which Chumayel says, "Lengthy drought is the burden of the katun." The accompanying glyphs on this page of Paris are largely evil.

Dresden 72c, fourth column, comprises three glyphs (fig. 46,6). This is a part of an almanac which appears to deal with rain and drought. This compartment, corresponding to 4 Manik, clearly holds ominous portents. The first glyph is a kin sign with brilliance prefix (p. 147) and with the number 3 attached. Here again, 3 must be read not numerically but as a superlative, giving to the whole glyph the meaning "intensely brilliant sun." There follow the tun sign with *il* postfix and, below, the kin and winged cauac. I think that it is not overly rash to assume that the four elements must be read together as *kintunyaabil,* despite the inverted sequence. The whole text would then be translatable as "intensely brilliant sun; severe drought." There are also occurrences of the kin and winged cauac combination on Madrid 21d–22d, but without the tun sign. Perhaps in those cases the winged cauac is to be read as *tun: kintun,* "drought," but not necessarily so severe or of such duration. There may be an example of the *kintunyaabil* glyph in Madrid 37, column C17. The *tun* and *il* postfix are clear; the details of the elements which should correspond to *kin* and *haab* (above) are rubbed, but what remains does not contradict this identification. The page deals with Ix years, when drought was expected, and the signs for evil and sun immediately precede the glyph in question.

So far as I know, there are no other examples of this *kintunyaabil* glyph. However, there is an example of a combination of kin and tun which should likewise represent *kintun. Kintunyaabil* is a drought affecting the whole year; *kintun* should, therefore, denote drought in general, without specifying the duration of its effect. A tun sign above a kin composes one of the glyphs on Madrid 34, which deals with Cauac years (fig. 43,64). These were assigned to the south and were expected to bring drought.

Glyphs for Seed and Seed Plot and Maize Seed (fig. 43,40–43). The main element has in the middle of the cartouche a small circle or oval, from which one line rises vertically to the top of the cartouche, while a second joins the circle to the base. Occasionally these lines are somewhat wavy, suggesting that the straight stroke developed to save time in writing. Prefixed to this there is an element which is the distinguishing feature of the maize god, and which I designate *te* (3), for there is good evidence that this affix has the phonic value *te* (p. 285). If this prefix is absent, the *te* (2) element is generally postfixed, but sometimes both affixes are missing.

There are four reasons for believing that this glyph has the general meaning of seed: (1) It is very frequently attached to the caban glyph, the sign for earth (fig. 43, 38,39). (2) In one example what is almost certainly a young maize plant, but in any case a plant of some kind, is sprouting from its top (fig. 43,43). (3) In very many instances the *te* (3) element, which is set in the head of the god of maize and vegetation and is his most important attribute in the codices, is prefixed or *te* (2) is postfixed. Both these elements have a vegetal connotation. (4) The glyph occurs in many contexts where agricultural activities are under discussion. Note, for example, its appearance in the divinatory almanac which deals with the newly planted maize on Madrid 26d–27d, where, however, the vertical lines are omitted. Mark, also, its frequency in the various almanacs on Dresden 71–73, dealing with weather (rain, drought, dark days etc.).

Although one could scarcely recognize the derivation of the glyph without confirmatory evidence, the circle with its two lines (one rising, the other descending) is a natural picture of germination. The one line could represent the developing stalk of the plant; the other, the root. Beyer (1928b) has identified this glyph as that of the *yaxche* (ceiba tree), but I do not consider that thesis sustainable. Indeed, the *yaxche* glyph has been identified (p. 58).

Pakal is the Yucatec term for sowing or seed; *pakalte* is seed plot. The question arises as to whether the *te* affixes are to be taken as indicating that the seed is maize or whether they translate the suffix *te* in *pakalte. Te* (3) is invariably prefixed and never appears when the *caban,* "earth," is adjoined; *te* (2) is invariably postfixed, and is used only when the caban sign is present (joined or in the preceding space). I think, therefore, that there can be little doubt that *te* (2) postfixed to the seed glyph converts it from *pakal* to *pakalte,* the caban sign serving to reinforce the meaning. Moreover, as *te* (3) is the symbol of the maize god *par excellence* and is never postfixed to the seed glyph, it presumably indicates that the seed in question is maize. *Pakalte* from the sixteenth century onward has signified the vegetable-seed plot as opposed to the milpa (*col*), but I think that glyphically its use must have covered both vegetable plot and milpa, unless *pakal* with *te* (3) prefix stood for milpa. Alternatively, the glyph by itself indicates seed; with the caban element, milpa.

Abundance of Maize (fig. 43,46–48). This sign consists of a combination of those for Kan and Imix. The Kan sign definitely represents maize; Imix is a sign of abundance (p. 72). The combination occurs in contexts which indicate benevolence. As already noted (p. 269), the sign for good luck, the 3 dog-ear glyph, not infrequently appears in the same passages as the glyph for abundance of maize. The latter is written thrice on Madrid 35, which deals with Kan years, which were believed to bring excellent crops, but it also appears three times on page 37, which is devoted to the Ix years during which drought was to be expected. Perhaps these occurrences refer to the possibility of changing drought into abundance by the required ceremonies to avert calamity, reported by Landa for some years. In the corresponding section of Dresden the sign occurs with the pages depicting the ceremonies prefatory to the Ben, Lamat, and Etz'nab years, which I have suggested correspond to north, east, and west. The first two were regarded as years of good crops; an Etz'nab year should be one of drought. Again, influences may have counteracted the general prognosis, for a straight average of two years of drought in four reflects extreme pessimism. Yucatan could not have flourished on such a record.

Dresden 27, which deals with the Akbal years, supplies some confirmation of the suggested identification. The top third of each of these four pages shows an animal carrying on his back a burden, which appears to be the burden or luck of the year. These drawings appear to supplement pictorially what is expressed glyphically above, for on each page the augural glyph and the cuch haab glyph are juxtaposed. The burden of page 27 is the maize god (fig. 64,1). Above, the burden glyph is adjacent to the Kan-Imix sign. If the suggested association of the glyphs with the pictures is correct, "abundance of maize is the burden" is a logical translation for these two glyphs, relating them to the picture of the maize god as the burden immediately below.

Maize God Symbol (fig. 43,44,45). Eight is the number of the maize god (p. 134). On Copan I, C6a, the coefficient of 8 is enclosed within an oval topped with a symbol of the young maize plant (figs. 13,1,2; 25,53). We have noted (p. 269) that a possible name for the maize god in Yucatan was Ah Uaxac-Yol-Kauil, "He-eight-heart-of-food." When, therefore, we find in the codices an augural glyph formed of the number 8 enclosed in a circle and surmounted by the maize symbol from the headdress of the maize god (not a hand with pointing finger, as has been suggested), we can be reasonably sure that we are dealing with a symbol for maize or for its patron. This glyph appears seven times in the codices. Of its six occurrences in Dresden, four appear above pictures which show rain falling (pp. 36b, 39c, 67a, 68a), and which, therefore, may be regarded as favorable to maize. In the first two of these cases the glyph seemingly replaces the normal Kan—maize symbol—for it follows the Imix glyph in one case and is combined with it in the other. On Dresden 65a, the sign follows the kin glyph, perhaps indicating the affect of excessive sun on the growing maize; on page 37b it has the *te* (1) prefix in place of the maize symbol. The glyph appears once in Madrid, on the page (35) devoted to auguries for the Kan years, where

the suggested interpretation fits well, as Kan years were expected to bring abundant harvests.

Dark Day (fig. 43,50). This common glyph, consisting of a kin sign in combination with Akbal, could be construed as "day and night" or "dark day" or "time of darkness." At first thought the translation "day and night" would seem the most logical, but I am inclined to think the interpretation "dark day" is the most probable. The glyph appears with considerable frequency above pictures which are rain-swept, and apparently unaccompanied by any other glyph to indicate rain; often, the sign is followed by the Imix sign of abundance (but note its association with drought; p. 270). A translation "time of darkness" in the sense that the sky is dark with approaching storms fits the context somewhat better than "day and night." That *akab*, "night," can be used in this sense is shown by such phrases as *akab yeeb*, "dark mist," *akab u uich ha*, "dark, black water." The expression could also be followed by the drought glyph, as the Maya paid some attention to storms which produced no rain.

Sun Darkened, Moon Darkened (fig. 43,51,52). The so-called eclipse glyphs, consisting of a sun or moon disk set against a background half black and half white, probably have the general meaning of sun darkened and moon darkened, or sun amidst black and white clouds, although they could refer specifically to eclipses. In a number of contexts where these glyphs appear, eclipses are almost surely not the subject of discussion. In fact, their appearance in divinatory almanacs cannot possibly refer to actual eclipses, since these do not occur at intervals of 52 or 65 days (the usual grouping of days in those almanacs). However, rain is often shown in pictures which accompany these eclipse glyphs: on Dresden 74, which deals with the great flood, a stream of water flows from this glyph, and the same composition can be seen on Dresden 37c, 39c, 66a, and 68a and on Madrid 32a, 33a, 71a. On Dresden 45b, the so-called Mars beast, identified as a water-bringer (p. 258), hangs from the sky, and this glyph appears above (fig. 64,4). Similarly on Madrid 17b, Chac, the rain god, falls from the glyph under discussion. On Paris 23b–24b the sun disks figure in the so-called zodiacal band, for the sundry creatures grasp them in their open jaws; on pages 4, 5, and 10 of the same codex the glyph figures in the auguries for Katuns 11 Ahau, 9 Ahau, and 12 Ahau. I think that there can be little doubt that the glyphs refer to the darkened sun and the darkened moon, the context indicating whether that was because of eclipses, rain storms, or lightning storms.

Rainy Sky. Not infrequently the first glyph in the almanacs which deal with weather is a sky sign with three lines of drops falling from it. The sky sign is usually tilted (fig. 46,1,9). That this indicates rain descending from the sky can hardly be doubted, especially as the compartment below is often filled with falling water. Probably the cleft sky-glyph with water affixes, so frequent on the monuments (fig. 43,*17–23*), has the same meaning. In the codices an element with a pattern perhaps representing thatch or turtle shell (a constellation?) can also be combined with the curving lines of drops to represent falling rain (Dresden 73c, cols. 2, 4).

Tentative Translations of Passages in Codex Dresden

There is a considerable body of augural glyphs in addition to those briefly treated above. I do not purpose to discuss these at the present time, for my intention has been to outline a more than probable structure of presentation and to illustrate it with typical examples of the glyphs; but to indicate how they function I give below a tentative translation of the augural glyphs of the seven compartments of Dresden 72c, and two of 71c (fig. 46,*1–9*), reserving, however, the right to change my mind on interpretations at any future date. Dubious interpretations are followed by one query mark; sheer guesses are marked by two query marks; elements apparently not represented in the glyphs are in brackets; sequence is right to left; semicolons divide translations of glyphs.

9. Raining sky; God *n;* his wind.
8. White wind (?); maize seed; evil tun.
7. Good tidings; of maize seed; its growth (??).
6. Intensely brilliant sun; severe drought.
5. Severe drought; [for] maize; its evil.
4. Maize year (?); evil; [for] the maize god.
3. ??; ??; relative to the tun.
2. Cloud-darkened days; great heaped-up abundance (?); seed in the earth, or in the milpa.
1. Raining sky; God *n;* his wind.

In Compartment 2 I have translated the second glyph as "great heaped-up abundance." *Chac,* "red," corresponding to the prefix, can mean both "red" and "giant" or "much"; I have preferred the second meaning. The postfix is the same as that which we found in the death glyph, and for which I suggested the tentative translation of "heap," and that meaning seems to fit the case here. For Compartment 3 I can not offer any translation, but for the others I feel reasonably confident that the general sense has been rendered. Roys calls my attention to the fact that *zac ik,* "white wind" (Compartment 8), is listed in Motul as a term for wind. There is little doubt that the composer of the dictionary got his lines mixed here, for he adds the world directions against the four entries of this term, but has them badly mixed both in Maya and in the translations. In Compartment 8 the literal translation of the compound would be *kaztunil;* the *tun* element might have an intensifying value as in

kintun, and have nothing to do with the 360-day tun.

In conclusion, I shall rehearse the section (Dresden 42c–45c) already discussed (fig. 61,*1–4*), giving as far as possible a free translation:

42c. 4 Ahau, etc. God B is set (??) to the south. The maize god [suffers from] prolonged drought.

43c. 4 Chicchan, etc. God B is set (??) to the east. Very good [for] the maize seed. Abundance of maize.

44c. 4 Oc, etc. God B stands (??) set (??) to the north. The maize god. Abundance of maize.

45c. 4 Men, etc. God B is set (??) to the west. The maize god [suffers from] prolonged drought. General death.

The only translations of which I am doubtful are the renderings "is set" and "stands." Those are sheer guesses, but the general meanings of the two glyphs in question can not be far removed from those suggested. The words in brackets are supplied to clarify the meaning.

There is a certain forthrightness in these texts which I deem to be in keeping with the Maya spirit. Drought and plenty are duly noted; adjectives or exclamations of woe or joy are not added in a string of glyphs. Moderation in all things. One is reminded of what Gilbert Murray has said of Greek literature, "It is all so normal and truthful; so singularly free from exaggeration, paradox, violent emphasis. . . ."

GLYPHIC GROUPS

A glyphic group or family consists of a varying number of complete glyphs, main elements, components of main elements used chiefly as affixes, or components of affixes, which are related either because they form a synonymous or near-synonymous family, or because they convey closely related ideas. Synonymous and near-synonymous glyphs or elements can be substituted for one another in some cases or in all cases, but not all the elements of a family are necessarily interchangeable. Interchangeability probably depended partly on meanings, partly on custom. Thus the jade water symbol can replace the *xoc,* "count," element, but the reverse is not the case. The glyph of the day Eb (mist, dew, frost) consists of a sign for death combined with one for water, presumably to indicate that mists and dew were regarded as baleful because they were believed to cause smut on the maize; the two elements together indicate destructive water (p. 81). However, the water element is always the same infix, the curve surrounded with circlets. So far as one can judge, any one of a dozen aquatic symbols could have served as this infix, but for reasons of clarity or because of tradition only the one symbol was used.

In assigning glyphs to groups I have been governed largely by interchangeability. Thus, if two or three elements could be substituted one for another without any apparent change in the meaning, I have placed them in the same group. This procedure is not without danger, for one runs the risk of designating as synonymous, elements which vary in meaning. For instance, had not the functions of the anterior and posterior date indicators been known, there would have been a distinct chance that their variable elements would have been classed as synonyms. The same might have been true of the postfixes of period glyphs, for until recently no one had realized that the postfix alters according to the manner in which the period glyphs are employed (p. 160). This danger has been guarded against as far as possible by seeking confirmation in more than one glyph of the interchangeability of any two elements.

The glyphic groups are not compact or closely knit; rather, they are of an amorphous character. Some elements form subgroups, the components of which tend to keep themselves apart from the rest of the family, perhaps with one member of the subgroup bridging the gap to the main group. The kan cross–yax–Chicchan–shell series, for instance, forms a subgroup in the water group. The shell element also appears in the underworld group, and there are other elements linking the water and underworld groups.

In bringing small elements, such as curls, into the discussion one runs the danger of overlooking convergence or similarities in design. A simple curl, to cite one case, is often used as a water symbol, both glyphically and pictorially, but it is also used under certain circumstances as an element denoting maize, and it may also indicate flames or smoke.

Two glyphic groups are discussed below in detail.

WATER GROUP

This is a very large and complex group which involves a number of different elements, several of which are also used in other senses. The following are direct water symbols: jade, circle or part of a circle surrounded with circlets, the "bunch of grapes" of the cauac element, X, hook or spiral, the god of number 3, the Moan bird, the serpent, the kan cross, the yax symbol, and shells. Some of these emblems have other symbolic values. The shell, for instance, is also a symbol of the underworld and night; the spiral and three dots seemingly can represent fire in some contexts.

Jade Symbol. This has already been discussed (p. 49). Jade is the precious substance, water, and is intimately associated with rain in Mexican mythology and probably in that of the Maya, too. Jade disks adorn the glyph for water in the codices (fig. 14,*3,5*) and frequently appear on the bodies of snakes (fig. 14,*6*) and of celestial dragons, in the latter case often grouped in threes (fig. 15,*12*).

There is, of course, a secondary association of jade with water in the color of both. A simple disk, or part of a disk with two smaller disks attached thereto, forms the symbolic glyph for Muluc, the day "water" (fig. 8,*4–7, 9–16*). This element reappears, surrounded by cirlets, as the sign for Mol, which apparently means rain clouds (fig. 17,*14–22*), and it is also one of the elements of the tun sign. Tun, which means "jade," is the year of 360 days, another name for which is haab, "the rainy season." The winged cauac sign, which comprises several water symbols, is a variant which under certain circumstances replaces the tun sign, and enters into the composition of the multiples of the tun (katun, etc.). It almost certainly corresponds to the word *haab,* although the uses of haab in the books of Chilam Balam do not quite parallel those of the cauac glyph. The most usual head form of the tun sign is that of the Moan bird, which also symbolizes water (p. 275; fig. 20,*10,11*). There is accordingly full evidence identifying the Muluc symbol as *tun,* "jade," a ritualistic expression for water.

The jade sign has at least one secondary use, and probably more will be discovered. It is the symbolic form corresponding to the head of the *xoc* fish, which is used to illustrate the homonymous verb *xoc,* "to count," in the posterior and anterior date indicators (p. 162; fig. 30,*37–44*). It functions principally as a substitute for the head of the *xoc* fish when that is the main element of a glyph; it does not normally replace the fish head when that is used as an affix or prefatory glyph. In such cases the comb element is the corresponding symbolic form, but in a few instances the jade symbol replaces the fish or comb as an affix (fig. 2,*56*).

Cauac Elements. Cauac, the basis of the winged cauac used as a variant of the tun sign, corresponds in meaning to rainstorm. The elements of which it may be composed are "the bunch of grapes" usually pendent from the top of the cartouche; an oval, curl, or quarter-circle (in early examples) surrounded with circlets, an X (codices), a long hook (codices), the jade beads (?) enclosed within a curving line of dots or circlets (codices), and what may be an Ik sign rendered very cursively (fig. 10,*33–45*). The "bunch of grapes" and the oval curl or quarter-circle surrounded with circlets frequently appear as ornaments on the bodies of celestial dragons, which are rain monsters (fig. 15,*11–13*) or occur on the bodies of snakes (Madrid 14). The X is a frequent symbol on the bodies and the pendulous snouts of snakes or celestial monsters, so plentiful on the facades of buildings in Yucatan. Indeed, the lattice motif of Puuc architecture is merely serried X's which adorn the body of the celestial monster (Seler, 1917, pl. 5). The snouts of these monsters are usually decorated with alternating X's and jade disks

(Seler, 1917, pl. 7*a*) and the same design appears on the supraorbital plate of feathered serpents (Morris, Charlot, and Morris, 1931, fig. 8). The long hook is probably an exaggeration of the earlier curl.

Whether some of these sundry elements are supposed to represent the markings on the bodies of snakes or celestial crocodiles and dragons or whether they were added to stress the pluvial character of those saurians, realistic or imaginative, does not much matter, for snakes and dragons were very intimately connected with rain and water in the conceptions of the Maya and all their neighbors (Thompson, 1939, pp. 152–61; 1943f).

Moan Bird. The Moan bird, a variety of owl, serves as the glyph for the month of Muan, which means showery weather. The Moan is without much doubt the bird perched on top of the celestial serpents (fig. 20,*10,11,17*). This bird with the flesh removed from its lower jaw is the usual head variant for the tun sign. There is a symbolic variant in Dresden for the month Muan, the main element of which is a curl which here presumably represents water (fig. 20,*18*). In one case, according to Miss Hunter's drawing, the Muan sign has a kan cross in its eye (Maudslay, 1889–1902, vol. 2, pl. 31), although the photograph is not sufficiently clear to confirm this. A representation of the Moan bird at Tikal has the Chicchan diagonal lines beneath its mouth; one at Copan has a triangle of dots in the same position (fig. 20,*10,17*). All of these are water symbols. The owl is intimately associated with the rain gods in the art of classical Teotihuacan (Armillas, 1945, pp. 10–12), thereby supplying yet more evidence for its pluvial rôle in the cosmology of Middle America. Through substitution the Moan owl is linked to the cauac and tun symbols of rain, and also to the spiral.

Serpent God of Number 13 (figs. 25,*9,10,14;* 28,*15*). The head of this creature sometimes replaces that of the Moan bird as the head variant of the tun glyph; in such cases to assure its identification the head is frequently surmounted by the tun sign (figs. 27,*28,30–33;* 28,*16,17;* other examples are on Copan I, K, 23, and HS; Quirigua E and Alt O and P; and Palenque HS).

On the Leiden plaque, on Quirigua B and Alt O, and on Copan HS this head is attached to the body of a snake. It has already been shown that this serpent or dragon is the god of the number 13, whose day is Muluc, "water" (p. 136). He is therefore a logical choice as a head variant of tun, which means jade, the precious water.

Kan Cross. This is the symbol which denotes the color yellow, but the glyph is frequently used in contexts where there is no reason to suppose any reference to that color. Furthermore, it is interchangeable with a number of elements which do not refer to yellow. Indeed, one of the

elements for which it can be substituted is yax, which signifies, among other things, a color; but that color is blue-green, not yellow. Kan is the Yucatec word for yellow, but it has various homonyms, among which is the root *kan*, "precious, highly esteemed or necessary." *Kanan* is a thing which is precious or highly esteemed or necessary; *kanan hal* and *kanan cunah* are verbal compounds with the same meanings, and *kan* is also the name for the beads used as money in Yucatan. The Motul dictionary gives one the impression that usually they were of stone, but from other sources we learn that they were normally of shell. The question arises whether these beads were called *kan* because they were precious or because they were of a yellowish hue. The shell apparently held in highest esteem by the Maya was *Spondylus princeps,* an inhabitant of the Pacific coast of Central America. This figures in Mendoza as tribute paid to the Aztec; numerous finds of *Spondylus princeps,* usually as containers for jade and other jewelry, in votive caches in the Maya area attest to the high esteem in which it was held (Boekelman, 1935, pp. 262–66). The outside of *Spondylus princeps* is a coral pink to deep red, but, according to Boekelman, there is a yellowish species of *Spondylus* which occurs on the Atlantic coast of Middle America. However, we have a definite statement that *kan* beads were red (Relaciones de Yucatan, 11:183). Lopez de Cogolludo and the Relacion de Valladolid speak of the beads used as currency (apart from jade) as being red; Lopez de Gomara, writing of the Peten, says necklaces of reddish pink shells were highly esteemed. The term *kan* can also apply to vermilion, but there is no reason why the Maya should have called red beads yellow. Accordingly, I think there is not much doubt that these beads were called *kan* because they were precious.

We have seen that the Maya used the glyph for jade to represent water because jade was the most precious substance they had, and water was the precious thing. That *kan*, "precious," may have likewise been a symbol for water is therefore not an unwarranted supposition. In reality, there is much evidence which converts the supposition into certainty.

In the Zapotec glyphs and in the art of classical Teotihuacan this kan cross is quite frequently worn in the headdresses of the rain gods (Caso, 1928, fig. 21; Armillas, 1945, pp. 17–18). The kan cross is prominent on the cheek of the only head variant of the day sign Muluc, "water" (fig. 8,*8*). It is a constant feature of the month glyphs Pop and Kayab, and the only obvious link between these two is that both represent objects connected with water, namely, reed mat and turtle. In a portrait of the old earth god on Dresden 37a, the kan cross is plainly drawn on the object on his back, which from other illustrations of that god we know to be a conch shell. This same cross is frequently set on or in streams of what appear to be water (fig. 44,3,4; Spinden, 1912, fig. 84a). It is also found sometimes on the forehead of a terrestrial monster; a good example of this is the head from which the maize plant grows on the Tablet of the Foliated Cross, Palenque (fig. 45,7). This reptile, of which Spinden (1924, p. 165) shows several examples, is often preceded by the number 7 (fig. 45,8). The creature is clearly a saurian or draconian monster, not improbably the earth monster itself, and perhaps the same as Ah Uuc-ti-Cab, "Lord seven earth," mentioned in the Ritual of the Bacabs. On the Tablet of the Sun, Palenque, he has as a water symbol the jade glyph surrounded with circlets, before his forehead; at Copan and Yaxchilan he appears with a variant of the Imix sign on his head (fig. 12,1,2). This earth monster is almost surely the crocodile which in Mexican belief floated in primeval waters, bearing on his back the world. His associations are with the earth, the underworld, fertility, vegetation, and water (pp. 70–71). The kan (precious) cross is therefore a logical attribute, stressing his connection with water and the production of food. See important change of opinion, page 252.

Interchangeability of Elements. In several glyphs there is an elbow-shaped prefix, clearly a water symbol as it is outlined with circlets, at the top of which there may be one of several elements, namely, the kan cross, the completion symbol, what may be a conventionalized shell, the Chicchan sign, and what may be a bone element. Among glyphs which take this prefix are the head of God C (fig. 43,1,3,6), the bat head with "Ben-Ich" superfix (fig. 43,9,10,12,14–16) the cleft-sky sign with "Ben-Ich" superfix (fig. 43,17–19,22), and the Kankin-on-side glyph. It is fairly clear that these elements can replace one another without in any way affecting the meaning. Sometimes the whole of this prefix is replaced with a jade symbol surrounded with dots, the whole being like a Mol sign, usually on its side (fig. 43,5,25,26,30,31). In other glyphs the yax prefix (Chicchan sign) is substituted (fig. 43,4,11,19,20,24) and in at least two cases the head of God Nine, the Chicchan god, replaces the yax symbol, of which it is an elaboration (figs. 3,7; 31,51). The connections of these sundry elements with water are discussed below.

The kan cross is joined to the cauac glyph in all five sections of the almanac on Madrid 22c (fig. 41,68). The only picture is the vulture, often associated with rain, set in a blue frame, and as the tidings in all sections seem to be good, it is a reasonable assumption that the kan-cauac glyph means something like precious storm (i.e. storm bringing precious rain), and does not refer to the color yellow. The same glyph with a prefix appears on

Madrid 21d, above a picture of the maize god. It is followed by the glyphs of the maize god and of abundance.

Very frequently the kan cross is joined to the yax-Chicchan prefix (fig. 45,13,14). Usually there is what resembles the number 2 above the compound, but it should be noted that there is always a cross between the two dots, whereas fillers are not commonly used with numbers in the codices. Furthermore, on Madrid 92a, the glyph with two dots and two crosses above it has a regular coefficient of 7 to the left. Accordingly, it is to be doubted that this superfix has numerical value. The glyph conceivably might denote the green precious thing, water. The two elements of which it is compounded appear together on what one supposes to be falling water (fig. 44,3) and serve as affixes interchangeable under certain conditions. On the other hand, the glyph appears above a shallow dish in Dresden 27b, as a new-year offering. Water is hardly an appropriate offering and is not likely to have been poured into a shallow dish. Another difficulty in regard to this compound lies in the fact that a kin sign replaces the kan sign in all four of the legible examples in Madrid, but in view of the careless and inaccurate manner in which this codex is drawn, it is not an unwarranted assumption that the kin element is due to the scribe's ignorance. The compound is in the hand of the principal figure of Seibal 3. The affix might be a numerical dot between two crescents, but is probably nonnumerical.

In an addition, made since this book went to press (p. 252), I have suggested that the kan cross may signify blue and, by extension, turquoise, hence water, "the blue-green, or precious thing." In that case this compound might mean jade and turquoise.

Not infrequently, snakes in Maya sculpture are decorated with the yax-Chicchan sign, the zero sign, the kan cross, or "shell" signs (fig. 44,6–8). In one case the body of the snake consists of linked yax-Chicchan signs (fig. 44,5); in other cases the reptilian markings consist of the pairs of slanting strokes of Chicchan set between jade disks (figs. 13,15; 28,17). In representation of what is apparently falling water most of these symbols recur (fig. 44,1–4).

The piers of the front of Room D of the Palace, Palenque, are of some importance in connection with the associations of these motifs. The first (a) is entirely gone, and of the last (g) one can only say that it carried a hieroglyphic inscription. The central designs of the preserved pillars are of interest, for they show pairs of individuals, one of whom holds a snake or axe (symbols of rain and storms), standing on representations of water and the underworld (the snake-bodied god of 13 and water lilies); the designs are clearly related in subject matter. Each design is enclosed within a frame consisting of linked water symbols of kinds already discussed, namely, bone ornament (Pier b), zero (Pier c), yax (Pier d), kan cross (Pier e), and the bone design (Pier f) (fig. 45,2,3,5,11). All alternate with jade disks. Thus once again these symbols are shown to be very intimately related.

There are other places in which the zero sign is rather clearly to be read not as 0, but as a symbol for water. In examples of Glyph X2 of the lunar series three circles in a line can be substituted for the zero sign above the double line of circlets (fig. 36,3,8,17,27,37). The number 3 has an aquatic connotation, for the god of that number is a storm god. In Glyph X5 of the same series the head with hooked nose has aquatic insignia, which may take the form of the cauac element as headdress or prefix, the Mol element, a simple jade disk or the zero sign (figs. 36,63; 37,3,13,19,25,29). In view of the range of affixes of Kan when not used as a day sign, I suspect that the zero sign as its prefix should also be read as an aquatic symbol, not as 0 (fig. 11,51–57).

These various relationships are shown in Table 19.

(Maudslay, 1889–1902, vol. 4, pl. 34), day sign Ik, and probably infix in cauac element.

X Symbol. Cauac element (codices), heads (snouts and eyebrows) of snakes (Yucatan).

Three Circles in Triangular Arrangement. This occurs on bodies of dragons (fig. 15,12) in the eye of the Moan bird used as tun (fig. 27,36–39), on the forehead of the frog head of uinal, on the shell symbol used as period glyph (figs. 32,46–55; 33,15–20), and occasionally as an infix of the yax sign (fig. 41,60). Once it appears below the mouth of a Moan bird (fig. 20,17), and rarely it replaces the usual infix of the Chicchan sign (fig. 42,37). The old goddess who is shown in Dresden pouring water from a vessel similarly has three dots in her eye. This element, which is not always arranged as a triangle, must be treated with caution, as it sometimes appears as a fire symbol (fig. 43,53–55), presumably in imitation of the three stones of the hearth (Thompson, 1930, p. 93). As a postfix it may perhaps have the value of heap (p. 268). Aquatically, it may represent the god of number 3, who, as a deity of the storm, could represent not only rain but also the fire of lightning.

TABLE 19—RELATIONSHIPS OF VARIOUS WATER SYMBOLS

Symbol	Muluc	Date Indicator	All Tun Glyphs	Muan	Count Affix	Ben-Ich Zotz'-Cauac	Ben-Ich Sky	Ben-Ich Bone	God C	Snakes and Crocodiles	Falling Water	Piers, Palenque House D
Jade	X	X	X	..	X	X	..	X	X	X	..	X
Xoc fish	..	X	..	..	X	..	..	..	..	..	..	..
Circlets	..	..	X	..	..	X	X	X	X	X	X	..
Serpent God of 13	..	..	X	..	..	..	..	..	..	X	..	..
Kan Cross	X	..	..	X	..	X	X	X	X	X	X	X
Yax	..	..	..	..	..	X	X	..	X	X	X	X
Zero	..	..	..	..	..	..	..	..	X	X	X	X
"Shell" or "Bone"	..	..	..	..	..	X	X	X	..	X	..	X
Moan bird	..	..	X	X	..	..	..	..	..	X	..	..
Spiral	..	..	X	X	..	..	..	..	..	X	X	..
Grapes	..	..	X	..	..	..	..	..	..	X	..	..

OTHER WATER SYMBOLS

Other symbols which occur in connection with water and the extended uses of some of those listed above are:

T Symbol. God of number 3 (storm god), God B (rain god), serpent god of earth, god of number 13

Ring of Circlets. This element appears on the forehead of god of number 3, the god of storms (fig. 24,12,13,17), on the forehead of the uinal frog (fig. 27,44,49,50), and around the Mol glyph (fig. 17,14–22). All of these are directly connected with water.

Spiral. I believe that the spiral in the eye denotes an

animal with aquatic associations. It is a constant feature of Gods B and K, the Moan bird, Chicchan, and most snakes and crocodiles. The occasional appearance of the spiral in the eye of the sun god in the codices may, I think, be attributed to careless copying by scribes unaware of the significance of this mark; the sun god is generally given a squint. On the other hand, it is also possible that the spiral symbolized fire, as Beyer believed, although I am not inclined to attach much importance to that identification. An important point connecting the spiral with rain is that it can be substituted for the two diagonal strokes of Chicchan in the yax prefix as generally drawn in the codices (figs. 17,*12,46;* 41,*23,24,26,73–76*). The spiral is commonly set in water as an identifying symbol, both in Maya and Mexican art (fig. 20,*30–34*).

The Chicchan God. This deity is the god of number 9, as can be seen by the yax symbol often on his forehead (p. 135; figs. 24,*50–52,54;* 25,*32,34,35;* 55,*3*) or before him (fig. 25,*46,49*). The profile of this deity occasionally replaces the yax affix, as with the Copan variant of the glyph of the sun at the horizon (fig. 31,*51*), or with the bound sky (fig. 3,*7*). Had a Maya artist wished to be a little fanciful, he might have drawn the month sign Yaxkin as two heads, those of the Chicchan god of number 9 and the sun god of number 4, and the meaning would have been clear to any Maya priest of moderate intelligence and education, but such practice would not have been conducive to clarity, any more than if someone said "with the mercurial velocity of a courser he absented himself" when he merely wished to remark "he departed rapidly."

Section of Shell. The element which frequently serves as a prefix and is interchangeable with the kan and water symbols (fig. 43,*15,16,22*) I take to be a section of a shell, probably a conch, the dots corresponding to the knobs on the circumference of the shell. The crescent or oval or indented circle I assume to be the mouth of the conch. This may appear a bold identification, but it has already been made by other students. This element is best seen in the headdress of a deity of the earth who combines symbols of death with a kin sign on his forehead, good examples of which are to be seen at Palenque E, and on the ball-court markers and stelae at Copan (fig. 21,*14–17*). This headdress appears to be the attribute of the rear head of the double-headed dragon. It also serves as a glyph (fig. 21,*18*). Seler (1915, p. 93) brings together a large series of these headdresses and concludes that the element in question is a section of a shell comparable to the *oyoualli* of the Mexicans; Spinden (1924, fig. 8) illustrates a number of examples and also identifies them as shells. It will be noted that several show three or more knobs. In naturalistic representations of conch

shells these knobs are frequently depicted with some prominence (fig. 21,*4–7*). The conch shell, as we have already seen (p. 173), is an attribute of gods of the underworld because the conch is a symbol of water, and the surface of the world is the back of the Cipactli monster resting in water. However, this is a secondary association, for the primary association of the conch is with water. For this reason we find conch shells prominently displayed in the so-called temple of Quetzalcoatl at Teotihuacan, a temple which seems to have been dedicated, however, to Tlaloc (Armillas, 1945, p. 26). One of the attributes of Quetzalcoatl himself was the ornament made from a section of conch shell; this he may have worn because he was primarily a god of the fresh vegetation which appears when the rains come, or because of his visit to the underworld (p. 172). That this section of conch is usually a symbol of the underworld is demonstrated, I think, by its use as a decoration of gods connected with that region. For example, on the Tablet of the Sun, Palenque, it is prominently displayed by the two jaguar gods of number 7 seated on the earth band who, like Bacabs, sustain the crossed double-headed monster. Earplugs representing this shell ornament blend imperceptibly into the inverted Ahau and bone motifs and are typically worn by gods of the underworld. That this element has a direct connection with water is amply shown, I think, by the fact that streams of water frequently descend or ascend from the headdress of which it forms a part. The long-nosed god with coefficient of 9, who is so frequently paired with the similar god with coefficient of 7, invariably has this shell ornament in his headdress (Spinden, 1924, fig. 46), and he is without doubt a god of the earth intimately associated with the growth of vegetation.

I am inclined to identify the prefix of the month Cumku and probably also Glyph G8 as variants of this same element. It also appears as part of Glyph X of the lunar series in a form following Glyph C5 on the Foliated Cross, Palenque, and, probably on Copan 9, the lower part of the glyph being the same in both cases (fig. 37,*34,38*). The kan cross, with which the shell element is under certain circumstances interchangeable, appears twice as Glyph X following Glyph C6 (fig. 37,*47,50*).

These associations of the shell ornament with water explain why this element could be logically used in place of other water attributes, such as the jade symbols or the kan cross, as a prefix of several glyphs.

Flattened-U Ornament. What may be a simplification of the shell element (cf. the shell on fig. 21,*15*) or may have a quite different origin is a flattened-*u* ornament, to which Kidder, Jennings, and Shook (1947, p. 225) call attention in their description of Serpent X, and which they identify as the supraorbital plate. It may be a head-dress, however, in view of the various cases in which similar monsters have shells as headdresses. It is often elaborated with the addition of two circles into a fantastic Ahau, and merges with the bone motif and the shell (fig. 43,*15,25*). The deity who wears this emblem is almost certainly one of the earth monsters, for on occasions he is adorned with vegetation (fig. 12,*4;* Kidder, Jennings, and Shook, 1947, fig. 98). As a glyphic element this flattened *u* appears as a prefix, generally at the top of a water symbol, in a number of glyphs, and in that combination it is almost certainly interchangeable with the kan cross, yax sign, and shell ornament. From its close connection with serpents or crocodiles, it is a fair assumption that it served as an aquatic symbol, an assumption which is partly confirmed by its substitution for elements known to have aquatic values.

Bone Ornament. An element like an inverted Ahau with pinched sides and often a nick in the top of the head sometimes serves as an ornament set in the earplug (figs. 23,*19,20;* 27,*6,12,13,31,55–57*) or as a nasal ornament. On occasions, it is indistinguishable from an inverted Ahau; at other times it blends with the shell ornament. It has been called a bone ornament, and I retain the name although I am not sure that it was made of that material. It is a fairly common decoration of earth monsters and snakes (figs. 12,*2;* 44,*5–7;* Spinden, 1912, figs. 115*e-g,i,k,* 118*b*). It appears, but not inverted and in a form more definitely that of Ahau, on a leaf of the maize plant of the Tablet of the Foliated Cross, Palenque, balancing a kan cross on the opposite leaf (Maudslay, 1889–1902, vol. 4, pl. 81). I do not know whether the inverted Ahau and the simple "bone" ornaments are two distinct elements which tend to converge, or whether they are the same element with varying amounts of elaboration, but as decorative motifs they do seem to be interchangeable. Small inverted Ahaus, grouped in twos or threes, form a common postfix (fig. 2,*25,26,29–31*), and sometimes they thus appear beneath the heads of earth monsters (fig. 45,*7*). The inverted position may not be significant because on occasion the Ahau is right side up (fig. 12,*1*). Because of the elusiveness of this element, it is impossible to list its functions with any certitude, but I would hazard that it serves to denote aquatic or terrestrial associations. Examples which blend with the shell and flattened *u* and which can be substituted for regular aquatic symbols are to be seen in figure 43,*1–32*.

The Maya sculptor or scribe wishing to indicate the aquatic character of any glyph or sculptural element had a wide choice of elements. In theory he could use any or all of them; in practice he was restricted by questions of space and tradition, and need of avoiding confusion.

The question of secondary meanings had also to be taken into consideration. In some cases the reader might be uncertain whether a kan cross referred to yellow or was to be read as connoting water; in the texts there might be doubt as to whether the muluc variant of the jade symbol referred to precious water or was to be taken as the geometric form corresponding to *xoc,* "count." Thus rules of correct usage in composition must have been established with sufficient latitude to allow the writer his own style. These allowable variations have been in the past a stumbling block to decipherment of the glyphs, but there is no reason why they should not be used to our glorious advantage, once their various groupings are established.

Underworld Group

The group of attributes which distinguish deities and concepts associated with the underworld and the surface of the earth is pretty extensive. Whether these can be further divided into subgroups, assignable respectively to the interior of the earth and its surface, is rather doubtful, for I think the two concepts merged in Maya thought. Among the attributes which belong to this group may be listed: water lilies, maize foliage, conch shells, black, the hair set with eyes of the death god, the gods of numbers 5, 7, and 13, the dog, and certain symbols specifically attributable to the death god, namely, bones, the percentage sign, and three circlets in a row.

Water Lily. This symbol, as the probable derivation of the Imix glyph, has already been discussed at length (pp. 72–73). It has also been demonstrated that its most common wearer is the jaguar god, the god of the interior of the earth, corresponding to the Mexican Tepeyollotl, who is at the same time the god of number 7 (fig. 12,*12,14,15*). The water lily sometimes adorns the headdress of the old god of number 5, blending with maize foliage, although this is not very clear in the illustrations of the god of number 5 on figure 24. The snake god of the number 13 is usually adorned with water lilies; they are particularly prominent on the full-figure representation of the snake god of number 13 on the west side of Quirigua D (fig. 28,*15*). In other cases this deity's headdress may be the Imix glyph, presumed to be derived from the water lily (figs. 12,*1–2;* 40,*1–3*), or water lilies grow from the god's head (fig. 12,*4*). The death god as lord of the number 10 sometimes wears a lily dangling from his earplug. On the murals of Bonampak the dancers, apparently all aquatic or terrestrial deities, are decked with water lilies, as are the three chiefs wearing jaguar skins.

Maize Foliage. As noted, maize foliage is often mingled with water lilies in the adornment of personages connected with the earth. When the sun god goes underworld and becomes the night sun and the ninth lord of the night, his glyph is changed to denote his altered status by the addition of a prefix or an infix. One of the commonest of these prefixes indicative of his terrestrial location is that of maize foliage or the maize spiral (figs. 38,48,50,51,56; 60,B4), but this is never present when the god is ruling in his celestial abode. Sometimes the old god of number 5 (fig. 21,3) or the jaguar god of number 7 (fig. 12,13 and jaguar headdresses at Bonampak) are similarly bedecked; once (Dresden 73b) the glyph of the death god has the maize foliage as its prefix. Naturally, the maize god himself usually has the same attribute. Again, a single element has more than one meaning, for the maize foliage or maize spiral may embellish the number 8, the maize god himself, or may serve to indicate a general relationship with the surface or the interior of the earth.

Conch Shell. This attribute has already been discussed, and it has been noted that in Mexican and Maya mythology the conch is the attribute of the gods of the interior of the earth (p. 278). Attention has also been called to the use of a section of conch as the main element of the glyph for south in the inscriptions (fig. 41,28,30,31,34,36) and for a variant of the kin sign believed to represent dawn or sunrise (fig. 31,1–11).

Black. Frequently the glyph of the sun as lord of the night is partly crosshatched, the conventional presentation of black in sculpture (fig. 34,48,51,53,57). The death god is usually depicted in the codices with a black area on the crown of his head and black spots on his body (fig. 13,11,19). The connection between black and the underworld is a natural one. It is probably because of the evil associations of the underworld, Metnal, the place of death and eternal cold, that the glyphs for misery and general death carry symbols of the underworld, such as the death eye, percentage sign, and the black infix (fig. 20,3–7).

Eyes of the Death God. The eyes or stars which adorn the hair of the death god and appear on his collar (fig. 13,11,19) or at his wrists or ankles have already been discussed in connection with the affix incorporating those elements, which has been translated as "death of" or "expiration of" (p. 189). Frequently, the glyph of the sun as lord of the night has his terrestrial rôle marked by a prefix which appears to consist of three eyes of the death god (fig. 34,46,49,52,54,55). As noted immediately above, the glyphs for misery and general death carry this element as a prefix.

Three Dots. Profiles on the monuments of the death god as Cimi often display three small dots or circles in a line across the brow (fig. 7,21,25,27), but they are absent from representations of Cimi in the codices. The death god, as lord of the number 10, usually has these three dots (fig. 24,56–59), and in some cases where they are no longer distinguishable, it is probable that they have been eroded. The glyph for general death has a postfix consisting of three dots arranged as a triangle, between two dots, which, to judge by an example on Madrid 40a, represent death eyes. I have made the tentative suggestion that this triangular arrangement as the postfix might indicate "heap" in the term *multun tzek* (p. 268). It will be noted that on the monuments Ix, the day sign corresponding to jaguar, invariably has three dots arranged in triangular fashion in the lower half. The jaguar, as already noted, is a god of the underworld.

It is not clear whether these three dots are the same water symbol already discussed, or whether they have an entirely different origin. A water symbol would not come amiss as a postfix for any deity connected with the surface or interior of the earth, for we have already seen lily flowers and maize foliage as identifying tags of that region.

Head for Completion. The head variant of the glyph for completion, with hand across lower jaw, has many attributes connecting him with the nether regions. Often the death eye adorns the forehead, as in the head for 10 (fig. 25,37–41), or on the collars of full-figure representations of that god (fig. 29,1–3,7). In other cases the three dots in a line or the percentage sign appear on the crown of the head (fig. 25,41,45). Quite commonly the head for completion has the scroll and flare pendant attached to the earplug (fig. 29,1,3,5,7). This pendant seems to indicate an association with the underworld, as it is frequently worn by the jaguar god of the underworld (fig. 12,13,15), by the death god but not in the codices where he wears a bone (fig. 28,12), by the snake god of number 13 (figs. 12,8; 28,15), and by other beings who move on or under the earth's surface. It is highly probable that this design is conventionalized maize foliage (cf. figs. 12,1,10; 40,2; 45,7).

I would not hazard a guess as to what connection there is between the completion glyph and the terrestrial regions, other than that this is quite probably an extension of the natural connection between death and finality, already expressed in Maya writing by employing the death eyes and hair or a skull as the ending sign "expiration of." As already noted, it is possible that the hand is used as a completion sign because *lahal* means to end or finish, and also to buffet with the palm of the hand or with two or three fingers held straight. Thus the hand, could be used as a homonym for end or finish, and this idea of ending would often be reinforced by the addition of symbols recalling death.

Bones. Bones are naturally an attribute of the death

god, who is often shown as a skeleton or, less frequently, wears a cloak painted with crossed bones (Dresden 28b). This same design of crossed bones is worn by the old red goddess who pours destructive rain (with Eb sign, p. 81) on the world as depicted on Dresden 74, and it once appears on the garment worn by the jaguar god of number 7 (Yaxchilan L 12). Pictures of the god of death in Dresden often show a long bone pendent from the earplug (fig. 13,*11,19*); the hieroglyph of the dog, whose connection with the underworld has been discussed, shows his vertebrae. In the divinatory almanac which extends from Dresden 64c to 69c God B appears above the skies and on the earth. In one case he is seated on a rectangle decorated with two pairs of crossed bones. One is probably justified in assuming that the picture indicates that the god is seated on the surface of the earth, the bones symbolizing Metnal beneath its surface. Crossed bones usually appear in the eye of the animal (jaguar or dog?) which occasionally serves as the kin in distance numbers, and which may represent the night, that is to say, the underworld (fig. 31,*22,24–27,29*). The short earplug pendant, perhaps of bones, with two little circles is another attribute of gods of the earth and the underworld, but as noted above, this is often hard to distinguish from the inverted Ahau on the one hand, and from the section of shell on the other (cf. fig. 27,*13*, with fig. 12,*2,4*).

The various attributes connected with the underworld are not too well segregated at present. Some of them, because of their aquatic associations, are also attributes of gods of the clouds and rain. That, however, while it does not make our task any easier, is in conformity with the religious ideas of the Maya and their neighbors, for rain-making snakes pass constantly from the interior of the earth or its surface springs, rivers, and lakes to the sky, or are divided into celestial and terrestrial groups (Wisdom, 1940, pp. 392–94).

A PAIR OF AFFIXES

Several groups of prefixes have been discussed (pp. 276–77), and it has been demonstrated that changes in postfixes can alter the meaning or the function of the whole glyph (pp. 163, 195), but the surface of the subject has hardly been scratched.

Postfix A

A very common affix is that which forms the postfix of the month glyphs Pop, Zec, Kankin, and Kayab. It is joined to the last only in Dresden; to the second only on the monuments (figs. 16,*1–9,45,47–51; 18,22–27,62–64*). The codical form differs slightly from that used on the monuments in that two black spots in the codices replace the shallow lines of the larger element on the monu-

ments. The postfix, which for the moment I shall designate Postfix A, usually, although not invariably, accompanies glyphs which have the "Ben-Ich" prefix. For example, it appears with "Ben-Ich" Ahau (fig. 11,*1–6,8*) and occasionally with Ahau when the "Ben-Ich" prefix is replaced by the centipede or crossed-bands prefixes (fig. 38,*5,6*). I think in such cases the "Ben-Ich" prefix is suppressed on spatial grounds, and is not synonymous with those other two prefixes, because it can occur with either of them (fig. 39,*1,3,4,6–8*).

Similarly when the "Ben-Ich" prefix is attached to the kin glyph to form the glyph for Kinich Ahau, Postfix A is also attached (figs. 42,*3;* 43,*66*), and the same is true of glyphs of the sun god on the monuments (Piedras Negras 25, Piedras Negras shell plaque, Copan Alt of 13). The only possible example of the glyph of God D with a "Ben-Ich" prefix also has Postfix A (Paris 6c). The same seems to hold true for the seed glyph (fig. 43,*38–43*), for the appearance of the "Ben-Ich" produces also Postfix A (Paris 5c), but not when the double wing as prefix and affix is present (Madrid 68a, 69b, 71a). The rare occurrence of a "Ben-Ich" prefix with an Imix glyph similarly leads to the addition of Postfix A (fig. 40,*16,36*).

The "Ben-Ich" prefix is not inseparable, however, from Postfix A, as in the case of the "Ben-Ich" katun glyph (fig. 33,*33,35–40*); in some glyphs with this prefix Postfix A may or may not be present (fig. 43,*9–16*). With the "Ben-Ich" prefix Postfix A usually accompanies a variant of the sign tentatively identified as the *hel,* "change," sign, and which is used as an augural glyph (fig. 30,*30*), this form far outnumbering in the codices the variant forms illustrated with it.

Postfix A replaces the jaw of a god who is one of the directional deities in the Venus table, and who resembles in other respects God D (fig. 42,*4*); joined to the Oc glyph and usually with the *ox* prefix to add emphasis, this postfix converts that glyph into a sign of good tidings (fig. 43,*33–35*).

Postfix A is usually attached to the Kan sign when the latter is used in the sense of maize food, and thereby appears to change the meaning of the glyph from ripe maize to green corn (fig. 13,*5,6*). Here we have a definite hint of the meaning of this affix. Let us see what confirmation we can find for this suggestion.

Postfix A appears prominently emerging from behind the earplugs on each side of the earth monster with kan cross on his forehead on the Tablet of the Foliated Cross, Palenque (fig. 45,*7*), and it is from the head of this monster that grows the foliated cross which, of course, is nothing more nor less than a highly conventionalized maize plant. The same design, although somewhat more like maize leaves, appears in the same positions on each side of the earth monster, from whose head grows the tree of the Tablet of the Cross, Palenque. Pairs of maize leaves are often arranged to take the shape of this motif, and the maize god himself frequently wears a headdress of conventionalized maize which is very like this affix, or he holds a maize plant of this form in his hand. These leaves may be a direct part of the headdress or rise from a Kan glyph set on the god's head (Lothrop, 1924, pl. 8; Dresden 9a, 11b, 12a, 13b, 14a, etc.). The only difference is that the two lines or black spots of the affix are replaced in representations of the maize god by a semicircle with two spots or squares or by spots on the outside of the design, but there are examples which approach closely the form of Postfix A (fig. 43,43). Actually, there would seem to be two distinct affixes derived from this foliage. One, already discussed, which has the values "maize" or "eight" (figs. 25,53,54; 43,41,42,44,45); the other, our Postfix A. I have wondered whether designs incorporating the circles refer directly to maize whereas those lacking them have a more general meaning of growth, but I do not place much confidence in this suggestion. Whether the elements of Postfix A are mutations of the maize foliage or not, we can at least be sure from the evidence of the Tablet of the Foliated Cross that these elements are associated with an earth monster who is a deity of vegetation and the young maize plant, and this surmise is strengthened by the variation of the affix which, attached to the kan, represents growing corn (fig. 43,43).

It is fairly obvious that Postfix A, when used with the month signs Pop, Zec, Kankin, and Kayab and with a very rare form of Muan (fig. 20,18) can carry no direct reference to maize. On the other hand, every one of these months has an association with water, and four of them are associated with kan. Pop and Kayab represent respectively (reed) mat and turtle, both of which have aquatic connections, and these two months carry the kan cross. Muan, which once is shown with the kan cross in its eye, is named for the Moan bird, whose connection with rain has been amply demonstrated (p. 114). Kankin embodies the word *kan*, and the Zec sign is not infrequently found in the headdress of the long-nosed earth monster, god of the number 13, who is a deity of water (fig. 25,10; see also fig. 33,53–56).

Similarly, the appearance of Postfix A with the "Ben-Ich" prefix in conjunction with Ahau to denote a position in the round of katuns or affixed to the kin sign to form the glyph of Kinich-Ahau cannot denote any connection with either maize, fresh vegetation, or water. In such cases Postfix A probably serves as a phoneme; with the month signs and with Kan it probably has an attributive value, that is to say, it has ideographic properties denoting the class to which the glyphs belong.

We must seek, therefore, a term which conveys the idea of green or fresh which will fit the meaning of new corn in the case of the Kan glyph with Postfix A, but which also embodies the concept of water to explain its presence with the month glyphs just cited. It seems possible that the word in question is *ak*. In Yucatec maize is *ixim* and *nal* is an ear of corn; *ak ixim* is green corn and *aknal* is an ear of green corn or a growing plant of young maize. *Ak* means not only fresh or tender or new, as in *ak zi,* "green wood for burning," *ak cay,* "fresh fish," *aklaahal* and *aktal,* both of which refer to vegetation turning green, and the examples just given, but it also carries the idea of humidity. *Akal* is to become humid, and *akacnac* is something humid; *akci* means the same or to pour water; *akzah* is to urinate; *akyaabil* is the rainy season, period of humidity, germination, and growth; and *akalche* is a swamp in the forest.

Interestingly enough *ak* has two other meanings, one of which perhaps serves to buttress weakly our identification, for the word is also used for tongue and liana. In many examples of serpents the bifurcated tongue is made to resemble foliage (figs. 12,1; 28,5,17; Spinden, 1911, figs. 24, 33, 49, 62). This might be taken as a conceit were it not that the little circles of the maize foliage are quite distinct on some examples. I am therefore inclined to think that as the artist strove to convey the associations of serpents with the rains, germination, and growth, he seized on the fact that *ak* meant both tongue and humidity or new growth to shape the tongue as a symbol of growth. In Tzeltal the term probably exists: *ghan* is ear of corn; *aghan* is new corn.

This identification of Postfix A with the sound *ak* is not satisfactorily established, for it does not at present account for the partnership of the postfix with the "Ben-Ich" prefix, but it can be offered as a good working hypothesis.

POSTFIX B

Another postfix which is perhaps even more common than Postfix A is to be seen in many glyphs, one of the best known of which is Glyph F of the lunar series (fig. 34,15–19,59–62,64–66). It is commonly subjoined to the sky glyph and is not apparently affected by changes of infix in that glyph (fig. 31,62–66). It is also found, although less commonly, with the earth glyph. It is the affix I designate *te* (2), but as the evidence for that identification has not been fully presented, I shall for the moment continue to speak of it as Postfix B. It accompanies the seed glyph, but not when that has the maize prefix (fig. 43,38–40). It has been shown (p. 271) that postfixed to seed, it converts *pakal* to *pakalte*. Occasionally it appears as a postfix to numerical heads. When the glyph of God D has the prefix consisting of an element which resembles the top of Akbal and which is surrounded with dots, Postfix B is usually added, although there are quite a few exceptions (fig. 42,*42*), but this postfix never accompanies any other form of God D. The prefix of God D has been identified as the head of a centipede by Tozzer and Allen (1910, p. 303) on the strength of the centipede which so frequently depends from the head-dress of that god. I do not think this identification can be challenged. *Chapat* is the general word in Yucatec for centipede, and there is a deity or mythological character called Ah Uuc-Chapat, "Lord seven centipede." The connection of God D with the centipede is not known.

Luckily, we are able to identify a personified form corresponding to Postfix B, for in six texts a head is substituted for this element as a component of Glyph F of the lunar series (fig. 34,*21,63,68*). These texts are on Copan 1, I, A, 6, and HS, Date 24, and on Quirigua K. That these heads correspond to Postfix B is evident from the fact that the other elements of Glyph F, namely, the prefix and the knot (in turn with its own head variants, one with prominent hooked nose or the froghead on its side), are present, and only Postfix B is missing. It will be recalled that this is not the only case of a postfix being replaced by a head variant.

In all six cases the head is that of a youthful deity, and the full figure which replaces Postfix B in Glyph F of Copan HS, Date 24, is almost certainly the youthful maize god. The characteristics of the head of Quirigua K, with the lock of hair on the cheek, confirm this identification. It follows that the corresponding head variant would indicate that Postfix B has some connection with maize or, perhaps, the more general concept of vegetation.

The occurrence of Postfix B with the supposed seed glyph again suggests a connection with the vegetal world. The fact that this postfix never appears with the seed glyph when the maize prefix is present (fig. 43,*41,42*) would indicate either that the two affixes are synonymous or that they differentiate sundry types of seed or seed plot (p. 271).

Another clue to the meaning of Postfix B is to be found in its rare use with head variants of numbers (figs. 24,*62; 25,20,36; 39,4–6;* Copan 19, IS; Xcalumkin IS, Glyph A). It occurs only with head numerals attached to month signs, to period glyphs, and to Glyph A of the lunar series. There is a probable example of it on Copan H', but with a coefficient of bar and dots, the 9 which belongs with Glyph A. It will be remembered that an element occurring between coefficients and month signs or period glyphs has already been noted, and identified as the numerical classifier *te* (1) (p. 55; fig. 2,*15–23*). As Postfix B here seems to function precisely as does

te (1), I believe that it must have the same sound value.

How can we reconcile an association with vegetation or maize with the sound *te*? In several of the lowland languages, namely, Manche Chol, Chontal, Tzeltal, and Tzotzil, the word for wood or tree is *te*; in Palencano Chol it is *tie*. In Yucatec, which often substitutes a *ch* for the *t* of Chiapas, the corresponding word is *che*. Nevertheless, in not a few compound names of trees in Yucatec the termination *te* is retained (e.g. *nicte, xchite, pucte, tahte, uzte,* and *poite*) and the same is true, although to a lesser extent, of objects of wood (*xolte,* "wooden staff," *ah nabte,* "lancer," *halabte,* "weaving sword," *popte,* "wooden bridge"). Halpern (1942) suggests that the shift was from *ch* to *t,* but Yucatec material does not bear this out, for it is in ritualistic words (*amte, amtun,* "wooden spider, stone spider," *uinicilte, uiniciltun,* "wooden man, stone man"), and compounds that the *t* is found. These are precisely the types of words in which old forms are most likely to be retained. I assume therefore that the shift was from *t* to *ch,* and that this was of fairly recent date. It is noteworthy that the sign for tree in Dresden is *te* (1), but once *te* (2) (p. 56).

Che has the general meaning of "tree" or "wood," but there are some grounds for believing that it may have had a more extended meaning of vegetation in general, for the Motul dictionary lists *u cheel pop,* "the leaves or branches of the reed called petate from which they make the mats." *Che* also means fresh, tender, youthful, or new as in *che cimil,* "to die very young," *che pa,* "bread of new and tender maize, and that same maize," *che cay,* "fresh, newly caught fish," and *che col,* "new milpa worked for the first time." If the shift from *te* to *che* in Yucatec was of fairly recent date, as would seem to be the case, it is a fair assumption that *te* formerly had the same range of meaning, and that therefore among its connotations were those of youth, newness, and vegetation. In that case it would not be surprising to find the head of a youthful god, probably the maize god, used as the head variant of a glyphic element (Postfix B) corresponding to the sound *te,* and to find that *te* has a linguistic affiliation with fresh vegetation, as indicated by its association with Postfix A, for which the word *ak* has been suggested. Indeed, in Palencano Chol, according to Sapper (1908), *tye* and *ti* mean maize stalk.

Besides *te* as a numerical classifier and as a suffix of verbs (added to some active verbs to form a future; added to some passive verbs to convert them to substantives), and *te,* "wood," and the assumed *che-te* term for fresh, new or tender, there is an adverb *te* signifying "there" or "toward," but this generally comes at the beginning of a sentence, and *e* is attached to the last word, e.g. *te bin u malel Cumkale,* "there by Cumkal he has to pass," *te caanalile,* "towards on high [the sky]." In connection with the last it is interesting to recall that Postfix B generally accompanies sky signs (fig. 31,62–66,72) and sometimes appears with earth signs. Such an identification, however, raises the question whether a postfix of a glyph can correspond to an adverb which normally precedes the word believed to correspond to the main element of the glyph. Should we expect the glyphic order of elements to correspond to the spoken order? I do not believe that as yet we have enough evidence to establish such a rule despite the fact that it appears logical (p. 51).

The uses of *te,* both orally and in general meaning, appear to correspond well with Postfix B, so that we can pair the two without, however, making any claim that the matter is settled. Postfix B must not be confused with the *il* affix (p. 285). As the first *te* affix has been designated *te* (1), I refer to Postfix B as *te* (2).

RELATIONS BETWEEN POSTFIXES A AND B

Under certain conditions Postfixes A and B are interchangeable. Either postfix may be used with the shell variant of the kin glyph or with the animal variant of the kin sign (fig. 31,1–8,22–29). These two variants of the kin are used in distance numbers and, as suggested, they may refer to a count by nights or by dawns. As there is no possibility that these two glyphs change their meaning when the postfix alters, it is clear that Postfixes A and B must be synonyms or near-synonyms or, if I may coin a word, ideonyms ("conveying the same idea"). Postfix B, as noted, usually accompanies sky glyphs, but in the case of the cleft-sky sign with "Ben-Ich" prefix, Postfix A sometimes replaces it (fig. 43,18–23). This is logical if this glyph with its water affixes means "rainy sky" (p. 273).

In the case of the glyph of the inverted fist, the postfix is commonly A (fig. 42,67) but the appearance of the prefix resembling an elephant's trunk in all 13 divisions of the divinatory almanac on Dresden 65b–69b, causes a shift to Postfix B (fig. 42,66). The only other occurrence of this prefix with the inverted fist (Dresden 33c) changes the Postfix from A to one with a spiral infix. However, this spiral postfix is nearly related to Postfix A, for it is substituted for the latter beneath the glyph Pop on Copan T 11 (figs. 16,6; 54,5), and below "Ben-Ich" Ahau on Chichen 12 (fig. 39,3).

In the case of the half-period glyph, Postfix B is usually under the shell part (fig. 32,46–50,54); with the glyph for 5 haab lacking, the postfix of the lacking element is always A (fig. 32,41–45). As previously noted the idea behind each glyph is that of a part lacking to the completion of a period. However, as Postfix B invariably accompanies the shell glyph with coefficient of 1 (fig. 33,15–20), it is possible that its appearance with the half-period is because

that shell element is also incorporated in the glyph for the half-period.

There is clearly a close connection between Postfixes A and B. The suggested interpretations of them, *ak* and *te,* conform to this connection, for both convey the idea of freshness and new growth.

The postfix, which for the moment we will call Postfix C, found with representations of Kayab on the monuments (fig. 18,53–61) must be synonymous with Postfix A, for it is replaced by the latter in Dresden. Postfix C resembles the affix for white or the *tu* affix save that it has an infix of three dots in a line. Postfix C occurs, although not with great frequency, at Chichen Itza and Halakal between the haab glyph and its coefficient (fig. 39,1,7,8). It is probable that Postfix C is a merger of a prefatory glyph, not uncommon at Chichen Itza, which is composed of a main element with three dots in a vertical line, a postfix of one or two inverted Ahaus, and the white prefix (fig. 38,1–6). This prefatory glyph, which Beyer identifies as an ending sign, appears only before the same haab glyph in combination with a CR date to indicate the tun in which the latter falls. On the assumption that this prefatory glyph and Postfix C are the same, the question arises whether it could occur before or after the coefficient without any change of meaning, or, as seems more probable, must we seek a term that could be used linguistically to correspond to the positions before and after the coefficient in the glyphic texts. *Te* appears to be the only possibility, for that word can be a locative ("there, in year *n*") or a numerical classifier usable with years. If we are justified in assigning to this affix and prefatory glyph the meaning *te,* we have established another link between Postfixes A and B. Postfixes B and C then would both represent the sound *te.* As Postfixes A and B are often interchangeable, the replacement of Postfix A by Postfix C in the Kayab glyph is understandable if, as may be the case, Postfixes B and C represent the same sound. Postfixes A, B, and C are prominent, but by no means the only, components of a group of affixes comparable in range, although not in meaning, to the kan cross, yax, and circlet group.

I have discussed Postfixes A and B as examples of the double problem of identifying pairs or groups of affixes which are interchangeable under certain conditions, and of attempting to pair them with Maya words. The approach to the second half of this problem is a particulary dangerous one because one has to rely largely on Yucatec Maya owing to the lack of extensive vocabularies in other lowland Maya languages. Even if it is assumed that the inventors of the glyphic writing spoke a language closer to Yucatec than to any other lowland language or dialect, we have no means of knowing how much the language changed between the invention of the glyphs and the sixteenth century. Those are perils which face any attempt to match words to glyphs. Nevertheless, I believe the danger is not so great as one might fear. The Yucatec word *ķintunyaabil* so closely matches the glyph for drought, that one feels some confidence that the ancient speech must have been close to Yucatec. Similarly, if *u* moon is used as a rebus for *u* the possessive (before consonants), one can exclude several Maya dialects which have a different form of the possessive.

Withal, the primary object of this demonstration has been not to make actual identifications, but to outline a new method which may lead to decipherments. Hitherto, affixes have been largely ignored in translating glyphs; until Beyer took up their study, they were accorded little more importance than is given to the frame of a picture, and the impression was rather widespread that in many cases they were meaningless adornments. Therefore, whether the suggested interpretations of these two post-fixes are correct or wide of the mark is beside the point, for what I would achieve is a system for examining the properties of each affix, questing for possible synonyms or near-synonyms, and then, if possible, pairing the affix with a Maya word. If the final step is a false one, the next student can start where I stumbled.

TE (3) AFFIX

Two affixes have already been assigned the meaning *te* with varying certainty; there is a third which seems to have the same phonic value, and which I call the *te* (3) affix. It has already been discussed, but a fuller review is called for. It is composed of two parts, the second of which is the same as the identifying characteristic in the codices of the maize god, and which is set on his head, a vegetal motif. The other is what may be a small face attached to the base of this vegetal motif. The whole would, accordingly, appear to be a symbol for the maize god, but that divinity was probably not restricted to a rulership over maize, for he was probably a deity of general vegetation, particularly of food plants, with special emphasis on his function as the spirit of maize.

This affix occurs as a prefix of the seed glyph (p. 271; fig. 43,*41,42*), and of the glyph eight maize (p. 272; fig. 43,*44,45*). One would be inclined to accept it as a symbol for maize alone were it not that it appears in a number of contexts where the restricted meaning of "maize" would hardly fit, but the more general term *te* is applicable.

In the case of the eight-maize glyph, there is one case (Dresden 37b) where *te* (1) replaces *te* (3) as the prefix (p. 272), a strong indication that the two affixes are synonyms. The brilliancy prefix (p. 147) pairs with

the *te* (1) affix when attached to the cauac glyph (fig. 43,*65–67*); it combines with the *te* (3) prefix when attached to the kin sign (fig. 43,*69*). This again suggests, although with less force, that *te* (1) and *te* (3) have the same value.

Attention has been called to the presence on Madrid 65–72, of a series of tun glyphs with coefficients, most of which have an affix identified as a numerical classifier, perhaps with the value *piz* or *p'el* or *tem* (p. 196). In one case, where this affix is missing, we find instead *te* (3) as a prefix (fig. 12,*19,23,24*). It is a fair conclusion that *te* (3) functions here also as a numerical classifier, and it will be recalled that *te* is used with the tun and other periods in the books of Chilam Balam as a numerical classifier. In this same almanac of Madrid thrice the uinal glyph has *te* (3) as a postfix, and each time there is a coefficient (fig. 12,*20*), and twice the same glyph in Dresden (13*c*, 21*b*), again with a coefficient, has the *te* (3) affix and the hand affix as prefixes. Here, too, one is, perhaps, justified in accepting the affix as the numerical classifier *te*. However, on Dresden 71a, there is an augural glyph composed of a Chuen sign, a *te* (2) prefix to the left, and above, according to Förstemann's edition, a *te* (3) prefix. The glyph is a little worn, and as on Dresden 72a, forming part of the same divinatory passage, what is apparently the same glyph has a clear hand with what is drawn as a kin infix instead of the *te* (3) prefix shown on page 71a, I think we are justified in supposing that the latter has been miscopied, and should be the same as the example on page 72a.

Te (3) occurs on the monuments affixed to a number of glyphs of unknown meaning, with and without co-efficients. It is particulary common at Palenque (fig. 53,*1*, Gl B14, C8, C16). One should not be surprised that at least three affixes apparently have the same phonic value; *te* is an important word with sundry meanings and uses. One has only to count the kin signs to realize how many glyphs could have the same meaning. Should Postfix C prove to have also the phonic value *te,* it would become *te* (4).

THE IL AFFIX

We will now discuss an affix of simpler use, for which I feel reasonably confident that I have discovered the meaning and the spoken equivalent. This is the *il* affix already briefly examined (p. 269), which has been identi-fied as a symbol for a knife (Seler, 1902–23, 1:392; Förstemann, 1904; Schellhas, 1904), apparently because of its use as a prefix of the death god, for a knife blade is not infrequently inserted in the nostrils of that deity, par-ticularly in Aztec art. Apart from the fact that the element bears no resemblance to a flint or an obsidian blade, its use as an affix to other glyphs precludes this interpretation.

In discussing the glyph for drought, I pointed out that as we had glyphic elements corresponding to *kin, tun,* and *yaab* (*haab*), the remaining element, the postfix in question, should correspond to the suffix *il* to complete the word *kintunyaabil*. In Yucatec *il* is a suffix which is of very frequent occurrence, particularly to denote attributive or gentilitious relationship, also to form comparatives and abstract nouns and certain verbal terminations (Tozzer, 1921, pp. 31, 36, 38). It is therefore one of the commonest suffixes in Yucatec; it is used in a similar way as a suffix in Manche Chol, in Yocotan, and probably in other Maya languages and dialects.

In the codices the *il* affix is largely found with head forms, at least two of which are of known gods, those of death and of maize. The glyph of the death god is the head corresponding to Cimi with the *il* prefix (fig. 42, *9,16,39*). It is not rash to suppose the whole represents the word *cimil*, "death," for a name for the death god was Yum-Cimil.

The name of the maize god in Yucatan has already been discussed; it may have been Ah Uaxac-Yol-Kauil (p. 269), and I have suggested that it is not improbable that the more generic name *kauil*, "foodstuff," may have been applied to the maize god, just as it was tacked on to Itzamna's name, probably to call attention to the rôle of those collective gods as providers of food. The head of the maize god's glyph with its maize details infixed and placed on top of the head surely stands for food, and the *il* prefix would refer to the *il* termination of the word *kauil*.

This affix appears both as a prefix and postfix with the glyph Ahau, which frequently appears in clauses of divinatory almanacs, often following the glyph of God D. I have suggested (p. 269) that this glyph corresponds to *ahaulil*, "rulership." If *ahaulil* is a contraction of *ahauilil*, the two glyphic affixes would correspond to the double *il* (fig. 43,*36*).

The *il* prefix not infrequently appears with the glyph of a water goddess (Gates' Glyph 123) of uncertain position in the Maya pantheon, and also with a head probably that of an animal, with kan or kin infix and a second infix of the two black bars found with the Oc glyph (Gates' Glyph 46). The same element serves as a suffix with Gates' Glyph 147, the lower part of which is an element in Akbal and other glyphs. There are a few scattered examples of this affix with common glyphs in the codices, but all are of rare occurrence save the tun glyph (fig. 46,*3,5,6,8*).

In the codices the tun glyph usually has the *il* element

as a postfix, but in the distance numbers on Dresden 61 and 69, this affix is missing and it does not appear in time counts on the monuments. Instead, the many examples of the tun with *il* postfix occur in divinatory almanacs and the divinations for the years. In most of these cases the tun glyph is followed by an augural glyph, and I think it is a fair assumption that the two go together to indicate a year of abundance or good crops or misery or whatever the augury may be. Thus, in the long divinatory almanac on Madrid 65–73b, the tun glyph with *il* postfix appears a number of times preceding or following such augural glyphs as the Kan-Imix sign, the Oc sign, or the death sign. I think that in such cases the glyph must represent *haabil*, for example *haabil numya*, "year of misery." How exactly the coefficient should be handled I do not know.

In the new-year pages of Dresden some interesting examples occur. On Dresden 27, above the picture of the death god, the regent of the entering year, is the glyph of that god followed by the tun with yax prefix and *il* postfix (fig. 64,*1*). The whole might be translated *Cimil yaxhaabil*, "the new year is associated with the death god." Here *il* indicates the gentilitious relationship of the year with the death god. On Dresden 28c the entering god is God D, and, above, appears the same yax-tun-il glyph, in this case followed, not preceded, by the glyph of God D. On Dresden 26c the entering god is K, and, above, his glyph follows the tun glyph with *il* postfix but with a double prefix, consisting of the yax element attached to a kan sign. These two passages surely must declare that the new years belong respectively to Itzamna and God K. On Dresden 25 the entering deity is the sun god, but neither his glyph nor the haabil combination appear.

On the monuments the *il* affix is commonly found in the lunar series, usually with Glyph D but occasionally with Glyph C. It will be remembered that the Yucatec word for moon is *u;* the Motul dictionary lists the term *uil*, "cosa de luna." It is a fair assumption that this postfix with Glyph C converts the moon sign from *u* to *uil*. With the up-ended frog the *il* and lunar affixes are interchangeable (fig. 11,*44–50*). As the lunar affix here is surely the possessive *u*, and *il* expresses attributive relationship, their interchangeability confirms the identification of the *il* affix. Other occurrences of this affix are with the sky sign, but it is not the usual affix (fig. 3,*5–8*), with "the seating of the day" glyph (fig. 19,*47,48*), and with a hand glyph (fig. 42,*55,56*).

The evidence, I think, is strong for accepting the meaning of this affix as *il*. If the affix has been correctly deciphered as *il*, this decipherment demonstrates that the position of affixes in the glyphs does not correspond to the order of the spoken word, for in the supposed Cimil glyph the element identified as *il* is prefixed to Cimi, whereas in the word itself *il* is a suffix. We had a hint of this in other cases in which an affix may be either a prefix or a postfix, notably in the case of Zec, which has the comb element as a prefix on the monuments but as a postfix in the codices, and in the cases of Gates' Glyphs 345.4, 7.4, 4.3.1 and 2, and 11.4.

THE ARITHMETICAL APPROACH

This method of seeking decipherments of glyphs involves segregating all known examples of a given glyph on the stelae, arranging them in chronological order, and computing the intervals between the dates with which they are associated. The system produces results if it can be shown that those intervals are multiples of a given number. In recent years three discoveries have resulted from this method. The glyphs of the lords of the nights were identified by finding that the intervals between recurrences of each member of the group were multiples of nine days (Thompson, 1929). By a similar method the cycle of 819 days was established (Thompson, 1943d). Likewise arithmetic was necessary to deduce the Yucatecan system of dating (Thompson, 1937) and to identify the 5-tun lacking glyph (Thompson, 1934a); it is used also to establish a relationship between the heads of Glyph C of the lunar series and Glyph X (p. 241).

Applied to dates and tables of supposed planetary significance, the arithmetical system is perilous; a single calculation has been identified as a multiple of the synodical revolution of two different planets. Clearly, with long intervals between dates and short synodical revolutions it is possible to reach agreement by adding or subtracting a hundredth of a day to the average length of the revolution in question. I do not believe that such calculations covering long spans of time can have much value until the correlation of the Maya calendar with our own is established beyond reasonable dispute, or until glyphs for the planets other than Venus have been identified.

There are still possibilities in this approach. It would seem that the meanings of a number of glyphs will be found only through an arithmetical solution. Among such glyphs might be cited the "Ben-Ich" katuns with coefficients usually ranging from 2 to 5 (p. 203) and the 1-shell period glyph (p. 194). The exact function of the world directional glyphs on the monuments can be established only arithmetically, and I suspect that the subject matter of the designs on stelae is governed by time cycles. Some glyphs will, I think, prove to be related to divisions of the 260-day cycle, and such associations can be proved only mathematically.

SUMMARY

In this chapter we have sent out reconnaissance patrols and probed the enemy's position, or, since we opened the chapter in terms of a siege of Clio, perhaps we should say that we have dallied with the muse, indulged in flirtation, and taken those first steps which may lead to conquest. In war, in love, or in Maya hieroglyphic research, one can learn from one's rebuffs how to conquer next time. I should not be among the least surprised should all the interpretations suggested in this chapter prove to be correct; in such pioneer work mistakes are to be expected. At present I am more interested in reconnoitering paths that may lead myself and others to success, than in battling in one small area to win an immediate but limited victory. The stronghold of Maya hieroglyphs can not be taken by an attack from a single direction. One must infiltrate at a dozen or more different points, and those points must first be tested.

We have discussed the glyphs which explain the divinatory almanacs in Dresden. It has been suggested that, contrary to general opinion, the glyphs do not explain the pictures, but that the pictures illustrate or supplement the glyphs. The opening glyphs of the clauses have been tentatively identified as verbal nouns and objects, and one or two guesses at meanings have been made; the closing glyphs of those clauses have been classed, with more justification, as augural signs which tell the luck of the day. Translation of a number of these has been offered. Among them are those for "good tidings," "evil," "abundance of food," "dark days" (storms), "drought," "rule," and "maize seed."

From the examination of glyphs accompanying the divinatory almanacs in the codices we passed to a review of two groups of associated elements, the water group and the underworld group. It was shown that there was in each case a considerable number of elements which under certain conditions were interchangeable. These associations were derived from community of idea rather than from linguistic similarities. Certain elements, such as the symbol for jade, the kan cross, and the Moan bird, have their primary and direct meanings, but all have also more extended use because all are connected with water. Just as water is a liquid, but a liquid is not necessarily water, so any of these symbols can stand for water, but it does not follow that a symbol for water can replace any one of them when it is used in its restricted sense, any more than we speak of liquid when we wish to treat specifically of water.

The various elements so far classified as belonging to these two groups have been enumerated, and it has been found that the boundaries between the groups are not well defined, for certain elements can have a foot in both camps.

A slightly different approach was followed in examining two affixes, for which the translations *ak* and *te* have been suggested. It was shown that they were interchangeable under certain conditions, and evidence was adduced that both elements were used both linguistically and ideographically, but the demonstration was primarily one of method. The decipherment of one of the affixes, the *te* element, is almost certainly correct, but here exact interpretation was a secondary consideration. There followed appraisements of two other affixes, the *te* (3) element and that corresponding to the relationship suffix *il* of spoken Yucatec.

The chapter concluded with a few suggestions concerning glyphs which may be solved arithmetically.

13

Glances Backward and a Look Ahead

Behold I see the haven nigh at hand,
To which I meane my weary course to bend;
Vere the main shete, and bear up with the land
The which afore is fairely to be kend.
——EDMUND SPENSER, *Faerie Queene*, Canto XII

THE METAPHOR shall be changed from Elizabethan to Maya; from sea lanes to forest trails. The *lubay* is reached; the time has come to put down our burden and look back over the course we have trodden. The way has been long, stony, and in places hard to follow. Floundering in more than one polemical morass, we have at times vainly thought to win salvation by grabbing the spiny trunk of that terror of travelers, the *kum* palm. What of the burden? We set forth with a triple *cuch:* to review what was previously known about Maya hieroglyphic writing; to set forth the properties of the glyphs and to expound such rules as govern the uses of affixes, the grammar, so to speak, of the written word; and to offer interpretations of glyphs hitherto undeciphered.

To this triple burden was added the *p'ic,* the extra load on top of the *cuch.* The poetical character of the hieroglyphic inscriptions, the mythological setting of the glyphs, and the general mentality and philosophical outlook of the Maya, as discernible in their literature, formed this weighty surcharge.

In this final chapter I shall not present a full summary, for the table of contents and the index are detailed and most chapters conclude with reviews of their contents. Instead, I purpose to outline what I regard as the most important contributions to our knowledge of these subjects in the preceding chapters, either made there for the first time or reproduced there in permanent form, although previously published by me in *Notes on Middle American Archaeology and Ethnology* or in *Theoretical Approaches to Problems.*

The remarkable feature of Maya hieroglyphic writing is its great flexibility. Because students have tended to concentrate on set ritualistic patterns, such as the IS, this has not been so apparent as wider research now reveals it to be. Nevertheless, even in those well-studied passages there is great diversity which familiarity causes us to overlook. Common words could be expressed by several glyphic elements and the choice could be expanded by the use of near-synonyms. The body of signs is greatly increased, perhaps doubled, by the Maya custom of having both a personified and a symbolic form for very many, per-

haps all, of their elements. Even wider latitude was permissible, for a glyph could be given a profile outline, which is conventionalized and does not resemble the true personification of the glyph (cf. fig. 40,*1–3* with fig. 40, *13,50*). This variability can be carried to great lengths: there are at least 10 distinct glyphs to depict the 360-day year, and considerable artistic latitude in depicting all of them was permitted; there are 13 distinct glyphs for the kin or period of 24 hours, and that number can be expanded to 20 if changes in affixes can be regarded as creating new glyphs.

This considerable range of interchangeability is further expanded by the groups of reciprocal synonymous and near-synonymous affixes. In Chapter 12 two of these groups have been discussed, and there are constant references to individual members throughout the book, for these affixes are the articulations of written Maya. The matter does not stop there; one meaning may be conveyed by a dozen glyphs, but any one of those dozen may have more than one meaning. The sign for jade not only represents that highly prized jewel, but stands for the day Muluc, "water," and is the symbolic form of the *xoc* fish, where it has the meaning of "count." Moreover, this jade symbol forms part of the normal glyph for the year of 360 days, which is called *tun,* "jade." As an element of the tun sign it has the extended meaning of "end" in the prefix or prefatory glyph of the twentieth day in the uinal, and it can also serve as the rebus of the suffix *tun* used to intensify the word to which it is attached, as in the glyph *kintunyaabil,* "prolonged drought." Finally, set in an oval of circlets the jade sign represents the month Mol and serves as an affix with the meaning of water. Thus, a very wide spread of meanings attaches to this single element.

Evidence is accumulating that the Maya used rebus writing to a considerable extent, employing a depictable object to represent a less easily reproduced homonym. Thus, the head of the *xoc* fish is used also to express the word *xoc,* "to count"; the sign of the moon, *u,* is employed as the possessive *u,* "of," or *u* as a means to convert a cardinal number to an ordinal; the glyph for the

360-day period called the tun can also stand for *tun,* "end," or *tun,* used for purposes of intensification. Other elements may represent two or more homonyms, as, for instance the affixes chac and yax. *Chac* signifies both "red" and "great," and the corresponding affix can be used in either sense; *yax* stands for "green" and "new," and again the one corresponding affix can be used with either meaning. A symbol may also have a secondary value. For example, the sign for black not only signifies swart, but can be extended to cover anything associated with the underworld, the land of darkness: the sun, as lord of the underworld, is given black markings to indicate not that he is a blackamoor, but that he is temporarily in the nether regions. To avoid in part the danger of misidentification because of the multiple use of a single element, not infrequently it was placed in an inverted position or on its side to express some restricted meaning. Thus, the shell symbol in one position and with a certain postfix represents day (more probably sunrise or perhaps even night); inverted and with different affixes it serves on the monuments as the symbol for south (figs. 31,*1–9;* 41,*28, 30,34,36*). The Ahau sign has a number of uses beside that of its common function as the twentieth day. It frequently appears as an affix and then it is almost invariably in the inverted position (fig. 2,*24–26*). That inversion of an element is primarily to indicate a specialized use is demonstrated by the Ahau glyph itself; in a certain compound the Ahau rests in the angle formed by the thumb and forefinger of an outstretched hand, but the Ahau may be upside down or in its normal position (fig. 46,*18–23*). Similarly, in the codical form of the glyph for east the Ahau is usually inverted but occasionally it is in the normal position.

Glyphs which belong to a single clause can be fused or the first can become an affix of the second, both of which processes are to be seen in examples of Glyphs G and F (fig. 34,*49,21*), or, where one element is normally fused with another or is its infix, the two can be separated (fig. 32,*47–53*). Similarly, the elements which form compound glyphs can stand as independent entities. The order of glyphs in some compounds and clauses can be reversed without any change of meaning (figs. 33,*36–38;* 40,*50–52;* 41,*6,20*).

From this brief outline of some of the complexities of Maya hieroglyphic writing it is clear that one must depend on the context in deciphering a passage. For instance, one must decide from the rest of the sentence whether the head of the god with dots on his chin is to be read as the number 9, as the Chicchan god, as *yax,* "green" or "new," or as water, the element which that snake god rules. This head appears with the tied glyph in a clause at Naranjo (fig. 3,*7,* Gl 4). We know that this glyph never takes a numerical coefficient, but in parallel clauses it has instead the kan cross and water symbol prefix (fig. 3,*3–6,8,9*), and so we are justified in reading the head in this text as a sign for water. This same head appears at Copan with the sunrise glyph (fig. 31,*51*). That glyph can take a coefficient, but apparently only when the number is 1. As the sunrise glyph at Copan frequently takes the yax prefix (fig. 31,*49,50*), we can rest assured that here the head stands for *yax,* "new." Attached to the baktun glyph at the start of an IS, the head clearly should be read as 9. In all three cases the context makes clear which meaning is to be given to the head, but in many other instances one is less certain.

Presumably to avoid confusion in the sundry usages of the glyph of this god, the personified form of the day Chicchan is given the reptilian form of the god, and the supraorbital plate is emphasized, but in the codical glyphs this crosshatched supraorbital plate is transferred to the region of the temple. Thus, to clarify ambiguous readings the Maya created new variants, which, however much they may have helped the Maya reader, hinder our work of decipherment.

So far we have confined ourselves to a summary discussion of the properties of the main elements of glyphs; a word should now be said about new knowledge concerning affixes and infixes, without the study of the meanings and functions of which little further progress in our subject can be made.

In discussing rules of Maya hieroglyphic writing we laid great stress on affixes and infixes, partly because of their importance as the articulations of the writing, and partly because they have been so generally ignored and in some cases even dismissed as ornamental additions. It was possible to establish eight new rules which apply to those particles:

1. Some affixes have personified forms, and it is not improbable that future research will show that all could be personified, although that practice was not commonly followed. As examples of personified forms of affixes may be mentioned: the flattened fish-head as the personified form of the bracket with line of dots (fig. 5,*48,49*); and the vulture with *ti* frontal ornament, the head of the *xoc* fish, the Chicchan god of number 9, the manikin death god, and what is probably the youthful maize god as personified forms corresponding respectively to the *ti;* comb, yax, death eye, and *te* (2) affixes (cf. figs. 4,*29;* 2,*30;* 31,*51;* 4,*7;* 34,*68* with figs. 2,*44,29;* 31,*49,50;* 4,*9;* 34,*66*).

2. Affixes and main elements can change places, the affix becoming the main element, and the main element a prefix or postfix. Usually when this occurs the affix is personified on changing to a main element (figs. 2,*29–31;* 34,*59–63*). An affix can become an infix (fig. 2,*4–7,9,10*), and an infix can be promoted to main element (fig. 32, *50,52*). The mastery of this rule is of value in decipher-

ment, as we can now decide what affixes are essential to the meaning of a glyph. For example, it was formerly supposed that the comb affix was not an essential part of the month sign Mac because it is not always present. We now know that although it is absent as a symbolic postfix, it is present as a personified main element or as an infix (fig. 18,*1–18*) and so it is an indispensable part of the sign.

3. Positions of affixes do not necessarily correspond to the order of words in the spoken language. For example, one affix, the *u* bracket, is nearly always a prefix, but another affix, the moon sign, with the same sound value is usually a postfix (fig. 11,*37–41*). In speech the possessive *u* precedes the object possessed and the possessor's name comes last. Accordingly, one affix corresponds in position to the spoken word; the other does not.

4. Under certain circumstances an affix can be transferred to an adjacent glyph (fig. 2,*58–61*). In some cases such shifts perhaps reflect slight variations in the spoken word, sometimes, perhaps, representing poetic license.

5. Usage had caused affixes commonly attached to glyphs in constant use to be generally restricted to either a prefixal or postfixal position, but they could be shifted from one position to another without any change in meaning. For example, on the monuments the comb is a prefix of the month Zec; in Dresden it is a postfix of the same glyph (fig. 16,*45–52*). Similarly, in a form of the hand glyph the "down-balls" affix is usually prefixed to the main element (fig. 42,*61*), but it can be postfixed (Dresden 15c), and the text indicates that there is no change in meaning. The double Imix glyph supplies another instance of a shift of this nature; the comb affix is normally a prefix of the second Imix, but it can be attached as a postfix to the first Imix (fig. 40,*13–15*). The crosshatched affix of the tun in Madrid, surely a numerical classifier, can similarly change from prefix to postfix (fig. 12,*23,24*).

6. Affixes, like main elements, can have varied meanings. The *te* (*1*) element is a good illustration of multiple usage. It may be the *te* numerical classifier (figs. 2,*13–23;* 12,*21*); it may have the meaning tree (*te* or *che*) (p. 56; fig. 62,*1,2*); it can stand for the grammatical suffix *te*, as in the glyph of Bolon-Yocte (fig. 12,*16–18*); and it can be an attributive affix to indicate a connection with vegetation or maize in particular (Dresden 37b). It is possible that it may also have been employed for the locative *te*. The positions of the affix in these sundry usages correspond to the spoken word: when used as a numerical classifier, it is correctly inserted between number and noun; when used as a grammatical suffix, it appears as a postfix; and when it is a substantive (tree), it is postfixed to the color, since in spoken Yucatec the adjective precedes the noun it qualifies. Thus we can conclude that sometimes the position of the affix corresponds to the spoken word; at other times it does not.

7. Affixes, like the proverbial flea, can have their own infixes or affixes, although the process can not be carried *ad infinitum* (cf. fig. 4,*21* with 22 Gl 3; and 41,*14–17* with *18,19,21*). The glyphs for *chac zac cimil,* "great faintings," supplies a good example of secondary meanings attached to affixes. In this compound *chac* means "great," not "red," and *zac* denotes not "white," but something which is not quite the same as the word it qualifies,

approaching our use of pseudo. *Zac cimil,* pseudo-death, is defined in the Motul dictionary as fainting or heart attack.

8. There are indications, perhaps hardly strong enough to justify the term "rule," that whereas a noun is normally the main element and the adjective which qualifies it is the prefix, a stress on the latter in speech could be reflected glyphically by converting the adjectival prefix into the main element and the noun into a postfix. Glyphs for the red, black, and yellow trees (fig. 62,*1,2*) supply an instance of this: the trees (substantives) are expressed glyphically as postfixes; the colors (adjectives) are the main elements. Here, however, the ritual of the directional colors is paramount; the tree is of secondary importance.

Affixes deciphered positively or with reservations comprise prepositions, relationship terms, numerical classifiers, attributive signs confirming the identity of the main sign, elements specifying a particular use of the main sign, adjectives, and nouns (particularly when these are also found as main elements). I suspect that affixes do not represent verbs, although that suspicion perhaps may never be confirmed or disproved because of the indistinct separation between verbs and nouns which is a feature of Maya speech.

The same multiplicity of meanings attaches to some affixes as to some main elements, and again we are often at a loss which way to turn in those mazes of anagogy. The problem is complex, indeed, when an affix with several meanings is attached to a main element with the same ambiguous properties. Happily, glyph decipherment, like the biography of Chaucer, "is built upon doubts and thrives upon perplexities." In such cases the doubts and perplexities which we are fain to shun mirror the train of thought which we should follow, for therein are imbedded the poetry and mysticism of the Maya.

This vast and important field of glyphic research has been neglected; students have turned to the arithmetical and calendarial aspects of Maya writing, treating those subjects more and more as though they were problems in ballistics or cryptography, soluble only by slide rule or calculating machine. Interesting as it is to speculate on methods the Maya may or may not have used to measure the length of a lunation or of the solar year, it is well to remember that in Maya eyes the moon was a vivid personality, whose unhappy story has shaped Maya thinking, and the sun was a hero, whose guises and contacts are embodied in the glyphs. The Maya attitude toward solar eclipses was far removed from that of the modern astronomer who checks his stop watch and the shutter of his camera as, businesslike, he awaits an event which may supply him with material for a new paper. Only by leaving the streamlined structure of modern research and knocking at the door of Maya mysticism and poetical fancy can one hope to understand Maya literature; one does not pursue Ariel with a repeating rifle.

One notable outcome of this study has been the establishment beyond serious question that the 13 days from Caban to Muluc inclusive are representations of the gods of the numbers 1–13. This is of transcendent importance not only because it yields many clues to the meanings of glyphic elements, but also because it is a reflection of the peculiar integration of the same divine elements in various combinations, so well typifying Maya thought and practice. No other people has developed toward time and its many divisions that mystical and spiritual attitude which the Maya evolved; nowhere else in the world, so far as I am aware, have the periods of time, from the day upward, been not only deified, but given active personalities and the most important parts on the divine stage.

The contrasting attitudes of Maya and Aztec to the days demonstrate the spiritual differences between those two cultures. Both peoples derived their sacred almanacs from a single source. The Maya held the days to be living gods, whereas the more materialistic Aztec regarded them as a string of names of animals and objects. The fourth Maya day was the day of the maize god; the fourth Aztec day was lizard: the twentieth Maya day was the sun god; the twentieth Aztec day was flower. The Maya days remained divinities; the Aztec days had been secularized. It is a situation comparable to that which has arisen in the western attitude toward St. Nicholas. To Latins and Slavs he is the patron saint of children and sailors, around whom many charming legends have clustered; to peoples of north European culture he has become a somewhat derisible and potbellied patron of extravagance, an unrespected tool of shopkeepers. The attitudes reflect the spiritual content of the two cultures.

The 13 day gods of the Maya, playing their collective and individual parts on the Maya stage, are seldom in the wings; as a reflection of those activities, they permeate the glyphic writing, for the hieroglyphs embody the thoughts, the beliefs, and the imagery of their users. The sun god is not only the sun; he is the day Ahau; he is the number 4; he is the patron of the month Yaxkin; he is the 24-hour day; he is the redundant sign which in Yucatan identifies the day glyph; and, with added attributes, he is one of the lords of the nights. Moreover, his profile can be used as part of the glyphs for east and west, for Yaxkin, and probably for the kin part of any glyph. In the form of Ahau he has many other functions, most of which are still unknown. Thus there is an extensive series of glyphic forms in which this one god appears, and in each case we are dependent on the context or affixes for indications as to how the glyph is to be read. Although the sun is probably the day god most

extensively used in glyphic writing, his 12 companions also reappear in numerous combinations. Only by careful scrutiny of every source on religion and folklore can we hope to follow the mental processes of the Maya who, to his way of thinking, logically assigned a wide range of subjects to the sway of each of these primary gods.

Maya mysticism is well exemplified by the poetical concept of the passage of time as a group of bearers, each with his period on his back, whose stages in the diuturnal march were the *lub,* the resting places of the porters. This charming fantasy, too, is preserved in the hieroglyphic texts, such as full-figure IS, and may also be retained in an abbreviated form in the use of the knot element, as in Glyph F. The combination of water symbols with the moon sign in some variants of Glyph D of the lunar series is another instance of a religious concept embodied in the glyphic writing, for it surely refers to the belief that at the time of conjunction the moon went "to her well," probably the Maya equivalent of the Mexican Tlalocan, "the land of rain." The dog, as a symbol of the underworld and of fire, supplies two more cases of the incorporation of religious belief and legend in the glyphs; the glyph of the Moan bird, both in its function as a rain symbol and in its variant form, the "13 layers of heaven," perpetuates the cosmological beliefs of its creators. The number of such instances could be greatly expanded. The need for spading among familiar glyphs to uncover their mythological and metaphoric roots is the reason for the lengthy and, I fear, arid discussion of day signs, month signs, and the component elements of the IS in Chapters 3, 4, and 6. In excuse, we may recall that arid soils commonly retain much mineral wealth.

The poetical character of the inscriptions is present not only in the origins and uses of individuals glyphs, but also in the construction of sentences. I am now convinced that the glyphic texts are a form of antiphony in blank verse. The redundant glyphs which I once regarded as evidence that the Maya were tautologists, are surely added to strengthen the melodic qualities of the verse. Those metrical qualities exist not only in the glyphic inscriptions of the monuments; they have survived in the books of Chilam Balam, and are particularly prominent in the texts which accompany the divinatory almanacs in the codices. The unvarying number of glyphs in each compartment of an almanac is not entirely governed by spatial considerations, for the Maya handled such problems easily with space-saving devices, such as placing two glyphs in one glyph block or fusing them. They seldom did this in the almanacs, thereby preserving the rhythmic beat of the blank verse. Mysticism, religion, and poetry completely dominate the hieroglyphic writing.

Among the general suggestions offered in the preceding

chapters the most far-reaching are those contained in the discussion of the glyphic texts which accompany the divinatory almanacs in Dresden. In Chapter 12 and elsewhere I have advanced the thesis that those passages, often consisting of four glyphs but frequently expanded to six or eight or reduced to three, record the influence of the regnant deity on each division of the almanac. I have assumed, not without reason I believe, that in the minimal texts the first glyph of each compartment is a verbal form which expresses the action of the god, that is to say his influence; the second glyph is that of the god then ruling, the subject of the verb; the third is the result of his influence, beneficial or otherwise, that is to say, the augural glyph. The enlargement of this minimal body of glyphs permits the recording of fuller data, such as information on world directions and colors, an expansion of the augury, or, in some cases, the object of the god's action.

A considerable body of augural glyphs has been deciphered with varying degrees of certitude, but less assurance bolsters the rendering of verbs of action. This investigation of the divinatory almanacs has established, to my satisfaction at least, that the supposed tables of the planets Mars, Jupiter, and Saturn have nothing to do with the revolutions of those planets, but are merely the preludes to more divinatory almanacs. The Mars beast, I feel reasonably sure, is not a symbol of that planet, but is a creature associated with the rains.

I am confident that it is now possible to offer approximate decipherments of a large proportion of the divinatory passages in Dresden and, to a lesser extent, in Madrid. One may not, at this point, be able to state positively what is the exact translation of some verbal glyph, but one can limit its possible meanings to a fairly short range. Whether a certain verbal glyph in combination with that of God B means "the rain god influences" or "the action of the rain god" is not of great consequence; the important step has been taken when the division into action of god and resultant luck of the day is recognized. As a result of the identification of a considerable group of augural glyphs, we now know that the great proportion of divinatory almanacs in Dresden (the range of subjects is wider in Madrid) deals with weather and its results on the crops. Abundance and drought, days of sunshine and rainy skies, days of darkness and days of storm, good tidings and evil, and days that are halfway good, planting and germination are the subjects chiefly discussed.

Progress is not confined to the divinatory almanacs, for a number of glyphs are identifiable on the pages of Dresden and Madrid dealing with the ceremonies for the new years. We can now assert that the accompanying glyphic texts give the prophecies for the incoming year along the lines described by Bishop Landa. It is a pleasant coincidence, of the kind that softens the asperities of our subject, that almost exactly one baktun (395 years) after Landa wrote his memorial on the calendar, research in original Maya sources confirms his statements. Now that we have a grasp of the subject matter, the work of decipherment should proceed more swiftly.

An outcome of this study, although one that has not always yielded direct results in decipherment, is the realization of the extent to which a single element may be used in widely separated glyphs. This, of course, can not be regarded as a discovery, but is the consequence of more careful examination of the component elements of each glyphic compound and of its variant forms. We have taken note of one such element, the jade symbol, which occurs in a large number of signs, but I have in mind the more complex forms which appear in several glyphic compounds.

An instance of this is the sign, perhaps a variant of the bundle device, which in various combinations forms the variant of Glyph X most commonly used when the coefficient of Glyph C is 5 or 6 (fig. 37,9,34,38,55,60,69) and once (erroneously?) when the coefficient is suppressed (fig. 36,13). At the top of this is usually added an element which resembles, but probably has nothing to do with, the inverted Ahau. There may also be present a fist, an element resembling the sign for white, an emblem vaguely reminiscent of an inverted hand, and Beyer's "serpent segment." An examination of these examples of Glyph X shows great variation in the compounds. In one case (fig. 37,43) the pseudo-white sign is the main element; it has two postfixes, one of which is the standard bundle affix. This bundle postfix may be a substitute for the main element which I have suggested may be a variant of it. Several of these factors reappear in the variable element of the IS introductory glyph corresponding to the month Pax (fig. 23,18–20,34). In three cases the dubious bundle element with "inverted Ahau" at top is before the head of the deity; on two occasions the outline resembling an inverted hand appears in the headdress; once the pseudo-white sign is set at the back of the head; and in two cases what appears to be the pad of a large member of the cat family is displayed at the back of the god's temple, perhaps corresponding to the closed fist of the Glyph X variant.

The same interchangeability of elements occurs in the case of Glyph G7 (fig. 34,32–37): the dubious bundle with "inverted Ahau" appears in two examples; the pseudo-white sign is the main element in one glyph and may be merged with the main sign in another (fig. 34,35); the clenched fist is the prominent headdress of a personified form of the glyph. In one case the glyph appears to have a coefficient of 7. One wonders whether this can symbolize the jaguar whose features seem to be incorporated in the portraits of the patron of Pax. It is quite consonant with Maya practice to record the number 7, not as a numerical factor, but as an attribute of the jaguar god, patron of that number.

We have, in short, identified a chain of related elements usable in three distinct glyphs, the general functions of which are known, but the precise meanings of which still escape us; but there is reason to believe that these related elements either have the same metaphrastic value or are related as members of a single body of attributive symbols. With that knowledge gained, we are on the alert for substitutions of one of these elements for another in other glyphic combinations, but disappointedly we realize that the number of glyphic elements which alone can represent some sound or idea is constantly shrinking. With a limited number of glyphic symbols to match with sounds or ideas, each new case of extravagance in interchangeability reduces the number of elements remaining to represent untranslated words. At the same time it is becoming apparent that unless the glyphs were incapable of reproducing Maya thought with some efficacy, most glyphic elements must have an extensive range of usages. Naturally, this makes decipherment more difficult, for each glyph in a context may have a series of meanings from which the most appropriate is to be chosen.

Decipherment of glyphs of unknown meaning is of secondary importance to comprehension of the structure of the glyphic writing, but is more perceptible evidence of progress. Among the reasonably certain decipherments here offered for the first time are glyphs for:

cuch (burden), the *cuch haab* (burden of year) compound, drought, continuous drought, abundance, heaped-up abundance, abundance of maize, sprouting maize, maize of various colors, seed and maize seed, seed plot (milpa), dark day, sun darkened, moon darkened, storm with lightning, brilliant sun, rainy sky, wind, *zac ik* (light? wind), evil, year of evil, *multun tzek* (heap of skulls), good tidings, *ahaulil* (rulership), drilling, *xoc* (count), fainting, tree, yaxche, rainy sky, and the glyph of Bolon-Yocte.

Tentative identifications include:

verbal glyphs, such as the hand forms for *etma* (hold in one's hand) or perhaps *machma* (take in one's hands, hence influence), *tz'a* (give) or *matan* (grace received); the *hel* (succeed or change places) element; the *bix* glyph used as a numerical classifier; two new signs to indicate the completion of a tun (figs. 32,56–60; 33,1–3); glyphs which may indicate counts to the seating of a tun and the seating of a day; a possible glyph for jade beads; and what may be a glyph for *uin* (set in order).

Among affixes identified are:

postfixes used with period glyphs to indicate a distance number and to call attention to katun and tun anniversaries; the locative *ti* affix; the forward prefix; the anterior postfix and the "eel" prefix with the same value; three affixes to denote *te* as a numerical classifier; *tu* prefix to denote an ordinal; the moon and bracket signs to indicate the possessive *u* or to convert a cardinal to an ordinal; the *il* relationship affix; the *kaz* (evil) sign as a modifier (halfway good etc.); the tun sign as an intensifier, as in the *kintunyaabil* (drought) glyph, and to denote end, as with the twentieth day of a uinal; the seating prefix used with month signs and the winged cauac; the *chac* prefix used in the sense of "great"; the kan cross, zero symbol, shell, and other signs signifying water; the maize prefix; the brightness (of sun and lightning) prefix; the dog as an affix to denote a connection with fire; Beyer's "owl plume" perhaps with the value *ak* and used with Ahau to indicate a period ending; and perhaps the "Ben-Ich" affix.

New variants of glyphs now first established include:

the personified forms of the propeller glyph (fig. 30,54); the *te* affix (fig. 34,21,63,68), the up-ended frog (cf. fig. 3,10, Gl 6; 12, Gl 5 with 11, Gl 5), the death eyes (fig. 4,7,8; note the manikin head alone replaces the death eyes in the Ahau-bundle compound; fig. 46,10–12,16); what may be a personified form of the distance number introductory glyph; the symbolic form of the day Chicchan on the monuments (firmly established and identified with yax symbol); a little head with an Olmec mouth as a personification of a postfix resembling, perhaps identical with, the *il* affix (fig. 3,3, Gl 2; 4, Gl 2; 9, Gl 5); the complete fish as a personified form of the comb; the vulture as a personified form of the *ti* affix; a personified form of the caban (non-day) glyph (fig. 5,24); a personified form of Etz'nab, as well as early forms of that day sign showing the flint blade; the symbolic form of the patron of the month Mol; a new variant of the baktun (fig. 26,19,22); the characteristic affix which distinguishes the kinchiltun from the calabtun; head variants for Kankin and Uo (fig. 35,8,10); and a head variant for the patron of the month Kankin.

Some connections have been established between Maya glyphs and those used by cultures to the north, although the search for such associations was incidental to the study and was not pursued. The kan cross, the Moan bird, and the spiral are used in both the Maya area and Teotihuacan with an aquatic value; jade is a Maya symbol for the year and turquoise is the Mexican equivalent; many day names have the same associations in the two areas (e.g. Akbal and Calli are days of the jaguar god of the interior of the earth, both Eb and Malinalli refer to the destructive effects of certain kinds of rains and mists, and both Men and Quauhtli are days of the old moon goddess); the moon glyph has water symbols added sometimes in both areas, a reference to the moon's residence in the land of the rain gods; and, finally, Mexican influences in Dresden, such as the presence of the gods Ixquimilli and Quetzalcoatl, the *oyoualli* ornament, and the opossum priest, were noted.

In the calendarial and arithmetical aspects of glyphic research our knowledge is increased by the identification of a cycle of 819 days, recorded on a number of monuments, which appears to have lunar and solar associations with the end of the current katun. Teeple's determinant thesis that the Maya calculated the discrepancy between their year of 365 days and the solar year receives confirmation from the discovery that there are records of such calculations giving a solar correction for 8 Cumku close to nearly all the CR anniversaries of 4 Ahau 8 Cumku which fell in the active period of stela erection.

In the field of astronomy a rearrangement of the table giving the starting points of the Venus cycle in the LC is offered, and there is a discussion of a possible combination of groupings of 405 and 361 lunations. The problem of the inauguration of the LC is newly explored, and a suggestion advanced to account for Imix not falling on the first day of each uinal. Evidence is given (expanded in App. IV) of the enormous periods of time covered by some Maya calculations into the past. Some of these amount to several million years; the longest covers a span of some 400,000,000 years. Tables which appear to deal with the burner ceremony and the *u sian chac*, "birth of Chac," ceremonies were uncovered in Dresden, and a contact was thereby made between that codex and the books of Chilam Balam, establishing the continuity of Maya ritualistic practice. A relationship between the heads of Glyph C of the lunar series and Glyph X was brought to light, together with some evidence that Glyph C refers to the current moon.

Enough has been written to give an idea both of the complexity of the subject and of such success as has attended this essay in decipherment.

Unfortunately, many of the mythological and lexical references on which the glyphs were based are now lost, with the result that associations of ideas, easily understood by an educated Maya, are incomprehensible to us. Sometimes such associations are discernible in Maya art, as, for example, in the use of the conch shell as a symbol of the underworld or the water lily as an emblem of the earth's surface or its interior; sometimes they have survived in the beliefs or folklore of the present-day Maya, as, for instance, the belief that the souls of the dead return to earth as insects on the day Cib, or the connection of the dog with fire and with the underworld, or the existence of snake deities called *chicchan;* sometimes the associations can be found in the writings of Landa and others of the sixteenth and seventeenth centuries, for ex-

ample, the assignment of death and drought to the south; often they can be inferred from ideas prevalent among the Mexicans, and that applies to derivations of the patrons of various days, notably those of Akbal, Ix, and Men. Nevertheless, the gaps in our knowledge of those subjects are lamentable. It is as though one were to read a political broadsheet or satire of the eighteenth century with little or no knowledge of the personalities, issues, and topical allusions of that period.

Manifestly, with many diverse meanings already established for glyphic elements and many more which escape us, one is confronted with a Herculean task. The glyphs are anagogical, but we have only a scant idea of the mysteries; even where we ken the inferences, gaps in our translation of the context make a choice between them difficult. Without a full understanding of the text one can not, for instance, tell whether the presence of a glyph of a dog refers to that animal's rôle as bringer of fire to mankind or to his duty of leading the dead to the underworld. That such mystical meanings are imbedded in the glyphs is beyond doubt, but as yet we can only guess as to the association the Maya author had in mind. Clearly, our duty is to seek more of those mythological allusions. Indeed, one can state unhesitatingly that without a thorough knowledge of all the source materials on Maya and Mexican religion, mythology, and folklore "we weave but nets to catch the wind."

Even when, in the distant future, the meanings of nearly all glyphic elements are known, there will ever be a certain looseness in translation, and for many short passages alternative renderings will always be possible; the translator will have to select from several choices the meaning which will best fit the context. This, really, is not discouraging, for our ultimate objective is not the literal word-for-word decipherment of the glyphs, but a fuller comprehension of the mentality, the poetic concepts, and the philosophical outlook of the Maya. That objective can be achieved even if we hesitate between two related interpretations of the difficult passage.

The decipherment of Maya hieroglyphic writing is not comparable to reading a difficult anagram, although I would be the last to deny either that the search is a fascinating task or that the mere increment of knowledge is not a worthy goal. With the anagram solved and the momentary glow of achievement extinguished, one forgets it to turn to something else, for one can proceed no further; the solution of the glyphic problem is something vastly different, for it leads us, key in hand, to the threshold of the inner keep of the Maya soul, and bids us enter. In truth, that simile is not all it might be in that it implies a complaisant acceptance of a right to enter in possession of the spiritual heritage of the Maya. That is not the case so far as I am concerned; the relationship is one which can best be expressed in terms of mediaeval and renaissance painting. The mystery is painted; the donor kneels in humility, a figure in the composition, yet aware that he is an intruder who has gained a privilege far greater than his meed.

The Maya rose to heights of spiritual grandeur, unfortified by which they could never have freed their culture from the shackles of a poor soil, a deleterious climate, inadequate methods of agriculture, and a pitifully restricted range of tools. Our own culture is the opposite of that of the Maya, for materially it has infinite wealth and resources, but spiritually it is desperately impoverished. In religious feeling and sense of duty, in happiness and tranquility, in painting and sculpture, in poetry and prose, in music, and in architecture, too, I think, but with less assurance, our present civilization is at low ebb, displaying vast mudflats of purposeless living and frustration. In such a sad plight we may well humble ourselves to inquire how and why the Maya, endowed with scant material resources, made a success of their life, whereas we, with all nature at our command, have fallen woefully short of that objective. The general answer to that inquiry, if we have the humility to make it, must lie in the greater spiritual wealth of the Maya, but the detailed story can be ours only if we busy ourselves in mastering the script in which the Maya classics are writ. Progress has been made, and "now at last the sacred influence of light appears, and from the walls of heaven shoots far into the bosom of dim night a glimmering dawn."

ADDENDUM

Through the courtesy of Señor Alberto Ruz L., I am able to refer to the magnificent hieroglyphic tablet found in the course of the first (1949) season's excavations at Palenque under his direction.

The text opens with an IS 9.10.11.17.0 11 Ahau 8 Mac expressed as full figures. The numerical coefficients are of particular interest in that the characteristic attributes are on the bodies or headdresses, not on the faces. Thus the heads for 11 have the caban element on arms and legs; the head for 10 is that of a youthful deity who wears a skull on his head and a death-head pectoral. There follows a date 9.10.10.11.2 1 Ik 15 Yaxkin, which is a base in the 819-day cycle (p. 212). Like that of the Cross, the accompanying glyphs do not conform to the usual pattern.

The most outstanding feature of the text is the presence of two complete lunar series (one somewhat damaged)

with CR dates; hitherto no lunar series has been found except with an IS. In two of the three lunar series Glyphs D and E are replaced by the head of God C with water affixes (Kan cross, shell, and circlets in elbow), and in both cases a kind of long V-shaped flare issues from the eye. This extends across the affixes to the left edge of the glyph, where there is a small circle between its arms. The design is similar to that on Copan N (fig. 36,*1*) save that in the Copan example the flare starts at the edge of the face, not from the eye (could it have been thought to have emerged from the hidden eye?). One is reminded of the legend that Sun plucked out one of Moon's eyes because the light she shed was too bright (Thompson, 1930, p. 132). The Pipil of Izalco say that Sun hits Moon so that one of her eyes is weak, and at Palopo there is a belief that the moon is blind in one eye (Redfield, 1946, p. 220). Sun and Moon fight, causing eclipses. However, the interval between the two associated dates is not correct for eclipses, so one can rule out that possibility. Accordingly, it is far from improbable that this glyph pictures the extinguishing of the moon's light at disappearance before conjunction. There are grounds for believing that God C's head may represent the sun at dawn (p. 171), and it is in the sun's morning rays that the old moon is lost to sight. Whether this be the correct explanation or not, we probably have in this glyph a pictorial representation of old moon's light lost to view at disappearance or conjunction (note the water emblems).

There is on this tablet an example of the "forward to sunrise" glyph, hitherto believed to have been confined to Piedras Negras and nearby El Cayo (p. 166). There is also an example of the "eel" affix as an anterior date indicator (p. 164), and another example of Glyph E used in a distance number with the value 20 (p. 167). Here, however, the shell-kin variant is interposed between the coefficient of 5 and the moon glyph; the whole records an interval of 25 days.

There are two examples of the dog (?) head variant of the kin used in distance numbers (p. 168). The crossed bones replace the eye in both cases; the coefficients are the completion affix and 18, respectively. It may be significant that this glyph is still unreported with a coefficient of less than 8. The one-shell-period glyph (p. 194) occurs with 9.10.10.11.2 1 Ik 15 Yaxkin. There is an example of Glyph G2 and two personified forms of G7; the shell-and-water variant of the tun (p. 193) appears.

A preliminary report by me on this text will have been published in Mexico as part of the report on the first season's excavations at Palenque before this publication is issued.

Divinatory Almanacs in the Books of Chilam Balam

Noble stock was graft with crab-tree slip.
—SHAKESPEARE, *Henry VI*, Pt. 2, Act 3, Scene 2

IN SEVERAL of the books of Chilam Balam and in Perez are the sorry remnants of the old art of prognostication of the days of the sacred almanac. These fall into three groups. Two examples (Perez 1 and Kaua 1) of days with their prognostications fitted to uinals of the old Maya calendar form the first, and least European, group; in Perez 1 degenerate examples of the day glyphs are given, but in no other case are any glyphs present. In the second group (Tizimin, Kaua 2, Ixil, Perez 2–4) the days are fitted to the Christian year starting with January 1, and there is varying emphasis on festivals of the Roman Catholic Church. Tizimin, for example, has few ecclesiastical notations; Kaua 2 has saints' names for practically all the days of the year. The names of the Maya months are given, with start of Pop correlated with July 16. Maya influence is even less apparent in almanacs of the third group (Nah and Tekax). Prognostications are confined to a bald statement whether the day is good or bad and even that is found with only the first three months; Maya day names are given, but the corresponding numerals are omitted. Maya month names are inserted.

All these almanacs appear to be traceable to two sources, or perhaps even to a single source. Perez 1 and Kaua 1 derive from an almanac fitted to a year 5 Kan. This could have been that of the years 1585, 1637, or 1689. I am inclined to think it may have been a sixteenth-century original. All the remaining almanacs must stem from a single source, for all start with 10 Oc on January 1, and have 11 Cimi as the year bearer on first of Pop. This is, of course, an impossible combination by orthodox Maya standards, and surely reflects the degeneracy of the calendar in colonial times. One explanation of its origin is given below. However, apart from the fact that 11 Cimi could not be the year bearer, it is inconceivable that compilers of six different almanacs should have independently chosen a year with 11 Cimi on first of Pop when there were fifty-one other choices. Furthermore, Kaua 2 and Perez 2 both pass from 6 Manik to 8 Lamat, and continue 9 Muluc, 10 Oc, 11 Chuen, 12 Eb, etc.; Kaua 1 jumps from 10 Chuen to 12 Eb, and that suggests strongly that the compiler of Kaua 1 was copying the day list from Kaua 2 or Perez 2 or a common ancestor, and

corrected his transcription to conform to the mistake in the original four places further down the list.

Furthermore, the sequence of good and bad days and the entries of "warnings and portents and evils imminent" agree so closely that there can be little doubt as to their common source.

PEREZ 1 (MANI)

Perez 1 (pages 96–99) once was part of Mani. It is a fragment consisting of a sequence of 80 days (one is accidentally omitted) which starts with 5 Kan and ends with 6 Akbal. As the starting point 5 Kan is said to be the year bearer, one can assume that the entries correspond to the uinals Pop, Uo, Zip, and Zotz', although there is no mention of those names. At the end of 20, 40, and 60 days are the phrases: "It turns back a second time," "It turns back a third time," and "It turns back a fourth time." As these entries precede what would be the starting points of the second, third, and fourth uinals, they serve to confirm the arrangement by uinals. On the left of each page are the day glyphs, woefully degenerate and, for the most part, unrecognizable. Each is enclosed within a square; coefficients are lacking. To the right of each glyph its name and number is written in European script, together with the luck of the day and sometimes a more specific divination. For example: *Uaxac Manik utz ma kazi utzul haab lae,* "8 Manik, Good, not evil. Good rain there."

An outline of the aspects of the days is given in Table 20. For the translation of the entries, not only of this almanac but of the rest of the series, I am indebted to Ralph L. Roys. Some of the passages are corrupt; others are in archaic language. All are abbreviated. These factors have made good translations difficult, and the absence of context is a serious drawback, for often more than one translation is possible. As an illustration of the difficulties, one might cite two entries which are of frequent occurrence. The first is the expression *balam haab,* which literally means balam (or jaguar) year. It seems unlikely that the expression can have this meaning here because it is referable to individual days. *Haab,* however, has the meaning of rain in several Maya languages and dialects, and it is therefore logical to apply that meaning to these entries, particularly since so many deal with rains and planting. This suggestion is largely confirmed by an entry in Kaua 1 where *balam hail* and *balam hab* occur together and seem to refer to the same thing. *Balam hail* is balam rain (or water).

We have no exact information as to what a balam rain may be. The balams are the guardians of the villages and milpas in the beliefs of the Yucatec Maya of the present day and are closely associated with the winds, but as they are coupled with the usual rain gods in prayers, almost as though *balam* and *chac* were synonymous, it is not unreasonable to suppose that a balam rain was one sent by the balams, but balam rains may be unfortunate, and in that case a different derivation is probable. Note jaguar glyphs in phrase at Yaxchilan which often contains the supposed glyph for rainy sky (fig. 46,*10–14,16*).

The second expression which can be translated in more ways than one is *u sian* or *u siyan,* which is often linked to the words *chaac* or *ku. Sian* can mean birth, or enchantment, or conjuring in witchcraft, or gift. The various contexts reveal that the meaning which will best fit all the entries is that of birh or beginning. This expression has already been fully discussed (p. 259). In the tabulation the comments have been made even briefer than in the originals.

The entries in Perez 1 are entirely of an agricultural nature with the possible exception of a notation to the effect that 10 Men is the day of the burner (p. 99); there are no social entries as in the Tizimin group of almanacs, and the sequence of good and bad days also is quite different from that of the almanacs composing that group.

Perez 1 is probably the most authentic source we now possess for sundry reasons. It is the only almanac which gives the glyphs. Perez 1 and Kaua 1 are the only two which correlate the almanac with the Maya year, and alone fail to list any Christian festivals. Perez 1 is much more reliable than Kaua 1 for reasons which will shortly appear. Nevertheless, I am suspicious of the value of the entries, for I should not be surprised to learn that they had been shifted from a year with a bearer of different name and number.

KAUA 1

Kaua 1 is a section of only 40 days correlated with two Maya uinals, the first entry, the day 9 Kan, being recorded as a year bearer. It is therefore clear that Kaua 1 seeks to correlate the sacred almanac with a Maya year.

The prognostications in Kaua 1, unfortunately, are nearly worthless, for if they are compared with the sequence in Perez 1 they will be found to be about the same. That is to say, Kaua 1 has the same entries for 9 Kan, 10 Chicchan, 11 Cimi etc. as Perez 1 has for 5 Kan, 6

Chicchan, 7 Cimi etc. Clearly, the compiler of Kaua 1 took the entries for a year with 5 Kan as the year bearer, and used them for a year 9 Kan, presumably under the impression that the luck of the day depended on its position not in the 260-day almanac, but in the months.

That the entries for a year 5 Kan were applied to a year 9 Kan and not vice versa is proved by internal evidence. Perez 1 correctly gives one entry concerning the burners, for the day 10 Men is said to be a burner's day. Kaua 1 lists as burner days: 2 Oc, 4 Chicchan, 9 Oc, and 1 Men (corrected from 2 Men) and perhaps 6 Ix. Of these only 4 Chicchan is correct. However, if the year 9 Kan had been formed from the entries for a year 5 Kan, 2 Oc and 1 Men would have been 11 Oc and 10 Men respectively in a year 5 Kan and those are true days of the burner (p. 99). On the supposition that 6 Ix was a slip for the following day, 7 Men, its equivalent in a year 5 Kan would have been 3 Men, which is in fact a burner day. 9 Oc is not a burner day either in a year 9 Kan or in a year 5 Kan. It is therefore clear that the author of Kaua 1 copied from the prototype of Perez 1 the entries for Pop and Uo, but changed the day sequence from 5 Kan 6 Cimi, etc., to 9 Kan 10 Cimi, etc., without realizing that thereby he made nonsense of all the entries. That Kaua 1 was not copied directly from Perez 1 is evident from the fact that there are details in the former which do not occur in the latter.

On the other hand, the resemblances between Perez 1 and Kaua 1 are so close, extending even to the same introductory paragraph, and to the same notes that the reckoning turns back at the end of 20 days, that it is apparent that there once existed two almanacs correlated with a year 9 Kan, or perhaps with a Christian year. One had what were probably correct entries; the other jumped the coefficient one place between 6 Manik and 12 Eb. The author of Kaua 1 copied the list of days from the latter, but set against them the entries from Perez 1. I am even inclined to believe that this may have been a piece of conscious antiquarianism, and that the author may have converted entries correlated with a Christian year back to a Maya year. The error in Kaua 2 suggests that that was the source of the day list of Kaua 1 if the latter is conscious antiquarianism. Whether that be the case or not, it is clear that the digits of the entries in Kaua 1 should be reduced by four (for those entries subsequent to 10 Chuen by five) places to obtain the correct prognostications.

TIZIMIN GROUP

The prognostications in Tizimin, Kaua 2, Ixil, and Perez 2–4, as already noted, are correlated with a Christian year. That the entries derive from a sacred almanac is abundantly clear. Items assigned to Maya days early in the year usually are associated with its second appearance, 260 days later. Thus January 13 and September 30 carry the same entry, *U kukum tok ch'apahal yani,* "Parade of the Warriors (?), there is sickness," in Tizimin and Perez 4, because 9 Ik falls on both positions. Other dates which carry the same prognostication for both appearances include 11 Kan, 13 Cimi, 1 Manik, 6 Eb, 12 Etz'nab, 1 Ahau, 7 Cimi, 12 Chuen, 1 Ben, 11 Akbal, 12 Kan, 4 Muluc, and 6 Chuen.

The entries in all cases start with 10 Oc on January 1. Maya month names are added, the seating of Pop occurring on 11 Cimi, July 16. This is an impossible situation, for the year bearer must be Kan, Muluc, Ix, or Cauac, and the seating of Pop should, if our theory be correct (p. 127), fall on Akbal, Lamat, Ben, or Etz'nab.

It cannot be coincidence that 9 Kan, which as we saw was the year bearer in Kaua 1, falls on July 14 in all the calendars of the Tizimin group. I suggest that the almanac was adjusted to a Maya year soon after the Spanish conquest when the year bearer fell on July 14. That would have been 1556 to 1560, a time at which the old calendar system was starting to decline, but before July 16 had been accepted as the permanent equivalent of first of Pop. With such a calendar Cimi would have corresponded to July 16. The author of the much later adjustment to a year starting with January 1 made 11 Cimi the year bearer because he had believed (most erroneously) that the Maya equivalent of July 16 was always first of Pop. He must have known that Kan, Muluc, Ix, and Cauac were the year bearers because the Tizimin almanac carries notations to the effect that 5 Ix and 6 Cauac (could) fall on first of Pop, but these entries are opposite the occurrences of those days, respectively, in June and September.

The arrangement of the prognostications, as they now stand, is at variance with what we know of the luck of the days. They are listed below in the order of their favorability, the numbers representing respectively good, bad, and uncertain days: Cimi (9, 3, 1); Oc and Etz'nab (8, 5, 0); Chicchan (7, 5, 1); Caban, Cauac, and Ahau (7, 6, 0); Cib (6, 6, 1); Men (6, 7, 0); Manik (5, 5, 3); Muluc (5, 8, 0); Imix and Eb (4, 8, 1); Ik, Akbal, Lamat, Chuen, and Ben (3, 10, 0); Kan (3, 9, 1); and Ix (2, 11, 0).

Cimi, day of death, and presumably a day of dire misfortune, stands at the head of the list! Most amazingly it is associated with rain. Oc and Etz'nab follow, yet both have low ratings on the monuments. Imix, which was second on the monuments, occupies twelfth place, and Kan, day of maize, is nineteenth on the list!

The luck of the day frequently disagrees with the activity for that day: 1 Kan, 2 Eb, 9 Imix, 12 Men, and 13 Etz'nab are listed as bad, yet they are days for planting; rain is usually welcome in Yucatan, yet days of rain are often listed as evil in these almanacs; clever men are born on 9 Ik and 12 Ik, but these are bad days. 1 Manik is a good day, but it brings punishment of boys and sickness. In our culture corporal chastisement of little wanton boys might well convert an indifferent day into one distinctly beneficial to the community, but one can be fairly certain that the prognostication refers to divine punishment, a far more serious matter. Indeed, it is not improbable that the entries concerning castigation of sundry groups (nobles, priests, officials, craftsmen, and boys) reflect the last stage of degeneration from the pattern of punishment inflicted by Venus at heliacal rising.

The whole scheme of prognostication is so mangled and so full of errors that it is next door to meaningless. There are many obvious errors and many more which one can infer. One almanac places an event on one day, another places it a day before or after; events that fall on days that repeat in the last 105 days of the year may recur after 259 or 261 days instead of 260. Obvious mistakes in spelling and mutilated and meaningless words and sentences are frequent in all but the simplest entries, and it is clear that the copyists had no idea of what they were copying in the more involved sentences.

One feels like averting one's face at the spectacle of this sad degeneracy. Can any good be gained by examining these monstrous abnormalities? The attempt has been worth while, for it has shown how little faith one can place in the historical reliability of compilers of the chronicles in view of their sorry efforts with the prognostics.

Even this Sodom and this Gomorrah have their Lot: one interesting set of entries, found with the days 1 Ahau, 6 Ahau, and 8 Lamat, surely refer, although in a sadly garbled way, to the Venus cult. The day 8 Lamat is said to be "the jaguar-faced 1 Ahau with the protruding teeth." 1 Ahau is the day of Venus, and undoubtedly serves also as a name for the Venus god at the moment of heliacal rising, when he emerges from the underworld, for 1 Ahau is the *lub* of the Venus cycle. We have seen that Lahun-Chan, who was the god of the planet Venus, had protruding teeth, and there are references to his jaguar features (pp. 77, 218). This passage, therefore, serves to confirm our deductions as to the nature of the Venus god, and at the same time indicates a weak tradition of the old cult which survived the many transcriptions of these 260-day almanacs. Lamat is the day of the planet Venus, although I know of no particular reason for expecting a coefficient of 8 except that it recalls the eight days of invisibility of the planet at inferior conjunction. For 1 Ahau, the day of Venus, we find in these almanacs the entry: "there comes forth a great putrescence from the underworld by day and night. Sudden death." I recall no direct connection between Venus and putrescence, but the underworld, the land of death, might well have such an association, and Cizin's name may derive from *ciz,* which has a parallel connotation of offensive odor. This prognostic, I should judge, must again refer to Venus at the moment of leaving the underworld at the end of the eight days of invisibility at inferior conjunction; sudden death would denote the death which Venus was believed to deal at the moment of heliacal rising. There is no known connection between Venus and the day 6 Ahau, yet monuments dedicated at 9.14.0.0.0 6 Ahau 13 Muan tend to be decorated with Venus symbols, so 6 Ahau may have been a Venus day of importance.

Notations of the days of the burner period are made in the various almanacs; the survival of this period long after the ceremonies connected therewith had fallen into desuetude bears witness to the former importance of this cycle of ceremonies. The *sian chac* entries seem to be entirely mixed up, but their presence, in however garbled form, testifies to the former prominence of that cycle.

The copyist responsible for Perez 3 is the most careless, for he has many entries a day before or after they should occur. Perez 2 advances the day coefficients by one place on jumping from 6 Manik to 8 Lamat on August 7, but corrects the error on September 18. The same jump occurs on October 5, where the count goes from 13 Cimi to 2 Manik, and again on November 15 where 5 Muluc follows 3 Manik. As a result, day coefficients are two places too great from November 15 to the end of the year. Such mistakes, and they occur in other almanacs on a smaller scale, indicate that the scribes no longer related the prophecies to the Maya number and name combination, but to positions in the Christian year. In Table 20 I have made allowances for these errors, entering the items under their correct days. I have omitted Kaua 1 from the tabulation because of the certainty that all the entries are those for a year 5 Kan changed to a year 9 Kan, and entries concerning the burners and the days on which Maya months were seated have likewise been excluded. I have somewhat simplified the translations and have read garbled words as though they were correctly given. I have also suppressed all entries concerning festivals of the Roman Catholic Church, although these are not without interest in revealing successive steps of degeneration in Maya wit and wisdom accompanied by an increasing interest in church festivals. The last stage in this unhappy descent from the Maya Helicon is reached in the almanacs of Nah and Tekax. In these the Maya day names without their numbers (as useful as a telephone number without the exchange name) are listed,

TABLE 20—PROGNOSTICATIONS FOR DAYS IN ALMANACS

Day Number	Day Name	Good or Bad	Event and Almanac in which recorded
9	Imix	B	Day of maize, P1
11		B	For Batabs, T, P4
1	Ik	G	For nobles, T, P2, P4
3		B	Strong wind, P2
4		B	Day of rain, P2; fish spawn, Ix
5		B	Strong wind, P2
6		B	Day of rain, K2, P2
9		B	Warriors parade, T, T,* P4; sickness, T,* K2, P2, P4; clever men born, P3 (twice)
11		G	Wind comes from the conch, T, K2, P2–4 (twice each); day of rain, T, K2, P4 (twice)
12		B	Clever men born, T, Ix, K2, P2–4
1	Akbal	B	Vigil, Ix
3		G	Heavy rains, T, T,† P4
5		B	Day of rain, P2
11		G	Ah kulel punished for sins, T, Ix, P2 (twice), P4 (twice)
12		G	Storm, rainy day, P3
13		B	Vigil, T, Ix, P2–4
1	Kan	B	Sultry weather, T, P2, P4; storm, P2; plant, T
4		G	Heavy rain, T, P4
6		G	Start of rains, T, Ix, K2,† P2–4 (last, twice); day of rain, P2†
9		G	Gifts, T, Ix, P3, P4 (twice); plant jicama, T
10		B	Vigil, Ix
11		G	Day of storm, P2; start of storm, P4; rain falls, T, P2, P3*; end of rainfall, T, Ix, P3
12		B	Lords punished for sins, T, Ix, K2, P4 (twice); lords die, T, Ix, K2, P2 (twice)
13		B	Day of fasting for god, T, Ix, P2 (twice), P3,† P4
6	Chicchan	B	Smoky sky, K2, P2
7		G	Rain, P2
1	Cimi	B	Cizin and death, K2, P2; deer pestilence, P1
4		G	Start of storm, T, Ix; birth of god (same?), P3, P4; rainy day, P2
6		G	Storm, K2, P2; birth of god, T, P4
7		G	Rain, T, P1, P3, P4; start of storm, T, P1, P3, P4; storm, P3, P4
8		G	Start of storm, heavy rains, P1
9		G	Strong wind, P2
13		G	Start of storm, T, Ix, P2–4 (last two, twice)
1	Manik	G	Boys punished, T (twice), K2, Ix, P2–4 (all twice); sickness, T, P3
8		G	Rain, P1, P4; for miserable ones, P2
12		G	For planting, T, Ix, K2, P2, P4
1	Lamat	B	Adhesion of leg of jaguar (?), T, P2, P4
3		B	Day for beans, limas, jicamas, P1
4		G	Water falls, very hard, Ix, P3, P4
6		B	Vigil, abundance, Ix; kills crops, P1
8		B	Jaguar-faced 1 Ahau with protruding teeth, T, Ix, P2–4
9		B	Milpa matters, P1

TABLE 20—PROGNOSTICATIONS FOR DAYS IN ALMANACS—*Continued*

Day Number	Day Name	Good or Bad	Event and Almanac in which recorded	Day Number	Day Name	Good or Bad	Event and Almanac in which recorded
10	Lamat	B	Jicamas, P1	4	Cib	B	Vigil, T (twice), K2, P2 (twice), P4
12		B	Encounter with Cizin, K2, P2	5		G	Jaguar rains, P1; planting, P3
1	Muluc	G	Calm for planting, T, P3, P4	6		B	Travel in woods (hunting?), T, Ix, K2, P2–4; call deer, T,† Ix,† P2,† P3, P4†
4		G	Thunder, T (twice), K2, P2, P4 (last two, twice), P3; clouds wander, P4	7		B	Continuous rain, K2, P4
5		B	Brings a rainy day, Ix, P2–4	13		G	Clouds scurry, K2, P2
6		G	Count of sunsets, T, Ix, P2, P4; day of heavy rain, P3	5	Caban	B	Sins of nobles (or craftsmen) punished, T, T,* Ix, P2, P2,* P3,* P4, P4*; sickness, K2
8		B	Close of vigil, T, Ix, P3, P4; calm sky, P3	10		G	Birth of Ahaus, T, P2–4
12		B	Penance, 3 nights of vigil, T, Ix, K2, P2–4; encounter with Cizin, K2, P2	12		B	Storm in west, T; bees, wild animals, P1
1	Oc	G	Great rain, Ix, K2, P3, P4; great storm, T, P2	13		G	Beekeeping, K2, P2
3		B	Jaguar year (rain), P3; wind, T	2	Etz'nab	G	Make settlements, T, P2
7		B	Thunder, P2	3		G	Banquets, gifts, T, P4
12		B	Thunder in west, Ix, K2, P2–4	6		B	Sickness, K2*?, P2
13		G	Day of rain, T, K2, P2–4	7		G	Plant, T, Ix, P2, P3,* P4; plant *noh uah*, T; day of *noh uah*, P2; perhaps (rain) will fall, P2; beginning of storm, good rain, P1
1	Chuen	B	Perhaps rain in east, K2, P2				
6		B	Conch closed, T (twice), Ix, P2, P4 (last two, twice), P3*	8		B	Holy men, T, Ix, K2, P2, P3,* P4
10		B	Start of sudden death, strong winds, T; sudden death, 5 days, K2, P2†; start of sudden death, 5 days, Ix, P3,† P4	12		B	Closing passage of conch (?), Ix, P2, P3, P3,* P4 (twice); sickness, T; death, K2, P2–4
12		G?	Punishment for sins of priests, vigil, T, Ix, P2–4 (all twice)	13		G	Plant, T (twice), Ix, P2 (twice), P3,* P4; rain, T, P2, P3,* P4; perhaps rain, P2; storm in west, P2, P4; thunder and rain, K2
13		B	If rain falls, sun, P1				
2	Eb	B	Plant crops, T	1	Cauac	B	Cold, T, Ix, K2, P2, P4 (twice); storm, K2
4		G	For deer hunters, T, Ix, P2, P3,† P4	3		G	Day of rain, K2, P2; start of rain, P3, P4
6		G	For deer hunting, T, Ix, K2, P2–4	5		B	Great wind, T
7		B	Wind, flooding rains, P1	8		G	Plant *noh uah*, T
11		B	Sudden death, for 5 days, K2, P2, P3 (see under 10 Chuen, 13 Ix, 1 Men)	9		G	For rulers of hives (?), T, P2, P4
13		B	Day of vigil, T, P4; sickness, K2	1	Ahau	B	Comes forth a great putrescence, T (twice), P2, P3,* P4 (last two, twice); from hell by day and night, P2, P3,* P4; sudden death, Ix, P3,* P4; fever, Ix
1	Ben	B	Sickness, T (twice), Ix, K2, K2,† P2, P2,† P3, P3,* P4				
3		B	Hunting, T, K2, P2–4	2		B	Cold, T, Ix, K2, P2; great cold, P4
5		G?	Strong wind for sowing, P3; shortness of breath, stabbing pain, T, Ix, P2, P4	6		B	There comes forth a great hellish putrescence, T, P4; great hellish fever from Metnal, K2; death, P2
1	Ix	B	Men die; end of men dying, Ix, P3, P4; birth of lords, T, K2, P2, P3,† P4				
4		B	Sins adhere to chiefs, T, Ix, K2, P2–4	8		B	Encounter with Cisin, T, Ix, K2, P2 (all except T, twice); sudden death, P2; vigil, K2
6		B	Vigil, Ix	9		G	Getting ready of the god, T, P2, P4 (each twice), P3; the birth of the god, P3
9		B	Sun also, P1				
12		G	Jaguar rains, T, K2, P2–4	10		B	Day of rain, P3, P4
13		B	Sudden death, P2	12		G	Wise men born, T, K2, P2, P3,† P4; writers born, P2
1	Men	B	End of sudden death, T, Ix, K2, P2–4	13		G	Wind, T
4		G	Drought, P1				
6		B	Rabbit rains, P4				
7		G	Great thunderstorm, Ix				
10		G	Thunderstorm, Ix, K2, P2, P2,* P4; sun, its burden, P1				
12		B	Great storm, planting, Ix; heavy rain, planting, P2–4				
13		G	Fortunate for traders, T, P3, P4; vigil, T, P2–4				
2	Cib	G?	Birth of god (Chac?), P4				
3		G	Bees hived, T, Ix, K2,† P2 (twice), P3, P3,† P4 (twice)				

*Listed one day early (e.g. 13 Cauac instead of 1 Ahau).
†Listed one day late (e.g. 13 Imix instead of 12 Ahau).
Ix, Ixil; K, Kaua; P, Perez; T, Tizimin.

starting with Oc (10 Oc as in the Tizimin group?) on January 1. The good or bad luck of the days in a sequence similar to that of the Tizimin group is noted for the first three months of the year; from April on, even that feature is omitted. There are no prognostications; the spaces they should occupy are devoted to the saints and festivals of the Roman Catholic church.

Max Beerbohm writes of "that quality of pathos which makes even unlovely relics dear to us—that piteousness which Time gives even to things robbed of their meaning and their use." It would not be just, but it would be charitable, to ascribe those qualities to these pitiful heirs of a great tradition.

The Correlation Question

I N A PREVIOUS publication (Thompson, 1935) I have reviewed the pros and cons of the various correlations which have been propounded. I have no desire to cross that swamp again, for I still adhere to the conclusion which I then reached, namely, that the 11.16.0.0.0 correlation is the most acceptable; but I still feel that the evidence in its favor is not irrefutable. Accordingly the discussion will be confined to examination of such new evidence as has accumulated in the past 14 years and of the new correlations proposed during that time.

All dates not otherwise specified are in the Gregorian calendar or, in the case of those prior to 1582, have been converted to that system from the Julian or old style reckoning by the addition of the requisite 10 days.

THE 260-DAY COUNT

Lincoln (1942) has investigated the calendar of the present-day Ixil Maya of the northwestern part of the highlands of Guatemala. The year bearers are I'k, Tche E, and Noh, corresponding to the Ik-Manik series. The year bearer 6 Noh (6 Caban) ran from sunset on March 10, 1940, or from midnight, six hours later, until sunset or midnight of March 11, 1940. This is not directly stated in the text, but the date can be recovered from the information that 6 Noh returned at sunset or at midnight of November 25, 1940, and continued through the day of November 26, 1940. The interval from March 10 to November 25 is 260. This is in exact agreement with La Farge's data from Jacaltenango, where a year bearer 7 Ah (Ben) entered at sunset of March 15, 1927, and ran through the day of March 16. The interval from that date to 6 Noh, sunset of March 10, 1940, is 4744, which is the distance from 7 Ah to 6 Noh (64 days and 18 × 260). It is also in agreement with La Farge's data from Santa Eulalia, where a year bearer 12 Chinax (Etz'nab) entered on the evening of March 13, 1932, and continued till sunset of March 14.

As this double dating is confusing, and as, moreover, it seems not impossible that the highland days actually are counted from midnight to midnight or perhaps from dawn to dawn, and may appear to start at sunset because of the guest system (p. 102), I shall not refer in future to the positions in our calendar on which a day may have entered, but that on which it was current. That is to say 6 Noh *entered* at sunset on November 25, 1940, but was *current* on November 26.

There has been some confusion in the discussion of the correlation of Aztec and Maya days of the 260-day period. The best Aztec-European double date is that of 1 Couatl for the surrender of Cuauhtemoc on August 23, 1521 (August 13 O.S.), because this is given by several sources. The distance from July 26, 1553, is 11,660 days. If those are subtracted from 13 Chicchan, the equivalent of July 26, 1553, according to the present-day calendars of Guatemala, the position 1 Chicchan is reached, and that is the Maya equivalent of 1 Couatl.

Sources disagree on the Aztec date for the entrance of the Spaniards in Tenochtitlan on November 18, 1519. Sahagun says it fell on 1 Eecatl on the eve of 10 Quecholli; Chimalpahin gives the position 8 Eecatl 9 Quecholli. Sahagun is surely wrong in giving the Aztec day as 1 Eecatl because the position 8 Eecatl for November 18, 1519, leads forward to 1 Miquiztli (Cimi) on July 26, 1553. To conform to the 1 Couatl and 13 Chicchan placements, 7 Cipactli must fall on November 18, 1519, and 8 Eecatl on November 19. These two dates have been fully discussed by Seler (1902–23, 1:177–83) and Caso (1939), both of whom conclude that November 18 should correspond to 7 Cipactli.

Spinden (1924, p. 100) calls attention to two other cases of double dating in the Annals of Tecamachalco. The equivalent of September 14, 1575, was a day Itzcuintli three days before 2 Acatl, and which must be 12 Itzcuintli; the second double dating gives February 11, 1576, as corresponding to 4 Tecpatl.

The first of these dates, projected backward, leads to 13 Couatl (Chicchan) on July 26, 1553; the second is not in agreement with the first. The interval in Aztec positions is 148 days; in the European calendar it is 150. Therefore, according to the first entry 4 Tecpatl would have to correspond to February 9. Should the second entry be the correct one, the equivalent of July 26, 1553, would be 2 Mazatl (Manik).

We have therefore four entries from Aztec records. The 1 Couatl date, given by three independent native sources, leads to 13 Couatl (13 Chicchan) on July 26, 1553; the first entry in the Annals of Tecamachalco does likewise. The second entry in the Annals of Tecamachalco leads to 2 Mazatl (Manik) on July 26, 1553; the better of two contradictory statements on the entry of the Spaniards into Tenochtitlan leads to 1 Miquiztli as the equivalent of the same Gregorian date.

This is pretty good evidence that the Aztec almanac was in line with those still functioning in the highlands of Guatemala, and that therefore Landa was probably wrong in placing 12 Kan 1 Pop on July 26, 1553. He should, I think, as La Farge has previously pointed out, have equated 12 Kan with July 25 and 13 Chicchan with July 26. Indirect support of this is perhaps deducible from evidence on the Chol calendar presented below.

There is a possible explanation of this one-day difference: Landa reached Yucatan in 1549; his calendar is securely dated as 1553, but it is extremely doubtful that Landa's native informant had enough knowledge of the European calendar to make the correlation of the two systems. It is possible, or even probable, that Landa had acquired sometime before 1553 the information that the year bearers fell on July 16 (O.S.), and when he came to set his Maya data against the European calendar, he utilized the information that he had gathered two or three years earlier, unaware of the fact that, because of the leap day in 1552, the position 1 Pop had moved from July 16 (O.S.) to July 15. It had stood at July 16 (O.S.) from 1548 to 1551. He might well have picked up the July 16 equation in 1550 or 1551, for at that time Christianity had made little impression in Yucatan (human sacrifice was still rampant 10 years later), and there is no reason why Landa should not have witnessed the year-bearer celebrations in some heathen community in 1550 or 1551, or casually heard of it from one of his colleagues, and made a note of the date in the European calendar. Probably at that time the complete integration of the Maya calendar with paganism was hardly apprehended, and therefore it had not yet been deemed a work of the devil meriting extirpation.

As we shall see in discussing the LC, there is indirect evidence which might support the above explanation of the apparent error of one day in Landa's correlation.

THE 365-DAY COUNT

In the annual report of the Division of Historical Research, Carnegie Institution of Washington, for 1945–46, F. V. Scholes gives advance notice of a hitherto unknown manuscript on the Manche Chol. This is Martin A. de Tovilla's *Relación histórica dyscreptiva de las provincias de la de Verapaz y de la del Manché de el Reyno de Guatemala*. Scholes presents an extract dealing with the Chol calendar from the manuscript, which is dated May 17, 1635. Tovilla states that the 360-day period ended June 28 and was followed by "the five days of great fast," which ended July 3. "Thus on July 4th begins the first day of the year according to their account."

It appears probable that this account was obtained from the Indians in the period 1631–33. If the latter date, 20 leap days had caused a backward slip in the Chol calendar of that amount, and new year in 1553 would have corresponded to July 24. This is one day before our corrected equation of 12 Kan 1 Pop = July 25, 1553. It will be remembered that Tovilla's dates are in Gregorian and that a leap day was intercalated in A.D. 1600. We do not know what set of year bearers the Manche Chol favored. If they used the Akbal-Lamat set that would account for the one-day discrepancy from the Yucatan position. That they so did is probable since the Kan-Muluc set stems from a Campeche-Yucatan innovation, and no other part of the Maya area, so far as we know, adopted the new system. In that case Chol 12 Kan 2 Pop would have fallen on July 25, 1553, and 11 Akbal 1 Pop would have been the year bearer on July 24, in agreement with our deduction.

It is probably more than a coincidence that the Chol calendar from the Alta Verapaz (Thompson, 1932) starts the year on July 14. If this is assumed to be Old Style dating, it would mean that the calendar had been frozen into the European between 1548 and 1555, depending on whether the Yucatec year started on July 15 or 16 (O.S.) in 1553 and on which set of year bearers the Chol used. The reductions in the Alta Verapaz culminated in the year 1549.

SHIFTS IN YEAR BEARERS

It has now been established fairly satisfactorily that the shift which caused, for example, the second, seventh, twelfth, and seventeenth positions in a month to coincide with Ahau, rather than the third, eighth, thirteenth, and eighteenth positions, took place at least as early as the middle of Cycle 9, in Campeche, and that it had no effect on the LC, for Etzna 18 and 19 give IS 9.12.0.0.0 10 Ahau 7 Yaxkin and 9.13.0.0.0 8 Ahau 7 Uo. Furthermore, a date 9 Ahau 17 Mol, which is followed by a head and then the katun sign with bracket, occurs on Stela 9 at that same site (fig. 35,*9–11*), and this almost surely corresponds to 9.19.0.0.0 9 Ahau 7 (8) Mol (Proskouriakoff and Thompson, 1947). None of these readings is absolutely certain, but they are all highly probable and, taken together, make a very strong case for this shift having occurred about the middle of the Classical or Initial Series Period.

The IS at Xcalumkin reads 9.15.12.6.9 7 Muluc (1 Kankin). Following Glyph A of the lunar series there is an unknown glyph with coefficient of 1. It is logical to assume that this is a head variant of Kankin, and that the coefficient of 1, accordingly, is evidence that by that date the shift had been adopted at that site (fig. 35,8). Miss Proskouriakoff has also noted a date 5 Ahau 2 Kayab, surely corresponding to 10.1.0.0.0 on Oxkintok 3 (fig. 35,*15*).

There are also two stelae (nos. 18 and 20) at Yaxchilan which record respectively 3 Eb 14 Mol and 6 Ix 16 Kankin, both of which are in the new system. Miss Proskouriakoff points out that these two stelae belong to a group of monuments at Yaxchilan which has stylistic affinities with the Puuc (fig. 35,*12,13*).

Lunar data from Etzna confirm that there was no break in the LC. Etzna 19 has a lunar series perhaps recording a moon age of 25 days, whereas one would expect about 27–28 days. The reading of 25 days is a little open to question. Both D and E are present. The former, of course, is without coefficient; the latter has an irregular bar in front of it, to the left of which there are two or three dots, probably weathering in the frame. The Xcalumkin IS conforms to the calculated moon age of that date. The date of Etzna 18 was chosen partly because the recorded moon age agreed with 9.13.0.0.0, but stylistic considerations (Stelae 19 and 18 are very similar in design) confirm the choice. The lunar series on this stela, accordingly, can also be used as evidence against a break in the LC.

The data from Etzna show clearly that the shift in month positions had no effect on the LC. It is necessary, therefore, to discard the possibility that this shift may have been accompanied by a break in the katun count, as Weitzel (1947) has supposed. Similarly, the one-day break which I had postulated at the time of the shift (Thompson, 1935) cannot have taken place. I think, therefore, that in view of the probability that Landa was one day off in placing 12 Kan on July 16 (O.S.), and the virtual certainty that there never was a break of one day in the LC, my original Ahau equation of 584,285 must be reduced to 584,283, making it two days greater than the Martinez-Hernandez equation.

LONG COUNT

No new information of a direct nature bearing on the engagement of tuns or katuns in the LC is forthcoming. It does seem almost certain that the author of the series of prophecies for the years in a Katun 5 Ahau which is given in Tizimin and Mani had access to the list of tun endings which was utilized by Don Juan Xiu when he made the entries on the famous page 66 of the Chronicle of Oxkutzcab. It would appear that the unknown author took the entry of a tun ending on 5 Ahau 17 Zec in a year 13 Kan beginning in 1541 and made it the start of a katun in 1593 by adding one CR. There seems to have been some doubt about the month position. Don Juan Xiu writes 5 Ahau 16 Zec; the Tizimin and Mani versions have 5 Ahau 15 Zec; it should be 5 Ahau 17 Zec. Later, the author inserts material which indicates that the katun ended on 5 Ahau in 1613, and it is obvious that he was not at all well acquainted with the workings of the katun count. The important point, however, is that he almost certainly had before him the sequence of tuns utilized by Juan Xiu, and therefore that series was an important source of material, and may have been in existence a long while before Juan Xiu copied it in A.D. 1685. We can be certain, however, that the statement that the series of prophecies was written in European script in Chetumal in 1544 is a falsification. Obviously no Maya could have written in European characters as early as 1544, a year before the arrival of the first Franciscan friars in Yucatan.

A puzzling feature in Landa's typical year is that the prophecies for the year were read on what would appear to have been 5 Zip, and this was followed in succession by the feasts of the doctors, hunters, and fishers, respectively, on 6, 7, and 8 Zip. One wonders why the prophecies for the year were read in Zip, rather than at the beginning of Pop, and why these other important festivals should have followed in quick succession. It struck me as possible that these entries refer to celebrations for the new tun rather than for the new year. Indeed, one gets the impression from Landa's account that the question of the prophecies for the year was settled during the ceremonies which began in Uayeb.

According to the 11.16.0.0.0 correlation (equation 584,283), tun endings between 1551 and 1553 were:

(11.16.12.0.0)	4 Ahau	7 Zip	August 31, 1551 (O. S.)
(11.16.13.0.0)	13 Ahau	2 Zip	August 25, 1552 (O. S.)
(11.16.14.0.0)	9 Ahau	17 Uo	August 20, 1553 (O. S.)

The festivals described by Landa were:

Prophecies for year	5 Zip	August 29 (O. S.)
Doctors' feast	6 Zip	August 30 (O. S.)
Hunters' feast	7 Zip	August 31 (O. S.)
Fishers' feast	8 Zip	September 1 (O. S.)

Plausibly, although one cannot be more positive than that, Landa collected data on these festivals in 1551, just as he may have obtained the 1 Pop = July 16 equation at that time, or perhaps in 1552. In the one case the festivals would have clustered about the new tun; in the other, they would have fallen in the first days of the new tun.

CERAMIC EVIDENCE

The evidence of pottery, I think, still continues to disbar the Spinden correlation and also any correlation that makes any position in the Maya LC prior to 11.0.0.0.0

coincide with the Spanish conquest. To discuss the matter at great length would not be advisable at this time, but one or two outstanding points can be reviewed.

In the Maya area plumbate pottery of the effigy type appears after the Initial Series Period, for it has been found in tombs at Copan built in refuse of buildings of the Great Period, and is nowhere found with deposits of that period in the Peten. It is absent from the Puuc except for one sherd at Uxmal (Brainerd, 1941), but it is associated with buildings of the Mexican Period at Chichen Itza and, on the evidence of one vessel purposely deposited in the debris of the Caracol, it was still in use when that city was abandoned. Apparently, it had disappeared by the time Mayapan had established itself firmly as the chief city of United Yucatan.

In the Valley of Mexico and surrounding areas plumbate occurs in the Mazapan Period, but it is wanting from Aztec II–IV, and from ceramic deposits earlier than Mazapan. Vaillant (1941) places the start of Aztec II around A.D. 1300; Caso (1941) has the same horizon commencing at approximately A.D. 1225. I am inclined to favor the Caso dating, but let us split the difference and consider A.D. 1260 as the inception of Aztec II.

The best reconstructions of Yucatecan history (Roys, 1933; Thompson, 1941b) place the abandonment of Chichen Itza in the last decade of the twelfth century. This, it will be seen, agrees well with information from central Mexico, for plumbate continued for a short while after the conquest of Chichen Itza, say until A.D. 1225, whereas it had disappeared in central Mexico before A.D. 1260.

The Mexican Period is said to have lasted 220 years and certainly started after 10.3.0.0.0, because hieroglyphic stone lintels at Chichen Itza belong to the pre-Mexican Period. We have therefore:

End of Initial Series Period	10. 3.0.0.0
220 years of Mexican Period	11.0.0.0
	10.14.0.0.0
Mayapan dominant 260 years	13.0.0.0
	11. 7.0.0.0
Post-Mayapan Period 80 years	4.0.0.0
Spanish conquest of Yucatan	11.11.0.0.0

This scheme, of course, is a rough one. If a hundred years on either side is allowed, the range of dates in the LC corresponding to the katun of the Spanish conquest would be from 11.6.0.0.0 to 11.16.0.0.0. Actually, there is some evidence that the Mexican conquest of Chichen Itza was not in 10.3.0.0.0, but in 10.8.0.0.0, and in that case the final date becomes 11.16.0.0.0. Adjustments might shorten these periods sufficiently to lead to an 11.3.0.0.0 correlation, but the periods can hardly be expanded to

agree with the 12.9.0.0.0 correlation, for there is then a displacement of plumbate or a gap of some 350 years between the end of the Initial Series Period and the appearance of effigy plumbate. Such a gap can hardly have existed in view of the certainty that the appearance of simple plumbate can not be set long after the close of the Initial Series Period; it may, in fact, be coeval with the final stages of that period (Thompson, 1948), and effigy plumbate probably followed close on simple plumbate.

The 12.9.0.0.0 correlation is clearly too long; is the 11.3.0.0.0 correlation too short? That depends on the estimated length of the Mexican Period at Chichen Itza. The end of plumbate (c. A.D. 1260), which we have seen was shortly after the fall of Chichen Itza, becomes 10.8.15.0.0 in that correlation; the start of the Mexican Period can not be earlier than 10.3.0.0.0 because at that date pre-Mexican buildings and hieroglyphic lintels were still being erected. At the outside, then, there are about 110 years into which to fit the Mexican Period, probably nearer 80 years, for one must allow some 20 years for the partial collapse of the Caracol after the abandonment of the site and before the deposit of the plumbate jar in its collapsed masonry, and the introducers of Mexican influences can hardly have walked into Chichen Itza the day after 10.3.0.0.0 was completed. The architects must tell us whether it is reasonable to suppose that the great mass of Mexican buildings could have been erected in that time, and, furthermore, whether or not at least three distinct styles or phases (Early Castillo, Warriors, and that group of late degenerate structures of which the Temple of the Initial Series, House of the Grinding Stones, Temple of the Interior Atlantean Columns, and the Casa Redonda are examples) could be compressed into a period of 80–110 years. Perhaps this ceramic and architectural frame can be garbed in the 11.3.0.0.0 correlation, but I fear the fit will be a bit tight around the hips and quite a lot of ankle may show.

THE MAKEMSON CORRELATION

The ingenious thesis of Dr. Makemson (1946) is that Landa never attempted a day-for-day correlation, but that the July 16 = 1 Pop equation was the work of a later copyist. Why Landa should have gone to the considerable trouble of placing the calendar for 1553 against the Maya year without attempting to correlate the two is hard to explain, but Dr. Makemson supposes that he did this. She further supposes that a copyist noted Landa's entry against 1 Imix 18 Yax, "Here begins the count of the calendar of the Indians, saying in their tongues 1 Imix," and that the copyist noted that this entry occurred opposite July 17; further, that the copyist supposed that the day began on sunset on July 16 and ran through July 17. She next assumes that the copyist, in view of the above entry, re-arranged the whole calendar to make 12 Kan 1 Pop coincide with July 16. To those suppositions yet others must be added. We must assume that only this copy or others made from it was available in Yucatan, that the Maya were so ignorant of their calendar that they accepted its start on July 16, in midsummer at a time when the maize was about a foot high, whereas they had known, according to the Makemson thesis, that new year fell late in the fall, long after the maize had been harvested. We must also suppose that the scribe—a member of a class of notorious hack writers—knew what no one else has ever reported from Yucatan, namely, that the Maya day ran from sunset to sunset, and that he corrected Landa in that respect. On the other hand, we must assume that he was so ignorant of the Maya calendar that he did not know that 1 Imix was the start of the 260-day almanac, although he had read it in Landa's manuscript, in the sentence before the place where he is supposed to have inserted the statement that 1 Pop was always on July 16.

Mrs. Makemson's idea that the Maya were so ignorant of their calendar that they accepted Landa's scribe's version of it is contradicted by Sanchez de Aguilar's statement that the attempts of the early friars to extirpate the Maya calendar were without success because most of the Maya knew it because it had been handed down to them from their forebears. Sanchez de Aguilar, who places first of Pop on July 17, surely did not take his material from Landa. His information on native customs does not repeat Landa; it supplements him. Moreover, in the use of the expression *cuch haab* and in the three names he gives for Uayeb he cannot be following Landa who used no such Maya terms. His spelling of month names differs from that of Landa. Accordingly, Aguilar is an independent source for the Maya year's having started with first of Pop in mid-July. If that is the case, Mrs. Makemson's elaborate explanation of the actions of this rascally scribe falls to the ground, but that is the cornerstone of the elaborate structure she has erected to house an astronomical correlation. Without it this towering mass of assumptions piled one upon another can ill withstand "from the lips of truth one mighty breath." Having dismissed Landa's correlation, Mrs. Makemson opts for an Ahau equation 489,138, which is just 246 days before the Spinden correlation. The result is that 12 Kan 1 Pop coincides with November 22, 1552 (Gregorian), and holds the LC position 12.9.17.9.4.

This correlation shares with that of Spinden the overwhelming disadvantage of leaving a great gap in the ceramic sequences of the Maya area and central Mexico, which has already led every person who has studied the pottery of either area to abandon it, but at the same time it does not partake of the one strong point in favor of the Spinden correlation, namely, agreement (with a one-day lag) with the almanacs of the Aztec and the present-day Maya of the highlands of Guatemala. Furthermore, all sources place the beginning of Pop during the sixteenth century in July, and, since Mrs. Makemson's paper was written, data on the Manche Chol calendar have confirmed this general equation. I can see no reason for supposing that all the sources which make 1 Pop coincide with July 16 (O.S.), or thereabouts, stem from Landa. Mrs. Makemson to the contrary, we have no certain information that Landa's manuscript was widely copied in Yucatan, nor is its influence apparent in all later historical documents written by Spaniards, although some of the authors of the Relaciones de Yucatan had access to it. Lopez de Cogolludo and Herrera probably studied a copy in Spain.

I do not think that much stock can be put in the Makemson thesis that the festivals detailed by Landa fit better a year starting in November than one starting in July. The descriptions of the rain-making ceremony in Mac and Pax have been shown by Long (1923a) to refer to the burner period, a celebration related not to the year, but to the 260-day period. Mrs. Makemson supposes that the reason for the absence of festivals in Ceh was that the men were busy in the fields at that time (June 29–July 18 in her correlation), but it is in February, March, April, and early May that the agriculturalists are most busy. Her correlation, of course, agrees very well with the lunar data and that concerning the planet Venus, but that was the basis on which it rested. The paper serves to illustrate the dangers of trying to establish a correlation on two or three lines of evidence instead of considering all evidence, that of the positions in the 260-day almanac, the years, the katuns, the moon, Venus, pottery sequences and architecture.

ESCALONA RAMOS CORRELATION

A correlation which makes the katun of the Spanish conquest occupy a position in the vicinity of 11.3.0.0.0 has had supporters for many years. Lehmann (1910) was probably the first to propose such a correlation, and Leslie Mitchell had a somewhat similar scheme. Escalona Ramos (1940) has published a day-for-day correlation using the Ahau equation 679,108 which makes 11.3.0.0.0 13 Ahau 13 (12) Pax correspond to March 11, 1543 (O.S.). This causes Landa's 12 Kan 1 Pop to fall on May 1 (O.S.), which means that it is 75 days out of conformity with the almanacs of all other groups, and in disagreement with what Landa himself writes. Escalona Ramos solves this problem to his own satisfaction by supposing that there were two different calendars, one the LC, the other the popular calendar. He supposes that in the popular calendar leap days were inserted, and cites a hodgepodge of long-since discredited references to the use of leap days by Aztec and Maya. I can see no evidence whatever for a second calendar which comprises a separate cycle of 52 years, with insertion of leap days every fourth year. If this was the popular calendar, why is it that the popular calendars of the present-day Maya of the Guatemalan highlands do not also insert leap days, and why should those almanacs without leap days check (with a one-day gap) with 12 Kan on July 26, 1553, which was in a cycle allegedly corrected by the insertion of leap days? Furthermore, we have the definite statement of Tovilla that the Manche Chol did not use leap days, and their new-year's day agrees within a day or so with Landa's date for 12 Kan 1 Pop by counting back the requisite multiple of 365 days, not a multiple of 365¼ days. The argument for this 52-year cycle with its leap days is against all the evidence, and represents an unsuccessful attempt by the author of the correlation to keep one foot in the camp of astronomy and the other in the Landa year. If Escalona Ramos accepts Landa, his lunar data are about nine days out. He must, therefore, ignore Landa's year or reconcile it by this strange method with his other data.

This correlation does not place Venus at heliacal rising after inferior conjunction on any of the possible dates in Dresden. Escalona Ramos chooses as his base 10.10.11.12.0 1 Ahau 18 Kayab, at which time, according to his calculations, Venus was 235 days past heliacal rising and about to be lost to sight, about 53 days before superior conjunction. However, the Maya and other peoples of Middle America were interested in heliacal rising of Venus four days after inferior conjunction at the end of the eight days of invisibility. The Venus table in Dresden ends at that point; there is no emphasis on heliacal setting nearly two months before superior conjunction.

Although I have not been averse to an 11.3.0.0.0 correlation, I can see very little to recommend this particular version of it.

10.10.0.0.0 (WEITZEL) CORRELATION

The latest correlation to be proposed makes 10.10.0.0.0 13 Ahau 13 Mol the katun of the conquest (Weitzel, 1947). Weitzel's thesis is that month positions were shifted forward one position, i.e. 4 Ahau 8 Mol shifted to 4 Ahau 7 Mol, in order to distinguish dates in a new calendar which was based on a concept of counting time by the day on which the period started rather than that on which it was completed, and this was achieved by subtracting 80 days, viz.:

Presumably Weitzel does not suppose that the katuns were given any LC position in his new calendar. He assumes that this new concept of counting by the beginning days of periods was due to Mexican influences, and cites the Mexican year of 365 days as being named for its beginning date, but that is not certain, for Caso (1939) brings forward good, although not irrefutable, evidence that the Aztec years were named not by the first day of the year then current but by the last day of the year (Caso, 1939). Even should he not be convinced by Caso's arguments, there is not a tittle of evidence for placing the Aztec year bearers at the start of the year. The alternative thesis places them at the start of Toxcatl (the sixth or seventh month).

Furthermore, texts from Etzna already cited (p. 305) make it clear that the shift of one day in month positions made no difference to the LC. The date 9.12.0.0.0 is recorded as 10 Ahau 7 Yaxkin at Etzna, whereas other cities wrote it 9.12.0.0.0 10 Ahau 8 Yaxkin. Nowhere is there any evidence for a backward shift of 80 days.

In an attempt to reconcile his correlation with the archaeological picture, Weitzel is forced to consider such purely Maya buildings as the Monjas and the Three Lintels as of the Mexican Period. No Maya hieroglyphic inscription at Chichen Itza can be safely referred to the Mexican Period. Weitzel cites an inscription on the tail of a serpent column in the definitely Mexican Temple of the Wall Panels in support of his ideas, but he omits to repeat what had been written on this subject by the excavator: "The portion belonging to the north column is plainly part of a hieroglyphic lintel which has been cut down to the proper size and the feathers and rattle treatment added, so that there is almost complete obliteration of the glyphs" (Ruppert, 1931, p. 124). The plate amply demonstrates the correctness of Ruppert's description, and in the caption repeats the information that the stone is re-used. The only other writer to treat of this inscription likewise notes that it is "a re-used inscription fashioned into a serpent's tail" (Beyer, 1937, p. 169). It is hard to see how the re-use of a piece of a lintel as part of the tail of a serpent can be taken as evidence for the contemporaneity of hieroglyphic stone lintels with buildings of that period. Nor is the presence of a snake with a human head in its jaws evidence that the lintel on which it occurs belongs in the Mexican Period, as Weitzel claims, since this motif is found throughout the Classical Period in the Central Area (e.g. Yaxchilan L 13, 14, 15, 25).

If the Initial Series Lintel was not re-used—and it almost certainly was because part of the inscription was

(10.5. 0. 0.0) 10 Ahau 8 Muan, katun ends May 18, 1448 (O.S.)
            4.0

(10.4.19.14.0) 8 Ahau 7 (8) Zac, katun begins February 28, 1448 (O.S.)

covered when it rested on the Atlantean columns—an extraordinary archaeological situation arises. It is known that Atlantean columns belong to the close of the Mexican Period and are later than buildings in the styles of the Temple of the Warriors, the Temple of the Jaguars, and the Temple of the Wall Panels. The Initial Series Lintel was dedicated in 10.3.0.0.0, but the lintels of the Monjas are admitted by Weitzel to have been dedicated in the same katun. In fact, the CR date of the Temple of the Initial Series is a year earlier than that on the various lintels in the Monjas, both readings again being accepted by Weitzel. There is some reason to believe the Monjas lintels may have been re-used because in some cases the width of the inscribed part of the lintel is too great for the doorway, and parts of glyphs are hidden under the masonry. Even ignoring that possibility and accepting the lintels as contemporaneous with that typically Maya construction the second story of the Monjas, Weitzel's scheme allows no time at all for the architectural and stylistic sequences which include such buildings as the sub-Castillo, the Castillo, and the Temples of the Chac Mool, the Warriors, the Jaguars, the Wall Panels, and the High Priest's Grave. This is so because this whole sequence and more besides lie between the second story of the Monjas and the Atlantean columns of the Initial Series Temple. Too much time may be allowed for the Mexican Period at Chichen Itza by other correlations, but one can not reduce that span to nothing.

Furthermore, in the Weitzel scheme Chichen Itza had not been abandoned by A.D. 1400, but we have seen that Chichen Itza had been deserted before the end of the plumbate horizon, which on evidence from the Mexican highlands almost surely ended about A.D. 1250. Weitzel's correlation also demands that the period of Mayapan's domination coincided with the occupation of Chichen Itza, which again is against the ceramic and architectural evidence. In addition to being at complete variance with the ceramic and architectural evidence, this correlation fails to agree with the data on the Aztec and highland Maya calendars which lead to the equation 12 Kan = July 25, 1553. His Ahau equation can be deduced to be 774,078.

Weitzel assumes that Christian influence in Yucatan was strong enough to cause the calendar to be frozen into the European year between 1528 and 1531; I deem that inconceivable, for at that time Yucatan was unconquered, and there were then no missionaries at work in the province. The attempts of the Montejos to conquer Yucatan from 1531–35 were never consolidated, and we can be sure that the calendar was not frozen at that time, and that no serious attempts had yet been made to evangelize the country. It was not until 1539 that Champoton became permanent Spanish territory, and not until 1541 that the final conquest of Yucatan was commenced and pushed with determination to its conclusion in 1546. It was not until 1545 that the friars arrived, and the first attempt was made to Christianize the country; even then the friars were too few to make much impression on the native way of life. The Maya certainly did not know enough about the European calendar to change their own to conform with it in or before 1532, and one can be reasonably certain that 1 Pop had not been frozen at July 16 even 20 years later.

Weitzel must also assume that the 260-day almanac was tied to the European year, and that is almost unthinkable. The Weitzel thesis requires us to assume that once every four years there was a nameless day (inserted at February 29, 1532, 1536, 1540, etc.?), but no such arrangement was ever followed in the 400 years of Spanish domination in Guatemala. If the last unfrozen year in Yucatan had started in 1530, the year bearer according to Weitzel would have been 2 Muluc on first of Pop equivalent to July 26, 1530 (Gregorian), but the present-day calendars of the Guatemalan highlands projected backwards and the Aztec almanac projected forward from 1521 make 10 Kan, not 2 Muluc, fall on that date.

Weitzel asserts that the Maya year was frozen into the European year so that from 1532 onwards 1 Pop always fell on July 16 (O.S.), but at the same time he uses an equation 2 Ix 1 Pop = July 13, 1543 (O.S.) to bring the 11 Chuen 18 Zac = February 15, 1544 (O.S.), equation into his scheme. Apart from the fact that the entry in question surely dates from much later than 1544, he can scarcely freeze the year between 1528 and 1532, and then get confirmatory evidence for his correlation in an unfrozen entry supposedly a dozen years later.

In brief, this correlation is based on two false premises: (1) the shift in month positions was a late innovation due to a wish to bring the Maya calendar into conformity with supposed Mexican practice, and (2) the shift in month positions was accompanied by a break of 80 days in the katun dates. The correlation is contrary to all archaeological evidence and fails to agree with the almanacs of the Aztec and present-day Maya peoples of the highlands of Guatemala. Moreover, the postulate that the Maya year was frozen into the European year before 1532 is untenable; a second postulate, that the Maya were naming their katuns for their opening days, is contrary to the general evidence (p. 182). One might also add that the evidence for a Katun 11 Ahau beginning late in 1546 is very poor.

If a new correlation is needed, we may have to discard the katun count, but at all costs keep the equation 12 Kan 1 Pop = July 25, 1553.

CONCLUSIONS

There is no prospect, I believe, that any of the three correlations just reviewed can be the right one. The 11.16.0.0.0 correlation with Ahau equation 584,283 still seems best to fit the sundry requirements. The possibility of a pre-Columbian break in the calendar becomes even more remote in the light of the new data on the Manche Chol and Ixil calendars. Moreover, the discovery that the shift in month positions was an early development and was not accompanied by any change in the LC is strong evidence against a break, since had there been one, that was the logical place to have made it.

The Ahau equation 584,283 requires that the Maya reckoned their moons not from the appearance of the new moon or from conjunction, but from disappearance of the old moon or conjunction, perhaps with both bases in use at different times and in different cities. However, we have seen that there is probably glyphic evidence for that thesis (p. 241).

Whorf's Attempts to Decipher the Maya Hieroglyphs

It is an old trait of human nature when in the mist to be very sure about its road.
—JOHN BUCHAN

IT HAD BEEN my intention to ignore Whorf's (1933, 1942) attempts to read the Maya hieroglyphic writing, supposing that all students of the subject would by now have consigned them to that limbo which already holds the discredited interpretations of Brasseur de Bourbourg (1869–70), de Rosny (1876), Charency (1876), Le Plongeon, Cresson (1894), and Cyrus Thomas (1886). Nevertheless, it seems advisable to examine his writings because of his position in the linguistic field and because of the air of certitude with which his interpretations are offered.

My objections to Whorf's writings are not against his conclusions as to the nature of Maya hieroglyphic writing, but against his lines of reasoning. I feel that he has built his structure on the shifting sands of false premises with the aid of a scaffolding of misidentifications. That the structure contains some good stone is not improbable. Whorf maintained that the glyphs are purely phonetic, and that each element represents a syllable or the single consonant with which that syllable commences. Glottal stops may be ignored. Obviously, with such a method, one can get almost any interpretation one likes out of the writing.

I propose to analyze very briefly the steps by which Whorf reaches two or three of his fundamental interpretations in order to show how shaky are the whole foundations.

Cumhu. Whorf's interpretation of the month sign Cumhu serves him both as proof of his arguments and as a base on which to build a whole series of interpretations. First, it should be noted that the month was almost certainly called Cumku in Yucatec, not Cumhu, for it is thus spelled in all the books of Chilam Balam and in the month list of Sanchez de Aguilar. The only source for Cumhu is our edition of Landa, which is notoriously weak in the transcriptions of Maya words; the *k* of Cumku might easily have been copied as *h* by the scribe who extracted the surviving version of Landa's writings. Secondly, it should be noted that in no other Maya language does the eighteenth month have a name resembling in any way Cumku.

Whorf (1933, p. 19) takes the superfix of Landa's drawing of Cumku as "a form of the day sign Ahau,"

which, he says, "was pronounced with the *a* scarcely sounded, and which would seem to represent the syllable *hu.* An examination of a series of Cumku glyphs would have shown Whorf that the superfix of Landa's glyph is not a sort of Ahau, but a poorly drawn example of the regular superfix which, whatever else it may be, is not a form of that day sign (fig. 19,*1–16*). Whorf next argues that the original name of the glyph may have been Cumhau. As he takes certain extraneous elements to the left as standing for *cum,* he reads the whole as Cumhau, completely ignoring the Kan sign which is the main element of the month glyph.

However, in 1942 a quite different derivation of Cumku appears: Whorf decides that the Kan sign does not stand for maize or ripeness, the fact that everywhere in the codices and on sculptures one finds the Kan sign associated with maize or the maize god being dismissed as secondary symbolism. Instead the Kan sign means *hu,* "iguana," apparently because the Aztec equivalent is Cuetzpalin, "lizard." The original meaning of the Kan sign, Whorf tells us, is *huun,* "a letter or book," and the sign shows us this book or letter folded up like a modern letter in its envelope! A glyph of an iguana above a Kan sign from Dresden is explained as "an example of the method of repeated affirmation, using the ordinary sign for *hu* [the Kan sign], topped by an iguana figure . . . . Here the formula which we use in transliterating is *hu-hu,* to be read or pronounced, of course, as *hu.*" On the same pages (29–31) as the iguana over the Kan sign, and occupying precisely the same positions, are pictorial glyphs showing respectively a turkey head and a haunch of venison, both above a Kan sign, and two fish, but these Whorf ignores. Obviously, they represent offerings, either turkey and maize, venison and maize, and iguana and maize, or, more probably, turkey tamales, venison tamales, and iguana tamales. The Kan sign cannot stand for *hu,* "iguana," in one place and not in the other; the pictures are so obviously related.

Whorf now returns to Cumhu (Cumku). Whereas before the *hu* had been represented by Ahau (elided to *hau*) as the superfix, now the *hu* is shown by the main element. A variant form of the superfix is identified as a feather (fig. 19,*15*), *"kukum,"* from which one drops the *ku* and obtains kumhu. The mere fact that kumhu (glottalized) and Cumhu are totally different sounds is not accepted by Whorf as a valid argument against his theory. Whorf does not mention that the superfix in question is extremely rare with Cumku, occuring only twice in Dresden and never in the inscriptions, and he gives nothing beyond his bare statement for accepting this highly conventionalized symbol as representing a feather.

Thus, two entirely different phonetic translations are offered for what is almost certainly a misspelled version of a Yucatecan month name. They are self-contradictory and based on a complete ignorance of Maya hieroglyphs.

One of the most important of Whorf's "proofs" derives from an identification of the hand as the symbol for the sound *ma* or *m*. First, Whorf, in a very roundabout and unconvincing way, shows how the sound *ma* might have been represented in Maya writing by a hand. Next, he calls attention to his drawing of Landa's sign for *m*, of which he says, "I regard it as a corrupted reproduction of a cursive Manik." I do not know whether he means that Landa's drawing or his own is the corrupted reproduction, for besides turning Landa's sign upside down, he has redrawn it in such a way that it appears about halfway between a Manik sign and Landa's *m*. Because the hand is the sign for the day called Manik only in Yucatec (other names in other dialects are ignored by Whorf), and because his drawing of Landa's *m* is identified by him as a hand (and of course *m* also covers *ma*), Whorf uses the definite identification of the hand as the symbol for *ma*. The hand completion sign is then given the sound *ma*, and we learn that in an IS this hand before a period glyph should be translated as *ma*, e.g. 9 baktuns, 15 katuns, *ma tun, ma uinal, ma ķin*. Although this interpretation is not implausible, it has, so far as I know, no parallel in the books of Chilam Balam. When used to translate the similar hand before a PE date, it makes nonsense: "9 Ahau 18 Mol, no 19 Katuns." If the sign means *ma* "no" or "not," it cannot precede a numeral.

Next, Whorf, rightly or wrongly, identifies the well-known prefix of Mac (Beyer's "down-balls" prefix) as two hands (fig. 18,*1–15,20*). He should at least have noted that in the scores of examples of this element in this and other glyphs not once do hands drawn in a naturalistic manner replace the elements he identifies as such; there is no mention of that fact. Instead, Whorf boldly states as a fact that the sign represents two hands wrist to wrist, and previous identifications of the element which are totally different are passed over in silence. The two hands are again given the sound *ma*. The fish head of Mac is identified as Cimi, "death," and given Landa's sound *ķ*, no attention being paid to the fact that the sound is *ķa* with a glottal, not *c*. Thus two doubtful hands (*ma?*) plus a wrongly identified Cimi (*ķa*) equal Mac.

The hand in Whorf's thesis can stand not only for *ma* but also for *m*. Thus in discussing Glyph C of the lunar series, Whorf assigns to the head of the death god, not the sound *ķa* as given by Landa, nor that of *c* which he used in the derivation of Mac, but that of *la*. To a kin sign which is not in the original, is ascribed the value *le*, although Landa assigns it the sound *te*. The hand below is given the sound *m* or *ma*, and the whole, together with the coefficients and the moon signs, reads "3 *Lama* lunations," "3 *lelemma* lunations," "5 *lemma* lunations." Next we are referred to Tozzer's grammar where, we are told, "a classifier used for periods of time is *lem*." Accordingly, if the Maya wrote these moon inscriptions *in the way they talked* they must have written not "six lunations," but "six *lem* lunations." It sounds very convincing, but if the reader will turn obligingly to Tozzer's grammar (1921, p. 291), he will find the entry "Lem. For times; hun lem, once." In other words, *lem* refers not to *time*, but to *times*. References to lunations in the books of Chilam Balam show the use of the numerical classifier *p'el* with moons. The least that can be said of such arguments is that they are unbelievably sloppy.

Rather than prolong this examination unwarrantedly, let us briefly discuss one of the two passages Whorf has translated from the codices. It is that on Madrid 113d [read 102d]. I give below Whorf's interpretation and my comment.

The action in the pictures is that of weaving. . . . The verbs for both pictures are alike and their second components are *ma*. The first component is a sign for which I have a body of evidence to show a phonetic value *ya*. Maya students will recall that it is the superfix of the glyphs of the months *Yax* (*Yac*) and *Yaxķin* (*Yack'in*) in the codices. The verb then reads *ya-ma*. *Yama* or *Yamah* would be a perfective or possibly an aorist of the transitive conjugation of a verb with stem *yam*. A common stem *yam* in the Perez dictionary means between, interstice, and as verb, interpose, insert, force between, get caught between. This is the action shown; the subject is *inserting* the shuttle and its thread into the warp, or *putting it between* the warp threads.

Comment: The first component, as every Maya student will recall, is definitely not the yax superfix. If, as I suppose, the body of evidence largely rests on this identification, it is of a wraithlike nature. Whorf completely ignores the postfix. The *ma* is our old friend the grasping hand.

I cannot understand the many meanings for verbs with the root *yam* which Whorf derives from Pio Perez. I find: *yambezah, mudar, diferenciar; dejar espacio entre dos cosas; interponer. Yamnaat, entrever, presuponer, calcular, prever. Yampahal, mudarse, diferenciarse, vomitar. Yampal, trocar suertes. Yamtah, poner intermedios.* Of these only the last could possibly correspond to the meanings assigned the stem by Whorf, although actually it means to set intervals. The word *yamtah* is not given in the Motul dictionary, but we find there a more precise definition of *yam: "la concavidad o espacio que hay entre dos cosas, e intervalo, o distancia de tiempo y lugar."* No word with the root *yam* in the Motul dictionary carries any meaning approaching that which Whorf implies. In fact, the action of inserting the shuttle seems to be the opposite of one main concept which is that of creating, not filling, a space in time or place which separates two objects. Whorf's translations from the Perez dictionary are grossly exaggerated and misleading. Taken in conjunction with the *lem* incident and Landa's *m*, they imply that Whorf considered that he could strain the evidence as much as he liked to gain his point.

Granting, even, that *yam* could be the root of a word meaning "to insert," I see no reason why that word should have been used to describe the act of weaving.

Whorf continues:

The first part of the object glyph is a sign that has phonetic values *sa* and *sak*. It appears here in the form it has as sign of the month Zac (Sak) and of the color white (sak), and so might have here the value *sak*. The second upper part of the glyph is the *a* of Landa. . . . The second lower part of the glyph is a form of the day-sign Ahau. My evidence is that Ahau is a polyphonic character and that one of its values besides *hau, hu* is *li, l.* Maya students will recall its use as superfix of the sign for east, *lik'in.* It is thus possible to read this object glyph as *sak-a-l.* But *sakal* [*sacal*] is the Maya word for woven cloth. . . . The two glyph blocks in the lower line are name-glyphs answering to the unknown name of the deity shown in the picture. We may denote them and this deity's name as $X_1 X_2$. We may now transliterate the

"verse" and translate it . . . *Yama sakal* X_1 X_2. Translation: X_1 X_2 inserts (it) into the cloth.

Comment: Unfortunately, Whorf is again in error. The element he reads as *zac* "white" is not that at all; the zac sign has two nubbins, and varies quite a lot from the element depicted on this page. One wants a lively imagination to recognize the superfix [my *te* (1) affix] as Landa's *a.* The main element is not an Ahau. Whorf elsewhere (1942, p. 487) identifies this same glyph as *e*, deriving it from Landa's sign for *e.* Thus, one must conclude that all three components of the glyph are wrongly identified.

Even had the elements been correctly translated, and even did the glyph compound actually represent the sounds *sakal* (admitting the dubious argument that the appearance of Ahau in the glyph for east permits its identification with *li* and thence *l*), it is very much to be doubted that such first-class weavers as the Maya would have used a word for woven cloth to represent the warp threads. I am neither a weaver nor a linguist, but such imprecision in nomenclature does not strike me as Maya.

Of the five elements which Whorf uses, four are wrongly identified; of the two words he obtains, one does not have the meaning he ascribes to it, whereas the other probably would not be used in the sense he attributes to it. Whorf's writings are a direful warning to those with a similarly uncritical approach to the hieroglyphic problems. For imprecision of a somewhat similar nature in Whorf's special field of linguistics, the reader is referred to a paper (Thompson, 1943g), in which I demonstrate that two words, *mis* and *tumin*, for which Whorf created an imposing Uto-Aztecan ancestry, are common Spanish words, introduced to the New World in post-Columbian times.

Maya Calculations Far into the Past and into the Future

Picked from the worm holes of long-vanish'd days.
—SHAKESPEARE, *Henry V*, Act II

IT SEEMS advisable to gather the most outstanding of Maya calculations into the past and into the future in order to illustrate how the Maya thought in vast expanses of time, and how they handled those great distances. It must be confessed that the Maya did not make those tremendous calculations without occasional mistakes, but they did calculate a date over 500,000,000 years in the past without error, a truly remarkable achievement.

For the sake of simplicity, I shall use the terms derived from Beltran to distinguish the higher periods, namely:

1 pictun	= 20 baktuns	(	8,000 tuns)
1 calabtun	= 20 pictuns	(	160,000 tuns)
1 kinchiltun	= 20 calabtuns	(	3,200,000 tuns)
1 alautun	= 20 kinchiltuns	(	64,000,000 tuns)

It should be remembered, however, that there is no direct evidence for the use of these compounds. They have been employed by Morley, Spinden and others, and thus have been legitimized, so to speak, by use.

One of the most interesting of the calculations into the past occurs on the Tablet of the Inscriptions, Palenque. It was Richard C. E. Long (1923) who first solved this equation by reading the tun coefficient as 2 instead of 1. With that change he was able to connect the dates satisfactorily:

```
1.13. 0. 9. 9. 2. 4.8   5 Lamat 1 Mol
   7.18. 2. 9. 2.12.1      Subtract
   ──────────────────────────────────
(1. 5. 2.)6.19.19.10.7   1 Manik 10 Zec
```

The coefficients of the two highest periods of the first date have been supplied from a possible arrangement of the inscription on Tikal 10. The calculation here covers 1,264,982 tuns, a little short of 1,250,000 years.

On this same tablet there is a calculation into the future which leads to the end of the current pictun:

```
(1.13. 0.) 9. 8. 9.13.0   8 Ahau 13 Pop
       10.11.10. 5.8         Add
    ──────────────────────────────────
(1.13.)1. 0. 0. 0. 0.8    5 Lamat 1 Mol
                     8        Subtract
    ──────────────────────────────────
(1.13.)1. 0. 0. 0. 0.0   10 Ahau 13 Yaxkin
```

As Long has noted, the pictun glyph has a coefficient of 1. This, I think, is fair evidence that the coefficient of the pictun which ended at 13.0.0.0.0   4 Ahau 8 Cumku

was 0, especially as the Maya priest had just been juggling with pictuns and calabtuns, and therefore desired that there should be no doubt as to the LC position of this date. On the other hand, it is possible that the 1 pictun merely records the distance from 4 Ahau 8 Cumku, although I regard this as a less plausible reconstruction. In any case, the record is positive proof that the Maya thought of the pictun as composed of 20, not 13, baktuns.

On Copan N there is a long calculation into the past (Thompson, 1944a), which again is incorrect as it stands. By changing the katun coefficient from 19 to 7 the distance number will connect the two dates:

```
(1.13. 0.) 9.16.10.0.0   1 Ahau 3 Zip
      14. 17. 7.10.0.0      Subtract
   ──────────────────────────────────
(1.12. 5.)12. 9. 0.0.0   1 Ahau 8 Zac
```

Here the distance is considerably less than in the example for the Temple of the Inscriptions, but reaches 118,950 tuns. Again, the coefficients above that of the baktun are here supplied in accordance with those which may have been in the minds of the astronomers of Tikal.

Tikal 10 has a most unusual inscription of early date. It opens with a day 8 Manik which is followed by three glyphs, any one of which might be the corresponding month position. There follows an IS introductory glyph and then an IS or distance number of eight periods, although the kin and its coefficient are suppressed.

The opposite side of the stela opens with a CR date 4? 13 Uo or Zip, for the downward extension of the reinforced cartouche argues against a month of the Cauac group. This I think may represent 9.2.0.0.0   4 Ahau 13 Uo. In that case the long series of period glyphs probably represents a distance number. Unfortunately, this number will not connect 8 Manik with 4 Ahau, for counted from 8 Manik and calling the kins 13, it leads to 1 Ahau. The variable element in the IS would agree reasonably well with the forms for Uo or Muan (fig. 23,*15*).

I am inclined to think that this sequence should be treated as a distance number because there seems no plausible reason for the base from which the IS would be counted. If a dot is added to the coefficient of the great-great cycle, that is to say, if it is read as 12 instead of 11, the distance number will connect 8 Manik to the date 4 Ahau 13 Uo:

```
(0. 0. 0.)19.18. 8.15. 7    8 Manik (10 Mol)
1.12.19. 9. 3.11. 2.(13)
─────────────────────────
(1.13. 0.) 9. 2. 0. 0. 0   4 Ahau 13 Uo
```

```
(1.12.19.)17.19.14.17.0   6 Ahau 18 Kayab
11.14. 5. 1.0
─────────────────────────
(1.13. 0.) 9.14. 0. 0.0   6 Ahau 13 Muan
```

This reconstruction is not offered with any assurance as to its validity, but as a possible alternative to the reading advocated by Morley. It has one advantage in that the pictun coefficient of the second date can be restored as 0 in accordance with the better interpretation of the 10 Ahau 13 Yaxkin, 1 pictun text at Palenque. It also connects, but with a correction, 8 Manik and the terminal date which is perhaps 4 Ahau 13 Uo. However, it should be noted that there is no evidence that the month position, 10 Mol, is recorded, and there is no apparent notation of 13 kins. Miss Proskouriakoff informs me that she believes on stylistic grounds that this is too early for this stela, but, of course, the count may have been carried forward to a later dedicatory date. The period glyphs of distance numbers are occasionally arranged in descending order, as would be the case were this a distance number. So far as the higher numbers are concerned, there is strong evidence at Quirigua, which will be reviewed, in favor of the suggested reconstruction. The distance number or IS, as it stands uncorrected, amounts to over 5,000,000 years, 5,115,671 tuns to be exact. One's mind reels at such stupendous spans of time.

The Stone of Chiapa has a distance number which, rearranged in descending order, reads 13.13.13.1.?.11.4. The equation can not be restored because the starting point is missing, although 6 Imix 9 Xul is perhaps the preferable reading. The distance is 2,189,220 tuns, well over 2,000,000 years.

A number of calculations, not of such startling magnitude, but of considerable range, occur on Dresden 61, 62. These have been discussed by a number of writers, and the LC position of 9 Kan 12 Kayab, the point of departure, has been established by Beyer (1943b). There are eight of these distance numbers, all of which have the same point of departure, and all of which consist of 4 pictuns, 6 baktuns, and an odd number of katuns, tuns, uinals, and kins. The longest which is correct as it stands can be transposed as follows:

```
(1.12.16.) 3.16.14.11.4   9 Kan 12 Kayab
4. 6.11.10. 7.2    Add
─────────────────────────
(1.13. 0.)10. 8. 5. 0.6   3 Cimi 14 Kayab
```

The interval is 34,630 tuns; the higher numbers in parenthesis are derived from the suggested reconstruction of the Tikal inscription.

A long distance number on Copan C is preceded by the calabtun glyph with a coefficient of 11, 12, or 13 and the date 6 Ahau 18 Kayab. The equation reads:

Conceivably the equation should be moved forward one CR. The association of the calabtun glyph with the earlier date would most logically indictate that the earlier date fell in a calabtun which was not the same as that current during Baktun 9. Should the coefficient of the pictun have been 0 at 13.0.0.0.0 4 Ahau 8 Cumku, as I believe, the coefficient of the calabtun would have been one digit less if a subtraction led back to the previous pictun, because as that pictun had a coefficient of 0, it was necessary to "borrow" from the calabtun, the next highest unit. If, as we have assumed, the coefficient of the calabtun during Cycle 9 was 13 and the pictun coefficient was 0, it follows that the calabtun coefficient corresponding to 6 Ahau 18 Kayab was 12. It is therefore highly probable that the number recorded with these calabtun glyphs on Stela C is 12, the insertion of 12 calabtuns serving as a warning that a calculation far in the past was to follow. This inscription therefore tends to confirm that the pictun coefficient was 0 during the period of the stela cult and is, to a lesser degree, evidence that the calabtun coefficient was 13 at the same time.

I now come to what may be the two greatest feats in calculation attempted by the Maya. On Quirigua F, C16b–C17a, there is a record which appears to read 0 pictuns, 13 kinchiltuns at 1 Ahau 13 Yaxkin (fig. 33,48). The kinchiltun glyph appears to be distinguished from the calabtun by a prefix to the left. In fact, 1 Ahau 13 Yaxkin does end 13 kinchiltuns:

```
( 0. 1.13.0.)9.16.10.0.0   1 Ahau 3 Zip
1. 8.13.0. 9.16.10.0.0    Subtract
─────────────────────────
(18.)13. 0. 0. 0. 0.0.0   1 Ahau 13 Yaxkin
```

Here the distance calculated is well over 90,000,000 years, to wit, 91,683,930 tuns. There is, apparently, another count far into the past in this inscription to reach the date 1 Ahau 13 Mol but the calculations elude me.

In a previous paper (Thompson, 1932b) I offered an entirely different decipherment for the date 1 Ahau 13 Yaxkin (Morley, 1937–38, 4:129) in reading the glyph at D16a not as 13 kinchiltuns, but as end of 13 baktuns. This latter reading is not acceptable, however; a hand as an ending sign cannot be placed between the coefficient and the period glyph. The glyph must be 13 kinchiltuns or 13 calabtuns; the prefix to the left suggests that it is the former.

The astronomers of Quirigua appear to have been interested in taking the current date of a monument and casting back until they found some great period far in the past which ended on the same day. Stela D at that city has the dedicatory date 9.16.15.0.0 7 Ahau 18 Pop. At C20 there is recorded 13 kinchiltuns, 7 Ahau 3 Pop (fig. 33,49). The calculation is:

```
( 0.  1.13.0.)9.16.15.0.0   7 Ahau 18 Pop
  6.  8.13.0. 9.16.15.0.0
───────────────────────────
(13.)13. 0.0. 0. 0. 0.0.0   7 Ahau 3 Pop
```

This is exactly 5 alautuns or 320,000,000 tuns before the extremely early date on Stela F, and some 400,000,000 years before the date at which Stela D was erected. The calculations to verify these positions are based on the very useful table published by Long (1919).

I feel reasonably confident that the two dates are correctly deciphered, because 1 Ahau 13 kinchiltuns next preceding the date of the IS end precisely on 1 Ahau 13 Yaxkin, and the 13 kinchiltuns which end on 7 Ahau prior to that fall on 7 Ahau 3 Pop. The chances of a date such as 1 Ahau 13 Yaxkin actually being that which marks the end of the first 1 Ahau kinchiltun preceding the IS are 1 in 73; the chances of 3 Pop being the month position of the next preceding 13 kinchiltuns ending on a day 7 Ahau are also 1 in 73.

There are, apparently, other calculations far into the past at Quirigua, notably on Stelae F and A where there are references to dates connected with periods which have coefficients of 19, but I have not been able to elucidate them.

I have throughout assumed that the baktuns were grouped, not in 13's but in 20's, for the evidence supporting a vigesimal count of baktuns in Dresden and at Palenque and Copan is too strong to be overridden. I assume that at an early date, when the LC was first invented, the highest period was the baktun and that baktuns were arranged in re-entering series of 13, but that a subsequent desire to extend the range of time led to the invention of the pictun and still greater periods. With that expansion of time, it was essential to fit the baktuns into a vigesimal count. Consequently, 20 baktuns were made the equivalent of one pictun, but by then 4 Ahau 8 Cumku was so strongly established as the cyclic ending of a round of 13 baktuns that it continued to be given that designation, although reckoned as the end of a cycle of 20 baktuns for the purposes of calculation. Should my reconstruction of the higher periods be correct, 4 Ahau 8 Cumku then became the end of 13 calabtuns, with the theoretical LC position 1.13.0.0.0.0.0.0.0 4 Ahau 8 Cumku.

In view of what has been written, I think there is reasonably good evidence that the Maya did not have great difficulty in handling numbers involving alautuns, each of which consisted of 64,000,000 tuns. For us, with modern facilities, it is not a simple matter to construct a table of alautun endings; for the Maya it must have been a formidable task. The desire to probe half a billion years into the past reveals a strange mental quirk. It was, perhaps, an attempt to grasp the intangible in order to show that infinity has no starting point. The Maya priest traveled 400 million years backward, but he was as far as ever from the beginning which still eluded him. If time consisted of larger and larger cycles, obviously there was no beginning. I feel reasonably confident that when these stelae came to be erected at Quirigua, the Maya priest-astronomers had accepted the idea that time had no beginning. Withal, there was, I think, in these elucidations of the day and month positions on which these periods ended millions of years ago a certain affinity to the spirit which leads campanologists to seek fresh combinations to extend the changes which can be rung. It is a subject which should also appeal to the psychologist.

Determinants

Gallop apace bright Phoebus, through the sky—
—CHRISTOPHER MARLOW, *Edward II*

THE DETERMINANT THEORY was first enunciated by Teeple (1930, pp. 70–85). A determinant is a date which is believed to record the gain of the Maya year of 365 days over the solar year of approximately 365.2422 days in the interval between 13.0.0.0.0 4 Ahau 8 Cumku and the date in question. Teeple showed that the Maya calculated the accumulated error in one of two ways: they either noted the month position at 13.0.0.0.0 4 Ahau 8 Cumku which by their calculation then occupied the same position in the solar year as the given date did at the time then current; or they recorded the anniversary in the solar year then current of the position which, according to their calculations, the month position in question had occupied in the year 13.0.0.0.0 4 Ahau 8 Cumku.

These calculations frequently dealt with the month position on which the current katun fell. Thus, shortly before 9.17.0.0.0 13 Ahau 18 Cumku the Maya priest might have been interested in calculating how great an interval there was between the solar anniversary of the original 18 Cumku at 13.0.0.0.0 and the position occupied by 18 Cumku in the year then current. The interval between 13.0.0.0.0 and 9.17.0.0.0 is 1,418,400 days which reduces to 3883 solar years of 365.2422 plus about half a year. However, in the course of 3883 years 940 leap days have been inserted. The subtraction of 730 (2×365) from this total of leap days, gives 210 as the number of days the Maya calendar is ahead of the solar year. By subtracting 210 days from 18 Cumku the position 8 Mol is reached. That date then held the same position in the solar year at 13.0.0.0.0 4 Ahau 8 Cumku as 18 Cumku does at 9.17.0.0.0. The equation could be reversed, and the Maya priest could pose this problem: "The current katun ends on 18 Cumku, but what was the position in the solar year of 18 Cumku at 13.0.0.0.0?" To find its anniversary in the current year, add 210. Then, 18 Cumku + 210 = 3 Zac; accordingly, 3 Zac current time is the solar anniversary of 18 Cumku at 13.0.0.0.0. Perhaps this can be expressed better in terms of our own calendar. If 9.17.0.0.0 13 Ahau 18 Cumku falls on January 24, then according to the tropical year 8 Mol fell on January 24 at 13.0.0.0.0. Similarly, if 18 Cumku fell on August 22 at 13.0.0.0.0, that position in the solar year is at 9.17.0.0.0 occupied by 3 Zac.

At Copan the date 9.16.12.5.17 6 Caban 10 Mol is repeated on half a dozen monuments, and its katun and 1½ katun anniversaries are also recorded; it is clearly the most important date at that city. Teeple identified it as a determinant of 9.17.0.0.0 13 Ahau 18 Cumku many years ago. As the date falls approximately eight years before 9.17.0.0.0, the correction should be two days less than for the latter date: 10 Mol + 208 = 18 Cumku. That is to say, 10 Mol occupied the same position in the solar year at 13.0.0.0.0 as 18 Cumku currently does (9.16.12.16.5 6 Chicchan 18 Cumku). It might be asked why the Maya chose 9.16.12 5.17 6 Caban 10 Mol rather than some other date, for instance 9.16.19.7.10 11 Oc 8 Mol, which has the advantage of being nearer the katun ending. I think that there were other factors which led to the election of 6 Caban 10 Mol, one of which is that Caban seems to have been a more popular day than Oc, but the choice may have been guided by a desire to establish a lunar relationship in harmony with that of the sun. The moon age of 9.16.12.5.17 is recorded on Temple 11 as 11 days. The Copanecs appear to have thought that 13.0.0.0.0 had a moon age of 22 days, and in that case the 10 Mol immediately following 4 Ahau 8 Cumku would also have had a moon age of 11 or 12 days. This may be coincidence, but I think there is enough evidence from other sources to suggest that the Maya sought to link the age of the moon with the solar relationships.

Copan, apparently, gave the reverse determinant of 9.17.0.0.0 on Altar Z, seeking the anniversary in current time of 18 Cumku at 13.0.0.0.0 4 Ahau 8 Cumku, as discussed above. The date is 9.16.18.9.19 12 Cauac 2 Zac which does not appear on the altar, but is implied by the following arrangement:

$$
\begin{array}{ll}
(9.16.18.9.19 & 12 \text{ Cauac } 2 \text{ Zac}) \\
\underline{1.8.\ 1} & \\
(9.17.\ 0.0.\ 0) & 13 \text{ Ahau } 18 \text{ Cumku}
\end{array}
$$

The correction should be 210 days; the equation is 18 Cumku + 209 = 2 Zac. It will be noted that 12 Cauac is the day before 13 Ahau. In this case there is no obvious lunar relationship.

At Piedras Negras 9.10.6.5.9 8 Muluc 2 Zip was carved on Stelae 33, 36, and 38, on L 2, and on MSS 1; its thirteenth tun and second katun anniversaries are declared respectively on Stelae 34 and 38. Of its importance, therefore, there can be no doubt. This date is the determinant of the current katun, 9.11.0.0.0 12 Ahau 8 Ceh, for it is the anniversary of 8 Ceh placed at 13.0.0.0.0 4 Ahau 8 Cumku. The interval is 3752 years requiring a correction of 179 days; the equation is 8 Ceh + 179 = 2 Zip. The moon age of 9.10.6.5.9 is recorded on Piedras Negras 36 as 4 days, and the moon age of 9.11.0.0.0 is given as four days by Pusilha K and as 5 days by Copan 13. The interval between the two dates (4931 days) is 167 moon less half a day. It therefore is probable that this date was chosen because it is linked to 8 Ceh both by solar and lunar calculations, although the lunar arrangement is different from that supposedly part of the 6 Caban 10 Mol equation.

On a jade in the Bishop collection occurs (9.10.10.6.14) 4 Ix 7 Zip. As this is followed by its katun anniversary, it is clearly a date of some importance. There is a possibility, however, that the date falls one CR later (Beyer, 1945). The interval of 3756 years requires a correction of 180 days. Here, the equation is the reverse of that just discussed. Instead of calculating the current anniversary of 8 Ceh placed at 13.0.0.0.0, the month position at 13.0.0.0.0 with the same solar position as 8 Ceh current time was sought: 7 Zip + 181 = 8 Ceh.

In the tun ending on 13.0.0.0.0 4 Ahau 8 Cumku 7 Zip should have had a moon age of 16 days, if 8 Cumku had a moon age of 22 days. The moon age of 9.10.10.6.14 4 Ix 7 Zip was 22 days, the same as for the original 8 Cumku.

The recession of 8 Cumku in the solar year was also of interest to the Maya. Again, the solar position at 13.0.0.0.0 equivalent to 8 Cumku current time or the month position in the current year which held the same position as 4 Ahau 8 Cumku at 13.0.0.0.0 might be given.

Dates which recorded the solar equivalents at 13.0.0.0.0 of 8 Cumku current time are given in Table 21.

Date 1 has no obvious lunar associations, but note that it recovers 4 Ahau of 4 Ahau 8 Cumku.

Date 2 is given a moon age of 22 days, which, according to Teeple, was that of 13.0.0.0.0 4 Ahau 8 Cumku in the opinion of the Copanec priesthood of that time. This date falls 191 days before 9.12.8.13.0 4 Ahau 8 Cumku, which is distant 73 CR from 13.0.0.0.0 4 Ahau 8 Cumku. The appearance of this CR anniversary of the original 4 Ahau 8 Cumku undoubtedly inspired calculation of the associated determinant. As we shall see, the Maya made a special point of noting determinants or anniversaries of 8 Cumku in the vicinity of CR anniversaries of 4 Ahau 8 Cumku.

Date 3 has a moon age calculable from 9.12.6.5.8 as 10 days. The moon age of 12.19.19.8.9 8 Muluc 17 Mol would have been 10 days if Palenque reckoned the moon age of 4 Ahau 8 Cumku as 24 days. Date 3 is just one vague year before Date 2, and is also related to the current 4 Ahau 8 Cumku.

Date 4 has a moon age which can be calculated from the base of 9.12.6.5.8 as 6 days. The moon age of 14 Mol at 12.19.19.8.6 5 Cimi 14 Mol would have been 7 days if Teeple was correct in supposing that Palenque reckoned the moon age of 13.0.0.0.0 as 24 days. Of course, it follows that 8 Cumku at 13.0.0.0.0 had the same moon age as at 9.12.18.15.10 1 Oc 8 Cumku.

Date 5. The moon age of this date can be calculated as 21 days from 9.14.0.0.0 given on Piedras Negras 3 as 17 days. It is plausible that this was an attempt to reach the same moon age for Date 5 as was calculated for 13.0.0.0.0 4 Ahau 8 Cumku.

Date 6 has no apparent lunar link with 8 Cumku. This date is one year and 201 days before 9.15.1.8.0 4 Ahau 8 Cumku, which is distant 74 CR from 13.0.0.0.0 4 Ahau 8 Cumku. Presumably a date one year and 201 days before the CR anniversary was chosen because the Maya did not wish to give the date 201 days before 9.15.1.8.0 4 Ahau 8 Cumku because that would have been a date posterior to 9.15.0.0.0 4 Ahau 13 Yax, that of the erection of the monument. The Maya generally eschewed the practice of recording on a monument dates subsequent to that of dedication.

TABLE 21—DETERMINANTS OF 8 CUMKU

No. of Inscription	Date		Equation	Solar
1. Copan 19	9.10.19.15. 0	4 Ahau 8 Ch'en	8 Ch'en + 180 = 8 Cumku	182
2. Copan H'	9.12. 8. 3. 9	8 Muluc 17 Mol	17 Mol + 191 = 8 Cumku	189
3. Palenque Cross	9.12. 7. 3. 4	7 Kan 17 Mol	17 Mol + 191 = 8 Cumku	189
4. Palenque Sun	9.12.18. 5.16	2 Cib 14 Mol	14 Mol + 194 = 8 Cumku	192
or	9.12.18. 5.17	3 Caban 15 Mol	15 Mol + 193 = 8 Cumku	192
5. Piedras Negras 8	9.14. 2.11. 9	6 Muluc 7 Mol	7 Mol + 201 = 8 Cumku	198
6. Calakmul 52	9.14.19.15.14	10 Ix 7 Mol	7 Mol + 201 = 8 Cumku	202
7. Yaxchilan L 14	9.15.10. 0. 1	4 Imix 4 Mol	4 Mol + 204 = 8 Cumku	204
8. Bonampak 2	9.17. 5. 8. 9	6 Muluc 17 Yaxkin	17 Yaxkin + 211 = 8 Cumku	213
9. Copan Q	9.17.19.11.17	5 Caban 15 Yaxkin	15 Yaxkin + 213 = 8 Cumku	215
10. Naranjo 8	9.18. 9.14. 3	11 Akbal 11 Yaxkin	11 Yaxkin + 217 = 8 Cumku	218

Date 7. There is again no obvious connection of a lunar character with 8 Cumku. The moon age of the current 8 Cumku for both Dates 6 and 7 is 7 days.

Date 8. 17 Yaxkin in the tun ending on 13.0.0.0.0 4 Ahau 8 Cumku (22 days) would have had a moon age of 17 days. The moon age of the current 7 Yaxkin can be calculated as 20 days.

Date 9 reveals no lunar associations.

Date 10 has no clear lunar basis, although the 11 Yaxkin *after* 4 Ahau 8 Cumku has a moon age of 22 days presumably the same as that calculated for 4 Ahau 8 Cumku.

Four of the ten determinants thus have both solar and lunar associations. In view of the various possibilities in-. volved in each date these lunar associations may be merely fortuitous, although one imagines that the Maya would have been interested in thus hitting two birds with one stone.

Two interesting anniversaries of 13.0.0.0.0 4 Ahau 8 Cumku appear, respectively, on Quirigua G and Palenque Cross. The seventy-fifth CR anniversary of the original 4 Ahau 8 Cumku fell on 9.17.14.3.0 4 Ahau 8 Cumku. The correction at that date should have been 214 days, which, added to the anniversary of 4 Ahau 8 Cumku, reach 9.17.14.13.14 10 Ix 17 Yax; we find 9.17.14.13.12 8 Eb 15 Yax recorded on Quirigua G. On the Cross at Palenque the date 8.19.6.8.8 11 Lamat 6 Xul appears. This is one vague year and 123 days after 8.19.5.2.0, the sixty-eighth CR anniversary of 13.0.0.0.0 4 Ahau 8 Cumku. The interval is 3535 years, which calls for a correction of 2 years and 126 days. The Maya cal-

may have been regarded as unlucky, for 10 is the number of death, and Akbal and Xul have associations with the underworld.

Copan 16 carries the date 5 Ahau 8 Yaxkin. The glyphs are carved in an early style which indicates that the date has the LC position of either 9.4.9.17.0 or 9.7.2.12.0 If the earlier position is accepted, the date becomes a determinant of the seventieth CR anniversary of 4 Ahau 8 Cumku, which fell on 9.4.10.10.0, again one year removed:

$$
\begin{array}{ll}
9.4.\ 9.17.\ 0 & \text{5 Ahau 8 Yaxkin} \\
7.\ 5 = & \textit{145 days subtract} \\
\hline
9.4.\ 9.\ 9.15 & \text{3 Men 8 Cumku} \\
1.\ 0.\ 5 & \textit{365 days add} \\
\hline
9.4.10.10.\ 0 & \text{4 Ahau 8 Cumku}
\end{array}
$$

The Maya equation is 8 Cumku + 145 = 8 Yaxkin; the true solar correction would be 8 Cumku + 151 = 14 Yaxkin. The accuracy is not remarkable, but the calculation was made at an early date. It was probably set one year earlier than the anniversary of 4 Ahau 8 Cumku so that the day Ahau might be recovered.

The manner in which determinants were calculated is not surely known, and it is obvious that more than one correction was used, for the Maya calculations may fall two or three days either side of the solar corrections. Teeple thought a solar-lunar equation was used; I am more inclined to think the correction was made in terms of the CR. Let us examine again those dates which are related to CR anniversaries of 4 Ahau 8 Cumku:

TABLE 22—DETERMINANTS OF 8 CUMKU NEAR CALENDAR ROUND ANNIVERSARIES

Anniversary of 4 Ahau 8 Cumku		Determinant Date	Correction	
Date	No.		Maya	Solar
A 8.19. 5. 2.0	68	8.19. 6. 8. 8 11 Lamat 6 Xul	+ 123 days and 1 vague year	126
B 9. 4.10.10.0	70	9. 4. 9.17. 0 5 Ahau 8 Yaxkin	+ 145 days less 1 vague year	151
C 9.12. 8.13.0	73	9.12. 8. 3. 9 8 Muluc 17 Mol	− 191 days	189
C′ 9.12. 8.13.0	73	9.12. 7. 3. 4 7 Kan 17 Mol	− 191 days and −1 vague year	189
C″ 9.12. 8.13.0	73	9.12. 8. 4. 5 11 Chicchan 13 Ch'en	+ 190 days less 1 vague year	189
D 9.15. 1. 8.0	74	9.14.19.15.14 10 Ix 7 Mol	− 201 days and −1 vague year	201
E 9.17.14. 3.0	75	9.17.14.13.12 8 Eb 15 Yax	+ 212 days]	214

culation is: 8 Cumku + 123 = 6 Xul. This is four days off, but may be a calculation made at an early date, before greater accuracy was attained. It is not clear why a date one year and 123 days after 8.19.6.8.8 4 Ahau 8 Cumku was chosen, although the earlier date, 10 Akbal 6 Xul,

Obviously different corrections are being applied, for no reasonably accurate system could lead to differences in corrections of 10 days in 52 vague years and 21 days in 104 vague years (differences between B and C, and B and D). Variations in the corrections at different times and at different cities are to be expected. It will be noted that the poorest (B) is on the earliest monument, and the next poorest on the second earliest monument. Dates C and E fall two days short of the solar calculations; Date D is the same as would be reached by using a correct solar year.

Most of the CR anniversaries of 4 Ahau 8 Cumku during the period of the inscriptions appear in the list, but the important seventy-second anniversary at 9.9.16.0.0 is absent. It is possible that this was recorded on the hieroglyphic stairway at Naranjo. On Glyph Block 7 there is a distance number of 13.1, followed by 13 ? 18 Zip. Morley hesitatingly supports 13 Men 18 Zip; Spinden reads the date as 9.9.15.13.10 13 Oc 18 Zip; Joyce reads it as 12 Oc 18 Zip. Personally, I should be inclined to read the day sign as Akbal, since the lower part definitely resembles the glyph for that day. If, however, Spinden's reading is used, the following relationship develops:

$$9.9.15.\ 3.10\quad 13\ \text{Oc}\ 18\ \text{Zip}$$
$$13.\ 1\qquad\qquad \textit{Subtract}$$
$$\overline{9.9.14.\ 8.\ 9\quad 12\ \text{Muluc}\ 2\ \text{Ch'en}}$$

The second date is $2 \times 365 - 179$ days before 9.9.16.0.0. The solar correction at this date is 177 days; the Maya calculation would be 8 Cumku $+$ 179 $=$ 2 Ch'en.

If this reading is accepted, nearly all the CR anniversaries of 4 Ahau 8 Cumku during the period of the stela cult were accompanied by their determinants or solar anniversaries, calculated within a year or two of the dates in question. Those missing fell in early or late periods when very few calculations were being made. It is a fair conclusion, I think, that the Maya deliberately recorded the determinant or anniversary of 4 Ahau 8 Cumku as each CR anniversary of that date approached. If such dates are accepted as deliberate, it follows that the many other determinants are almost certainly the result of Maya calculations for the correction of their year, and are not coincidences.

The subject is vast and complex. I do not purpose to enter into further detail; enough has been written to outline the determinant theory, and for fuller information, the writer is referred to Teeple's discussion of the matter in *Maya Astronomy*.

Hieroglyphic Glossary and Index

And though a linguist should pride himself to have all the tongues that Babel cleft the world into, yet,
if he have not studied the solid things in them as well as the Words & Lexicons, he were nothing so much
to be esteem'd a learned man as any Yeoman or Tradesman completely wise in his Mother Dialect only.
—JOHN MILTON, *A Tractate on Education*

The primary purpose of this hieroglyphic glossary and index is to supplement the references in the text to illustrations; more important are the other uses which grew out of its compilation, for it drives home the constant appearance of many of the fundamental glyphic forms, and emphasizes the rarity of others. Some glyphic elements are rare; others are as frequent as rosy-fiingered dawns in the writings of that other blind poet. Indeed, I have sometimes wondered whether it might not be advisable to try to match the commonest glyphic elements with the commonest words in the spoken tongue, for we have seen that a correspondence in frequency of use in the spoken and written word applies to some elements, namely *u, ti,* and *te.*

Many elements listed in the glossary and index have not been discussed in the body of the text or have been accorded but passing mention. A study of the illustrations listed for such elements, often dubbed with somewhat bizarre names, will supplement discussions in the text on many matters. For example, the glossary brings to light further cases of interchangeability of postfix and prefix, notably in the case of the bundle postfix (cf. fig. 58,3,–Z3 with fig. 58,4,–C'5). It also reveals more clearly how elements in clauses occur in other combinations; those in the clauses at Yaxchilan illustrated in figure 46 are a case in point. Through the glossary and index the components can be traced in other textual arrangements. The same is true of affixes which appear almost to be integral parts of specific glyphs, but which through the glossary can be found in other com-

binations (e.g. the 8-shaped affix with the kinchiltun glyph). The glossary also stresses the many variants of common glyphic elements; the haab glyphs well illustrate this use. It also augments the bulk of personified variants, as for example in the case of personifications of the sky sign (fig. 52,2–H8), and hints at new synonyms. For instance, it now seems possible that the postfix with eyelash infix (figs. 36,25,39; 37,59,67), to which I was inclined to attach the meaning of death, may be a synonym of the *il* affix, for the one can substitute for the other in other glyphs, as for example the Ahau-Ik compound. Indeed, the compilation of this glossary and index has taught me much; my regret, if I may be permitted the Irishism, is that it was not undertaken before the text was written.

The hieroglyphic glossary and index is also an invitation to readers to experiment in decipherment, for the uses and range of some element or glyph therein contained may suggest an examination of what Sylvanus Morley lovingly termed the Corpus Inscriptionum Mayarum for all examples of the element in question. There is an undoubted need for a complete dictionary of Maya glyphic elements, but its compilation would be a formidable task.

The general index should also be consulted, particularly for hieroglyphs of Maya deities. In a few cases possible variants of rare elements are grouped under the same heading, although the evidence that they are identical is weak. *Semblant* applies to appearance, not necessarily to functional value.

References

Most of these entries are of works cited in the text, but I have included some of the most important writings of the great pioneers of our field, such as Förstemann. Their discoveries now mingle with more recent tributaries in the stream of glyphic research; the fountainheads are half-forgotten. It is, therefore, meet and right that we should make this pilgrimage to do homage to mighty men.

The principal vocabularies in lowland Maya languages are listed; for the most part those of the highland Maya are omitted, because the few references to highland vocabularies are specific and the attention paid to highland languages does not warrant a listing of those not cited.

AMRAM, D. W.
1942 The Lacandon, last of the Maya. *El México Antiguo*, 6: 15–26. Mexico.

ANDRADE, M. J.
1946 Materials on the Mam, Jacalteca, Aguacatec, Chuj, Bachajon, Palencano, and Lacandon languages. *Microfilm Coll. MSS. on Middle Amer. Cultural Anthropol.*, no. 10. Chicago.

ANDREWS, E. W.
1934 Glyph X of the supplementary series of the Maya inscriptions. *Amer. Anthropol.*, 36: 345–54. Menasha.
1938 The phonetic value of Glyph C of the Maya supplementary series. *Amer. Anthropol.*, 40: 755–58. Menasha.
1940 Chronology and astronomy in the Maya area. In *The Maya and their neighbors*, pp. 150–61. New York.
1942 The inscription on Stela 38, Piedras Negras, El Petén, Guatemala. *Amer. Antiquity*, 7: 364–68. Menasha.
1943 The archaeology of southwestern Campeche. *Carnegie Inst. Wash.*, Pub. 546, Contrib. 40. Washington.

APENES, O.
1936 Possible derivations of the 260 day period of the Maya calendar. *Ethnos*, 1: 5–8. Stockholm.

ARMILLAS, P.
1945 Los dioses de Teotihuacan. *Univ. Nac. de Cuyo, Anales del Inst. de Etnología Amer.*, 6: 35–61. Mendoza.
1947 La serpiente emplumada: Quetzalcoatl y Tlaloc. *Cuadernos Americanos*, 6: 161–78. Mexico.

AULIE, E., and H. W. AULIE
1947 Chol-English dictionary. MS. in possession of the authors. (Palencano-Chol.)
1947a Jini wen t'an jini ch'ujul bü tsa' bü ts'ijbunti cha'an jini ch'ujul bü Markos. (Palencano version of St. Mark.) American Bible Society. Mexico.

BARBACHANO, F. C.
1946 Monografía sobre los tzeltales de Tenejapa. *Microfilm Coll. MSS. on Middle Amer. Cultural Anthropol.*, no. 5. Chicago.
1946a Monografía de los tzotziles de San Miguel Mitontik. *Microfilm Coll. MSS. on Middle Amer. Cultural Anthropol.*, no. 6. Chicago.

BARRERA VASQUEZ, A.
1937 Problemas que ofrece la traducción de los documentos mayas postcortesianos. *El México Antiguo*, 5: 83–86. Mexico.
1939 El códice Pérez. *Rev. Mex. de Estudios Antropol.*, 3: 69–83. Mexico.
1939a La identificación de la deidad "E" de Schellhas. *Cuadernos Mayas*, no. 2. Merida.
1941 Sobre la significación de algunos nombres de signos del calendario maya. In *Los Mayas antiguos*, pp. 79–86. Mexico.
1943 Horóscopos mayas ó el pronóstico de los 20 signos del tzolkin según los libros de Chilam Balam, de Kaua y de Mani. *Registro de Cultura Yucateca*, vol. 1, no. 6, pp. 4–33. Mexico.
1944 Canción de la danza del arquero flechador. *Tlalocan*, 1: 273–77. Sacramento.

BASAURI, C.
1931 Tojolabales, tzeltales y mayas. Breves apuntes sobre antropología, etnografía y lingüística. Mexico.

BECERRA, M. E.
1933 El antiguo calendario chiapaneco. Estudio comparativo entre este i los calendarios precoloniales maya, quiche i nahoa. Mexico.
1935 Vocabulario de la lengua chol que se habla en el Distrito de Palenque del Estado de Chiapas . . . acopiado en Noviembre y Diciembre de 1934. *Anales del Mus. Nac. de Arqueol., Hist., y Etnog.*, Epoca 5, 2: 249–78. Mexico.

BELTRAN DE SANTA ROSA, M. P.
1859 Arte de el idioma maya reducido a sucintas reglas y semilexicon yucateco. Merida. (1st ed., Mexico, 1746.)

BERENDT, C. H.
Vocabulario comparativo de las lenguas pertenecientes a la familia maya-quiche 6 a 700 vocablos en 24 idiomas. (MS. was in hands of E. Rockstroh. This was not used by Stoll in his comparative word list as Gates [in Morley, 1920] has stated. The present location of this MS. is unknown.)
1870 Apuntes sobre la lengua chaneabal con un vocabulario. Tuxtla Gutierrez. (MS. in Berendt Collection, Philadelphia. Photographic copy in Peabody Museum, Harvard University.)

BERLIN, H.
1943 Notes on Glyph C of the lunar series at Palenque. *Carnegie Inst. Wash., Div. Hist. Res., Notes on Middle Amer. Archaeol. and Ethnol.*, no. 24. Cambridge.
1944 Un templo olvidado en Palenque. *Rev. Mex. de Estudios Antropol.*, 6: 62–90. Mexico.
1944a A tentative identification of the head variant for eleven. *Carnegie Inst. Wash., Div. Hist. Res., Notes on Middle Amer. Archaeol. and Ethnol.*, no. 33. Cambridge.
1945 A critique of dates at Palenque. *Amer. Antiquity*, 10: 340–47. Menasha.

BEYER, H.
1908 The symbolic meaning of the dog in ancient Mexico. *Amer. Anthropol.*, 10: 419–22. Lancaster.
1913 Ueber die mythologischen Affen der Mexikaner und Maya. *Proc. 18th Int. Cong. Amer.*, pp. 140–54. London.
1921 El color negro en el simbolismo de los antiguos mexicanos. *Revista de Revistas*, July 10. Mexico.
1921a El llamado "calendario azteca." Mexico.
1921b La aleta de Cipactli. *El México Antiguo*, 1: 199–203. Mexico.
1925 Apuntes sobre el jeroglífico Ek "negro." *Anales del Museo Nac. de Arqueol., Hist., y Etnog.*, Epoca 4, 3: 209–13. Mexico.
1926 Apuntes sobre el jeroglífico maya Muluc. *Mem. Soc. Cient. "Antonio Alzate,"* 45: 143–46. Mexico.
1926a La cifra tres en el simbolismo maya. *Mem. Soc. Cient. "Antonio Alzate,"* 45: 459–66. Mexico.
1926b Einige zusammengesetzte Mayahieroglyphen. *Internat. Archiv für Ethnog.*, 27: 91–93. Leiden.
1926c Die Verdopplung in der Hieroglyphenschrift der Maya. *Anthropos*, 21: 580–82. St. Gabriel Mödling bei Wien.
1926d La inscripción del Dintel 30 de Yaxchilan. *El México Antiguo*, 2: 251–58. Mexico.
1927 La cifra diez en el simbolismo maya. *Rev. Mex. de Estudios Hist.*, 1: 3–7. Mexico.
1927a Las dos estelas mayas de Tila, Chis. *Mem. Soc. Cient. "Antonio Alzate,"* 47: 123–43. Mexico.
1927b Dos fechas del Palacio de Palenque. *Rev. Mex. de Estudios Hist.*, 1: 107–14. Mexico.
1927c Review of Morley, "The inscriptions at Copan." *El México Antiguo*, 2: 313–18. Mexico.
1928 Symbolic ciphers in the eyes of Maya deities. *Anthropos*, 23: 32–37. St. Gabriel Mödling bei Wien.
1928a El origen del jeroglífico maya Akbal. *Rev. Mex. de Estudios Hist.*, 2: 5–9. Mexico.

BEYER, H.—(*continued*)

1928b El jeroglífico maya Yaxche. *Rev. Mex. de Estudios Hist.*, 2: 179–83. Mexico.

1929 The supposed Maya hieroglyph of the screech owl. *Amer. Anthropol.*, 31: 34–59. Menasha.

1930 The analysis of the Maya hieroglyphs. *Internat. Archiv für Ethnog.*, 31: 1–20. Leiden.

1930a The infix in Maya hieroglyphs—infixes touching the frame. *Proc. 23d Int. Cong. Amer.*, pp. 193–99. New York.

1931 Mayan hieroglyphs: the variable element of the introducing glyphs as month indicator. *Anthropos*, 26: 99–108. St. Gabriel Mödling bei Wien.

1931a The Maya day-signs Been and Kan. *Amer. Anthropol.*, 33: 199–208. Menasha.

1931b Die Ziffer Eins in den Mayahieroglyphen. *El México Antiguo*, vol. 3, no. 7, pp. 25–41. Mexico.

1932 The stylistic history of the Maya hieroglyphs. *Middle Amer. Res. Ser.*, Pub. 4, pp. 71–102. New Orleans.

1932a Mayan hieroglyphs: some tuns signs. *Middle Amer. Res. Ser.*, Pub. 4, pp. 103–30. New Orleans.

1932b An Ahau date with a katun and a katun ending glyph. *Middle Amer. Res. Ser.*, Pub. 4, pp. 131–36. New Orleans.

1933 A discussion of the Gates classification of Maya hieroglyphs. *Amer. Anthropol.*, 35: 659–94. Menasha.

1933a Emendations of the "Serpent Numbers" of the Dresden Maya Codex. *Anthropos*, 28: 1–7. St. Gabriel Mödling bei Wien.

1933b The relation of the synodical month and eclipses to the Maya correlation problem. *Middle Amer. Res. Ser.*, Pub. 5, pp. 301–19. New Orleans.

1934 The position of the affixes in Maya writing: I. *Maya Res.*, 1: 20–29. New York.

1934a The position of the affixes in Maya writing: II. *Maya Res.*, 1: 101–08. New York.

1934b Die Mayahieroglyphe "Hand." *Proc. 24th Int. Cong. Amer.*, pp. 265–71. Hamburg.

1935 On the correlation between Maya and Christian chronology. *Maya Res.*, 2: 64–72. New York.

1935a The date on the long-nosed mask of Labná. *Maya Res.*, 2: 184–88. New York.

1935b The dates on Lintel 10 of Yaxchilan. *Maya Res.*, 2: 394–97. New York.

1935c Zur Konkordanzfrage der Mayadaten mit denen der christlichen Zeitrechnung. *Zeit. für Ethnol.*, 65: 75–80. Berlin.

1935d The date on the cornice of House C of the palace at Palenque. *El México Antiguo*, vol. 3, nos. 9–10, pp. 53–55. Mexico.

1936 The position of the affixes in Maya writing: III. *Maya Res.*, 3: 102–104. New Orleans.

1936a Another Maya hieroglyph for day. *Amer. Antiquity*, 2: 13–14. Menasha.

1936b *See* 1935d.

1936c The lunar glyphs of the supplementary series at Quirigua. *El México Antiguo*, vol. 3, nos. 11–12, pp. 1–11. Mexico.

1936d Mayan hieroglyphs: Glyph G8 of the supplementary series. *Amer. Anthropol.*, 38: 247–49. Menasha.

1936e Note concerning the moon-count at Palenque and Tila. *Maya Res.*, 3: 110–11. New Orleans.

1936f The relation of two dates on Altar U, Copan. *Maya Res.*, 3: 193–94. New Orleans.

1936g The true zero date of the Maya. *Maya Res.*, 3: 202–04. New Orleans.

1936h Decipherment of a greatly damaged inscription at Palenque. *El México Antiguo*, 4: 1–6. Mexico.

1936i Eine weitere Mayahieroglyphe für "Tag." *El México Antiguo*, 4: 7–10. Mexico.

1937 Studies on the inscriptions of Chichen Itza. *Carnegie Inst. Wash.*, Pub. 483, Contrib. 21. Washington.

1937a Lunar glyphs of the supplementary series at Piedras Negras. *El México Antiguo*, 4: 75–82. Mexico.

1938 Two high period series at Palenque. *El México Antiguo*, 4: 145–54. Mexico.

1938a Das Zeichen für Zwanzig in den Maya-Inschriften. *El México Antiguo*, 4: 155–61. Mexico.

BEYER, H.—(*continued*)

1938b Die Tagesdaten auf dem Maya-Altar des Mexikanischen National Museums. *Zeit. für Ethnol.*, 70: 88–93. Berlin.

1939 Elucidation of a secondary series on Lintel 2 of Piedras Negras. *El México Antiguo*, 4: 289–92. Mexico.

1939a Remarks on some Maya hieroglyphs from Piedras Negras. *Ethnos*, 4: 105–11. Stockholm.

1940 Rectification of a date on Stela 12 of Piedras Negras. *El México Antiguo*, 5: 7–8. Mexico.

1941 A discussion of J. Eric Thompson's interpretations of Chichen Itza hieroglyphs. *Amer. Antiquity*, 6: 327–38. Menasha.

1941a The variants of Glyph D of the Supplementary Series. In *Los Mayas antiguos*, pp. 63–72. Mexico.

1943 Algunos datos sobre los dinteles mayas de Tikal en el Museo Etnográfico de Basilea. *Proc. 27th Int. Cong. Amer.*, 1: 338–43. Mexico.

1943a The Maya hieroglyph "ending day." *Proc. 27th Int. Cong. Amer.*, 1: 344–51. Mexico.

1943b The long count position of the serpent number dates. *Proc. 27th Int. Cong. Amer.*, 1: 401–05. Mexico.

1945 An incised Maya inscription in the Metropolitan Museum of Art, New York. *Middle Amer. Res. Records*, vol. 1, no. 7. New Orleans.

1945a The Maya hieroglyph Chicchan derivative. *Middle Amer. Res. Records*, vol. 1, no. 8. New Orleans.

BLOM, F.

1929 Preliminary report of the John Geddings Gray Memorial Expedition. *Tulane Univ., Dept. Middle Amer. Res.* New Orleans.

1935 The Pestac stela. *Maya Res.*, 2: 190–91. New York.

——, and O. LA FARGE

1926–27 Tribes and temples. *Middle Amer. Res. Ser.*, vols. 1 and 2. New Orleans.

BOEKELMAN, H. J.

1935 Ethno- and archaeo-conchological notes on four Middle American shells. *Maya Res.*, 2: 257–77. New York.

BOTURINI, B. L.

1746 Idea de una nueva historia general de la América Septentrional. Madrid.

BOWDITCH, C. P.

1900 The Lords of the Night and the Tonalamatl of the Codex Borbonicus. *Amer. Anthropol.*, 2: 145–54. New York.

1901 Was the beginning day of the Maya month numbered zero (or twenty) or one? Cambridge.

1901a A method which may have been used by the Mayas in calculating time. Cambridge.

1901b Memoranda on the Maya calendars used in the Books of Chilam Balam. *Amer. Anthropol.*, 3: 129–38. New York.

1901c On the age of Maya ruins. *Amer. Anthropol.*, 3: 697–700. New York.

1901d Notes on the report of Teobert Maler in Memoirs of the Peabody Museum, Vol. II, no. I. Cambridge.

1903 Notes on the report of Teobert Maler in Memoirs of the Peabody Museum, Vol. II, no. II. Cambridge.

1903a A suggestive Maya inscription. Cambridge.

1906 Mayan nomenclature. Cambridge.

1906a The Temples of the Cross, of the Foliated Cross and of the Sun at Palenque. Cambridge.

1909 The dates and numbers of pages 24 and 46 to 50 of the Dresden Codex. In *Putnam Anniv. Vol.*, pp. 268–98. New York.

1910 The numeration, calendar systems and astronomical knowledge of the Mayas. Cambridge.

BRAINERD, G. W.

1941 Fine Orange pottery in Yucatan. *Rev. Mex. de Estudios Antropol.*, 5: 163–83. Mexico.

BRASSEUR DE BOURBOURG, C. E.

1862 Gramática de la lengua quiche. Grammaire de la langue quichée, espagnole-française, mise en parallèle avec ses deux dialectes, cakchiquel et tzutuhil. . . . Paris.

1864 Relation des choses de Yucatan de Diego de Landa . . . accompagné de documents divers historiques et chronologiques. . . . Paris.

1869 *See* Codex Madrid.

BRINTON, D. G.
1882 The Maya chronicle. *Brinton's Library of Aboriginal Amer. Lit., no. 1.* Philadelphia.
1882a The graphic system and ancient records of the Mayas. Introduction to C. Thomas, 1882.
1882b American hero-myths. A study in the native religions of the western continent. Philadelphia.
1885 The annals of the Cakchiquels. The original text with a translation, notes and introduction. *Brinton's Library of Aboriginal Amer. Lit., no. 6.* Philadelphia.
1890 Essays of an Americanist. Philadelphia.
1893 The native calendar of Central America and Mexico. A study in linguistics and symbolism. *Proc. Amer. Philos. Soc., 31:* 258–314. Philadelphia.
1895 A primer of Mayan hieroglyphics. *Univ. Pa. Ser. in Philol., Lit. and Archaeol.,* vol. 3, no. 2. Philadelphia.
1900 Catalogue of the Berendt linguistic collection. *Bull. Free Mus. of Science and Art, Univ. Pa., 1:* 1–18. Philadelphia.

BUNTING, E. J. W.
1932 Ixtlavacan Quiche calendar of 1854. *Maya Soc. Quart., 1:* 72–75. Baltimore.

BURKITT, R.
1902 Notes on the Kekchi language. *Amer. Anthropol., 4:* 441–63. New York.
1918 The hils [*sic*] and the corn. *Mus. Jour., 9:* 274–89. Philadelphia.
1930–31 The calendar of Soloma and other Indian towns. *Man,* vol. 30, no. 80; vol. 31, no. 160. London.

CAHCOH, DICTIONARY OF
c. 1700 Fragments of three vocabularies; about 300 pp. survive. In Berendt Collection, Philadelphia. Photostat in Peabody Museum, Harvard University. (Gates attributes part, at least, of this to Fray Dionysio de Zuñiga.)

CALENDARIO CAKCHIQUEL
1685 Berendt MS. no. 57. In library, University of Pennsylvania Museum.

CASO, A.
1928 Las estelas zapotecas. Mexico.
1937 Tenían los teotihuacanos conocimiento del tonalpohualli? *El México Antiguo, 4:* 131–43. Mexico.
1939 La correlacion de los años azteca y cristiano. *Rev. Mex. de Estudios Antropol., 3:* 11–45. Mexico.
1940 El entierro del siglo. *Rev. Mex. de Estudios Antropol., 4:* 65–76. Mexico.
1941 El complejo arqueológico de Tula y las grandes culturas indígenas de Mexico. *Rev. Mex. de Estudios Antropol., 5:* 85–95. Mexico.
1946 El calendario matlatzinca. *Rev. Mex. de Estudios Antropol., 8:* 95–109. Mexico.
1947 Calendario y escritura de las antiguas culturas de Monte Alban. *In* Obras completas de Miguel Othón de Mendizabal. Mexico.
——, M. W. STIRLING, et al.
1946 ¿Conocieron la rueda los indigénas mesoamericanos? *Cuadernos Americanos, 5:* 193–207. Mexico.

CHANEABAL LANGUAGE
See Toholabal language.

CHARENCY, C. F. H. G. DE
1884 Recherches sur le calendrier zotzil. *Revue d'Ethnographie, 3:* 398–401. Paris.
1885 Vocabulaire de la langue tzotzil. *Memoires de l'Academie Nationale des Sciences, Arts et Belles-Lettres de Caen.* Caen. (Extracted from MS. attributed to Fr. Manuel Hidalgo, probably 1735. Original in La Bibliothèque Nationale, Paris.)
1889 Vocabulario tzotzil-espanol. Dialecto de los indios de la parte oriental del Estado de Chiapas (Mexico). Orleans.
1899 Noms des points de l'espace dans divers dialectes americains. *Jour. Soc. des Amer. de Paris, 2:* 109–78. Paris.

CHILAM BALAM OF CHUMAYEL
See Roys, 1933.

CHILAM BALAM OF IXIL
See Roys, 1946.

CHILAM BALAM OF KAUA
Original thought to be in Merida. There is a photographic reproduction by Gates, a copy of which is in Peabody

CHILAM BALAM OF KAUA—(*continued*)
Museum, Harvard University. A partial copy is in the Berendt Collection, Philadelphia.

CHILAM BALAM OF MANI
Original lost. Copious extracts in Codex Perez.

CHILAM BALAM OF TIZIMIN
Original in Mexico City. Photographed by T. Maler. Gates reproduction, a copy of which is in Peabody Museum, Harvard University. Copy made in 1868 in Berendt Collection, Philadelphia.

CHOL LANGUAGE
See Moran. For Palencano Chol, see Andrade, Aulie and Aulie, Becerra, Berendt (no date), and Fernandez and Fernandez.

CHONTAL LANGUAGE
See Blom and La Farge, and Scholes and Roys.

CHORTI LANGUAGE
See Girard, Ruano Suarez, and Wisdom.

CHRONICLE OF CHICXULUB
1882 Crónica de Chicxulub. *In* Brinton, 1882. (*See also* Crónica de Yaxkukul.)
1936 Historia y crónica de Chac-xulub-chen. Prólogo, versión y notas de H. Pérez Martínez. Mexico.

CLINE, H. F.
1944 Lore and deities of the Lacandon Indians, Chiapas, Mexico. *Jour. Amer. Folklore, 57:* 107–15. Menasha.

CODEX CHIMALPOPOCA
1945 Códice Chimalpopoca. Anales de Cuauhtitlan y leyenda de los soles. Translation by Primo F. Velásquez. *Universidad Nacional Autónoma de México, Instituto de Historia.* Mexico.

CODEX DRESDEN
1880 Die Maya-Handschrift der Königlichen Bibliothek zu Dresden; herausgegeben von Prof. Dr. E. Förstemann. Leipzig. (2d ed., 1892.)

CODEX MADRID (Cortesiano section)
1892 Códice maya denominado Cortesiano que se conserva en el Museo Arqueologico Nacional (Madrid). Reproducción fotocromolitográfica ordenada en la misma forma que el original. Hecha y publicada bajo la dirección de D. Juan de Dios de la Rada y Delgado y D. Jeronimo López de Ayala u del Hierro. Madrid.

CODEX MADRID (Troano section)
1869–70 Manuscrit Troano. Etudes sur le système graphique et la langue des Mayas. By C. E. Brasseur de Bourbourg. 2 vols. Paris.

CODEX MENDOZA
1938 Codex Mendoza. The Mexican MS. known as the Collection of Mendoza and preserved in the Bodleian Library, Oxford. Edited and translated by James Cooper-Clark. 3 vols. London.

CODEX PARIS
1887 Codex Peresianus manuscrit hiératique des anciens Indiens de l'Amérique Centrale conservé à la Bibliothèque Nationale de Paris, avec une introduction par Léon de Rosny. Publié en couleurs. Paris.

CODEX PEREZ
(c. 1837) *See* Barrera Vasquez, 1939; Roys, 1949a; Solis Acala, 1949.

CODICES, MEXICAN
See Noguera, 1933, for full listing.

CORDOVA, J. DE
1886 Arte del idioma zapoteca. Morelia. (Written in late 16th century.)

CORDY, N.
1936 The cardinal point South in Maya language and glyph and its implications. *Maya Res., 3:* 326–29. New Orleans.
1946 Examples of phonetic construction in Maya hieroglyphs. *Amer. Antiquity, 12:* 108–17. Menasha.

CORONEL, J.
1620 Arte en lengua de maya recopilado y enmendado. Mexico. (2d ed. as preface to Motul dictionary, 1929.)

CRÓNICA DE CALKINI
1935 The Maya Calkini chronicle or documents concerning the descent of the Ah-Canul, or men of the serpent, their arrival and territory. In facsimile. Introduction by W. E. Gates. *Maya Soc.,* Pub. 8. Baltimore.

CRÓNICA DE YAXKUKUL
1926 Crónicas mayas. Crónica de Yaxkukul. With Spanish translation and notes by J. Martínez Hernández. Merida.

CRÓNICA DE OXKUTZCAB
1657–1817 Original in Peabody Museum, Harvard University. Reproduction by Gates and Bowditch. Only page 66 is of importance in connection with this study. (Also known as Xiu Chronicles).

DIBBLE, C.
1940 El antiguo sistema de escritura en México. *Rev. Mex. de Estudios Antropol.*, 4: 105–28. Mexico.

DIESELDORFF, E. P.
1926–33 Kunst und Religion der Mayavölker im alten und heutigen Mittelamerika. 3 vols. Berlin.

DITTRICH, A.
1936 Die Korrelation der Maya-Chronologie. Reprinted from *Abhandlungen der Preussischen Akademie der Wissenschaften*. Berlin.
1937 Der Planet Venus und seine Behandlung im Dresdener Maya-Kodex. Reprinted from *Sitzungsberichten der Preussischen Akademie der Wissenschaften*. Berlin.
1939 Die Finsternistafel des Dresdener Maya-Kodex. Reprinted from *Abhandlungen der Preussischen Akademie der Wissenschaften*. Berlin.

ESCALONA RAMOS, A.
1940 Cronología y astronomía maya-mexica (con un anexo de historias indígenas.) Mexico.
1943 Cronología y astronomía maya-mexica. Un nuevo sistema de correlación calendarica. *Proc. 27th Int. Cong. Amer.*, 1: 623–30. Mexico.

FERNANDEZ GUARDIA, R., and J. FERNANDEZ FERRAZ
1892 Lenguas indígenas de Central América en el siglo XVIII según copia del Archivo de Indias hecha por León Fernandez. San Jose de Costa Rica.

FÖRSTEMANN, E. W.
1886 Erläuterung zur Mayahandschrift der Königlichen öffentlichen Bibliothek zu Dresden. Dresden.
1887 Zur Entzifferung der Mayahandschriften. Dresden.
1891 Zur Maya-Chronologie. *Zeit. für Ethnol.*, 23: 142–55. Berlin.
1891a Zur Entzifferung der Mayahandschriften, II. Dresden.
1892 Zur Entzifferung der Mayahandschriften, III. Dresden.
1893 Die Zeitperioden der Mayas. *Globus*, 63: 30–32. Brunswick.
1894 Zur Entzifferung der Mayahandschriften, IV. Dresden.
1894a Die Mayahieroglyphen. *Globus*, 60: 78–80. Brunswick.
1895 Zur Entzifferung der Mayahandschriften, V. Dresden.
1897 Zur Entzifferung der Mayahandschriften, VI. Dresden.
1901 Commentar zur Mayahandschrift der Königlichen öffentlichen Bibliothek zu Dresden. Dresden. (English translation in Förstemann, 1906.)
1901a Der Mayagott des Jahresschlusses. *Globus*, 80: 189–92. Brunswick.
1902 Commentar zur Madrider Handschrift. Danzig.
1902a Eine historische Maya-Inschrift. *Globus*, 81: 150–53. Brunswick.
1903 Commentar zur Pariser Handschrift. Danzig.
1904 Various papers. *Bur. Amer. Ethnol.*, Bull. 28, pp. 393–590. Washington. (Contains translations of most of the papers listed above, as well as others not listed.)
1906 Commentary on the Maya manuscript in the Royal Public Library of Dresden. *Papers Peabody Mus. Harvard Univ.*, vol. 4, no. 2. Cambridge. See Tozzer, 1907a for full bibliography.

FULTON, C. C.
1947 Elements of Maya arithmetic with particular attention to the calendar. *Carnegie Inst. Wash., Div. Hist. Res., Notes on Middle Amer. Archaeol. and Ethnol.*, no. 85. Cambridge.
1948 Did the Maya have a zero? The meanings of our zero and the Maya "zero" symbols. *Carnegie Inst. Wash., Div. Hist. Res., Notes on Middle Amer. Archaeol. and Ethnol.*, no. 90. Cambridge.

GADOW, H.
1908 Through southern Mexico. London.

GANN, T. W. F.
1900 Mounds in northern Honduras. *Bur. Amer. Ethnol.*, 19th Ann. Rept., pt. 2, pp. 655–92. Washington.

GANN, T. W. F.—(*continued*)
1918 The Maya Indians of southern Yucatan and northern British Honduras. *Bur. Amer. Ethnol.*, Bull. 64. Washington.
1924 In an unknown land. London.
1926 A new Maya stela with Initial Series date. *Man*, vol. 26, no. 37. London.
1928 Recently discovered Maya temples in Yucatan with date sculptured on wooden lintel. *Man*, vol. 28, no. 5. London. See Thompson, 1940c, for full bibliography.
——, and J. E. S. THOMPSON
1931 The history of the Maya. New York and London.

GATES, W.
1910 Commentary upon the Maya-Tzental Perez Codex with a concluding note upon the linguistic problem of the Maya glyphs. *Papers Peabody Mus. Harvard Univ.*, vol. 6, no. 1. Cambridge.
1931 An outline dictionary of Maya glyphs. *Maya Soc.*, Pub. 1. Baltimore.
1931a The thirteen Ahaus in the Kaua manuscript. . . . *Maya Soc. Quart.*, 1: 2–20. Baltimore.
1931b Glyph studies. *Maya Soc. Quart.*, 1: 32–33. Baltimore.
1931c A Lanquin Kekchi calendar. *Maya Soc. Quart.*, 1: 29–32. Baltimore.
1932 Glyph studies. *Maya Soc. Quart.*, 1: 68–70. Baltimore.
1932a Pokonchi calendar. *Maya Soc. Quart.*, 1: 75–77. Baltimore.
1932b Eras of the thirteen gods and the nine gods. *Maya Soc. Quart.*, 1: 78–92. Baltimore.
1932c The Mayance nations. *Maya Soc. Quart.*, 1: 97–106. Baltimore.
1932d Glyph studies. *Maya Soc. Quart.*, 1: 153–82. Baltimore.
1937 Yucatan before and after the conquest, by Friar Diego de Landa, with other related documents, maps and illustrations. Translated with notes. *Maya Soc.*, Pub. 20. Baltimore.
1940 A grammar of Maya. *Maya Soc.*, Pub. 13. Baltimore.

GAUMER, G.
1917 Monografía de los mamíferos de Yucatán. Mexico.

GENET, J.
1934 Notes sur l'écriture maya-quichée. *Revue des Etudes Mayas-Quichées*, 1: 1–22. Paris.
1934a Les glyphes symboliques dans l'écriture maya-quichée. Le glyphe symbolique de la guerre. *Revue des Etudes Mayas-Quichées*, 1: 23–32. Paris.
1934b L'écriture maya-quichée et les glyphes phonétiques. *Revue des Etudes Mayas-Quichées*, 1: 37–63. Paris.

GIRARD, R.
1940 El Chorti. *Revista del Archivo y Biblioteca Nacionales*, vol. 19, starting with no. 2. Tegucigalpa.

GOODMAN, J. T.
1897 The archaic Maya inscriptions. *In* appendix to Maudslay, 1889–1902.
1905 Maya dates. *Amer. Anthropol.*, 7: 642–47. Lancaster.

GORDON, G. B.
1896 Prehistoric ruins of Copan, Honduras. A preliminary report of the explorations by the Museum, 1891–1895. *Mem. Peabody Mus. Harvard Univ.*, vol. 1, no. 1. Cambridge.
1902 The Hieroglyphic Stairway, ruins of Copan. Report on explorations by the Museum. *Mem. Peabody Mus. Harvard Univ.*, vol. 1, no. 6. Cambridge.
1902a On the use of zero and twenty in the Maya time system. *Amer. Anthropol.*, 4: 237–75. New York.
1905 The serpent motive in the ancient art of Central America and Mexico. *Transactions, Dept. Archaeol., Univ. Pa.*, 1: 131–63. Philadelphia.
1913 An unpublished inscription from Quirigua, Guatemala. *Proc. 18th Int. Cong. Amer.*, pp. 238–40. London.

GOUBAUD C., A.
1935 El "Guajxaquíp Báts"—ceremonia calendárica indígena. *Anales Soc. de Geog. e Hist. de Guatemala*, 12: 39–52. Guatemala.
1937 The Guajxaquíp Báts. An Indian ceremony of Guatemala. Guatemala. (Translation of Goubaud, 1935.)
——, J. de D. ROSALES and S. TAX
1947 Reconnaissance of northern Guatemala, 1944. *Microfilm*

GOUBAUD C., A., J. de D. ROSALES and S. TAX—*(continued)*
Coll. MSS. on Middle Amer. Cultural Anthropol., no. 17.
Chicago.

GRUYTER, W. J. DE
1946 A new approach to Maya hieroglyphs. Amsterdam.

GUITERAS HOLMES, C.
1946 Informe de San Pedro Chenalhó (Chiapas). *Microfilm Coll.
of MSS. on Middle Amer. Cultural Anthropol.*, no. 14.
Chicago.

GUTHE, C. E.
1921 A possible solution of the number series on pages 51 to
58 of the Dresden Codex. *Papers Peabody Mus. Harvard
Univ.*, vol. 6, no. 2. Cambridge.
1932 The Maya lunar count. *Science*, 75: 271–77. Lancaster.

HAGAR, S.
1917 The American Zodiac. *Amer. Anthropol.*, 19: 518–32.
Lancaster.

HALPERN, A. M.
1942 A theory of Maya tš-sounds. *Carnegie Inst. Wash., Div.
Hist. Res., Notes on Middle Amer. Archaeol. and Ethnol.*,
no. 13. Cambridge.

HERNANDEZ SPINA, V.
1854 Kalendaryo conservado hasta el dia por los sacerdotes
del sol en Ixtlavacan, pueblo descendiente de la nación
quiché. (A partial translation of this by E. J. W. Bunting
is in *Maya Soc. Quart.*, 1: 72–75. Baltimore, 1932.)

HEWETT, E. L.
1911 Two seasons' work in Guatemala. *Bull. Archaeol. Inst.
Amer.*, 2: 117–34. Norwood.
1912 The excavations at Quirigua in 1912. *Bull. Archaeol. Inst.
Amer.*, 3: 163–71. Norwood.
1913 The excavation of Quirigua, Guatemala, by the School of
American Archaeology. *Proc. 18th Int. Cong. Amer.*,
pp. 241–48. London.
1916 Latest work of the School of American Archaeology at
Quirigua. In *Holmes Anniv. Vol.*, pp. 157–62. Washington.

HOLMES, W. H.
1907 On a nephrite statuette from San Andres Tuxtla, Vera
Cruz, Mexico. *Amer. Anthropol.*, 9: 691–701. Lancaster.

JAKEMAN, M. W.
1945 The origins and history of the Mayas. In three parts.
Part 1, introductory investigations. Los Angeles.

JOYCE, T. A.
1912 A short guide to the American antiquities in the British
Museum. British Museum, London.
1914 Mexican archaeology. London and New York.
1923 Guide to the Maudslay collection of Maya sculptures
(casts and originals) from Central America. British Museum, London.
1925 The Hieroglyphic Stairway at Naranjo, Guatemala. *Proc.
21st Int. Cong. Amer.*, pt. 2, pp. 297–304. Göteborg.
1929 Report on the British Museum Expedition to British
Honduras, 1929. *Jour. Royal Anthropol. Inst.*, 59: 439–59.
London.

——, T. GANN, E. L. GRUNING, and R. C. E. LONG
1928 Report on the British Museum Expedition to British
Honduras, 1928. *Jour. Royal Anthropol. Inst.*, 58: 323–50.
London.

KIDDER, A. V.
1947 The artifacts of Uaxactun, Guatemala. *Carnegie Inst.
Wash.*, Pub. 576. Washington.
1948 Kaminaljuyu, Guatemala: addenda and corrigenda. *Carnegie Inst. Wash., Div. Hist. Res., Notes on Middle
Amer. Archaeol. and Ethnol.*, no. 89. Cambridge.

——, J. D. JENNINGS, and E. M. SHOOK
1946 Excavations at Kaminaljuyu, Guatemala. *Carnegie Inst.
Wash.*, Pub. 561. Washington.

——, and J. E. THOMPSON
1938 The correlation of Maya and Christian chronologies. In
Carnegie Inst. Wash., Pub. 501, pp. 493–510. Washington.

KINGSBOROUGH, E. K.
1831–48 Antiquities of Mexico. London. 9 vols. (Codex Dresden
is reproduced in vol. 3.)

KREICHGAUER, D.
1914 Uber Sonnen- und Mondfinsternisse in der Dresdener
Mayahandschrift. *Anthropos*, 9: 1019. San Gabriel
Mödling bei Wien.
1927 Anschluss der Maya-Chronologie an die julianische.
Anthropos, 22: 1–15. San Gabriel Mödling bei Wien.
1932 Über die Maya-Chronologie. *Anthropos*, 27: 621–26. San
Gabriel Mödling bei Wien.

KROEBER, A. L.
1934 Native American population. *Amer. Anthropol.*, 36: 1–25.
Menasha.

LA FARGE, O.
1934 Post-Columbian dates and the Mayan correlation problem.
Maya Res., 1: 109–24. New York.
1947 Santa Eulalia. The religion of a Cuchumatán Indian town.
Univ. Chicago Pub. in Anthropol. Chicago.

——, and D. BYERS
1931 The year bearer's people. *Middle Amer. Res. Ser.*, Pub. 3.
New Orleans.

LANDA, D. DE
See Brasseur de Bourbourg, 1864; Gates, 1937; and
Tozzer, 1941.

LARSEN, H.
1936 The 260 day period as related to the agricultural life of
the ancient Indian. *Ethnos*, 1: 9–12. Stockholm.

LEHMANN, W.
1906 Traditions des anciens mexicains. Texte inédit et original
en langue nahuatl avec traduction en latin. *Jour. Soc. des
Amer. de Paris*, n.s., 3: 239–97. Paris.
1910 Ergebnisse einer Forschungreise in Mittelamerika und
Mexico, 1907–1909. *Zeit. für Ethnol.*, 42: 687–749. Berlin.
1920 Zentral-Amerika. 1 Teil. Die Sprachen Zentral-Amerikas.
2 vols. Berlin.

LEON Y GAMA, A.
1792 Descripción histórica y cronológica de las dos piedras . . .
que se hallaron . . . el año de 1790. Mexico.

LINCOLN, J. S.
1942 The Maya calendar of the Ixil of Guatemala. *Carnegie
Inst. Wash.*, Pub. 528, Contrib. 38. Washington.
1946 An ethnological study of the Ixil Indians of the Guatemala
highlands. *Microfilm Coll. MSS. on Middle Amer. Cultural Anthropol.*, no. 1. Chicago.

LIZANA, B. DE
1893 Historia de Yucatán. Devocionario de Ntra. Sra. de Izamal
y conquista espiritual. Mexico. (1st ed., Valladolid, 1633.)

LIZARDI RAMOS, CESAR
1936 Recurrencias de las fechas mayas. Mexico.
1937 El orden de los katunes de la cuenta corta. Mexico.
1941 El glifo B y la sincronología maya-cristiana. In *Los Mayas
Antiguos*, pp. 243–69. Mexico.

LONG, R. C. E.
1919 The highest known Maya number. *Man*, vol. 19, no. 20.
London.
1919a The date of the Maya ruins at Santa Rita, British Honduras. *Man*, vol. 19, no. 29. London.
1923 Maya high numbers. *Man*, vol. 23, no. 39. London.
1923a The burner period of the Mayas. *Man*, vol. 23, no. 108.
London.
1925 Some Maya time periods. *Proc. 21st Int. Cong. Amer.*,
pp. 574–80. Göteborg.
1931 The correlation of Maya and Christian chronology. *Jour.
Royal Anthropol. Soc.*, 61: 407–12. London.
1934 The dates in the Annals of the Cakchiquels and a note
on the 260-day period of the Maya. *Jour. Royal Anthropol.
Inst.*, 64: 57–68. London.
1935 Maya and Mexican writing. *Maya Res.*, 2: 24–32. New
York.
1936 Maya writing and its decipherment. *Maya Res.*, 3: 309–15.
New Orleans.
1940 The dates on Altar 5 at Tikal. *Amer. Antiquity*, 5:
283–86. Menasha.
1942 The payment of tribute in the Codex Mendoza. *Carnegie
Inst. Wash., Div. Hist. Res., Notes on Middle Amer.
Archaeol. and Ethnol.*, no. 10. Cambridge.
1948 Some remarks on Maya arithmetic. *Carnegie Inst. Wash.,
Div. Hist. Res., Notes on Middle Amer. Archaeol. and
Ethnol.*, no. 88. Cambridge.

Lopez de Cogolludo, Diego
1867–68 Historia de Yucatan. 3d ed. Merida. (1st ed., Madrid, 1688.)
Lothrop, S. K.
1924 Tulum. An archaeological study of the east coast of Yucatan. *Carnegie Inst. Wash.*, Pub. 335. Washington.
1929 Sculptural fragments from Palenque. *Jour. Royal Anthropol. Inst.*, 59: 53–63. London.
1930 A modern survival of the ancient Maya calendar. *Proc. 23d Int. Cong. Amer.*, pp. 652–55. New York.
Ludendorff, H.
(The series of papers listed below are reprinted from the *Sitzungsberichten der Preussischen Akademie der Wissenschaften*, Berlin, and are numbered, except the first and second, in a series denominated Untersuchungen zur Astronomie der Maya.)
1930 Über die Entstehung der Tzolkin-Periode im Kalender der Maya. [No. 1.]
1930a Über die Reduktion der Maya-Datierungen auf unsere Zeitrechnung. [No. 2.]
1931 Die astronomische Bedeutung der Seiten 51 und 52 des Dresdener Maya-Kodex. No. 3.
1931a Das Mondalter in den Inschriften der Maya. No. 4.
1931b Die Venustafel des Dresdener Kodex. No. 5.
1933 Über die Seiten 51 and 52 des Dresdener Kodex und über einige astronomische Inschriften der Maya. No. 6.
1933a Die astronomischen Inschriften in Yaxchilan. No. 7.
1934 Weitere astronomische Inschriften der Maya. No. 8.
1935 Die astronomische Inschrift aus dem Tempel des Kreuzes in Palenque. No. 9.
1936 Zur astronomischen Deutung der Maya-Inschriften. No. 10.
1937 Zur Deutung des Dresdener Maya-Kodex. No. 11.
1938 Astronomische Inschriften in Palenque. No. 12.
1940 Astronomische Inschriften in Piedras Negras und Naranjo. No. 13.
1942 Die astronomischen Inschriften in Naranjo. No. 14.
1943 Die astronomischen Inschriften in Quiriguá. No. 15. (Prepared for publication by A. Dittrich.)
Makemson, M. W.
1943 The astronomical tables of the Maya. *Carnegie Inst. Wash.*, Pub. 546, Contrib. 42. Washington.
1944 The enigma of Maya astronomy. *Dyn*, vol. 1, nos. 4 and 5, pp. 47–52. Mexico.
1946 The Maya correlation problem. *Pub. Vassar College Observatory*, no. 5. Poughkeepsie.
1947 The Maya new year. MS.
Maler, T.
1901 Researches in the central portion of the Usumatsintla Valley. [Piedras Negras, Chinikiha, etc.] *Mem. Peabody Mus. Harvard Univ.*, vol. 2, no. 1. Cambridge.
1903 Researches in the central portion of the Usumatsintla Valley. [Yaxchilan, El Cayo, etc.] *Mem. Peabody Mus. Harvard Univ.*, vol. 2, no. 2. Cambridge.
1908 Explorations of the Upper Usumatsintla and adjacent region. Altar de Sacrificios; Seibal; Itsimté-Sacluk; Cankuen. *Mem. Peabody Mus. Harvard Univ.*, vol. 4, no. 1. Cambridge.
1908a Explorations in the Department of Peten, Guatemala, and adjacent region. Topoxté; Yaxhá; Benque Viejo; Naranjo. *Mem. Peabody Mus. Harvard Univ.*, vol. 4, no. 2. Cambridge.
1910 Explorations in the Department of Peten, Guatemala, and adjacent region. Motul de San José; Peten–Itza. *Mem. Peabody Mus. Harvard Univ.*, vol. 4, no. 3. Cambridge.
1911 Explorations in the Department of Peten, Guatemala. Tikal. *Mem. Peabody Mus. Harvard Univ.*, vol. 5, no. 1. Cambridge.
Martínez Hernández, J.
1909 El Chilam Balam de Mani ó Códice Pérez. With introduction. Merida. (Colegio San José de Artes y oficios.)
1912 Los grandes ciclos de la historia maya según el manuscrito de Chumayel. *Proc. 17th Int. Cong. Amer.*, pp. 180–213. Mexico.
1926 Paralelismo entre los calendarios maya y azteca. Su correlación con el calendario juliano. Merida. (Compañia Tipográfica Yucateca.)

Martínez Hernández, J.—(continued)
(1927) Crónicas mayas. Merida. (Compañía Tipográfica Yucateca.)
1928 Significación cronológica de los ciclos mayas. Merida.
1944 La tabla maya de eclipses. *Diario de Yucatán* (Jan. 1). Merida.
Martyr, Peter
1612 De nouo orbe or the historie of the West Indies, contayning the actes and aduentures of the Spanyardes, which haue conquered and peopled those countries, inriched with varietie of pleasant relation of the manners, ceremonies, lawes, gouerments, and warres of the Indians. Translations by R. Eden and M. Lok. London.
Mason, J. A.
1940 The native languages of Middle America. In *The Maya and their neighbors*, pp. 52–87. New York.
Maudslay, A. P.
1889–1902 Archaeology. Biologia Centrali-Americana. 5 vols. London.
1898 A Maya calendar inscription interpreted by Goodman's tables. *Proc. Royal Soc.*, 62: 67–80. London.
Meinshausen, M.
1913 Über Sonnen- und Mondfinsternisse in der Dresdener Mayahandschrift. *Zeit. für Ethnol.*, 45: 221–27. Berlin.
Merrill, R. H.
1945 Maya sun calendar dictum disproved. *Amer. Antiquity*, 10: 307–11. Menasha.
Moran, F.
1935 Arte y diccionario en lengua cholti. *Maya Soc.*, Pub. 9. Baltimore. (Original composed c. 1650. Additions made in Belem c. 1690. Converted from Chol-Spanish to Spanish-Chol, perhaps by Franciscan fathers, and Lacandon words added c. 1695, presumably at Nuestra. Señora de los Dolores.)
Morley, F. R., and S. G. Morley
1938 The age and provenance of the Leyden plate. *Carnegie Inst. Wash.*, Pub. 509, Contrib. 24. Washington.
Morley, R. K.
1918 On computations for the Maya calendar. *Amer. Anthropol.*, 20: 49–61. Lancaster.
Morley, S. G.
1910 The correlation of Maya and Christian chronology. *Amer. Jour. Archaeol.*, 14: 193–204. Norwood.
1915 An introduction to the study of the Maya hieroglyphs. *Bur. Amer. Ethnol.*, Bull. 57. Washington.
1916 The Supplementary Series in the Maya inscriptions. In *Holmes Anniv. Vol.*, pp. 366–96. Washington.
1917 The rise and fall of the Maya civilization in the light of the monuments and the native chronicles. *Proc. 19th Int. Cong. Amer.*, pp. 140–49. Washington.
1917a The hotun as the principal chronological unit of the old Maya Empire. *Proc. 19th Int. Cong. Amer.*, pp. 195–201. Washington.
1918 Archaeology. *Carnegie Inst. Wash.*, Year Book 17, pp. 269–76. Washington.
1920 The inscriptions at Copan. *Carnegie Inst. Wash.*, Pub. 219. Washington.
1922 The foremost intellectual achievement of ancient America. *Nat. Geog. Mag.*, 41: 109–30. Washington.
1925 Archaeology. *Carnegie Inst. Wash.*, Year Book 24, pp. 247–70. Washington.
1937–38 The inscriptions of Peten. *Carnegie Inst. Wash.*, Pub. 437. 5 vols. Washington.
1938 The Maya new empire. In *Carnegie Inst. Wash.*, Pub. 501, pp. 533–65. Washington.
1939 Recent epigraphic discoveries at the ruins of Copan, Honduras. In *So live the works of men*, pp. 277–93. Albuquerque.
1945 Combinations of Glyphs G and F in the Supplementary Series. *Carnegie Inst. Wash.*, Div. Hist. Res., *Notes on Middle Amer. Archaeol. and Ethnol.*, no. 49. Cambridge.
1945a The Initial and Supplementary Series of Stela 5 at Altar de Sacrificios, Guatemala. *Carnegie Inst. Wash.*, Div. Hist. Res., *Notes on Middle Amer. Archaeol. and Ethnol.*, no. 58. Cambridge.
Morris, E. H., J. Charlot, and A. A. Morris
1931 The Temple of the Warriors at Chichen Itzá, Yucatan. *Carnegie Inst. Wash.*, Pub. 406. 2 vols. Washington.

MOTUL DICTIONARY
1929 Diccionario de Motul, maya-español, atribuido a Fray Antonio de Ciudad Real y Arte de lengua maya por Fray Juan Coronel. J. Martínez Hernández, ed. Merida. (Original 16th century MS. missing; copy, said to be 17th century, in John Carter Brown Library, Providence. This contains also Spanish-Maya sections not published in Martínez Hernández edition.)

NILSSON, M. P.
1920 Primitive time-reckoning. A study . . . of the art of counting time among the primitive and early culture peoples. Lund.

NOGUERA, E.
1927 Ruinas de Tizatlan. Los altares de sacrificios de Tizatlan. *Secretaría de Educación Pública.* Mexico.
1933 Bibliografía de códices precolombinos y documentos indígenas posteriores a la conquista. *Anales del Mus. Nac. de Arqueol., Hist., y Etnog.,* Epoca 4, vol. 8, pp. 583–602. Mexico.

NOLL-HUSUM, H.
1937 Grundlegendes zur Zeitbestimmung der Maya. Eine Aufgabe der geschichtlichen Himmelskunde. *Zeit. für Ethnol.,* 69: 53–63. Berlin.

NOTTEBOHM, K. H.
1944 A possible lunar series on the Leyden plate. *Carnegie Inst. Wash., Div. Hist. Res., Notes on Middle Amer. Archaeol. and Ethnol.,* no. 34. Cambridge.

NOYES, E.
1935 Notes on the Maya day-count. *Maya Res.,* 2: 383–93. New York.

NUÑEZ DE LA VEGA, F.
1702 Constituciones dioecesanas del obispado de Chiappa. Rome.

NUTTALL, Z.
1903 A suggestion to Maya scholars. *Amer. Anthropol.,* 5: 667–78. Lancaster.
1928 Nouvelles lumières sur les civilisations américaines et le système du calendrier. *Proc. 22d Int. Cong. Amer.,* pp. 119–48. Rome.

ORDOÑEZ Y AGUIAR, R. DE
1907 Historia de la creación del cielo y de la tierra, conforme al sistema de la gentilidad americana. In *Bibliografía mexicana del siglo XVIII,* sect. 1, pt. 4. Mexico. (Written c. 1790.)

OVIEDO Y VALDÉS, G. F. DE
1851–55 Historia general y natural de las Indias, islas y tierra-firme del mar océano. 4 vols. Madrid. (Written c. 1550.)

PACHECO CRUZ, S.
1939 Léxico de la fauna yucateca. Merida.
1947 Usos, costumbres, religión i supersticiones de los mayas. Merida.

PALACIOS, E. J.
1928 En los confines de la selva lacandona. Exploraciones en el Estado de Chiapas, 1926. *Secretaría de Educación Pública.* Mexico.
1933 El calendario y los jeroglíficos cronográficos mayas. Mexico.
1935 Guia arqueológica de Chichen-Itza. *Secretaría de Educación Pública.* Mexico.
1936 Inscripción recientemente descubierta en Palenque. *Maya Res.,* 3: 2–17. New Orleans.
1937 Mas gemas del arte Maya en Palenque. *Anales del Mus. Nac. de Arqueol., Hist. y Etnog.,* Epoca 5, vol. 2, pp. 193–225. Mexico.

PAVÓN ABREU, R.
1943 Cronología maya. *Mus. Arqueol., Etnog. e Hist. de Campeche.* Campeche.
1945 Morales, una importante ciudad arqueológica en Tabasco. *Mus. Arqueol., Etnog., e Hist., de Campeche,* Cuaderno, no. 6. Campeche.

PEÑAFIEL, A.
1885 Nombres geográficos de México. Catálogo alfabético de los nombres de lugar pertenecientes al idioma "nahuatl." Mexico. (Secretaría de Fomento.)

PEREZ DICTIONARY
1866–77 Diccionario de la lengua Maya. (Compiled by J. Pio Perez; completed by C. H. Berendt.) Merida.

PINEDA, E.
1845 Descripción geográfica del Departamento de Chiapas y Soconusco. Mexico.

PINEDA, V.
1888 Historia de las sublevaciones indígenas habidas en el estado de Chiapas. Gramática de la lengua Tzel-tal y diccionario de la misma. Chiapas.

PIO PEREZ, J.
1843 Ancient chronology of Yucatan; or, a true exposition of the method used by the Indians for computing time. In Stephens, 1843, 1: 434–59; 2: 465–69.
1864 Cronología antigua de Yucatán y examen del método con que los indios contaban el tiempo. In Brasseur de Bourbourg, 1864, pp. 366–429.
1898 Coordinación alfabética de las voces del idioma maya que se hallan en el arte y obra del Padre Fr. Pedro Beltrán de Santa Rosa. . . . Merida.

POGO, ALEXANDER
1937 Maya astronomy. *Carnegie Inst. Wash.,* Year Book 36, pp. 24–25. Washington.

POPOL VUH
1927 Manuscrito de Chichicastenango (Popol Buj). . . . Texto indígena fonetizado y traducido al castellano. . . . by J. Antonio Villacorta C. and Flavio Rodas N. Guatemala.

POUSSE, A.
1884 Nouvelles recherches pour l'interprétation des caractères hiératiques de l'Amérique Centrale. Rapport sur un memoire de M. A. Pousse adressé a la Société Américaine de France. *Archives de la Soc. Amér. de France,* 2d ser., 3: 118–27. Paris.

POZAS ARCINIEGA, R.
1947 Monografía de Chamulá. *Microfilm Coll. MSS. on Middle Amer. Cultural Anthropol.,* no. 15. Chicago.

PROSKOURIAKOFF, T.
1944 An inscription on a jade probably carved at Piedras Negras. *Carnegie Inst. Wash., Div. Hist. Res., Notes on Middle Amer. Archaeol. and Ethnol.,* no. 47. Cambridge.
1946 An album of Maya architecture. *Carnegie Inst. Wash.,* Pub. 558. Washington.
——, and J. E. S. THOMPSON
1947 Maya Calendar Round dates such as 9 Ahau 17 Mol. *Carnegie Inst. Wash., Div. Hist. Res., Notes on Middle Amer. Archaeol. and Ethnol.,* no. 79. Cambridge.

RANDS, R. L.
1946 Some manifestations of water in Mesoamerican art. MS.

RAYNAUD, G.
1893 Les manuscrits precolombiens. *Archives du Comité d'Archéologie Américaine,* ser. 3, 1: 1–176. Paris.

REDFIELD, R.
1936 The coati and the ceiba. *Maya Res.,* 3: 231–43. New Orleans.
1946 Notes on San Antonio Palopó. *Microfilm Coll. MSS. on Middle Amer. Cultural Anthropol.,* no. 4. Chicago.
——, and A. VILLA R.
1934 Chan Kom, a Maya village. *Carnegie Inst. Wash.,* Pub. 448. Washington.
1939 Notes on the ethnography of Tzeltal communities of Chiapas. *Carnegie Inst. Wash.,* Pub. 509, Contrib. 28. Washington.

RELACIONES DE YUCATAN
1898–1900 In Colección de documentos inéditos relativos al descubrimiento, conquista y organización de las antiguas posesiones españolas de ultramar. 2d ser., vols. 11 and 13. Madrid.

RITUAL OF THE BACABS
MS. of 237 pages of medical incantations. Original belonged to William Gates. Photostatic copy in Peabody Museum, Harvard University; transcription and partial translation by Ralph L. Roys.

RODAZ, J. DE
1688 Arte de la lengua Tzotzlem o tzinacanteca con explicación del año solar y un tratado de las quentas de los indios en lengua Tzotzlem. Lo todo escrito el año de 1688. Present copy made by Fr. Dionisio Pereyra. Comitlan, 1723. (Used by Charency, 1884; original in La Bibliothèque Nationale, Paris.)

ROSNY, L. DE
1876 Essai sur le déchiffrement de l'écriture hiératique de l'Amérique Centrale. Paris.
1883 Codex cortesianus. Manuscrit hiératique des anciens indiens de l'Amérique Centrale. Paris.

ROYS, L.
1933 The Maya correlation problem today. *Amer. Anthropol.*, 35: 403–17. Menasha.
1945 Moon age tables. *Carnegie Inst. Wash., Div. Hist. Res., Notes on Middle Amer. Archaeol. and Ethnol.*, no. 50. Cambridge.

ROYS, R. L.
1922 A new Maya historical narrative. *Amer. Anthropol.*, 24: 44–60. Menasha.
1931 The ethno-botany of the Maya. *Middle Amer. Res. Ser.*, Pub. 2. New Orleans.
1933 The book of Chilam Balam of Chumayel. *Carnegie Inst. Wash.*, Pub. 438. Washington.
1939 The titles of Ebtun. *Carnegie Inst. Wash.*, Pub. 505. Washington.
1940 Personal names of the Maya of Yucatan. *Carnegie Inst. Wash.*, Pub. 523, Contrib. 31. Washington.
1943 The Indian background of colonial Yucatan. *Carnegie Inst. Wash.*, Pub. 548. Washington.
1944 The Vienna dictionary. *Carnegie Inst. Wash., Div. Hist. Res., Notes on Middle Amer. Archaeol. and Ethnol.*, no. 41. Cambridge.
1946 The book of Chilam Balam of Ixil. *Carnegie Inst. Wash., Div. Hist. Res., Notes on Middle Amer. Archaeol. and Ethnol.*, no. 75. Cambridge.
1949 The prophecies for the Maya tuns or years in the books of Chilam Balam of Tizimin and Mani. *Carnegie Inst. Wash.*, Pub. 585, Contrib. 51. Washington.
1949a Guide to the Codex Perez. *Carnegie Inst. Wash.*, Pub. 585, Contrib. 49. Washington.

RUANO SUAREZ, A.
1892 Vocabulario de las lenguas pokoman y chorti. MS. 121 pp. Photostat in Peabody Museum, Harvard University. Said to contain 1500 Chorti words. Jilotepeque.

RUPPERT, K.
1931 The Temple of the Wall Panels, Chichen Itza. *Carnegie Inst. Wash.*, Pub. 403, Contrib. 3. Washington.
1935 The Caracol at Chichen Itza, Yucatan, Mexico. *Carnegie Inst. Wash.*, Pub. 454. Washington.
——, and J. H. DENISON
1943 Archaeological reconnaissance in Campeche, Quintana Roo, and Peten. *Carnegie Inst. Wash.*, Pub. 543. Washington.

RUZ LHUILLIER, A.
1944 Extensión geográfica del dialecto maya-chontal. *Escuela Nac. de Antropol.*, Pub. 2. Mexico.

SAHAGUN, B. DE
1938 Historia general de las cosas de Nueva España. Pedro Robredo, ed. 5 vols. Mexico.

SANCHEZ DE AGUILAR, P.
1892 Informe contra idolorum cultores del Obispado de Yucatan. *Anales del Mus. Nac. de México*, Epoca 1, vol. 6, pp. 13–122. Mexico. (1st ed. Madrid, 1639.)

SAN FRANCISCO DICTIONARY
17th century. Original missing. Copy by Juan Pio Perez. Photographic copy of this by W. E. Gates in Peabody Museum, Harvard Univ. Maya-Spanish and Spanish-Maya.

SAPPER, K.
1897 Das nördliche Mittel-Amerika nebst einem Ausflug nach dem Hochland von Anahuac. Brunswick.
1904 Der gegenwärtige Stand der ethnographischen Kenntnis von Mittelamerika. *Archiv für Anthropol.*, 3: 1–38. Brunswick.
1908 Choles und Chorties. *Proc. 15th Int. Cong. Amer.*, pp. 423–65. Quebec.
1925 Über brujeria in Guatemala. *Proc. 21st Int. Cong. Amer.*, pp. 391–405. Göteborg.
1936 Die Verapaz im 16. and 17. Jahrhundert. Ein Beitrag zur historischen Geographie und Ethnographie des nördöstlichen Guatemala. *Bayerischen Akademie der Wissenschaften*, 37: 1–46. Munich.

SATTERTHWAITE, L.
1940 Another Piedras Negras stela. *Univ. Mus. Bull.*, vol. 8, nos. 2–3, pp. 24–27. Philadelphia.
1942 Opposed interpretations of dates and hieroglyph styles at Chichen Itza. *Rev. Mex. de Estudios Antropol.*, 6: 19–35. Mexico.
1943 New photographs and the date of Stela 14, Piedras Negras. *Carnegie Inst. Wash., Div. Hist. Res., Notes on Middle Amer. Archaeol. and Ethnol.*, no. 28. Cambridge.
1947 Concepts and structures of Maya calendrical arithmetics. *Joint Publications, Univ. Pa. Mus., Phila. Anthropol. Soc.*, no. 3. Philadelphia.

SCHELLHAS, P.
1904 Representation of deities of the Maya manuscripts. *Papers Peabody Mus. Harvard Univ.*, vol. 4, no. 1. Cambridge.
1926 Der Ursprung der Mayahandschriften. *Zeit. für Ethnol.*, 58: 1–16. Berlin.
1929 Die Madrider Mayahandschrift. *Zeit. für Ethnol.*, 61: 1–32. Berlin.
1945 Die Entzifferung der Mayahieroglyphen ein unlösbares Problem? *Ethnos*, 10: 44–53. Stockholm.

SCHOLES, F. V., and E. B. ADAMS
1938 Don Diego Quijada, Alcalde Mayor de Yucatán, 1561–1565. *Biblioteca Historica Mexicana de Obras Inéditas*, vols. 14, 15. Mexico.
——, and R. L. ROYS
1948 The Maya Chontal Indians of Acalan-Tixchel: a contribution to the history and ethnography of the Yucatan Peninsula. *Carnegie Inst. Wash.*, Pub. 560. Washington.

SCHULTZE JENA, L.
1946 La vida y las creencias de los indígenas quiches de Guatemala. Translated by A. Goubaud C. and H. D. Sapper. *Publicaciones Especiales del Instituto Indigenista Nacional*, 1. Guatemala. (Original published in Jena, 1933.)

SCHULZ, R. P. C.
1933 Zur Korrelation des Mayakalenders mit der europäischen Zeitrechnung. *Zeit. für Ethnol.*, 65: 396–99. Berlin.
1935 Zur Chronologie der Maya. *Zeit. für Ethnol.*, 67: 49–68, 321–31. Berlin.
1936 Beiträge zur Chronologie und Astronomie des alten Zentralamerika. *Anthropos*, 31: 758–88. St. Gabriel-Mödling bei Wien.
1940 Las fechas de la "cuenta larga" en las páginas 51a y 52a del códice de Dresde. *El México Antiguo*, 5: 195–97. Mexico.
1942 Apuntes sobre cálculos relativos al calendario de los indígenas de Chiapas. *El México Antiguo*, 6: 6–14. Mexico.
1944 Los sistemas cronológicos de los libros del Chilam Balam. *El México Antiguo*, 6: 239–60. Mexico.

SELER, E.
1889 Chronologie der Cakchiquel-Annalen. *Zeit. für Ethnol.*, 21: 475–76. Berlin.
1901 Die alten Ansiedelungen von Chaculá. Berlin.
1902–23 Gesammelte Abhandlungen zur amerikanischen Sprach- und Alterthumskunde. 5 vols. Berlin.
1904 The Mexican chronology with special reference to the Zapotec calendar. *Bur. Amer. Ethnol.*, Bull. 28, pp. 11–55. Washington. (Also in Seler, 1902–23.)
1904a Venus period in the picture writings of the Borgian codex group. *Bur. Amer. Ethnol.*, Bull. 28, pp. 353–91. Washington. (Also in Seler, 1902–23.)
1904–09 Codex Borgia, eine altmexikanische Bilderschrift der Bibliothek der Congregatio de Propaganda Fide. 3 vols. Berlin.
1905 On the present state of our knowledge of the Mexican and Central American hieroglyphic writing. *Proc. 13th Int. Cong. Amer.*, pp. 157–70. New York.
1915 Beobachtungen und Studien in den Ruinen von Palenque. From *Abhandlungen der Königl. Preussischen Akademie der Wissenschaften, Jahrgang, 1915. Phil.-Hist. Klasse*, Nr. 5. Berlin.
1917 Die Ruinen von Uxmal. From *Abhandlungen der Königl. Preussischen Akademie der Wissenschaften, Jahrgang 1917. Phil.-Hist. Klasse*, Nr. 3. Berlin.

SERNA, J. DE LA
1892 Manual de ministros de indios. *Anales Mus. Nac. de México*, Epoca 1, vol. 6, pp. 263–475. Mexico.

SIEGEL, M.
1941 Religion in western Guatemala: a product of acculturation. *Amer. Anthropol.*, 43: 62–76. Menasha.

SMITH, G. E.
1924 Elephants and ethnologists. London.

SMITH, R. E.
1936 Ceramics of Uaxactun: a preliminary analysis of decorative technics and design. Photoduplicated. *Carnegie Inst. Wash., Div. Hist. Res.* Guatemala.

SOLANA DICTIONARY
1632 Vocabulario muy copioso en lengua española y maya de Yucatan. (Original was in Gates collection, not in the Library of the Hispanic Society of America, as previously thought. Now in the library of Brigham Young University, Provo, Utah. 115 ff.)

SOLIS ALCALA, E.
1927 El canhel. *Bol. Univ. Nac. del Sureste*, Jan.-June, pp. 245–47. Merida.
1927a 11 Ahau katun 13 nicte-katun. *Bol. Univ. Nac. del Sureste*, Jan.-June, pp. 355–57. Merida.
1929 Estudios acerca del idioma maya. El nombre maya del signo para denotar el cero. *Bol. Univ. Nac. del Sureste*, July 1929–Jan. 1930, pp. 81–85. Merida.
1949 Códice Pérez. Traducción libre del Maya al Castellano. Merida.
——, and E. SOLIS MENDIBURU
1925 Los Ahau-katunes del manuscrito de Mani. *Nueva traducción e interpretación. Bol. Univ. Nac. del Sureste.* Supplement. Merida.

SOUSTELLE, J.
1936 Mexique, terre indienne. Paris.

SPINDEN, H. J.
1913 A study of Maya art. Its subject matter and historical development. *Mem. Peabody Mus. Harvard Univ.*, vol. 6. Cambridge.
1916 The question of the zodiac in America. *Amer. Anthropol.*, 18: 53–80. Lancaster.
1924 The reduction of Mayan dates. *Papers Peabody Mus. Harvard Univ.*, vol. 6, no. 4. Cambridge.
1928 Maya inscriptions dealing with Venus and the moon. *Buffalo Soc. of Natural Sciences Bull.*, vol. 14, no. 1. Buffalo.
1928a The population of ancient America. *Geog. Rev.*, 18: 641–60. New York.
1930 Maya dates and what they reveal. *Brooklyn Inst. of Arts and Sciences*, vol. 4, no. 1. Brooklyn.
1930a The eclipse table of the Dresden Codex. *Proc. 23d Int. Cong. Amer.*, pp. 140–48. New York.
1940 Diffusion of Maya astronomy. In *The Maya and their neighbors*, pp. 162–78. New York.
1942 Time scale for the New World. *Proc. Eighth Amer. Scientific Cong.*, 2: 39–44. Washington.

STADELMAN, R.
1940 Maize cultivation in northwestern Guatemala. *Carnegie Inst. Wash.*, Pub. 523, Contrib. 34. Washington.

STARR, F.
1902 Notes upon the ethnography of southern Mexico, pt. II. *Davenport Acad. of Nat. Sciences*, 9: 63–172. Davenport.

STEGGERDA, M.
1938 The Maya Indians of Yucatan. In *Carnegie Inst. Wash.*, Pub. 501, pp. 567–84. Washington.

STEPHENS, J. L.
1843 Incidents of travel in Yucatan. 2 vols. New York and London.

STIRLING, M. W.
1940 An Initial Series from Tres Zapotes, Vera Cruz, Mexico. *Nat. Geog. Soc. Contrib. Technic. Pap., Mex. Archaeol. Ser.*, vol. 1, no. 1. Washington.
1943 Stone monuments of southern Mexico. *Bur. Amer. Ethnol.*, Bull. 138. Washington.

STOLL, O.
1884 Zur Ethnographie der Republik Guatemala. Zurich.
1887 Die Sprache der Ixil-Indianer, ein Beitrag zur Ethnologie und Linguistik der Maya-Völker. Leipzig.
1938 Etnografía de la Republica de Guatemala. Guatemala. Translated by A. Goubaud Carrera from German edition of 1884.

STRÖMSVIK, G.
1941 Substela caches and stela foundations at Copan and Quirigua. *Carnegie Inst. Wash.*, Pub. 528, Contrib. 37. Washington.

TAX, S.
1946 The towns of Lake Atitlan. *Microfilm Coll. MSS. on Middle Amer. Cultural Anthropol.*, no. 13. Chicago.
1947 Notes on Santo Tomás Chichicastenango. *Microfilm Coll. of MSS. on Middle Amer. Cultural Anthropol.*, no. 16. Chicago.
1947a Miscellaneous notes on Guatemala. *Microfilm Coll. of MSS. on Middle Amer. Cultural Anthropol.*, no. 18. Chicago.

TEEPLE, J. E.
1925 Maya inscriptions: Glyphs C, D, and E of the Supplementary Series. *Amer. Anthropol.*, 27: 108–15. Menasha.
1925a Maya inscriptions: further notes on the Supplementary Series. *Amer. Anthropol.*, 27: 544–49. Menasha.
1926 Maya inscriptions: the Venus calendar and another correlation. *Amer. Anthropol.*, n.s. 28: 402–08. Menasha.
1927 Maya inscriptions, IV. *Amer. Anthropol.*, 29: 283–91. Menasha.
1927a Maya inscriptions: Stela C at Copan. *Amer. Anthropol.*, 29: 278–82. Menasha.
1928 Maya inscriptions. VI. The lunar calendar and its relation to Maya history. *Amer. Anthropol.*, 30: 391–407. Menasha.
1930 Maya astronomy. *Carnegie Inst. Wash.*, Pub. 403, Contrib. 2. Washington.

TERMER, F.
1930 Zur Ethnologie und Ethnographie des nördlichen Mittelamerika. *Ibero-Amerikanisches Archiv*, vol. 4, no. 3. Berlin and Bonn.
1930a Über die Mayasprache von Chicomucelo. *Proc. 23d Int. Cong. Amer.*, pp. 926–36. New York.

THOMAS, C.
1882 A study of the manuscript Troano. *U. S. Dept. of Interior, Contrib. to North Amer. Ethnol.*, 5: 1–237. Washington.
1894 The Maya year. *Bur. Amer. Ethnol.*, Bull. 18. Washington.
1897 Day symbols of the Maya year. *Bur. Amer. Ethnol.*, 16th Ann. Rept., pp. 199–265. Washington.
1900 Mayan time systems and time symbols. *Amer. Anthropol.*, 2: 53–62. New York.
1901 Numeral systems of Mexico and Central America. *Bur. Amer. Ethnol.*, 19th Ann. Rept., pp. 853–955. Washington.
1901a Mayan calendar systems. *Bur. Amer. Ethnol.*, 19th Ann. Rept., pt. 2, pp. 693–819. Washington.
1904 Mayan calendar systems. II. *Bur. Amer. Ethnol.*, 22d Ann. Rept., pp. 197–305. Washington.

THOMPSON, J. E. S.
1929 Maya chronology: Glyph G of the Lunar Series. *Amer. Anthropol.*, 31: 223–31. Menasha.
1930 Ethnology of the Mayas of southern and central British Honduras. *Field Mus. Nat. Hist., Anthropol. Ser.*, vol. 17, no. 2. Chicago.
1931 Archaeological investigations in the southern Cayo District, British Honduras. *Field Mus. Nat. Hist., Anthropol. Ser.*, vol. 17, no. 3. Chicago.
1932 A Maya calendar from Alta Vera Paz, Guatemala. *Amer. Anthropol.*, 34: 449–54. Menasha.
1932a The humming bird and the flower. *Maya Soc. Quart.*, 1: 120–22. Baltimore.
1932b The solar year of the Mayas at Quirigua, Guatemala. *Field Mus. Nat. Hist., Anthropol. Ser.*, vol. 17, no. 4. Chicago.
1934 Sky bearers, colors and directions in Maya and Mexican religion. *Carnegie Inst. Wash.*, Pub. 436, Contrib. 10. Washington.
1934a Maya chronology: the fifteen tun glyph. *Carnegie Inst. Wash.*, Pub. 436, Contrib. 11. Washington.
1935 Maya chronology: the correlation question. *Carnegie Inst. Wash.*, Pub. 456, Contrib. 14. Washington.
1935a The dates on Altar U, Copan. *Maya Res.*, 2: 11–13. New York.
1936 The dates of the Temple of the Cross, Palenque. *Maya Res.*, 3: 287–93. New Orleans.
1936a Lunar inscriptions in the Usumacintla Valley. *El México Antiguo*, 4: 69–73. Mexico.

THOMPSON, J. E. S.—(*continued*)

1937 A new method of deciphering Yucatecan dates with special reference to Chichen Itza. *Carnegie Inst. Wash.*, Pub. 483, Contrib. 22. Washington.

1938 Sixteenth and seventeenth century reports on the Chol Mayas. *Amer. Anthropol.*, 40: 584–604. Menasha.

1939 The moon goddess in Middle America with notes on related deities. *Carnegie Inst. Wash.*, Pub. 509, Contrib. 29. Washington.

1940 Archaeological problems of the lowland Maya. In *The Maya and their neighbors*, pp. 126–38. New York.

1940a Late ceramic horizons at Benque Viejo, British Honduras. *Carnegie Inst. Wash.*, Pub. 528, Contrib. 35. Washington.

1940b Apuntes sobre la estela número 5 de Balakbal, Q. R. *Rev. Mex. de Estudios Antropol.*, 4: 5–9. Mexico.

1940c Bibliografías de antropólogos. Thomas William Francis Gann. *Bol. Bibliográfico de Antropol. Amer.*, 4: 158–60. Mexico.

1941 Apuntes sobre las supersticiones de los mayas de Socotz, Honduras Británica. In *Los Mayas Antiguos*, pp. 99–110. Mexico.

1941a Dating of certain inscriptions of non-Maya origin. *Carnegie Inst. Wash., Div. Hist. Res., Theoretical Approaches to Problems*, no. 1. Cambridge.

1941b A coordination of the history of Chichen Itza with ceramic sequences in central Mexico. *Rev. Mex. de Estudios Antropol.*, 5: 97–111. Mexico.

1941c Maya arithmetic. *Carnegie Inst. Wash.*, Pub. 528, Contrib. 36. Washington.

1942 Observations on Glyph G of the Lunar Series. *Carnegie Inst. Wash., Div. Hist. Res., Notes on Middle Amer. Archaeol. and Ethnol.*, no. 7. Cambridge.

1943 Some sculptures from southeastern Quezaltenango, Guatemala. *Carnegie Inst. Wash., Div. Hist. Res., Notes on Middle Amer. Archaeol. and Ethnol.*, no. 17. Cambridge.

1943a The Initial Series of Stela 14, Piedras Negras, Guatemala, and a date on Stela 19, Naranjo, Guatemala. *Carnegie Inst. Wash., Div. Hist. Res., Notes on Middle Amer. Archaeol. and Ethnol.*, no. 18. Cambridge.

1943b Representations of Tlalchitonatiuh at Chichen Itza, Yucatan, and at El Baul, Escuintla. *Carnegie Inst. Wash., Div. Hist. Res., Notes on Middle Amer. Archaeol. and Ethnol.*, no. 19. Cambridge.

1943c Maya epigraphy: directional glyphs in counting. *Carnegie Inst. Wash., Div. Hist. Res., Notes on Middle Amer. Archaeol. and Ethnol.*, no. 20. Cambridge.

1943d Maya epigraphy: a cycle of 819 days. *Carnegie Inst. Wash., Div. Hist. Res., Notes on Middle Amer. Archaeol. and Ethnol.*, no. 22. Cambridge.

1943e A trial survey of the southern Maya area. *Amer. Antiquity*, 9: 106–34. Menasha.

1943f Las llamadas "Fachadas de Quetzalcouatl." *Proc. 27th Int. Cong. Amer.*, 1: 391–400. Mexico.

1943g Pitfalls and stimuli in the interpretation of history through loan words. *Middle Amer. Res. Inst., Philol. and Documentary Studies*, vol. 1, no. 2. New Orleans.

1944 The fish as a Maya symbol for counting and further discussion of directional glyphs. *Carnegie Inst. Wash., Div. Hist. Res., Theoretical Approaches to Problems*, no. 2. Cambridge.

1944a Jottings on inscriptions at Copan. *Carnegie Inst. Wash., Div. Hist. Res., Notes on Middle Amer. Archaeol. and Ethnol.*, no. 38. Cambridge.

1944b The dating of seven monuments at Piedras Negras. *Carnegie Inst. Wash., Div. Hist. Res., Notes on Middle Amer. Archaeol. and Ethnol.*, no. 39. Cambridge.

1944c Variant methods of date recordings in the Jatate drainage, Chiapas. *Carnegie Inst. Wash., Div. Hist. Res., Notes on Middle Amer. Archaeol. and Ethnol.*, no. 45. Cambridge.

1944d La correlación mas probable entre las cronologías maya y cristiana. *Diario de Yucatán*, c. February 9. Merida.

1945 Un vistazo a las "ciudades" mayas: su aspecto y función. *Cuadernos Americanos*, vol. 4, no. 2, pp. 133–49. Mexico.

1945a A survey of the northern Maya area. *Amer. Antiquity*, 11: 2–24. Menasha.

1945b The inscription on the altar of Zoomorph O, Quirigua. *Carnegie Inst. Wash., Div. Hist. Res., Notes on Middle Amer. Archaeol. and Ethnol.*, no. 56. Cambridge.

THOMPSON, J. E. S.—(*continued*)

1945c Escritura jeroglífica, aritmética y astronomía de los mayas. *Enciclopedia Yucatanense*, 2: 308–42. Mexico.

1946 The dating of Structure 44, Yaxchilan, and its bearing on the sequence of texts at that site. *Carnegie Inst. Wash., Div. Hist. Res., Notes on Middle Amer. Archaeol. and Ethnol.*, no. 71. Cambridge.

1948 An archaeological reconnaissance in the Cotzumalhuapa region, Escuintla, Guatemala. *Carnegie Inst. Wash.*, Pub. 574, Contrib. 44. Washington.

——, H. E. D. POLLOCK, and J. CHARLOT

1932 A preliminary study of the ruins of Coba, Quintana Roo, Mexico. *Carnegie Inst. Wash.*, Pub. 424. Washington.

TICUL DICTIONARY

1690 Original missing. Printed in Pio Pérez, J., 1898, pp. 123–296.

TOHOLABAL LANGUAGE

Also called Chaneabal. *See* Basauri, Berendt, Blom and La Farge, Fernandez y Fernandez, and Seler (1901).

TOSCANO, S.

1947 Mitos y leyendas del antiguo México. *Secretaría de Educación Pública.* Mexico.

TOVILLA, M. A. DE

1635 Relación histórica dyscreptiva de las provincias de la Verapaz y de la del Manché de el Reyno de Guatemala. MS. photostated by F. V. Scholes. Original in Seville.

TOZZER, A. M.

1907 A comparative study of the Mayas and the Lacandones. New York.

1907a Ernst Förstemann. *Amer. Anthropol.*, 9: 153–59. Lancaster.

1911 Prehistoric ruins of Tikal, Guatemala. *Mem. Peabody Mus. Harvard Univ.*, vol. 5, no. 2. Cambridge.

1913 A Spanish manuscript letter on the Lacandones, in the Archives of the Indies at Seville. *Proc. 18th Int. Cong. Amer.*, pp. 497–509. London.

1921 A Maya grammar with bibliography and appraisement of the works noted. *Papers Peabody Mus. Harvard Univ.*, vol. 9. Cambridge.

1941 Landa's relación de las cosas de Yucatan. A translation. Edited with notes. *Papers Peabody Mus. Harvard Univ.*, vol. 18. Cambridge.

——, and G. ALLEN

1910 Animal figures in the Maya codices. *Papers Peabody Mus. Harvard Univ.*, vol. 4, no. 3. Cambridge.

TZELTAL DICTIONARY

Bocabulario en lengua Tzeldal. 2 vols. Tzeltal-Spanish and Spanish-Tzeltal. (Original in Bancroft Library, Univ. of Cal. Gates photographic copy. Gates says the author was Domingo de Ara; Barrera Vasquez maintains the dictionary was written by Antonio Aguilar. For other Tzeltal material see: Blom and La Farge; V. Pineda; and Fernandez and Fernandez.)

TZOTZIL DICTIONARY

[Vocabulario] Tzotzil-Castellano. 351 pp. folio. (Gates lists this as Diccionario grande del siglo XVI.) Photographic reproduction in Peabody Museum. (For other Tzotzil material see Charency, 1885; Fernandez and Fernandez; and Seler, 1901.)

VAILLANT, G. C.

1935 Chronology and stratigraphy in the Maya area. *Maya Res.*, 2: 119–43. New York.

1941 Aztecs of Mexico. New York.

VALENTINI, P. J. J.

1880 The Landa alphabet; a Spanish fabrication. *Proc. Amer. Antiquarian Soc.*, 75: 59–91. Worcester.

VASQUEZ, F.

1937–44 Crónica de la Provincia del Santisimo Nombre de Jesus de Guatemala. *Biblioteca Goathemala*, vols. 14–17. Guatemala. (1st ed. 1714–16.)

VIENNA DICTIONARY

c. 1625 Bocabulario de Mayathan por su abecario. MS. in the National Library in Vienna. Attributed to Diego Lejon. 199 pp. (*See* R. L. Roys, 1944.)

VILLA ROJAS, A.

1945 The Maya of east central Quintana Roo. *Carnegie Inst. Wash.*, Pub. 559. Washington.

VILLA ROJAS, A.—(*continued*)

1946 Notas sobre la etnografía de los indios tzeltales de Oxchuc. *Microfilm Coll. of MSS. on Middle Amer. Cultural Anthropol.*, no. 7. Chicago.

VILLAGUTIERRE SOTO-MAYOR, J. DE

1933 Historia de la conquista de la Provincia de el Itza. *Biblioteca Goathemala*, vol. 9. Guatemala. (1st ed. Madrid, 1701.)

WAGLEY, C.

1941 Economics of a Guatemalan village. *Mem. Amer. Anthropol. Assoc.*, no. 58. Menasha.

WAUCHOPE, R.

1947 An approach to the Maya correlation problem through Guatemala highland archaeology and native annals. *Amer. Antiquity*, 13: 59–66. Menasha.

WEITZEL, R. B.

1930 Maya chronological systems. *Amer. Jour. Archaeol.*, 34: 182–89. Washington.

1935 Maya moon glyphs and new moons. *Maya Res.*, 2: 14–23. New York.

1945 Inscriptions at Chichen Itza and the Maya correlation problem. *Amer. Antiquity*, 11: 27–31. Menasha.

1947 Yucatecan chronological systems. *Amer. Antiquity*, 13: 53–58. Menasha.

1948 An astronomical test of Caso's correlation. *Amer. Antiquity*, 13:323. Menasha.

WHORF, B. L.

1932 A central Mexican inscription combining Mexican and Maya day signs. *Amer. Anthropol.*, 34: 296–302. Menasha.

1933 The phonetic value of certain characters in Maya writing. *Papers Peabody Mus. Harvard Univ.*, vol. 13, no. 2. Cambridge.

WHORF, B. L.—(*continued*)

1935 Maya writing and its decipherment. *Maya Res.*, 2: 367–82. New York.

1942 Decipherment of the linguistic portion of the Maya hieroglyphs. *Smithsonian Inst.*, Report for 1941, pp. 479–502. Washington.

WILLOUGHBY, T. T.

c. 1908 Catalogue of glyphs in the Maya codices. (Glyphs drawn on separate cards under supervision of C. P. Bowditch. Used extensively by Gates in compilation of his Outline Dictionary of Maya Glyphs. Original in Peabody Museum, Harvard University.)

WILLSON, R. W.

1924 Astronomical notes on the Maya codices. *Papers Peabody Mus. Harvard Univ.*, vol. 6, no. 3. Cambridge.

WIRSING, P.

1930 Qu'ec Chi–German vocabulary. MS. in six parts in Library, Peabody Museum, Harvard University.

WISDOM, C.

1940 The Chorti Indians of Guatemala. *Univ. Chicago Pub. in Anthropol., Ethnolog. Ser.* Chicago.

XIMENEZ, F.

1929–31 Historia de la Provincia de San Vicente de Chiapa y Guatemala de la orden de Predicadores. *Biblioteca Goathemala*, vols. 1–3. Guatemala. (Written c. 1721.)

YDE, J.

1938 An archaeological reconnaissance of northwestern Honduras. Copenhagen.

YUCATEC LANGUAGE

See entries under Beltran de Santa Rosa, Coronel, Gates (1940), Motul dictionary, Perez dictionary, Pio Perez (1898), San Francisco dictionary, Solana dictionary, Ticul dictionary, Tozzer (1921), and Vienna dictionary.

General Index

Glyphic elements are listed in the Hieroglyphic Glossary and Index, hereinafter abbreviated to HGI, and in many cases supplement entries in this General Index. To save space all references to archaeological sites and monuments are omitted; because of the prevalence of Yucatec in linguistic discussion, the many citations of specific words in that language are also excluded from the index. Numbers in boldface refer to illustrations.

Abacus, 256
Adultery, associated with day Oc, 79, 89; associated with Katun 9 Ahau, 181; by Venus, 218
Agriculture, 3–5, 8, 24–26, 104; almanacs for, 258–62, 271; days for activities, 300–01
Aguacatec, 87; day names, 69
Akanchob, 133
Albinos, 143
Alligators, two-headed, as celestial monsters, 11, 21. *See also* Crocodile
Almanacs, divinatory, *see* Two-hundred-and-sixty-day cycle
Altars, 20; modern Indian, 94–95
Amatl, "paper," 97; *analte* probably corruption of, 23, 125
Andrade, M. J., 16, 249
Andrews, E. W., 34, 242
Architecture, 6, 9, 22; bearing on correlation, 306, 308–09
Arithmetic, checks, 157–58; computing year, 256; long distance calculations, 314–16; Maltese cross, 247; multiples of Venus revolutions, 225–27; multiplication tables, 24, 252–61; **64,2,3;** ring numbers, 154, 225, 253–54; **64,2;** short cuts, 124–25, 150, 221, 247–49, 256; vigesimal, 51, 141, 316; wheels for counting, 161, 247–48, 250. *See also* Numbers; Two-hundred-and-sixty-day cycle
Arts and crafts, *see* (both HGI) Men; Monkey
Astrology, 63–64, 92
Astronomy, constellations, 80, 111, 116. *See also* Moon; Stars; Venus
Aulie, W., iii, 17, 47, 52, 81
Axe, represents thunderbolts, 276; symbol of God B, 134, 276
Ayopechtli, 116
Aztec, *see* Mexican

Bacabs, 10, 85, 86, 89, 109, 116, 124, 161
Balam, 298; -cab, 84; rain, 297–98; 300–01
Ball courts, 22–23
Barrera Vasquez, A., 29, 34, *passim* 70–87, 252
Becerra, M. E., 51, 52
Bees, 84, 301; almanacs for, 26; keeping, 109; once people, 85; **14, 22**
Beltran de Santa Rosa, M. P., 52
Berendt, C. H., 29
Berlin, H., 34, 158
Beyer, H., iv, 33, 35, 38, 41, 42, 43, 45, 57–58, 71, 74, 105, 107, 111, 112, 113, 117, 119–20, 122, 135, 142, 144, 167, 169, 172, 188, 189, 190, 198, 199, 203, 210, 212, 236, 238, 239, 243, 266, 268, 271, 278, 284, 285, 308, 315
Bird deities, 138, 146; associated with world directions, 147; **42,2,23.** *See also* Macaw; Moan bird (HGI); Quetzal
Birds representing periods, 146, 147, 148
Black, affix or infix, *see* Ek affix (HGI); associated with hunting gods, *see* God M; markings on dog, 78, 113, 142; markings on Moan birds, 145; represented by crosshatching, 113, 145, 173, 280; worn by gods of west, 224, 251. *See also* Glyph G9 (HGI); God L; God M
Bleeding, medicinal, 87
Blom, F., and O. La Farge, 52, 165, 249
Blood, offerings of, 13
Blowgun, 87
Blue, utensils painted, 110. *See also* Green; Turquoise
Bolon, "nine," extended meanings of, 54, 129
Bolon-ti-Ku, "9 gods," 12, 54, 210
Bolon-Tz'acab, 54, 60, 124, 129

Bolon-Yocte, 47, 54, 56, 291, 294; **12,16–18**
Bowditch, C. P., iii, 31–32, 105, 216, 247
Brasseur de Bourbourg, Abbé C. E., 25, 28–29, 52, 69, 78, 311
Brinton, D. G., 30, 31, 73, 130
Bukxoc, discussion, 161
Burden concept, *see* Time, burden of
Burkitt, R., 34, 52, 69
Butterflies, souls of dead warriors, 85

Cacao, 41, 110; associated with day Manik, 77; counting of, 52, 53; god of, 76–77
Cakchiquel, 16, 27, 49, 51–53, 97, 122, 143, 170, 178, 238; day names, 68–69; Long Count, 27, 151, 183
Calendar, 400-day, 27, 151, 183; origin of, 98; time needed to construct, 150
Calendar Round, 123–24; anniversaries, 318–19; combined with lords of nights, 211–12; defined, 123; development of, 150–53; harmonized with Venus revolution, 153, 221–27
Capstones, hieroglyphic, 22
Cardinal points, *see* World directions
Caso, A., 28, 33, 84, 96, 125, 303, 308
Cason, J., 185
Caves, worship in, 175
Ceiba tree, connection with Imix, 71–72; glyph of, 56, 271, 294; **62,4;** symbolism, 10, 71
Ceilings, hieroglyphic, 22
Celestial bands, *see* Planetary bands
Celestial monsters, 11, 87, 148–49, 171, 219, 260, 274; God C in jaws of, 171; cauac element representing, 110–13, 148; decorative elements, 192, 274–75; **15,11–13;** Moan bird, perches on, 114. *See also* Itzamna
Cenote, defined, 4; moon in, 236, 238
Central Area, Maya, 3–4, 6–8, 16
Ceremonial centers, abandonment of, 6; description of, 8; use by modern Maya, 20, 95
Ceremonies, duration, 175; of almanac, 92, 94–96; of 8 Batz, 94–95, 175; propitiatory, 63, 124. *See also* Burner period; New-year ceremonies
Chacs, rain gods, 10, 11, 73, 108, 193–94, 270, 272; Ah Lelem-Caan-Chac, 147; birth of, 259, 295, 298; moon in abode of, 238; *Uo* frogs, their musicians, 144
Chac-uayab-xoc, 162
Chaneabal, 16–17, 47, 49, 52, 53, 84, 87, 122, 142
Character of Maya, 7, 13–15, 66, 252, 262, 273, 291, 295–96, 316
Charency, C. F. H. G. de, 31, 249, 311
Charlot, J., iii, 61
Chiapan, 16–17, 84, 88. *See also* Chaneabal; Tzeltal; Tzotzil
Chiapanec, 97
Chicchan snake gods, 11, 45, 75, 88, 89, 135, 144, 153, 259, 264, 276, 278, 290; **13,12,17,18; 31,51; 9,64; 41,90; 42,37; 63,3.** *See also* (all HGI). Chicchan; God One Chicchan; Personified numbers, nine; Yax affix
Chicomuceltec, 78, 109
Chieftainship, days of, 300, 301; mat symbol of, 48
Chilam Balam, books of, iv, 14, 29, 31, 109, 110, 119, 121, 158, 165, 191, 219; almanacs in, 263, 297–302; description of, 34; errors in, 34, 182, 183; parallels to date recording, 199, 259; quotations from, 54
Chilam Balam of Chumayel, 14, 34, 77, 96, 147, 202, 247, 266; burner period in, 99; creation myths in, 86, 90, 96, 97, 99, 176, 183, 210, 214, 218, 248; katun prophecies in, 56, 60, 181–82, 183, 203, 218, 219, 270–71; quotations from, 55, 60,

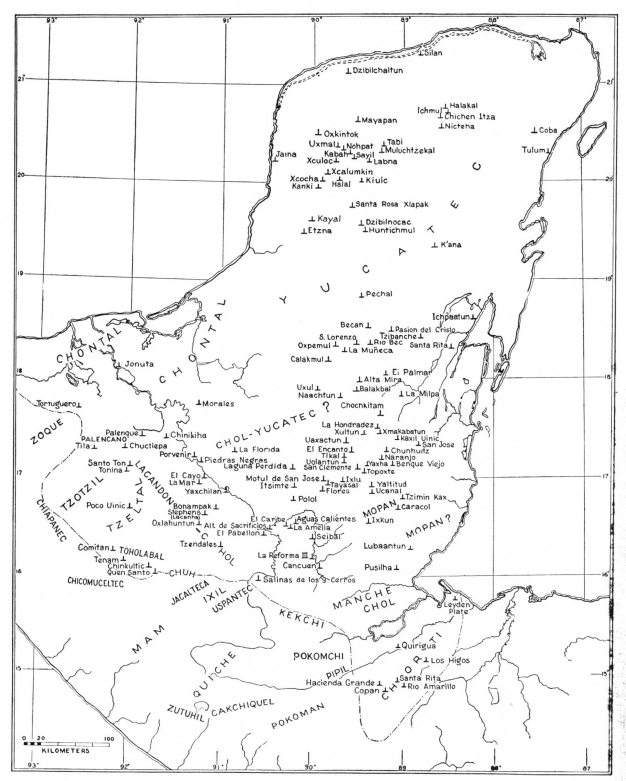

FIG. 1—MAP OF THE MAYA AREA

Showing archaeological sites with hieroglyphic texts, and main
linguistic divisions as they probably were in the sixteenth century.
Some minor sites in Yucatan and Campeche omitted to avoid
crowded lettering. The broken line marks the approximate area of
lowland Maya speech. Note how all sites with hieroglyphic inscriptions are within that area.

Fig. 2—GLYPH FORMATIONS

(see p. iv for list of abbreviations)

INFIXES, PREFIXES AND POSTFIXES:

1. Imix glyph. P.N. L 2, C1.
2. Imix with Ahau as infix. P.N. Thr 1, B1.
3. Ch'en with prefix above. Pal. Cross, U14.
4. Ch'en with prefix to left. Yax. L. 30, F2.
5. Ch'en with infix replacing prefix. Tik. T 4, L 2, H3.
6. Uo with prefix to left. Tila C, A6.
7. Uo with prefix above. Hatz. Ceel Alt 1, B1.
8. Posterior date indicator with "forward" prefix to left. Chinik. Thr 1, E1.
9. Posterior date indicator with "forward" prefix above. P.N. 3, C2a.
10. Posterior date indicator with "forward" element as infix. Cop. Q, B6.
11. Posterior date indicator with postfix pointing to left and prefix to left. Seib. HS, I2.
12. Posterior date indicator with postfix pointing to right and prefix above. Quir. F, B11a.
13. Katun with postfix below. Yax. L 25, L1.
14. Katun with postfix to right. Yax. L 30, G4.
15. One tun with *te* to left; circle above. Yax. 11, M3.
16. Fourth of Zec with *te* to left; circle above. Cop. HS, Date 23.
17. First of Mol with *te* to left; circle below. Cop. J, Gl 47.
18. Eighth of Cumku with *te* above; circle to left. Cop. C, B3a.
19. Third of Pop with *te* above; circle to left. Inverted. Pal. Olvidado.
20. Third of Zotz' with *te* above; circle to right. Inverted. Cop. 7, B7a.
21. Second (of Pop) with *te* attached to head for two. Yula 1, B1.
22. Two tuns with *te* above. Cop. T 11, E door, S jamb, C2.
23. Six (uinals) with *te* below numerical head. Xcal. IS, A6–B6.
24. Inverted Ahau above earth, when used as kin. Single. Quir. C, I1.
25. Inverted Ahau as postfix below. Double. Cop. J (N), A7b.
26. Inverted Ahau as postfix to right. Single. Cop. J (S), D2.
27. Inverted Ahau above earth when used as kin. Double. P.N. 8, B24.
28. Inverted Ahau on side as prefix. Cop. 9, B6.
29. Comb as postfix to crosshatched glyph. Pal. House C, cornice.
30. Crosshatched glyph becomes prefix, head variant of comb serving as main glyph. Pal. Inscr. (M), F8.
31. Head variant of crosshatched glyph. Pal. Inscr. (W), N2.
32. Sunrise glyph. Tik. T 4, L 3, C4.
33. "Forward to sunrise" combination. P.N. Thr 1, J'1.

OVERLAPPING AND FUSING OF GLYPHS:

34. Tun overlapping uinal. Quir. E (W), B11.
35. Glyph G9. P.N. 6, A8.
36. Glyph F. Pal. 1, A6b.
37. Glyphs G9 and F fused. Cop. T 11, N door, W panel.
38. Introductory glyph to 819-day cycle with lunar element as postfix. Yax. L 30, E3.
39. Introductory glyph to 819-day cycle with lunar element as infix. Quir. K, A7b.
40. Kayab with two postfixes below. Quir. A, B9.
41. Kayab with one postfix to side. Pal. Fol. Cross, O5.
42. Kayab with two postfixes fused. Nar. HS, V1b.
43. Anterior date indicator with two postfixes below. Quir. K, B6a.
44. Anterior date indicator with one postfix to left; other below. Cop. U, J1.
45. Anterior date indicator with fused postfixes. Cop. A, B2b.

SUPPRESSION OF ELEMENTS:

46. Katun glyph with one comb suppressed. Quir. E (W), B13b.
47. Two-legged sky glyph with both prefixes above. Quir. E (W), A8b.
48. Two-legged sky glyph with one prefix to left; one above. Quir. C (W), D13.
49. Two-legged sky glyph with one "leg" suppressed. Quir. D (E), D22a.
50. Glyph B standard form. Quir. E (E), C8.
51. Glyph B with oval element as infix of animal. P.N. 1, C1.
52. Glyph B with head of God C replacing animal head and oval element suppressed. Cop. 19, B10.
53. Glyph B with top arm of sky sign suppressed. Quir. P, B4.
54. Glyph B with lower arm of sky sign suppressed. Cop. J, 11b.
55. Glyph B with geometric variant in place of head form. Pal. Fol. Cross, B11.
56. Glyph B with muluc "count" symbol replacing bracket prefix. Head and oval elements suppressed. Pal. Cross, B12.
57. Normal form of sky sign. Cop. U, C2.

TRANSFER OF AFFIXES:

58. Action glyph of hand type and maize glyph. Dresden 13b.
59. Same with affix of maize glyph transferred to first glyph and prefix of latter replaced by *u* postfix with second glyph. Dresden 14b.
60. Hand action glyph and God B. Dresden 31c.
61. Same pair with postfix become a prefix and change in second postfix. Dresden 31c.

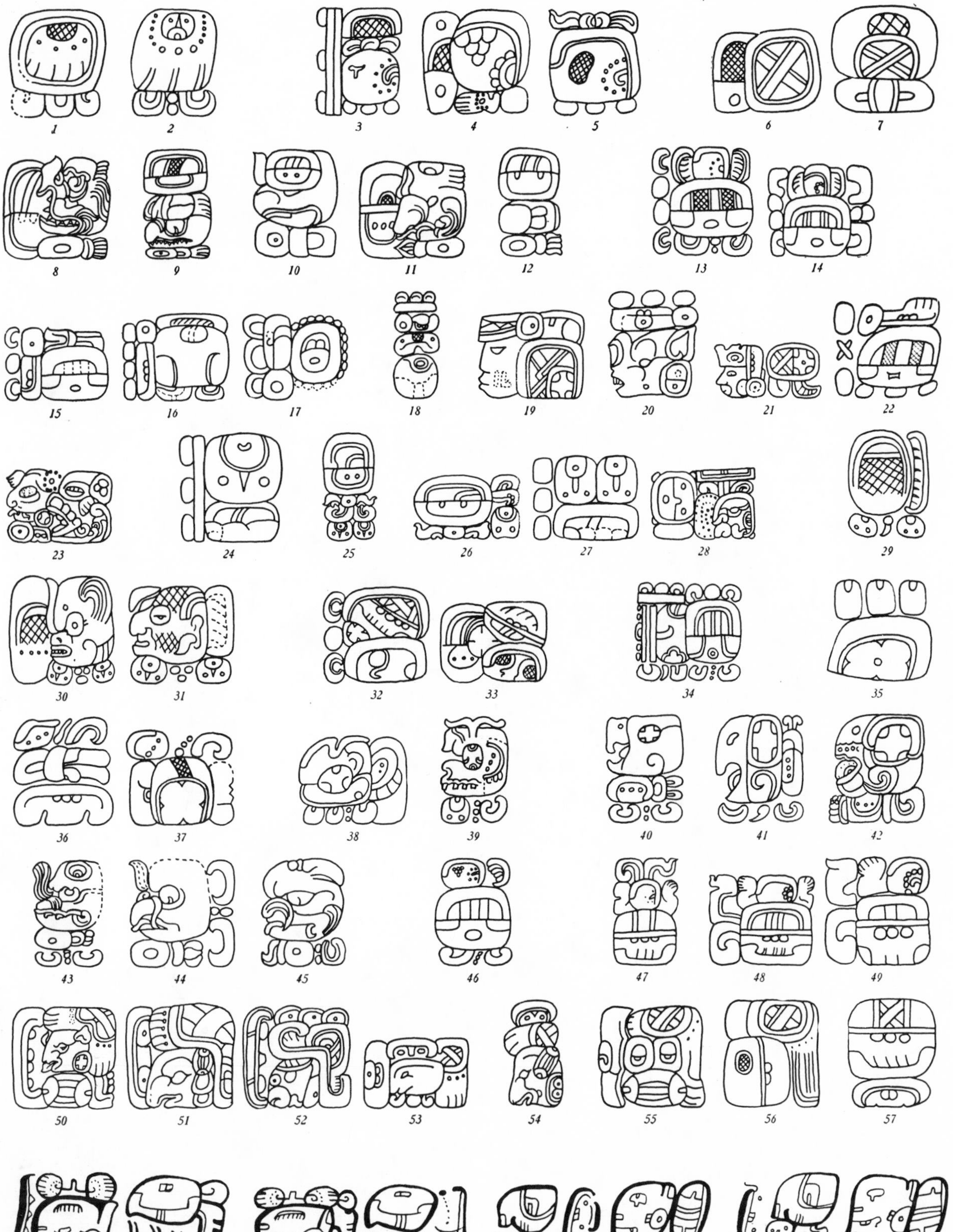

Fig. 2

Fig. 3—CLAUSES

1. Six tuns as distance number with both regular and distance number postfix. Pal. Sun, P1.
2. Prefatory glyph. "Forward to completion of 2 baktuns." Pal. Fol. Cross, C7–D7.
3. Clause of three glyphs. Nar. 29, H13–H14.
4. Clause of three glyphs. Nar. 29, I17–I18.
5. Clause of five glyphs. Nar. 24, A5–A9.
6. Clause of eight glyphs. Nar. 24, E5–D9.
7. Clause of five glyphs. Nar. 24, E16–E18.
8. Clause of four glyphs with intervening glyphs. Nar. 24, C7, C9–C10.
9. Clause of six glyphs with intervening glyphs. Nar. 29, F8–F9, G10–G11.
10. Clause of seven glyphs. Pal. Inscr. (M), I4–I7.
11. Clause of six glyphs. Pal. Inscr. (M), L9–M2.
12. Clause of six glyphs. Pal. Inscr. (M), K3–L5.
13. Clause of two glyphs. Quir. F, A9.
14. Clause of three glyphs. Pal. Inscr. (E), S6–S7.
15. Clause of four glyphs. Note expansion of material of first two glyph blocks of adjacent clause to four glyph blocks. Chichen 4, H1–G3.

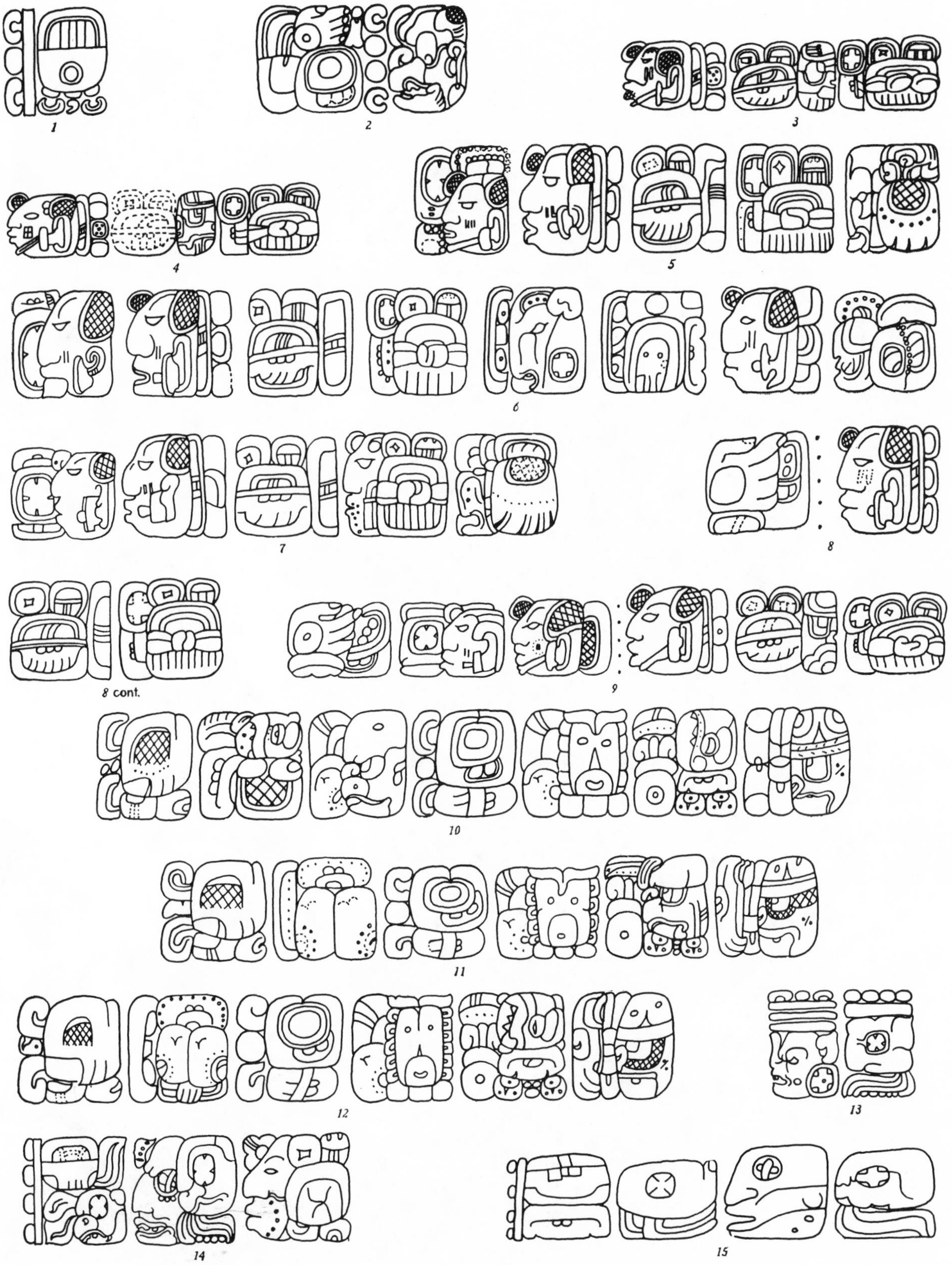
1
2
3
4
5
6
7
8
8 cont.
9
10
11
12
13
14
15

Fig. 3

Fig. 4—CLAUSES AND VARIABLE AFFIXES

"COUNT OF THE HAAB" CLAUSES:

1. East. Cop. Q, D3–C4.
2. North? Cop. 6, C5.
3. West. Nar. 24, E9–D10.
4. South. Quir. J, C9–D9.

AFFIXES DENOTING "EXPIRATION":

5. Distance number introductory glyph with flattened fish-head prefix; death eyes and hair postfix. Cop. A, B11a.
6. Head form of distance number introductory glyph with death eyes and hair as prefix and postfix. Cop. T 11, E door, N panel, A1.
7. Distance number introductory glyph with skull as prefix; hair and eyes as postfix. Cop. N, B9.
8. God C in sky elbow with skull as prefix. Pal. Cross, W panel of entrance.
9. Glyph B of lunar series with death eyes and hair as prefix; with oval as postfix. Quir. I, A6a.
10. Head of death god with death or night eye before forehead. Cop. I, C1.

SUFFIXES WITH PERIOD GLYPHS:

11. Normal form of symbolic variant of tun. Pal. Cross, B5.
12. Tun and katun, former with distance number postfix. Quir. C, C11.
13. "Expiration 5 tuns" with anniversary form of postfix. Yax. L 2, D1.
14. "First katun" with anniversary form of postfix. P.N. L 3, G1.
15. "Completion of count of 15 katuns" without postfix. Cop. 4, B7.

MOON AS SYMBOL FOR TWENTY IN DISTANCE NUMBERS:

16. With coefficient of 11: 31 days. Balak. 5, D10.
17. With coefficient completion sign: 20 days. Pal. Cross, B13.
18. With coefficient of 3: 23 days. P.N. L 3, Z1.

WEST:

19. Dresden 45c.

"TU" PREFIX:

20. Usual winged cauac as haab. Quir. E, C11b.
21. "Tu haab" anniversary glyph. Cop. 8, E1.
22. "In 5 tu haab in katun 1 Ahau." Yula 1, B2–A4.
23. "On the twelfth of Cumku." Chichen 27, B1.

SNAKE OR EEL AFFIX AS ANTERIOR DATE INDICATOR:

24. Pal. Inscr. (W), E8.
25. Pal. Inscr. (E), M7.
26. Xcal. North Building.

HEAD FORMS OF TUN SIGNS:

27. Personified cauac with "tail." Quir. F, C11.
28. Moan-bird variant. Pal. Inscr. (E), R3.

VULTURE HEAD REPLACING "TI" ELEMENT IN ANTERIOR DATE INDICATORS:

29. *Xoc* main element becomes prefix; *"ti"* postfix becomes main element as head of vulture with *"ti"* element above beak. Quir. J, E3.
30. Vulture head with *"ti"* element apparently as main element. Cop. HS, fragment (Gordon, pl. 13, row D).

KIN GLYPH AS INDICATOR OF DAY SIGNS:

31. 9 Lamat, kin. Chichen 2, A1–B1.
32. 8 Manik, kin, tu. Chichen 4, A1–B1.
33. 7 Muluc, kin. Xcal. IS, A8–B8.
34. 2 Chuen, end kin. Kabah jamb, A1–B1.

PHRASES:

35. "9 Lamat, kin, tu buluc Yax ichil 13 haab, ichil 1 Ahau." Chichen 5, A1–A4.
36. "6 Ahau 13 Muan, completion of count of 14 katuns, the count of the tun." Tik. 16, A1–A5.
37. "Completion of the haab. 1 Ahau 8 Kayab, the seating of the haab. The tenth katun, half a period completed, a tun." Pal. Inscr. (E), R12–T3.

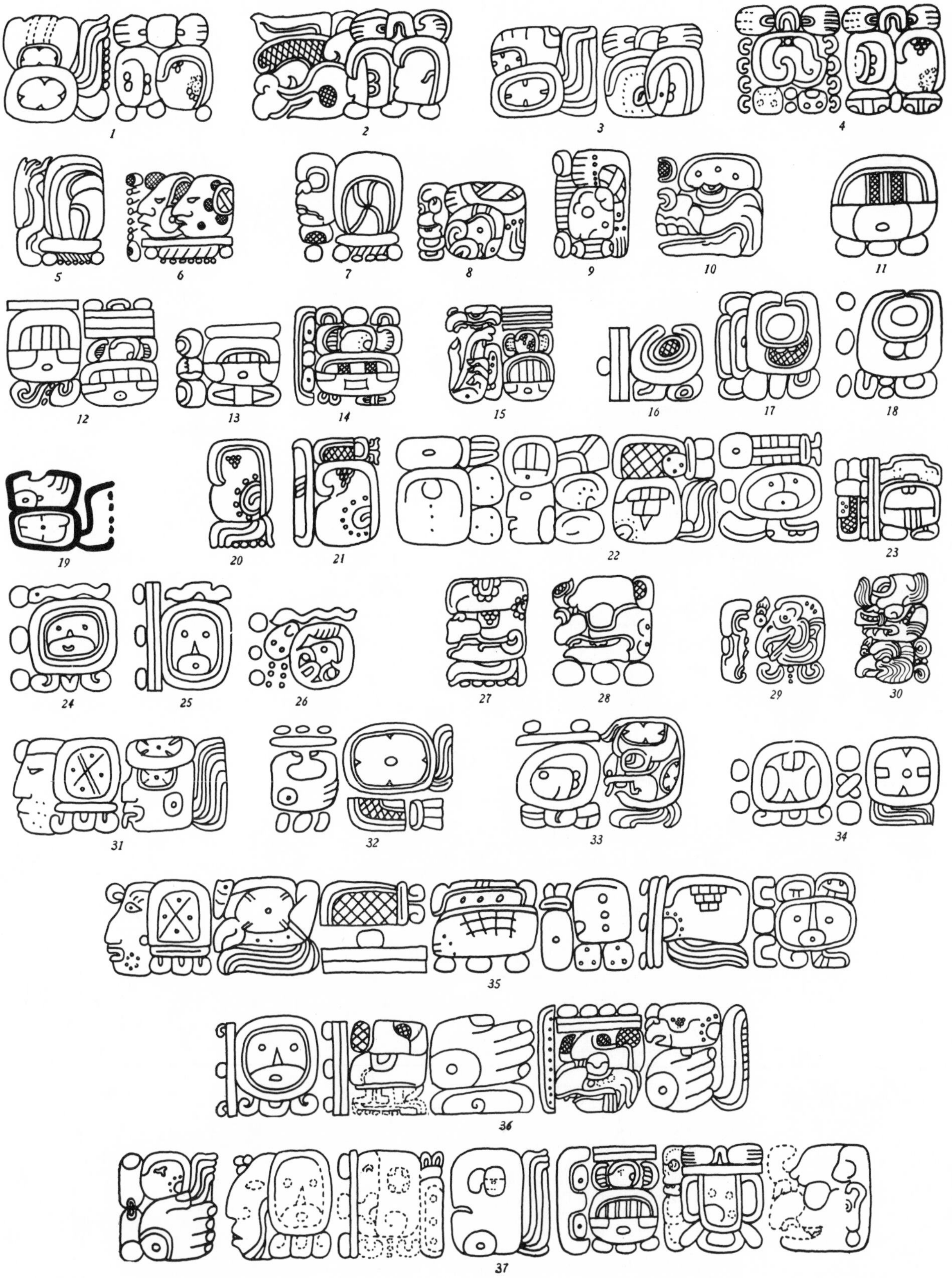
1
2
3
4
5
6
7
8
9
10
11
12
13
14
15
16
17
18
19
20
21
22
23
24
25
26
27
28
29
30
31
32
33
34
35
36
37

Fig. 4

Fig. 5—INTERCHANGEABILITY OF ELEMENTS OF THE COUNT GROUP OF AFFIXES

NATURALISTIC REPRESENTATIONS OF FISH:
1. Pottery. Chajcar, Alta Verapaz.
2. Ball court. Chichen.
3. Pottery. Chajcar, Alta Verapaz.
4. Cop. N.

FLANKING ELEMENTS OF IS INTRODUCTORY GLYPH:
5. Realistic fish. Cop. C.
6. Head of fish. Cop. P.
7. Head of fish. Cop. 16.
8. Conventionalized design. Cop. E.
9. Conventionalized fish head. Cop. 2.
10. *U* bracket with additions. Cop. P.
11. Conventionalized design. Cop. 7.
12. Comb with additions. Cop. A.
13. Katun with *u* brackets. Jade. Tzibanche.

PREFIXES WITH DOUBLE IMIX GLYPH:
14. Comb. Quir. A, D11.
15. Dots. Yax. L 56, L2b.
16. Fish. Yax. L 2, Q1.

PREFIXES WITH DISTANCE NUMBER INTRODUCTORY GLYPH:
17. *U* bracket. Quir. D, A21b.
18. Dots. Cop. I', F1b.
19. Head of fish. Cop. 4, A5b.
20. Head of fish. Cop. 5, B1a.
21. Death eyes and hair. Nar. 35, E7.
22. Death's head. Cop. N, B9.

PREFIXES WITH CABAN (NON-DAY SIGN) GLYPH:
23. *U* bracket. Quir. E, B15b.
24. Flattened fish head. Quir. E, D11.
25. Water. Cop. I, C4b.
26. Skull or fish. P.N. Thr, A'4–B'4.
27. Death eyes. Nar. 35, D5.

PREFIXES WITH GLYPH B, LUNAR SERIES:
28. *U* bracket. P.N. L 3, E1.
29. Dots. Pal. 1, A8.
30. Flattened fish-head. Pal. Fol. Cross, B11.
31. Fish head. Cop. 6, A6, l.h.
32. Water. Pal. Cross, B12.
33. Death eyes and hair. Quir. I, A6a.

PREFIXES WITH GOD C IN CELESTIAL ELBOW:
34. Flattened fish head. Nar. HS, Inscr. 12.
35. Water postfix. Cop. I, A9a.
36. Skull. Pal. Cross, W jamb.
37. Skull and eyes. Yax. L 56, G2b.
38. Dots. Pal. Cross, C12.
39. Dots. Pal. Inscr. (W), S12a.

PREFIXES WITH HAAB COMPLETED:
40. *U* bracket. Pusil. K, B2.
41. Flattened fish-head. Pal. Inscr. (E), M1.
42. Fish head. Pal. Inscr. (E), L5.
43. Skull. P.N. Alt 2, L1.
44. Death eyes. Cop. 13, B9.
45. Death eyes. Uax. 12, A2.
46. Link. Pal. Inscr. (E), R12.

PREFIXES AND PREFATORY GLYPHS WITH PERIOD GLYPHS:
47. *U* bracket 15 katuns. P.N. Alt 2, H2.
48. Dots 13 katuns. Pal. Fol. Cross, O15.
49. Flattened fish-head 15 katuns. P.N. Thr, M.
50. Hand fish-head 2 katuns. Quir. D, B17a–B17b, u.h.
51. Death eyes 19 katuns. Quir. Str 1, Y'.
52. Death eyes 13 tuns. Cop. U, A2.

SUNDRY GLYPHS:
53. Yax with coefficient of 18, formed of bar and three dots and head for 10. Tik. 6, A10.
54. Haunch of venison on dish. Dresden 35a.
55. Offering of fish. Dresden 31b.
56. Iguana. Madrid 3b.
57. So-called Mars beast. Dresden 45b.
58. Kan, "ripe maize," in dish. Dresden 25b.
59. Iguana tamales or iguana and maize. Dresden 30b.
60. Turkey tamales or turkey and maize. Dresden 34a.
61. Germination. Seeds sprouting from earth symbol. Madrid 28b.
62. Shield as probable symbol for war. Madrid 16b.
63. Shield with "stone" as prefix. Dresden 60a.

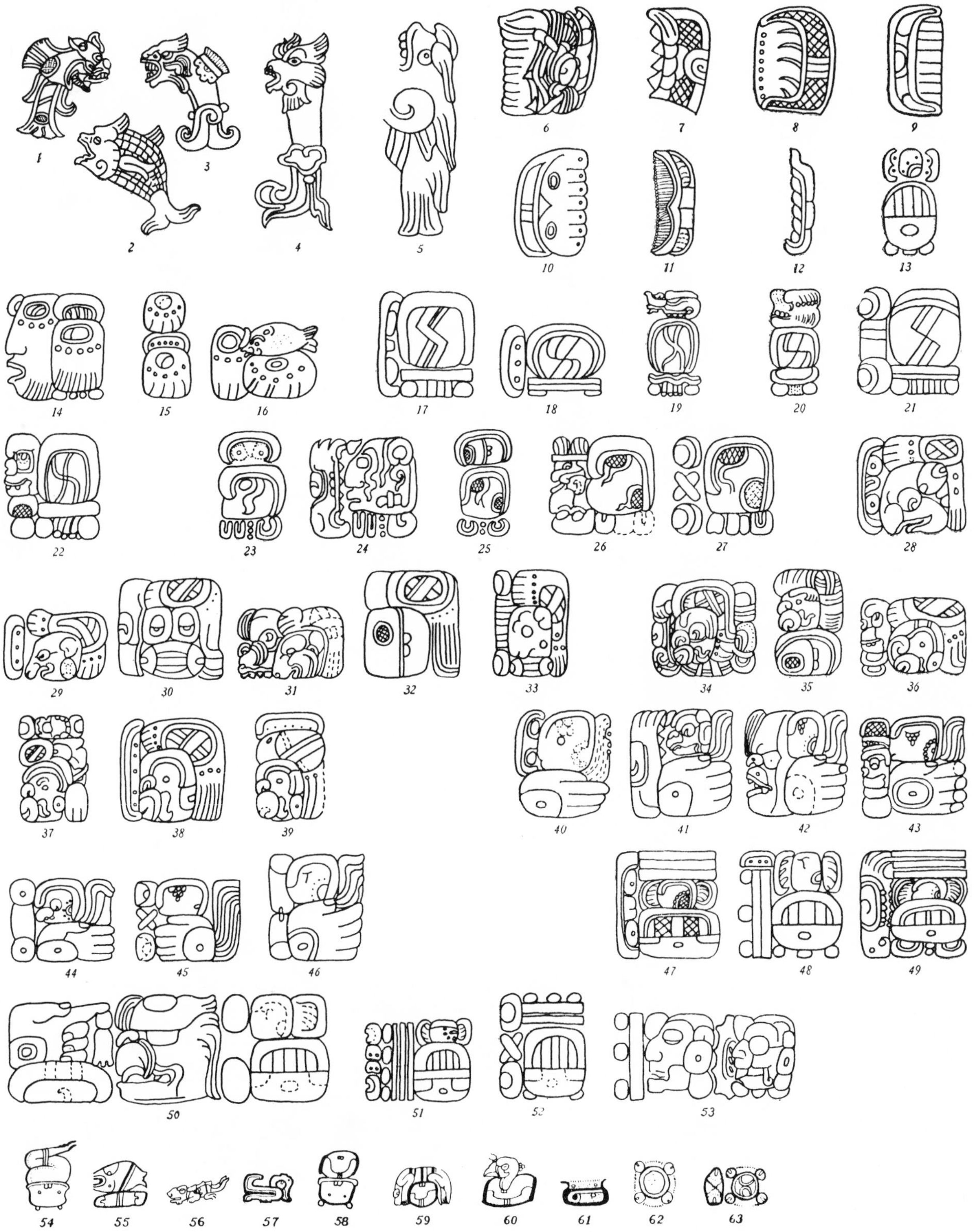
1 2 3 4 5 6 7 8 9 10 11 12 13 14 15 16 17 18 19 20 21 22 23 24 25 26 27 28 29 30 31 32 33 34 35 36 37 38 39 40 41 42 43 44 45 46 47 48 49 50 51 52 53 54 55 56 57 58 59 60 61 62 63

Fig. 5

Fig. 6—DAY SIGNS: IMIX TO KAN

IMIX:
1. Uax. fresco, Gl 41.
2. Uax. fresco, Gl 61.
3. P.N. L 2, C1.
4. Pal. Cross, U5.
5. Yax. L 41, A1.
6. Yax. L 25, O1.
7. P.N. 1, G8.
8. P.N. 3, E2.
9. Nar. 32, Y1.
10. Yula 2, A1.
11. Chichen 27, Bl 18.
12. Chama Vase.
13. Ratinlixal Vase.
14. Perez 21.
15. Dresden 35b.
16. Madrid 14b.
17. Landa.

IK:
18. Uax. fresco, Gl 42.
19. Uax. fresco, Gl 62.
20. Nar. HS, V1a.
21. Pal. Cross, E9.
22. Pal. Inscr., Pier C.
23. P.N. 8, C19.
24. Tik. T 4, L 3, B3.
25. Pal. 96 Gl., F2.
26. Quir. G, K'1.
27. Cop. U, L5.
28. Ratinlixal Vase.
29. Perez 21, column 5.
30. Dresden 15b.
31. Dresden 2b.
32. Madrid 99b.
33. Madrid 13b.
34. Landa.

AKBAL:
35. Uax. fresco, Gl 43.
36. Uax. fresco, Gl 63.
37. Pal. Sun, E1.
38. Pal. Sun, P6.
39. Pal. Cross, G1.
40. Tik. T 4, L 3, D4.
41. Tik. T 4, L 3, E2.
42. Morales 2, C9.
43. Polol 4, B5.
44. Ratinlixal Vase.
45. Chichen 20.
46. Perez 20.
47. Dresden 5c.
48. Dresden 22b.
49. Madrid 63c.
50. Landa.

KAN:
51. Uax. fresco, Gl 64.
52. Uax. fresco, Gl 44.
53. Nar. 25, D9.
54. Chinik. Thr, N1.
55. Pal. Cross, R17.
56. Pal. Cross, U10.
57. Pal. death's head.
58. P.N. Thr 1, H'2.
59. Cop. Q, E6.
60. Quir. Alt O, J'4b.
61. Chichen 23, Bl 16.
62. Chichen 34.
63. Chama Vase.
64. Perez 21, column 5.
65. Dresden 6b.
66. Madrid 83b.
67. Madrid 47c.
68. Landa.

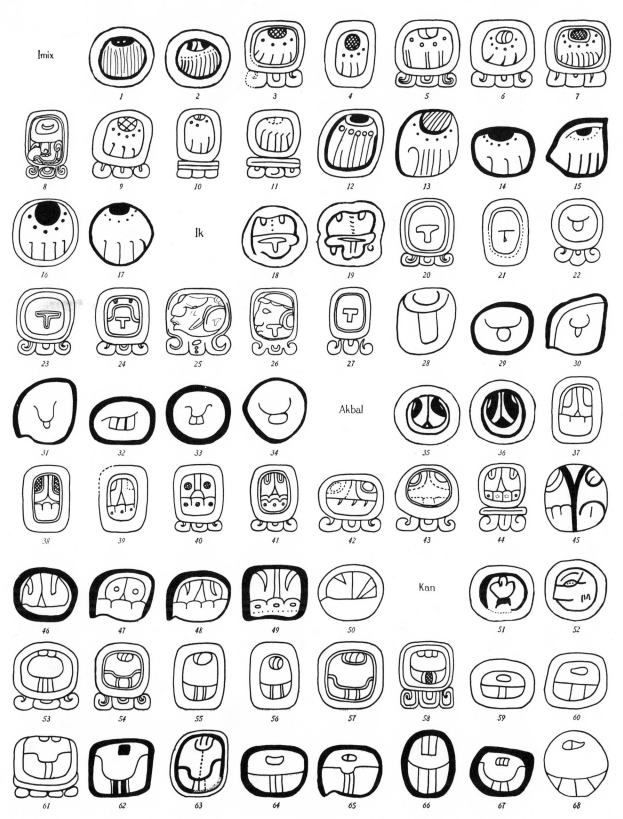

Imix

Ik

Akbal

Kan

Fig. 6

FIG. 7—DAY SIGNS: CHICCHAN TO LAMAT

CHICCHAN:
1. Uax. fresco, Gl 25.
2. Uax. fresco, Gl 65.
3. Pal. Cross, T14.
4. Cop. H, L, u.h.
5. Nar. 22, E15.
6. P.N. 9, C8.
7. Yax. L 27, A1.
8. Cop. HS, Date 26.
9. Cop. T 11.
10. Chama Vase.
11. Perez 21, column 7.
12. Dresden 43c.
13. Dresden 9c.
14. Dresden 61c.
15. Madrid 45a.
16. Madrid 16b.
17. Landa.

CIMI:
18. Uax. fresco, Gl 26.
19. Uax. fresco, Gl 66.
20. Yax. L 35, C4.
21. Yax. L 10, A1.
22. Yax. 18, A2.
23. Pal. tablet in Madrid.
24. Tik. Alt 5.
25. Quir. J, H2.
26. Cop. pectoral on statue.
27. Cop. HS.
28. Quir. E, A12b.
29. Perez 21, column 5.
30. Dresden 12a.
31. Dresden 10b.
32. Madrid 47b.
33. Madrid 85c.
34. Landa.

MANIK:
35. Uax. fresco, Gl 27.
36. Uax. fresco, Gl 67.
37. Tik. 10, A2.
38. Pal. House C, substructure.
39. Ton. 7, Side A.
40. Pal. 96 Gl, H1.
41. Pal. 96 Gl, H7.
42. P.N. Thr 1, O1.
43. P.N. 12, A20.
44. Chichen 14, A1.
45. Chichen 12, A1.
46. Chama Vase.
47. Perez 21, column 7.
48. Dresden 4c.
49. Madrid 89c.
50. Landa.

LAMAT:
51. Uax. fresco, Gl 28.
52. Uax. fresco, Gl 68.
53. Pusil. D, E9.
54. P.N. L 4, O1.
55. Cop. I, C7.
56. Pal. Inscr. (W), E6.
57. Cop. J, Gl 27.
58. Nar. 24, A1.
59. Cop. HS, Date 24.
60. Cop. HS, Date 3.
61. Pal. 96 Gl., D4.
62. Chichen 4, A1.
63. Chama Vase.
64. Perez 21, column 5.
65. Dresden 47b.
66. Dresden 47a.
67. Dresden 17c.
68. Landa.

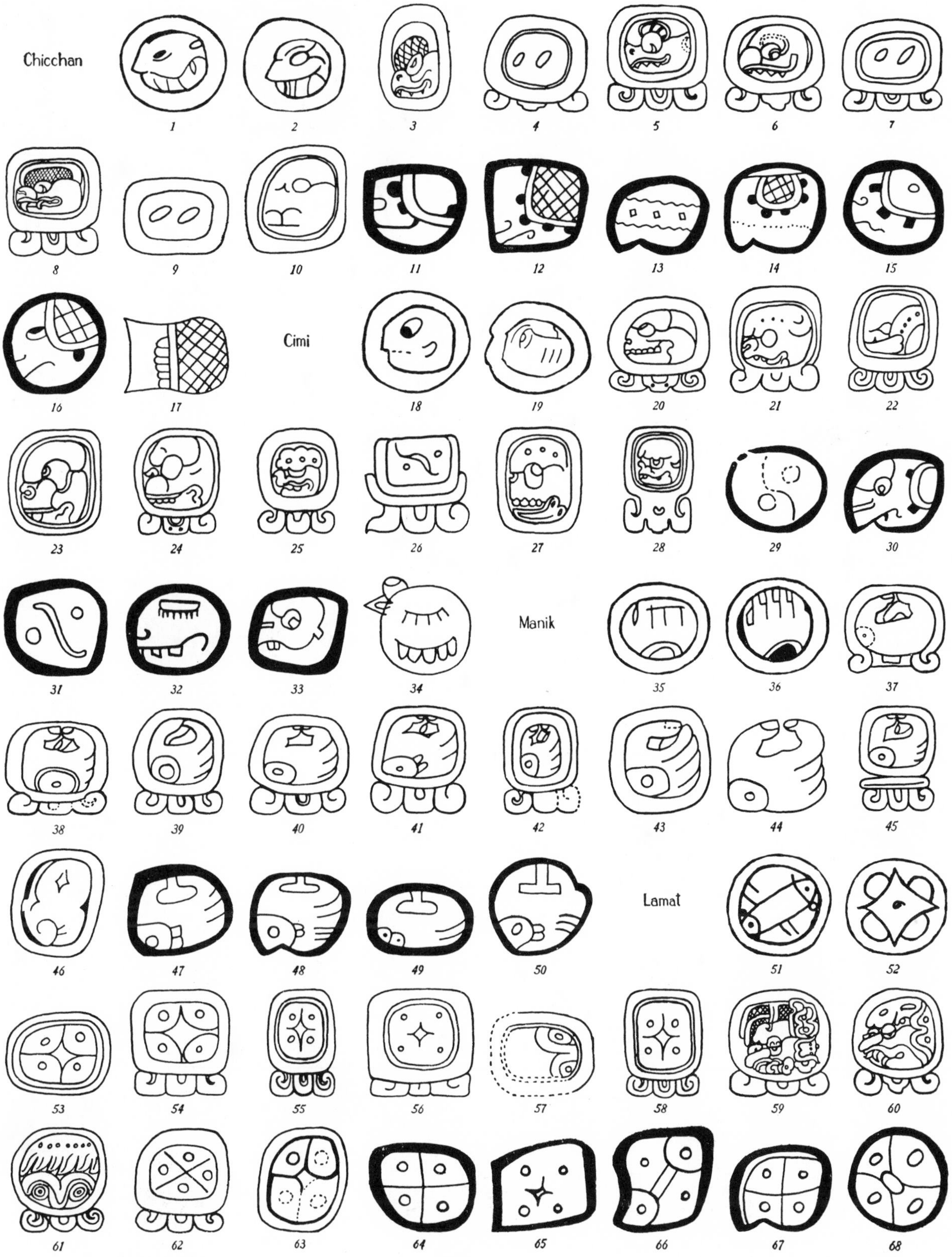
Chicchan
1
2
3
4
5
6
7
8
9
10
11
12
13
14
15
16
17
Cimi
18
19
20
21
22
23
24
25
26
27
28
29
30
31
32
33
34
Manik
35
36
37
38
39
40
41
42
43
44
45
46
47
48
49
50
Lamat
51
52
53
54
55
56
57
58
59
60
61
62
63
64
65
66
67
68

Fig. 7

FIG. 8—DAY SIGNS: MULUC TO EB

MULUC:
1. Uax. fresco, Gl 29.
2. Uax. fresco, Gl 49.
3. Uax. fresco, Gl 69.
4. Tik. Alt 5, Gl 1.
5. Tik. Alt 5, Gl 27.
6. Xcal. IS, A8.
7. El Cayo L 1, K14.
8. Cop. HS, Step L, A.
9. Yax. L 21, C5.
10. Ton. 20.
11. Chichen 1, C2.
12. Perez 21, column 7.
13. Dresden 58b.
14. Madrid 15b.
15. Madrid 15b.
16. Landa.

OC:
17. Uax. fresco, Gl 10.
18. Uax. fresco, Gl 30.
19. Uax. fresco, Gl 50.
20. Pal. Sun, L1.
21. Pal. Fol. Cross, N5.
22. Pal. Fol. Cross, E1.
23. Pal. Olvidado.
24. Cop. HS, Step P, M.
25. Cop. HS, Step Q, M.
26. Yax. L 29, A4.
27. Quir. K, B6.
28. Perez 17.
29. Dresden 47a.
30. Dresden 45a.
31. Dresden 22a.
32. Madrid 64a.
33. Madrid 45a.
34. Landa.

CHUEN:
35. Uax. fresco, Gl 11.
36. Uax. fresco, Gl 51.
37. Uax. fresco, Gl 71.
38. Pal. HS, C4b.
39. P.N. shell, E2.
40. Cop. altar of 1.
41. Cop. F', B1b.
42. Pal. 96 Gl., B6.
43. Ixlu 2, A1.
44. Kabah jamb, Gl 1.
45. Perez 21, column 7.
46. Dresden 2a.
47. Dresden 55a.
48. Dresden 6c.
49. Madrid 15b.
50. Landa.

EB:
51. Uax. fresco, Gl 12.
52. Uax. fresco, Gl 52.
53. Leiden Plaque, A7.
54. P.N. L 12, B4.
55. Pal. Palace, balustrade.
56. Pal. Tablet 2.
57. Yax. L 24, X1.
58. Yax. L 26, F'1.
59. Tik. T 4, L 2, B3.
60. Nar. 10, A1.
61. Quir. C, E1.
62. Cop. U, O3.
63. Nar. 32, A'3.
64. Uxmal capstone.
65. Dresden 12a.
66. Madrid 39b.
67. Madrid 13b.
68. Landa.

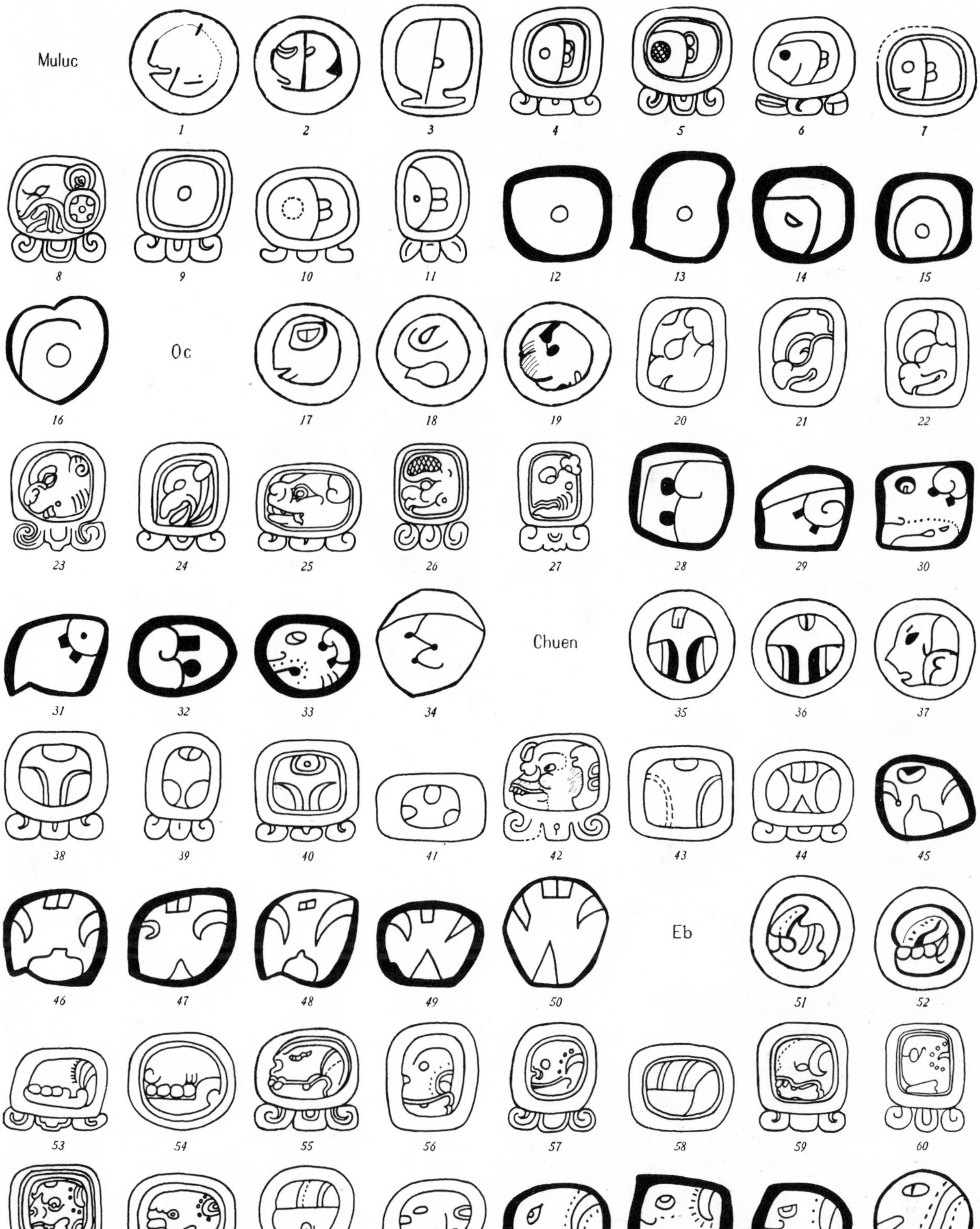
Muluc
Oc
Chuen
Eb
1 2 3 4 5 6 7
8 9 10 11 12 13 14 15
16 17 18 19 20 21 22
23 24 25 26 27 28 29 30
31 32 33 34 35 36 37
38 39 40 41 42 43 44 45
46 47 48 49 50 51 52
53 54 55 56 57 58 59 60
61 62 63 64 65 66 67 68

Fig. 8

Fig. 9—DAY SIGNS: BEN TO CIB

BEN:
1. Uax. fresco, Gl 53.
2. Uax. fresco, Gl 33.
3. Pal. House A, A1.
4. Tik. T 4, L 2, B7.
5. P.N. L 9, P2a.
6. P.N. Alt 2, E1.
7. Yax. L 53, A1.
8. Yax. L 30, A2.
9. P.N. L 3, A13.
10. Cop. Q, C1.
11. Nar. 35, D8.
12. Chichen 10.
13. Chama II Vase.
14. Perez 19, Gl 6.
15. Dresden 4a.
16. Madrid 24d.
17. Landa.

Ix:
18. Uax. fresco, Gl 14.
19. Uax. fresco, Gl 34.
20. Yax. L 10, E5b.
21. Chinkul. ball court.
22. Yax. 20, E1b.
23. Nar. 22, F17.
24. Yax. L 43, D2.
25. Xcal. column.
26. Yax. L 59, J.
27. Yax. L 27, E2a.
28. Chama II Vase.
29. Perez 17, bottom.
30. Dresden 4b.
31. Dresden 44b.
32. Madrid 45c.
33. Madrid 81a.
34. Landa.

MEN:
35. Uax. fresco, Gl 55.
36. Uax. fresco, Gl 35.
37. Tik. 17, A4.
38. Stone of Chiapa, C4.
39. Nar. 29, G18.
40. Nar. 23, F17.
41. Cop. N, pedestal, A1.
42. P.N. L 3, K2.
43. Perez 21, column 7.
44. Dresden 57b.
45. Dresden 30b.
46. Dresden 36c.
47. Madrid 89a.
48. Madrid 14b.
49. Landa.

CIB:
50. Uax. fresco, Gl 16.
51. Uax. fresco, Gl 56.
52. Yax. L 48, C5.
53. Pal. Fol. Cross, L1.
54. Pal. Fol. Cross, N16.
55. P.N. 3, A4.
56. P.N. 3, C2b.
57. Tik. T 4, L 2, L8.
58. Cop. T 11, H7.
59. Cop. T 11, E door, N panel, A2b.
60. P.N. L 3, H'4.
61. Poco Uinik 3, C21.
62. Chama II Vase.
63. Perez 23b.
64. Dresden 6b.
65. Dresden 42c.
66. Dresden 54a.
67. Madrid 30a.
68. Landa.

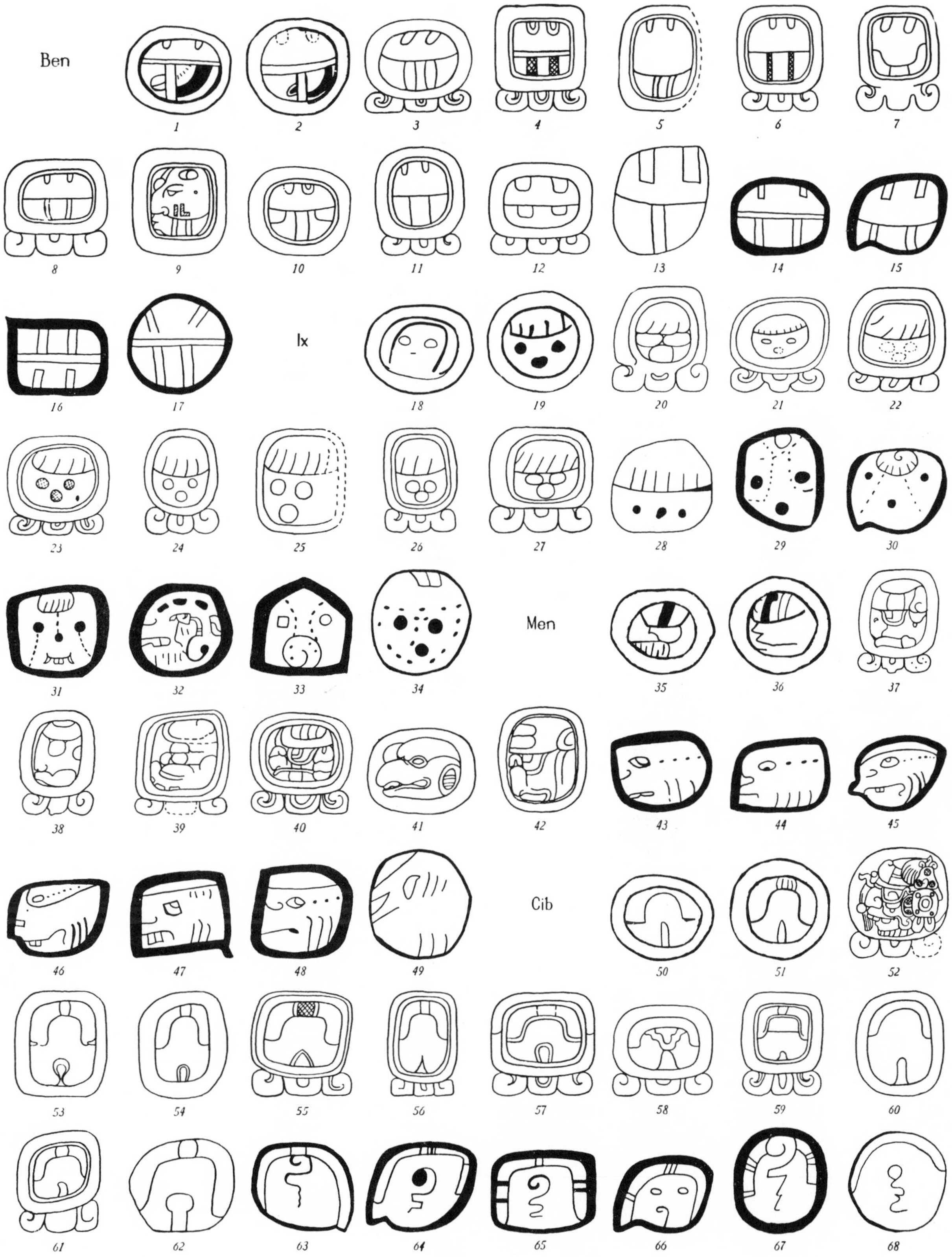
Ben
1 2 3 4 5 6 7
8 9 10 11 12 13 14 15
16 17
Ix
18 19 20 21 22
23 24 25 26 27 28 29 30
31 32 33 34
Men
35 36 37
38 39 40 41 42 43 44 45
46 47 48 49
Cib
50 51 52
53 54 55 56 57 58 59 60
61 62 63 64 65 66 67 68

FIG. 9

Fig. 10—DAY SIGNS: CABAN TO AHAU

Caban:
1. Uax. fresco, Gl 37.
2. Uax. fresco, Gl 57.
3. Pal. Inscr. (W), K11.
4. Pal. Sun, O7.
5. Seib. HS, J2.
6. Quir. F, A18b.
7. Quir. D, AB13.
8. Cop. R, A1.
9. Cop. T, front.
10. Chama II Vase.
11. Perez 21, column 7.
12. Dresden 15b.
13. Dresden 57a.
14. Madrid 10b.
15. Landa.

Etz'nab:
16. Uax. fresco, Gl 18.
17. Uax. fresco, Gl 38.
18. Uax. fresco, Gl 58.
19. Balak. 5, A4.
20. Cop. X, A1.
21. Pal. Inscr. (W), Q11.
22. Pal. Inscr. (W), T5.
23. Pal. Cross, R7.
24. Tik. T 4, L 2, G3.
25. Tik. T 4, L 2, I1.
26. Perez 21, column 5.
27. Dresden 5c.
28. Dresden 22c.
29. Madrid 103b.
30. Landa.

Cauac:
31. Uax. fresco, Gl 39.
32. Uax. fresco, Gl 59.

33. Yax. L 37, C6a.
34. Pal. Palace, House C, K1.
35. Pal. Fol. Cross, B13.
36. Cop. T 11, N door, W panel.
37. P.N. L 3, F'6.
38. P.N. 12, A16b.
39. Perez 21, column 6.
40. Dresden 10b.
41. Dresden 56a.
42. Madrid 15b.
43. Madrid 10a.
44. Madrid 14b.
45. Landa.

Ahau:
46. Uax. fresco, Gl 20.
47. Uax. fresco, Gl 60.
48. Uax. 20, A1.
49. P.N. L 12, C1.
50. Cop. 16, A3b.
51. Nar. HS, 13.
52. Chinik. Thr 1, A1.
53. Pal. Cross, D3.
54. Tik. T 4, L 3, A1.
55. Cop. M, B2b.
56. Yax. L 31, C4.
57. Cop. T 11, S door, E panel.
58. P.N. Thr 1, K'a.
59. Quir. P, B3, u.h.
60. Quir. Str 1, A'.
61. Seib. 10, A1.
62. Flores 2, A.
63. Tzibanche jade. Gl 1.
64. S. Rita. Gann, pl. 29, no. 2.
65. S. Rita. Gann, pl. 31, no. 3.
66. S. Rita. Gann, pl. 29, no. 8.
67. S. Rita. Gann, pl. 30, no. 8.
68. S. Rita. Gann, pl. 29, no. 4.

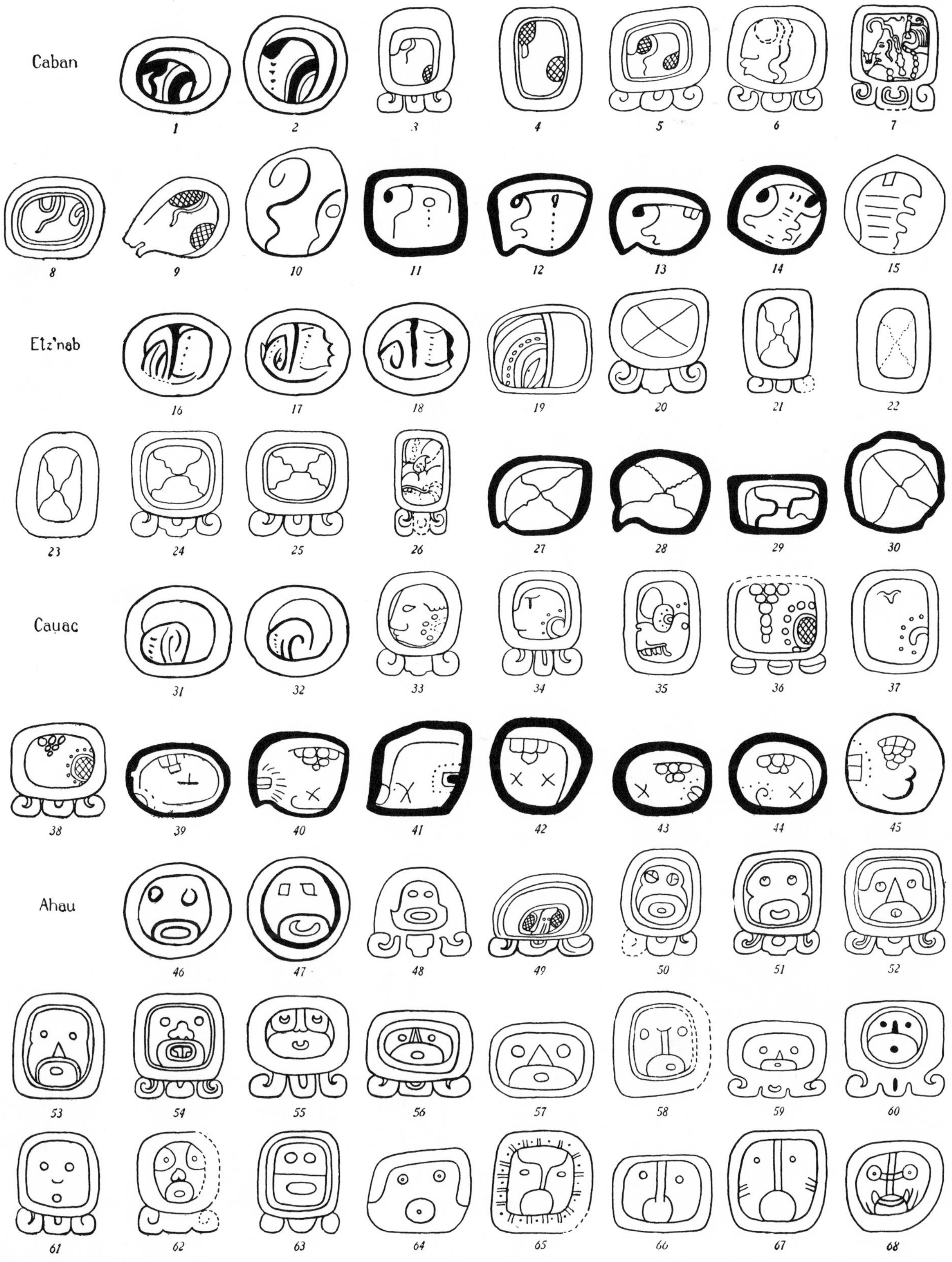
Caban
Etz'nab
Cauac
Ahau

Fig. 10

Fig. 11—AHAU (*CONTINUED*) AND SUNDRY GLYPHS

SYMBOLIC FORMS:
1. Chichen 19, B1.
2. Chichen 20, Gl 12.
3. Chichen 20, Gl 19.
4. Chichen 5, A4.
5. Chichen 3, D5.
6. Chichen 14, D.
7. Yula 1, A4.
8. Chichen 27, B1.
9. Perez 5, top center.
10. Dresden 24.
11. Dresden 24.
12. Dresden 6b.
13. Dresden 47a.
14. Madrid 48b.
15. Landa.
16. Chumayel, p. 72.

PROFILES:
17. Tik. 8, A7.
18. Tik. 7, A8.
19. Cop. 24, B5.
20. Cop. 9, B5.
21. Pal. HS, A4.
22. Pal. Inscr. (E), S8.
23. La Florida 9, A1.
24. Cop. C, A2b.
25. P.N. Alt 2, H1.
26. Quir. J, B11.
27. Cop. Review Stand, Qb.
28. Quir. C, B5.
29. Pal. 96 Gl, A1.
30. P.N. L 3, V4.
31. P.N. 15, on pouch.
32. Quir. Str 1, U.

33. Cop. D, A4b.
34. Quir. D, D14.
35. Cop. D′, Side D, A.
36. Cop. T 11, lowest step.

"SUBJECT INDICATOR":
37. Lunar postfix. Quir. E, D9.
38. Lunar infix. Quir. D, D17a.
39. Lunar postfix. Cop. M, B4b.
40. *U* bracket prefix. Quir. C, C7.
41. *U* bracket prefix. Quir. C, B7.
42. Same glyph? Quir. F, C9a.
43. Parrot head. Cop. N, A16.

"FROG" GLYPH:
44. Pal. HS, A5a.
45. P.N. 1, B3.
46. Pal. Cross, E7.
47. Pal. Fol. Cross, C5.
48. Forward prefix. Pal. Cross, C17.
49. Forward prefix. Pal. Inscr. (W), K9b.
50. Pal. Inscr. (W), K12.

KAN GLYPH:
51. Cop. B, A9.
52. Pal. Inscr. (W), B12.
53. Pal. Inscr. (W), B7.
54. Tik. 5, A12.
55. Chichen 19, front, B2.
56. Chichen 19, under, A4.
57. Chichen 19, front F2b.

VARIOUS:
58. 4 Ahau katun. Ocosingo jade.
59. 8 Ahau with *ak* postfix. Cop. 6, B7a.
60. Double Imix with fish replacing comb. Nebaj vase.

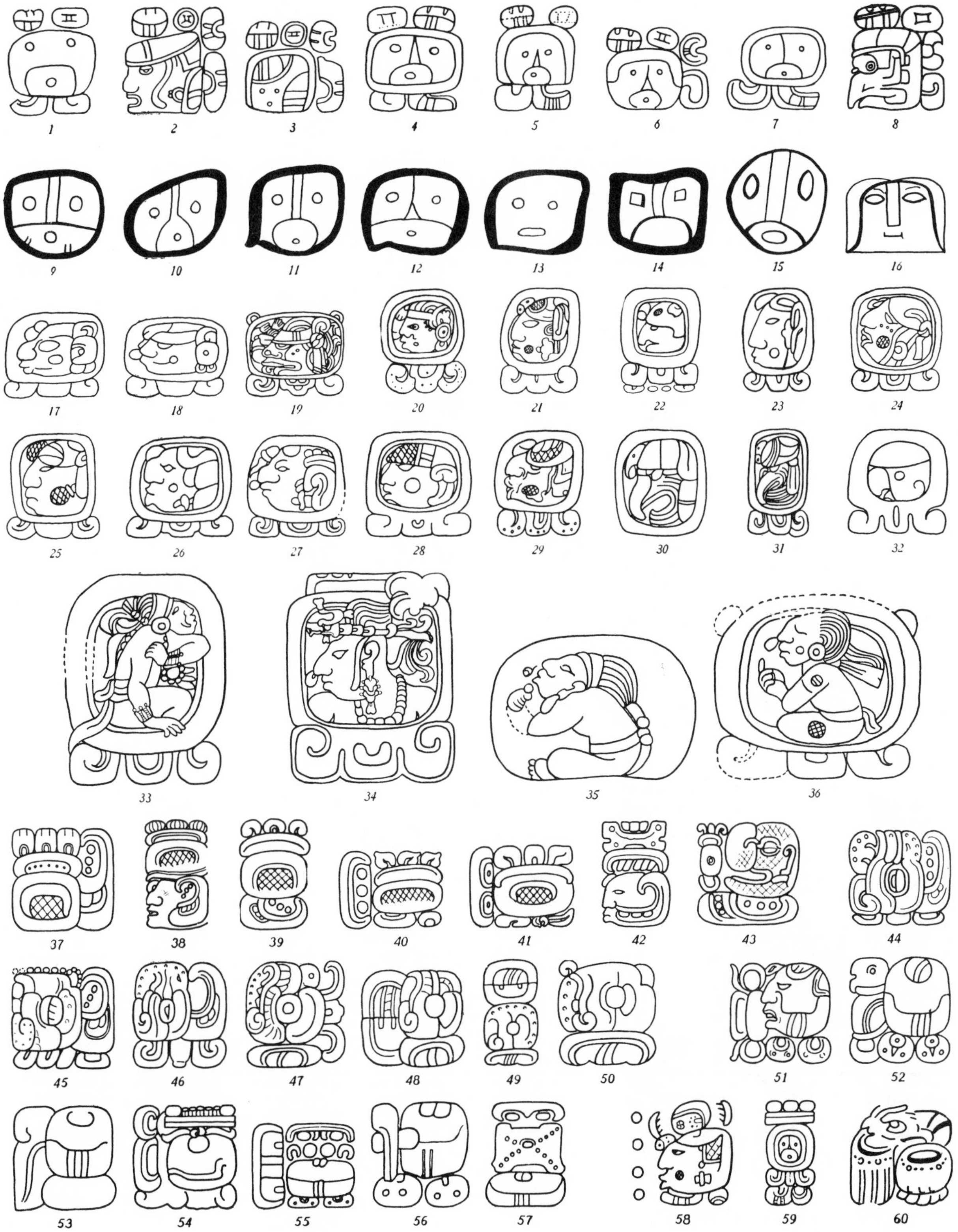

Fig. 11

Fig. 12—DERIVATIONS OF DAY SIGNS: IMIX TO AKBAL. AFFIXES

1. Earth crocodile with Imix headdress and naturalistic water lilies. Yax. 7.
2. Earth crocodile with Imix headdress. Cop. T 11.
3. Earth crocodile resting on Imix sign. Headdress on individual on Cop. U.
4. Water lilies emerging from head of earth crocodile. Pal. Palace, House D.
5. Water lily, Pal. Palace, House D.
6. Water lily, Chichen ball court.
7. Water lily on bowl from Calcetok, Yucatan. After Spinden.
8. Fish nibbling at water lily. Ixkun 1.
9. Ik sign with plant growing from it held by maize god. Madrid 97d.
10. Ik sign with maize growing from it. Cop. H.
11. Glyph of God B. Dresden 43c.
12. Jaguar with water lily in headdress. Dresden 8a.
13. Jaguar god. Tik. T 4.
14. Jaguar god with water-lily design. Pal. Sun.
15. Jaguar god. P.N. MSS 16.
16. Glyph of Bolon-Yocte. Dresden 60b.
17. Glyph of Bolon-Yocte. Paris 7.
18. Glyph of Bolon-Yocte. Pal. Palace, House C, cornice.
19. 13 *te* tuns. Madrid 66a.
20. 4 uinals with *te* (3) postfix. Madrid 72a.
21. Moon with coefficient of 5, prefix and *te* (1) postfix. 25 days? Dresden 27a.
22. Moon with coefficient of 16 and prefix. 36 days? Dresden 27c.
23. 9 tuns with numerical classifier prefixed. Madrid 66a.
24. 7 tuns with numerical classifier postfixed. Madrid 70b.

FIG. 12

Fɪɢ. 13—DERIVATIONS OF DAY SIGNS: KAN TO MANIK

1. Maize god with maize sprouting from Kan sign in headdress. Dresden 9b, left figure.
2. Maize god with maize headdress. Cop. H.
3. Maize growing from Kan sign, and God B sowing seed. Madrid 28b.
4. Glyph of maize god. Quir. P.
5. Glyph for maize offering. Dresden 30b.
6. Glyph for new maize. Dresden 31b.
7. Glyph for red maize. Dresden 41c.
8. Glyph for yellow maize. Dresden 36a.
9. Glyph for white maize. Dresden 66b.
10. Kan-Imix, abundance of maize. Madrid 21b.
11. Death god. Dresden 14a.
12. Chicchan god. Dresden 7b.
13. Glyph of death or *multun tzek,* "heap of skulls." Dresden 10a.
14. Glyph of death god. Dresden 11a.
15. Serpent with Chicchan markings. Madrid 30a.
16. Glyph of death god. Quir. P.
17. Glyph of Chicchan god. Madrid 104b.
18. Glyph of Chicchan god. Dresden 21c.
19. Death god with leg terminating in flower. Dresden 15a.
20. Black god with deer as headdress and carrying spear. Madrid 51c.
21. Black god with spear, the butt of which is shaped as a hand. Madrid 32a.
22. Black god with axe and torch. Scorpion claws emerge from his waist. Madrid 33b.
23. Black god with head of God M at waist and scorpion tail ending in hand. Madrid 79a.
24. Scorpion with deer held by rope which it grasps in its tail. Madrid 44b.

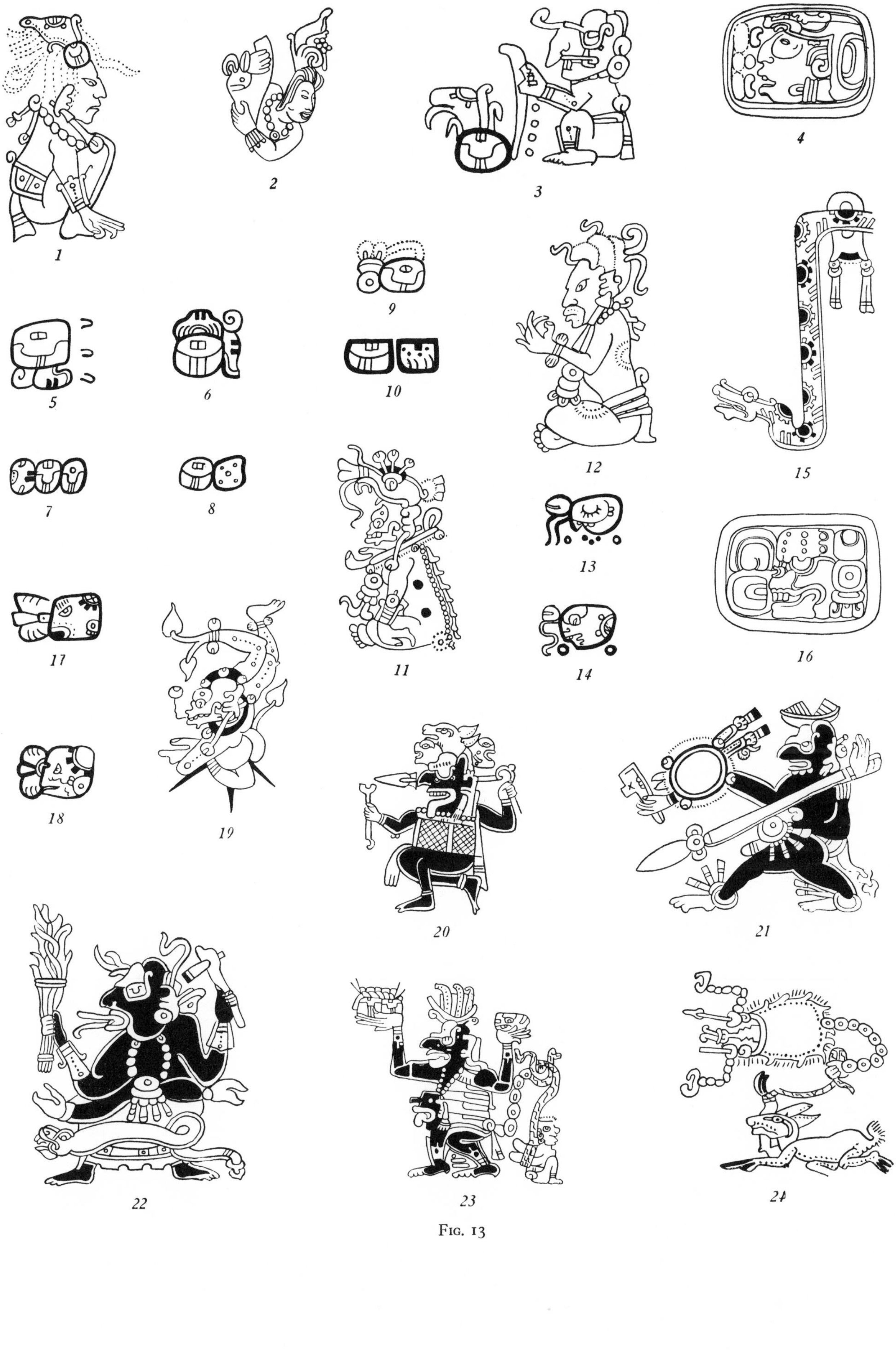
1
2
3
4
5
6
7
8
9
10
11
12
13
14
15
16
17
18
19
20
21
22
23
24

Fig. 13

Fig. 14—DERIVATIONS OF DAY SIGNS: LAMAT TO CABAN

1. Lahun-Chan Venus God. Dresden 47b.
2. Glyph of Lahun-Chan. Dresden 47b.
3. Glyph for water. Paris 16.
4. Glyph of Lahun-Chan. Chichen 34.
5. Picture of water decorated with jade disks. Dresden 36c.
6. Serpent with jade disks on body and head of God B. Dresden 35b.
7. Xolotl, the canine deity, with symbols of death. Greenstone idol in Stuttgart Museum.
8. Dog playing drum. Madrid 37a.
9. Dog with tips of ears missing. Dresden 13c.
10. Glyph for dog. Dresden 13c.
11. So-called glyph of God C, "the black craftsman, the black creator." Dresden 29c.
12. God C. Dresden 5a.
13. God C in celestial band. Madrid 25.
14. Eb glyph set in deluge. Dresden 74.
15. Ear of jaguar used as day Ocelotl and jagged ear of dog as day Itzcuintli. Fejervary-Mayer 39, 15.
16a. Glyph of old goddess. "The red weaver, craftswoman." Dresden 69, E3.
16b. Glyph of old goddess. "The red goddess." Dresden 39b.
16c. Glyph of old goddess. "The red goddess." Dresden 74.
16d. Glyph of old goddess. "The weaver, the craftswoman." Madrid 102d.
17. Goddess Ilamatecutli-Ciuacoatl. Bourbon 28.
18. Goddess I. Dresden 18b.
19. Caban (earth) with plant growing from it. Madrid 24a.
20. Caban (earth) with maize god seated on it. Madrid 24d.
21. God B seated on terrestrial monster with Caban signs. Dresden 30a.
22. Glyph for bee. Madrid 105b.
23. Glyph of Goddess I. Dresden 18b.
24. Glyph of Goddess I. Dresden 16c.
25. Part of terrestrial monster with Caban signs. Pal. Sun.

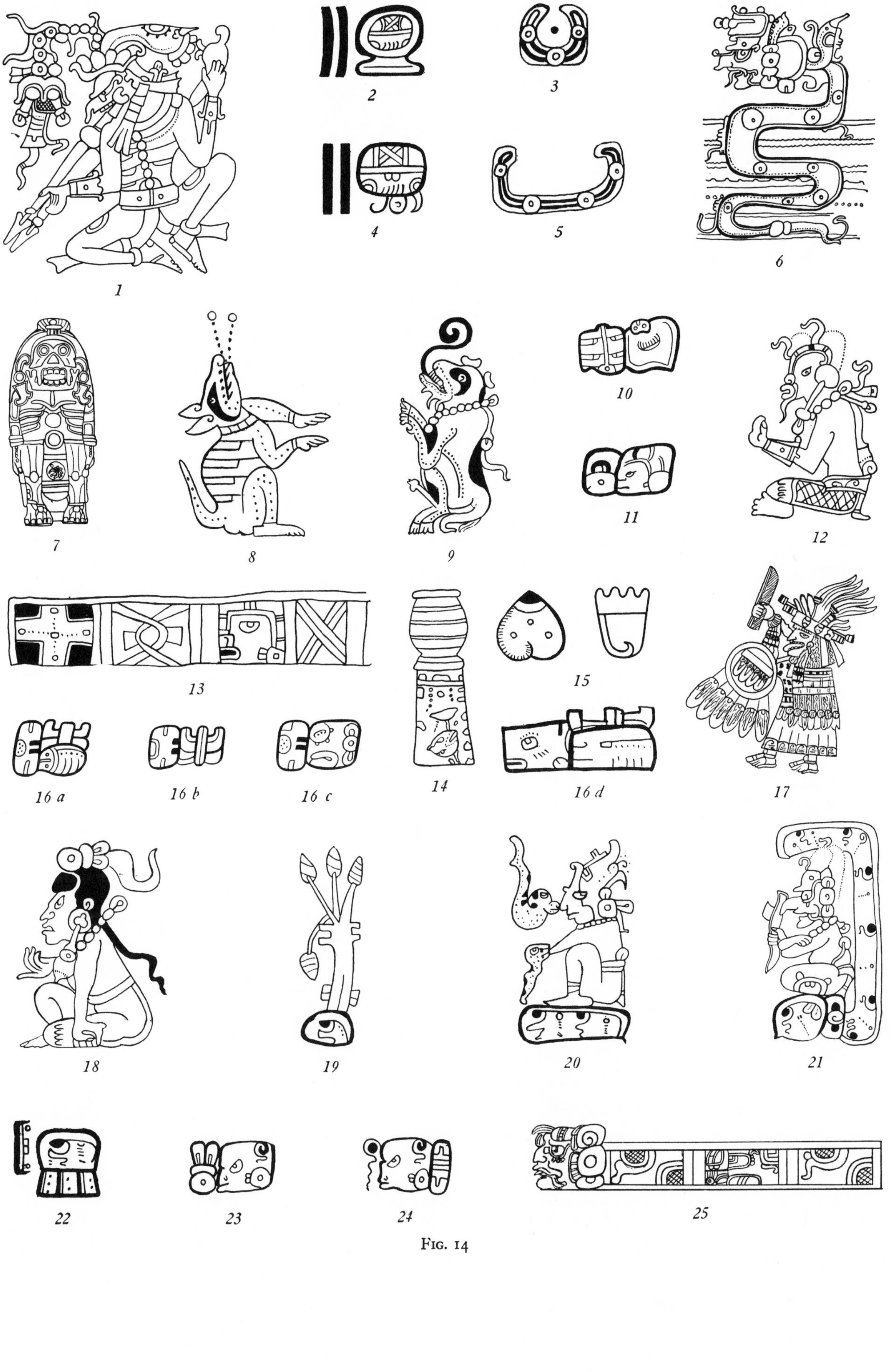
1
2
3
4
5
6
7
8
9
10
11
12
13
14
15
16 a
16 b
16 c
16 d
17
18
19
20
21
22
23
24
25

Fig. 14

Fig. 15—DERIVATIONS OF DAY SIGNS: ETZ'NAB TO AHAU

1. God Q. Madrid 27d.
2. God Q. Madrid 86c.
3. God Q at human sacrifice. Madrid 76.
4. God R. Dresden 5b.
5. God R. Madrid 107b.
6. Glyph of God Q. Madrid 38c.
7. Glyph of God Q. Madrid 86b.
8. Head of Xipe. Vatican A 43.
9. Glyph of God R. Dresden 5b.
10. Glyph of God R. Madrid 112c.
11. Face of celestial dragon with cauac symbols. Quir. P. After Maudslay.
12. Celestial dragon with cauac symbols. Cop. Alt. M. After Spinden.
13. Foreleg of celestial dragon. Pal. Cross. After Maudslay.
14. God B seated on conventionalized head of God D. Dresden 41a.
15. Sun god. Dresden 26b.
16. Sun god. Cop. A.

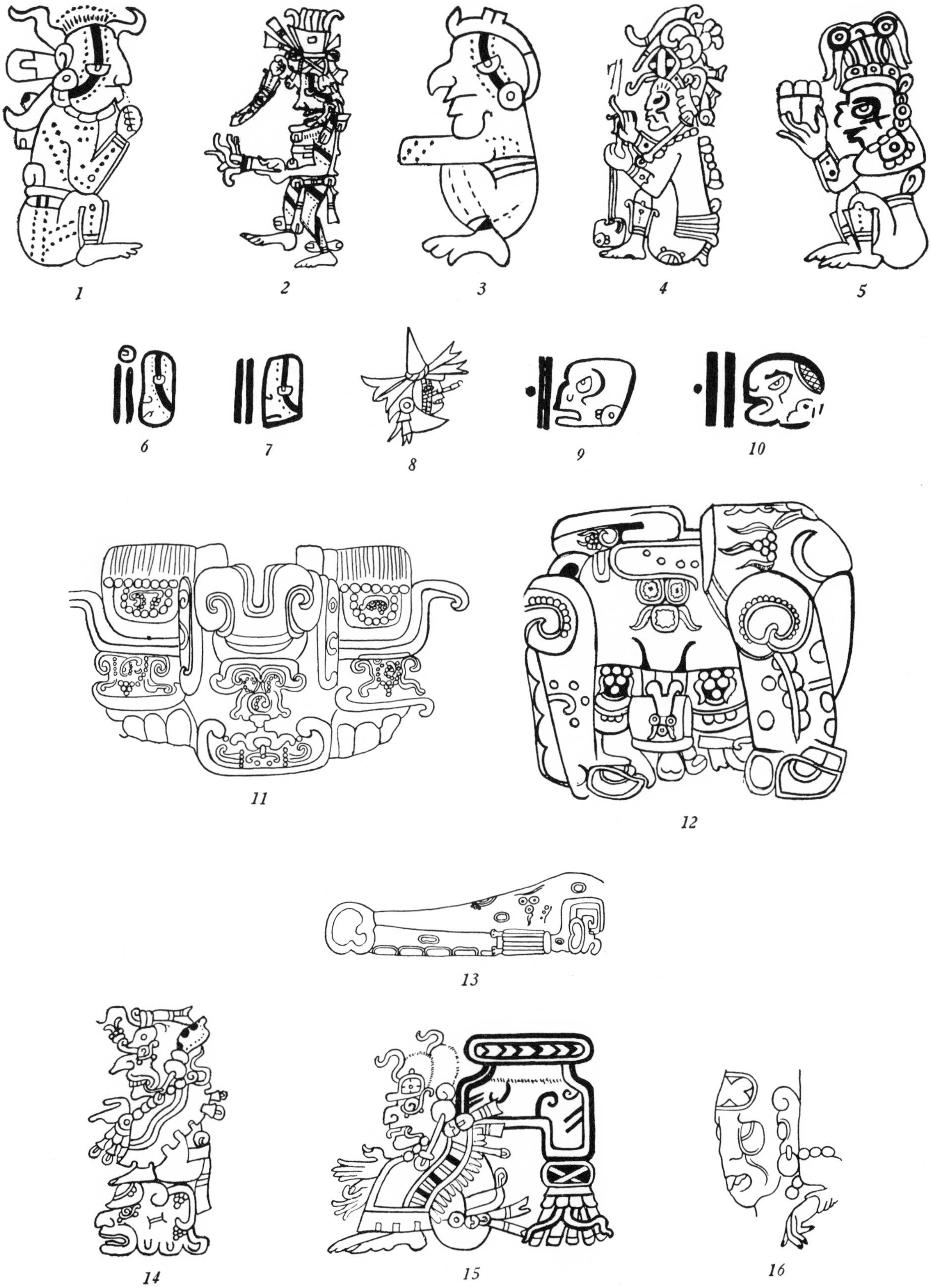

FIG. 15

FIG. 16—MONTH SIGNS: POP TO XUL

POP:
1. P.N. L 12, K1.
2. Pal. House A, pier, D3.
3. Pal. 1, B9.
4. Tik. T 4, L 2, A4.
5. Tik. T 4, L 2, H1.
6. Cop. HS, Q, A.
7. Yula 2, H2.
8. Dresden 70d.
9. Landa.

Uo:
10. Pal. House A, B2.
11. Tila C, A6.
12. P.N. 3, C6.
13. Ton. 7, C2.
14. Yax. L 31, I4.
15. Pal. 96 Gl., G2.
16. Nar. 12, B9b.
17. Hatz. Ceel 1, B1.
18. Chichen 16, B1.
19. Dresden 62d.
20. Dresden 49c.
21. Dresden 48c.
22. Landa.

ZIP:
23. Yax. L 10, A2a.
24. Nar. HS, P1b.
25. Pal. Inscr. (W), H11.
26. Yax. L 56, G1.
27. Quir. F, D8.
28. Cop. Review Stand, B1.
29. Cop. T 11, E door, N panel, B3.
30. Tila A, B5.
31. Uax. IS Vase.
32. Dresden 48a.

33. Dresden 62c.
34. Landa.

ZOTZ':
35. Chinkul. ball court.
36. Cop. 6, B6.
37. Pal. Cross, R13.
38. Yax. L 54, B1.
39. Yax. L 3, C1.
40. Quir. J, B15.
41. Nar. 32, Z1.
42. Dresden 47a.
43. Dresden 46b.
44. Landa.

ZEC:
45. Pal. House A, Pier A.
46. Yax. L 41, B1.
47. Yax. 12, D1.
48. Cop. HS (Gordon, pl. 13q).
49. Cop. HS, Step Sn.
50. Quir. J, G3.
51. Yax. L 30, G5.
52. Dresden 46c.
53. Landa.

XUL:
54. P.N. 39, B1b.
55. Pal. Madrid Tablet 2, B1.
56. Pal. Sun, F1.
57. Tik. Alt 5, Gl 11.
58. Pal. 96 Gl., C5.
59. Quir. Str 1, B'1.
60. Palmar 14, A2.
61. Dresden 63b.
62. Dresden 49c.
63. Dresden 46d.
64. Landa.

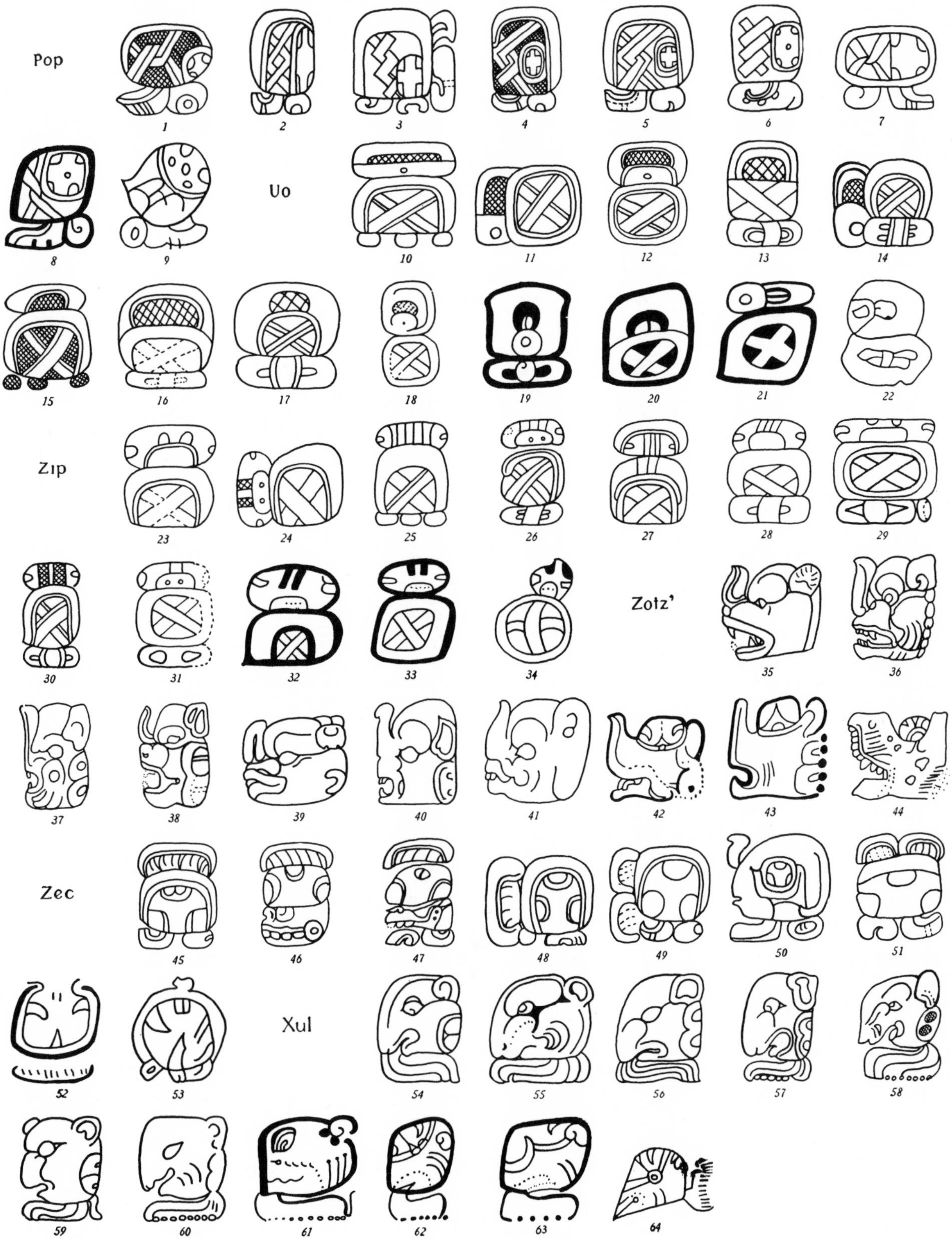
Pop
1
2
3
4
5
6
7
8
9
Uo
10
11
12
13
14
15
16
17
18
19
20
21
22
Zip
23
24
25
26
27
28
29
30
31
32
33
34
Zotz'
35
36
37
38
39
40
41
42
43
44
Zec
45
46
47
48
49
50
51
52
53
Xul
54
55
56
57
58
59
60
61
62
63
64

Fig. 16

Fig. 17—MONTH SIGNS: YAXKIN TO CEH

YAXKIN:
1. Yax. L 37, S6b.
2. Cop. 10, A9.
3. Pusil. K, D11.
4. Nar. 23, E18.
5. Tik. 5, C4.
6. Cop. HS, Date 26.
7. El Cayo, L 1, F3.
8. Quir. D, A17b.
9. P.N. Thr 1, J'2.
10. Cop. Q, B1.
11. Dresden 60b.
12. Dresden 70b.
13. Landa.

MOL:
14. P.N. 36, C8.
15. Pal. Fol. Cross, M1.
16. Yax. L 14, E1.
17. Tik. T 4, L 2, B1.
18. Cop. T, front.
19. Ton. 20, C4.
20. Quir. Str 1, V.
21. Dresden 47b.
22. Landa.

CH'EN:
23. Pal. Inscr. (W), L11.
24. Pal. HS, C4a, l.h.
25. Yax. L 25, N2.
26. Cop. D, A5.
27. Tik. T 4, L 2, H3.
28. Tik. T 4, L 3, F2.
29. P.N. L 3, E2.
30. Sacchana 2, A5.
31. Chichen 20, Gl 29.
32. Dresden 47c.
33. Landa.

YAX:
34. Uax. 26, B6.
35. P.N. L 12, G1.
36. Pal. Inscr. (W), T5b.
37. La Florida 9, C4.
38. P.N. Alt 2, G2.
39. Yax. L 27, B1.
40. Yax. L 30, G1.
41. Quir. F, A17b.
42. Comitan 1, B2.
43. Chichen 5, B2.
44. Chichen 23, Bl 18.
45. Dresden 46d.
46. Dresden 48a.
47. Landa.

ZAC:
48. Nar. 22, F15.
49. Calak. 89, B6b.
50. Cop. 4. A6b.
51. Cop. altar from river, D1.
52. P.N. 12, B16.
53. Chichen 1, A6.
54. Dresden 46a.
55. Landa.

CEH:
56. P.N. L 2, G1.
57. Cop. 2, C6.
58. Pal. Inscr. (W), R1b.
59. Pal. 96 Gl., B1.
60. Quir. Alt P, H2a, l.h.
61. P.N. 12, B11.
62. Quir. Str 1, A"b.
63. Dresden 49b.
64. Dresden 45a.
65. Landa.

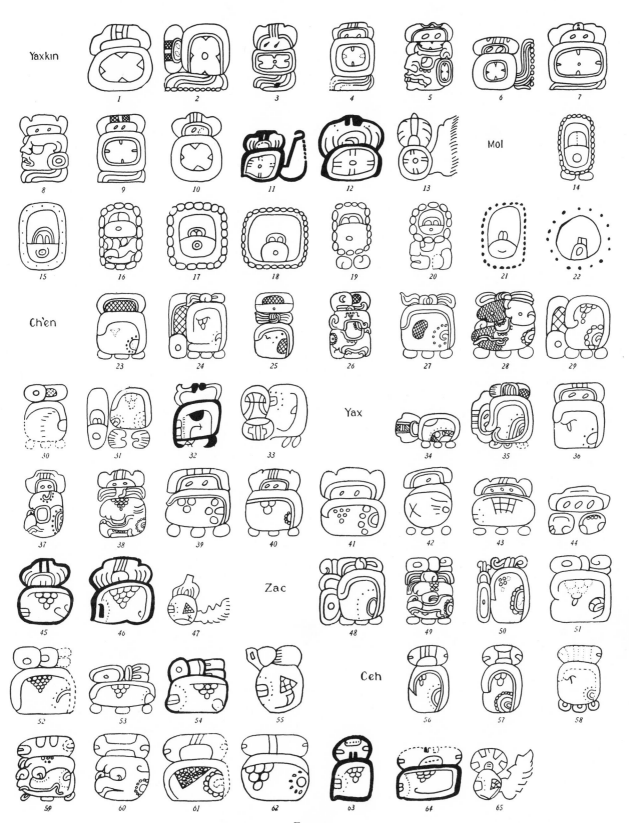

Yaxkin

Mol

Ch'en

Yax

Zac

Ceh

Fig. 17

FIG. 18—MONTH SIGNS: MAC TO KAYAB

MAC:
1. P.N. 25, A8.
2. Pusil. D, G10.
3. Pal. Inscr. (E), N7.
4. Pal. Fol. Cross, C15.
5. Tik. Alt 5, Gl 25.
6. Palmar 8, A2.
7. Yax. L 25, F1a.
8. Yax. L 24, Y1a.
9. Yax. L 43, B1.
10. P.N. 16, D4b.
11. Pal. 96 Gl., A7.
12. Nar. 14, A2.
13. Aguas Cal. 1, E10.
14. Cop. W, B.
15. Cop. I″, B1.
16. Yaxha 13, A2.
17. Dresden 49c.
18. Dresden 49d.
19. Dresden 48c.
20. Landa.

KANKIN:
21. Cop. X, B1.
22. Nar. HS, V1b.
23. Pal. Sun, H2.
24. Chinik. Thr B1.
25. P.N. Alt 2, D2.
26. P.N. Alt 2, B1.
27. Seib. HS, K1a.
28. Uxmal Monjas, Capstone 1, B1.
29. Dresden 50a.
30. Landa.

MUAN:
31. Yax. L 35, X4.
32. Nar. 22, F17.

33. Nar. 23, H17.
34. Tik. Alt 5, Gl 2.
35. Mor. 2, D9.
36. Cop. A, C2b.
37. Pal. 96 Gl., L2.
38. P.N. Thr 1, K′1b.
39. Quir. G, N1.
40. Kabah jamb, B1.
41. Chichen 23, Bl 16.
42. Dresden 48b.
43. Dresden 48a.
44. Dresden 47b.
45. Landa.

PAX:
46. Pal Palace, House C.
47. Yax. 21, F4.
48. Nar. 13, F9.
49. Pal. 96 Gl., G8.
50. P.N. L 3, U5.
51. Dresden 46c.
52. Landa.

KAYAB:
53. Nar. HS, V1b.
54. Pal. Tablet 2, D2.
55. Pal. Cross, S17.
56. Cop. C, A3.
57. Cop. ball court.
58. Quir. F, B18a.
59. Quir. K, A7a.
60. Flores 2, B1.
61. Ucanal 4, B1.
62. Dresden 61b.
63. Dresden 62d.
64. Landa.

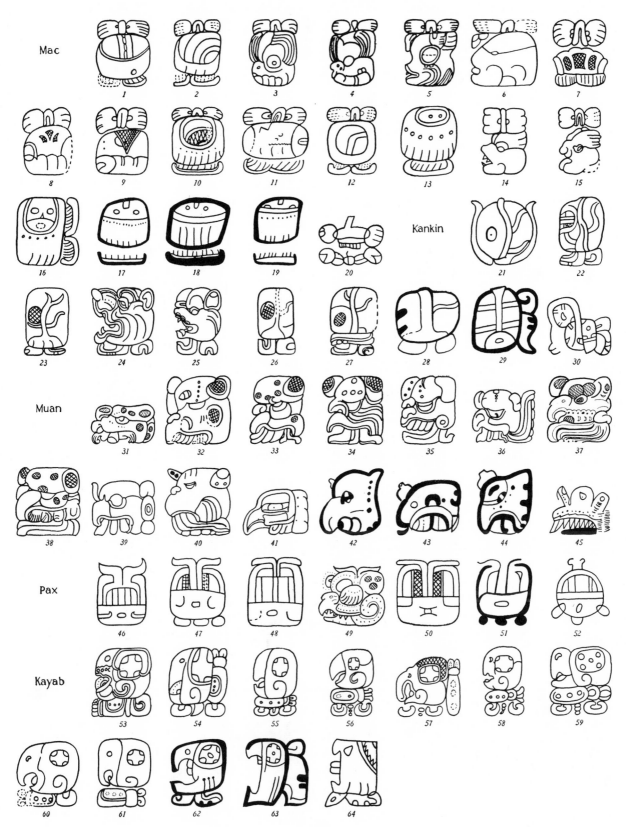

Mac

Kankin

Muan

Pax

Kayab

Fig. 18

CUMKU:
1. Balak. 5, D2.
2. Cop. 3 (W), A7a, l.h.
3. P.N. 35, B10.
4. Pal. Cross, C4.
5. Nar. 24, D16.
6. Quir. E, A17b.
7. Cop. T 11, S door, E panel.
8. Cop. Review Stand, R1.
9. Cop. G3, B2.
10. Tila A, B7.
11. Chichen 27, B1.
12. Dresden 63b.
13. Dresden 69d.
14. Dresden 58e.
15. Dresden 62e.
16. Landa.

UAYEB:
17. Pal. Inscr. (E), E5.
18. Pal. Inscr. (W), Q4.
19. Pal. Fol. Cross, D8.
20. Dresden 50b.

ENDS OF MONTHS:
21. 13 Ik, End Mol. Pal. Cross, C9–D9.
22. 1 Caban, End Yaxkin. P.N. shell, K2.
23. 1 Eb, End Yaxkin. Yax. L 9, A1–A3.
24. 13 Manik, End Yaxkin. Pal. House C, G1.
25. 9 Eb, End Yaxkin. Nar. 19, C1–C3.
26. 8 Manik, End Ceh. P.N. MSS 16, A1–B1.
27. 2 Eb, End Uayeb. Nar. HS, A1.

SEATINGS:
28. Seating of Zac. Pal. House E.
29. Seating of Pop. Pal. Cross, P3.
30. Tik. T 4, L 2, A4.
31. Seating of Kayab. Nar. 29, I7.
32. Seating of Zac. P.N. 12, B20a.
33. Seating of Zotz'. Pal. Cross, R13.
34. Seating of Pop. Cop. U, B1.
35. Seating of Zac. Pal. Cross, F9.
36. Seating of Uayeb. Dresden 50.
37. Seating of haab. Chinik. Thr 1, C1.
38. Seating of haab. Pal. Inscr. (W), E9.
39. Seating of haab. Pal. Inscr. (W), B9.
40. Forward from Seating of haab, Pal. Inscr. (W), H8.
41. Its Seating of haab. Pal. Inscr. (M), B1.
42. Indicator, Count to Seating of haab. Pal. Inscr. (E), L3.
43. Indicator, Count to Seating of haab. Pal. Inscr. (E), L10.
44. Indicator, Count to Seating of haab. Pal. Inscr. (E), G6.
45. Seating of haab. Cop. T 11, step, P1.
46. Indicator, Seating day. Pal. Fol. Cross, N7.
47. Indicator, Seating day. Pal. Inscr. (W), R8.
48. Indicator, Seating day. Pal. Inscr. (W), T7.
49. Indicator, Seating day. Tik. T 4, L 2, L9.
50. Indicator, Seating day. Pal. Sun, A14.
51. Seating of haab. Cop. U, O4.

Cumku

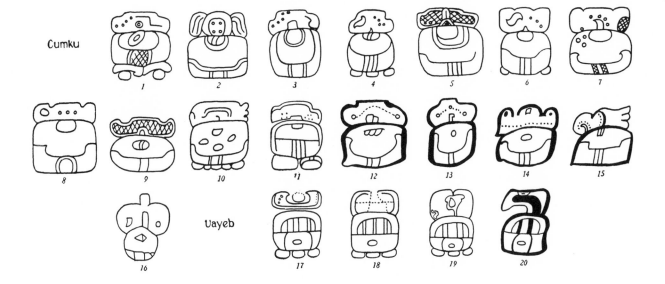

Uayeb

Fig. 19

Fig. 20—SYMBOL FOR BLACK AND THE ASSOCIATIONS OF
THE MOAN BIRD AND SPIRAL WITH WATER

BLACK:
1. Glyph for black. Dresden 30b.
2. Glyph for black. Dresden 53b.
3. Glyph for misery with black infix. Dresden 6c.
4. Glyph of death god with black infix. Dresden 20b.
5. Glyph of death god with black infix. Dresden 28a.
6. Glyph of death god without black markings. Dresden 13b.
7. Glyph for misery without black markings. Dresden 73b.
8. Moon glyph with black infix outlined with crosshatching. Pal.
   Cross, B13.
9. Moon glyph without black outlining. Quir. A, A7.

MOAN BIRD AS CELESTIAL BIRD OF RAIN:
10. Moan bird above celestial dragon. Tik. T 4.
11. Moan bird on celestial dragon with planetary symbols. Pal.
    House E.
12. Moan bird. Yax. 4.
13. Moan bird with vegetation on head and spiral in eye. Dresden
    10a.
14. Moan bird with maize sprouting from Kan glyph on head and
    spiral in eye. Dresden 11a.
15. Planetary band with bird's head, probably of the Moan, at ends.
    Nar. 32.
16. God B with spiral in eye. Dresden 29b.
17. Moan bird perched on planetary band. Cop. H.
18. Spiral variant of month glyph Muan. Dresden 46c.
19. Glyphs of Moan bird. Dresden 16c.
20. Glyphs of Moan bird. Dresden 18b.
21. God D holding spiral. Dresden 4c.
22. Glyph associated with God D holding spiral. Dresden 4c.
23. Glyph for Moan bird. Dresden 8b.
24. Glyph for 13 layers of heaven above picture of Moan bird.
    Dresden 7c.

GLYPHS WITH SPIRALS:
25. Glyph of hand with spiral. Tik. 17, H5.
26. Glyph of hand with spiral. Pal. Inscr. (W), O11.
27. Spiral glyph. Nar. 8, B1.
28. Spiral glyph. Nar. 13, H4.
29. Cauac "storm" glyph with spiral infix. Madrid 34.
30. Glyph 9 spiral associated with God B as lord of the storage
    tank of rain. Dresden 35b.
31. Glyph for Atezcahuacan. Tribute roll, pl. 44.
32. Glyph of Anencquilco. Tribute roll, pl. 26.
33. Glyph for Atzacan. Tribute roll, pl. 18.
34. Glyph for Acozpa. Tribute roll, pl. 51.
35. Long-nosed god with spiral in eye. Cop. D.

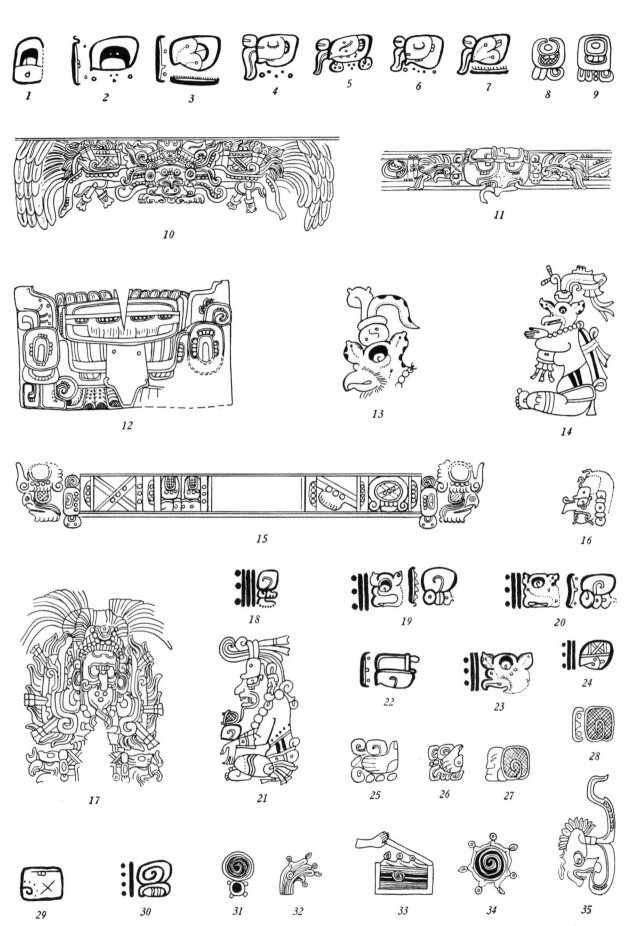

FIG. 20

Fig. 21—OLD EARTH GOD AND OTHER DEITIES ASSO-
CIATED WITH THE CONCH SHELL

1. God N with tun headdress. Dresden 48a.
2. God N with tun headdress. Paris 4b and D3. Glyph of God N.
   Dresden 21c.
3. God N seated in conch and wearing maize headdress and
   associated glyph. Dresden 41b.
4. Old god wearing conch. On pottery vessel, Alta Verapaz. After
   Dieseldorff.
5. Old god wearing deer headdress seated in conch. Design on
   gold disk from cenote, Chichen. (Courtesy of Peabody Museum,
   Harvard University.)
6. Old god wearing conch. On pottery vessel, Alta Verapaz. After
   Dieseldorff.
7. Old god emerging from conch. On pottery vessel, Alta Verapaz.
   After Dieseldorff.
8. Earth deity emerging from conch and holding maize stalk.
   Pal. Cross.
9. Tepeyollotl, as lord of night, before temple in which reposes
   conch shell. Vatican B 22.
10. Tecciztecatl, "He of the conch," regent of week 1 Miquiztli.
    Seated on symbol of night with conch shell before him. Aubin
    Tonalamatl 6.
11. Conch shell and eye of darkness before Tepeyollotl and Xolotl
    as regents of week 1 Mazatl. Bourbon 6.
12. Conch and darkness symbols associated with regent of week 1
    Miquiztli. Bourbon 6.
13. Tepeyollotl, the jaguar god of the interior of the earth, as
    regent of week 1 Mazatl. Conch and what may be eye of dark-
    ness before his face. Aubin Tonalamatl 3.
14. Shell group of symbols worn by long-nosed god. Pal. Cross.
15. Shell group of symbols worn by long-nosed god. Pal. Palace,
    House E.
16. Shell group of symbols worn by long-nosed god. Pal. Palace,
    House A.
17. Shell group of symbols worn by long-nosed god. Cop. 1.
18. Glyph of shell and kin elements. Pal. Inscr. (M), J8, D5.

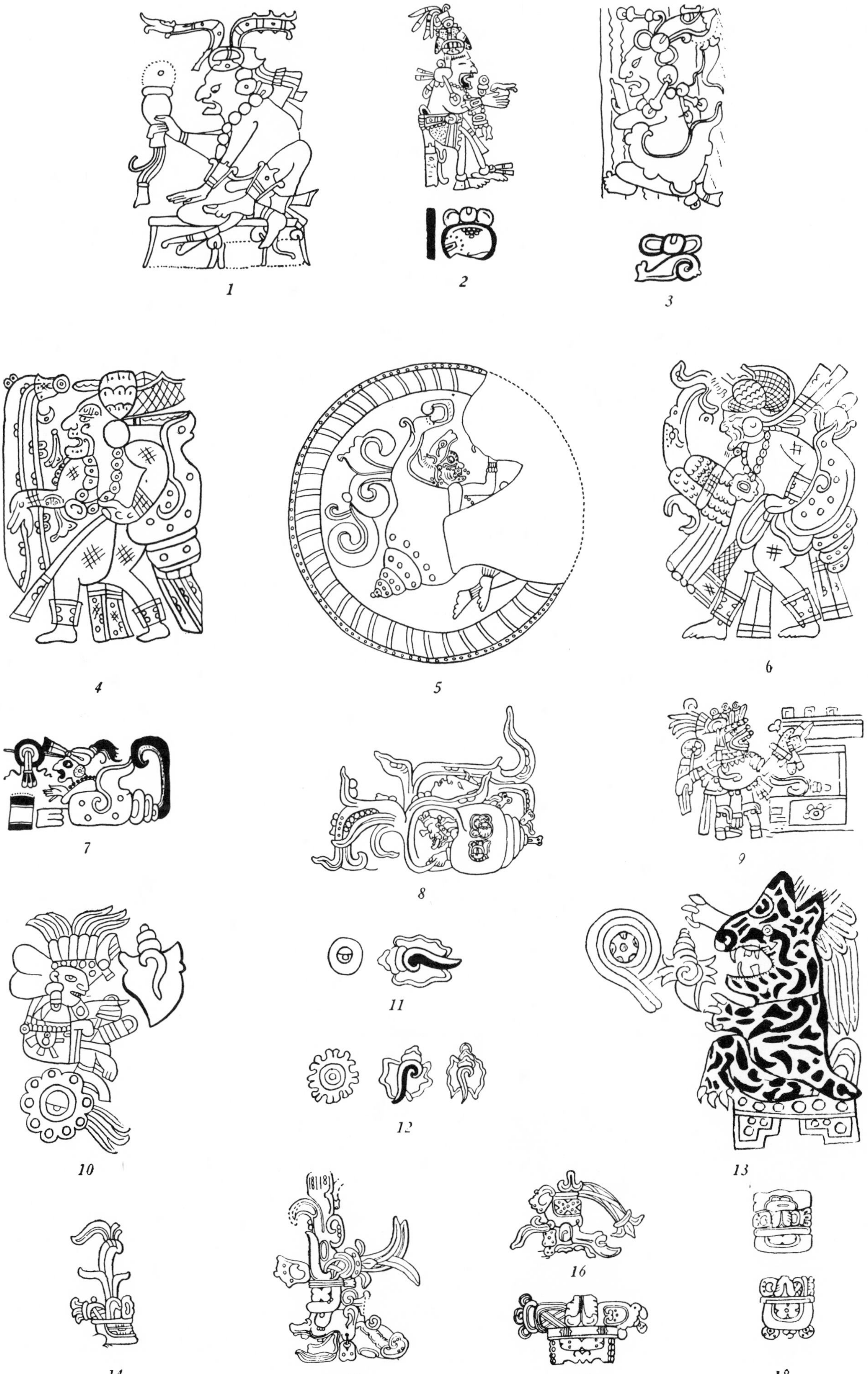
1
2
3
4
5
6
7
8
9
10
11
12
13
14
15
16
17
18

Fig. 21

FIG. 22—INITIAL SERIES INTRODUCTORY GLYPHS:
VARIABLE ELEMENTS POP TO YAX

POP:
1. Pal. HS.
2. Cop. P.
3. Cop. P.
4. Pal. Olvidado.
5. Yax. Str 44.
6. P.N. 16.
7. Quir. D.

Uo:
8. Cop. I.
9. Cop. I'.
10. Tila C.

ZIP:
11. P.N. 36.
12. Yax. L. 26.
13. Yax. 1.
14. Quir. F.
15. Cop. N.
16. Tila A.

ZOTZ':
17. P.N. 29.
18. Cop. 7
19. Cop. 7
20. Cop. 1.
21. Cop. 6.
22. Quir. J.

ZEC:
23. P.N. L 12.
24. Pal. Cross.
25. Mor. 2.
26. Yax. 11.
27. Quir. H.
28. Los Higos 1.

XUL:
29. P.N. 39.

YAXKIN:
30. Leiden Plaque.
31. Cop. 16.
32. Cop. 23.
33. Pusil. K.
34. P.N. 3.
35. Cop. HS, Date 26.
36. Quir. D (W).
37. Quir. C (W).

MOL:
38. Cop. 15.
39. Uxul 2.
40. P.N. 10.
41. El Cayo, L 1.
42. Quir. Str 1.
43. Uax. 7, left.

CH'EN:
44. Cop. 17.
45. Ichpatun 1.
46. Alt. de Sac. 6.
47. Cop. D.
48. P.N. L 3.
49. Sacchana 2.

YAX:
50. Uax. 26.
51. Pusil. E.
52. Nar. 24.
53. Cop. B.
54. Cop. S.
55. Cop. HS, Date 24 (perhaps Yaxkin).
56. Yax. L 21.
57. Yax. L 29.
58. Quir. K.
59. Sacchana 1.

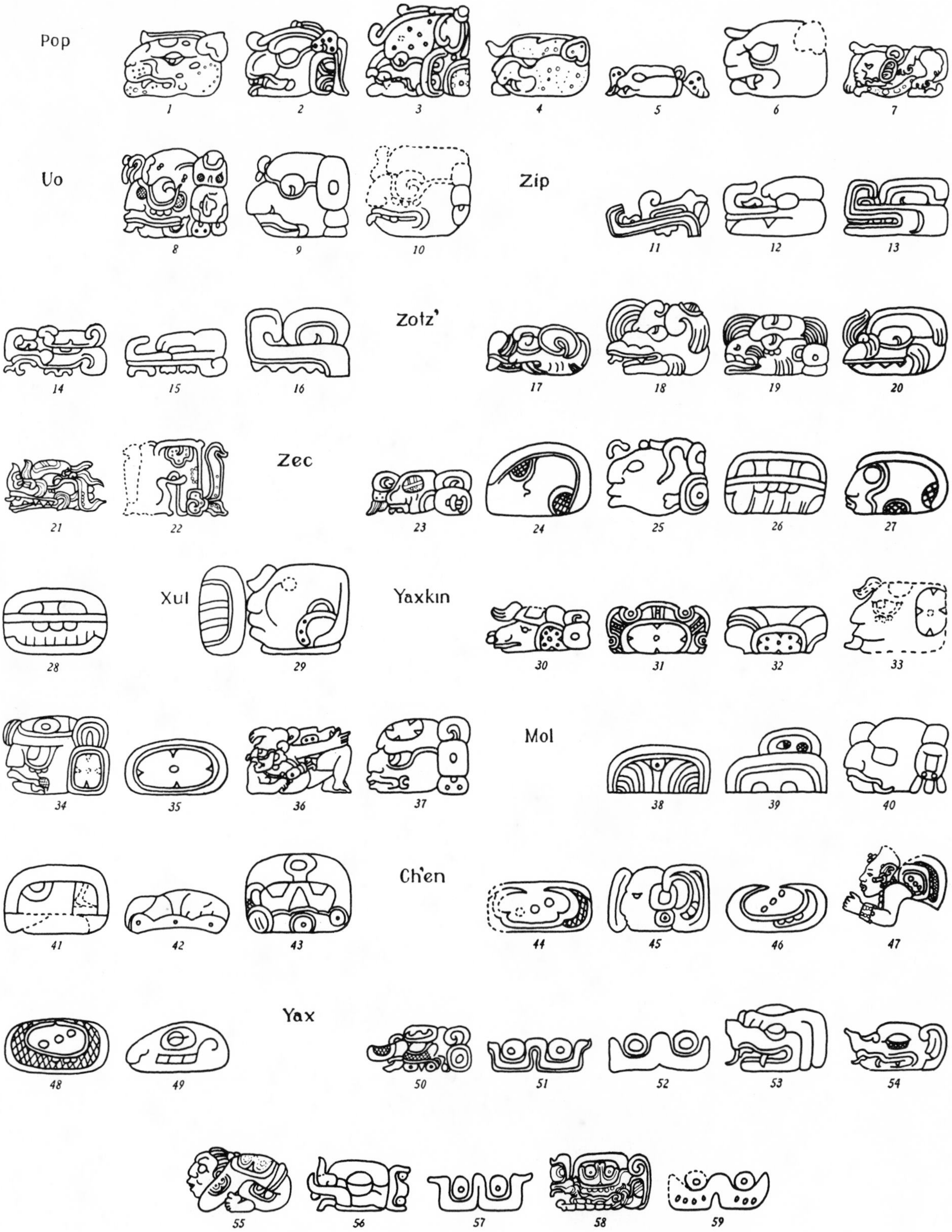
Pop
1 2 3 4 5 6 7
Uo
8 9 10
Zip
11 12 13
14 15 16
Zotz'
17 18 19 20
21 22
Zec
23 24 25 26 27
28
Xul
29
Yaxkin
30 31 32 33
34 35 36 37
Mol
38 39 40
41 42 43
Ch'en
44 45 46 47
48 49
Yax
50 51 52 53 54
55 56 57 58 59

FIG. 22

FIG. 23—INITIAL SERIES INTRODUCTORY GLYPHS:
VARIABLE ELEMENTS ZAC TO CUMKU AND EXAMPLES
OF COMPLETE GLYPHS

ZAC:
  1. P.N. 23.
  2. Quir. I.
  3. Chichen 1.

CEH:
  4. P.N. L 2.
  5. Pal. Sun.
  6. Quir. P.
  7. Quir. Alt P.

MAC:
  8. Pal. Fol. Cross.
  9. Cop. 2.

KANKIN:
  10. Nar. HS.
  11. Pusil. P.
  12. Xcal. IS.
  13. Quir. Alt O.
  14. Uax. IS Vase.

MUAN:
  15. Tik. 10, A6. (?)
  16. P.N. 3.
  17. Quir. G.

PAX:
  18. Yax. L 48.
  19. Cop. 9.
  20. Quir. B.

KAYAB:
  21. Cop. 3 (E).
  22. Cop. 5.
  23. Cop. C (W).
  24. Quir. F (W).
  25. Quir. E (W).
  26. Quir. A (E).
  27. Ixkun 2.

CUMKU:
  28. Cop. 3 (W).
  29. Cop. A.
  30. Cop. C (E).
  31. Quir. E (E).
  32. Quir. C (E).

COMPLETE GLYPHS:
  33. Yaxkin. Leiden Plaque.
  34. Pax. Oxkin. L 1.
  35. Zec? Cop. 21.
  36. Pax? Pal. stucco in Madrid.
  37. Ch'en. Cop. D.
  38. Yaxkin. Cop. HS, Date 26.
  39. Ch'en. P.N. L 3.
  40. Ch'en. Sacchana 2.

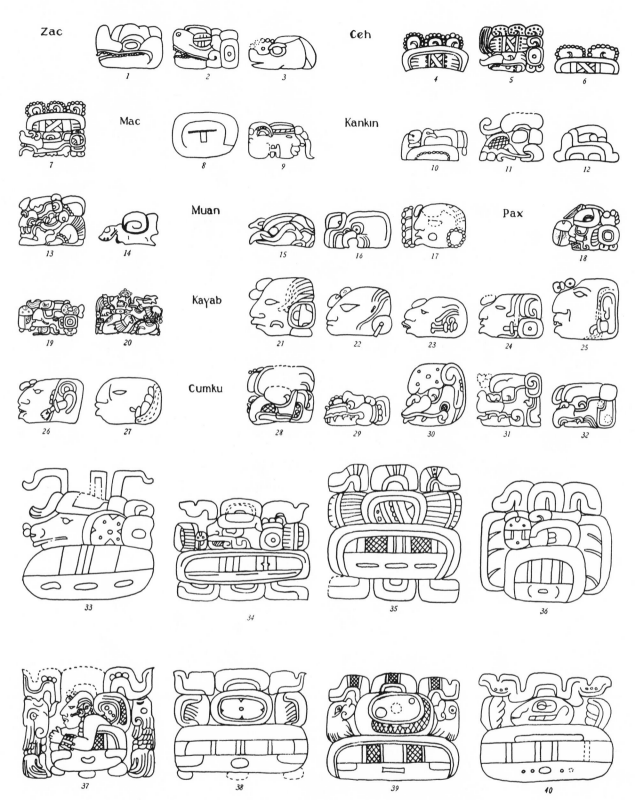

Zac

Ceh

Mac

Kankin

Muan

Pax

Kayab

Cumku

Fig. 23

FIG. 24—HEADS FOR NUMBERS 1 THROUGH 10

ONE:
1. Pal. Madrid stucco.
2. Pal. Sun, A3.
3. Pal. Fol. Cross, A8.
4. Quir. F, D5a.
5. P.N. Thr, G'2.
6. P.N. Thr screen, B1.
7. Pal. 96 Gl., H6.

TWO:
8. P.N. L 2, A9–A10.
9. Pal. Inscr. Pier A.
10. Pal. 96 Gl., E8.
11. Pal. 96 Gl., F8.

THREE:
12. Pal. Sun, A6.
13. Pal. Inscr. (E), Q3.
14. Pal. Olvidado.
15. Pal. Olvidado.
16. Quir. F, D8a.
17. Chichen 23, Band 18.

FOUR:
18. Yax. L 48, A3.
19. Cop. 15, A4.
20. Pal. Fol. Cross, A6.
21. Pal. Cross, A6.
22. Pal. Madrid stucco.
23. Quir. F, B4a.
24. Quir. Alt P, F1a.
25. Halakal 1, F1.

FIVE:
26. Pal. Tab. 1, C3.
27. Pal. Tab. 1, B2.
28. Cop. I, B5.
29. Quir. J, A8.
30. Pal. 96 Gl., D4.
31. P.N. 15, front.

SIX:
32. P.N. L 2, A7–A8.
33. Pal. Inscr., Pier A.
34. Pal. Tab. 1, B3.
35. Pal. Olvidado.
36. Quir. A, B5a.
37. Pal. 96 Gl., C5.

SEVEN:
38. P.N. 4, A7.
39. Pal. 96 Gl., H7.
40. P.N. Thr, I'2.
41. Quir. D, C13–C14.

EIGHT:
42. Yax. L 48, B1.
43. Pal. Cross, A8.
44. Pal. HS, A2.
45. Quir. J, A11.
46. Cop. C, B7b.
47. Cop. T 11, S door, W panel.
48. Pal. 96 Gl., B1.
49. Pal. 96 Gl., C3.

NINE:
50. Yax. L 48, A2.
51. Cop. drain cover.
52. P.N. L 2, A2.
53. Quir. J, A6.
54. P.N. L 3, A2.
55. Pal. 96 Gl., H1.

TEN:
56. Nar. HS, I2a.
57. Cop. 6, B6a.
58. Cop. I, C6b.
59. Pal. Fol. Cross, A12.
60. Quir. F, C8b.
61. Quir. F, C4a.
62. Quir. A, A9b.

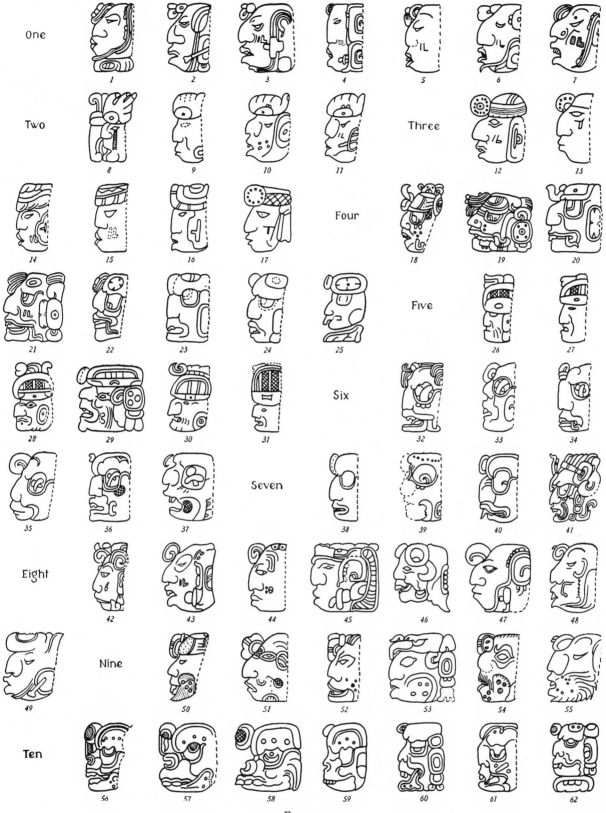

One   1   2   3   4   5   6   7

Two   8   9   10   11   Three   12   13

14   15   16   17   Four   18   19   20

21   22   23   24   25   Five   26   27

28   29   30   31   Six   32   33   34

35   36   37   Seven   38   39   40   41

Eight   42   43   44   45   46   47   48

49   Nine   50   51   52   53   54   55

Ten   56   57   58   59   60   61   62

Fig. 24

Fig. 25—HEADS FOR NUMBERS 11 THROUGH 19 AND FOR COMPLETION,
NUMERICAL HEADS IN CODEX DRESDEN, AND SYMBOLS FOR NUMBERS

ELEVEN:
1. Yax. L 48, A4.
2. P.N. L 2, A5–A6.

TWELVE:
3. Pal. Cross, A3.
4. Tila B, B3.
5. Pal. 96 Gl., A1.
6. Quir. F, B5a.
7. Chichen 3, A1a.

THIRTEEN:
8. Pal. Str 18.
9. Pal. HS, A3.
10. Pal. Sun, A8.
11. Pal. Cross, A5.
12. Tila B, A4.
13. Cop. HS, Qa.
14. Quir. F, A4a.

FOURTEEN:
15. Quir. F, B3a.
16. Quir. Alt O, E2–F2.

FIFTEEN:
17. P.N. 9, B4a.
18. Pal. 96 Gl., G2.
19. Quir. G, E1.
20. Chichen 12, A3.

SIXTEEN:
21. Yax. L 48, B2.
22. Pal. Inscr. (E), T6a.
23. Quir. J, A4.
24. Quir. F, D3a.
25. Quir. Alt O, G1a.

SEVENTEEN:
26. P.N. 14, A5.
27. Quir. F, A5a.
28. Quir. G, C2.

EIGHTEEN:
29. Pal. Cross, A9.
30. Pal. Sun, A4.
31. Quir. Str 1, V.

NINETEEN:
32. Cop. 10, A3a.
33. Cop. 3, B3, u.h.
34. Pal. House A, Pier A.
35. Pal. Cross, A4.
36. Cop. T 11, S door, E panel (reversed).

COMPLETION:
37. Nar. HS, J2a.
38. Nar. HS, K2a.
39. Cop. 1, A5a.
40. Pal. Fol. Cross, A7.
41. Quir. J, A9.
42. Quir. F, C5a.
43. Quir. F, D4a.
44. Quir. Alt P, D2a.
45. Quir. Alt P, E1a.

NUMERICAL HEADS IN DRESDEN:
46. Head for 9. Dresden 70.
47. Head for 18. Dresden 69.
48. Head for 16. Dresden 61.
49. Head for 19. Dresden 61.

SYMBOLS FOR NUMBERS:
50. Thumbs representing 1. Nar. HS, Bl 6, B3b; Quir. F (E), D10.
51. Sign used for 3. Dresden 9b.
52. Kin sign used as 4. Cop. 1, D6a.
53. Bar and three dots with maize foliage, representing 8. Cop. I, C6.
54. Bar and three dots with *te* (3) headdress. Dresden 36b.
55. Completion or zero signs. Pusil. O, B4a; Yax. L 25, K1.
56. Completion or zero signs. Cop. M, A2b; P.N. Thr 1, A'2.
57. Hand and shell as completion sign or zero. Pal. Cross, A7.
58. Hand and shell as completion sign or zero. Quir. A, B4a.
59. Shells as symbols of completion. Dresden 64, 70.
60. Moon as symbol for 20. Dresden 4c.

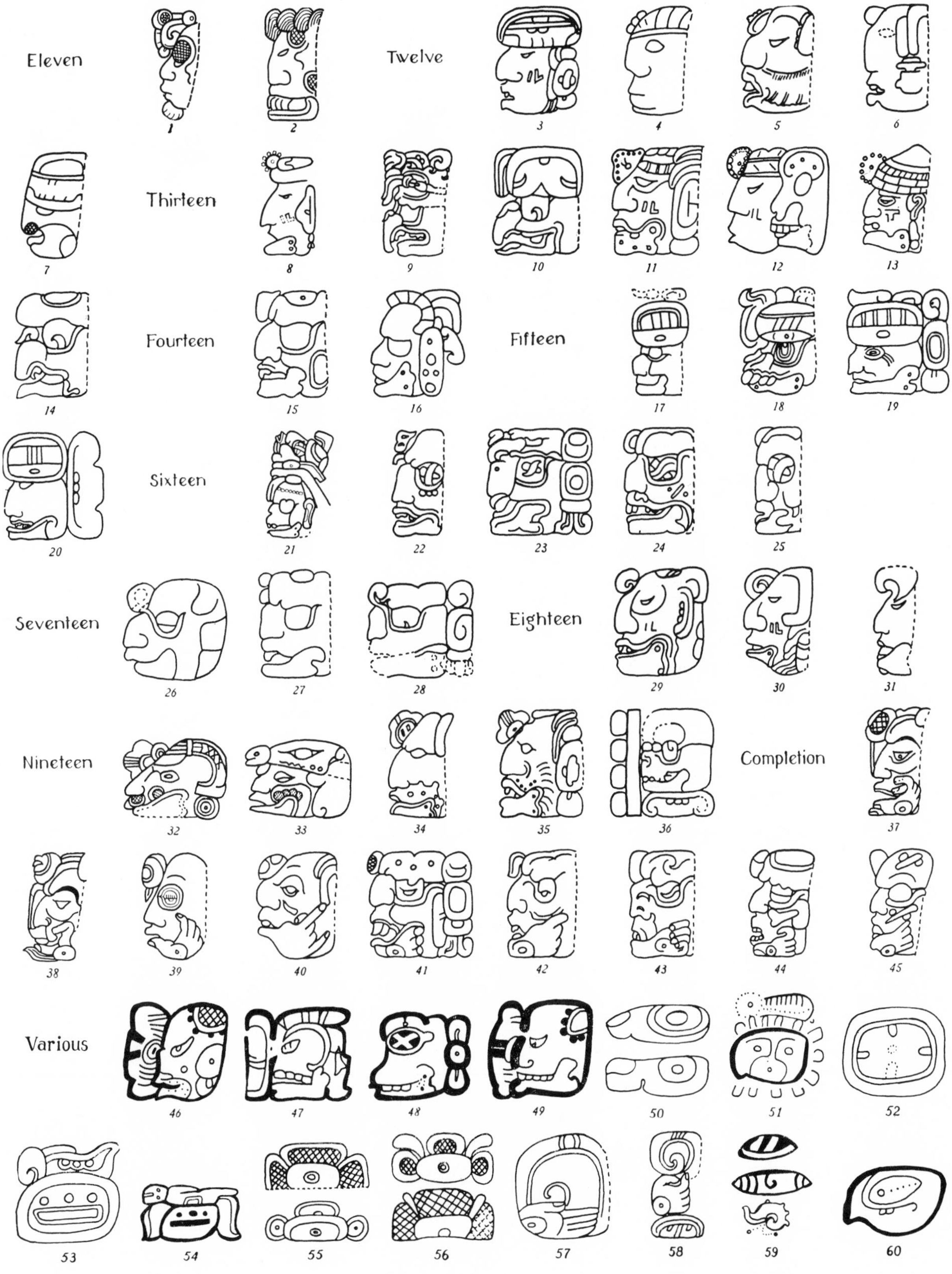

Eleven
1
2
Twelve
3
4
5
6
7
Thirteen
8
9
10
11
12
13
14
Fourteen
15
16
Fifteen
17
18
19
20
Sixteen
21
22
23
24
25
Seventeen
26
27
28
Eighteen
29
30
31
Nineteen
32
33
34
35
36
Completion
37
38
39
40
41
42
43
44
45
Various
46
47
48
49
50
51
52
53
54
55
56
57
58
59
60

Fig. 25

FIG. 26—GEOMETRIC (OR SYMBOLIC) FORMS OF PERIOD GLYPHS

CALABTUN AND KINCHILTUN:
1. Calabtun. Tik. 10, A8.
2. Calabtun. Pal. House E, band.
3. Calabtun. Pal. Inscr. (W), E12.
4. Calabtun. Stone of Chiapa, B3.
5. Calabtun. Cop. C, A2.
6. Calabtun. Cop. C, B2.
7. Kinchiltun. Quir. F, D16a.

PICTUN:
8. Tik. 10, A9.
9. Pal. House E, band.
10. Pal. Inscr. (W), F11.
11. Pal. Inscr. (M), L3.
12. Quir. F, C16b.
13. Dresden 69, center column.
14. Dresden 61, A13.

BAKTUN:
15. Uax. 26, A4.
16. Pal. Inscr. (W), J2.
17. Pal. Cross, B3.
18. Cop. S, H.
19. Cop. T 11, E door, S panel, B5.
20. Quir. O, A1.
21. Quir. I, A3.
22. Hatz. Ceel 2, B1.
23. Uax. IS Vase, A2.

KATUN:
24. Balak. 5, D9.
25. Pal. Cross, B4.
26. Cop. J (W), Gl 24.
27. Yax. L 30, C4.
28. Cop. T 11, E door, S panel, C1.

29. Nar. 13, A2.
30. Pal. 96 Gl., H6.
31. Sacchana 1, B3.
32. Dresden 61, A14.

TUN:
33. Uax. 26, A5.
34. Pal. stucco in Madrid.
35. Nar. 24, D14.
36. Quir. J, E2.
37. P.N. Thr 1, B'2.
38. Cop. U, O2.
39. Nakum C, A5.
40. Dresden 61, B14.

UINAL:
41. Balak. 5, D8.
42. Cop. 26.
43. Pal. Cross, B6.
44. Tila C, B4.
45. Stone of Chiapa, D2.
46. Cop. HS, Date 22.
47. Chichen 1, B4.
48. Dresden 61, A15.

KIN:
49. Uax. 26, A6.
50. Pusil. K, C5.
51. Cop. I, A5b.
52. Pal. Fol. Cross, D17.
53. Cop. M, C2.
54. Quir. O, E1.
55. Quir. P, A3b.
56. Quir. I, A4b.
57. Dresden 61, B15.

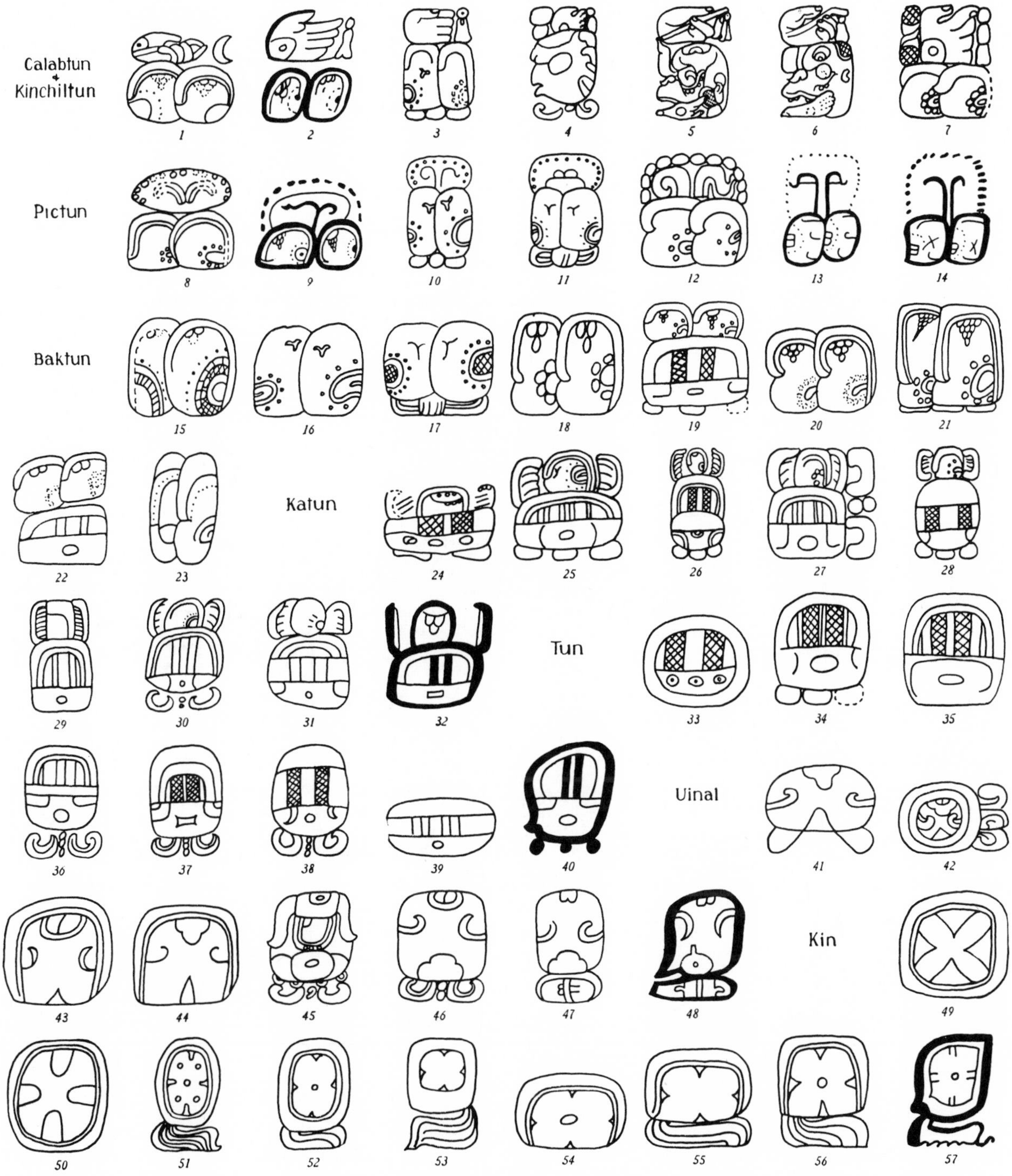
Calabtun
Kinchiltun
Pictun
Baktun
Katun
Tun
Uinal
Kin
1
2
3
4
5
6
7
8
9
10
11
12
13
14
15
16
17
18
19
20
21
22
23
24
25
26
27
28
29
30
31
32
33
34
35
36
37
38
39
40
41
42
43
44
45
46
47
48
49
50
51
52
53
54
55
56
57

Fig. 26

Fig. 27—HEAD (PERSONIFIED) FORMS OF PERIOD GLYPHS

PICTUN:
  1. Chiapa Stone, A3.
  2. Cop. N, B14.

BAKTUN:
  3. Leiden A2.
  4. Oxkin. L 1, A2.
  5. P.N. L 12, A2.
  6. Pusil. O, A3.
  7. Pal. stucco in Paris.
  8. Pal. Olvidado.
  9. Yax. L 56, B1.
  10. P.N. 10, A3.
  11. Cop. HS, Date 25.
  12. Quir. E, A3.
  13. P.N. L 3, B2.
  14. Sacchana 1, A3.

KATUN:
  15. Leiden A3.
  16. Oxkin. L 1, A3.
  17. P.N. L 12, B2.
  18. Pusil. O, B3.
  19. Pal. stucco in Madrid.
  20. Cop. I, B3.
  21. P.N. 1, A3.
  22. Yax. L 56, A2.
  23. Xcal. IS, B4.
  24. Cop. HS, Step K, Db.
  25. Quir. F, B3b.
  26. P.N. L 3, B3.
  27. Chichen 1, B3.

TUN:
  28. Leiden A4.
  29. P.N. L 12, A3.
  30. Yax. L 48, A4.
  31. Pusil. O, A4.
  32. Nar. HS, M3b.

  33. Pal. Inscr., Pier A, 46.
  34. Cop. J (E), A4.
  35. Yax. L 56, B2.
  36. P.N. 10, A4.
  37. Cop. HS, Date 26.
  38. Quir. J, B5.
  39. Sacchana 1, A4.

UINAL:
  40. Leiden A5.
  41. P.N. L 12, B3.
  42. Pusil. O, B4.
  43. Cop. drain cover.
  44. Nar. HS, J2.
  45. Pal. stucco in Madrid.
  46. Yax. L 56, C1.
  47. Mor. 2, B4.
  48. Cop. HS, Step K.
  49. P.N. 14, B5.
  50. Quir. E (W), B4.
  51. Uax. 7, B4.
  52. Sacchana 1, B4 (with unusual zero coefficient).

KIN:
  53. Leiden A6.
  54. P.N. L 12, A4.
  55. Pusil. O, A5.
  56. Cop. drain cover.
  57. Nar. HS, K2.
  58. Yax. L 56, D1.
  59. P.N. 10, A5.
  60. Cop. HS, Date 1.
  61. P.N. 14, B6.
  62. Quir. K, B4b.
  63. Quir. Str 1, K-L.
  64. Uax. IS Vase, B3.
  65. Sacchana 2, A5.
  66. Chichen 1, A5.

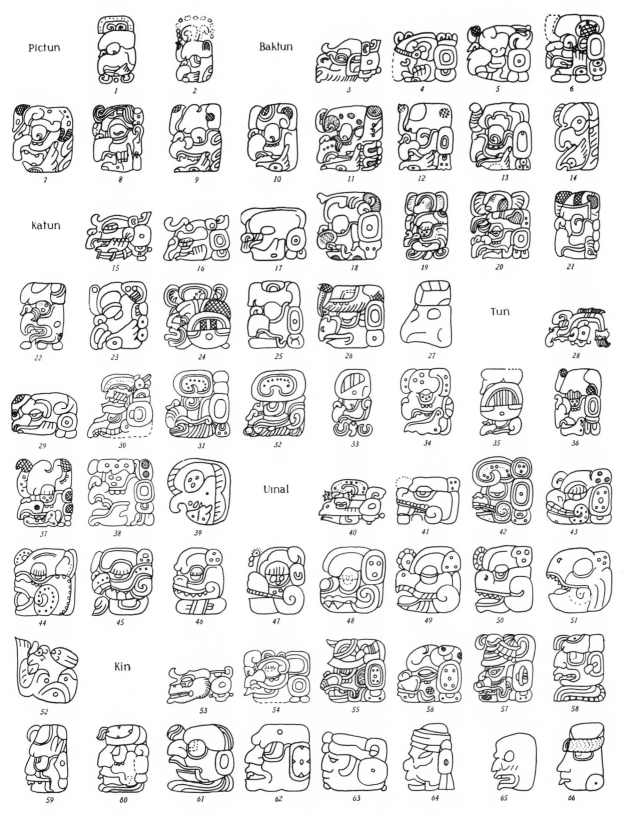

Pictun Baktun katun Tun Uinal Kin

Fig. 27

FIG. 28—FULL-FIGURE GLYPHS OF BAKTUN, KATUN,
AND TUN, AND COEFFICIENTS

1. 9 baktuns. Quir. B.
2. 9 baktuns. Quir. D (E).
3. 9 baktuns. Cop. D.
4. 9 baktuns. Quir. D (W).
5. 9 baktuns. Quir. Alt O.
6. 17 katuns. Quir. B.
7. 16 katuns. Quir. D (E).
8. 15 katuns. Cop. D.
9. 16 katuns. Quir. D (W).
10. 17 katuns. Quir. Alt O.
11. 10 katuns. Cop. HS, Date 24.
12. 10 tuns. Quir. B.
13. 15 tuns. Quir. D (E).
14. 5 tuns. Cop. D.
15. 13 tuns. Quir. D (W).
16. 1 tun. Cop. HS, Date 24.
17. 14 tuns. Quir. Alt O.

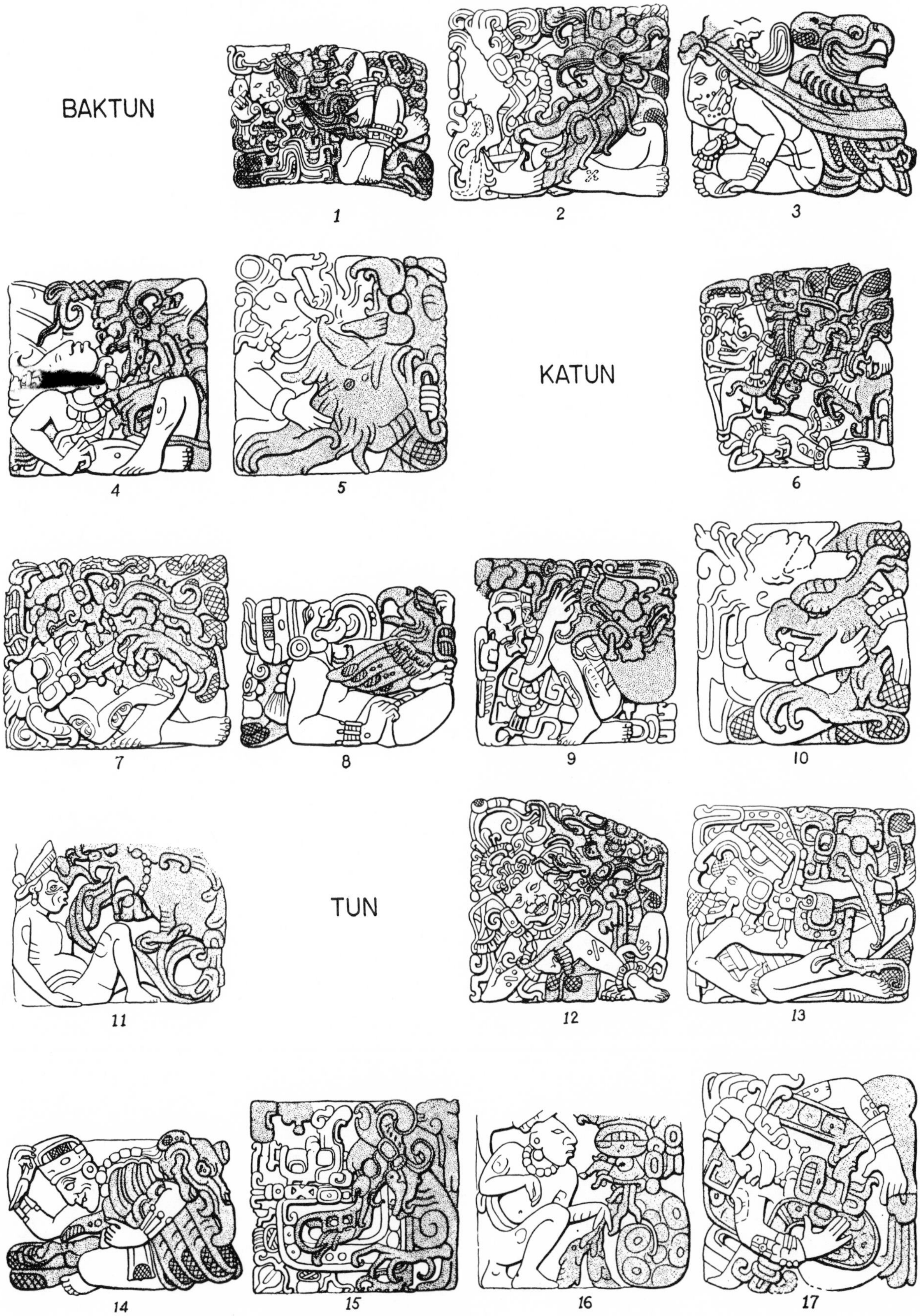
BAKTUN
KATUN
TUN
1
2
3
4
5
6
7
8
9
10
11
12
13
14
15
16
17

Fig. 28

FIG. 29—FULL-FIGURE GLYPHS OF UINAL, KIN, AND
LUNAR SERIES, AND COEFFICIENTS

1. 0 uinals. Quir. B.
2. 0 uinals. Quir. D (E).
3. 0 uinals. Cop. D.
4. 4 uinals. Quir. D (W).
5. 0 kins. Quir. B.
6. 0 kins. Quir. D (E).
7. 0 kins. Cop. D.
8. 17 kins. Quir. D (W).
9. 8 kins. Cop. HS, Date 24.
10. 16 kins. Yax. L 48.
11. Glyphs G9 and F. Quir. B.
12. 7 animal head E, D. Quir. B.
13. 1C. Quir. B.
14. Glyph B with Glyph X in carrying pack. Quir. B.
15. A9 with added elements not identified. Quir. B.
16. Glyphs G3 and F. Cop. HS, Date 24.
17. Count 4 moons (Glyph C). Cop. HS, Date 24.

UINAL

KIN

LUNAR SERIES

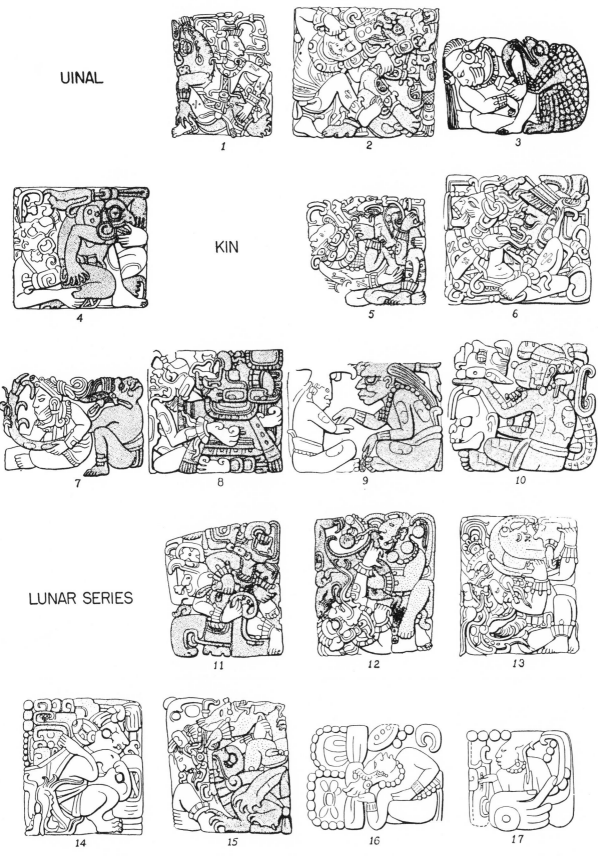

Fig. 29

Fig. 30—SPECIALIZED GLYPHS IN DISTANCE NUMBERS

SUPPRESSION OF GLYPHS:
1. Kin coefficient attached to uinal glyph. Quir. M, A1.
2. Kin coefficient attached to uinal glyph. Yax. L 25, K1.
3. Kin coefficient attached to tun. Uinal and coefficient (o) suppressed. Yax. 12, A6.
4. Kin and tun glyphs. Uinal and coefficient (o) suppressed. Cop. J (E), Gl 18.
5. One katun, 10 tuns. Tun coefficient attached to katun; o uinals and o kins suppressed. Cop. U, I1.
6. 3 tuns. o uinals, o kins suppressed. Tik. T 4, L 3, F1.
7. Reversed coefficients: 4 uinals, 19 kins. Quir. E (W), B16b.
8. Distance number of nothing: o uinals o kins. Quir. K, C3b.

DISTANCE NUMBER INTRODUCTORY GLYPH—SYMBOLIC AND HEAD FORMS:
9. Yax. L 25, J.
10. Cop. I, C6b.
11. Pusil. D, C8.
12. Cop. HS (Gordon, pl. 12), J3.
13. Cop. HS, Step P1.
14. Cop. A, B11a.
15. Quir. Str 1, K′.
16. Cop. T 11, E door, S panel, A1.
17. Pal. 96 Gl., G6.
18. Pal. 96 Gl., C2.
19. Pal. 96 Gl., D8.

"HEL," SUCCESSION, GLYPH:
20. Count of 3 "hel." Pal. Cross, O8.
21. 1 or 3 "hel." Pal Inscr. (W), R5.
22. The 9-16-9 "hel" count. Pal. Inscr. (E), S6–S7.
23. The 9-16-9 "hel" count. Pal. Inscr. (M), G10–J1.
24. 5 "hel." Pal. Sun, Q7.
25. 13 "hel." Cop. B, B11a.
26. 14 "hel." Quir. J, C16.
27. 14 "hel." Cop. N, pedestal, D5.
28. 16 "hel." Quir. I, B9a.
29. Dresden 10b.
30. Dresden 5a.
31. Dresden 25b.
32. Madrid 70a.
33. Madrid 66b.

34. Madrid 68a.
35. Madrid 72a.
36. Glyph for feast. Mendoza 19.

ANTERIOR DATE INDICATORS:
37. P.N. L 2, X3.
38. P.N. 12, A16a.
39. Cop. U, P2.
40. Quir. P, E9b.
41. Cop. C, A7a.

POSTERIOR DATE INDICATORS:
42. Pal. Inscr. (W), R12.
43. Yax. L 25, N1.
44. Quir. E. (W), S5.
45. Pal. Inscr. (W), S5.
46. Pal. 96 Gl., G1.
47. Cop. T 11, E door, S panel, C5.

"SNAKE" PREFIX AS ANTERIOR DATE INDICATOR:
48. With 13 Ahau. Pal. Inscr. (E), M7.
49. With 3 Ahau. Pal. Inscr. (W), R3.
50. With 1 Manik. Pal. 1, A10.
51. With 13 Ahau. Pal. 96 Gl., K2.

"PROPELLER" GLYPH:
52. Symbolic form. Pal. Inscr. (W), O2.
53. Symbolic form. Pal. Inscr. (M), C4.
54. Personified. Pal. 96 Gl., B3.

LONG-NOSED GOD WITH FLARE IN FOREHEAD:
55. Personified. Cop. K, P2b.
56. Symbolic form. Pal. Fol. Cross, A15.
57. Full figure. Pal. Fol. Cross, D2.
58. Full figure. Pal. Fol. Cross, C6.
59. Personified. Cop. R, F2.

FISH-IN-HAND AND SKY CLAUSE:
60. Pal. Fol. Cross, M10–L11.
61. Intervening glyphs not shown. Pal. Sun, O13, N15.
62. Pal. Cross, O9–O10.
63. Fish not certain. Personified sky sign. Bonam. 2, C1–D1.

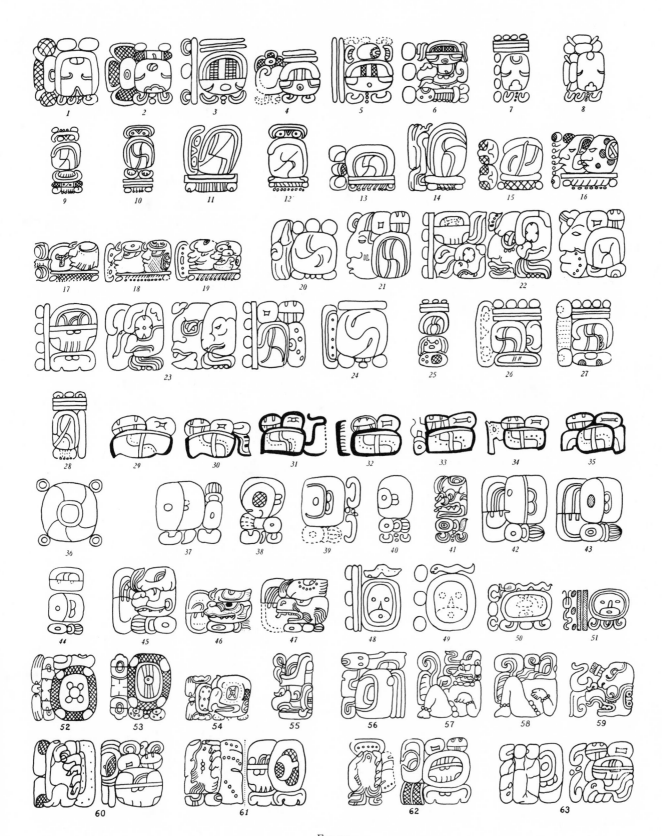

FIG. 30

FIG. 31—SPECIALIZED GLYPHS FOR KIN AND SKY SYMBOLS

SHELL VARIANT OF KIN:
1. Nar. HS, B3.
2. Cop. I, C6a.
3. Pal. Fol. Cross, B12.
4. Cop. HS, Date 22.
5. Cop. HS, fragment.
6. Yax. L 31, K3a.
7. Seib. HS, I1b.
8. Nar. 32, M1.

"GLYPH Z":
9. Yax. Str 44.
10. Yax. L 46, C"1.
11. With Y. Yax. L 21, A5.

INVERTED AHAU:
12. P.N. 1, F3.
13. P.N. 8, B24.
14. P.N. shell, H1.
15. Quir. C, I1.
16. P.N. L 3, L1.
17. P.N. L 3, U4.
18. Nar. 12, C8b.
19. Quir. Alt O, U1a.
20. Yax. L 10, E5a.
21. On side. Cop. 9, B6.

ANIMAL VARIANT:
22. Pal. Inscr. (E), M6.
23. Pal. Inscr. (W), G8.
24. Pal. Sun, C14,
25. Pestac 1, C6.
26. Cop. J (W), Gl 17.
27. Quir. H, S2.
28. Cop. HS, S11.
29. Nar. 32, X5.
30. With lunar series. Yax. L 29, C1.
31. With lunar series. Quir. E (W), B6a.
32. With lunar series. Quir. B, Gl 8.

QUINCUNX GLYPHS:
33. Pal. 96 Gl., L1.
34. Glyph Y. Pal. Cross, B10.

35. Glyph Y. Yax. 4, fragment.
36. Glyph Y and moon. Yax. L 21, B5.
37. Glyphs Y and Z. Yax. L 56, E1.
38. Glyph Y. Yax. L 29, A5.
39. Pal. Inscr. (W), Q12.
40. P.N. Alt 2, I1.

SUN-AT-HORIZON GLYPHS:
41. 1 kin. Tik. T 4, L 3, C4.
42. 1 kin. Tik. T 4, L 2, A7.
43. 1 kin. Nar. 32, T2.
44. Without prefix. P.N. 36, C7.
45. Forward to. P.N. 1, E3.
46. Forward to. P.N. L 3, T2.
47. Forward to. P.N. Thr 1, N1.
48. Forward to. P.N. Thr 1, I'–J'1.
49. Yax prefix. Cop. N, pedestal, A4.
50. Yax prefix. Cop. R, K2a.
51. Chicchan head. Cop. N, A17.

SKY ELEMENTS IN VARIOUS GLYPHS:
52. Cop. A, C11.
53. Yax. 1, C9.
54. Yax. L 31, J4.
55. Nar. 23, H16.
56. Pal. Inscr. (W), D12.
57. Pal. Fol. Cross, O14.
58. Pal. Sun, A1–B2.
59. P.N. L 2, A1–B2.
60. P.N. L 3, E1.
61. Quir. P, B4.
62. Quir. E, D6.
63. Cop. B back, 2.
64. Cop. Q, E4.
65. Cop. U, C2.
66. Cop. U, L3.
67. Quir. E, A18b.
68. Yax. L 35, A6.
69. Yax. L 31, J4.
70. P.N. L 3, K1.
71. Quir. C, B15.
72. Dresden 56a.

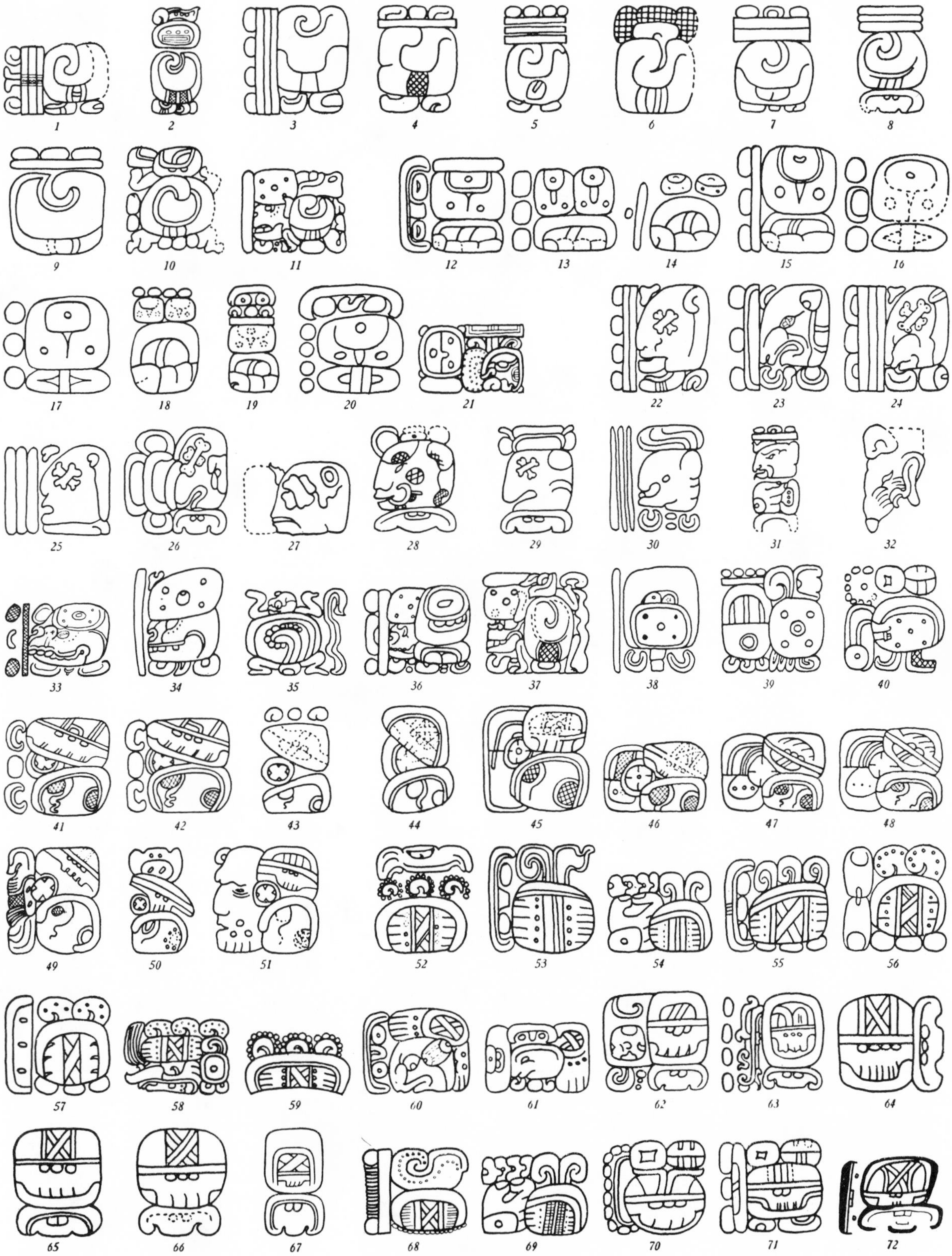
1
2
3
4
5
6
7
8
9
10
11
12
13
14
15
16
17
18
19
20
21
22
23
24
25
26
27
28
29
30
31
32
33
34
35
36
37
38
39
40
41
42
43
44
45
46
47
48
49
50
51
52
53
54
55
56
57
58
59
60
61
62
63
64
65
66
67
68
69
70
71
72

FIG. 31

Fig. 32—PERIOD ENDING SIGNS

1. Completion 13 baktuns. Pal. Cross, D4–C5.
2. Completion of fifteenth baktun. Mor. 2, E8–F8.
3. Completion of third katun. Uax. 12, A6–B6.
4. Completion of fifteenth katun. Cop. B, B5–B6.
5. Completion count of fifteenth katun. Cop. 4, B7.
6. Completion of twelfth katun. Cop. Altar of I.
7. Completion of fifteenth katun. Pusil. E, A11–B11.
8. Completion of fourteenth katun. P.N. 3, F9–F10.
9. Completion 10 katuns. Nar. L 1, F3.
10. Completion period of fifteenth katun. Cop. A, B12b–C12a.
11. Forward to completion of second baktun. Pal. Fol. Cross, C7–D7.
12. Tenth katun. Pal. Inscr. (E), T2.
13. Fifteenth katun. P.N. Alt 2, H2.
14. Count of 11 katuns. Pal. Inscr. (M), A3.
15. Count of 9 katuns. Pal. Inscr. (E), P3.
16. Tenth baktun. Cop. 8, E2.
17. Expiration of 11 katuns. Pal. 96 Gl., B2.
18. Expiration of 19 katuns. Quir. Str 1, Y'.
19. Expiration of 10 tuns. Ixlu Alt of 2, A3.
20. Count of succession (?) of 9 baktuns. Pal. Cross, S1–R2.
21. Succession (?) of count of 11 katuns. Pal. Inscr. (W), O3–P3.
22. Completion of expiration of 19 katuns. Quir. Str 1, W1–X1.
23. Count of succession of 14 katuns. P.N. 3, G10–H10.
24. Completion of haab. Nar. 25, D4.
25. Completion of count of new haab. P.N. Alt 2, G3.
26. Completion of count of haab. Pal. Inscr. (E), L5.
27. Completion of expiration of haab. Nar. 10, A8.
28. Completion of haab. Nar. 24, E15.
29. Completion of haab. Cop. N, B18a.
30. Haab. Quir. E, C11.
31. Haab. Quir. F, C11a.
32. Tun. Pal. Inscr. (E), R3.
33. Tun. Pal. Inscr. (E), T8.
34. Count of 13 tuns. Tik. 5, C4.
35. 13 haabs. Pal. 96 Gl., K3.
36. Fifth haab. Quir. J, A16.
37. Fifth haab. Quir. C, D12.
38. Fifth haab. Quir. A, B11.
39. Fifth haab. P.N. 12, A12.
40. Fifth haab. Yax. L 3, D1a.
41. 5 haabs lacking. P.N. 25, I14.
42. 5 haabs lacking. P.N. 36, D8.
43. 5 haabs lacking. P.N. L 2, X12.
44. 5 haabs lacking. Quir. D, C22b, u.h.
45. 5 haabs lacking. P.N. Thr 1, K'2.
46. Half of period. Uax. 22, B3.
47. Completion of half period. Cop. P, A7–B7a.
48. At its half period. Cop. 6, A7b.
49. Completion of half period. Calak. 9, C3.
50. Half period. Cop. J (W), Gl 34.
51. Half period. Cop. J (S), C2, l.h.
52. At half period. Nar. 22, H20.
53. Half period of a katun. Tik. T 4, L 3, A2.
54. Half period. Ixlu Alt of 2, B3.
55. Half period (forward) to 13 Ahau. Quir. F, B19.
56. Forward to haab completed (?) Cop. Z, B3.
57. Haab completed (?) Cop. Q, F1.
58. Haab completed (?) Cop. Review Stand, T1a.
59. Haab completed (?) Cop. 11, B1.
60. Haab completed (?) Cop. G2, B2.

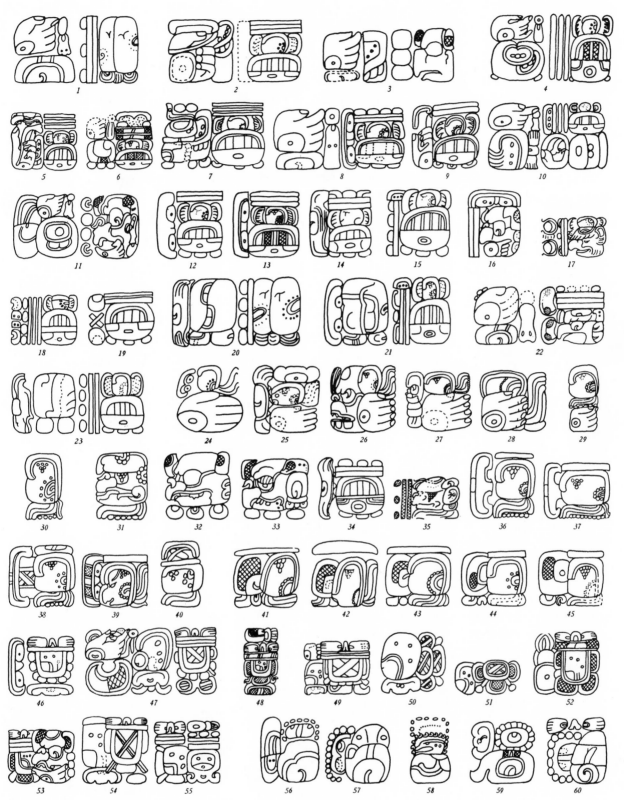

FIG. 32

FIG. 33—GLYPHS ASSOCIATED WITH PERIOD ENDINGS AND ANNIVERSARIES

POSSIBLE GLYPHS FOR TUN:
1. Cop. U, N5.
2. Cop. G1, A2.
3. Cop. S, I1b.

HAND SPRINKLING WATER:
4. Cop. B, B7.
5. Quir. C, C13.
6. Nar. 14, E12.
7. Cop. 6, A7a.
8. Quir. A, D5.

SHELL, HAND, AND AFFIXES:
9. Quir. A, C6b.
10. Quir. E, C12.
11. Quir. A, D7.
12. Pal. Inscr. (M), D3.
13. Quir. P, C7b.
14. Quir. E, D19a.

ONE SHELL PERIOD:
15. Pal. Fol. Cross, N17.
16. Pal. Inscr. (M), F7.
17. Pal. Inscr. (W), S11.
18. Nar. 24, D8.
19. Tik. T 4, L 2, K1.
20. Pal. 96 Gl., I8.

ANNIVERSARIES:
21. First katun. P.N. L 3, F1.
22. Expiration 5 tuns. Yax. L 2, D1.
23. Completion of third katun. P.N. 8, C20.
24. Expiration 13 tuns. Cop. U, A2.
25. Completion of first katun. Pal. 96 Gl., I1.
26. Completion count of 2 katuns. Quir. D, B17.
27. Sixth haab, third katun. P.N. 12, A20.
28. Completion of fifth haab, 1 katun. P.N. 3, F4–E5.
29. 5 haabs, 3 katuns (reversed). Cop. T 11, N door, W panel.
30. 5 haabs, third katun. Cop. 8, E1–F1.
31. Haab glyph with coefficient destroyed. P.N. Thr 1, L.
32. 2 haabs, fourth tun. Cop. U, M4.

"BEN-ICH" KATUN:
33. With coefficient of 1. P.N. 3, A9.
34. With coefficient of 1, but without "Ben-Ich." P.N. 1, C3.
35. 2 "Ben-Ich" katuns. P.N. 37, D12.
36. 3 "Ben-Ich" katuns with lunar prefatory glyph. Yax. L 31, J1.
37. 3 "Ben-Ich" katuns with lunar prefatory glyph. Yax. L 31, K2.
38. 3 "Ben-Ich" katuns followed by lunar glyph. Yax. L 21, C8–D8.
39. 4 "Ben-Ich" katuns. P.N. shell plaque, F3.
40. 5 "Ben-Ich" katuns. Pal. 96 Gl., D1.
41. 5 katuns, without "Ben-Ich." Pal. 96 Gl., L6.
42. 5 katuns and shell-hand glyph. Quir. C, C14–D14.
43. 6 katuns. Yax. L 27, D1a.
44. Glyph of Kinich Ahau. Dresden 11c.
45. 1 "Ben-Ich" Ahau. Chichen 19, B1.
46. Glyph with "Ben-Ich" prefix. Yax. L 37, B7.
47. Glyph with "Ben-Ich" prefix, showing Lamat derivation. Yax. L 35, B1.

13 KINCHILTUNS:
48. 13 kinchiltuns, at 1 Ahau 13 Yaxkin. Quir. F, D16–C17a.
49. 13 kinchiltuns, 7 Ahau 3 Pop. Quir. D, C20.

BAKTUN GLYPH WITH AFFIXES:
50. Nar. 29, I12.
51. Cop. N, pedestal, 22.
52. Tik. T 4, L 2, G2.

LONG-NOSED GOD WITH UINAL HEADDRESS AND COEFFICIENT OF ONE:
53. Quir. F, D15a.
54. Pal. Inscr. (W), G12.
55. Cop. N, pedestal, 20.
56. Yax. L 13, E2.

TRIPLE CAUAC GLYPH:
57. Pal. Cross, C7.
58. Quir. C, A14.
59. Seib. 10, C2.
60. Seib. HS, Panel B, L2.

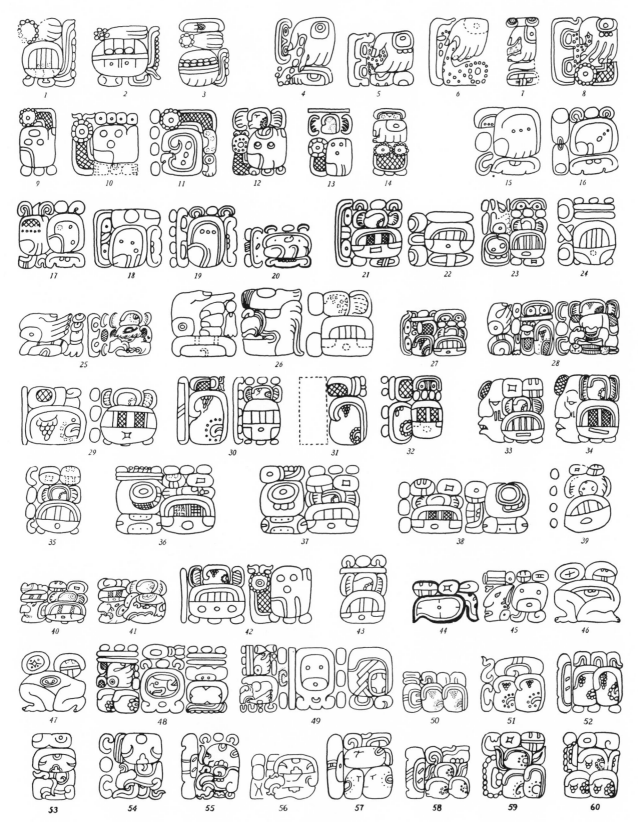

FIG. 33

FIG. 34—GLYPHS G AND F OF THE LUNAR SERIES

GLYPH G1:
1. P.N. 25, A9.
2. P.N. 36, A5.
3. Cop. 1, B5a.
4. Cop. I, A6a.
5. Cop. I, C7b.
6. Cop. HS, fragment.
7. P.N. L 3, B13–14.

GLYPH G2:
8. Chinkul. marker.
9. Ton. 30.
10. Yax. L 26, T′1a.
11. Ton. 7.
12. P. Uinik 3, A16.
13. Chichen 1, B6.

GLYPH G3:
14. Yax. L 10, B1a. With F.
15. Pal. Palace, House C. With F.
16. Pal. Sun, A9. With F.
17. Pal. tablet. With F.
18. Tzendales 1, A3. With F.
19. Yax. L 46, B″3. With F.
20. Xcal. IS, A9.
21. Cop. HS, Date 24. With F.

GLYPH G4:
22. Nar. 24, C4.
23. Nar. 29, G4.
24. Ixkun 2, A6.

GLYPH G5:
25. Leiden A8a, u.h.
26. Balak. 5, D1.
27. Yax. L 48, B4a, u.h.
28. P.N. L 2, D1.
29. Calak. 89, B4, u.h. With F
30. Los Higos 1, A6.

GLYPH G6:
31. Cop. H′, Ea, l.h.

GLYPH G7:
32. Pal. Palace, House E, fresco.
33. Ton. (?) round altar.
34. P.N. 3, B4.
35. Cop. A, A5.
36. Cop. HS, Date 10. With F.
37. Quir. D (W), A15.
38. Quir. E (W), A6. With F.

GLYPH G8:
39. P.N. L 12, A5.
40. Cop. 10, B4. With F.
41. Cop. 12, A6.
42. Pal. Cross, A10a. With F.
43. Pal. Fol. Cross B9. With F.
44. P.N. 14, B7.
45. Yax. L 21, B4. With F.

GLYPH G9:
46. Pusil. D, G7.
47. Pal. 1, A6a.
48. Cop. I, C2a.
49. Nar. 30, B4. With F.
50. Yax. 11, O1. With F.
51. Yax. L 3, B1. With F.
52. Ton. 7, C1.
53. Quir. F (E), C6a.
54. Quir. E (E), D5a.
55. Nar. 13, F4.
56. Quir. K, A5b.
57. Comitan 1, B4.

GLYPH F:
58. Pal. Palace, House E, fresco.
59. Yax. L 48, B4b, u.h.
60. P.N. 25, A10.
61. Pal. 1, A6b.
62. Yax. L 56, D2b. Knot personified.
63. Cop. 1, B5b. *Te* (2) personified.
64. Yax. 11, O1b.
65. Cop. N, A9. Knot personified.
66. Nar. 13, E5.
67. Quir. F (E), C6b.
68. Quir. K, A6. *Te* (2) personified.

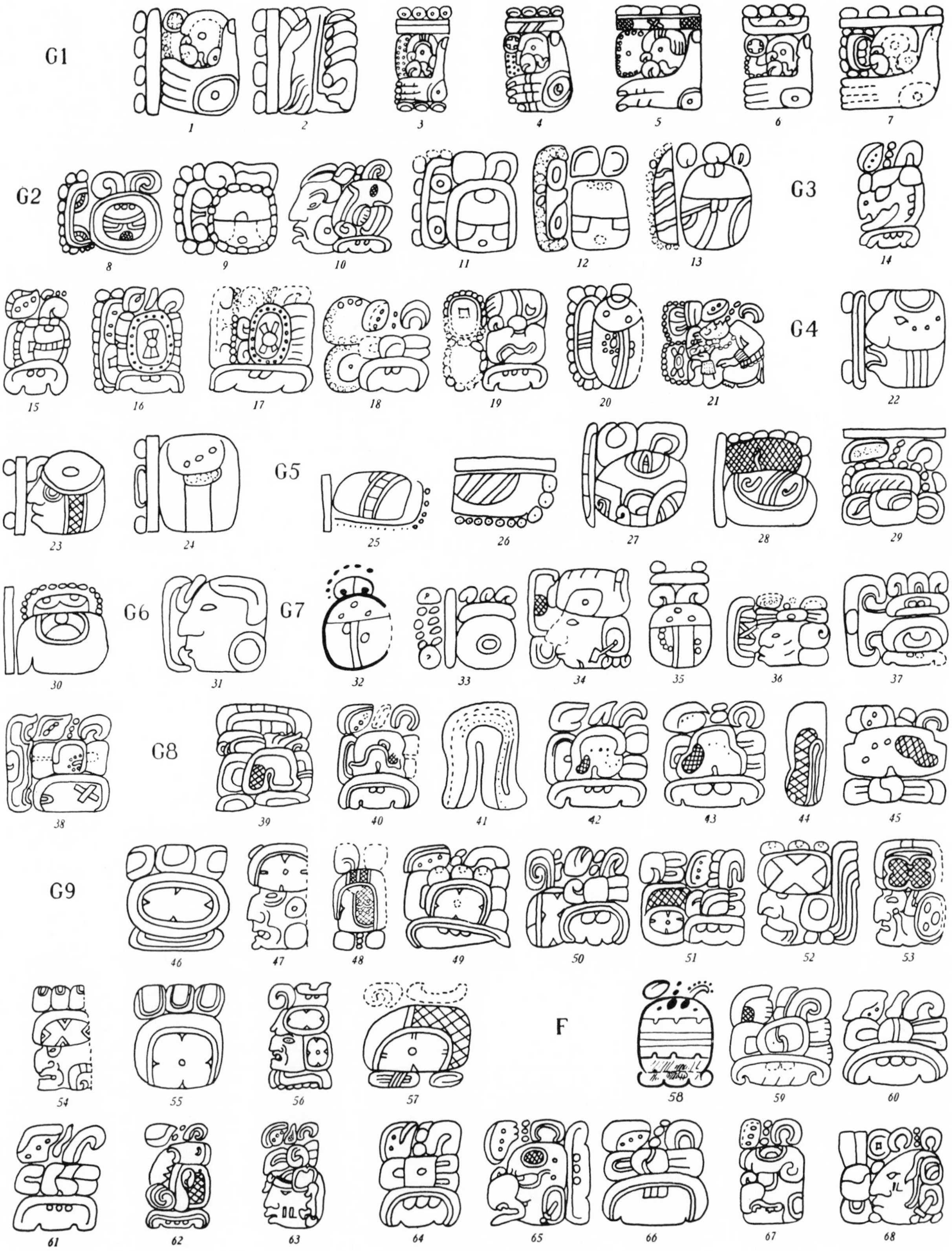
G1
G2
G3
G4
G5
G6
G7
G8
G9
F

Fig. 34

Fig. 35—819-DAY COUNT AND MONTH POSITION SHIFT

CLAUSES DEALING WITH 819-DAY COUNT:
1. Pal. 1, A11–B11.
2. Yax. L 30, E3–F5.
3. Yax. 11, D'6–C'9.
4. Yax. 1, E3–F6.
5. Quir. K, A7b–C2a.
6. Yax. L 29, C4–D5. Supplementary.
7. Yax. 1, C8–D9. Supplementary.

SHIFT IN COEFFICIENT OF MONTH:
8. 7 Muluc 1 Kankin. Xcal. IS, A8a, A14a.
9. 10 Ahau 7 Yaxkin. Etzna 18, A7, D2.
10. 8 Ahau 7 Uo. Etzna 19, A4–B4.
11. 9 Ahau 17 Mol. Etzna 9, A1–B1.
12. Kin, 6 Ix 16 Kankin. Yax. 20, E1–E2.
13. Kin, 3 Eb 14 Mol. Yax. 18, A1–A3.
14. 2 Chuen, kin, third of Muan. Kabah, Str 1, A1–C1.
15. 5 Ahau, kin, 2 Kayab. Oxkin. 3.

DIRECTIONAL COUNTING GLYPHS:
16. *"Hel"* glyph, 6 kins, 14 uinals, 11 tuns counted from the anterior position 11 Ahau is counted forward to 6 Cimi 4 *te* Zec. Cop. HS, Dates 22 and 23.

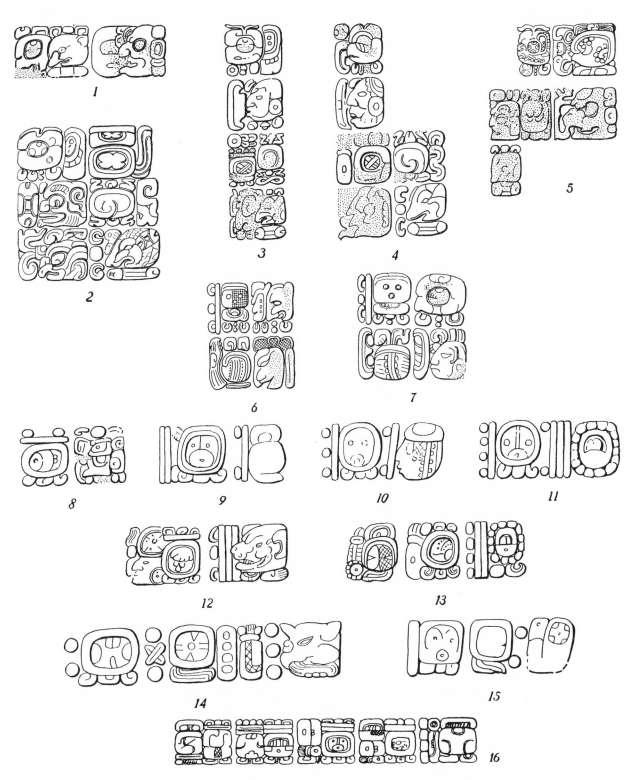

FIG. 35

FIG. 36—LUNAR SERIES: GLYPH C COEFFICIENTS ABSENT OR 2 TO 4

    1– 5. Cop. N. 1D, 0C, X, B, 10A.
    6–10. P.N. L 3. 9D, 0C, X, B, 10A.
   11–14. Cop. J. 18D, 0C, X, B, 10A.
   15–18. Yax. L 48. 12D, 2C, X, 9A.
   19–24. Pal. Cross. 5 *"bix"*(?) D, 2C, X, B, 9A.
   25–28. P.N. 3. 7E, D, 2C, X, 9A.
   29–33. Quir. E (East). "Moon completed" (?), 2C, X, B, 9A.
   34–38. Quir. A. 6E, D, 2C, X, 10A.
   39–43. Ixkun 2. 5D, 3C, X, B, 10A.
   44–48. P.N. 1. 8E (written 8D), 3C, X, B, 10A.
   49–53. Yax. L 46. 14D, 3C, X, B, 10A.
   54–56. Yax. L 21. 7 *"bix"*(?) D, 3C, X, 9A.
   57–60. P.N. 36. 4D, 4C, X, 9A.
   61–65. Quir. P. 3E(?), D, 4C, X, B, 9A.
   66–71. Nar. 13. 7E, D, 4C, X, B, 9A.
      72. Nar. 14, 9A.

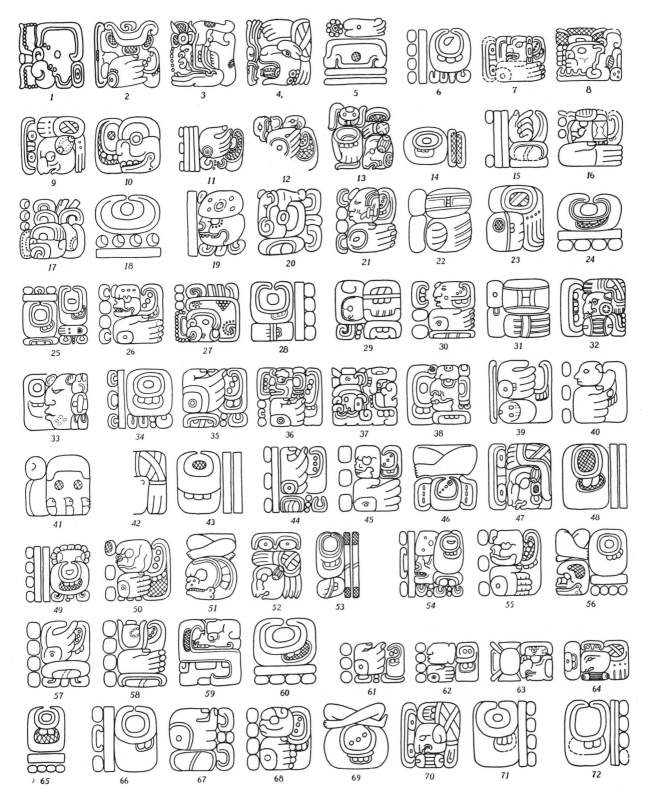

FIG. 36

Fig. 37—LUNAR SERIES: GLYPH C COEFFICIENTS 5 AND 6

1- 5. Yax. 11. 12D, 5C, X, B, 10A.
6-10. P.N. L 2. 19 days, D, 5C, X, 9A.
11-15. Pal. 1. 19 days, D, 5C, X, B, 10A.
16-22. Quir. G. 3E, D, 5C, X, B variant, B variant, 10A.
23-25. Yax. L 56. 11D, 5C, X, B, 10A.
26-31. Quir. Alt O. End D, 5C, X, B, 10A.
32-35. Cop. 9. 5E, 5C, X, 10A.
36-40. Pal. Fol. Cross. 10D, 5C, X, B, 10A. Coefficient of C omitted in drawing.
41-45. Cop. M. 2D?, 5C, X, B, 10A.
46-47. Pusil. O. 5E, D, 6C, X, 9A.
48-52. Cop. A. 15D, 6C, X, B, 9A.
53-57. Nar. 29. 19D, 6C, X, 9A, B.
58-62. Quir. J. 4D, 6C, X, B, 9A.
63-66. Quir. F (E), 0D, 6C, X, 10A.
67-71. P.N. 12. 3E, D, 6C, X, B, 10A.

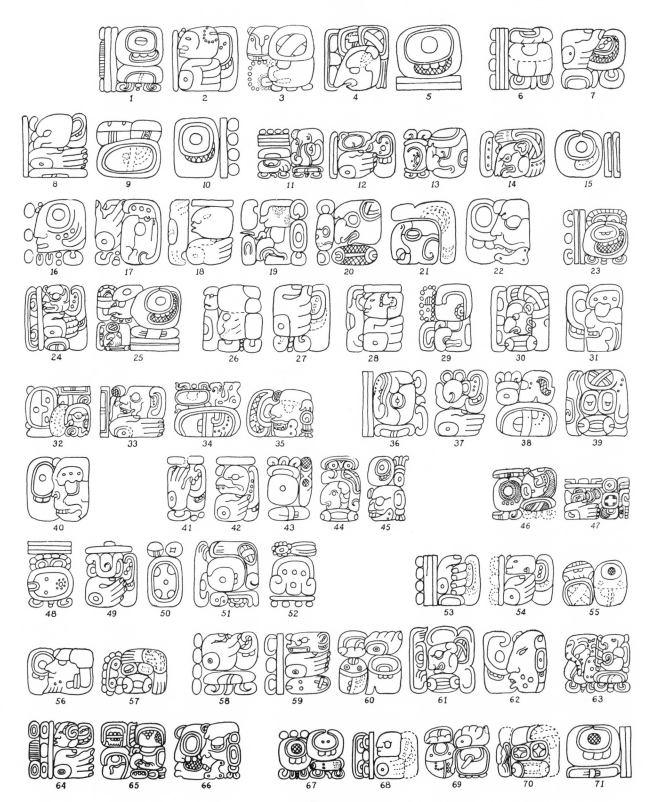

FIG. 37

Fig. 38—DATES AT CHICHEN ITZA AND NEIGHBORING SITES

1. 9 Lamat, the day, 11 Yax, in the journey of (?) Tun 13 within (?) (Katun) 1 Ahau. 10.2.12.1.8. Chichen 2, A1–B3.
2. 9 Lamat, the day, 11 Yax, in the journey of (?) Tun 13 (within Katun 1 Ahau), the day. 10.2.12.1.8. Chichen 4, H3–H6.
3. 9 Lamat, the day, on eleventh of Yax, in the journey of (?) Tun 13 within (?) (Katun) 1 Ahau. 10.2.12.1.8. Chichen 5, A1–A4.
4. 12 Kan, the day, on seventh of Zac, in the journey of (?) Tun 13 within (?) (Katun) 1 Ahau, the day. 10.2.12.2.4. Chichen 3, A1–B2, C4–D5.
5. 8 Kan 2 Pop, in the journey of the fifth tun (the katun) at 1 Ahau. 10.2.4.8.4. Yula 1, A1–A4.
6. 3 Eb, the day, tenth of Pop, in the journey of (?) Tun 5, (the katun) at 1 Ahau. 10.2.4.8.12. Yula 2, G1–H4.
7. 11 Ben, the day, on eleventh (?) of Cumku, in the journey of (?) Tun 18, within (the katun) 3 Ahau. 10.1.17.5.13. Chichen 27, A1–D1.
8. 3 Imix 9 Yax, Tun 1, within (Katun) 12 Ahau. Perhaps an error for 10.3.0.2.1 3 Imix 4 Ch'en. Chichen 23, Bl 18.

"Ben-Ich" here translated "within" might be rendered "its countenance."

(After H. Beyer. Original, shows characteristic T element on cheek of head for three, first glyph of eight.)

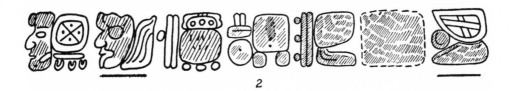

1

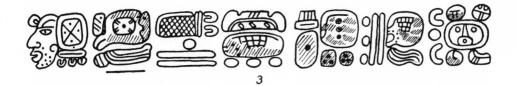

2

3

4

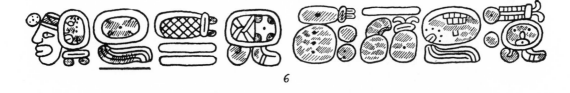

5

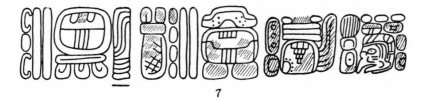

6

7

8

FIG. 38

Fig. 39—DATES AT CHICHEN ITZA AND NEIGHBORING SITES (*CONTINUED*)

1. Possibly 9 Muluc on seventh of Pop, in the journey of (?) Tun 1, within (Katun) 1 Ahau, the day. 10.2.0.7.9. However, month sign and winged cauac are transposed. Furthermore, the day sign and its head coefficient are unreliable. Halakal L 1.

2. 9 Muluc on seventh of Zac. Tun 10. (The Katun) day (?) 1 Ahau. 10.2.9.1.9. Chichen 1.

3. 8 Manik, the day, on fifteenth of Uo, in the journey of (?) Tun 11, within (Katun) 1 Ahau, the day. 10.2.10.11.7. Chichen 12.

4. 8 Manik, the day, on fifteenth of Uo. Forward to completion of 11 tuns, within (the katun) on Ahau. 10.2.10.11.7. Chichen 14.

5. 8 Manik, the day, on fifteenth of Uo, in the journey of (?) Tun 11, within (the katun) on 1 Ahau. 10.2.10.11.7. Chichen 15.

6. 8 Manik, the day, on fifteenth of Uo, in the journey of (?) Tun 11, within (katun) 1 Ahau, the day. 10.2.10.11.7. Chichen 16.

7. 6 Muluc (??), the day, on twelfth (?) of Mac, in the first tun, within (Katun) 1 Ahau, the day. 10.2.0.1.9 (??). Chichen 20, Gl 2–4, 10–12.

8. 7 Akbal, the day, on first of Ch'en, in the first tun, within (the katun) on 1 Ahau. 10.2.0.15.3. Chichen 20, Gl 27–29, 33–35.

"Ben-Ich" here translated "within" might be rendered "its countenance."

(After H. Beyer.)

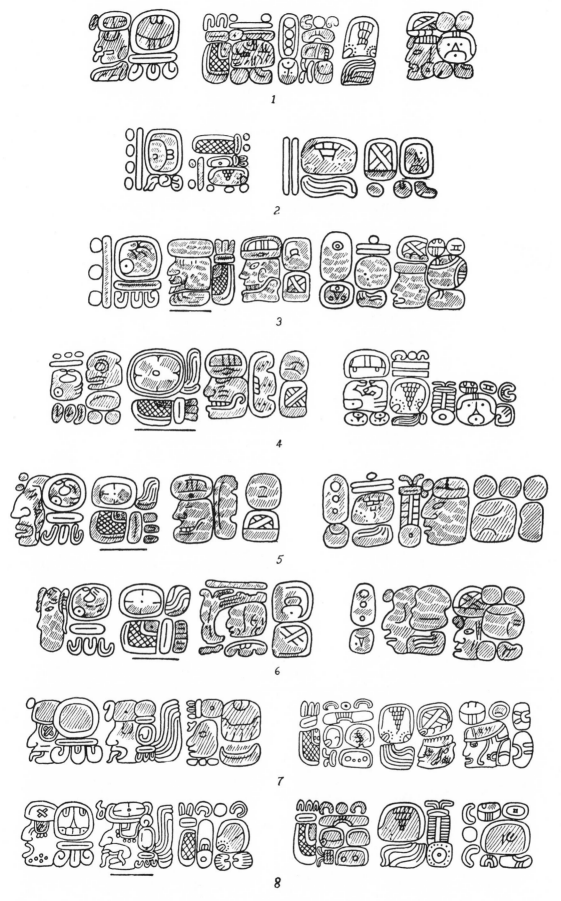

FIG. 39

FIG. 40—IMIX WITH VARYING AFFIXES AND IN COMPOUND GLYPHS

1. Pal. Inscr. (E), N8.
2. Cop. 1, D3.
3. P.N. Alt 2, E3.
4. Pal. HS, B2 (tun).
5. Yax. L 37, B3.
6. Cop. J south, C4, u.h.
7. Nar. 23, H15.
8. Nar. 32, Y3.
9. Pal. Tower, E4.
10. Cop. A, C7a.
11. Yax. L 46, F″5.
12. Yax. L 41, C3.
13. Quir. A, D11.
14. Cop. A, C10b.
15. Pal. Tower, D3.
16. Cop. P, A9b.
17. P.N. Thr 1, F′5.
18. Cop. C″, D1.
19. Chichen 3.
20. Cop. U, S3.
21. Carved Shell, Tuxtla Museum.
22. Cop. U, R3.
23. Pal. Cross, D6.
24. Pal. Cross, E2.
25. Pal. Fol. Cross, M14.
26. Pal. Sun, O14.
27. P.N. 15, C15.
28. P.N. L 3, P1.
29. Pal. 96 Gl., G6.
30. Cop. HS (Gordon, pl. 13m).
31. Yax. L 18, A5.
32. Cop. M, B7b.
33. P.N. Thr 1, A1.
34. Cop. J (S), D4.
35. Cop. A, D11a.
36. Cop. A, B6b.
37. Pal. Tablet of Creation, A1.
38. Cop. S, G1b.
39. Quir. P, Cartouche 4, B2.
40. P.N. 1, F2.
41. P.N. shell, E3.
42. Chichen 10.
43. Yax. 18, D2.
44. P.N. L 3, Incised Gl.
45. Quir. C, B6.
46. Cop. T 22, E1.
47. Cop. P, D11a.
48. Cop. U, S2.
49. Yax. L 18, B5.
50. P.N. L 2, U1–V1.
51. Quir. C, A13.
52. Quir. C, D7.
53. Pal. HS, D3a.
54. Cop. J (S), D7b.
55. Cop. T 11, step, Gl 20.
56. Cop. 10, D13a.
57. Cop. HS fragment (Gordon, pl. 13i).
58. Pal. Inscr. (W), N8.
59. Cop. E, C10b.
60. Cop. C, A4a.
61. Pal. Inscr. (M), H9.
62. Yax. 11, S3.
63. Pal. Inscr. (W), N10.
64. Yax. L 24, A4a.
65. Quir. J, C8.
66. Yax. L 25, R2–S2.
67. Pal. Cross, J1.
68. Nar. 24, E18.
69. Quir. F, A10.
70. P.N. Thr 1, Z3.

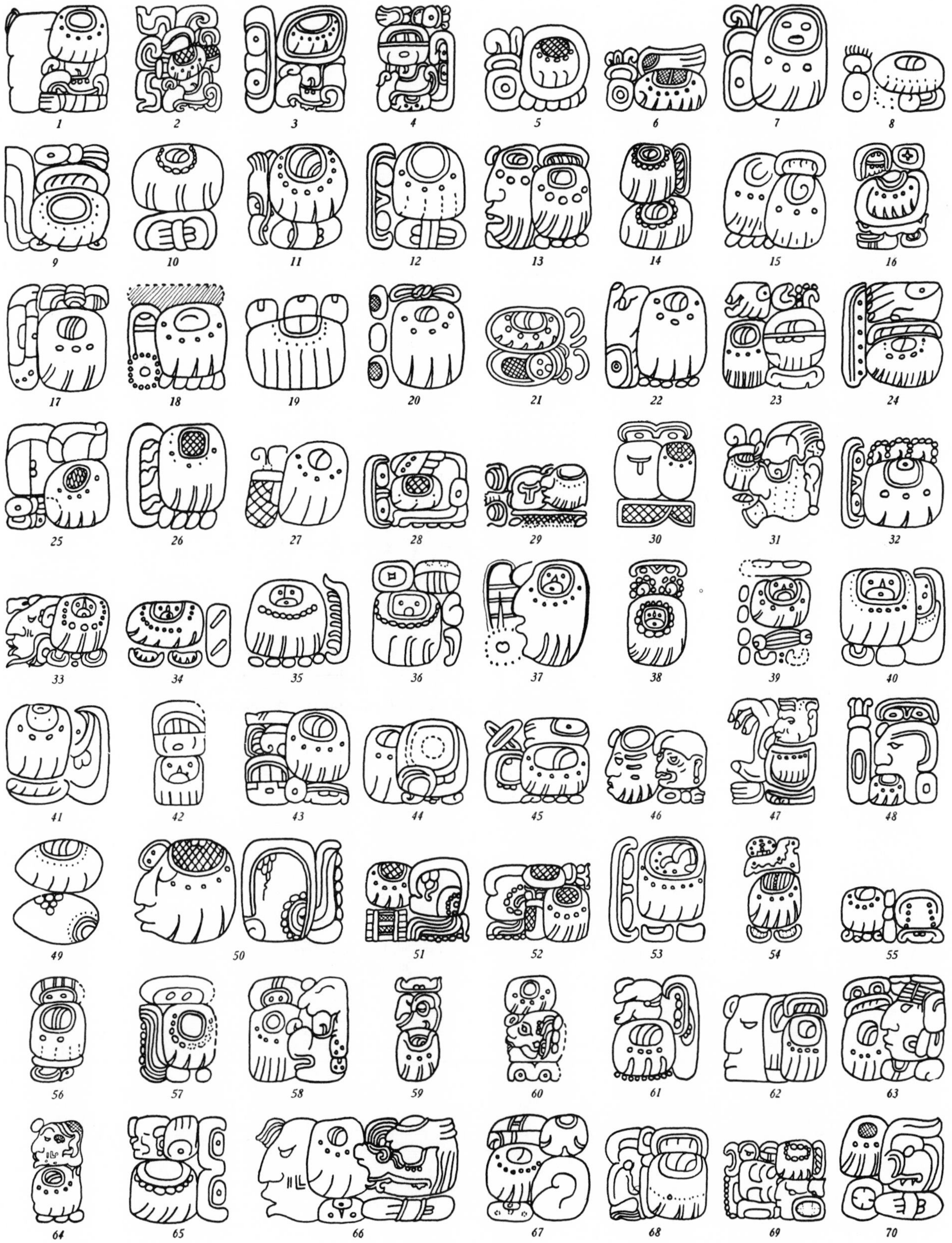

Fig. 40

Fig. 41—DIRECTIONAL AND COLOR GLYPHS

EAST:
1. Dresden 43c.
2. Dresden 30c.
3. Madrid 25d.
4. Madrid 50a.
5, 6. To east count of the year. Nakum D, E1–F1.
7, 8. To east count of the year. Cop. P, D14.
9. Pal. Inscr. (M), H7.

NORTH:
10. Dresden 44c.
11. Dresden 31c.
12. Madrid 25d.
13. Madrid 50a.

WEST:
14. Dresden 45c.
15. Dresden 31c.
16. Madrid 25d.
17. Madrid 50a.
18. Pal. Inscr. (M), H8.
19, 20. To west count of the year. Nar. 24, E9–D10.
21, 22. To west count of the year. Cop. E, D3–D4.

SOUTH:
23. Dresden 42c.
24. Dresden 31c.
25. Madrid 25d.
26. Madrid 50a.
27. Dresden 26c.
28, 29. To south count of the year. Cop. T, C8–C9.
30. Quir. M, D4.
31. Cop. J, Gl 15.

SUNDRY DIRECTIONAL GLYPHS:
32. East. Cop. A, D8a.
33. West. Cop. A, D8b.
34. South. Cop. A, D9a.
35. North? Cop. A, D9b.
36. South. Cop. 6, C5a.

RED OR GREAT:
37. Dresden 30c.
38. Madrid 43b.
39. Madrid 20d.
40. Red god. Dresden 30c.
41. Red old goddess. Dresden 2b.
42. Pal. Inscr. (M), M7.
43. Red god of rain. Dresden 42a.
44. Red god of rain. Dresden 25c.
45. Yax. L 37, D1. Affix probably bone semblant, not *chac*.

WHITE OR ARTIFICIAL:
46. Dresden 31c.
47. Madrid 43b.
48. Madrid 20d.
49. White god. Dresden 29c.
50. White moon goddess. Dresden 20c.
51. White god. Pal. Inscr. (M), N1.
52. White god of rain. Dresden 38b.
53. White earth. Dresden 67b.
54. Great fainting (*chac zac cimil*). Dresden 18c.

BLACK:
55. Dresden 31c.
56. Madrid 43c.
57. Madrid 20d.
58. Black god. Dresden 29c.
59. Black sky. Dresden 74.
60. Dresden 73a.
61. Black god of rain. Dresden 43a.
62. Black earth. Dresden 74.
63. Black maize god. Madrid 26d.

YELLOW OR WATERY, PERHAPS BLUE:
64. Dresden 31c.
65. Madrid 43c.
66. Madrid 21d.
67. Yellow god. Dresden 29c.
68. Yellow or watery haab. Madrid 22c.
69. Yellow maize seed. Madrid 27d.
70. Yellow rain god. Dresden 43a.
71. Yellow or water dog. Pal. Cross, S15.
72. Cop. T, S side.

GREEN OR NEW OR STRONG:
73. Madrid 43b.
74. Madrid 34a.
75. Dresden 71b.
76. Dresden 71b.
77. Dresden 56b.
78. Green or new Imix. Dresden 42b.
79. Green rain god. Dresden 26c.
80. Madrid 94d.
81. Pal. Inscr. (M), N2.
82. Its strong sun. Dresden 60b.
83. Quir. E, C10.
84. Pal. Fol. Cross, D12.
85. Quir. C, L1.
86. Triple haab. Pal. Cross, C7.
87. Green God C. Pal. Palace.
88. Quir. J, D8.
89. New moon? Cop. J, Gl 13.
90. Chicchan god with green on forehead. Pal. Inscr. (M), M10.

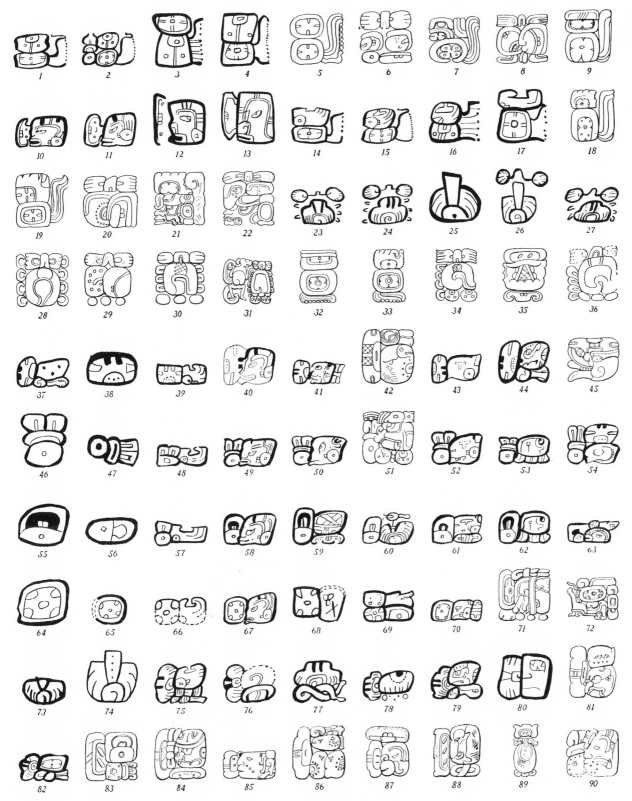

FIG. 41

FIG. 42—GLYPHS OF DEITIES, PERIODS, AND ACTION IN CODICES

GODS OF WORLD DIRECTIONS WITH VENUS TABLE, DRESDEN 46–50:
1–5. Associated with north.
6–10. Associated with west.
11–15. Associated with south.
16–20. Associated with east.
21–23. Variant forms of nos. 12, 17, and 2.

GLYPHS OF GODS ASSOCIATED WITH VENUS:
24–31. With introductory glyphs to table. Dresden 24.
    32. Dresden 57b.
    33. Red or great Venus. Dresden 50.

GLYPHS OF GODS:
34–41. Associated with divinatory almanac. No. 36 is the *ahaulil* glyph. Dresden 23b.
    42. God D. Dresden 5c.

PERIOD GLYPHS:
    43. Pictun. Dresden 69.
    44. Baktun. Dresden 70.
45–47. Katuns. Dresden 69, 70, 70.
    48. Tun? Dresden 69.
    49. Uinal. Dresden 69.
50–53. Kins. All Dresden 69.

GLYPHS WITH HANDS, MAINLY GLYPHS OF ACTION:
    54. Dresden 66b.
    55. Dresden 50b.
    56. Dresden 50b.
    57. Dresden 31c.
    58. Dresden 14b.

59. Dresden 12c.
60. Dresden 15b.
61. Dresden 13b.
62. Dresden 10b.
63. Dresden 5c.
64. Dresden 10a.
65. Dresden 29c.
66. Dresden 68c.
67. Dresden 33c.
68. Madrid 39a.
69. Madrid 66b.

GLYPHS MAINLY OF ACTION GROUP:
70. Dresden 50c.
71. Dresden 48c.
72. Dresden 23b.
73. Dresden 10b.
74. Dresden 23a.
75. Dresden 20c.
76. Dresden 5b.
77. Dresden 8b.
78. Dresden 16b.
79. Madrid 98b.
80. Dresden 35a.
81. Dresden 21b.
82. Dresden 11b.
83. Dresden 11c.
84. Dresden 8a.
85. Dresden 6b.
86. Dresden 18b.
87. Dresden 45b.

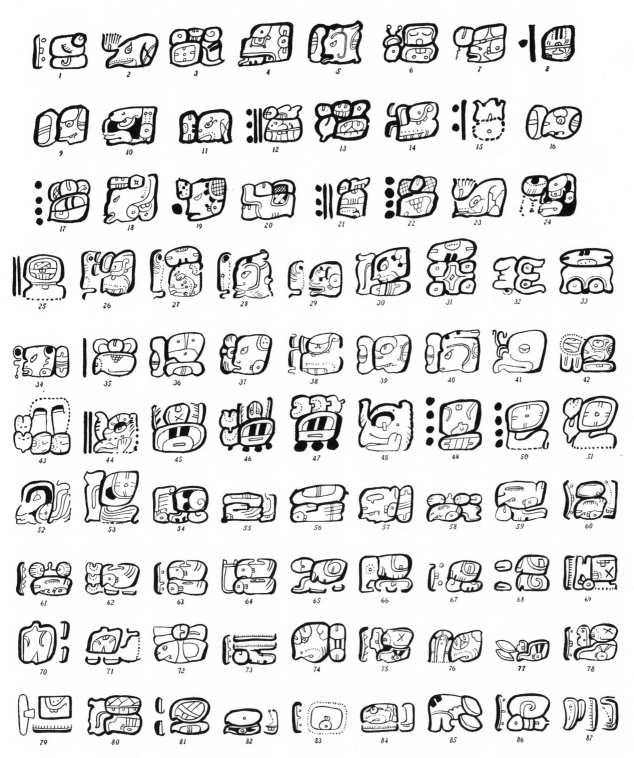

FIG. 42

FIG. 43—AFFIXES OF WATER GROUP AND GLYPHS FROM CODICES

AFFIXES WITH GOD C:
1. Completion and water. Gl X. Cop. N, A12.
2. Completion. Gl X. Quir. A, B8.
3. Kan cross and water. Yax. L 25, Q2.
4. Yax and jade. Pal. Palace, House C, Eaves.
5. Mol. Cop. 7, B12a.
6. Water. El Cayo L 1, A8.
7. Snake element? Cop. P, C7.
8. Shell and water. Quir. D (E), C18b.

AFFIXES WITH "BEN-ICH" BAT:
9. Kan cross and water. Cop. 11, A7.
10. Kan cross and water. Cop. A, D4b.
11. Yax. Cop. U, Q1.
12. Bone (?) and water. Cop. HS (Gordon, pl. 12c).
13. Mol (?) and other element. Cop. I, D6.
14. Water. Cop. 9, D6b.
15. Bone (?) and water. Cop. 8, E7.
16. Shell and water. Cop. 1, D4.

AFFIXES WITH "BEN-ICH" SKY (RAINY SKY?):
17. Kan cross and water. Yax. L 26, C″2.
18. Kan cross and water. Yax. L 25, W2.
19. Yax and water. Yax. L 16, F5.
20. Yax and water. Yax. 12, C6.
21. Water. Yax. L 10, A7b.
22. Shell and water. Yax. L 24, C′3.
23. God C and water. Yax. Str 44, X4, l.h.

AFFIXES WITH LONG-SNOUTED ANIMAL WITH "BEN-ICH":
24. Yax and water (?). Pal. Cross, O13.
25. Mol and bone (?). Pal. Cross, E15.
26. Shell (?) and water. Pal. Inscr. (M), G4.

AFFIXES WITH "BEN-ICH AND BONE" GLYPH:
27. Kan cross and water. Pal. Palace, House A, Balustrade.
28. Kan cross and water (?). Pal. Palace, House C, Eaves.
29. Yax. Pal. Fol. Cross, O17.
30. Mol and bone (?). Pal. Inscr. (M), E9.
31. Mol and shell. Pal. Inscr. (E), Q9.
32. Water and bone (?). Pal. Sun. K3.

GLYPHS, PRINCIPALLY AUGURAL, IN CODICES:
33. Very good fortune. Three dog. Dresden 13b.
34. Very good fortune. Three dog. Dresden 65b.
35. Medium good fortune. Three dog qualified by *kaz* glyph. Dresden 69a.
36. *Ahaulil*. Dresden 20b.
37. *Kuch,* "burden," glyph. Dresden 18c.
38. Earth-seed compound. Dresden 71.
39. Seed-earth compound. Dresden 66a.
40. Seed with affix. Dresden 55a.
41,42. Maize seed. Dresden 40b, 44b.
43. Sprouting seed. Perez 22.
44. Eight as maize symbol. Dresden 67a.
45. Eight as maize symbol with Imix. Substitute for Imix-Kan. Dresden 39c.
46,47. Kan-Imix compound. Dresden 43b, 7c.
48,49. To be read together. *Kan-Imix u cuch,* "abundant food its charge." New-year prophecy. Dresden 27a.
50. Kin-Akbal, "darkness," compound. Dresden 71.
51. Sun darkened. Dresden 66a.
52. Moon darkened. Dresden 66a.
53. Fire drill. Madrid 38c.
54. Drill jade (?). Dresden 8b.
55. Drill with head of dog (fire symbol). Dresden 5b.
56. Pseudo-Men glyph. Dresden 7c.
57–59. *Kintunyaabil,* "drought," glyphs. Dresden 42c, 45c, 72c.
60,61. To be read together. *Kintunyaabil u cuch,* "drought its charge." New-year prophecy. Dresden 26a.
62,63. To be read together. *Yaxhaabil kintunyaabil,* "for the new-year drought." New-year prophecy. Dresden 27c.
64. *Kintun,* "burning suns," New-year prophecy. Madrid 34.
65. Cauac with "brilliance" and *te* (1) prefixes, probably indicating lightning storm. Above picture of dog with torch. Dresden 36a.
66. Glyph of sun god followed by cauac with brilliance and *te* (1) affixes. Dresden 11b.
67. Glyph of God B followed by cauac with brilliance and *te* (1) affixes. Dresden 31b.
68. Head of sun god with brilliance prefix. Dresden 53b.
69. Very brilliant sun with *te* (3) affix substituted for *te* (1). Dresden 72c.
70. Sky symbol with brilliance prefix. Madrid 15b.

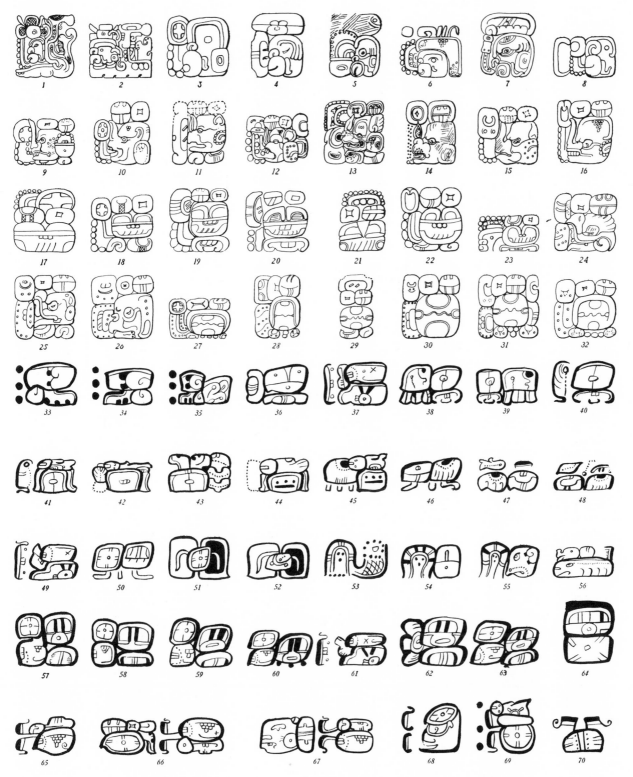

FIG. 43

FIG. 44—KAN CROSS, YAX, AND COMPLETION SIGNS
ASSOCIATED WITH SNAKES AND WATER (?)

1. Stream of water (?) with completion sign on it which falls from
   long-nosed god with death markings in hand of figure. Pal.
   Cross, west side of entrance to sanctuary.
2. Stream of water (?) with kan cross and completion sign. Quir. H.
3. Stream of water (?) with kan cross and Yax symbol alternating.
   Yax. 7.
4. Stream of water (?) with kan cross falling from vessel (?)
   decorated with glyphic element held by long-nosed monster.
   Quir. P.
5. Part of snake with body formed of yax signs alternating with
   jade beads and with what may be shell element at back of head.
   Pal. Cross.
6. Head of two-headed snake with yax and bone elements. Tik.
   T 4, L 3.
7. Yax ornament with shell outline and jade bead with bone appendages attached to body of snake belonging with no. 6. Tik.
   T 4, L 3.
8. Fretlike upper jaw of serpent with kan cross attached. Pal.
   Palace, House D, Pier C.

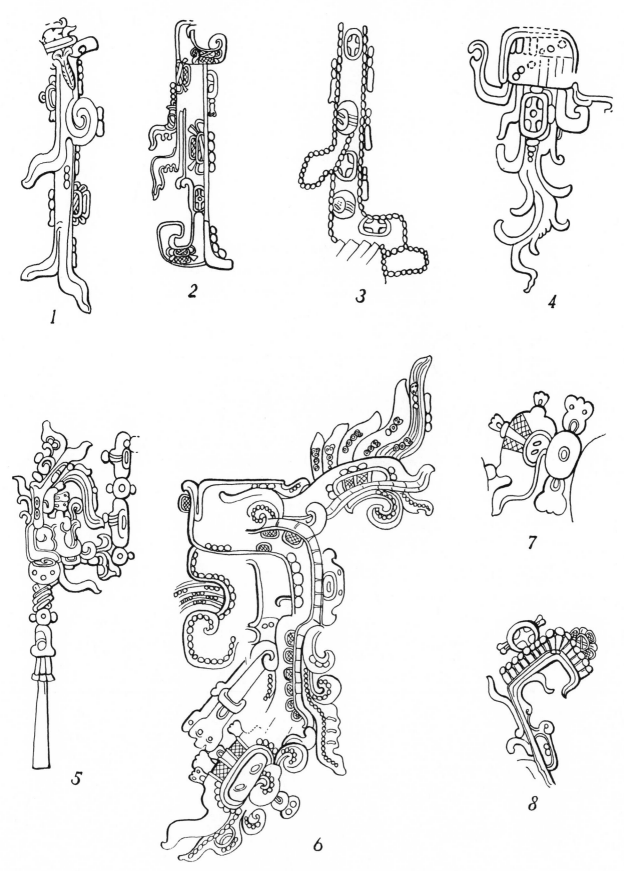

FIG. 44

FIG. 45—KAN CROSS, COMPLETION, YAX, BONE, AND JADE SYMBOLS

1. Jade and bone with water (?) falling from them. Pal. Fol. Cross.
2. Bone and jade alternating to form frame. Pal. Palace, House D, Pier f.
3. Completion and jade alternating to form frame. Pal. Palace, House D, Pier c.
4. Kan cross with jade and bone attachments. Pal. Fol. Cross, side of sanctuary.
5. Yax and jade alternating to form frame. Pal. Palace, House D, Pier d.
6,9. Flower elements attached to kan cross. Pal. Palace, House E, mural in west room.
7. Head of earth monster with kan cross on forehead, from which grows maize plant. Pal. Fol. Cross.
8. Head of long-nosed earth monster of no. 7 with kan cross, jade, bone, and yax symbols.
10. Long-nosed monster joined to completion sign. Tik. 1, base of south side.
11. Kan cross and jade alternating to form frame. Pal. Palace, House D, Pier e.
12. Flower element attached to jade bead. Pal. Palace, House E, mural in west room.
13. Yax and kan cross symbol. Dresden 18c.
14. Goddess carrying yax and kan cross in pack on her back. Dresden 18c.

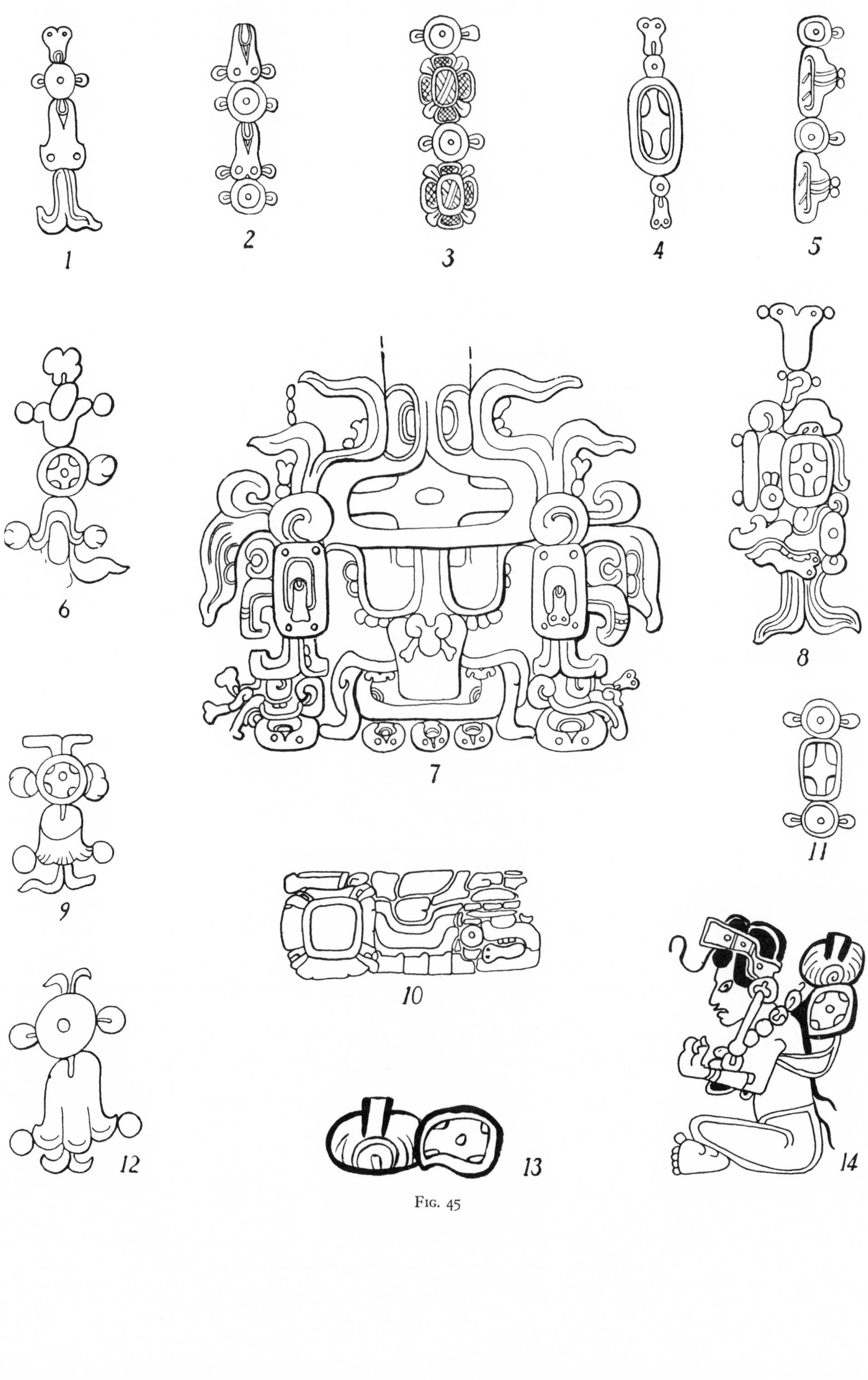
1
2
3
4
5
6
7
8
9
10
11
12
13
14

Fig. 45

Fɪɢ. 46—DIVINATORY TEXTS, CLAUSES, AND MULTIPLICATION TABLE

1–9. Glyphs accompanying nine sections of a divinatory almanac
with 65-day intervals on Dresden 71c–72c.

Vᴀʀɪᴀᴛɪᴏɴꜱ ᴏɴ ᴀ ᴄʟᴀᴜꜱᴇ ᴀᴛ Yᴀxᴄʜɪʟᴀɴ:
10. Yax. L 25, A1–A4. Glyphs reversed to conform to standard
presentation.
11. Yax. 12, F2–F4.
12. Yax. L 56, K1–L2.
13. Yax. 11, Z5–A′8.
14. Yax. L 2, M1–Q1.
15. Yax. L 42, G1–G4.
16. Yax. L 46, F″5–F″7.
17. Schematization of 91 and 364 multiplication table together
with IS which precede it. Dresden 31a–32a.

Aʜᴀᴜ ᴇʟᴇᴍᴇɴᴛ ɪɴ ᴄᴏᴍᴘᴏᴜɴᴅ ɢʟʏᴘʜꜱ:
18. Ahau in hand. Cop. J, B7a.
19. Ahau in hand. Cop. J, D7a.
20. Ahau in hand with *ti* prefix. Yax. L 3, C2a.
21. Ahau in hand with *u* bracket prefix. P.N. 3, E3a.
22. Inverted Ahau in hand with *u* bracket prefix. Cop. Q, F6a.
23. Inverted Ahau in hand with prefix. Bonam. 1, Gl band.
24. Ahau with flamelike prefix. Cop. 9, D7a.
25. Ahau with flamelike prefix. Rio Amarillo, Alt 1, D1a.
26. Ahau with flamelike prefix. Bonam. 1, Gl band.
27. Kan. Perez prophecies for a Katun 5 Ahau.
28. Muluc. Perez prophecies for a Katun 5 Ahau.
29. Ix. Perez prophecies for a Katun 5 Ahau.
30. Cauac. Perez prophecies for a Katun 5 Ahau.
31. Cauac. Perez prophecies for a Katun 5 Ahau.
32. *Cuch*, "burden." Perez prophecies for a Katun 5 Ahau.

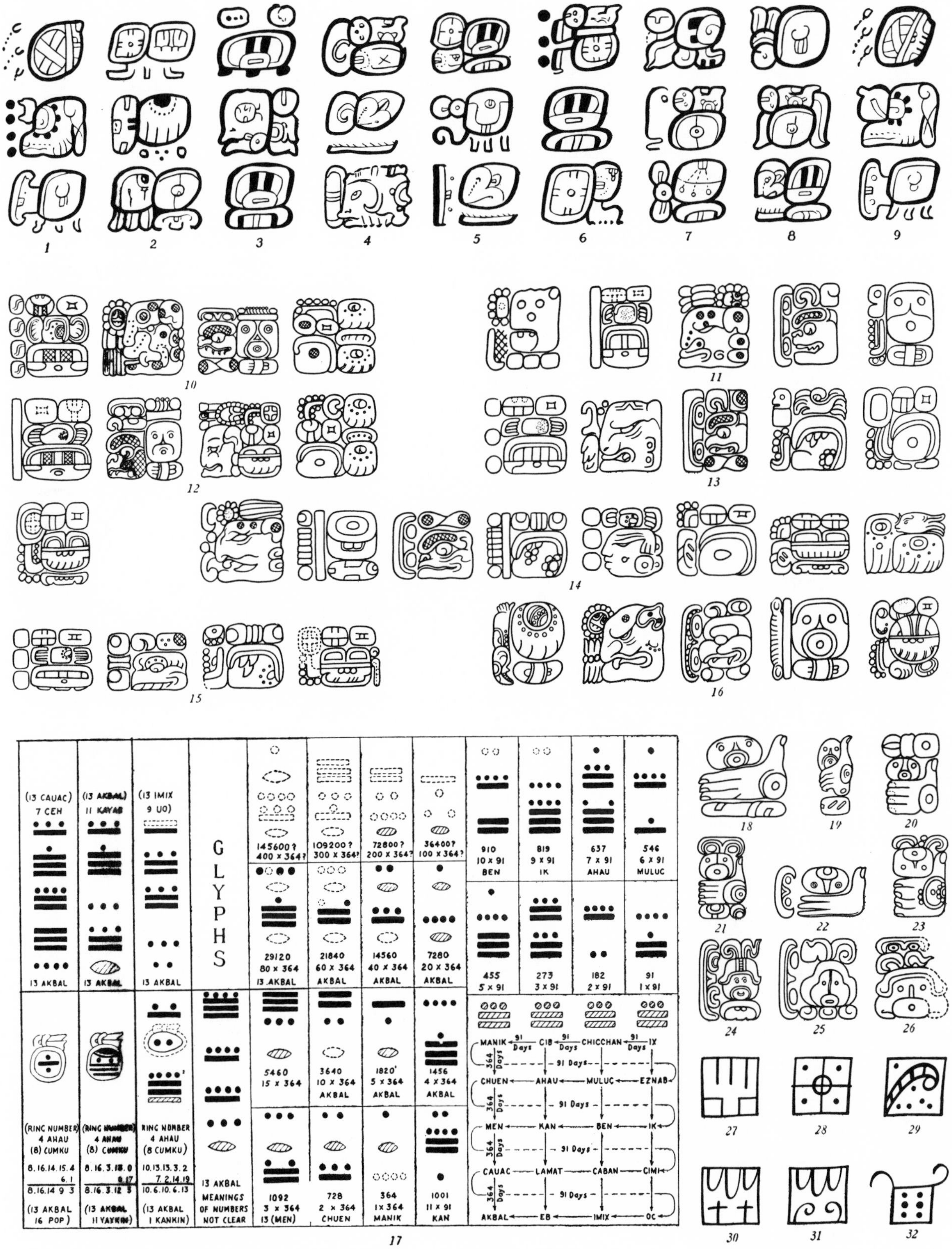

1
2
3
4
5
6
7
8
9
10
11
12
13
14
15
16
(13 CAUAC) 7 CEH
13 AKBAL
(13 AKBAL) 11 KAYAB
13 AKBAL
(13 IMIX 9 UO)
13 AKBAL
GLYPHS
145600? 400 x 364?
109200? 300 x 364?
72800? 200 x 364?
36400? 100 x 364?
29120 80 x 364 13 AKBAL
21840 60 x 364 AKBAL
14560 40 x 364 AKBAL
7280 20 x 364 AKBAL
910 10 x 91 BEN
819 9 x 91 IK
637 7 x 91 AHAU
546 6 x 91 MULUC
455 5 x 91
273 3 x 91
182 2 x 91
91 1 x 91
(RING NUMBER) 4 AHAU (8) CUMKU
8.16.14.15.4
6.1
8.16.14 9 3
(13 AKBAL 16 POP)
(RING NUMBER) 4 AHAU (8) CUMKU
8.16.3.13.0
0.17
8.16.3.12 3
(13 AKBAL 11 YAXKIN)
RING NUMBER 4 AHAU (8 CUMKU)
10.13.13.3.2
7.2.14.19
10.6.10.6.13
(13 AKBAL 1 KANKIN)
13 AKBAL MEANINGS OF NUMBERS NOT CLEAR
5460 15 x 364
3640 10 x 364 AKBAL
1820 5 x 364 AKBAL
1456 4 x 364 AKBAL
1092 3 x 364 13 (MEN)
728 2 x 364 CHUEN
364 1 x 364 MANIK
1001 11 x 91 KAN
MANIK 91 Days CIB 91 Days CHICCHAN 91 Days IX
364 Days
91 Days
CHUEN AHAU MULUC EZNAB
364 Days
91 Days
MEN KAN BEN IK
364 Days
91 Days
CAUAC LAMAT CABAN CIMI
364 Days
91 Days
AKBAL EB IMIX OC
17
18
19
20
21
22
23
24
25
26
27
28
29
30
31
32

FIG. 46

FIG. 47—EARLY INSCRIPTIONS

1. P.N. L 12. IS and following glyphs. 9.3.19.12.12 9 Eb 10 Zec, Gl G8 (error for G9), Gl F. Possible date (9.4.0.0.0) 13 Ahau 18 Yax, count of tun (C1, E1, G1), but arrangement most irregular. (Courtesy of University Museum, Philadelphia.)

2. Yax. L 48. IS with full-figure period glyphs and personified numbers. Read to bottom of Column A before passing to Column B. 9.4.11.8.16 2 Cib (19 Pax), Gl G5 and F. Note monkey serving as kin with end of tail shaped as head of serpent. Also note coefficient of 16 formed by holding head for 6 above that for 10.

3. Pusil. O. IS and lunar series. 9.7.0.0.0 7 Ahau (3 Kankin), Gl G9, F, 5E, D, 6C, X, 9A. (Courtesy of British Museum.)

4. Cop. 24. Part of IS. 9.2.10.0.(0) 3 Ahau (8 Cumku). Note centipede element projecting from cartouche of day sign.

5. P.N. 29. Part of IS. 9.5.5.(0.0 4 Ahau 13 Zotz'). The kins and uinals can be safely restored as zero because the IS introductory glyph is the form for Zotz'. Distance number 1.1.10.19 (C1–D1) leads to 9.6.6.10.19 9 Cauac 7 Yax (C4–D4).

6. P.N. MSS 19. Seating glyph and glyph with coefficient of 1 shown as a thumb. (Courtesy of University Museum, Philadelphia.)

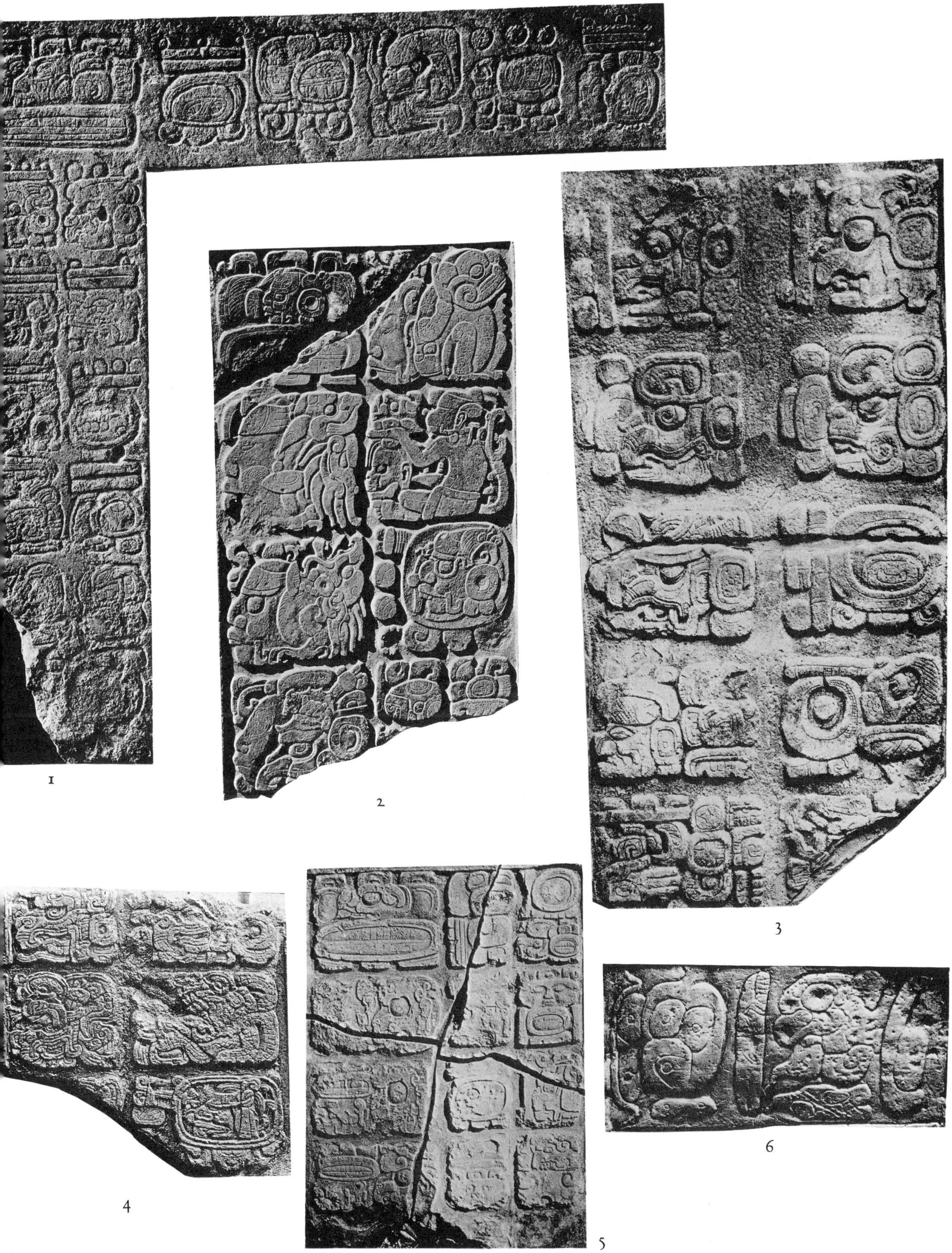
1
2
3
4
5
6

Fig. 47

1

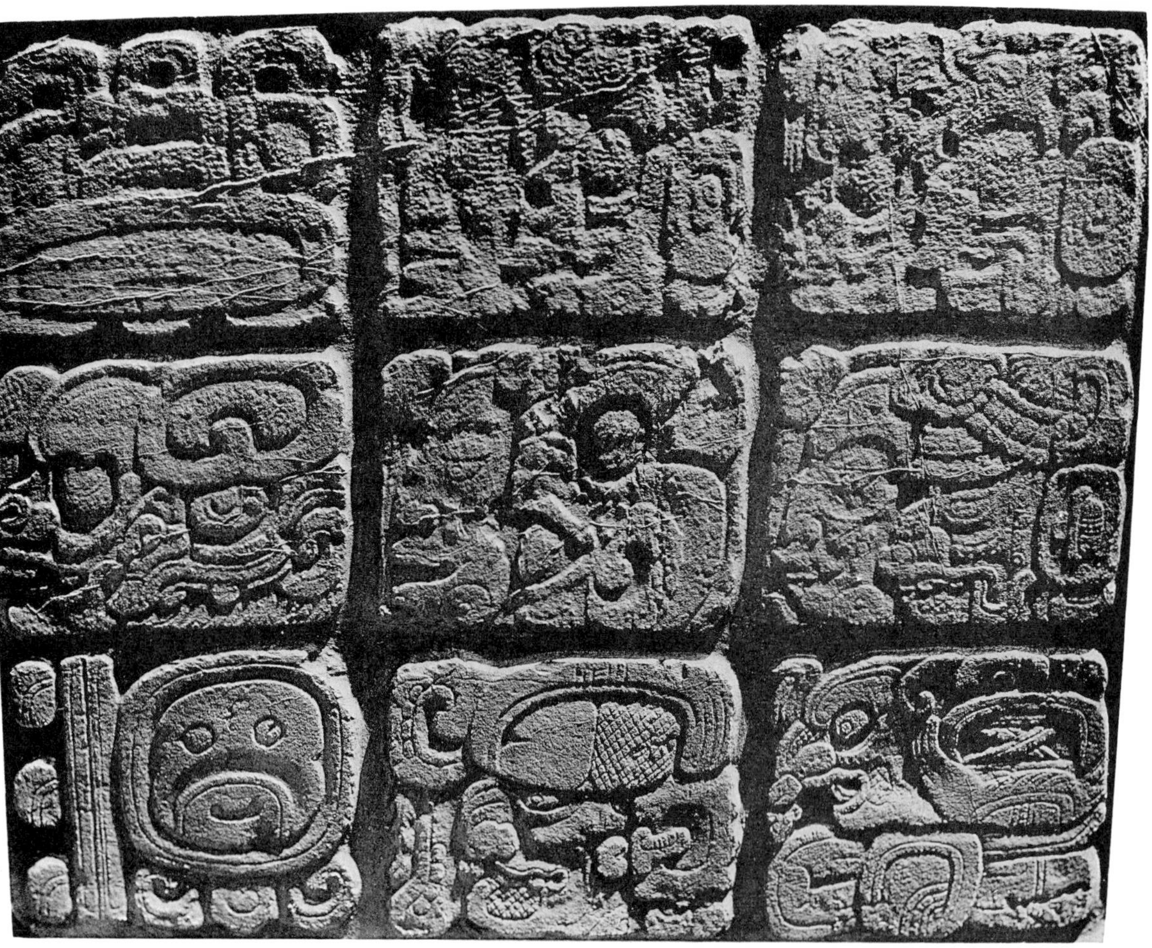

2

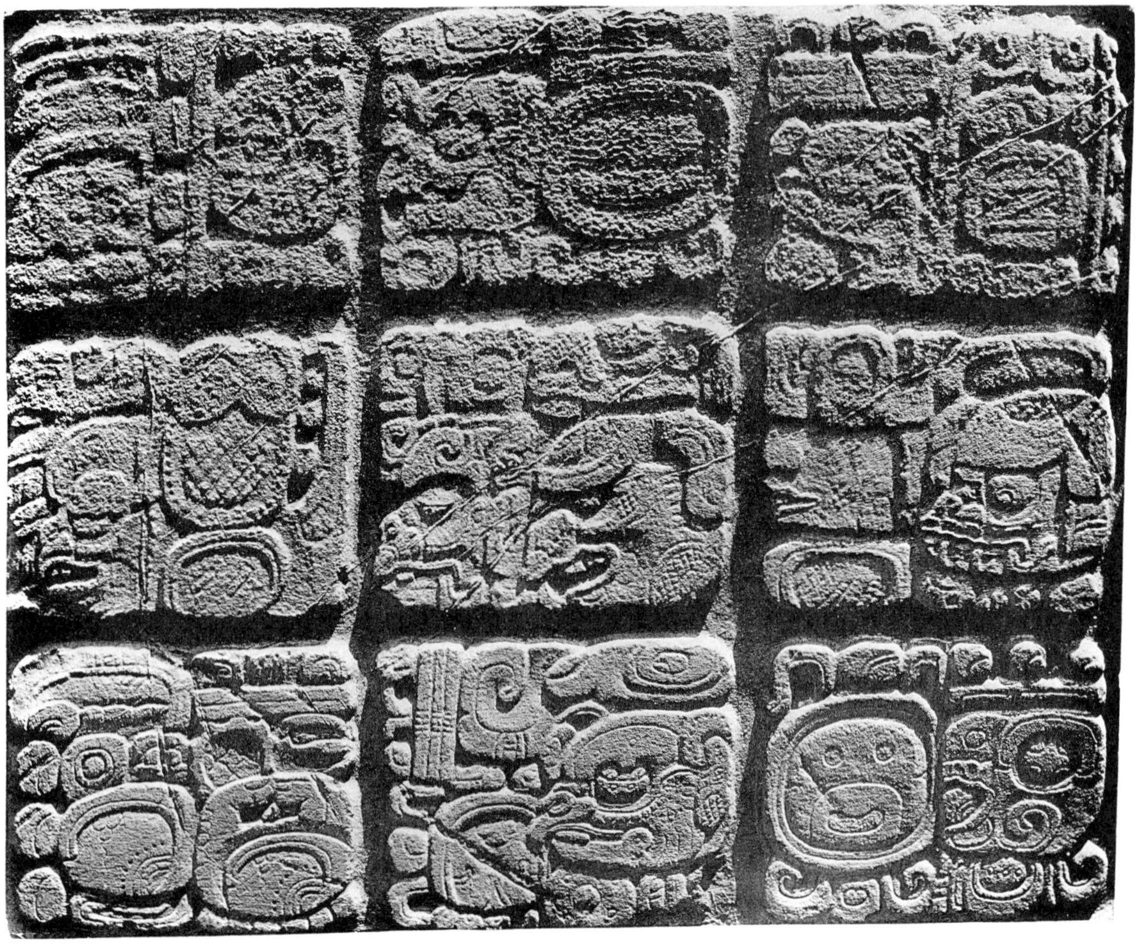

Fig. 48

Fɪɢ. 48—PART OF THE HIEROGLYPHIC STAIRWAY, NARANJO

1. Bl 5. IS with personified glyphs. Read across rows. 9.10.10.0.0 13 Ahau (18 Kankin), Gl G9, glyph of unknown meaning. Columns lettered I, J, K,
2. Bl 6. Dates and distance numbers. Read across rows. Columns lettered L, M, N. Distance number 9 kins, 4 uinals, 1 tun (L1b–M1a); (9.9.18.16.3) 7 Akbal 16 Muan (M1b–N1a); sundry glyphs of unknown meaning; distance number 17 kins, 1 uinal, 1 tun (M3); (9.10.0.0.0) 1 Ahau 8 Kayab (N3). Note use of thumb to designate number 1 at M1a and M3b.

(Courtesy of Peabody Museum, Harvard University)

Fig. 49—TEXTS FROM THE USUMACINTA BASIN

1. Yax. L. 25. Date and distance number. Distance number o kins, 7 uinals, 2 tuns, 2 katuns leading from (9.12.9.8.1) 5 Imix 4 Mac, recorded on under side of lintel, count forward to (9.14.11.15.1) 3 Imix 14 Ch'en. (Courtesy of British Museum.)

2. Yax. L. 27. Dates and distance number. (9.13.13.12.5) 6 Chicchan 8 Zac (written 8 Yax); distance number 9 kins, 5 uinals, 17 tuns, 1 katun count forward to (E1–F1) (9.15.10.17.14) 6 Ix 12 Yaxkin; distance number o kins, 17 uinals, 6 tuns (H2). The calculation continues on L. 59. Note 6 katuns (D1a), 5 "Ben-Ich" katuns (G1a), Venus monster with Ahau-like Ik compound (A2–B2 and F2; see also Yax. 12, A2–B2).

3. Chinik. Thr 1. Dates and distance number. (9.7.0.0.0) 7 Ahau 3 Kankin, seating of haab; 1 uinal counted forward to (D1–E1) (9.7.0.1.0) 1 Ahau 3 Muan (F1–G1). Note personified form of Kankin (B1) and unusual prefix to uinal. (Courtesy of Peabody Museum, Harvard University.)

4. Chinik. Thr 1. Distance number and date. Distance number of 4 kins (eroded), 14 uinals, 5 tuns, 1 katun (H1–J1), counted forward to (M1) 2 Kan (N1). The month position 17 Uo is missing. The starting point is 1 Ahau 3 Muan, recorded on the first part of this text. Note rare personified form of Kan. (Courtesy of Peabody Museum, Harvard University.)

5. La Florida, 9. Lunar series. (9.15.0.0.0) 4 Ahau 13 Yax; Gl G9, F, 11D, 3C, X, B, 10A. Note personified form of Yax.

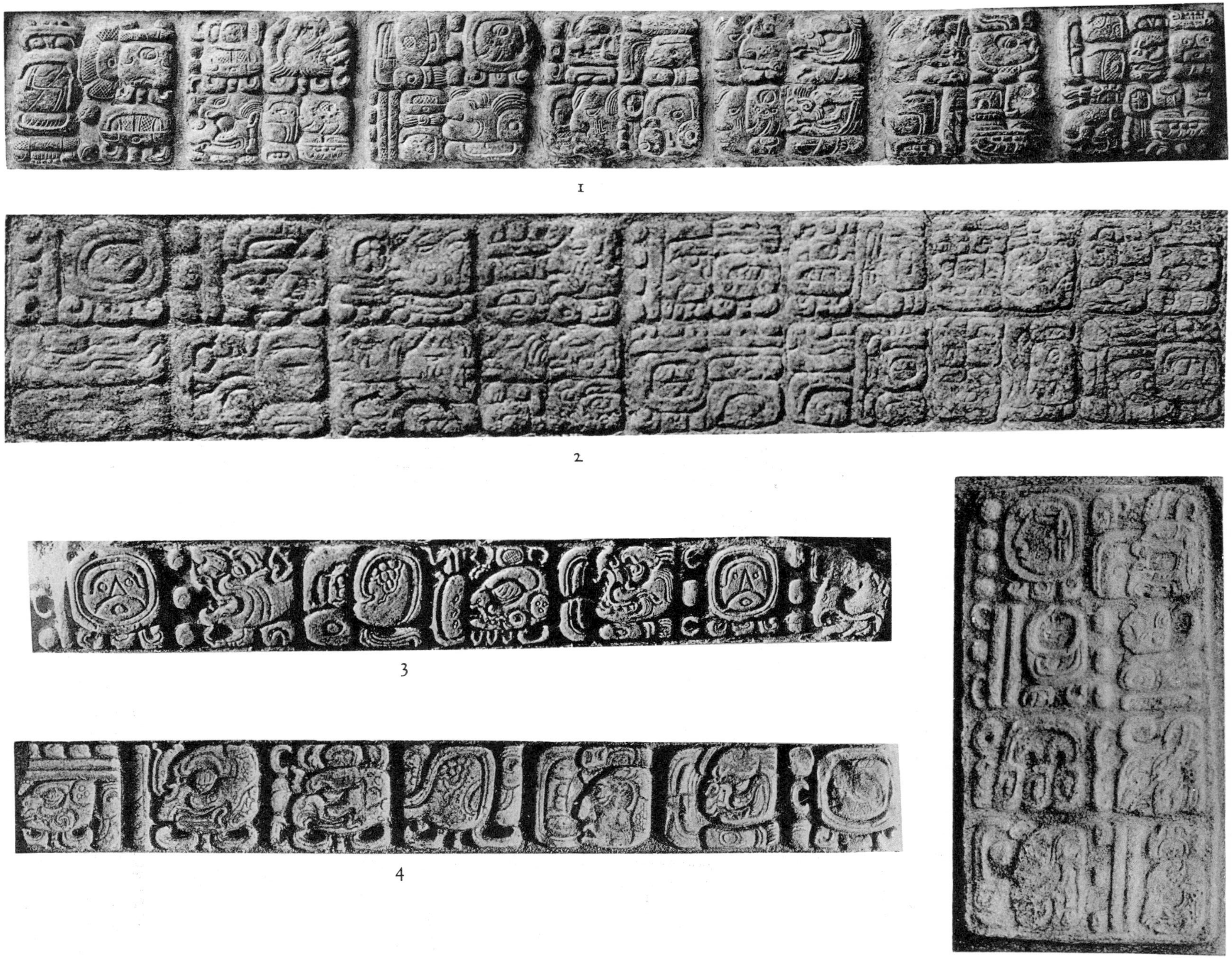

Fig. 49

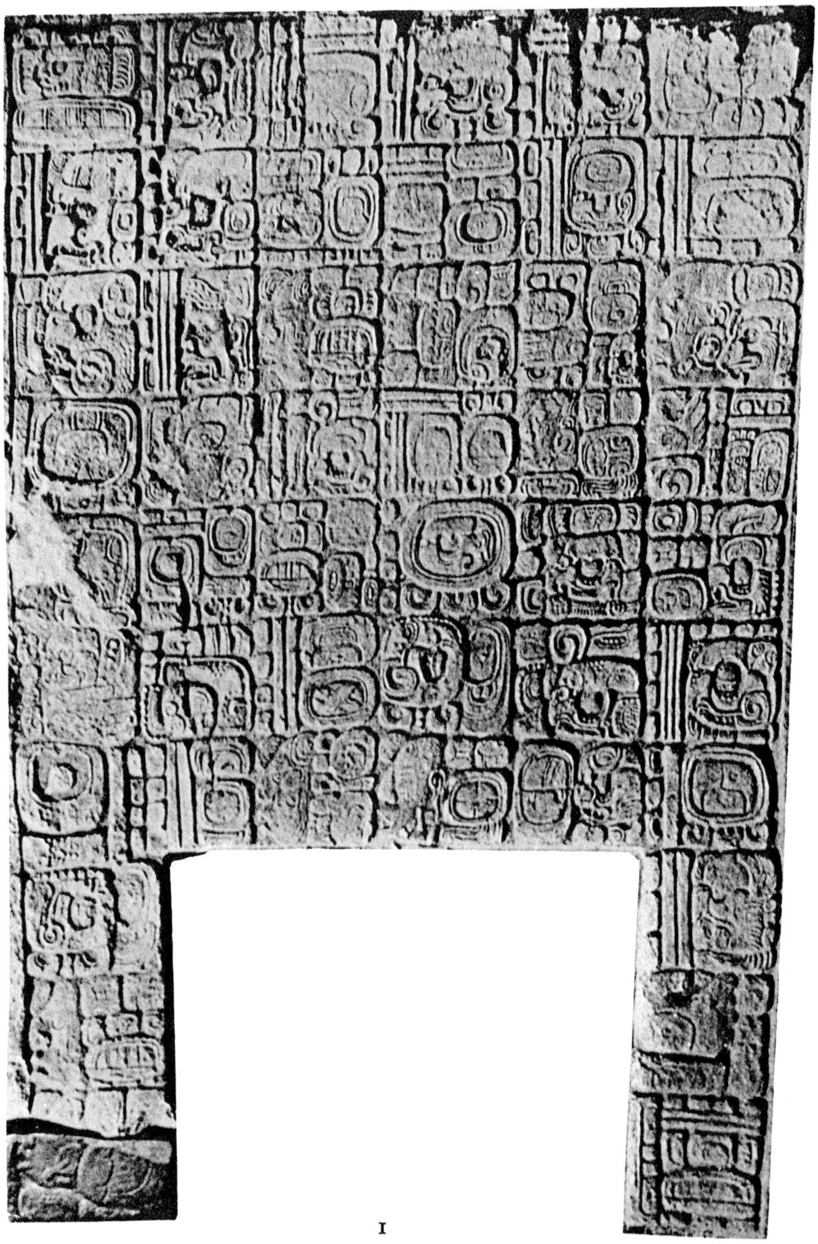

1

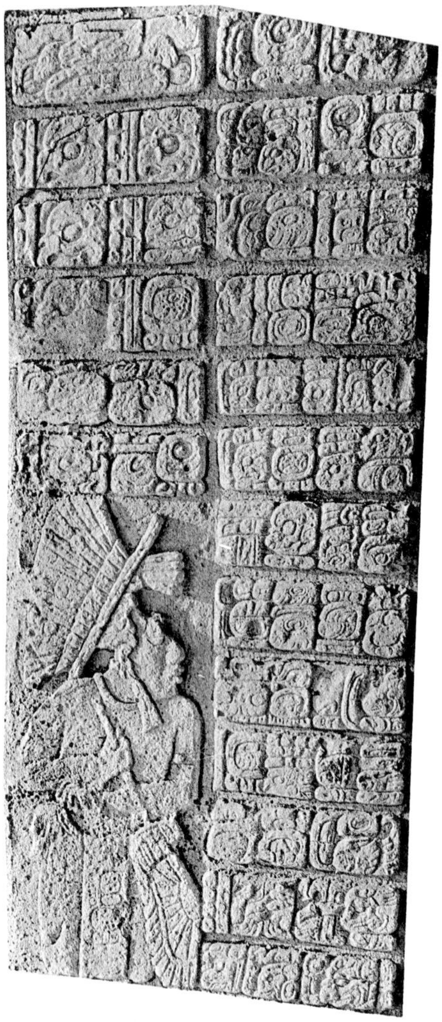

2

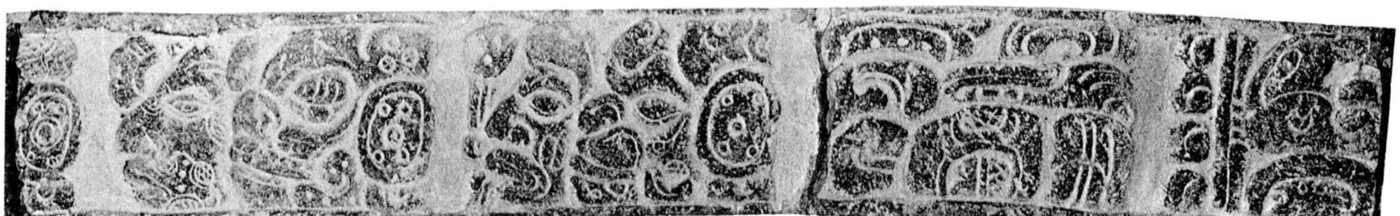

3

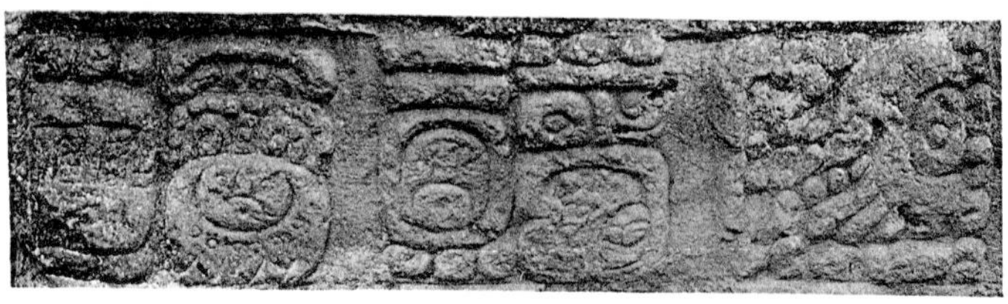

4

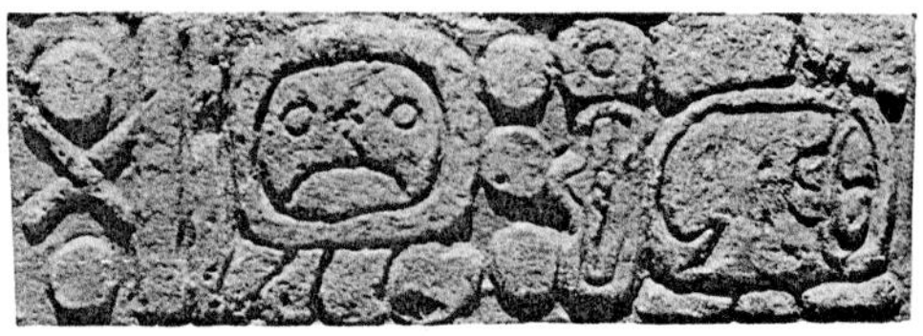

5

Fig. 50

FIG. 50—TEXTS OF VARIOUS PERIODS

1. P.N. 3. IS and PE. 9.12.2.0.16 5 Cib, G7, unknown, 7E, D, 2C, X, 9A, 14 Yaxkin (A1–B7); frog with moon postfix (A8); 1 (?) "Ben-Ich" katun (A9); 0 kins, 10 uinals, 12 tuns, count forward to (9.12.14.10.16) 1 Cib 14 Kankin (C1-D2a); 10 kins, 11 uinals, 1 tun, 1 katun, count forward to (D4–C5) (9.13.16.4.6) 4 Cimi 14 Uo (D5–C6); 15 kins, 8 uinals, 3 tuns, count forward to (E1–F1) (9.13.19.13.1) 11 Imix 14 Yax (E2–F2); completion of fifth haab 1 katun (F4–E5; this declares an anniversary of a date given elsewhere on this stela); 19 kins, 4 uinals, count forward to (F6–E7) (9.14.0.0.0) 6 Ahau 13 Muan, completion of fourteenth katun (F7–F10). (Courtesy of Peabody Museum, Harvard University.)

2. Yax. Str 44, middle door. 9.12.8.14.1 12 Imix, G2, F, 7E, D, (4)C, X, B, 9A, 4 Pop (A1–D2); distance number 0 kins, 12 uinals (D8b–C9a); count forward to (9.12.9.8.1) 5 Imix 4 Mac (D9b–C10).

3. Cop. Stone re-used as cover of drain. Glyphs are of early style, of about 9.7.0.0.0. Part of an IS recording 9 uinals, ? kins and perhaps Glyph G1. Note clear yax ornament on head of 9. Glyphs covered with paper to bring out detail.

4. Cop. Fragmentary stone recovered from Copan river. Three tuns, Imix-Ahau with u bracket, (9.18.10.0.0) 10 Ahau 8 Zac, hand scattering water.

5. El Amparo 1. 12 Ahau, 3 te with unidentified month glyph. Ornamental cross in coefficient of Ahau indicates a late text. Note unusual postfix of Ahau. (Photograph by Richard Ceough.)

Fig. 51—TEXTS AT YAXCHILAN, COPAN, AND PALENQUE

1. Yax. Str 44, southeast doorway, upper step. The columns are
   lettered V to Y. (9.6.10.14.15) 4 Men 3 Mac (V1–W1); 19
   kins, 2 uinals, 11 tuns, 7 katuns (V5–W5), leading to
   (9.14.1.17.14) 5 Ix 17 Kankin, declared elsewhere in this text;
   17 kins, 15 uinals, 15 tuns (Y4b–X5a), leading to (9.14.17.15.11)
   2 Chuen 14 Mol (Y5b–X6a). Note 5 katuns (X3a). (Photographs
   by Giles G. Healey.)
2. Yax. 12. (9.15.10.17.14) 6 Ix 14 Yaxkin; 6 kins, (0 uinals),
   10 tuns, count forward to (A6–B6) (9.16.1.0.0) 11 Ahau 8
   Zec (C1–D1). Note Venus glyph and "Ahau"-Ik compound
   (A2–B2), as on Yax. L 27, 5 "Ben-Ich" katuns (B3), variant
   form of distance number introductory glyph with lunar postfix
   (B5). (Photograph by Giles G. Healey.)
3. Cop. Review Stand. Last two glyphs recording (9.17.0.0.0) 13
   Ahau 18 Cumku.
4. Pal. Lápida de Creación, incised glyphs. (Courtesy of Museo
   Nacional de Antropología, Mexico.)

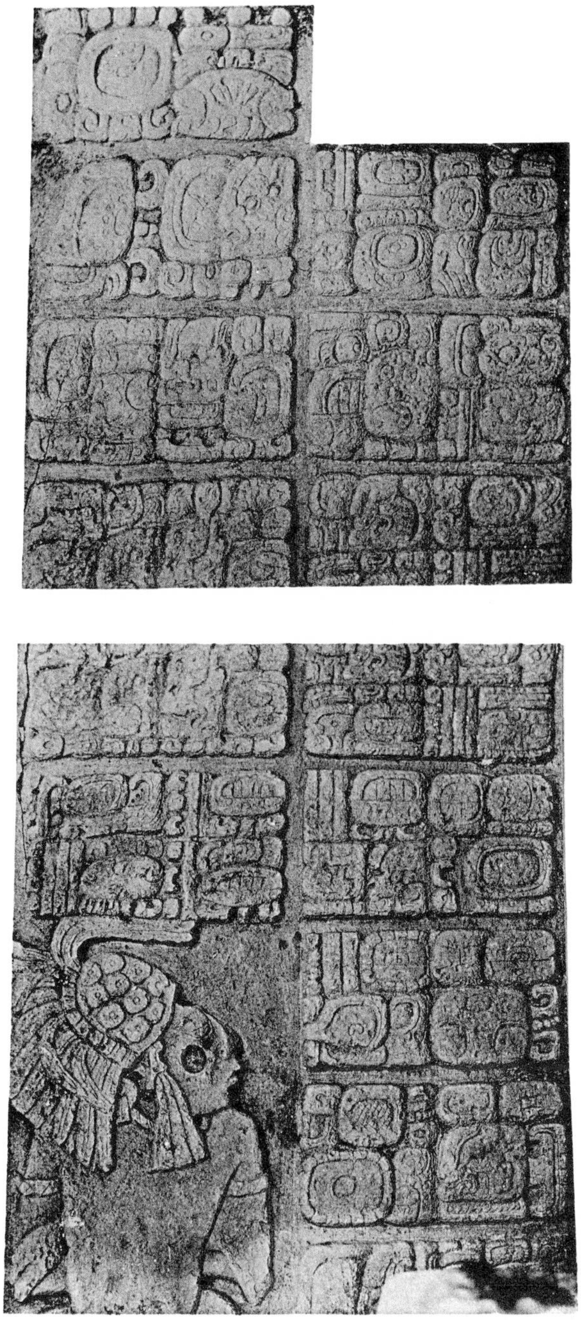

1

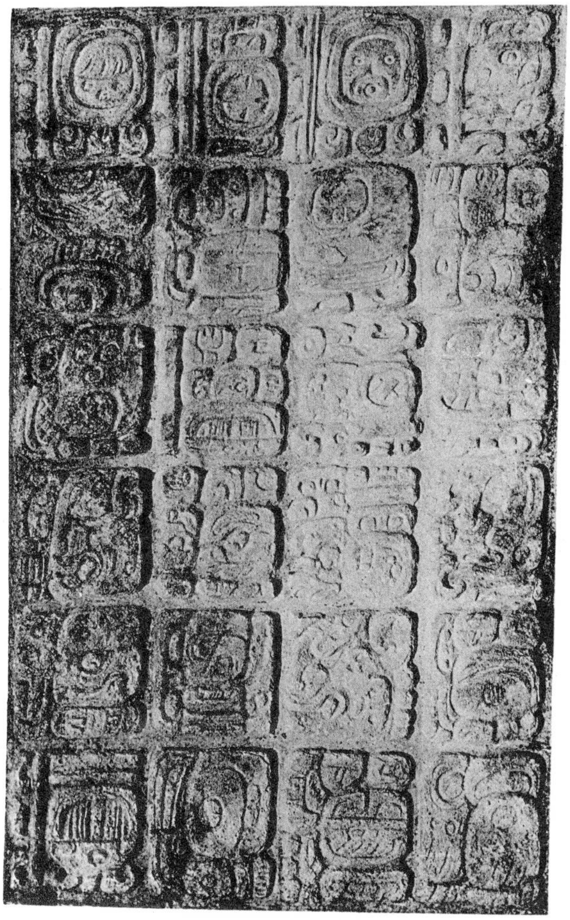

2

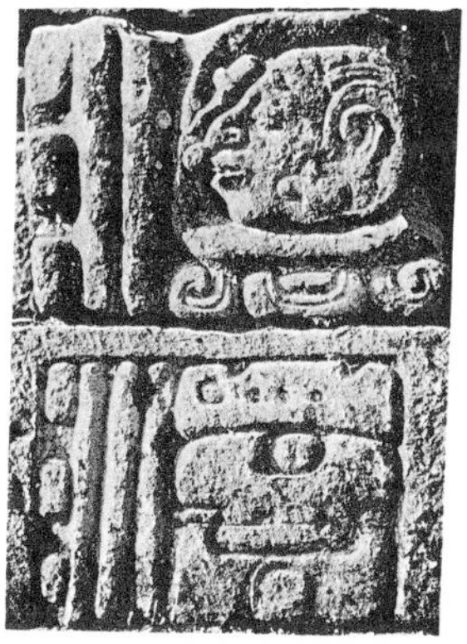

3

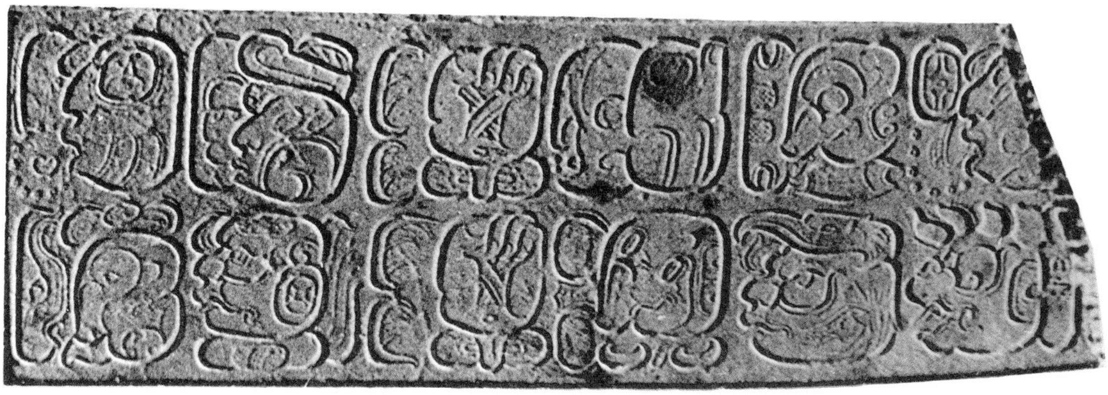

4

Fig. 51

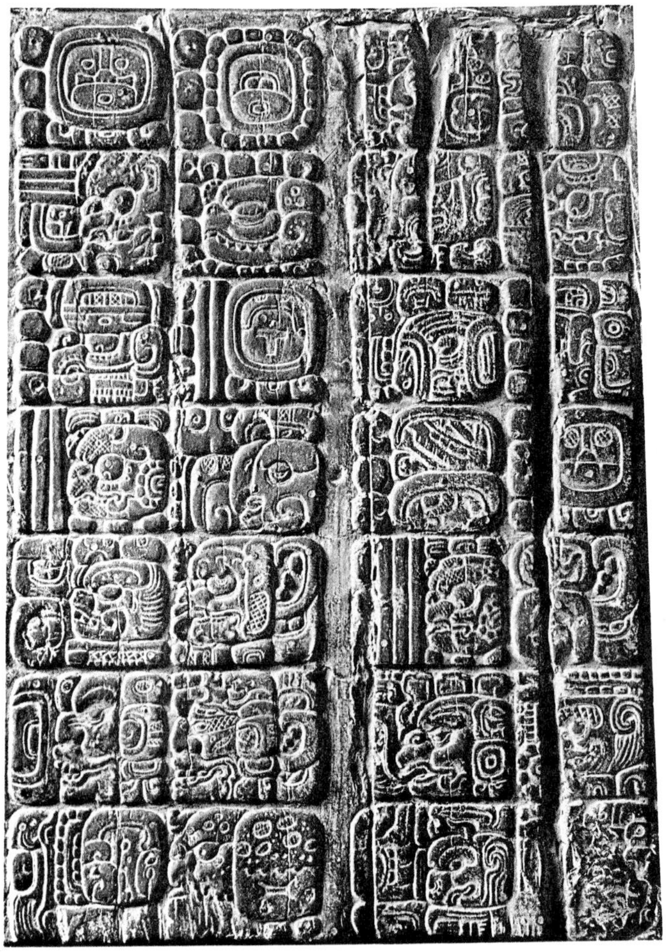

1

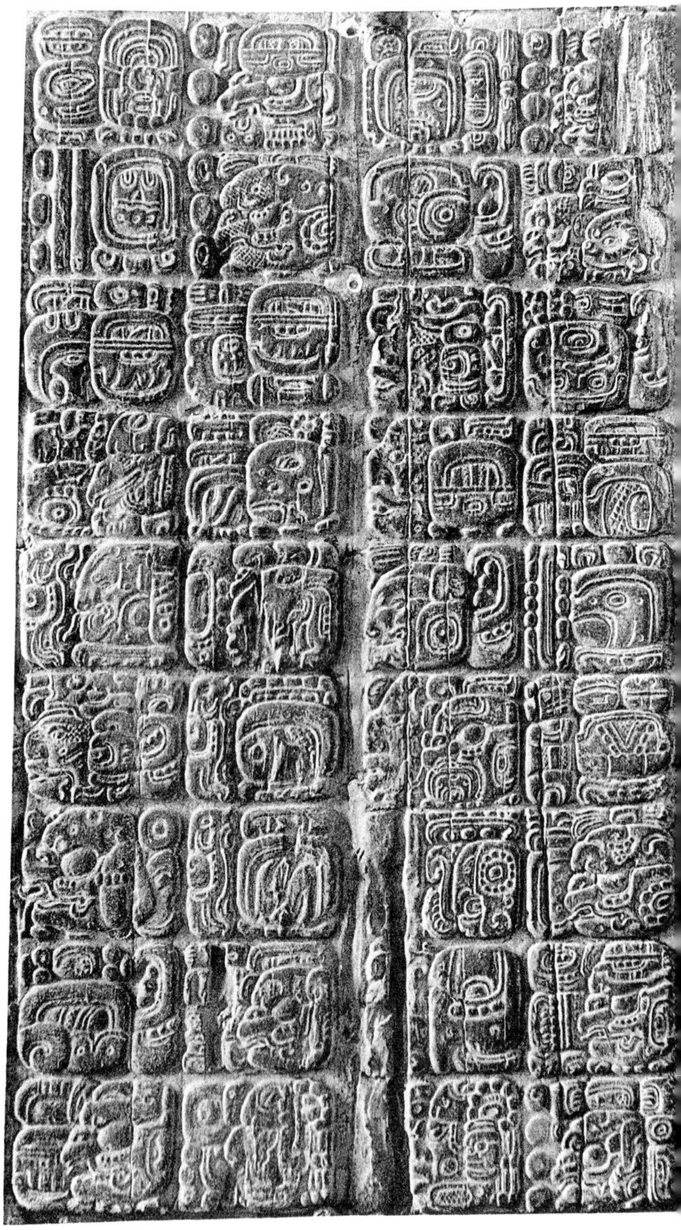

2

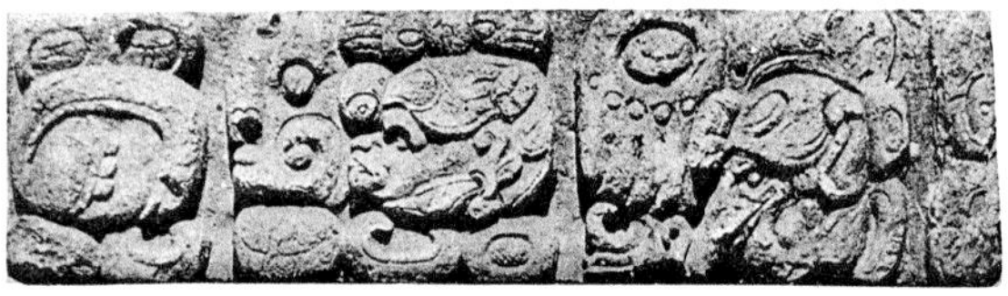

3

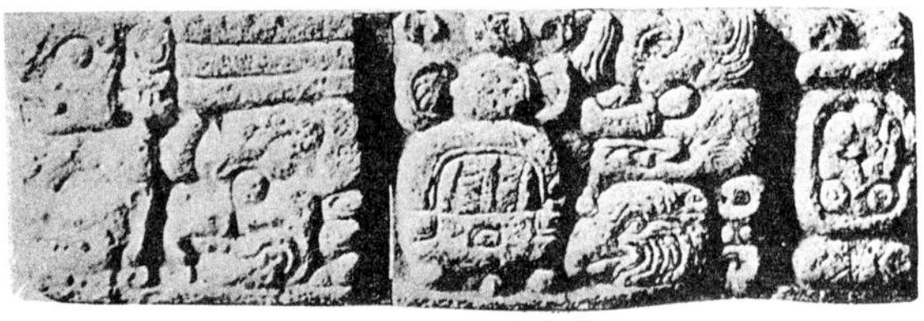

4

Fig. 52

FIG. 52—TEXTS AT TIKAL AND COPAN

1, 2. Tik. T 4, L 3. One of the few surviving texts in wood. The arrangement is:

A1–A2	9.15.10. 0.0	3 Ahau 3 Mol. Half period of katun
B2–A3	2. 2.2	
B3–A4	9.15.12. 2.2	11 Ik 15 Ch'en
C4	1	1 sun at horizon
D4–C5	9.15.12. 2.3	12 Akbal 16 Ch'en
F1	3.(0.0)	
E2–F2	9.15.15. 2.3	13 Akbal 1 Ch'en

Note Venus glyph as prefix (B4a), unusual postfix of tun glyphs at A3 and F1, and possible record of 4 katuns at H9, but the hand holding axe against the cheek makes this identification doubtful. (Photographed from a cast in Peabody Museum, Harvard University.)

3, 4. Cop. HS, fragments. The first fragment illustrates non-calendarial glyphs of the best period of carving at Copan (c. 9.16.0.0.0.); the second has an incomplete distance number of 1.15. ?. ? leading back to a day 7 Lamat. Note the anterior date indicator with *ti* element personified as vulture with *ti* on his forehead (cf. fig. 4,29). (Courtesy of Peabody Museum, Harvard University.)

FIG. 53—TEXTS AT PALENQUE, QUIRIGUA, AND XCALUMKIN

1. Left side of Cross, Pal. The dates are:

A1–B9	12.19.13. 4. 0	8 Ahau 18 Zec (IS).
A10–A13		Five *bix* days, D, 2C, X, B, 9A
B13	1. 0	Moon glyph with zero coefficient
A16–B16	12.19.13. 3. 0	1 Ahau 18 Zotz' (819-day count)
D1–C2	8. 5. 2	Written 8.5.0. Joins first date with 13 Ik, end of Mol, given below
D3–C5	13. 0. 0. 0. 0	4 Ahau 8 Cumku, completion 13 baktuns
D5–C6a	1. 9. 2	
C9–D9	13. 0. 1. 9. 2	13 Ik, end of Mol
D13–C15	1.18. 3.12. 0	
E1–F1	1.18. 5. 3. 2	9 Ik 15 Ceh
	(12.19.13. 3. 0)	1 Ahau 18 Zotz') not repeated
E5–F6	2. 1. 7.11. 2	
E9–F9	2. 1. 0.14. 2	9 Ik 0 Yax (written 0 Zac)
E10–F11	3. 6.10.12. 2	
E12–F12		9 Ik starting point of count
F15–F16	(5. 7.11. 8. 4 1. 6. 7.13	1 Kan 2 Cumku)
Rt. tablet	5. 8.17.15.17	11 Caban 0 Pop

It is possible that the last three dates should be shifted forward about 24 CR. (Courtesy of British Museum.)

2. Quir. F, east side. Personified numbers and periods in IS:

C1–D5, D8 C6–C8	9.16.10.0.0	1 Ahau 3 Zip G9, F, moon completed (?), 6C, X, 10A
D10–C11 C13a	(0.12.10. 0. 0. 0.0.0) 11. 1. (0. 0.0.0)	1 Ahau, tun?? ?
D14 C14	(0.11.18.19. 0. 0.0.0)	1 Ahau 13 Mol Completion 19 baktuns (?)
D16–C17	18.13. 0. 0. 0. 0.0	1 Ahau 13 Yaxkin
D16a		Completion 13 kinchiltuns

The dates from D10 to C14 are dubious. The record of 1 Ahau, tun, may refer to 9.16.10.0.0; the glyph with coefficient of 19 is not a known form of the batktun; the glyph read as 11 pictuns 1 baktun would normally be read as 11 baktuns 1 katun. (Courtesy of British Museum.)

3. Xcal. Temple of Initial Series. Personified numbers and periods:

A1–A8	9.15.12.6.9	7 Muluc (1 Kankin on part not shown)
B8–B12		Kin, G3, unknown, 2D, 2C, X, B

(Photograph of cast in Peabody Museum, Harvard University.)

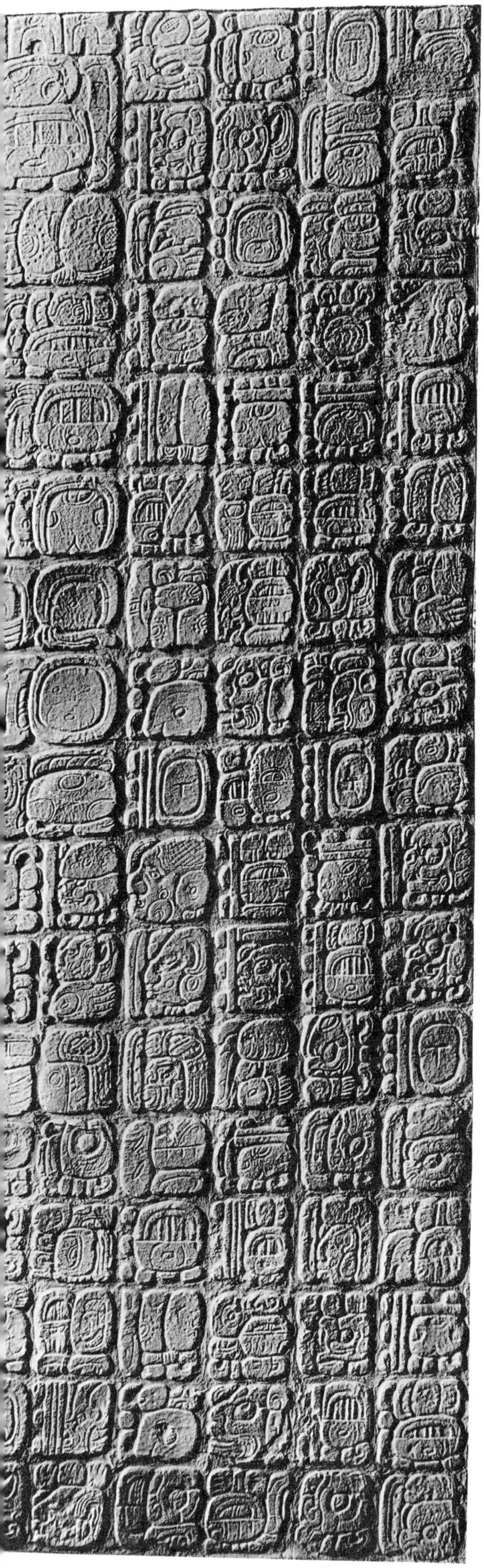

1

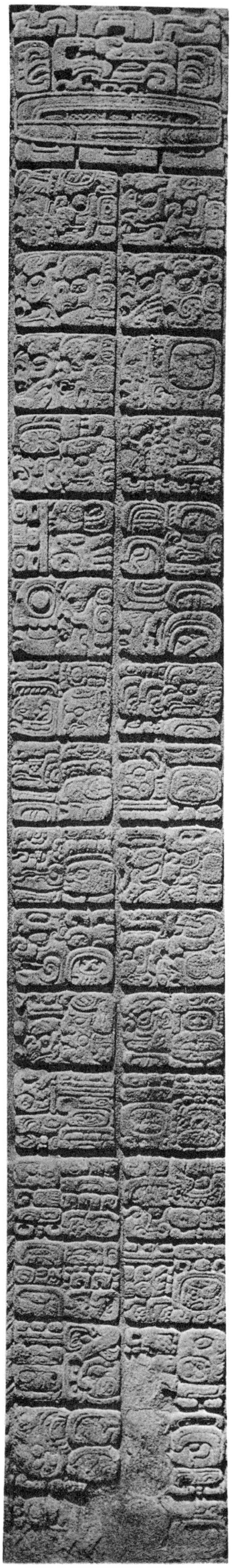

2

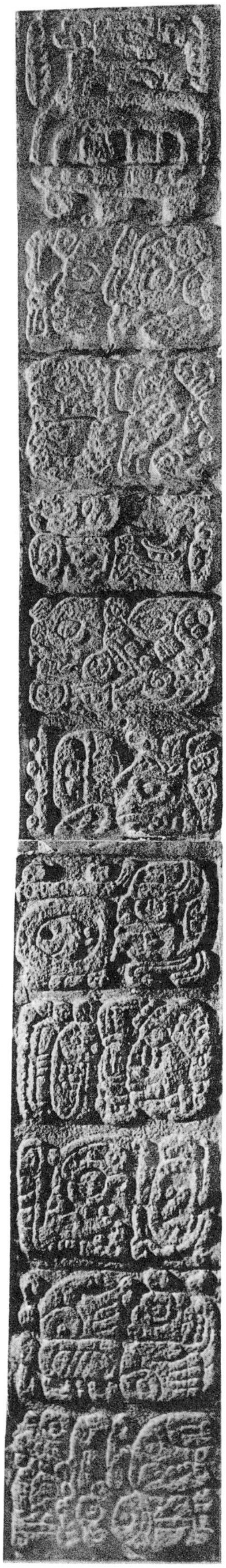

3

Fig. 53

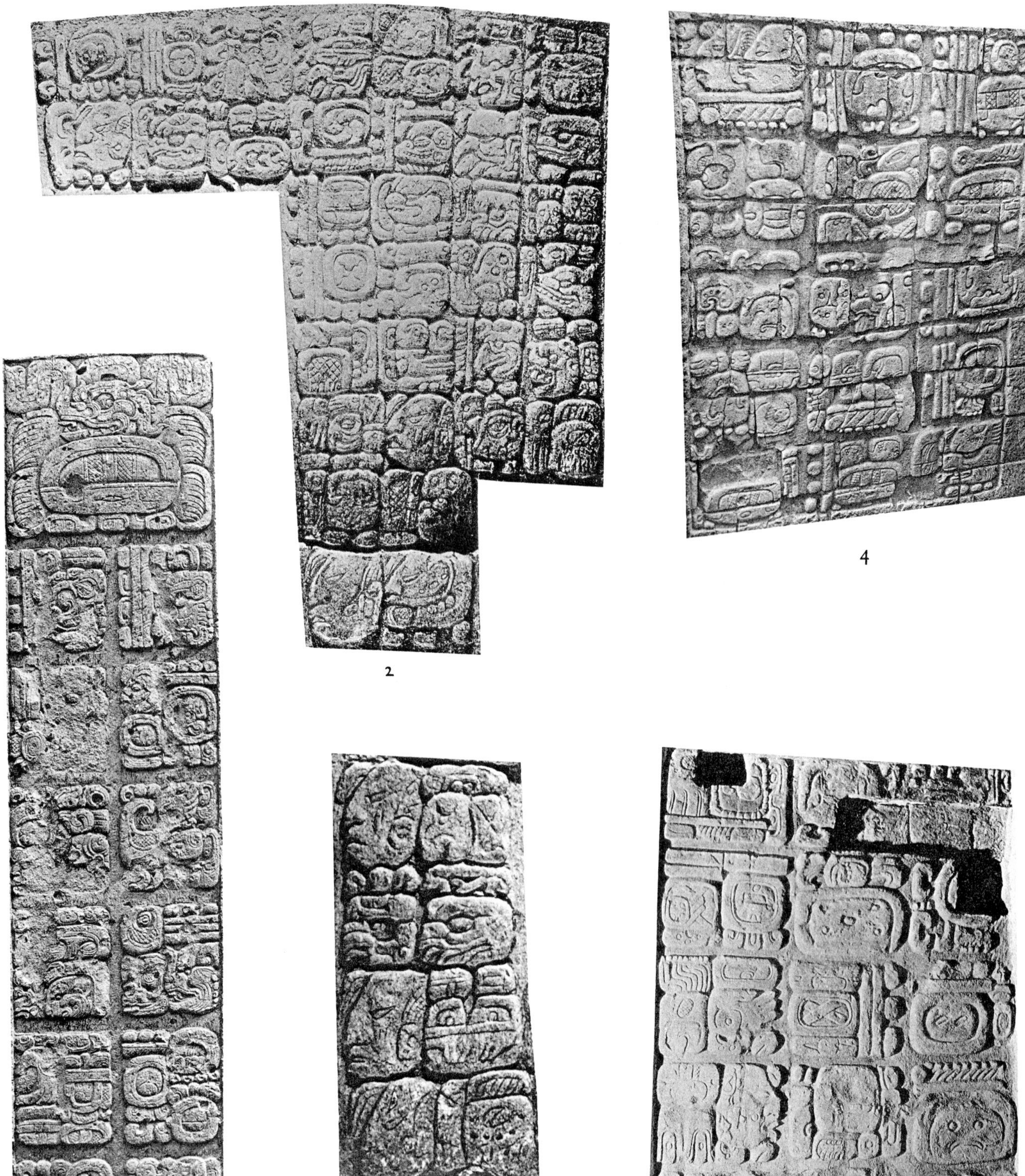
1
2
3
4
5

Fig. 54

Fig. 54—TEXTS AT COPAN AND BONAMPAK

1. Cop. 6. IS and lunar series recording 9.12.10.0.0 9 Ahau, G9, F (personified postfix converted into main element, 2E, D, 2(?)C, (coefficient obliterated), B with *xoc* head, X, 10A, 18 Zotz', completion half period, 8 Ahau (postfix indicating a katun ending, that is 9.13.0.0.0 8 Ahau 8 Uo).

2,3. Bonam. 2. CR dates, position of first fixed by Gl G. Arrangement:

A1–B1	9.17. 5. 8. 9	6 Muluc 17 Yaxkin
A2–B2		Gl G7, F
D2–E3	13. 7. 9	Count forward to
D4–E4	9.17.18.15.18	12 Etz'nab 1 Ceh
E5		Completion of haab (meaning?).

(Photograph by Giles G. Healey.)

4. Cop. T 11, E door, S panel. Arrangement:

B1	3.12	Distance number. Position uncertain
A2–B4		Glyphs apparently of an 819-day cycle
A5–C4	9.17.2.12.16	IS written 9.17.2.11.16, but one uinal later reaches 1 Cib 19 Ceh given on south doorway, but not at start of panel.
C5		Count forward to

Note unusual form of baktun and rare occurrence of "count forward to" glyph after IS. Also personified form of distance number introductory glyph.

5. Cop. T 11, E door, N panel. Arrangement:

A3–B3	(9.17.1.3.5)	9 Chicchan 13 Zip
C2		5 Cib 10 Pop [*sic*]

Direction of glyphs reversed to face outward in doorway. Partly obliterated A1–B1 apparently give a distance number which is best as 1.9.11. A distance number of 1.9.11 would connect the first date with the IS (amended) on the south panel. The combination 5 Cib 10 Pop is impossible. Note great Venus glyph at C4b.

FIG. 55—TEXTS AT PALENQUE AND QUIRIGUA

1. Pal. 96 Gl.:

A1–B1	9.11. 0. 0. 0	12 Ahau 8 Ceh,
B2		Expiration of 11 katuns
A5–A6	2. 1.11	Count forward to
B6–A7	9.11. 2. 1.11	9 Chuen 9 Mac
D2–C4	2. 8. 4.17	Count forward to
D4–C5	9.13.10. 6. 8	5 Lamat 6 Xul
E1–E2	19.15.14	Count forward to
F2–E3	9.14.10. 4. 2	9 Ik 5 Kayab
F7–G1	2. 2.14. 5	Count forward to
H1–G2	9.16.13. 0. 7	9 Manik 15 Uo
H6–G7	1.(0. 0. 0)	Count forward to
H7–G8	9.17.13. 0. 7	7 Manik 0 Pax
H8–I1		Completion of first katun
L1	7	
K2–L2	9.17.13. 0. 0	13 Ahau 13 Muan. Anterior
		date of pair
K3		13 tuns.
L3–K4a		Forward to completion of
		katun (?).

Note Venus and lunar glyph as part of what is possibly the distance number introductory glyph (E7), unusual variants Lamat and Pax (D4b, G8), the cauac glyph with affixes (A8, C8, F6, H5), one shell completion glyph (I8), five katuns (L6), winged cauac with kan cross infix (L4b), "elephant trunk" prefix as in Dresden (E5).

2–4. Opening sentences of Quir. Alt P:

A1–B2		IS introductory glyph for
		month Ceh
C1–F1, H2	9.18. 5. 0. 0	4 Ahau 13 Ceh, fifth haab.
E2–G2		Glyphs G, F, 3E, D, 4C,
		X, B, 9A

Note the unusual form of Glyph A with coefficient inside the crescent and head forms for Ceh and haab.

(Photographs specially taken for this publication by Giles G. Healey.)

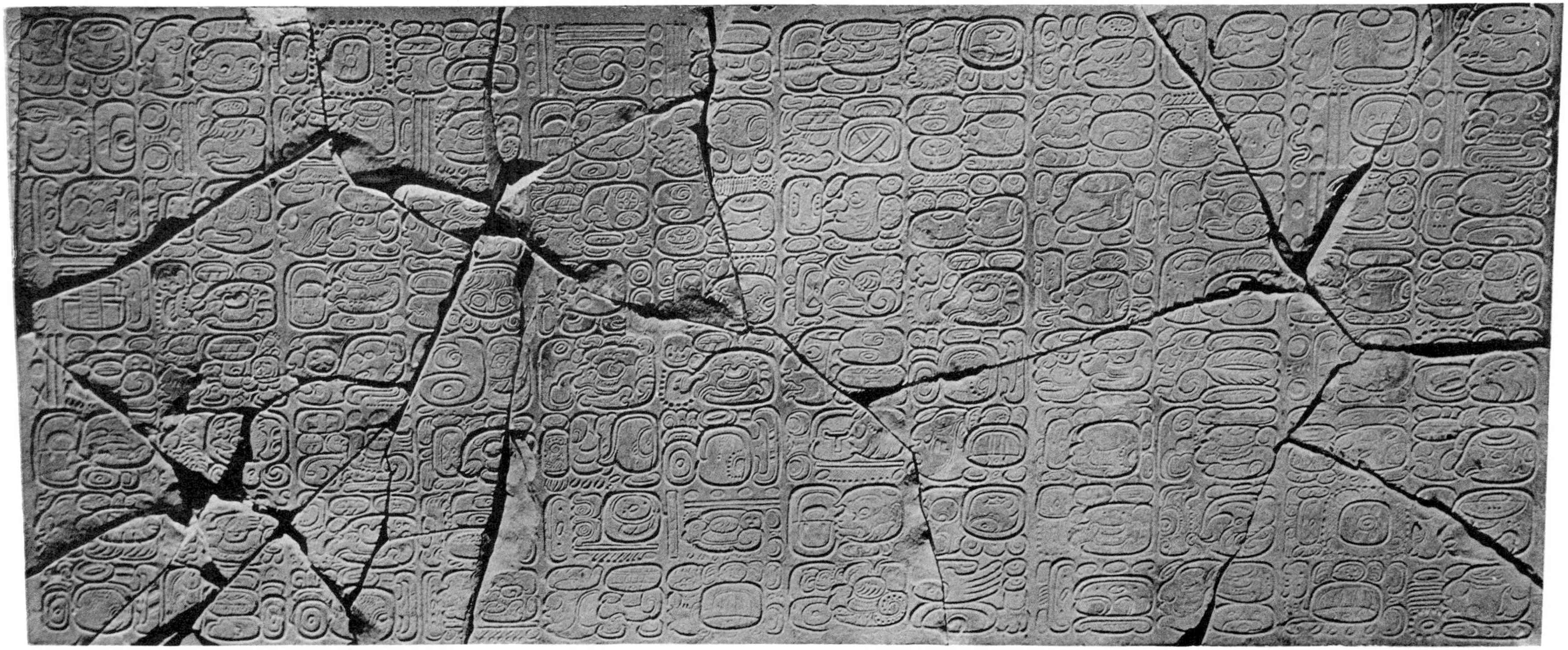

1

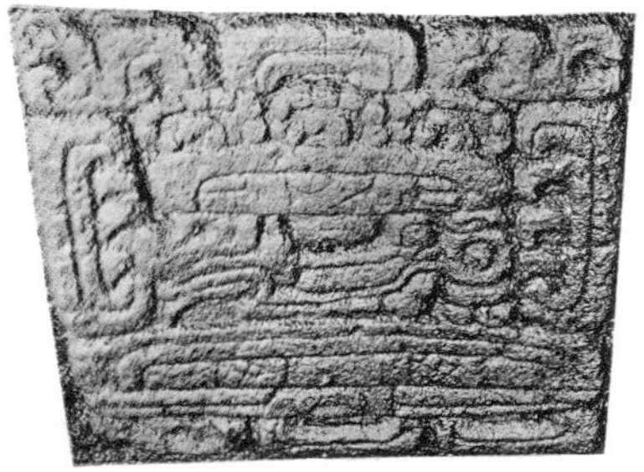

2

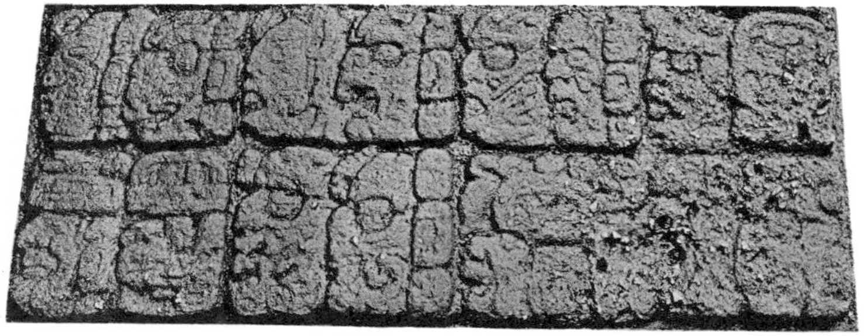

3

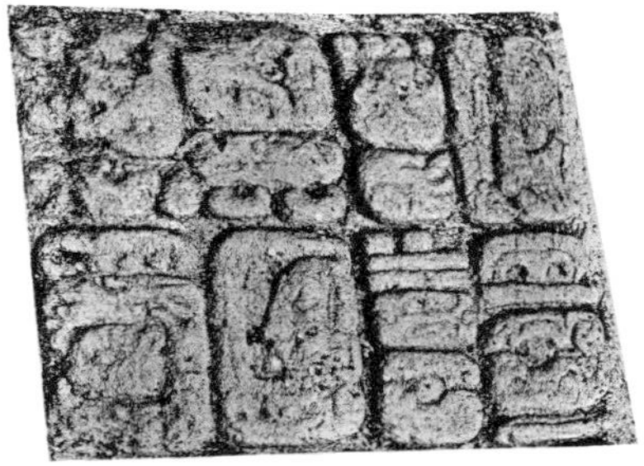

4

Fig. 55

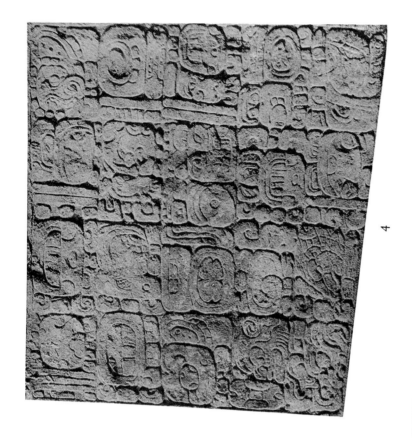

FIG. 56

FIG. 56—TEXTS FROM CHIAPAS AND CAMPECHE

1. Xcal. north temple, east column. First two glyphs may record: Haab 1, 13 Ahau, probably a reference to a date falling in tun ending on 9.14.1.0.0. Note style of glyphs.

2. Yax. 7. Noncalendarial glyphs on front.

3. Tila C. IS 9.13.0.0.0 8 Ahau 8 Uo.

4. Yax. L. 30. The text is carried forward from L 29 and the first column is E. There is recorded a base in the 819-day count at 1 Ben 1 Ch'en:

Lintel 29	9.13.17.12.10	8 Oc (IS)
E1–F1	1. 1.17	(Subtract)
E2–F2	9.13.16.10.13	1 Ben 1 Ch'en
E3–F5		Glyphs of 819-day count
G1	(9.13.17.12.10)	13 Yax, month of IS
H3–H4a	2. 3. 5.10	Its count to
H4b–G5	9.16. 1. 0. 0	11 Ahau 8 Zec

5. Yax. L 14. Opening pair of glyphs are 4 Imix 4 Mol, probably referable to 9.15.10.0.11. They are followed by the glyph of the hand grasping fish. Note half-speckled Ahau with *u* postfix at B4.

6. Yax. 11. IS records 9.16.1.0.0 11 Ahau 8 Zec with glyphs G9, F, 6Y, 12D, 5C (perhaps 4C), X, B, 9A. Note tied-up lunar glyph as on L 30 and *te* (t) prefix with tun and 8 Zec. "Ben-Ich" katun with possible coefficient of 5 is also recorded. (Courtesy of Peabody Museum, Harvard University.)

Fig. 57—TEXTS AT PIEDRAS NEGRAS AND PALENQUE

1–6. P.N. L 3. The text has been rearranged and a part omitted. 1, A1–H2; 2, I1–N2, originally to the right of no. 1; 3, O1–T2, originally to the right of no. 2; 4, U1–V12, originally the right edge of lintel, joining no. 3 at top; 5, glyphs at right edge of bench; 6, some of glyphs at bottom of lintel. The text runs:

1.	A1–A14, E2	9.15.18. 3.13	5 Ben 16 Ch'en (IS)
	B14–F1		G1, F, 9D, C completed, X, B, 10A
	G1		One katun anniversary (note postfix)
2.	L1	2	(Inverted Ahau variant)
	K2–L2	9.15.18. 3.15	7 Men 18 Ch'en
3.	S1–T1	8. 8. 2	
	S2–T2		From earlier date forward to sunrise
4.	U1–V1	9.16. 6.11.17	7 Caban 0 Pax
	U4	3	(Inverted Ahau variant)
	V4–U5	9.16. 6.12. 0	10 Ahau 3 Pax
	U7–U8	1. 4.12. 1	Forward to sunrise
	V8	9.17.11. 6. 1	12 Imix 19 Zip

5,6. These contain no chronological matter. (Courtesy of University Museum, Philadelphia.)

7. P.N. 10, left side. The text runs:

A1–B5, A9	9.15.10.0.0	3 Ahau 3 Mol
A6–B8		GF, 9D, 3C, X, B, 10A
B9		Glyph for half period completed

8. Stucco glyphs from Olvidado, Pal. They form an incomplete IS, the parts lacking being in parentheses: 9.10.(14).5.10 3 Oc 3 Pop (G), F, (D), 6C (X, B, A). The variable element of the IS introductory glyph is the head of a jaguar, which is correct for this IS which falls in Pop. (Courtesy of National Museum of Anthropology, Mexico.)

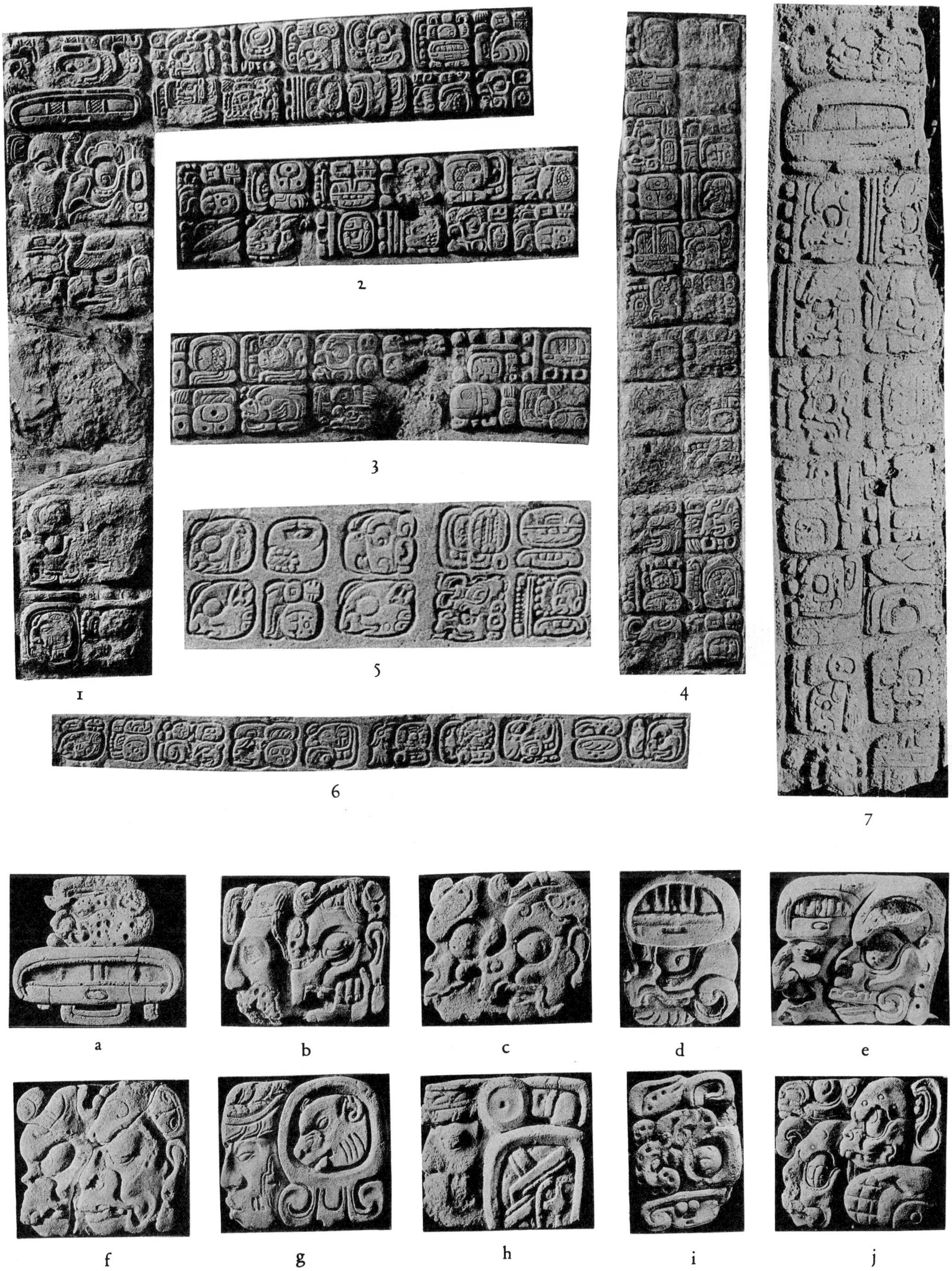
1
2
3
4
5
6
7
a
b
c
d
e
f
g
h
i
j

FIG. 57

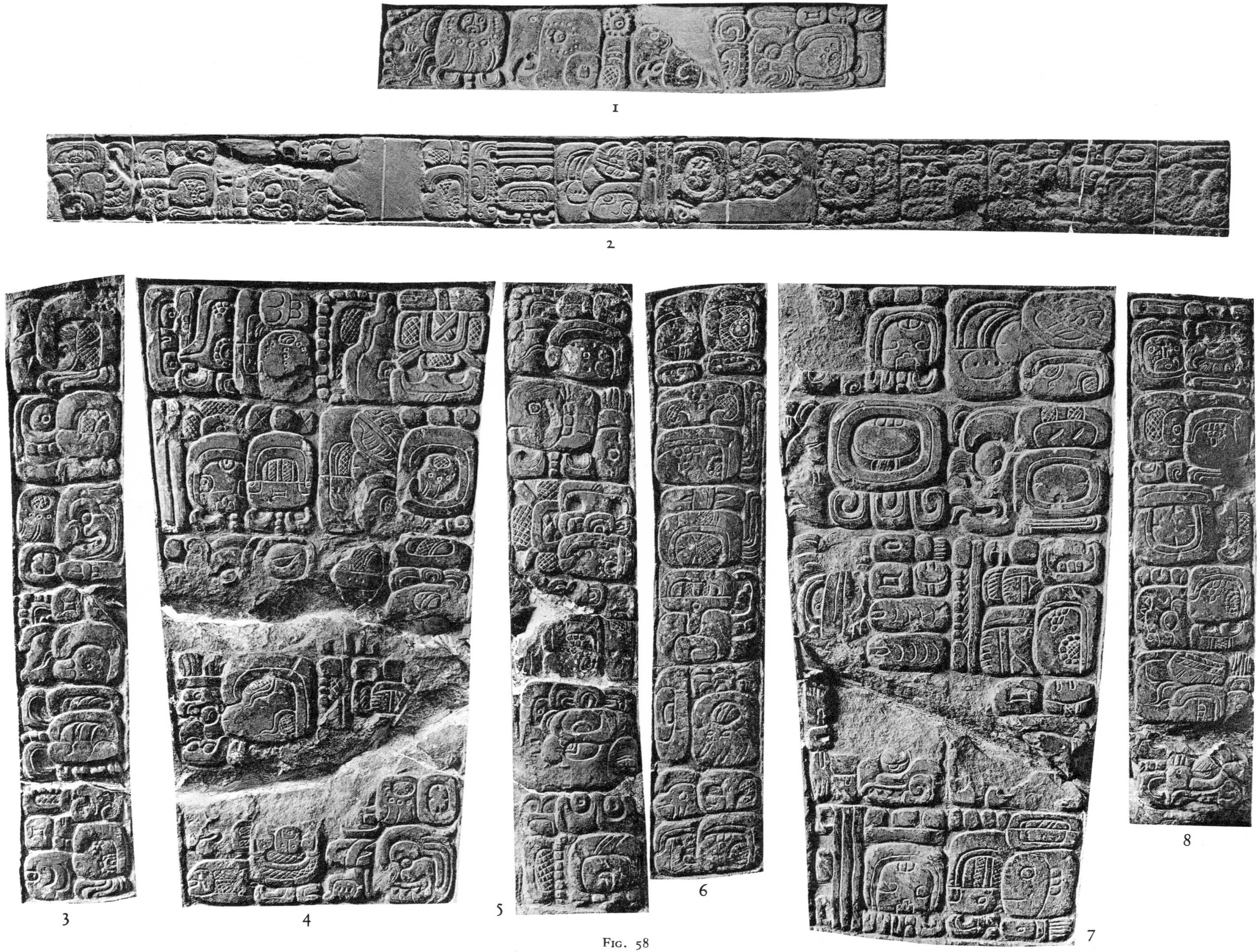

1 2 3 4 5 6 7 8

Fig. 58

F<small>IG</small>. 58—PIEDRAS NEGRAS, THRONE 1: TEXT ON TOP, FRONT, AND LEGS OF SCREEN

1. Top of screen (B–E).

2. Front (H–U).

3–5. Left leg (Z–E').

6–8. Right leg (F'–K').
The chronological parts of the text run:

		L1–M1	
			Count of 15 katuns distance, ? haab
A	O1–P1	9.15.18.16. 7	12 Manik 5 Zotz'
B		(9.17. 9. 5.11	10 Chuen 19 Zip)
			Suppressed
	A'2–C'2	1. 0.10	Forward to day (sunrise)
C	D'2–A'3	9.17.10. 6. 1	3 Imix 4 Zotz'
	G'1–J'1	3. 3	Forward to day (sunrise)
D	G'2–J'2	9.17.10. 9. 4	1 Kan 7 Yaxkin
	G'5–J'5	4. 8.16	Count forward to
E	K'1	9.17.15. 0. 0	5 Ahau 3 Muan
	K'2		5 haab lacking

Various glyphs are of interest: 1 Imix-Ahau (B1), double sky glyph with death-eye prefix followed by cauac glyph (R1, C'4, I'3), Venus prefix (E'6), kin with crosshatching (Z1, F'3), sundry cauac glyphs (I1, R1b, Z6, A'1, E'1, E'3, E'4, F'2, F'6, J'3, K'4, and beaked head (J, H'4, K'6). The anniversary of Date A, 2 katuns, 6 tuns later, is given on Stela 12 (fig. 59,6) and Date A, in turn, is the 13-tun anniversary of (9.15,5.16.7) 12 Manik 10 Yaxkin recorded on the leg of another altar. Date D is one katun later than 9.16.10.9.4 3 Kan 7 Ceh which may be recorded on L 10. Date C is 1 tun before a date on L 3 (fig. 57.4). (Courtesy of University Museum, Philadelphia.)

Fig. 59—TEXTS AT OXLAHUNTUN AND PIEDRAS NEGRAS

1. Glyphs incised in stucco at Oxlahuntun. Column to left destroyed. Text reads:

A1–B1	(9.11. 0. 0.0	12 Ahau 8 Ceh) seating of haab
A2–B2	1.11.(6.5)	
A3–B3	(9.12.11. 6.5)	13 Chicchan 18 Yax
A4–B5	9.13. 0. 0.0	8 Ahau (8 Uo). Completion of haab. Count 13 katuns

(Photographs by Giles G. Healey.)

2–5. Glyphs on legs of P.N. Alt 2:

A1–B1	9.13. 9.14.15	7 Men 18 Kankin
C1–D1	1. 8. 6.18	Forward to day (sunrise)
E1–D2	9.14.18. 3.13	at 7 Ben 16 Kankin
F3–G1	1.14. 7	
H1–G2	9.15. 0. 0. 0	4 Ahau 13 Yax
H2–G3		Fifteenth katun. Count haab completed
I2–K1	1. 0. 0. 0	Forward to day (sunrise)
J2–K2	9.16. 0. 0. 0	at 2 Ahau 13 Zec
J3–L2		Completion of sixteenth katun, expiration of haab completed, the tun

(Courtesy of University Museum, Philadelphia.)

6. Surviving glyphs on right side of P.N. 12, the IS of which is destroyed:

A1–A8, B11	(9.18. 5. 0. 0)	4 Ahau 13 Ceh
A9–A11		3E, D, 6C, X, B, 10A
A12–B12		Fifth haab. Count of haab completed
B15–A16a	8. 3. 1	Count backward to
A16b–B16	9.17.16.14.19	1 Cauac 12 Zac
A20a	1.13	(Counted backward from IS)
A20b–B20	9.18. 4.16. 7	10 Manik 0 Zac
A21		Sixth haab, third katun

The last record calls attention to the last date being the 3-katun and 6-tun anniversary of a date, the first katun anniversary of which is given on Thr 1 (fig. 58,2). (Courtesy of University Museum, Philadelphia.)

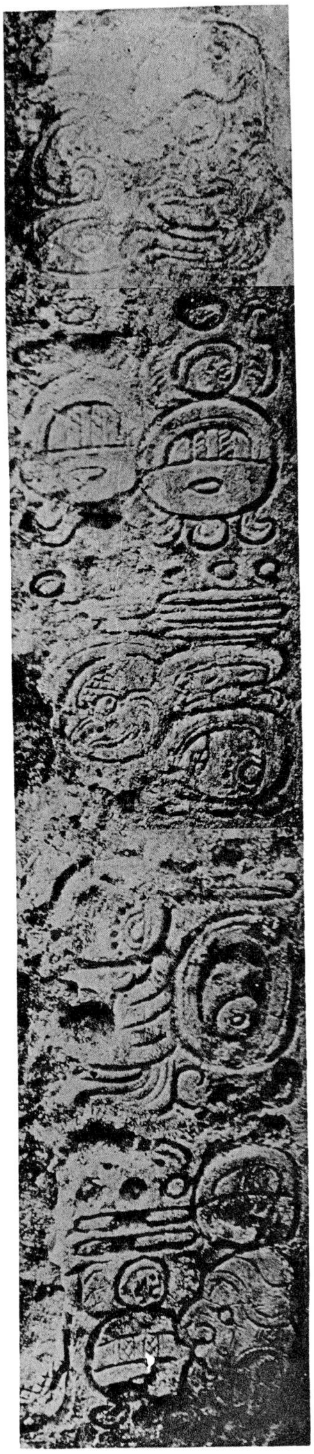

1

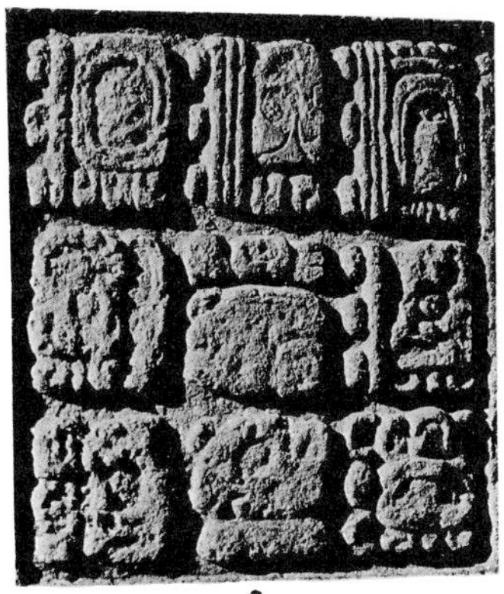

2

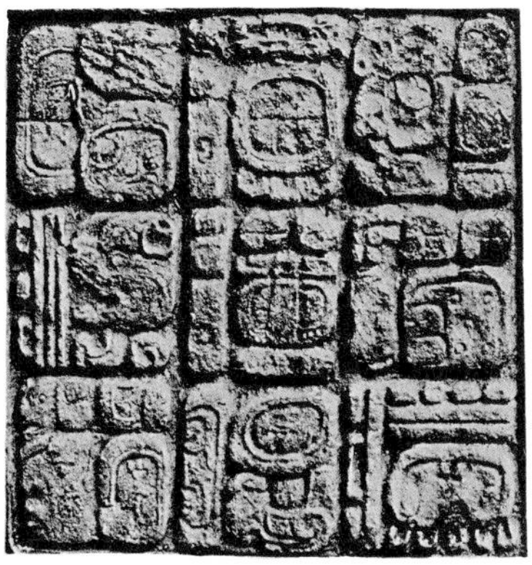

3

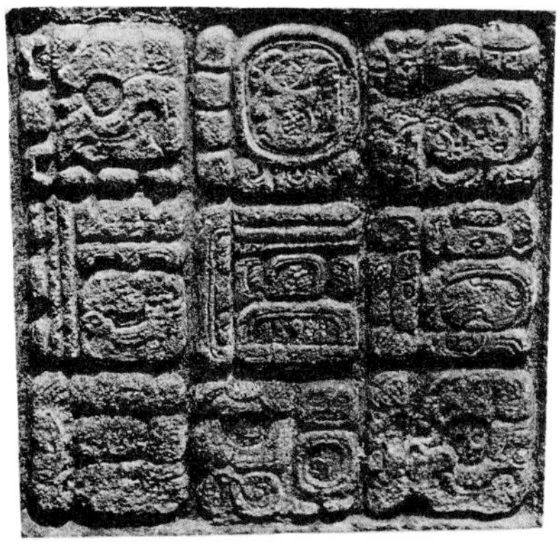

4

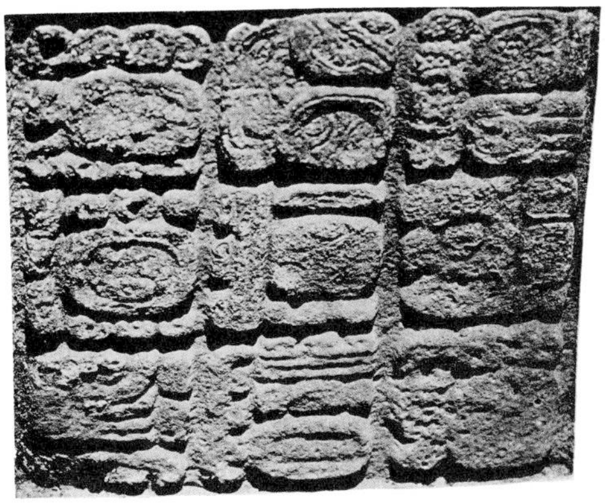

5

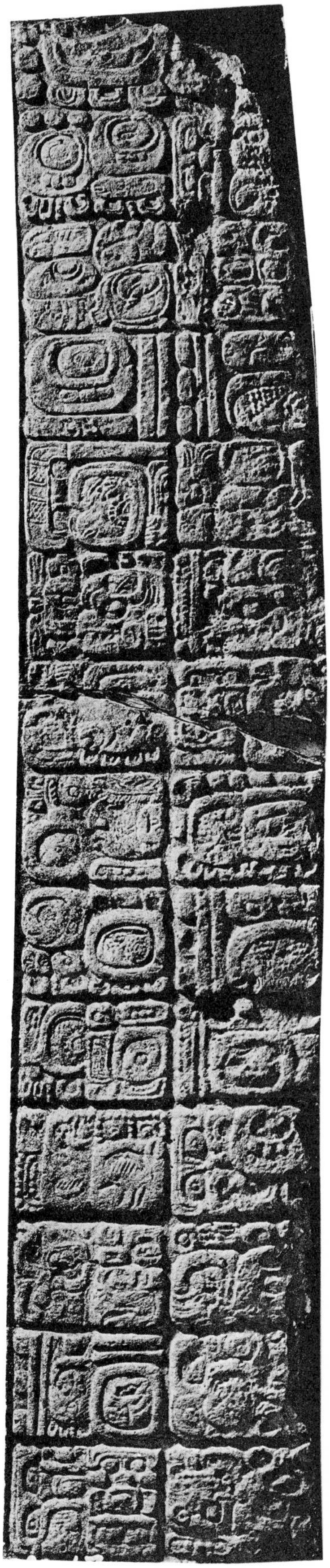

6

Fig. 59

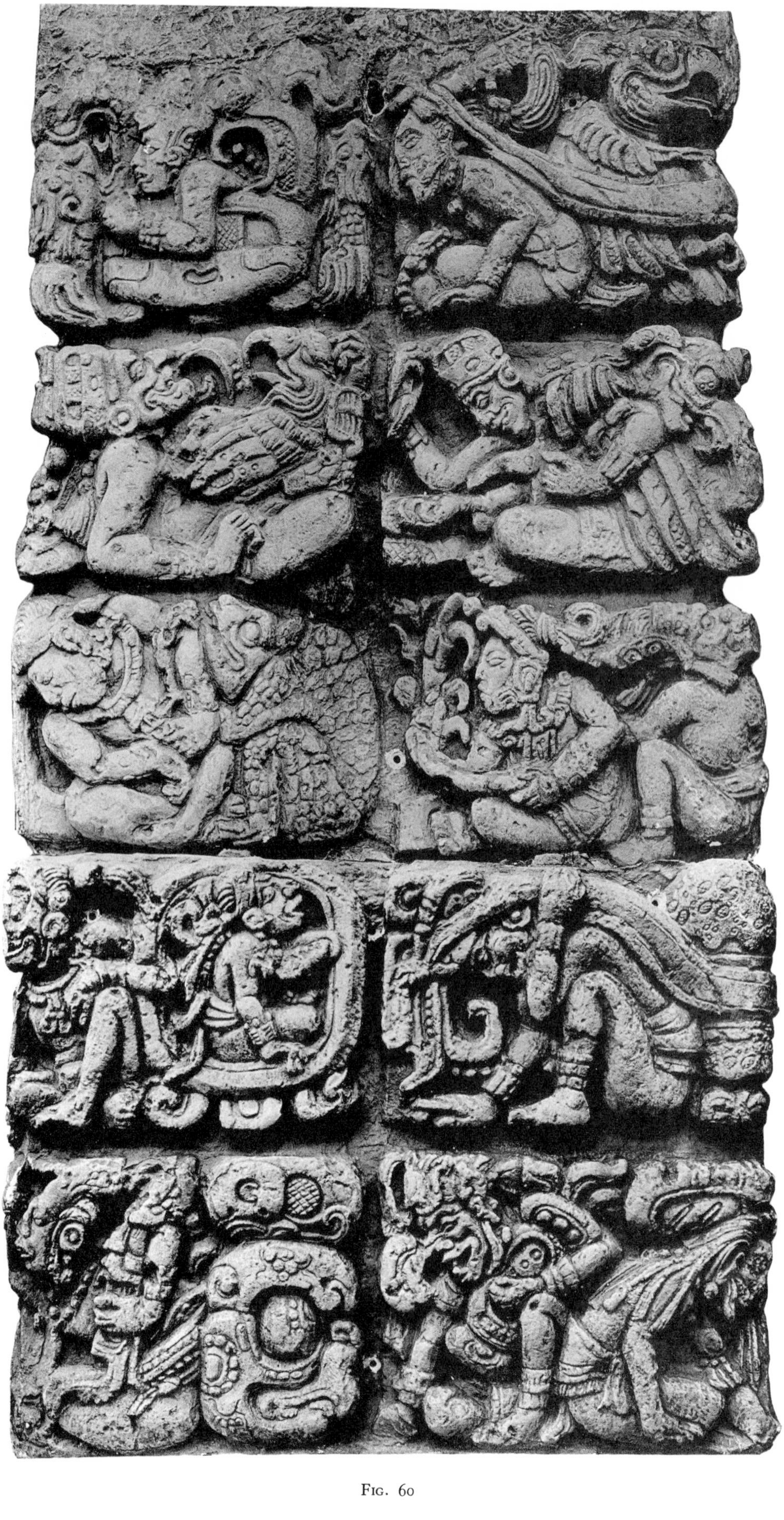

Fig. 60

Fig. 60—FULL-FIGURE GLYPHS, COPAN, D

The IS reads 9.15.5.0.0   10 Ahau 8 Ch'en. Compare with frontispiece which is an adaptation from this text. (Photograph of cast specially taken for this publication by Department of Ethnography, British Museum.)

Fig. 61—TWO DIVINATORY ALMANACS, CODEX DRESDEN

1–4. Divinatory almanac on Dresden 42c–45c divided into four sections of 65 days each and probably connected with burner ceremony, as the sections start with the days 4 Ahau, 4 Chicchan, 4 Oc, and 4 Men. These are "the rulers," the days on which the burners let the fire run. Each division is associated with a world direction and contains the dog glyph, which among other things is a fire symbol. There are also prognostications. The days within each section are at intervals of eight days, with 17 days to carry to the start of the next section (6 × 8+17=65).

1. 4 Ahau, 12 Lamat, 7 Cib, 2 Kan, 10 Eb, 5 Ahau, 13 Lamat. South, God B, fire dog, maize god, drought.

2. 4 Chicchan, 12 Ben, 7 Imix, 2 Muluc, 10 Caban, 5 Chicchan, 13 Ben. East, fire dog, God B, good tidings, maize seed, abundance of maize.

3. 4 Oc, 12 Etz'nab, 7 Cimi, 2 Ix, 10 Ik, 5 Oc, 13 Etz'nab. Glyph for set up (?), north, fire dog, God B, maize god, abundance of maize.

4. 4 Men, 13 Akbal, 7 Chuen, 2 Cauac, 10 Manik, 5 Men, 13 Akbal. West, fire dog, God B, maize god, drought, death. First 13 Akbal is error for 12 Akbal.

5–6. Divinatory almanac on Dresden 13b–14b divided into five sections of 52 days each. Sections start with 6 Ahau, 6 Eb, 6 Kan, 6 Cib, and 6 Lamat. Arrangement is:

+ 13 = 6 Ben,	+ 9 = 2 Ik,	+ 7 = 9 Muluc,	+ 7 = 3 Cib,	+ 7 = 10 Akbal,	+ 9 = 6 Eb.
6 Chicchan,	2 Ix,	9 Imix,	3 Lamat,	10 Men,	6 Kan.
6 Caban,	2 Cimi,	9 Ben,	3 Ahau,	10 Manik,	6 Cib.
6 Muluc,	2 Etz'nab,	9 Chicchan,	3 Eb,	10 Cauac,	6 Lamat.
6 Imix,	2 Oc,	9 Caban,	3 Kan,	10 Chuen,	6 Ahau.
Death god,	Maize god,	God C,	Old god,	God Q,	God D.
Multuntzek (?)	Succession (?)	Good tidings,	?	Misery,	His rule.

First pair of glyphs show hand action-glyph and green-corn glyph. Note shifting of affixes in these two glyphs in last three columns. The pairs have a meaning such as "his influence on the maize" (p. 266). (Photographs specially taken for this report by Giles G. Healey.)

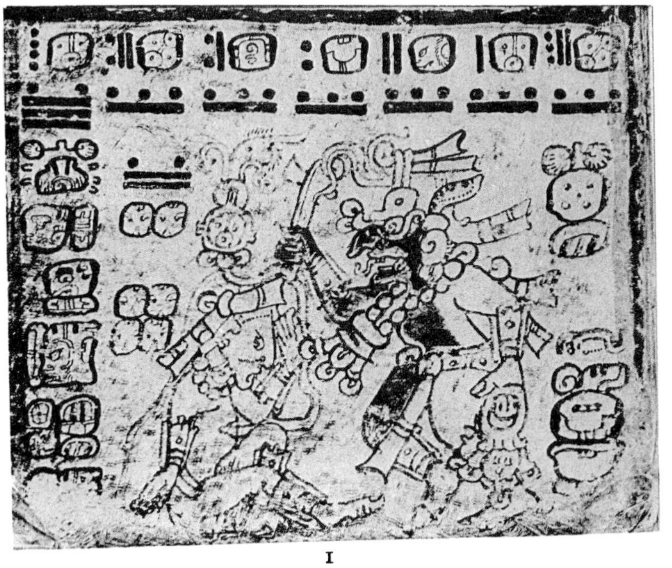

1

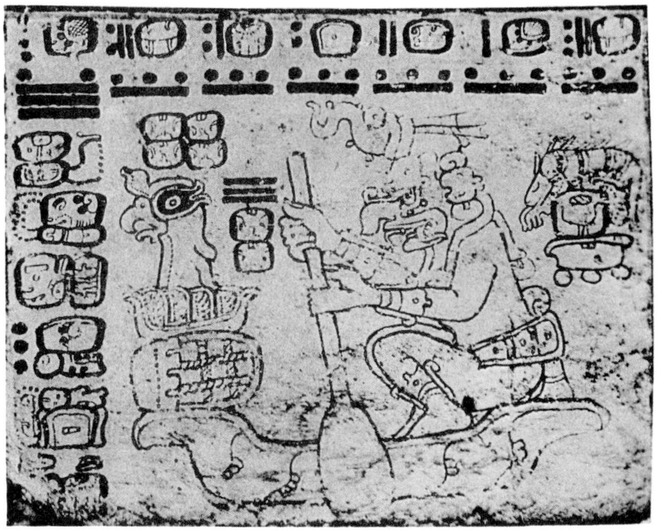

2

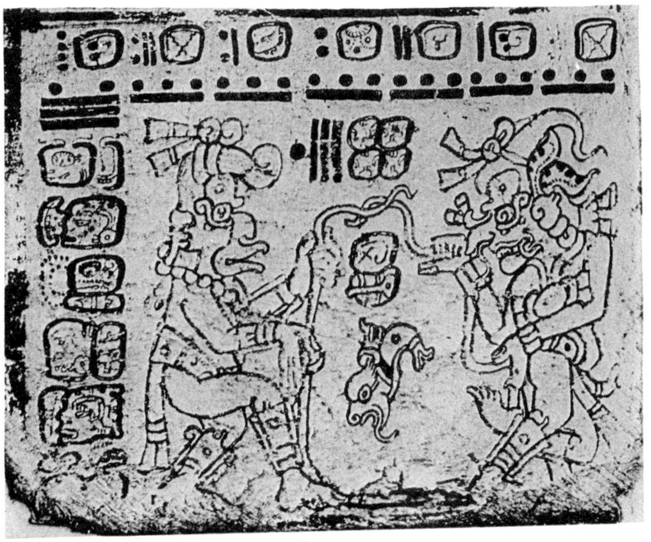

3

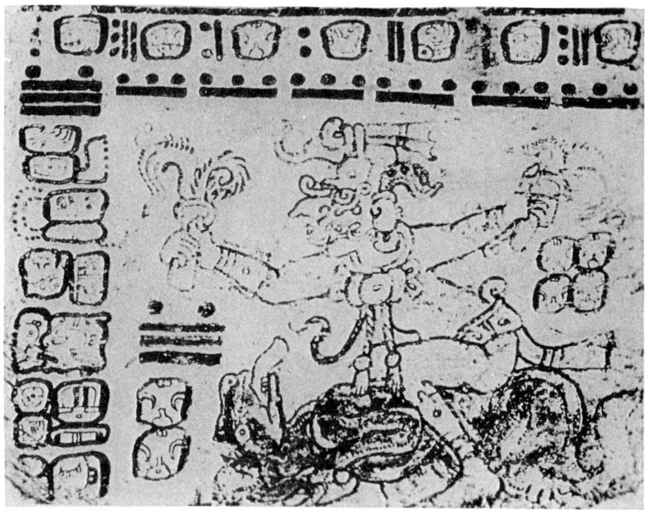

4

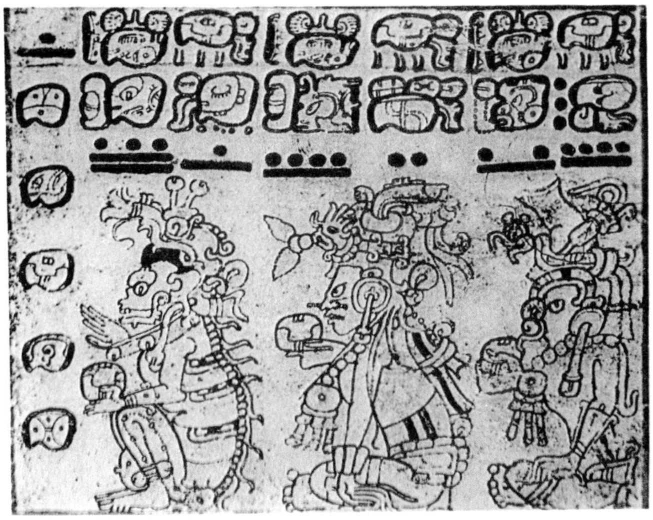

5

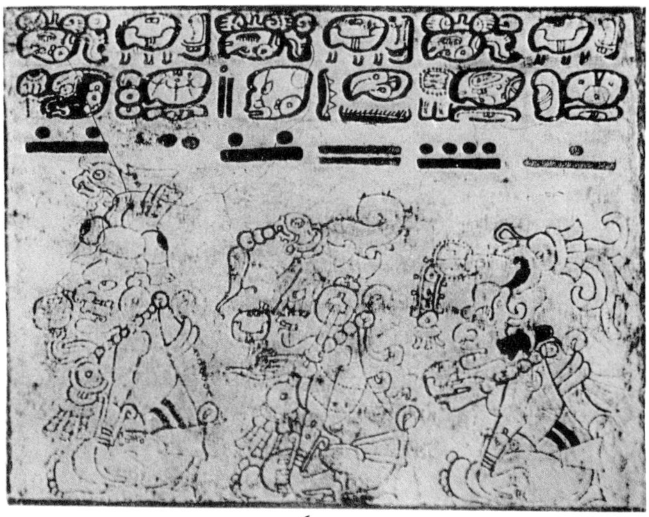

6

Fig. 61

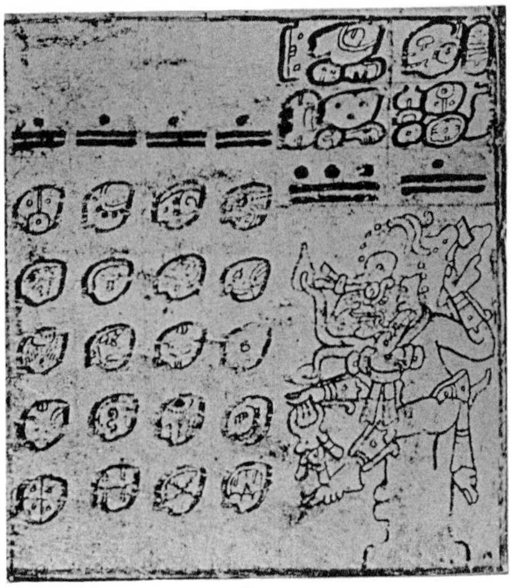

1

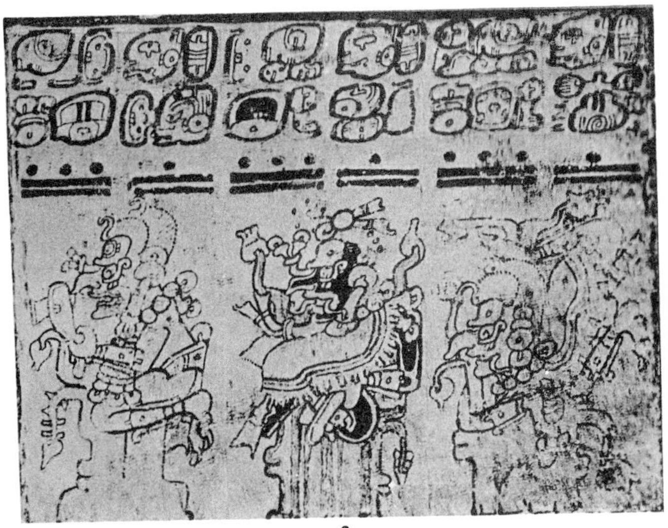

2

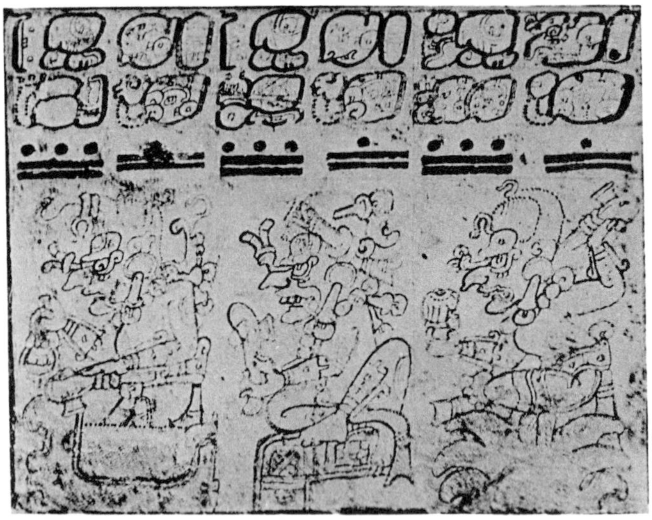

3

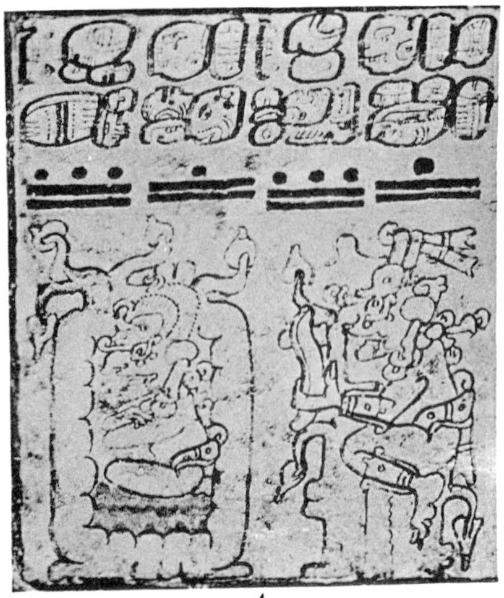

4

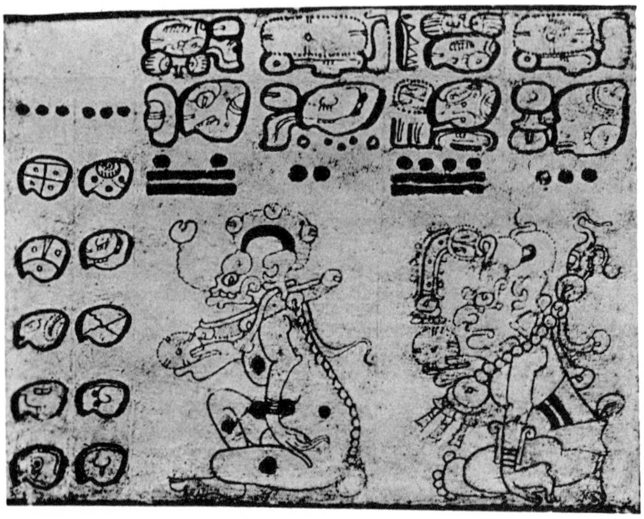

5

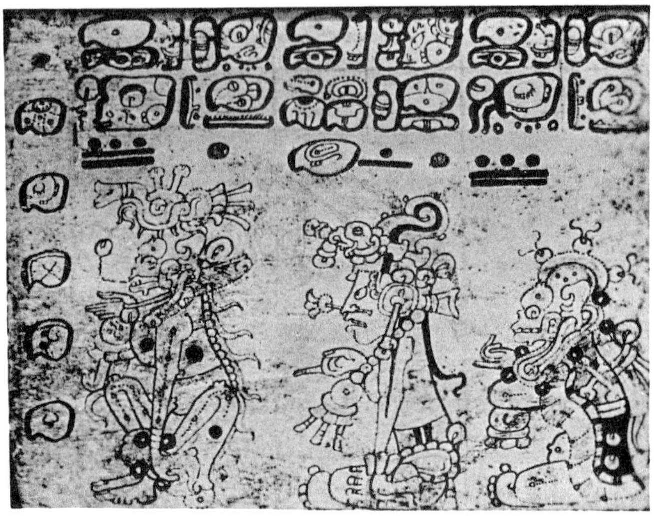

6

Fig. 62

Fɪɢ. 62—THREE DIVINATORY ALMANACS, CODEX DRESDEN

1-4. Divinatory almanac on Dresden 30c–33c covering 2340 (9×260) days and probably formed to relate the cycle of the nine lords of the nights with the 260-day cycle. Starting and ending point 11 Ahau with nine intervals of 13 days (117) to reach 11 Caban, then 11 Ix, 11 Chuen, 11 Lamat, 11 Chicchan, etc., decreasing three places until all 20 day names have headed the division (20×117=2340), and each day with coefficient of 11 has appeared once in every column. World directions and colors are in each of the first four compartments in the sequence: red, east; white, north; black, west; yellow, south. First glyph in all compartments is a hand of the action group; the second glyph that of God B. Note *te* (1) postfix, here meaning "tree," with three colors; God B is posed on world trees in pictures below.

5. Divinatory almanac on Dresden 15c divided into 10 sections, of 26 days each, with 3 Lamat as starting and finishing point. Only two subdivisions with intervals of 12 and 14 days. Hand glyph of the action group opens each compartment (note postfix switch to prefix); kin sign with dotted outline the second glyph; glyphs of death god and God D occupy the third place in their respective compartments; the death (*multuntzek*?) glyph and the glyph of a goddess.

6. Divinatory almanac on Dresden 12b divided into five sections, of 52 days each, with three subdivisions (intervals of 13, 26, and 13 days). Same action glyph, a Muluc variant, opens each section; second glyph that of deity—death god, a goddess, and death god again; last pair of glyphs in each compartment the luck of the day: death and misery; abundance its rule; death (*multuntzek*?) and misery.

(Photographs specially taken for this report by Giles G. Healey.)

Fig. 63—FIVE DIVINATORY ALMANACS, CODEX DRESDEN

1. Almanac on Dresden 12c divided into four sections of 65 days
   each with 13 Chuen starting and finishing point. There are
   three subdivisions with intervals of 26, 26, and 13 days so
   that all days have coefficients of 13. Arrangement:

+ 26 = 13 Caban	+ 26 = 13 Akbal	+ 13 = 13 Cib
13 Ik	13 Lamat	13 Imix
13 Manik	13 Ben	13 Cimi
13 Eb	13 Etz'nab	13 Chuen
Picture: God D	Earth god	Sun god
Third glyph: Chicchan	Earth god	Sun god
Fourth glyph: rulership	Maize god	Lightning

   Opening glyph in each compartment is a hand glyph of the
   action group; second glyph is the dotted kin sign with *te* (1)
   postfix (controls?, gives? light).

2. Divinatory almanac on Dresden 13a divided into five sections
   of 52 days each with obliterated Imix as starting and finishing
   point, and two subdivisions, each of 26 days, but coefficients
   of days omitted. Portraits of terrestrial snake and death god.

3. Divinatory almanac on Dresden 14a–15a divided into five
   sections of 52 days each, with 8 Ahau as starting and finishing
   point, and four subdivisions, each at an interval of 13 days so
   that every day in cycle appears once with coefficient of 13.
   Portraits are of maize god, Chicchan god, death god, and sun
   god. Note repetition of head with Etz'nab infix.

4. Double almanac of 520 days on Dresden 12a divided into 10
   sections of 52 days each, with 8 Ahau as starting and finishing
   point, and two subdivisions with intervals of 27 and 25 days.
   Coefficients of days are omitted. Auguries for first subdivision,
   maize and good tidings; for second subdivision, 13 skies
   and death (*multuntzek?*).

5, 6. Divinatory almanac on Dresden 13c–14c divided into 10 sections of 26 days each, with 2 Men as starting and finishing
   point, and four subdivisions with intervals of 7, 3, 3, and
   13 days. Augural glyphs are: misery, ?, ?, good tidings, and
   abundance.

   (Photographs specially taken for this report by Giles G.
   Healey.)

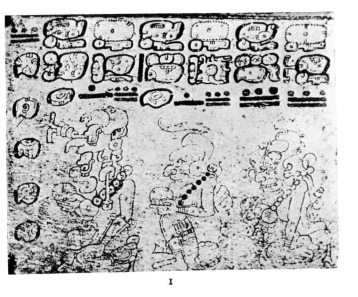

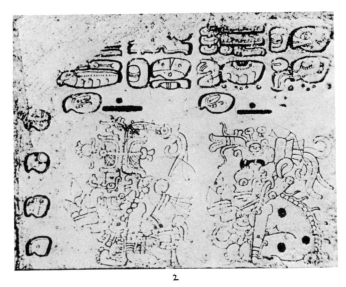

1

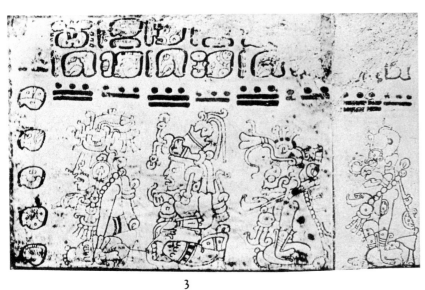

2

3

4

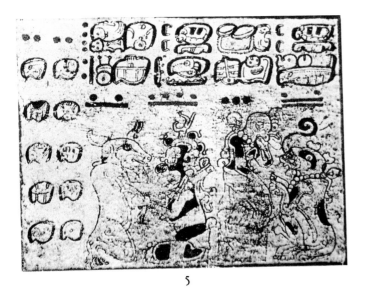

5

6

Fig. 63

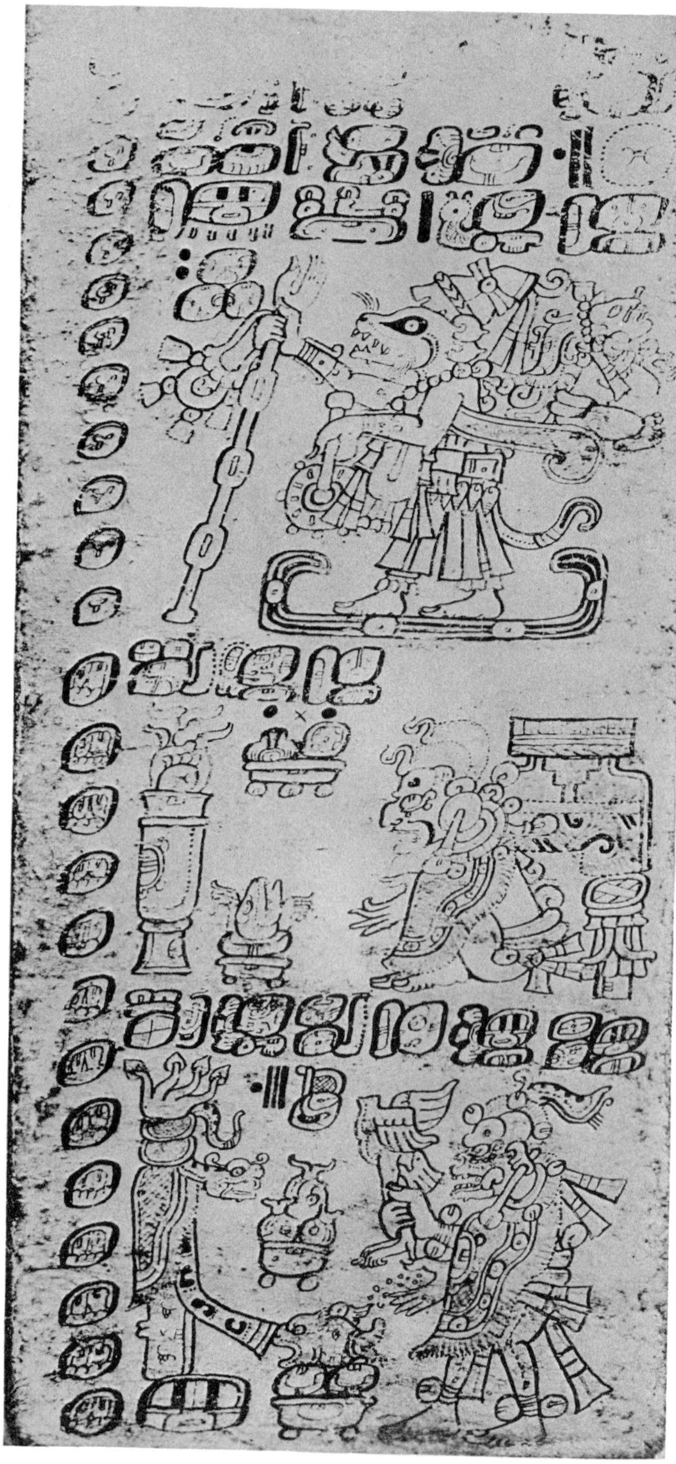

I

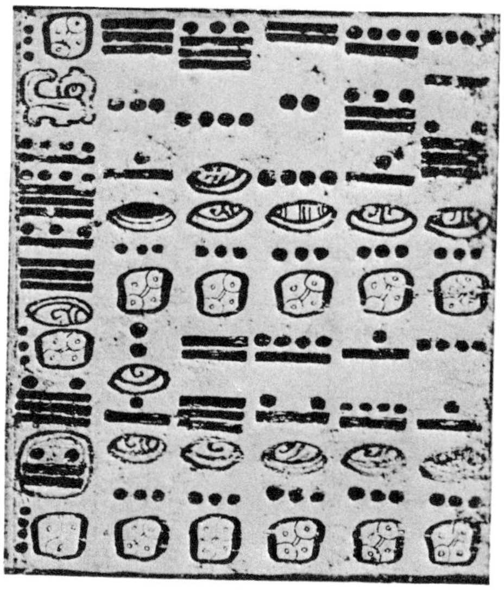

2

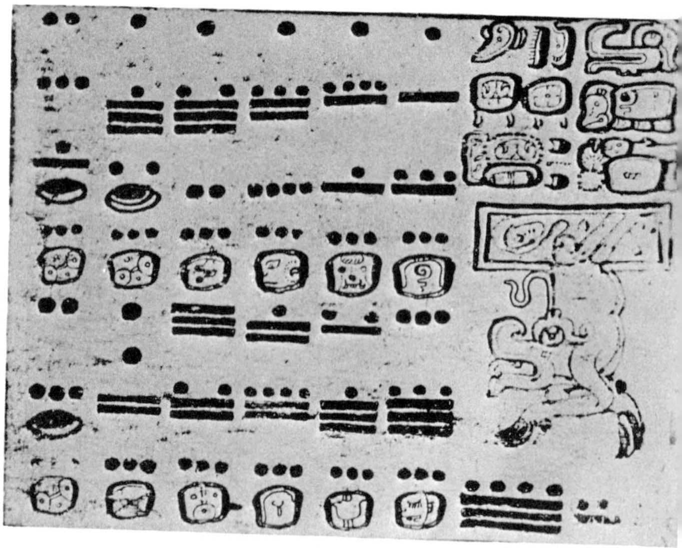

3

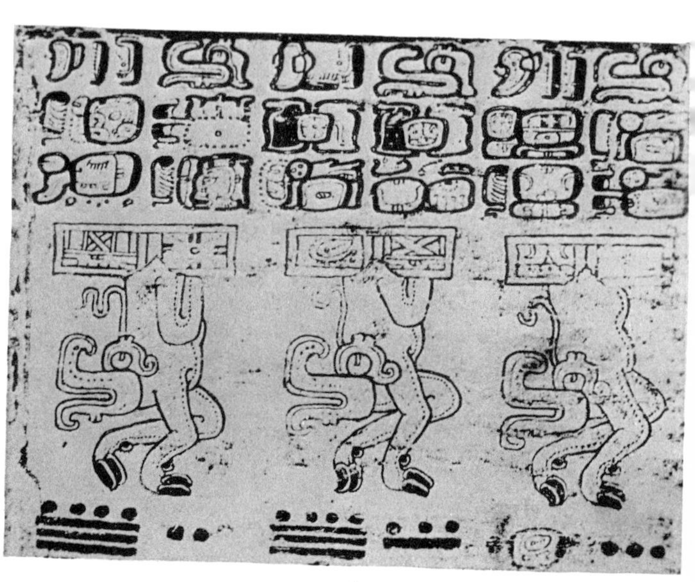

4

Fig. 64

FIG. 64—CEREMONIES FOR NEW YEAR AND AN ALMANAC AND TABLES

1. Ceremonies held in Uayeb for a new year with Akbal as year bearer on Dresden 27. Note glyph for abundance followed by the *cuch haabil* glyphs at top and, at bottom, glyphs for west, death god, new tun, and drought.

2–4. IS, multiplication table, and divinatory almanac forming single chapter, Dresden 43b–45b. On left IS 9.19.8.15.0 reckoned from base at 3 Lamat, 17 uinals and 12 kins before 13.0.0.0.0 4 Ahau 8 Cumku. This gives it the LC position 9.19.7.15.8 3 Lamat (6 Zotz'). Multiplication table is based on same position 3 Lamat. It proceeds at intervals of 78 days until 780 (3×260) days are reached. Some, but not all, subsequent numbers are multiples of 780, but we must not assume that numbers which are not multiples of 780 contain errors, for some are important multiples of 260. Table starts at bottom right on page 44b:

3.18	3 Cimi	(1 × 78)	
7.16	3 Kan	(2 × 78)	
11.14	3 Ik	(3 × 78)	
15.12	3 Ahau	(4 × 78)	
1. 1.10	3 Etz'nab	(5 × 78)	
2. 3. 0	3 Lamat	(10 × 78)	
1. 5. 8	3 Cib	(6 × 78)	
1. 9. 6	3 Ix	(7 × 78)	
1.13. 4	3 Eb	(8 × 78)	
1.17. 2	3 Oc	(9 × 78)	
4. 6. 0	3 Lamat	(2 × 780)	(6 × 260)
6. 9. 0	3 Lamat	(3 × 780)	(9 × 260)
9. 7. 0	3 Lamat	(13 × 260)	
10.15. 0	3 Lamat	(5 × 780)	(15 × 260)
1.16. 2. 0	3 Lamat	(50 × 260)	
2. 3. 6. 0	3 Lamat	(20 × 780)	(60 × 260)
4. 6.12. 0*	3 Lamat	(40 × 780)	(120 × 260)
8.13. 6. 0†	3 Lamat	(80 × 780)	(240 × 260)
10. 2. 4. 0	3 Lamat	(280 × 260)	
18. 4. 0. 0	3 Lamat	(168 × 780)	(504 × 260)
15. 3. 6. 0	3 Lamat	(140 × 780)	(420 × 260)
1. 1. 0. 6. 0	3 Lamat	(194 × 780)	(582 × 260)

* Written 4.5.17.0, 260 days earlier.
† Written 9.13.6.0.

Some rearrangement has been made. The question remains open whether 13×260 is intentional or an error for 8.12.0 (4×780) and whether 4.5.17.0 should be corrected to 4.6.12.0. Similarly, the addition of 260 days to 1.16.2.0 produces 1.16.15.0 (17×780).

This table leads up to a divinatory almanac with pictures of the so-called Mars beasts, which, however, are probably rain animals. The almanac is a triple cycle of 260 days divided into 10 sections, each of 78 days, and the starting days of the sections are those given in the 10 multiples of 78 in the table. Various augural glyphs are given, largely connected with maize, as discussed in the text. The darkness glyph is prominent and probably refers to stormy weather, having no connection here with eclipses.

(Photographs specially taken for this report by Giles G. Healey.)